Law and Institutions
of the European Union

This book is dedicated to the memory of Dominik Lasok

Law and Institutions of the European Union

Seventh Edition

K P E Lasok QC Middle Temple, MA (Cantab), LLM, PhD (Exeter)

and

the late **D Lasok** LenDr, LLM, PhD, Dr Juris, LLD, Dhc
of the Middle Temple, one of Her Majesty's Counsel,
Emeritus Professor of European Law and former
Director of the Centre for European Legal Studies at
the University of Exeter. Visiting Professor at Marmara University (Istanbul)

*Scire leges non hoc est verba earum tenere,
sed vim ac potestatem*, Celsus, 1.3.17

Butterworths
A Member of the LexisNexis Group

Members of the LexisNexis Group worldwide

United Kingdom	Butterworths Tolley, a Division of Reed Elsevier (UK) Ltd, Halsbury House, 35 Chancery Lane, LONDON, WC2A 1EL, and 4 Hill Street, EDINBURGH EH2 3JZ
Argentina	Abeledo Perrot, Jurisprudencia Argentina and Depalma, BUENOS AIRES
Australia	Butterworths, a Division of Reed International Books Australia Pty Ltd, CHATSWOOD, New South Wales
Austria	ARD Betriebsdienst and Verlag Orac, VIENNA
Canada	Butterworths Canada Ltd, MARKHAM, Ontario
Chile	Publitecsa and Conosur Ltda, SANTIAGO DE CHILE
Czech Republic	Orac sro, PRAGUE
France	Editions du Juris-Classeur SA, PARIS
Hong Kong	Butterworths Asia (Hong Kong), HONG KONG
Hungary	Hvg Orac, BUDAPEST
India	Butterworths India, NEW DELHI
Ireland	Butterworths (Ireland) Ltd, DUBLIN
Italy	Giuffré, MILAN
Malaysia	Malayan Law Journal Sdn Bhd, KUALA LUMPUR
New Zealand	Butterworths of New Zealand, WELLINGTON
Poland	Wydawnictwa Prawnicze PWN, WARSAW
Singapore	Butterworths Asia, SINGAPORE
South Africa	Butterworths Publishers (Pty) Ltd, DURBAN
Switzerland	Stämpfli Verlag AG, BERNE
USA	LexisNexis, DAYTON, Ohio

© Reed Elsevier (UK) Ltd 2001

ISBN 0 406 901 864

Typeset by Doyle & Co, Colchester
Printed by The Bath Press Ltd

Visit Butterworths LexisNexis *direct* **at www.butterworths.com**

Preface to the Seventh Edition

The previous, and this, edition of this book are a continuation of Lasok and Bridge, *Law and Institutions of the European Communities* and Lasok, *The Law of the Economy in the European Communities*.

The purpose of this work is to present both the institutional and the substantive aspects of the law relating to the European Union in what is hoped to be an approachable form. In these days, such an objective is difficult to achieve successfully due to the broad legislative compass of the Union and due to the constant pressure of change.

In view of those difficulties, one way of attempting to achieve the desired result would be to describe the law in the form of abstract propositions backed up by footnoted references to the relevant legal provisions and decided cases. However, such a solution would not be entirely satisfactory. Being removed from the context in which the law operates and presented in a factual vacuum, the result would convey little impression of the real impact of the provisions being described. The reader would be confronted with a miasma of rules and principles.

In previous editions, as in this one, the authors of this work have taken the view that the law and institutions of the European Community and, later, the European Union, are best observed, described and understood in the factual and economic context of the Community and, now, the Union. In order to do that, it is necessary to give some explanation of how and why it is that the European Union has reached its present state of evolution. In addition, it is desirable, if not essential, to illustrate the operation of the law by reference to the problems thrown up in particular cases.

Unfortunately, in a work of this size, it is not always possible both to describe and to illustrate the operation of every principle and rule of law. Some compromise must be reached. In some instances, the basic principles can be stated and described and the detailed implementation of the principles omitted. In others, more detailed explanation is necessary. It is hoped that the end result will prove a satisfactory one for readers.

I would like to thank P A Stone, MA, LL.B, Barrister and Reader in Law in the University of Essex for his help with Chapter 36 and Mrs Audrey Thorp who helped with the preparation of the manuscript.

Preparation of this edition was disrupted and delayed by the illness and death of my father, who had started work on this edition and asked me to complete it. In the circumstances, it is fitting that it should be dedicated to him. Although he did not complete this edition, it retains his imprint and his particular views about the development of the European Communities into the European Union.

It has been possible to include some developments in the law that took place in the first few months of 2001 but, in more general terms, this edition states the law as it stood on 31 December 2000.

K P E L
Monckton Chambers
Gray's Inn
May 2001

Preface to the first edition

Ubi Societas Ibi Jus

To understand the nature of the law one must understand the nature of the society from which it emanates and which it purports to govern.

We are used to the concepts of national and international law. The former is the law of a sovereign state and as such it governs the society comprised in a state that is a group of people living within a defined area under a government which has executive, legislative, judicial and administrative powers. International law, on the other hand, is the body of rules which governs relations between states and such international organizations as are set up and recognized by states as bearers of rights and duties. In exceptional situations individuals may be regarded as subjects of international law. As a body of rules international law is derived partly from custom and state practice, partly from the will of states expressed in treaties and partly generated by institutions (eg the United Nations Organization) set up by states and based on a treaty.

The object of this book is to define and analyse a nascent body of law which can be described as the law of the European Community. It is neither a national nor an international system of law in the accepted sense of these terms but a *sui generis* system emanating from the will to create a European Community. It reflects, of course, the nature of this design. At this stage we can speak of the European Community only in general political terms as an organization with limited, mainly economic objectives and a potential for development towards a federal organization. In strictly juristic, institutional terms we have to speak of the European Communities, that is the European Coal and Steel Community, the European Atomic Energy Community and the European Economic Community and, therefore, a distinction between 'Community' and 'Communities' has to be borne in mind. The law of the European Community, as we understand it, comprises consequently elements of international and national law as well as the rules generated by the Communities, of which the European Economic Community may be regarded as a cornerstone of future developments. This we shall endeavour to emphasize.

The genesis of this book lies in the authors' experience of teaching European Community Law in the University of Exeter. They wish to express their thanks to their students, both undergraduate and post-graduate, for the patience and forbearance with which they endured the authors' experimental first steps in this field. The authors claim to have written no more than an introduction to the complex system of Community law. In order to explain its working to the reader it was thought necessary to stress the institutional aspects of the Community and matters of principle at the expense of the details of the law of the economy which is still at a formative stage. It is hoped, however, that it is informative and provocative in that by setting out the rudiments it will make the reader aware of the unprecedented challenge facing Europe, the United Kingdom and the citizen, be he lawyer or layman. The aim throughout has been to approach the subject from the standpoint of the United Kingdom joining a continental Community which is already a going concern and this explains the emphasis placed on the political background of the Community and the civil law framework within which it functions. The authors owe a considerable debt to the numerous pioneer writers on the Communities and their law and pay them generous tribute.

This is a joint work. Chapters 1, 3, 4, 10, 11, 13 and 14 were drafted by D Lasok; chapters 5, 6, 7, 8, 9 and 12 were drafted by J W Bridge; chapter 2 was drafted jointly. The work of each author has been subject to the comments and criticisms of the other and both authors are in agreement on and each accepts responsibility for the form and content of the whole book.

The authors' gratitude is due to all the members of the secretarial staff of the Faculty of Law of the University of Exeter who, with their accustomed cheerfulness and efficiency, undertook the typing of the manuscript; to the Publishers; and to their wives and families to whom this book is dedicated.

D L
J W B
Exeter
Michaelmas 1972

Contents

PART I   THE NATURE OF THE EUROPEAN UNION AND OF
COMMUNITY LAW

Chapter 1
The birth and growth of the European Community   3

Chapter 4
The nature and challenge of Community law 101

Chapter 5
Sources of Community law 122

PART II   THE LAW OF THE INSTITUTIONS

Chapter 6
The European Council 207

Chapter 7
The European Parliament 214

Chapter 8
The Commission 230

Chapter 9
The Council of the European Union   246

Chapter 10
The Court of Auditors and budgetary procedure   265

Chapter 11
Ancillary Community institutions

Chapter 12
The Court of Justice and the Court of First Instance   289

PART III   THE RELATIONSHIP BETWEEN COMMUNITY LAW
AND THE MUNICIPAL LAW OF THE MEMBER STATES

Chapter 13
Implementation of Community law in the legal systems of the Member States   331

Chapter 14
Enforcement of Community law   371

Chapter 15
Community law in the United Kingdom 399

PART IV   THE LAW OF THE ECONOMY

Chapter 16
The Law of the Economy: concept and scope 423

Chapter 17
EC trade law: external market 433

PART V   THE LAW OF THE ECONOMY:
COMMUNITY POLICIES

Chapter 27
Competition: general principles   608

Chapter 28
Competition: practices contrary to Article 81 (ex Article 85)

Chapter 29

Competition: abuse of a dominant position and mergers 685

Chapter 30

State aid (EC Articles 87–89 (ex Articles 92–94)) 705

Chapter 31

Intellectual property rights 721

Chapter 32

Social policy 756

Table of statutes

Table of European legislation

RESOLUTIONS

Table of international legislation

Table of other enactments

List of cases

li

PAGE

J

K

M

PAGE

U

W

Decisions of the European Court of Justice are listed below numerically. These decisions are also included in the preceding alphabetical list.

c List of cases

PAGE

Part I

The nature of the European Union and of Community Law

Chapter 1

The birth and growth of the European Community

A. The formation of the European Community

The recurrent dream of a unified Europe is part of our cultural heritage. Students of history are familiar with the attempts to create a united Europe mainly by force, for conquest and universalism often go hand in hand. Only within living memory have two powerful ideologies, Communism and Nazism, endeavoured to unify Europe in their own fashion. In August 1920 the advance of the Red Army 'through the heart of Poland to the conquest of Europe and world conflagration'[1] was brought to a halt at the gates of Warsaw in what was described[2] as the eighteenth decisive battle of world history. In 1945 ended the Second World War, unleashed by one Adolf Hitler who dreamed of a millennium of German domination over Europe. After six years of struggle most of Europe was reduced to smouldering heaps of rubble, physically and politically. The old Europe became just a phase in the Continent's saga and history began to work towards a different concept of unification.

　　Students of political thought are familiar with the rivalries for excellence between the concept of the sovereign state and federal ideas. From the Middle Ages right up to our time the state was regarded as an ideal self-sufficient unit, capable of securing protection and self-fulfilment of individuals. The nineteenth and the first half of the twentieth centuries witnessed the apotheosis of the sovereign state as the supreme and sublime goal of human organization. Everything was to be subordinated to the state. This Hegelian ideal, no doubt rooted in Plato's philosophy, being an element of the explanation of the universe and of historical determinism, was eagerly adopted by modern dictatorships both of the fascist and communist type and soon brought into disrepute. The Second World War did not solve Europe's problems but resulted in a new division based

1　General Tukhachevski in an order to his armies quoted by Umiastowski, R, *Russia and the Polish Republic 1918–1941* (1944), p 84.
2　By Lord D'Abernon; Fuller, J F C, *The Decisive Battles of the Western World, 1792–1944*, Vol 2 (1970), p 411.

on the conquest of its eastern half and generating mutual distrust between the West and the East. In a sense it contributed to the creation of two European Communities: of the West (which is the subject of the present study) and of the East (the so-called Council for Mutual Economic Co-operation). The two Communities reflected the political reality of the divided Europe and the relationship of the countries they represented. They also depicted a process of integration along different lines. Whilst the East European Community reflected the leading rôle of the Soviet Union and the common political ideology of the bloc, the West European Community reflected, structurally, vague federalist ideas[3] of the nineteenth and twentieth centuries and, politically, the fear of the other side expressed in the statement that Stalin was the chief architect of West European solidarity.[4] The former collapsed in 1989, the latter continues to consolidate its structure moving from the concept of 'Community' to a 'European Union'.

The Second World War demonstrated the futility of conquests and the vulnerability of the sovereign state concept. The sovereign state could no longer guarantee the protection of the citizen and so the traditional concept of allegiance based on a *sui generis* contract broke down. Interdependence of states rather than independence became the key to post-war international relations, and was reflected in current trends of international law, especially in the ideology and structure of the United Nations. The slogan *si vis pacem para bellum* had to give way to the quest for justice among men and nations and *si vis pacem para pacem* had to become the order of the day. An admirable example of co-operation and a practical application of the call for peace in the European Coal and Steel Community, built on the premise that, if the basic raw materials for war (coal and steel) are removed from national control, wars between the traditional enemies, France and Germany, will become virtually impossible as long as both are prevented from developing a substantial war industry. A corollary benefit of the international control of these resources, accruing not only to France and Germany but also to the other members of the Community, was brought about by the rationalization of the coal and steel industries and the economic stimulus created by an enlarged market.

With the demise of the state ideology, federalism found a new lease of life. Federal doctrines have, in the past, set their face against the idolatry of the state, but they were Utopian rather than realistic whilst physical, territorial federalism in Western Europe proved politically impossible. Federalism had to search for other, more realistic forms. Harold Laski, in an introduction to his book, *Liberty in the Modern State*,[5] argued that the Second World War and its antecedents had shown that 'the principle of national sovereignty has exhausted its usefulness'. He wrote further: 'it is through supranational planning in fields like electric power, transport, or an integrated economy of coal and steel, that we can best hope to attain this end [ie to make liberty possible]. It is, of course, impossible to leave such planning in private hands.' Laski dubbed his idea 'functional federalism' because he was opposed to the concept of territorial federalism, that is to say a United States of Europe or a Federal Western Europe, an enlarged version of Switzerland, which he regarded as both obsolete and impractical.

Whilst 'functional federalism' has been accepted by the architects of the West European Community, Laski's pessimism about territorial federalism may yet

---

3 Delmas, C, *Le Fédéralisme et l'Europe* (1969).
4 Spaak, H-P, *Combats Inachevés* (1969), pp 249–250.
5 Republished in 1948.

prove unfounded. It is clear that economic co-operation and legal integration will tighten the political and organizational bonds between states and from this reality new political forms will emerge. Territorial federalism is not just round the corner but is not as remote as it may seem. It may well be that it will not be heralded by political theory but will grow up as a child of evolution. In the Community institutions, which we shall examine in detail, the stage seems to have been set for such a development.

The post-war practical exercise in international co-operation in Western Europe has proved that nations can live together and work together, that they can solve their differences amicably and, where need be, through appropriate legal and judicial process. It has demonstrated that the concept of a Community is not only viable but also capable of growth and development. The Community institutions have already been working for two generations and their very existence and practical usefulness will inevitably lead to their refinement.

If we cast our minds back to the early post-war we will realize that a Community approach was the practical answer to many problems. Europe was in ruins politically and economically; the European colonial empires faced liquidation; the importance of the single European states which dominated the League of Nations was diminished; the 'dollar-gap' resulted in great influence of the USA not only as a benevolent saviour but also as a potential master; an 'iron curtain' was drawn across Europe and the world cowered in the shadows of great powers, the USA and Soviet Russia, facing each other menacingly across Europe. Only rapid recovery in concert could restore Europe's self-respect. What is more it became only too obvious that economic reconstruction had to match political aspirations. Thus the idea of a European Community was forced upon Europeans as an economic and political necessity. As for grand designs, the architects of the Community soon realized that great ideologies and elaborate blueprints were of little practical use and that nothing could be achieved at one stroke. Robert Schuman,[6] the great French European, said: 'L'Europe ne se fera pas d'un coup dans une construction d'ensemble, elle se fera par des réalisations concrètes créant d'abord une solidarité de fait ...'

This factual solidarity can be traced to events of great importance to Europe and the world at large, as the work of world recovery and reconstruction began to create a fabric of international economic co-operation. We should mention, if only briefly, these events and forms of co-operation because they too contributed to European solidarity and in a sense paved the way for the institutional framework of the European Community.

B.　The International Monetary Fund and the World Bank

The IMF was created at a conference at Bretton Woods in 1946, with the object of maintaining the stability of national currencies, reducing restrictions on currency exchange and helping countries to maintain a balance of payments. The subscribing countries participate on a share basis: USA 28%, USSR 12.5% and Europe only 16%. The size of the share determines the voting power of the subscribers. Countries (including the United Kingdom) often borrow money to maintain their solvency. The World Bank was also created at Bretton Woods.

6　Quoted by Lorette, L de Sainte, *Le Marché Commun* (1961), p 17; Patjin, S (ed), *Landmarks in European Unity* (1970), p 46.

Here again states participate on a share basis. The USA alone provides 38% of the capital. The Bank offers not only financial assistance but also provides experts in various fields. It has been useful to finance projects incapable of being financed otherwise, especially in the developing countries.

C.   The Havana Charter and GATT

Representatives of 55 countries, assembled at Havana on the initiative of the USA in 1947–48, drafted a Charter of International Commerce which envisaged a gradual reduction of customs tariffs; proposed suppression of import quotas (except in the case of agricultural produce) and imbalance of payments; prohibited discrimination in commerce (except in the case of former colonies, customs unions and free exchange areas); encouraged investments in the developing countries and suggested an International Trade Organization. Liberia was the only country which ratified the Charter.

The idea of this Charter was nevertheless accepted by 23 countries which in October 1947 signed the General Agreement on Tariffs and Trade (GATT). It is concerned with customs and commercial policy. The Agreement has been in operation without being ratified between countries which subscribe to its principles and countries which apply its principles without having formally signed it. With the United Arab Emirates joining recently the number of members rose to 117, and 119 countries participated in 1994 in the Uruguay Round of negotiations. Under the auspices of GATT frequent meetings of experts are held and many rules of customs and trade laws have been modified.

The members of GATT have set up a Council of Representatives with a secretariat in Geneva. Moreover, member countries adhere, as a rule, to the principles propounded by GATT in the matter of customs, import quotas and preferences and enter into bilateral agreements in these fields. It is significant that the so-called Schuman Plan and the European Economic Community Treaty were submitted to GATT to ensure conformity with its principles. As from 4 May 1964 the EC, representing the Member States, has been taking part in negotiations within GATT and has since played a significant role as one of the largest world trade partners.

The outcome of the protracted negotiations with GATT from 1986 to 1994, known as the Uruguay Round, was the creation of the World Trade Organisation (WTO). This provides a common institutional framework for the conduct of trade relations among its members. The WTO consists of a Ministerial Conference composed of representatives of the members, who have authority to take decisions under any of the Multilateral Trade Agreements made between them, and various councils, including councils concerned specifically with trade in goods, services and trade-related aspects of intellectual property rights.[7]

D.   The UN Economic Commission for Europe

This Commission was established in 1947 in Geneva for the purpose of exchanging information and statistical data on coal, electricity and transport in Western and

7   See further Lasok, D, *The Trade and Customs Law of the European Union* (3rd edn, 1998), pp 19-26.

Eastern Europe. Twenty-eight countries, including the USA, are involved. The Commission has published analytical studies of the economic situations of several European countries but, as the division between the Western and Eastern blocs deepened, it failed as an instrument of European co-operation. However, since 1989, a new chapter of European history has opened.

E. The Marshall Plan and the Organization for European Economic Co-operation

In a speech at Harvard on 5 July 1947 General George Marshall, the US Secretary of State, announced a plan for European relief. Instead of loans to individual countries the USA offered economic aid on the sole condition that the Europeans work out a common programme for the relief of poverty and for economic reconstruction. His appeal was addressed to Europe as a whole, stating that '... our policy is not directed against any country or against any doctrine but against hunger, poverty, despair and chaos; its aim is the renewal of active economy throughout the world'.[8] The Plan was welcomed in Western Europe and the Foreign Secretaries of France and the United Kingdom invited the USSR to join them. Ten days later Molotov scorned the invitation and enjoined Czechoslovakia, Poland and Finland, who expressed interest, to have nothing to do with the Plan. Subsequently, in January 1949, a specifically East European regional organization emerged, allegedly not as a response or counterweight[9] to the Marshall Plan but to meet the needs of the region and to 'strengthen the unity and the brotherly alliance of independent and equal socialist countries'.[10] Thus the division of Europe became further accentuated.

Only Western Europe benefited from the Marshall Plan economically and politically as the Plan, in a practical way, contributed to European integration. The significance of Marshall's gift to Europe is rarely appreciated.

Sixteen West European countries participated in the conference and the ensuing Committee of Economic Co-operation which led to the creation of the Organization for European Economic Co-operation[11] in April 1948. More than 13 million dollars were poured into Europe out of the American bounty. This was undoubtedly the first substantial move towards economic co-operation in Europe and the Americans quite rightly take pride in their contribution. Indeed European economic cohesion and strength was in the political interest of the USA even if Europe was to become a competitive force to be reckoned with. Thus American willingness to protect Western Europe from communist expansion contributed towards European unity.[12]

At first the OEEC examined the various national plans of economic reconstruction and then worked out a programme of distribution of the American aid. From a legal point of view the important feature of the OEEC was its inter-governmental structure. The sovereignty of each country was safeguarded and no political strings were attached, so much so that even Switzerland, sworn to perpetual neutrality, could participate. The Organization, which consisted of a

---

8   Lorette, op cit, p 22.
9   Ciamaga L, *Od wspolpracy do integracji* (1965), p 13.
10 Fikus, D *RWPG-Fakty* (1966), p 16.
11 See the Convention of 16 April 1948, TS 59 (1949); Cmnd 7796.
12 Grosser, A, *Les occidentaux, le pays d'Europe et les Etats-Unis depuis la guerre* (1978), p 224.

Council of Ministers, an Executive Committee and a Secretariat, survived the completion of the Marshall Plan. It embraced 18 countries, including West Germany since 1949 and Spain since 1959 and Yugoslavia represented by an observer. The OEEC could take decisions which were binding on members. It endeavoured to co-ordinate national economic policies and provide experts who serve in an advisory capacity in special fields, ie transport, electricity, textiles, etc. It even tried to bring together rival groups like the EEC and the EFTA.

From its inception the OEEC endeavoured to liberalize European trade. It brought about a reduction of import quotas without tampering with the customs laws, which resulted in a short-lived trade boom. In 1952 the United Kingdom and France, contrary to the OEEC's advice, lapsed into import quotas and so exposed the weakness of the Organization. As new forms of economic co-operation began to take shape, the OEEC exhausted its usefulness. In 1961 it was transformed into an Organization for Economic Co-operation and Development (OECD)[13] for the purpose of assisting the developing countries. The European countries were joined by the USA and Canada as well as the EEC in its corporate capacity, ie independently of its members.

F.   The Council of Europe

Parallel to this economic co-operation there was a movement towards political and military integration. The various European movements joined forces in a Congress of Europe held in May 1948 in The Hague under the presidency of Winston Churchill. This resulted in the Council of Europe, inaugurated in 1949 at Strasbourg. It started with the five countries of the Brussels Military Alliance (now the Western European Union), viz the UK, France, Belgium, Holland and Luxembourg, and now embraces 26 countries of Western Europe including Spain and Portugal, which were originally excluded; Greece, suspended from membership in 1967 and readmitted in 1974; San Marino, which joined in 1989, and East European countries. Political changes in Eastern Europe towards the end of 1989, opened the way for further enlargement and for making the Council of Europe truly 'European'.

The Council of Europe[14] consists of a Consultative Assembly composed of parliamentary delegates of the Member States, a Committee of Ministers and a Secretariat. It has a permanent seat at Strasbourg. As a political design it has proved a failure since it has not developed beyond the nuclear stage of a federal organization. Its main achievements lie in the field of human rights, having established a Commission and a Court of Human Rights. But, above all, it has kept the idea of a United Europe alive.

In the economic field the Consultative Assembly in 1951 formulated proposals to turn Europe into a 'low tariff club' through the lowering of customs barriers. It also put forward, under the name of the 'Strasbourg Plan', ideas for the economic development of the former colonies of the European powers and for the adoption of preferential tariffs between these territories; the British Commonwealth on the one hand and the European countries on the other. Further initiatives aimed at the organization of European agriculture (the so-called 'green pool') and transport. However the economic initiatives of the Council of Europe

---

13   See the Convention of 14 December 1960. TS 21 (1962); Cmnd 1646.
14   See the Statute of the Council of Europe, TS 51 (1949); Cmnd 7778.

have been superseded by the EC and its political initiatives remained in an embryonic stage, though the Council provides a forum for cultural and political contacts extending beyond the membership of the EC and so preserves the concept of European unity.

G.   The North Atlantic Treaty Organization and transport

NATO developed from the North Atlantic Treaty of 1949[15] which was an extension of the Brussels Treaty of 1948.[16] It now embraces all the West European countries (except Austria, Ireland, Sweden and Switzerland) as well as the USA, Canada, Greece and Turkey. France has withdrawn from NATO but remains party to the North Atlantic Treaty. It is important to note that, without a surrender of sovereignty, decisions[17] within NATO are taken collectively and that this co-operation, though confined to military matters, contributes to the cohesion of Western Europe.

In another technical field, that of transport, the Conference of European Ministers of Transport has for some years now achieved rationalization of railway transport and, incidentally, enabled the 17 countries involved to make substantial economies. This means that railway carriages marked EUROP can be used and repaired anywhere within the organization and need not be returned empty to their countries of origin. Complementing EUROP is EUROFIMA (*Société de financement de matériel ferroviaire*), which by international agreement is entitled to exemption from customs and taxes in respect of railway equipment no matter where it is ultimately used within the organization. The more complex problem of the rationalization of transport by road, sea and air has recently been tackled by the EEC.

However, following the radical changes in West-East relations and the mutual reduction of arms programme, NATO is being adapted to a new rôle. When it has outlived its usefulness defence may well fall within the domain of the European Community as mooted in the Maastricht Treaty.

H.   The Benelux union

For the purpose of customs, the three countries (Belgium, Netherlands, Luxembourg) have become one. This has been achieved by stages in spite of the disparity of their economic systems and policies. As from 1 January 1948 they removed customs barriers between themselves and agreed upon common customs tariffs vis-à-vis the outside world. In 1951 they adopted a common scheme of customs and excise duties, with the exception of excise on alcohol, sugar and petrol. In 1954 they authorized a free flow of capital, which meant a freedom of investment and unrestricted transfer of currency within the three countries. Since 1956 they have entered into common commercial treaties with other countries and accepted a free movement of labour among themselves. In 1958 they signed a treaty of economic union which came into force on 17 November 1960. From

---

15   See the Treaty of 4 April 1949; TS 56 (1949); Cmnd 7789.
16   See the Treaty of Economic, Social and Cultural Collaboration and Collective Self-Defence of 17 March 1948; TS 1 (1949); Cmnd 7599.
17   NATO handbook (1978), p 39.

that date the economy of the Benelux countries was geared to the basic assumptions of an internal market, that is the removal of customs barriers, resulting in free movement of goods and the free movement of capital and manpower. These three elements were adopted later on for the formation of the EEC by the Treaty of Rome.

The Benelux union did not destroy the national sovereignty of the three countries or affect their identity as subjects of international law. Though economic integration led inevitably to a greater cohesion in a political and military sense, each country has preserved its political and legal system. The economic integration of the Benelux countries was not a painless operation, for there were rival interests of industries across the borders. However, as a result, the internal trade of these countries increased by 50% whereas their external trade jumped to fifth place after the USA, the UK, West Germany and Canada, thus surpassing France even though the population of France was twice that of the Benelux countries.

From 1948 to 1956 the national revenue of Belgium and the Netherlands increased considerably and so did their trade with the outside world. This minute Common Market proved to be profitable, not only to the three countries but also to others. Its unqualified success whetted the appetites of neighbouring states and led to the projection of the experiment on a European scale.

I.   The Schuman Plan

Robert Schuman and Count Sforza thought that a customs union between France and Italy would be beneficial to both countries. A customs treaty was signed in 1949 but both countries lacked the will to see it through. This failure indicated that a less ambitious approach, limited perhaps to one basic industry, should be attempted. Thus coal and steel was selected as the industry basic to many other industries and one especially relevant to the business of war. If war were to be eliminated coal and steel must be put under international control and if economic progress were to breach national frontiers this basic industry must be made to serve a community of nations.

This was not a novel philosophy, for back in 1948 the European Movement proclaimed at The Hague the need for an industrial programme especially for the production and distribution of coal. A year later, at Westminster, the European Movement proposed a scheme for several basic industries, ie coal, steel, electricity and transport, envisaging a European institution responsible for a general policy in respect of each of these four industries, especially in the field of investments, the volume of production and prices and a consultative body consisting of employers and employees as well as representatives of the public interest.

This, in turn, led to the so-called Schuman Plan. In May 1950 France, through its Minister of Foreign Affairs, Robert Schuman, proposed to place all the Franco-German production of coal and steel under a common authority and invited other countries to do the same. Schuman declared: '... Par la mise en commun de productions de base et par l'institution d'une Haute Autorité nouvelle, dont les décisions lieront la France, l'Allemagne et les pays qui adhéreront, cette proposition réalisera les premières assises concrètes d'une Fédération Européenne indispensable à la préservation de la paix ...'[18]

18   Lorette, op cit, p 38.

J. The European Coal and Steel Community

On 18 April 1951 the Ministers representing France, Germany, Italy, Belgium, Holland and Luxembourg signed in Paris a treaty which established the European Coal and Steel Community (*Communauté Européenne du Charbon et de l'Acier*). The Treaty was ratified, not without national opposition, eg it was ratified by the French Chamber of Deputies by 377 votes against 235 and by the Senate by 182 votes against 32. The industries concerned were unhappy as the Treaty was imposed upon them without prior consultation but it was, without doubt, a wise scheme.

The Treaty of Paris, this first instrument of European integration, was concluded for a period of fifty years from its entry into force and consists of 100 articles, three annexes, three protocols and a convention of transitory provisions. The most important feature of the Coal and Steel Community is its supra-national character. It is no longer an inter-governmental but a truly supra-national organization. It was aptly described[19] as a 'quasi federation in an important economic sector, the Member States retaining their sovereignty in all other sectors'.

Apart from supra-national organs the Community enjoyed a faculty of self-administration manifested in the choice and recruitment of officials, a financial autonomy marked by the power of levying taxes and a measure of self-control vested in a parliamentary assembly.

The Community was endowed with five organs:

(1) an executive, called the High Authority;
(2) a Consultative Committee attached to the High Authority;
(3) a Special Council of Ministers;
(4) an Assembly; and
(5) a Court of Justice.

The High Authority was the permanent executive of the Community. It consisted of nine members, eight chosen unanimously by the six governments and the ninth co-opted by the eight members to emphasize the supra-national character of the Community. A third of the High Authority retired every second year and was replaced by new members irrespective of nationality. The functions of the High Authority included the launching and management of a common market in coal and steel, development and control of investments and scientific research, action to curb unemployment, discrimination and restrictive practices, the imposition of common taxes upon the production of coal and steel; all this without reference to the governments of the Member States, subject only to responsibility to the Court and the Assembly. It is true that the field of independent action of the High Authority was restricted, but where it could act it took decisions which were binding upon the Member States.

The High Authority was assisted by a Consultative Committee consisting of representatives of employers, trade unions and consumers designated by the Special Council of Ministers on the advice of the trade unions and the producer and consumer organizations.

The Special Council of Ministers represented the sovereign power of the Member States. Its function was to harmonize the national economies on the

19 By Guy de Carmay, *Fortune d'Europe* (1953).

recommendation of the High Authority in the fields of coal and steel. Political control was in the hands of the Assembly of the Coal and Steel Community, which consisted of 68 members, of which France, Germany and Italy provided 18 each and the remaining 24 represented the Benelux countries. Members were elected by their national Parliaments though they could have been elected directly. The Assembly could dismiss the High Authority by a two-thirds majority and together with the Member States could propose amendments to the Treaty.

The Court consisted of seven members. Its function was to act as a watch-dog over the application of the Treaty, examine the decisions of the High Authority in the light of the Treaty provisions and adjudicate upon the alleged breaches of the Treaty. During the seven years of its existence the Court gave 137 decisions which were of considerable importance to the Community. These decisions had a binding force in the Member States. They are still relevant to Community law.

Several lessons could be drawn from this experiment. It proved that supra-national institutions could function in spite of diverse national interests; that far from being an economic disaster this first European common market greatly contributed to the economic progress of the Member States. The enlarged market activated industries far beyond those directly connected with coal and steel. The greatest benefit accrued to Italy, the economically weakest member. However, all was not well all the time. In 1959 there was a crisis in the coal industry caused mainly by over-production and an increase in the use of oil which rendered coal mines, especially in Belgium and Germany, redundant. The High Authority endeavoured to finance stock-piling, to reduce production and even to lower wages, but the Council of Ministers refused to sanction these measures clearly because national interests were at stake. The High Authority was, therefore, forced to provide a special aid to Belgium, which was hit very badly, for the rehabilitation and retraining of miners and to restrict imports from outside the Community. The very existence of the Community enabled it to relieve at least one country but it also became clear that there must be a common European policy in the field of energy. Whilst the Community was successful in its field it was not able to cope with other economic problems and its limited success certainly did not satisfy those who worked for a United Europe in their lifetime.

K.   Towards the Treaties of Rome

The greater integration of Europe owes a great deal to military considerations for it is evident that military alliances have political and economic consequences.

The problem of the defence of Western Europe, especially the American insistence on the participation of Germany in the defence of the Continent, raised delicate political and economic questions. The Germans were doing well without having to spend vast sums on defence, yet there was an aversion to their having a finger on the common trigger and some fear of the revival of German military might. These fears were assuaged partly by the international control of coal and steel, partly by the pacific stance of the German people. However, in view of the cost of defence, it was quite inequitable that Germany should be shielded by her neighbours at their expense. A German contribution had to be sought within an international framework. France, especially, insisted on supra-national control of the armed forces and so in 1952 the European Defence Treaty was signed.

The Treaty envisaged a European Defence Community as a kind of federation without a central federal government. The organization was to consist of a

Commissariat, an Assembly, a Council of Ministers and a Court of Justice, all modelled upon the Coal and Steel Community. It is interesting to note that whilst internationalist France actively promoted the idea it was nationalist France which wrecked the edifice, as on 30 August 1954 the French National Assembly refused to ratify the treaty already ratified by the other countries.

The failure to create a European Army led to the London Conference in September 1954 which resulted in turn in the admission of Italy and West Germany to the alliance by virtue of the Protocols to the Brussels Treaty signed in Paris in October 1954. The Final Act of the London Conference gave birth to yet another organization, the Council of Western European Union embracing the United Kingdom, Belgium, Holland, Luxembourg, France, Germany and Italy. It has subsequently passed through certain mutations but achieved no prominence apart from defence in the NATO setting though logically it brought the United Kingdom into the process of West European integration. However, it is likely to be revived if the reforms of NATO result in lesser dependence on the USA and the Maastricht provisions are developed.

For a while the unionist movement lay dormant, though on the Continent there were encouraging stirrings among the various industries, especially agriculture and the trade unions. The idea was resurrected at the meeting of the Foreign Ministers of the six members of the Coal and Steel Community in June 1955 at Messina. They were unanimous in their resolve to pursue the concept of an economic union and they were encouraged to do so by the governments of the Benelux countries.

At the outset of the Conference the Ministers proclaimed their intention to 'pursue the establishment of a United Europe through the development of common institutions, a progressive fusion of national economies, the creation of a Common Market and harmonization of social policies'.[20] During the Conference the Ministers became more precise as they considered that a 'constitution of a European Common Market must be their objective' though they realized that this could only be achieved by stages. To do this, again on the advice of the Benelux countries, the Ministers set up an Inter-Governmental Committee to study the various problems. The United Kingdom was invited to attend and indeed a minor official from the Board of Trade took part in the preliminary discussions.

In July 1955 the Committee met in Brussels with the object of co-ordinating the work of the various sub-committees set up to study the problems of investment, social policy, fuel and power, atomic energy and transport. The work continued during the summer and autumn of 1955 and among the sixty or so experts there were representatives of the Coal and Steel Community, the Organization for European Co-operation, the Council of Europe and, for a while, of the United Kingdom. Then followed a period of considerable activity and several meetings of the Foreign Ministers of the six countries. Reports of experts were considered, and finally a treaty was drafted and signed in Rome on 25 March 1957. This was the first Treaty of Rome which established the European Economic Community. The Treaty consists of 248 articles, four appendices, nine protocols and a convention relating to the association with the Community of the Overseas Countries and Territories which have special relations with Belgium, France, Italy and the Netherlands.

The second Treaty of Rome, setting up the European Community of Atomic Energy (Euratom) was signed on the same day. It consists of 225 articles, five appendices and one protocol.

---

20   Quoted by Lorette, op cit, p 60.

Both treaties had to be ratified by the parliaments of the signatory states. The respective reactions of these parliaments are worthy of comparison. In Germany both Houses of Parliament ratified the Treaties unanimously. In Belgium in the Chamber of Deputies 174 voted for and four against ratification; in the Senate 134 for and two against. In France in the Chamber of Deputies 342 voted for and 239 against the ratification; in the Senate 222 for and 70 against. In Italy in the Chamber of Deputies 311 voted for and 144 against the ratification; the Senate voted unanimously for ratification. In Luxembourg 46 votes were cast for and three against ratification. In the Netherlands in the Chamber of Deputies 114 votes were cast for and 12 against ratification; in the Senate 44 for and five against. The numerical opposition in France and Italy is significant but can easily be explained by the existence of large Communist Parties in those countries and the attitude of the mother-country of Communism to European Unity.[1]

The Treaties became operative on 1 January 1958.

L.   The three communities

The two Treaties of Rome added two new Communities to the Coal and Steel Community.

The European Atomic Energy Community (Euratom) was created as a specialist market for atomic energy. Atomic energy is a relatively new source of power with a virtually unlimited potential. It is hoped, therefore, that it will satisfy the demands of our technological era. In the 1960s the Six imported about a quarter of their energy from countries outside the Community. By 1975, it was considered, they would have to import 40% of their needs unless atomic energy took over from the traditional sources of power. However this target was not realized as in 1973 the Community was importing some 63% of its energy and the oil crisis aggravated the situation. A common energy policy embracing Euratom for which the Community has been striving, albeit without success, has become not only a matter of economic urgency but also a factor in European integration.

The object of Euratom is to develop nuclear energy, distribute it within the Community and sell the surplus to the outside world. In view of the development costs involved the Community must collectively engage in the necessary research and disseminate the accumulated knowledge. It must develop industry in a rational way ensuring a fair distribution within the Community and, finally, it must, as a body, consider the international implications of the peaceful use of nuclear energy. In many respects Euratom corresponds to the Coal and Steel Community.

The objectives of the European Economic Community (EEC) are wider than the objectives of the remaining two Communities, for the EEC is not a mere specialist organization but an instrument of progressive economic integration with a corresponding political potential. Therefore, whilst bearing in mind the three separate juristic entities, the EEC is by far the most important and may be regarded as a prototype of an integrated European Community.

M.   The merger of the communities' institutions

The main institutions of the ECSC, as we have seen, were five in number: an executive body known as the High Authority; a Consultative Committee; a Special

---

1   'Soviet unease over UK entry', *European Community* (February 1972), p 16.

Council made up of the representatives of the governments of the Member States; a Parliamentary Assembly made up of representative parliamentarians of the national parliaments of the Member States; and a Court of Justice. When the EEC and Euratom were established, their institutions were modelled upon those of the ECSC and this naturally suggested the merger of the separate institutions so as to avoid a multiplicity of institutions responsible for the achievement of similar tasks. This merger has taken place in two stages.

A Convention relating to certain institutions common to the European Communities was concluded simultaneously with the Rome Treaties and provided for the establishment of a single Court of Justice and a single Parliamentary Assembly to serve all three Communities. The completion of this process of institutional merger was not immediately realized, with the result that for some years each of the Communities retained its own executive body (High Authority in the case of the ECSC and Commissions in the case of the EEC and Euratom) and Council. This institutional separatism resulted from the adoption of a functional approach to European integration; three Communities were established by separate treaties and charged with the achievement of specific objectives. Further, the role of the Commissions and Councils in relation to the EEC and Euratom differed significantly from that of the High Authority and Special Council in relation to the ECSC, and so in 1957 separate institutions seemed appropriate. In practice this separation was found to be unsatisfactory. Whilst the objectives of each Community are distinct they also overlap and form part of a larger economic whole. In several fields, such as coal and steel and atomic energy, it was desirable for the Communities to coordinate their policy; the existence of separate institutions, each with its own personnel with different views and ideas, militated against this. Eventually a treaty was signed in May 1965 and took effect on 1 July 1967, providing for further fusion of the Communities. This treaty instituted a single Commission to replace the High Authority of the ECSC and the Commissions of the EEC and Euratom, and a single Council to replace the separate Councils of the three Communities.

This 'Merger Treaty', which completed the institutional merger of the three Communities, represented a further step towards the eventual merger of the Communities to form a single European Community.

N.   The United Kingdom and European solidarity

The United Kingdom has contributed to European solidarity (particularly in the field of military co-operation) but has tended to remain aloof. It is true that in 1946 in his famous Zurich speech Winston Churchill urged the establishment of a United States of Europe based on a partnership between France and Germany. But the rôle which he assigned to the United Kingdom was that of a friend and sponsor of the new Europe, clearly a rôle which fell far short of full participation.[2]

Successive British post-war governments adopted a lukewarm and sceptical attitude towards developments on the Continent. There were, perhaps, two main reasons for this. In the first place, unlike her continental allies, Britain had not endured defeat and enemy occupation. Although she had suffered economically

---

2   Kitzinger, U, *The European Common Market and Community* (1967), p 37.

as a result of the war, British institutions and the British way of life were not only preserved intact but could in a sense be said to be triumphant. From such a standpoint the prospect of compromising British independence in favour of union with continental Europe was not very attractive. In addition, at that time Britain was still in possession of a considerable colonial empire to which, as well as to the independent members of the Commonwealth, she looked rather than to the Continent. There was also the special relationship which had been forged during the Second World War between Britain and the United States. The British attitude to European integration in the years immediately following the Second World War is, perhaps, summed up by the reaction of Ernest Bevin, when Foreign Secretary, to the proposal that Britain should participate in a European Assembly as part of the Council of Europe: 'I don't like it. I don't like it. If you open that Pandora's Box you will find it full of Trojan horses.'[3]

By the late 1950s exclusion from the advantages which became apparent within the Community and the fear that she might lose political influence made her realize that the idea of the European Community, far from being a failure, was a force to be reckoned with. The United Kingdom never joined the Coal and Steel Community (although she did establish a form of association with it) and cold-shouldered the Common Market negotiations. In 1957 Britain proposed a 'free trade area' (the so called Maudling Plan) and, when this failed, created a rival organization, the European Free Trade Association (EFTA) in 1959. However, in some respects EFTA, which embraced Austria, Denmark, Norway, Portugal, Sweden, Switzerland and the United Kingdom, proved less successful than the European Economic Community and a positive policy towards the European Community emerged.

In 1961 the Macmillan Government applied for membership of the EEC. The negotiations (the British team was headed by the Lord Privy Seal, Mr Edward Heath) dragged on, but when the British side, leaving some minor problems to further negotiations, was ready to sign in 1963 the French President, General de Gaulle, vetoed the British entry. In 1967 the Wilson government renewed the application but it was vetoed again by France before negotiations could take place. The third attempt was made by the Heath government in 1970 and the negotiations for entry were successfully concluded in January 1972.

Grand debates were held in Parliament and elsewhere during the summer and autumn of 1971 and the government mounted a massive information service. Opinion polls revealed a considerable opposition to British entry into Europe and party politics obscured the discussion on the merits of the entry. It transpired that the Labour Party, who would have been happy to accept the terms of the British accession when in power, was opposed to the terms when in opposition. The declared reasons that the situation had changed and that the country's economy did not warrant accession at this time, though hardly convincing, were vigorously advanced by the Labour Party opposition. Opponents in principle argued that there was little advantage in accession to the Community, whilst the surrender of sovereignty was an unforgivable folly. On 28 October 1971 the government secured a reasonable majority[4] with the support of the Liberals and Labour dissenters from the official party policy who voted for the entry in principle but pledged themselves to oppose the consequential legislation. The

---

3 Robertson, A H, *The Council of Europe* (2nd edn, 1961), p 6, n 23.
4 823 HC Official Report (5th series) col 2212.

historic decision, which merited a national unity, was soured by the antics of party politics. On 20 January 1972 the eleventh-hour attempt to prevent the signing of the Treaty of Accession until the full text 'has been published and its contents laid before the House' failed, but the vote on the motion produced a majority of only 21 for the government,[5] the Conservative opponents abstaining and the Labour members voting under a three-line whip.

Because of the lack of bi-partisan policy the British participation in the Community depends much upon the party political game. Indeed the Labour Party opposition announced, in its electoral manifesto of 1974, that when returned to power it would embark upon 'fundamental re-negotiations' of the condition of entry.[6] Such negotiations did take place though it was difficult to see the real purpose other than to keep faith with the electorate and to placate the opposition within the party. The government advice that, on balance, Britain should remain in the Community was endorsed by a two-thirds majority of the electorate in what became a novel constitutional experiment: a 'consultative referendum' of 1975. However the party never adopted any constructive attitude whilst the Labour government failed to play a positive role or to demonstrate a European conviction. Moreover, when, again in opposition, the party at its annual conferences in 1980, 1981 and 1982 voted for withdrawal from the Community this, according to a Shadow Foreign Secretary in 1981, was to be done without a referendum. Only after the general election of 1983 some leading members of the Labour Party recognized, at the 1983 annual conference, that withdrawal might not be a realistic proposition. Indeed the question of membership was no longer a prominent issue at subsequent conferences, though in 1985 the leader of the 32-strong British Labour Party in the European Parliament declared that 'as a committed anti-marketeer, I will continue to campaign for withdrawal'.[7]

However, making party political capital of the unpopularity of the Thatcher government in the late 1980s the Labour Party, in opposition, turned to Europe partly out of conviction, but also to resume the traditional role of the opposition. At last, the two major parties appeared to be broadly in agreement, subject to dissenting factions, either in principle or detail.

Conservative governments proved in the past more positive though quite reticent on the question of political integration and reluctant, for example, to join the European Monetary System so essential for the achievement of the Common Market. They wrenched out of the Community a correction of the disproportionate British budgetary contribution but have managed so far to achieve only a partial reform in the two areas of major British concern: the Community Budget and the Common Agricultural Policy.

The United Kingdom has proved a difficult and somewhat cool partner. Both major political parties are much to blame, primarily for the lack of a national policy for Europe and the lack of a clear vision of the Community as well as of the rôle this country ought to play in European integration. Mr Major's claim that 'Britain is in the heart of Europe' and Mr Blair's assurance of a positive stand on Europe remain yet to be proved to the satisfaction of continental Europeans. In fact, in view of the self-imposed isolation of the United Kingdom the leadership of European integration got into the hands of the Franco-German alliance.

5   829 HC Official Report (5th series) col 800.
6   Lasok, D, 'Some Legal Aspects of Fundamental Re-negotiations' (1976) 5 EL Rev 375.
7   As reported in *Europe*, 13 June 1985, p 4.

O.   The Treaties of Accession

In simple legal terms the first Treaty of Accession,[8] signed on 22 January 1972 on behalf of the six Member States, the Communities (represented by Mr Gaston Thorn, Foreign Minister of Luxembourg and President of the Council of Ministers) and the four prospective members Denmark, Ireland, Norway and the United Kingdom, is a Treaty signifying admission of new members to the three Communities. However, only three joined since Norway, in view of the adverse result of the national referendum, was unable to accede. The Treaty, being a prototype of subsequent accession treaties, consists of three articles stating that the new members accede to the existing Communities and accept all their rules. A lengthy Act, signed at the same time, confirmed the results of the negotiations and gave details of what membership entailed. Full membership as from 1 January 1973 was conditional upon the incorporation of the Community law into the municipal laws of the new members. The period of transition was completed on 1 July 1977, which meant that as from that date the Community of Nine was fully established.

We shall discuss elsewhere the effects of the Treaty for the United Kingdom and the Community. It will suffice to say, at this stage, that neither the texts of the founding Treaties nor the institutions established under these Treaties were radically changed, though they were adjusted to give effect to the enlarged membership.

The second Treaty of Accession[9] heralded the admission of Greece as the tenth member as from 1 January 1981, the period of transition to be completed in the main by 1 January 1991.

The third Treaty of Accession,[10] signed on 12 June 1985, brought Spain and Portugal into the Community of Twelve. Subject to a complex transitory regime, these two countries, associated with the Community since 1970 and 1972 respectively, became full members as from 1 January 1986.

Austria formally applied to join the Communities in July 1989, followed by Sweden (July 1991), Finland (March 1992), Switzerland (May 1992) and Norway (November 1992). Norway (once an applicant in the first enlargement), Sweden, Finland and Austria were all four deserting EFTA and the European Economic Area (EEA) which they formed with the EEC only in October 1991. In the event, the applications of Norway and Switzerland proved abortive (the former only after a referendum in which 52.2% voted against membership). Austria, Sweden and Finland formally joined with effect from 1 January 1995. Ironically the United Kingdom, which championed the enlargement of the Community (in preference to 'deepening' the process of integration), mounted a lacklustre opposition to the emerging pattern of the voting system in the enlarged Community by insisting that, as hitherto, 23 votes ought to be sufficient to block decisions of the qualified majority instead of 27 as arithmetic would suggest. It had to back down.

The applications of Turkey and Morocco were met by a negative opinion of the Commission in 1989 nearly two years after they were made. Cyprus and Malta too were disappointed, Cyprus[11] because it was considered that the two communities of the divided island would have to be reconciled (which is unlikely to happen in

8   TS 16 (1979); Cmnd 7461.
9   OJ 1979, L2 91/9; EC 18 (1979); Cmnd 7650.
10   OJ 1985, L302/1; EC 27 (1985); Cmnd 9634.
11   Bull 6–1993 point 1.3.6; Suppl 5/93 and xxiv Gen Report point 722.

the near future) and Malta because her economy was found deficient.[12] The applications of Hungary and Poland (31 March and 8 April 1994, respectively) appear to be too optimistic to prognosticate an early or even eventual success. Nonetheless, accession negotiations with those countries and Cyprus, the Czech Republic, Estonia and Slovenia began in March 1998. In the case of Bulgaria, Latvia, Lithuania, Romania and the Slovak Republic, it was decided in 1997 that the Commission should re-examine the case for accession on an annual basis. In October 1999, the Commission proposed opening accession talks in 2000 and that Turkey should be regarded as a candidate for accession. Thus the Community/Union appeared to be poised for consolidation come the end of the millennium.

P.   Towards European Union

Over the years the outward expansion of the Community was accompanied by inner growth and consolidation though not at the speed and on the scale the integrationists would have liked. Indeed the projected evolution from the stage of the Common Market to that of the Economic Union has proved slow and disappointing since not even all the objectives of the Common market have been achieved as planned. The Monetary Policy, mooted as early as 1964[13] and proposed in earnest in 1971 and 1972[14] to be completed by 31 December 1980, failed to produce a European Monetary System indispensable to a coherent policy and economic integration. In 1985[15] the White Paper from the Commission to the European Council drew particular attention to the scale of unachieved Treaty objectives and pointed the way to their achievement by 1992, that is, 35 years since the signing of the Treaty of Rome.

However, on the positive side, there has been a growing awareness of the Community spirit and hitherto unprecedented political co-operation. The constitution of the Community has also experienced change. The decision of the Council of Ministers of 20 September 1976[16] to carry out the Treaty promise of direct elections to the European Parliament resulted in 1979 in a fundamental reform of that institution. Instead of being a body of delegates from national legislatures the Parliament is now truly representative of 'Euro-constituencies' and the national political parties. This has enhanced the legitimacy of that institution and, having raised its prestige, opened up the way to a more active and influential participation in the life of the Community.

The process of integration initiated by the institutional merger proved to be a harder task than imagined. An evolutionary approach was advocated in this respect in the Tindemans Report[17] published in January 1976. It postulated a gradual development towards European Union building on the existing institutions and the practices which have evolved outside the Treaty framework. The Report envisaged a closer co-operation between the Member States, notably a co-ordination of their foreign policy and regular meetings of heads of

---

12   Bull 6–1993 point 1.3.7; Suppl 4.93 and xxiv Gen Report 724.
13   Council Decision 64/301; OJ 1964, p 1207; (Sp Ed 1963–64, p 143).
14   Council Resolutions, Compendium of Community Monetary Texts, 1979, pp 25, 30, 33.
15   COM (85) 310 Final.
16   OJ 1976, L278/1.
17   Based on the recommendation of the Heads of State or Government meeting in Paris in December 1974; EC Bull Supp 1/76; Mitchell, J D B, 'The Tindemans Report – Retrospect and Prospect' (1976) 13 CML Rev 455.

government acting as the 'European Council'. It proposed 'to put an end to the distinction which still exists between ministerial meetings which deal with political co-operation and those which deal with the subjects covered by the Treaty'. It proposed to strengthen the rôle of the European Council by making the Council of Ministers for Foreign Affairs responsible for the preparation of its meetings and by the European Council indicating the institution or organization responsible for the execution of its decisions.

The Report emphasized further the need to develop a common foreign policy together with extended external economic relations and a common defence policy and to convert policy commitments into 'legal obligations'. It advocated recourse to majority voting in the Council as a 'normal practice of the Community'. Avoiding any rigid timetable or development by stages, the Report suggested a 'two-speed plan of economic integration' in which the so-called 'weaker members', ie Ireland, Italy and the United Kingdom, should proceed at a slower pace than the others. The idea proved quite unrealistic.

The failure of the Tindemans Report prompted the Brussels European Council of 1978 to ask 'The Three Wise Men'[18] to prepare another report on the political reform of the European Community.[19] This Report,[20] presented to the European Council in October 1979, listed the failures of the Community in carrying out its original and new policies. 'The reasons', it held, 'lie rather in political circumstances and attitudes that sometimes produced conflicting conceptions of the right way forward, and sometimes produced no clear conceptions at all ...'[1] Only the European Council had made a significant contribution towards an improvement of the Community decision-making procedure in so far as it became 'an escape from the bureaucracy weighing down the other institutions in order to provide leadership and guidance'.[2] The Three Wise Men thought that 'the principle needs to be affirmed yet again that the Commission is the natural executive organ of the Community'.[3] They rejected the idea of a 'two-speed integration' and appealed for solidarity in the face of economic recession.[4]

These and other initiatives had no real impact but the bold 'Draft Treaty establishing the European Union',[5] triggered off action which ultimately resulted in the passing of the Single European Act in 1986. The Draft Treaty, also known by its chief architect as the Spinelli Report, revived the idea of European federalism but was clearly ahead of its time. It consisted of 87 articles divided into five parts dealing with the Union; the objectives, methods of action and competences of the Union; institutional provisions; the policies of the Union; and the finances of the Union, respectively. Reflecting a federalist concept, the Draft Treaty purported to move the Community to the status of a European Union as envisaged in the Treaties establishing the European Communities and confirmed by the Conference of the Heads of State or Government of 20 October 1972 and in the Solemn Stuttgart Declaration of 19 June 1983. In order to achieve this objective the Draft proposed a redistribution of powers, especially the law-making function, from the Council of Ministers to the Parliament and the Commission, a diminution of

---

18   Borend Biesheuval, Edmund Dell, Robert Marjolin.
19   EC Bull 12/78, p 97.
20   Duff, A N, 'The Report of the Three Wise Men', Jo Common Market Studies, Vol XIX (1981), 237 et seq.
1   At p 19.
2   At p 9.
3   At p 72.
4   At pp 89–91.
5   Capotorti, F, et al, *Le Traité d'Union Européenne* (1985) (Text and Commentary).

the blocking powers of Member States in the decision-making process, and the imposition of sanctions on the Member States for serious and persistent breaches of their duties. The federalist shift was marked by the enhanced status of the Union in relation to the Member States; increased powers of the Parliament; increased supervisory powers of the Court of Justice (including appeals against the decisions of national courts); the adoption of the European Monetary System; and a common citizenship of the Union for the citizens of the Member States coupled with effective protection of fundamental rights derived from the common principles of the Member States' constitutions and the European Convention for the Protection of Human Rights and Fundamental Freedoms.

The Draft Treaty was welcomed by six of the ten national parliaments; the Danish Folketing rejected it, whilst a non-committal attitude pending parliamentary scrutiny was adopted in Greece, Ireland and the United Kingdom. At the Fontainebleau European Council in the summer of 1984 two ad hoc committees, one on 'institutional affairs' and another on a 'people's Europe', were set up. Known by the names of their chairmen as the Dooge and the Adonnino Committee, respectively, these Committees presented their reports and recommendations to the Milan European Council of June 1985. The former proposed, in particular, that decisions should normally be taken by a qualified or simple majority; that the Commission's powers should be strengthened; that the Parliament should be given a wider rôle in the decision-making process; and that the Court of Justice's extended powers should include the protection of fundamental rights guaranteed within the Community's legal framework. It recommended the convention of an inter-governmental conference 'to negotiate a Draft European Union Treaty'. Despite the British, Danish and Greek opposition the Council decided by a majority to convene such a conference by reference to Article 236 of the EEC Treaty. It also accepted the Commission's White paper (mentioned above) containing recommendations for the completion of the internal market and the strengthening of Community technological co-operation.

At the General Affairs Council of July 1985 Foreign Ministers agreed the details of the inter-governmental conference under the Luxembourg Presidency with the twin objectives defined by the Milan Council, ie the revision of the Rome Treaties and the drafting of a treaty on political co-operation and European security. However, the results of the many years of debate are disappointing since the Single European Act,[6] which emerged in 1986, far from advancing the federal concept of the Spinelli Report, consists merely of a number of significant, but nevertheless cosmetic, reforms.

Since the effects of the Single Act shall be mentioned in the relevant chapters it will suffice to observe that it is merely one of the landmarks in the long road towards the European Union. Structurally, its main merit was the simultaneous reform of the three Treaties establishing the Three Communities for it further advanced the concept of one Community. It affirmed the fine resolution to progress towards European unity but it remained silent as regards its meaning and scope and, in its contents, fell short of the Spinelli Report.

However, it made certain adjustments to the powers and functions of the institutions, laid down a 'co-operation procedure' which enhanced the influence of the Parliament on the Council's decisions and, whilst retaining the principle of unanimity, it moved further towards qualified majority in the decision-making

---

6 Single European Act and Final Act, European Communities No 12 (1986); HMSO, Cmnd 9578; See H C Foreign Affairs Committee, Session 1985–86, HMSO 442; H L Select Committee on the European Communities, Session 1985–86, 12th Report, HMSO (HL 149).

process of the Council. It provided for a more efficient functioning of the internal market and laid down foundations for a joint formulation and implementation of European foreign policy, linking it with security.

The founding Treaties were amended by the Single European Act 1986 and the process continued as a result of the summit meetings held in Madrid (26–27 June 1989), Strasbourg (December 1989) and Dublin (25–26 June 1990) at which it was decided (not without opposition) to move towards the Economic and Monetary Union and to call an inter-governmental conference on the Political Union, respectively.

The Madrid meeting revealed considerable disagreement over the Commission's proposals for the Economic and Monetary Union as well as the Social Charter. In view of the British opposition a compromise was reached on the former but the latter was shelved. It was agreed, though, at Dublin, to implement the Economic and Monetary Union by stages and to call two parallel inter-governmental conferences on 14 December 1990, immediately after the Rome summit: one on the Political Union and the other on the Economic and Monetary Union; both, it was hoped, producing results by the end of 1992.

The reunification of Germany on 3 October 1990, preceded by the dramatic changes in Eastern Europe towards the end of 1989 and the collapse of the Soviet empire, had a profound impact on Europe as a whole. The cold war ended officially on 21 November 1990 with the signing in Paris by 32 European countries, the USA and Canada of the 'Paris Charter' on the occasion of the Conference on Security and Co-operation in Europe. By signing the 45-page Charter the signatories committed themselves to the principles of democracy, human rights, co-operation, social justice and economic freedom. The Charter incorporates also a promise to end coercion and discrimination, a joint effort to combat terrorism and to achieve a mutual and balanced force reduction.

The joining forces between the EEC and the EFTA (albeit without Switzerland which by national referendum on 6 December 1992 decided against ratification) to form a European Economic Area[7] was a promising venture. The agreement between these originally rival blocs begins an economic partnership between the free trade and common market philosophy as it extends most of the single market principles to the whole area. The political benefit of such a partnership is evident as it contributes in a significant measure to the construction of a United Europe.

Q.   The Maastricht Treaty and beyond

The Maastricht Treaty of the European Union (TEU) was signed in February 1992 with the hope that its ratification would coincide with the completion of the internal market by the end of 1992. However, following the negative referendum (50.7% against, 49.3% for) in Denmark the ratification had to be postponed so that the Danes, having gained concessions at the meeting of the European Council on 11–12 December 1992 in Edinburgh, could be coaxed into a more conciliatory mood. Thus on 18 May 1993 they reversed their previous decision by 56.7% voting for and 43.3% voting against. Only countries which expected to be the net beneficiaries of the new Treaty showed enthusiasm for the new order.[8] The United Kingdom lived through a court[9] case and bizarre scenes in the House of

7   Signed on 21 October 1991, entered into force on 1 January 1994.
8   France the self-proclaimed leader of Europe, managed only a 51.5% majority of the national referendum held in September 1992.
9   *R v Secretary of State for Foreign and Commonwealth Affairs, ex p Rees-Mogg* [1994] 1 All ER 457, QB.

Commons during the debates on the Bill of ratification where the opposition of the so-called Eurosceptics combined forces to embarrass the government whose leader proclaimed 'Britain to be in the heart of Europe'. Eventually the government succeeded on a vote of confidence and in the final voting the House of Commons approved the Bill by 292 votes to 112. The last country to complete the ratification process was Germany, following a positive judgment of the Constitutional Court on 12 October 1993, a year behind schedule.

The Maastricht Treaty, as the constitution of the Union,[10] is an inelegant document accompanied by some 17 Protocols and 33 Declarations, most of which aim to preserve certain national interests reflecting close negotiations. The most prominent of the latter are the Protocols concerning the derogations from the Treaty by Denmark and the United Kingdom.

The TEU consists of seven Titles with articles originally identified by capital letters to distinguish the numbering of the Treaties founding the three Communities. Title I (Articles A to F) contains Common Provisions. Title II (Article G) sets out amendments and additions to the EEC Treaty. Title III (Article H) and Title IV (Article I) respectively comprise amendments to the ECSC and Euratom Treaties. Title V (Articles J.1 to J.11) contains provisions on a common foreign policy and security policy and Title VI (Articles K.1 to K.9) provisions on co-operation in respect of justice and home affairs. Title VII (Articles L to S) contains the Final Provisions.

The Union rests on three 'pillars': amendments to the existing Community Treaties; provisions on a Common Foreign and Security Policy and provisions on Co-operation in the Fields of Justice and Home Affairs.

Founded on the European Communities,[11] the Union intends to build upon the *acquis communautaire*,[12] whilst being governed by the Community institutions[13] with the exception of the European Council, which is an institution of the Union and not of the Community.[14] Certain competences of the Union are outside the Community legal system and thus expressly excluded from the jurisdiction of the Court of Justice.[15] Justice and home affairs are reserved for co-operation among the Member States and common foreign and security policy are matters left to the Member States and to the Member States and the Union. They remain subject to inter-governmental relations of the Member States. The Treaty creates new institutions and extends the competences of the Community.

As from 1 January 1995 the Union of the twelve has become the Union of fifteen countries. By virtue of the fourth enlargement Austria, Finland and Sweden joined the Union but, in the case of Norway, history repeated itself as, like on the occasion of the first enlargement, the Norwegians in a national referendum invalidated their government's signature to the Treaty of Accession.

In the meantime work on Maastricht II continued with the object of improving the flawed Treaty. It was carried out through the mechanism of the Intergovernmental Conference acting under the auspices of the Madrid European Council (1995), followed in Turin (March 1996), Florence (June 1996) and Dublin (December 1996). The results were approved by the Amsterdam Council

---

10　For general critical comments see Everling, 'Reflections on the structure of the European Union', 29 CML Rev 1053–1077.
11　Art A (now 1).
12　Arts B and C (now 2 and 3). The acquis communautaire is the accumulated volume of Community law at any one time.
13　Arts C and E (now 3 and 5).
14　Art D (now 4).
15　Art L (now 46).

(June 1997) and on 2 October 1997 the Treaty of Amsterdam amending the Treaty on European Union, the Treaties establishing the European Communities and certain Related Acts was signed.

The Amsterdam Treaty is as unwieldy as its predecessor.[16] It consists of the amendments on the Treaty on European Union,[17] amendments of the Treaty establishing the European Community,[18] 13 Protocols, 51 Declarations, eight Declarations of which the Conference of Amsterdam took notice and a Declaration on the amendment of Article K.7 of the Treaty of European Union.

The specific provisions of the Treaty are comprised in six sections, ie Freedom, Security and Justice; the Union and the Citizen; Effective and Coherent External Policy; and Simplification and Consolidation of the relevant Treaties, including the Treaty on European Union. Since the parties have signed the treaty and not its consolidated version prepared by the Secretariat of the Council for 'illustrative purposes', the Treaty remains the formal source of law.

The Treaty of Amsterdam continues a dual approach to European integration distinguishing between 'the Union' which has no legal personality and the 'Community' whose legal personality has been impressed on the Treaties founding the three original Communities, although the same countries constitute both organizations. Thus separate provisions concerning the Union are marked by letters whereas the provisions concerning the Community are marked by numbers. The consolidated texts of the Treaty on European Union[19] and of the European Community[20] are numbered thus, replacing the lettered articles of the former and changing the numerical order of the latter. As a result of the consolidation the re-organised texts display a certain order but consolidation is likely to confuse the provisions concerning the Union and the Community since both are not numbered and the new numerical order no longer corresponds to the old one. It will therefore be necessary to identify the consolidated and the old order. Moreover, confusion arises from cross-references between the Union and the Community particularly where provisions regarding the Community refer to 'institutions of the Union'.

The main thrust of the new Treaty reflects a desire to present an attractive image of the Union to the peoples of Europe emphasising citizens' rights and concern with social problems, mainly unemployment. Looking forward to the next millennium the Treaty endeavours to strengthen the notion of the Union, improve its foreign policy and defence mechanism, develop co-operation in the field of justice and internal affairs and face the prospect of the enlargement of the Union. It also contains a divisive element in the shape of the new Title VI which encourages the Member States to develop close co-operation between themselves where the objectives of the Treaties cannot be achieved by applying the relevant Treaty procedures. Such action implies a greater degree of solidarity between certain countries but also undermines the process of European integration at equal pace and according to common constitutional principles.

The Protocol concerned with Institutions leaves the reform of the institutional structure to a later date when the membership of the Union has exceeded twenty. This is likely to occur early in the millennium. So far 11 countries are lined up

16   Kortenberg, H (pseudonym), 'La negotiation du Traité. Une vue cavalière,' Rev Trim de Droit Europeén, 4/1997 p 709 et seq.; Dehousse, F 'Le Traité d'Amsterdam, Reflet de la Nouvelle Europe', Cahiers de Droit Europeén, 3–4/1997, p 205 et seq; Lasok, D 'Special Commentary on the Treaty of Amsterdam'; Vaughan: Law of the European Communities (1997) p 1 et seq.
17   OJ 1997, C 340/145.
18   OJ 1997, C 340/173.
19   OJ 1997, C 340/152–172.
20   OJ 1997, C 340/181–302.

for negotiations. Of these, six countries (Czech Republic, Hungary, Poland, Estonia, Slovenia and Cyprus) were selected by the Luxembourg Council (December 1997) to begin negotiations in the Spring of 1998. Despite the political division of the island consisting of two de facto republics, Cyprus was included in the first wave of negotiations as one unit represented by the southern division as the Republic of Cyprus. Turkey, despite the Association Agreement of 1964, which envisaged membership of the Community,[1] though considered by the Luxembourg Council as 'eligible' was not included among either of the first or the second wave of applicants (ie Bulgaria, Romania, Slovakia, Latvia and Lithuania).

Verbose and repetitious, the Treaty of Amsterdam is studded with declarations of intent and proposed legislation but, although it lacks the quality expected of a constitutional instrument, it marks another milestone on the path leading to European unification. In the view of the French Conseil Constitutionnel it is unconstitutional[2] as it conflicts with the exercise of national sovereignty. However, the last instrument of Ratification of the Amsterdam Treaty was deposited on 30 March 1999 and the Treaty came into force on 1 May 1999. Barely had that been done when the European Council announced the convening of an Intergovernmental Conference in early 2000 in order to resolve outstanding institutional issues that need to be settled before any further enlargement of the European Union. The Conference opened formally in February 2000 with the intention of adopting amendments to the Treaties by December 2000. The amendments were at the time of writing intended to be set out in a new Treaty to be signed at Nice and would include a charter of fundamental rights.[3]

Speculation about the future of Europe reflects two broad questions, ie whether the Community should continue as an organization of sovereign states or should become a community of peoples disregarding national boundaries and sovereignties and thus adopt a federal form. There is also a question of the method to be applied. Here we can see a sharp conflict between the evolutionary-pragmatic approach rooted in the common law philosophy and the doctrinaire-formalistic approach of the civil law system. Both reflect different historical experiences and different constitution-making processes. The former insists on a gradual step-by-step development building upon the completion of the programmes laid down in the Treaties; the latter takes a more radical and imaginative view, contending that a constitution is not merely a record of achievements but also an expression of a vision and aspirations. Although the former lacks the drama and the rhetoric of the Latin races, it may prove more realistic, because politics is the art of the possible. On the other hand, behind the smokescreen of idealism there lurks the hard reality of national interests and the fact that implementation and enforcement of obligations is more onerous than a declaration of intent or expectations.

With the still unfinished programme of the Maastricht Treaty it is a matter of conjecture whether the Amsterdam Treaty will speed up or retard the consolidation of the Union of today and whether further enlargement, diluting the present concept of the Community, will replace it with a larger vision of a united Europe from the straits of Gibraltar to the Urals or, perhaps, will lead to a Europe of varied geometry, consisting of an inner club and peripheral membership. At the start of a new millennium we have the world's largest trading unit with a population of some 370 million, consisting of 15 states of different sizes, common yet diverse, cultural heritages, wealth and aspirations, and still a European Union in the making.

1   Lasok, D, et al, *Turkey and the European Community* (1993), p 23 et seq.
2   Chaltiel, F, 'Commentaire de la decision du Conseil Constitutionnel relative au Traité d'Amsterdam', Rev. du Marché Commun No 415 (1998) p 73 et seq.
3   See the Appendix.

Chapter 2

The concept and status of the European Communities and of the European Union

A. The European Community and the Union

(1) WHAT IS IN THE NAME?

The European Community is a result of international solidarity which we have considered in the light of post-war developments in international relations, and of the conscious effort to create a kind of unity in Western Europe. When political unification proved premature the architects of the Community seized upon the economic elements of inter-state relations and built these into the three 'Communities' (Coal and Steel, Euratom and EEC), so much so that within the vague notion of a political Community we have three legally definable treaty-based 'Communities'.

The Single European Act (1986) by simultaneously amending the three founding Treaties (ECSC, EEC and EURATOM) contributed to the notion of a single European Community but, formally, by virtue of TEU Article 1 the High Contracting parties established among themselves a European Community. Thus it is legitimate to consider that the three Communities have been absorbed in the notion of the European Community (EC), and the ECSC, EEC and EURATOM Treaties should be cited only in a historical context. Moreover, the EC has become the substratum of the European Union, since, according to the Treaty on the Union[1] 'the Union shall be founded on the European Communities, supplemented by the policies and forms of co-operation established by the Treaty'. Thus the trinitary concept of the Community has been remodelled simply by enlarging its competences and creating new ones which transcend the economic vocation of the Community and which are in the gestion of the Union established by

---

1   Art 1, para 3 (ex Art A, para 3). Where the Amsterdam Treaty has renumbered a Treaty provision, the original number of the provision will be referred to in brackets preceded by 'ex': The Treaty in question will be indicated by the initials of the Treaty preceding the number of the provision.

TEU Article 1.[2] As a result the Community and the Union co-exist in the peculiar process of European integration.

'This Treaty marks a new stage in the process of creating an ever closer union among the peoples of Europe, in which decisions are taken as closely as possible to the citizen'.[3] In the context of Article 1 the Union signifies the emerging polity but the word 'union' emphasizes the alliance or co-operation of the peoples of Europe. In the context of the Community the decision-making process results from the inter-institutional co-operation regulated by the Treaty but in the context of the Union decisions are taken by the intergovernmental conference, also regulated by the Treaty. As for the decisions in the context of the Union to be taken 'closely to the citizen' the provision appears ambiguous if not couched in the vacuous language of public relations.

The relationship between the Community and the Union has been defined by the Treaty[4] which provides that 'The Union shall be served by a single institutional framework which shall ensure the consistency and the continuity of the activities carried out in order to attain its objectives while respecting and building upon the *acquis communautaire*'. This implies an evolving concept of the Community and of the Union leading eventually to the transmutation and consolidation of the Union as the ultimate form of European integration assuming, of course, that neither inner stagnation nor a global calamity shall frustrate the process.

Political scientists[5] who are always ahead of political reality, offer a variety of ideas of the emerging polity, but a blueprint, which can become the basis of discussion at a government level, has yet to come to light. Statesmen, unless constitution-makers, shall continue groping in the dark of negotiating corridors adjusting the existing Treaties. The result is a bizarre creature unlikely to have been designed by the Almighty but rather by a committee; though, like the unsightly camel, it is well adapted to survive in the desert of political ideas.

General de Gaulle spoke of a Europe of States and President Pompidou,[6] commenting on the challenge of the enlarged Community, spoke guardedly about a confederation. Monnet, one of the spiritual fathers of the Community, although a federalist at heart, was more guarded in his predictions, placing his optimism in a natural evolutionary process. If either of these statesmen were pressed to define their vision of Europe they probably would have taken refuge from the quip attributed to Napoleon that 'a constitution ought to be brief but ambiguous'.

Amsterdam, and for that matter Maastricht, does not make us wiser as Article 6(3)[7] simply states that 'The Union shall respect the national identities of its Member States', thus vaguely referring to a 'Europe of States'. Such identity can be accommodated in a concept of federation.

Occasionally the Community is described as a federation, the idea favoured by the Court of Justice, but the adjective 'federal' (though not the reality) was excised from the drafts of the Maastricht TEU.[8] Nevertheless the evolution of

---

2 Amsterdam, ex Art A.
3 Ibid.
4 Art 3(1), Amsterdam (ex TEU Art C(2)).
5 For a summary see: Pentland, C C, 'Political Theories of European Integration: Between Science and Ideology; in Lasok, D and Soldatos, P (ed), *Les Communautés en Fonctionnement* (1981), pp 546 et seq.
6 The Times, 12 May 1972.
7 Ex Art F(1).
8 See Art A(3) of the Draft 'Treaty on the Union', Working Document prepared by the Netherlands Presidency of the Council of Ministers on 12 and 13 November 1991: 'The Treaty marks a new stage in the process leading gradually to a Union with a federal goal'.

the Community, in view of the extended competences in the economic area and single currency and of the Union in the field of external policy and defence as well as in internal affairs and justice, points clearly towards a federal plan.

(2)   THE TASKS AND ACTIVITIES OF THE COMMUNITY

EC Articles 2 and 3 in the Amsterdam Version have reformulated and extended the tasks and activities of the Community originally set out in the corresponding provisions of the EEC Treaty. EC Article 2 (ex Art 2) adds to the establishment of the common market:

(1)   an economic and monetary union;
(2)   the implementation of common policies or activities set out in Articles 3 and 4;
(3)   the promotion of a harmonious, balanced and sustainable development of economic activities;
(4)   a high level of employment and social protection;
(5)   equality between men and women;
(6)   sustainable and non-inflationary growth;
(7)   a high degree of competitiveness and convergence of economic performance;
(8)   a high level of protection and improvement of the quality of the environment;
(9)   the raising of the standard of living and quality of life; and
(10) economic and social cohesion and solidarity among Member States.

EC Article 3 reiterates and considerably expands the activities of the Community providing for:

(a)   the prohibition, as between Member States, of customs duties and quantitative restrictions on the import and export of goods, and of all other measures having equivalent effect;
(b)   a common commercial policy;
(c)   an internal market characterised by the abolition, as between Member States, of obstacles to the free movement of goods, persons, services and capital;
(d)   measures concerning the entry and movement of persons as provided for in Title IV;
(e)   a common policy in the sphere of agriculture and fisheries;
(f)   a common policy in the sphere of transport;
(g)   a system ensuring that competition in the internal market is not distorted;
(h)   the approximation of the laws of Member States to the extent required;
(i)   the promotion of co-ordination between employment policies of the Member States with a view to enhancing their effectiveness by developing a co-ordinated strategy for employment;
(j)   a policy in the social sphere comprising a European Social Fund;
(k)   the strengthening of economic and social cohesion;
(l)   a policy in the sphere of the environment;
(m)   the strengthening of the competitiveness of Community industry;
(n)   the promotion of research and technological development;
(o)   encouragement for the establishment and development of trans-European networks;
(p)   a contribution to the attainment of a high level of health protection;
(q)   a contribution to education and training of quality and to the flowering of the cultures of the Member States;
(r)   a policy in the sphere of development of co-operation;

(s) the association of the overseas countries and territories in order to increase trade and promote jointly economic and social development;
(t) a contribution to the strengthening of consumer protection;
(u) measures in the spheres of energy, civil protection and tourism.

The Amsterdam Treaty adds a rider to Article 3 to the effect that in all the activities comprised therein 'the Community shall aim to eliminate inequalities, and to promote equality, between men and women'. New EC Article 6[9] provides that 'Environmental protection requirements must be integrated into the definition and implementation of the Community policies and activities referred to in Article 3, in particular with a view to promoting sustainable development'.

Most of these activities have already reached a high level of Community policy but the new and challenging economic and monetary policies are to be accomplished according to a timetable laid down in EC Article 4 (ex Art 3a). We shall endeavour to discuss most of these activities and add comments, where appropriate, to the innovations brought about by the Maastricht and Amsterdam Treaties.

(3) FEDERATION OR CONFEDERATION?

In the long history of mankind only a few confederations can be recorded: Switzerland 1291–1848; the Netherlands 1581–1795; the USA 1776–1788; Germany 1815–1866. Since these confederations developed either into unitary states or federations it is worthwhile contrasting the confederal with the federal type of constitution. In a federal state the sovereign power is apportioned between a central government and a number of Member States. There are basically two models of power arrangement: from the base to the centre and from the centre to the base. For example, the US Constitution is so arranged that power flows from the states to the federal government which has no powers, apart from those delegated to it by the states. It is more difficult to find a classic example of the opposite, though Canada is sometimes quoted as being one where the power flows from the dominion government to the provinces. This was, no doubt, the scheme convenient to colonial rule and to some of the fathers of the Canadian state, but constitutional developments, whilst safeguarding the federal 'peace, order and good government', have confirmed that the provinces were created by the British parliament with original and sovereign powers. Therefore Canada only partially fits the model of centralized federation. For the purpose of international relations a federal state is represented by a central government. Internally, the legislature, the judiciary, the administration and indeed the law can be divided into federal and state.

In a confederation the sovereignty enjoyed by the individual Member States is said to be complete. It can be defined as a relationship of sovereign states, each Member State retaining its status as a subject of international law. In a federation, on the other hand, the sovereignty of the individual Member States merges into the one sovereignty of the federation. In a confederation the central government acts directly on the Member States but only through the Member States upon individuals. It follows that outwardly each member of a confederation can enter into separate relations with foreign states and, of course, may of its own right be a member of the United Nations, whereas members of a federation, as a rule,[10]

---

9 Ex Art 3c.
10 Cf the anomalous position of two member republics of the USSR: Ukraine and Belorussia; Dolan, E, 'The Member-Republics of the USSR as Subjects of the Law of Nations' [1955] ICLQ 629–36.

cannot enter into separate relations with foreign states. Inwardly, members of a confederation maintain their independent and separate form of government, legislature, judiciary, administration and system of law, their relation to the central government being contractual rather than organic. A confederation has no distinct legal order for it is a political association of states rather than a composite state.

On balance the emerging European Union fits, in the light of the EEC Treaty as amended by the TEU, better into a federal than a confederal form.[11]

Since, of the three Communities, the EEC is the prototype of the legal structure of the European Union, it is essential to examine its legal status, for it reflects the relationship between the Member States inter se, the Member States to the Community and the Community to the outside world. The status of the Union rests upon its constitution, ie the Treaty of Rome as amended by the Treaty of Maastricht and Amsterdam, and the appropriate rules of international law, as well as the constitutional laws of the Member States.

It is clear that neither the Community nor the Union is not a state[12] in a classical sense for it has no territory of its own except as defined in the Treaties for the purpose of their application, no population which is not a citizenry of the Member States though EC Article 17 (ex Art 8(1)) proclaims that 'every person holding the nationality of a Member State shall be a citizen of the Union', while its 'government' has no powers except those defined by the Treaty. However, it would be quite inadequate to define the EC or the Union as the association of states which subscribe to the Treaty of Maastricht, since the Treaty lays down a foundation for something more than a loose partnership of states involved in a joint economic enterprise. The Treaty is not a mere contractual compact, it is an institutional stage of European unity.

The Community/Union, though consisting of sovereign states, is a separate, albeit supra-national, entity and, in this respect, it is governed by the law of international institutions in general and its own constitution in particular. In this context the law of international institutions, an offshoot of public international law, applies to the Community/Union as a regional arrangement.

It is perfectly legitimate for sovereign states in their capacity as the makers of international law to act in concert in setting up institutions and organizations furthering the interests of mankind. Of these the most impelling precedent is the UN which, though universal in character and purpose, does not exclude regional organizations. Indeed it has been pointed out[13] that the difficulty of developing global institutions raised the hope of a greater success in the field of regional organizations. Unlike its predecessor, the League of Nations, which was conceived merely to be an association,[14] the United Nations Organization[15] has the status of a legal person, ie it is a bearer of rights and duties pertinent to legal personality

---

11   See further Ipsen, H P, *Europäisches Gemeinschaftsrecht* (1972), pp 182 et seq.

12   According to Art 1 of the Montevideo Convention of 1933 on the Rights and Duties of States, 'the state as a person of international law should possess the following qualifications: (*a*) a permanent population, (*b*) a defined territory, (*c*) a government and (*d*) a capacity to enter into relations with other states'.

13   Jenks, C W, 'World Organization and European Integration', *European Yearbook*, Vol I, p 173; see also Scheuner, U, 'Europe and the United Nations', *European Yearbook*, Vol VIII, pp 67–90.

14   Although the Covenant did not confer juristic personality upon the League of Nations it was often argued that such personality was necessary for the League to fulfil its functions; cf Jenks, C W, [1945] BYIL, p 267.

15   United Nations Charter, Art 104; Advisory Opinion on Reparation for Injuries suffered in the Service of the United Nations, ICJ Reports (1949), p 174.

because it was so willed by the founder states. The same is the position of the EC. In their terse statement that 'the Community shall have legal personality'[16] the founder states unequivocally created a new international entity independent of its component parts and endowed it with the status and attributes of a legal person. Oddly enough, the Treaties do not credit the Union with legal personality, although in some respects the Union can be identified with the Community, and vice versa.

By virtue of customary international law two attributes, viz the treaty-making power and the capacity of sending and receiving envoys, mark out an entity as a sovereign body and a subject of international law. The Holy See[17] was a classic example of this doctrine from 1870 when it lost territorial sovereignty until 1929 when it regained a symbolic territory by the Lateran Treaty. The EC need not resort to custom to support its claim for the Treaty provides for both the legal personality and the treaty-making power.[18] The capacity to enter into diplomatic relations derives generally from the legal personality of the EC and specifically from art 17 of the protocol on the Privileges and Immunities of the European Communities of 1965. By the end of 1990 the EC, as a legal person distinct from its members, had established diplomatic relations with more than 130 countries including the Holy See, China and the USSR, and maintains a delegation at the UNO. The German Democratic Republic too, in the last days of its life, appointed an ambassador but, as a result of the reunification of Germany, this appointment has lapsed.

The EEC was set up by a treaty of unlimited duration (EC Art 312, ex Art 240), and so was the EAEC (Art 208), but the ECSC only for fifty years (art 97).[19] By its design the Community is committed to a continuous progress, by its nature it appears irreversible. Theoretically it is possible for a Member State to withdraw as long as it remains sovereign, that is as long as the political integration or transformation of the economic community into a more homogeneous body politic has not materialized. However, in reality the economic structure of the Member States and their national interests may become so intertwined in the course of time that a breakaway may prove impracticable. On the other hand it is always possible to maintain the status quo and so reduce the Union to political stagnation. The Community/Union itself has a built-in system which may either advance it towards political and institutional integration or preserve the self-contained units of sovereign states whilst developing the economy and creating wealth within the existing institutions. This depends on whether the Community/Union institutions are strengthened at the expense of sovereignty or whether the sovereign element keeps the institutions in the servile role of functional bureaucracy.

EC Article 236 which provided for the revision[20] of the EEC Treaty has been replaced by TEU Article 48 (ex Art N) (now EC Art 309) which lays down an

---

16 EEC Art 210; ECSC Art 6(1); EAEC Art 184.
17 Kunz, J L, 'The Status of the Holy See in International Law; (1952) 46 AJIL 308 et seq.
18 EEC Arts 113, 114, 131, 228, 237, 238; ECSC Arts 6, 71; EAEC Arts 101 and 206. The treaty-making power of the ECSC was implicitly recognized by the UK in the agreement of 1954 between the UK and the ECSC, 258 UNTS 322.
19 When the ECSC Treaty expires, it will not be replaced. The intention is that the EC Treaty shall apply in full to the coal and steel industries. The assets and liabilities of the ECSC will be transferred to the EC on 24 July 2002: see the Protocol on the financial consequences of the expiry of the ECSC Treaty and on the research fund for coal and steel attached to the Treaty of Nice (OJ 2001, C 80/1 at 67).
20 ECSC Art 96; EAEC Art 204.

elaborate procedure. Thus the initiative lies with the governments of the Member States or the Commission which may submit to the Council proposals for the amendment of the Treaties on which the Union is founded. If the Council, after consulting the European Parliament and, where appropriate, the Commission, delivers an opinion in favour of a conference or representatives of the governments of the Member States, the conference shall be convened by the President of the Council for the purpose of determining by common accord the amendments to be made to those Treaties. The European Central Bank shall also be consulted in the case of institutional changes in the monetary area.

It is not clear whether the opinion favouring the calling of the conference has to be taken unanimously or by a majority vote though it is clear that 'common accord' is required to the amendments agreed by the conference. Amendments shall enter into force after being ratified by all the Member States in accordance with their respective constitutions.

Enlargement of the Union is also subject to a unanimous decision of the Member states followed by the amendment of the Treaty duly ratified by all contracting states in accordance with their respective constitutions.[1]

The Member States of the Union are the Member States of the three European Communities. It is not possible for a country to be a member of the Union without being at the same time a member of the EC, ie of all three original Communities. Article 49[2] lays down the conditions of the membership of the Union providing that 'any European State which respects the principles set out in Article 6(1) (below) may apply to become a member' according to the procedure laid down therein.

Thus both amendments to the Treaty and the composition of the Union shall remain in the power of the Member States, negotiations and unanimity in a classic form of international law safeguarding their sovereign rights.

(4)   THE EUROPEAN UNION

According to TEU Article 1 (ex Art A3) 'The Union shall be founded on the European Communities supplemented by the policies and forms of co-operation established by this Treaty'. The EEC Treaty, amended by the Single European Act, became the foundation of the Community and the Community has simply changed its name by dropping the adjective 'Economic'.[3] However, though the main body of the TEU is that of the EEC, the two sectoral Communities continue their separate existence, albeit as integral components of the Union.

The objectives of the Union are stated in TEU Article 2 (ex Art B) which reflects the activities supported by the different 'pillars' including the *acquis communautaire*, which can be described as the achievements reached under the founding Treaties including legislation and case law. A dynamic development was predicted by the provisions for a conference of representatives of the Member States in 1996 to examine 'those provisions of the Treaty for which revision is provided, in accordance with the objectives set out in Articles A and B' of the Maastricht Treaty;[4] a timetable for the achievement of the objectives[5] and assurance that 'The Union shall provide itself with the means necessary to attain its objectives and carry through its policies'.[6] Moreover the Council may transfer to the

---

1   TEU Art 49 (ex Art O).
2   (Ex Art O), repealing EEC Art 237.
3   TEU Art 8 (ex Art G(11)).
4   TEU Art B first para, 5th indent, and Art N(2), as originally worded.
5   TEU Art 2 (ex Art B para 2).
6   TEU Art 6(4)(ex Art F(3)).

European Community matters pertaining to police and judicial co-operation[7] though such a decision, being in the competence of inter-governmental conference, shall need to be adopted by the Member States in accordance with their respective constitutions.[8]

Specifically the Union set itself the following objectives:

(1) to promote economic and social progress and a high level of employment ... through the strengthening of economic and social cohesion and ... monetary union, ultimately including a single currency;
(2) to assert its identity on the international scene, in particular through the implementation of a common foreign and security policy;
(3) to strengthen the protection of the rights and interests of the nationals of its Member States through the introduction of a citizenship of the Union;
(4) to maintain and develop the Union as an area of freedom, security and justice, in which the free movement of persons is assured in conjunction with appropriate measures with respect to external border controls, asylum, immigration and the prevention and combating of crime;
(5) to maintain in full the *acquis communautaire* and build on it with a view to considering to what extent the policies and the forms of co-operation introduced by this Treaty may need to be revised with the aim of ensuring the effectiveness of the mechanisms and the institutions of the Community.

These objectives are to be achieved according to the Treaty while respecting the principle of subsidiarity as defined in EC Article 5.[9]

The nature of the Union is reflected in TEU Article 6[10] which provides that 'the Union is founded on the principles of liberty, democracy, respect for human rights and fundamental freedoms, and the rule of law, principles which are common to the Member States'. The Union shall respect fundamental rights, as guaranteed by the European Convention as 'general principles of Community law' and shall also 'respect the national identities of its Member States'.

TEU Article 7[11] defines the procedure in the event of 'serious and persistent' breach by a Member State of principles on which the Union is based. In such a case the European Council shall consider a proposal by one-third of the Member States or by the Commission and, after obtaining the assent of the European Parliament expressed by a two-thirds majority of the votes cast, representing a majority of its members, shall, unanimously, determine the existence of such a breach. The Member State concerned is invited to submit its observations. Where such a determination has been made, the Council, acting by a qualified majority in accordance with EC Article 205(2),[12] without taking into account the vote of the representative of the State in question, may suspend 'certain rights deriving from the application of this Treaty to the State in question, including the voting rights of that State in Council'. Nevertheless the obligations of the State in question shall continue to be binding on it. The Council, acting by a qualified majority (presumably without the votes of the State in question), may decide to vary or revoke the measures imposed. It is not clear whether the Council shall act alone or with the assent of the European Parliament and what specific 'rights' shall be

---

7 TEU Art 29 (ex Art K.1).
8 TEU Art 42 (ex Art K.14).
9 TEU Art 2 (ex Art B).
10 Ex Art F.
11 Ex Art F.1.
12 Ex Art 148(2).

affected. This procedure is patently different from the procedure for breaches of the EC Treaty[13] since the determination of breaches of the TEU is in the hands of political institutions and not in the Court of Justice and so is the sanction since suspension of Member States of the EC or their rights has not been envisaged in the founding Treaties.[14]

New EU Title VII[15] inserted by the Amsterdam Treaty contains general provisions enabling Member States, which intend to establish 'closer co-operation' between themselves, to make use of the institutions, procedures and mechanisms laid down by the Treaties establishing the Union and the Community.[16] This co-operation ought to aim at furthering the objectives of the Union and at protecting its interests. It should be used as a last resort, where the objectives of the Treaties could be attained by applying the relevant procedures laid down in the Treaties. It shall not affect the '*acquis communautaire*' and the measures adopted under the other provisions of the Treaties or the competences, rights, obligations and interests of those Member States which do not participate in this process. The Member States shall apply, as far as they are concerned, the acts and decisions adopted for the implementation of the co-operation in which they participate. Those which do not participate in such co-operation shall not impede the implementation thereof by the participating Member States.

For the adoption of acts and decisions necessary for the implementation of the co-operation envisaged above, the relevant institutional provisions of the Treaty shall apply.[17] However, while all the Members of the Council shall be able to participate in the deliberations, only those representing participating Member States shall take part in the decision-making process. The qualified majority shall be defined as the same proportion of the weighted votes as laid down in EC Article 205(2)[18] and unanimity will apply to only the members of the Council concerned.

These provisions amplify in a selective manner the solidarity principle of EC Article 10[19] but, at the same time, set the stage for a division within the Union into two classes of Member States: those who continue the process of integration at the level of their Treaty obligations and those who intend to form a close-knit elite of forerunners of European federation.

(5)   INSTITUTIONAL FRAMEWORK

More than the European Community the Union exhibits features of a federal design. This is reflected in all three pillars of the Union. The Union was endowed with extended or new competences, which can be found in classical forms of federal political systems though there is lack of coherence and some of these provisions remain yet to be refined. The most striking are the provisions which have converted the Community into an Economic Union. The many other competences comprise economic and social cohesion (subject to the British Protocol, see infra), education and vocational training, culture and public health, consumer protection, environment, industry, development co-operation, energy, civil protection and tourism.

---

13   See infra.
14   But see Art 88 of the ECSC Treaty.
15   Ex Title VIa.
16   TEU Art 43 (ex Art K.15).
17   TEU Art 44 (ex Art K.16).
18   Ex Art 148.
19   Ex Art 5.

The institutional arrangements under the first pillar represent a single set of organs acting for all three pillars.[20] The functions of the Community are carried out by the European Parliament, the Council, the Commission, the Court of Justice and the Court of Auditors, each institution acting within the limits of powers conferred upon it by the Treaty.[1] As hitherto the dominant organ is the Council of Ministers representing the sovereign power of the Member States, though with the erosion of unanimity and the expansion of the competences of the Union the rôle of the individual Member States in the decision-making process tends to diminish.

The European Council (originally the Council of Heads of State or of Governments) which was officially promoted by the Single European Act to the status of one of the principal institutions of the Community has become under the new arrangement an institution of the Union rather than of the Community.[2] However, as hitherto, it has been assigned a leading role in so far as it 'shall provide the Union with the necessary impetus for its development and shall define its general political guidelines'. It meets at least twice a year under chairmanship of the Head of State or Government of the Member State which holds the Presidency of the Council.

The European Parliament has gained an enhanced status as a deliberative and consultative body with a modicum of political and budgetary control and increased participation in the legislative process.

The Commission, a truly Community institution, with a power of initiative, preparation and decision, also gained more power as far as administration of Community policies is concerned, though the principle of subsidiarity may curb its ambition. The Commission participates in the work of the Council and the Parliament. It also has certain executive and quasi-judicial powers and, particularly as regards the enforcement actions, it may apply to the Court of Justice for a financial sanction to be imposed upon a Member State in default of its Treaty obligations.

The Court of Auditors has now been promoted to the rank of principal institution.

In furtherance of the objectives of the Economic and Monetary Union a European System of Central Banks (ESCB) and a European Central Bank (ECB) shall be established in accordance with the procedures laid down in the Maastricht Treaty and shall act within the limits of the powers placed upon them by the Treaty and the relevant Protocols.[3]

The judicial power of the Community is in the hands of the Court of Justice (ECJ) and the Court of First Instance (CFI). If anything the Court resembles more a federal court than the International Court of Justice at The Hague. In fact it is an internal court of the Community with the power of arbitration, adjudication, repression and advice. It is not a substitute for the jurisdictions of the national courts of the Member States and it has no power of appeal over the national courts, but it has exclusive jurisdiction over the Community institutions. The power of interpretation of the Treaties, of the acts of the Community institutions and of the bodies established under the Treaties enables the Court to exercise a quasi-legislative function and thus build up a body of case law which

---

20 TEU Arts 3 and 4 (ex Arts C and E).
 1 EC Art 7 (ex Art 4).
 2 TEU Art 4 (ex Art D).
 3 EC Art 8 (ex Art 4a) and Protocols 3 and 4 and see ch 24 infra.

contributes to the development of the law. The Court of Justice can be credited with an unparalleled contribution to European integration. Though its competence has been enlarged, it has no jurisdiction in matters which the TEU has reserved to the inter-governmental decisions except that, as amended by the Amsterdam Treaty, the Court of Justice shall be competent to make preliminary rulings on the validity and interpretation of Conventions made in the context of Police and Judicial Co-operation in criminal matters,[4] as well as in the context of 'closer co-operation enabling the Union to develop more rapidly into an area of freedom, security and justice'[5] and with regard to the operation of the founding Treaties.[6] Thus the demarcation line between the Union and the Community begins to be blurred.

'The Community is a new legal order ... comprising not only the Members but also their nationals.'[7] In this dictum the Court of Justice unmistakenly alluded to the federal complexion of the Community and its law. Indeed Community law is distinct from the municipal laws of the Member States but it is administered by both the national authorities and Community institutions. In the terms of the Treaties the states have created the institutions and endeavour to build a uniform body of law to regulate their economic and social activities. Although surrender of a certain portion of national sovereignty is necessary to achieve these objectives, the pooling of sovereignty even in a Treaty of such magnitude as the Treaty of European Union is not explicit enough to create a federal state or government. Therefore at this stage the Union is merely an organization of sovereign states with a strong federal potential.

(6) CITIZENSHIP OF THE UNION

Furthering the notion of a 'People's Europe' the EC Treaty established 'citizenship of the Union'[8] to which every person holding the nationality of a Member State is entitled. The Amsterdam Treaty adds a rider to the effect that 'Citizenship of the Union shall complement and not replace national citizenship' and that 'Citizens of the Union shall enjoy the rights conferred by this Treaty and shall be subject to the duties imposed thereby'. The citizenship of the Union entails the right to move freely and reside within the territory of the Member States, the right to vote and to stand as a candidate at municipal elections as well as the right to vote and stand in elections to the European Parliament in the country in which the citizen resides. However these principles are subject to implementation by the Council acting unanimously on a proposal from the Commission after consulting the European Parliament. There is as yet no proposal for the right (active or passive) to participate in national general elections.

Every citizen of the Union may write to any Community institution in one of the official languages and have an answer in the same language.

Every citizen of the Union shall have the right to petition the European Parliament and to apply to the European Ombudsman[9] who is to be appointed in accordance with EC Article 195 (ex Art 138e).

---

4   TEU Art 35 (ex Art K.7).
5   TEU Art 40(4) (ex Art K.12(4)).
6   TEU Arts 46–53 (ex Arts L–S).
7   Case 26/62 *Van Gend & Loos NV v Nederlandse Administraitie der Belastingen* [1963] ECR 1 at 29, [1963] CMLR 105 at 129.
8   EC Art 17 (ex Arts 8–8b).
9   EC Art 21 (ex Art 8d and 138d). Mr Jacob Söderman (Finnish Parliamentary Ombudsman) was sworn as Community Ombudsman on 27 September 1995.

In fact the appointment of the first Ombudsman was delayed and Parliament was challenged in this respect by an individual.[10] The President of the Court of First Instance dismissed his application for interim measures. On appeal, the Court of Justice ruled that the application was not 'sufficiently precise'[11] and confirmed the principle that the Court has no power to issue directions to the Institutions.[12]

Whilst in a third country, every citizen of the Union shall be entitled to diplomatic and consular protection of any Member State on the same conditions as the nationals of that state (if his own State is not represented in that third country). To implement this objective the Member States must establish between themselves the necessary rules and to secure this protection by means of appropriate international negotiations.[13]

(7)   THE SECOND PILLAR OF THE UNION: COMMON FOREIGN AND SECURITY POLICY

(a)   Foreign Policy
Perhaps the most promising achievement of the TEU (which replaced the corresponding provisions of the Single European Act) lies in the development of a Common Foreign and Security Policy as the second pillar of the Union. In the Amsterdam version the objectives of such policy shall be:[14]

(1)   to safeguard the common values, fundamental interests, independence and integrity of the Union in conformity with the principles of the UN Charter;
(2)   to strengthen the security of the Union in all ways;
(3)   to preserve peace and strengthen international security in accordance with the principles of the UN Charter as well as the principles of the Helsinki Final Act and the objectives of the Paris Charter; including those on external borders;
(4)   to promote international co-operation;
(5)   to develop and consolidate democracy and the rule of law and respect for human rights and fundamental freedoms.

The Union shall pursue these objectives by:

–   defining the principles of and general guidance for the common foreign and security policy;
–   deciding on common strategies;
–   adopting joint actions;
–   adopting common positions;
–   strengthening systematic co-operation between Member States in the conduct of policy.[15]

In order to achieve these objectives the Union shall establish systematic co-operation between Member States and implement joint actions in which the Member States have essential interests in common. The Member States for their part shall 'support the Union's external and security policy actively and unreservedly in a spirit of loyalty and mutual solidarity. They shall refrain from

10   Case T-146/95R: *Giorgio Bernardi* [1995] ECR II-2255.
11   Case C-303/96P: *Giorgio Bernardi v European Parliament* [1997] ECR I-1239.
12   See Case T-56/92: *Koelman v Commission* [1993] ECR I-1267 (para 19).
13   EC Art 20 (ex Art 8c).
14   TEU Art 11 (ex Art J.1).
15   TEU Art 12 (ex Art J.2).

any action which is contrary to the interests of the Union or likely to impair its effectiveness as a cohesive force in international relations. The European Council[16] shall define the principles and general guidelines, decide on common strategies to be implemented by the Union whilst the Council shall take implementing decisions. The Council shall also recommend common strategies to the European Council and shall implement them, in particular by adopting joint actions and common positions. The Council shall ensure the unity, consistency and effectiveness of action by the Union.

Joint actions[17] shall address specific situations where operational action by the Union is deemed to be required. They shall lay down their objectives, scope, the means to be made available to the Union, if necessary their duration, and the conditions for their implementation. They are subject to review by the Council if there is a change in circumstances having a substantial effect upon the joint action in question.

Thus the functions are divided: the Union shall provide leadership and the Member States their co-operation. Joint actions, decided upon by the Council, shall commit the Member States in the positions they adopt and in the conduct of their activity. If there is any plan to adopt a national position or take national action pursuant to the joint action information shall be provided in time to allow, if necessary, for prior consultations within the Council. In cases of 'imperative need' (undefined in the Treaty) arising from changes in the situation and failing a Council decision, Member States may take the necessary measures as a matter of urgency having regard to the general objectives of the joint action and have to inform the Council accordingly. Should there be any 'major difficulties' (undefined in the Treaty) in implementing a joint action, a Member State shall refer them to the Council which shall discuss them and seek appropriate solutions.[18] The vagueness of the undefined 'imperative need' and 'major difficulties' seems to provide the Member State with a loophole whilst the Treaty gives no answer to the problem arising from the fact that a Member State may consider it impossible to overcome the difficulties in question and the Council may think otherwise.

'Common positions'[19] shall define the approach of the Union to a particular matter of a geographical or thematic nature. Member States are obliged to ensure that their national policies conform to the common positions adopted by the Council. They also have to inform and consult one another within the Council on any matter of foreign and security policy of general interest in order to ensure that the Union's influence is exerted as effectively as possible by means of concerted and converged action.[20]

As can be seen the Union has not reached as yet the stage of having its own autonomous external policy. The union has the capacity to conduct external relations within the scope of the Treaties but the Member States have not relinquished all their original powers in this field in favour of the Community, and consequently, despite the increased powers of the Union, bicephalous conduct of external relations continues.

(b) Security
Following the disintegration of the USSR and of the Warsaw Pact the security position in Europe has changed dramatically. NATO, with its American protective

16 TEU Art 13 (ex Art J.3).
17 TEU Art 14 (ex Art J.4).
18 TEU Art 14(5–7).
19 TEU Art 15 (ex Art J.5).
20 TEU Art 16 (ex Art J.6).

umbrella, has to be adapted to a new role. This, coupled with developing political integration and the growing awareness of Europe's responsibility for its own safety, has led to the linkage of a Common Foreign and Security Policy in the Maastricht Treaty.[1] Thus the common foreign and security policy shall include all questions relating to the security of the Union, including the progressive framing of a common defence policy, which might lead to a common defence, should the European Council so decide. In fact the Western European Union (WEU) is an integral part of the development of the Union and, as such, has an operational capacity which supports the Union in framing the defence aspects of the common foreign and security policy. The Union shall accordingly foster closer institutional relations with the WEU with a view to the integration of the WEU into the Union, should the European Council so decide. It shall, in that case, recommend to the Member States the adoption of such decision in accordance with their constitutional requirements.[2] However, according to the agreement to be reached with the WEU (which includes nine of the EC countries), the Union shall respect the NATO obligations of certain Member States and shall not prevent any bilateral arrangements within the framework of the WEU and NATO (eg Franco-German co-operation in the field of land forces or Franco-British co-operation in the field of air force).

Questions of security policy shall include humanitarian and rescue tasks, peace-keeping tasks and tasks of combat forces in crisis management, including peacemaking. The progressive framing of a common defence policy entails co-operation between Member States in the field of armaments.

(c)   The machinery
In matters covered by the common foreign and security policy the Union shall be represented by its Presidency,[3] assisted, if need be, by the next Member State to hold the Presidency,[4] presumably by invitation of the President in office. In particular the Presidency shall be responsible for the implementation of the decisions of the Council and in that capacity shall in principle articulate the position of the Union in international organizations and international conferences.[5]

The Presidency shall be assisted by the Secretary-General of the Council who shall exercise the function of High Representative for the common foreign and security policy.[6] More specifically, the High Representative shall in that capacity contribute to the formulation, preparation and implementation of policy decisions and, when appropriate and acting on behalf of the Council at the request of the Presidency, conduct political dialogue with third parties.[7] The Commission shall be 'fully associated' in the tasks of the Presidency,[8] though neither the Amsterdam Treaty nor its predecessor, the Maastricht Treaty, which contain identical provisions, elaborate on the role of the Commission in this respect. The Presidency shall consult the European Parliament on the main aspects and basic choices of the common foreign and security policy and shall be kept regularly informed by the Presidency and the Commission. The European Parliament may ask questions of the Council, debate the issues and make recommendations to the Council.[9] Any Member State or the

---

1   TEU Art 17(1) (ex Art J.7(1)).
2   TEU Art 17(2) (ex Art J.7(2)).
3   TEU Art 18(1) (ex Art J.8(1)).
4   TEU Art 18(4).
5   TEU Art 18(2).
6   TEU Art 18(3).
7   Art 26 (ex Art J.16).
8   Art 18(4) (ex Art J.8(4)), see also Art 27 (ex Art J.17).
9   Art 21 (ex Art J.11).

Commission may refer to the Council any question in this field and may submit proposals to the Council.[10] However the general principles and guidelines will be defined by the European Council whilst the Council will, by decisions, carry out the implementing tasks. In cases requiring a rapid decision, the Presidency, of its own motion, or at the request of the Commission or a Member State, shall convene an extraordinary Council meeting within 48 hours or, in an emergency, within a shorter period.[11]

Decisions shall be taken by the Council unanimously but abstentions by members present or represented shall not prevent the adoption of such decisions.[12] When abstaining, any member may qualify its abstention by making a formal declaration in which case it shall not be bound by the decision but shall accept that the decision commits the Union. The Member State concerned shall refrain from any action likely to conflict with the decision or impede Union action based on that decision and the other Member States shall respect its position. However the decision shall not be adopted if the members of the Council qualifying their abstention represent more than one-third of the votes weighted in accordance with EC Article 205(2).

By derogation from the above provisions the Council shall act by qualified majority[13] when adopting joint actions, common positions or taking any other decision on the basis of a common strategy as well as when adopting any decision implementing a joint action or a common position. In such cases decisions shall require at least 62 votes in favour, cast by at least ten members. If a member of the Council declares that, for important and stated reasons of national policy, it intends to oppose the adoption of a decision to be taken by qualified majority, a vote shall not be taken. However the Council may, acting by a qualified majority, request that the matter be referred to the European Council for decision by unanimity. The provisions of this paragraph shall not apply to decisions having military or defence implications.

In procedural matters the Council shall act by a simple majority of its members.[14]

To conclude an agreement in the context of foreign and security policy with a third country or an international organization the Council, acting unanimously, may authorise the Presidency, assisted by the Commission, as appropriate, to open negotiations to that effect.[15] Such agreements shall be concluded by the Council unanimously on a recommendation from the Presidency. However, no agreement shall be binding on a Member State whose representative in the Council states that it has to comply with the requirements of its own constitutional procedure. In such a situation the other members of the Council may agree that the agreement shall apply provisionally to them. These provisions shall also apply to judicial co-operation in criminal matters.

Without prejudice to EC Article 207,[16] which concerns the Committee of the Permanent Representatives,[17] a Political Committee (established by the Single European Act) which consists of senior civil servants of the Member States, shall monitor the international situation covered by the common foreign and security

10   Art 22(1) (ex Art J.12(1)).
11   Art 22(2) (ex Art J.12(2)). For military matters, the Council is assisted by a Military Committee and a military staff: see the Decisions of 22 January 2001 (OJ 2001, L27/4 and 27/7). A rapid reaction mechanism is provided for in Regulation 381/2001, OJ 2001, L57/5.
12   Art 23(1) (ex Art J.13(1)).
13   Art 23(2).
14   Art 23(3).
15   TEU Art 24 (ex Art J.14).
16   Ex Art 151.
17   See Infra.

policy. It shall contribute to the definition of policies by delivering opinions to the Council at the request of the Council or on its own initiative. It shall also monitor the implementation of agreed policies, without prejudice to the responsibility of the Presidency and the Commission.[18] It remains to be seen how this additional procedure shall improve the efficacy of the already complicated Treaty arrangements.

Administrative expenditure, which the provisions on foreign and security policy entail for the institutions, shall be charged to the budget of the European Communities. Operational expenditure arising from the implementation of the policy shall also be charged to the budget except those which have military or defence implications and cases where the Council acting unanimously decides otherwise. Where the expenditure is not charged to the budget it shall be charged to the Member States in accordance with the gross national product scale, unless the Council acting unanimously decides otherwise. As for expenditure arising from operations having military or defence implications, Member States whose representatives in the Council have made a formal declaration under TEU Article 23(1), shall not be obliged to contribute to the financing of such operations.[19]

The apportionment of the financial burden of the common foreign and security policy seems fair enough but the provisions enabling Member States to opt out of the common action seem to encourage the shifting of the burden onto those countries which shall be determined that the Union's policy is not confined to mere verbal posturing.

(8)   THE THIRD PILLAR OF THE UNION: POLICE AND JUDICIAL CO-OPERATION IN CRIMINAL MATTERS

The grandiose title of 'Co-operation in the Field of Justice and Home Affairs' of the Maastricht Treaty has been replaced by Title VI under the caption of 'Provisions on Police and Judicial Co-operation in Criminal Matters'.

TEU Article 29[20] states that the objective of a high level of safety of the citizen shall be achieved by preventing and combating crime, in particular terrorism, trafficking in persons and offences against children, illicit trafficking in drugs and arms, corruption and fraud. The mechanism envisaged includes closer co-operation between police forces, customs authorities and other competent authorities in the Member States, both directly and through the European Police Office (Europol); closer co-operation between judicial and other competent authorities and approximation of criminal law.

Details of common action in this field are laid down in TEU Article 30.[1] These include: operational co-operation between the above-mentioned authorities and other specialised law enforcement services of the Member States in relation to the prevention, detection and investigation of criminal offences, the collection, storage, processing, analysis and exchange of relevant information, including information on suspicious financial transactions, subject to the protection of personal data; co-operation and joint initiatives in training, the exchange of officers, the use of equipment; forensic research; and the common evaluation of particular investigative techniques in relation to the detection of serious forms of organized crime.

---

18   TEU Art 25 (ex Art J.15). The 'standing formation' of the Committee is the Political and Security Committee established by Decision of 22 January 2001: OJ 2001, L27/1.
19   TEU Art 28(2–3) (ex Art J.18(2–3)).
20   Ex Art K.1.
  1   Ex Art K.2.

The Council shall promote co-operation through Europol to enable Europol to facilitate the performance of its tasks; adopt measures allowing Europol to ask the competent authorities of the Member States to conduct and co-ordinate their investigation in specific cases and to develop specific expertise which may be put at the disposal of Member States to assist them in investigating cases of organised crime; promote liaison arrangements between prosecuting/investigating officials specializing in combating organized crime in close co-operation with Europol, and establish a research, documentation and statistical network on cross-border crime.

Common action on judicial co-operation in criminal matters shall include facilitating and accelerating co-operation between competent ministries and judicial or equivalent authorities of the Member States in relation to proceedings and the enforcement of decisions; facilitating extradition; ensuring compatibility of rules of co-operation; preventing conflicts of jurisdiction and adopting measures establishing minimum rules relating to the constituent elements of criminal acts and penalties in the fields of organised crime, terrorism and drug trafficking.[2]

TEU Article 32[3] provides that the Council shall lay down conditions and limitations under which the competent authorities referred to in TEU Articles 30 and 31 may operate in the territory of another Member State. However TEU Article 33[4] stipulates that the new provisions shall not affect the exercise of the responsibilities incumbent upon Member States with regard to the maintenance of law and order and the safeguarding of internal security.

TEU Article 34[5] details the procedure to be adopted by the Council for the implementation of its new responsibilities. Thus, acting unanimously on the initiative of any Member State or of the Commission, it may adopt common positions defining the approach of the Union to a particular matter; adopt framework decisions and establish conventions which it shall recommend to the Member States for adoption in accordance with their respective constitutional requirements.

Where the Council is required to act by a qualified majority, the votes of the Member States shall be weighted in accordance with EC Article 205,[6] and for their adoption at least 62 votes, cast by at least ten Member States shall be required. For procedural questions the Council shall act by a majority of its members.

TEU Article 35[7] provides that the Court of Justice shall have jurisdiction to give preliminary rulings on the validity and interpretation of framework decisions and decisions as well as of the conventions and the measures implementing them. It shall also have jurisdiction to review the legality of framework decisions and decisions in actions brought by a Member State or the Commission on the same basis as EC Article 230(1).[8] Moreover the Court of Justice shall have jurisdiction to rule on any dispute between the Member States regarding the interpretation or the application of acts adopted under TEU Article 34, above, wherever such dispute cannot be settled by the Council to rule on any dispute between Member States and the Commission regarding the interpretation or the application of conventions established under TEU Article 34. However, the Court of Justice shall have no jurisdiction to review the validity or proportionality of operations carried out by the police or other law enforcement services of a Member State or

2   TEU Art 31 (ex Art K.3).
3   Ex Art K.4.
4   Ex Art K.5.
5   Ex Art K.6.
6   Ex Art 148(2).
7   Ex Art K.7.
8   Ex Art 173(1).

the exercise of the responsibilities incumbent upon Member States with regard to the maintenance of law and order and the safeguarding of internal security.

TEU Article 36[9] provides for the setting up of a co-ordinating committee consisting of senior national officials which, in addition to co-ordination at the Union level, shall proffer opinions and contribute to the preparation of the Council's discussions in the areas referred to in TEU Article 29. The Commission shall be associated with work of the committee.

At international conferences and within international organizations in which Member States participate they are obliged to defend the common position reached in the Council.[10]

Agreements reached in the field of common foreign and security policy may also cover matters falling under this title.[11]

Before adopting any measures envisaged in TEU Article 34(2)(b), (c) and (d) (ie measures concerned with the approximation of national decisions in related matters which have no direct effect and conventions) the Council is obliged to consult the European Parliament. The latter ought to respond within the time-limit set by the Council, but not later than within three months. In the absence of Parliament's opinion, the Council is free to act.[12] The Presidency and the Commission shall regularly inform the European Parliament of discussion within the Council and the European Parliament may ask questions of the Council or make recommendations.[13]

The TEU, as amended by the Amsterdam Treaty[14] encourages Member States to establish 'closer co-operation' between themselves and, in this context, they may be authorised to avail themselves of the institutions, procedures and mechanisms laid down by the Treaties with the aim of enabling the Union to develop more rapidly into an area of freedom, security and justice.[15] Such authorization may be granted by the Council acting by a qualified majority at the request of the Member States concerned and after inviting the Commission to present its opinion. The request shall be forwarded to the European Parliament, presumably, for information only since its opinion is not required. If a member of the Council declares that, for important and stated reasons of national policy, it intends to oppose the granting of an authorization by qualified majority, a vote shall not be taken. However the Council may, acting by a qualified majority, request that the matter be referred to the European Council for decision by unanimity.[16]

Any Member State which wishes to become a party to co-operation in the area of police and judicial co-operation in criminal matters as aforesaid shall notify its intention to the Council and to the Commission, which shall give an opinion to the Council possibly accompanied by a recommendation for specific arrangements. The Council shall decide on the request and the specific arrangements. The decision shall be deemed to be positive unless the Council, acting by a qualified majority, decides to hold it in abeyance, in which case the Council shall state its reasons and set a deadline for re-examining its decision.[17]

---

9   Ex Art K.8.
10   TEU Art 37 (ex Art K.9).
11   TEU Art 38 (ex Art K.10).
12   TEU Art 39(1) (ex Art K.11(1)).
13   TEU Art 39(2), (3).
14   TEU Arts 43–45 (ex Arts K.15–K.17).
15   TEU Art 40(1) (ex Art K.12(1)).
16   TEU Art 39(2).
17   TEU Art 39(3).

The provisions set out in TEU Article 40(1–3) shall be subject to the jurisdiction of the Court of Justice.[18] However TEU Article 40 is without prejudice to the provisions of the Protocol integrating the Schengen *Acquis* into the framework of the European Union.[19]

Administrative expenditures which are incurred by the institutions shall be charged to the budget of the European Communities.[20] Operational expenditure arising from the implementation of the policy shall also be charged to the budget, except where the Council unanimously decides otherwise. In the latter case it shall be charged to the Member States in accordance with the gross national product scale, unless the Council unanimously decides otherwise.[1]

The Council, acting unanimously on the initiative of the Commission or a Member State and after consulting the European Parliament, may decide that matters covered by TEU Article 29 (police and judicial co-operation in criminal matters) shall fall under EC Title IV (visas, asylum, immigration and other policies related to the movement of persons, see infra). In such a case the Member States shall adopt that decision in accordance with their constitutions.[2]

(9)   CLOSER CO-OPERATION AND THE SCHENGEN *ACQUIS*

Title VII of the TEU contains provisions permitting Member States to establish closer co-operation between themselves, consistently with the Treaties, even though that co-operation involves only some of the Member States. That development in Community law was prompted in part by a growing divergence in a number of areas between the existing Member States (originating in what is now referred to as 'the Schengen *Acquis*' and culminating in the 'opt-outs' from various parts of the Maastricht and Amsterdam Treaties, negotiated in particular by the United Kingdom) and in part by the realisation that any new members of the European Union would have a far harder task in adapting to the Community system than hitherto. The conclusion reached was that the European Union could not act as a monolithic block and that some degree of flexibility had to be built into it. Particular provision had to be made for the Schengen *Acquis*, which was an existing example of closer co-operation between some, but not all, Member States.

In 1985, the governments of the States of the Benelux Economic Union, the Federal Republic of Germany and France signed an agreement at Schengen, in Luxembourg, on the gradual abolition of checks at their common borders.[3] Supplemented by an Implementation Convention adopted in 1990, the Schengen Agreement provided for a more advanced form of liberalisation of internal frontier controls between the signatories than existed at that time within the Community. The Schengen Agreement and the various other measures adopted under its aegis proved a success; and the original signatories were joined by Italy (1990), Spain and Portugal (1991), Greece (1992), Austria (1995) and Denmark, Finland and Sweden (1996). The resulting body of law became known as 'the Schengen *Acquis*'. Iceland and Norway became associated with the implementation of the Schengen *Acquis* and its further development pursuant to an agreement made in

18   TEU Art 40(4).
19   TEU Art 40(5). As to the Schengen *Acquis*, see the next section.
20   TEU Art 41(2) (ex Art K.13(2)).
 1   TEU Art 41(2)(3) (ex Art K.13(2) (3)).
 2   TEU Art 42 (ex Art K.14).
 3   Agreement on the Gradual Abolition of Controls of the Common Frontiers, 14 June 1985, English text, HL Paper 90 (1989), Border Controls of People, Select Committee of the European Communities, Session 1988-89, 22nd report, 35.

1996. Only two Member States remained outside those arrangements: Ireland and the United Kingdom. With effect from the entry into force of the Amsterdam Treaty, the Schengen *Acquis* was formally integrated into the framework of the EU through what is now Protocol 2 to the TEU.

The provisions of the Schengen *Acquis* are applicable as part of the framework of the EU only to the extent that they are compatible with the EU and Community law; and their integration does not affect the position of Ireland and the United Kingdom.[4] The effect of integration is that the parties to the Schengen *Acquis* are authorised to establish closer co-operation between themselves within the scope of the Schengen *Acquis*. That co-operation is to be conducted within the institutional and legal framework of the EU and subject to the relevant provisions of the TEU and the EC Treaty. The Schengen *Acquis* is applicable to the parties thereto as a matter of Community law from the date of entry into force of the Amsterdam Treaty; and, as from that date, the Council has replaced the Executive Committee provided for in the Convention implementing the Schengen Agreement. In addition, the jurisdiction of the ECJ, as defined in the EC Treaty, extends to the Schengen *Acquis* (save that the ECJ has no jurisdiction over measures or decisions relating to the maintenance of law and order and the safeguarding of internal security).[5]

Since the Schengen *Acquis* is integrated into the EU only to the extent that it is compatible with the EU and Community law, the Council must determine what is the legal basis in Community law for each of the provisions and decisions that constitute the *Acquis*.[6] The determination of the Council is not a condition of the incorporation of the *Acquis*: the relevant Treaty provisions (whatever they are) apply automatically, even in the absence of a determination of the Council;[7] and, if there is no relevant Treaty provision, the relevant part of the *Acquis* cannot be integrated. Subject to that, and in the absence of a determination of the Council, provisions or decisions forming part of the Schengen *Acquis* are regarded as acts based on Title VI of the TEU (Police and Judicial Co-operation in Criminal Matters).[8] Proposals and initiatives building upon the Schengen *Acquis* (that is, measures adopted after the integration of the *Acquis* into the framework of the EU) are subject to the relevant provisions of the Treaties and may be adopted and applied by the parties to the Schengen *Acquis*, without the involvement of other Member States (although they may participate if they wish).[9] For the purpose of identifying the legal basis of the *Acquis* in Community law (and excluding any parts of the *Acquis* that were no longer operative), the contents of the Schengen *Acquis* were defined by Council Decision 1999/435 and the legal basis for each part of the *Acquis* was determined in Council Decision 1999/436.[10]

---

4 Provision is made for the participation of Ireland and the United Kingdom in the Schengen *Acquis*: see the Protocol integrating the Schengen *Acquis* into the framework of the European Union, Arts 4, 5(1) and 8. In 1999, the United Kingdom submitted a request to participate in certain provisions of the Schengen *Acquis*. The Council decided in May 2000 that the United Kingdom could do so: see Council Decision 2000/365 (OJ 2000, L131/43).
5 Ibid, Arts 1 and 2.
6 Ibid, Art 2(1), second sub-para.
7 Ibid, Art 5(2).
8 Ibid, Art 2(1), fourth sub-para.
9 Ibid, Art 5(1), which refers to the authorisation given by TEU Art 40 (ex Art K.12) and EC Art 11 (ex Art 5a).
10 OJ 1999, L176/1 and 17, respectively. Provision was made for Iceland and Norway by Council Decision 1999/437 and by an agreement made with those countries (see OJ 1999, L176/31 and 35 respectively). The agreement came into effect on 26 June 2000 (see OJ 2000, L149/36). Further arrangements for applying the Schengen *Acquis* to the Scandinavian countries were made by Decision 2000/777 (OJ 2000, L309/24).

The Schengen *Acquis* provided an example of how some Member States could develop closer co-operation between themselves, consistently with the objectives of the Treaties; but it also indicated the potential disadvantages of such a development taking place independently. Accordingly, TEU Articles 43-45 (ex Art K.15-17) provide for the development of such forms of closer co-operation that do not involve all the Member States within the framework of the TEU and the EC Treaty.

TEU Article 43 (ex Art K.15) permits Member States to make use of the institutions, procedures and mechanisms laid down by the TEU and the EC Treaty for the purpose of establishing closer co-operation between themselves[11] provided that such co-operation meets eight criteria: it must be aimed at furthering the objectives of the Union and at protecting and serving its interests; it must respect the principles of the TEU and the EC Treaty and the single institutional framework of the Union; it must be used only as a last resort, where the objectives of the Treaties could not be attained by applying the procedures laid down in them; it must concern at least a majority of Member States; it must not affect the '*acquis communautaire*' and the measures adopted under the other provisions of the Treaties; it must not affect the competences, rights, obligations and interests of non-participating Member States; it must be open to all Member States and allow them to become parties to the co-operation at any time, provided that they comply with the basic decision and the decisions taken with that framework of co-operation; and it must comply with additional criteria laid down in EC Article 11 (ex Art 5a) and TEU Article 40 (ex Art K.12), depending upon the area of co-operation, and be authorised by the Council.[12]

EC Article 11(1) (ex Art 5a(1)) provides that the co-operation envisaged must satisfy five additional criteria: it must not concern areas which fall within the exclusive competence of the Community; it must not affect Community policies, actions or programmes; it must not concern the citizenship of the Union or discriminate between nationals of Member States; it must remain within the limits of the powers conferred upon the Community by the EC Treaty; and it must neither constitute a discrimination or a restriction of trade between Member States nor distort competition in such trade. TEU Article 40 (ex Art K.12) is concerned with closer co-operation regarding police and judicial co-operation in criminal matters.[13]

A permitted form of co-operation must be authorised by the Council, which acts by a qualified majority on a proposal from the Commission and after consulting the European Parliament. The Commission's proposal is made after the Commission has received a request from the States concerned. If the Commission does not make a proposal in response to a request, it must inform the Member States concerned of its reasons for not doing so. If, for important reasons of national policy (which must be stated when the objection is raised), a member of the Council objects to the grant of authorisation by qualified majority vote, a vote shall not be taken. The proposal for closer co-operation may be abandoned at that stage. If it is not abandoned, the Council may, acting by a qualified majority, refer the matter to the Council (composed, for these purposes, of the heads of State or of Government of the Member States) for decision by unanimity.[14] A Member State wishing to join authorised co-operation between

---

11   TEU Title VII appears to apply to the Schengen *Acquis* but EC Art 11 operates without prejudice to the Protocol integrating the Schengen *Acquis* into the framework of the European Union: see EC Art 11(5).
12   TEU Art 43(1).
13   See p 44 above.
14   EC Art 11(2).

other Member States must notify its intention to the Council and to the Commission. The latter must give an opinion to the Council within three months of receipt of the notification and, within four months of the date of the notification (which may not be the same as the date of its receipt by the Commission), the Commission must decide on it and on any specific arrangements that may be necessitated by the participation of the State in question.[15]

The relevant institutional provisions of the TEU and the EC Treaty apply to the procedure for the adoption of the acts and decisions necessary for the implementation of an authorised form of co-operation (that is to say, the act or decision in question must be adopted in accordance with the procedure indicated for the making of acts or decisions under the Treaty provision that is capable of providing the legal basis for the act or decision in question). However, although all members of the Council are able to take part in the deliberations leading up to the making of the act or decision, only those members who represent Member States participating in the authorised co-operation may be involved in the actual adoption of decisions.[16] Acts and decisions that are necessary for any form of authorised co-operation are subject to all relevant provisions of the EC Treaty, save where it and the TEU expressly provide otherwise.[17] Accordingly, the normal procedures for challenging the lawfulness of such measures apply unless expressly excluded.[18] When a Member State participates in authorised co-operation, it is obliged to apply relevant acts and decisions adopted for the implementation of the co-operation. Non-participating Member States are obliged not to impede the implementation of those acts and decisions by participating States.[19] Expenditure resulting from implementing any form of authorised co-operation, other than administrative costs incurred by the Community institutions, are borne by the participating states unless the Council unanimously decides otherwise.[20]

(10)   RELATIONSHIP BETWEEN THE COMMUNITY, THE UNION AND THE MEMBER STATES

(a)   Attributed powers and the occupied field
The relationship between the Community and the Member States is based on the attribution (or delegation) of state powers to the Community institutions and the division of functions. Thus, within the specific domain of the Community the institutions are provided with exclusive authority whilst outside the domain of the Community the Member States retain their powers and responsibilities but the demarcation line is neither clear not precise.[1] Indeed it keeps shifting in favour of the Community/Union. In fact the Community institutions exercise portions of the original powers of sovereign states and in that sense act in a subsidiary capacity. However, to the extent of that delegation, by virtue of the Treaty, a common domain has been created and within that domain the Member States' action has been sublimated to that of the Community. This domain, originally implied in the founding Treaties, tends to expand through the combined

---

15   EC Art 11(3).
16   TEU Art 44(1) (ex Art K.16(1)). Provision is made adjusting the definitions of qualified majority and of unanimity where not all Member States participate in the adoption process.
17   EC Art 11(4).
18   TEU Art 46 (ex Art L) in fact provides expressly that the ECJ's powers extend to TEU Title VII.
19   TEU Art 43(2).
20   TEU Art 44(2).
1   See Case 30/59: *De Gezamenlijke Steenkolenmijnen in Limburg v High Authority* [1961] ECR 1 at 23 (full quotation p 333, infra).

effect of the preamble to the EC Treaty which lists in general terms the political, economic and social objectives of the Treaty and EC Article 308 (ex Art 235)) which enables the Council to legislate on the recommendation of the Commission and in consultation with the European Parliament in matters relevant to the Common Market which have not been expressly dealt with by the Treaty. However, quite apart from the express limitation arising from the reference to the Common Market, the function of Article 308 is purely residual. 'It follows from the very wording of Article [308] that ... its use as a legal basis for a measure is justified only where no other provision of the Treaty gives the Community institutions the necessary power to adopt the measure in question'.[2] It cannot by itself alone provide the necessary authority for specific legislative measures and also cannot be used as a substitute for Treaty provisions which, in view of their specific purpose, provide the correct legal basis for implementing legislation.[3] Within these limitations new policies, ie on energy, industry, regional development, the protection of the environment and of the consumer, science and technology, education and culture, have evolved.

Once delegated, the power cannot be withdrawn[4] or, as stated by the ECJ on several occasions,[5] where the Community has acted within its competence the Member States must refrain from taking concurrent action. It follows that where 'the Community has established a common organization in a particular sector, the Member States must refrain from taking any unilateral measure even if that measure is likely to support the common policy of the Community'.[6] However, until the Community has claimed its competence by using it the Member States are free to act as sovereign states.[7] This is the doctrine of the 'occupied field' which, recently, has prevented the United Kingdom from enacting legislation which would extend the number of lighting devices compulsory for motor vehicles beyond the list comprised in a Community directive.[8] Thus the Community determines the extent of the legal integration and does not permit the Member States to be out of step either by exceeding the limit or failing to reach it. It will not, of course, interfere in situations wholly internal to a Member State.[9]

By analogy, the above observations apply to the Union as the TEU concerns the competences of the Member States hitherto retained by them as being outside the TEC. However, notwithstanding the principle of solidarity which pervades both the Community and the Union, the delegation of powers attributed to the Union has not reached the degree of intensity enjoyed by the Community. Whilst the delegation to the Community is nearly complete and perfect as the

---

2   Case 56/88: *United Kingdom v Council* [1989] 2 CMLR 789; at para 13, [1989] ECR 1615.
3   See Case 45/86: *Commission v Council, Re Generalized Tariff Preferences* [1987] ECR 1493, [1988] 2 CMLR 131 based on Case 56/88.
4   Case 24/83: *Gewiese v Mackenzie* [1984] ECR 817.
5   Eg Case 22/70, infra p 52 note 1, Opinion 1/75, supra.
6   Case C-249/91: *Commission v France*, [1994] ECR I-787.
7   Cases 3, 4, 6/76: *Officer van Justitie v Kramer* [1976] ECR 1279, [1976] 2 CMLR 440. Case 76/86: *Commission v Germany, Re milk substitutes* [1989] ECR 1021, [1991] 1 CMLR 741. See also Case C-49/89: *Corsica Ferries France v Direction Générale des Douanes Françaises* [1989] ECR 4441, [1991] 2 CMLR 227.
8   Case 60/86: *Commission v United Kingdom* [1988] ECR 3921, [1988] 3 CMLR 437. See also Case C-35/88: *Commission v Greece, Re KYDEP (organization of agricultural market is an occupied field)* [1990] ECR I-3125, [1992] 1 CMLR 548.
9   See eg Case 44/84: *Hurd v Jones (HM Inspector of Taxes)* [1986] ECR 29, [1986] 2 CMLR 1; Case 238/82: *Duphar BV v Netherlands, Re regulation of medical prescriptions without discriminating against imports* [1984] ECR 523, [1985] 1 CMLR 256; Case C-333/88: *Tither v IRC, Re income tax mortgage relief* [1990] 2 CMLR 779.

competences of the Member States are carried out by the institutional mechanism, the Union operates mainly through the mechanism of the inter-governmental conference. The difference is not only a matter of degree and form but, more importantly, a matter of substance as far as the efficacy and binding force of the decisions are concerned. Moreover the Union cannot rely on implied powers as is the case of the Community. The judicial control, in the case of the Community, is complete as far as the conduct of the institutions and of the Member States is concerned whereas, in the case of the Union, it is only proportional to the commitment of the Member States to the Union.

(b) Subsidiarity

'Subsidiarity', inserted into the Maastricht Treaty, has a philosophical[10] and a practical[11] significance. As a concept it is derived from the Catholic doctrine of Thomas Aquinas followed by papal encyclicals through the ages[12] in which the Popes have endeavoured to assert human values in face of abuse of these values by social or political evils of their times. In Community vocabulary 'subsidiarity' can be related to the 1931 Encyclical in which Pius XI, addressing the danger of the individual being smothered under the increasing weight of the corporate state (especially of a fascist or communist type), sought to reaffirm the unique nature of man as a responsible being and a founder of social groups of ascending order. Thus local or municipal authorities ought not to impede the individual's initiative in matters he can best cope with and the central government of the state ought not to impose its will upon the local or municipal governments acting in the field of their competence. To enable the individual and the lower echelons of society to fulfil their part in the social groupings decisions should always be taken at the lowest practical level. In this sense subsidiarity is opposed to centralism and the unnecessary exercise of power downwards. However it also means that, in practical terms, the higher echelons ought to focus their attention on what is essential and appropriate to their function. Applied to the European Union subsidiarity ought to contribute to a sensible distribution of powers or functions as regards the individual, the Member State and the Union's institutions. A lesson in that respect has been learned by the Community when it was concluded that in dealing with standardization only essential standards ought to be regulated by Community legislation.

Subsidiarity has not been invented at Maastricht[13] though it has excited a deal of literature and speculation as to its meaning and portent under the Maastricht provisions.

EC Article 5 (ex Art 3b) provides:

'The Community shall act within the limits of the powers conferred upon it by this Treaty and of the objectives assigned to it therein. In areas which do not fall within its exclusive competence, the Community shall take action, in accordance with the principle of subsidiarity, only if and in so far as the

---

10 Beale, A, and Geary, R, 'Subsidiarity comes of age?' New Law Journal, 7 January 1994, p 12.
11 Lasok, D, 'Subsidiarity and the Occupied Field' New Law Journal, 11 September 1992, p 1230.
12 Eg *Rerum Novarum* of Leo XIII; *Quadragesimo Anno* of Pius XI; *Centensimus Annus* of John Paul II.
13 See Report on Economic Union, EC Bull Supp 5/75; Draft Treaty establishing the European Union, EC Bull Supp 6/83; Principle of Subsidiarity, EP Committee on International Affairs, Rapporteur Valery Giscard d'Estaing; DOC EN/RR/91692 and DOC EN/RR/98228; See Cass, 'The Word that saves Maastricht? The principle of subsidiarity and the division of powers within the European Community' 29 CML Rev 1107–1136.

objectives of the proposed action cannot be sufficiently achieved by the Member States and can therefore, by reason of the scale or effects of the proposed action, be better achieved by the Community. Any action by the Community shall not go beyond what is necessary to achieve the objectives of this Treaty.'

The operative meaning and scope of ECS Article 3b is not easy to grasp. The Commission, explaining the principle, stated that:

'In the Community context subsidiarity means that the functions handed over to the Community are those which the Member States, at the various levels of decision-making can no longer discharge satisfactorily.'[14]

The Edinburgh European Council (11–12 December 1992) accepted this formulation and instructed the Council of Ministers to seek an inter-institutional agreement in this matter. The inter-institutional conference convened in Luxembourg before the TEU came into force adopted a declaration on 'democracy, transparency and subsidiarity'[15] binding the Council, the Parliament and the Commission. In particular the Commission undertook to demonstrate that the principle has been observed in the explanatory memorandum accompanying each of its proposals and to submit an annual report to Parliament and the Council. Moreover the Commission decided to withdraw a number of proposals considered at Edinburgh. The Commission also adopted a report analysing existing legislation in the light of subsidiarity and identifying a number of areas where the measures can be recast, simplified or repealed.[16] The Protocol on the application of the principles of subsidiarity and proportionality attached to the Amsterdam Treaty purports to explain the working of the principle in practice. Thus in exercising the powers conferred on the Community each institution shall ensure that the principles of subsidiarity and proportionality are complied with. It shall also ensure that action by the Community shall not go beyond what is necessary to achieve the objectives of the Treaty. The application of the principles shall respect the general provisions and the objectives of the Treaty, particularly as regards the maintaining of the *acquis communautaire* and the institutional balance. It shall not affect the principles developed by the Court of Justice regarding the relationship between national and Community law and it should take into account TEU Article 6 (ex Art F(4)), according to which 'the Union shall provide itself with the means necessary to attain its objectives and carry through its policies'.

Whilst the principle of subsidiarity does not call into question the powers conferred on the EC as interpreted by the Court of Justice, the criteria of subsidiarity shall relate to areas for which the Community does not have exclusive competence and provide a guide as to how those powers are to be exercised at the Community level. 'Subsidiarity is a dynamic concept and should be applied in the light of the objectives set out in the Treaty. It allows Community action within the limits of its powers to be expanded where circumstances so require, and conversely, to be restricted or discontinued where it is no longer required.'

In the light of the Protocol subsidiarity is not a static concept but, since it is applied to areas in which the Community does not have exclusive competence, its effect is akin to implied powers going, in effect, beyond the scope of EC Article 308

---

14   The Principle of Subsidiarity: Communication of the Commission to the Council and the European Parliament, SEC(92) 1990 Final, para 2.
15   EC Bull 10–1993, points 1.6.2 and 2.2.1; and points 1.6.3 and 2.2.2.
16   COM(93) 545; EC Bull 11–1993, point 1.7.2.

(ex Art 235). It seems unlikely that the Community would restrict or relinquish powers acquired on the basis of subsidiarity. If anything, it would probably cling to *acquis communautaire* in accordance with the doctrine of occupied field.

The protocol requires justification of Community legislation in compliance with the principles of subsidiarity and proportionality; and the reasons that a Community objective can be better achieved by the Community than by the Member States must be substantiated. The following guidelines should indicate whether the proposed action cannot be sufficiently achieved by Member States in the framework of their constitutional systems:

– the issue in question has transnational aspects which cannot be satisfactorily regulated by Member States;
– actions by Member States alone or lack of Community action would conflict with the requirements of the Treaty (eg the need to correct distortion of competition or to avoid disguised restrictions on trade or strengthen economic or social cohesion) or otherwise significantly damage Member States' interests;
– action at Community level would produce clear benefits by reason of its scale or effects compared with action at the level of the Member States.

The Protocol stresses that the Community action shall be as simple as possible and consistent with effective enforcement. The Community shall legislate only where necessary. Directives should be preferred to regulations and framework directives to detailed measures leaving as much scope for national decision as possible. While respecting Community law, care should be taken to respect well established national arrangements and the organization and working of Member States' legal systems. Where appropriate and subject to the need of proper enforcement, Community measures should provide Member States with alternative ways to achieve the objectives of the measures.

Without prejudice to its right of initiative, the Commission should:

– except in cases of particular urgency or confidentiality, consult widely before proposing legislation and publish consultation documents;
– justify the relevance of its proposals with regard to the principle of subsidiarity;
– take into account the burden, whether financial or administrative, falling upon the Community, national governments, local authorities, economic operators and citizens;
– submit an annual report to the European Council, the European Parliament and the Council on the application on the principle of subsidiarity.

While observing the relevant procedures, the European Parliament and the Council shall, as an integral part of the overall examination of the Commission proposal, consider their consistency with the principle of subsidiarity. In the course of procedures referred to in EC Article 251 and 252,[17] the European Parliament shall be informed by the Council of its reasons to adopt its common position in relation to the principle of subsidiarity and proportionality.

The Protocol goes a long way to explain the working of the principle of subsidiarity.

Subsidiarity, as a principle of law, joins the ranks of general principles of the Treaty like the principle of solidarity (EC Article 10 (ex Art 5)) which underpins

17   Ex Art 189b and Art 189c.

the Member States' duties in the Community, the principle of non-discrimination (EC Article 12 (ex Art 6)) which has been used extensively to combat the social evil of inequality (equality being an essential ingredient of justice) or the principle of implied powers (EC Article 308 (ex Art 235)) which enables the Council to act sensibly in furtherance of the objectives of the Treaty and also to check the legal basis of Community legislation, ie whether the Council acted according to the principle of unanimity or qualified majority.[18] While these principles have enriched the case law they have not been applied in isolation or in abstract. In this sense they can be said to be 'non-justiciable' but, when invoked in an auxiliary capacity in specific situations they become subject to judicial interpretation. Thus, when the Court of Justice considered the allegation that the Commission has infringed the principle of subsidiarity by imposing a fine for breach of competition rules, it dismissed the claim as unfounded since before the entry into force of the Maastricht Treaty Article 3b did not 'constitute a general principle of law by reference to which the legality of Community acts should be reviewed'.[19]

Subsidiarity is a signal to the Community legislator and to the Member States to exert vigilance over what is done on their behalf. Given the basic assumption of the Community, that Community powers have derived from the delegation of sovereignty of the Member States, subsidiarity may serve to check an excessive tendency towards centralism and, in that sense, it may act as a brake on the adventurism of Community institutions and on the ambitions of their bureaucracy but not on the development of policies mapped out in the Treaties.

Subsidiarity is a reflection of federalism as indeed is the Community design. Therefore the relationship between the Member States and the Community, given the delegation or attribution of power, reflects on another general principle, that of occupied field. As a result of that delegation, by virtue of the Treaties, a common domain has been created and, within that domain the original powers of the Member States have been sublimated to the Community institutions. This domain tends to expand due to the inherent dynamism of the Community. Once delegated the power cannot be withdrawn[20] or, as stated by the Court of Justice, where the Community has acted within its competence the Member States must refrain from taking concurrent action.[1] Thus subsidiarity shall not enable the Member States to claw back the powers already lost or likely to be lost by virtue of the TEC, as some have hoped.

Similarly, subsidiarity shall not justify the Member States legislating in excess of the Community measures[2] though there should be more room for Member States' discretion by means of derogations written into Community legislation.

The principle of subsidiarity does not conflict with the occupied field but ought to sharpen the discussion on the use of powers attributed to the Community institutions. Its main challenge lies in the Community legislation and it remains yet to be seen what contribution it will make to the shaping of the Union.

---

18   See Case 45/86: *Commission v Council, Re Generalized Tariff Preferences* [1987] ECR 1493.
19   Case T-29/92: *SPO v Commission* [1995] ECR II-289 (para 331).
20   Case 24/83: *Gewiese v Mackenzie* [1984] ECR 817.
 1   Case 22/70: *Commission v Council* [1971] ECR 263 at 2775; Opinion 1/75, *Re the OECD Understanding on the Local Cost Standard* [1975] ECR 1355 at 1364.
 2   See eg Case 60/86: *Commission v United Kingdom* [1988] ECR 3921, [1988] 3 CMLR 437; Case 195/84: *Denkavit Futermittel GmbH v Land Nordrhein-Westfalen* [1985] ECR 3181, [1987] 3 CMLR 585; Case 29/87: *Dansk Denkavit ApS v Landbrugsministeriet* [1990] 1 CMLR 203; Case 255/86: *Commission v Belgium* [1988] ECR 693, [1989] 3 CMLR 91.

(c)   Member States' duties to the Community

By a net of duties, transcending the contractual obligations of states in international law, the Treaty integrates the Member States and their peoples into the Community. These duties are general and particular, explicit and implicit, horizontal and vertical.

The duty to comply with Community law is addressed to the states as a whole. Thus it is no excuse that the government is without fault when another organ, even a constitutionally independent institution of the state, like the parliament, is liable.[3]

The Community too is bound by the principle of solidarity.[4]

The most important general duties are expressed in forms of solidarity[5] whereby the Member States undertake to take all appropriate measures to promote the objectives of the Treaties and to refrain from any measures which could jeopardize the achievements of these objectives, and non-discrimination on the ground of nationality.[6] The former is often cited in cases where states are prosecuted for the failure to comply with their obligations; the latter, coupled especially with the social provisions of the Treaty, has been developed by case law of the Community Court not only into a shield of protection of the rights of individuals but also as a weapon against discriminatory national legislation.[7]

The duty of solidarity does not permit Member States to adopt measures that could render a Community law impotent[8] or to retain on their statute book a national measure inconsistent with Community law. Thus it is not enough, for example, for the Constitutional Court of a Member State to order the judiciary to disregard statutory provisions of that kind, for the state ought to repeal the offending legislation.[9] Similarly a municipal legislative provision cannot be set up against the direct effect of a regulation without compromising the fundamental principle of supremacy of Community law.[10] As for directives, these have to be transposed into national law as binding provisions, not merely as advisory circulars.[11]

The principle of non-discrimination on the ground of nationality applies to all persons in all situations covered by Community law. Therefore, for example, a British tourist mugged in France could not be denied compensation under the French scheme which provided compensation for the victims of crime but limited it to French citizens only.[12]

---

3   Case 77/69: *Commission v Belgium* [1970] ECR 237.
4   See Case C-2/88 Imm: *Re FF Zwartveld* [1990] ECR I-4405, [1990] 3 CMLR 457.
5   EC Art 10 (ex Art 5); EAEC Art 192; ECSC Art 86.
6   EC Art 12 (ex Art 6); EAEC Arts 96 and 97; ECSC Art 69.
7   See eg Cases 61/81: *Commission v United Kingdom* [1982] ECR 2601, [1982] 3 CMLR 284; 165/82 *Commission v United Kingdom* [1983] ECR 3431, [1984] 1 CMLR 44; Case 248/83: *Commission v Germany* [1985] ECR 1459, [1986] 2 CMLR 588; Case 163/82: *Commission v Italy* [1983] ECR 3273, [1984] 3 CMLR 169; Case 167/73: *Commission v France* [1974] ECR 359, [1974] 2 CMLR 216.
8   See eg Case 231/83: *Cullet v Centre Leclerc* [1985] ECR 305, [1985] 2 CMLR 524.
9   Case 104/86: *Commission v Italy* [1988] ECR 1799, [1989] 3 CMLR 25.
10 Case 34/73: *Variola SpA v Administrazione Italiana della Finanze* [1973] ECR 981 at para 15.
11 Case 239/85: *Commission v Belgium* [1986] ECR 3645, [1988] 1 CMLR 248. See also Case C-240/89: *Commission v Italy, Re Directive on the Protection of Workers from Asbestos* [1990] ECR I-4853. Cases C-13/90 and C-14/90: *Commission v France*; [1991] ECR I-4327 and 4331; Case C-381/92: *Commission v Ireland* [1994] ECR I-215.
12 Case 186/87: *Cowan v Trésor Public* [1989] ECR 195, [1990] 2 CMLR 613.

Explicit duties are expressed in the form of a command (eg that customs duties must be abolished) whilst implicit duties can be inferred from the provisions of the Treaties which envisage a certain action (eg adjustment of national monopolies or obligations arising from treaties with non-member countries) or the control of the state apparatus in its executive, legislative and judicial functions in order to facilitate the execution of explicit duties.

There is also an implied duty of vigilance exemplified by the right of the Member States to challenge the validity of acts of the institutions even if they are party to the act in question (for example a regulation made by the Council). Such challenge can be taken on the grounds of lack of competence, misuse of powers, breach of Community law or of any essential procedural requirement. Recently this enabled the United Kingdom to obtain annulment of two directives, one for the use of certain hormones in livestock farming,[13] and another providing for minimum standards of comfort for battery hens.[14] In both cases the text of the directive differed from the draft on which the vote was taken, the irregularities having been perpetrated in the secretariat of the Council.

Horizontal duties reflect the international law principle of reciprocity coupled with the Community principle of solidarity enshrined in EC Article 10 (ex Art 5). Sometimes these duties are expressed in the direct language of command or prohibition, sometimes in the indirect language of a provision which entrusts a specific task to the Community institutions implying that it will be carried out through co-operation between the Member States and reciprocal respect. For example, in the field of the movement of goods there is a duty not to discriminate against foreign goods by hindering their movements,[15] discriminatory taxes, reliance on derogations to protect national products and, even in government-sponsored advertising, by exhorting the public to buy national products.[16] In brief a Member State cannot unilaterally opt out of its obligations. Indeed, 'in permitting the Member States to profit from the Community the Treaty imposes on them also the obligation to respect its rules ... The failure in the duty of solidarity accepted by Member States by the fact of their adherence to the Community strikes at the very root of the Community legal order'.[17]

Vertical duties comprise the Member States' duties to the Community itself and to the citizens of all the Member States including their own. Thus the executive of a Member State must adopt the administrative measures necessary to carry into effect the Community policies, the legislature must enact implementing laws and make sure that the national system is in line with the rules of Community law and the judiciary must ensure not only the correct application of Community law but also the legal protection which individuals, irrespective of their nationality, derive from the Community legal order.

The rights of individuals are enshrined not only in the principle of the free movement of persons, ie workers, self-employed persons and the providers of

---

13 Case 68/86: *United Kingdom v Council* [1988] ECR 855, [1988] 2 CMLR 543. See also Case C-331/88: *R v Minister of Agriculture, ex p Fédération Européenne de la Santé Animale* [1990] ECR I-4023; [1991] I, CMLR 507 where the ECJ held valid Directive 88/146 prohibiting the use in livestock farming of hormonal substances.

14 Case 131/86: *United Kingdom v Council, Re Battery Hens* [1988] ECR 905, [1988] 2 CMLR 364. See also Case C-128/94: *Hans Hönig v Stadt Stockach* [1995] ECR I-3389.

15 See Lasok, D, *The Customs Law of the EEC* (3rd edn, 1998) chs 3–6.

16 Case 249/81: *Commission v Ireland, Re Buy Irish Campaign* [1982] ECR 4005, [1983] 2 CMLR 104.

17 Case 128/78: *Commission v United Kingdom* [1979] ECR 419, [1979] 2 CMLR 45 at paras 9 and 12.

services and their families and the social security protection, but also various other safeguards. These safeguards include equal treatment in the case of similar offences committed by citizens and aliens,[18] due process of the law[19] and the so-called Eurodefences, ie defences from criminal prosecution under national law which is inconsistent with Community law[20] and individual rights protected under Community legislation.[1]

(d) Enforcement of Member States' duties
The uniqueness of the Community legal order lies in the control and enforcement of legality to which sovereign states together with the institutions and individuals are subject. Member States have undertaken unconditionally the obligation of submitting the differences arising from the interpretation and application of the Treaties to no other method or authority but the Community Court.[2] Having submitted to a compulsory adjudication by the ECJ they have also delegated to the Commission the power of prosecution.[3] This measure of confidence and integration was hailed by the ECJ as 'far exceeding the rules heretofore recognized in classical international law' and the procedure as 'the *ultima ratio* enabling the Community interests enshrined in the Treaty to prevail over the inertia and resistance of Member States'.[4] However individuals are not in a position of compelling the Commission to act.[5]

The procedure, laid down in EC Article 226 (ex Art 169), consists of an administrative and judicial stage. Thus the Commission must engage in a dialogue with the state concerned in order to establish the facts and, where warranted, issue a reasoned opinion giving the accused state the opportunity to submit its observations. The purpose of the pre-litigation procedure is to enable the State in question to explain its position and ward off the accusation.[6] Failure to address itself to the observation submitted by the State renders the action of the Commission inadmissible.[7] The opinion that there is a prima facie case against the State itself cannot be challenged with the object of securing its annulment since the State can defend its position at the judicial stage of the proceedings.[8] However, if the Commission fails to substantiate its accusation in the administrative stage the case will not proceed to the judicial stage.[9]

---

18 Eg Case 8/77: *Sagulo, Brenco and Bakhouche* [1977] ECR 1495, [1977] 2 CMLR 585. Case 36/75: *Rutili v Ministère de l'Interieur* [1975] ECR 1219 at 1232, [1976] 1 CMLR 140.
19 Eg Case 98/79: *Pecastaing v Belgium* [1980] ECR 691, [1980] 3 CMLR 685.
20 Eg Case 83/78: *Pigs Marketing Board v Redmond* [1978] ECR 2347, [1979] 1 CMLR 177.
1   See eg Case C-6, 9/90: *Francovich v Italy* [1991] ECR I-5357, [1993] 2 CMLR 66; Case C-479/93: *Francovich v Italy* [1995] ECR I-3843; Joined Cases C-178/94, C-179/94, C-188/94, C-189/94 and C-190/94: *Erich Dillentoffer v Germany* [1996] ECR I-4845.
2   EC Art 292 (ex Art 219); EAEC Art 193; ECSC Art 87.
3   EC Art 226 (ex Art 169); EAEC Art 141; ECSC Art 88.
4   Case 25/59: *Netherlands v High Authority* [1960] ECR 355.
5   See Case 247/87: *Star Fruit v Commission* [1989] ECR 291; Case C-371/89: *Emrich v Commission* [1990] ECR I-1555. Joined Cases T-479/93 and T-559/93: *Bernardi v Commission* [1994] ECR II-1115; Case C-87/89: *Société Nationale Interprofessionelle de la Tomate v Commission* [1990] ECR I-1981; [1991] 3 CMLR 439; Case T-117/96: *Intertronic F Cornelis GmbH v Commission* [1997] ECR II-141; Case T-201/96: *Smanor SA v Commission* [1997] ECR II-1081.
6   Case C-293/85: *Commission v Belgium* [1988] ECR 305 (para 13).
7   Case C-266/94: *Commission v Spain* [1995] ECR I-1975.
8   Joined Cases 6 and 11/69: *Commission v France* [1969] ECR 523 at para 36, [1970] CMLR 43.
9   Case C-296/92: *Commission v Italy* [1994] ECR I-1.

Having established a prima facie breach the Commission must inform the state of the measures which the Commission considers necessary to bring the failure to an end.[10] If these measures are taken within the specified time the action shall be discontinued but compliance after the deadline does not prevent the Commission from continuing the action.[11] In the view of the ECJ this is justified since the judgment of the Court 'may be of substantive interest as establishing the basis of a responsibility that a Member State may incur as a result of its default, as regards Member States, the Community or private parties'.[12]

The function of the judicial process in cases against the Member States is to declare the legal position and thus bring the erring state back on the path of legality. It is assumed that, motivated by the rule of law, the states will comply with the judgment. Should they fail to do so the Commission may bring another action, this time for the declaration that the Member States concerned has failed to fulfil an obligation under the Treaty,[13] but such cases are relatively rare.

If the Commission considers that the Member State concerned has not taken the requisite measures it shall, after giving that state the opportunity to submit its observations, issue a reasoned opinion specifying the points on which the state has not complied with the judgment of the Court of Justice. If the state fails to take the necessary measures within the time limit laid down by the Commission, the latter may bring the case before the Court. In doing so it shall specify the amount of the lump sum or penalty payment to be paid by the defaulting state and, in the case of non-compliance with the judgment, the Court may impose a lump sum or penalty payment as appropriate.[14] The sanction has been introduced by the TEU and its effectiveness remains to be evaluated.

(e) Derogations

There are two examples of derogation from the standard procedure laid down in EC Articles 226 and 227 (ex Arts 169 and 170)[15] in the case of supervision of state aids[16] and in the case of improper use by Member States of the power to enact national measures on grounds of 'major needs' referred to in EC Article 30 (ex Art 36) or relating to the protection of the environment or the working environment in accordance with Article 100a.[17] In such cases the Commission and any other Member State may, by-passing the administrative stage, bring the matter directly before the Court of Justice.[18]

---

10 Case 7/61: *Commission v Italy* [1961] ECR 317 at 334; [1962] CMLR 39.
11 Case C-362/90: *Commission v Italy* [1992] ECR I-2353.
12 Case 39/72: *Commission v Italy* [1973] ECR 101 at para 11, [1973] CMLR 439; Case C-29/90: *Commission v Greece* [1992] ECR I-1917 para 12; Case C-361/88: *Commission v Germany* [1991] ECR I-2567 and C-59/89: *Commission v Germany* [1991] ECR I-2607.
13 Eg see Case 160/85: *Commission v Italy* [1986] ECR 3245; Cases 227–230/85: *Commission v Belgium* [1988] ECR 1, [1989] 2 CMLR 797; Case 169/87 *Commission v France (No 2)* [1988] ECR 4093, [1990] 1 CMLR 49; Case C-375/89: *Commission v Belgium* [1991] ECR I-383; Case C-19/91: *Commission v Belgium* [1991] ECR I-5937; Case C-328/90: *Commission v Greece* [1992] ECR I-425; Case C-75/91: *Commission v Netherlands* [1992] ECR I-549; Case C-101/91: *Commission v Italy* [1993] ECR I-191; Case C-345/92: *Commission v Germany* [1993] ECR 1–1115; Case C-266/89: *Commission v Italy* [1991] ECR I-2411, [1993] 1 CMLR 188; Case C-334/94: *Commission v France* [1996] ECR I-1307.
14 EC Art 228(2) (ex Art 171(2)).
15 EC Art 226 (ex Art 169) and EC Art 227 (ex Art 170).
16 See ch 29, infra.
17 EC Art 95(4) (ex Art 100a).
18 EC Art 95(9) (ex Art 100a).

(f) Procedure under TEU Article 7[19]

As we have already noted[20] complaints against members of the Union that they have failed to respect the principles on which the Union is founded, are subject to a special procedure and special sanctions in the hands of the political institutions, without involving the Court of Justice.

(g) Compensation for state's breach of duties

Under Community law a Member State guilty of a breach of a Treaty obligation or of Community legislation is liable to make good any damage suffered by private parties as a result of its action.[1]

B.   The status of the Communities

(1)   CORPORATE CAPACITY

The provisions of the three Treaties constituting the Communities are identical and quite explicit on the legal status of the Communities in the Member States. Thus EC Article 282 (ex Art 211) provides that 'in each of the Member States, the Community shall enjoy the most extensive legal capacity accorded to legal persons under their laws; it may, in particular, acquire or dispose of movable and immovable property and may be party to legal proceedings'.

It is clear from the Treaties that it is only the Communities themselves and not their separate institutions which have legal personality. In a case arising under the ECSC Treaty, *Algera v Common Assembly of the ECSC,*[2] the Court of Justice laid it down in as many words: 'only the Community and not its institutions possess legal capacity'. Although the Court in that case was referring to the institutions of the ECSC, it is equally applicable to the merged institutions which serve the three Communities. It is clear that the legal personality and capacity of the Communities, following the classic theory of the personality of corporations, is quite distinct from those of the Member States. In a case before an Italian court in 1963 it was argued that the acts of the ECSC should be regarded by Italian law as the acts of the Italian state so that the ECSC could enjoy the preferential status in the Italian law of bankruptcy which is enjoyed by the Italian state. But the Court rejected that argument and held 'that the Community, while it is composed of the Member States is ... a distinct and autonomous corporation which cannot be identified with them ... [It is] a free and autonomous private corporation, under no control from the State institutions'.[3] Despite the Commission's argument to the contrary the principle was affirmed by the ECJ in a similar case.[4]

---

19   Ex Art F.1.
20   See supra, pp 33–34.
1   Joined Cases C-6/90 and C-9/90: *Francovich v Italy* [1991] ECR I-5357 (para 40); Case C-334/92: *Wagner Miret v Fondo de Garantia Salarial* [1993] ECR I-6911 (paras 22 and 23); Joined Cases C-46/93 and C-48/93: *Brasserie du Pêcheur SA v Germany* and *R v Secretary of State for Transport, ex p Factortame Ltd* [1996] ECR I-1029; Joined Cases C-178/94, C-179/94, C-188/94, C-189/94 and C-190/84: *Erich Dillenkofer et al v Germany* [1996] ECR I-4845. See also Case C-392/93: *R v HM Treasury, ex p British Telecommunications plc* [1996] ECR I-1631; Case C-5/94: *R v Ministry of Agriculture, ex p Hedley Lomas (Ireland) Ltd* [1996] ECR I-2553, [1996] 2 CMLR 391.
2   Cases 7/56 and 3–7/57: [1957–58] ECR 39; cf Case 63–69/72: *Wilhelm Werhahn Hansamühle v Council* [1973] ECR 1229 at 1246.
3   *ECSC High Authority v C O Elettromeccaniche Merlini* [1964] CMLR 184 at 194.
4   Case 168/82: *ECSC v Liquidator of Ferrière Sant 'Anna SpA* [1983] ECR 1681 at 1696.

Whilst the Communities are 'private' corporations in the sense that they are autonomous and quite distinct from the Member States because they regard themselves to be in a similar position towards the Communities as the promoters of a joint stock company towards the company itself, the Court of Justice of the Communities has held that the legal personality of the Communities is governed by public law. Thus in *Von Lachmüller v Commission*[5] the Court stated that the legal personality of the Community is a personality which 'exists in public law by virtue of the powers and functions which belong to the Community'. This statement was made in accordance with the continental practice of classifying corporate bodies. Thus in French law, for example, the category of *personnes morales de droit public* includes the state itself, administrative sub-divisions of the state and state enterprises such as universities, hospitals and nationalized industries. The competence of such corporate bodies is governed by public law and not by the civil law which would govern the competence of *personnes morales de droit privé*, such as commercial companies.[6] In the *Von Lachmüller* case the Court held that contracts of employment between the EEC and its employees were governed by public law and as such were subject to the procedures of administrative law.

This is a distinction quite unknown to English law, which has a single concept of contract. Thus in English law whether a contract is between John Brown and Bill Smith or between John Brown and the Department of the Environment or between John Brown and the National Coal Board, all will be subject to the jurisdiction of the High Court. But in French law, which makes a distinction between the public sphere and the private, contracts to which at least one of the parties is a *personne morale de droit public* tend to be subject to the jurisdiction of the administrative courts, whereas contracts between private individuals or *personnes morales de droit privé* are subject to the jurisdiction of the civil courts. This jurisdictional distinction is thus reflected in Community law.

Since 1 January 1973, and by virtue of section 2(1) of the European Communities Act 1972, the Communities have enjoyed corporate status under the laws of the United Kingdom. But this was no innovation, for such a status is already enjoyed by other international organizations of which the United Kingdom is a member under the terms of the International Organizations Act 1968. That Act makes it possible for a special statutory status of a body corporate to be conferred upon such organizations.[7]

Given that it is the Communities themselves which possess legal personality and not the individual institutions, this raises the practical question of how the Communities are represented in law. The Treaties answer this question. In the case of the ECSC, Art 6 of the Treaty provides that 'the Community shall be represented by its institutions, each within the limits of its powers'. This has been interpreted in the sense that the ECSC may be represented by its institutions each within the limits of the field of competence given it by the Treaty. The Court of Justice has also held that the term 'institutions' means the institutions named in the Treaty and does not include the departments into which those institutions may be divided for administrative purposes.[8] In the cases of the EC and Euratom the position is much simpler since, at EC Article 282 (ex Art 211) and EAEC

---

5   Cases 43, 45 and 48/59: [1960] ECR 463; see also Case 1/55: *Kergall v Common Assembly* [1954–56] ECR 151.
6   See Amos and Walton, *Introduction to French Law* (3rd edn, 1967), pp 47 et seq.
7   Cf Bridge, J W, 'The United Nations and English Law' (1969) 18 I & CLQ at 694 and 702.
8   Case 66/63: *Netherlands Government v High Authority of the European Coal and Steel Community* [1964] ECR 533, [1964] CMLR 522.

Article 185, it is stated that 'the Community shall be represented by the Commission'.[9] This is a rôle which the Commission, with its expert Legal Service, is particularly well equipped to fill.

While the Communities enjoy an extensive legal capacity in the territories of the Member States, they also enjoy privileges and immunities of the type usually accorded to the premises and officers of the international organizations. Article 28 of the Merger Treaty provides that the European Communities shall enjoy in the territories of the Member States 'such privileges and immunities as are necessary for the performance of their tasks'. The terms and conditions of those privileges and immunities are set out in a Protocol annexed to the Merger Treaty though the Treaty itself was repealed and most of its content was incorporated by Article 9 of the Amsterdam Treaty. The protocol provides that the premises, buildings and archives of the Communities shall be inviolable.[10] The assets and revenues of the Communities shall be exempt from taxation.[11] Customs duties and restrictions shall not apply to either goods intended for official use or to Community publications.[12] The official communications of the Communities shall enjoy the treatment accorded to diplomatic missions and shall not be subject to censorship.[13] The members and servants of Community institutions shall be issued with *laissez-passer* for the purposes of travel.[14] The members of the European Parliament shall enjoy freedom of movement to and from the meetings of the Parliament and their opinions expressed or votes cast in the course of parliamentary proceedings shall not be the subject of inquiry or legal proceedings[15] though the privilege belongs to the institution (which can waive it) and not to the individual concerned. Both representatives of the Member States taking part in the work of Community institutions and the officials and servants of such institutions shall enjoy the customary privileges and immunities which include, inter alia, exemption from national taxation of allowances paid to Community officials[16] as well as payments made by the European Parliament to its members.[17] The Community Court, distinguishing between private and official business, held in *Sayag v Leduc*[18] that a Euratom official, not being employed as a chauffeur by the Commission, was not entitled to immunity in respect of liability arising from a road traffic accident caused whilst carrying guests of the Commission in his own car.

New institutions, notably the European Central Bank and the European Monetary Institute, have been granted privileges and immunities necessary for

---

9   On the power to serve a garnishee order on the Commission see Case 1/87: *SA Universe Tankship v Commission* [1987] ECR 2807. See also Case C-182/91: *Forabrique Burkinabe v Commission* [1993] ECR I-2161; Case C-1/94SA: *Dupret SA v Commission* [1995] ECR I-1; Case 2/94SA: *Empresa Nacional de Uranio SA v Commission* [1995] ECR I-2767.
10   Protocol on Privileges and Immunities, 1965, Arts 1 and 2.
11   Ibid, Art 3.
12   Ibid, Art 4.
13   Ibid, Art 6.
14   Ibid, Art 7.
15   Ibid, Arts 8–10. See Case 149/85: *Wybot v Foure* [1986] ECR 2391, [1987] 1 CMLR 819. See also Case C-201/89: *Jean-Marie Le Pen v Detlef Puhl* [1990] ECR I-1183.
16   Ibid, Art 13; Case 85/85: *Commission v Belgium, Re Property Tax on Community Civil Servants* [1986] ECR 1149, [1987] 1 CMLR 787.
17   Case 208/80: *Lord Bruce of Donington v Eric Gordon Aspden* [1981] ECR 2205, [1981] 3 CMLR 506.
18   Ibid, Arts 11–16; see Case 5/68: *Sayag v Leduc* [1968] ECR 395, [1969] CMLR 12. Case 9/69: *Sayag v Leduc* [1969] ECR 329.

the performance of their tasks by Protocol 7 annexed to the TEU. The Protocol supplements Article 23 of the Protocol annexed to the Merger Treaty as it extends the privileges and immunities to the members of the organs and the staff of the ECB, ie exemption 'from any form of taxation or imposition of a like nature on the occasion of any increase in its capital and the various formalities which may be connected therewith in the State where the Bank has its seat. The activities of the Bank and of its organs carried on in accordance with the Statute of European System of Central banks and of the ECB shall not be subject to any turnover tax'. The same principles apply to the European Monetary Institute.

The diplomatic missions of non-Member States to the Communities shall equally enjoy such privileges and immunities.[19] Finally, the Protocol stresses that all these privileges, immunities and facilities are accorded solely in the interests of the Communities and that immunity should be waived whenever waiver is not contrary to Community interests.[20]

(2)   CONTRACTUAL AND NON-CONTRACTUAL LIABILITY OF THE COMMUNITY

(a)   Contractual obligations
In its corporate capacity the Community assumes liability for contracts and non-contractual obligations. The EC and the Euratom Treaties[1] provide that the Community's contractual liability is to be governed by the law applicable to the contract in question. Though the formula begs the question it must be assumed that a national municipal law rather than a national private international law is involved. Such contracts may be concerned with the acquisition and disposal of property, as well as goods to be delivered and work to be carried out. Obligations arising from the employment with the Community fall into a special category.

The jurisdictional provisions are in this respect contained in EC Articles 238 and 240 (ex Arts 181 and 183). The former confers jurisdiction upon the Court of Justice pursuant to an arbitration clause contained in a contract concluded by or on behalf of the Community irrespective of whether or not it is governed by public or private law. The latter confirms jurisdiction of the national courts in the absence of such a clause.

Since there is no Community substantive law of contract as such it is assumed that the governing law will be expressly designated in cases in which the Community is a party; otherwise, in the light of the provisions of the 1980 Convention[2] one would assume it to be the municipal law of a Member State with which the contract is most closely connected.

The case law on the subject remains yet to be developed. In the *Pellegrini*[3] case a contract for the expert cleaning of Community atomic energy installations situated in Italy was expressly subjected to Italian law and the Commission's claim for breach of the contract was decided accordingly. The case sets a precedent for the proposition that where the governing law is the law of a Member State no expert evidence regarding the same shall be called. This accords with the

---

19   Ibid, Art 17.
20   Ibid, Art 18.
 1   EC Art 288 (ex Art 215 (1)); EAEC Art 188 (1); there is no equivalent provision in the ECSC Treaty though the Community is contractually liable, see Case 1/55: *Kergall v Common Assembly* [1954–56] ECR 151.
 2   Convention on the Law applicable to Contractual Obligations; for details see Lasok, D and Stone, P A, *The Conflict of Laws in the European Community* (1987), ch 9.
 3   Case 23/76: *Pellegrini v EC Commission* [1976] ECR 1807, [1977] 2 CMLR 77. See also Case 232/84: *Commission v Tordeur* [1985] ECR 3223 – the ECJ knows the law even if the system involved is not represented by a ECJ judge.

continental principle that *curia novit jura* reinforced, no doubt, by the fact that the Community Court consists of judges eligible to hold judicial offices in their own countries. Besides, legal points may well be elucidated in the course of the written procedure and the Court can, of its own motion, inquire about the matter with the Ministry of Justice or an equivalent department of the state concerned.

In a case[4] concerning building contracts brought on the basis of EAEC Article 153 and EC Article 238 (ex Art 181) the ECJ had to decide not only on the merits of the conflicting claims but also whether Belgian law (chosen by the parties for the major aspects of the contract) or Italian law (designated for some minor aspects but claimed by the Italian parties to be the 'natural law' of the whole contract) was the governing law. The ECJ held that the law expressly chosen was to be applied whilst the references to Italian law constituted merely a derogation justifiable in the specific circumstances of the contract which was being executed in Italy. In order to determine the Commission's rights arising from the breach of the contract the Commission was required to prove a causal relationship between its loss and the unilateral interruption in accordance with 'the general principles of the law of liability'. The Commission failed under this head though it succeeded under the three remaining heads, ie compensation for the inferior quality of the executed work; the difference between the contract price and the actual value of the executed work; and the cost of bringing the completed work up to the specifications laid down in the contract. The case demonstrates the problem of the choice of law but also demonstrates a tendency to rely on general principles which can be found in the laws of the Member States rather than the technicalities of the governing law.

Of the other recorded cases one[5] entailed a claim against the Commission for reimbursement of certain expenditure on research equipment incurred in the performance of a market research contract in pursuance of a Commission regulation, the other[6] a claim for goods delivered and work carried out for the Commission. The former failed upon the interpretation of the terms of the contract entailing matters of fact rather than the governing law. The latter succeeded in accordance with Belgian law.

In yet another case[7] the Commission, in pursuance of an arbitration clause, successfully claimed damages for non-performance of a contract by a journalist together with interest at the various statutory rates applicable in Belgium at the relevant time.

A more abstract statement of a claim will not suffice as the Rules of Procedure of the Court of Justice require a substantiation of any claim.[8] Similarly, it is not sufficient to allege that, in view of an under priced contract, the Community was unduly enriched at the expense of the contractor.[9]

There is no express provision in the Treaties with regard to quasi-contract though the concept is well known in national systems. However, in the case law, contractual obligation covers quasi-contracts.[10]

---

4   Case 318/81: *Commission v CO DE MI SpA* [1982] ECR 1325, [1985] ECR 3693, [1987] 3 CMLR 516.
5   Case 251/84: *Centrale Marketinggesellschaft der deutscher Agrarwirtschaft GmbH v Commission* [1986] ECR 217, [1987] 2 CMLR 788.
6   Case 220/85: *Fadex NV v Commission* [1986] ECR 3387.
7   Case 426/85: *Commission v Zoubek* [1986] ECR 4057, [1988] 1 CMLR 257.
8   Joined Cases 19/60–21/60; 2/61 and 3/61: *Fives Lille Cail v ECSC High Authority* [1961] ECR 281 (295).
9   Case C-330/88: *Alfredo Grifoni v EAEC Commission* [1991] ECR I-1045. [1993] 1 CMLR 337.
10 Cases 4–13/59: *Mannesmann AG v High Authority* [1960] ECR 113; Case 18/63: *Wollast (née Schmitz) v Commission* [1964] ECR 85 Case 80/63: *Degreef v Commission* [1964] ECR 391; Case 110/63: *Willame v Commission* [1965] ECR 649; Case 26/67: *Danvin v Commission* [1968] ECR 315.

(b)   Community servants and others

Employment[11] with the Community institutions is subject to a special regime governed by the Staff Regulations[12] supplemented by contracts for auxiliary and local staff and massive case law. The Staff Regulations which govern the Community Civil Service, constitute a *sui generis* unitary code of law binding and applicable in all the Member States.[13] Each institution acts as employer and therefore, has to be sued in that capacity rather than the Commission which represents the Community generally. Thus, eg, the Court librarian sues the ECJ in its administrative capacity and the ECJ in its judicial capacity hears and disposes of the case.[14] All disputes between the Community and its servants, including the employees of the European Investment Bank,[15] were originally subject to the exclusive jurisdiction of the Court of Justice.[16] The jurisdiction of the ECJ in this field was transferred to the CFI subject to appeals to the ECJ on points of law only. These appeals are governed by the procedure laid down by the ECJ.[17]

A distinction must be made between Community civil servants and auxiliary[18] and local[19] staff. Civil servants enjoy a status entailing a career structure and pension rights governed by the Staff Regulations, the others have contractual rights and obligations governed by the proper (national) law of the contract. Staff Regulations govern the appointment, promotion, working conditions and emoluments, rights and duties (including the duty of confidentiality which extends beyond the period of service) and protection[20] of the servants as well as their discipline (with the right of appeal to the CFI), personal liability and the termination of office. The application of Staff Regulations may, however, lead to the application of national law where, for example, collateral rights are concerned. Thus in cases[1] involving pension rights of the surviving, divorced wives, reference had to be made to relevant national laws determining the financial effects of the decrees of divorce and, consequently, of the status of the claimant vis-à-vis the decreased Community official. Similarly, where children's rights based on the Staff Regulations are claimed, their status in relation to the parent will have to be determined by the relevant national law.

Where the Staff Regulations do not apply, the contents of the contract of employment with the Community shall be governed by national law. Thus, it was held,[2] that where Italian law was the governing law in relation to auxiliary

---

11   For details see Lasok, D, *The Professions and Services in the European Economic Community* (1986), ch 7.

12   Enacted in 1968, amended and consolidated in 1981: see Regulations 187/81, 397/81, 2780/81, 371/82, 372/82, 3139/82, 3332/82, 440/83, 1819/83, 2023/83, 2074/83, 3681/83, 420/85, 1578/85, 3856/86, 793/87, 3019/87, 2339/88, 3736/90, 2232/91, 3832/91, 3834/91, 571/92, 3947/92, 3161/94, 626/95. The Council lays down the Staff Regulations: EC Art 283 (ex Art 212).

13   See Case 137/80: *Commission v Belgium* [1981] ECR 2393.

14   See Case 15/60: *Simon v Court of Justice* [1961] ECR 115; Case 2/80: *Dautzenberg v Court of Justice* [1980] ECR 3107, See also Case 125/87: *Brown v Court of Justice* [1989] ECR 3489.

15   See Case 110/75: *Mills v European Investment Bank* [1976] ECR 955 (admissibility); 1613 (merits).

16   EC Art 236 (ex Art 179); ECSC Art 40 (2) (3); EAEC Art 152.

17   OJ 2001, C 34/1, Rules of Procedure, Arts 110–123.

18   See Case 17/78: *Deshormes (née La Valle) v Commission* [1979] ECR 189.

19   See Case 105/80: *Desmedt v Commission* [1981] ECR 1701.

20   See Case 18/78: *Mrs V v Commission* [1979] ECR 2093; see also Case 180/87: *Hamill v Commission* [1988] ECR 6141 [1990] 1 CMLR 982.

 1   Case 24/71: *Meinhardt (née Forderung) v Commission* [1972] ECR 269, [1973] CMLR 136; Case 40/79: *Mrs P v Commission* [1979] ECR 3299, [1981] ECR 361.

 2   Case 109/81: *Pace (née Porta) v Commission* [1982] ECR 2469.

staff recruited locally the applicant was entitled to the full benefits of permanent employment granted by Italian law in the specific circumstances including the pension rights which would have been earned had the Commission paid the appropriate contribution under the Italian social security system. Similarly, in the case of a medical person,[3] who contracted to provide services to the Commission on an hourly basis, the position was governed by Belgian law as designated in the contract and, therefore, in the circumstances the claim to a pension was held unfounded.

A principle of confidentiality applies to the members of the institutions of the Community, the members of committees and the officials and servants even after their duties have ceased. Thus they are not at liberty to disclose information of the kind covered by the obligation of professional secrecy, in particular information about undertakings, their business relations or their cost components.[4] This is a personal obligation. However in the case of breach committed in the course of their duties the Commission should be responsible for the damage by virtue of its vicarious liability.[5]

(c)   Non-contractual liability

In the case of non-contractual liability the Treaties[6] provide that 'the Community shall, in accordance with the general principles common to the laws of the Member States, make good any damage[7] caused by its institutions or by its servants in the performance of their duties'. This applies to damages caused by the ECB or its servants in the performance of their duties. Thus the Court of Justice is required to apply these general principles as an additional source of law in much the same way that the International Court of Justice can resort to 'the general principles of law recognized by civilized nations' as a source of international law.[8]

A fundamental question which arises here is whether in order to be recognized and applied by the Court of Justice such general principles must be known to the municipal laws of all the Member States. Certainly in the jurisprudence of the International Court of Justice such an exacting condition has not been applied. Sir Hersch Lauterpracht has defined general principles of law as 'those principles of law, private and public, which in contemplation of the legal experience of civilized nations lead one to regard as obvious maxims of jurisprudence of a general and fundamental character'.[9] Thus the International Court of Justice must inquire of 'the way in which the law of States representing the main systems of jurisprudence regulates the problem in the situations in question'.[10]

---

3   Case 123/84: *Klein v Commission* [1985] ECR 1907, [1987] 2 CMLR 799.
4   EC Art 287 (ex Art 214). See Case 180/87: *Hamill v Commission* supra.
5   See EC Art 288(2) (ex Art 215(2)).
6   EC Art 288(2) (ex Art 215(2)); EAEC Art 188(2) but see a different formulation of the principle in ECSC Arts 40(1) and 34; see also Lord Mackenzie Stuart, 'The Non-Contractual Liability of the European Economic Community' (1975).
7   Cf Cases 5, 7 and 13–24/66 *Kampffmeyer v Commission* [1967] ECR 245, (1967–68) 5 CML Rev 208; Case 153/73; *Holtz and Willemsen GmbH v Council and Commission* [1974] ECR 675, [1975] 1 CMLR 91; Case 169/73: *Compagnie Continentale France v Council* [1975] ECR 117, [1975] CMLR 578; Case 74/74: *Comptoir National Technique Agricole (CNTA) SA v Commission* [1975] ECR 533. Cases 83, 94/764, 15, 40/77: *Bayerische HNL Vermehrungsbetriebe GmbH & Co KH v Council and Commission* [1978] ECR 1209, [1978] 3 CMLR 566.
8   See Art 38(1)(c) of the Statute of the International Court of Justice.
9   *International Law, being the Collected Papers of Hersch Lauterpracht* (1970), Vol 1, p 69.
10   Ibid, p 71. For an account of the practice of the International Court also, see ibid, pp 68–77.

The ECJ has adopted a similar approach. As one commentator has put it, 'whilst it is not necessary ... that *all* states concerned agree on a certain principle of law, it is equally true that such a principle must not merely exist in the law of one country or only in a minority of legal systems ... [It] is not desirable to have a *brouillard* consisting of diverse national legal systems, but rather an adequate solution which is germane to the legal order of the Communities. This result will be reached only after thorough comparative analysis of the legal systems. To the extent that such research reveals a common core, it is not unlikely that the solutions adopted will readily be approved by the Member States in their national laws as well'.[11] In the words of Advocate-General Lagrange the spirit which has guided the Court has been 'not simply [to] take a more or less arithmetical average of the different municipal solutions, but [to] choose those solutions from among the various legal systems prevailing in the different Member States as, having regard to the objectives of the Treaty, appeared to it the best or, if one may use the word, the most progressive'.[12] This must be so because a comparative study would reveal that there is no uniformity between Member States as regards the detailed principles governing the liability in tort.

In recent years the ECJ has made a similar use of general principles of law for the interpretation of Community law and the recognition of human rights.[13] The Court has interpreted its duty to ensure that the law is observed as permitting it to apply as part of Community law a body of unwritten, fundamental legal principles which are common to the national legal and political systems of the Member States. The function of these fundamental principles in the Community legal order is, in the words of Advocate-General Dutheillet de Lamothe, 'to contribute to forming that philosophical, political and legal substratum common to the Member States from which emerges through the case law an unwritten Community law, one of the essential aims of which is precisely to ensure respect for the fundamental rights of the individual'.[14] The Court has demonstrated its willingness to test the validity of Community acts against such criteria.

(d)   The principles
Regarding the principles governing the non-contractual liability of the Community it has to be borne in mind that the concept cannot be construed in the sense of 'tort' or unlawful act of private law giving rise to a civil remedy of damages and/ or injunction but has to be seen in the context of the activities of the Community institutions. These activities include the exercise of administrative and legislative functions and, like in any state system, may fall occasionally below the standard of sound and efficient administration expected in the West European political culture. Such malfunctioning would reveal a fault of the system (*faute de service*) for which the state should be responsible. Moreover, in narrowly defined circumstances, the system may be liable in the absence of fault or blameworthiness. Thus, for example, although under French law a statute may not be challenged

---

11 Lorenz, K, 'General Principles of Law: Their Elaboration in the Court of Justice of the European Communities' (1964) 13 AJCL at 9, 10, 11.
12 Case 14/61: *Hoogovens v High Authority* [1963] ECR 253, [1963] CMLR 73 at 85, 86.
13 See generally Pescatore, P, 'Fundamental Rights and Freedoms in the System of the European Communities' (1970) 18 AJCL 343; Zuleeg, M, 'Fundamental Rights and the Law of the European Communities' (1971) 8 CML Rev 446; Bridge, J W, et al, *Fundamental Rights* (1973), ch 20.
14 Case 11/70: *Internationale Handelsgesellschaft GmbH v Einfuhr-und Vorratsstelle für Getreide und Futtermittel* [1970] ECR 1125 at 1146, [1972] CMLR 255 at 271.

in the courts, the administration may incur liability in accordance with the principle of *'égalité devant les charges publiques'* if, as a result of a legislative measure, an individual has suffered damage in excess of the sacrifice borne by the citizenry in a comparable situation.[15] However at the present state of Community law there is no liability without unlawfulness.[16]

Similarly, under the German *Grundgesetz* the principle of proportionality (*Verhältnismassigkeit*) protects the citizens from excessive burdens without necessarily imputing fault to the state.[17]

Whilst it can be said that the concept of Community liability has been modelled upon that of state liability, one would look in vain for a direct reference to a particular system in the judgments of the Court of Justice, since the Court contents itself with a synthetic and unattributed statement of the general principle. However, the Advocates-General[18] do occasionally, albeit briefly, refer to national laws relevant in this respect.

It is common ground that Community liability cannot be imputed to a Treaty concluded between Member States.[19] The same principle applies to a claim of compensation for the damage suffered by customs agents who become redundant as a consequence of the abolition of tax and customs frontiers attributed to the implementation of the internal market by the Single European Act.[20] They claimed compensation on the basis of the Community's strict liability or, in the alternative, on the Community's liability for fault. The Court ruled their action inadmissible on both counts because, firstly, the subject-matter of the proceedings is not defined sufficiently precisely by reference to the Statute of the Court or the Rules of Procedure, secondly, the application does not concern the SEA alone and does not make its legal basis clear and, thirdly, EC Article 288 (ex Art 215) allows the issue of liability of only the Community institutions or its servants to be raised.

On substance, the Court ruled that '... the claim based on the strict liability of the Community seeks to impute liability to the Community for damage whose source is to be found in the Single Act, which is an instrument of primary Community law. It is thus neither an act of the Community institutions nor an act of the servants of the Community ... and cannot, therefore, give rise to strict non-contractual liability on the part of the Community'.

Having recited the established case law the Court disposed of the claim based on the basis of fault emphasising that, firstly, liability of the Community arises 'only the institutions have infringed a legal obligation to act under a provision of

15 See Cases 9 and 11/71: *Compagnie d'Approvisionnement v Commission (No 2)* [1972] ECR 391, [1973] CMLR 529 (per A-G Mayras at 422–423) and Case 26/81: *Oleifici Mediterraanei SA v EEC* [1982] ECR 3057 (per A-G Verloren van Themaat at 3089–3090).
16 Case 59/83: *Biovilac NV v Commission* [1984] ECR 4057 at para 28.
17 See Case 11/70: *Internationale Handelsgesellschaft v EVGF* [1970] ECR 1125 (per Adv/Gen Dutheillet de Lamothe at 1146), [1972] CMLR 255; Case 5/73: *Balkan-Import-Export v HZA Berlin-Packhof* [1973] ECR 1091; Case 114/76: *Bela-Mühle v Grows-Farm* [1977] ECR 1211, [1979] 2 CMLR 83; Case 116/76: *Granaria v HAP* [1977] ECR 1247, [1979] 2 CMLR 83; Cases 119, 120/76: *Ölmühle Hamburg v HZA Hamburg-Waltershof* [1977] ECR 1269, [1979] 2 CMLR 83.
18 See eg Adv-Gen Verloren van Themaat in Case 26/81, note 15, supra; A-G Reischl in Cases 56–60/74: *Kampfmeyer v Commission and Council* [1976] ECR 711 at 752–753; A-G Roemer in Case 5/71: *Aktien-Zuckerfabrik Schöppenstedt v Council* [1971] ECR 975 at 989; A-G Gand in Case 4/68: *Firma Schqarzwaldmilch v Einfuhr-und Vorratsstelle für Fette* [1968] ECR 377, [1969] CMLR 406.
19 Case 169/73: *Compagnie Continentale France v Council* [1975] ECR 117 (para 16) and Joined Cases 31/86 and 35/86: *LAISA and CPC España v Council* [1988] ECR 2285.
20 Case T-113/96: *Edovard Dubois et Fils SA v Council* [1998] ECR II-125, para 47.

Community law' (para 56) and, secondly 'even if a legal obligation to act had been infringed in this case, that failure would certainly not, in the circumstances, be such as to entail the liability of the Community' (para 58).

(e)   Institutional liability

In the terms[1] of the EC and Euratom Treaties the Community must make good any damage caused by its institutions or by its servants in the performance of their duties. The ECSC Treaty requires, in addition, an element of fault. However in practice so far no-fault liability has to be considered only a remote possibility. The question did arise in Cases 9 and 11/71 cited above where compensation was claimed in respect of subsidies on imports of cereals following the devaluation of the French currency in 1969. However the ECJ rejected the claim without addressing itself to the contention of no-fault liability. A decade later, in Case 26/81 cited above, the ECJ was quite prepared to consider the argument but dismissed the claim as arising from a commercial risk rather than the Community rules which purported to reform the organization of the common market in oil and fats. It observed that 'the alleged damage, even assuming it to have been substantiated, is attributable entirely to the applicant's conduct'. The Court took the opportunity of restating the principle that in order to succeed the applicant must prove 'unlawfulness of the conduct of which the institutions are accused, the reality of the damage and the existence of a causal connection between the conduct and the damage in question'.[2] In doing so the Court re-emphasized the requirement of fault which underlies the unlawful nature of the conduct for which the Community is responsible.

The rules were laid down in *Schöppenstedt v Council*[3] where the ECJ dismissed a claim for compensation for loss of income alleged to have been caused by a Council regulation laying down the measures needed to offset the difference between national and Community sugar prices. Addressing itself to the problem of liability, the Court held that where legislative action involving measures of economic policy is concerned the Community will not incur non-contractual liability for damage suffered by individuals in consequence of such action unless a 'sufficiently flagrant violation of a superior rule of law for the protection of the individual has occurred'. The Court did not elucidate the meaning of the 'superior rule of law' it had in mind. However it drew a distinction between a claim for compensation and an action for annulment of the measure in question and emphasized the autonomous nature of these two remedies. However, as ruled subsequently,[4] the autonomous nature of the claim for compensation is concerned with procedure, ie the action can be brought in its own virtue without it being collateral to the action for annulment. Yet in practice claims for compensation

---

1   See note 6, supra.

2   Note 15, Case 26/81 at para 16; see also Case 353/88: *Briantex v Commission* [1989] ECR 3623.

3   Case 5/71: [1971] ECR 975 at para 11. Joined Cases 83/76, 94//76, 4/77, 15/77 and 40/77: *Bayerische HNLV v Council and Commission* [1978] ECR 1209; see also Case 50/86; *Les Grands Moulins de Paris v Commission* [1987] ECR 4833 and C-282/90: *Industrie-en Handelsonderneming Vreugdenhil BV v Commission* [1992] ECR I-1937.

4   Cases 197–200, 243 and 245, 247/80: *Ludwigshafener v Council and Commission* [1981] ECR 3211; see also Case 52/81: *Faust v Commission* [1982] ECR 3745; Case 256/81: *Paul's Agriculture Ltd v Council and Commission* [1983] ECR 1707, [1983] 3 CMLR 176.

are linked with the illegality of the act complained[5] of as the self-evident proof of wrongfulness or fault of the system.

Failure to act may also provide a cause of action for compensation where the relevant Community institution is in breach of a duty[6] to act and such failure is a direct cause of loss or damage. Here again failure to execute a duty is tantamount to a fault of the system.

The action under EC Article 288(2) (ex Art 215(2)) is an autonomous action and has to be distinguished from the application for annulment of a Community act though, in practice, the action implies an allegation of illegality.[7] If illegality has been established in absence of a domestic remedy a direct action against the Community is in order, but, in absence of a ruling of the ECJ declaring the act illegal, no action would be permitted.[8] However, even if the Community act is declared illegal by the ECJ, the annulment of the act in question is in itself insufficient to incur Community liability.[9]

(f) Vicarious liability

In the terms of the Treaties the Community is vicariously liable for non-contractual obligations incurred by Community servants in the course of their official duties. This kind of liability is another aspect of the *faute de service* or of the malfunctioning of the system since the Community selects its servants, details their duties and controls their activities. However the act of the servant must be attributable[10] to the Community because the Community is liable only for those acts which are the necessary extension of the tasks given to the institutions.[11] Therefore, should the servant act outside the scope of his duties or engage in activities which are *ultra vires* the institutions, the Community would not be vicariously liable but the servant would be by virtue of *faute personnelle*.

Cases involving the Community in vicarious liability for misdeeds of its servants are rare. In the case of what was described as 'reciprocal assaults'[12] the Commission was condemned to pay a symbolic ECU to a female official in compensation of non-material damage resulting from a failure to investigate her complaints against a male colleague. In another[13] case the indiscretion of an official

---

5 See eg Case 5/71, supra; Case 9 and 11/71, supra; Case 59/72: *Wünsche v Commission* [1973] ECR 791; Cases 63–69/72: *Werhahn v Council* [1973] ECR 1229; Case 153/73: *Holtz v Council and Commission* [1974] ECR 675, [1975] 1 CMLR 91; Case 74/74: *CNTA v Commission* [1975] ECR 533, [1977] 1 CMLR 171; Case 99/74: *Société des Grands Moulins v Commission* [1975] ECR 1531; Cases 54–60/76: *Compagnie Industrielle et Agricole v Council and Commission* [1977] ECR 645; Cases 83 and 94/76, 4, 15, 40/77: *Bayerische HNL v Council and Commission* [1978] ECR 1209, [1978] 3 CMLR 566; Case 238/78: *Ireks-Arkady v Council and Commission* [1979] ECR 2955; Cases 241, 242 and 245–250/78: *DGV v Council and Commission* [1979] ECR 3017.

6 See Case 30/66: *Becher v Commission* [1967] ECR 285; Case 43/72: *Merkur v Commission* [1973] ECR 1055; Case 40/75: *Société des Produits Bertrand v Commission* [1976] ECR 1, [1976] 1 CMLR 220; Case 90/78: *Granaria BV v Council and Commission* [1979] ECR 1081.

7 Case 4/69: *Lütticke GmbH v Commission* [1971] ECR 325; Cases 9 and 11/71 at paras 4, 5 and 6, supra. Case 5/71, supra. See also Case C-87/89: *Société Nationale Interprofessionnelle de la Tomate v Commission* [1990] ECR I-1981, [1991] 3 CMLR, 439 Case C-97/91: *Oleificio Borelli SpA v Commission* [1992] ECR I-6313.

8 Case 20/88: *Roquette Frères v Commission* [1989] ECR 1553, [1991] 2 CMLR 6.

9 Case C-282/90: *Industrie Vreugdenhil BV v Commission* [1992] ECR I-1937; [1994] 2 CMLR 803. See also Case T-478/93: *Wafer Zoo Srl v Commission* [1995] ECR II-1479, [1996] 2 CMLR 750.

10 Case 9/69: *Sayag v Leduc* [1969] ECR 329.

11 Ibid, at 336.

12 Case 18/78: *Mrs V v Commission* [1979] ECR 2093.

13 Cases 145/83, 53, 84: *Adams v Commission* [1985] ECR 3539, [1986] 1 CMLR 506.

led to a series of calamities which fell upon a person who supplied information to the Commission in the course of the investigations of breaches of Community competition rules. The information helped to find the undertaking[14] concerned guilty of breaches of Community law but the disclosure of the informer's identity led to the latter's resignation from his employment; prosecution and conviction in Switzerland for offences under Swiss law which prohibits the passing of commercial secrets to an unauthorized body (ie the Commission, *in casu*); his financial ruin and his wife's suicide. The ECJ dismissed a rather extravagant claim against the Commission[15] for its failure to prevent his prosecution and imprisonment in Switzerland but found the Commission liable for the breach of confidentiality by the Commission official and awarded damages for mental anguish and economic loss plus costs without actually identifying the specific heads of damage. The Count also considered contributory negligence of the plaintiff.[16]

As a general principle of law claimants for damages ought to mitigate their loss and where they themselves contributed to the loss they will have their compensation reduced to the extent of their negligence. Thus for example in the Adams claim[17] the contributing factor to his misfortune was the fact that he supplied the documents which compromised his employers but took no precaution against being identified.

The Community may also be vicariously liable for the acts of an agency or body under its control. However the liability will depend upon the status[18] of the agency or body in question vis-à-vis the Community. The *Worms*[19] case illustrates the point. Worms, a scrap-metal agent, sued the High Authority of the Coal and Steel Community for damages, because having exposed fraud in the scrap-metal business, he was ostracized by dealers and consequently himself went out of business. He argued that the High Authority was at fault because it failed to protect him from the boycott which ruined his business or to end the fraud and prosecute the wrongdoers. He failed because the High Authority was not considered responsible for the agencies it established under Belgian law, one to purchase scrap-metal on behalf of the Coal and Steel Community and another to collect the scrap equalization levy imposed upon scrap-metal dealers to subsidize imported scrap. Worms failed because the purchasing agency was said to be an autonomous private body for which the Community was not vicariously liable. He should have sued before Belgian courts, under Belgian law, the persons and bodies responsible for his loss.

(g)   Concurrent liability and choice of jurisdiction
Where Community policy requires implementation by national authorities and the applicant alleges damage resulting from such implementation the question of liability and jurisdiction arises since the applicant may embark on a direct action at the Court of First Instance or in a national court. In the latter case a reference to the ECJ may be made under EC Article 234 (ex Art 177). A concurrent action in both jurisdictions is not impossible but appears to be inadvisable. In view of the autonomous nature of the action under EC Article 288(2) (ex Art 215(2))

14   Case 85/76: *Hoffman-LaRoche v Commission* [1979] ECR 461, [1979] 3 CMLR 211.
15   Case 53/84: *Adams v Commission* [1985] ECR 3539, [1986] 1 CMLR 506.
16   Case 145/83: *Adams v Commission* [1985] ECR 3539, [1986] 1 CMLR 506.
17   Adams' personal troubles later reached a climax in his being sentenced to ten years' imprisonment for plotting to have his second wife assassinated so that he could collect a substantial benefit from an insurance policy on her life: The Times, 15 March 1994.
18   See Cases 32 and 33/58: *SNUPAT v High Authority* [1959] ECR 127.
19   Case 18/60: *Worms v High Authority* [1962] ECR 195.

the applicant must have *locus standi* by virtue of EC Article 230(4) (ex Art 173(4)), ie direct and individual concern, but the claimant may have to exhaust any causes of action which lie in national jurisdiction.[20] If the cause of the action is attributable to national authorities he has to pursue his rights on the home ground, eg where the Commission refused to make FEOGA reimbursements to a trader in agricultural produce. The Court confirmed[1] this to be the correct course of action because EC Article 288(2) (ex Art 215(2)) is inapplicable to cases involving damage caused by national institutions even if they apply Community rules. If the cause falls within the Community competence and cannot be attributed to the state the ECJ has jurisdiction[2] but it does not seem necessary to exhaust any national remedies.

In Case C-152/88[3] the *locus standi* of an importer of Chilean apples was not in question for the suspension by the Commission of import licences was a Community act. Thus the suspension without derogation in respect of products en route on the ocean was held to be in breach of the relevant regulation leading to a direct action for damages under EC Article 288(2) (ex Art 215(2)).

(h)   Proof of damage, causation and remoteness
Since there are no specific Community rules governing the proof and heads of damage, causation or remoteness the Community Court applies what might be termed the general principles of the law of damage common to the Member States. It insists that the claimant proves his claim in the light of the Community obligations drawing a distinction between admissible claims and claims arising from 'commercial risks' for which the Community cannot be liable. It also dismisses 'speculative' claims and, as we have noted in the *Adams* cases, claims which are too remote. The case law, beginning with the *Schöppenstedt*[4] ruling that 'a claim for an unspecified form of damages is not sufficiently concrete and must, therefore, be regarded as inadmissible', lays down the rules for the practice of the Court.

In *Kampffmeyer v Commission*[5] the ECJ held that compensation was payable where, as a result of an unlawful act of the Commission, the claimant sustained losses from cancellation of transactions following the refusal of import licences.

In *CNTA v Commission*[6] compensation for losses following currency fluctuations was possible in view of the abolition of monetary compensatory amounts (MCAs) in respect of colza and rape seeds and oils produced therefrom for export. However the claimant produced no proof and the ECJ held that he could not be regarded as having suffered loss if he was not exposed to any exchange risk at all, or was so exposed but no actual loss occurred.

In *Lesieur v Commission*,[7] the claimant failed to make out a case for the abolition of MCAs in the oil and fats sector which, he argued, resulted in the loss

20   See Case 175/84: *Krohn v Commission* [1986] ECR 753 at para 27, [1987] 1 CMLR 745.
 1   Cases 89/86 and 91/86; *L'Etoile v Commission* [1987] ECR 3005 [1988] 3 CMLR 564; Case C-55/90: *Cato v Commission* [1992] ECR I-2533, [1992] 2 CMLR 459. See also Cases 106–120/87 *Asteris AE v Greece* [1990] 1 CMLR 575. C-66/91 and C-66/91R: *Emerald Meats Ltd v Commission* [1991] ECR I-1143 [1994] 2 CMLR 697.
 2   See Case 175/84 supra and Case 20/88: *Roquette Frères v Commission* [1989] ECR 1553 at para 15, [1991] 2 CMLR 6.
 3   *Sofrimport Sarl v Commission*: [1990] ECR I-2477, [1990] 3 CMLR 80. See also Case C-51/95P: *Unifruit Hellas EPE v Commission* [1997] ECR I-727.
 4   Case 5/71, supra, at para 9.
 5   Cases 5–7, 13–24, /66: [1967] ECR 245.
 6   Case 74/74, supra.
 7   Cases 67–85/75: [1976] ECR 391, [1976] 2 CMLR 185.

of cheap supplies on the international markets and deprived him of expected profits. The ECJ ruled that, although a sudden abolition of the MCAs constituted an infringement of the principle of protection of legitimate expectations, the object of the measure was to prevent disturbances in the trade, rather than secure profits for traders. Besides, no actual damage was proved.

In *Société Roquette v Commission*[8] the claim, based on the loss arising from the fixing of the MCAs in respect of the importation of amyloid products into France contrary to a regulation on the conjunctural policy in agriculture resulting from the widening gaps of currency values, failed. Neither actual loss nor causal connection was proved.

In *Kampffmeyer v Commission and Council*[9] a claim in respect of anticipated loss in 1975 based on prices and aids for cereals during 1974 failed. The ECJ held that, although it was not prevented from making a declaration regarding future losses, it could not award damages *in casu* since no liability was established.

In *Milch v Commission*[10] the claimant obtained export certificates for certain North African countries fixing in advance refunds for the export of butter stored by the German Agricultural Intervention Board. He sold a quantity of the product to his Belgian partner. The German customs authorities paid a part of the refund but rejected further demands on the ground that there was no proof of marketing in the countries concerned. Thereupon he brought an action against the Commission on the ground that the Commission had led him to believe that the payment of the refunds fixed in advance depended merely upon proof that the product had left the country. The ECJ ruled, however, that he had to show that the product not only left the country but was also marketed in the territory for which it was destined.

In *Pool v Council*[11] an English cattle breeder, who claimed compensation for the damage caused to him by fixing the conversion rates of the pound sterling applicable specifically to the agricultural sector, failed as his calculations to prove the alleged damage were based on speculative and unrealistic comparisons and did not support his claim. There was no causal connection.

In *Julius Kind v Commission*[12] a German butcher sought, unsuccessfully, compensation for alleged losses suffered as a result of the market organization for sheepmeat following the Anglo-French controversy in that field. As an importer of meat from Britain, where the prices were lower than elsewhere, he was hit by the claw-back rule to offset the variable slaughter premium which as from 1980 imposed levies upon the British products. He claimed damages as his business declined, especially that he was unable to penetrate the Swiss market. However he proved no actual loss and revealed that he attempted to enter the Swiss market only after the coming into force of the regulation which he blamed for his alleged loss.

Following the earlier *Quellmehl* and *Gritz* cases[13] a successful claim[14] was made in cases where the ECJ held that, by abolishing subsidies for the production of

8   Case 26/74: [1976] ECR 677, also Case 253/84: *GAEC v Council and Commission (re reduction of MCAs)* [1987] ECR 123.
9   Cases 56–60/74: [1976] ECR 711; see Adv-Gen Reischl at 753 on the nature of damage.
10   Case 44/76: [1977] ECR 393.
11   Case 49/79: [1980] ECR 569, [1980] 3 CMLR 279.
12   Case 106/81: [1982] ECR 2885.
13   Cases 238/78: *Ireks-Arkady v Council and Commission* [1979] ECR 2955; Cases 241, 242 and 245–250/78: *DVG v Council and Commission* [1979] ECR 3017; Cases 261 and 262/78: *Interquell Stärke-Chemie and Diamalt v Council and Commission* [1979] ECR 3045 and [1982] ECR 3271.
14   Joined Cases 64 and 113/76, 167 and 239/78, and 27, 28 and 45/79: *Dumortier Frères v Council* [1982] ECR 1733.

maize gritz used in the brewing industry, whilst maintaining production subsidies for starch used in the bakery industry, the Commission had infringed the principle of equality, ie a 'superior rule of law' for the protection of the individual. In these cases the producers of quellmehl and gritz were entitled to compensation based on the subsidy they would have received had they been treated equally with the producers of starch.

A similar conclusion was reached in the milk quota cases. The legislation establishing milk quotas in 1984 omitted to grant quotas to milk producers who agreed to refrain from marketing milk for a limited period under an earlier scheme entitling them to premiums. It was annulled as contravening legitimate expectations.[15] The Council responded by allowing the producers a quota, valid from 1989, set at 60% of the milk deliveries in the year preceding the application for a non-marketing premium. Subsequently the ECJ[16] held the 40% reduction invalid and upheld the claims for compensation under EC Article 288(2) (ex Art 215(2)) in the first of batch of cases.[17] The Court felt that the violation was serious enough to justify damages since, without stating any overriding grounds of public interest, the legislature had failed to consider the situation of the producers.

In a recent case[18] arising from the progressive dismantling of the system of MCAs, the Court reiterated the three conditions of a successful action in this respect, ie unlawful act, damage and causal link connecting unlawfulness with damage, but warned that undue emphasis on illegality of the act without establishing the other factors may be fatal to the action. In other words, the object of the action is not to punish the institution in default but to compensate the claimant for genuine loss directly attributable to such an act. However a causal connection has to be established. Thus a claim based on the fishing agreement between the Community and Senegal was dismissed because the claimant failed to establish a causal connection between alleged breach of Community law and his loss.[19]

Heads of damage and limitation
Regarding the heads of damage it seems the Court will award damages for actual loss (*damnum emergens*)[20] as well as the consequential loss (*lucrum cessans*) in accordance with the practice established in the Member States. In claims of a personal nature the ECJ may award compensation for material as well as moral damage.[1] The quantum has to be worked out and substantiated by the claimant assuming, of course, that he has proved infringement of a substantive right. Where the quantum is in dispute the parties ought to negotiate a settlement but, where

---

15 Case 120/86: *Mulder v Minister of Agriculture* [1988] ECR 2321, [1989] 2 CMLR 1; Joined Cases C-104/89 and C-37/90: *Mulder v Council and Commission* [1992] ECR I-3061; see also Joined Cases T-195/94 and T-202/94: *Friedhelm Quiller and Johann Heusmann v Council* [1997] ECR II-2247.

16 Cases C-189/89: *Spagl v HZA Rosenheim* and C-217/89 *Pastätter v HZA Bad Reichenhall* [1990] ECR I-4539 and ECR I-4585, resp.

17 Joined Cases C-104/89 and C-37/90: *Mulder v Commission and Council* [1992] ECR I-3061.

18 Case 253/84: *Groupement Agricole v Council and Commission* [1987] ECR 123, [1988] 1 CMLR 677; see also Cases 353/88: *Briantex v Commission* [1989] ECR 3623; 122/86: *Epicheiriseon v Commission and Council* [1989] ECR 3959; C-358/90; *Compagnia Italiana Alcool v Commission* [1992] ECR I-2457, [1992] 2 CMLR 876 at para 47.

19 Case T-572/93: *Odigitria AAE v Council and Commission* [1995] ECR II-2025, [1996] 2 CMLR 59. See also Case T-168/94: *Blackspur v Council and Commission* [1995] ECR II-2627 and (on appeal) Case C-362/95P: *Blackspur etc* [1997] ECR I-4775.

20 Joined Cases C-104/89 and C-37/90: *Mulder v Council and Commission* [1992] ECR I-3061.

1 See Cases 18/78 supra, p 67 note 12 and 145/83 supra, p 67 note 13.

they are unable to agree, the Court may appoint expert assessors to assist in the process.[2]

However, recently the ECJ,[3] following its interlocutory judgment, gave a detailed breakdown of compensation in respect of an accidental fall from the roof of the atomic establishment, into expenditure caused by the accident, total temporary incapacity and permanent invalidity and included in the final sum interest and an allowance for inflation.

Claims against the Community for compensation arising from non-contractual liability are subject to a limitation period of five years,[4] the time beginning to run from the date on which the event giving rise to damage had occurred.[5] This, in the case of refunds, is the moment of the actual loss, not the date on which the refunds were instituted.[6]

---

2   See Case 59/83: *Biovilac v Commission* [1984] ECR 4057 at para 28.
3   Case C-308/87: *Alfredo Grifoni v EAEC* [1990] ECR I-1203 (interlocutory): final judgment [1994] ECR I-341.
4   Protocol on the Statute of the ECJ, Art 43.
5   Cases 5–7, 13–24 and 30/66, supra; Case 11/72: *Giordano v Commission* [1973] ECR 417.
6   Joined cases 256, 265 and 267/80 and 5/81: *Birra Wührer v Council and Commission* [1982] ECR 85 at 106; Case 51/81: *De Franceschi v Council and Commission* [1982] ECR 117 at 134.

Chapter 3

External relations

A. External relations or foreign policy?

A policy implies a defined objective and means of its implementation and enforcement. The European Communities as conceived in the founding Treaties had no foreign policy as such but, within their scope, were endowed with powers to develop relations with the outside world. It will suffice to mention the treaty-making powers, the Common Commercial Policy and external extension of certain policies laid down in the Treaties. In that sense the external relations of the Communities reflected certain internal policies and represented a reaction to events affecting the Communities. It can be said that the external relations, based on the express powers written into the Treaties, were the natural extension of the internal policy, ie actions in *foro interno* were complemented by actions in *foro externo*. Moreover, with the development of the Community as an international trading unit and the consolidation of the common market the necessity of life dictated a broader approach, so much so that in the opinion of the Court of Justice[1] 'the authority to enter into international relations may not only arise from express attributions by the Treaty but may also flow implicitly from its provisions'. However even such a broad interpretation of the existing powers could not cover the existing deficit.

As we have observed the development of the European Political Co-operation was to give an answer to the problem. Thus the Single European Act[2] linked foreign policy with security stressing that co-operation in the latter would contribute to the development of the former. Whilst recognizing the weakness of the Community and the advantages of co-operation in the international arena the Act has advanced towards a single European policy in so far as it strengthened the institutional framework within which such a policy can be promulgated and set up a machinery for moving from consultations to joint action in which the Member States and the institutions would be associated. It paved the way for the adoption of the 'second pillar' of the Maastricht Treaty. However the TEU has accentuated the dichotomy between external economic relations (which are managed by the

---

1   Opinion 2/91: *Re ILO Convention 170 on Chemicals at Work* [1993] ECR I-1061, [1993] 3 CMLR 800 at para 7.
2   SEA Art 30.

institutions) and foreign policy *stricto sensu* to which the institutional mechanism of the Treaty does not apply. So, despite the 'ever closer union' the Treaty can do no more than proclaim that 'the Union shall assert its identity in the international scene'. It cannot, as yet claim exclusive competence in this field. Thus it is premature to conclude that the Union has its own foreign policy and security policy though, proceeding in a bicephalous manner, it is moving in that direction.

B.   The power base

It has already been pointed out that the Communities have personality and capacity under international law. Their personality and capacity may be classified as of the functional sort referred to by the International Court of Justice in its advisory opinion in the *Reparation for Injuries* case arising from the assassination by terrorists of a United Nations' mediator in Palestine.[3] That is to say that the Communities at international law have the degree of personality and capacity which is necessary to enable them to carry out their functions on the international plane. This general view is substantiated by the terms of the Treaties themselves.

ECSC Article 6 states clearly that 'in international relations the Community shall enjoy the legal capacity it requires to perform its functions and attain its objectives'. The EC and Euratom Treaties, on the other hand, merely state that the Communities have legal personality but do not refer to any specific attribution of capacity in international law.[4] Nevertheless such latter capacity may not only be inferred from the nature of the Communities as the creatures of treaties but it has also been expressly confirmed by the Court of Justice in its judgment in *Re ERTA, Commission v Council*.[5] There the Court observed that EC Article 281 (ex Art 210), by stating that the Community has legal personality, 'means that in its external relations the Community enjoys the capacity to establish contractual links with non-Member States over the whole field of the objectives defined in Part One of the Treaty'.[6]

This, as we shall see later, is merely a power base from which spring the two attributes of legal personality in international relations, ie the treaty-making power (*jus tractatus*) and the capacity to engage in diplomacy (*jus missionis*). Quantitatively, however, the European Community falls short of the powers characteristic of a federal state in this field. In other words, though having an incipient potential for the creation of its own external policy, the Community can act only within the limits of the founding Treaties. However the scope of the action necessary to achieve the Treaty objectives may require powers which have not been expressly granted, in which case the founding Treaties themselves authorize recourse to implied powers. In the terms of the EC[7] Treaty 'if actions of the Community should prove necessary to attain, in the course of the operation of the common market, one of the objectives

---

3   ICJ Reports 1949, 174. See generally Henig, S, *External Relations of the European Community* (1971) and Costonis, J J, 'Treaty Making Powers of the EEC' (1967) *European Yearbook 31*; Coffey, P, *The External Relations of the EEC* (1976); Soldatos, P, 'La politique extérieure' in Lasok, D and Soldatos, P, *Les Communautés Européennes en Fonctionnement* (1981), pp 477 et seq.
4   EC Art 281 (ex Art 210) and EAEC Art 184.
5   Case 22/70: [1971] ECR 263, [1971] CMLR 335.
6   Ibid, at para 14.
7   EC Art 308 (ex Art 235); ECSC Art 95 (1); EAEC Art 203.

of the Community and this treaty has not provided the necessary powers, the EC Council shall, acting unanimously on a proposal from the EC Commission and after consulting the Parliament, take the appropriate measures'. This, however, is not a blanket provision increasing the existing powers but an auxiliary lever to be operated for the definite purpose of the common market and strictly within the spirit of the Treaty and in accordance with the procedure laid down therein. In the opinion of the ECJ it can be used in the field of external relations.[8]

A new lever has been provided by the Single European Act mainly at the initiative of the British Government which considers a common approach to foreign policy to be one of the mainsprings of European integration. Article 30 of the Act provided for regular quarterly meetings of the Ministers of Foreign Affairs of the Member States within the framework of European Political Co-operation; insists on a joint formulation and implementation of a European foreign policy and consistency of the external policies of the European Community and the policies agreed in European Political Co-operation. It charges the Presidency of the Council (which assumes the function of the Presidency of European Co-operation) with the management of Political Co-operation and with the tasks of initiating action and representing the positions of the Member States in relations with the outside world as far as the activities of European Political Co-operation are concerned. It provides further for a Secretariat to assist the Presidency and to work with the European Correspondents' Group and Working Groups as regards the preparation of the meetings of Ministers and the monitoring of the implementation of policies decided by Ministers. The new approach to Political Co-operation within the Community and the formulation of external policy involves also the Commission and the European Parliament. The former shall be fully associated with the proceedings of Political Co-operation, the latter will be informed of the issues which are being examined within the framework of Political Co-operation and given an opportunity of presenting its point of view which shall be taken into consideration within the framework of Political Co-operation.

Thus the SEA paved the way for the formulation of the Foreign and Security Policy (comprised in the 'second pillar' of the Union) complementing the Community capacity in the field of the economic external relations.[9]

C. *Jus tractatus*

(1) COMMUNITY COMPETENCE

According to the founding Treaties each Community has the capacity to establish relations with certain international organizations and to conclude certain types of international agreements. Thus each of them is competent to establish relations with the organs of the United Nations[10] and its specialized agencies and the Organization for European Economic Co-operation[11] as well as the Council of Europe.[12] Moreover the EC and the Euratom can maintain relations with the World Trade Organization (and formerly GATT) and also such relations as are

---

8   Case 22/70, supra [1971] ECR 263 at 283, [1971] CMLR 355 at 362; Joined Cases 3, 4, 6/76: *Officier van Justitie v Kramer* [1976] ECR 1279, [1976] 2 CMLR 440; Opinion 1/76, [1977] 2 CMLR 279.
9   See supra, pp 37 ff.
10 EC Art 302(1) (ex Art 229(1)); ECSC Art 93; EAEC Art 199.
11 EC Art 304 (ex Art 231); ECSC Art 93; EAEC Art 201.
12 EC Art 303 (ex Art 230); ECSC Art 94; EAEC Art 200.

appropriate with all international organizations,[13] including the International Labour Office.[14]

Since the treaty-making power is limited to specific types of treaties the Communities may use it only to conclude treaties and agreements envisaged in the founding Treaties. Thus each Community is competent to make accession[15] treaties which have the object of admitting new members' and in the case of the EC and Euratom,[16] association agreements, which have the object of establishing a special relationship short of full membership of the Community. Moreover, the EC has power to make trade[17] agreements and Euratom[18] can enter into agreements or contracts with a non-Member State, an international organization or even an individual from a non-Member State in the context of the common market for atomic energy. However the ECSC[19] Treaty limits the Community competence in the context of the common market for coal and steel to a general supervision of the commercial policy of the Member States in this sector, including tariffs and import and export licences, to ensure compliance with the Treaty.

Accession is now subject to the Treaty on the European Union which means that a new Member State joins the Union as well as the three[20] Communities. Since the Community competence is a power attributed to it by the founding Treaties at the expense of the Member States we are confronted with interaction between attributed (Community) and original (state) competence. It is, therefore, possible to distinguish in the field of external relations between exclusive Community competence, concurrent competence, and joint competence.[1] However, irrespective of the existence of Community competence, the consequence of attribution is that the Member States, being sovereign, enjoy their original right until the exclusive Community competence has been used.[2]

Accession Treaties, though concluded by the Community, have to be signed by all the existing and the acceding Member States and they can, of course, be aborted by the veto of an existing member or frustrated by the EP refusing to give its assent. Because of their constitutional nature they are a class apart but from a Community point of view can be regarded as emanating from the joint competence; though from the point of view of the acceding state as well as the existing Member States, they represent an exercise of sovereign power which, in the case of the latter, is not limited merely to a vote.

Association agreements emanate from the joint competence of the Community, the Member States and the associate country.

As emphasized in the case law[3] the Community enjoys exclusive competence in the field of commercial policy. The point was made in the Opinion[4] of the

13   EC Art 302(1)(2) (ex Art 229(1)(2)); EAEC Art 199.
14   See Case 217/86: *Commission v Council* (OJ 1986, C 242/8) (re Council resolution refusing the Commission authority to negotiate an agreement on the use of asbestos) removed from the Register; see Opinion 2/91, Re Convention No 170 of the ILO concerning safety in the use of chemicals at work [1993] ECR I-1061 (joint competence).
15   EC Art 237 replaced by TEU Art 49 (ex Art O); ECSC Art 98; EAEC Art 206.
16   EC Art 182–188 and 310 (ex Arts 131–136a and 238); EAEC Art 206.
17   EC Art 133 (ex Art 113).
18   EAEC Art 101.
19   Arts 71–75.
20   TEU Art 49 (ex Art O).
1   Waelbroeck, M et al, *Le droit de la Communauté Européenne* (1981), Vol 12, pp 103 et seq.
2   Joined cases 3, 4, 6/76, p 75 note 8, supra.
3   See especially Case 22/70, p 74 note 5, supra and cases below.
4   Opinion 1/75: [1975] ECR 1355 at 1364, [1976] 1 CMLR 85 at 93; see also Case 41/76: *Criel (née Donckerwolke) v Procureur de la République* [1976] ECR 1921 at 1936, [1977] 2 CMLR 535 at 551; Case 52/77: *Cayrol v Rivoira* [1977] ECR 2261, [1978] 2 CMLR 253; Case 179/78: *Procureur de la République v Rivoira* [1979] ECR 1147, [1979] 3 CMLR 456.

ECJ ruling that export credit agreements within the Organization for Economic Co-operation and Development were closely connected with export trade and, therefore, within the EEC Treaty, thus disposing of the contention that there may still be a parallel (or concurrent) competence vested in the Member States. Consequently, held the Court, the Member States must refrain from taking concurrent actions.

In its ruling on the Draft Convention of the International Atomic Energy on the Physical Protection of Nuclear Materials, Facilities and Transport[5] the ECJ held[6] that the Community had exclusive competence to join the Convention not only by virtue of its international legal personality and the treaty-making power but also because of the objectives of the founding Treaty. Since the business of the Convention was within the Community competence the Member States no longer had any concurring powers but, in the spirit of Community solidarity, had to co-operate. However there was a practical problem because the Convention had to be implemented through the co-operation between the Community and the Member States. This problem was resolved by apportioning specific tasks as between the Community and the Member States. The Community assumed responsibility for the supply arrangements and management of the common market in nuclear energy as well as the execution of the security provisions and the management of property rights whilst the remaining tasks were undertaken by the Member States.

With the growing integration within the Community the area of concurrent competence has been in decline. However there are still areas of potential exclusive competence which have not been appropriated by the Community. This is so in cases where the financial commitments cannot be discharged from the Community budget and, therefore, call for further participation of the Member States. Besides this there are problems with the trade agreements of the Member States where their partners in trade do not recognize the legal personality of the Community or, for reasons better known to themselves, they prefer to deal with the Member States directly.

The ECJ's opinion on the Draft International Agreement on Natural Rubber[7] exemplifies the first problem for, whilst the Community was competent to become party to the Agreement in its own right, the management of the rubber resources, being within the scope of trade or commercial policy, the lack of own funds to contribute towards this expensive international project necessitated an involvement of the Member States in their individual capacity. The second problem (today merely of a historical interest) is well illustrated in relations with the former USSR and the COMECON countries. Despite repeated overtures the two parts of the divided Europe have kept apart. Whilst the COMECON until the Convention of 1985[8] had no autonomous legal personality its members were reluctant to recognize the personalities of the European Communities. As a result trade between the Member States of the EEC and the COMECON countries continued on a bilateral basis.

Certain agreements reflect as their central feature a concept of joint competence of the Community and the Member State. They also reflect various forms of co-operation between the contracting parties. The word 'co-operation' has several meanings and its precise scope has to be examined in the light of the

---

5 Vienna and New York Convention of 3 March 1980; Misc 27 (1980); Cmnd 8112.
6 Ruling 1/78: [1978] ECR 2151, [1979] 1 CMLR 131.
7 Opinion 1/78: [1979] ECR 2871, [1979] 3 CMLR 639.
8 See Warsaw Convention of 27 June 1985 on the legal capacity, privilege and immunities of COMECON.

terms of the agreement in question. Thus, for example, the agreement with Canada[9] is a 'framework agreement of commercial and economic co-operation'; the agreements with Sri Lanka, Pakistan and Bangladesh[10] are each a 'commercial co-operation agreement'; agreements with the ASEAN[11] Group (ie Indonesia, Malaysia, the Philippines, Singapore and Thailand) refer to 'commercial, economic and development co-operation'; whilst agreements with the Mediterranean[12] countries as well as the 1975 Lomé[13] Convention are simply 'agreements of co-operation'. We should mention in this context the co-operation agreements with two state-trading countries (which were not members of the COMECON), Yugoslavia[14] and China.[15] Co-operation agreements enable the Member States to enter into bilateral agreements with the Community partners within the scope of these agreements. However, to ensure Community supremacy, they expressly provide that the bilateral agreements are subordinate to the framework agreements and the Community text prevails 'even if the terms of the two were identical'.[16] Another feature, exemplified by the EC-Canada agreement, is the joint Co-operation Committee set up by the EC and the other party (without a direct involvement of the Member States) to oversee the implementation and, presumably, to deal with conflicts arising therefrom.

We should also mention in the context of competence the so-called mixed agreements,[17] ie international treaties in which the contracting parties comprise the Community and one or more Member States on the one side and one or more non-Community signatories on the other. Such treaties are not expressly provided for in the EC Treaty but are envisaged in Article 102 of the Euratom Treaty, and therefore, acceptable to the whole Community. Such treaties were considered by the ECJ in the Opinion on Natural Rubber[18] which thought that they were particularly useful to embody multilateral arrangements in cases where the subject matter concerned the Community and individual Member States in such a way that it would be impracticable to negotiate a collective agreement and then sub-divide it into a number of agreements each relating to a particular party.

The area we have touched upon is vast and still expanding. What needs to be said in conclusion is that, whilst the founding Treaties provide a framework for Community external relations and lay down rules regarding exclusive Community competence, the process is still evolving and the original competence of the Member States retained outside the founding Treaties remains to a degree relevant to Treaties within the Community competence. The panorama of Community

---

9   OJ 1976, L260; Lasok, D, 'Involvement with the European Economic Community: Some Canadian Considerations' (1976) 22 McGill Law Jo No 4 575.
10   Sri Lanka, OJ 1975, L247/2; Pakistan, OJ 1976, L168/2; Bangladesh, OJ 1976, L319/2. The new agreement with Pakistan, OJ 1986, L113/86, is a 'commercial economic, development and co-operation agreement', see Council Reg 1196/86, OJ 1986, L108/1 annexed thereto.
11   OJ 1980, L144/2.
12   Algeria, OJ 1978, L263/2; Morocco, OJ 1978, L264/2; Tunisia, OJ 1978, L265/2; Egypt, OJ 1978, L266/2; Lebanon, OJ 1978, L267/2; Jordan, OJ 1978, L268/2; Syria, OJ 1978, L269/2.
13   Ts 105 (1979); Cmnd 7751; OJ 1976, L25/2; see p 84 note 16, infra.
14   OJ 1973, L224/1, renewed 1980. See Gen Report 1980, p 276. Spent as a result of the disintegration of Yugoslavia.
15   OJ 1978, L123/1; see also OJ 1985 C 250/2; see Kapur, H, *China and the EEC: The New Connection* (1986).
16   EEC–Canada Agreement, Art IV.
17   See further O'Keefe, D and Schermers, H G, *Mixed Agreements* (1983).
18   Opinion 1/78 [1979] ECR 2871, [1979] 3 CMLR 639.

Treaties[19] reflects a variety of relations ranging from bilateral or multilateral agreements, various forms of co-operation, preferential and non-preferential trade arrangements, comprehensive agreements as well as commodity agreements. The global strategy for multilateral agreements reflects trade relations on a regional basis as well as related to groups of countries and other 'Communities'. Hence the European extension of free trade to the European Free Trade Area (EFTA) countries, culminating in the creation of the EEA,[20] association agreements with certain Mediterranean countries,[1] co-operation agreements with the Mediterranean countries of Africa and Asia, agreements of the South-East Asian countries (ASEAN) and certain individual Latin American countries and countries associated in the Cartagena Agreement.[2] However the most spectacular in numbers and geographical extension is the Lomé Association Convention embracing 69 African, Caribbean and Pacific countries (ACP).

The Community is also involved in tariff negotiations within GATT and participates in the work of the OECD, using the world and regional platform for trade in order to promote and defend its interests.

(2)   TREATY-MAKING PROCEDURE

The founding Treaties lay down the procedures for the exercise of the treaty-making power of the Community. These involve interaction of the Community institutions and agreement between the Member States in Council. Bearing in mind the nuances between the three Treaties the position under the EC Treaty as amended by the TEU is as follows:

(a)   Accession Treaties
Accession of new members to the Union (which entails membership of the three Communities) is available to European countries that respect the principles of liberty, democracy, respect for human rights and fundamental freedoms and the rule of law without any further qualifications.[3] However it can be assumed that further (unwritten) conditions apply, viz that the applicant country must be in the eyes of the existing members a parliamentary democracy capable and willing to carry out the Community obligations. This can be inferred from the experience so far suggesting that the admission of Greece, Spain and Portugal was delayed mainly for political reasons and that Turkey is facing similar difficulties. Indeed the negative opinion[4] regarding the latter suggests further qualifications, viz that the applicant's economy has been aligned to that of the Community, that it

---

19   See further, Raux, J, *Les accords externes de la CEE* (1977); Flaesch-Mougin, C, *Les accords externes de la CEE, Essai d'une typologie* (1979) and McGovern, E, Stanbrook, C and Hawkes, L W N, 'External Relations', Law of the European Communities, *Halsbury's Laws of England* (4th edn) Vol 51, 477. Bury, C, et al, *European Community External Relations*, Law and Practice (1995).

20   Austria, OJ 1972, L300/2; Finland, OJ 1973, L328/2; Iceland, OJ 1972, L301/2; Norway, OJ 1973, L171/2; Portugal, OJ 1972, L301/167; Sweden, OJ 1972, L300/97; Switzerland, OJ 1972, L300/189; See General Report 1978, p 264. See Case 218/83: *Les Rapides Savoyards Sàrl v Directeur Général des Douanes et Droit Indirects* [1984] ECR 3105, [1985] 3 CMLR 116.

1   Ie Cyprus, Malta, Turkey (Greece 1963–1981).

2   Ie Bolivia, Columbia, Ecuador, Peru and Venezuela, OJ 1064, L153/1.

3   TEU Art 49 (ex Art O) cross-referring to TEU Art 6(1) (ex Art F); ECSC Art 98; EAEC Art 205.

4   Press Conference of Sr Matutes on 18 December 1989, announcing the Commission's opinion.

has a satisfactory record of human rights and no quarrels with the existing Member States.

The procedure for admission begins with an application to the Council which has to be accepted unanimously and referred to the Commission for its opinion. Since the Treaty does not require expressly a positive opinion it seems that the Council may decide to open negotiations despite an adverse opinion of the Commission. Conversely, any Member States may block the proceedings despite a positive opinion of the Commission. Negotiations that follow are conducted by the Commission under the negotiation mandate imposed by the Council. These negotiations may take a long time. Thus the negotiations on the first British application lasted nearly two years only to be vetoed by France when the United Kingdom was prepared to sign. The negotiations with Greece were long and protracted, ending in 1979, with Greece becoming the tenth Member State on 1 January 1981. The negotiations with Portugal and Spain began formally in 1978 and 1979, respectively, after earlier overtures and favourable opinions of the Commission, the two countries becoming members as from 1 January 1986. The results of the negotiations are enshrined in the Act of Accession which accompanies the Treaty of Accession which signifies, on the one hand, the positive decision of the Council and the agreement of the applicant state on the other, and which has to be ratified by all the contracting states in accordance with their respective constitutions. The Treaty is an instrument of international law whilst being at the same time a 'Community act'. The Treaty and the Act of Accession entail also an amendment of the constituent (founding) Treaty and the Community law as appropriate. Where the ratification is subject to a referendum the Accession Treaty may be frustrated, as it was twice in the case of Norway, by the adverse decision of the electorate.

Accession is a political act the consequences of which are determined by the states themselves.[5] As such it is not open to challenge in court but, as a legal act, it is subject to judicial interpretation.[6] In this process the Council acts in a dual role, ie that of an institution representing the collective will of the Member States and that of a gathering of Ministers each representing the interests of its own country. The Commission acts as a purely Community institution as the initiator of policy and the executor of the negotiating mandate laid down by the Council. The Parliament is not formally involved in negotiations but its assent by an absolute majority of its component members is required.

(b)   Association agreements

So far two kinds of association agreements have come to light, ie those with European countries by virtue of EC Article 310 (ex Art 238) and those with non-European countries specifically envisaged in EC Article 182 (ex Art 131).

Association with European countries may be expressly designed to lead to full membership or leave the matter open. However, there is no automatic transition from association to accession. Thus association agreements with Greece of 1963 and Turkey of 1964 offered a prospect of membership but the agreements with Malta and Cyprus left the question open. Greece became a Member State on 1 January 1981 but Turkey's application of 14 April 1987 was turned down on 18 December 1989.[7] Malta and Cyprus applied for membership

---

5   See Case 93/78: *Mattheus v Doego* [1978] ECR 2203, [1979] 1 CMLR 551.
6   See eg Case C-27/96: *Danisco Sugar AB v Allmänna Ombutet* [1997] ECR I-6653; Case C-138/95P: *Campo Ebro v Council* [1997] ECR I-2027.
7   Commission Opinion and Press Conference on 18 December 1989 of Sr Matutes, at that time member of the Commission responsible for the Mediterranean Policy of the EC.

but in 1994 their application was turned down. Cyprus applied again and was placed in the first group of applicants to begin negotiations in the Spring of 1998.

Although the terms of the European association differ in detail, the object is to create close economic relations between the Community and the associated country and to enable the latter to adjust its economy and so to prepare itself for the assumption of duties consequent upon accession.

Association agreements with East European countries, exemplified by the agreement with Poland signed on 16 December 1991,[8] follow a common pattern. The preamble details the main assumptions of the agreement, in particular the Community's respect for the rule of law, respect of human rights and free trade, and concludes that the ultimate objective is the admission of Poland to the Community. However, there is no guarantee of admission. The scope of the agreement is wide as it purports to establish a political dialogue, facilitate development of trade and harmonious economic relations between the parties, set up a framework of financial and technical assistance of the Community, gradual integration of Poland with the Community and support for co-operation in the field of culture.[9]

The political dialogue is to unfold at three levels, ie involving the President of the Republic together with the President of the Commission and the President of the Council; the Ministers at the level of the Council[10] and within the framework of the parliamentary Committee of the Association.[11] Moreover the parties shall maintain contact through diplomatic channels, exchange of information and any other useful methods,[12] such as through the meeting of 'political directors' (ie higher officials of the ministry of foreign affairs). Such an arrangement is unprecedented but, no doubt, reflects the development of the Community into the Union.

The substantive provisions of the agreement touch upon the objectives of the EC Treaty and thus indicate the path of the harmonization of the economic system of the associated country with that of the Community and the implementation of the agreement with the object of joining the Community. The process of implementation has been planned in two consecutive periods of five years, the first period being 'transitional'. During the last twelve months of the transitional period the Council shall review the situation and shall take a decision, in the light of the achievements of that period, as regards the movement to the second period. The achievements to look at are the achievements in transformation of the associated country to the system of the market economy.[13]

The main plank of the association is the free exchange of goods subject to protective measures safeguarding the interests of the Community as regards produce of agriculture and fishery. Without proceeding to a customs union the parties have agreed to eliminate customs duties and quantitative restrictions at an unequal rate favouring the associated country[14] except as regards textiles;[15] steel and coal[16] and produce of agriculture[17] and fisheries.[18]

  8   Lasok, D, *Zarys Prawa Unii Europejskiej* (1995) p 201 et seq.
  9   Art 2.
10   Art 3.
11   Art 5.
12   Art 4.
13   Art 6.
14   Art 9.
15   Art 15 and Protocol 1.
16   Art 16 and Protocol 2.
17   Arts 18–21.
18   Arts 22–23.

Further details reflect provisions analogous to the EC Treaty envisaging however, a programme of limited concessions by the Community and reform of the system of the associated country. Specific provisions affect access to the labour market;[19] economic activities;[20] services,[1] liberalization of payments[2] in the context of economic activities in the framework of the association agreement; competition;[3] and the harmonization of laws. Article 68 contains a list of areas within which the associated country has to adjust its laws to the principles applicable in the Community.

In certain areas the Community committed itself to render assistance to the associated country. These areas include: co-operation in economic development taking into consideration regional co-operation and the integration of Central and Eastern Europe,[4] co-operation in the industrial sector,[5] promotion and protection of investments;[6] co-operation in the field of standardisation;[7] research and technology,[8] and education;[9] co-operation in the agricultural and alimentary sector;[10] energy[11] and nuclear safety;[12] protection of natural environment;[13] modernisation and development of transport;[14] modernization of communicating services;[15] banking, insurance and financial services;[16] technical assistance leading to the acceptance of the Polish currency on international markets[17] and co-operation in combating of the laundering of gains from crime especially from trafficking in drugs;[18] co-operation in regional policy and town and country planning;[19] co-operation in the social policy sector;[20] tourism;[1] support for small and medium enterprise;[2] support for the information industry and access to data bases;[3] co-operation in the field of customs services;[4] statistical techniques[5] and mutual information about economic developments and integration.[6]

The association agreement was buttressed by generous financial assistance comprised in the two PHARE programmes.[7]

19 Art 37.
20 Arts 44–54.
 1 Art 55.
 2 Art 59.
 3 Art 63.
 4 Art 71.
 5 Art 72.
 6 Art 73.
 7 Art 74.
 8 Art 75.
 9 Art 76.
10 Art 77.
11 Art 78.
12 Art 79.
13 Art 80.
14 Art 81.
15 Art 82.
16 Art 83.
17 Art 84.
18 Art 85.
19 Art 86.
20 Art 87.
 1 Art 88.
 2 Art 89.
 3 Art 90.
 4 Art 91.
 5 Art 92.
 6 Art 93.
 7 Art 97.

The institutions established in the framework of the association comprise the Council of Association, the Committee of Association and the Parliamentary Committee. The Council of the Association consists of members of the Polish government and members of the Council, Ministers of the European Union and of the European Commission.

The functions of the Council of Association include the supervision of the implementation of the objectives and programmes of the agreement,[8] legislation necessary to carry into effect the provisions of the agreement in the form of decisions and recommendations[9] and the solution of disputes.[10] The Council functions according to its own regulation. The meetings of the Council are chaired alternatively by the representative of Poland and the minister from the Member State of the Community which currently carried the Presidency of the Community.[11] In the absence of a specific provision it is assumed that decisions are carried unanimously.

The Committee of the Association, whose main function is the preparation of the meeting of the Council of Association, consists of senior officials representing the Polish government, the Council of Ministers and of the Commission.[12]

The Parliamentary Committee[13] consists of representatives of the Polish parliament and of the European Parliament. Its main function is to organize meetings and exchange views. It is chaired alternatively by representatives of the two Parliaments in accordance with a regulation which it formulates. It is entitled to receive information from the Council of the Association on the progress of the implementation of the agreement.[14]

As mentioned earlier the political dialogue at the level of the President of the Republic, the President of the Council of the European Union and the President of the Commission fulfils the function of a 'summit meeting' in analogy to the European Council of the European Union.

It seems that the agreement outlined above admirably serves the object of association leading to membership of the Union.

The object of the other form of association is, according to EC Article 182(2) (ex Art 131(2)), to promote the economic and social development of certain non-European countries and territories listed in EC Annex II which, in view of their former colonial dependency, have retained a special relationship with some of the Member States or, as critics would have it, to promote a form of neo-colonialism.[15] The developments to date negate the latter suggestion. Indeed according to EC Article 182(3) (ex Art 131(3)) associations shall serve primarily to further the interests and prosperity of the inhabitants of these countries and territories in order to lead them to the economic, social and cultural development to which they aspire. More precisely, in the light of EC Articles 183–186 (ex Arts 132–135) the object is to create a customs union between the Community and the associated states, to encourage investment and economic and commercial co-operation and to regulate on a non-discriminatory basis the right of establishment of nationals and corporations.

---

8   Art 102.
9   Art 104.
10   Art 105.
11   Art 103.
12   Art 106.
13   Arts 108 and 109.
14   Art 110.
15   Curzon, V, *Yearbook of World Affairs* (1971), p 118.

Referring specifically to this form of association EC Article 187 (ex Art 136) as originally worded, provided that multilateral agreements should be made by an implementing convention attached to the Treaty for an initial period of five years to be reviewed and renewed from time to time. However this model was replaced by a negotiated one, which took its name from the capital city where it was signed. The process has gone through six stages of development, ie Yaoundé I (1964), Yaoundé II (1969), with modifications for anglophonic countries, Arusha (1968 and 1969), Lomé I (1975), Lomé II (1984) and Lomé IV (1989) concluded for ten years.[16] This reflects an evolution of the relationship between the EC and, as of now, 69 'developing' African, Caribbean and Pacific Ocean (ACP) countries. The trading position has reached, at present, an almost non-reciprocal level, the only restrictions affecting a fraction of agricultural exports to the EC, from the ACP countries. Apart from that there are no customs duties and no quantitative restrictions on imports or exports between the parties. The sugar-producing countries have a guarantee regarding the volume of exports and the price, thus contributing to stability in this sector. For the purpose of the origin of goods the EC treats the ACP countries as one trading unit, thus recognizing the principle of cumulative origin in this respect. The ACP countries grant the EC the most-favoured-nation treatment in trade and undertake not to discriminate between the Member States. The EC economic aid, mainly in the form of grants to develop small and medium-sized industries and stabilize the export earnings as well as industrial expertise,[17] is channelled through the Convention to individual countries. The ACP countries receive financial aid from the European Development Fund.

As the relations under the Convention develop, the Community, apart from increasing its financial contributions, is able to pinpoint certain priorities such as the environment, the rôle of women, decentralized co-operation and promotion of the private sector and, in view of the poor record of human rights in certain countries, reaffirm the universal and indivisible human rights.[18]

The Convention has established three institutions – a Council of Ministers, a Committee of Ambassadors and a Consultative Assembly – to direct the relations between the Community and the associated states. Any disputes arising under the Convention are initially referred to the Council of Ministers and, in the last resort, to a specified arbitration procedure. The organization has certainly stimulated trade and contributed to the stabilization of the export earnings of the ACP states by protecting them against fluctuations in commodity prices.

Irrespective of the type of association the procedure for the making of the association agreements is uniform. Such agreements[19] are concluded by the Council acting unanimously and after receiving the assent of the European Parliament which shall act by an absolute majority of its component members. In practice negotiations are conducted by the Commission under the Council's direction. The Parliament

16 Lomé II TS 105 (1979); Cmnd 7751; The Courrier, No 58, Special Issue Nov 1979; Kirkpatrick, C H, 'Lomé II', (1980) Journal of World Trade, 35; Lomé III EC 19 (1985); Cmnd 9511; The Courrier, Jan–Feb 1985; Lomé IV The Courrier, March–April 1990, pp 56 et seq. The Lomé Convention has now been replaced by a 'Partnership Agreement' signed in Cotonou on 23 June 2000. Pending ratification, transitional measures are provided for in Decision 1/2000 (OJ 2000, L195/46).
17 See Case 114/86: *United Kingdom v Commission, Re Lomé II Service Contracts* [1988] ECR 5289, [1989] 1 CMLR 32. But see Case 126/83: *STS Consorzio per Sistemi di Telecomunicazione via Satellite SpA v Commission* [1984] ECR 2769; See Case C-316/91: *European Parliament v Council Re validity of the Financial Regulation for development of ECP countries* [1994] ECR I-625.
18 Twenty-seventh General Report (1994) p 279.
19 EC Art 300(2) (ex Art 228(2)); EAEC Art 206(2) amended by SEA Art 9.

takes no part in the negotiations but has to give its assent as in the case of accession of new members. Association agreements are subject to ratification by the Member States and the associated country.

(c)   Trade agreements

The most numerous international agreements made by the EC are, of course, the trade agreements concluded in the context of the Common Commercial Policy and, as observed earlier, there is a great variety of these corresponding to the Community policy and the interests of the other contracting parties. In accordance with EC Article 133 (ex Art 113) the Common Commercial Policy shall be based on uniform principles particularly in regards to changes in tariff rates, the conclusion of tariff and trade agreements, the achievement of uniformity in measures of liberalisation, export policy and measures to protect trade such as those to be taken in the event of dumping or subsidies. Where trade agreements with third countries or international organizations have to be negotiated, the Commission shall make recommendations to the Council which shall, in turn, authorize the Commission to open negotiations. These negotiations are conducted by the Commission in consultation with a special committee appointed for the purpose by the Council within the framework of directives issued by the Council. The mandate and the directives require a decision by a qualified majority of the Council. The Parliament is not involved formally in the formation of trade agreements but, of course, is free to discuss the issues involved and express opinions. It may also question the members of the Commission and of the Council in the context of the political supervision of the working of the Community. To conclude such agreements the Council acts by a qualified majority.

(3)   IMPLIED POWERS

In view of its limited treaty-making power the Community has the capacity to enter into international agreements strictly within the limits of the Treaty, each type of agreement being governed by specified Treaty provisions. However where the relevant article appears insufficient to carry out the intention of the parties EC Article 308 (ex Art 228) may be called in aid. Thus, for example, the conclusion of the framework agreement with Canada and the international rubber agreement was supported by reference to EC Article 228 (now Art 308) under which unanimity is required.

(4)   AGREEMENTS IN GENERAL: RÔLE OF COUNCIL COMMISSION AND PARLIAMENT

EC Article 300 (ex Art 228) contains a general formula regarding the procedure for the conclusion of agreements between the Community and one or more states or an international organization where such agreements are envisaged by the Treaty. The Commission shall make recommendations to the Council which shall authorize the Commission to open the necessary negotiations. The Commission shall conduct these negotiations in consultation with a special committee appointed by the Council to assist it in this task and within the framework of such directives as the Council may issue.

In exercising its powers in this respect the Council shall act by a qualified majority on a proposal from the Commission as required by the Treaty. However the Council shall act unanimously where the agreement covers a field for which unanimity is required for the adoption of internal rules or for association agreements.[20]

20   See pp 75 ff, supra.

Except in the case of trade agreements, the Council shall conclude agreements after consulting the European Parliament, including cases where the agreement covers a field for which the procedure[1] laid down in EC Article 251 (ex Art 189b) and EC Article 252 (ex Art 189c) is required for the adoption of internal rules. The European Parliament shall deliver its opinion within a time limit laid by the Council. The Council shall go ahead in the absence of an opinion delivered in time.

By way of derogation association agreements, other agreements establishing a specific institutional framework by organizing co-operation procedures, agreements having important budgetary implications for the Community and agreements entailing amendment of an act adopted under the procedure of EC Article 251 (ex Art 189b) shall be concluded after the assent of the European Parliament has been obtained.

The respective rôles of the Council and the Commission under the terms of EC Article 300(1) (ex Art 228(1)) have been settled in Court in the ERTA[2] case.

In January 1962, under the auspices of the UN Economic Commission for Europe, a European Road Transport Agreement (ERTA) was signed by a number of European states including the five original members of the Community. That Agreement has not yet come into force because of an insufficient number of ratifications. In 1967 negotiations were resumed to revise the ERTA. In 1969 the Council of the Communities made a regulation dealing with the harmonization of certain social provisions in the field of road transport. In March 1970 at a meeting of the Council the attitude to be taken by the Member States of the Communities in the final stage of the ERTA negotiations to be held in April 1970 was discussed. Those negotiations were then undertaken and concluded by the Member States in the light of that discussion and the Economic Commission for Europe declared that the ERTA would be open for signature from July 1970. In May 1970 the Commission of the Communities instituted proceedings seeking an annulment of the Council's discussion of March 1970 on the grounds that the Council had acted in breach of Article 228 of the EEC Treaty. This challenge raised the wider issue of the relative rôles of Council and Commission in the conduct of the Community's external relations.

The Court stated that under EC Article 228 (now Art 300) the right to conclude an agreement with non-Member States lay with the Council, with the Commission cast in the rôle of negotiator. But those institutions could only play those rôles under the authority of either an express Treaty provision or a decision taken under the Treaty. The bulk of the negotiations for the ERTA had been concluded before the Community had a developed transport policy, therefore the Community as such had no authority to negotiate and ratify the ERTA. At the time of the Council discussions which were in issue, the ERTA negotiations had already reached such an advanced stage that it would have jeopardized the whole Agreement to have attempted to reopen them. Thus the Court held that the procedures specified in EC Article 228 (now Art 300) were clearly inapplicable. The only obligation on the Member States was to ensure that nothing was done to prejudice the interests of the Community and so that the Council in co-ordinating the attitudes of Member States to the ERTA in the light of Community interests had acted quite properly. Thus even where the provisions of the Treaties are not directly applicable to the external relations of the Member States they are nevertheless under a continuing

1   See pp 261 ff, infra.
2   Case 22/70: *Commission v Council, Re European Road Transport Agreement* [1971] ECR 263, [1971] 3 CMLR 335.

obligation, under the terms of EC Article 10 (ex Art 5), to 'abstain from any measure which could jeopardize the attainment of the objectives of the Treaty'.

(5) SIGNING OF TREATIES

Community external Treaties or agreements negotiated in accordance with the requisite procedures are signed on behalf of the Community by the President of the Council who is usually the Minister of External Affairs of the Member State holding the presidency at the time of the signing. Accession Treaties and association agreements have to be signed and ratified on behalf of all Member States.

(6) JUDICIAL CONTROL

The Court of Justice plays no part in the exercise of the Community treaty-making power though within its overall mission of ensuring that the law is observed it has the power of judicial review of Community acts. Indeed the Council, the Commission or a Member State may obtain from the ECJ an opinion whether an agreement envisaged is compatible with the Treaty.[3] Should the opinion be adverse the agreement would enter into force only following an amendment of the Treaty in accordance with TEU Art 48 (ex Art N) which provides that:

> The government of any Member State or the Commission may submit to the Council proposals for the amendment of the Treaties on which the Union is founded. If the Council, after consulting the European Parliament and, where appropriate, the Commission, delivers an opinion in favour of calling a conference of representatives of the governments of the Member States, the conference shall be convened by the President of the Council for the purpose of determining by common accord the amendments to be made to those Treaties. The European Central Bank shall also be consulted in the case of institutional changes in the monetary area. The amendments shall enter into force after being ratified by all the Member States in accordance with their respective constitutional requirements.

So far the Treaties have not been amended following the negative opinion of the Court of Justice. The following opinions (rulings in the case of the Euratom) have been handed down by the Court: 1/75: *Re OECD Understanding on Local Cost Standard;*[4] 1/76: *Re Draft Agreement on the Establishment of a European Laying-up Fund for Inland Water Vessels;*[5] 1/78: *Re Draft International Agreement on Natural Rubber;*[6] 1/91: *Re EEC-EFTA Agreement;*[7] 1/92: *Re EEC-EFTA Agreement;*[8] ruling 1/78: *Re International Convention on Nuclear Materials;*[9] Opinion 2/91:P *Re I.L.O. Convention 170 on Chemicals at Work;*[10] 1/94: *Re Agreement Establishing World Trade Organization;*[11] 2/92: *Re Competence of the Community or One of its Institutions to participate in the Third Revised Decision of the OECD on national treatment;*[12] 3/94: *Re GATT (WTO) Framework Agreement on Bananas;*[13] 2/94:

---

3   EC Art 300(6) (ex Art 228(6)); EAEC Art 103(3).
4   [1975] ECR 1355, [1976] 1 CMLR 85 – positive.
5   [1977] ECR 741 – negative.
6   [1979] ECR 2871 – ambiguous.
7   [1991] ECR I-6079, [1992] 1 CMLR 245 – negative.
8   [1992] ECR I-2821, [1992] 2 CMLR 217 – positive.
9   [1978] ECR 2151 – positive.
10 [1993] ECR I-1061, [1993] 1 CMLR 800 – positive.
11 [1994] ECR I-5267 – positive.
12 [1995] ECR I-521 – positive.
13 [1995] ECR I-4577 – positive.

Re Accession of the Communities to the Convention for the Protection of Human Rights and Fundamental Freedoms.[14]

(7)   SUBSTITUTION

The Community may also assume obligations under an international agreement without actually negotiating and signing it. This occurs in international law by virtue of substitution with the consent of all parties concerned. The example of the GATT springs to mind in this respect as the Community has assumed the rights and duties vested in the Member States of the Community though strictly it was not a member of that organization.[15] Indeed formal accession would reduce its voting power to one whilst in the present situation the Community, being the spokesman for the whole collective, can count on as many as there are Member States. It is arguable that the Community should also become party to the European Convention on Human Rights but there are several obstacles to formal accession, one of which is that the Convention is open only to states and the Community is not a state as yet. However in practice the ECJ applies the Convention by substition and, since the Maastricht Treaty, in its own right, as one of the sources of general principles of law.[16]

(8)   EAEC AND ECSC TREATIES

The negotiation and conclusion of Euratom agreements is in the hands of the Commission acting under the direction of the Council[17] which signifies its consent by a qualified majority. However agreements or contracts whose implementation does not require action by the Council and can be effected within the limits of the relevant budget are negotiated and concluded solely by the Commission though the Commission must keep the Council informed.

There are no provisions in the ECSC Treaty regarding the formation of international agreements. In practice the Commission negotiates and concludes such agreements on behalf of the Community within the framework of the Treaty and Part II of the Convention on the Transitional Provisions attached to the Treaty.

D.   The European Economic area (EEA)

A major development of the European economic integration is due to the creation of the EEA. Thus, without actually enlarging the Community the combined strength of the EC and the EFTA represent a population of some 380 million. This represents a considerable economic power.

The Agreement between the two blocs was reached in October 1991 and it was expected to be ratified by the end of 1992 to coincide with the completion of the internal market. However the EP considered it necessary to have an Opinion of the Court of Justice on the compatibility of the draft Agreement with the EC Treaty. On the request of the Commission the ECJ ruled[18] that

---

14   [1996] ECR I-1759, [1996] 2 CMLR 265 – negative.
15   See Joined Cases 21–24/72: *International Fruit Co NV v Produktschap voor Groenten en Fruit (No 3)* [1972] ECR 1219, [1975] 2 CMLR 1. See also Case C-469/93: *Amministrazione delle Finanze v Chiquita Italia SpA* [1995] ECR I-4533.
16   See TEU Art 6(2) (ex Art F(2)), infra.
17   EAEC Art 101.
18   Opinion 1/91: *Re Draft Treaty on a European Economic Area* [1991] ECR I-6079, [1992] 1 CMLR 245.

certain provisions of the Agreement, notably the proposed judicial system, would conflict with the foundations of the Community and its legal order. The Court followed its Opinion 1/76[19] where it found a less ambitious scheme unacceptable. A rapid rescue operation resulted in an amendment whereby the offending parts of the Agreement were removed and a non-judicial conflict-solving method was adopted. This consists of a conciliatory procedure and ad hoc arbitration by a body of arbitrators drawn from both sides. The Court, in its second Opinion,[20] approved the amendment and the EEA Agreement was signed on 2 May 1992. However there was a setback since Switzerland, by national referendum,[1] decided against ratification. Thereupon the parties negotiated an adjusting protocol[2] which would enable the Agreement to be implemented without Switzerland which, nevertheless, can join at a later date. This enabled the parties to ratify and put the Agreement into force by 1 January 1994.

(1) STRUCTURE OF THE EEA[3]

At the head of the EEA is the Council[4] which consists of the EC Council of Ministers and a member of the EC Commission and of one member of the government of each of the EFTA States. The office of President[5] is held alternately for six months by a member of the Council of the European Union and a member of the government of an EFTA State. Decisions of the Council shall be taken by 'agreement by the EC on the one hand and the EFTA States on the other'.[6] This means unanimity on both sides and unanimity in Council between the two sides. The Council is to provide leadership[7] since its role is to give political impetus to the implementation of the Agreement and to lay down the general guidelines for the EEA Joint Committee. The Contracting Parties and the EC Member States in their respective fields of competence may, after discussion in the EEA Joint Committee, or directly in exceptionally urgent cases, raise matters in the EEA Council.

The EEA Joint Committee consists of representatives of the Contracting Parties.[8] The office of President[9] is held alternately, for a period of six months by the EC (represented by a member of the Commission) and the representative of one of the EFTA countries. It meets regularly at least once a month or, as circumstances demand, at the initiative of its President or one of the Contracting parties. It may appoint sub-committees and working groups.

The Joint Committee shall take decisions by 'agreement between the EC and the EFTA States', the latter 'speaking with one voice'. How that 'one voice' will be arrived at is a matter for the EFTA States to decide. The same applies to the

---

19 Opinion 1/76: *Re Draft Agreement on European Laying-up Fund for Inland Waterway Vessels* [1977] ECR 741, [1977] 2 CMLR 279.
20 Opinion 1/92: [1992] ECR I-2821, [1992] 2 CMLR 217.
1 National Referendum on 6 December 1992.
2 EC Bull 3/1993 point 1.3.2.
3 Laredo, A T, 'The EEA Agreement: An Overall View', CMLRev (29) p 1200; O'Keefe, D, 'The Agreement on the EEA', Legal Issues of European Integration, 1992/I, p 12; Raymond, 'Institutions, decision-making procedure and settlement of disputes in the European Economic Area' CMLRev 1993, p 449; Laursen, F, 'EFTA and the EC: Implications of 1992' (190).
4 EEA Agreement Art 90.
5 Art 91.
6 Art 90(2).
7 Art 89.
8 Art 93.
9 Art 94.

EC as it is not clear whether the Commission shall obtain a blanket authority or shall act in accordance with the mandate received beforehand from the Council of Ministers.

By virtue of Article 95 an EEA Joint Parliamentary Committee consisting of equal numbers of the members of the European Parliament and members of Parliament of the EFTA States shall be established. It shall hold sessions alternately in the EC and in an EFTA State in accordance with Protocol 36 which, incidentally, determines the size of the Committee. Its function is to 'contribute to a better understanding between the EC and EFTA ... through dialogue and debate'. It shall adopt its own rules of procedure.

In order to bring together the advisory bodies concerned with social and economic matters an EEA Consultative Committee representing the EC Economic and Social Committee and the EFTA Consultative Committee has been established.[10] It shall express its views in the field of its competence by means of reports and resolutions. It shall adopt its own rules of procedure.

(2) THE DECISION-MAKING PROCEDURE

Decisions within the EEA shall be taken in accordance with the rules contained in Articles 97 to 104 of the Agreement which acknowledges, in the first place, the legislative autonomy of the Contracting Parties. Thus each Contracting Party is free to amend, subject to informing the other and subject to the principle of non-discrimination, its internal legislation in the areas covered by the Agreement. However, in view of the acceptance of the *acquis communautaire*, ie the acceptance of the EC legislation and case law governing the operation of the common market up to the coming into force of the Agreement, any further development of EC law is of vital importance to the EEA. After all, the EEA is an aspect of European integration in which the law plays a constructive part. Therefore the legislative autonomy of the Contracting Parties is subject to two conditions, ie that the EEA Joint Committee concludes that the legislation in question does not affect adversely the good functioning of the Agreement and procedures laid down in Article 98 have been followed. The latter provides that the Annexes to the Agreement and certain Protocols may be amended by a decision of the EEA Joint Committee as described below.

The EC Commission which, as a rule, initiates EC legislation shall, informally, seek advice from the EFTA experts on any proposal within the scope of the EEA Agreement.[11] The object of this exercise is to take into account the views of the EFTA experts before the Commission proposal is submitted to the Council of Ministers. When the project goes to the Council copies thereof have to be transmitted to the EFTA States. At that stage preliminary exchange of views may take place in the EEA Joint Committee at the request of one of the Contracting Parties. Thereafter, during the process of the enactment of the project into a Community measure, the Parties will be engaged in the exchange of information and consultations within the EEA Joint Committee with the object of bringing the matter to a satisfactory conclusion in the spirit of good faith and co-operation.

Whenever the EC adopts legislation on an issue governed by the Agreement it must, as soon as possible, inform the other Contracting Parties in the EEA Joint Committee. Thereupon the Joint Committee shall take a decision 'as close as possible' to the EC measure amending an Annex in order to achieve a

10 Art 96.
11 Art 100.

simultaneous application of the measure as well as the amendment of the Annex in question.

If no agreement on the amendment of an Annex can be reached the EEA Joint Committee shall examine other ways and means to ensure the good functioning of the Agreement. These can include equivalent legislation.

Unless otherwise provided therein the decisions of the EEA Joint Committee shall be binding upon the Contracting Parties who must take the necessary steps to ensure their implementation.

(3)   HOMOGENEITY, SURVEILLANCE AND SETTLEMENT OF DISPUTES

In order to arrive at a uniform interpretation of the Agreement and of the Community legislation the EEA Joint Committee shall keep under constant review the case law of the Court of Justice and of the EFTA Court.[12] The two Courts shall transmit their judgments to that body. If a difference in the case law of the two Courts cannot be reconciled the matter shall be resolved under the procedure for the settlement of disputes governed by Article 105. Article 106 completes this process as it provides detailed rules for the transmission of judgments, their classification and communication of the relevant documents to the competent authorities of the Contracting Parties by the Registrar of the Court of Justice.

By virtue of EC Article 234 (ex Art 177) the Court of Justice is competent to make preliminary rulings on points of Community law (including international agreements to which the EC is a party) for the benefit of national courts. The EEA Agreement falls into that category as far as the courts of the EC Member States are concerned. Now, by virtue of Article 107 the courts of the EFTA States shall be allowed to ask the Court of Justice for interpretation of EEA rules in accordance with the procedure laid down in Protocol 34.

By a separate agreement between the EFTA States they shall establish a Court of Justice (EFTA Court) charged with the application of the Agreement and having competence, in particular, in respect of actions concerning the surveillance procedure regarding the EFTA States, appeals against decisions in the field of competition made by the EFTA Surveillance Authority and the settlement of disputes between EFTA States. Following the example of the Community the EFTA States shall establish an independent Surveillance Authority which, like the Commission, shall be charged with the duty of enforcing the obligations arising from the Agreement as well as the rules of competition.[13]

In order to ensure a uniform surveillance throughout the EEA the EFTA Surveillance Authority and the Commission shall co-operate, exchange information and consult each other on surveillance policy and in individual cases. They shall receive complaints concerning the application of the Agreement and inform each other of such complaints. Each shall examine complaints falling within its jurisdiction and pass to the other body complaints concerning the latter. In case of disagreement between them either may refer the matter to the EEA Joint Committee.[14]

---

12   See eg Case E8-9/94: *Forbrukerombudet v Mattel Scandinavia* [1996] 1 CMLR 313; Case E-1/95: *Samuelsson v Svenska Staten* [1995] 3 CMLR 813; Case E-2/94: *Scottish Salmon Growers v EFTA Surveillance Authority* [1995] 1 CMLR 851; Case E-5/96: *Ullensaker Kommune v Nille AS* [1997] 3 CMLR 236; Case E-3/96: *ASK v ABB Offshore Technology AS* [1997] 2 CMLR 954; Case E-3195: *Langeland v Norske Fabrikom AS* [1997] 2 CMLR 966; Case E-2/96: *Ulstein v Möller* [1997] 2 CMLR 878; Case E-2/95: *Eidesund v Starvanger Catering AS* [1997] 2 CMLR 672.

13   Art 108.

14   Art 109.

Pecuniary obligations imposed upon persons other than states by the EC Commission, the EFTA Surveillance Authority, the Court of Justice and the EC Court of First Instance and the EFTA Court shall be enforceable by the relevant authority of the state in which enforcement is to be carried out.

Article 111 (as revised after negative Opinion of the ECJ) lays down the following rules under which the EC and EFTA States may bring a dispute regarding the interpretation or application of the Agreement before the EEA Joint Committee:

'(a)   The EEA Joint Committee may settle the dispute after examining the relevant facts and concerning the food functioning of the Agreement;

(b)   If the dispute concerns the provisions of the Agreement which are identical in substance to the corresponding provisions of the EC and ECSC Treaties or the Community legislation enacted by virtue of these Treaties and has not been settled within three months after it has been submitted to the EEA Joint Committee, the Contracting Parties to the dispute may agree to refer the matter to the Court of Justice for a ruling on the interpretation of the rules involved.

If the EEA Joint Committee has not reached an agreement on the settlement of the dispute within six months from the date on which it was seised or if, by then, the Contracting Parties to the dispute have not decided to refer the matter to the Court of Justice, a Contracting Party may take a safeguard measure in accordance with Article 112(2)[15] and 113 or apply Article 102.

If a dispute concerns the scope or duration of safeguard (ie situations different from disputes envisaged in the preceding paragraph) taken in accordance with Articles 112 and 114 and, if the EEA Joint Committee after three months has not settled the matter any Contracting party may refer the dispute to arbitration envisaged in Protocol 33. The arbitration award shall be binding upon the parties concerned.'

(4)   THE SCOPE OF THE EEA AGREEMENT

The Agreement[16] purports to promote a continued and balanced strengthening of trade and economic relations between the Parties with equal conditions of competition and the respect of the same rules, with a view to creating a homogeneous European Economic Area through the achievement of the basic aims of the common market (ie the free movement of goods, persons, services and capital), the rules of competition and closer co-operation in certain fields, notably research and development, education and social policy. However there is more to it since it covers coal and steel products, and in the field of agriculture and fisheries it attempts to find a compromise between the protection objectives of the CAP and free trade within the EEA. It purports to eliminate discriminatory internal taxation, state aids and monopolies, co-ordinate transport and promote social policy, consumer protection and the environment on the lines of the European Community. Article 3, echoing identical provisions of the EC Treaties, enshrines the principle of solidarity which is the foundation of the EC and now has become a principle of the EEA. Thus the Contracting Parties have a duty of taking all appropriate measures, whether particular or general, to ensure fulfilment of the obligations arising out of the Agreement and to refrain from

15   In respect of societal or environment problems.
16   Art 1.

taking any measures which would jeopardize the attainment of the objectives of the Agreement. The many details written into the Agreement and its Annexes and Protocols, including the acceptance of the achievements of the Community epitomized in the *acquis communautaire*,[17] emulate the European Community without actually involving membership of the EC. Moreover the EFTA countries offer to share the financial burden of the Community. No other association agreement opens up such a close relationship.

(5)   THE FUTURE OF THE EEA

With the defection of Austria, Finland and Sweden the prospects of the EEA appear bleak though it may function with diminished numbers of EFTA countries. On the other hand EFTA may be rejuvenated by new countries joining the organization if their hopes of joining the European Union are dashed. Turkey is in that position; though not a member of EFTA she has negotiated an agreement with EFTA. Eastern Europeans have an ambition to join the Union but, if disappointed with the prospect of a prolonged waiting period, may seek their fortune in the membership of EFTA and become part of the EEA. Whatever the future may hold for the EEA it will remain a historical witness to an imaginative contribution to European integration.

E.   Effects of Community External Treaties

(1)   EFFECT ON THE COMMUNITY LEGAL ORDER

External Community Treaties are binding upon the institutions and the Member States.[18] Though no such provision can be found either in the EAEC or the ECSC Treaties it is assumed that the EC formula has a universal application within the Community legal order. Consequently there is a duty of compliance with the terms of the Treaties both upon the institutions and the Member States. Thus in ensuring respect for commitments arising from an agreement concluded by the institutions, the Member States fulfil an obligation not only in relation to the non-member country concerned but also for due performance of the agreement.[19]

Community Treaties are published in the Official Journal and, being in the nature of legal acts, they form an integral part of the Community legal order[20] and may be cited before the ECJ as well as the national courts. In the hierarchy of the Community legal norms they can be placed in a middle position between the founding Treaties with which they ought to be compatible and the Community legislative acts over which they may claim superiority by virtue of international law. However their effect depends upon their specific provisions, ie whether or not they are directly applicable. The problem did arise in connection with claims based upon the GATT and association agreements.

---

17   Art 6.
18   EC Art 300 (ex Art 228(7)).
19   Case 104/81: *HZA Mainz v Kupferberg* [1982] ECR 3641 at 3662, [1983] 1 CMLR 1 at 20; see also Case 253/83: *Sektkellerei Kupferberg v HZA Mainz, Re Sherry Wine from Spain* [1985] ECR 157, [1987] 1 CMLR 36.
20   See Ruling 1/78 [1978] ECR 2151 at 2180, [1979] 1 CMLR 131 at 160. See Case C-182/89: *Commission v France,* [1990] ECR I-4337 where the ECJ held the importation of feline skins in contravention of the Convention on International Trade in endangered species of wild fauna and flora to be a breach of EC Arts 5 and 189 (now EC Arts 10 and 249).

Faced with a claim that an EC regulation restricting the importation of fruit from a non-Community country contravened the rules of the GATT the ECJ held that the supremacy of international law should be respected but concluded that, *in casu*, the relevant provision of the GATT was neither binding nor capable of conferring any directly enforceable rights upon the private party concerned.[1] In such a case any conflict should be resolved between the Community and the GATT institutions. The Court also held in another case[2] that an EC regulation providing for compensatory amounts to offset the fluctuations in the value of currency did not contravene the GATT and, therefore, was valid. Clearly the ruling would have been different had the GATT rules imposed a duty upon the Community and conferred a corresponding right upon the party concerned.

Decisions taken by the Council of the Association within the scope of an Association Agreement form an integral part of the Community legal order and are binding upon the Community and the Member States.[3]

(2) EFFECT ON MEMBER STATES

Two questions arise as regards the effect upon the Member States of the Community, ie whether in their relations between themselves they can derogate from their duties to the Community by virtue of prior international obligations and whether their existing international obligations to third countries falling within the scope of the founding Treaties have been affected by their Community obligations.

In the *Radio Valves*[4] case Italy claimed that she was free to apply customs duties established under an agreement[5] made within the framework of the GATT and thus evade the duty of reducing the tariff rates imposed by the EC Treaty. The ECJ ruled that Italy was unable to do so because within its specific domain the founding Treaty takes precedence over agreements concluded between the Member States before they have set up the Community and these include agreements made under the auspices of the GATT. However the scope of this ruling is limited since it applies only to agreements made between the Member States themselves and not between the Member States and non-Community countries. The latter are subject to specific provisions of the founding Treaties.[6]

The *Radio Valves* case has to be distinguished from the *Plants Inspection*[7] case where the Netherlands successfully pleaded the International Plant Protection Convention[8] against the contention that, by imposing phytosanitary inspection of plants exported to other Member States as well as certificates and fees, that Member State has introduced charges having equivalent effect to customs duties prohibited in inter-state trade under the EC Treaty. Far from being incompatible

1   See Joined Cases 21–24/72, p 88 note 15, supra and also Joined Cases 267–269/81: *Amministrazione delle Finanze dello Stato v SPI* [1983] ECR 801, [1984] 1 CMLR 354; Case 266/81: *Siot v Ministero delle Finance* [1983] ECR 731, [1984] 2 CMLR 231; Case 38/75: *Nederlandse Spoorwegen v Inspecteur der Invoerrechten en Accijnzen* [1975] ECR 1439, [1976] 1 CMLR 167.
2   Case 9/73: *Schlüter v HZA Lörrach* [1973] ECR 1135.
3   Case 204/86: *Greece v Council, Re budgetary allocation of financial aid to Turkey* [1988] ECR 5323, [1990] 1 CMLR 481 and Case 30/88: *Greece v Commission, Re Aid to Turkey* [1989] ECR 3711, [1991] 2 CMLR 169.
4   Case 10/61: *Commission v Italy* [1962] ECR 1, [1962] CMLR 187.
5   Geneva Protocol 6 of 23 May 1956.
6   EC Art 307 (ex Art 234); but see EAEC Art 106 and ECSC Art 75.
7   Case 89/76: *Commission v Netherlands* [1977] ECR 1355, [1978] 3 CMLR 630.
8   Rome Convention of 1951, TS 16 (1954); Cmnd 9077.

with the Community law the Convention was considered by the ECJ to perform a function similar to that of the public health and phytosanitary measures adopted by a Community directive whilst the fees were acceptable as long as they did not exceed the actual costs of the operation. Moreover the simultaneous application of the Convention would promote rather than hinder Community trade. However in the *Van Wesemeal*[9] case the Court held that Belgium could not rely on an International Labour Organization Convention[10] sanctioning fee-charging employment agencies in order to derogate from the free movement of services in the Community. Similarly, concerning the labelling of cheese in intra-Community trade, the ECJ held that multilateral treaties cannot be pleaded against Community law if only the EC Member States are involved.[11] These cases show that in the relations inter se the Member States must give precedence to their Community obligations over the rights they may claim under international instruments.

The answer to the second question is to be found in EC Article 307 (ex Art 234) which is both a guarantee of stability and a harbinger of change. Stability of the established international relations and respect for vested rights is assured by the first paragraph, which has adopted the principle of *inter alios facta* of classic international law enshrined in Article 30 of the 1969 Vienna Convention on Treaties. Accordingly the membership of the Community leaves undisturbed the rights and obligations arising from Treaties to which the Member States and third countries are parties. Whilst the relations with third parties are safeguarded 'only in matters governed by the EEC Treaty that Treaty takes precedence over agreements concluded between Member States before its entry into force'.[12]

The second paragraph contains a harbinger of change as it enjoins the Member States to adjust their existing international obligations to their duties to the Community and their fellow members. Thus they ought to use their opportunity, when such Treaties come up for revision or renewal, in order to eliminate incompatibilities. They are not expected to break their Treaties but to renegotiate their terms and, when doing so, adopt a common stance where appropriate. In this process they are assisted by Council Decision 69/494[13] which provides for the progressive standardization of agreements concerning commercial relations between Member States and third countries and rules on the negotiation of Community agreements. This Decision gives the Commission the necessary supervisory and co-ordinating powers but also enables it to recommend to the Council the express or tacit extension of the existing agreements. It has postulated the replacement of national bilateral agreements by Community bilateral agreements by the end of 1972. This, however, has proved a forlorn hope since the deadline has already been extended[14] several times and uniformity is not yet in sight. The problem is more difficult than it might seem because trade agreements usually form part of a complex package deal in which Community obligations cannot be easily isolated.

With reference to EC Article 307 (ex Art 234) the ECJ[15] conceded that it did not alter the nature of private rights or duties derived from pre-membership or pre-accession Treaties between the Member States and third countries. It held,

---

9 Joined Cases 110, 111/78: *Ministère Public v Van Wesemae* [1979] ECR 35, [1979] 3 CMLR 87.
10 Convention No 196; Geneva 1949, Cmnd 7852.
11 Case 286/86: *Ministère Public v Déserbais* [1988] ECR 4907, [1989] 1 CMLR 516.
12 Case 10/61, supra, ECR at 10.
13 OJ Sp Ed 1969, p 603.
14 Recent extension, Council Decision 90/224, OJ 1990, L120/72.
15 Case 812/79: *A-G v Burgoa* [1980] ECR 2787, [1981] 2 CMLR 193.

accordingly, that the London Fisheries Convention of 1964 which governed maritime relations between Ireland and Spain, when Spain was outside the Community, prevailed over Community law. Since, however, the national law was held to be applicable in the circumstances the penalties for illegal fishing prescribed by it and imposed upon a Spanish trawlerman were not incompatible with the interim fishery regime imposed by the Council Regulation 1376/78 designed to promote a framework of the relations between Spain and the Community. As from the accession of Spain the matter has been subject to the Common Fisheries Policy.

(3)   EFFECT ON INDIVIDUALS

Since the Community embraces not only the Member States but also their citizens Community external treaties affect individuals too. Being part of the Community *corpus juris* these treaties may be pleaded not only before the ECJ but also before national courts and thence referred to ECJ for interpretation should a national court find this necessary. Individual rights depend, of course, upon the nature of the Treaty, ie whether it is an accession or association or trade agreement and also on the specific provision contained therein, that is, whether or not it has a direct effect.

Thus a Belgian[16] importer of wine from Greece could not be absolved from the payment of a countervailing charge imposed by Belgian law by virtue of a Community regulation because the association agreement with Greece upon which he relied, although providing for free access of the product to the common market, did not exempt levies designed to eliminate disturbance of the market. Similarly a German[17] importer of tomato concentrates from Greece could not successfully challenge a Community regulation designed to protect the industry in Italy by raising the price since the association agreement allowed the Community to regulate the import and the price of the product. However, a French[18] importer of bananas could rely on the Yaoundé Convention (a predecessor of the Lomé Convention) not only to have his case referred to the ECJ for a preliminary ruling but also to defeat the preference of his government for suppliers of bananas from former French colonies. The organization of the banana market, sensitive to the ACP countries, has recently caused some controversy, especially in Germany which is a large importer of bananas. Regulation 404/93[19] established a single market in the sector, a system of grants to the producers and supported the traditional patterns with the ACP countries. Consequently European importers of bananas (mainly German) have to pay import levies on products from the ACP countries. The German government[20] and the German importers[1] failed to have the Regulation declared void. An Italian[2] importer of hide from Senegal was afforded protection under the Lomé Convention from the imposition of health inspection fees chargeable

16   Case 181/73: *Haegeman v Belgium* [1974] ECR 449 at 459, 460, [1975] 1 CMLR 515 at 530.
17   Case 40/72: *Schroeder v Germany* [1973] ECR 125, [1973] CMLR 824.
18   Case 48/74: *Charmasson v Minister of Economic Affairs* [1974] ECR 1383, [1975] 2 CMLR 208.
19   OJ 1993, L47/1.
20   Case C-280/93: *Germany v Council* [1994] ECR I-4973.
 1   Case C-288/93R: *Comaco v Council* order of 21 June 1993 (unreported, no final judgment was delivered). See also Joined Cases C-429/92 and C-25/93: *ASSOBACAM v Commission* [1993] ECR I-3991; Cases C-257/93: *Leon Van Parijs v Council and Commission* [1993] ECR I-3335; C-276/93: *Chiquita Banana Co BV v Council* [1993] ECR I-3345; Case C-478/93: *Netherlands v Commission* [1995] ECR I-3081; Joined Cases C-9/95, C-23/95, and C-156/95 *Belgium and Germany v Commission* [1997] ECR I-645.
 2   Case 87/75: *Bresciani v Amministraazione delle Finanze dello Stato* [1976] ECR 129, [1976] 2 CMLR 62. See also *A Co Ltd v Republic of X* [1993] 2 CMLR 117, QBD.

under Italian law. Not so fortunate was a Madagascan[3] lawyer with French professional qualifications as he was unable to practise law at the Paris Bar because the Lomé Convention did not provide for free access to the professions or freedom to offer services in the Community for the nationals of the ACP countries. Similarly unfortunate was a Turkish wife who came to join her husband in Germany but could not rely on Article 12 of the Ankara Agreement which provides that the parties are to be 'guided' by the provisions of the EC Treaty for the purpose of securing freedom of movement for workers. Since the Agreement was not in the nature of 'self-executing treaties' its efficacy depended upon the decisions taken by the Council of Association, the provision was held to have no direct effect, ie it created no enforceable rights. Although the decisions of the Council of Association were held to be binding upon the parties their effects upon the individuals were determined by their specific provisions.[4] Therefore, as exemplified in an English reference for a preliminary ruling arising from the EEC–Portugal[5] free trade agreement, it is essential to consider the nature and scope of the agreement in order to ask the Court the relevant questions and, indeed, assess its impact upon the rights of individuals or, as put by the ECJ,[6] account must be taken of the whole agreement in order to focus attention on the real issues before the Court.

In the English jurisdiction judicial notice was taken of the EEC–Portugal Agreement of 1972 as the Court of Appeal[7] held that it was directly applicable by virtue of section 1(2) of the European Communities Act 1972. However the Court referred to the ECJ the question whether Article 14 of the Agreement prohibiting quantitative restrictions on imports and exports had a direct effect so as to prevail over section 16(2) of the UK Copyright Act 1956. The ECJ,[8] citing its own judgment in the *Terrapin*[9] case held that the enforcement by the proprietor of the copyright protected by national law was justified within the terms of Article 23 of the EEC–Portugal Agreement which provided that 'The Agreement shall not preclude prohibitions or restrictions on imports, exports or goods in transit justified on grounds of ... the protection of industrial and commercial property ...'. Therefore the enforcement did not constitute any restriction on trade envisaged in Article 14(2) of the said Agreement. The reference seemed unnecessary since the relationship between the EEC and Portugal did not create a common market or a custom union and the case had to be so distinguished.

---

3   Case 65/77: *Re Jean Razanatsimba* [1977] ECR 2229, [1978] 1 CMLR 246, but see Case C-18/90: *Office National de l'Emploi v Kziber* [1991] ECR I-199; Case C-58/93: *Zoubir Yousfi v Belgium, Re social security rights under EC–Morocco Agreement* [1994] ECR I-1353.
4   Case 12/86: *Demirel v Stadt Schwäbisch Gmünd* [1987] ECR 3719, [1989] 1 CMLR 421; Case C-192/89: *Sevince v Staatsecretaris van Justitie* [1990] ECR I-3461; but see Case C-237/91: *Kus v Landeshauptstadt Wiesbachen* (notion of regular employment) [1992] ECR I-6791; [1993] 2 CMLR 887; Case C-355/93: *Hayriye Eroglu v Land Baden Würtemberg* [1994] ECR I-5113; Case C-434/93: *Ahmet Bozkurt v Staatssecretaris van Justitie* [1995] ECR I-1475; Case C-277/94: *Z Taflan-Met v Besteuer van de Social Verzekereingsbank* [1996] ECR I-4085; Case C-171/95: *Recep Tetik v Land Berlin* [1997] ECR I-329; Case C-386/95: *Suleyman Eker v Land Baden-Würtemberg* [1997] ECR I-2697; Case C-36/96: *Faik Günaydin v Freistaat Bayeru* [1997] ECR I-5143; Case C-98/96: *Kasim Ertanir v Land Hessen* [1997] ECR I-5179; and *R v Secretary of State for the Home Department, ex p Narin (expulsion of a Turkish national from the UK)* [1990] 2 CMLR 233, CA.
5   OJ 1972, L301/165; Council Reg 2844/72.
6   Case 253/83, supra [1987] 1 CMLR 36 at 55.
7   *Polydor Ltd v Harlequin Record Shops Ltd* [1980] 2 CMLR 413.
8   Case 270/80: [1982] ECR 329, [1982] 1 CMLR 677.
9   Case 119/75: *Terrapin v Terranova* [1976] ECR 1039 at 1061, [1976] 2 CMLR 482 at 526.

The ECJ took a formal view of the Association Agreement with Cyprus and did not take notice of the de facto partition of the island, as it refused to recognise phytosanitary certificates issued by the authorities of the Turkish Republic of Northern Cyprus.[10]

Another aspect of an EC trade agreement was raised in the English jurisdiction in a case[11] involving the export of oil to a destination inconsistent with the United Kingdom policy. In a contract A agreed to sell to B a quantity of British North Sea crude oil, 'the destination is to be free but always within the exporting country's government policy'. When A learned that the oil was intended for Israel A and the supplier refused to load the oil aboard the ship nominated by B on the ground that delivery to Israel was contrary to the UK policy. After arbitration and protracted litigation in the UK during which the EC law and the EEC–Israel Agreement were considered the matter came before the ECJ for a preliminary ruling. The ECJ held that the Agreement did not prohibit the imposition of new quantitative restrictions or measures having equivalent effect on exports from a Member State to Israel and that the Council Regulation 2603/69 establishing common rules for exports likewise did not prohibit such restrictions. Moreover Articles 34 and 85 (concerning exports and restrictive practices, respectively) (now EC Arts 29 and 81) did not prevent a Member State from adopting a restrictive policy, subject to certain conditions as the trade involved was not a trade between Member States. If the conditions under which restrictions contrary to Articles 34 and 85 were not observed, when for example the Member State concerned failed to give notice to the Commission in accordance with the established procedure, such a failure on the part of a Member State would not create individual rights which national courts were required to protect.

As in the previous cases the rights of individuals depend on the terms of the Agreement.

F. *Jus missionis*

To carry out their functions in the international setting the Communities have to maintain contacts with non-Member States and international organizations. Customarily these contacts are effected through diplomatic missions accredited to foreign sovereigns. Their main task is to represent the sending sovereign and articulate his position, gather intelligence and pass it on to the authorities at home. The *jus missionis*, an attribute of legal personality at international law, is governed by time-honoured custom supplemented by bilateral Treaties and modern Conventions. However the latter are of little use to the Communities because the 1961 Vienna Convention on Diplomatic Relations applies only to states whilst the 1975 Vienna Convention applicable to world organizations only has not as yet been accepted by the Member States of the Community. Therefore the exercise of the *jus missionis* of the Communities rests upon their claim to international legal personality and the recognition by the countries and international organizations with whom they have established relations. International customary and conventional law applies only by analogy whilst the established practice tends to create precedents and rules of conduct.

---

10 Case C-432/92: *R v Minister of Agriculture, ex p SP Anastasiou (Pissoure) Ltd* [1994] ECR I-3087, [1995] 1 CMLR 569.
11 Case 174/84: *Bulk Oil (Zug) v Sun International* [1986] 2 All ER 744, [1986] ECR 559, [1986] 2 CMLR 732.

In the sense of the 'internal' Community law the right to enter into diplomatic relations is based on the Community's legal personality complemented by the Protocol on the Privileges and Immunities of the European Communities attached to the Merger Treaty of 1965.[12] Article 17 of the Protocol provides that the Member States in whose territory the Communities have their seat shall accord the customary diplomatic immunities and privileges to missions of third countries accredited to the Communities. Since diplomatic relations are normally conducted on the basis of reciprocity it is common ground that the countries concerned have not only recognized the legal personality of the Community but will also extend the same courtesy to its representatives who will enjoy diplomatic immunity and rank according to the diplomatic list.[13] In the course of time a network of diplomatic relations has been established either informally or by formal agreements. In 1998 the number of diplomatic missions from non-Member countries (including the Vatican) rose to 165[14] establishing relations with all three or any one of the Communities. Their representatives are stationed in Brussels, the unofficial capital of the Communities, but most of these are also accredited to Belgium. Therefore Belgium accords them the same status.[15]

The principle applies to Community civil servants. Therefore Belgium[16] was in breach of Art 12(b) of the Protocol (and consequently of EC Article 10 (ex Art 5)) by not taking the necessary measures to ensure that the byelaws of certain municipalities exempt Community civil servants and other officials and the members of their families from the requirement of registration and tax on their properties situated in these municipalities. Similarly, in a subsequent case,[17] Belgium was condemned for refusing to grant reductions in tax on income from immovable property where, by virtue of Art 13(2) of the Protocol the tenants or their spouses are exempt from national taxes on salaries, wages and emoluments paid by the Community. However, the denial of mortgage relief (available in the United Kingdom to taxpayers irrespective of their nationality) to Community civil servants who are exempt from UK taxation and so ineligible for mortgage relief, does not constitute a breach of EC privileges and immunities.[18]

Historically the United Kingdom and Sweden in 1952 were the first countries to send a permanent delegation to the High Authority of the ECSC,[19] followed by Japan in 1954. The US Ambassador was the first diplomat accredited to the EEC[20] in 1958.

The procedure of accreditation is at present governed by the Accords de Luxembourg.[1] The decision to establish diplomatic relations is taken by the Council unanimously, each Member State having a right of veto regarding every mission and every individual representative. The letters of credence are submitted separately to the President of the Council and the President of the Commission.

12 Ie the Treaty of Brussels establishing a Single Council and a Single Commission of the European Communities; repealed by the Amsterdam Treaty except the Protocol.
13 See Case 5/68: *Sayag v Leduc* [1968] ECR 395, [1969] CMLR 12; Case 9/69: *Sayag v Leduc* [1969] ECR 329.
14 1998 General Report (1999), para 958.
15 Virally, M, Gerbet, P, Salmon, J, *Les missions permanentes auprès des organisations internationales* (1971), p 722. See also Case C-88/92: *X v Staatssecretaris van Financiën (Re tax domicile)* [1993] ECR I-3315.
16 Case 85/85: *Commission v Belgium (Re registration of Community officials for municipal tax on residencies)* [1986] ECR 1149, [1987] 1 CMLR 787 at para 27.
17 Case 260/86: *Commission v Belgium* [1988] ECR 955, [1989] 3 CMLR 103 at para 12.
18 Case C-333/88: *Tither v IRC* [1990] ECR I-1133, [1990] 2 CMLR 779.
19 First General Report ECSC, points 14 and 15.
20 First General Report EEC, point 168.
 1 Ninth General Report, EEC, pp 31–33; EC Bull 3/66.

The doyen of the diplomatic corps accredited to the Community is the Apostolic Nuncio as has been the tradition in relations between Christian countries.

The representatives of the Community abroad have no uniform status; even their official titles and the designation of the missions differ from country to country. The first mission was installed in London following the agreement with the ECSC in 1955 though the first diplomatic representative of the three Communities was accredited to the United Kingdom only in 1968. The second mission was set up in Washington in 1972 and then in 1974 in Tokyo by virtue of a formal agreement between the Commission and Japan. In 1998 the Commission maintained 128 delegations abroad.[2]

The first mission to an international organization was installed in Geneva in 1964 to cover the GATT, the ILO, the United Nations Economic Commission for Europe and later UNCTAD. The originally unofficial mission to the United Nations Organization HQ in New York has enjoyed diplomatic status since 1976. There is also a mission to OECD and UNESCO in Paris and to the International Atomic Energy Agency in Vienna.

The existence of diplomatic missions has not only enhanced the international status of the Community and facilitated the negotiations of trade agreements but also contributed to the development of the base for the Community external relations.

2   1998 General Report (1999) para 559.

Chapter 4

The nature and challenge of Community law

A. The meaning of Community law

It is axiomatic that a body which itself is a distinct legal entity will have its own law either infused into its forms by a superior legislator or generated by its organs or both. In the Community legal order both elements are present: the law of the Treaty and the law generated by the Community organs. Moreover, a certain area of the law will be enacted by the Member States themselves in accordance with the Treaty and, although this law is, strictly speaking, a product of the sovereign legislatures of the Member States it should be included in the wider concept of Community law.[1] These are the dimensions of Community law in the light of its sources. However, before analysing the sources of Community law it seems necessary to consider its nature and scope. This is particularly important from a British point of view, bearing in mind that at accession there was a wholesale reception of Community law and that since accession we have participated in a legislative process which differs considerably from our own.

Community law defies the accepted classifications of law; it is both international and municipal, public and private, substantive and procedural, enacted and formulated in precedents. It is a *sui generis* law and must be treated as such. Therefore it has to be studied in its international setting with due attention to its impact upon the laws of the Member States and the quasi-autonomous law-making capacity of the Community organs.

In the opinion of the European Court of Justice,[2] the Community 'constitutes a new legal order in international law for whose benefit the states have limited their sovereign rights, albeit within limited fields, and the subjects of which

---

1 The Second European Conference of Law Faculties held in April 1971 in Strasbourg under the aegis of the Council of Europe recommended that the authorities in Member States be urged to introduce or reinforce the teaching of (1) the law of European Organizations, (2) the substantive law created by or within the European Organizations, and (3) the law of European states.

2 In Case 26/62: *Van Gend en Loos v Nederlandse Administraatie der Belastingen* [1963] ECR 1 at 29, [1963] CMLR 105 at 129.

comprise not only the Member States but also their nationals'. It corresponds to the territorial law of a state.

By incorporation of the Treaties into the municipal law of the Member States Community law becomes part of the internal legal structure of the Member States. Moreover, in the process of the approximation of laws a wide area of economic law has become uniform throughout the Community. However, although Community measures enacted into the national systems are both Community and municipal law the ECJ[3] insists that they must not lose their identity, and their Community character in the process for, should this happen, the ECJ's power to give a preliminary ruling upon the validity or interpretation of a measure 'lost' in the national system, would be frustrated.

The once (so it seemed)[4] clear-cut distinction between public and private law has been blurred in the course of time. If we consider that public law is concerned with the organization of the state and the relations between the citizen and the state whilst private law governs relations between individuals and/or corporations we shall observe that Community law contains both elements. It has an impact upon the constitutions and public powers of the Member States, it is concerned with the creation of a supra-national organization out of the pooled sovereignty of the Member States and brings the citizen politically and in his economic activities face to face with a supra-national authority and a new 'European' allegiance. Private law relations (and here we can safely discard the controversy whether 'commercial law' is 'private law' or a separate branch of the law) are affected too but only to a degree, that is to say in so far as the economic policies enforced by Community law impinge upon such relations. As legal machinery is used for the execution of the economic policies enshrined in the Treaty some aspects of Community law can be described for the want of a better term as 'economic law' or the law of the economy. This phenomenon, characteristic of the Community, will be considered in detail.[5] The bulk of private law relations comprised in the law of contract, tort, property, family relations (though family status determined by national law is relevant to immigration and social security rights) and succession remains outside the scope of Community law. So does criminal law, though criminal sanctions will have to be developed in order to check abuses of the Community system in the context of the third pillar of the Union.[6] In the meantime Community obligations are backed up, where appropriate, by national penal laws.

True to the civil law tradition the corpus of Community law has been laid down in treaties and derivative legislation but it would be a mistake to assume that precedent plays no active role in the Community law-making process. We shall discuss the sources of Community law in detail and it may suffice to say that the European Court of Justice, like the French Counseil d'Etat to which it has some resemblance, often has an opportunity of explaining the law and laying down rules in precedents and it has not refrained from using this power. As practice

---

3 See Case 34/73: *Variola SpA v Amministrazione delle Finanze dello Stato* [1973] ECR 981 at para 11.
4 Publicum jus est, quod ad statum rei Romanae spectat, privatum quod ad singulorum utilitatem: sunt enim quaedam publice utilia, quoadem privatim, *Digesta* 1, 1, 1, 2; cf Llewellyn, K, *The Bramble Bush* (1960), p 18.
5 See Part IV, below.
6 See Bridge, J W, 'The European Communities and the Criminal Law', *Criminal Law Review*, February 1976, p 88; Wood, J, 'The Communities and the Criminal Law', in *In Memoriam J D B Mitchell* (1983), pp 211 et seq; Lasok, D, *The Customs Law of the European Economic Community* (3rd edn, 1998) ch 7.

develops both Community Courts tends to follow their own decisions in the spirit of *jurisprudence constante*[7] but will not hesitate to deviate for good reason.[8] And so the Court considers itself free to decide in a different way the same legal point if it arises between different parties and in a different context.[9]

Without attempting a definition of Community law (which, incidentally, cannot be found in the Treaties) we should reiterate that Community law consists of that portion of public international law which governs treaties and international institutions, of the Treaties and their Annexes, of the rules generated by the Community organs and those portions of the municipal laws of the Member States which they are bound to enact in the execution of their obligations. These are not distinct branches but merely the dimensions of Community law.

B. The challenge of Community law

Community law is a new legal order but to a British lawyer it is also an alien order because it has emanated from the civil law systems and, despite the British participation in the legislative process, remains under the civil law influence. This does not necessarily mean that it is inferior or oppressive, as has been suggested from time to time in the passion of debate, but that it is simply different from ours. It should be borne in mind that in its background lies the philosophy of sophisticated, long-established legal systems and the will to create a Community through legal integration of which the enacted law is the preferred instrument. Being intertwined with the legal systems of the founder states Community law cannot be isolated from these but historically and philosophically has to be seen as a child of civil law and as more civil law countries join the Community its influence continues and grows.

In order to make a valid comparison between civil law and common law and thus elicit some general features of the Community legal system it will first be necessary to debunk some popular myths. There is in England some, albeit unfounded, aversion to codes of law and even the code Napoléon, of which the French are justly proud, does not escape criticism as if no branch of English law had been codified or codification had not been the long-term aim of the Law Commission. Critics believe that codes of law stultify the growth of the law and turn it into a pool of stagnant water whilst common law for ever remains a stream of fresh water. Forgetting that codes are essentially a work of compromise they assume that they are the tools of autocracy. Moreover, it is readily assumed that, whilst in this country we are governed by the wisdom of judges contained in precedents, the continentals are denied this privilege and, because of their rejection of *stare decisis*, suffer from the uncertainty of the law. It would be futile to recite the various misconceptions in order to rebut them. What has to be recognized is the fact that despite their common Romano-Christian roots the evolution of the civil law and common law systems happens to differ and that as a result two different legal styles have developed. Comparative studies help one to understand these differences but, not being engaged in a comparative study, we have to content ourselves with a few generalities. Because we have joined the Community as a

---

7 Eg Case 32, 33/58: *Société Nouvelle des Usines de Pontlieue Aciéries du Temple v High Authority of the European Coal and Steel Community* [1959] ECR 127.

8 Eg Case 48/72: *Brasserie de Haecht v Wilkin-Janssen* [1973] ECR 77, [1973] CMLR 287.

9 Eg Cases 28–30/62: *Da Costa en Schaake NV v Nederlandse Administratie der Belastingen* [1963] ECR 31, [1963] CMLR 224. Cf Case C-10/89: *SA CNL-SUCAL NV v HAG GF AG* [1990] ECR I-3711 and Cases C-267/91 and C-268/91: *Keck and Mithouard* [1993] ECR I-6097, in which the ECJ diverged from its earlier case law.

going concern, with a legal system well on its way, the British lawyer has to face the unprecedented challenge of the continental legal style.[10]

Codes of law are not mere comprehensive, systematically arranged statutes. In a sense they are also codes of morals for in their legal institutions, especially general principles of the law, they offer guidelines to a way of life. The law tends to proceed from general principles to particular rules of conduct and so the administration of justice tends to be deductive rather than inductive. Contrast the British fragmentary legislation and tightly drafted statutes which, according to Lord Scarman,[11] 'are elaborate to the point of complexity; detailed to the point of unintelligibility; yet strangely uninformative on matters of principle'. The English administration of justice tends, therefore, to be inductive, so much so that one can say that we have a system of remedies established by precedent and statute rather than a plain statement of rights and duties from which remedies can be deduced. Community law follows this latter style as it tends to prescribe the right conduct for governments and individuals and grants remedies in the event of deviation.

The codes of law, being systems of generalities, provide but a façade for case law, because decided cases are the real witness and the living law. However, in view of the supremacy of legislation and the constitutionally limited lower of judges to adjudicate not *legislate*, precedents have only a persuasive authority and cannot be cited as the source of law or superior authority. The theory that codes have no gaps enables the courts to legislate by way of extensive interpretation from analogy or simply through *equitas*. The European Court of Justice is in a similar position though its scope for legislative activities is wider than that of the civil courts of the Member States.

In England the judge comes, as a rule, from the Bar and remains a member of his Inn of Court even when elevated to the Bench. On the Continent the judge is a product of special training and a judicial career, he stands aloof from the Bar and resembles more an academic lawyer than an advocate. The English administration of justice has a strong personal flavour because as a rule the judge sits alone and delivers a personal judgment of 'his court'. In the Court of Appeal or the House of Lords, though no longer alone, he still delivers his personal, concurring or dissenting, judgment which often conceals an advocate in judicial robes. The continental judge, as a rule, sits as a member of a team, does not deliver his individual judgment whether or not he agrees with the judgment of his brethren and so preserves a kind of judicial anonymity. The European Court of Justice is a 'continental' court in all respects, sits as a team and delivers a single judgment. It is assisted by Advocates-General (an office unknown in this country), whose functions shall be considered elsewhere.[12]

The style of the administration of justice is greatly influenced by the scope and rules of judicial interpretation. As compared with their continental brethren and the European Court, English judges seem to have a narrower scope in the field of interpretation. The *Bosch*[13] case is a good illustration. Whilst our judges are not allowed to study the '*travaux préparatoires*', that is the materials and debates

---

10   See Lord Denning MR in *H P Bulmer Ltd v J Bollinger SA* [1974] 2 All ER 1226 at 1231–1232, [1974] 2 CMLR 91 at 119 and 120; Scarman, Sir Leslie, *English Law: The New Dimension*, Hamlyn Lectures, Twenty-sixth Series, 1974, pp 21 et seq.

11   BBC Third Programme, *The Listener*, 9 January 1969, pp 44–46.

12   See Chapter 12.

13   Case 13/61: *Kledingverhoopbedrijf de Geus en Uitdenbogerd v Robert Bosch GmbH* [1962] ECR 45, [1962] CMLR 1; D Thompson, 'The Bosch Case' (1962) 11 ICLQ 721; Case 14/70: *Deutsche Bakels GmbH v Oberfinanzdirektion München* [1970] ECR 1001, [1971] CMLR 188; Case 42/72: *Alfons Lütticke GmbH v Hauptzollamt Passau* [1973] ECR 57 at 74–75, [1973] CMLR 309 at 316–317.

in Parliament leading to the passing of legislation, in order to find out the mind of the legislature,[14] the continental judges are allowed to do so and base their judgment on their study. The *Bosch* case was concerned with restrictive practices contrary to EC Article 81(1) (ex Art 85(1)) but the question was whether the said article could be applied before the enactment of the procedural rules envisaged by EC Article 83 (ex Art 87). Pending such enactment national law was to apply. The Dutch court of first instance ruled that EC Article 81 (ex Art 85) was not operative before Regulation 17 of 1962 was made; the Court of Appeal referred the case to the Community Court under EC Article 234 (ex Art 177) and the plaintiff appealed to the Dutch Supreme Court which upheld the reference. The final ruling of the Community Court was that it was the intention of the EEC that EC Article 81 (ex Art 85) shall be operative only in respect of agreements and decisions which the national authorities considered prohibited and incapable of exemption. Other agreements could be saved in accordance with Article 5 of the Regulation. An English Court would probably have applied national law by virtue of EC Article 83 (ex Art 87).

Another attribute of the continental courts is the power to resort to teleological interpretation of codes and statutes which enables them to apply old law in the context of social change or give the rules of law a dynamic and functional effect.[15] In this country (perhaps with the exception of the House of Lords) courts have no such power and, indeed, should an iconoclast judge venture into such practices he would soon find his judgments overruled by higher courts. The Community Court, it seems, enjoys this attribute of judicial power in the best traditions of continental courts and, having established its authority, does occasionally resort to this kind of interpretation. Unlike literal interpretations the Court puts into the mouth of the legislator the meaning of words he should have used rather than words he has actually used to express his intention.[16]

The Courts' role is much coloured by the rules of procedure. The predominant feature of continental procedural law is the inquisitorial power of the court. This system places a heavy duty on the court to inquire into the facts of the case in order to ascertain the objective truth. Unlike the English judge the continental judge is not an impartial umpire watching the contest of the parties and seeing merely that the rules of the game are observed. This requires a greater involvement of the court which, among other things, manifests itself in the examination of witnesses and parties by the judge. Although these inquisitorial powers have not been expressly spelt out in the founding Treaties they can be found in the Protocol on the Statute of the Court of Justice and the Rules of Procedure.[17] It is clear that the European

---

14   Save under the principle in *Pepper v Hart* [1993] AC 593, [1993] 1 All ER 42.

15   Cf Pescatore, P, Interpretation of Community Law and the Doctrine of Acte Clair, in Bathurst, M, et al (eds), *Legal Problems of an Enlarged European Community* (1972) p 27 at pp 32–34.

16   Eg Case 14/63: *Forges de Clabecq v High Authority* [1963] ECR 357, [1964] CMLR 167; Case 9/73: *Schlüter v Hauptzollamt Lörrach* [1973] ECR 1135 at 1153; Case 6/72: *Europemballage Corpn and Continental Can Inc v Commission* [1973] ECR 215, [1973] CMLR 199; Case 8/73 *Hauptzollamt-Bremerhaven v Massey Ferguson* [1973] ECR 897; Case 37–38/73: *Sociaal Fonds voor de Diamant arbeiders v N V Indiamex and Association defait De Beler* [1973] ECR 1609; Case 151/73: *Government of Ireland v Council* [1974] ECR 285 at 296 and 297, [1974] 1 CMLR 429 at 446–447. Most prominent examples of teleological interpretation include *Van Gend*, supra; Case 93/71: *Leonesio v Italian Ministry of Agriculture and Forestry* [1972] ECR 287, [1973] CMLR 343; Case 43/75: *Defrenne v SABENA* [1976] ECR 455, [1976] 2 CMLR 98.

17   Statute, Arts 17 et seq; ECSC Statute, Art 20 et seq; EAEC Statute, Art 17 et seq; Rules of Procedure, present codified version OJ 2001, C 34/1 and 39, Arts 45–54ᵃ (Court of Justice) and 64–75 (Court of First Instance). See further Lasok, K P E, *The European Court of Justice: Practice and Procedure* (2nd edn, 1994), pp 30 et seq.

Community Court functions like any continental court and this involves a tight control of the proceedings, powers to require parties to produce documents and supply the information the court deems necessary as well as the examination of witnesses and parties by the court.

Other salient features of continental procedure are the predominance of written pleadings which contain mainly legal arguments, hence the art of written advocacy somewhat similar to our Chancery proceedings; the absence of drama in court engineered in this country by the public examination and cross-examination of witnesses. Oral procedure consists of the hearing of any witnesses or experts followed by succinct summary of the main points submitted by the advocates of each party to the proceedings. Then follows a collective judgment of the court, after due deliberations in private, usually read in open court on the appointed day together with other judgments. The report of the court is brief and concise based on the draft prepared by the reporting judge. All the features of a civil law court are attributable to the European Community Court and offer a challenge our lawyers have to meet in practice.

Because of its wide dimensions, Community law offers a challenge to three types of lawyers: lawyers in government service, lawyers in commerce and industry, and lawyers in private practice.

Government lawyers of all the Member States together with the Community draftsmen bear co-responsibility for the drafting of the Community legislation. They also play their part in litigation in which the government is involved in cases either before the ECJ or the national courts.

In-house lawyers are particularly concerned with the impact of Community economic law, especially in the field of restrictive practices, intellectual property, corporations, establishment, social security and labour relations, taxation, customs and movement of goods and capital, agriculture in addition to the mass of the Community rules and regulations which affect investments and commercial operations in their various ramifications as well as subsidies to industry, consumer protection and environment.

Lawyers in private practice, both in advice and litigation, face the problem not only of the Community law as such but also of its impact in the various areas of national law, including criminal law. Since by virtue of the European Communities Act 1972 Community law has become part of the British legal system it can no longer be regarded as 'foreign' law left to specialists engaged in marginal practice. Thus expertise in Community law has become an essential ingredient of the quality of legal service; its neglect may result in claims for professional negligence.[18]

Turning now to a more daunting, through not impossible proposition: EC Article 43 (ex Art 52) gives lawyers the 'right of establishment' on the basis of free movement within the Community. So far this right has not resulted in a migration of lawyers within the Community simply because the practice of law is essentially national. However, difficulties have come to light because admission to practise is, in most countries, governed by law and restrictive practices of the profession. In accordance with EC Article 43 (ex Art 52) ECJ held, in *Reyners v Belgium*,[19] that a Dutch national living in Belgium and having appropriate Belgian professional qualifications was unlawfully excluded from the exercise of

---

18 See judgment of the Oberlandesgericht Koblenz in *Re a Lawyer's Professional Negligence* [1990] 3 CMLR 415. See also Lloyd J (in *Matrix Ltd v Theodore Goddard* [1998] STC 1 at 26f to 27j: lawyers practising in specialised fields have a duty to exercise reasonable skill and care).
19 Case 2/74: [1974] ECR 631, [1974] 2 CMLR 305.

the profession of *avocat* on the ground that according to Belgian law only Belgian nationals were admitted to practice. The principle was applied to remove a disqualification on the ground of the lack of habitual residence of a Dutch lawyer who lived in Belgium but wished to practise in the Netherlands.[20] The same ruling was made with regard to a Belgian who acquired French professional qualification and wished to practise in Paris.[1] In the *Klopp*[2] case a national rule of practice prohibiting an advocate from maintaining chambers in two different areas was held illegal when applied to a German lawyer wishing to practise in Paris whilst keeping his practice in Düsseldorf, the lawyer being qualified in both countries. The judgment of the ECJ has been applied[3] in France.

There is at present no rule to prevent an alien, as an alien, becoming a member of the Bar. Solicitors, allegedly on the basis of section 3 of the Act of Settlement 1700 (which declared aliens incapable of enjoying certain offices or places of trust) and a counsel's opinion of some vintage and doubtful weight, had to be British subjects but this discrimination has now been removed.[4] As far as practice is concerned solicitors must observe the general code of their profession whether they handle 'domestic' or 'foreign' business. A foreign lawyer wishing to practise in England and Wales must, subject to professional qualifications, elect to practise either as a barrister or a solicitor. He cannot do both.

Under the freedom of establishment British lawyers are entitled to set up in practice abroad on an equal footing, their success depending, of course, on their proficiency in foreign and Community law. There is a theoretical and practical side to it. In theory the right of establishment and the principle of non-discrimination apply. By EC Article 43 (ex Art 52) the freedom of establishment includes the right to engage in and carry on self-employed occupation under the conditions laid down by the law of the country of establishment for its own nationals. The Treaty is clear – free movement of persons – but how does it affect lawyers? EC Article 50(d) (ex Art 60(d)), defining the term 'service', refers to 'professions' and this, traditionally, includes the legal profession. But lawyers are, in some respects, involved in the administration of justice which is a public process and an exercise of the authority of the state, not just commercial enterprise or service with which the Common Market is concerned. English solicitors are designated as 'Officers of the Supreme Court' and barristers are supposed to be 'assisting' the court in its work. German *Rechtsanwälte*, who combine the work of the English barrister and solicitor, are too 'officers of the court'. The French have a diversified profession but those who are involved in court work are regarded as 'auxiliaries of justice' or of 'tribunals'. The *avocats*, who are the aristocracy of the French legal profession, may be called to the Bench or replace public prosecutors, so there is too a considerable involvement in the administration of justice.

---

20 Case 33/74: *J H M Van Binsbergen v Bestuur van de Bedrijfsvereniging voor de Metaalnijverhied* [1974] ECR 1299, [1975] 1 CMLR 298.
1 Case 71/76: *Thieffrey v Conseil de l'Ordre des Avocats à la Cour de Paris* [1977] ECR 765, [1977] 2 CMLR 373.
2 Case 107/83: *Ordre des Avocats au Barreau de Paris v Klopp* [1984] ECR 2971, [1985] 1 CMLR 99; see also Case C-55/94: *Reinhard Gebhard v Consiglio dell' Ordine degli Avvocate* [1995] ECR I-4165; see further Lasok, D, *The Professions and Services in the European Economic Community* (1986), pp 161 et seq.
3 *Maitre Cammarata v Conseil de l'Ordre des Avocats au Barreau de Marseille* Court d'Appel, Aix-en-Provence [1988] 1 CMLR 243; *Conseil de l'Ordre des Avocats au Barreau de Nice v Raynel* Supreme Court [1990] 2 CMLR 190.
4 Solicitors Amendment Act 1974, s 1; Solicitors' Act 1974, s 29.

One can, of course, envisage difficulties,[5] eg in France and Germany where only specially appointed lawyers may appear before the Supreme Court; in England the position is rather complicated because of the relations between the two branches of the profession and the existence of Queen's Counsel and Juniors. To face these problems the Bar Council[6] has relaxed the rules by allowing a barrister to accept a brief from a foreign lawyer directly without the intermediary of an English solicitor and a Queen's Counsel to act without a Junior, originally in Community matters only. However these rules are not meant to change the nature of the practice at the Bar in England and Wales or allow the barrister to do the solicitor's work. A barrister may enter into any association including partnership with any lawyer (except solicitors practising in the UK) for the purpose of sharing any office or services abroad but in the UK cannot undertake work not normally performed by a practising barrister in England and Wales, receive or handle clients' money or accept the status of an employee or of a commercial agent or business agent.

In December 1975 an agreement[7] between the Paris Bar and the English Bar was made to the effect that members of one may appear and plead before the Courts of the other provided they are led by members of the local Bar. In England and Wales this rule applies to all courts where only barristers may plead. This arrangement may well lead to similar bilateral agreements between the English Bar and the corresponding branches of the profession of the remaining Member States of the Community.

Discrimination and restrictive practices apart the stumbling block to the harmonization of the legal profession has been the lack of recognition of professional qualifications obtained abroad. Pending the solution of this problem Council Directive 77/249[8] was passed to 'facilitate the effective exercise by lawyers of freedom to provide services'. However, until the acceptance of mutual recognition of diplomas and professional qualifications the persons to whom the Directive applied had to qualify and obtain the professional title used in the Member State in which they intend to become established. In the spirit of the Directive the Consultative Committee of the Bars and Law Societies of the European Community (CCBE) has introduced, as from October 1978, lawyers' 'Euro-Cards' to enable their holders to identify themselves before the national authorities as persons qualified to practise the law. This was a general rule which did not exclude bilateral arrangements across the frontiers. However, the privilege was available only to lawyers established in the EC. Thus an East German lawyer was not eligible, since during its existence the GDR was not part of the EC and the Protocol on Internal German Trade, being applicable only to the movement of goods, was irrelevant to the provision of services.[9]

The privilege enabled foreign lawyers to gain access to their clients, provide advice and appear in court in company with a local lawyer. However, warned the

---

5   See Case 138/80: *Re Jules Borker* [1980] ECR 1975, [1980] 3 CMLR 638 and *Public Prosecutor of Cologne v Lischka* (Cologne Court of Appeal) [1981] 2 CMLR 189.

6   *Law Society's Gazette*, Vol 68 (1971), pp 187, 193, 194; Vol 70, p 1568; Vol 71, p 378; *Guardian Gazette*, 27 April 1974, p 114.

7   *Times*, December 1975; the relationship between the Paris Bar and the Law Society of England and Wales is governed by an agreement signed on 12 April 1976. In Case 269/80: *R v Tymen* [1981] 2 CMLR 544, the British judge expressed his appreciation of the skill with which the French advocate pleaded his case in English.

8   OJ 1977, L78/17, see European Communities (Service of Lawyers) Order 1978 SI 1978 No 1910. See Case C-294/89: *Commission v France, re lawyers' service* [1991] ECR I-3591; [1993] 3 CMLR 569.

9   *Re an East German Lawyer*, Supreme Federal Court [1990] 2 CMLR 185.

ECJ, the requirement that a foreign lawyer must work in conjunction with a local lawyer in relation to court proceedings must not be too restrictive lest the objectives of the Directive become frustrated.[10]

Moreover, the condition was that only lawyers permitted to practise in one Member State could take advantage of the Directive in order to provide services in another Member State. Thus the Directive could not be interpreted in such a way as to enable a lawyer disbarred for reasons relating to 'dignity, good repute and integrity' to gain access to the profession abroad.[11]

However, to ensure complete mobility of lawyers it was essential to establish principles of universal recognition of professional qualifications so that lawyers admitted to practise in one Member State could practise in the entire Community. This was achieved by Council Directive 89/48[12] which completes the work of the ECJ, whose judgments have removed various restrictions based on national laws and practices of the profession.[13] The Directive applies to professions regulated by national laws except those (eg the medical professions) already governed by Community legislation. It is particularly relevant to the legal profession.

The Directive aims at introducing a general system of recognition unrelated to any specific profession. It assumes comparability of educational courses of a university level existing in the Member States. However, such courses should be available only to persons holding a certificate awarded on successful completion of a full-time course of higher education.

The Directive proceeds from a broad definition of professional qualifications consisting of the award of a formal diploma, certificate or equivalent evidence by a competent national authority designated for the purpose by a Member State's laws, regulations or administrative provisions. This award must show that its holder has successfully completed a post-secondary course of at least three years' duration and has also successfully completed the requisite professional training which enables him to take up and pursue a regulated profession in the Member State concerned. This recognition will also be extended to awards obtained in non-Community countries (eg Switzerland), if a Member State, in accordance with Recommendation 89/49 appended to the Directive, accords such recognition in its own territory.

Adaptation comprises apprenticeship under the supervision of a qualified lawyer, possibly accompanied by further training. Aptitude testing, on the other hand, is limited to a test of professional knowledge of the applicant by the competent authorities of the host country with the aim of assessing the ability of the applicant to practise in that country. In principle the host country must give the applicant the right to choose either an adaptation period or an aptitude test. However, for professions whose practice requires knowledge of national law and in respect of which the provision of advice and/or assistance concerning national law is an essential and constant aspect of the professional activity, the host country must decide whether the adaptation or the aptitude test must be applied, though it may not apply both cumulatively. Adaptation has been accepted for the legal profession in the United Kingdom.[14]

---

10   Case 427/85: *Commission v Germany, Re Lawyers' Services* [1988] ECR 1123, [1989] 2 CMLR 677.
11   Case 292/86: *Gullung v Conseil de l'Ordre des Avocats* [1988] ECR 111, [1988] 2 CMLR 57.
12   OJ 1989, L19/16. See further ch 20, infra.
13   See pp 520 et seq, infra.
14   Lasok, D, 'Lawyers Facing 1992', Law Society Gazette, 25 October 1989; Wallace, R M M, 'Freedom to Practise in the EEC', New Law Journal, vol 139, No 6417 (1989) p 1004.

Whilst a Member State must recognize professional qualifications obtained in fellow Member States it may also require the applicant for such recognition to provide evidence of professional experience where the duration of his education and training is at least one year less than that required in its territory, or to complete an adaptation period not exceeding three years, or to take an aptitude test where the applicant's education or training differs substantially from those covered by the diplomas required in its own system.

The Directive is limited to the recognition of foreign qualifications necessary for the exercise of the right of establishment leaving to the Member States the details of implementation. However, it reserves to the Member States the right to regulate and to ensure respect of the rules of personal conduct and etiquette of the members of the professions. It also provides for the documentation and proof of good character or good repute.

The Directive came into effect on 4 January 1990. During the subsequent five years its implementation and application were to be monitored by the Commission who would report to the European Parliament and the Council of Ministers. Its impact in practice remains to be evaluated as regards both the formation of the legal profession and the practice of the law in the Community.

As for the right of audience before the Court of Justice, some rules have been laid down in Article 17 of the Protocol on the Statute of the Court of Justice which provides that parties must be represented by a lawyer entitled to practise before a court of one of the Member States and this includes also university teachers if, as in Germany, they have the right of audience before the national courts. This means that English solicitors can appear before the Court during the whole process, written and oral, provided they have the right of audience before the courts in this country. In practice solicitors have not been barred from appearing before the Court of Justice and, indeed, some have made a practice of it.

The Court of Justice has recently ruled[15] inadmissible proceedings brought by a litigant in person as expressly precluded by the Protocol. Finally, academic lawyers, responsible for the formation of the lawyers of tomorrow, have to tune their professional skills and their curricula to the challenge of Community law.

C.   The language of Community law

Language is the main tool in the legal workshop and it is common ground that each legal system has its own technical language. So it is with Community law. Within the Community of the Six the problem of the legal language was magnified sixfold as lawyers from the six countries tried first to frame the Treaty and then establish a common interpretation of the texts of Community law. In the enlarged Community the problem has been further magnified and has been complicated through the accession of two common law countries and the Scandinavian Countries with their peculiar legal styles.

The problem of language has a special bearing upon the legislative process, the interpretation and administration of the law and harmonization of national laws. It will be considered in relation to these three areas.

---

15   Case C-174/96P: *Orlando Lopez v Court of Justice of the European Communities* [1997] ECR I-6409, [1997] 3 CMLR 294.

(1)   THE TREATY AND COMMUNITY LEGISLATION

The EC Treaty was drawn up in a single document in the German, French, Italian and Dutch languages, all four texts being equally authentic.[16] By contrast the ECSC Treaty is in one authentic version in the French language.

The Treaty of Brussels, concerning the accession of Denmark, Ireland, Norway and the United Kingdom, was also drawn up in a single document in the Danish, Dutch, English, French, German, Irish, Italian and Norwegian languages, all texts being equally authentic.[17] The same principle was adopted on the accession of Greece, Greek being the eighth authentic Treaty language, and Spain and Portugal, Spanish and Portuguese being the ninth and the tenth authentic languages, to be increased to 12 on accession of Finland, Sweden and Austria, the latter being a German-speaking country.

The Maastricht and Amsterdam Treaties were drawn up in a single original in the official language of the Member States, the text of each of these languages being equally authentic.

This is an accepted form of a multilateral, multilingual treaty for which the United Nations Charter is one of the outstanding precedents. The effect of the formula 'equally authentic' is that all texts, having an equal status, can be cited as the authoritative statement of the law and that no one text takes precedence over the others. This does not solve the problem of the discrepancies in the various texts which inter se are nothing but translations. With the greatest care and skill expended on the formulation of treaties discrepancies are inevitable because the translation of a legal text is not merely a matter of language. The question of interpretation of authentic texts which reveal a discrepancy in the meaning of words attributable to legal concepts and institutions resolves itself into the question of the intention of the parties. The rule of international law, which has evolved to deal with this problem, is that there is a presumption against an interpretation which is contrary to any one of the equally authentic texts. It follows that it is necessary to find a meaning which is compatible with all the texts. In order to achieve this object it is necessary first to establish the meanings of each text and then select the meaning which is not contrary to any particular text. A practical illustration of the application of this rule is the *Mavrommatis* case,[18] in which the Permanent Court of International Justice explained that 'when considering two equally authentic texts, one of which appears to have a wider meaning than the other, it is the duty of the Court to apply the narrower text since such an interpretation is compatible with both texts and, no doubt, corresponds to the common intention of the parties'.

In *Fédération Charbonnière de Belgique v High Authority*[19] the Community Court considered the argument that the ECSC Treaty being an international treaty was subject to restrictive interpretation and broadly agreed with the principle, though it considered that rules of interpretation used in both international law and national laws were perfectly acceptable. However, in later cases a broader formula has evolved. In *Milchwerke Heinz Wöhrmann & Sohn KG v Commission*[20]

---

16   Art 248; the languages are listed in alphabetical order in accordance with the French nomenclature of the four countries.

17   Art 3; the languages are listed in alphabetical order according to Cmnd 4862, but since Norway failed to ratify the Treaty there were in the Community seven official languages; see Adaptation Decision, Art 2; ten since the admission of Greece, Spain and Portugal and 12 since admission of Austria, Finland and Sweden.

18   [1924] PCIJ Rep Ser A, No 2, p 12.

19   Case 8/55: [1954–1956] ECR 245.

20   Case 31 and 33/62: [1962] ECR 501, [1963] CMLR 152.

Advocate-General Roemer submitted that where three texts revealed a clear meaning but the fourth was inconsistent with them the latter should follow suit. In *de Geus v Bosch*[1] Advocate-General Lagrange submitted that where all four texts conveyed different meanings the Court should decide the issue according to the spirit of the text. In *Mij PPW International NV v Hoofdproduktschap voor Akkerbouwprodukten*,[2] concerning the issue of certificates for export refunds, the Court held that no argument could be drawn either from any linguistic discrepancies between the various texts or from the number of the verbs used in one or other version because the meaning of the relevant provisions had to be determined in the light of their objectives.

Moreover in a case[3] concerning the application of rules governing the grant of aid for skimmed milk the ECJ held that 'the elimination of linguistic discrepancies by way of interpretation may in certain circumstances run counter to the concern for legal certainty in as much as one or more of the texts involved may have to be interpreted in a manner at variance with the natural and usual meaning of the words. Consequently it is preferable to explore the possibilities of solving the point at issue without giving preference to any one of the texts involved'. However where the word 'spouse' used in all other languages was rendered into Dutch as 'wife'[4] the ECJ preferred a 'sexually neutral construction' meaning either 'wife' or 'husband', as the case may be, thus giving weight to legislative policy rather than language and ensuring at the same time uniformity throughout the Community.

In view of the discrepancy between the various language versions the Court of Justice ruled out the possibility of accepting one version of the text in isolation and stressed that a text should be interpreted on the basis of 'both the real intention of its author and the aim he seeks to achieve, in the light in particular of the versions in all … languages'.[5]

Since the Treaties of Paris, Rome, Brussels, Maastricht and Amsterdam are 'self-executing' there is no need of their being 'transformed' by statute into the domestic law of the Member States. Consequently, as far as the authentic texts are concerned, the Treaties have to be taken as they stand. The danger of producing a different text for the purpose of legislation, not uncommon in the process of translation of international conventions, has been excluded. This does not solve the problem of Community law in the countries whose language has not been included in the authentic texts or, as in the case of the United Kingdom, countries which have subsequently adhered to the Treaties. The general rule of international law may be too narrow and so the spirit rather than the letter of the Treaty should prevail.

In their endeavour to give effect to the common intention of the parties comprised in a multilingual treaty the draftsmen try to exclude discrepancies and potential conflicts of interpretation but this is a quite impossible task. The end product must be a compromise if not a synthesis of the systems involved. Where this is impossible they have to choose consciously the technical language which

---

1   Case 13/61: [1962] ECR 45, [1962] CMLR 1 at 23.
2   Case 61/72: [1973] ECR 301; see also (re family allowances) Case 6/74: *Moulijn v Commission* [1974] ECR 1287.
3   Case 80/76: *North Kerry Milk Products Ltd v Minister for Agriculture and Fisheries* [1977] ECR 425, [1977] 2 CMLR 769 at 781.
4   Case 9/79: *Wörsdorfer (née Koschniske) v Raad van Arbeid* [1979] ECR 2717, [1980] 1 CMLR 87.
5   See Case 55/87: *Moksel v BALM* [1988] ECR 3845; see also Case C-259/95: *European Parliament v Council* [1997] ECR I-5303.

seems most appropriate or most commonly used or the language of the legal system which has the greatest influence in the deliberations. The Treaties unmistakably bear the imprint of French law for the French have the uncanny knack of assisting the international law-making process with their texts as the starting point of deliberations and, hopefully, the wording to be adopted.[6] However the ECJ need not be perturbed by textual discrepancies for, in the best traditions of continental jurisprudence, it can rely on teleological interpretation. In other words, when in doubt, the spirit rather than the letter of the law should prevail, thus giving weight to the legislative policy aimed at by the law-maker. Or, as put by Judge Kutscher[7] 'the difficulties of interpretation arising from the multilingual nature of Community law are frequently resolved not through a grammatical interpretation but by resorting to an examination of the objects of the provision and its place in the system of the Treaty ...'. Indeed committed to a dynamic and evolutionary interpretation of Community law[8] the Court on its own admission 'cannot ... be content with a literal interpretation ...'.[9] Moreover the objective envisaged may prompt a liberal interpretation as was, eg the case of 'identification' of persons on social security to their entitlement of butter at reduced price without injury to their pride.[10]

This attitude appears to be reflected in certain dicta of Lord Denning MR[11] who, in his iconoclastic way, may have given the impression that teleological interpretation should be adopted generally, not merely in respect of Community law. When referring to an English statute which incorporated the International Convention on the Carriage of Goods by Road 1956, he said that 'by interpreting the Treaty of Rome ... we must certainly adopt the new approach'.[12] For that he was duly rebuked since 'membership of the EC does not involve abandonment of national construction of multilateral conventions ...'.[13] No doubt this is correct as regards international treaties other than the Community Treaties. However, taken out of context, the dictum that ... 'no assistance from methods said to be used in interpreting the Treaty of Rome by the European Court of Justice ...'[14] may become a source of mischief. There is no way of denying that Community law, whether comprised in Treaties or derivative legislation, is a *sui generis* law and has to be interpreted by national courts in the light of the jurisprudence of the Community Court. Should there be a difficulty in this respect the matter ought to be referred to the Community Court for a preliminary ruling under EC Article 234 (ex Art 177).

Whilst the Treaty is a 'once and for all' exercise the Community legislation is a continuous process. The techniques have already been perfected through common effort of the Community lawyers and here, perhaps, the lawyer no longer feels a champion of his own system (which, as every lawyer knows, is the best system in the world!) or suffers under the limitations of his national training and the inhibitions acquired from his legal language becoming his second nature. The

---

6 See *Bell Concord Educational Trust Ltd v Customs and Excise Comrs* [1989] 1 CMLR 845 in which the English Court of Appeal used the French text of the 6th VAT Directive to elucidate the meaning of the Directive and of the English implementing statute.

7 Kutscher, H, *Methods of Interpretation as seen by a Judge at the Court of Justice*, Judicial and Academic Conference 27–28 September 1976, p 20.

8 Ibid, p 39.

9 Case 6/60: *Jean E Humblet v Belgium* [1960] ECR 559.

10 Case 29/69: *Stauder v City of Ulm* [1969] ECR 419, (paras 4 and 5), [1970] CMLR 112.

11 *H P Bulmer Ltd v J Bollinger SA* [1974] Ch 401 at 419–425.

12 *James Buchanan Co Ltd v Babco Forwarding and Shipping (UK) Ltd* [1977] 2 CMLR 455 at 459, CA.

13 Ibid [1978] 1 CMLR 156 at 161, HL.

14 Ibid.

newcomers to this task are at a certain disadvantage and their contribution initially must perforce be rather limited. This is a special practical challenge to any civil servant joining the legal service of the Community.

EC Article 254 (ex Art 191) provides that regulations 'shall be published in the Official Journal of the Communities' and that (as a rule) directives and decisions 'shall be notified to those to whom they are addressed'. At first the Official Journal was published in Dutch, French, German and Italian but Article 155 of the first Act of Accession, as amended by the Adaptation Decision, provided that 'the texts of the Acts of the Institution of the Community adopted before the accession and drawn up by the Council or the Commission in the Danish and English languages shall, from the date of accession, be authentic under the same conditions as the texts drawn up in the four original languages'.[15] The same principle was adopted in Article 147 of the second Act of Accession regarding Greece and Article 397 of the third Act of Accession regarding Spain and Portugal and Decision 95/1.

Since directives and decisions have to be 'notified' but, apparently, need not be 'published' difficulties arose in the past[16] and these prompted the Community Court to suggest that publication be improved. As a result directives and decisions are now, as a rule, published in the Official Journal.

Let us turn now to some specific pitfalls of the technical language of Community law, problems known only too well to British translators of the Community texts who soon discovered that 'corresponding' legal terms in two languages seldom correspond *exactly*.[17]

In the drafting of conventions the generalizations about the civil law system are brought to the test and, usually, to grief. Illusions of the oneness of the system based on Roman Law and codes are quickly exposed and we are left with a vague notion of a common core of the law, a common historical heritage, and a similarity of styles. As in a large family there are traces of common genes but also manifestations of mutations and acquired differences. As in a family the stronger members prevail and so one can trace in multilingual texts the influence of a particular system. It is not surprising that the French legal language provides a starting point for the consideration of the problems of language in the Community texts.

The student of Community law must from the start familiarize himself with the problem of language known only too well to the student of comparative law, whilst the practitioner may find support for his argument from a comparison of the texts, bearing in mind that he is confronted with a conceptual rather than purely linguistic problem. Such problems are reflected in the growing volume of case law, examples of which have been listed in the previous editions of this book.

(2)   LANGUAGE IN THE INSTITUTIONS

Deliberations within the institutions are conducted in the official languages of the Community, which necessitates a system of simultaneous interpretation and explains the number of interpreters and translators employed by each institution.

---

15   Reg 857/72 of 24 April 1972 establishing special editions of the Official Journal; JO L101, 1972.

16   Joined Cases 73 and 74/63: *Internationale Crediet-en Handelsvereniging 'Rotterdam' NV v Minister van Landouw et Visserij* [1964] ECR 1 at 13–14, [1964] CMLR 198; Case 69/69: *Alcan v Commission* [1970] ECR 385 at 396, [1970] CMLR 337 at 340.

17   Hall, D F, 'Translating the Treaties', *European Review*, Spring Issue 1972; Héraud, G, 'La Communauté Européenne et La Question Linguistique' (1981) 5 *Rev d'Integration Européenne*, p 5 et seq.

The Community is a multi-language organization, the respect of the language of each Member State remaining one of the aspects of national sovereignty. Whilst the Union proclaims respect for the national identity[18] of the Member States the rules governing the languages of the institutions shall, without prejudice to the provisions contained in the rules of procedure of the Court of Justice, be determined by the Council, acting unanimously.[19] So far there has been no attempt to rationalize the use of languages though the problem continues to dog the efficiency of Community proceedings.[20]

(3) LANGUAGE IN THE COURT OF JUSTICE AND IN THE COURT OF FIRST INSTANCE

The requirement that judges must be fit to occupy the highest judicial offices in their respective countries is both an advantage and a handicap. The advantage is obvious in the quality of the judicial body and the potential of having the best legal traditions of the Member States in the service of the Community Court. The handicap is that judges, perhaps more than any other lawyers, are conditioned by their own system. However, until truly Community judges emerge the national judges will continue to enrich and shape the Community judiciary with their native skills and characters. Judge Donner thus summarized the position of the national judge: 'I remember one of my colleagues saying at the end of a long debate in which he had tried to win us over to his national solution on a particular point, "Well, gentlemen, if you do not want to adopt my approach, you will at least have to admit that it is the only reasonable one".'[1]

In order to assist the Court with the linguistic problems the Rules of Procedure enabled the Court to set up a language department consisting of experts, combining the knowledge of several of the official languages of the Court and law.[2] Originally the official languages of the Court were French, German, Italian and Netherlands[3] but with the enlargement of the Community the rules of procedure[4] had to be adapted to include the new official languages. At present the official languages of the Court are: Danish, English, French, German, Italian, Netherlands and, since 1 January 1981, Greek, since 1 January 1986, Spanish and Portuguese and since 1 January 1995, Finnish and Swedish; but Irish (though not official) may also be used. These changes resulting in an increased number of the official languages will no doubt further multiply the problems involved.

The present position is that only one of the official languages may be used as the procedural language.[5] The choice is, in principle, left to the applicant. However, if the defendant is a Member State or a person or corporation subject to a Member State the procedural language will be the official language of

---

18 TEU Art 6(3) (ex Art F(3)).
19 Convention relating to Certain Institutions common to the European Communities of 27 March 1957 annexed to the EEC and EAEC Treaties and amending the ECSC Treaty. See TEC Art 290 (ex Art 217).
20 See Stark, F, 'Faszination Deutsch: Die Wiederentedeckung eine Sprache für Europe' (1993) and contrast Gueriviere, J, 'Belgique: la revanche des langues' (1994).
1 Donner, A M, *The Role of the lawyer in the European Communities* (1968), p 43.
2 Rules of Procedure (codified version, OJ 1999, C 65/1) Art 22.
3 Ibid, Art 29(1). Dutch, as the language of Holland, is not synonymous with the 'Netherlands language' which is also spoken in certain parts of Belgium. Such Belgians enjoy two 'official languages': French and Netherlands. On the problem of translation from Greek see Case C-168/91: *Christos Konstantinidis v Staadt Altensteig* [1993] ECR I-1191, [1993] 3 CMLR 401.
4 Case 1/60: *FERAM SpA v High Authority* [1960] ECR 165 at 170; see further Lasok, K P E, op cit, p 54.
5 Rules of Procedure, Art 29(2).

that state. Should there be more than one official language involved the applicant would be able to choose one from these, which led the Court to rule that unless the defendant is a Community institution the language of the case is that of the defendant. If the parties to the case so desire, the Court, upon their joint application, may designate the use of another official language as the procedural language. In exceptional circumstances the Court may authorize the total or partial use of another official language as the procedural language if so requested by one of the parties. Such a request has to be considered in the light of the comments by the other party and the Advocate-General but is not open to any of the organs of the Community.

In the proceedings involving a preliminary ruling under EC Article 234 (ex Art 177)[6] on matters of the interpretation of the Treaty, the validity and interpretation of the act of the Community organs and the interpretation of the statutes of bodies established by the Council, the procedural language shall be that of the court or tribunal which requests the preliminary ruling in question.

The procedural language is used to procure written evidence and pleas before the Court. Documents produced in another language must be accompanied by a translation in the procedural language. These documents are regarded as 'authentic', which means in practical terms that they cannot be challenged merely on linguistic grounds (RP 31).

Witnesses and experts ought to use the procedural language or one of the official languages but, if unable to do so the Court will allow them to use another language. The witness or expert is allowed to speak through an interpreter or address himself to a judge of his native language[7] but at the end a record will be made under the direction of the Court's Registrar in the procedural language.

The President of the Court, the Presidents of Chambers when directing the proceedings, the Judge-Rapporteur when making his preliminary report and judges and Advocates-General when asking questions and the Advocates-General when making their submissions may use an official language in preference to the procedural language. However, their utterings will be translated into the procedural language under the direction of the Registrar.

The Registrar will also, on the application of a judge, Advocate-General or one of the parties, ensure that a translation into the official languages of his choice is made of what has been said or recorded during the proceedings before the Court or Chamber (RP 30), is delivered in the procedural language (RP 29(2)) and then published by the Registrar in all the official languages (RP 68). Since the final version of the judgment will generally be in French the authentic text is usually a translation into the language of the case and it is vetted by a judge whose mother tongue is the same.[8] This may occasionally produce difficulties as eg the inaccurate translation of the German *Gefährdungen der öffentlichen Ordnung* into its French equivalent *des menaces à l'ordre public* into English *breaches of the peace*.[9]

In spite of the tremendous language problem only few cases have so far involved the technical question of the use of language. In *De Gezamenlijke Steenkolenmijnen*

---

6   Statutes of the Court: EC Statute, Art 20; EAEC Statute, Art 21; ECSC Treaty, Art 41 RP, 29/2.

7   Case 18/63: *Wollast (née Schmitz) v Commission* [1964] ECR 85, where the witness and the President of the Court were Italians but the counsel was French, and the President acted virtually as an interpreter.

8   Lasok, K P E, 'Practice and Procedure before the ECJ' (1981) ECLR, 92.

9   Case 67/74: *Bonsignore v Oberstadtdirektor de Stadt Köln* [1975] ECR 297, [1975] 1 CMLR 472 and Case 30/77: *R v Bouchéreau* [1977] ECR 1999, [1977] 2 CMLR 800, respectively.

in Limburg v High Authority[10] the Court had to rule on the use of the procedural language by an intervener. The Court held that 'it is only as from the moment that he is admitted to intervene that the intervener is obliged to use the language required for the procedure in the main action, without prejudice to the application of' RP 29 (2) (*c*).

In *FERAM v High Authority of the European Coal and Steel Community*[11] the admissibility of documents drawn up in languages other than the procedural language was challenged. The Court held that: 'The documents in question were deposited at the Registry before the oral procedure had ended and therefore they were known to the Court before judgment was given. The fact that a document drawn up in one of the official languages of the Community is produced means that the Court has knowledge not merely of its existence but also of its contents. For, like all the institutions of the three Communities, the Court is cognizant of four languages [now 12] by virtue of an irrebuttable presumption of law.' The provisions concerning the language of procedure cannot be regarded as being of public policy (*ordre public; zwingendes Recht; openbare orde; ordine pubblico*) –

(1) because the language of procedure is that of the applicant, unless the defendant is one of the Member States of the three Communities or a legal person subject to the jurisdiction of one of the Member States;
(2) because, both on the joint application of the parties and on the application of a single party and without the consent of the other party being necessary, the Court can authorize the use of an official language other than the language of the procedure.

The challenge failed.

The rules governing the language of procedure are fairly clear but they do not explain what actually happens when the multilingual Court retires for deliberations in private before proceeding to judgment. Judge Donner[12] explained the problems the judges have to face and stressed how difficult it is for a lawyer to shed his second nature acquired in the practice of his national law and to sublimate his experience to a Community concept of law which must perforce savour of a synthesis of the laws of the Member States. No doubt the personality of the individual judge and the authority of his national law play a part in the deliberations.

The deliberations are entirely private and in the absence of interpreters. Practice established French to be the *lingua franca* with the consequent disadvantage to judges whose fluency in French is not as good as might be desired. To get round this difficulty former Judge Riese[13] used to state his position in his native German and then restate it in French. In this way he endeavoured to have his say as best he could first in the legal jargon of his own country, and then give his brethren the benefit of an authentic translation into the 'working' language. It is clear that the Court must live with the problem (further aggravated by the enlargement of the Community) until the relevant portion of the law has become uniform and a new generation of truly Community lawyers has replaced the judges schooled in their native lands.

10   Case 30/59: [1961] ECR 1 at 48 but see Case 45/81: *Alexander Moksel Import-Export GmbH v Commission* [1982] ECR 1120: procedural language was German but intervener allowed to present submissions at the hearing in English.
11   Case 1/60: [1960] ECR 165 at 170–171.
12   Donner, op cit, p 44.
13   Riese, O, 'Erfahrungen aus der Praxis des Gerichtshofes der Europäischen Gemeinschaft für Kohle und Stahl', *Deutsche Richterzeitung* (1958), 270–272.

Still more complex is the jurisprudence of the language of the law. On more than one occasion the Community Court had to turn its mind to the interpretation of technical terms only to confirm that similarities conceal divergencies and nuances in the legal systems. The following examples illustrate the point.

(a) *Détournement de pouvoir*[14] A notion of French administrative law to cover a variety of cases of misuse of power has been before the Court on several occasions. In *Associazione Industrie Siderurgiche Italiane (Assider) v High Authority of the European Coal and Steel Community*[15] Advocate-General Lagrange reviewed painstakingly the concept of the misuse of power in each of the six Member States. In that case an association of Italian steel enterprises complained of being adversely affected by certain decisions[16] of the High Authority of the Coal and Steel Community which concerned the publication of price lists and conditions of sale by the steel industry. The plaintiffs contended that the general decisions of the High Authority in these matters constituted a threat to Italian steel enterprises, and that they were vitiated by the *détournement de pouvoir*. Moreover, since those enterprises which had infringed the previous regulations were not subjected to any sanction, the plaintiffs considered this to be a manifest injustice, and thus a misuse of power in respect of those enterprises which had observed the Treaty. The Court held that since decision 2/54 was annulled by the judgment in the case of *French Government v High Authority of the European Coal and Steel Community*[17] and decision 3/54 repealed by the High Authority it was unnecessary for the Court to define *détournement de pouvoir*. Decision 1/54, having been upheld by the Court in the case of *Italian Government v High Authority of the European Coal and Steel Community*,[18] could not be regarded as misuse of power in the absence of new arguments. In the circumstances the Court was able to fall back on the classical dodge of not having to define an awkward concept. The plaintiffs fared no better in their request for an interpretation of the judgment[19] as the Court held that the judgment, being free from obscurities, presented no occasion for interpretation.

The saga of the *détournement de pouvoir* is likely to continue in spite of the attempts by the Court to offer an objective definition of *détournement* as 'the use made by a public authority of its powers for an object other than that for which a power was conferred upon it ...'[20] simply because of the variations of the use and abuse of public power. In view of Advocate-General Warner 'misuse of power is often pleaded but seldom proved ...' In that case it was proved.[1]

(b) *Faute de service* In several cases the Community Court considered grievances arising from alleged 'default of the administration' (*faute de service*). On one occasion a Belgian corporation[2] complained that it was unable to sell coal in France because of the refusal of a licence by French authorities which, in effect, impeded the free flow of coal within the Community. Repeated requests to the Coal and

---

14 *Ermessemissbrauch, sviamento de potere, misbruik van bevoegdheid.*
15 Case 3/54: [1954–56] ECR 63.
16 Case 1/54: JO, 13 January 1953, 217; Case 2/54; ibid, 218; Case 3/54, ibid, 219.
17 Case 1/54: [1954–56] ECR 1.
18 Case 2/54: [1954–56] ECR 37.
19 Case 5/55: [1954–56] ECR 135.
20 Case 8/55: *Fédération Charbonnière de Belgique v High Authority* [1954–56] ECR 245 at 272–273.
 1 Case 105/75: *Giuffrida v Council* [1976] ECR 1395 at 1405. See cases under EC Art 288 (ex Art 215) supra.
 2 Cases 9–12/60: *Société Commerciale Antoine Vloeberghs SA v High Authority of the European Coal and Steel Community* [1961] ECR 197.

Steel Community were of no avail and the corporation suffered damage as a result of inaction of the Community. The Court held that the plaintiff was entitled to redress for *faute de service* without insisting that the act complained of had to be annulled first. However, in *Plaumann & Co v EEC Commission*[3] damages were refused in the absence of a declaration of nullity but the decision turned upon different considerations, mainly the *locus standi* of the claimant. In subsequent cases[4] the Court recognized the independent nature of the action in accordance with EC Articles 288 and 235 (ex Arts 215 and 178), but considered that where a claim is made in respect of injury attributable to a legislative act of the Community involving choices of economic policy the claimant can succeed only if there is a 'sufficiently flagrant infringement of a superior rule of law protecting the individual'.[5]

Several other cases[6] threw light on the concept of *faute de service* but perhaps the most instructive are the cases involving grievances of Community employees. It was held[7] that failure to renew a contract of employment in an irregular fashion constituted *faute de service* and so would an unlawful activity of an organ of the Community preventing a person from carrying on his normal occupation and causing him material and moral damage.[8]

The many aspects of *faute de service* were considered from a comparative point of view in *Algera v Common Assembly*,[9] a case concerning the disputed validity of a decision affecting employees. The Court stated:[10]

'... A study of comparative law reveals that in the six Member States an administrative act creating substantive rights in a particular party cannot in principle be revoked, provided that it amounted to a legal act. In such a case, the substantive right having been acquired, the necessity of ensuring confidence in the stability of the situation thus created outweighs the interest of the administration which might wish to revoke its decision. This applies particularly in the appointment of an official.

If, on the contrary, the administrative act is illegal, the law of all the Member States recognizes the possibility of revocation. The lack of an objective legal basis for the act affects the substantive right of the party concerned and justifies the revocation of the said act. It is appropriate to emphasize that this principle is generally recognized and that it is only the conditions for its exercise which vary.

---

3 Case 25/62: [1963] ECR 95, [1964] CMLR 29. Contrast Case C-229/88 *Cargill BV v Commission* [1990] 2 CMLR 753 (reduction of agricultural subsidy) with Case C-152/88: *Sofrimport Sarl v Commission* [1992] ECR I-153, [1990] 3 CMLR 80 (suspension of import licence).

4 Case 5/71: *Aktien-Zuckerfabrik Schöppenstedt v Council* [1971] ECR 975; Cases 63–69/72: *Werhahn v Council* [1973] ECR 1229.

5 *Werhahn*, supra.

6 Eg Cases 19/60, 21/60, 2–3/61: *Société Fives Lille Cail v High Authority of the European Coal and Steel Community* [1961] ECR 281 at 295–296, [1962] CMLR 251 at 281–282; Cases 5–7/66, 13–24/66: *Firma E Kampffmeyer v Commission* [1967] ECR 245; Case 36/62: *Société des Aciéries du Temple v High Authority of the European Coal and Steel Community* [1963] ECR 289, [1964] CMLR 49 at 56; Case 3/65: *Société Anonyme Métallurgique d'Espérance Langdoz v High Authority of the European Coal and Steel Community* [1965] ECR 1065, [1966] CMLR 146 at 167; 11 Rec. 1321.

7 In Case 1/55: *Kergall v Common Assembly* [1954–56] ECR 151.

8 Cf Case 18/60: *Worms v High Authority of the European Coal and Steel Community* [1962] ECR 195, [1963] CMLR 1 where an independent body was involved and, therefore, the Community was not liable.

9 Cases 7/56, 3–7/57 [1957–58] ECR 39.

10 Valentine, D G, *The Court of Justice of the European Communities*, Vol 2 (1965), pp 757–758.

French law requires that the revocation of the illegal act must occur before the expiration of the time limit for bringing an appeal, or if an appeal is brought, before judgment. Belgian, Luxembourg and Dutch law, with certain differences, appear to follow analogous rules.

On the other hand, German law does not recognize a time limit for the exercise of the right of revocation unless such a limit is provided by a special provision. Thus, the Federal law concerning public officials, by Article 13 thereof, allows the withdrawal of an appointment only within a period of six months. However, it is generally recognized that the principle of good faith (*Treu und Glauben*) is opposed to an unduly delayed withdrawal ...

... Italian law is particularly precise upon this question. Any administrative act is vitiated by incompetence, violation of the law or *ultra vires (eccesso di potere)* can be annulled *ex tunc* by the administration which enacted it, independently of the substantive rights to which it might have given rise ...

The revocability of an administrative act tainted with illegality is therefore, recognized in all the Member States ...'

Faute de service was proved and the earlier decision in *Kergall v Common Assembly* was cited with approval.

(c) Exception d'illégalité The defence of illegality, which is often resorted to in order to contest the legality of an administrative act, in national jurisdictions can also be pleaded before the Community Court. In a leading case[11] Advocate-General Lagrange thus summarized the contribution of the six legal systems to the concept of *exception d'illégalité*.

'... In three of the Member States, France, Belgium and Italy, this *exception* is freely admitted, being considered as forming part of the normal sphere of application of the claim for annulment. This is due to the fact that in these three countries, rules made by the executive power are considered, as far as the right to appeal against them is concerned, from the formal point of view, that is to say being administrative acts they are liable to be annulled if they are contrary to the law. Given that the direct claim for annulment is possible with regard to them, there is no objection in principle to the [judicial] control of their legality being also exercised when individual claims are made of which they are the object. The advantage is that the *exception* may be set up at any time, even when the time limit for a claim against the regulation or the general decision has expired. On the other hand, if the claim is successful only the individual decision is annulled, which avoids the grave consequences of the annulment of the regulation itself, declared with retrospective effect *erga omnes*.'

These few examples invite a comparative approach to the interpretation of the Community law concepts. Indeed, as stressed by Advocate-General Roemer,[12] the Court has to 'call upon the law of the different Member States in order to arrive at a meaningful interpretation of Community law'. However, faced with the pluralist linguistic and legal background of the Community legal order the

---

11 Case 2/57: *Compagnie des Hauts Fourneaux de Chasse v High Authority of the European Coal and Steel Community* [1957–58] ECR 199 at 203–205. See also Case 9/56: *Meroni & Co Industrie Metallurgiche SpA v High Authority of the European Coal and Steel Community* [1957–58] ECR 133; Cases 31, 33/62: *Milchwerke Heinz Wöhrmann & Sohn KG v Commission* [1962] ECR 501, [1963] CMLR 152.

12 Case 6/54: *Netherlands Government v High Authority* [1954–56] ECR 103.

Court has maintained a discreet distance from the national systems.[13] Whilst displaying a certain 'comparative attitude'[14] the Court has in fact embarked on an autonomous interpretation of the Community law emphasizing in this way its autonomous nature. The attractive idea of 'applied comparative law'[15] emerging from Luxembourg remains a theoretical rather than practical proposition.

13 See especially Case 145/83: *Adams v Commission* [1985] ECR 3539, [1986] 1 CMLR 506.

14 Pescatore, P, 'Les recours, dans la Jurisprudence de la Cour de Justice des Communautés Européennes, à des normes déduites de la comparaison des droits des Etats Membres', RIDC, 1980, p 337.

15 Cf Jolowicz, A, 'Some Practical Aspects and the Case for Applied Comparative Law', in *New Perspectives for a Common Law of Europe* (ed Cappelletti, M) (1978), pp 237 et seq.

Chapter 5

Sources of Community law

A. Introduction

The phrase 'source of law' can be used in several senses. It can mean the causes of law, that is to say the creative elements which contribute to the making of the law and thus can be the law itself. These may be historical facts devoid of any authority or political, social and economic conditions of the society which may, or may not, be regarded by the law as authoritative. The European Community owes its existence to international solidarity and the will to create a better Europe through economic cohesion. As 'causes', or sources of Community law they are rather remote and only of a passing interest to lawyers though lawyers ought to make themselves aware of 'the "grand design" underlying the European construction which was proclaimed in 1611 by Henri Navarre and accomplished only during the cold war.[1] In their work lawyers are concerned more with formal sources, that is authorities which may be cited in court and which are thus judicially cognizable. When analysing these we look to their authors and places where they can be found.

B. The origins of Community law

Unlike the International Court of Justice at The Hague, which is directed to apply international conventions, international custom, the general principles of law recognized by civilized nations and judicial decisions and the teachings of the most highly qualified publicists of the various nations,[2] the Community Court is left without specific guidance. Each of the relevant Treaties is content with the direction that 'the Court of Justice shall ensure that in the interpretation and application of this Treaty the law is observed',[3] without actually defining the *law*

---

1 Pescatore in Bathurst et al, op cit at pp 32–34.
2 Statute of the International Court of Justice, Art 38.
3 EC Art 220 (ex Art 164); Euratom Art 136; ECSC Art 31 – words 'and of rules laid down for the implementation thereof', added.

or its sources. In spite of this the Court has functioned vigorously applying Community law from a variety of sources.[4]

In the sense of the author or authority from which Community law is derived we can distinguish between *primary* and *secondary* sources. The distinction is important for theoretical and practical reasons because primary sources, being hierarchically superior, generate derivative (secondary) law and provide the criteria by which the validity of the latter is tested.

(1) PRIMARY SOURCES

(a) Constitutional Treaties
They are the *Constitutional Treaties* because together they form the organizational law of the Community. They constitute the basis of the Community legal order and the *fons et origo* of all Community law; they are its primary sources.

The primary sources of Community law consist of the three founding Treaties (ECSC, EAEC and EC) with their Annexes and Protocols, which supplement the Treaties; the Convention on Certain Institutions Common to the European Communities (1957); the Merger Treaty (1965); the Luxembourg Treaty on Budgetary Matters (1970); the first Treaty of Accession and its Annexes (1972); the Second Budgetary Treaty (1975), the Act of the Council concerning direct elections to the European Parliament (1976), the second Treaty of Accession and its Annexes (1979), the third Treaty of Accession and its Annexes (1985), the Single European Act (1986), the Maastricht Treaty on European Union (1993) with its Protocols and Declarations, the Fourth Treaty of Accession (1994), and the Amsterdam Treaty on European Union with its Protocols and Declarations.

The founding Treaties are 'self-executing'[5] treaties which means that, when ratified, they become law automatically within the Member States. In contrast with 'non-self-executing' treaties (which constitute international obligations but require implementing legislation before they become applicable in internal law), 'self-executing' treaties must be applied directly by the municipal courts as the law of the land. A treaty is, by its nature, a contract between two or more states; it is not a legislative act. However, it may be regarded as a legislative act whenever it is designed by the signatory states as a declaration of their understanding of what a particular rule of law is, or an expressly formulated norm of future behaviour, or a constitution of an international organization. The legislative nature of the EC Treaty is indicated by its purpose and specific provisions (EC Articles 299 and 313 (ex Arts 227 and 241)), and confirmed by the 'Act concerning the Conditions of Accession and the Adjustment of the Treaties' (Article 2).[6] The status of the Protocols is the same, as by virtue of EC Article 311 (ex Art 239) they 'form an integral part' of the Treaty.

The content of the EC Treaty is complex not only because it creates institutions and defines the objectives of the Community, but also because it provides the basis and authority for Community legislation. It provides for an Executive, a Bureaucracy, a Parliament and a Court and charges these institutions with the execution of the Treaty. The Treaty remains a treaty, that is an agreement between the signatory states, but it differs from a classical treaty not only because it creates

---

4   See Bebr, G, *Judicial Control of the European Communities* (1962), p 26.
5   On self-executing treaties see the judgment of Chief Justice Marshall in *Foster and Elam v Neilson* 2 Pet 253 (US 1829).
6   Attached to the Treaties of Accession.

supranational institutions but, more importantly, because, unlike a typical treaty, its execution has been taken out of the hands of the parties. The institutions it creates, notwithstanding their imperfections and limitations, can be likened to the corresponding institutions of the internal law. Their strength lies in the fact that certain important powers have been transferred or delegated by the states to these institutions, making them quasi-autonomous. Their weakness lies in the fact that their functioning is contingent upon the continuous discharge of the Treaty obligations by the Member States. Thus, if a country adopts an obstructive attitude the Community will continue to function though its dynamism shall be stunned.[7] If a country withdraws from the Community havoc could be caused but the Community would not come to an end and the institutions could not cease to function. But if a number of states withdrew the Community would cease to be a practical possibility.

If we apply a juristic construction to the Treaty modelled upon internal law it can be argued that the Treaty is the Constitution of the Community[8] or, to use Judge Donner's phrase, that the Member States have undertaken obligations 'not simply on a reciprocal basis but primarily towards the new collectivity they set up'.[9] The authors of this book subscribe to the constitutional theory in spite of arguments advancing an opposite opinion, namely that the Treaty is merely a bundle of contractual obligations.

In addition to the Constitution of the Community the Treaty contains what continental lawyers would term 'ordinary legislation', implying thereby a hierarchy of legal norms.[10] The relationship between 'constitutional' provisions and the 'ordinary legislation' of the Treaty, obvious to continental lawyers but rather obscure to British lawyers, who are not familiar with the theory of hierarchy of legal norms, is of some practical importance as far as the legislative function of the Community organs is concerned. The point is whether the Treaty alone can provide sufficient authority for legislation by these organs or whether the growth of Community law must depend on its original source, ie the power delegated by the Member States. The answer seems to be in the affirmative, ie that the Treaty is sufficient for a dynamic and orderly development, assuming, of course, that the Community organs do not act *ultra vires*. The Treaty could not have envisaged all the eventualities but provided[11] a wide scope for Community initiatives, safeguarding at the same time the principle of legality through the instrumentality of the Court and the vital interests of the Member States through the instrumentality of the Council. Thus, in order to attain the Community objectives the Council by a unanimous decision may take the appropriate measures (which, presumably, include appropriate legal measures) on the recommendation of the Commission and in consultation with the Parliament. These powers are wide but circumscribed by the Treaty and so it was argued[12] correctly that the provisions of EC Article 308 (ex Art 235) constitute no blanket authority for 'implied powers'. The problem

---

7   As during the 'constitutional crisis' of 1965, see infra pp 209–212.
8   Eg Wagner, H, op cit, p 24 and Pescatore, P, *L'Ordre Juridique des Communautés Européennes* (1971), pp 36 et seq; for some opinion see German Federal Constitutional Court (First Chamber), Decision of 18 October 1967, [1967] AWD 477–8 (1980) Europarecht, 134–7.
9   'The Constitutional Powers of the Court of Justice of the European Communities', 11 CML Review, 1974, p 128.
10 Ie the Constitution, Acts of Parliament, legislative acts of the Executive and delegated legislation.
11 EC Art 308 (ex Art 235); EAEC Art 203; ECSC Art 95.
12 Wohlfarth, E, Everling, H, Glässner, H J, Sprung, R, 'Die Europäische Wirtschafts-gemeinschaft', *Kommentar zum Vertrage* (1960), comment (7) on Art 235.

did arise under the ECSC Treaty and the Community Court considered *ultra vires* the delegation of powers vested in the High Authority to an agency in Brussels set up for the purpose of operating a system of subsidies to equalize the cost of scrap iron.[13] More recently the ECJ,[14] ruling on the validity of a Community action programme for the vocational training of young people, held (citing its decision in another case)[15] that the use of EC Article 308 (ex Art 235) as a legal base for a measure is justified only where no other provision of the Treaty gives the Community institutions the necessary power. In the instant case EC Article 128 (as originally worded – see now EC Article 150) provided a sufficient base for the measure in question.

In order to supplement the powers of the Community organs (and thus, presumably, curtail the temptation to rely on 'implied powers') a practice under the ECSC Treaty was established whereby a certain amount of law-making power was exercised by assembled representatives of the Member States.[16] The practice spread to the EEC, the most interesting example of this being the decisions which resulted in the acceleration of the setting up of the customs union.[17] The legal nature of these devices (described as 'acts of representatives')[18] is obscure. They are regarded as 'international agreements in simplified form'[19] and the 'borderline of international law and Community law'.[20] These 'acts of representatives', no doubt, contribute to the development of Community policy and law and in a sense provide a substitute for the revision of the Treaty. A further dynamic application of EC Article 308 (ex Art 235) can be seen in the implementation of the Dublin agreement of 1975 on the adoption of the correcting mechanism in respect of the budgetary obligations of the Member States.[1]

The view that the Treaty provides the Constitution of the Community is fortified by the fact that so far recourse has been taken to the Community Court and Community law rather than international law sources for the purpose of the interpretation of the Treaties and legislative acts made under the Treaties. The Court itself, through the Advocate-General Lagrange,[2] considered the role of general international law as a source of Community law rather limited because:

---

13 Case 9/56: *Meroni & Co Industrie Metallurgiche SpA v High Authority of the ECSC* [1957–1958] ECR 133 at 149–154.

14 Case 56/88: *United Kingdom v Council, Re Vocational Training Programme* [1989] ECR 1615, [1989] 2 CMLR 789 at para 5. See also Case 242/87: *Commission v Council, Re Erasmus* [1989] ECR 1425 and Cases C-51/89, C-90/89 and C-94/89: *United Kingdom, France and Germany, Re the COMETT II Programme* [1991] ECR I-2757, [1992] 1 CMLR 40.

15 Case 45/86: *Commission v Council, Re Generalized Tariff Preferences* [1987] ECR 1493 [1988] 2 CMLR 131 see also Case C-295/90: *European Parliament v Council, Re mobility of students*, [1992] ECR I-4193.

16 ECSC Art 69, concerning free movement of skilled labour (JO 586/55 and 1647/63); ECSC Art 70, concerning international railroad tariffs (JO 607/55, 701/55, 130/56 and 431/59); see Kaiser, 'Die im Rat vereinigten Vertreter der Regierungen der Mitgliedstaaten', *Festschrift Ophüls* (1965), pp 107–124.

17 JO 1217/60 and 1284/62.

18 Brinkhorst, L J, 'Implementation of (non-self-executing) Legislation of the European Economic Community, including Directives', *Legal Problems of an Enlarged European Commuity* (ed Bathurst, M E, et al) (1972), p 72.

19 Pescatore, P, 'La personalité internationale de la Communauté', *Les relations extérieures de la Communauté unifiée* (1969), p 585.

20 Resolution following the parliamentary report by Burger (EP doc 215/1968–69) concerning collective acts of the Member States of the Community (JO 1969, C).

1 *Bulletin of the European Communities* 1975, No 3, p 6.

2 In Case 8/55: *Fédération Charbonnière de Belgique v High Authority* [1954–56] ECR 245 at 277.

'... our Court is not an international tribunal, but is concerned with a community which has been created by six states and which resembles more a federation than an international organization ... The Treaty ... although concluded in the form of international treaties and undoubtedly being one, nevertheless also constitutes, from a substantive point of view, the character of the Community and as a consequence the legal provisions derived from the Treaty must be viewed as the internal law of the Community. ...'

An international treaty creating rights and obligations of states may be regarded as special law within the general compass of international law. The point which concerns the EC Treaty as a source of law is whether the obligations contained therein can be derogated from by reference to general principles of international law. One of such general rules (albeit discredited through abuse) is the doctrine of necessity,[3] which suggests that states in cases of extreme emergency may resort to breaches of international law. As states are rather prone to resort to legal subterfuge under the guise of real or imagined emergency,[4] EC Article 226 (as originally worded) provided a specific procedure to deal with such situations during the transitional period of the Common Market. Accordingly, as decreed by the Community Court,[5] the plea of necessity cannot succeed in face of EC Article 226. Furthermore, having safeguarded certain state interests (eg EC Articles 30, 46(1), 119, 134, 146 (ex Arts 36, 56(1), 108, 115, 123)), the Treaty has reduced[6] the scope of arbitrary 'emergency' action states may be tempted to take in protection of their 'sovereign rights'. EC Article 226 was designed to correct matters arising during the transitional period and was repealed by the Amsterdam Treaty.

There is, however, no reason why a rule of international law recognized by the Member States as a general rule of law should not be applied in the interpretation of the Treaties or Community legislation. Thus, eg, in *Van Duyn v Home Office*[7] the Community Court upheld the principle of international law that, whilst a state has a duty of receiving its own nationals, it has no such duty in respect of the nationals of another state though Community nationals may claim a right of entry by virtue of a directly applicable provision of the EC Treaty. In *Nold v Commission* the Court considered that 'international agreements in which the Member States have participated or to which they have adhered contain indications which have to be taken into account within the framework of Community law'[8] but in an earlier case[9] the Court held that 'the validity of acts of the institutions within the meaning of EC Article 177 [now 234] of the Treaty cannot be tested against a rule of International Law unless that rule is binding on the Community and capable of creating rights of which interested parties may avail themselves in a court of law'.

Recently the Court had to decide whether Council Regulation 3300/91 (OJ 1991, L315/1) suspending certain tariff concessions based on the Co-operation Agreement with Yugoslavia of 1980 (Council Regulation 314/83, OJ 1983, L41/1),

3 Oppenheim, L, *International Law*, Vol 1 (8th edn, 1955), pp 297 et seq, and Brownlie, I, *International Law and the Use of Force by States* (1963), pp 40–44.
4 Cf the measures taken by the Labour Government in the UK when coming to power in 1967 which resulted in breaches of several treaties.
5 Case 7/61: *Commission v Italy* [1961] ECR 317 at 328–329, [1962] CMLR 39 at 52.
6 Commission decision of 23 July 1968, No 68/301/EEC, authorizing the French Government to take certain measures under Art 108(3) (now EC Art 119(3)).
7 Case 41/74: [1974] ECR 1337, [1975] 1 CMLR 1.
8 Case 4/73: [1974] ECR 491 at 507, [1974] 2 CMLR 338 at 354.
9 Case 9/73: *Schlüter v Hauptzollamt Lörrach* [1973] ECR 1135 at 1157.

was valid as a consequence of armed conflict and disintegration of that country. The *clausula rebus sic stantibus* of customary international law applied.[10]

In the light of the above it seems that the Community, being an autonomous organization created within the framework of international law, is governed by its own law and its Court will apply the rules of international law only if such rules are relevant to the definition of Community rights[11] or obligations (such as eg good faith[12]) arising from the international status of the Community. Regarding the Member States' position in the Community and vis-à-vis each other they have to bear in mind that, in accordance with the general rule of international law (now enshrined in Article 30 of the 1969 Vienna Convention on the Law of Treaties though the Community as such is not a party to the Convention), 'by assuming a new obligation which is incompatible with rights held under a prior treaty a state ipso facto gives up the exercise of these rights to the extent necessary for the performance of its new obligations'.[13] Member States are locked in a system of reciprocal duties and duties to the collective which they themselves have created.

(b) Duration and amendment of the treaties

Whilst the ECSC Treaty (Article 97) was concluded for fifty years the EC (EC Article 312, ex Art 240) and the EAEC Treaty (Article 208) were concluded for an unlimited period. There was no provision for withdrawal, suspension or expulsion of a Member State. However a precedent for negotiated withdrawal was set up in the case of Greenland, which became part of the Community as a Danish dependency but relinquished its privileges on reaching a further autonomy. This necessitated an amendment of the Treaties constituting the three Communities.[14]

The Treaties[15] provide a procedure for their amendment which reflects the status of the Community as a creature of international law and safeguards the sovereign rights of the Member States. Thus an amendment of the ECSC Treaty must be proposed by a Member State or the High Authority to the Council and if accepted by a two-thirds majority the President of the Council will convene an inter-governmental conference to consider the proposal. Amendments accepted by common accord by the conference become effective when ratified by the Member States in accordance with their constitutions.

A slightly different procedure, entailing the participation of the Parliament, applies to amendments of the two other Treaties. Accordingly a proposal emanating either from a Member State or the Commission goes before the Council and, if the Council after consulting the Parliament and, where appropriate, the Commission, delivers an opinion in favour of calling a conference of the representatives of the governments, such a conference must be convened to determine by common accord the amendments to be made. The amendments enter into force after being ratified by the Member States. The Single European Act, which amended all three Treaties, was enacted in that way, the decision to convene the conference having been reached by a majority of seven to three.[16]

10 Case C-162/96: *A Racke & Co v HZA Mainz* [1998] ECR I-3655.
11 *Van Duyn*, supra; Cases 21–24/72: *International Fruit Co v Produktschap voor Groenten en Fruit (No 3)* [1972] ECR 1219 at 1226; Case 36/75: *Rutili v Ministère de L'Interieur* [1975] ECR 1219, [1976] 1 CMLR 140.
12 See Case 104/81: *HZA Mainz v Kupferberg* [1982] ECR 3641 para 18 and also Case C-286/90: *Anklagemindigheden v Poulsen and Diva Navigation* [1992] ECR I-6019 and Case T-115/94: *Opel Austria v Council* [1997] ECR II-39.
13 Case 10/61: *Commission v Italy* [1962] ECR 1 at 10, [1962] CMLR 187 at 203.
14 Treaty of Brussels, EC, 19 (1985); OJ 1985, L29/1.
15 TEU Art 48 (ex Art N, ex EC Art 236, as originally worded); ECSC Art 96; EAEC Art 204.
16 On the enactment of the TEU see supra, p 22 et seq.

The Treaty on European Union too has been concluded for an unlimited period (Article 51, ex Art Q) and can be amended according to the procedure outlined above, except that the European Central Bank has to be consulted in the case of institutional changes in the monetary area (TEU Article 48, ex Art N). For good measure the EC Treaty is also concluded for an unlimited period (EC Article 312 (ex Art 240)) and its amendment is governed by the same procedure as the amendment of the Treaty on European Union.

The Amsterdam Treaty envisages the possibility of suspension of certain rights arising from the membership of the Union (TEU Article 7, ex Art F.1) and of the Community (EC Article 309 (ex Art 236)) in accordance with the procedure laid down in TEU Article 7[17] where the decision to suspend the voting rights of the representative of the government of a Member State has been taken in accordance with TEU Article 7(2). The Council may also suspend certain of the rights deriving from the application of the EC Treaty.

We should observe in this context that accession of new members entails amendments of the founding Treaties (such amendments being comprised in the Acts of Accession and the relevant Protocols) which require unanimity of decision and ratification by all the contracting states.[18]

Association agreements and other international agreements incompatible with the founding Treaties cannot be entered into unless the Treaty concerned has previously been amended in accordance with the procedure laid down therein.[19]

(c)   Application of the Treaties
The founding Treaties,[20] as amended by the Acts of Accession, circumscribe their territorial application thus defining a Community territory. They apply not only to the mass land of the Member States and the territories for which they are internationally responsible (like the self-governing territory of Gibraltar) but also to the territorial waters[1] of the Member States and, presumably, to their contiguous zone and the continental shelf – a matter of great importance not only for fishery rights but also for the exploitation of mineral wealth.

The Protocol[2] on German Internal Trade and Connected Problems (now only of historical interest) granted a special status to the German Democratic Republic (recognizing implicitly the concept of 'one Germany') as a territory which, though not part of the Community territory, was not a non-Member State in relation to the German Federal Republic.[3] The Treaty applies to the French overseas departments, the Azores, Madeira and the Canary Islands. However, in view of the peculiar conditions of these regions the Council, acting by a qualified majority on a proposal from the Commission and after consulting the European Parliament,

---

17   See pp 33-34, supra.
18   ECSC Art 98; Euratom Art 205; EC Art 300(5) (ex Art 228(5)) and TEU Art 48 (ex Art N).
19   EC Art 300(5) (see EC Art 238 as originally worded), EAEC Art 206(3); TEU Art 48 (ex Art N); see also Opinion 1/75 [1975] ECR 1355, [1976] 1 CMLR 85; Opinion 1/76 [1977] ECR 741, [1977] 2 CMLR 279; Ruling 1/78 [1978] ECR 2151, [1979] 1 CMLR 131; Opinion 1/78 [1979] ECR 2871, [1973] 3 CMLR 639. Opinion 1/91 [1992] 1 CMLR 245; Opinion 1/92 [1992] 2 CMLR 217; Opinion 2/91 [1993] 3 CMLR 800.
20   ECSC Art 79(1); Euratom Art 198(1); EC Art 299(1) (ex Art 227(1)).
 1   See Case 61/77: *Commission v Ireland* [1978] ECR 417 at 446, [1978] 2 CMLR 466 at 513–514; Case 63/83: *R v Kirk* [1984] ECR 2689, [1984] 3 CMLR 522, [1985] 1 All ER 453. Case C-146/89: *Commission v United Kingdom, re territorial sea* [1991] ECR I-3533, [1991] 3 CMLR 649.
 2   Protocol attached to EC Treaty Art 1 repealed by Amsterdam Treaty.
 3   See Case 23/79: *Geflügelschlachterei Freystadt GmbH v HZA Hamburg-Jonas* [1979] ECR 2789.

shall adopt specific measures aimed in particular, at laying down the conditions of application of the present Treaty to those regions, including common policies.[4]

The Treaty applies to the Aland Islands by virtue of Protocol No 2 to the Act of Accession of Austria, Finland and Sweden.[5]

The Treaty does not apply to the Faeroe Islands or the sovereign British bases in Cyprus.[6]

As regards the Channel Islands and the Isle of Man the Treaty applies only to the extent necessary to ensure the implementation of the arrangements for those islands in accordance with the Act of Accession of 1972.[7]

As regards substance the unity application was breached by the TEU which enabled the United Kingdom and Denmark to opt out of certain crucial provisions.[8]

The Treaties have also extra-territorial effect, which is especially pertinent to the operation of the Community competition policy. The principle was established by the ECJ in the ICI[9] case in which a British multi-national company, together with its associates, claimed, albeit unsuccessfully, immunity from liability for restrictive practices contrary to EC Article 81(1) (ex Art 85(1)) on the ground that it had no physical presence in the Community at a time when the United Kingdom was not a member. The jurisdiction over overseas entities can be claimed either in accordance with the so-called 'effects doctrine' favoured by the Commission or the more pragmatic approach of the ECJ which held that the fact that one of the parties to an agreement prohibited by the Treaty is situated outside the Community does not prevent the application of the rules since the agreement is operative in the territory of the Common Market.[10]

(d)   Conventions between Member States
According to EC Article 293 (ex Art 220) Member States ought to negotiate conventions to secure for the benefit of their nationals the protection of rights, abolition of double taxation, mutual recognition of companies and reciprocal recognition and enforcement of judgments of municipal courts and arbitration awards. It goes without saying that such conventions shall have the force of treaties and be binding accordingly. By these conventions the Member States can create new laws and, in view of the sovereign power of states, these laws can go far beyond the scope of the founding Treaties. Should this be the case the Community Court might have to rule whether such laws, being in excess of the founding Treaties, are cognizable by the Court as a source of Community law. Rules seem to be evolving both by the Community Court and the national courts of the Member States. Thus it was held by the Paris Court of Appeal that Community law superseded rights and obligations arising from previous bilateral social security

---

4   EC Art 299(2) (ex Art 227(2)).
5   EC Art 299(5).
6   EC Art 299(6)(a), (b).
7   EC Art 299(6)(c); See Case C-355/89: *Department of Employment v Barr and Montrose Holdings* [1991] ECR I-3479; see also Case C-171/96: *Pereira Roque v Lieutenant Governor of Jersey, Re deportation of a Portuguese national* [1998] ECR I-4607.
8   See Protocol 8 on the Statute of the ESCB, Protocol 10 on the Third Stage of the Economic and Monetary Union; Protocol 12 on Danish participation in the Third Stage of the Economic and Monetary Union; and Protocol 14 on UK opting out of the Social Charter.
9   Case 48/69: *ICI Ltd v Commission* [1972] ECR 619, [1972] CMLR 557; see also Joined Cases 89, 104, 114, 116, 117 and 125–129/85: *A Ahlstrom Oy v Commission, Re Wood Pulp Cartel* [1988] ECR 5193, [1988] 4 CMLR 901; Case T-102/96: *Gencor Ltd v Commission* [1999] ECR II-753.
10 Case 22/71: *Béguelin Import Co v SA GL Import-Export* [1971] ECR 949 at 959, [1972] CMLR 81 at 95.

conventions between Member States inconsistent with the founding Treaty,[11] though the Community Court[12] held that Community law would not prevent additional social benefits arising under municipal law.

Conventions between Member States subsequent to the founding Treaty were held by the Community Court unable to alter the existing Community law[13] though doubts were cast on the position in the submission of Advocate-General Roemer in *Germany v Commission*.[14]

Since the position is somewhat uncertain, a cautious approach should be adopted to the problem of conventions between Member States as a source of Community law. If they are within the scope of EC Article 293 (ex Art 220) no question will arise for the conventions should be regarded as an instrument of harmonization or approximation of national laws. They will be negotiated and concluded within the Community spectrum, the Commission taking an active part in the process. The scope of the conventions envisaged in EC Article 293 (ex Art 220) is wider than the scope of the harmonization of laws under EC Articles 94–99 (ex Arts 100–102). However, little progress has been achieved to date. In fact only four such Conventions have been signed: the 1968 Convention on Jurisdiction and the Enforcement of Judgments in Civil and Commercial Matters, signed in 1969,[15] in force between the original six Member States as from 1 February 1973;[16] the Convention on the Law Applicable to Contractual Obligations,[17] signed in 1980 and in force; the 1968 Convention on the Mutual Recognition of Companies and Bodies Corporate, signed in 1968 by the original six Member States but not yet in force;[18] the European Patent for the Common Market Convention[19] of 1975, signed but not yet in force; and the Convention on the Elimination of Double Taxation in connection with the adjustment of profits of associated companies signed on 23 July 1990.

In accordance with the Acts of Accession the new Member States are bound to accede to the Conventions subject to adjustments which may be necessary in individual cases. Further Conventions, ie on Bankruptcy (1970)[20] and Mergers of Companies (1973),[1] are in a draft form.

If the subject matter of a convention is outside the scope of EC Article 293, (ex Art 220) but nevertheless within the scope of the Community as laid down in the founding Treaties such a convention may well be regarded as a source of Community law. An example to the point is the Luxembourg Convention for the

---

11 *Nani v Caisse d'Assurance Vieillesse des Travailleurs Salariés de Paris* [1964] CMLR 334, 4 CMLR Rev 70–71.

12 Case 92/63: *Nonnenmacher (or Moebs) v Bestuur der Sociale Verzekeringsbank* [1964] ECR 281 at 288, [1964] CMLR 338 at 347.

13 Case 33/64: *Betriebskrankenkasse der Heseper Torfwerk GmbH v Koster (née van Dijk)* [1965] ECR 97 at 104, [1966] CMLR 191 at 208.

14 Case 24/62: [1963] ECR 63, [1963] CMLR 347 at 361–362.

15 OJ 1972, L299/32, amended final text OJ 1983, C 97/2 (and amended by subsequent conventions; see Sch 1 to the UK Civil Jurisdiction and Judgments Act 1982 (as amended by the Civil Jurisdiction and Judgments Act 1991); Lasok and Stone, op cit, chs 5, 6, 7.

16 Denmark, Ireland and the United Kingdom signed the convention on 9 October 1978 (OJ 1978, L304); Greece in 1982; Spain and Portugal 1989; Austria, Finland and Sweden by a Convention signed in 1996.

17 OJ 1980, L266 and supplementary Convention on the accession of Greece, OJ 1984, L146; signed by ten Member States final text of 1984, L 146.

18 See EC Bull Supp 2/69; Lasok D, and Stone, PA, Conflict of Laws in the European Community (1987) 89 et seq.

19 OJ 1976, L17/1; Lasok and Stone, op cit, pp 85 et seq.

20 See 1980 Draft, EC Bull Supp 2/82; Lasok and Stone, op cit, ch 10.

1 Resurrected in the form of the Draft Tenth Directive on Cross-border Mergers; OJ 1985, C 23/11; EC Bull Supp 3/85.

European Patent for the Common Market of 1975.[2] It has been signed, though not yet ratified, by the Member States with the object of creating one patent territory and establishing a uniform legal regime applicable to patents in the whole of the Common Market. It has been actively encouraged by a resolution of the Council of Ministers[3] and the Commission had a hand in it. The Convention, in its preamble, claims to have accomplished one of the Community objectives and, in Article 73, enables the national courts to refer matters of its interpretation to the ECJ for a preliminary ruling in accordance with EC Article 234 (ex Art 177). Finally it states expressly, in Article 93, that none of its provisions 'may be invoked against the application of any provision' of the EC Treaty.

The Luxembourg Convention (not yet in force) is a companion to the Munich European Patent Convention of 1973[4] which is already in force comprising not only the Member States but also other countries, ie Lichtenstein and Switzerland. Both Conventions purport to establish a system of law common to the contracting parties.[5] However European patents, governed by the Munich Convention, except in so far as is otherwise provided in the Convention, have in each of the contracting states for which they are granted the effect of a national patent granted by the state concerned whilst Community patents, governed by the Luxembourg Convention, are to have a unitary character. Having an autonomous character, Community patents are subject only to the Community Patent Convention and to those provisions of the European Patent Convention which are binding upon every European patent. The two Conventions are interrelated but, strictly speaking, only the Luxembourg Convention creating Community patents is a Community legislative act, the Munich Convention not being in a technical sense a Community instrument. However, having said that, one has to bear in mind that the two Conventions have adopted a uniform system for the granting and the contesting of patents but left the enforcement of patent rights to national jurisdictions. This enables the national courts to request preliminary rulings and the Community Court to rule on the interpretation of both Conventions and the validity and interpretation of implementing provisions.[6]

Though a classical instrument of international legislation, conventions have not proved to be an attractive instrument of Community legislation. Ruled by the principles of international law, they have to be negotiated, signed and, where appropriate, ratified. They may contain a denunciation clause and have to be expressly adopted on accession of new Member States. They are slow to enact, invite reservations and delays in coming into force. They do not seem to have any prominent future in the law-making process of the Community.

The TEU envisages the adoption of conventions binding the Member States in the field of Police and Judicial Co-operation in Criminal Matters (Article 34(2)(d), ex Art K.6(2)(d)) which shall be subject to the jurisdiction of the Court of Justice as far as their interpretation and application is concerned.[7]

(e) Community external Treaties

In addition to Conventions which, as we have noted, represent an internal development of Community law, there is a substantial volume of law engendered

---

2   OJ 1976, L17/1; see also Community Patent Agreement, OJ 1989, L401/1 and Patent Litigation Protocol (OJ 1989, L401/34); Common Appeal Court Statute (OJ 1989, L401/48) and Common Appeal Court Privileges Protocol (OJ 1989, L401/45).
3   OJ 1976, L17/43.
4   International Legal Materials, Vol XIII (1974), pp 270 et seq.
5   Munich Convention Art 1; Luxembourg Convention Art 1.
6   Luxembourg Convention Art 73.
7   See pp 41–44, supra.

by Community external treaties.[8] Both sources have an international flavour and both are procedurally linked with international law but, whilst the former is concerned primarily with the Community internal market, the latter reflects the Community's position as a world trading unit and a power base for the Community's own external policy.

However, the treaty-making power of the Community, unlike that of a state, is not unlimited, for by virtue of EC Article 300 (ex Art 228) the Community can enter into agreements with the states and international organizations where so provided by the Treaty. It provides further that such agreements shall be binding upon the Member States if concluded in accordance with the procedure laid down therein.

It follows that by submitting to the Treaty the Member States delegate to the Community an important portion of their sovereign power to create international obligations and new laws in as far as the external treaty agreement with a state or international organization may be a source of law.[9] The delegation is not absolute for it is exercised subject to the participation of each Member State in Council and the recourse to the Court. However, the Court acts as the watchdog of the Community legality but not of the interests of the Member States.

All these agreements, in so far as they shape the trade pattern between the Community and the outside world and thereby affect both the internal arrangement of the Community and the legal obligations of the Member States, can be regarded as a source of Community law from which individual rights may be derived.[10] However, both Conventions and external Community treaties or agreements, while sources of Community rights and obligations, defy the classification into primary and secondary sources of Community law and, therefore, should be placed between the founding Treaties and the Community legislation discussed below.

(2)   SECONDARY SOURCES

By secondary sources of Community law we understand the law-making acts of the Community organs which result in a body of law generated by the Community itself in its quasi-autonomous capacity. We regard these sources as secondary because their authority is derived from the provisions of the founding Treaties. Moreover in the hierarchy of legal norms they rank second to Treaty provisions. Their scope is circumscribed and their validity can be tested against the criteria laid down in the Treaties. To all intents and purposes they resemble delegated legislation. The importance of the law-making power of the Community cannot be over-emphasized because, as stated by a distinguished jurist, 'the first and most essential means by which a supra-national organization endeavours to carry out its objectives ... resides in the law-making power'.[11]

Legislation denotes rules of law made deliberately in the prescribed form by some competent authority. The founding Treaties carefully avoid the term *legislation* and refer instead to *regulations*,[12] apparently, as has been suggested,[13] to

---

8   See p 73 et seq, supra.
9   Cf Sir Gerald Fitzmaurice, 'Some Problems Regarding the Formal Sources of International Law', *Symbolae Verzijl*, p 160, quoted by Morand, C A, *La législation dans les Communautés Européennes* (1968), p 16.
10 See p 96 et seq, supra.
11 Guggenheim, P, 'Organisations économiques supranationales, independance et neutralité de la Suisse', *Rev de droit suisse*, Vol 82 (1963) II, p 247.
12 EC Art 249 (ex Art 189), 2nd para; EAEC Art 161(2); ECSC Arts 31 and 35(1) and (2).
13 Pescatore, P, 'Les aspects fonctionnels de la Communauté économique européenne', *Les aspects juridiques du marché commun* (1958), p 67; cf Catalano, N, 'La fusion des voies de droit', *Colloquium at Liège* (1965), p 284.

ward off the wrath of the national parliaments likely to be provoked by the suggestion that an outside body shall usurp their legislative function. The Community Court also preferred to refer to *pouvoirs réglementaires*,[14] although on another occasion[15] references were made to *compétence réglementaire* (p 687), *normative* (p 688) and *légiférante* (p 692). Without going into semantic niceties[16] the law-making power of the Community organs can be identified as one corresponding to a general accepted notion of legislation. This means that it results in rules of conduct addressed to subjects of Community law which emanate from a definite organ, are made in a set form and, by virtue of the authority vested in the organ, have an obligatory character.

(a) Obligatory acts

These consist of regulations, directives and decisions made by the European Parliament acting jointly with the Council, by the Council or by the Commission in order to carry out their task in accordance with the Treaty (EC Article 249, (ex Art 189), 1st para).

The nomenclature adopted in the EC and EAEC Treaties is identical but it differs in the ECSC Treaty. Thus under Article 14 of the ECSC Treaty we have decisions, recommendations and opinions. 'Decisions' under the ECSC Treaty correspond to regulations under the remaining two Treaties because they are said to be 'binding in their entirety'. However, the ECJ, depending on the scope of the given act, distinguishes between 'general decisions'[17] which are equivalent to regulations and 'individual decisions'[18] which are equivalent to decisions under the EC and EAEC Treaties. 'Recommendations' under the ECSC Treaty correspond to directives under the other two Treaties. 'Opinions' correspond to opinions and, as under the EC and EAEC Treaties, they have no binding force. Bearing in mind these nuances we shall examine the position in terms of the EC Treaty as amended by the TEU.

(i) Regulations

Concept and scope   Regulations have a general scope, are 'binding in their entirety' and are 'directly applicable' in all Member States (EC Article 249, ex Art 189, para 2). The principle applies also to Staff Regulations which, though being a code of employment rules of Community civil servants, have a binding force in the Member States.[19] It follows that, apart from their applicability without the intermediary of the state, regulations are meant to be an instrument of uniformity within the Community. Uniformity is the desired aim but cannot always be achieved and so it may be necessary to leave implementation to the Member States. The agricultural regulations illustrate the point and the problem, for they leave it to each state to execute in its own fashion the system of levies and restitutions,

---

14 Case 15/57: *Compagnie des Hauts Fourneaux de Chasse v High Authority of the ECSC* [1957] ECR 211.
15 Case 20/59: *Italy v High Authority of the ECSC* [1960] ECR 325 terms taken from Rec (1960) 662 at 687, 688, 692.
16 Morand, C A, *La législation dans les Communautés Européennes* (1968), pp 7–17.
17 Case 18/57: *Nold KG v High Authority of the ECSC* [1957] ECR 121; Case 18/62: *Barge v High Authority of the ECSC* [1963] ECR 259, [1965] CMLR 330.
18 Case 20/58: *Phoenix-Rheinrohr AG v High Authority of the ECSC* [1959] ECR 75; Cases 22 and 23/60: *Raymond Elz v High Authority of the ECSC* [1961] ECR 181; Cases 23, 24, 52/63: *Usines Émile Henricot v High Authority of the ECSC* [1963] ECR 217, [1964] CMLR 119.
19 Case 189/85: *Commission v Germany, Re Family Allowances for Community Officials* [1987] ECR 2061, [1988] 2 CMLR 86; Case 186/85: *Commission v Belgium, Re Family Benefits for Community Civil Servants* [1987] ECR 2029, [1988] 2 CMLR 759.

to establish the necessary procedures and impose sanctions. In some cases, eg the free movement of workers[20] and social security of migrant workers,[1] the function of the regulations is to co-ordinate the national systems within the scope of the Treaty provisions regarding the Community rights of free movement or social protection for the Community nationals, their dependants and certain other categories of persons. However these regulations define neither 'workers' nor 'nationality', though both are Community concepts. The former is politically 'neutral' but the latter emanates from the sovereign prerogative of the Member States. It follows that the definition of 'workers' is ultimately a matter for the Community Court[2] but, within the notion of the citizenship of the Union (EC Article 17 (ex Art 8)), each Member State is free to determine who has the privilege of its citizenship and how its citizenship is lost or acquired.

The regulation authorizing Germany to accept the importation of cattle from Denmark, before Denmark joined the Community, exemplifies the use of a regulation otherwise than as a general instrument of Community legislation as it concerns one country only and simply gives leave to take measures appropriate to the situation in hand.[3]

The term 'regulation' is also used to describe measures whereby the Commission imposes 'provisional' and the Council 'definitive' anti-dumping duties in specific situations and in respect of individual parties.

Substantive and procedural requirements In order to constitute a regulation the act of the Community organ must comply with certain conditions. In the first place regulations must rest upon the authority of the Treaty which means that they are made where so provided by the Treaty; if not so provided by the Treaty that act cannot have the character of a regulation.[4] Regulations have to be reasoned (*motivés*) or 'substantiated' in the terms of the Treaty[5] which, in the submission of Advocate-General Lagrange[6] means that they indicate in general terms the aims pursued by the regulations, the reasons which justify the regulations and the outlines of the system adopted.

However, as stated by the ECJ,[7] 'the extent of the requirement laid down by Article 190 [now Art 253] ... to state the reasons on which measures are based depends on the nature of the measure in question', which means, in effect, that a statement of the authority and an intelligible exposition of the policy behind the given measure should suffice. In practice regulations (as well as other measures) contain in their preambles not only a recital of the relevant Treaty provisions but also, often, a lengthy statement of the objectives aimed to be achieved as well as the justification required by the principle of subsidiarity.[8] The latter are particularly useful for the analysis of the text.

---

20 Reg 1612/68 (OJ 1968, L257/2), Art 4(12), (13), (15). ch 19 infra.
1   Reg 1408/71 (OJ 1971, L149/1). Amended and consolidated OJ 1980, C 138/1. See ch 22, infra.
2   See Case 75/63: *Hoekstra (née Unger) v Bestuur der Bedriffsvereniging voor Detailhanded en Ambachten* [1964] ECR 177, [1964] CMLR 319.
3   Reg 15/64 (JO 573/64).
4   This can be inferred from the judgment of the ECJ in Cases 1 and 14/57: *Société des Usines à Tubes de la Sarre v High Authority of the ECSC* [1957–58] ECR 105, referring to 'decision' under the ECSC Treaty.
5   EC Art 253 (ex Art 190); ECSC Art 15; EAEC Art 162.
6   Case 18/62: *Barge v High Authority of the ECSC* [1963] ECR 259, [1965] CMLR 330.
7   Caser 5/67: *W Beus GmbH & Co v HZA München* [1968] ECR 83 at 95, [1968] CMLR 131.
8   See Case 154/83: *Firma Josef Hoche v Bundesanstalt für Landwirtschaftliche Marktordnung* [1985] ECR 1215, [1986] 2 CMLR 632.

Since regulations have to be based on specific articles of the Treaty a general reference to the Treaty or to EC Article 308 (ex Art 235) which deals with the implied powers of the Community,[9] will not suffice. This principle was upheld by the ECJ where the Council regulation on Generalized Tariff preferences was challenged by the Commission[10] and where the UK challenged the Vocational Training Programme approved by the Council.[11]

In the former case there was a conflict of opinion between the Commission and the Council, as the Commission wished to enact the measure in question by virtue of EC Article 113 (now 133), which meant that it could have been passed by a qualified majority in Council. However, the Council amended the proposal hoping to pass it by virtue of EC Article 235 (now 308) for which unanimity is required. Since there was no agreement in the Council the regulation was enacted on the basis of a general reference to the Treaty. The ECJ annulled the regulation for lack of substantiation. In its view, the regulation fell squarely within the ambit of EC Article 113 (now 133) as it was a measure taken in furtherance of the Common Commercial Policy and so EC Article 235 (now 308) would have been inappropriate. However, without reference to any specific article of the Treaty there was no substantiation which is necessary for derivative legislation.

In the latter case the scheme authorized by the Council fell within the ambit of EC Article 128 (now 150(1), as amended) and the budgetary appropriations governed by common policies. Therefore the reference to EC Article 235 (now 308), whose function is 'residual' in the sense that it enables the Member States acting unanimously to supplement insufficient Community powers (as argued by the United Kingdom), would have been clearly inappropriate. Budgetary consideration did not affect the legal basis of the measure involved. It was held equally inappropriate, or rather, superfluous, to include EC Article 308 (ex Art 235) where in a matter of tariff classification a combination of EC Articles 26 and 133 (ex Arts 28 and 113) was the correct legal basis. However the regulation on harmonized commodity description was not annulled since only a technical defect was revealed.[12]

In this context it is apposite to mention the juxtaposition of general and specific provisions of the Treaty, for it is relevant to the exercise of delegated powers and the substantiation of derivative legislation. In principle *lex specialis derogat legis generali*. Thus, for example, EC Article 94 (ex Art 100) stands to EC Article 37 (ex Art 43) as *lex generalis* stands to *lex specialis*. In other words, while the former provides the general basis and procedure for the harmonization of national laws, EC Article 37 (ex Art 43) provides specifically for a common agricultural policy and, within the latter, EC Article 34 (ex Art 40) for a common organization of agricultural markets. It follows that EC Article 37 (ex Art 43) provides a sufficient basis for consumer protection within the general scheme of agricultural policy,[13] or for animal welfare legislation,[14] while EC Article 34(2) (ex Art 40(3)) enables the Commission to issue a regulation for the sale of intervention butter cheaply at Christmas even though it undercuts the sales of margarine. Thus the complaint

---

9 See p 48.
10 Case 45/86: *Commission v Council* [1987] ECR 1493, [1988] 2 CMLR 131 at para 13.
11 Case 56/88: *United Kingdom v Council* [1989] ECR 1615, [1989] 2 CMLR 789.
12 Case 165/87: *Commission v Council* [1988] ECR 5545, [1990] 1 CMLR 457. On the application of Art 308 (ex Art 235) see supra, p 125 notes 14 and 15.
13 Case 68/86: *United Kingdom v Council, Re Agricultural Hormones* [1988] ECR 855, [1988] 2 CMLR 543.
14 Case 131/86: *United Kingdom v Council, Re the protection of battery hens* [1988] ECR 905, [1988] 2 CMLR 364.

of margarine traders that the regulation is invalid because it is discriminatory cannot be sustained since the common organization of the market for milk (butter) based on intervention is different from that for fats (margarine) based on production aid. On that ground the case can also be distinguished from the Isoglucose cases mentioned below.

The justification for substantiation is clear for it is a safeguard against arbitrary exercise of authority. It is also essential for the parties concerned to know their legal position and to be able to defend their rights. In other words, as explained the ECJ (in a case involving a decision)[15] 'In imposing upon the Commission the obligation to state reasons for its decisions, Article 190 [now 253] is not taking mere formal considerations into account but seeks to give an opportunity to the parties of defending their rights, to the Court of exercising its supervisory functions and to Member States and to all interested nationals of ascertaining the circumstances in which the Commission has applied the Treaty.' What the Court said about the Commission can equally be said about the Council and what can be said about a decision can equally be said about a regulation. Therefore, where, in the circumstances of the case, the reasons turn out to be insufficient, the sanction of nullity may be applied on substantive grounds and also on the ground of the infringement of an essential procedural requirement.[16] Perhaps the most instructive examples of the annulment on that ground are the *Isoglucose* cases[17] which have incidentally raised important questions concerning the Parliament's participation in Community legislation and the right of intervention before the ECJ. At issue was the validity of Council Regulation 1293/79 (OJ 1979, L162/10) fixing quotas for the production of isoglucose and imposing a tax on this product. The Regulation was successfully challenged by isoglucose producers since it discriminated in favour of sugar producers. However the Regulation was also bad because in the circumstances the essential requirement, ie consultation with Parliament in accordance with EC Article 37(2) (ex Art 43(2)), was not observed.

Regulations are presumed valid and effective unless and until they have been declared invalid by the Community Court.[18] The temporal effect of the declaration of nullity is within the discretion of the ECJ subject to the guidelines laid down in a case concerning social security rights.[19] In principle, the judgments of the ECJ have a retrospective effect but, exceptionally, they may have prospective effect only.[20]

Regulations have to be published in the Official Journal of the Community. They become binding on the date specified therein or, in the absence of a commencing date, on the twentieth day following their publication.[1]

---

15 Case 24/62: *Germany v Commission* [1963] ECR 63 at 69.
16 EC Art 230 (ex Art 173): Case 18/57: *Nold K G v High Authority of the ECSC* [1959] ECR 41 at 52; Case 6/72: *Europemballage Corpn and Continental Can Co Inc v Commission* [1973] ECR 215, [1973] CMLR 199; Case 73/74: *Groupement des Fabricants de Papiers de Belgique v EC Commission* [1975] ECR 1491, [1976] 1 CMLR 589.
17 Joined Cases 103/77 and 145/77: *Royal Scholten-Honig (Holdings) Ltd v Intervention Board for Agricultural Produce* [1978] ECR 2037, [1979] 1 CMLR 675; Case 138/79: *S A Roquette Frères v Council* [1980] ECR 3333; and Case 139/79: *Maizena GmbH v Council* [1980] ECR 3393; Jacobs, F, *Isoglucose Resurgent: Two Powers of the European Parliament upheld by the Court*, 18 CML Rev (1981), p 219.
18 Case 101/78: *Granaria BV v Hoofdproduktschap voor Akkerbouwprodukten* [1979] ECR 623, [1979] 3 CMLR 124.
19 Case 41/84: *Pinna v Caisse d'Allocations Familiales de la Savoie* [1986] ECR 1, [1988] 1 CMLR 350; see also Case 112/83: *Société de Produits de Mais SA v Administration des Douanes et Droits Indirects* [1985] ECR 719, [1988] 1 CMLR 459.
20 See eg Case 309/85: *Barra v Belgium and City of Liège, Re Education Fees* [1988] ECR 355, [1988] 2 CMLR 409.
1 EAEC Art 163(1); EC Art 254 (ex Art 191(2)).

By virtue of EC Article 254(1) (ex Art 191(1)) regulations, directives and decisions adopted in accordance with the procedure laid down in EC Article 251 (ex Art 189b) shall be signed by the President of the European Parliament and by the President of the Council and published in the Official Journal. They shall enter into force on the date specified therein or, in the absence thereof, on the twentieth day following that of their publication. However, neither the publicity nor the form of the act will be decisive in determining the nature of the act, that is, whether or not it is a regulation. The ECJ took the view that it was necessary to consider the contents and nature rather than the form of the act to determine its legal nature.[2] Should this be otherwise, improper acts dressed up as regulations would enable the Community organs to exercise their powers arbitrarily and so would erode the legal protection under the Treaty.

The effect of regulations   As we have observed earlier, regulations have a mandatory effect. They bind the states and have the force of law in their territories without the need of transformation or confirmation by their legislatures. Thus it was held by the ECJ[3] that Council Regulation 1975/69 and Commission Regulation 2195/69, which provided for the payment of a premium in respect of slaughtered dairy cows, were 'directly applicable' and required no domestic provisions to make them effective in Italy so as to create rights vested in the individuals concerned. They left no discretion to Member States. Therefore Italy was in default because she failed to meet her obligation, the inefficiency of the national apparatus affording no defence.[4] In the literature the power to legislate in this way reflects the 'institutional autonomy'[5] of the Community and the concept of 'delegated legislation'.[6] The Member States are at the receiving end and it is their duty to see that the regulation is carried out. 'Consequently', held the ECJ,[7] 'all methods of implementation are contrary to the Treaty which would have the result of creating an obstacle to the direct effect of Community Regulations and jeopardizing their simultaneous and uniform application in the whole of the Community.'

Implementation and derogations   The obligatory nature of the regulation and the duty to implement it are well illustrated in the *Tachograph*[8] case where the British Government unsuccessfully contended that it was free to enact a permissive measure when Council Regulation 1463/70 insisted that the installation of recording equipment in certain vehicles was compulsory and subject to sanction

---

2   Cf Cases 16 and 17/62: *Confédération Nationale des Producteurs des Fruits et Légumes v Council* [1962] ECR 471 at 478–479, [1963] CMLR 150 at 173–74. Case 250/81: *Greek Canners Association v Commission* [1982] ECR 3535, [1983] 2 CMLR 32. Case 26/86: *Deutz und Gelderman v Council* [1987] ECR 941, [1988] 1 CMLR 668; Cases 97/86, 193/86 and 215/86 *ASTERIS and Greece v Commission* [1988] 3 CMLR 493 at paras 13, 14 [1988] ECR 2181.
3   Case 93/71: *Orsolina Leonesio v Italian Ministry of Agriculture* [1972] ECR 287 at 295, [1973] CMLR 343.
4   Case 39/72: *Commission v Italy* [1973] ECR 101, [1973] CMLR 439. See also Case 309/84: *Commission v Italy* [1986] ECR 599.
5   Rideau, J, *Le rôle des états membres dans l'application du droit communautaire*, AFDI, 1972, p 864 (884–5).
6   Pescatore, P, *L'ordre juridiques des Communautées européennes* (2nd edn, 1975), pp 192–193.
7   Note 4, supra, ECR at 114.
8   Case 128/78: *Commission v United Kingdom* [1979] ECR 419, [1979] 2 CMLR 45 at para 9, citing its own judgment in Case 39/72: *Commission v Italy* [1973] ECR 101, [1973] CMLR 439.

for non-compliance. Holding the United Kingdom liable for a breach of the Treaty the ECJ ruled that it would be inconceivable to allow a Member State to implement a regulation 'in an incomplete or selective manner ... so as to render abortive certain aspects of Community legislation which it has opposed or which it considered contrary to its national interest ...'.

Earlier the ECJ[9] defended the integrity of Community law by pointing out that a Member State, when passing a regulation into the national law, must not disguise its Community character by altering, for example, the date on which the regulation came into force. However for practical reasons, a regulation may have to be implemented in the terms of domestic law (as was, for example, the case of the EC Egg Marketing Regulations 2772/75 and 95/69 on labelling and quality control) in which case a national measure would be permitted if not incompatible with the terms of the regulation.[10] In other words, in the absence of any provision in the Regulations regarding the purchase of bands and labels to be affixed to egg packs, the Member States are free to make arrangements for the issue of bands and labels and charge for the supervision of the marketing system.

Indeed the regulation may expressly provide for a national implementing measure[11] indicating a time limit for doing so but as repeatedly emphasized by the ECJ it cannot be overridden by national legislation.[12] Although its validity may be challenged albeit indirectly in the course of proceedings at the national level[13] it can be annulled only by the Community Court.[14] However the finding of illegality of a regulation by the ECJ in one case may be relied upon by national courts in other proceedings.[15]

The Court of Justice has the power to review the legality of acts adopted jointly by the European Parliament and the Council, of acts of the Council, of the Commission and of the European Central Bank other than recommendations and opinions, and of acts of the European Parliament intended to produce legal effects vis-à-vis third parties (EC Article 230(1) (ex Art 173(1))). The 'acts' include, of course, regulations. However individuals may challenge only decisions addressed to them or decisions which, although in the form of regulation or a decision addressed to another person, are of direct and individual concern to the former (EC Article 230(4), ex Art 173(4)). The meaning of regulation or decision in the context of actions brought by individuals has given rise to a problem of interpretation. Thus in Case 138/79,[16] in which the applicant sought the annulment

---

9   Case 34/73: *Variola SpA v Amministrazione Italiane delle Finanze* [1973] ECR 981 at para 15.
10   Case 31/78: *Bussone v Italian Ministry for Agriculture and Forestry* [1978] ECR 2429 at 2444, [1979] 3 CMLR 18 at 30. See also Case 272/83: *Commission v Italy, Re Agricultural Producer Groups* [1985] ECR 1057; [1987] 2 CMLR 426.
11   Eg Reg 1463/70 (OJ 1970, L164/1), Art 21(1) – re tachograph.
12   Case 6/64: *Costa Flaminio v ENEL* [1964] ECR 585 at 586–587, [1964] CMLR 425 at 456; Case 43/71: *Politi SAS v Italian Ministry of Finance, Re statistical levies* [1971] ECR 1039 at 1048–1049, [1973] CMLR 60, *Simmenthal Cases* 35/76: [1976] ECR 1871, [1977] 2 CMLR 1; 106/77 (No 2) [1978] ECR 629, [1978] 3 CMLR 263; 70/77 (No 3) [1978] ECR 1453, [1978] 3 CMLR 670.
13   See Case 199/86: *Raiffeisen Hauptgenossenschaft v Bundesanstalt für landwitschaftliche Marktordnung* [1988] ECR 1169, [1989] 2 CMLR 999.
14   Cases 119 and 120/76: *Ölmühle Hamburg A-G v HZA Hamburg-Waltershof* and *Becher v HZA Bremen-Nord* [1977] ECR 1269, [1979] 2 CMLR 83; see also Case 273/81: *Société Laitière de Gacé SA v FORMA* [1982] ECR 4193, [1984] 1 CMLR 542.
15   See Case 66/80: *International Chemical Corpn Sp A v Amministrazione delle Finanze dello Stato* [1981] ECR 1191, [1983] 2 CMLR 593.
16   See p 136 note 17, supra; see also Case C-229/88: *Cargill BV v Commission* [1990] ECR I-1303; [1990] 2 CMLR 753 (no *locus standi*), and Case C-152/88 *Sofrimport Sarl v Commission* [1990] ECR I-2477.

of a Council Regulation fixing a production quota for isoglucose, the defendant unsuccessfully contended that the application was inadmissible because it was directed against a regulation and, therefore, outside the scope of Article 173(4) (now 230(4)). The Court ruled that the Regulation was a measure in which the undertakings manufacturing isoglucose had a direct and individual concern.

In an earlier case[17] the applicants sought the annulment of Council Regulation 1692/72 concerning protective measures on the importation of motor cycles from Japan but the Court found that it was not of direct and individual concern to them. It would only be so if the applicants, pursuant to that measure, were refused an import authorization. In that case they would be able to raise the matter before the national court, which should, where appropriate, refer the question of its validity to the ECJ by virtue of EC Article 234 (ex Art 177). The Court added that 'the possibility of determining more or less precisely the number or even the identity of the persons to whom a measure applies by no means implies that it must be regarded as being of individual concern to them'. Indeed the Regulation could not produce effects in individual cases until it had been implemented by the national authorities. Similarly Council Regulation 3781/85 establishing a system of penalties for infringements of the provisions concerning fishing in the Act of Accession of Spain and Portugal was held to be of no individual concern to an association of fishermen. Its members would be affected only by a national decision which should only be taken if several conditions are complied with, and provided that decision is confirmed by the Commission.[18]

Apart from providing for implementation by national authorities a regulation may provide for derogation, in which case national law will apply in the area specifically reserved for deviation from the general scope of the regulation. A derogation grants the Member States a discretion whether to apply the specific provision of the regulation or substitute for it a national rule. However, derogations have to be construed restrictively and applied strictly within the permissiveness of the regulation. Thus, for example, Regulation 171/83 concerned with conservation of fishery resources provided that although, according to Community rules, fishing for plaice was allowed to the minimum size of 25cm in length of the species, national rules could restrict the size to 27cm. However, complying with the Community rules, a Dutch fisherman was correctly prosecuted for the breach of national rules, such rules being applicable to Dutchmen by virtue of the derogation.[19]

Council and Commission regulations   Since the Council and the Commission are empowered to make regulations, a theoretical and practical question as to the standing of the Commission regulations vis-à-vis regulations made by the Council may arise. Indeed Advocate-General Roemer argued in a case[20] concerning regulations issued by the Council that they should override regulations issued by the Commission. In principle, where each legislates in its own right, there should be no conflict because the two institutions operate in their respective sphere of

17 Case 123/77: *Unione Nazionale Importatori e Commercianti Motoveicoli Esteri (UNICME) v Council* [1978] ECR 845.
18 Case 55/86: *Association Provincial de Armadores de Buques de Pesca de Gran Sol de Ponteverda (Arposol) v Council* [1988] ECR 13 at s 13 [1990] 3 CMLR 80.
19 Case 53/86: *Officer van Justitie v Romkes* [1987] ECR 2691, [1988] 3 CMLR 126.
20 Case 32/65: *Italian v Council and Commission* [1966] ECR 389 at 415, [1969] CMLR 39 at 46.

competence and one is not hierarchically superior to the other. In practice, however, the Commission exercises substantial powers delegated to it by the Council, notably in the fields of agricultural policy, customs and competition, and makes regulations accordingly. The procedure of delegation itself was challenged, albeit unsuccessfully, in the *Köster*[1] case involving the setting up and operation of management committees to administer the common market in cereals. The objections that, despite the requirement of consulting Parliament under EC Article 37(2) (ex Art 43(2)) the Council alone made the relevant regulation and that, by delegating its powers to the Commission, it debilitated its decision-making power, were overruled as the Council retained control and could substitute its own measures for those taken by the Commission. The Court, following an earlier case,[2] held that the delegation did not contravene the Treaty.

Another leading case[3] was concerned with the organization of the common market in sugar. Under the relevant regulation the Commission was empowered to take measures to prevent disturbances in the market resulting from price fluctuations. Its powers were to be exercised under the management committee procedure. However the Commission delegated to Italy the power to control the Italian market and the Italian Government, in turn, enacted a decree imposing a levy on sugar stockholders. The latter challenged the validity of the decree before Italian courts which, on reference, led the Community Court to pronounce upon the validity of the sub-delegation of the Commission's powers to Italy. The ECJ ruled that, whilst the delegation to the Commission was in order, the sub-delegation to Italy was not. It acknowledged the need of 'wide powers of discretion and action'[4] in the hands of the Commission to carry out its mandate but ruled, in effect, that even an extensive interpretation of the task of implementation could not entail a further delegation going out of control of the Council.[5] The principle that *delegatus non potest delegare* has been vindicated.

The third leading case illustrates the operation of delegated powers in the implementation of EC Article 83 (ex Art 87) concerned with the enforcement of the competition policy. By Regulation 17/62[6] the Council provided for the procedure to investigate and adjudicate violations of EC Articles 81 and 82 (ex Arts 85 and 86) and laid down sanctions to be administered by the Commission. It delegated to the Commission the power to lay down implementing provisions including provisions governing the hearing of alleged violations before the Commission. The accused firm challenged the legality of such wide powers delegated to the Commission and argued that, since they included the power of legislation, they went beyond the scope of the exercise of powers conferred on the Commission by the Council for the implementation of the rules laid down by the Council by virtue of the 4th indent of EC Article 211 (ex Art 155). The ECJ, explaining the scope of EC Article 211 (ex Art 155), stressed that the function of implementation entails the taking of the appropriate measures which includes measures of a legislative nature, such as regulations.

1   Case 25/70: *EVGV v Köster* [1970] ECR 1161, [1972] CMLR 255. See also Case 278/84: *Germany v Commission, Re Revaluation of the Green Mark* [1988] 1 CMLR 632; Cases 167/88: *Association Générale de Producteurs de Blé v Office national Interprofessionel des Céréales* [1991] 2 CMLR 61; C-365/89: *Cargill BV v Produktschap voor Marganine* [1991] ECR I-3045.
2   Case 9/56: *Meroni & Co v High Authority* [1957–58] ECR 133.
3   Case 23/75: *Rey Soda v Cassa Conguaglio Zucchero* [1975] ECR 1279, [1976] 1 CMLR 185.
4   At paras 10 and 11.
5   Case 41/69: *ACF Chemiefarma v Commission* [1970] ECR 661.
6   OJ 1959–1962/87.

The position of delegated legislation has been clarified by Article 10 of the Single European Act which, by supplementing the provisions of EC Article 145 (now 202), conferred on the Commission, in the Acts which the Council adopts, powers for the implementation of the rules which the Council lays down. The Council may impose certain requirements in respect of the exercise of these powers and may also reserve the right, in specific cases, to exercise directly implementing powers itself. The procedure for the exercise of implementing powers must comply with principles and rules to be laid down in advance by the Council, acting unanimously on a proposal from the Commission and after obtaining the opinion of the European Parliament.

Thus Council regulations and Commission regulations fulfil different functions and their validity has to be tested in the light of the Treaty provisions governing the respective powers and functions of the two institutions. If the Commission issues regulations in its capacity as the executor of the decisions of the Council its regulations have to conform to the letter and the spirit of the delegation but, as can be inferred from the cases mentioned above, the delegated powers have to be wide enough to give effect to the provisions of the Treaty.

In exercising its powers, whether original or delegated, the Commission has to act *infra vires* for the measures it enacts will be interpreted narrowly.[7]

However, the scope of the delegation will determine the Commission's freedom of action. Thus in the Christmas butter scheme case[8] the relevant regulation was held to be valid because of the wide implementing powers granted to the Commission, while in the tuna case[9] there was no scope for the Commission to use its imagination in providing additional rules. Therefore both the implementing and the tertiary regulation fixing compensation were void.

In the event of conflict between a Council regulation and implementing Commission decision the former (assuming it is valid per se) must prevail simply because the exercise of the delegated power has to conform with the scope of the delegation, but the competence to strike out the latter is within the functions of the ECJ. This is an aspect of the exclusive jurisdiction of the Court and of the judicial control of the acts of the Institutions. A Council regulation, which provided that customs duties which have not been recovered because of a mistake of the customs authorities, enabled such authorities to waive the duties if the importer was an innocent party to the mistake. A Commission decision regarding the post-clearance recovery of duties provided for a delayed recovery which clearly contradicted the intention of the regulation. A German court faced with the protests of an importer asked the ECJ whether it could, in the circumstances, declare the Commission decision invalid. The ECJ reiterated the principle that it was only competent to exercise the judicial control over Community acts. Thus national authorities must hold such acts valid and, in case of doubt, seek a preliminary ruling from the ECJ.[10]

---

7   Case 61/86: *United Kingdom v Commission, Re Clawback on Export of Sheep* [1988] ECR 431, [1988] 2 CMLR 98; see also Case C-212/94: *FMC plc & Others v Intervention Board for Agriculture* [1996] ECR I-389; Cases 305/85 and 142/86: *Re Ewe Slaughter Premiums, United Kingdom v Commission* [1988] ECR 467, [1988] 2 CMLR 169 and Case 162/86: *Livestock Sales Transport Ltd v Intervention Board for Agricultural Produce* [1988] ECR 489, [1988] 2 CMLR 186.

8   Cases 279–280/84 and 285–286/84: *Walter Rau Lebensmittelwerke v Commission* [1987] ECR 1069, [1988] 2 CMLR 704.

9   Case 264/86: *France v Commission, Re Tuna Producers* [1988] ECR 973, [1989] 1 CMLR 13.

10   Case 314/85: *Foto-Frost v HZA Lübeck-Ost* [1987] ECR 4199, [1988] 3 CMLR 57.

(ii)   Directives[11]

Concept and scope   As compared with regulations which are, in principle, 'binding in their entirety', directives issued by the Council and the Commission are 'binding as to the result to be achieved, upon each Member State to which they are addressed' and the choice of the method is left to the state concerned (3rd sentence of EC Article 249 (ex Art 189); but under ECSC, Article 14 recommendations correspond to directives). We can see that, unlike regulations, directives are not meant to be an instrument of uniformity even if the same objective is aimed at when a directive is addressed to several states simultaneously unless, of course, the wording of a particular directive leaves no discretion.[12] In practice, directives are used mainly to effect approximation of national laws in accordance with EC Article 94 (ex Art 100). In this respect EC Article 94 (ex Art 100) delimits both the scope and the methods providing for directives 'for the approximation of such laws, regulations or administrative provisions of the Member States as directly affect the establishment or functioning of the common market'.

Like regulations directives have to be reasoned or 'motivated' and based on the Treaty. Indeed, they are subordinated to the Treaty provisions.[13] They have to be notified to the addressees and will take effect upon such notification.[14] They may be addressed in the language of the addressee state.[15]

Directives must be addressed to states, they cannot be addressed to individuals.[16] Being in the nature of commands directives impose specific obligations upon the Member States. In the first place they have to be implemented completely[17] and in the most effective way. It follows that directives must be implemented by 'binding acts', not by 'advisory circulars'. Thus, held the ECJ,[18] 'mere administrative practices which by their nature may be changed at the whim of the authorities and which lack appropriate publicity do not constitute proper implementation ...'. Moreover, the duty to implement is the responsibility of the state or states to which the directive has been addressed even if within that state (or states) the constituent units (eg provinces) have legislative powers.[19]

The duty to implement is enforceable within the discretion of the Commission under EC Article 226 (ex Art 169), but not by a private party. Moreover the Commission cannot be forced to proceed under the pressure of a private party.[20]

---

11   See generally Prechal, S, *Directives in European Community Law* (1995).
12   See Case 38/77: *Enka BV v Inspecteur der Invoerrechten* [1977] ECR 2203. See also the ASTERIS case, p 137, note 2, supra.
13   Case 103/84: *Commission v Italy, Re Subsidy for Municipal Transport* [1986] ECR 1759, [1987] 2 CMLR 825.
14   EC Art 254(2) (ex Art 191(2)); EAEC Art 162(2).
15   Council Reg 1/58, Art 3, JO, 6 October 1958, p 385/58 (Sp edn 1952–1958, p 59).
16   Cases 56, 58/64: *Etablissements Consten and Grundig v Commission* [1966] ECR 299 at 337, [1966] CMLR 418 at 468.
17   See Case 239/85: *Commission v Belgium, Re Toxic and Dangerous Waste* [1986] ECR 3645; [1988] 1 CMLR 248; see also Case 235/84: *Commission v Italy, Re Business Transfer Legislation* [1986] ECR 2291, [1987] 3 CMLR 115.
18   Case 160/82: *Commission v Netherlands* [1984] 1 CMLR 230. See also Case 291/84: *Commission v Netherlands, Re Groundwater Directive* [1987] ECR 3483; Case C-381/92: *Commission v Ireland* [1944] ECR I-215 (para 7); and Case C-311/95: *Commission v Greece* [1996] ECR I-2433, [1989] 1 CMLR 479.
19   Case 1/86: *Commission v Belgium, Re the Groundwater Directive* [1987] ECR 2797; [1989] 1 CMLR 474. See also Case C-290/89: *Commission v Belgium* [1991] ECR I-2851.
20   Case 247/87: *Star Fruit Co SA v Commission* [1989] ECR 291, paras 11 and 12, [1990] 1 CMLR 733.

It has been suggested[1] that the choice of the method permitted by the Treaty implies the choice of the instrument and the choice of the contents of the instrument. It seems, however, that the choice of the method implies a procedural discretion, ie the choice of the type of instrument or machinery of implementation that suits best the given national system. As regards the contents (or substance) the discretion clearly depends upon the particularity or the degree of detail of the directive in question as well as the state of the existing national law involved. Thus in the eyes of the ECJ[2] it is not sufficient that the existing national law fulfils the aims of the directive for its details must also be implemented if not already covered unequivocally. This does not preclude creation of rights for individuals or pleading the directive before the municipal courts,[3] as emphasized in the *Francovich* case.[4]

Whilst the choice of the method is left to the addressee the Community usually sets a time limit upon the implementation of directives. The reason for this is that time is needed in order to adapt the municipal law accordingly. Even so states are not always able to comply promptly. The speed with which the Value Added Tax was introduced in Italy is a good example of this, showing, incidentally, that a directive is less effective than a regulation in so far as its availability to individuals may depend upon implementation. Therefore there are many enforcement actions concerned with inadequate or untimely implementation of directives. In most cases a threat of action will suffice and, where the Member State complies, the action will be withdrawn. However no Member State can plead the complexity of the implementation or the necessity of wide consultations in defence of non-compliance,[5] or even a terrorist[6] act, if the damage caused thereby had not been repaired with due diligence.

As in the case of regulations only the ECJ is competent to rule on the validity of directives. Therefore, in case of doubt raised within a national jurisdiction, reference to the ECJ for a preliminary ruling ought to be made.[7]

Implementation and derogations Directives vary considerably in their scope and the precision of their text, especially where they are used as an instrument of harmonization of national laws. There they have to overcome the inbuilt resistance of often well-entrenched national rules. Consequently for political, not legislative reasons, in order to have the measure enacted they often reflect a compromise at the level of the lowest common denominator. Since, unlike instruments of international legislation, they cannot be enacted subject to reservations, they may be riddled with derogations giving effect to the residual force of national law. Here again the doctrine of the 'occupied field' comes to the fore since the scope of a particular directive will delineate the respective Community and national

1 Easson, A J, 'EEC Directives for the Harmonisation of Law', Y E L (1981) p 1 (at 33).
2 Case 91/81: *Commission v Italy (Re Collective Redundancies)* [1982] ECR 2133, [1982] 3 CMLR 468 followed by Case 131/84: *Commission v Italy* [1985] ECR 3531.
3 Eg Dir 64/221/EEC (JO 850/64) Art 4(3): 'The Member States cannot introduce new measures or acts which are of a more restrictive nature than those in force at the time of notification of this directive'; Case 41/74: *Van Duyn v Home Office* [1975] Ch 358, [1975] ECR 1337; cf Case 28/67: *Molkerei-Zentrale v Hauptzollamt Paderborn* [1968] ECR 143, [1968] CMLR 187; see also Case 9/70: *Grad v Finanzamt Traunstein* [1970] ECR 825, [1971] CMLR 1 (decision and directives on turnover tax).
4 Infra p 148.
5 See Case 58/81: *Commission v Luxembourg (Re Head of Household Allowance)* [1982] ECR 2175, [1982] 3 CMLR 482.
6 Case 101/84: *Commission v Italy (Re Failure to provide Transport Statistics due to Destruction of Data Processing Centre)* [1985] ECR 2629, [1986] 2 CMLR 352.
7 *R v Minister of Agriculture Fisheries and Food, ex p Fédération Européene de la Santé Animale* [1988] 3 CMLR 207, QB.

competence. Indeed, if the directive is drafted so tightly that it leaves no doubt as to its scope, and if the business regulated therein is exhaustively treated, there will be no gaps and, therefore, no room for manœuvre, not even for a permissive rule indicating the option of derogation left to Member States.[8] But this may not be so.

Thus, while directives have to be implemented 'completely', their 'complete' implementation in substance may, nevertheless, entrench divisive elements of national laws. This is well illustrated by the derogations in the directives on consumer protection, for example the directive on the safety of toys[9] and product liability.[10] After nine years of labour in enacting the latter it is obvious that concessions to national laws had to be made. Many other examples can be quoted: for example, the directive on the labelling of products distinguishing between dangerous substances and dangerous preparations imposed Community rules with regard to the former but not on preparations containing dangerous substances. In respect of the latter, Member States are free to apply their own laws though they have no discretion as far as the aims of the directives which have to be achieved.[11] Similarly the directives on environmental protection;[12] company law;[13] public works.[14]

A directive may also include a special derogation clause whereby the permissive rule cannot be applied unilaterally but its exercise is conditional upon permission granted by the Council.[15]

Interpretation of directives   Interpretation of directives involves not only the construction of the Community text[16] but also of the national implementing legislation and the residual national law. It is common ground that the implementing legislation ought to be so interpreted as to give effect to the intention of the Community legislator expressed in the directive itself.[17] It is also common ground that derogations must be interpreted strictly otherwise the whole object of the

---

8 See eg Case 195/84: *Denkavit Futtermittel GmbH v Land Nordhein-Westfalen (Re Directives on Additives to Animal Foodstuffs)* [1985] ECR 3181, [1987] 3 CMLR 585; Case 29/87: *Dansk Denkavit v Landbrugsministeriet* [1988] ECR 2965, [1990] 1 CMLR 203; Case 130/85: *Wulro BV v Tuchtgerecht van de Stichting Scharreleieren-Controle (Re labelling of Eggs)* [1987] ECR 675, [1988] 1 CMLR 496; Case 306/84: *Commission v Belgium* [1987] ECR 675; [1988] 1 CMLR 768; Case 60/86: *Commission v United Kingdom* [1988] 3 CMLR 437; Case 264/86: *France v Commission* [1988] ECR 973, [1989] 1 CMLR 13; Case 255/86: *Commission v Belgium, Re Labelling of Bulk Fruit and Vegetables* [1988] ECR 693, [1989] 3 CMLR 91.
9 OJ 1988, L187.
10 OJ 1985, L210.
11 Case 187/84: *Italy v Caldana, Re Motor Oil* [1985] ECR 3013; [1989] 1 CMLR 137.
12 Case 302/86: *Commission v Denmark, Re Disposable Beer Cans* [1988] ECR 4607, [1989] 1 CMLR 619; Case 228/87: *Pretura Unifacata di Torino v Persons Unknown (Re Purity of Drinking Water)* [1988] ECR 5099, [1990] 1 CMLR 716.
13 Case 112/86: *AMRO Aandelen Fonds v Inspecteur der Registrar Successie (Re Company Taxation)* [1987] ECR 4453, [1989] 1 CMLR 789; Case 136/87: *Ubbink Isolatie BV v Dak-en Wandtechniekl BV (Re Company Liability to Third Parties)* [1988] ECR 4665, [1990] 1 CMLR 262.
14 Cases 27–29/86: *Constructions et Entreprises Industrielles SA v Association Intercommunale pour les Autoroutes des Ardennes (Re Tenders Specifications)* [1987] ECR 3347, [1989] 2 CMLR 224.
15 Case 203/87: *Commission v Italy, Re Zero Rating for Earthquake Victims* [1989] ECR 371, [1989] 2 CMLR 461.
16 Case 81/87: *R v HM Treasury, ex p Daily Mail and General Trust plc* [1988] ECR 5483, [1988] 3 CMLR 713; Case C-106/89: *Marleasing SA v La Commercial Internacional de Alimentación SA* [1990] ECR I-4135.
17 Case 31/87: *Gebroeders Beentjes BV v Netherlands (Re Public Works Contract)* [1988] ECR 4635, [1990] 1 CMLR 287.

directive might be frustrated.[18] It is interesting to note that the directives to combat sex discrimination have provided a fertile ground for litigation and, consequently, for the interpretation of the relevant Treaty provisions,[19] the directives themselves and of the implementing legislation. It goes without saying that questions concerning all three aspects are referable to the ECJ for a preliminary ruling, the last one, because national implementation raises the question of supremacy of Community law in face of its conflict with national law. In the light of their interpretation the effects of the directives are revealed.

The effect of directives   Directives, being commands addressed to Member States, have a direct effect upon their addressees. It is the duty of the latter to give effect to their obligation in this respect. In principle, a directive takes effect only through the domestic measures implementing it;[20] and, once implemented, the directive remains as a guide to the interpretation of the domestic measures but not as a distinct source of rights.[1] Failure to enact within the specified time or incomplete enactment constitutes a breach of the solidarity principle and exposes the state concerned to enforcement proceedings.[2] Once the obligation has been perfected, for example by the effluction of time, there is no defence except the invalidity of the directive itself (on the ground of procedural or substantive defect), which would have to be declared by the ECJ since Member States have no competence to do so.

The plea that the failure to implement has had no adverse effect on the functioning of the Common Market, tantamount to saying that the directive was superfluous, would be of no avail.[3]

Various other excuses have been offered, albeit without success, for non-implementation of directives, for example: difficulties in appreciating all relevant issues and complexity of national procedures;[4] lack of technical facilities to institute appropriate procedures;[5] the fact that only few combined rail/road and road/inland waterway operations, regulated by a relevant transport directive, occur.[6] It is clear that the burden of proof in showing why the given directive has not been implemented into the national system lies on the defaulting country. Such a burden is not easy to discharge bearing in mind that all the Member States are involved in the legislative process. Since each Member State is responsible for its own

---

18   See Case 237/84: *Commission v Belgium, Re the Business Transfer Directive* [1986] ECR 1247, [1988] 2 CMLR 865; see also Case 324/86: *Foreningen of Arbejdsledere i Danmark v Daddy Dance Hall (Re Employees' Rights on Transfer of Undertaking)* [1988] ECR 739, [1989] 2 CMLR 517.

19   See ch 32, infra.

20   Eg Case 8/81: *Becker v Finanzamt Münster-Innenstadt* [1982] ECR Art 53, paras 17–25.

 1   Case C-106/89: *Marleasing* [1990] ECR I-4135. Hence, when a directive has been properly implemented, reliance upon the directive as a source of rights has been described as having no purpose: eg Case 270/81: *Felicitas Rickmers-Linie v Finanzamt für verkehrsteuern Hamburg* [1982] ECR 2771, paras 24–27; Case 222/84: *Johnson v Chief Constable of the RUC* [1986] ECR 1651, paras 51 and 56–59; Cases C-253/96 to C-258/96: *Kampelmann v Landschaftsverband Westfalen-Lippe* [1997] ECR I-6907, paras 40–47.

 2   See eg Case 147/77: *Commission v Italy (Re Animal Slaughter Directive)* [1978] ECR 1307, [1978] 3 CMLR 428; Case 124/81: *Commission v United Kingdom, Re Ultra Heat Treated Milk* [1983] ECR 203, [1983] 2 CMLR 1.

 3   See Case 95/77: *Commission v Netherlands* [1978] ECR 863.

 4   Case 390/85 *Commission v Belgium: Re Stock Exchange Listing Directives* [1987] ECR 761, [1988] 1 CMLR 146.

 5   Case 419/85: *Commission v Italy, Re the Community Driving Licence* [1987] ECR 2115, [1988] 3 CMLR 461.

 6   Case 420/85: *Commission v Italy, Re Combined Transport* [1987] ECR 2983, [1989] 1 CMLR 490.

default reciprocity is not required. Therefore the fact that some other fellow Member State has failed to implement provides no lawful excuse or defence for a state in default.[7]

The bulk of the enforcement cases consists of failures to implement directives. It reflects the efficacy of the national legislative machinery and, perhaps, the commitment to the cause of integration.

Rights of individuals   While directives are binding upon the Member States the rights of individuals arising therefrom depend on the scope of any particular directive. By their designation they have, in principle, no direct effect upon individuals unless implemented into national legislation. However, in substance they may well be sufficiently explicit and detailed to make transformation (or transposition) a mere formality and thus take effect in the absence of implementation. In such a case they should have an overriding effect on inconsistent national law. This was the tenor of the decision of the Belgian Counseil d'Etat which held[8] that Directive 64/221 purporting to co-ordinate the special measures concerning the movement and residence of workers on the grounds of public policy, public security and public health, had such effect in Belgium. The ECJ confirmed this principle in the *Van Duyn* case[9] but a few years later the French Conseil d'Etat denied the direct effect of the same directive.[10] However, in contrast with regulations and Treaty provisions, an essential condition for the direct effect of a directive is that the directive has not been implemented, properly or at all, by the Member State concerned within the time fixed for doing so.[11] The direct effect of Directives is distinct from that of other provisions of EC law.[12]

In *Grad v Finanzamt Traunstein*[13] the ECJ stated that 'if, in accordance with Article 189, regulations are directly applicable and consequently are, by their very nature, capable of producing direct legal effects, it does not follow that the other acts mentioned in this article can never have similar effects' and concluded that 'the provisions of the decision and of the directives, taken together, produce direct effects in the relations between the Member States and their citizens and create for the latter the right to enforce them before the Courts'. Grad, a haulage contractor, was caught in a tax law confusion. By Council Decision 65/271[14] a uniform turnover tax system to promote competition in transport was introduced. Later two Council directives[15] provided for the introduction of the Value Added

---

7   Case C-38/89: *Ministère Public v Blanquernon* [1990] ECR I-83 [1990] 2 CMLR 340.
8   *Corvelyn v Belgium* (7 October 1968, unreported); (1969) Cahiers de droit européen 343, at 345–346.
9   Case 41/74: *Van Duyn v Home Office (No 2)* (direct effect of Directive 64/221) [1974] ECR 1337, [1975] 1 CMLR 1. Case C-188/89: *Foster v British Gas plc* (direct effect of Directive 76/207) [1990] ECR I-3313, [1990] 2 CMLR 833.
10   *Minister of the Interior v Cohn-Bendit* (1979) Dalloz 155, [1980] 1 CMLR 543.
11   See Case 8/81: *Becker v Finanzamt Münster-Innenstadt* [1982] ECR 53, paras 20 and 24; Case 270/81: *Felicitas Rickmers - Linie v Finanzamt fur Verkehrsteuern Hamburg* [1982] ECR 2771, paras 24-27; Case 80/86: *Kolpinghuis Nijmegen* [1987] ECR 3969, paras 1-8 of the A-G's opinion, paras 6-9 and 15 of the judgment; Case C-221/88: *Busseni* [1990] ECR I-495, para 52 of the A-G's opinion; Cases C-140/91, C-141/91, C-278/91 and C-279/91: *Suffritti v INPS* [1992] ECR I-6337, para 13; Case C-346/97: *Braathens Sverige AB v Riksskatteverket* [1999] ECR I-3419, para 29.
12   Eg Case C-91/92: *Dori v Recreb Srl* [1994] ECR I-3325.
13   Case 9/70: [1970] ECR 825 at 837, see also on turnover tax Case 20/70: *Transports Lesage & Cie v Hauptzollamt Freiburg* [1970] ECR 861, [1971] CMLR 1; Case 23/70: *Haselhorst v Finanzamt Düsseldorf-Altstadt* [1970] ECR 881, [1971] CMLR 1.
14   OJ Sp edn 1965, p 67.
15   Dir 67/227 (OJ Sp edn, 1967, p 13) amended by Dir 69/463 (OJ Sp edn, 1969, p 551).

Tax as from 1 January 1972. Germany brought the VAT into operation ahead of the Community schedule and as from 1 January 1968 applied it to transport in lieu of the previous tax system. However it imposed a new tax on road transport as from 1 January 1969 providing that it would cease to apply by 31 December 1970. Grad objected to this new tax which, in turn, raised the question of the effect of the decision in Germany. The ECJ held that the decision was directly applicable and so were the two directives. At the end there was no consolation for Grad because the relevant provision of the decision applied only from 1 January 1972, ie the date of the introduction of the VAT in the Community and, therefore, the internal tax system prevailed in the interim. However the case broke new ground as regards the effectiveness of measures other than regulations.

The second important case in this respect was *SACE*.[16] In order to accelerate the process of the removal of customs duties ahead of the Treaty schedule, Directive 68/31[17] required Italy to abolish certain administrative charges imposed on imports by 1 July 1968. The directive was prompted by Decision 66/532.[18] The point was whether, in order to benefit SACE, the combined effect of the decision and the directive overruled the Italian law which authorized the charges imposed after the date fixed by the directive but before the expiry of the transitional period envisaged by the Treaty. The ECJ held that Italy was under obligation to accelerate the process in accordance with the directive and, therefore, SACE had a directly enforceable right in this respect.

In *Re Forestry Reproductive Material*[19] the Court reaffirmed its position, saying that 'if in respect of Member States to which it is addressed, the provisions of a directive have no less binding an effect than that of any other rule of Community law, such an effect applies all the more to provisions relating to the time limits for implementing the measures provided for'. Further decisions along the same lines followed.

In *Van Duyn v Home Office*[20] the ECJ held Directive 64/221 together with Article 48(3) of the EEC as having a direct effect as far as the right of entry of a worker and the derogation on the ground of public policy on the part of a Member State were concerned. Thus the directive explained and complemented the relevant provision of the Treaty.

In the second *Defrenne* case[1] the combined effect of EC Article 141 (ex Art 119) of the EEC Treaty (directly applicable as from the end of the transition period) and directive 75/117[2] to implement the principle of equal pay for equal work (laid down in the above-mentioned article) vindicated the right of a Belgian air hostess to equal treatment with her male colleagues but only as far as their pay was concerned. The decision was much criticized[3] as one stretching the teleological

---

16 Case 33/70: *SACE SpA v Italian Ministry for Finance* [1970] ECR 1213, [1971] CMLR 123.

17 JO 1968, 12/8.

18 JO 1966, 2971.

19 Case 79/72: *Commission v Italy* [1973] ECR 667 at 672, [1973] CMLR 773 at 781; see also Case 93/79: *Commission v Italy (Re Weighing Machines)* [1979] ECR 3837, [1980] 2 CMLR 647; Case 91/79: *Commission v Italy (Re Detergents)* [1980] ECR 1099, [1981] 1 CMLR 331; Case 102/79: *Commission v Belgium (Re Type Approval)* [1980] ECR 1473, [1981] 1 CMLR 282.

20 Case 41/74: [1974] 1337, [1975] 1 CMLR 1.

1 Case 43/75: *Defrenne v SABENA* [1976] ECR 455, [1976] 2 CMLR 98. See also Case C-262/88: *Barber v Guardian Royal Exchange Assurance Group* [1990] ECR I-1889, [1990] 2 CMLR 513, see further ch 32, *infra*.

2 OJ 1975, L45/19.

3 Hamson, C J, Methods of Interpretation – A Critical Assessment of the Results; *Judicial and Academic Conference*, 27–28 September 1976.

interpretation too far and virtually usurping a legislative function which the Court does not possess but, it seems, it cannot be faulted on that ground. However in subsequent proceedings[4] the Court felt unable to stretch the point to cover all conditions at work. The *Defrenne* case stands out not only as an example of extensive interpretation of a directive made in aid of a Treaty provision but also of direct effect of a directive on the rights of individuals. It has not only exposed sex bias in the employment laws[5] but also led to an enforcement action to eliminate inconsistency of national laws with the Community principle of the equality of the sexes in employment.[6]

The Sex Discrimination (Social Security) Directive (79/7) has proved equally effective[7] to extend invalidity care allowance to married women and to eliminate the inconsistency in the UK law that, while a non-contributory invalidity pension was denied to women capable of performing normal household duties it was available to men in similar circumstances.[8] However, Directive 76/207 was held incapable of extending the benefit of compulsory maternity leave to fathers.[9]

The *Francovich*[10] case raises the question of state responsibility to individuals for failure to implement a directive protecting their rights in the event of their employer's bankruptcy. Italy failed to implement Directive 80/987 which required the state to provide specific guarantees for the payment of unpaid wages and to that end enact appropriate national legislation ensuring the setting up of a guarantee fund. In the enforcement proceedings brought by the Commission[11] it was clear that Italy was in breach of Community law. The next point was whether the state's failure triggered off state liability grounded in Community law in the absence of a remedy under the national law. This question was answered in the affirmative in the subsequent case[12] in which certain employees sued the state, in the national jurisdiction, for compensation in respect of wages owed to them by the bankrupt employer on the ground of the state's failure to implement the Directive. The ECJ ruled that for the state to be liable to make good the resultant damage suffered by the employees three conditions had to be satisfied, ie the result intended by the

4   Case 149/77: *Defrenne v SABENA* [1978] ECR 1365, [1978] 3 CMLR 312.
5   See Cases: 129/79: *Macarthys Ltd v Smith* [1980] ECR 1275, [1980] 2 CMLR 205; 69/80: *Worringham and Humphreys v Lloyds Bank* [1981] ECR 767, [1981] 2 CMLR 1; 96/80: *Jenkins v Kingsgate* ibid, 24; 12/81: *Garland v British Rail Engineering Ltd* [1982] ECR 359, [1982] 1 CMLR 696; 19/81: *Burton v British Railways Board* [1982] ECR 555, [1982] 2 CMLR 136; 222/84: *Johnston v Chief Constable of the RUC* [1986] ECR 1651, [1986] 3 CMLR 240; 152/84: *Marshall v Southampton and South West Hampshire Area Health Authority* [1986] ECR 723, [1986] 1 CMLR 688. See also Case 14/83: *Von Colson and Kamann v Land Nordrhein-Westfahlen* [1984] ECR 1891, [1986] 2 CMLR 430 and Case 79/83: *Hartz v Deutsche Tradux GmbH* [1984] ECR 1921, [1986] 2 CMLR 430; Case 170/84: *Bilka-Kaufhaus GmbH v Von Harz* [1986] ECR 1607, [1986] 2 CMLR 701.
6   Case 61/81: *Commission v United Kingdom* [1982] ECR 2601, [1982] 3 CMLR 284; Case 165/82: *Commission v United Kingdom* [1983] ECR 3431, [1984] 1 CMLR 44; Case 163/82: *Commission v Italy* [1983] ECR 3273, [1984] 3 CMLR 169; Case 248/83: *Commission v Germany* [1985] ECR 1459, [1986] 2 CMLR 588.
7   Case 150/85: *Drake v Chief Adjudication Officer* [1986] ECR 1995, [1986] 3 CMLR 43; Case 286/85: *McDermott and Cotter v Minister for Social Welfare* [1987] ECR 1453, [1987] 2 CMLR 607.
8   Case 384/85: *Clarke v Chief Adjudication Officer* [1987] ECR 2865, [1987] 3 CMLR 277.
9   Case 184/83: *Hofman v Barmer Ersatzkasse* [1984] ECR 3047, [1986] 1 CMLR 242. See also Case 163/82, supra, note 6.
10 Cases C-6/90 and 9/90 *Francovich v Italy* [1991] ECR I-5357, [1993] 2 CMLR 66; Case C-479/93: *Francovich v Italy* [1995] ECR I-3843.
11 Case 22/87: *Commission v Italy* [1989] ECR 143.
12 See supra, note 10 at para 38.

Directive had to entail the grant of rights to the individuals concerned, the contents of their rights had to be identifiable from the Directive itself and there had to be a causal connection between the State's breach of duty and damage suffered by the individuals. These conditions were satisfied in the instant case. The Court conceded that the Directive was not directly effective because the institutions to guarantee the wages were not identified but, following its own judgment in the *Factortame*[13] case, ruled that the State was obliged to provide an effective remedy to safeguard the rights of individuals guaranteed by the Directive. Such conclusion was inherent in the Treaty since the state was in duty bound to carry out its obligations. The potential of the *Francovich* ruling is quite wide since, bearing in mind the three conditions, it opens up the possibility of individuals claiming compensation in the event of the state failing to implement a directive or, even, implementing it incompletely or incorrectly.[14] The directive was transposed into national law in 1992 but the application of the directive posed some problems to the Italian court. Answering the question concerning the scope of the directive the ECJ replied that its scope was expressly limited so that the protection of employees does not cover those whose contract or relation of employment is with the employer who cannot, under national law, be subject to proceedings to satisfy collectively the claims of creditors. Such an employer cannot be in a 'state of insolvency' within the specific meaning of that phrase as used in the directive.

The above interpretation has not affected the claimants in the instant case who have already experienced several years of litigation but has focused attention on the discrepancies in the national systems regarding insolvency.[15] However, the *Francovich* case is an important landmark in the interpretation of directives. Clearly, failure to transpose in the time set in the directive or to transpose incorrectly, sets in motion the enforcement proceedings taken by the Commission against the state in question but the action for compensation taken by an individual in the national jurisdiction parallel to the enforcement proceedings may prove more effective as demonstrated by subsequent cases.

Joined Cases C-46/93 and C-48/93[16] concern the conditions under which a Member State may incur liability for damage caused to individuals by breaches of Community law attributed to the State in question. *Brasserie du Pêcheur,* a French company, claimed compensation because it was forced to discontinue exports of beer which did not comply with purity requirements of the German Biergesetz. The ECJ ruled that the law in question was incompatible with the Treaty[17] and consequently the French company brought an action against the German Government. In the *Factortame* case Spanish fishing companies claimed compensation from the British Government since, in consequence of the changes in the Merchant Shipping Act 1988 which was incompatible with EC Article 43 (ex Art 52),[18] they suffered a loss. Following the second *Factortame* case the House of Lords directed the claimants to give particulars of their loss.[19]

In the *Francovich* case,[20] the ECJ held that Member States are obliged to make good loss and damage caused to individuals by breaches of Community

---

13 Case C-213/89: *R v Secretary of State for Transport, ex p Factortame Ltd (No 2)* [1990] ECR I-2433, [1990] 3 CMLR 1.

14 See Case C-334/92: *Wagner Miret v Fondo de Guarantia Salarial* [1993] ECR I-6911.

15 Case C-479/93: *Francovich v Italy* [1995] ECR I-3843.

16 [1996] ECR I-1029.

17 Case 178/84: *Commission v Germany* [1987] ECR 1227,.

18 Case C-246/89: *Commission v United Kingdom* [1991] ECR I-4585.

19 Case C-221/89: *Factortame (No 3)* [1991] ECR I-3905 and *R v Secretary of Stae, ex p Factortame (No 5)* [2000] 1 AC 524.

20 Cases C-6/90 and C-9/90, supra, para 37.

law for which they can be held responsible. It was contended that Member States are required to make good loss or damage caused to individuals *only* where the provisions breached are *not* directly effective. The Court rejected this contention saying that the principle of State liability in this respect is *inherent* in the system of the Treaty.[1] In *Factortame*, following its own judgment in the *Francovich* case, the ECJ laid down the following criteria for the determination of the State's liability:

(1) the breach of Community law attributable to the national legislature acting in a field in which it has wide discretion must be sufficiently serious;
(2) there must be a direct causal link between the breach and the damage sustained by the individuals;
(3) the State must make good the loss or damage in accordance with its national law on liability provided that the conditions laid down in national law must not be less favourable than those relating to similar domestic claims;
(4) the national court cannot, under the national legislation which it applies, make reparation conditional upon a requirement of fault, whether intentional or negligent, on the part of the State organ responsible for the breach;
(5) reparation by Member States must be commensurate with the loss or damage sustained;
(6) the obligation of the Member States to make good the loss cannot be limited to damage sustained after the delivery of a judgment of the Court finding the infringement in question.

Following Joined Cases C-46-93 and C-48/93 the ECJ ruled that the Government of Germany which failed to transpose in time Directive 90/314 on package travel, package holidays and package tours, was liable to pay compensation to individuals who suffered loss as a result of the insolvency of the travel organizers.[2] Consequences of the *Francovich* case provided consolation to disappointed consumers.

An individual may rely on a directive not only to claim a right rooted in Community law but also to bring a valid defence to prosecution under national law which is at variance with it. The point is well illustrated in the *Ratti* case.[3] Ratti was prosecuted for offences against Italian law in respect of packaging and labelling of certain products. His defence was that he complied with Directive 73/173[4] and Directive 77/728[5] on the packaging and labelling of solvents and varnishes respectively, neither directive having been implemented in Italy. He both succeeded and failed. The former was to be implemented by 8 December 1974, the latter by 9 November 1979 but Ratti anticipated both and in doing so was in collision with Italian law which remained unamended. On reference for a preliminary ruling the ECJ held that a directive can become directly effective when the time limit set for its implementation has been reached. Thus Ratti was protected under the former but not under the latter directive and, therefore,

---

1   Ibid, para 35.
2   Joined Cases C-178/94, C-179/94, C-188/94, C-189/94 and C-190/94: *Erich Dillenkofer v Germany* [1996] ECR I-4845.
3   Case 148/78: *Pubblico Ministero v Ratti* [1979] ECR 1629, [1980] 1 CMLR 96; see also Case 79/72: *Commission v Italy* [1973] ECR 667 at 672, [1973] CMLR 773 at 781; Case C-194/94: *CIA Security International v Signalson SA* [1996] ECR I-2201.
4   OJ 1973, L189/7.
5   OJ 1977, L303/23.

had a defence to charges in respect of solvents but none in respect of varnishes. The fact that he imported some of the varnishes from Germany where the relevant directive had been implemented afforded him no defence under Italian law. It follows that the date of the entry into force of the directive according to Community law is decisive.

A private law aspect of a directive came to light in the UHT milk products case.[6] There, a breach of contract to import these products was caused by the UK government restrictions because, inter alia, they were pre-packed in France in metric containers. The defence, that the traditional pint rather than the continental litre was the only lawful measure for liquids such as milk, was successful because the UK had negotiated a temporary stay of the coming into force of the relevant directives.[7] However, as the ban continued the Commission brought a successful enforcement action against the United Kingdom in which the defence on the ground of public health failed, whilst the formal defence on the ground of the national market regulation for liquids was no longer available.[8]

The ghost of *Grad* appeared in a case[9] where a German taxpayer claimed exemption from VAT in respect of credit negotiation transactions based on Directive 77/388 concerning the harmonization of turnover taxes which at that time had not been implemented in Germany. The ECJ, repeating virtually verbatim its dictum on the nature of directives expressed in *Grad*, concluded that, especially in the light of the *Ratti* case, the taxpayer may rely on the provisions of a directive if they are unconditional and sufficiently precise if the directive has not been implemented properly or at all in domestic legislation. In such a case the state cannot take advantage of its failure to implement the directive. This clarified the law. Such clarification was needed especially since the German Federal Fiscal Court, relying expressly upon the decision of the French Conseil d'Etat in a similar case[10] denied the direct effect of Directive 77/388 on the ground that it had not been enacted into a national statute. It thought that whilst the directive was binding upon Member States it could not create 'directly applicable law in those states'.[11]

Next to the question of direct applicability/direct effect is the question of vertical and horizontal effect of directives. The phrase 'vertical effect' is used to describe the relationship between the state and a legal or natural person. 'Horizontal effect' describes the relationship between legal or natural persons. Some directives are concerned only with the former; others with the latter. Here again the question whether a directive is concerned with vertical or horizontal relationships depends on the intention of the legislator to be divined from its wording. Most of the cases discussed above involve a vertical effect.[12] Irrespective of the intended effect of the directive (whether it applies to vertical or horizontal relationships), the interpretation of the national law involved must be carried out within the parameters of the wording and purpose of the directive whether or not the national rules have been enacted in order to implement the directive in

---

6   Case 244/78: *Union Laitière Normande v French Dairy Farmers Ltd* [1979] ECR 2663, [1980] 1 CMLR 314.
7   Ie 71/316, JO 1971, L207/1; 71/354. JO 1971, L243/29; 75/106, OJ 1975, L42/1.
8   Case 124/81: *Commission v United Kingdom* [1983] ECR 203, [1983] 2 CMLR 1.
9   Case 8/81: *Becker v Finanzamt Münster-Innenstadt* [1982] ECR 53, [1982] 1 CMLR 499 at 512.
10   25.2.1981 (Re la diréctive 77/388) (1981) Dalloz I R 33.
11   Case VB 51/80: *Re Value Added Tax Directives* [1982] 1 CMLR 527 at 529.
12   Case 80/86: *Officier van Justitie v Kolpinghuis Nijmegen BV* [1987] ECR 3969, [1989] 2 CMLR 18; see also Case 14/86: *Pretore di Salò v X* [1987] ECR 2545, [1989] 1 CMLR 71.

question.[13] However, the obligation to construe national law consistently with a directive does not mean that the former must be given a meaning that, as a matter of language, it is incapable of bearing.[14] Where a directive is relied on not as an aid to the interpretation of national law but as a source of rights independent of national law, the distinction between horizontal and vertical relationships becomes of critical importance. A directive can be regarded as a source of rights only if it has not been implemented properly or at all within the time for doing so and, even then, it can be invoked for that pupose only in the context of a vertical relationship, not a horizontal one. In short, a legal or natural person may rely upon an unimplemented directive as against the state, not as against another legal or natural person (although, so far as reliance against the state is concerned, it does not matter in what capacity the state is acting).[15]

Marleasing concerned the interpretation of the First Company Directive. *In casu*, a Spanish company claimed that the Memorandum and Articles of another Spanish company were devoid of any legal purpose and therefore, violated the Spanish Code of Civil Law. The respondent relied on Article 11 of the Directive which contains a list of grounds upon which the nullity of a company may be declared but the 'legal purpose' does not figure in the list. However, Spain had failed timeously to implement the Directive. On reference, the ECJ answered in the negative the question whether a private party could plead the provisions of an unimplemented Directive against another private party. However for the interpretation of national law the Court relied on the *Von Colson*[16] case where it held that 'in applying the national law ... national courts are required to interpret their national law in the light of the wording and purpose of the Directive'; consequently the Spanish court was obliged to interpret the provisions of the Code so as to preclude a declaration of nullity of a company based on a ground which is not listed in the First Company Directive.

In Case C-91/92[17] the ECJ clarified the position as regards the horizontal effect of directive 85/577 covering contracts negotiated away from business premises. Miss Dori concluded at Milan railway station a contract for an English correspondence course. Four days later she cancelled the contract and informed the other party accordingly. However the other party assigned its claim to the respondent. Miss Dori advised the respondent that she had the right to cancel according to the directive. However the directive was not transposed into Italian law at the time of the contract in question. The ECJ concluded that, in the absence of transposition, Miss Dori could not rely on the directive.

When Case C-192/94[18] was brought, Directive 87/102 on consumer credit protection was not implemented in Spain but the directive intended to confer rights of action against the lender. The directive, not being transposed into national rules, could not be relied on. However, it seems that the consumer can rely on the *Francovich* precedent if the conditions underlying state liability are fulfilled.

---

13   See especially Case C-208/90: *Emmott v Minister for Social Welfare* [1991] ECR I-4269, [1991] 3 CMLR 894.
14   Case C-106/89: *Marleasing SA v La Comercial Internacional de Alimentación SA* [1990] ECR I-4135, [1992] 1 CMLR 305.
15   Case 152/84: *Marshall v Southampton and Hampshire Area Health South West Authority* [1986] ECR 723, [1986] 1 CMLR 688.
16   Case 14/83: *Von Colson and Kamann v Land Nordrhein-Westfalen* [1984] ECR 1891, [1986] 2 CMLR 430.
17   Case C-91/92: *Paola Faccini Dori v Recreb Srl* [1994] ECR I-3325.
18   Case C-192/94: *El Corte Inglés SA v Rivero* [1996] ECR I-1281, [1996] 2 CMLR 507.

As mentioned earlier, directives are meant to be different from regulations. In a sense they are because they allow a defined objective to be achieved by diverse methods. However some directives are drafted in considerable detail, leaving little discretion for the Member States and, where they provide a blueprint for entirely novel legislation, they are indistinguishable from regulations in so far as they are addressed to the Member States and not to the whole world generally; they rule the states but not *erga omnes*; and where they affect individuals they do it by perfecting otherwise incomplete Community rights[19] or affording Community defences against prosecutions by the States in default.[20] In that sense directives are 'indirectly applicable'.[1]

Since directives have become the main instrument of harmonization or approximation of national laws their potential as a source of Community law is quite considerable. However in practice the clear-cut distinction between regulations and directives implied in the Treaty has been blurred.

(iii) Decisions

Concept and scope A decision[2] of the Council or the Commission is binding in its entirety upon those to whom it is addressed. It may be addressed either to Member States or to individuals or corporations. It differs from a regulation which is formulated in an abstract manner. However a regulation does not become a decision merely because the addressees can be identified or, in other words, because its scope can be individualized.[3] Recently the ECJ distinguished decisions from directives in the context of the powers exercised by the Commission.[4]

Like a regulation or a directive a decision has to be 'substantiated', ie based on a Treaty provision. However, mere references to an article of the Treaty, eg to EC Article 87(1) (ex Art 92(1)) on state aids, will not suffice.[5] Indeed, it would be against the principle of the due process of law to allow an unsubstantiated decision to have a binding effect. It has to be notified to whom it is addressed though no particular form of notification is needed.[6] It takes effect upon notification.[7]

Unlike a regulation a decision is binding upon the addressee only, but, unlike a directive, it is 'binding in its entirety', leaving no discretion in the manner in which it is to be carried out. However, a decision may be the result of an obligation imposed on the Commission by a regulation.[8] The term 'decision' has of course a special meaning to denote one of the binding Community acts and sometimes a source of Community law. It is not, therefore, a mere conclusion of a process of reasoning or settlement or solution of a problem. Furthermore it is not a mere

---

19 Eg *Defrenne*, supra.
20 Eg *Ratti*, supra.
1 Cf Opinion of A-G Reischl in *Ratti*, op cit ECR at 1650; Warner, J-P, The Relationship between European Community Law and the National Law of the Member States [1979] 93 LQR 349 at 359; but see Leitao, A R, 'L'effet direct des directives: une mystification?' [1981] RTDE 425.
2 EC Art 249(4) (ex Art 189(4)): EAEC Art 161(4); ECSC Art 14(2).
3 Case 789, 790/79: *Calpak SpA v Commission* [1980] ECR 1949, [1981] 1 CMLR 26.
4 Cases C-48/90 and 66/90: *Netherlands v Commission, re Netherlands express delivery services*. [1992] ECR I-565.
5 Case 248/84: *Germany v Commission (Re Regional Aid Plans)* [1987] ECR 4013, [1989] 1 CMLR 591.
6 Case 6/72R: *Europemballage Corpn Continental Can Co Inc v Commission* [1972] ECR 157 at 221, [1972] CMLR 690 at 691.
7 Cases 98/78: *Racke v Hauptzollamt Mainz* [1979] ECR 69 and 99/78: *Decker KG v Hauptzollamt Landau* [1979] ECR 101.
8 Case 16/65: *Schwarze v Einfuhr-und Vorratsstelle für Getreide und Füttermittel* [1965] ECR 877, [1966] CMLR 172.

repetition of an established rule[9] or a stage in internal procedure,[10] or an instruction to an agency set up by the Community.[11] The many cases under ECSC Article 14 provided an opportunity for the Community Court to define the meaning of 'decision' and the definition in one of such cases seems apposite to the position under the EC Treaty. The Court held that a decision must appear as an act originating from the competent organization intended to produce juridical effects, constituting the ultimate end of the internal procedure of this organization and according to which such organization makes its final ruling in a form allowing its nature to be identified.[12]

Whether an administrative act of the organs of the Community is a regulation, directive or decision is determined not by its form but by its content and object,[13] or, as put by Advocate-General Roemer,[14] it is the function of the act rather than the process of its formation which should be primarily examined.

Under ECSC Article 33 a distinction is made between general and individual decisions depending on the manner in which the addressees are affected.[15] General decisions are 'quasi-legislative acts made by a public authority and having a rule-making effect *erga omnes*'.[16] Individual decisions were held to be decisions in which the competent authority had to 'determine such concrete cases as are submitted to it'.[17]

The EC and EAEC Treaties distinguish between plain decisions which may be challenged by individuals (or corporations) to whom they are addressed, and decisions in the form of regulations which may be challenged by individuals upon proof that they are of direct and individual concern to them. In the latter cases the Court has to examine the substance of the measure to determine its true nature.[18]

Challenging a decision   Decisions, being binding acts, are subject to judicial review within the terms of EC Article 230(1) (ex Art 173(1)). The grounds of review include infringement of essential procedural requirements.[19] Individuals are competent to challenge decisions under the conditions laid down in EC Article 230(4) (ex Art 173(4)).

The question of *locus standi* arose in a dispute concerning state aids in which the Commission found a French parafiscal tax to be unlawful. Challenged by

9 Case 9/56: *Meroni & Co, Industrie Metallurgiche SpA v High Authority of the ECSC* [1957–58] ECR 133.
10 Cases 53–54/63: *Lemmerz-Werke GmbH v High Authorty of the ECSC* [1963] ECR 239 at 247, 248, [1964] CMLR 384 at 399.
11 Case 21/58: *Felten und Guillaume Carlswerke Eisen- und Stahl AG v High Authority of the ECSC* [1959] ECR 99.
12 Case 54/65: *Compagnie des Forges de Châtillon, Commentry et Neuves-Maisons v High Authority of the ECSC* [1966] ECR 185 at 195, [1966] CMLR 525 at 538.
13 Cases 16–17/62: *Confédération Nationale des Producteurs de Fruits et Légumes v Council* [1962] ECR 471 at 477–479, [1963] CMLR 160 at 173–174.
14 Case 40/64: In *Sgarlata v Commission* [1965] ECR 215 at 231, [1966] CMLR 314 at 318.
15 Case 18/57: *Nold KG v High Authority of the ECSC* [1959] ECR 41 at 49–50; Cases 55–59/63, 61–63/63: *Modena v High Authority of the ECSC* [1964] ECR 211 at 227, 228 [1964] CMLR 401 at 413.
16 *Nold*, supra at 50.
17 Case 20/58: *Phoenix-Rheinrohr AG v High Authority of the ECSC* [1959] ECR 75 at 88–89.
18 Case 101/76: *Koninklijke Scholten Honig NV v Council and Commission* [1977] ECR 797, [1980] 2 CMLR 669.
19 Case C-304/89: *Estabelecimento Isodoro Oliveira v Commission* [1991] ECR I-2283, [1993] 2 CMLR 774.

a state-appointed trade association the Commission successfully contended that such a body had no standing to challenge its decision.[20]

The problem under the EC Treaty is one of 'mixed acts', that is to say acts with the character of regulations[1] and decisions or directives[2] and decisions. Such mixed measures seem impossible under the ECSC Treaty[3] but they came to light under the EC and the EAEC Treaties. Assuming that such measures are valid *per se* the practical question of the scope of their application arises or, more precisely, whether they affect individuals apart from states and whether they can be challenged by individuals under EC Article 230 (ex Art 173(2)). It was held[4] that a measure that could be classified as a regulation could contain provisions applicable to individuals and thus enable them to take action under EC Article 230 (ex Art 173). On the other hand, a Commission decision merely to reject a claim for amendment of a regulation will be treated as analogous to a regulation[5] with the result that an individual may not have the necessary *locus standi* under EC Article 230 (ex Art 173).

The problem[6] of a directive and decision was raised by the *Finanzgerichte* (Finance Courts) of Munich (Case 9/70), Baden-Würtemberg (Case 20/70) and Düsseldorf (Case 23/70) which moved the Community Court to rule whether article 4 of *Decision* 65/271/EEC, JO 1500/65, read together with article 1 of the first *Directive* on Turnover Tax, JO 1301/67 'are directly binding in the relations between Member States and private persons and create individual rights which can be invoked before municipal courts'. The Community Court ruled that EC Article 249 (ex Art 189), does not prevent private individuals from founding their actions before municipal courts upon *Directives* and *Decisions* addressed to Member States. Concluding that these measures can have, in appropriate cases, an internal effect, a learned jurist remarked that, as a result, an important barrier against the legal protection of private parties against these Community measures has been removed.[7]

Terminological confusion   In the course of time certain categories of 'decision' having diverse effects have emerged. These include:

Executive decisions, eg to engage the Community in external relations whether within the EC framework (ie conclude trade agreements and association agreements or to establish diplomatic relations) or in the context of the TEU in

---

20   Case 282/85: *Comité de Développement et de Promotion du Textile et de l'Habillement v Commission* [1986] ECR 2469, [1988] 2 CMLR 156.

1   Eg Case 25/62: *Plaumann & Co v Commission* [1963] ECR 95, [1964] CMLR 29, where the ECJ held that to be a decision an act ought to be addressed to a particular person and have a binding effect upon that person.

2   Eg *Consten v Grundig*, supra, p 142, note 16. See also *Grad*, supra, p 143, note 3.

3   *Nold*, above, and Case 8/55: *Fédération Charbonnière de Belgique v High Authority of the ECSC* [1954–56] ECR 245 at 247, also A-G Lagrange in Case 30/59: *De Gezamenlijke Steenkolenmijnen in Limburg v High Authority of the ECSC* [1961] ECR 1.

4   In Case 30/67: *Industria Molitoria Imolese v Council* [1968] ECR 115, 5 CML Rev 480; see also Case 123/77: *UNICME v Council* [1978] ECR 845 at 851.

5   Case 42/71: *Firma Nordgetreide GmbH & Co KG v Commission* [1972] ECR 105, [1973] CMLR 177.

6   Brinkhorst, L J, 'Implementation of (non-self-executing) Legislation of the European Economic Community, including Directives', *Legal Problems of an Enlarged European Community* (ed Bathurst, M E, et al) (1972), p 75; and Mitchell, J D B, 'Community Legislation', ibid, p 100.

7   Brinkhorst, L J, op cit, p 76.

the sphere of external policy, security or police and judicial co-operation. The former create rights and obligations vested in the Member States and individuals; the latter are governed by political considerations.

In the area of organizational law, eg the Commission by Decision 73/351[8] set up an Advisory Committee on Customs Matters. By a series of Council decisions the monetary policy such as it is has been put into operation. These acts of the Institutions do not resemble exactly the definitions of decisions so far elicited from the judgments of the ECJ mentioned above.

Administrative decisions comprise the internal acts of the Community such as the appointment, promotion and dismissal of officials or the distribution of functions within the Community bureaucracy. They also comprise Commission decisions in the field of dumping, state aids and allocation of funds in the execution of certain policies, eg regional, social.

In the latter context the administration of the European Social Fund came under judicial scrutiny as the United Kingdom complained of the lack of consistency in the execution of the policy.[9] At issue was a Commission decision expressed in the annual declaration of the Fund's assistance to Member States for the ensuing year. Since these decisions have reflected, in the past, a certain consistency, it was argued that a legitimate expectation was created which enabled the Member States to make their commitments. The Commission, having altered the basis of the allocation of assistance after the Member States had made their commitments, was declared to have acted improperly.

Two other examples reflect the judicial control of Commission's administrative decisions.

Commission decision 94/871 of 21 December 1994 on the clearance of the EAGGF accounts was annulled by the ECJ because the Commission failed to recognize certain items chargeable to the EAGGF (in case expenditure related to leaf tobacco – no corresponding refunds).[10] Decision 93/625 of 22 September 1993 concerning aid granted by national authorities to an economic interest group consisting of a racecourse undertaking was also annulled and the French government was ordered to require repayment.[11]

Quasi-judicial decisions in their classical forms comprise the decisions of the Commission in a process of adjudication of the behaviour of Member States (ie preliminary to enforcement proceedings) or enterprises in the field of competition (ie negative clearance, exemptions, determination of infringements).

The variety of 'decisions' is confusing for some are, some are not, legally binding. However, a distinction can be made between binding and non-binding decisions. The former are made within the legal framework of the Treaty in the sense of EC Article 249 (ex Art 189). They are formal acts complying with procedural requirements; they impose rights or obligations upon the Institutions, or the Member States or individuals, and are subject to judicial control by the ECJ. The latter do not constitute formal acts of the Institutions, do not comply

---

8   OJ 1973, L321/37 amended by Decision 76/921 (OJ 1976, L362/55), and Customs Code, arts 247–249.
9   Case 84/85: *United Kingdom v Commission (Re the European Social Fund)* [1987] ECR 3765, [1988] 1 CMLR 113.
10   Case C-61/95: *Greece v Commission* [1998] ECR I-207. Cf Cases: C-342/89: *Germany v Commission* [1991] ECR I-5031; Case C-346/89: *Italy v Commission* [1991] ECR I-5057.
11   Case T-67/94: *Ladbroke Racing Ltd v Commission* [1998] ECR II-1.

with strictly legal and formal Treaty requirements and, therefore, are not subject to judicial control. They are taken within the political framework of the Community to conduct or settle Community affairs and, consequently, do not impose rights or obligations upon the Institutions, or the Member States or individuals.

In the light of these criteria the ECJ judgment in Case 114/86,[12] that Commission instructions for nationality quotas for shortlists of tenderers for public service contracts under Lomé Convention II were not 'decisions' and, therefore, not subject to judicial review, is rather surprising. These instructions constituted an exercise of power and did affect individual rights as far as the allocation of contracts according to nationality quotas was concerned. It would seem that, rather than dismissing the case for inadmissibility, the Court should have addressed itself to the question whether or not the power was properly exercised. In the light of this case it is not surprising that the Commission was held not to be liable in damages to an unsuccessful tenderer for a lost public contract under Lomé Convention I. The question was, of course, different as the Commission acted according to discretion by giving advice on the selection of the contractors.[13]

Like any other binding acts, decisions have to be carried out by their addressees. In the case of the Member States, failure to abide by a decision will trigger off an enforcement action. Such actions cannot be defended by the plea that the decision in question is unlawful[14] but the ECJ has the inherent power to review the legality of the disputed measure in such proceedings. However, the better view seems that a decision of doubtful character ought to be challenged in attack rather than in defence.

(b)   Non-obligatory acts

It is debatable whether recommendations[15] and opinions[16] can be regarded as sources of Community law. These are listed in EC Article 249 (ex Art 189), as attributes of the power of the Council and Commission[17] necessary for the execution of their task but, unlike regulations, directives and decisions, are said to have 'no binding force'.

Taking the binding force as a criterion of the authority of the acts of the Community organs, *opinions* cannot be regarded as a source of Community law but *recommendations* can only in so far as they are made under the ECSC Treaty. *Recommendations*[18] under the EC Treaty have no force of law.

The existence of 'non-binding' acts is not exclusive to the European Community. Such acts are typical of international organizations of sovereign states,[19] which in theory cannot take orders from outside. The European Community, in spite of some measure of cohesion, still remains a community of

---

12   Case 114/86: *United Kingdom v Commission (Re Lomé II Service Contracts)* [1988] ECR 5289, [1989] 1 CMLR 32.
13   Case 267/82: *Dévelopment SA v Commission* [1986] ECR 1907, [1989] 1 CMLR 309.
14   Case 226/87: *Commission v Greece (Re Public Sector Insurance)* [1988] ECR 3611 [1989] 3 CMLR 569.
15   Eg *Re Luxembourg Agricultural Policy* 65/300/EEC 26 May 1965, [1965] CMLR 355.
16   Eg Case 7/61: *Commission v Italy* [1961] ECR 317 at 326, [1962] CMLR 39 at 50.
17   See EC Arts 53, 77, 97 (ex Arts 64, 81, 102).
18   Eg recommendation 84/549 (OJ 1984, L298/49) for the introduction of services on the basis of common harmonized approach in the field of telecommunications.
19   Cf Sloan, B, 'The Binding Force of a "Recommendation" of the General Assembly of the United Nations', (1948), 25 BYBIL 1; Johnson, D H, 'The Effect of Resolutions of the General Assembly of the United Nations', (1955–56) 32 32 BYBIL 97.

sovereign states and so it has to be recognized that the Community organs have to carry out a variety of functions, some of which call for legislation, others for guidance.[20] Therefore, neither recommendations nor opinions of the Council and Commission should be ignored. Their role is persuasive and constructive in the formulation and execution of the policies of the Community. Though they cannot be formally cited as sources of Community law they ought to be regarded, in the light of their potential, as auxiliary elements of the law-making process of the Community.[1] In that sense the ECJ conceded (in the field of social security) that recommendations are not entirely void of any legal effect.[2] They are reviewable if adopted in the context of international commitments of the Community as, eg under the EEC-EFTA Convention of 1987.[3]

(c)   Non-Treaty acts
In addition to the listed non-binding acts, various other instruments, such as memoranda,[4] communications,[5] deliberations,[6] programmes,[7] guidelines[8] and resolutions may be adopted. These are non-Treaty acts descriptive of the various actions or procedures undertaken or carried out in the life of the Community. They have no binding legal effect unless, despite their nomenclature, they meet the criteria laid down in the Treaty for binding Community acts. Such acts must, in the opinion of the Community Court[9] constitute 'the exercise, upon the conclusion of an internal procedure laid down by law, of a power provided for by law which is extended to produce legal effects of such a nature as to affect adversely the interests of the applicant by modifying its legal position ...'. Thus 'deliberations' in the Council of Ministers were held to be capable of annulment (though they were valid in the instant case) because in the particular circumstances they were intended to bind the Member States.[10] In *Commission v Luxembourg and Belgium*[11] the ECJ held that a resolution of the Council had no binding effect because it was merely an expression of intention. Similarly,[12] the Council Resolution of 22 March 1971, which is primarily an expression of the policy

---

20   Cf ECJ judgment in joint Cases 1/57 and 14/57; *Sociétée des Usines à Tubes de la Sarre v High Authority of the ECSC* [1957–58] ECR 105 at 115.
 1   Soldatos, P, and Vandersanden, G, 'La recommandation, source indirecte du rapproachement' in De Ripainsel-Landy, D et al, *Les instruments du rapprochement des législations dans la communauté Economique Européenne* (1976), pp 95 et seq.
 2   See Case 322/88: *Grimaldi v Fonds des Maladies Professionnelles* [1989] ECR 4407, [1991] 2 CMLR 265.
 3   Case C-188/91: *Deutsche Shell G v HZA Hamburg-Harburg* [1993] ECR I-383.
 4   Eg Commission's Memorandum to Council of 18 March 1970 on the establishment of Industrial Policy, Fourth Gen Report 1970 item 205 et seq; Commission to Council on action in the cultural sector EC Bull Supp 6/77, p 5, Commission White Paper 1985; Com (85) 310 Final.
 5   Communication by an official: Case 48/69: *ICI Ltd v Commission* [1972] ECR 619, [1972] CMLR 557; Case 56/72: *Goeth-Van der Schueren v Commission* [1973] ECR 181; Commission's Communication to the Council on Admission to Institutions of Higher Education (Com) (78) 468 and 469, both of 22 September 1978.
 6   Case 81/72: *Commission v Council* [1973] ECR 575, [1973] CMLR 639.
 7   Eg Council Decision 77/294 (OJ 1977, L101/1) adopting the Fourth Medium-term Programme. Council action programme to implement the Environmental Policy (JO 1977, C 139/1).
 8   Eg Council Resolution laying down guidelines for the Regional Policy (OJ 1979, C 36/10).
 9   Case 182/80: *H P Gauff v Commission* [1982] ECR 799, [1982] 3 CMLR 402 at para 18.
10   ERTA case, note 6, supra.
11   Case 90, 91/63 [1964] ECR 625, [1965] CMLR 58.
12   Case 9/73: *Schlüter v Hauptzollamt Lörrach* [1973] ECR 1135 at para 40, supra.

favoured by the Council and Government Representatives of the Member States concerning the establishment of an economic and monetary union within the next ten years following 1 January 1971, cannot for its part, either, by reason of its content, '… create legal consequences of which parties might avail themselves in court …'. Probably in the same category would be the joint resolution of the Parliament, the Commission and the Council[13] which proclaims that:

'1. The European Parliament, the Council and the Commission stress the prime importance they attach to the protection of fundamental rights, as derived in part from the constitutions of the Member States and the European Convention for the Protection of Human Rights and Fundamental Freedoms.

2. In the exercise of their powers and in pursuance of the aims of the European Communities they respect and will continue to respect these rights.'

The exhortation to respect Human Rights and Fundamental Freedoms as 'general principles of Community law' has been translated by the TEU into a Treaty obligation.[14]

A resolution may not be binding or creative of rights but, it seems, can be pleaded in support of a Treaty policy. It is doubtful though, whether, like a directive or a regulation, it is a legislative act, but it can convert a programmatic provision of the Treaty into a binding obligation. Such might have been the position in the *Manghera* case.[15] Manghera, in defiance of a state monopoly for the manufacture, import and sale of tobacco, imported a quantity of the product directly from another Member State without paying the duties due under Italian law. This occurred after a resolution[16] of the Council of Ministers which endorsed the undertaking of two states in default (ie France and Italy) to abolish the existing commercial state monopolies by a certain date. On reference, the ECJ considered that Manghera had a good defence not by virtue of the resolution, which the Court found incapable of engendering private rights, but by virtue of the direct effect of EC Article 31(1) (ex Art 37(1)), as from the end of the period of transition.

However the most striking example of a resolution[17] having a binding effect is the Council of Ministers Hague Resolution of 3 November 1976 adopted for the regulation of fishery conservation pending the finalization of the Common Fishery Policy. It provided for consultations with the Commission prior to the enactment of national measures in this field. Unilateral measures taken by the United Kingdom in contravention of the procedural requirement of the said resolution resulted in three enforcement actions: one by France[18] and another two by the Commission.[19] The resolution, like a directive, provided also a valid defence in Community law for an individual charged with the violation of the UK legislation enacted in contravention thereof.[20]

---

13 OJ 1977, C 103/1.
14 TEU Art 6 (ex Art F(2)); see further p 184, infra.
15 Case 59/75: *Pubblico Ministero v Flavia Manghera* [1976] ECR 91, [1976] 1 CMLR 557.
16 JO 1970, C 50.
17 EC Bull 1976/10 item 1502; summarized in the Irish Fisheries case, Case 61/77: *Commission v Ireland* [1978] ECR 417, [1978] 2 CMLR 466; see further Churchill, R, 'Revision of the EEC's Common Fisheries Policy' (1980) ELRev 3 and 95.
18 Case 141/78: *France v United Kingdom* [1979] ECR 2923, [1980] 1 CMLR 6.
19 Case 32/79: *Commission v United Kingdom (Re Fishery Conservation Measures)* [1980] ECR 2403, [1981] 1 CMLR 219; Case 804/79: *Commission v United Kingdom* [1981] ECR 1045, [1982] 1 CMLR 543.
20 Case 269/80: *R v Tymen* [1981] ECR 3079, [1982] 2 CMLR 111.

A striking feature of the Amsterdam Treaty is the number of declarations related to both the Treaty on the Union and the Community. These declarations range from the endorsement of the abolition of the death penalty envisaged in Protocol No. 6 to the European Convention for the Protection of Human Rights, the emphasis of the social significance of sport to, inter alia, aspects of foreign policy, security, the quality of the drafting of Community legislation, and the observation that 'the Treaty of Amsterdam does not meet the need for substantial progress towards reinforcing the institution'.

The legal status of declarations appended to the Treaty is uncertain particularly because some are confined to an observation of facts, others offer an explanation of Treaty provisions and yet others unfold future development. It is submitted that declarations as such do not constitute binding acts but rather an aid to interpretation of certain Treaty provisions or an affirmation of a particular concern of the Union.

(d)   Control of the Community legislation
All the acts of the Community organs are subject to the principle of legality as is the case with the executive and administrative acts of a law-abiding state. This principle imposes a certain limit upon the Community organs as they have to operate within the scope of their attributed powers (*infra legem*) or within the scope of their delegated powers. The Treaties are quite explicit in this respect. EC Article 7 (ex Art 4) provides that the functions of the Community shall be carried out by the Parliament, the Council, the Commission, the Court of Auditors and the Court of Justice and that 'each institution shall act within limits of the powers conferred upon it by this Treaty'.

If we accept the analogy of the TEU to a state constitution we can construe a system of control of the acts of the Community organs parallel to that of the acts of state organs. In most systems we can note a triple form of control: constitutional, political (or parliamentary) and judicial, to which we can add for good measure the control by what passes for 'public opinion'. The EC Treaty has, as we have noted[1] earlier, added a possible controlling factor in the shape of the subsidiarity principle. However the potentiality of this new general principle has yet to be tested.

Thus the constitution (Treaty) sets up the system and defines the functions and powers of the state (Community) organs. The constitutional control is a strictly legal control in so far as it rests upon the assumption that the state itself is governed by law (*Rechtstaat*, see Bracton on the Rule of Law) and that the machinery of the state operates according to law. Since all the Member States of the Community subscribe to the notion of the *Rechtstaat* there is no reason to suppose that the Community would be different.

Political or parliamentary control of the executive takes various forms: debate, questions, censure. The legislative acts of the executive are subject to parliamentary scrutiny and where breaches of the constitution are alleged the matter may be considered by a constitutional tribunal or (as in the case of the United Kingdom) parliament itself. This does not preclude a judicial review. The European Parliament can hardly be regarded as a parliament in the accepted sense of the word. It is a deliberative body and in a limited sense a controlling body. Its control is confined to the control of the Commission as the chief bureaucratic body but, not being a fully-fledged parliament, it neither legislates (although it participates

---

1   See supra, p 49 et seq.

in the legislative process) nor controls the legislative acts of the Community organs.[2]

In the Community the control of legality is in the hands of the Community Court.[3] Thus, within the duty of ensuring that the law is observed in the interpretation and application of the Treaty, the Court has the power of judicial review of the legality of acts of the Community Institutions. These include regulations, directions and decisions which are 'binding' but exclude recommendations and opinions which are 'not binding'. The legal status of the Community acts determines the scope of judicial control. It follows that only the 'binding acts' may, in accordance with the Treaties,[4] be subject to judicial control.

Recently various 'Acts' of the European Parliament came under judicial scrutiny, the phenomenon being a reflection of the ascendancy of the European Parliament and of the extent of the judicial control in the Community. While the European Parliament is the master in its own house, ie in control of its own proceedings,[5] certain Acts, particularly those which are not merely regulating procedure and may have legal effects outside the Parliament's domain, have to conform to the principle of legality as understood in the Community system. Thus, in principle, decisions of the European Parliament are subject to judicial review, as, for example, was the resolution to allocate staff, which was *ultra vires*,[6] financial aid to political parties fighting an election to the European Parliament, which was declared to be outside the scope of the Community budget since the matter was exclusively within the power of the Member States.[7] However, the setting up of a parliamentary committee of inquiry[8] or the decision to hold a plenary session away from Strasbourg,[9] though 'decisions' of a kind, were not justiciable as they were taken within the notion of parliamentary procedure and were not intended to produce external legal effects.

The making, the notification and the publication of the binding acts are subject to the Court's scrutiny from the point of view of legality, form and publicity of these acts. The Court has jurisdiction[10] 'to review the legality of acts adopted jointly by the European Parliament and the Council, of acts of the Council, of the Commission and of the European Central Bank and of the European Parliament intended to produce legal effects' vis-á-vis third parties.

Actions for review are brought by 'a Member State, the Council or the Commission' on grounds of lack of competence, infringement of an essential procedural requirement; infringement of this Treaty or of any rule of law relating to its application or misuse of powers.[11] It has jurisdiction 'under the same conditions in actions brought by the European Parliament, by the Court of Auditors and by the European Central Bank for the purpose of protecting their prerogatives'.[12]

---

2 However, see the *Isoglucose* cases, supra; see also Case 230/81: *Luxembourg v European Parliament* [1983] ECR 255, [1983] 2 CMLR 726.
3 EC Arts 220, 230, 234 (ex Arts 164, 173, 177).
4 TEC Art 230 (ex Art 173); EAEC Art 146; ECSC Art 33; but see Case 182/80, supra, p 158, note 9.
5 See Cases 230/81 and 108/83: *Luxembourg v European Parliament* [1983] ECR 255 and [1984] ECR 1945.
6 Case 108/83: *Luxembourg v European Parliament* [1984] ECR 1945, [1986] 2 CMLR 507.
7 Case 294/83: *Partie Ecologiste, 'les Verts' v European Parliament* [1986] ECR 1339, [1987] 2 CMLR 343.
8 Case 78/85: *Group of the European Right v European Parliament* [1986] ECR 1753, [1988] 3 CMLR 645.
9 Cases 358/85 and 51/86: *France v European Parliament, Re Meetings Facilities in Brussels* [1988] ECR 4821, [1990] 1 CMLR 309.
10 EC Art 230(1) (ex Art 173(1)).
11 EC Art 230(2).

A natural or legal person can also institute proceedings but only for the annulment of a decision addressed to that person or a decision which, 'although in the form of a regulation or a decision addressed to another person, is of direct and individual concern to [the complainant]'.[13] Therefore, held the ECJ,[14] an application for annulment of a decision was unfounded if the applicant had no longer any legally recognized interest in the matter. Indeed it would constitute an abuse of the judicial process to pursue the action when a judgment of the ECJ concerning the same parties and a similar question was already given in another case. Thus the application for annulment of a Commission decision fixing the minimum price of frozen beef put up for sale by the intervention agency had to be dismissed when the applicant, having offered a lower price (which was rejected), brought an action for annulment of the decision rejecting his offer.

It must be emphasized that national courts are not competent to rule on the validity of Community Acts. If such Acts are challenged in a national jurisdiction a reference for a preliminary ruling ought to be made but pending such ruling they have to be considered valid. It was so held by the ECJ in a case of attempted post-clearance recovery of customs duties where the imported goods were mistakenly regarded as duty-free. The Commission decision ordering recovery out of time was held invalid.[15]

Similarly, while reviewing a Commission decision addressed to a Member State with regard to state aid, the ECJ held that pending the judicial determination the decision had internal validity, was binding on the addressee and had to be complied with unless compliance was impossible or suspended by ECJ's order.[16]

(e) Judicial legislation

(i) The powers of the ECJ

The Court has the duty of ensuring observance of the law and whilst doing so may explain and complement the Treaties and Community legislation. This gives the Court an opportunity of laying down or defining Community law. The powers and functions of the Court will be analysed elsewhere[17] and it will suffice here to investigate the ways in which the Court may contribute to the sources of Community law. Jurisdiction to decide certain matters at first instance has been allocated to the court of first instance (the CFI) which is attached to the ECJ.

The Court, as a fully-fledged judicial body, has the power necessary to carry out its duties as specified in the Treaties. Its jurisdiction is exceptional in the sense that it is not a substitute for the national courts of the Member States. It is exclusive and also circumscribed by the Treaties. In all aspects it is the internal Court of the Community and as far as legal style is concerned it is a continental court modelled upon the French Conseil d'Etat.

The jurisdiction of the ECJ combines a variety of judicial functions extending over a number of specialist fields: 'federal' (adjudicating upon the relations between the Member States and the Community), constitutional (on the institutional balance, the institutional competence and the compatibility of Community legislation with the constituent Treaties), administrative (on the

---

12   EC Art 230(3).
13   EC Art 230(4) (ex Art 173).
14   Case 243/78: *Simmenthal SpA v Commission* [1980] ECR 593.
15   Case 314/85: *Foto-Frost v HZA Lübeck-Ost* [1987] ECR 4199, [1988] 3 CMLR 57; see also *R v Minister of Agriculture, Fisheries and Food, ex p FEDESA* [1988] 3 CMLR 207, QB and 661, QB.
16   Case 63/87: *Commission v Greece* [1988] ECR 2875, [1989] 3 CMLR 677.
17   See ch 9, infra.

validity of administrative orders and decisions), economic and commercial (on the various economic policies of the Community and commercial activities or enterprises), social (social justice and equality of the sexes), and labour (relationships between the Community and its servants). In relation to some of these matters, the ECJ's jurisdiction is original and in relation to others it is appellate. The appellate jurisdiction comprises supervision over the quasi-judicial decisions of the Commission (ie in the field of competition, state aids, dumping, economic protective measures, financial sanctions imposed by the Commission under the ECSC Treaty), appeals in intellectual property matters[18] and appeals from judgments of the CFI.

There are no appeals to the ECJ from national courts which, within their jurisdiction, administer Community law; though the ECJ has the power of advising the national courts by means of reference for preliminary ruling on points of Community law.[19]

In so far as the Court has to ensure observance of the law it acts as an instrument of sovereignty; in so far as it has to ensure the correct interpretation and application of the law as regards both the functioning of the Community and the development of the Community law, it exercises a law-making function appropriate to a judicial body. We shall address ourselves to the latter.

It is axiomatic that, given the requisite power, the lesser the precision of the law the greater the scope for judicial legislation. The Community Treaties are far from being precise and tightly drafted. In so far as they represent the Community framework it is the task of the Court to complete the system and fill the gaps.

(ii) Judicial interpretation

Interpretation is the principal method of laying down judge-made law and since the Court is a continental court it has adopted what we have termed the 'continental style'. In the civil law systems the court has no law-making power and precedent is not regarded as a source of law. However, through the instrumentality of interpretation judges are in the position of filling the gaps in the legal system and, through the definition of rights and duties in judgments, they create a body of rules which, without any statutory authority, has a persuasive force. The Community Court is in a unique position: it has the power to review the legality of the acts of the Community organs, has no parliament to look up to as a sovereign source of law and, above all, has to interpret Treaties which comprise general policies alongside precise rules of law.[20] In the circumstances the Community Court cannot help contributing to the growth of Community law.

In the absence of any established canons of interpretation[1] the Court is free to draw on rules evolved in the Member States and will do so not only in the spirit of the Community but also for practical reasons, because Community law, in order to command general respect and acceptance, has to be a synthesis of the laws of the Member States and, at every stage of its growth, has to draw strength from the practices and principles already well established.

---

18 Community Patent Agreement, EEC Member States [1990] 2 CMLR 194; Reg No 40/94 on the Community Trade Mark (OJ 1994, 11 of 14 January 1994 p1); Reg No 2100/94 (OJ 1994, L227 p 1) on Community plant variety rights.
19 See ch 10, infra.
20 Cf opinion of A-G Roemer in Case 13/60: *Geitling Ruhrkohlen Verkaufs-GmbH v High Authority of the ECSC* [1962] ECR 83, [1962] CMLR 113 at 125, 128.
 1 Kutscher, K, *Methods of Interpretation as seen by a Judge at the Court of Justice* (1976); Lasok, K P E, in 'Law of the European Communities' (looseleaf edn, 1993) (Vaughan, D, (gen ed)) Part 2(7).

Literal, or grammatical, interpretation is always the basic method and where the meaning of the text is clear there is no need of interpretation for *clara non sunt interpretanda*. However, in the Community set-up Community legislation must conform to the relevant treaty, so much so that the clear language of an act of a Community organ must not be allowed to prevail if, in the light of the Treaty, it leads to absurdity or illegality.[2]

On the question of linguistic differences and inconsistencies between the different provisions of the Treaty, Advocate-General Roemer submitted in *Internationale Crediet- en Handelsvereniging NV 'Rotterdam' v Ministry of Agriculture and Fisheries*[3] that the same standard of draftsmanship as that in the national legislation cannot be expected in Treaties.[4] Literal interpretation must take this into account.

Next to literal interpretation comes the logical interpretation which requires the Court to consider the text within the context of the system. In *Simon v Court of Justice of the European Communities*[5] the Court held that where the text is ambiguous the most reasonable solution must be sought, and in *Société Technique Minière v Maschinenbau Ulm GmbH*[6] the Court restricted prohibitions in the Treaty to matters which it considered detrimental to the aims of the Community. In *Germany v Commission*[7] Advocate-General Roemer submitted that the Court should be guided by considerations which make good sense both politically and administratively, and in *Costa Flaminio v ENEL*[8] Advocate-General Lagrange stated that excessive formalism should give way to the Community spirit in relations between the Community and the Member States. In a more technical sense Advocate-General Lagrange put in a nutshell the purpose of logical interpretation when he stressed in *de Geus v Bosch*[9] that the Court must not be defeated by obscurities or contradictions in the wording of the text for the real meaning can be deduced from the context or spirit of the text. In this vein several cases have been decided, illustrating both the technique and law-making potential of logical interpretation.[10]

2 Case 14/63: *Forges de Clabecq v High Authority of the ECSC* [1963] ECR 357 at 372, 373 [1964] CMLR 167 at 176; Case 2/67: *De Moor v Caisse de Pension des Employés Privés* [1967] ECR 197, [1967] CMLR 223 at 230–31, 325. See also Case 67/79: *Fellinger v Bundesanstalt für Arbeit* [1980] ECR 535 at 550, [1981] 1 CMLR 471 at 478.
3 Cases 73–74/63: [1964] ECR 1, [1964] CMLR 198 at 206.
4 Cf Lord Denning in *HP Bulmer Ltd v J Bollinger SA* [1974] 2 All ER 1226 at 1231–1232.
5 Case 15/60: [1961] ECR 115 at 125. See also Case 9/70: *Grad v Finanzant Traustein* [1970] ECR 825 at 839, [1971] CMLR 1 at 25; Case 67/79, supra.
6 Case 56/65: [1966] ECR 235 at 248, 249, [1966] CMLR 357 at 371, 376.
7 Case 34/62: [1963] ECR 131 at 156, [1963] CMLR 369 at 380.
8 Case 6/64: [1964] ECR 585 at 609, [1964] CMLR 425 at 448.
9 Case 13/61: [1962] ECR 45 at 70, [1962] CMLR 1 at 23. See also Case 118/79: *Gerbrüder Knauf v HZA Hamburg-Jonas* [1980] ECR 1183 at 1190–1191; Case 143/82: *Lipman v Commission* [1983] ECR 1301 at 1310; Case 136/80: *Hudig en Pieters BV v Minister van Landbouw en Visserij* [1981] ECR 2233 at 2241–2242, [1983] 1 CMLR 582 at 593.
10 Eg case 10/61: *Re Italian Customs Duty on Radio Valves Commission v Italy* [1962] CMLR 187 at 201–202; ref. to Arts 12, 14 (1) and 19 (2) (III); Case 75/63: *Hoekstra (née Unger) v Bestuur der Bedriffsvereniging voor Detailhandel en Ambachten* [1964] ECR 177, [1964] CMLR 319, ref to Art 51; Case 24/62: *Germany v Commission* [1963] ECR 63, [1963] CMLR 347 at 336–367, ref to Arts 25 (3) and 29; Case 10/65: *Deutschmann v Germany* [1965] ECR 469, [1965] CMLR 259, ref to Arts 13 and 95; Case 27/67: *Fink-Frucht GmbH v Hauptzollamt München* [1968] ECR 223, [1968] CMLR 187 at 299, ref to Arts 30 and 95; Case 29/68: *Milch-Fett- und Eierkontor GmbH v Hauptzollamt Saarbrücken (No 2)* [1969] ECR 165, [1969] CMLR 390, ref to Arts 9, 12, 13; Case 13/72: *Re Food Aids: Netherlands v Commission* [1973] ECR 27 at 40–42; see also the opinion of A-G Roemer in Case 5/71: *Aktien-Zuckerfabrik Schöppenstedt v Council* [1971] ECR 975 and A-G Warner in Case 81/72: *Re Civil Service Salaries Commission v Council* [1973] ECR 575 at 595–596, [1973] CMLR 639 at 652–653.

Courts are notoriously reticent about the use of teleological interpretation which, though basically literal, brings out the intention of the legislator in the light of the conditions prevailing at the time of the judgment.[11] Teleological interpretation is necessary where literal interpretation would lead to absurd results.[12] The Treaties have not existed long enough to have, in the absence of a fundamental revision, their lives extended by interpretation, but references to the spirit or the aims of the Treaties[13] enable the Court to fill the gaps in the system and so 'update' the text. In doing so the Court has consciously acted not only as the 'Constitutional Court' of the Community but also as an architect of European integration.[14]

The Court does not act arbitrarily but judicially, which means that it has to see that its interpretation reflects the intention of the parties to the Treaties and the *ratio legis* of the text.[15] In tracing the intention of the legislator the Court is free to consult materials extraneous to the Treaty. These consist of the *travaux préparatoires* leading to the conclusion of Treaties and statements on behalf of the Community. The former are the various publications which reflect the substance of the negotiations and the attitudes of the negotiating parties from the inception to the conclusion of the Treaties. One could single out in this context official communiques and minutes of meetings, should these be available, and the official views of the negotiating governments. In view of the nature of the negotiations and the way governments work in their international relations the materials are not readily available. They have, according to a learned jurist,[16] 'a certain value, though their precise juristic meaning is arguable'. Though the Advocates-General have referred to *travaux préparatoires* in their opinions,[17] the court has effectively ceased to use the

---

11 See Case 33/69: *Commission v Italy* [1970] ECR 93 at 101, [1971] CMLR 466 at 475; Case 43/75: *Defrenne v SABENA* [1976] ECR 455 at 472, [1976] 2 CMLR 98 at 123–124.
12 See Cases 7/56 and 3–7/57: *Algera v Common Assembly* [1957–58] ECR 39.
13 Eg Case 56/65: *Société Technique Minière v Maschinenbau Ulm GmbH* [1966] ECR 235, [1966] CMLR 357; Case 34/62: *Germany v Commission* [1963] ECR 131, [1963] CMLR 369; Case 6/64: *Costa Flaminio v ENEL* [1964] ECR 585, [1964] CMLR 425; Case 13/61: *de Geus v Bosch* [1962] ECR 45, [1962] CMLR 1; Case 6/54: *Netherlands Government v High Authority* [1954–56] ECR 103; Case 6/60: *Jean Humblet v Belgium* [1960] ECR 559; Case 8–11/66: *Re Noordwijks Cement Accord* [1967] CMLR 77 at 104–105; Case 8/55: *Fédération Charbonnière de Belgique v High Authority of the ECSC* [1954–56] ECR 245; Case 16/61: *Modena v High Authority of the ECSC* [1962] ECR 546, [1962] CMLR 221 at 241; *Continental Can,* supra [1973] ECR at 143–245; [1973] CMLR at 223–225, 233–235; Case 151/73: *Ireland v Council* [1974] ECR 285, [1974] 1 CMLR 429 at 446–447. Ormand, R, 'L'utilisation particulière de la méthode d'interprétation des traites selon leur "effet utile" par la cour de Justice' 12 RTDE (1976) pp 624 et seq; Bleckmann, A, 'Teleologie and dynamische Auslegung der Europaischen Gemeinschaftsrechts' 14 EuR (1979) pp 239 et seq; Mortelmans, K, 'Les lacunes provisoires en droit communautaire' 17 CDE (1981) pp 410 et seq.
14 Schermers, H, 'The European Court of Justice: Promoter of European Integration' 22A JCL (1974) pp 459 et seq; Lasok, D, 'La Cour de Justice, instrument de l'integration communautaire' Rev d'integration europénne, II (1979) pp 391 et seq.
15 Case 6/60: *Jean-E Humblet v Belgium* [1960] ECR 559, supra at p 1154.
16 Reuter, P, *La CECA* (1953), p 30.
17 Cf Lagrange in Case 8/55: *Fédération Charbonnière de Belgique v High Authority of the ECSC* [1954–56] ECR 245; Roemer in Case 6/54: *Netherlands Government v High Authority of the ECSC* [1954–56] ECR 103; Cases 90–91/63: *Re Import of Milk Products, Commission v Luxembourg and Belgium* [1964] ECR 625 at 640, [1965] CMLR 58 at 65; Case 13/60: *Geitling Ruhrkohlen-Verkaufs-GmbH v High Authority of the ECSC* [1962] ECR 83 at 140, [1962] CMLR 113 at 146; Cases 73–74/63: *Internationale Crediet- en Handelsvereniging 'Rotterdam' v Minister von Landbowwen Visserij* [1964] ECR 1 at 20, [1964] CMLR 198 at 207; and in Case 38/69: *Re Customs Duties on Lead and Zinc Commission v Italy* [1970] ECR 47 at 62, [1970] CMLR 77 at 85; Case 42/72: A G Roemer in *Alfons Lütticke GmbH v Hauptzollamt Passau* [1973] ECR 57 at 74–75, [1973] CMLR 309 at 316–317.

travaux préparatoires of the Treaties, preferring to rely upon their content and purposes.[18]

Statements on behalf of the Community may[19] elucidate the Community legislation but the views of the Community officials on the interpretation of the Treaties are hardly relevant.[20] They are equally ineffective as far as the interpretation of the Community legislation is concerned.[1]

It follows that *travaux préparatoires*, as explained by Advocate-General Lagrange[2] have no compulsory place in the interpretation of the Treaties, but it is universally accepted that judges may turn to them for information in order to clarify the thoughts of the legislator. The judges are entirely free in their evaluation of these materials. However, *travaux préparatoires* are useful only if they clearly express the intention of the draftsman[3].

Preparatory materials are more likely to be used in the interpretation of Community legislation[4] or a Convention[5] since these are often preceded by working papers or explanatory memoranda accessible to the public. In this respect much can be expected of the application of the principle of subsidiarity to the drafting of Community legislation.[6]

In addition to interpretation in a technical sense further elements play an auxiliary part in the development of Community law. Of these we shall mention briefly references to the municipal laws of the Member States, references to general principles of law and references to learned writings.

The Treaties, like the rules of public international law, are influenced by the rules of municipal law. More than that they are derived from the laws of the Member States. As submitted by Advocate-General Roemer[7] the Court has to 'call upon the law of the different Member States in order to arrive at a meaningful interpretation of our Community law'. As a result some early cases comprise a detailed comparative study. Perhaps the best examples are the cases involving misuse of power and withdrawal, with retrospective effect, of an illegal administrative act.[8]

18   Case 2/74: *Reyners v Belgium* [1974] ECR 631 at 666, [1974] 2 CMLR 305 at 324, A-G Mayras.

19   Cases 2–10/63: *Società Industriale Acciaierie San Michele v High Authority of the ECSC* [1963] ECR 327 at 342-343, [1964] CMLR 146 at 165.

20   A-G Roemer in Cases 90–91/63: *Re Import of Milk Products Commission v Luxembourg and Belgium* [1964] ECR 625 at 640, [1965] CMLR 58 at 65; Cases 8–11/66: *Re Noordwijks Cement Accoord Society Anonyme Cimenteries CBR v Commission* [1967] ECR 75, [1967] CMLR 77 at 87.

 1   Cases 53–54/63: *Lemmerz-Werke GmbH v High Authority of the ECSC* [1963] ECR 239 at 247, [1964] CMLR 384 at 398.

 2   Case 8/55: *Fédération Charbonnière de Belgique v High Authority of the ECSC* [1954–56] ECR 245.

 3   Case 15/60: *Simon v Court of Justice* [1961] ECR 115 at 125; Cases C-68/94 and C-30/95: *France v Commission* [1998] ECR I-1375, para 167.

 4   Case 29/69: *Stauder v City of Ulm* [1969] ECR 419 at 425, [1970] CMLR 112 at 118; Case 83/78: *Pigs Marketing Board v Redmond* [1978] ECR 2347, [1979] 1 CMLR 177; Case 107/80: *Adorno v Commission* [1981] ECR 1469 at 1484, [1983] 2 CMLR 310 at 325; Case 38/81: *Effer SpA v Kantner* [1982] ECR 825 at 834, [1984] 2 CMLR 667 at 674–675.

 5   Case 14/70: *Deutsche Bakels v Oberfinanzdirektion München* [1970] ECR 1001; Case 30/71: *Kurt Siemers v HZA Bad Reichenhall* [1971] ECR 919, [1972] CMLR 121; Case 159/80: *Wünsche v Bundesanstalt für landwirtschaftlicheMarktordnung* [1981] ECR 2161 at 2175.

 6   Protocol on the application of the principle of subsidiarity annexed to the Treaty of Amsterdam, see pp 47–48, supra.

 7   Case 6/54: in *Netherlands Government v High Authority of the ECSC* [1954–56] ECR 103.

 8   See also Cases 7/56 and 3–7/57: *Algera v Common Assembly* [1957–58] ECR 39; Case 14/61: *Hoogovens v High Authority of the ECSC* [1962] ECR 253 at 281–284 and 287, [1963] CMLR 73 at 90–91, 96; further examples: Campbell, A, *Common Market law* (1969), Vol I, 7/258, pp 531–532.

In the latter case the Court came to the conclusion that 'a study of comparative law shows that whenever an administrative act is wrong in law, the laws of the Member States admit the possibility of revocation', and in accordance with this finding decreed that such an act was revokable with a retrospective effect. It does not follow, however, that the laws of all the Member States must be consulted. If the problem is peculiar to two countries a consideration of the two systems may be sufficient,[9] and on occasions even reference to one country only may suffice.[10] The other extreme, which the Court is free to adopt, is that sometimes a national system cannot be regarded as apposite.[11] More intriguing is the possibility of reference to the law of a non-Member State, but this must be regarded as a special case.[12] Indeed the Community law of competition, being modelled upon American law, invites such a reference.[13] Before the British accession the English law of estoppel[14] was considered whilst Advocate-General Warner made a significant British contribution to the discussion of natural justice.[15] The meaning and scope of professional privilege[16] applicable to lawyers in the process of investigation of the alleged breaches of competition rules was defined by reference to national systems.

However reference to national laws is exceptional and serves a purely auxiliary purpose where the Community judge cannot, through independent interpretation, identify in Community law or its general principles the elements which would enable him to construe the content or scope of the Community rule in question.[17] It is not normally made without express direction[18] to that effect. Moreover a concept of Community law must be construed in the context of the Community system by reference to national legislation rather than judgments of national courts[19] and in a manner compatible with the objectives of the Community measure in

9   A-G Lagrange in Case 5/55: *Associazione Industrie Siderurgiche Italiane v High Authority of the ECSC* [1954–55] ECR 135.

10 French law: Cases 7 and 9/54: *Groupement des Industries Siderurgiques Luxembourgoises v High Authority of the ECSC* [1954–55] ECR 175; Case 12/74: *Commission v Germany* [1975] ECR 181 at 209; German law: Case 18/57: *Nold KG v High Authority of the ECSC* [1959] ECR 41 pp 110–111; Cases 17 and 20/61: *Klöeckner-Werke und Hoesch v High Authority of the ECSC* [1962] ECR 325 at 351–353.

11 Eg Case 1/64: *Glucosiéries Réunies v Commission* [1964] ECR 813, [1964] CMLR 596 at 599.

12 See eg Case 12/73: *Muras v HZA Hamburg-Jonas* [1973] ECR 963 at 974.

13 Case 13/60: A-G Roemer in *Geitling Ruhrkohlen Verkaufs-GmbH v High Authority of the ECSC* [1962] ECR 83 at 126, [1962] CMLR 113 at 141; Case 16/61: *Modena v High Authority* [1962] CMLR 221 at 229–230, 232 [1962] ECR 546.

14 A-G Roemer in Cases 41 and 50/59: *Hamborner Bergbau AG v High Authority of the ECSC* [1960] ECR 493. Cf Case 48/72: *Brasserie de Haecht v Wilkin-Janssen* [1973] ECR 77 at 87, [1973] CMLR 287 at 302; Case 84/85: *United Kingdom v Commission (Re European Social Fund)* [1987] ECR 3765, [1988] 1 CMLR 113.

15 Case 17/74: *Transocean Marine Paint Association v Commission* [1974] ECR 1063, [1974] 2 CMLR 459.

16 Case 155/79: *A M & S Europe Ltd v Commission* [1982] ECR 1575 at 1610–1612, [1982] 2 CMLR 264 at 322–324.

17 Cases T-43/90: *Diaz Garcia v European Parliament* [1992] ECR II-2619 and Case T-85/91: *Khouri v Commission* [1992] ECR II-2637.

18 Case 51/76: *Verbond van Nederlandse Ondernemingen v Inspecteur der Invoerrechten en Accijnzen* [1977] ECR 113 at 124–125, [1977] 1 CMLR 413 at 427; Case 154/80: *Staatssecretaris van Financiën v Coöperatieve Aardappelenvewaarplaats GA* [1981] ECR 445 at 453, [1981] 3 CMLR 337 at 345; Case 64/81: *Corman et Fils SA v HZA Gronau* [1982] ECR 13 at 24.

19 Case 1/77: *Robert Bosch GmbH v HZA Hildesheim* [1977] ECR 1473 at 1481, [1977] 2 CMLR 563 at 578.

question.[20] Consequently the process may not result in a restrictive interpretation of Community law.[1]

Echoing Article 38 of the Statute of the International Court of Justice the Community Court also refers to 'general principles of law'. These can be traced to doctrines developed within the context of public international law[2] or the municipal law of the Member States, but others remain untraceable.[3] No doubt the reference to 'general principles of law' has a certain scope as such principles may mean general doctrines of the law, eg justice, the right to be heard, etc, or rules of law expressed in general terms, eg contractual freedom, liability for wrongful act, non-discrimination, etc. Learned commentators[4] recognize the competence of the Court to take recourse to 'general principles of law'. Their views have been summarized as follows: 'il semble que lorsqu'une notion juridique existe, identique, dans le droit interne de tous les Etats membres, celle-ci s'impose aux organes de la Communauté comme un principe général qui doit être appliqué sous peine de la violation d'une règle de droit relative a l'application du traité'.[5]

Finally we should note the contribution of learned writers (the so-called *doctrine*) to the *Jurisprudence*[6] of the Community Court. Here again an analogy to Article 38 of the Statute of the International Court of Justice comes to mind where reference is made to 'the teachings of the most highly qualified publicists'. Continental courts are familiar with the contribution of learned writers to the development of the law and these, to command authority, need not necessarily be dead. Community law is still a relatively undeveloped system, a law in books rather than fully entrenched in life and, therefore, offers a challenge and scope for creative comments. *Doctrine* represents, of course, well-founded opinions on what the law should be, not any piece of 'creative writing', by those who have established a reputation in their field. Its influence should not be exaggerated but viewed from the perspective of the standing of the academic lawyer in the civil law countries and the closer affinity of continental judges to the academic world rather than the Bar. The fact that, in spite of the abundance of academic writings on Community law, the Court only in few cases, albeit through the Advocates-General, referred to juristic writings indicates both the scope and limitations of their contribution.

20 Case 75/63: *Hoekstra (née Unger) v Bestuur der Bedrijfsvereiniging voor Detailhandel en Ambachten* [1964] ECR 177 at 184–185; [1964] CMLR 319 at 347.
1 Case 149/79: *Commission v Belgium* [1980] ECR 3881 at 3903, [1981] 2 CMLR 413 at 435.
2 Eg on equality and discrimination, A-G Lagrange in Case 13/63: *Re Electric Refrigerators Italy v Commission* [1963] ECR 165 at 190, [1963] CMLR 289 at 303, on the status of international administrative tribunals; A-G Roemer in Case 1/56: *Bourgaux v ECSC Common Assembly* [1954–56] ECR 361.
3 Eg on the meaning of 'discrimination' and 'comparable price conditions to consumers in comparable circumstances' in Cases 3–18, 25, 26/58: *Barbara Erzbergbau v High Authority* [1960] ECR 173.
4 Reuter, P, 'Le recours de la Cour de justice des Communautés européennes à des principes généraux de droit', in *Mélanges Henri Rolin* (1964), p 263.
5 Mathijsen, P, *Le droit de la CECA* (1958), p 142.
6 A-G Roemer in Case 13/60: *Geitling Ruhrkohlen-Verkaufs-GmbH v High Authority of the ECSC* [1962] ECR 83 at 135–136, [1962] CMLR 113 at 159; in Cases 106–107/63: *Toepfer KG v Commission* [1965] ECR 405 at 436 [1966] CMLR 111 at 118, on the power of intervention of the Council of Ministers by Wohlfart, E, Everling, U, Glaesner, H J, and Sprung, R, 'Die Europäische Wirtschaftsgemeinschaft', *Kommentar zum Vertrag* (1969); A-G Roemer in Case 67/63: *Sorema v High Authority of the ECSC* [1964] ECR 151 at 170, [1964] CMLR 350 at 352, on the definition of an association of undertakings by Reuter, P, *La Communauté Européenne du Charbon et de l'Acier* (1953); A-G Warner in Case 31/74: *Filippo Galli* [1975] ECR 47 att 70 on the direct applicability of regulations by Winter, J A in 9 CML Rev, 1972 p 425 at 435–436; A-G Reischl in Case 72/74: *Union Syndicale-Service Public Européen v Council (No 2)* [1975] ECR 401 at 416 cites several writers on Administrative Law.

(iii)   Community precedents[7]

Since *Jurisprudence* represents the body of case law evolved through interpretation of the texts a few comments on the role of precedents in the Community system seem necessary. The judgment of the Court can be divided into two parts: the *motifs* (reasons) and the *dispositif* (the ruling). From the parties' point of view the ruling is of primary interest because, after all, it decided the issue. Indeed, under the doctrine of *res judicata* the judgment is binding upon the Court where there is an identity of parties, cause and object.[8] Apart from *res judicata* the Court is not bound by its previous decisions but this does not mean that precedents are ignored.

In the eyes of the continental lawyer precedents have only a persuasive force in the sense that they reflect the application of the law in practice. However they must be taken into account when assessing the likely impact of arguments in court or prognosticating the outcome of litigation. Assuming that courts do not administer justice in an erratic manner the concept of *jurisprudence constante* suggests that their decisions provide a reliable guide. Under the doctrine of separation of powers the judges have no law-making function and indeed by Article 5 of the French Civil Code they are prohibited from deciding cases in a general and rule-making manner. Their decisions must be based on the law, not on previously decided cases. Should the latter be the case the decision in France would probably be quashed by the Cour de Cassation because of *défaut de base légale*.[9] However, there is no harm in considering cases and citing precedents in the *motifs* of the judgment. Judges who study reports of cases cannot fail to notice the interpretation adopted by the Courts. They have the benefit of learned comments and opinions expressed in the *doctrine*, and during oral arguments counsel do not neglect the opportunity of impressing upon the Court the fact that a certain decision was reached on similar facts in previous cases. However, by tradition, when deciding a case judges must arrive at the particular interpretation by themselves just in case the Court which decided the previous case made a mistake. Therefore, judgments are substantiated by reference to the law comprised in codes and statutes. In the absence of a code or statute the case will be decided according to custom and in the absence of custom according to 'equity, reason, justice, tradition', but never according to 'precedent'.[10]

The scope for the persuasive influence of precedent is very great indeed in the uncodified areas of the law, notably administrative law. Here in addition to statutes the 'general principles of the law' play a considerable part and these, in turn, can often be found applied in precedents. The French Conseil d'Etat not only administers a body of law derived from precedents but also endeavours to relate its decisions to the pattern of case law.

The Community Court, modelled upon the Conseil d'Etat, fulfils a similar function and relies on its own decisions in a similar manner. On several occasions it either followed or referred to its previous decisions[11] in the *motifs*, which

---

7   Koopmans, T, '*Stare Decisis* in European Law', in O'Keefe and Schermers (eds), *Essays in European Law and Integration*, (1982), pp 11–27.

8   Cases 28–30/62: *Da Costa en Schaake NV v Nederlandse Administratre der Belastingen* [1963] ECR 61, [1963] CMLR 224; A-G Lagrange at 229–233.

9   David, R, *Le Droit Français* (1960), p 161.

10   Ibid, p 162.

11   Cases 28–30/62: *Da Costa en Schaake NV v Netherlands Revenue Department* [1963] ECR 31, [1963] CMLR 224; Case 44/65: *Hessische Knappschaft v Maison Singer* [1965] ECR 965, [1966] CMLR 82; Case 28/67: *Mölkerei-Zentrale Westfalen-Lippe GmbH v Hauptzollamt Paderborn* [1968] ECR 143 at 153, [1968] CMLR 187 at 216–219; *Filippo Galli*, supra,

correspond to the *ratio decidendi* of the common law doctrine of precedent. The tendency of citing precedents not only by the Court but also, and to a greater extent, by the Advocates-General has grown in the course of time.[12]

Advocate-General Roemer[13] thus stated the position 'it is natural that as the Common Market develops facts may appear which by reason of their novelty and the impossibility of foreseeing them may compel us to modify hitherto well established legal opinions' and he concluded that previous decisions cannot have the binding force of precedents. In another case[14] involving the interpretation of EC Article 85 (now 81) in which the parties abundantly cited previous decisions, he said: 'It is, therefore, appropriate ... to resort to these decisions with discretion, even where the general terms of propositions suggest their application to problems not arising in the case before the Court when they were formulated.' Indeed the question whether a previous judgment was binding upon another national court would be held inadmissible.[15]

Whilst the judgments of the ECJ are precedents in their own right because they have settled important points of law and in many cases broken a new ground the question arises whether they are *precedents* in the accepted sense of the word or, more precisely, within the common law doctrine of *stare decisis*.

The doctrine of *stare decisis* rests upon the hierarchy of courts and the style of judgments and reports. The ECJ is a unique court of first and last instance (save to the extent that jurisdiction at first instance has been allocated to the CFI), but since it has become a court of appeal from the CFI precedents are likely to be more widely used in the Community adjudication system, at least to the extent that the CFI considers itself bound by previous judgments of the ECJ. Although it is the internal court of the Community it is not an exact replica of a supreme federal court; still less it resembles the Court of International Justice. However it functions like a supreme court of a federation as well as the only judicial organ of an inter-state organization. In that capacity it has to decide matters of principle and policy. In the latter context the ECJ has been using its Olympian position in furtherance of a legal integration of the Community.[16] Nevertheless, the ECJ's technique is to decide each case on its specific merits rather than in the light of the historical experience enshrined in precedents. Therefore it avoids using the theory of *acte clair* in this respect preferring a fresh approach to the issues before

123; Case 12/74: *Commission v Federal Republic of Germany* [1975] ECR 181, [1975] 1 CMLR 340; Case 67/74: *Bonsignore v Oberstadtdirektor der Stadt Köln* [1975] ECR 297, [1975] 1 CMLR 472; *Union Syndicale* op cit, 123; Case 94/74: *IGAV-Industria Gomma Articoli Vari v Ente Nazionale* [1975] ECR 699 at 701, 705, 708; Case 7/75: *F v Belgium* [1975] ECR 679 at 684; Case 21/75: *Schroeder KG-Hamburg v Oberstadtsdirektor der Stadt Köln* [1975] ECR 905 at 910, to name some older cases.

12   *Fillipo Galli* at 68; *Angelo Alaimo* at 113; *Commission* at 206 et seq; *Bonsignore* at 310; *Union Syndicale* at 708; case 79/74: *Berthold Küster v European Parliament* [1975] ECR 725 at 734; *IGAV-Industria Gomma Articoli Vari v ENCC-Ente Nazionale etc* at 715; *Fracas*, supra, at 692; Case 8/75: supra. *Caisse Primaire d'Assurance Maladaise Sélestat (Bas-Rhin) France v Association du Football Club Andlau (Bes-Rhin) France* [1975] ECR 739 at 757; *Schroeder KG* op cit at 915; Case 112/76 *Manzoni v Fonds National de Retraite des Ouvriers Mineurs* [1977] ECR 1647, [1978] 2 CMLR 416 to name only some older cases.

13   In Case 1/64: *SA Glucosiéries Réunies v Commission* [1964] ECR 413 at 419, [1964] CMLR 596 at 598.

14   Case 23/67: *Brasserie de Haecht v Wilkin* [1967] ECR 407, [1968] CMLR 26.

15   See Case 24/66 (*bis*)L *Gesellschaft für Getreidehandel mbH v Commission* [1973] ECR 1599 at 1603; per A-G Reischl at 1606.

16   Lasok, D, 'La Cour de Justice, instrument de l'intégration communautaire' (1979), *Rev d'intégration européenne*, pp 391 et seq.

it. However, in the *CILFIT*[17] case the Court, albeit hesitantly, recognized the force of precedent in Community law, repeating its dictum in an earlier case[18] that '... the authority of an interpretation ... already given by the Court may deprive the obligation (to refer under Article 177) of its purpose and thus empty it of its substance ...'.

Like a supreme court it is not and cannot be bound by its own decisions.[19] Indeed in the Community context it is doubtful whether it has the power, let alone the wish, to declare itself bound by its own decisions.[20] However it may wish to cite its own decisions either to indicate a continuing line of reasoning or, simply, to cut corners. This is a matter of the style of citation.

There is a rather haphazard approach to citation in the ECJ decisions. Originally, in the few cases in which a previous ruling was adopted, there was no trace of the pedigree of the new ruling. Whole sentences or paragraphs were incorporated in the judgment without reference to or acknowledgement of the source. The famous dictum that 'the Community is a new legal order etc' taken from the *Van Gend* case appeared often in the reports.[1] As of late the formula 'As the Court has already stated in ...' with reference to the cited case,[2] or words to that effect, has been adopted. No doubt this is an improvement but we still have to wait for the Court's express acknowledgement[3] of the persuasive authority of its own decisions and for the Court distinguishing rulings inconsistent with the previous ones and giving the reasons for the distinction. So far the Court has tended to ignore previous decisions from which it has deviated.[4] However it did not hesitate to apply the tenor of its judgment in an enforcement action[5] to a

---

17 Case 283/81: *CILFIT Srl v Ministry of Health* [1982] ECR 3415 at para 13, [1983] 1 CMLR 472.

18 Cases 28–30/62: *Da Costa v Nederlandse Belastingadministratie* [1963] ECR 31, [1963] CMLR 224.

19 See Case 112/76: *Manzoni v Fonds National de Retraite des Ouvriers Mineurs* [1977] ECR 1647 at 1662, [1978] 2 CMLR 416 at 429 (per A-G Warner).

20 Cf the British House of Lords ruled to be so bound in *London Street Tramways Co Ltd v LCC* [1898] AC 375 but discarded the rule per Lord Gardiner LC, reported at [1966] 3 All ER 77, [1966] 1 WLR 1234.

1 Case 26/62: *Van Gend en Loos v Netherlands Amministratie der Belastingen* [1963] ECR 1 at 29, [1963] CMLR 105 at 129.

2 Eg Case 70/77: *Simmenthal SpA v Administrazione delle Finanze dello Stato* [1978] ECR 1453 at 1469, [1978] 3 CMLR 670 at 684; Case 50/76: *Amsterdam Bulb BV v Produktschap voor Siergewassen* [1977] ECR 137 at 146, [1977] 2 CMLR 218 at 240; Case 128/78: *Commission v United Kingdom, Re Tachograph* [1979] ECR 419 at 428, [1979] 2 CMLR 45 at 55; Case 153/78: *Re Health Control on Imported Meat: Commission v Germany* [1979] ECR 2555 at para 5 (p 2564), [1980] 1 CMLR 198 at 207; Cases 66/79, 127–128/79: *Amministrazione delle Finanze v Meridionale Industria Salumi SRL* [1980] ECR 1237 at 1261, [1981] 1 CMLR 1 at 17; Case 811/79: *Amministrazione delle Finanze dello Stato v Ariete SpA* [1980] ECR 2545 at 2553, 2555, [1981] 1 CMLR 316.

3 In this respect Case 54/80: *Procureur de la République v Wilner* [1980] ECR 3673, [1983] 2 CMLR 444, at paras 6 and 7, citing Case 65/79: *Procureur de la République v Chatain* [1980] ECR 1345, [1981] 3 CMLR 418 as a source of Community law. See also Case 283/81, note 17, supra citing Cases 28–30/62, note 18 supra; Case C-70/88: *European Parliament v Council, re E P prerogatives* [1990] ECR I-2041 citing Case 302/87: *European Parliament v Council, re comitology* [1988] ECR 5615.

4 However, in Cases 240–242/82, 261–262/82 and 268–269/82 *Stichting Sigarettenindustrie v Commission* [1985] ECR 3831, [1987] 3 CMLR 661, the ECJ distinguished its judgment in Cases 209–215 and 218/78: *Heintz van Landewyck Sàrl v Commission* [1980] ECR 3125, [1981] 3 CMLR 134. See also Cases C-267 and C-268/9: *Keck and Mithouard, Proceedings against* [1993] ECR I-6097.

5 Case 152/78: *Commission v France* [1980] ECR 2299, [1981] 2 CMLR 743.

subsequent reference[6] arising from a prosecution under national law regulating the advertisement of alcoholic beverages inconsistent with Community law. Yet, in the terms of the judgment it was not a question of applying a precedent but of interpreting the relevant Community law as well as the judgment which explained the law. However, more recently the Court disposed of a case which revealed no new issues simply by reference to its earlier decisions.[7]

The doctrine of binding precedent must be supported by a comprehensive system of law reporting. The decisions of the ECJ are reported systematically whether in the private collections (eg CMLR) or the Court's own Reports (ECR). However not all cases are so reported and the ECR, though an official publication of the Court, does not carry the seal of authenticity. Probably no such guarantee can be given in view of the linguistic problems of translation but, in view of the quality of the reports, there is no reason to suppose that they are not a faithful reproduction of the Court's records.

There is no hierarchical relationship between the national judiciary and the ECJ. Even in the field of references for preliminary rulings the ECJ does not operate as a court of appeal or review but simply as a court of reference, albeit with the unique and supreme power of interpretation. Therefore the essential condition upon which the doctrine of *stare decisis* rests is not present. The judgments of the ECJ are not subject to appeal or *exequatur* within national jurisdictions and their executive authority, except in the case of judgments against the Member States, is assured by Treaty provisions.[8] However since their status ranks no higher than a *res judicata* it depends upon the given national system whether they are treated as precedents or otherwise. Thus the curious result of section 3(2) of the European Communities Act 1972 is that their status in the United Kingdom appears to be higher than that in the civil law countries.[9]

Despite the arguments against the '*government of judges*',[10] the status of preliminary rulings appears to be different from the judgments in contentious proceedings. Here the Court makes a ruling on an abstract point of law which, in a sense, becomes the property of the whole Community in view of the procedure in which the Commission and all the Member States may participate and the general interest the point should have for the entire Community legal system. Therefore, as argued Advocate-General Warner,[11] these rulings should have effect *erga omnes*. In reality they can be so regarded despite the fact that national courts are free to raise similar if not identical questions repeatedly and that the ECJ too is free to change its mind.

In conclusion the creative role of the ECJ in the interpretation and formulation of the principles of Community law has to be recognized without necessarily ascribing to its case law the status of a formal source of law.

---

6   Joined Cases 314–316/81 and 83/82: *Procureur de la République v Waterkeyn* [1982] ECR 4337, [1983] 2 CMLR 145.
7   Cases 271–274/84 and 6–7/85: *Procureur de la République v Chiron* [1986] ECR 529, [1988] 1 CMLR 735.
8   EC Art 244 (ex Art 187); ECSC Arts 44 and 92; EAEC Arts 159 and 164.
9   Wall, E A, European Communities Act 1972 (1973), p 28.
10 Lecourt, R, *Le juge devant le marché commun* (1970), p 57; *L'Europe des Juges* (1976).
11 Case 112/76: *Manzoni v Fonds National de Retraite des Ouvriers Mineurs* [1977] ECR 1647 at 1661–1663, [1978] 2 CMLR 416 at 429–430. See also Joined Cases 28–30/62: *Da Costa en Schaake NV v Nederlandse Belastingadministratie* [1963] ECR 31 at 38, [1963] CMLR 224 at 235–236; Case 283/81: *CILFIT Srl v Minister of Health* [1982] ECR 3415 at 3429–3430, [1983] 1 CMLR 472 at 477–478; Case 112/83: *Société des Produits de Maïs SA v Administration des Douanes* [1985] ECR 719, [1988] 1 CMLR 459.

(iv)   Basic doctrines
In furthering 'the intention of the contracting states ... to create a Community designed for progressive integration'[12] the Court developed certain doctrines which characterize the Community legal order as an original system and determine its relationship to the municipal law of the Member States:

Unity   From an early stage the Court advanced the idea of a functional unity of the three Communities[13] which, in the jurisprudence of the Court, meant that one founding Treaty should be interpreted with the aid of the others.[14] Of these cases one involving a Community official merits a special attention.[15] Sr Campolongo, who was employed by the High Authority of the Coal and Steel Community, was discharged and took up an appointment with the European Investment Bank instituted under the EC Treaty. He claimed various benefits including a reinstallation allowance, but the Court decreed that he was not entitled to it because the 'functional unity' of the Communities does not permit accumulation of payments due on the termination of employment with one and commencement of employment with another institution of the Communities. The Court recognized the separate legal personalities of the Communities according to Articles 6, 210 (now EC Article 281) and 184 of the Treaties which founded the ECSC, EC and EAEC, respectively, but emphasized that through the Merger Treaty a strong legal bond between the Communities has been established. Advocate-General Roemer, whose submissions in this respect were followed by the Court, stated that 'the European Treaties are nothing but a partial implementation of a grand general programme, dominated by the idea of a complete integration of the European States'.

The idea of unity in the uniform interpretation and application of the Community and the equal acceptance of Treaty obligations by the Member States was emphasized by the Court on several occasions. In the *Gingerbread*[16] cases the Court underlined the unitary and mandatory nature of Community law without which it would be impossible to establish the Common Market. This theme was followed in the *Costa*[17] case where, inter alia, the compatibility of the nationalization of the Italian electricity industry with the EC Treaty was raised and cases in which the Court insisted that certain key terms of Community law such as *scrap equalization charge*;[18] *rediscount rate*;[19] *public policy*;[20] to give just a few examples, have a 'Community meaning' and must be interpreted and applied as such. In respect of the Member States' duties the Court stressed that a state 'cannot ... unilaterally opt out of ... its obligations' and that 'non-compliance ...

---

12   Kutscher, op cit, p 32.
13   Colon, J-P, *Le gouvernement des juges dans les Communautés Européennes* (1966) 74 et seq.
14   Case 6/60: *Humblet v Belgium* [1960] ECR 559; Case 30/59: *De Gezamenlijke Steenkolenmijnen in Limburg v High Authority of the ECSC* [1961] ECR 1; Case 9/59: (1959), 6 Rec 27; Case 13/60: *Geitling v High Authority* [1962] ECR 83; Case 230/81: *Luxembourg v European Parliament* [1983] ECR 255, [1983] 2 CMLR 726.
15   Cases 27/59 and 39/59: *Alberto Campolongo v High Authority of the ECSC* [1960] ECR 391.
16   Cases 2–3/62: *Commission v Luxembourg and Belgium (Import Licences for Ginger Bread)* [1962] ECR 425, [1963] CMLR 199.
17   Case 6/64: *Costa v ENEL* [1964] ECR 585, [1964] CMLR 425.
18   Case 26/66: *Koninklijke Nederlandsche Hoogovens v High Authority of the ECSG* [1967] ECR 115.
19   Cases 6–11/69: *Commission v France* [1969] ECR 523, [1970] CMLR 43.
20   *Van Duyn*, p 147, note 20, supra; Case 30/77: *R v Bouchereau* [1977] ECR 1999, [1977] 2 CMLR 800.

strikes at the very root of the Community legal order ...' and 'brings into question the equality of Member States before Community law ...'.[1]

The unity of the three Communities was strengthened by the Single European Act and the Treaties of Maastricht and Amsterdam.[2]

Autonomy The doctrine of the autonomy of Community law rests, on the one hand, on the concept of unity and on the principle of the separation of powers or functions, on the other. The constitutional principle of separation means, in the Community context, a division of functions between the Community Institutions and the Member States[3] and, in the administration of justice, between the Community Court and national courts.[4]

The autonomy of Community law means that it is 'quite independent of the legislation passed by the Member States'.[5] It is derived from an extraneous source, albeit an organization created by the Member States themselves, it extends equally and uniformly over their territories, and has to be applied by their courts in its original form. The uniformity of its interpretation is assured by the obligation to seek preliminary rulings from the Community Court.

The practical application of the doctrine of autonomy has manifested itself in areas where the integrity and efficacy of Community law has to be safeguarded[6] or where it has to be distinguished from national law as, for example, in the field of competition where the two systems overlap.[7] Thus held the ECJ: the efficacy of the Treaty would be impaired if, in the context of partial integration with national law, the specific tasks entrusted to the Community were not interpreted as totally independent.[8] It follows that the Member States are in no position of taking unilateral measures to carry out the mandatory provisions of Community law.[9] The concept of the autonomy of Community law, first mentioned by the ECJ in *San Michele v High Authority of the ECSC*,[10] sets it apart from national law as a separate and independent legal order yet ruling directly over the territories of the Member States. It reflects a federal legal system.

Supremacy of Community law The supremacy of Community law when in conflict with national law is the logical consequence of the federal concept of the Community.[11] The doctrine itself is nowhere mentioned in the Treaties but can

---

1 Case 128/78: *Commission v United Kingdom, Re Tachographs* [1979] ECR 419, [1979] 2 CMLR 45.
2 TEU, Art 1 (ex Art A).
3 ERTA Case, p 86, note 2, para 12, supra; Case 30/59: *De Gezamenlijke Steenkolenmijnen in Limburg v High Authority of the ECSC* [1961] ECR 1 at 23.
4 A-G Roemer in Case 6/54: *Government of the Netherlands v High Authority of the ECSC* [1954–56] ECR 103.
5 Case 28/67: *Mölkerei-Zentrale Westfalen/Lippe GmbH v Hauptzollamt Paderborn* [1968] ECR 143 at 152, [1968] CMLR 187 at 217 (this version differs from ECR).
6 *Variola*, p 138, note 9, supra.
7 Case 14/68: *Wilhelm v Bundeskartellamt* [1969] ECR 1, [1969] CMLR 100.
8 Case 30/59: supra.
9 Eg Case 13/68: *Salgoil Spa v Italian Ministry of Foreign Trade (Re Import quotas)* [1968] ECR 453, [1969] CMLR 181; Cases 90–91/63: *Commission v Luxembourg and Belgium (Re Special Import Licence of Milk Products)* [1964] ECR 625, [1965] CMLR 58; Case 52/77: *Cayrol v Rivoira and Figli (Re import Licence)* [1977] ECR 2261, [1978] 2 CMLR 253; Case 128/78: *Commission v United Kingdom, Re Tachographs* [1979] ECR 419, [1979] 2 CMLR 45.
10 Case 9/65: [1967] ECR 27 at 30.
11 Ipsen, H P, 'Rapport du droit des Communautés Européennes avec le droit national', *Le Droit des Affaires* (1964), No 47.

be deduced from the Member States' constitutional law,[12] in so far as the national constitutions[13] and practice recognize the primacy of international obligations without necessarily stating *expressis verbis* that in the case of conflict Community law prevails, and their readiness to make the Community function. In other words, since the creation of the Community and the endowment of its Institutions with executive, legislative and judicial functions implies a delegation of sovereignty, the Community could not function as a supranational organization if the delegated powers were insufficient or capable of being withdrawn. Therefore supremacy does not reflect any inherent superiority of Community Law but merely a working relationship.

Supremacy was first mentioned by the ECJ in a case involving the effect of the ECSC Treaty on previously enacted Belgian tax law.[14] On that occasion the Court saw the relationship between the two systems in the light of the monist theory of international law. In *Van Gend*, that most important constitutional case, the Court saw the 'new legal order' in the light of a federalist concept.[15] Thus the base of the doctrine was shifted but firmly established in *Costa v ENEL*[16] in which, inter alia, the question of compatibility of the Italian decree nationalizing the electricity industry with the Community legal order was raised. The Court held that '(The Treaty) ... has created its own legal system which, on the entry into force of the Treaty, became an integral part of the legal systems of the Member States and which their courts are bound to apply ... because of its special and original nature ... (it) could not be overridden by domestic legal provisions, however framed, without being deprived of its character as Community law and without the legal basis of the Community itself being called into question'.

Commenting specifically on the impact of the Community upon national legislation the Court thought that 'the transfer by the States from their domestic legal system to the Community legal system of the rights and obligations arising under the Treaty carries with it a permanent limitation of their sovereign rights, against which a subsequent unilateral act incompatible with the concept of the Community cannot prevail'.[17]

In the same vein, in the *Second Art Treasures*[18] case, the Court, condemning Italy's attempt to introduce a tax on the export of art treasures, held that 'the Member States' assignment of rights and powers to the Community in accordance with the provisions of the Treaty entails a definitive limitation of their sovereign rights against which no provisions of municipal law, whatever their nature, can be legally invoked'.

In another case the Court held that, where the lowest minimum export price of flower bulbs has been fixed by the Community, the exporting country 'may neither adopt nor allow national organizations having legislative power to adopt any measure which would conceal the Community nature and effects' of such provisions, even if the minimum price would render the transaction unprofitable.[19] Implying that a national provision inconsistent with a binding

---

12 Cf European Communities Act 1972, s 2(1).
13 See ch 10, infra.
14 Case 6/60: *Humblet v Belgium* [1960] ECR 559 at 569.
15 Case 26/62: [1963] ECR 1 at 12, [1963] CMLR 105.
16 Case 6/64; [1964] ECR 585 at 593 and 594, [1964] CMLR 425 at 455, 456.
17 Ibid, ECR at 594.
18 Case 48/71: *Commission v Italy* [1972] ECR 527, para 9, [1972] CMLR 699 at 708.
19 Case 50/76: *Amsterdam Bulb BV v Produktschap voor Siergeqassen* [1977] ECR 137 at 151, [1977] 2 CMLR 218 at 243.

Community rule must be void the Court held that such a Community rule would 'preclude the valid adoption of new legislative measures to the extent to which they would be incompatible with Community provisions'.[20] Addressing itself to the national judicature the ECJ ruled that 'A national court which is called upon ... to apply provisions of Community law is under a duty to give full effects to those provisions, if necessary refusing of its own motion to apply any conflicting provisions of national legislation, even if adopted subsequently, and it is not necessary for the court to request or await a prior setting aside of such provision by legislative or other constitutional means'.[1] As a matter of Community law, the duty of the national court is simply to disapply the inconsistant provision of domestic law in the case before it; but that does not preclude the application to that situation of domestic concepts of nullity, invalidity or inexistence.[2] The ECJ has no express power to declare void national legislation but can achieve the same effect through the doctrine of supremacy since its ruling in this respect may emphasize that it is not sufficient for the national (supreme) court to disapply inconsistent national law because such law must be specifically repealed by the national legislature. Failure to do so would infringe the principle of solidarity written into the Treaty.[3]

However the most dramatic assertion of supremacy occurred in the case of an alleged violation of the German Basic Law by a Community regulation.[4] The Court ruled that 'no provisions of municipal law, of whatever nature they may be, may prevail over Community law ... lest it be deprived of its character as Community law and its very legal foundation be endangered. The validity of a Community act or its application in a Member State remains, therefore, unimpaired even if it is alleged that the basic rights ... of the national constitution were violated'.

Direct applicability and direct effect Like the doctrines of autonomy and supremacy the doctrine of direct applicability of Community law has been enunciated in the *Van Gend* case. On that occasion the ECJ held that EC Article 12 (now 25) was applicable to the Member State and the citizen alike and that it created rights which the citizen could rely on and which his national courts were bound to uphold even against national legislation. The doctrine holds the key to the relationship between Community law and national law and unmistakably points to a federal character of the former because in a federal system federal law bears directly upon the citizens of the component states. We shall see this when assessing the impact of Community law upon the national systems. At this stage it will suffice to consider its theoretical implications. In the literature a distinction is made between 'direct applicability' and 'direct effect' of Community law. The former

---

20 Case 106/77: *Amministrazione delle Finanze dell Stato v Simmenthal SpA* [1978] ECR 629 at 643, [1978] 3 CMLR 263 at 283. See also Case C-13/91 and C-113/91: *Criminal proceedings against Debus* [1992] ECR I-3617 and Cases C-228/90–C-234/90, C-339/90 and C-353/90: *Simba SpA v Minister of Finance* [1992] ECR I-3713; Case C-3/91: *Exportur v LOR SA and Confiserie du Tech* [1992] ECR I-5529.

1 Ibid, ECR at 647, CMLR at 283. See also Case C-213/89: *R v Secretary of State for Transport, ex p Factortame Ltd (No 2)* [1990] ECR I-2433, [1990] 3 CMLR 1.

2 Cases C-10/97 to C-22/97: *Ministero delle Finanze v IN CO GE '90 Srl* [1998] ECR I-6307, paras 20–21.

3 Case 104/86: *Commission v Italy, Re Repayment of Illegal Taxes* [1988] ECR 1799, [1989] 3 CMLR 25, at para 12; see also Case 815/79: *Proceedings against Cremonini and Vrankovich* [1980] ECR 3583 at 3607, [1981] 3 CMLR 49.

4 Case 11/70: *Internationale Handelsgesellschaft mbH v Einfuhr-und-Vorratsstelle für Getreide und Futtermittel* [1970] ECR 1125 at 1127, [1972] CMLR 255 at 283.

refers to the source of the law, the latter to its range of application or, more precisely, to the capacity of a Community measure to create rights available to individuals which can be invoked before national institutions.[5] This is a valid distinction but not exclusive to Community law. As pointed out by Advocate-General Warner[6] the distinction is known to national statutes 'some provisions of which impose obligations on the state or public authorities without conferring rights on citizens'. Indeed one has to distinguish not only between the contents of legal rules but also between the addressees of these rules. In the *Van Gend* case the argument on behalf of the state concerned (incidentally accepted by Advocate-General Roemer) was that the obligation contained in the relevant Treaty provision concerned the state involved and did not give rise to any claim on behalf of the importer. However the Court, in its famous dictum, enclosed both the state and the importer and concluded that the provision was applicable in litigation before national courts and that, because of its content and purpose, is generated remedies available to the importer. In other words, a directly applicable provision had, as its effect, an enforceable Community right.

The doctrine, as we shall see later,[7] is of an immense practical importance as far as individuals are concerned since they can deduce support for their claims from the text of the Treaties, international arrangements, regulations and directions if such is the intention of the legislator expressed in presence and unconditional wording of the relevant text. It also strengthens the federal concept of the Community.

General principles of law   Next to the basic doctrines the Court has to be credited with the development of general principles of Community law. To these we have already alluded in the context of interpretation. It remains now to discuss these in the context of the legal integration through the Court's jurisprudence.

By a doctrine, as distinguished from a principle or a rule of law, we understand a general proposition or guidance relating to a fundamental issue such as the nature of Community law or the conflict between the Community and national law. A principle, or a rule of law, on the other hand, can be construed more narrowly as a rule of conduct prescribed in the given circumstances and carrying a sanction for non-compliance. Thus a principle or rule of law consists of a hypothesis, a disposition and a sanction. The hypothesis postulates a factual situation which ought to be responded to in accordance with the disposition or prescribed conduct. The law as a normative system is vindicated by the appropriate sanction which is, on the one hand, civil, ie nullity of the act in question, damages or both, and punitive, on the other. A punitive sanction often serves to vindicate a civil obligation.

Codified systems consist of general and particular rules. The former come close to doctrines in the sense the term has been used above. However, though they can be vindicated like any particular rule, they serve a dual purpose: as pointers to interpretation by the courts and as indications of policy to legislators. Thus such general rules as eg public policy or equality indicate the limits of interpretation in particular cases and also enable the courts to fill the gaps which

---

5   Winter, J, 'Direct Applicability and Direct Effect: Two Distinct and Different Concepts in Community law' (1972) CML Rev p 425; Wyatt, D, 'Directly applicable Provisions of EEC law' (1975) 125 NLJ, pp 458, 575, 669, 793. The distinction drawn in the literature is not always reflected in the case law.

6   In Case 31/74: *Filippo Galli* [1975] ECR 47 at 70, [1975] 1 CMLR 211.

7   See further p 146 et seq supra.

are not supposed to exist in codes of law but, in reality, do become exposed because life is more imaginative than the most astute legislator. With reference to the same examples a particular application of public policy or equality may be subject to separate legislation, eg to restrict the sale of firearms or combat racial or sex discrimination, or, simply, a general principle to be further developed in the code.

The above-mentioned legislative techniques are well exemplified in the text of the EC Treaty. There we find general principles such as the principle of subsidiarity (EC Article 5 (ex Art 3(b))), solidarity (EC Article 10 (ex Art 5)) which governs the relationship between the Member States and the Community and the principle of non-discrimination on the ground of nationality (EC Article 12 (ex Art 6)) applicable to matters governed by the Treaty. In these two articles the Court found a powerful support in the interpretation of the Treaty provisions as well as a formal source to complement inadequately expressed intentions of the makers of the Treaty.

The principle of the freedom of movement of persons (EC Article 39 (ex Art 48)) within the Community has been not only partly elaborated in the Treaty but also carried into effect in considerable detail by derivative legislation comprising rules on migration and social security. The right of establishment of liberal professions (EC Article 43 (ex Art 52)) too has been developed partly in the text, partly outside the text of the Treaty by derivative legislation. The same technique has been adapted to all Treaty policies, some of which remain still in their embryonic stage.

Faced with this kind of enacted law the Court, in the absence of interpretation clauses, has to resort to every method of interpretation known to national judiciaries. It also has to dip into the treasury of national tradition in order to adopt for the Community some well-established and universally recognized principles of national law. In the EC Treaty there is only one reference to 'general principles common to the laws of the Member States' in EC Article 288(2) (ex Art 215(2)) according to which the non-contractual liability of the Community should be judged. However, in practice, the Court may take recourse to EC Article 230(2) (ex Art 173(2)), which enables it to annul Community acts which 'infringe the Treaty or any rule of law relating to its application'. These other 'rules of law' begin to emerge as follows:

(a) *Due process and natural justice* In civilized societies the existence and observance of procedural rules provide a safeguard and protection of substantive rights. The making and enforcement of rules of conduct have to conform to a notion of 'due process' where the authorities do not act arbitrarily but give reasons for their acts.[8] Where a person is accused of an offence he has a right to be informed of his charges, be heard and represented by an independent advocate. However the right to be heard is not applicable to any situation just because a person wants to be heard, eg in the case of medical examination carried out by a medical board.[9]

Thus the sanction of nullity applies to Community acts made in contravention of 'an essential procedural requirement'.[10] The Court, following the Advocate-General's strong plea for the recognition of the principle *audi alteram partem* even in the absence of express legislation to that effect, held in a competition

---

8 See eg Case 248/84: *Germany v Commission (Re Regional Aid Plans)* [1987] ECR 4013; [1987] ECR 1493, [1988] 2 CMLR 131.
9 See Case T-154/89: *Vidrányi v Commission* [1990] ECR II-455.
10 EC Art 230(2) (ex Art 173(2)).

case[11] that 'a person whose interests are perceptibly affected by a decision taken by a public authority must be given the opportunity to make his point of view known'.[12] This implies that the party concerned must be informed of the conditions under which the Treaty has been applied.[13]

The right of defence also implies the right to be represented by counsel even in disciplinary proceedings where parties need not and are not normally represented.[14] The principle of *non bis in idem* applies not only in the case of two disciplinary sanctions for a single transgression but also to multiple disciplinary proceedings following a single occurrence.[15] It does not apply to parallel proceedings in competition cases under two different systems.[16]

Double jeopardy was pleaded, albeit unsuccessfully, in respect of forfeiture of returnable deposits.[17] In view of the failure to export in time, two deposits were forfeited: one for exportation and another for advance-fixed refund. The ECJ held both forfeitures correct and lawful since they resulted from an administrative procedure which was well founded and the sanction was proportionate to the failure of the applicant. Although it is in the nature of penalty a forfeiture bears no criminal features and, therefore, does not attract criminal safeguards. The principle of double jeopardy does not apply.

The Commission's investigative powers do not override the protection afforded by the privilege of confidentiality of communications between an independent lawyer practising in the Community and his client relating to a case investigated by the Commission.[18]

(b) *Equality* Equality before the law is, next to due process, an essential ingredient of justice. In the EC equality is to be achieved through suppression of discrimination on the ground of nationality (EC Article 12 (ex Art 6)); as between consumers and producers of agricultural produce (EC Article 34(2) (ex Art 40(2))) and as between employees on account of their sex (EC Article 141 (ex Art 119)). The Court, however, deduced from these scanty provisions a general principle of Community law.[19]

---

11 Case 17/74: *Transocean Marine Paint Association v Commission* [1974] ECR 1063 at 1079, [1974] 2 CMLR 459 at 477. Cases 46/87 and 227/88: *Hoecht AG v Commission (re competition)* [1989] ECR 2859, [1991] 4 CMLR 410; Case C-49/88: *Al-Jubail Fertilizer Co v Council (re anti-dumping)* [1991] ECR I-3187, [1991] 3 CMLR 377.

12 See also Case 75/77: *Mollet v Commission* [1978] ECR 897.

13 Case 24/62: *Germany v Commission* [1963] ECR 63 at 69, [1963] CMLR 347; see also Case 34/77: *Oslizlok v Commission* [1978] ECR 1099; Case 85/76: *Hoffmann-La Roche v Commission* [1979] ECR 461, [1979] 3 CMLR 211. Joined Cases 209–215, 218/78: *Heintz van Landewyck Sarl v Commission* [1980] ECR 3125 at 3237, [1981] 3 CMLR 134 at 215; Joined Cases 100–103/80: *Musique Diffusion Française SA v Commission* [1983] ECR 1825 at 1880, 1881, 1887, [1983] 3 CMLR 221 at 315, 320; Case 222/86: *UNECTEF v Heylens* [1987] ECR 4097 at para 15.

14 Case 115/80: *Demont v Commission* [1981] ECR 3147, paras 11 and 12.

15 Joined Cases 18, 35/65: *Gutmann v Euratom Commission* [1966] ECR 103 at 119, [1967] ECR 61.

16 Case 14/68: *Walt Wilhelm v Bundeskartellamt* [1969] ECR 1 at 15, [1969] CMLR 100 at 120–121; Case 7/72: *Boehringer Mannheim GmbH v Commission* [1972] ECR 1281 at 1289, [1973] CMLR 864 at 887.

17 Case 137/85: *Maizena GmbH v Bundesanstalt für Landwirtschaftliche Marktordnung* [1987] ECR 4587, [1989] 2 CMLR 336.

18 Case 155/79: *A M & S Europe Ltd v Commission* [1982] ECR 1575 at 1610–1613, [1982] 2 CMLR 264 at 322–325; Duffy, P J, 'Legal Privilege and Community Law' 132 NLJ (1982) 580–582.

19 See Case 1/72: *Frilli v Belgium* [1972] ECR 457, [1973] CMLR 386; Case 152/73: *Sotgiu v Deutsche Bundespost* [1974] ECR 153.

In developing the theme the Court made a start under the ECSC Treaty by combating discriminatory practices expressly prohibited by Articles 4(b) and 60.[20] More significant is the development under the EC Treaty where the Court applied the principle of non-discrimination to goods, persons and states. However it made it plain in the case of a discriminatory reception of Italian refrigerators in France[1] that 'the different treatment of non-comparable situations does not lead automatically to the conclusion that there is discrimination'.

Thus the principle of equality in identical or in comparable[2] situations forms the basis of the Common Market. Indeed the free movement of goods is assured by enforcing the prohibition of discriminatory measures whether they are equivalent to customs duties[3] or quantitative restrictions[4] or whether they are fiscal measures designed to protect a national produce at the expense of a similar imported one.[5]

EC Article 32(2) (ex Art 40(3)) (second sub-paragraph) provides that, in the context of the CAP, the organization of agricultural markets must 'exclude any discrimination between producers or consumers within the Community'. In the jurisprudence of the ECJ that prohibition of discrimination is merely 'a specific enunciation of the general principle of equality which is one of the fundamental principles of Community law'.[6]

However prohibition of any discrimination between producers in the Community refers to the objectives of the common organization but not to various conditions of production resulting from national rules which are general in character and pursue other objectives.[7]

Equality of treatment was also vindicated in cases involving subsidies to producers in the context of the Common Agricultural Policy. Thus the Court declared invalid Commission Regulation 563/76 which, in order to reduce the stocks of skimmed milk powder, obliged animal feed producers to purchase skimmed milk powder instead of soya used as protein ingredient with the consequent result that the cost of animal feed had increased and upset farmers. The Court held the regulation contrary to the principle of equality in so far as it made the producers purchase skimmed milk powder 'at such a disproportionate

---

20   Eg Case 8/57: *Groupement des Hauts Fourneaux et Aciéries Belges v High Authority of the ECSC* [1958] ECR 245 at 256; see also Case 234/82: *Ferrière di Roé Volciano SpA v Commission, Re fines for infringement of production quotas in steel* [1983] ECR 3921.
1   Case 13/63: *Italy v Commission* [1963] ECR 165, [1963] CMLR 289.
2   Case T-48/89: *Beltrantre v Council* [1990] ECR II-493 at para 34; see also Case C-37/89: *Weises v Caisse Nationale des Barreaux Français* [1990] ECR I-2395.
3   See ch 13, post.
4   See ch 13, post.
5   Eg Cases 52 and 55/65: *Germany v Commission (tax on imported meat)* [1966] ECR 159, [1967] CMLR 22; Case 28/67: *Mölkerei-Zentrale Westfalen-Lippe GmbH v Haupzollamt Paderborn (powdered milk)* [1968] ECR 143, [1968] CMLR 187; Case 232/78: *Commission v France (Sheepmeat)* [1979] ECR 2729, [1980] 1 CMLR 418; Case 168/78: *Commission v France (tax on alcoholic drinks)* [1980] ECR 347, [1981] 2 CMLR 631; Case 169/78: *Commission v Italy (tax on alcoholic drinks)* [1980] ECR 385, [1981] 2 CMLR 673; Case 171/78: *Commission v Denmark (tax on alcoholic drinks)* [1980] ECR 447, [1981] CMLR 688 but see also Case 140/79: *Chemical Farmaceutici SpA v DAF SpA* [1981] ECR 1, [1981] 3 CMLR 350; Case 46/80: *Vinal SpA v Orbat SpA* [1981] ECR 77, [1981] 3 CMLR 524.
6   Case C-309/96: *Daniele Annibaldi v Sindaco del Comune di Guidonia* [1997] ECR I-7493, para 18. See Joined Cases 201/85 and 202/85: *Klensch v Secrétaire d'Etat* [1986] ECR 3477 (para 9); and Case C-2/92: *R v Ministry of Agriculture, ex p Bostock* [1994] ECR I-955 (para 23).
7   See Joined Cases 141/81, 142/81 and 143/81: *Holdijk* [1982] ECR 1299 (para 12); and Case 118/86: *Openbaar Ministerie v Nertsvoederfabriek Nederland* [1987] ECR 3883 (para 12).

price that it was equivalent to a discriminatory distribution of the burden of costs between the various agricultural sectors'.[8]

A similar attitude was adopted in the *Quellmehl* and *Gritz*[9] cases. Quellmehl is a product of maize or wheat used in the production of bread, gritz is a product of maize used in brewing. A Community subsidy was provided in order to enable starch to compete with synthetic products. However the unexpected result was that subsidized starch (because it is up to a point interchangeable with quellmehl and gritz) obtained an unfair advantage over these products and began to replace quellmehl in bakeries and gritz in breweries. To even up the competitive position subsidies were extended to quellmehl and gritz. However, subsequently, by a resolution the Council withdrew the subsidies from quellmehl and gritz but not from starch. The quellmehl and gritz producers obtained a judgment against the Council on the ground of discrimination[10] but subsidies were reinstated only as from the date of the judgment. The claim for compensation under EC Article 288 (ex Art 215(2)) covering the period during which subsidies were withdrawn was recognized by the Court on the ground that the producers of quellmehl and gritz were a small, clearly definable group and that the loss they suffered exceeded the normal risk pertinent to their business. Therefore they were entitled to compensation based on the subsidy they would have received had they been treated equally with the producers of starch. The quantum (left to be determined in later proceedings) was to be reduced by the proportion of the loss they were able to pass to their customers.

The third instance of equal treatment of products is exemplified by the *Isoglucose*[11] cases which, as noted elsewhere,[12] released the potential powers of the European Parliament. Again, to reduce the surplus of sugar, a substantial levy was imposed by regulation on isoglucose, a recently produced sweetener in heavy competition with sugar. According to the complainants this levy was of such a deterrent proportion that it would have made the production of isoglucose uneconomical. The Court restored the balance between the competing products on the ground that discriminatory regulation offended the principle of equality. The levy was eliminated with retrospective effect. However the claim for compensation failed, the Court in an almost perfunctory manner concentrating on the nature of the offending legislation rather than the consequential loss suffered by the producers of isoglucose.[13]

---

8 Cases 83, 94/76, 4, 15, 40/77: *Bayerische HNL Vermehrungsbetriebe GmbH & Co KG v Council and Commission* [1978] ECR 1209, [1978] 3 CMLR 566; see also Case 114/76: *Bela-Mühle KG v Grows-Farm GmbH* [1977] ECR 1211, [1279] 2 CMLR 83; Case 116/76: *Granaria BV v Hoofdproduktschap voor Akkerbouw-Produkten* [1977] ECR 1247, [1979] 2 CMLR 83; Cases 119, 120/76: *Ölmühle Hamburg AG v Hauptzollamt Hamburg Waltershof (First Skimmed Milk Powder Cases)* [1977] ECR 1269, [1979] 2 CMLR 83.

9 Cases 64, 113/76, 167, 239/78, 27, 28, 45/79: *Dumortier Frères SA v Council* [1979] ECR 3091; Case 238/78: *Ireks-Arkady v Council and Commission* [1979] ECR 2955; Cases 241, 242, 245–250/78: *DGV v Council and Commission* [1979] ECR 3017; Cases 261, 262/78: *Interquell Stärke-Chemie GmbH & Co KG and Diamalt AG v Council and Commission* [1979] ECR 3045.

10 Cases 117/76, 16/77: *Firma Albert Ruckdeschel & Co v Hauptzollamt Hamburg-St Annen* [1977] ECR 1753 [1979] 2 CMLR 445; Cases 124/76, 20/77: *Moulins et Huileries de Pont-a-Mousson SA v Office National Interprofessionnel des Céréales* [1977] ECR 1795, [1979] 2 CMLR 445.

11 Cases 103, 145/77: *Royal Scholten-Honig (Holdings) Ltd and Tunnel Refineries Ltd v Intervention Board for Agricultural Produce (first Isoglucose cases)* [1978] ECR 2037, [1979] 1 CMLR 675; and *Second Isoglucose Cases* 116, 124/77: *Amylum NV and Tunnel Refineries Ltd v Council and Commission* [1979] ECR 3497; Case 143/77: *Koninklijke Scholten-Honig NV v Council and Commission* [1979] ECR 3583.

12 See p 136, supra. See also Jacobs, F, 'Isoglucose Resurgent: Two Powers of the European Parliament' (1981) 18 CMLRev 219.

13 *Second Isoglucose Cases*, supra, note 11.

There is as yet no equality between Community citizens in a general sense but only in the context of the freedom of movement of workers and the right of establishment and in the context of enforceable Community rights. As held in the *Van Duyn*[14] case a Member State cannot, in accordance with the rules of international law, refuse entry to its own citizens but may do so according to the EC Treaty to the citizens of the fellow Member States only if the Community right of entry falls within the exception of public policy. However, once admitted a Community citizen must not be discriminated against whether it concerns his freedom of movement;[15] employment;[16] or the whole variety of social rights including the rights under a national scheme for the protection of the victims of crime.[17] Security for the costs of judicial proceedings exacted from citizens of another Member State where it is not required from citizens of that State and where the action is connected with the exercise of Community rights is incompatible with the principle of non-discrimination under the Treaty.[18] A mere threat of discrimination contained in national law is incompatible with Community rules.[19]

However Community law does not allow 'positive discrimination' or 'affirmative action' as Americans have it, in order to promote female candidates in areas where women are under represented in preference to men who hold the same qualification.[20]

The hard-won Community right to equal pay within the national systems[1] has provided an opportunity for broadening up national rules in the name of equality between the sexes.[2] Some problems involving sex equality arose in

---

14   Case 41/74: *Van Duyn v Home Office (No 2)* [1974] ECR 1337, [1975] 1 CMLR 1.
15   Eg Case 36/75: *Rutili v Ministère de l'Intérieur* [1975] ECR 1219, [1976] 1 CMLR 140,
16   Eg Cases 44/72: *Marsman v Rosskamp* [1972] ECR 1243, [1973] CMLR 501: 152/73: *Sotgiu v Deutsche Bundespost* [1974] ECR 153; 15/69: *Württembergische Milchverwertung-Südmilch AG v Ugliola* [1969] ECR 363, [1970] CMLR 194; 36/74: *Walrave and Koch v Association Union Cycliste Internationale* [1974] ECR 1405, [1975] 1 CMLR 320; 13/76: *Donà v Mantero* [1976] ECR 1333, [1976] 2 CMLR 578.
17   Case 186/87: *Cowan v Trésor Public* [1989] ECR 195, [1990] 2 CMLR 613.
18   Case C-43/95: *Data Delecta v MSL Dynamics* [1996] ECR I-4661; Case C-323/95: *David Charles Hayes and Jeanette Karen Hayes v Kronenberger GmbH* [1997] ECR I-1711.
19   Case 167/73: *Commission v France* [1974] ECR 359, [1974] 2 CMLR 216 followed by Case C-334/94: *Commission v France* [1996] ECR I-1307.
20   Case C-450/93: *Kalanke v Freie Hansestadt Bremen* [1995] ECR I-3051, [1996] 1 CMLR 175.
1   Case 43/75: *Defrenne v SABENA* [1976] ECR 455, [1976] 2 CMLR 98. See also Case 109/88: *Handels-Og Kontor-Funktionaerernes Forbund I Danmark v Dansk Arbejdsgiverforening, ex p Danfoss A/S* [1989] ECR 3199, [1991] 1 CMLR 8; Case 9/88: *Da Veiga v Staatssecretaries van Justitie* [1989] ECR 2989, [1991] 1 CMLR 217; Case 33/88: *Allué and Coonan v University of Venice, Re Employment of Foreign Language Teachers* [1989] ECR 1591, [1991] 1 CMLR 283.
2   Eg Cases 129/79: *Macarthys Ltd v Smith* [1980] ECR 1275, [1980] 2 CMLR 205; 69/80: *Worringham and Humphreys v Lloyds Bank Ltd* [1981] ECR 767, [1981] 2 CMLR 1; 96/80 *Jenkins v Kingsgate (Clothing Productions) Ltd* [1981] ECR 911, [1981] 2 CMLR 24; *Garland v British Rail Engineering Ltd* (reference to ECJ) [1981] 2 CMLR 542; Case 12/81: (ECJ) [1982] ECR 359, [1982] 1 CMLR 696; *Burton v British Railways Board* (reference to ECJ) [1981] 3 CMLR 100; Case 152/84: *Marshall v Southampton and South West Hampshire Area Health Authority* [1986] ECR 723, [1986] 1 CMLR 688; Case 150/85: *Drake v Chief Adjudication Officer* [1986] ECR 1995, [1986] 3 CMLR 43; Case 237/85: *Rummler v Dato-Druck GmbH (Re Sex Discrimination)* [1986] ECR 2101, [1987] 3 CMLR 127; Case 286/85: *McDermott and Cotter v Minister for Social Welfare* [1987] ECR 1453, [1987] 2 CMLR 607; Case 262/84: *Beets-Proper v Lanschot Bankiers NV* [1986] ECR 773, [1987] 2 CMLR 616; Case 157/86: *Murphy v Bord Telecom Eireann* [1988] ECR 673, [1988] 1 CMLR 879; Case 312/86: *Commission v France, Re Protection of Women* [1988] ECR 6315, [1989] 1 CMLR 408; Case C-262/88: *Barber v Guardian Royal Exchange Assurance Group (Re Occupational Pension Scheme)* [1990] ECR I-1889, [1990] 2 CMLR 513.

connection with employees of the Community but these cases had to be decided in the light of the interpretation of contractual rights in Community service. Thus an Italian official of the European Parliament who married a Luxembourg national was to be deprived of an expatriation allowance unless she was the head of the family. The Court refused to accept the principle that the entitlement should depend on sex and annulled the decision depriving her of the allowance.[3] Similarly an expatriation allowance of a Belgian employee at a Euratom centre in Italy, who married an Italian and thereby automatically acquired Italian citizenship without relinquishing her Belgian citizenship, was preserved since citizenship acquired involuntarily should not be the determining factor.[4] However in a slightly different situation, where a French Community official working in Belgium married a Belgian citizen and would not have acquired Belgian citizenship if she had made a declaration that she wished to retain her old one, the inaction on her part was interpreted as her acquiescence. Therefore she had to take the consequences, the Court saying that 'there are no reasons associated with equal treatment why her Belgian nationality should not be taken into account in applying the provision concerned'.[5]

Even computerized rules of procedure are not allowed to discriminate since access to the summary proceedings for the prosecution of debts expressed in foreign currency cannot be denied to a creditor resident in another Member State if such claims can be pursued in ordinary legal proceedings.[6]

In matters involving the conduct of the Member States the Court has often emphasized their duties vis-à-vis each other and the Community they have created, such duties being a reflection of equality and reciprocity. A breach 'strikes at the very root of the Community legal order' and 'brings into question the equality of Member States before Community law and creates discrimination at the expense of their nationals'.[7]

However the principle does not apply in Community trade relations with third countries and individuals or corporations cannot demand equal treatment in that respect.[8]

(c) *Fundamental human rights* Fundamental human rights whether expressed in a solemn declaration (French system), a constitutional guarantee (German system) or case law (British system), whether extensive or fragmentary, form part of West European legal heritage. This heritage was enriched by the European Convention on Human Rights of 1950 to which all the Member States of the Community adhere in principle though not in every detail. The Community itself, through a joint declaration of the Commission, Council of Ministers and Parliament[9] of 5 April 1977, echoed by the European Council[10] on 7/8 April 1978, proclaimed its respect for fundamental human rights and postulated their observance in the work of its institutions though the Community is not subject to

---

3 Case 20/71: *Sabbatini v European Parliament* [1972] ECR 345, [1972] CMLR 945. See Case 59/85: *Netherlands v Anne Florence Reed* (cohabiting Community citizens have to be treated like the cohabiting citizens of the host state) [1986] ECR 1283, [1987] 2 CMLR 448.
4 Case 21/74: *Airola v Commission* [1975] ECR 221.
5 Case 37/74: *Van den Broeck v Commission* [1975] ECR 235.
6 Case 22/80: *Boussac Saint-Frères SA v Gerstenmeier* [1980] ECR 3427, [1982] 1 CMLR 202.
7 ECJ Court in the *Tachograph* case, p 174, note 1, at para 12, supra. See also Case 231/78: *Commission v United Kingdom* [1979] ECR 1447 at 1462.
8 Case 55/75: *Balkan-Import-Export GmbH v HZA Berlin-Packhof* [1976] ECR 19 at 31–32; Case 52/81: *Faust v Commission* [1982] ECR 3745 at 3762; Case 245/81: *Edeka Zentrale v Germany* [1982] ECR 2745 at 2756.
9 OJ 1977, C 103/1; EC Bull 3/1977, p 5. See TEU Art F.
10 EC Bull 3/1978, p 5. Forman, J, 'The Joint Declaration on Fundamental Rights' (1977) 2 E L Rev pp 210 et seq.

the jurisdiction of the European Commission on Human Rights.[11] Human rights and representative democracy, stressed the European Commission, are the essential conditions of the membership of the Community.[12] In 1979[13] the Commission urged the Community to adhere to the Convention in its corporate capacity. It participated in the Helsinki discussions on human rights. The Helsinki Final Act was signed by Aldo Moro as the President of the Council (assassinated by terrorists) on the basis of the Community competence in the field of commercial policy.[14]

Prompted by the conclusions of the European Council at Copenhagen in 1993 the Council of Ministers referred to the Court of Justice the question of whether accession to the Convention is compatible with the Treaty.[15] The ECJ answered in the negative.[16] In its opinion EC Article 308 (ex Art 235) does not provide an appropriate legal basis and only an amendment of this Treaty would make accession possible. Besides, accession to the Convention would necessitate substantial changes in the present Community arrangements for the protection of human rights as it would mean the Community becoming subject to a separate institutional system created by the Convention. In view of their constitutional implications for the Community and the Member States, such changes would have constitutional consequences which could not be accommodated within the powers contained in the legal order of the Community.

The Maastricht Treaty[17] raised the concern for human rights to the rank of 'general principles of Community law', thus confirming the position taken by the Court of Justice. The Amsterdam Treaty[18] repeated the principle that:

'The Union shall respect fundamental rights, as guaranteed by the European Convention for the Protection of Human Rights and Fundamental Freedom signed in Rome on 4 November 1950 and as they result from the constitutional traditions common to the Member States, as general principles of Community law.'

This has formalised the position.

Originally the Court of Justice did not recognize the arguments based on fundamental human rights of Member States[19] but in the course of time admitted that the protection of fundamental rights forms part of the general principles common to the laws of the Member States. It held that:

'... In fact, respect for fundamental rights forms an integral part of the general principles of law protected by the Court of Justice. The protection of such rights, whilst inspired by the constitutional traditions common to the Member States, must be ensured within the framework of the structure and objectives of the Community.'[20]

11 *Re the European School in Brussels, D v Belgium and the European Communities* [1987] 2 CMLR 57.
12 See Commission Opinion on Application of Turkey, 1989, p 79, note 4 supra.
13 EC Bull 4/1978, p 16 and Commission Memorandum on the Accession to the European Convention on Human Rights, EC Bull Supp 2/1979, pp 5 et seq.
14 The European Parliament and the World at Large (Feb 1981), p 5 (18).
15 OJ, 1994, C 174/8; Bull 4–1994, point 1.1.4.
16 Opinion 2/94, *Re The Accession of the Community to the European Human Rights Convention* [1996] ECR I-1700, [1996] 2 CMLR 265.
17 TEU Art 6(2) (ex Art F(2)).
18 Art 6(2) (ex Art F(2)).
19 Case 1/58: *Stork v High Authority* [1959] ECR 17 (36–38); 40/59: *Präsident Ruhrkohlen-Verkaufsgesellschaft mbH v High Authority* [1960] ECR 423; 40/64: *Sgarlata v Commission* [1965] ECR 215.
20 Case 11/70: *Internationale Handelsgesellschaft v EVGF* [1970] ECR 1125 (1134); [1972] CMLR 255 (271); Cases 25–26, 30/70: *EVGF v Köster, Berodt & Co; Henck and Scheer* [1970] ECR 1161 (para 22), [1972] CMLR 255.

As can be seen the text of the Treaty on European Union has been inspired by the Court of Justice whilst the latter seems to have taken aboard the principle of substitution known to International Law. In other words the Community/Union is substituted, in certain respects, to the principles common to its constituent Member States. However, in spite of the emotive sound of 'fundamental human rights', because of the nature of its jurisdiction and the subject-matter of the Treaties, the Court of Justice has so far encountered few genuine human rights cases.

In *Stauder v Stadt Ulm*[1] the ECJ rejected as unfounded the claim of a German citizen that the Community scheme to provide butter at a reduced price to certain persons was invalid because, having required him to reveal his identity, it hurt his dignity and this constituted an infringement of his fundamental human rights. The Court held that the Community scheme did not insist that his identity must be revealed and suggested that the clumsy method of proving the entitlement, for which the national authorities were responsible, could have been replaced by a more sophisticated code.

In *Nold v EC Commission*[2] the Court was at pains to show its faith in fundamental human rights but refused to annul a Commission decision on the marketing of coal which, in effect, denied direct access to sources of supply to wholesale dealers whose turnover fell below the minimum laid down by the Commission. The plea of discrimination and of the denial of economic opportunities made no impact upon the Court when measured against market rationalization pursued under the Coal and Steel Treaty.

In *National Panasonic (UK) Ltd v EC Commission*[3] the Court, citing Nold, held that there was no violation of the right to privacy guaranteed by the Convention in the Community procedures governing search and seizure for the purpose of enforcing the Community competition law. It is clear that a human rights argument cannot be allowed to frustrate the legal process necessary for the enforcement of the Community obligations of a corporation engaged in restrictive practices.

However in *Dow Benelux*[4] the Court ruled that Article 8 protected the private home of any individual but not business premises of a company though the investigative powers of the Commission were subject to the principle of proportionality; and in *Hoechst*[5] it held that the Commission cannot carry out its investigations at an individual's private home.

In *FEDETAB*[6] the ECJ, rejecting an application for the annulment of a competition decision, denied the suggestion that the Commission failed to apply Article 6(1) of the Convention stressing that 'the Commission is bound to respect the procedural guarantees provided for by Community law and has done so ...'.

In *Prais v EC Council*[7] the Court, whilst acknowledging the freedom of religion guaranteed by the European Convention, refused to annul a process of selecting Community employees in favour of a person who complained of unfair treatment because the selection process, held simultaneously in the Community capital cities, happened to coincide with a holy day in the calendar of her religious persuasion.

1   Case 29/69: [1969] ECR 419, [1970] CMLR 112.
2   Case 4/73: [1974] ECR 491, [1974] 2 CMLR 338 at para 13.
3   Case 136/79: [1980] ECR 2033, [1980] 3 CMLR 169.
4   Case 85/87: *Dow Benelux NV v Commission* [1989] ECR 3137.
5   Joined Cases, 46/87 and 227/88: *Hoechst AG v Commission* [1989] ECR 2859 at para 17, [1991] 4 CMLR 410.
6   Cases 209–215, 218/78: *Heinz Van Landewyck Sàrl v Commission* [1980] ECR 3125, [1981] 3 CMLR 134.
7   Case 130/75: [1976] ECR 1589, [1976] 2 CMLR 708.

In *Hauer v Land Rheinland-Pfalz*[8] the Court, following *Nold*, drew a distinction between rights to property guaranteed by the Convention and the EC Treaty and the exercise of such rights which can be interfered with by virtue of the Protocol to the Convention, Community law as well as the constitutions of the Member States. In the circumstances it refused to annul a Council regulation concerned with agricultural planning the effect of which was a restriction on the planting of vines for commercial purposes. The Court thought that where there is a conflict between a Community objective of a general nature (ie implementation of the CAP structural policy) and a right to property guaranteed by national law such a conflict must be resolved according to the principle of proportionality. To decide whether the restrictions on the use of property were lawful the Court considered whether they corresponded to the general interest pursued by the Community and concluded that they were not unlawful.[9] However in another case[10] the special position of a farmer engaged in farming as his main occupation was recognized but it was emphasized that corporate entities would not be able to benefit from such concession.

In *Valsabbia*[11] reference was made to the first Protocol of the Convention as well as the *Nold* case when the Court explained that the minimum price system was not an infringement of property rights and that the Community guarantee cannot be extended to cover commercial risks.

In two cases involving the Member States' rights to control the movement of persons within the Community system the ECJ ignored the plea of a 'right to privacy' without reference to the Convention. In order to enjoy their right of free movement the persons concerned had to comply with the rules for the control of foreign nationals, the sanctions for the breach of such rules being proportionate to the gravity of the offence.[12]

However, in two other cases involving the expulsion and prohibition of re-entry on the ground of public policy of certain ladies of alleged loose morals, the ECJ declined to comment on the Convention right of access to courts and fair hearing because such rights were already safeguarded in the Community system.[13] Dealing specifically with the question of public policy it held that, given the procedural safeguards, the Member State was within its rights to take certain anti-prostitution measures even though prostitution as such was not a criminal offence, provided that certain public manifestations of the trade were prohibited and that these measures were applicable to Belgian nationals as well.

In a reference from a French court the ECJ held that an order confining an Italian trade union agitator to a certain area was contrary to the Community principles of the equality of treatment and free movement. Referring specifically to certain provisions of the Convention it concluded: 'no restrictions in the

8 Case 44/79: [1979] ECR 3727, [1980] 3 CMLR 42. See also Case 5/88: *Wachauf v Germany* [1989] ECR 2609, [1991] 1 CMLR 328.
9 At paras 23 and 30; see also A-G Van Gerven in the Irish Abortion Case: Case C-159/90 *Society for the Protection of Unborn Children Ireland Ltd v Grogan* [1991] ECR I-4685, [1991] 3 CMLR 849 paras 32–38.
10 Case 312/85: *Villa Banfi SpA v Regione Toscana* [1988] 1 CMLR 72; see also Case 5/88: *Wachauf v Germany* [1989] ECR 2609 [1991] 1 CMLR 328.
11 Cases 154, 205, 206, 226–228, 263, 264/78; 39, 31, 83, 85/79: *Ferriera Valsabbia SpA v Commission* [1980] ECR 907, [1981] 1 CMLR 613.
12 Case 118/75: *Re Watson and Belmann* [1976] ECR 1185, [1976] 2 CMLR 552; Case 48/75 *Re Royer* [1976] ECR 497, [1976] 2 CMLR 619.
13 Case 98/79: *Pecastaing v Belgium* [1980] ECR 691, [1980] 3 CMLR 685; Cases 115 and 116/81: *Rezguia Adoui and Dominique Cornuaille v Belgium* [1982] ECR 1665, [1982] 3 CMLR 631.

interests of national security or public safety shall be placed on the rights secured by the above quoted articles other than such as are necessary for the protection of those interests in a democratic society ...'.[14] The Court emphasized that the Community right of movement must be interpreted in the light of the guarantees of individual freedom secured by the Convention. The same sentiment was expressed by the Court when interpreting the public policy provisions relating to the rights of the establishment and of provisions of services as it ruled that the limitations of these rights had to be evaluated in the light of Article 10 of the Convention on the freedom of expression.[15]

Referring again to fundamental human rights, the ECJ interpreted a provision of the Community Social Security Regulation to the effect that such rights were not violated when three Italian unemployed workers had forfeited their right to unemployment benefit because in their search for employment abroad they were absent from their host country for a period longer than that allowed by the Regulation. The rule was reasonable and they were informed of the position in their own language.[16]

However, citing the right to family life enshrined in Article 8 of the European Convention on Human Rights, the ECJ considered that a Member State had a duty under Article 9 of Regulation 1612/68 to provide housing accommodation to family members of a migrant worker who were allowed to join him. The proviso that such duty was conditional upon the availability of accommodation was valid only on first entry. Such right could not be lost if the housing position had subsequently deteriorated.[17]

The Court has heard so far not only actions against the Community alleging breaches of fundamental human rights including trade union rights[18] and the protection from expropriation without compensation[19] but also actions against the Member States alleging breaches of Community rights through non-observance of fundamental human rights.[20] However no Community measure has been struck down to date. No doubt this reflects the weakness of the claims but also, some may fear, the readiness of the Court to assert the supremacy of Community law. Indeed, dismissing as unfounded the argument that regulations which imposed a forfeitable deposit for the grant of export licences had violated fundamental rights (ie the right of economic freedom and proportionality) guaranteed by the German Constitution, the Court held that 'no provisions of municipal law, of whatever nature they may be, may prevail over Community law ... lest it be deprived of its character as Community law and its very legal foundations be endangered. The validity of a Community act or its application in a Member State remains, therefore, unimpaired even if it is alleged that the basic rights ... of the national constitution were violated'.[1]

14 Case 36/75: *Rutili v Ministère de l'Intérieur* [1975] ECR 1219 at 1232, [1976] 1 CMLR 140.
15 Case C-260/89: *Elliniki Radiophonia-Tileorassi v Dimotiki* [1991] ECR I-2925.
16 Cases 41, 121 and 796/79: *Testa v Bundesanstalt für Arbeit* [1980] ECR 1979, [1981] 2 CMLR 552 at 578.
17 Case 249/86: *Commission v Germany, Re Housing of Migrant Workers* [1989] ECR 1263, [1990] 3 CMLR 540, (paras 10, 11, 12).
18 Cases 175/73: *Union Syndicale etc, Massa and Kortner v Council* [1974] ECR 917, [1975] 1 CMLR 131; 18/74: *Syndicat Général du Personnel des Organismes Européens v Commission* [1974] ECR 933, [1975] 1 CMLR 144.
19 Cases 56–60/74: *Kurt Kampffmeyer v Commission and Council* [1976] ECR 711.
20 *Rutili*, supra; Case 149/77: *Defrenne v SABENA* [1978] ECR 1365, [1978] 3 CMLR 312 – sex discrimination contrary to EC Art 141 (ex Art 119), the ILO Convention No 111 of 1958 and the European Social Charter of 1991; Case 98/79: *Pecastaing v Belgium* [1980] ECR 691, [1980] 3 CMLR 685 (fair hearing in deportation proceedings).
1 *Handelsgesellschaft*, p 184, note 20, supra [1970] ECR at 1127, [1972] CMLR at 283.

This dictum has to be seen in the context of a weak case in which the Court, nevertheless, like in *Stauder* and later in *Nold* and *Hauer*, repeatedly asserted its adherence to fundamental human rights as 'the general principles of law ... which should be followed within the framework of Community law'.[2] However the ECJ operates under the limitations of its own status and functions in so far as it has to consider the argument of non-conformity of Community measures with fundamental human rights in the light of Community law and not in the light of national constitutions.[3] The ECJ is not a court of human rights as such but the Court of the Community whose law has been fashioned according to the laws of the Member States. Since the Community legal order, albeit limited in its scope, is derived from a delegation of sovereignty, it is, as pointed out by Advocate-General Warner,[4] unthinkable that the delegation would exceed the powers contained in their constitutions. It follows that fundamental rights so guaranteed must be respected in the Community. However for the time being they cannot rank higher than 'general principles of law'[5] which have to be asserted in individual cases without the benefit of a charter of fundamental rights entrenched in the system.

Even if we postulate a charter of fundamental rights for the Union such a charter, at present, can only reflect the current structure and objectives of the Union. These objectives revolve around the economic-social concept of the Community (the political goal being still on the horizon) and, therefore, arguments based on human rights have to be related to the economic activity of the Union. Such arguments evoke little sympathy, generally. Thus, for example, human rights pleas directed against Community rules on the labelling of wine[6] can be easily dismissed on the ground that the use of the labelling terminology has been exhaustively regulated and that the prohibition of any innovative terminology constitutes no infringement of the freedom of commerce guaranteed by the national constitutional law. Similarly it is futile to argue that the organization of agricultural markets, which can operate unfairly against the interest of individual traders, infringes their fundamental rights (ie the right to property and the freedom of commerce) when, in fact, traders have to take ordinary commercial risks foreseeable in the course of this business.[7] Therefore, rather than resorting to the emotive invocation of human rights, it would seem more apposite to appeal to equitable remedies which the Court has been developing and which, in the discretion of the Court, may mitigate the harshness of the law.

(d) *Equitable Remedies* It seems convenient to group under a general title of *Equity* several principles which have been applied by the ECJ or put forward in order to mitigate hardship arising from a strict application of the law. Apart from this common feature these principles can be traced to the municipal law of one or several Member States.

(e) *Protection of vested rights* The protection of 'vested rights' has a long tradition in Western Europe. It is based on certain premises such as the impartiality and independence of the judiciary, the running of the affairs of the state according to law and non-retrospective legislation. In exercising its general function the ECJ has endeavoured to incorporate these postulates into the Community legal order and in doing so protect vested rights by recourse to certain general principles of law.

2 See *Nold* p 185, note 2, supra at ECR 507.
3 Cases 41, 121, 796/79: *Testa, Maggio and Vitale v Bundesanstalt für Arbeit* [1980] ECR 1979, [1981] 2 CMLR 552 at para 18.
4 Case 7/76: *IRCA v Amministrazione delle Finanze dello Stato* [1976] ECR 1213 at 1237.
5 See *Nold*, supra and Case 63/83: *R v Kirk* [1984] ECR 2689 at 2718, [1984] 3 CMLR 522.
6 Case 234/85: *Staatsanwalt Freiburg v Keller* [1986] ECR 2897, [1987] 1 CMLR 875.
7 Case 59/83: *Biovilac NV v Commission* [1984] ECR 4057, [1987] 2 CMLR 881.

Vested rights, that is rights acquired within the society's legal framework and according to legal process, need a climate of legal certainty. This means, on the one hand, stability of the legal system and predictability, on the other. One ought to know one's legal position and, when a change occurs in the law, one should not be affected adversely as far as one's existing rights are concerned. In more technical terms one's rights should not be taken away or forfeited by retrospective legislation and one's legitimate expectations, built upon the existing legal system, should not be frustrated.

Thus, in principle, Community law is not retrospective. Where it is retrospective it has to be expressly stated to be so and justified on the ground that the legitimate objective could not be attained otherwise.[8] It is not quite clear what the legitimate objective means in abstract. It seems to mean an objective of the Treaty as a superior rule of law which has to be carried into effect by Community legislation. Such legislation may, therefore, have to be enacted with a retrospective effect.[9] Observing that penal provisions may not have a retrospective effect is one of the principles common to legal orders of the Member States and is enshrined in Article 7 of the European Convention, the ECJ[10] held that retrospective Community legislation could not, in effect, validate a national measure that would invest with penal sanction an act that was not a crime when it was committed. The position remains yet to be clarified by the ECJ since the judicial authority on the subject is still rather scanty and ambiguous.[11] It seems that the need for a retrospective measure has to be substantiated by the legislator and, where questioned, approved by the Court within its power of review of the legality of Community acts. In brief, it has to be justified convincingly on the ground of common good.

There appear to be two safeguards of the non-retrospective principle: interpretation and the protection of legitimate expectations. Thus, in the absence of a clear provision to the contrary, legislation is presumed to regulate future relations, that is, not to be retrospective.[12] The principle is well illustrated in a case involving the operative date of a regulation.[13] On 30 June 1976 the Commission passed a regulation curtailing the right of exporters of sugar to have their export licences cancelled. The regulation was to enter into force on 1 July 1976. However the publication of the measure in the Official Journal was delayed until 2 July. On 1 July the applicant applied for cancellation of licences he held at that time but this was refused by virtue of the regulation. Therefore he moved for the annulment of the regulation. This the Court found unnecessary holding that the regulation must be construed to have come into force on the date of its publication, ie 2 July, and thus protecting the rights vested in the applicant. The Court inferred that the Commission did not intend the regulation to have a retrospective effect.[14]

8   Case 98/78: *Racke v Hauptzollamt Mainz* [1979] ECR 69; Case 99/78: *Weingut Gustav Decker KG v Hauptzollamt Landau* [1979] ECR 101. See also Case 159/82: *Verli-Wallace v Commission* [1983] ECR 2711 at 2718–2719 and Case C-143/88 and C-92/89: *Zuckerfabrik Südermitmarschen AG v HZA Itzehoe* [1991] ECR I-415, [1993] 3 CMLR 1.

9   Case 99/78: *Weingut Gustav Decker v HZA Landau* [1979] ECR 101 at para 8.

10 See Case 63/83, supra, p 188, note 5.

11 See case 37/70: *Rewe-Zentrale des Lebensmittel-Grosshandels GmbH v Hauptzollamt Emmerich* [1971] ECR 23, [1971] CMLR 238.

12 See Case 100/63: *Kelsbeck v Bestuur der Sociale Verzekeringsbank* [1964] ECR 565 at 575; see also A-G Mayras in Case 70/72: *Commission v Germany* [1973] ECR 813 at 844 and A-G Warner in case 7/76, supra; see also *Rewe-Zentrale*, supra, *Decker*, supra.

13 Case 88/76: *Société pour Exportation des Sucres v Commission* [1977] ECR 709.

14 See also Case 112/77: *Töpfer & Co GmbH v Commission* [1978] ECR 1019.

Legitimate expectations A prudent person's reliance on the certainty of the law ought to be rewarded by the protection of his confidence in the system.[15] Hence the principle of 'legitimate expectations'[16] (derived from German law), which requires eg that 'the rules imposing charges on the taxpayer must be clear and precise so that he may know without ambiguity what his rights and obligations are and may take steps accordingly'.[17] However, there can be no legitimate expectation where a prudent trader would have foreseen the developments.[18]

The principle was first applied in the *Staff Salaries*[19] case where the Commission sought annulment of a Council decision which reversed a previous decision fixing criteria for the remuneration of Community civil servants and substituting a new formula. The previous decision was a result of negotiations and was to remain in force for three years. It created a legitimate expectation that the Community would pay its employees according to the agreed scales. The Court upheld this contention and annulled the offending measure but ruled, in accordance with EC Article 231 (ex Art 174, 2nd paragraph), that it should remain in force until a new one has been enacted, thus safeguarding the interim pay regime.

The most illuminating examples of the application of the principle can be found in the jungle of the Common Agricultural Policy.[20] To begin with the *Deuka*[1] case: in order to reduce the surplus of wheat and yet maintain the market prices the Commission adopted a system of premiums to encourage the process of denaturing, ie rendering the produce in question unfit for human consumption. The amount of the premium was fixed for each crop on an annual basis subject to adjustments in response to market fluctuations. To qualify for a premium the processor had to obtain a prior authorization from the relevant authority, carry out the process and its completion. By a new regulation coming into force on 1 June 1970 the Commission abolished the relevant regulation, which provided for an increased premium for the denaturing of wheat of a certain grade.

During June and July 1970 Deuka had denatured a quantity of wheat which the company had purchased before 1 June 1970. It then claimed the increased premium in accordance with the now abolished regulation arguing that the new regulation was invalid. On reference from a German court the ECJ did not annul the regulation but, in the name of legal certainty, held that it ought to be so interpreted as to make the increased premium payable even if the denaturing process occurred after 1 June, provided that the wheat was purchased and the authorization to process it was obtained before 1 June. Deuka had embarked on a venture which had the backing of the law and its expectations had to be protected.

---

15 Vertrauensschutz, protéction de la confiance légitime. See Case 289/81: *Mavridis v European Parliament* [1983] ECR 1731 at 1744.
16 Usher, J A, 'The Influence of National Concepts on Decisions of the European Court' [1976] 1 ELRev 359 at 363; Sharpston, E, 'Legitimate Expectations and Economic Reality' (1991) 15 ELRev 103 et seq.
17 Case 169/80: *Administration des Douanes v Gondrand Frères* [1981] ECR 1931 at 1942.
18 Case T-336/94: *Efisol SA v Commission* [1996] ECR II-1343 [1997] 3 CMLR 298.
19 Case 81/72: *Commission v Council* [1973] ECR 575, [1973] CMLR 639.
20 Case T-472/93: *Campo Ebro Industrial SA v Council* [1995] ECR II-421, [1996] 1 CMLR 1038; Cases T-466/93, T-469/93; T-473/93, T-474/93 and T-477/93: *O'Dwyer v Council* [1995] ECR II-2071 [1996] 2 CMLR 148; Case C-22/94: *Irish Farmers Association v Minister for Agriculture* [1997] ECR I-1809, [1997] 2 CMLR 621.
1 Case 78/74: *Deuka etc v Einfuhr-und Vorratsstelle für Getreide und Futtermittel* [1975] ECR 421, [1975] 2 CMLR 28.

The stress is, therefore, on the requirement that the expectation is 'legitimate',[2] that is, conceived in the mind of a prudent person who acts according to the letter and the spirit of the law in confidence that his fidelity to the law will be reciprocated. Mere speculation will not do. This is illustrated by the *Mackprang*[3] case. In the spring of 1969 the fall in the forward rate of the French franc opened up a prospect of a profit on the exchange rate to dealers in cereals who purchased the produce in France and sold it to the German Agricultural Intervention Agency (EVGF). Under the CAP such national agencies are bound to purchase agricultural produce. The intensified market activities posed a threat to the German intervention system as well as the storage capacity of the Agency. In the circumstances the Commission by Decision 69/138[4] authorized the German Government to restrict intervention purchases to wheat and barley grown only in Germany. Identical decisions were adopted for Belgium and the Netherlands. The Decision was issued on 8 May 1969, took effect on the same day but exempted offers made before that date. On 6 May Mackprang, a German dealer in cereals, offered to the EVGF eight lots of wheat purchased in France stating that the produce was situated in various parts of Germany whilst in actual fact it was still in transit from France to Germany. On 8 May the EVGF accepted the offer but subsequently declined to accept deliveries to its warehouses. Mackprang's claim to compensation on the ground of a legitimate expectation failed. The ECJ, on reference, conceded that the Decision being a derogation from the relevant Regulations had to be interpreted in the light of the objectives pursued by those Regulations but held it was 'a justified precaution against purely speculative activities'.[5] Therefore it did not constitute an infringement of the principle of protection of legitimate expectation. Advocate-General Warner, holding that the transaction was 'subversive to the intervention system', thus disposed of the argument:

> 'No trader who was exploiting that situation in order to make out of the system profits that the system was never designed to bestow on him could legitimately rely on the persistence of the situation. On the contrary, the only reasonable expectation that such a trader could have was that the competent authorities would act as swiftly as possible to bring the situation to an end. Nor ... could he expect particular tenderness at their hands.'

If a loss occurs as a result of frustrated legitimate expectations an action for damages may be brought under EC Article 288(2) (ex Art 215 (2)). In such a case the claimant must prove not only that he had such an expectation on which he had acted reasonably but also a causal link between his loss and the relevant Community act. The case of *CNTA v Commission*[6] provides an interesting example. By Regulation 974/71 the Council had established a system of monetary

---

2 Eg Cases 95–98/74, 15, 100/75: *Union Nationale des Coopératives Agricoles de Céréales v Commission* [1975] ECR 1615; Cases 44–51/77: *Union Malt v Commission* [1978] ECR 57, [1978] 3 CMLR 702; Case 78/77: *Lührs v Hauptzollamt Hamburg-Jonas* [1978] ECR 169, [1979] 1 CMLR 657; Case 130/78: *Salumificio di Cornuda SpA v Amministrazione delle Finanze dello Stato* [1979] ECR 867, [1979] 3 CMLR 561; Case 12/78: *Italy v Commission* [1979] ECR 1731, [1980] 2 CMLR 573 (*Re Monetary Compensatory Amounts for Durum Wheat*); and Case 84/78: *Tomadini SNC v Amministrazione delle Finanze* [1979] ECR 1801, [1980] 2 CMLR 573; Case 49/79: *Pool v Council* [1980] ECR 569, [1980] 3 CMLR 279.
3 Case 2/75: *Einfuhr-und Vorratsstelle für Getreide und Futtermittel v Mackprang* [1975] ECR 607, [1977] 1 CMLR 198. See also Case 49/79, supra.
4 OJ 1969, L112.
5 Case 2/75, note 3, supra, para 4.
6 Case 74/74: [1975] ECR 533, [1977] 1 CMLR 171 and [1976] ECR 797.

compensatory amounts in order to make good losses arising from fluctuations in exchange rates. The system was extended to colza seed by Commission Regulation 1471/71, further extended to France by Commission Regulations 17/72 and 144/72. By Regulation 189/72 made on 26 January 1972 the Commission abolished the system as from 1 February 1972. The CNTA (a French company) was in the colza business which was covered by both Regulations. Before the second Regulation was enacted the CNTA made a number of export contracts which were to be performed after the scheme had been abolished. It claimed that it had suffered loss as a result of the sudden and unexpected abolition of the scheme without there being any provision in respect of transactions entered into during the lifetime of the scheme. CNTA's claim was further strengthened by reference to a scheme of export refunds whose rates fluctuated but could be fixed in advance in respect of any particular transaction. To that end the exporter had to lodge a deposit which would be forfeited if he failed to export as arranged. CNTA, having obtained advance fixing of the refunds in respect of certain transactions before 26 January, claimed that it entered these on the assumption that monetary compensatory amounts would be payable and calculated its profits accordingly.

In order to establish liability under Article 288(2) (ex Art 215(2)) CNTA had to prove that 'in accordance with general principles common to the laws of the Member States', the Commission had acted wrongly. CNTA argued, accordingly, that Regulation 189/72 constituted an act envisaged by the said article because it infringed the principle of legal certainty and frustrated its legitimate expectations. The Court conceded the force of this argument and held that:

'In these circumstances, a trader may legitimately expect that for transactions irrevocably undertaken by him because he has obtained, subject to a deposit, export licences fixing the amount of the refund in advance, no unforeseeable alteration will occur which could have the effect of causing him inevitable loss, by re-exposing him to the exchange risk.

... The Community is therefore liable if, in the absence of an overriding matter of public interest, the Commission abolished with immediate effect and without warning the application of compensatory amounts in a specific sector without adopting transitional measures which would at least permit traders either to avoid the loss which would have been suffered in the performance of export contracts, the existence and irrevocability of which are established by the advance fixing of the refunds, or to compensation for such loss.

... In the absence of an overriding matter of public interest, the Commission has violated a superior rule of law, thus rendering the Community liable, by failing to include in Regulation 189/72 transitional measures for the protection of the confidence which a trader might legitimately have in the Community rules.'[7]

Having said that, the Court did not declare Regulation 189/72 invalid. Thus the wrongful act was not the Regulation itself but the omission to issue a warning to traders and to institute a transitional regime to protect transactions already in progress. This omission constituted a violation of a 'superior rule of law', ie the protection of legitimate expectations.

Turning to the question of damages the Court held that, in the circumstances, the Community was not liable to compensate the claimant for all the losses incurred. It held that 'it is necessary to take into consideration the fact that the

---

7   Ibid, paras 42–44; see also Case 12/78: *Re Monetary Compensatory Amounts for Durum Wheat*, p 191, note 2, supra.

maintenance of the compensatory amounts was in no way guaranteed ... and that it could not therefore legitimately expect under all circumstances to make the profits which would have accrued to it from the contract under the system of compensatory amounts ... The protection which it may claim by reason of its legitimate expectation is merely that of not suffering loss by reason of the withdrawal of those amounts.'[8]

In subsequent proceedings to determine the actual damages the claimant was unable to prove any loss arising from the withdrawal of the scheme within the limits stated above because payments for the shipments were made in French currency. Any loss of anticipated profits was covered by the commercial risk involved.[9] However the principle of the protection of legitimate expectations has been established.

Other examples of frustrated legitimate expectations: in Case 120/86[10] by a milk regulation the Commission withdrew non-marketing premiums for five years including the reference year for the calculation of milk quota. The applicant, who planned his production on the basis of the existing quota, was disappointed when allotted a nil quota. The ECJ thought to rectify the position by allowing him to receive his quota from the national reserve for the year in question.

In another case,[11] where the state aid involved was not duly notified, the Commission delayed for 26 months the decision to declare the aid illegal and to order repayment of the aid. However, the beneficiary of the aid had the decision annulled for breach of his legitimate expectation.

Good faith was pleaded in *Meganck v Commission*[12] where a temporary official drew certain family allowances to which strictly he was not entitled. When faced with the demand for repayment he claimed, successfully, that he received these in good faith not knowing from his salary slips that he was in fact overpaid.

Fairness or equity appeared in several cases. Mr Costacurta's[13] application for admission to an internal competition for a position in the Community service was rejected without sufficient reasons being given by the relevant selection board. The ECJ annulled the decision of the board on the ground that in the circumstances, it was *unfair* to the official.

Force majeure In the *Reich*[14] case the claimant failed to observe the time limit provided for in a licence for the importation of maize from a Member State. He argued that this was due to *force majeure*, ie the delay in importation due to a fault of the railway authority and not his own. The ECJ held that, since *force majeure* was a valid excuse under the regulation governing imports from non-Community countries, there was no reason why *in equity* this principle should not apply to imports from a Member State of the Community.

---

8 Ibid, paras 45–46.
9 Case 74/74, p 191, note 6, supra, [1976] ECR 797.
10 Case 120/86: *Mulder v Minister for Agriculture and Fisheries* [1988] ECR 2321, [1989] 2 CMLR 1 followed by claims under Art 215(2): Cases C-104/89 and C-37/90: *Mulder v Council and Commission*, [1992] ECR I-3061.
11 Case 223/85: *Rijn-Schelde-Verolm Maschinefabrieken en Scheepswerven NV v Commission* [1987] ECR 4617, [1989] 2 CMLR 259.
12 Case 36/72: [1973] ECR 527 at 534. See also Case 92/82: *Gutmann v Commission (Re Resettlement Allowance)* [1983] ECR 3127.
13 Case 31/75: *Costacurta v Commission* [1975] ECR 1563 at 1570.
14 Case 64/74: *Reich v Hauptzollamt Landau* [1975] ECR 261, at 268, [1975] 1 CMLR 396 at 405.

Lührs,[15] an exporter of potatoes in Sweden, who in the circumstances could not rely on the plea of legitimate expectations, claimed that he was nevertheless unfairly treated because of the uncertainty inherent in the regulations governing the exchange of the tax on exports into national currency. The ECJ held that *natural justice* required that of the two rates of exchange which could have been applied in his case the one, which at the material time was less onerous to the taxpayer, should be applied.

Force majeure was pleaded both in the *Handelsgesellschaft*[16] and the third *Kampffmeyer* case.[17] Both were concerned with the operation of the system of export/import licences and advance fixing certificates for agricultural produce. The issue of licences was subject to a forfeitable deposit in the event of the authorization to export/import not being exhausted within the stated period. If, as a result of *force majeure*, the transaction was not completed the national authority operating the system could either refund the deposit or extend the period for completion. The system was challenged in the *Handelsgesellschaft* case on several grounds including *force majeure* in so far as the referring court inquired whether, on the proper construction of the regulation in question, the forfeiture of the deposit was excluded only in cases of *force majeure*. Should this be the case the ground would be too narrow to do justice to the appellant. The ECJ answered in the negative but gave a broad definition of *force majeure*. It held: 'The concept of *force majeure* is not limited to absolute impossibility but must be understood in the sense of unusual circumstances outside the control of the importer or exporter, the consequences of which, in spite of the exercise of all due care, could not have been avoided except at the cost of excessive sacrifice. The concept implies a sufficient flexibility regarding not only the nature of the occurrence relied upon but also the care which the exporter should have exercised in order to meet it and the extent of the sacrifice which he should have accepted to that end' (at para 23).

In the *Kampffmeyer* case the issue was whether the loss of an import licence following despatch by non-registered letter constituted *force majeure* so as to absolve the trader from the forfeiture of his deposit. It was basically a matter of fact, that is, whether a diligent trader fulfils his duty of care in the context of his business and the Community licensing system if he sends his licence by ordinary post. Holding that 'in the absence of any express provision of Community law, it is for the national court to say whether such a trader has or has not exercised all reasonable care', the ECJ ruled that the matter was one of application, not of interpretation and left the decision to the referring court. In German law the responsibility lay with the trader.

Another abortive attempt to take advantage of *force majeure* occurred in *IFG v Commission*[18] where a trader sought from the Community compensation in respect of a transaction which, due to floods in Rumania, was not completed within the period of his import licence. His claim was supported by the argument that due to a change in the Community law his legitimate expectations were frustrated. The ECJ, whilst recognizing *force majeure* to be a cause 'of derogation from the strict requirements of the law', could not find any reason why the Community should be liable under EC

15 Case 78/77: *Lührs v Hauptzollamt Hamburg-Jonas* [1978] ECR 169 at 180, [1979] 1 CMLR 657.
16 Case 11/70, p 184, note 20, supra.
17 Case 158/73: *Kampffmeyer v Einfuhr-und Vorratsstelle für Getreide und Futtermittel* [1974] ECR 101. See also Case C-200/94: *Anglo Irish Beef Processors v Minister for Agriculture* [1996] ECR I-1925.
18 Case 68/77: *Intercontinentale Fleischhandelsgesellschaft mbH & Co KG v Commission* [1978] ECR 353, [1978] 2 CMLR 733.

Article 288 (ex Art 215, 2nd paragraph) in the present case. Indeed, held the Court, remedy should be sought from the other contracting party.

However a French exporter of wheat to the United Kingdom was successful.[19] His cargo perished in the North Sea but his claim for 'accession compensatory amounts' due under Regulation 269/73 was refused on the ground that he was unable to prove that the goods had reached their destination. The Regulation, unlike Regulation 192/75 governing export refunds for agricultural produce, did not contain the *force majeure* formula. Therefore, on reference, the ECJ rectified the position by applying by analogy Regulation 192/75. It held that 'Regulation 269/73 is to be interpreted as meaning that where goods exported from an old Member State to a new Member State have perished in transit as a result of *force majeure*, the exporter is entitled to the same compensatory amounts as would have been due to him if the goods had reached their destination and if import formalities had been completed there'.[20] Thus the Court not only applied an equitable general principle to mitigate hardship but also in doing so filled a lacuna in the Community system.

Another French[1] exporter dealing in animal feed had not received back from the British customs authorities the original T5 control form which would enable him to claim monetary compensation amounts from the French authorities. Instead he claimed on the ground of *force majeure* and proportionality. However the ECJ found the refusal of the French authorities to entertain his claim justified, pointing out the procedural remedies available for such maladministration of customs formalities.

Force majeure was pleaded unsuccessfully by an Irish exporter of agricultural intervention produce which was stolen from the company's depot in England while on its way out of the Community. The exporter suffered forfeiture of security for non-performance. Since exportation of the procedure was the exporter's principal obligation the forfeiture of the security was not held disproportionate while the loss of the goods was not regarded as being due to *force majeure* which was defined by the Court. Moreover, the innocence or non-negligence of the exporter was held irrelevant.[2]

Similarly the inability to export because of the purchaser's refusal to take delivery of the goods was not regarded as *force majeure*. Consequently, forfeiture of the deposit to secure export licence was held justified.[3]

Holding that the undertaking not to produce milk runs with the farmland the ECJ ruled that a forced sale of the farm by the mortgagee did not absolve the original farmer from the duty of repaying the whole of the non-marketing premium. In the circumstances the loss of his farm was not caused by *force majeure* which would justify him not facing the penalty for the breach of his obligation.[4]

Greece was also unsuccessful in claiming that the payment of her contribution to the Community budget was prevented by *force majeure*, ie a strike at the Bank of Greece. The Community was entitled to moratory interest.[5]

19 Case 6/78: *Union Française de Céréales v Hauptzollamt Hamburg-Jonas* [1978] ECR 1675.
20 Ibid, para 6.
1   Case 266/84: *Denkavit France Sarl v FORMA* [1986] ECR 149, [1987] 3 CMLR 202.
2   Case 296/86: *Anthony McNicholl Ltd v Minister for Agriculture* [1988] ECR 1491, [1988] 2 CMLR 275. See also Case C-109/95: *Astir AE v Greece (re refund for agricultural products)* [1997] ECR I-1385.
3   Case 109/86: *Ioannis Theodorakis Viomikhania Eleou AE v Greece* [1987] ECR 4319, [1989] 2 CMLR 166.
4   Case 199/87: *Mads Peder Jensen v Landbrugsministeriet* [1988] ECR 5045, [1989] 3 CMLR 64.
5   Case 70/86: *Commission v Greece* [1987] ECR 3545, [1989] 1 CMLR 441.

Belgium fared no better when she blamed *force majeure* for delayed payments of the monetary compensatory amounts. The complexity of Community legislation was not so unusual as to provide an excuse while the sudden increase in applications was due to the Belgian administration which reintroduced the MCAs. The resulting staffing problem was a matter for Belgian policy and could not be attributed to *force majeure*.[6]

We can conclude, therefore, that the ECJ had adhered to the classic concept of *force majeure* as 'unusual circumstances outside the control' of those who plead it defined in Case 68/77.[7]

Proportionality The principle of *proportionality*, which is an aspect of the Aristotelian distributive justice, embodied in the German Constitution, made an early debut[8] before the Community Court but was most dramatically, though unsuccessfully, pleaded in the *Handelsgesellschaft* case. In simple terms the principle means that social burdens should be distributed fairly according to the capacity of the members of the society. According to Advocate-General Dutheillet de Lamothe[9] it means that such burdens may be imposed only for the purposes of the public interest to the extent that is strictly necessary for the attainment of such purposes.

Dealing with the argument that forfeitable deposits instituted under Regulation 120/67 infringed the principle of proportionality (as persistently claimed by the trader and maintained by the Verwaltungsgericht at Frankfurt) the ECJ held that it was a matter of Community law which could not be overriden by principles of national law even of a constitutional character. The system itself was justified as it served the purposes of the Treaty in supporting the common organization of agricultural markets.

Explaining the notion of proportionality in another case[10] the ECJ said:

'In order to establish whether a provision of Community law is consonant with the principle of proportionality it is necessary to establish, in the first place, whether the means it employs to achieve the aim correspond to the importance of the aim and, in the second place, whether they are necessary for its achievement.'

Thus proportionality reflects the duty of defining specific objectives and the choice of means to attain these objectives within the framework of the Treaty. The test of proportionality may also be applied to see whether the given measure is appropriate. However the suitability of a measure ought to be disproportionate to a substantial degree in order to be invalid or, as stated by the Court: 'the legality of a measure can be adversely affected only if the measure is manifestly unsuitable for achieving the aim pursued by the competent Community institution'.[11] The severity of the test can be explained in so far as the claimant sought, on a non-fault basis, compensation from the Community for a loss sustained as a result of the application of a valid agricultural regulation.

6　Case 145/85: *Denkavit BelgiëNV v Belgium* [1987] ECR 565, [1988] 2 CMLR 679.
7　Supra, p 194, note 18.
8　Case 8/55: *Fédération Charbonnière de Belgique v High Authority of the ECSC* [1954–56] ECR 292 at 299.
9　Case 11/70: *Internationale Handelsgesellschaft* [1970] ECR 1125 at 1146.
10　Case 66/82: *Fromonçais SA v Fonds d'Orientation* [1983] ECR 395 at para 8.
11　Case 59/83: *Biovilac NV v Commission* [1984] ECR 4057 at para 17.

The reverse does not seem to apply since a private party claiming a Community gain cannot rely on the principle of proportionality if he had not complied with the standards laid down, eg for denaturing an agricultural product. Although the sanction was hard the Court dismissed the claim holding that the Commission was justified in laying down strict conditions to ensure compliance. It held that the Commission 'was not obliged to vary the severity of the measure in question according to the gravity of the (claimant's) failure to comply with that obligation. Such a measure cannot be regarded as out of proportion to the objective pursued'.[12]

The system was more positively defended by the ECJ in another case,[13] since the burdens it imposed were not 'manifestly out of proportion to the object in view'[14] whilst 'the competent authorities must be in a position constantly to follow trade movements in order to assess market trends and apply the measures laid down in the Regulation'.[15] However whilst the forfeiture of a deposit for not complying with the licensing system is fully justified[16] it is not so justified on the ground of failing to comply with purely bureaucratic requirements such, for example, as the delay in submitting a proof of imports of tomato concentrates.[17] The principle of proportionality has been applied with diverse results in several other cases dealing with such problems as: the movement of goods[18] and persons[19] and state responsibility for the implementation of the CAP.[20]

Proportionality continues to be a favourite plea in order to save the forfeiture of deposits under the Community regulations. We have seen it above coupled, albeit unsuccessfully, with *force majeure*. The question which arose was whether in Case 38/86 (No 2) forfeiture was a proportional penalty.[1] Forfeiture of security for non-completion of sales of intervention produce was disputed as the purchaser repudiated the contract in order to benefit from the new exchange rate of 'green' currency. However, the ECJ held that the vendor had to bear the consequences which were not out of proportion to his failure to conclude the sales. However, in an earlier case[2] only partial forfeiture was held to be justified on the principle of proportionality. It appears in a rather confused factual situation that the carrier of intervention food aid to Ethiopia had not complied with the tender requirements. His ships sailed later than the deadline and they were more than 15 years old. The main question was whether compliance with the time limit for sailing was

---

12 Case 272/81: *Société Ru-Mi v Forma* [1982] ECR 4167 at para 14.
13 Case 5/73: *Balkan-Import-Export GmbH v Hauptzollamt Berlin-Packhof* [1973] ECR 1091 at 1112.
14 See also Cases 119 and 120/76: *Ölmühle Hamburg AG v Hauptzollamt Hamburg Waltershof and Becher v HZA Bremen-Nord* [1977] ECR 1269, [1979] 2 CMLR 83.
15 ECJ reciting a preamble to Regulation 120/67 in the third *Kampffmeyer* case, p 194, note 17, supra.
16 Case 85/78: *Bundesanstalt für Landwirtschaftliche Marktordnung v Jacob Hirsch & Sohne GmbH* [1978] ECR 2517, [1979] 2 CMLR 631.
17 Case 122/78: *Buitoni SA v Fonds d'orientation et de Regularisation des Marches Agricoles* [1979] ECR 677, [1979] 2 CMLR 665.
18 Case 62/70: *Bock KG v Commission* [1971] ECR 897 at 909, [1972] CMLR 160; Case 52/77: *Cayrol v Rivoira and Figli* [1977] ECR 2261 at 2281, [1978] 2 CMLR 253.
19 Case 67/74: *Bonsignore v Oberstadtdirektor der Stadt Köhn* [1975] ECR 297; Case 36/75: *Rutili v Ministère de l'intérieur* [1975] ECR 1219, [1976] 1 CMLR 140; Case 8/77: *Re Sagulo, Brenca and Bakhouche* [1977] ECR 1495 at 1506, [1977] 2 CMLR 585. Case 30/77: *R v Bouchereau* [1977] ECR 1999.
20 Case 166/78: *Italy v Council* [1979] ECR 2575 at 2601.
1 Case 38/86: *Firma Karl-Heinz Neumann v Bundesanstalt für Landwirtschaftliche Marktordnung (No 2)* [1987] ECR 1675, [1988] 1 CMLR 523.
2 Case 21/85: *A Maas & Co v Bundesanstalt für Landwirtschaftliche Marktordnung* [1986] ECR 3537, [1987] 3 CMLR 794.

the principal obligation since no ships used for the purpose were close to the required category. As the latter was regarded to be a secondary obligation only partial forfeiture of the security seemed justified. Still in the maze of the CAP, a dairy company, supplying skimmed milk as animal feed for calves, lost only a part of the subsidy involved. It was duty bound to keep accurate records and submit these to the authority promptly since the amount of the subsidy depended upon the maximum number of calves on individual holdings during the relevant month. Since a number of customers of the dairy company were in default the repayment of the subsidy in full was considered disproportionate.

Conclusions   In the context of the Community justice proportionality is a reflection of the rule of law. It has a twofold effect: it works for the protection of the individual from the harshness of administration and contributes to the fair distribution of burdens in society; and it restrains the Community and national institutions from deviating from the basic principles of Community law which include not only the founding Treaties but also equitable principles embodied in the national systems.

While it is an open question how far equitable principles can be developed to enrich the Community legal system, it has to be appreciated that the CAP has proved to be one of the main areas of their application. A reform of the CAP into a more rational system might have a sobering effect. The ECJ too has shown concern that the development does not get out of hand. Dealing once more with the plea that forfeiture of a deposit under the CAP in respect of intervention sales was an excessive penalty the Court refused to recognize the principle of 'objective unfairness'[3] (apparently derived from the German system) holding it to be non-existent in the Community law. It stressed that a principle of national law has no obligatory application in the Community system while the uniform application of Community rules throughout the Community is an overriding feature of the Community system. A national judge hard pressed by arguments from the national jurisdiction ought to take refuge in the procedure for a preliminary ruling, thus leaving to the ECJ the task of ensuring the uniformity within the Community system.

Reflecting on the use and development of general principles of law at the hands of the Community Court one should not underestimate their potential for the interpretation of Community law and for the closing of gaps which the system reveals in practice. However one should not overestimate this potential or attribute to it the character of a Community 'common law' system[4] implying thereby a new body of rules superimposed upon the law derived from the Treaties.

Opinions of the Advocates-General   The Advocate-General participates in every case before the ECJ[5] and his opinion forms an obligatory part of the adjudicating process though not of the judgment itself. In the light of his function and the nature of the Community Court the Advocate-General can be likened to a judge of a first instance court within the Community administration of justice. Therefore, if he is followed by the Court his opinion may be regarded as a concurring judgment by analogy to individual judgments of a collegiate common law court. If he is not followed, by the same analogy, his opinion may be regarded as a dissenting judgment.

---

3   Case 299/84: *Firma Karl-Heinz Neumann v Bundesanstalt für Landwirtschaftliche Marktordnund* [1985] ECR 3663, [1987] 3 CMLR 4.
4   Cf A-G Dutheillet de Lamothe in the *Handelsgesellschaft* case, supra, at 1146–1147.
5   There are no Advocates-General in the First Instance Court but judges may act as such where appropriate.

In the common law system dissenting and concurring judgments are studied with equal interest since at the ultimate instance a dissent in a court below may become the final ruling of a superior court. Even without that change of fortune a dissenting judgment may be used in argument on another occasion in the hope that a fresh approach may sharpen its force. In the Community system, on the other hand, the opinion of the Advocate-General has to be seen as a personal judgment and an invitation to the Court to follow suit. It is fully reasoned and it tends to relate the proposed solution to the pattern of case law established by the Court. One can therefore discern a greater appreciation of Community precedents in the opinions of Advocates-General than in the judgments of the Court.

The Advocates-General have made a significant contribution to the development of Community law. Their opinions, in view of their personal style, appear by and large to be more readable than the judgments of the Court. However, no matter what their weight as a persuasive force or part of dynamic jurisprudence, they lack the authority of the *res judicata*.

C. Where to find Community law

(1)   TREATIES AND RELATED INSTRUMENTS

The authentic and official English texts of the Community Treaties are available in a variety of forms:

(a)   Editions published by the Community:
(i) *Treaties establishing the European Communities: Treaties amending these Treaties: Documents concerning the Accession* (European Communities Office for Official Publications, 1978). This volume contains all the Treaties and their annexes in force on 1 July 1978. See also abridged edition, 1987.
(ii) *Documents concerning the accession of the Hellenic Republic to the European Communities (Official Journal of the European Communities, 1979,* L291).
(iii) *Documents concerning the accession of Spain and Portugal* (OJ 1985, L302).
(iv) *Collected agreements concluded by the European Communities.* The volumes contain the texts of agreements with non-Member States and international organizations.
(v) *Treaty on European Union* (Maastricht), OJ 1993, C 244/1.
(vi) *Treaty on European Union* (Amsterdam), OJ 1997, C 340/1.

(b)   HM Stationery Office Editions of the Treaties are also available as follows:
(i) *Treaty establishing the European Coal and Steel Community, Paris 18 April 1951* (Amended text: Cmnd 7461). The sole authentic text of this Treaty is in French which is printed together with an English translation; the latter has no official standing.
(ii) *Treaty establishing the European Economic Community, Rome 25 March 1957; Treaty establishing the European Atomic Energy Community, Rome 25 March 1957* (Amended text: Cmnd 7460).
(iii) *Treaty concerning the Accession of the Kingdom of Denmark, Ireland, the Kingdom of Norway and the United Kingdom of Great Britain and Northern Ireland to the European Economic Community and the European Atomic Energy Community and Decision of the Council of the European Communities concerning the Accession of the said States to the European Coal and Steel Community, Brussels 22 January 1972* (Amended text: Cmnd 7463).
(iv) *Single European Act 1986* (Cmnd 9758).

(c) The texts of the principal Treaties and of some other Community instruments are also available in Sweet and Maxwell's Encyclopaedia of European Union Law (Constitutional Texts) looseleaf.

(d) Annotated texts of the Treaties and of related Community instruments are to be found in *Halsbury's Statutes of England* (3rd edn), Volume 42A, European Continuation Volume 1, 1952–72 and in Sweet and Maxwell's *Encyclopaedia of European Community Law* – Secondary Legislation. Both of these works are kept up to date by Supplements.

(2) COMMUNITY LEGISLATION

The legislation of the Communities, ie decisions and recommendations in the case of the ECSC and regulations, directives and decisions in the cases of the EC and Euratom, are published in the *Official Journal of the European Communities*. This appears, almost daily, in each of the official languages of the Communities. An English edition has been published since 9 October 1972.

Annotated texts of Community secondary legislation are to be found in *Halsbury's Statutes of England* (3rd edn), Volume 42A and Supplements and in the *Encyclopaedia of European Community Law*, Volumes CI to VI. Community and national legislation relating to economic activities is summarized in *European Law Digest* (1973 and continued). The TMC Asser Institute's *Guide to EEC Legislation* (1979), in two volumes with an annual cumulative supplement, provides an invaluable subject index to past and current Community legislation.

(3) CASE LAW

The texts of its judgments and opinions with the submissions of the Advocates-General are published in periodical parts by the Court of Justice in each of the official languages of the Communities. The version in the procedural language in respect of a particular case is the only authentic version. The French version, which was commonly used in the United Kingdom before accession, is entitled *Recueil da la Jurisprudence de la Cour*. An English version entitled *European Court Reports* has been published in periodical parts since 1973. English translations of the pre-accession volumes of reports of cases before the Court from 1953 to 1972 have been published.

Since 1962 English translations of the judgments of both the Court of Justice and of some of the courts of the Member States on points of Community law and decisions of the Commission on restrictive practices have been published under the name *Common Market Law Reports* (also available on CD-ROM). Since 1970 these Reports have also included on occasion the texts of the judgments in the procedural language. English translations of the judgments of the Court of Justice prior to the commencement of the *Common Market Law Reports* are to be found in Volume 2 of Valentine's *Court of Justice of the European Communities* (1965).

Since the establishment of the Court of First Instance, cases decided by the Court of Justice bear the prefix 'C' (Cour) and those by the Court of First Instance prefix 'T' (tribunal). Appeals from the Court of First Instance to Court of Justice bear the prefix 'P' (pourvoi).

English translations of the judgments of the Court of Justice are also to be found in *Common Market Reports* published by the Commerce Clearing House Inc of Chicago. Since May 1972 leading cases have been published in the *Times* newspaper. Community and national case law relating to economic activities is summarized in *European Law Digest* (1973 and continued) and European Current Law. Eversen, Sperl and Usher's *Compendium of Case Law relating to the European Communities* covers the years 1973–1976 and has been replaced by a *Digest of Case Law* prepared under the auspices of the Court of Justice.

(4)   SUBSIDIARY SOURCES

(a)   Official papers of Community institutions
There is a vast amount of such material covering all the activities of the Communities. It ranges from general reports and journalism to highly specialized monographs on detailed aspects of Community activity. Most of this material appears in all the official languages and some of the pre-accession papers are also available in unofficial English versions. From the lawyer's point of view the most significant and informative include the following:

Reports and opinions of the Commission and the consultative committees published in the Official Journal. Discussion documents and draft legislative proposals are available in mimeographed form with the prefixes COM (for Commission) and SEC (for Secretary General).

The Debates and Working Documents (*Documents de Séance*) of the European Parliament. The Debates are published as an annexe to the Official Journal and the Working Documents are published individually by the Parliament itself.

The Bulletin of the European Communities published in periodical parts by the Secretariat of the Commission. In addition to giving a monthly account of current activities and developments the Supplements to the *Bulletin* are convenient sources of the texts of important reports and proposals for legislation.

The annual *General Report on the Activities of the Communities* and since the establishment of the Union, the *General Report on the Activities of the European Union*, submitted by the Commission to the European Parliament. The General Secretariat of the Council also publishes an annual *Review of the Council's Work*.

(b)   Journals
There are three English-language journals devoted to Community matters. The *Common Market Law Review* (1963/1964 and continued), the *European Law Review* (1975/1976 and continued) and *Legal Issues of European Integration* (1974 and continued) are all concerned with the law. There are also specialist journals: *European Competition Law Review, European Intellectual Property Law Review* and *European Taxation. The Journal of Common Market Studies* (1962 and continued) is not exclusively legal and also covers economic and political aspects of Community activities. Articles on Community legal topics are also to be found in the *International and Comparative Law Quarterly*, the *Journal of Business Law* and the *International Company and Commercial Law Review*. Articles may also be found in the *British Yearbook of International Law* and, more particularly, in the *Yearbook of European Law*.

(c)   General Works
Arnull.   The General Principles of EEC Law and the Individual (1990)
Barking and Brealey (eds).   Practitioners' Handbook of EC Law (1998)
Brealey and Hoskins.   Remedies in EC Law (1998)
Brown.   The Court of Justice of the European Communities (4th edn, 1994)
Collins.   European Community Law in the United Kingdom (5th edn, 1999)

De Burca and Scott. The Constitution of the European Union (1999)
Hartley. The Foundations of European Community Law (4th edn, 1998)
Kapteyn & Verloren Van Themaat. Introduction to the Law of the European
 Communities (3rd edn by Gormley, 1998)
Lasok, K.P.E. The European Court of Justice (2nd edn, 1994)
Lasok & Soldatos (eds) The European Communities in Action containing 24
 contributions (1981)
Lenaerts and others. Constitutional Law of the European Union (1999) and
 Procedural Law of the European Union (1999).
Mathijsen. A Guide to European Community Law (7th edn, 1999)
Plender and others. European Courts Practice and Precidents (1996, supplement,
 1998)
Schermers & Waelbroeck. Judicial Protection in the European Communities
 (5th edn, 1992)
Shaw. European Community Law (1993)
Steiner. Textbook on EEC Law (4th edn, 1994)
Toth. Legal Protection of Individuals in the European Communities (1978)
Toth. The Oxford Encyclopaedia of Community Law (1990)
Wyatt & Dashwood. European Community Law (3rd edn, 1993)
Halsbury's Laws of England (4th edn) Vol 51, Law of the European Communities
 (ed by Vaughan 2nd edn, 1991) containing 21 contributions covering the whole
 area of Community Law.
Isaac. Droit Communautaire General (3rd edn, 1992)
Cerexe. Le Droit Européen (1979)
Druesne. Droit Materiel et Politiques de la Communauté Europenne (2nd edn, 1992)
Rideau, J. Droit Institutionnel de l'Union et des Communaute's Europeénnes
 (2nd edn, 1996)
Craig, P. & De Burca Grainne. EU Law, Text, Cases, Materials (2nd edn, 1998)
Rideau & Charrier. Code de Procedures Européennes (1990)
Louis. L'Ordre Juridique Communautaire (2nd edn, 1983)
Philip. Les Institutions Européennes (1981)
Grisoli. L'Europe del Mercato Commune (1983)
Tridimas T. The General Principles of EC Law (1999)

(d) Monographs
Bellamy & Child. Common Market Law of Competition (2001)
Cawthra. Industrial Property Rights in the EEC (2nd edn, 1986)
Easson. Taxation in the European Community (1993)
Goyder. EEC Competition Law (3rd edn, 1998)
Greaves. Transport of the European Community (1991)
Kerse. EEC Antitrust Procedure (4th edn, 1991)
Korah. An Introductory Guide to EEC Competition Law and Practice (4th edn,
 1990)
Kramer. EC Environmental Law (1999)
Lasok (D). The Professions and Services in the EEC (1986)
Lasok (D). The Trade and Customs Law of the EEC (3rd edn, 1998)
Lasok & Stone. Conflict of Laws in the European Community (1987)
O'Keeffe, Twomey. Legal Issues of the Maastricht Treaty (1994)
Oliver. Free Movement of Goods in the EEC (3rd edn, 1995)
Prechal S. Directives in European Community Law (1995)
Stone. Copyright in the UK and the EC (1990)
Usher. Legal Aspects of Agriculture in the European Community (1988)

Van Kraay.   Tourism and the Hotel and Catering Industries in the EC (1993)
Portwood.   Mergers under EEC Competition Law (1994)
Watson.   Social Security Law of the European Communities (1980)
Whish.   Competition Law (2nd edn, 1989)
Woolridge.   Company Law in the UK and the European Community (1991)

(e)   Treaties, Cases and Materials
Sweet & Maxwell.   European Community Treaties (4th edn, 1980)
Plender & Usher.   Cases and materials on the Law of the European Communities
    (3rd edn 1993)
Weatherhill.   Cases and Materials on EEC Law (1992)
Foster.   Blackstone's EC Legislation (6th edn, 1995–6)
Ruddent & Phelan.   Basic Community Cases (2nd edn, 1997)
Rudden & Wyatt.   Basic Community Laws (7th edn, 1999)

(5)   ELECTRONIC SOURCES

CELEX is the European Union's official inter-institutional database. It can be
accessed through the Europa server on the Internet (http://europa.eu.int/ and
http://europa.eu.int/celex/). CELEX is also distributed through the office or
Official Publications of the European Communities, subscriptions through a
network of official agents, which act as gateways, and 24 licence-holders who
disseminate derived reviews of CELEX on-line or on CD-ROM.
The EUR-Lex service (hittp://europe.eu.int/eur-lex/) offers simple, user-friendly
access free of charge to legal information produced by the institutions.
    The EUR-Lex gives access to documents published daily in the 'L' and 'C'
Official Journals, treaties currently in force or in the process of ratification, the
Directory of Community Legislation in force, consolidated versions of legislative
instruments and recent Court judgments. The Official Journal is also available
on CD-ROM. The Court of Justice and Court of First Instance can be accessed
on the Internet (http://europa.eu.int/cj/en/index.htm). Sweet & Maxwell provide
the European Legal Information CD-Rom and the EU News Online, a service
available free of charge on the Internet. Butterworths provides European Union
materials in the LEXIS-NEXIS service.

Part II

The law of the institutions

Chapter 6

The European Council

According to TEU Article 3 (ex Art C) 'the Union shall be served by a single institutional framework'. According to TEU Article 5 (ex Art E) this framework consists of the principal institutions, ie the European Parliament, the Council, the Commission, the Court of Justice and the Court of Auditors (the Commission and the Council being assisted by the Economic and Social Committee and the Committee of the Regions – see EC Article 3 (ex Art 4)), supplemented by the European Council (TEU Article 4 (ex Art D)).

Within the concept of the union the European Council, which has evolved in the course of time, assumes a leading role as a unique institution of the Union.

Since the founding Treaties were basically concerned with economic matters it became clear quite early that they were lacking another essential ingredient of integrated Europe, ie political cohesion. There were also certain matters of principle (eg Community budget contributions) which had to be sorted out at the highest political level. Such concerns were originally aired informally in 'summit' meetings of European Community leaders. As the Community developed it became evident that such meetings had to be formalized. The first attempt to do so was the Davignon Report presented to the Council of Ministers in 1970.[1]

In the Davignon Report the desire is expressed to make progress towards political unification through co-operation on foreign policy. The object of this co-operation is to achieve a better mutual understanding on major problems of international policy and to strengthen the sense of common purpose by harmonizing ideas, concerting attitudes and taking common action whenever this is possible and desirable.[2] To those ends it was proposed that the Foreign Ministers of the Member States should meet regularly at least at six-monthly intervals.[3] Preparations for these meetings should be undertaken by a Political Committee made up of the Heads of the Political Departments of the respective Foreign Ministries, the Committee itself should meet at least four times a year and may

---

1 The report is reproduced in the *Bulletin of the European Communities*, Vol 3 (1970), No 11, at pp 9 et seq. Also see the *Report of the Political Affairs Committee on the Political Future of the European Community* (European Parliament Working Document 118/70).
2 *Davignon Report*, Part Two, sections I and IV.
3 Ibid, section II.

set up working groups responsible for specific tasks.[4] The Report also proposed that if the circumstances are sufficiently grave or the subject matter sufficiently important a ministerial meeting may be replaced by a conference of Heads of State or Government.[5] These proposals were implemented and a regular pattern of ministerial meetings in May and November of each year was established.[6] At these meetings such matters as East-West relations, the European security conference and the Middle East were discussed.

At the Paris Summit Meeting in October 1972, in the context of their declared aim to achieve European Union by 1980, the Heads of State or Government agreed to intensify the level of political consultation and asked their Foreign Ministers to prepare a further report on methods to improve political co-operation.[7] That report was completed in July 1973 and subsequently approved by the Heads of State or governments.[8] As a result the Foreign Ministers of the Member States have met regularly at least four times a year. The report also confirmed the role of the Political Committee and established the so-called 'Group of Correspondents' to assist it in its work.[9] The machinery for political consultation between the Member States of the Community was given a further dimension by a decision of the Heads of Government at their meeting in Paris in December 1974 to meet regularly three times a year accompanied by their Foreign Ministers.[10] These institutionalized summit meetings are known as meetings of the European Council and quickly became a regular feature of Community life.

The European Council has been hailed as an example of 'the Community's capacity for self-renewal in difficult circumstances'.[11] By the early 1970s a new political impetus was needed as the Community moved from the shelter of the Treaties into largely uncharted waters. It is the European Council's role to supply that impetus. As the *Three Wise Men's Report* has observed,[12] the European Council (i) provides a forum for free and informal exchange of views between the Heads of Government; (ii) it can range over matters of Treaty competence, of political co-operation and of common concern to the Member States; and (iii) it can generate an impetus for the progressive development of the Community.

By the creation of machinery for political consultation distinct from yet parallel to the institutions of the Communities the Governments of the Member States distinguished between matters of international politics at the inter-governmental level on the one hand and the activities of the Communities based on legal obligations contained in the Treaties on the other.[13] Matters of mutual political concern to the Member States which did not directly relate to the Treaties were discussed by the Foreign Ministers outside the Community structure and assisted by the Political

---

4   Ibid, ss II(3) and III. In practice the Political Committee met much more frequently; see Annex to the Second Report on European political co-operation, *Seventh General Report on the Activities of the European Communities* (1974) at p 509.
5   Ibid, s Ii(1)(*b*).
6   Meetings were held in May and November commencing in November 1970.
7   See the declaration issued at the end of the Summit Meeting, paras 14 and 15, *Sixth General Report on the Activities of the European Communities* (1973) pp 15, 16.
8   The report is printed in *Seventh General Report on the Activities on the European Communities* (1974) at p 502.
9   See Part II of the report, ibid at p 504.
10 See the communiqué issued at the end of the Meeting, para 3, *Eighth General Report on the Activities of the European Communities* (1975) at p 297.
11 *Report on European Institutions* (1979), p 15.
12 Ibid, pp 16, 17.
13 See Second Report on European Political Co-operation, *Seventh General Report on the Activities of the European Communities* (1974) at p 507.

Committee; matters which did directly relate to the Treaties were discussed within the Council of the Communities assisted by the Committee of Permanent Representatives. By the same token the European Council was a hybrid which if discussing non-Community matters was no more than a Summit Conference and if discussing Community matters could be regarded as a manifestation of the Council of the Communities.[14] The type of matter discussed by the European Council in the field of political co-operation is illustrated by its activities in April 1990.[15] During that month the following items featured on the agenda: the reunification of Germany and relations with Central and Eastern Europe; the relations between Lithuania and the USSR; hostilities in Angola; tension between India and Pakistan; a dispute between Senegal and Mauritania; the threatened use of weapons of mass destruction in the Middle East; the assassination of the President of Colombia; and the civil war in Liberia.

Through these important developments the Community may be seen to have been striving for an external identity in a general political sense over and above its character as a trading bloc. That objective was given a new status and a fresh impetus by the Single European Act. First, the European Council lost its hybrid status and became a treaty-based Community institution which brings together the Heads of State or Government and the President of the Commission.[16] It is also provided that the European Council should in future meet at least twice a year.[17] This reduction in the frequency of meetings reflects the Dooge Committee's concern to prevent the European Council from becoming 'simply another body dealing with the day-to-day business of the Community' but rather that it 'should play a strategic role and give direction and political impetus [to] the Community'.[18] Second, on the foundation of existing undertakings and practices,[19] European co-operation in the sphere of foreign policy was also given treaty status and the authority which flows from it. It is now a formal legal obligation of the members of the Community 'to endeavour jointly to formulate and implement a European foreign policy'.[20] Through a process of mutual information and consultation the Member States undertake to maximize the impact of their combined influence on foreign affairs through co-ordination, convergence, joint action and the development of common principles and objectives.[1] It is expressly provided that there must be consistency between the Community's external policies and the policies agreed in the field of foreign affairs.[2] Particular emphasis is placed on closer co-operation on the political, economic, technological and industrial aspects of European security.[3] Common positions in relation to international institutions and at international conferences is another aim.[4] Further provisions deal with the institutional arrangements for co-operation in the sphere of foreign policy.

---

14 There is no reason why the Council should not be made up of Heads of Government; see Merger Treaty, Art 11. For confirmation of this analysis of the European Council as a hybrid see *Report on European Institutions* (1979), pp 17, 18.
15 See *Bulletin of the European Communities* (1990) No 4, points 1.1–1.11 and 1.3.1–1.3.9.
16 Single European Act, Art 2 (now TEU Art 4, 2nd para (ex Art D)).
17 Ibid.
18 See EC Commission, *An Ever Closer Union* (1985) Annex II, p 337.
19 Single European Act, Art 1, para 3.
20 Ibid, Art 30(1).
 1 Ibid, Art 30(2) and (3)(c).
 2 Ibid, Art 30(5), which gives the Presidency and the Commission special responsibilities in this respect.
 3 Ibid, Art 30(6) without derogation from either the Western European Union or the Atlantic Alliance.
 4 Ibid, Art 30(7); as are relations with third countries, regional groupings and international organizations; ibid, Art 30(8) and (9).

The foreign ministers of the Member States are given a new mandate to meet at least four times a year within the framework of European political co-operation with the added authority to discuss foreign policy matters also at the meetings of the Council.[5] Both the Commission and the European Parliament are fully and closely associated with this new dimension of Community activity and the practice of seeking the views of the latter and of keeping it regularly informed on current foreign policy issues are expressly continued.[6] The presidency for the purposes of European political co-operation will rotate with the Presidency of the Council,[7] assisted by the existing Political Committee[8] and European Correspondents Group.[9] Meetings of either the Political Committee or at ministerial level may be convened within 48 hours at the request of at least three Member States.[10] A European Political Co-operation Secretariat is also established in Brussels to assist in preparing and implementing these activities.[11]

These provisions mark a major advance in the development of the Community as a political force. By removing the earlier distinction between Community matters proper and matters of political co-operation and making the latter legitimate matters of Community concern the Community has signalled its intention to become a full participant in foreign affairs. The opportunity has now been provided to develop a coherent foreign policy consistent with the overall policy objectives of the Community. An opportunity to review progress was provided five years after the entry into force of the Single European Act.[12]

The European Council took at Strasbourg in 1989 the momentous decision to convene an inter-governmental conference on the Economic and Monetary Union and in June 1990 at Dublin on the Political Union. At Maastricht in December 1991 it paved the way for the British Protocol which enabled the United Kingdom to opt out of the Social Charter and, again in December in Edinburgh, smoothed negotiations for concessions which enabled the Danish electorate to reverse their rejection of the TEU and thus, at the end, saved the Treaty.

The European Council elevated to be an institution of the EC by virtue of Article 2 of the SEA has become an institution of the Union by virtue of TEU Article 4 (ex Art D). However it is a hybrid because, though formally it is no longer subject to the EC Treaty, it remains concerned with the process of European integration, of which the EC is a substratum.

TEU Article 4(1)[13] re-emphasizes the leading role of the European Council as the body that 'shall provide the Union with the necessary impetus for its development and shall define the general political guidelines thereof'.

After each of its meetings the European Council shall submit to the European Parliament a report of its proceedings and a yearly written report on the progress achieved by the Union. Thus with the involvement of the European parliament a systematic review of the Union's affairs has been established, adding the democratic element of the debate on the future of European integration.

However it has to be borne in mind that the decisions or resolutions of the European Council, being political in nature and general in substance, have no

---

5   Ibid, Art 30(3)(a).
6   Ibid, Art 30(3)(b) and (4).
7   Ibid, Art 30(10)(a) and (b).
8   Ibid, Art 30(10)(c) and (f).
9   Ibid, Art 30(10)(e).
10 Ibid, Art 30(10)(d).
11 Ibid, Art 30(10)(g) and (11).
12 Ibid, Art 30(12).
13 Ex Art D.

force of law and not being enforceable acts, are not subject to the controlling power of the Court of Justice. To be effective, where appropriate, they have to be transformed into binding legislation in accordance with the procedures laid down in the EC Treaty.

The business of the Union and of the Community cannot be easily separated. For example under EC Article 99(2)[14] the European Council is involved in the co-ordination of economic policies of the Member States and of the Community whilst under EC Article 113(3)[15] the President of the European Central Bank presents an annual report to the European Council. On the other hand the Council under TEU Article 7(1)[16] (but meeting composed of heads of state or of government, that is, like the European Council with the absence of the President of the Commission) determines the existence of a breach of a duty to the Union committed by a Member State and under TEU Article 13[17] the European Council defines the principles and guidelines for the common foreign and security policy which the Member States shall put into effect on the basis of the Council's implementing decisions. Derogations in the field of external policy and security[18] and judicial co-operation in criminal matters[19] are also subject to determination of the European Council.

Unlike the other institutions the European Council acts without any internal regulations. This lack of formality is characteristic of this 'senior' body, which is convened by the Member State which holds the Presidency of the Union/Community, its meetings are normally held in that country and the agenda is prepared by the Presidency. The agenda reflects the most important current problems of the Union and the Community. For example the presidency conclusions on the occasion of the acceptance of the Amsterdam Treaty touched the following issues:

(1) Implementation of the provisions of the second pillar of the Maastricht Treaty including the implementation of the Schergen Conventions concerning the abolition of controls of the movement of persons within the Community;
(2) Enlargement of the Community in accordance with the Agenda 2000 taking into consideration of the Union's policies including the agricultural and structural policies as well as the future financial implications of the enlargement;
(3) Resolutions with regard to the Economic and Monetary Union including commitments of the Member States, the Commission and the Council regarding the implementation of the Stability and Growth pact showing the common determination to keep employment on the top of the political agenda of the Union; resolutions of the Council to ensure budgetary discipline of the Member States, resolution of the European Council endorsing the principles of a new exchange rate mechanism and regulations constituting the legal framework for the Euro;
(4) Employment, competitives and economic growth in the Community, are primary concerns of the Union;
(5) Environment: its commitment of the Union to the Earth Summit on Environment and Development and to a leading role in the implementation

---

14 Ex Art 103(2).
15 Ex Art 109b(3).
16 Ex Art F.1.
17 Ex Art J.3.
18 TEU Art 23 (ex Art J.13(2)).
19 TEU Art 40(2) (ex Art K.12(2)).

of the various initiatives in this field. With regard to development the Union ought to aim at the eradication of poverty and the change of consumption and production patterns and the integration of economic, environmental and social policies. Noting that the growth of new technologies in the area of genetic engineering poses acute ethical problems the European Council has adopted a declaration on banning the cloning of human beings;

(6) Freedom, Security and Justice: endorsement by the Council of Ministers of the Action Plan to combat organized crime, drug abuse and of the joint action in those areas including implementation of the policy of approximation of the laws and practices of police, customs services and judicial authorities; endorsement of the adoption of the Convention on Corruption by Justice and Home Affairs Ministers; of the ratification of the Convention on the Protection of the European Communities' Financial Interests, the ratification by the Member States of the Convention on Asylum and the approval of the agreement establishing the European Monitoring Centre on Racism and Xenophobia in Vienna;

(7) External Relations concerning trade, relations with countries and groups of countries and control of arms exports; implementation of the New Transatlantic Agenda and Joint EU–US Action plan recalling the contribution of the 1947 Marshall Plan to European integration; endorsement of the dialogue between the EU and the Russian Federation especially of the signing of the Founding Act on Mutual Relations, Co-operation and Security between NATO and the Russian Federation; expression of concern over the Middle East peace process, the turmoil in former Yugoslavia and expression of hope in regard to the developments in relations with Mediterranean countries, in the internal situation of South Africa, Albania and the Republic of Congo; and expression of optimism following the transfer of Hong-Kong and the forthcoming return of Macau to China.

These conclusions reflect a wide range of issues facing the Union in Europe and elsewhere, a mixture of Union and Community business which concerns the European Council. We can say that the European Council is concerned with the internal and external aspects of the European integration of both economic and political nature. Its main concern is the development of the Union as a European entity and its status in the world. The present stage can be described as a stage of transition from the Communities via the EC towards the European Union and in this process the European Council has assumed a strategic role. Hence the references to 'impetus' and 'general guidance' in the Treaty.[20] This has, in the first place, constitutional implications both for the Union and the Member States. The constitution of the Union is in the making. It involves the institutional framework of the organization itself and the adjustment of the constitutional position of the Member States, mainly their sovereignty.

Next comes the international implication, ie further enlargement of the Union, relations with NATO and Russia and the countries associated with her, as well as the position of the Union as a single partner in the World Trade Organization.

Inside the organization itself the European Council has a role in the development of the economic and social integration and in this area the functions of the Union and the Community overlap.

Finally the European Council functions as a leveller of differences between Member States in areas which are not subject to the jurisdiction of the Court of

20 TEU Art 4(1) (ex Art D(1)).

Justice. In the past as at summit meetings, now as the European Council, it uses its authority to smooth over differences which threatened to split the Community and to work out a compromise solution. The TEU[1] has formalised the process of determination of alleged breaches of principles on which the Union is founded.

The strategic role of the European Council can be summarized in the initiation of general policies and response to initiatives articulated by the Council of Ministers.

---

1   Art 7 (ex Art F).

Chapter 7

The European Parliament

A. Evolution of the European Parliament

None of the institutions has undergone as much change as the European Parliament. From a modest role of supervising the High Authority under the ECSC Treaty[1] it graduated, under the EEC and the Euratom Treaties,[2] to a supervisory and advisory function and gradually acquired more power reflecting the evolution of the Community. The new powers include participation in the legislative process,[3] budgetary procedure,[4] participation in the election of the Commission[5] and in the decision-making process including assent to accession and association treaties.[6] Naturally, it aspires to the status of a fully-fledged parliament of a democratic state.

The original designation as 'Assembly' reflected its lowly status and the French influence.[7] No doubt, to enhance its prestige, the Assembly at first adopted the title of 'European Parliamentary Assembly'[8] and then renamed itself 'European Parliament'.[9] Although the latter designation was used in its working papers and the Council documents, the original title was used officially[10] until it was formally replaced by Article 3(1) of the Single European Act 1986.

---

1   Art 20.
2   Art 137 (now 189) and Art 107 respectively.
3   See pp 260–264.
4   See pp 267–273.
5   See pp 230–231.
6   See pp 80–85.
7   Under the *ancien régime*, Parlements were courts subservient to the executive.
8   Resolution of 20 March 1958 (OJ 1958, p 6).
9   Resolution of 30 March 1062 (OJ 1962, p 1045).
10 See Council Decision 76/787 (OJ 1976, L278/5) on direct suffrage.

B. Elections and membership of the European Parliament

The founding treaties provided, in identical terms, that the Assembly is the representative of the peoples of the States brought together in the Community.[11] The formula has been retained both in the Maastricht and Amsterdam amendments of the Treaty[12] though the latter limits the number of Members of the European Parliament to 700 which provides for the increase of the present strength of the EP in the event of further enlargement of the Community.

At the beginning these representatives were the delegates of the respective national parliaments, appointed according to national procedures, in numbers laid down by the Treaties.[13] The Treaties also provided that the Assembly was to draw up proposals for direct universal suffrage in accordance with a uniform procedure in all Member States, the Council of Ministers laying down the appropriate provisions for adoption by the Member States.[14] In 1975 the EP submitted its proposals for direct elections[15] but they were accepted by the Member States. Therefore in 1976 the Council adopted a decision on the Act concerning direct elections,[16] in accordance with which the first direct election was held in 1979. According to the decision[17] national procedures are to be used pending the entry into force of a uniform electoral procedure. Thus elections in 1984, 1989 and 1994 were held according to national rules.[18]

The EC[19] Treaty, as amended, reiterated the principle that the EP is in charge of elaborating a proposal for elections 'by universal suffrage in accordance with a uniform procedure in all Member States or in accordance with principles common to all Member States'. The Council, acting unanimously on the proposal voted by a majority of the EP's component members, shall lay down the appropriate provisions which it shall recommend to Member States for adoption in accordance with their respective constitutions. Bearing in mind the variety of electoral systems the task set before the EP is by no means a simple one.

Parliament shall also lay down internal regulations and general conditions governing the performance of its members for which it shall seek an opinion from the Commission and obtain the unanimous approval of the Council.[20]

The Treaty[1] allocated the number of seats to which the Member States are entitled, broadly according to the size of their population, as follows: Germany, 99; France, Italy and the United Kingdom, 87 each; Spain, 64; the Netherlands, 31;

---

11 ECSC Art 20; EC Art 189 (ex Art 137); EAEC Art 107. By the Merger Treaty (now Amsterdam 9(2)), a single institution, the EP, exercises the functions of the parliaments created by the following Treaties.
12 EC Art 189 (ex Art 137).
13 ECSC Art 21(1); EC Art 138(1) (as originally worded); EAEC Art 108(1)(2).
14 ECSC Art 21(3); EC Art 138(3) (as originally worded); EAEC Art 108(3).
15 Text, Bull of the European Communities (1975), Part I, p 95 et seq.
16 Decision 76/787 (OJ 1976, L278/5, amended by the Acts of Accession (1979, 1985, 1995) and Parliamentary decision 93/81 (OJ 1993, L33/15).
17 Art 7(2).
18 UK: see European Parliamentary Elections 1984 (SI 1984, No 137) replaced by the European Assembly Election Regulations 1986 (SI 1986, No 2209); European Parliamentary Elections Act 1993 (1993 C41). For the current position, see the European Parliamentary Elections Act 1999.
19 EC Art 190(4) (ex Art 138(4)).
20 EC Art 190(5) (ex Art 138(5)).
 1 EC Art 190(2) (ex Art 138(2)).

Belgium, Greece and Portugal, 25 each; Sweden, 22; Austria, 21; Denmark and Finland, 16 each; Ireland, 15 and Luxembourg, six.

The EP is elected for a term of five years.[2] According to the EC Treaty[3] citizens of the Union who are resident in a Member State have the right to vote and to stand as a candidate in elections to the EP under the same conditions as nationals of that State.[4] However, at present, the Member States determine the electoral procedure,[5] the division of their territories into constituencies,[6] the right to vote and the verification of contested polls. Thus, for example, under the British system persons who are disqualified for membership of the House of Commons and Lords of Appeal in Ordinary are ineligible.[7] However, peers, ordained clergy and ministers of religion are nonetheless eligible to stand for election to the EP.[8]

Although the precise date of the election is to be fixed by each Member State, it ought to be held within the same period of four days between a Thursday and a Sunday[9] but counting of the votes may not start until the close of the polling in the state which voted last within the prescribed period.[10]

Members of the EP are true representatives, not mere delegates, of the electorate and, therefore, they perform their duties independently and cannot be bound by instructions or act under a binding mandate.[11]

A double mandate, that is the simultaneous membership of the national parliament, is not incompatible with the membership of the EP[12] but membership of a national government is incompatible,[13] and so is the service with the Community as a member of the Commission, the Court of Auditors, the Economic and Social Committee and other committees, a judge, advocate general or registrar of the Court of Justice, certain officials of the European Investment Bank or any active official or servant of the Community institutions or the specialised bodies attached to them.[14]

Whilst in office the members of the EP are entitled to the privileges and immunities befitting the dignity of the institution they serve.[15] Accordingly during the parliamentary sessions, they enjoy, in the territory of their own State, the immunities accorded to members of the national parliament and, in the territory of any other Member State, immunity from any form of detention and from legal

2   EC Art 190(3) (ex Art 138(3)); dec 76/787, Art 1, supra.
3   Art 19(2) (ex Art 8b(2)).
4   See Dir 93/109 (OJ 1993, L329/94); see also resolution of the EP implementing the dir OJ 1994, C44/159.
5   Dec 76/787, Art 7(2) supra; See eg the *Belgian Cour d'Arbitrage* in *Re Application de Gerolf Annemans* [1990] 3 CMLR 341 and the same *(No 2)* [1990] 3 CMLR 353; and the *French Conseil d'Etat* in *Re Nicolo* [1990] 1 CMLR 173. In 1999, the United Kingdom introduced election by reference to party lists: See the European Parliamentary Elections Act 1999.
6   Eg the UK is divided into 12 electoral regions, nine in England and one each in Scotland, Wales and Northern Ireland; See European Parliamentary Elections Act 1978, as amended by the European Parliamentary Elections Act 1999.
7   European Parliamentary Elections Act 1978, Sch 1, para 5(1).
8   Ibid, Sch 1, para 5(3).
9   Act concerning the election of the EP Art 9(1).
10 Ibid, Art 9(2).
11 Ibid, Art 4(1).
12 Ibid, Art 4(1).
13 Ibid, Art 6(1); but see the position of a former President of the French Constitutional Council – see *French Conseil d'Etat* in case *Ange Sitbon* [1990] 2 CMLR 633.
14 Ibid, Art 6(1).
15 Ibid, Art 4(2); See case 149/85: *Wybot v Faure* [1986] ECR 2391, [1987] 1 CMLR 819 and Case 208/80: *Bruce v Aspden* [1981] ECR 2205, [1981] 3 CMLR 506.

proceedings in respect of the opinions expressed or votes cast in the performance of their duties.[16] Immunity applies also to members while they are travelling to and from meetings of the EP, but immunity cannot be claimed when a member is found committing an offence. Since immunity belongs to the EP, it is free to exercise its right of waiver[17] in accordance with the procedure laid down in the Rules of Procedure.[18]

C. Modus operandi

The EP, being an autonomous body within the institutional framework of the Community, determines its internal organization and *modus operandi* governed, at present, by the Rules of Procedure.[19] In this respect the EP successfully asserted its independence claiming that in the absence of Treaty provisions it was free to choose the place of its proceedings.[20] Eventually the matter was settled by the Protocol on the location of the seats of the institutions attached to the Amsterdam Treaty which confirmed the EP as a travelling circus since the EP has its seat in Strasbourg where the 12 periods of monthly plenary sessions, including the budgetary session, is to be held. The periods of additional sessions are to be held in Brussels and the General Secretariat of the EP and its departments remain in Luxembourg – a costly and time-consuming procedure.

The EC Treaty contains only a few general rules affecting the EP, its own organization and working order being laid down in the Rules of Procedure. The EP must hold an annual session which has to meet, without requiring to be convened, on the second Tuesday in March.[1] It may meet in extraordinary session at the request of a majority of its members or at the request of the Councillor of the Commission.[2] The EP is considered to be in session (even if it is not actually sitting) until the closure of an annual or extraordinary session.[3]

The EP elects its President and officers from among its members[4] and adopts its own rules of procedure[5] acting by a majority of its members. Save, as otherwise provided in the Treaty, the EP acts by an absolute majority of the votes cast[6] but the quorum is determined by the Rules of Procedure.[7] The quorum has been fixed at one-third of the entire Parliament.[8] If fewer than 32 members are present the President may rule that there is no quorum.[9]

---

16 Merger Treaty, Protocol on the Privileges and Immunities of the European Communities, Arts 9 and 10; See Case C-201/89: *Le Pen and National Front v Puhl* [1990] ECR I–1183.
17 Ibid, Art 10.
18 OJ 1999, L202/1, Rule 6.
19 OJ 1999, L202/1.
20 Case 230/81: *Luxembourg v European Parliament* [1983] ECR 255, [1983] 2 CMLR 726 and Case 108/83: *Luxembourg v European Parliament (No 2)* [1984] ECR 1945, [1986] 2 CMLR 507.
1 EC Art 196(1) (ex Art 139(1)).
2 EC Art 192(2) (ex Art 139(2)).
3 Rules of Procedure, 10.
4 EC Art 197(1) (ex Art 140(1)).
5 EC Art 199(1) (ex Art 142(1)).
6 EC Art 198(1) (ex Art 141(1)).
7 EC Art 198(2) (ex Art 141(2)).
8 Rule 126(2).
9 Rule 126(5).

The Rules deal with such matters as privileges and immunities,[10] attendance of members:[11] payment of expenses and allowances:[12] verification of credentials:[13] term of office of members:[14] code of conduct:[15] convening of Parliament:[16] venue of sittings and meetings:[17] officers of Parliament:[18] parliamentary bureaux and other offices in the Parliament:[19] political groups:[20] relations with other Institutions which include nomination of the President of the Commission and the vote of approval of the Commission:[1] motion of censure on the Commission;[2] appointment of members of the Court of Auditors;[3] appointment of the members of the European Central Bank:[4] statements by the Commission, Council and European Council:[5] statements by the Court of Auditors:[6] statements by the European Central Bank:[7] questions to the Council and Commission:[8] annual general report of the Commission:[9] resolutions and recommendations:[10] relations with national parliaments:[11] legislative procedures:[12] assent procedure:[13] dialogue between management and labour;[14] supervisory powers:[15] budgetary procedures:[16] treaties and international agreements:[17] common foreign and security policy:[18] co-operation in the fields of justice and home affairs:[19] determination of breach by a Member State of principles common to the Member States;[20] order of business:[1] rules for conduct of sittings:[2] quorum and voting:[3] interruptive and procedural motions:[4] public records of proceedings:[5] parliamentary committees:[6] interparliamentary

10   Rule 3 and Rule 6.
11   Rule 4.
12   Rule 5.
13   Rule 7.
14   Rule 8.
15   Rule 9.
16   Rule 10.
17   Rule 11.
18   Rules 12–20.
19   Rules 21–28.
20   Rules 29–31.
1   Rule 32 and following.
2   Rule 34.
3   Rule 35.
4   Rule 36.
5   Rules 37 and 38.
6   Rule 39.
7   Rule 40.
8   Rules 42–44.
9   Rule 45.
10   Rules 48–54.
11   Rules 55–56.
12   Rules 57–84.
13   Rule 86.
14   Rule 87.
15   Rules 88–91.
16   Rules 92–94.
17   Rules 95–98.
18   Rules 99–104.
19   Rules 105–107.
20   Rule 108.
1   Rules 110–115.
2   Rules 116–125.
3   Rules 126–140.
4   Rules 141–147.
5   Rules 148–149.
6   Rules 150–167.

delegations:[7] petitions:[8] the ombudsman:[9] application and amendment of the Rules of Procedure:[10] secretariat of the Parliament:[11] accounting[12] and unfinished business.[13] These comprehensive rules reflect the parliamentary practice of the Member States adapting to the function of the EP, they amplify and complement the rudimentary Treaty provisions.

The governing bodies of the EP consist of the Bureau of the Parliament which consist of the President and 14 Vice-Presidents, five Quaestors, the Conference of Presidents and the Conference of Committee Chairman, assisted by a Secretary General and a Secretariat comprising, in December 1998, 3,489 permanent and 603 temporary posts.[14]

For the election of the President of the Parliament the Chair is taken by the oldest member present. The President, Vice-President and Quaestors are elected by secret ballot for a term of two-and-a-half years. The President represents the EP in international relations, on ceremonial occasions and in administrative, legal and financial matters. He directs all the activities of Parliament and its bodies. He opens, suspends and closes sittings, maintains order and presides over the proceedings of Parliament ensuring that the Rules are respected. Vice-Presidents deputise for the president during the latter's absence or inability to discharge his duties. The Quaestors are members of the Bureau in advisory capacity. They are responsible for administrative and financial matters directly concerning members in accordance with guidelines laid down by the Bureau. The Bureau takes decisions by a majority vote but in the event of a tie the President is entitled to a casting vote.

The Bureau carries out the duties assigned to it under the Rules of Procedure to wit to take financial, organizational and administrative decisions concerning the members and the internal organization of the Parliament, its Secretariat and its bodies; it draws up Parliament's preliminary draft estimates, appoints the Secretary General, adopts guidelines for Quaestors and takes decisions relating to the conduct of sittings.

The Conference of Presidents consists of the President of Parliament and the chairmen of the political groupings. The non-affiliated members delegate two of their number to attend meetings of the Conference of Presidents, without having the right to vote. The Conference of Presidents endeavours to reach a consensus on matters referred to it but where a consensus cannot be reached, the matter is put to vote subject to a weighting in accordance with the number of members in each political group. The Conference of Presidents decides on the organization of Parliament's work and legislative planning as well as the allocation of seats in the chamber among the political groups, the non-affiliated members and the institutions of the European Union. It is the authority responsible for the relations with the other institutions and bodies of the Union and with the national parliaments as well as with relations with non-member countries and with non-Union institutions and organisations. It is also responsible for the composition and competence of committees and temporary committees of inquiry and of joint parliamentary committees, standing delegations and ad hoc delegations. It draws

7   Rules 168–170.
8   Rules 174–176.
9   Rules 177–179.
10   Rules 180–181.
11   Rule 182.
12   Rules 183–184.
13   Rule 185.
14   General Report 1998 (1999) para 1079.

up the agenda of part-session of the Parliament and submits proposals to the Bureau on administrative and financial matters concerning the political groups.

The Conference of Committee Chairmen consists of the chairmen of all standing or temporary committees and elects its chairman. It may make recommendations to the Conference of Presidents concerning the work of committees and the drafting of the agenda of part-sessions.

The Conference of Delegation Chairmen consists of the chairmen of all standing interparliamentary delegations and elects its chairman. It may make recommendations to the conference of Presidents concerning the work of delegations.

D. Political Groups and Parliamentary Committees

The EP functions through its political groups and standing committees. The rationale and object of political groupings has been expressed by the EC Treaty, Article 191:[15]

'Political parties at European level are important as a factor for integration within the Union. They contribute to forming a European awareness and to expressing the political will of the citizens of the Union.'

In the chamber the members are not seated in national groups but in multi-national groups representing similar political philosophy across the national boundaries. The seating, arranged by the Conference of Presidents, is more than symbolic.

The formation of political groups is regulated by the Rules of Procedure. According to Rule 29 a political group must comprise members from more than one Member State and must consist of at least 23 members if they come from two Member States, 18 if they come from three Member States and 14 if they come from four or more Member States. A member may not belong to more than one group. The formation of a group is notified to the President of the Parliament. A statement to that effect is published in the Official Journal specifying the name of the group, its members and its bureau. Members who are not affiliated to any group are provided with a secretariat and detailed arrangements are laid down by the Bureau which determines the status and parliamentary rights of such members.

Following the 1999 elections, the distribution of seats among the political parties was as follows: European People's Party and European Democrats (EPP/ED), 233; Party of European Socialists (PES), 180; European Liberal, Democratic and Reform Party (ELDR), 50; Greens/European Free Alliance (Greens/EFA), 48; Confederal Group of the European United Left/Nordic Green Left Group (EUL/NGL), 42; Union for a Europe of Nations (UEN), 30; Europe of Democracies and Diversities Group (EDD), 16; Independents (Belgian and French National Front Members, Italian radicals, regionalist members from the Freedom Party in Austria, one Spanish regionalist, Ian Paisley), 27. The composition and denomination of political groups may change.

At present the EP consists of 17 standing committees[16] each specialising in a particular area of Union and Community policy. Committee members are elected during the first part-session following the re-election of Parliament and again

---

15 Ex Art 138a.
16 Rule 150 and Annex VI of the Rules of Procedure.

two-and-a-half years thereafter. Powers and responsibilities of standing committees are defined in Annex VI as follows:

(1) Committee on Foreign Affairs, Human Rights, Common Security and Defence Policy;
(2) Committee on Budgets;
(3) Committee on Budgetary Control;
(4) Committee on Citizens' Freedoms and Rights, Justice and Home Affairs;
(5) Committee on Economic and Monetary Affairs;
(6) Committee on Legal Affairs and the Internal Market;
(7) Committee on Industry, External Trade, Research and Energy;
(8) Committee on Employment and Social Affairs;
(9) Committee on Environment, Public Health and Consumer Policy;
(10) Committee on Agriculture and Rural Development;
(11) Committee on Fisheries;
(12) Committee on Regional Policy, Transport and Tourism;
(13) Committee on Culture, Youth Education, the Media and Sport;
(14) Committee on Development and Co-operation;
(15) Committee on Constitutional Affairs;
(16) Committee on Women's Rights and Equal Opportunities;
(17) Committee on Petitions.

The titles of the Committees generally describe their particular concerns but a further brief comment may relate their responsibilities to the provisions of the treaties and inter-institutional relations, ie:

(1) relations with the WEU, monitoring the negotiations concerning human rights and democracy in non-Community countries; co-ordination of the work of the inter-parliamentary delegations and joint parliamentary committees;
(2) exercise of the EP's budgetary powers; consideration of estimates; co-operation with the Committee on Budgetary Control; implementation, management and control of budgets;
(3) responsibility for control of financial, budgetary and administrative implementing measures, in relation to the General Budget; the financial regulations; the closure, presenting and auditing of the accounts and balance sheets of the Communities; monitoring the implementation of current budgets; the preparation of legislative opinions on the regulation of budgetary procedure, examination of cases of fraud and irregularities; the consideration of reports and opinions of the Court of Auditors and exercising these duties in co-operation with the Committee on Budgets;
(4) responsibility for matters relating to the rights of citizens of the Union, matters relating to the maintenance and development of an area of freedom, security and justice;
(5) monitoring of the completion of the internal market; questions of monetary policy, balance of payments, capital movements, reform of the world monetary system;
(6) responsibility for matters relating to the creation, interpretation and application of Community Law, co-ordination at Community level of national legislation in the sphere of the internal market, the Staff Regulations, the protection of the EP's rights and prerogatives;
(7) industrial policy; monitoring of the common commercial policy; research programmes and energy policy;

(8) employment and social policy, the European Social Fund, vocational training and the free movement of workers;

(9) monitoring the implementation of the Community policy in respect of the Environment, Health and Consumer Protection;

(10) covers matters relating to CAP; opinions arising in related fields such as public health, economic policy, external economic relations, relations with European and other associated countries;

(11) responsibility for the operation and development of the Common Fishery Policy including the Financial Instrument for Fishery Guidance;

(12) responsibility for the development of regional policy, the impact of the other Community policies on the regions and the impact of any enlargement of the Union and association agreements on regional policy, transport policy, tourism and postal services;

(13) consideration of proposals relating to the establishment of a cultural Community, education policy, the development of policy on sports and leisure;

(14) examination and monitoring of Community policy particularly as regards the North-South dialogue, the application of the ACP-EC Convention; humanitarian and food aid; industrial, agricultural and rural development; technical, financial and educational development and relations with international organizations;

(15) responsibility for matters related to the political union and drafting of relevant acts; the development of European integration; the working of the institutional structure; the implementation and assessment of the operation of the Treaty on European Union; the drawing up of uniform electoral procedure;

(16) responsibility for the definition and evolution of women's rights in the Union, based on the EP's resolutions on this subject; the implementation of the EC directives, consideration of the status of migrant women and partners of migrant workers; problems relating to professional activities of women and their family role; women in the institutions of the EU;

(17) responsibility for matters relating to petitions and for relations with the Ombudsman.

The main function of the Committees is to examine questions referred to them and draw up reports according to the continental parliamentary practice, which forms the basis for debates translated into all the official languages of the Community.[17] However, only the resolution arising from the reports is subject to vote. In practice the Committees have not only drawn up reports for parliamentary debates but also maintained contact with the Commission and the Council, thus ensuring cohesion and continuation of the Community process, a flow of information as well as the effectiveness of parliamentary control. The EP assumed responsibility for monitoring, and supervision of the activities of the Community institutions and for the implementation for the obligations of the Member States.

As standing committees, they can meet at any time at the call of their chairmen or the President of the Parliament,[18] which means that Parliament can remain vigilant at all times.

---

17 Rules 154–163.
18 Rule 166.

E. Powers and functions

The EP is not a replica of national legislatures. Indeed it was conceived as such but its advisory and supervisory functions have only in the course of time been supplemented by participation in the Community legislative process and budgetary procedure where it acts together with other institutions.

Whilst the EP is the master of its own procedure[19] its acts which have an external effect are, in accordance with the principle of legality, subject to judicial control. Thus, for example, the setting up of a parliamentary committee of inquiry,[20] or the decision regarding the meeting facilities and work of Parliament[1] were not judicable since such decisions were taken within the notion of parliamentary procedure. However such decisions as allocation of staff[2] or grant of financial aid to political parties fighting in elections to the EP were declared *ultra vires* of the EP because such expenditure, being exclusively within the power of the Member States, could not be covered by the Community budget.[3]

Under the EC Treaty the EP had no *locus standi* generally to challenge directly the acts of the institutions by virtue of EC Article 173(1)[4] as originally worded, but was not precluded from taking action to establish infringements of the Treaty if the Council or the Commission, in dereliction of their duty, failed to act.[5] However, even though unable to bring action for annulment of a Community act,[6] where other legal remedies in the hands of the Member States, the institutions or individuals were available, the Court of Justice would consider the action of the EP admissible, provided that the action in question was the safeguard of Parliament's prerogative.[7] The Court ruled:

'The absence in the Treaties of any provision for annulment may constitute a procedural gap, but it cannot prevail over the fundamental interest in the maintenance and observance of the institutional balance laid down in the Treaties establishing the European Communities'.[8]

The amendment of the EC Treaty[9] closed the gap providing that:

'The Court of Justice shall review the legality of acts adopted jointly by the European Parliament and the Council, of acts of the Council, of the Commission and of the ECB, other than recommendations and opinions, and of acts of the European Parliament intended to produce legal effects vis-à-vis third parties.'

---

19 Case 230/81: *Luxembourg v European Parliament,* supra; Case 108/83: (No 2), p 217, note 20 supra and Case C-213/88 and C39/89: *Luxembourg v European Parliament* [1991] ECR I–5643.
20 Case 78/85: *Group of European Right v EP* [1986] ECR 1753, [1988] 3 CMLR 645. See also Case C-681/90: *Blot v EP* [1990] ECR I-2101.
1 Joined Cases 358/85 and 51/86: *France v EP* [1988] ECR 4821, [1990] 1 CMLR 309.
2 Case 108/83, p 217, note 20 supra.
3 Case 294/83: *Parti Ecologiste 'Les Verts' v EP* [1986] ECR 1339, [1987] 2 CMLR 343.
4 Case 216/83: *Parti Ecologiste 'Les Verts' v Commission and Council* [1984] ECR 3325; See also Case 295/83 *Parti Ecologiste v EP* [1984] ECR 3331; Case 297/83: *Parti Ecologiste v Council* [1984] ECR 3339; See also Joined Cases C-181/, C-248/91: *EP v Council and Commission (re aid to Bangladesh)* [1993] ECR I-3685, [1994] 3 CMLR 317; Case C-187/93: *EP v Council (re the shipment of waste regulation)* [1994] ECR I-2857, [1995] 2 CMLR 309.
5 Case 13/83: *EP v Council (re Transport policy)* [1985] ECR 1513, [1986] 1 CMLR 138.
6 Case 302/87 *EP v Commission (Comitology)* [1988] ECR 5615.
7 Case C-70/88: *EP v Council (re Chernobyl disaster)* [1990] ECR I-2041, [1991] ECR I-4259, [1992] 1 CMLR 91; Case C-189/97: *EP v Council* [1999] ECR I-4741.
8 Case 70/88, supra, para 26.
9 EC Art 230(1) (ex Art 173(1)).

It also added[10] that:

'The Court shall have jurisdiction ... in actions brought by the European Parliament, by the Court of Auditors and by the ECB for the purpose of protecting their prerogatives.'

By amending Article 175[11] the Treaty included the EP among the Member States and the other institutions of the Community which may bring an action to establish infringements of the Treaties.

These amendments have raised further the status of the EP as a potential litigant and the EP, no doubt, shall take advantage of this opportunity to prove its vigilance.[12]

The amended EC Treaty has extended the powers of the European Parliament. Article 193[13] authorises the EP to set up a temporary Committee of Inquiry to investigate alleged contraventions or maladministration in the implementation of Community law. Such a Committee may be set up at the request of a quarter of Parliament's strength. It acts without prejudice to the powers conferred by the Treaty on other institutions or bodies except where allegations are examined before a court and whilst the case is *sub judice*. The Committee shall cease to exist on the submission of its report. The constitution and *modus operandi* of a Committee of Inquiry are governed by the Rules of Procedure[14] and by the decision of the EP, the Council and the Commission.[15]

Although the power of setting up committees of inquiry is limited to writing a report it implies investigation and the fact of such inquiry and the publicity it attracts is in itself significant since it enables the EP to censure the malfunctioning of the Community institutions. Of the inquiries instituted in recent times we shall mention the inquiry into BSE (the so-called 'mad cow' disease)[16], that concerning alleged mismanagement in the application of Community law and the inquiry on fraud in the customs transit procedures.[17] Probably the best known investigation initiated by the EP took the form of a Committee of Independent Experts convened jointly by the EP and the Commission in January 1999 to investigate fraud, mismanagement and nepotism in the Commission. Following publication of the Committee's first report in March 1999, the entire Commission resigned.[18]

Another novel attribute of the EP enables it to hear petitions.[19] Such petitions may be formulated by any citizen of the Union and any natural or legal person residing or having its registered office in a Member State. The petition may be formulated individually by or in association with other citizens or persons on a

---

10   Ibid, para 3.
11   Now Art 232.
12   See Case C-295/90: *EP v Council (re Students Residence directive)* [1992] ECR I–4193, [1993] 3 CMLR 281; Case C-187/93: supra, Case C-65/90: *EP v Council* [1992] ECR I–4953; Case C-388/92: *EP v Council* [1994] ECR I–2067.
13   Ex Art 138c.
14   Rule 151.
15   OJ 1995, L113/2, Annex VIII attached to the Rules.
16   General Report 1996, para 504.
17   1995 General Report, para 1009.
18   First Report on Allegations regarding Fraud, Mismanagement and Nepotism in the European Commission, 15 March 1999 (available on the Internet at http://www.europarl.eu.int/experts/ en/default.htm). The second report was published on 10 September 1999. The Committee consisted of a former head of the Swedish Audit Office, a former Judge at the European Court of Human Rights, a former President of the EC Court of Auditors and a former Advocate General of the ECJ.
19   EC Art 194 (ex Art 138d).

matter which comes within the Community activity and which affects him, her or it directly. The Rules of Procedure[20] amplify the Treaty provisions. Petitions cannot be anonymous. They should show the name, occupation, nationality and permanent address of the petitioner. They must be written in one of the official languages of the Union. They are entered in the register and forwarded by the President to the committee responsible which first has to ascertain whether the petition in question falls within the sphere of activities of the European Union. If they are declared inadmissible the petitioner must be advised accordingly. In such cases the committee may suggest that the petitioner contacts the competent authority of the Member State concerned or of the Union. Where the committee deems it appropriate it may refer the matter to the Ombudsman.

Petitions of persons who are neither citizens of the Union nor reside nor have a registered office in a Member State are filed in a separate register and are dealt with by the appropriate committee.

The committee responsible may decide to draw up a report or otherwise express its opinion on petitions it declared inadmissible. When considering petitions the committee may organize a hearing or despatch members to establish facts of the situation *in situ*. It may also request the Commission to submit relevant documents, supply information and grant access to its facilities. At the end of the proceedings it submits motions for resolutions to Parliament and informs Parliament every six months of the outcome of its deliberations. It informs Parliament of the measures taken by the Council or the Commission on the petitions.

The EP has also the power to appoint an Ombudsman.[1] He is authorized to receive complaints from any citizen of the Union or any natural or legal person residing, or having a registered office in a Member State, concerning alleged maladministration in the activities of the Community's institutions or bodies, with the exception of the Community judicial organs acting in their judicial functions.

The Ombudsman shall be appointed after each election of the EP for the duration of its term of office. He is eligible for reappointment. He may be dismissed by the Court of Justice at the request of the EP if he no longer fulfils the conditions required for the performance of his duties or if he is guilty of serious misconduct. He is completely independent in the performance of his duties. In his office he shall neither seek nor take instructions from anybody. He may not, during his term of office, engage in any other occupation, whether gainful or not.

The Ombudsman may act on his own initiative or on the basis of complaints submitted to him directly or by a member of the EP, except where the matter is subject to judicial proceedings. Where he is satisfied that the allegations have been proved, he will refer the matter to the institution complained against, which will have three months to respond. He will then pass his report to the EP and the institution concerned, and the complainant will be informed of the outcome.

The Rules of Procedure[2] amplify the provisions of the Treaty regarding the appointment, dismissal and activities of the Ombudsman. Nominations for the appointment of the Ombudsman must be supported by a minimum of 32 members of the EP, who are nationals of at least two Member States. Nominations have to be supported by documentary evidence regarding the qualifications of the nominee. The Committees concerned may hear the nominees, such hearing being open to all members. A short list will be submitted to the vote of Parliament

---

20 Rules 174–176.
1 EC Art 195 (ex Art 138e).
2 Rules 177–179.

in a secret ballot, the President making sure that at least half of the Parliament's component members are present. The decision is taken by a majority of the votes cast. The person appointed takes an oath before the Court of Justice.[3]

One tenth of the Parliament's component members may request the dismissal of the Ombudsman. The request is submitted to the committee responsible which, if it decides by a majority of its members that the reasons for dismissal are well founded, shall submit a report to Parliament. If he so requests, the Ombudsman shall be heard before the report is put to the vote. Parliament shall, following a debate, take a decision by secret ballot, the President making sure that half of Parliament's members are present. If the Ombudsman does not resign despite a decision dismissing him the President shall apply to the Court of Justice for confirmation of the dismissal.

The activities of the Ombudsman are subject to the Rules of Procedure. The Ombudsman receives a substantial number of complaints but, since his remit covers only maladministration of Community institutions, a large proportion of complaints had to be dismissed.[4] Acting on his own initiative the Ombudsman has initiated inquiries into such things as the access of the public to Community institutions' documents, competition procedures and into the Commission's internal procedures for handling cases of infringement of Community law.[5]

F. Political control, budget and legislation

The EP is now directly involved in the appointment of the Commission[6] and has to be consulted in the appointment of the Court of Auditors which is the responsibility of the Council.[7] This, in itself, is significant as a growing influence of parliamentary democracy on the evolution of the institutional framework of the Union. Apart from that the EP exercises a degree of political control through the supervision of the Commission and the Council.

The founding Treaties provided that Parliament was to discuss, in open session, the annual general report to it by the Commission.[8] The Report was not a mere record of the work of the Commission but a general synthesis of the life of the Communities, their achievements and failures, their record and prospects.

Since the establishment of the Union the General Report of the Activities of the European Union includes also a report of the European Council after each of its meetings and a yearly report on the progress achieved by the Union.[9] The Commission also reports annually of the application of Community law in the Member States. Those Reports are referred to parliamentary committees which may submit specific and fundamental questions to the plenary session.[10] The committees may also invite the members of the Commission to elaborate the parts

---

3   Mr Jacob Söderman, former Parliamentary Ombudsman in Finland was sworn in as the first EP Ombudsman on 27 September 1995.
4   By the end of 1997 he had received 1,412 complaints, of which 196 were admissible; see 1998 General Report, para 22.
5   See 1996 General Report, para 23.
6   EC Art 214 (ex Art 158), see infra, pp 230–231.
7   EC Art 247(3) (ex Art 188b(2)), see infra, p 265.
8   ECSC Art 24; EC Art 200 (ex Art 143); EAEC Art 113.
9   TEU Art 4 (ex Art D).
10 Rules 45–47.

of the report for which they are responsible and to answer questions. The General Report has to be published not only as a public record but also as a publication informative of the state of the Union. It has to be discussed in open session of the EP.[11] This enables the EP to discuss and comment upon the entire range of Community activity. The Commission also presents to the EP its annual legislative programme. After a debate the Commission and the EP draw up a joint plan pinpointing the priorities in the legislative field and fixing a timetable for the submission by the Commission of all its proposals.[12] Such a device is designed both to stress inter-institutional co-operation and to promote efficiency and expedition of the legislative procedure. Initial experience has been positive[13] and the practice continues.

In its supervisory capacity the EP possesses the power of censure over the Commission. According to the founding Treaties such motions may be tabled at any time in general terms of the conduct on Community affairs by the Commission.[14] The Treaties attach no conditions to the motion. However, according to the Rules of Procedure, the motion may be tabled by at least one-tenth of the membership of the Parliament[15] and must be in writing under the title 'motion of censure' and be substantiated. It must be directed against the whole Commission. The vote on the motion must be taken in public, not earlier than 48 hours after the beginning of the debate;[16] the motion is carried by a two-thirds majority of the entire Parliament and, as a result the entire Commission must resign as a body[17] and be replaced. The Commission shall attend to the current business until replaced according to EC Article 214 (ex Art 158). In such a case, the term of office of the new Commission shall expire on the date on which the term of office of the replaced Commission would have expired.[18] Although motions of censure have been tabled on several occasions, none as yet has been carried.[19] Nevertheless the power of censure appears effective.

The EP has the means of exercising a degree of supervision over the day-to-day activities of the Commission and Council through its power of asking questions.[20] Written questions can be put to the Commission and the Council which, together with the answers, are published in the Official Journal. Oral questions may also be put to the Commission during a plenary session and these may be followed by debate. In addition, at each part-session a period is set aside for Question Time during which oral questions may be put. This provides an opportunity for short questions to be put followed by supplementary questions, thus leading to a dialogue between the members of the Parliament and the members of the

---

11 EC Art 200 (ex Art 143).
12 Rule 57.
13 See European Parliament: The Work of the European Parliament: July 1988–June 1989 (1989) p 13.
14 ECSC Art 24; EC Art 201 (ex Art 144); EAEC Art 114.
15 Rule 34.
16 Rule 34(5); EC Art 201(1) (ex Art 144(1)) says three days.
17 EC Art 201(2) (ex Art 144(2)).
18 EC Art 201(2) (ex Art 144(2)).
19 The last occasion on which a motion of censure was proposed was in 1999 as a result of criticisms of financial mismanagement and nepotism by the Commission. After building up a good head of steam, the process degenerated into chaos. However, the Commission had been so badly damaged politically by the process and by the report of a Committee of Independent Experts (see note 18 on p 224) that it resigned without there being a vote by the EP on the motion.
20 EC Art 197 (ex Art 140), Rules of Procedure, rr 42–44 and Annex II.

Commission and the Council. During 1998[1] the EP addressed 5,573 questions to the Commission and the Council, ie 4,114 written questions (3,737 to the Commission and 377 to the Council), 204 oral questions with debate (125 to the Commission and 79 to the Council), and 1,255 during question time (788 to the Commission and 467 to the Council).

The right to ask questions enables an eye to be kept on developments and implementation of Community policy both generally and in relation to particular topics including matters of political co-operation discussed by Foreign Ministers of the Member States. The TEU expressly involved the EP in discussions of foreign and security policy as well as justice and internal affairs. Thus:

'The Presidency shall consult the European Parliament on the main aspects and the basic choices of the common foreign and security policy and shall ensure that the views of the European Parliament are duly taken into consideration. The European Parliament shall be kept regularly informed by the Presidency and the Commission of the development of the Union's foreign and security policy. The European Parliament may ask questions of the Council or make recommendations to it. It shall hold an annual debate on progress in implementing the common foreign and security policy.'[2]

Likewise in the field of police and judicial co-operation in criminal matters.[3] The Rules of Procedure[4] reflect these provisions.

Any member may table a motion for a resolution on a matter falling within the sphere of activities of the European Union.[5] Such motions are addressed to the appropriate committee which decides whether the motion is to be adopted and result in a report which is then subject to debate.

At least 32 members or a political group may table a proposal for a recommendation to the Council concerning subjects in the fields of foreign relations and security and police and judicial co-operation in criminal matters which are referred to the appropriate committee. Where the Committee presents a report, it submits to Parliament a proposal for debate.[6]

Rules 91–94 govern consultations with the Commission and Council in the fields referred to above. The process of consultation may take place at either or both of two stages in the decision-making process: the Council may consult the EP after it has received a proposal from the Commission: the Commission itself may consult the EP when it is in the process of drafting its proposals.

Resolutions, proposals for a recommendation and consultation reflect the advisory function of the EP. The right of consultation is not a power of decision but, at least in the legislative process, it forms an important element of the decision. Where the Treaties require the Council to consult the EP before an act is adopted, the opinion of the EP must be sought and obtained otherwise the act in question may be annulled because an essential procedural requirement has been infringed.[7]

In practice the influence of the EP depends on the subject matter in hand[8] and the process towards the elimination of the so-called 'democratic deficit' of

1 1998 General Report, para 1078.
2 TEU Art 21 (ex Art J 11).
3 TEU Art 39 (ex Art K 11).
4 Rules 103–104.
5 Rule 48(1).
6 Rule 49.
7 See Case 138/79: *SA Roquette Frères v Council* [1980] ECR 3333.
8 See *The Impact of the European Parliament on Community Policies* (Research and Documentation Papers. Political Series, No 5, 1983 and Action Taken Series No 3, 1988).

the Community as witnessed by the Single European Act 1986 and the Treaties on European Union 1993 and 1997. As a result the EP not only strengthened its position in areas of exclusive competence outlined above but also in areas of joint competence, notably in the area of legislation[9] and budgetary procedure[10] where it acts within the framework of inter-institutional procedures. Judging by the formulation of the Rules of Procedure, the EP regards itself as an institution of the Union, not merely of the Community.

9   See infra, pp 260–264.
10   See infra, pp 267–273.

Chapter 8

The Commission

A. Composition and appointment

The Commission consists at present of 20 members 'chosen on the grounds of their general competence and whose independence is beyond doubt'.[1] The number of members of the Commission may be altered by unanimous decision of the Council. Only nationals of Member States are eligible. The Commission must include at least one, but not more than two nationals of each State. France, Germany, Italy, Spain and the United Kingdom provide two Commissioners each and each of the remaining countries one.

Whilst the nominees have to be appointed by common accord of the governments of the Member States after approval of the EP, each country adopts its own criteria of selection. Consequently the Commission reflects a variety of talents and vocations: politicians, civil servants and academics. Traditionally the British commissioners represent the ruling party and the opposition.

The procedure of appointment is governed by EC Article 214 (ex Art 158). Members of the Commission are appointed for a period of five years (which coincides with the term of office of the EP), the term of office being renewable. Since 1994 the Commission has been appointed according to the new procedure. Thus the governments of the Member States nominate by common accord, after consulting the EP, the person they intend to appoint as the President of the Commission. Then the governments of the Member States nominate, in consultation with the nominee for President, the other persons whom they intend to appoint as members of the Commission. The President and the other members of the Commission nominated in this manner are subject as a body to a vote of approval by the EP. By approval by the EP, the President and the other members of the Commission shall be appointed by the common accord of the governments of the Member States.[2] The procedure was tested at the meeting of the Council in Corfu (June 25–26, 1994) when the United Kingdom vetoed the nomination of a candidate for President put forward by France and Germany without previous consultation and thus a precedent distorting the Treaty provisions was averted.

1   EC Art 213 (ex Art 157).
2   Eg Decision 1999/499 (OJ 1999, L194/45).

The Rules of Procedure of the EP[3] govern the procedure for the nomination of the President of the Commission and the vote of approval of the Commission. Thus the President of the EP requests the nominee to make a statement to Parliament which is followed by a debate in which the Council is invited to take part. Parliament approves or rejects the nomination by a majority of the votes cast. The President then forwards the result of the vote to the President of the European Council and to the governments of the Member States. Should the result of the vote in Parliament be negative, the President would request the governments of the Member States to withdraw their nominations and submit a new one.

When the Member States have agreed on the nomination of the other members of the Commission the President of the EP, after consulting the nominee for President of the Commission, will request the nominees to appear before the appropriate committees according to their prospective fields of responsibility. The committee may invite the nominee to make a statement and answer questions and report its conclusions to the President. This presents an opportunity to test the nominee's 'general competence' and suitability for discharging the functions allocated to him.

The nominee for President presents the programme of a nominated Commission, presumably with the allocation of portfolios to individual members of the Commission, at a meeting of Parliament which the whole Council is invited to attend. The statement is followed by a debate. In order to wind up the debate, any political group may table a motion for a resolution which shall contain a statement as to whether Parliament approves or rejects the nominated Commission. Parliament then votes on the motion by a majority of the votes cast. If Parliament approves the nominated Commission, the President shall notify the governments of the Member States that the appointment of the Commission may now take place.

We should note not only the respective functions in this exercise of the EP and the Member States but also the enhanced power of the EP in this respect. Thus the EP has acquired an effective veto over the nomination whilst the Member States cannot force their nominees down the Parliament's throat. Moreover the required 'common accord' implies not only unanimity but also absence of bullying tactics on the part of a Member State or group of States.

The procedure enables the President-elect to influence the selection of his team since he has to be consulted, albeit without the power of veto, in the composition of the whole Commission. He also controls the distribution of the portfolios within the Commission.

The linkage with Parliament is also significant as it emphasizes the close working relations between these two institutions which, in the struggle for power, are the natural allies against the Council, the EP aspiring to a status of a fully fledged parliament and the Commission to be the government of the Community.

The Commission may appoint a Vice-President or two Vice-Presidents.[4] The second option was applied when the Commission was installed in office in 1995 and 1999.

A Commissioner may resign or may be compulsorily retired by the Court of Justice on application by the Council or the Commission if he no longer fulfils the conditions required for the performance of his duties or if he has been guilty

---

3   Rules 32–34.
4   EC Art 217 (ex Art 161).

of serious misconduct.[5] Neither the Treaty nor the Rules of Procedure of the Commission[6] define the grounds of resignation or serious misconduct or the procedure for compulsory retirement.[7]

A vacancy caused by death, resignation or compulsory retirement is to be filled for the remainder of the Commission's term of office by a new member appointed by common accord of the governments of the Member States but the Council, acting unanimously, may decide that such vacancy need not be filled.[8] Parliamentary approval does not seem to be required either for the replacement or the decision not to fill the vacancy. In the event of resignation, compulsory retirement or death, the President shall be replaced for the remainder of his term of office, in which case the procedure outlined above shall be applied.[9] Save in the case of compulsory retirement, members of the Commission who have resigned shall remain in office until they have been replaced.[10]

B. Status of members of the Commission

Because of the collegiate nature of the Commission, the President occupies the position of *primus inter pares* among his colleagues. Otherwise the only difference consists of special duties and a higher remuneration enjoyed by the President and Vice-Presidents.[11] In the absence of Treaty provisions their duties are subject to the Commission's own constitution.[12] Accordingly the President establishes the commission's political guidelines; allocates responsibilities to individual commissioners; represents the Commission; convenes its meetings; lays down the agenda; and, subject to the possibility of delegation, signs or authenticates the minutes and acts of the Commission.[13] Together with the President of the Council, he receives the letters of credence of foreign diplomats since the Community is represented by the Commission.[14]

The order of precedence among the Vice-Presidents is by their appointment to office and their age in the case of equal seniority. A Vice-President deputises for the President during his absence.[15] There is a functional equality among the Vice-Presidents as they exercise presidential duties in rotation.

---

5   EC Art 216 (ex Art 160).
6   93/492 (OJ 1993, L230/15).
7   A Commissioner has been compulsorily retired because of permanently incapacitating illness: see Bulletin of the European Communities (1976), Part 7/8, points 2.4.41 and 2.4.43 and Decision 76/619 (OJ 1976, L201/31). A Commissioner has also been asked by the EP to answer allegations of misconduct; see European Parliament – EP News, 20–26 October 1990, p 2.
8   EC, Art 215(2), ex Art 159(2). Eg Council Decision 1999/493 (OJ 1999, L192/53): when the whole Commission resigned in 1999, the procedure for appointing a future Commission was commenced immediately and, in the meantime, the old Commission remained in office save for three members, one of whom had decided to take up a post in industry, the other two being elected to the EP.
9   EC Art 215(3) (ex Art 159(3)).
10 EC Art 215(4) (ex Art 159(4)).
11 See Council Reg (EEC 422/67), (Euratom) 5/67, (OJ 1967, 187), amended by Council Regs (ECSC, EEC, Euratom) 2163/70; 1546/73; 1416/81; 3822/81; 3875/87; 4045/88; 3911/90; 2426/91; 3835/92.
12 See Commission Rules of Procedure (OJ 2000, L308/26).
13 Ibid, Arts 1–3, 5, 6, 11 and 18.
14 EC Art 282 (ex Art 211).
15 Rules of Procedure, Art 22.

Members of the Commission receive remuneration befitting the dignity of their office as well as allowances for themselves and their families, including a compensation for three years after having relinquished their office and a pension for life starting at the age of 65.[16] They also enjoy immunity from local jurisdiction, exemption from immigration rules, freedom from currency restrictions and exemption from import and export control of their movable property and vehicles,[17] exemption from national taxation subject, however, to Community tax on their Community salaries and emoluments,[18] and to certain social security benefits.[19] They are treated as diplomats of the highest rank.

The Treaty provides that Members of the Commission are persons 'whose independence is beyond doubt'.[20] This means that although nominated by the Member States, they are not their delegates. Being truly Community servants they must be completely independent in the performance of their duties. Therefore, in the performance of their duties, they must neither seek nor take instructions from any government or from any other body, and must refrain from any action incompatible with their duties.[1] Each Member State undertakes to respect this principle and not to seek to influence the members of the Commission in the performance of their tasks.[2] Independence of the members of the Commission is further ensured by the fact that they are appointed to a full-time well-paid job with compensation when leaving and pension rights. Therefore they must refrain from engaging in any other occupation, whether gainful or not, and, when entering into office, they must give a solemn undertaking that both during and after their term of office they will respect the obligations arising from it and, in particular, their duty to behave with integrity and discretion as regards the acceptance, after they cease to hold office, of certain appointments or benefits. In the event of any breach of these obligations, the Court of Justice may, on application by the Council or the Commission, rule that the member concerned be either compulsorily retired or deprived of his right to a pension or other benefits in its stead.[3]

Concerning the conflict of interests, the Commission replied to parliamentary questions that activities in science and teaching as well as the membership of political, professional and cultural organizations serving a general public interest should not be incompatible with the status of a member of the Commission.[4] Membership of a national parliament would be incompatible, but not the membership of a local or municipal council.[5] Standing for election to the Parliament should not disqualify, because the membership of the Commission does not imply a renunciation of a passive electoral right though, in such a case the member of the Commission

---

16 Council Reg 422/67 as amended, supra.
17 See, Protocol on the Privileges and Immunities of the European Communities annexed to the EC, ECSC and EAEC Treaties (and formerly annexed to the merger Treaty), Arts 12 and 20.
18 Ibid, Arts 13, 14, 20.
19 Ibid, Arts 15, 20.
20 EC Art 213(1) (ex Art 157(1)).
1   EC Art 213(1) (ex Art 157(1)).
2   EC Art 213(1) (ex Art 157(1)).
3   EC Art 213(2) (ex Art 157(2)). Eg Council Decision 1999/494 (OJ 1999, L192/55), by which the Council referred to the ECJ the case of a Commissioner who had resigned in order to take up a post with a company operating in a sector over which he had responsibility as a Commissioner. The case was later settled: See Council Decision 2000/44 (OJ 2000, L16/73).
4   Answers to written questions 32–34 (OJ 1960, pp 1105, 1107, 1108).
5   Answers to written questions 657/73 (OJ 1974, C 39 p 26) and 54/74 (OJ 1974, C 97 p 2).

concerned must abstain from the meeting of the Commission during his electoral campaign.[6]

The Treaty[7] also provides that the members of the institutions of the Community, the members of committees and officials and other servants of the Community are prohibited from divulging confidential information acquired in office, even after their duties have ceased.

In the absence of a prescribed form of solemn undertaking, it has become a tradition that it is given in public at a special session of the Court of Justice. It is also possible to make a declaration in private before the other members of the Commission at its first meeting or when, upon a new term of office, the Commission is presented by its President to the Parliament.

C.   Organization

(1)   COLLEGIALITY

The principle of collegiality has been enshrined in the provisions of the founding Treaties[8] and the Rules of Procedure which provide tersely that 'The Commission shall act collectively in accordance with these Rules'.[9] Although EC Article 219(1) provides that 'The Commission shall work under the political guidance of its President', it functions as a collegiate body in the sense that it, collectively, and not the Commissioners individually, bears responsibility for its acts.[10]

The Commission acts by a majority of its members.[11] Although in practice most decisions of the Commission are unanimous, Article 7 of the Rules of Procedure provides for a quorum equal to a majority of the number of members specified in the Treaty, ie 11 at present. A meeting of the Commission is valid only if the number of members laid down in the Rules of Procedure is present.[12]

Within the framework of collegiality the Commission may authorize 'one or more of its Members to take, on its behalf and under its responsibility, clearly defined management and administrative measures'.[13] The principle was approved by the Court of Justice under the previous Rules[14] and again in more recent cases,[15] the Court limiting the delegation to management and administrative matters, which restriction became part of the Rules in force at present.[16] Powers conferred in this way may be sub-delegated unless the empowering decision expressly provides otherwise[17] without prejudice to the rules concerning delegation in respect of financial matters or the

---

6   Answers to written questions 124/68 (OJ 1968, C 83 p 17), and 858/76 (OJ 1976, C 70, p 28).
7   EC Art 287 (ex Art 214).
8   ECSC Art 16(4); EC Art 219 (ex Art 163); EAEC Art 131.
9   Art 1.
10   See Case C-327/91: *France v Commission* [1994] ECR I-3641.
11   EC Art 219(2) (ex Art 163(2)).
12   EC Art 219(3) (ex Art 163(3)).
13   Rules, Art 13 (first sentence).
14   Cases 8–11/66: *Re Noordwijks Cement Accord* [1967] ECR 75, [1967] CMLR 77.
15   Cases 43/82 and 63/82: *VBVB v Commission* [1984] ECR 19 and Case 5/85: *AKZO Chemie BV and AKZO Chemie UK v Commission* [1986] ECR 2585, [1987] 3 CMLR 716.
16   See further Joined Cases T-79/89, T-84/89 and 86/89, T-91/89, T-92/89, T-94/89, T-96/89, T-98/89, T-102/89, T-104/89: *BASF AG v Commission* [1992] ECR II-315; and also Case C-137/92P: *Commission v BASF* [1994] ECR I-2555.
17   Rules, Art 13 (third sentence).

powers conferred on the appointing authority or the authority empowered to conclude contracts of employment.[18]

(2)   MEETINGS OF THE COMMISSION

Meetings of the Commission are convened by the President as a rule at least once a week, and, additionally, whenever necessary.[19] The President assumes responsibility for the agenda which reflects the annual programme adopted by the Commission and a quarterly rolling programme and which includes any items requiring a Commission decision.[20] The agenda and the necessary working documents are circulated to the Members of the Commission in the working languages prescribed by the Commission. Any Member may request to withdraw from the agenda any item which will be held over for a later meeting. The Commission may also, on a proposal from the President, discuss any item which is not on the agenda or by majority vote, may decide not to discuss an item on the agenda.[1]

The Commission takes decisions on a proposal from one or more of its Members and a vote shall be taken if any Member so requests. Decisions are adopted if a majority of the number of Members specified in the Treaty vote in favour.[2]

Meetings of the Commission are not open to the public and discussions are confidential.[3]

(3)   THE PATTERN OF A 'GOVERNMENT'

The Commission is organized on the pattern of a government. Each Commissioner has an area of responsibility within which he has to prepare the Commission's business and implement its decisions.[4] The distribution of portfolios is not static and may change with the Commission.

Each Commissioner is assisted by a *cabinet* of his own choice, headed by the *chef de cabinet* who is usually of the same nationality as the Commissioner himself. The Cabinet consists of a small group of counsellors (usually about five) who assist him in the preparation of Commission decisions.[5]

In addition to the cabinets, the Commission's personnel is organized into auxiliary services and specialist departments or Directorates General, divided in turn into Directorates and then into Units.[6] At the head of each department there is a Director General responsible to the relevant Commissioner. The Commission may also set up temporary structures to deal with specific assignments,[7] such as inter-service groups and task forces (concerned with eg human resources concentrations, enlargement of the Community).

Formerly, the Commission's directorates-general were known by a roman numeral and a title (for example: DG IV – Competition). At the time of writing, the Commission was in the process of a fundamental reorganisation. Its departments can roughly be divided into three groups: those concerned with providing

---

18   Ibid, Art 13 (last sentence).
19   Ibid, Art 5. The Commission normally meets on Wednesdays.
20   Ibid, Art 6.
 1   Ibid.
 2   Ibid, Art 8.
 3   Ibid, Art 9.
 4   Ibid, Art 3 and 16 (second sentence).
 5   Ibid, Art 16.
 6   Ibid, Art 19.
 7   Ibid, Art 20.

services to the Commission; those pursuing the policies entrusted to the Commission; and those concerned with the EU's external relations[8]. The first group comprises the following: the Secretariat General; the Legal Service; the Press and Communication service[9]; the Joint Interpreting and Conference Service; the Translation Service; the Publication Office; Eurostat (the Statistical Office); the Inspectorate General (which is concerned with promoting the efficiency, effectiveness and functioning of the Commission's services); the European Anti-Fraud Office (which conducts administrative anti-fraud investigations, both internally – within the Community institutions – and externally, for the purpose of protecting the financial interests of the EC); the Personnel and Administration Directorate-General (which is concerned with the Commission's own staff); the Budget Directorate-General (which is concerned with administering the EC's budget, promoting good financial management and managing the process of formulating and adopting the budget); and the Financial Control Directorate-General (which is concerned with examining and auditing the implementation of Community policies and the like). The second group of departments comprises the following directorates-general: Economic and Financial Affairs; Enterprise (covering such matters as industrial policy); Competition; Employment and Social Affairs; Agriculture; Transport and Energy; Environment; Research (covering essentially non-nuclear research, such as life sciences and the eco-system); Joint Research Centre (that is, the nuclear research centres created under the EAEC Treaty and any additional functions carried out at those centres); Information Society (information technology generally); Fisheries; Internal Market (covering such things as free movement of goods and services, public procurement, and so forth); Regional Policy; Taxation and Customs Union; Education and Culture; Health and Consumer Protection; Justice and Home Affairs (free movement of persons, citizenship, immigration, asylum, police and judicial co-operation and so forth). The third group of departments comprises the Humanitarian Aid Office and the following directorates-general: External Relations; Trade (covering such things as dumping, trade protection, access to third country markets, the WTO); Development (that is, development co-operation policy in relation to developing countries and overseas countries and territories having a special link with particular Member States); Enlargement (dealings with applicants for membership of the EU); and the Common Service for External Relations (which essentially manages all aspects of aid to third countries).

In 1998 the personnel of the Commission comprised 16,344 permanent posts (including 1,903 in the language service) and 750 temporary posts (including 13 in the language service); 1,518 permanent posts and 114 temporary posts paid out of research appropriations; 525 permanent posts in the Publications Office; 51 permanent posts at the European Centre for the Development of Vocational training and 83 at the European Foundation for the Improvement of Living and Working Conditions.

The Secretariat General consists of the Secretary General, a deputy, an administrative unit and six directorates covering the following: the Commission's registry; co-ordination of 'horizontal matters' (that is, matters potentially affecting most of the Commission's spheres of activity), institutional aspects, Community law and information; internal co-ordination of Commission departments and

8   The Commission itself has used a four part division between: general services; policies; external relations; and internal services.
9   It is not officially described as a 'service'.

relations between the Commission and the citizen; relations with the Council; relations with the EP, the European Ombudsman, the Economic and Social Committee and the Committee of Regions; and the forward studies unit (which monitors and evaluates European integration, establishes permanent relations with bodies involved in forecasting and works on specific briefs). A special unit has also been set up to prepare and conduct the work of the Inter-Governmental Conference on the reform of the institutions.

The Secretary-General assists the President in the preparation of the proceedings and meetings of the Commission, ensures that decision-making procedures are implemented; ensures the departmental co-ordination in preparing the proceedings of the Commission and that the requisite documents are submitted.[10] He takes care that official notifications and publication of Commission instruments are duly published in the Official Journal. To co-ordinate the activities within the Commission he chairs the meetings of the *chefs de cabinet* which he convenes. Except where otherwise decided by the Commission he attends the meetings of the Commission. Together with the President he authenticates instruments (ie proposals of legislation) adopted by the Commission.[11]

The Secretary-General is responsible for the official relations with the other institutions and he monitors the proceedings of the other institutions and keeps the Commission informed.[12] Acting on behalf of the Commission he negotiates with the Member States through the COREPER and acts as a go-between in the Commission's dialogue with the Council and the Parliament.

The Legal Service performs an important function in the service of the Commission. According to a former Director-General there are three main tasks of the legal service: advice to the Commission; general institutional responsibility; and a special responsibility for CELEX.[13] Advice to the Commission consists of consultation on legal questions concerning the exercise of the powers of the Commission, advice before it takes a decision and defence of the decision. According to the Rules of Procedure[14] 'the Legal Service shall be consulted on all drafts or proposals for legal instruments and on all documents which may have legal implications'. The Commission, having to enforce the Treaties, consults the Legal Service in order to determine whether an alleged breach by the Member States or legal or natural persons has occurred and, where there is a prima facie case of breach, instructs the Legal Service to prepare a reasoned opinion and, ultimately, institute proceedings.

In direct actions before the Court of Justice, the Commission appears either as the plaintiff or the defendant represented by an agent chosen from the appropriate team of the Legal Service. Since it represents the Commission the Service has to consult the Commissioner responsible for the portfolio involved and submit the draft of the arguments for his consideration.

In references for preliminary rulings the Commission intervention is facultative,[15] but the Commission appears in practice as the 'guardian of the Treaties'.

The Legal Service, as the advisor to the Commission plays an important part in inter-institutional relations. Thus it is involved in the preparation of amendments

---

10 Rules, Art 17.
11 Ibid, Art 18.
12 Ibid, Art 17.
13 C–D Ehlermann, 'The Role of the Legal Service of the Commission of the European Communities in the Creation of Community Law' (Exeter Lecture 1981) p 6.
14 Art 21, second para.
15 Protocol on the Statute of the Court of Justice, Art 20.

to the Treaties, the formation in specialist committees of the Parliament and the working groups of the Council, the enlargement of the Community, international treaties and the implications for the Community of the European Convention of Human Rights.[16]

The Legal Service is also involved in the setting up of CELEX, an automated documentation system which covers the Treaties and Community legislation as well as parliamentary questions and answers and working documents preliminary to Community legislation.

D.   Functions and powers

(1)   TREATY PROVISIONS

Article 9 of the Merger Treaty (now Amsterdam 9(2)) provides that the Commission shall exercise the powers and competences bestowed by the founding Treaties upon the High Authority of the ECSC and the Commissions of the EEC and Euratom. Thus functions and powers of the merged Commission vary from Treaty to Treaty. The Treaties on the European Union have further extended the Commission's competence.

EC Article 211 (ex Art 155) summarizes the functions and powers of the Commission as follows:

> 'In order to ensure the proper functioning and development of the common market, the Commission shall:
> − ensure that the provisions of this Treaty and the measures taken by the institutions pursuant thereto are applied;
> − formulate recommendations or deliver opinions on matters dealt with in this Treaty, if it expressly so provides or if the Commission considers it necessary;
> − have its own power of decision and participate in the shaping of measures taken by the Council and by the European Parliament in the manner provided for in this Treaty;
> − exercise the powers conferred on it by the Council for the implementation of the rules laid down by the latter.'

These powers and functions may be summarized as the powers of enforcement of the Treaty provisions, powers of initiation of a Community policy including the implementing legislation, and powers of administering the Community budget and Community Funds. According to their nature these powers reflect administrative, executive and quasi-judicial functions.

As the 'guardian of the Treaties',[17] the Commission has the necessary powers to institute inquiries into alleged infringements of the Treaties and Community law, whether by the Member States or private parties, to evaluate the evidence and to take action as appropriate. To that end the Commission is empowered to collect information[18] and the Member States are in duty bound to furnish it in accordance with the Treaty. A similar duty of a selective scope has been imposed upon corporations and individuals.[19] Having evaluated the evidence the

---

16 Ehlermann, op cit p 13.
17 Kovar, R, *La Commission, gardienne des traités* (1974) pp 3–33.
18 EC Art 284 (ex Art 213).
19 Eg investigation of transport discrimination: EC Art 75 (ex Art 79(4)); investigation of infringement of competition rules: EC Art 85 (ex Art 89).

Commission may enter into a dialogue with the alleged offender and a issue warning to prevent infringements of the Treaty. Where the preventive measures fail the Commission shall exercise a repressive function.[20]

As the initiator of policy the Commission formulates a programme of action[1] and recommendations or opinions on matters laid down in the Treaties or on its own initiative. Therefore, through its specialist departments the Commission is continuously engaged in the study of matters falling within the scope of the Treaties and formulates proposals to the Council and, where appropriate, to the Member States. The EC Treaty provides specifically for recommendations to be made to the Member States in respect of measures to harmonize national laws in order to prevent distortion of the conditions of competition[2] and to avoid malfunctioning of the common market and of economic policy;[3] to avoid excessive government deficit;[4] and to the Council concerning the opening of negotiations of trade agreements with third countries[5] and the implementation of the common commercial policy.[6]

Opinions are specifically to be addressed to the Member States concerning the movement of capital to and from third countries;[7] co-operation in the social field[8] and the failure to fulfil Treaty obligations.[9] Opinions to be addressed to the Council concern safeguard measures to be taken by a Member State facing difficulties in implementing economic policy or excessive government deficits which are monitored by the Commission.[10] Moreover the Commission, may, by virtue of its position, exercise its power of initiative whenever it considers that the Council ought to act in order to further the objectives of the Treaty.

The executive function of the Commission consists of ensuring that the rules of the Treaties and the decisions of the Council are applied in particular cases, whether concerning the government of a Member State or commercial undertakings. Under the ECSC Treaty it deals directly with coal and steel undertakings and monitors some of their activities. The Treaty enables it to promote and co-ordinate their capital spending and to prohibit the financing of any scheme which is incompatible with the Treaty.[11] It may provide financial assistance to these industries for their restructuring and for miners and steel workers facing redundancy.[12] Under the EAEC Treaty the Commission has direct supervisory responsibilities similar to those in respect of the coal and steel industries, relating in particular to safety and the protection of the health of the workers in the nuclear energy industry,[13] and the supply and use of fissile materials.[14] Under the EC Treaty the Commission has similar powers, in particular

20 On the enforcement of State obligations see supra, pp 298 et seq.
1 See eg the Commission White Paper on the Completion of the Internal Market, COM(85) 310, or the Commission initiative under Presidency of Mr. Delors in relation to the Economic and Monetary Union and Social Charter.
2 Arts 96 and 97 (ex Arts 101 and 102).
3 Arts 98 and Art 99 (ex Arts 102 and 103).
4 Art 104 (ex Art 104c); See also Protocol No 5 on the excessive deficit procedure annexed to the Maastricht Treaty.
5 Art 133 (ex Art 113).
6 Art 133 (ex Art 113).
7 EC Art 57 (ex Art 73c).
8 Art 140 (ex Art 118c).
9 Arts 226 and 227 (ex Arts 169 and 170).
10 Arts 99 and 104 (ex Arts 103 and 104c).
11 See ECSC, Art 54.
12 ECSC, Art 56.
13 See EAEC Treaty, Arts 30–39.
14 EAEC, Arts 52–76.

in respect of state aids and subsidies;[15] discriminatory taxation;[16] and competition[17] as well as certain common policies.[18]

The Commission exercises a number of representative, financial and administrative functions. It represents the legal persona of the Community.[19] Where the Treaty provides for the conclusion of agreements between the Community and one or more states or international organizations, the Commission shall have recommendations to the Council, which may authorise the Commission to open negotiations.[20] The Commission is authorized to maintain relations with organs of the United Nations Organization, of its specialized agencies and the World Trade Organization as well as with international organizations.[1]

The Commission is responsible for the administration of Community Funds which form part of the Community budget: the European Social Fund which is used to redeploy and retrain workers and to promote social welfare;[2] the European Development Fund which provides grants and loans to overseas territories and countries associated with the Community;[3] the European Agricultural Guidance and Guarantee Fund which is used to cover agricultural market support costs and to assist farm modernisation schemes;[4] the European Regional Development Fund which has been set up to correct imbalances with the Community;[5] and the Cohesion Fund to provide financial contributions to projects in the fields of environment and trans-European networks in the area of transport infrastructure[6] and funds to foster co-operation in the field of research and technological development within the framework of Treaty provisions.[7]

Under the Treaty on the European Union the Commission is associated with the work carried out in the common foreign and security field[8] and the Commission may refer to the Council any question in this area[9] and request that the Presidency convenes an extraordinary Council meeting.[10] In the field of police and judicial co-operation in criminal matters the Commission may use its initiative to propose relevant legislation and conventions[11] being 'fully associated with work in this area.[12]

(2)   LEGISLATIVE POWERS OF THE COMMISSION

In certain rare cases the Commission can legislate in its own right using the Community instruments, regulations, directives and decisions. For example, by virtue of EC Article 39(3)(d) (ex Art 48(3)(d)) the Commission can issue regulations laying down the conditions under which workers have the right to remain in a Member State in which they have been employed.[13]

---

15   EC Arts 87–89 (ex Arts 92–94).
16   EC Art 90 (ex Art 95).
17   EC Arts 81–86 (ex Arts 85–90).
18   Eg Agriculture, Transport, Common Commercial Policy.
19   EC Art 282 (ex Art 211).
20   EC Art 300(1) (ex Art 228(1)).
 1   EC Art 302 (ex Art 229).
 2   EC Arts 146–148 (ex Arts 123–125).
 3   EC Arts 177–181 (ex Arts 130u–130y).
 4   EC Arts 37 (ex Arts 43 and 148, ex Art 125 respectively).
 5   See reg 1787/84 (OJ 1984, L169) and EC Art 160 (ex Art 130c).
 6   EC Art 161 (ex Art 130d).
 7   EC Arts 163–173 (ex Arts 130f–130p).
 8   TEU Art 27 (ex Art J 17).
 9   TEU Art 22(1) (ex Art J 12(i)).
10   TEU Art 22(2) (ex Art J 12(2)).
11   TEU Art 34(2) (ex Art K 6(2)).
12   TEU Art 36(2) (ex Art K 8(2)).
13   See eg Reg 1251/70 (OJ 1970, Sp Ed).

By virtue of EC Article 86(3) (ex Art 90(3)) the Commission can issue directives or decisions to regulate the grant to public undertakings special or exclusive rights by Member States. Commission directive 80/723[14] on the transparency of financial relations between the Member States and public corporations the object of which was to check upon hidden state aid in contravention of the Treaty, was challenged unsuccessfully on the ground that the Commission had no general power to legislate but only power of surveillance and implementation.[15]

The Court of Justice held that EC Article 189 (now 249) did not make any distinction between directives which have general application and others which lay down only specific measures. The limits of the Commission's power have to be inferred not from general principles but from specific provisions of the Treaty, in this case from EC Article 90(3) (now 86(3)).

In Case C-202/88[16] France challenged the validity of Commission directive 88/301 on telecommunication terminal equipment which had been enacted by virtue of EC Article 90(3) (now 86(3)) alleging that the Commission was acting *ultra vires* and that the directive was contrary to EC Article 87 (now 83) and should have been enacted under EC Article 100a (now 95), ie enacted by the Council in accordance with the procedure provided for Community legislation. The Court dismissed the challenge confirming the powers of the Commission to act alone and that, as regards the contents of the directive, 'the Commission merely determined in general terms obligations which are binding on the Member States under the Treaty' (paras 17 and 18).

The Commission may issue decisions by virtue of EC Article 86(3) (ex Art 90(3)) as above.[17]

The Commission is also authorized to legislate by virtue of EC Article 202 (ex Art 145) which enables the Council to delegate its powers of implementation of the rules which the Council lays down.[18] Notable examples of the exercise of this power can be seen in relation to the Common Agricultural Policy, customs laws under the Customs Code, and competition.

(3) DELEGATION OF COUNCIL FUNCTIONS

The Council has no obligation to delegate but does so within its discretion.[19] However the Council cannot create new powers by delegation but will merely authorize the Commission to act within the scope of its own competence and according to its directions. Thus the delegated measures are governed by the more general and hierarchically superior treaty rules which determine the scope of the delegation.[20]

On the principle that *delegatus non potest delegare* the Commission could not authorise a Member State to impose a pecuniary charge on sugar stocks held in

---

14 OJ 1980, L195/35.
15 Joined Cases 188–190: *France, Italy and United Kingdom v Commission* [1982] ECR 2545, [1982] 3 CMLR 144.
16 C-202/88: *France v Commission* [1991] ECR I–1223; [1992] 5 CMLR 552.
17 See Cases C-48 and 66/90: *Koninklijke PTT Nederland NV v Commission* [1992] ECR I–565.
18 See EC, Art 211 (ex Art 155), which enables the Commission to exercise the powers conferred on it by the Council.
19 Case 25/70: *EVGF v Koster Berodt Co* [1970] ECR 1161, [1972] CMLR 255; See also Opinion 1/78, *Re Natural Rubber* [1979] ECR 2871, [1979] 3 CMLR 639.
20 See Case 38/70: *Deutsche Tradax GmbH v EVGF* [1971] ECR 145(154), [1972] CMLR 213 (236); Case 58/70: *Compagnie Continentale v Hoofsdproduktschap voor Akkerbouwprodukten* [1971] ECR 163, [1972] CMLR 213; Joined Cases 279, 280, 285, 286/84: *Walter Rau v Commission (re Christmas butter scheme)* [1987] ECR 1069, [1988] 2 CMLR 704; Case C-303/90: *France v Commission* [1991] ECR I-5315.

that State as it could upset the balance of power between the Council and the Commission and relieve the latter of its responsibility.[1]

(4) MODUS OPERANDI

As we have already noted decisions of the Commission are taken at the Commission's meetings which take place in accordance with the Rules of Procedure.

The *chefs de cabinet* are responsible for the preparatory work. They meet each Monday under the chairmanship of the Secretary General or the *chef de cabinet* of the President in order to review and finalize the draft agenda for the Commission's meeting on Wednesday. Non-controversial issues can be disposed of at that stage.

The decision-making process has been simplified and improved by means of written procedure, internal delegation and recourse to committees. Under the written procedure draft proposals that have been agreed by the Directorates-General directly involved and endorsed by the Legal Service, are circulated by the Secretariat among the Commissioners at the request of the proposer.[2] In the absence of objections or amendments within a specified period the proposal is deemed to have been accepted and the Secretariat will record it accordingly in a note that will in turn be recorded in the minutes of the next meeting of the Commission.[3]

Internal delegation takes two forms: delegation of decision-making power to individual members of the Commission; and delegation to Commission officials. Provided that the principle of collective responsibility among Commissioners is observed, one or more members of the Commission can be empowered to take clearly defined management or administrative measures or to adopt the definitive text of an instrument or a proposal to be presented to the other institutions (where the substance of the proposal has already been determined in discussion within the Commission). The enabling decision may also provide that this delegated power may be sub-delegated.[4] Powers may be delegated to senior officials[5] in the administration of certain policies, eg competition under Council Regulation 17 of 1962;[6] the Common Agricultural Policy; and the control in the Member States of the Community Agricultural Policy;[7] and the control in the Member States of the Community of receipts and expenditure.[8] The procedure can be justified on the ground that it covers narrowly defined executive decisions rather than matters of policy[9] and that it remains under the collegiate control of the Commission.[10]

---

1   Case 23/75: *Rey Soda v Casa Conguaglio Zucchero* [1975] ECR 1279 (1300), [1976] 1 CMLR 185 (208); See also Case 100/74: *Société CAM, SA v Commission and Council* [1975] ECR 1393 (1401); Case 37/75: *Bogusat KG v HZA Berlin-Packhof* [1975] ECR 1339.

2   Rules of Procedure (OJ 2000, L308/26), Art 12.

3   Ibid.

4   Ibid, Art 13.

5   See Commission Decision 72/21 (OJ 1972, L7), on delegation of signature.

6   See eg Case 8/72: *Vereeniging van Cementhandelaren v Commission* [1972] ECR 977(989), [1973] CMLR 7(22); See also Case 48/69: *Imperial Chemical Industries v Commission* [1972] ECR 619, [1972] CMLR 557; Case 52/69: *Geigy AG v Commission* [1972] ECR 787, [1972] CMLR 557; Case 53/69: *Sandoz AG v Commission* [1972] ECR 845, [1972] CMLR 557; Case 55/69: *Cassella Farbwerke Mainkur AG v Commission* [1972] ECR 887, [1972] CMLR 557; Case 56/69: *Farbwerke Hoecht AG v Commission* [1972] ECR 927, [1972] CMLR 557.

7   See Commission Decisions 67/424, 67/425, 67/526 and 68/83, amended by Commission decisions 68/273, 72/144, 73/298, 73/334 and 73/357.

8   Commission Decision 74/55 (OJ 1974, L34).

9   First General Report on the Activities of the European Communities, p 468.

10 Rules of Procedure, Arts 13–14.

There are two kinds of committees assisting the Commission in its specific tasks: the management (*gestion*) and rule-making (*réglementation*) committees. They are composed of the representatives (civil servants) of the Member States chaired by a non-voting senior official of the Commission. They take decisions by a qualified majority in accordance with the voting system in the Council.[11]

The procedure of management committees was first introduced by a Council regulation concerning the regulation of agricultural markets for cereals[12] which set up a precedent for similar committees established for the main groups of agricultural products. According to this procedure the Commission submits its proposal to the committee which ought to give its opinion within the specified time.[13] However, the Commission is not bound by the opinion. If the committee rejects the proposal, the proposed measure can be adopted by the Commission but in any event has to be referred to the Council, which may within a month adopt its own decision on the matter. In the meantime, the Commission may defer application of the measure that it has adopted.[14] If, however, the committee fails to respond to the Commission's request, there is no recourse to the Council in order to invoke its power in substitution of the delegated power of the Commission[15] and the proposed measure shall take effect.

The procedure was challenged and its legality was upheld by the Court of Justice.[16]

The procedure of rule-making committees was first introduced in 1968 by a Council regulation concerning the determination of the origin of goods.[17] It operates in the field of customs law and the Common Commercial Policy. The procedure is the same as in the case of management committees except that the Commission may put into effect the proposed measure only if approved by a weighted majority. If the proposal is disapproved or if there is no reaction to the request within the set time the Commission may refer the matter directly to the Council. Within three months the Council has to take a decision by a weighted majority either adopting the proposed measure or substituting its own. If, however, the Council fails to act within three months the Commission is free to put into effect its original proposal. The legality of this procedure was challenged and confirmed.[18]

In addition to the above a number of technical committees for the implementation of the Treaties were created. Some of these were set up directly under Treaty provisions, others were set up by the Council or the Commission. Their composition reflects their objectives but, generally, they are composed of national civil servants and independent experts chaired by a Commission official. They may devise their own rules of procedure.

The Commission's power of implementation of Treaty provisions was enhanced by Article 10 of the Single European Act, which supplements the provisions of EC Article 202.[19] To put into operation this power, the Commission

---

11 EC Art 205 (ex Art 148).
12 Reg No 19 of 4 April 1962 (see now reg 1766/92 (OJ 1992, L181/29), as amended).
13 Reg 1766/92, Art 23(2).
14 Ibid, Art 23(3).
15 See Case 35/78: *GNJ Schouten BV v Hoofdproduktschap voor Akkerbouwprodukten* [1978] ECR 2543 (2558).
16 Case 11/70: *Internationale Handelsgesellschaft mbH v EVGF* [1970] ECR 1125, [1972] CMLR 255; Case 25/70: *EVGF v Köster, Berodl & Co* [1970] ECR 1161, [1972] CMLR 255; Case 26/70: *EVGF v Günther Henck* [1970] ECR 1183, [1972] CMLR 255; Case 30/70: *Sheer v EVGF* [1970] ECR 1197, [1972] CMLR 255; See also Case 23/75, p 242, note 1, supra.
17 Reg 802/68, repealed by Reg 2913/92 (Community Customs Code).
18 Case 5/77: *Tedeschi v Denkavit Commerciale* [1977] ECR 1555, [1978] 1 CMLR 1.
19 Ex Art 145.

together with the Parliament[20] suggested a procedure for setting up advisory committees but the Council, in the so-called 'comitology decision'[1] significantly departed from the proposal. It provided that the implementing powers conferred upon the Commission shall be exercised either independently, or by one of the advisory, management or regulatory committee procedures, or by a special emergency procedure.[2]

The comitology decision was not welcomed by the Commission, apprehensive that it would impose constraints of its freedom of action and that it would impede the process of implementation.[3] The EP contended that the decision was unlawful but the Court of Justice ruled that the action was inadmissible on the ground that the Parliament lacked the necessary *locus standi* to bring such an action.[4] The Commission, also, failed as its contention that recourse to the management committee procedure would impinge upon its exclusive competence was dismissed on the merits.[5] Thus the procedure was confirmed to stay.

E.   Reforming the Commission?

The Commission, like any other institution is subject to change in the light of experience and the pressure for a model of a constitution. In the life of the Community the Commission acquired greater powers as the competences of the Community have expanded and, in the procedure of appointment of the President and the Commissioners, influence of the governments of the Member States has been reduced whilst the influence of the European Parliament has been increased. The changes do not reflect any particular model of constitutionalism though political writers have much to say on the subject. The evolution of the Commission follows a pragmatic line as, indeed, does the evolution of the Community/Union. Discussions reflect three different tendencies: to reduce the Commission to an administrative institution; to retain the status quo; and to promote the Commission to a *sui generis* government of the evolving Union. The starting point of the pragmatic approach is the status quo which, however, implies a compromise and reflects the inner dynamism of the Community.

In the course of time reforms ranging from cosmetic changes (eg the reduction of the size of the Commission) to fundamental remodelling of its functions have been suggested. Conventional critique sees the Commission as a bureaucratic body, which has become too large and unwieldy, dissipating its efforts on adventurous schemes and inconsequential legislation. Nevertheless, not only by design but also in reality, the Commission has been endowed with the potential of becoming the power engine of European integration.

The TEU, whilst keeping the size and nature of the Commission unchanged, adopted some of the ideas on the appointment of the Commission from the EP in the context of the Draft Treaty on European Union.[6] However, it did not follow

20   See Commission's proposal COM(86) 35 and EP opinion DOC A2–138/86.
1   Dec 87/373 (OJ 1987, L197/33).
2   Ibid, Arts 1–3. See now Council Decision 1999/468 (OJ 1999, L184/23) and the Declarations published in OJ 1999, C 203/1.
3   See EC, Bull (1987) Part 6, point 2.4.14.
4   Case 302/87: *EP v Council* [1988] ECR 5615.
5   Case 16/88: *Commission v Council* [1989] ECR 3457.
6   OJ 1984, C 77/33.

through the idea that the Commission should be an executive body with real authority and that, when constituted, it would submit its programme and be invested by the EP to which it would be responsible.

The idea that the Commission is (or should be) the government of the Community was advocated by Hallstein, once President of the Commission,[7] for which he was duly rebuked by President de Gaulle who favoured a 'nationalist' as against a 'federal' Europe. Nevertheless, Hallstein's prophetic words: 'When we had first harmonized our policy on heavy industry, we thought the time has come to a common defence policy and even for a "Political Community"'[8] have become a reality in the Treaties on European Union. In this transformation of the Europe of the 'common market' to a Europe of 'political unity' with a federal design the role of the Commission may change. As indicated by a former President of the Commission, Mr. Delors, the Commission 'should be turned into a proper executive answerable for its actions'; and 'appointed democratically'.[9] Clearly such a transformation would considerably change the status quo and move European integration further in the federalist direction with attractive prospects for the Commission.

7 Hallstein, W, *True Problems of European Integration* p 10.
8 Hallstein, W, *Unity of the Drive for Europe* p 24.
9 Address to the EP, 17 January 1990, EC Bull Supp 1/90: *The Commission's Programme for 1990's*, pp 12–13.

Chapter 9

The Council of the European Union

A. Concept and powers

The Merger Treaty (now Amsterdam 9(2)) established a Single Council of the European Communities in substitution for the corresponding institutions acting under the founding Treaties. In the institutional structure of the European Community it represents the element of sovereignty of the Member States. In that forum the Member States defend their interests. In matters concerning the Community it acts as a supranational institution but in matters which have not been completely transferred to the Community jurisdiction (ie external policy and security and co-operation in the field of internal affairs and justice) it acts de facto as an inter-governmental conference.

According to its nature it is a Council of Ministers representing the Member States but, following the establishment of the Union, it assumed the name of the Council of the European Union,[1] though it is commonly referred to as 'The Council'[2] in contradistinction to the European Council. As a legal institution the Council is a kind of fiction because it does not function as a permanent homogenous body but there are as many Councils as there are gatherings of Ministers meeting on the business of the Treaties. Although the Ministers carry out Community business as representatives of their governments their meetings cannot be regarded as international gatherings or diplomatic conferences. They act as an institution within the framework of the Community constitution.

The powers of the Council are succinctly but vaguely stated as follows:[3]

'To ensure that the objectives set out in this Treaty are attained the Council shall . . .
- ensure co-ordination of the general economic policies of the Member States;
- have power to take decisions;

---

1 Council Decision 93/591 (OJ 1993, L281/18).
2 See EC Treaty, title of sec 2, ch 1, title 1 of Part V.
3 EC Art 202 (ex Art 145).

   – confer on the Commission, in the acts which the Council adopts, powers
    for the implementation of the rules which the Council lays down . . .'

The main functions of the Council comprise co-ordination of the general economic
policies of the Member States and the taking of decisions, both powers being
circumscribed by the Treaties. Although, broadly speaking, the Council fulfils
the same functions in all three Communities there are nuances. The EC and
EAEC Treaties are principally framework treaties whilst the ECSC appears to
be a self-contained closely defined legal order. Under the ECSC Treaty, the
Commission generally has the power to take decisions subject to consultations
with the Council, whereas under the EC and the EAEC Treaties the power of
decision lies principally with the Council acting upon a proposal from the
Commission. Though under the ECSC Treaty, the Commission has wide powers
of independent decision it has made a practice of seeking approval of the Council.[4]

   The substantive parts of the Treaties consist of specific policies, some of which
have been sketched in only rudimentary terms. Therefore these policies have to be
put into effect by the Council through the co-operation with the Commission thus
resulting in co-ordination of the economies of the Member States. The duty imposed
on the Council to ensure co-ordination and take decisions, by itself establishes only
a power base from which derive specific measures by virtue of and in conjunctions
with more detailed dispositions.[5] Therefore the object of that provision is to seize
upon the relevant provisions of the Treaty and to enable the Council to make
decisions for their implementation in accordance with the procedures provided for
in the Treaty. For example, with the object of promoting the Economic and
Monetary Union, ahead of Maastricht, by virtue of decision 90/141[6] the Council
was entrusted with the responsibility of conducting, at least twice a year, a general
examination of the economic policies and the performance of the Member States
during the first stage of EMU.[7] During the second and the third stages the Council
has to exercise a greater power of intervention notably to prevent Member States
falling into excessive government deficits.

   The power to 'take decisions' is central to the concept of the Community
and, vested in the Council, it accentuates the role of the Council in the institutional
framework, especially as regards its relations with the Commission. The term
'decision' has several meanings and generally describes, internally, the Council's
competence in the legislative process, implementation of Treaty provisions and
the enactment of the Community budget, and externally, the participation in the
foreign relations of the Community. Whilst it plays a decisive role in the life of
the Community, the Council shares in various degrees with the other institutions
its power of decision.

   The Council's power of decision under the EC and Euratom Treaties has
been blunted by the principle that, in general, the Council can act only upon a
proposal from the Commission.[8] Moreover, in this process the Commission's
position is further strengthened by the rule of voting in Council, in particular, in
view of the gradual restriction of unanimity.

---

4   von Lindeiner-Wildan, K, *La Supernationalité en tant que principe du droit* (1970), pp 104–105.
5   A-G Warner in Case 81/72: *Commission v Council* [1973] ECR 575 (592), [1973] CMLR
    639 (647).
6   OJ 1990, L78/;23.
7   See Ch 24, infra.
8   See Case C-301/90: *Commission v Council* [1992] ECR I-221.

B. Composition

The Council consists of representatives of the Member States authorised to commit the government.[9] In principle each Member State designates its representative but they must be of a ministerial rank. The status of the representative is determined by the constitution of a Member State. Thus, a civil servant cannot act as a member of the Council but it appears that members of the executive of the component parts of certain countries (ie of the Länder of Germany and regions and communities of Belgium) may, if a particular matter falls within their competence.

The Treaty[10] allows any member of the Council to cast a vote on behalf of only one other Member State. The representation cannot be extended to substitutes who do not hold ministerial rank, though they may attend and participate in the deliberations without a right to vote. In such rare cases the right to vote would be entrusted to another member of the Council.

Being representatives of their governments the Ministers are bound by instructions which depend on the style of the government and the importance of the issue to national interests. A minister may also consent to a decision of the Council subject to consultation with his government.[11]

The composition of the Council varies depending upon the title of the ministers and the subject matter to be discussed. One has to distinguish between general and specialized Council meetings. In the first category are the General Affairs Council meetings attended by the Ministers of Foreign Affairs and the Financial Affairs Council (ECOFIN) meetings attended by the Ministers of Economic and Financial Affairs. The Ministers of Foreign Affairs meet once a month and their agenda may include not only matters relating to external affairs but also matters of general concern such as those relating to the working of the institutions. The ECOFIN, like the General Council, holds a regular meeting every month except in August. The ECOFIN is in charge of the legislative programme implementing the economic policies of the Community by the Member States including the completion of the Single Market. In the context of the EMU the ECOFIN takes crucial decisions not reserved to the European Council.[12]

The specialized Council meetings are attended by those Ministers whose portfolios relate to specific subjects on the agenda, for example agriculture, industry, transport, labour or culture etc and the preparation of meetings of the European Council. They meet as required (normally once a month in the case of ECOFIN, the General Affairs and Agricultural Councils; the Transport, Environment and Industry Councils meeting two to four times a year) except that Ministers of Agriculture must meet at least once a year in July to determine prices of agricultural products for the forthcoming agricultural year.

The Council meets when convened by its President on his own initiative or at the request of once of its members or of the Commission.[13] The office of the President of the Council rotates among the Member States for terms of six months in the order decided by the Council unanimously.[14]

9   EC Art 203(1) (ex Art 146(1)).
10   EC Art 206 (ex Art 150).
11   See Council's reply to Written Question 246/68 of Mr Vredeling (OJ 1968, C 13 p 12).
12   EC Art 111(2–4) (ex Art 109(2–4)) and Declaration 3 attached to the Maastricht Treaty.
13   EC Art 204 (ex Art 147).
14   EC Art 203(2) (ex Art 147).

The Presidency plays a vital role not only in the business of the Community but also in the business of the Union. Although the office is only transitory, the Presidency is engaged in the continuous process, therefore, the achievements of a Presidency very often bear witness to the work of its predecessors. Nevertheless the success of a particular Presidency depends not only on the weight and diplomacy of the country holding the office but also on the efficacy of the infrastructure comprising the Secretariat, COREPER on the one hand and the Ministries of the President's country on the other.

On the substantive plain it is essential to distinguish between the Council acting in the context of the Community[15] and the Union.[16]

C. The Secretariat and COREPER

The founding Treaties[17] provided for a General Secretariat to assist the Council. With the establishment of the European Union the work of the General Secretariat expanded[18] and the Secretary General assumed a new role assisting the Presidency as High Representative for the common foreign and security policy.[19]

The Secretary-General is responsible for the General Secretariat as its administrative head and for the functions of the High Representative in the field of the common foreign and security policy.[20] He is assisted by the Deputy Secretary-General responsible for the running of the General Secretariat. The Secretary-General and the Deputy Secretary-General are appointed by the Council acting unanimously, the Council deciding upon the organization of the General Secretariat.

The General Secretariat carries out the necessary tasks in furtherance of the activities of the Council, the Permanent Representatives Committee (COREPER) and all the committees and working parties set up by the Council.[1] It has its own Legal Service and ten Directorates-General each covering a more or less homogenous group of activities. In addition to a research and documentation division and a group of lawyer linguists, the Legal Service is divided into five teams:

– Team I covers internal market, industry, telecommunications, tourism, energy, civil protection, research, trans-European network, transport, social affairs, culture, education, youth, regional policy, environment, food harmonization, health and consumer protection.

– Team II covers agriculture, fisheries, economic and monetary policy, taxation, free movement of capital and matters for consideration of ECOFIN prepared by COREPER II.[2]

---

15 EC Art 203 (ex Art 146).

16 TEU Art 13(3) to Art 26 (ex Arts J 3(3) to J 16), in the fields of external relations and security and Art 30 (ex Art K 2); Art 31 (ex Art K 3); Art 34 (ex Art K 6); Art 39 (ex Art K 11); Art 40 (ex Art K 12); Art 41 (ex Art K 13); Art 42 (ex Art K 14) in the field of police and judicial co-operation; and Art 43 (ex Art K 15) and Art 44 (ex Art K 16) in the context of provisions on closer co-operation between Member States.

17 EC Art 207(2) (ex Art 151(2)); ECSC Art 30(2); EAEC Art 121(2).

18 TEU Art 18 (ex Art J 8) and EC Art 207 (ex Art 151).

19 TEU Art 18 (ex Art J 8); see supra, p 39.

20 1996 General Report on the Activities of the European Union (1997) p 424.

1 EC Art 207(2) (ex Art 151(2)).

2 As to COREPER II, see infra, p 251.

- Team III covers external relations and all matters relating to international agreements and relations with international organizations.
- Team IV covers institutional affairs, justice and home affairs, budget and staff regulations.
- Team V covers justice and home affairs.

The Directorates General cover the following areas:
- Directorate-General A: administration, personnel, infrastructure, translation and documentation and finances of the Secretariat;
- Directorate-General B: agriculture and fisheries;
- Directorate-General C: internal market, customs union, industrial policy, telecommunications and information society;
- Directorate-General D: research, energy and transport;
- Directorate-General E: external economic relations and the common foreign and security policy;
- Directorate-General F: institutional affairs, budget and staff regulations, relations with the European Parliament and the Economic and Social Committee and the Committee of the Regions, information policy and public relations;
- Directorate-General G: economic and monetary and financial affairs and EMU;
- Directorate-General H: justice and home affairs;
- Directorate-General I: environment and consumer policy, civil protection, health and food legislation; and
- Directorate-General J: economic and social cohesion, regional policy, employment, social policy, social dialogue, education and youth, audio-visual and culture.

The Secretary-General attends the meetings of the Council. There is a cabinet supporting him in the execution of his duties. By the end of 1998 the staff serving the Council comprised 2,441 permanent posts and 18 temporary posts.[3]

The Legal Service represents the Council in litigation, provides legal advice and makes it sure that acts having legal effects are drafted correctly in substance and in form. The Secretariat is responsible that the text of the acts faithfully reflect the conclusions reached in Council. Failure to do so would enable the Court of Justice to annul the acts in question on the ground of breach of an essential procedural requirement.[4]

The COREPER[5] ranks among the most important committees established under the Treaties. Its main function is to ensure a permanent presence of the Member States among the Community institutions. It fills the gap in the system caused by the transitory character of the Council. The common experience of European organisations set up since 1945 has been that, where they have institutions made up of ministerial representatives of governments which, because of other demands on their time and attention, can only meet infrequently, a permanent representative body of ambassadorial rank is necessary not only to carry out routine matters of administration but also to undertake preparatory work for meetings of the ministers and ensure an element of continuity in their action.

---

3 1998 General Report [1999], para 1085.
4 See eg Case 68/86: *United Kingdom v Council (re agricultural hormones)* [1988] ECR 855, [1988] 2 CMLR 543; Case 131/86: *United Kingdom v Council (re battery hens)* [1988] ECR 905, [1988] 2 CMLR 364.
5 French acronym of 'Comite des representants permanents'.

This has been the experience of the OEEC, the Council of Europe, the Western European Union and NATO.[6] There was no provision for such a body in the ECSC Treaty but, in 1953, the Special Council established a Co-ordinating Committee of senior officials of the governments of the Member States to prepare the Council's meetings and to undertake ad hoc tasks at the Council's request.[7] The experiment was carried into the EC and EAEC Treaties which gave the Council the power to create a committee of the representatives of the Member States and to determine its functions. The Merger Treaty completed the process by assigning to the COREPER the work of preparing the meetings of the Council and carrying out the specific tasks entrusted to it by the Council.[8] The reason why these functions have not been transferred to the Secretariat (manned by Community officials) seems to be that the Member States preferred to keep control of the business through their own civil servants[9] who are the eyes and ears of their governments.[10] However, in the course of time the Committee has acquired a Community character and has come to play a distinctive and important part in the institutional machinery of the Communities. The fear that it may upset the Community's institutional balance[11] in so far as it might effectively put more power in the hands of the Council and thus erode the Commission-Council dialogue by requiring the Commission to deal with a group of subordinate Permanent Representatives instead of the ministers themselves, was assuaged by the Council's assurance that it had no intention of delegating its power of decision to the Permanent Representatives.[12] At the end of the day the position of the COREPER has been accepted as a body which strengthens the dialogue between the Council and the Commission and ensures that Ministers do not waste time on matters which can be settled without controversy.

The Court of Justice[13] explained that the COREPER is not an institution invested by the Treaties with inherent powers but rather an auxiliary organ of the Council performing tasks of preparation and execution without exercising powers of decision which belong to the Council.

The COREPER consists of resident representatives of the Member States with ambassadorial rank. Its chairmanship rotates together with the Presidency of the Council.[14] It operates at two levels ie Ambassadors (COREPER II) and their deputies (COREPER I). COREPER II deals with institutional matters, economic and financial problems, external relations and international negotiations. COREPER I deals with routine and technical matters.[15] Decisions are taken in accordance with the voting system of the Council.

The main functions of the COREPER are to act as a channel of communication between the Commission and the national governments, to prepare the work of the Council and carry out any tasks assigned to it by the Council, and to act as the forum for negotiation of the Council's decisions. Thus the COREPER is directly involved in the work of the Community institutions.

---

6 See Palmer, N, et al, *European Unity* (1968).
7 See *Les Nouvelles: Droit des Communaute's Européennes* (1969), p 241 et seq.
8 Merger Treaty, Art 4; replaced by EC Art 207(1) (ex Art 151(1)).
9 Bleckman, A, *Europarecht* (3rd edn, 1980), p 25.
10 Noel, E, 'The Committee of Permanent Representatives' (1967) 5 Journal of Common Market Studies 219, 220.
11 Mayne, R, *The Institutions of the European Community* (1968), p 37.
12 See Noel, op cit, pp 228, 229.
13 Case C-25/94: *Commission v Council* [1996] ECR I–1469.
14 Council's Rules of Procedure, Art 19(4); see OJ 2000, L149/21.
15 See Guide to the Council of the European Communities (1990) pp 39–43.

The COREPER meets at least once a week preparing the way for the meeting of the Council and easing the burden by disposing of certain business. The agenda for the meeting of the Council consists of Part A and Part B. Part A includes items on which agreement has been reached within the COREPER; items in part B require a decision at the ministerial level.[16] The former may be adopted without discussion though ministers (and the Commission) are free to express an opinion and make statements which shall be included in the minutes (an item will be withdrawn from Part A if a position taken on the item would lead to further discussion or if a member of the Council or the Commission so requests). Items in Part B will be discussed by the ministers but the ground work would have been prepared by the COREPER. In both cases a formal adoption by the Council is necessary in order to give the decision the legal force of an act of the Council.

D. Modus operandi

According to the Amsterdam Treaty the Council shall have its seat in Brussels but during the months of April, June and October it shall hold its meetings in Luxembourg.[17] It functions within the framework of the Treaties according to its own Rules of Procedure.[18]

The President of the Council convenes the meetings of the Council on his own initiative or the request of the Commission or a Member State and draws up the provisional agenda for each meeting.[19] The agenda is sent to the Member States and to the Commission who may transmit to the Secretariat items they wish to include in the agenda. As we mentioned the agenda is divided into Part A and Part B, the former comprising items on which there is agreement established at COREPER, the latter comprises items which the Council decides after discussion or which are referred to another meeting. Apart from the current business which is transacted at meetings in private the Council holds public debates on the six-monthly programme submitted by the Presidency and, if appropriate, on the Commission's annual work programme. The Secretariat is responsible for the keeping of the minutes.[20]

The acts adopted by the Council and acts adopted jointly by the European Parliament and the Council are signed by the President and the Secretary-General or Deputy Secretary-General; but the latter may delegate their signature to the Director General of the General Secretariat.[1]

The Rules of Procedure determine the format and the citation of the various acts issuing from the Council, ie regulations, directives and decisions, common positions and joint actions adopted under TEU Articles 12 (ex Art J 2) and 10 (ex Art J 3), joint actions and conventions adopted under TEU Article 31 (ex Art K 3).[2] The Secretary General passes authentic copies of Council directives other than those referred to in EC Article 254(1) and (2) (ex Art 191(1) and (2)) and Council decisions and

---

16 Rules of Procedure, Art 3(7)–(8).
17 See also Rules of Procedure, Art 1(3).
18 See Council Decision 2000/396 (OJ 2000, L149/21) and Case 68/86: *United Kingdom v Council* [1988] ECR 855.
19 Rules of Procedure, Arts 1 and 3.
20 Rules, Arts 5, 8 and 13.
 1 Ibid, Art 15.
 2 Ibid, Annex II.

recommendations on to the governments of the Member States and the Commission.[3] Certain acts of the Council, conventions and international agreements concluded by the Community must be published in the Official Journal. Others are so published unless the Council or COREPER objects. In other cases, the decision whether or not to publish is decided on an ad hoc basis.[4]

The Council meets in private[5] but policy debates, referred to in Article 8 of the Rules of Procedure, may be subject to public transmission by audiovisual means. The Commission (and, where it exercises the right of initiative, the European Central Bank) must be invited to take part in meetings, though the Council may decide to deliberate on its own.[6] Members of the European Parliament are not invited to attend. Therefore, the Council does not admit the public or observers and the publicity of its acts and debates are subject to authorization. The deliberations of the Council are confidential, and so are the records unless the Council decides otherwise.[7] Apart from the publication of legislative acts in the Official Journal the Council may authorize press releases and issue official communiques. The Council may also allow the publication of copies or extracts from its records for the purpose of judicial proceedings.[8] Relying on what is now Article 10 of the Rules of Procedure the Council has decided that the public shall have access to Council documents upon application in writing to the General Secretariat.[9] However, access shall not be granted if disclosure could undermine the protection of the public interest; the protection of the individual and of privacy; commercial and industrial secrecy, the Community's financial interests; and confidentiality as requested by natural and legal persons.[10] Moreover, access may be refused in order to protect the confidentiality of the Council's proceedings.[11] To complete the transparency rules the Council adopted on 2 October 1995 a 'code of conduct'[12] concerning the publication of minutes and declarations of the Council acting as legislator.

EC Article 205 (ex Art 148) provides that 'Save as otherwise provided in this Treaty, the Council shall act by a majority of its members' and lays down rules for decisions to be taken by qualified majority. 'The presence of the majority of the members of the Council who are entitled to vote is required to enable the Council to vote'.[13]

The Treaty provides for three voting methods, by simple majority, qualified majority and unanimity, but the choice of a method does not belong to the Council. It reflects the complexity of the legal order of the Community and of the Union as well as the tendency to restrict unanimity in accordance with the federalist evolution of the Union.

As mentioned earlier the Treaty provides that, save otherwise stipulated, the Council shall act by a majority. However there are very few occasions, albeit of

3   Ibid, Art 18(3).
4   Ibid, Art 17.
5   Ibid, Art 5(1).
6   Ibid, Art 5(2).
7   Ibid, Art 6.
8   Ibid, Art 6(2).
9   Council Decision 93/731 (OJ 1993, L340/43), as amended by Decision 96/705 (OJ 1996, L325/19) and by Decision 2000/23 (OJ 2000, L9/22).
10 Decision 93/731, Art 4(1).
11 Ibid, Art 4(2); See also Case T-194/94: *Carvel and Guardian Newspapers Ltd v Council* [1995] ECR II–2765, [1995] 3 CMLR 359; Case C-58/94: *Netherlands v Council* [1996] ECR I–2169.
12 Bull UE 10/95, point 1.9.1.
13 Rules of Procedure, Art 11(4).

minor importance, when the Council decides by simple majority.[14]

According to the principle of qualified (or weighted) majority the Treaty allocates to each Member State a number of votes corresponding more or less to the population, ie Luxembourg 2 votes, Denmark, Finland and Ireland 3 votes each; Austria and Sweden 4 votes each; Belgium, Greece, The Netherlands and Portugal 5 votes each; Spain 8 votes; and France, Germany, Italy and the United Kingdom 10 votes each. Where a Council decision is required to be taken upon a proposal from the Commission, a qualified majority of at least 62 (out of the total of 87 votes) will suffice but where the Council acts in other cases the qualified majority of 62 votes must be cast by at least ten Member States.[15] In neither case can the five largest countries commanding 48 votes alone impose their will upon the Community, nor can the smaller countries. To reach a majority a combination of smaller and larger countries is required and this maintains a certain balance of power among the Member States.

Taking into account the amendments arising from the Amsterdam Treaty the Council decides by a qualified majority in the following matters: establishment of closer relations between Member States;[16] guidelines for the completion of the internal market;[17] market organization within the common agricultural policy;[18] definition of exceptions to the right of establishment;[19] professional qualifications within the right of establishment;[20] freedom to provide services by nationals of third countries;[1] liberalization of specific services;[2] free movement of capital with third countries and the Member States;[3] dealing with a sudden inflow of nationals of third countries;[4] discrimination by carriers charging different transport rates;[5] provisions applicable to transport by rail, road and inland waterway;[6] rules of competition;[7] rules applicable to state aids;[8] charges other than various forms of indirect taxation;[9] Member States' legislation leading to distortion of competition;[10] guidelines for economic policy;[11] assessment of Member States' excessive deficit;[12] recommendations regarding monetary policy;[13] recommendations of the central rates of the ECU within the exchange-rate system;[14] composition of the Economic and Financial Committee;[15] protective measures regarding balance of payments;[16] derogations regarding economic

---

14 EC Art 207(3) (ex Art 151(3)); EC Art 208 (ex Art 152); EC Art 209 (ex Art 153); EC Art 284 (ex Art 213); and TEU Art 48(2) (ex Art N(2)).
15 EC Art 205(2) (ex Art 148(2)).
16 EC Art 11(2) (ex Art 5a(2)).
17 EC Art 14(3) (ex Art 7a(3)).
18 EC Art 37(3) (ex Art 43(3)).
19 EC Art 45(2) (ex Art 55(2)).
20 EC Art 47(2) (ex Art 57(2)).
1 EC Art 49(2) (ex Art 59(2)).
2 EC Art 52 (ex Art 63).
3 EC Art 57(2) (ex Art 73c(2)) and EC Art 60(2) (ex Art 73g(2)).
4 EC Art 64(2) (ex Art 73.1(2)).
5 EC Art 75(3) (ex Art 79(3)).
6 EC Art 80(2) (ex Art 84(2)).
7 EC Art 83(1) (ex Art 87(1)).
8 EC Art 89 (ex Art 94).
9 EC Art 92 (ex Art 98).
10 EC Art 96 (ex Art 101).
11 EC Art 97(2) and (4) (ex Art 103(2) and (4)).
12 EC Art 104(6) (ex Art 104c(6)).
13 EC Art 107(6) (ex Art 106(6)).
14 EC Art 111 (ex Art 109).
15 EC Art 114(3) (ex Art 109(c)(3)).
16 EC Art 120(3) (ex Art 109(i)(3)).

and monetary union;[17] guidelines for employment policy;[18] employment incentive measures;[19] aids for exports to third countries;[20] management and labour agreements;[1] policy for education, vocational training and youth;[2] public health;[3] adoption of the research framework programme;[4] joint undertakings in research and technology development;[5] determination of salaries of the President and Members of the Commission, of the President, Judges, Advocates-General and Registrar of the Court of Justice;[6] the measures applicable to outermost regions;[7] sanctions implementing decisions taken under the provisions of the Treaty on Union in the field of foreign and security policy[8] and sanctions for breaches of fundamental rights.[9]

A certain modification of the voting system became necessary as a result of the provisions of the TEU concerning the monetary union and the social charter. Thus, in the context of the former, the Council acting on the recommendation of the Commission concerning excessive deficit of a Member State shall take the appropriate decision by a majority of two-thirds of votes of its members weighted in accordance with Article 205(2), excluding the votes of the country concerned.[10] Member States which shall not participate in the third phase of the monetary union will not vote on the decisions relevant to that phase and the qualified majority shall correspond to two-thirds of the votes of the Member States which shall not be subject to derogation whilst the unanimity provided for shall apply solely to those States.[11]

The Protocol on social policy attached to the Maastricht Treaty regulates the position arising from the British refusal to accept the Social Charter of 1989. Accordingly the remaining Member States are authorized to put the Charter into force without British participation in the relevant deliberations and the decision-making process.

The principle of unanimity enables a Member State to veto the decisions of the Council which, according to the treaty, require a consensus among the members of the Council. However abstentions by members present or represented do not prevent the adoption by the Council of acts which require unanimity.[12] After the period of transition, due to the progress of European integration, the instances of unanimity tend to diminish giving way to qualified majority. Unanimity has been reserved for the most important issues such as amendment of the Treaty,[13] the enlargement of the Community,[14] association agreements,[15] exercise of implied

---

17   EC Art 122(2) and (5) (ex Art 109k(2) and (5)).
18   EC Art 128(2) (ex Art 109q(2)).
19   EC Art 128(4) (ex Art 109q(4)).
20   EC Art 132(1) (ex Art 112(1)).
 1   EC Art 139(2) (ex Art 118b(2)).
 2   EC Art 149(4) (ex Art 126(4)).
 3   EC Art 152(4) (ex Art 129(4)).
 4   EC Art 166(4) (ex Art 130i(4)).
 5   EC Art 172 (ex Art 130o).
 6   EC Art 210 (ex Art 154).
 7   EC Art 299(2) (ex Art 227(2)).
 8   EC Art 301 (ex Art 228a).
 9   EC Art 309(2) and (3) (ex Art 236(2) and (3)).
10   Art 104(13) (ex Art 104c(13)).
11   Art 122(5) (ex Art 109K(5)).
12   Art 205(3) (ex Art 148(3)).
13   TEU Art 48 (ex Art N).
14   TEU Art 49 (ex Art O).
15   EC Art 310 (ex Art 238) and EC Art 300(2) (ex Art 228(2)).

powers by the Council;[16] the increase of the number of judges and advocates general;[17] approval of the Court's Rules of Procedure;[18] the exercise of the rights of citizens of the European Union;[19] social security rights;[20] recognition of professional qualifications of self-employed persons;[1] certain aspects of the Common Transport Policy;[2] the harmonization of turnover taxes, excise duties and other forms of indirect taxation;[3] decisions in the field of Common Foreign and Security Policy;[4] and when adopting framework decisions and conventions in the field of Police and Judicial Co-operation in criminal matters.[5] Unanimity is also applied when the Council, acting on a proposal from the Commission, intends to adopt an act which constitutes an amendment to that proposal.[6] The Council acts unanimously on the amendment on which the Commission has delivered a negative opinion on an act adopted in the form of a common position[7] but shall act by a qualified majority if subsequently the Conciliation Committee approves the proposed act.[8]

In practice the President, when putting a proposal to vote, endeavours to steer the Council towards consensus with or without formal voting.[9]

In some cases the problems facing the Communities have proved insoluble, even after recourse to a marathon session to reach a consensus. Intransigence on the part of one or more Member States claiming that vital national interests are at stake may provoke a constitutional crisis in the Community. The precedent was set up by France during the crisis of the 'empty chair' in 1965 which resulted in the Luxembourg Accords of 1966. The crisis began with the French veto of the British application for membership in 1963[10] and continued during the French Presidency in 1965.[11] In 1965 the Commission, in an attempt to solve a number of outstanding problems, proposed a package deal embracing three unconnected items: (1) the completion of farm price regulations demanded by France in particular; (2) a Commission proposal for the independence of the financing of the Communities out of their own resources instead of contributions from the Member States, and (3) the granting of greater powers to the European Parliament which was sought by the Parliament itself with the support of the Netherlands. This package-deal was opposed by France ostensibly on the ground that the Commission had disclosed its proposals to the European Parliament before the French government had an opportunity to consider them. The other Member States were willing to consider the package deal as a whole, but France insisted that only farm finance should be dealt with. A deadline of 30 June 1965 had been fixed by the Council for the settlement of this issue but when no agreement had been reached by midnight on that date the French Foreign Minister, who happened to be the current President of the Council, refused to overrun the time-limit and brought

---

16 EC Art 308 (ex Art 235).
17 EC Art 221(4) (ex Art 165(4)) and EC Art 222(3) (ex Art 166(3)).
18 EC Art 225(4) (ex Art 168a(4)).
19 EC Art 18(2) (ex Art 8a(2)).
20 EC Art 42 (ex Art 51).
 1 EC Art 47(2) (ex Art 57(2)).
 2 EC Art 71(2) (ex Art 75(2)).
 3 EC Art 93 (ex Art 99).
 4 TEU Art 23(1) (ex Art J 13(1)).
 5 TEU Art 34(2) (ex Art K 6(2)).
 6 EC Art 250(1) (ex Art 189a(1)).
 7 EC Art 251(3) (ex Art 189b(3)).
 8 EC Art 251(4 and 5) (ex Art 189b (4 and 5)).
 9 XXVI General Report 1992, point 1986.
10 VI General Report (1963), see Introduction.
11 IX General Report (1966) see Ch 1.

the meeting to an end. Thereafter France refused to take part in any meetings of the Council. The Council continued to meet in the absence of France, but eventually at a private meeting in Luxembourg, a compromise was reached, commonly, albeit erroneously, called the 'Agreement, or Accord of Luxembourg'. It provides, inter alia:

'I. Where in the case of decisions which may be taken by majority vote on a proposal of the Commission, very important interests of one or more partners are at stake, the Members of the Council will endeavour, within a reasonable time, to reach solutions which can be adopted by all the Members of the Council while respecting their mutual interests and those of the Community, in accordance with Article 2 of the EEC Treaty.

II. With regard to the preceding paragraph, the French delegation considers that where very important interests are at stake the discussion must be continued until unanimous agreement is reached.'

Thus, in effect, the Luxembourg formula is merely an agreement to disagree,[12] and provides no solution in the event of failure to reach agreement. It should be borne in mind that it is relevant only to decisions where the Treaty provides for a majority vote; it does not affect the power of veto in cases where unanimity is required by the Treaty. The legality of the Accords de Luxembourg is highly questionable since they do not constitute an amendment of the Treaty although they have distorted the voting system. They have led to a practice that the Council, instead of counting votes, takes its decisions generally by consensus. However the possibility of a Member State opposing a decision of the Council has become part of the *acquis communautaire*.[13]

So be it, but the Accords de Luxembourg are in direct conflict with EC Article 7(1)[14] imposing the obligation that 'each institution shall act within the limits of the powers conferred upon it by this Treaty'. Although the validity of the Accords has not been formally considered by the Court of Justice, the above-stated conclusion is supported by its case law on the extent of the authority of the institutions of the Community. The Court stressed, for example, that the institutional balance established by the Treaties must not be disturbed.[15] Similarly, it held that attempts by the Council to act in derogation from the express provisions of the Treaties can have no legal effect.[16]

The Commission, whilst never expressly approving of the Accords, has nevertheless acquiesced and co-operated in their application. Although the Accords have not affected the legal relations and powers of the Commission and Council they had in practice a limiting effect on the process of integration,[17] especially that recourse to unanimity where Treaties did not require it, did, as a result, slow down the decision-making process.[18] The Commission considering the dangers of insisting on unanimity in the Council in an enlarged Community

---

12 IX General Report (1966) pp 31–33.
13 See Rideau, J, *Droit Institutionnel de l'Union et des Communautés Européennes* (2nd edn, 1966), p 283.
14 Ex Art 4(1).
15 See Case 25/70: *EVGF v Köster* [1970] ECR 1161: and Opinion 1/78 *Draft International Agreement on Natural Rubber* [1979] ECR 2871.
16 See Case 59/75: *Pubblico Ministero v Manghera* [1976] ECR 91, [1976] 1 CMLR 557; and Case 43/75: *Defrenne v SABENA* [1976] ECR 455, [1976] 1 CMLR 98.
17 See Second General Report (1969), pp 14 et seq.
18 See Bull (1964) No 9/10, suppl pp 33, 34.

urged the acceptance of two principles: (1) that decisions by majority vote should again be the normal practice of the Council except where Treaties provide otherwise; and (2) that where unanimity in the Council is required it should only apply to outline policy decisions and majority voting should then be the rule in connection with the decisions necessary to implement such policies.[19] These principles received a measure of recognition by the Council when the United Kingdom opposed the Commission's proposal for fixing farm prices for reasons connected with the budgetary problem. However the President of the Council concluded that the conditions laid down in the Treaty for taking a decision had been reached and the Council adopted the proposal by qualified majority.[20] This was important because it was the first time that farm prices had not been fixed by unanimity[1] and it showed that the Council acknowledged that the vital interests at stake were those of the Community itself and the credibility of its decision-making process.

With the evolution of the Community the forthcoming institutional reforms provided an opportunity for a revision of the voting system. However, the Parliament's Draft Treaty for a European Union[2] envisaged the retention of a national right of veto for a transitional period of ten years.[3] *The Three Wise Men's* Report considered an insistence on unanimity available to a Member State when, in its judgment, its very important interests are at stake[4] and the Dooge Committee in its report of 1985[5] thought that unanimity should be retained in exceptional cases of a limited number.

Neither the Single European Act nor the Treaties on European Union have effected a significant change of the voting system. The Single European Act, with the object of completing the internal market relaxed in the relevant areas the Treaty's requirement for unanimity in favour of a qualified majority[6] and a similar technique had been adopted in the Treaties on Union. It seems that the majority of Member States are reluctant to give up the right of veto as one of the last attributes of sovereignty.[7]

The present practice suggests that Member States have become more willing to abstain rather than to insist on exercising a right of veto.[8] Recent changes in the voting method seems also to have contributed to a more restrained use of veto. Thus it is now standard practice for the *tour de table* procedure, where Council members vote in alphabetical order of the Member States starting with the member who, in that order, follows the member holding the office of President.[9] The question of a vote is no longer left to the President of the Council,[10] for in addition to voting on his initiative, the President is required to open a voting procedure

19 See Bull of the European Communities (1974) Part I, p 5, and Eighth General Report (1975), p 9.
20 See Bull of the European Communities, (1981) Part 5, pp 7, 8.
1 See Thirtieth Review of the Council's Work (1984), p 175.
2 OJ 1984, C 77, Art 23(3).
3 See EC Commission, An Ever Closer Union (1985) Annex I, p 312.
4 Report on European Institutions (1979), p 51.
5 See Bull EC 3/85, points 3, 5, 1 et seq.
6 Arts 13–19.
7 See House of Commons Debates, 6th Series, 1985–86, Vol 96, col 320.
8 See Noel, E, *Working Together: The Institutions of the European Community* (1988), p 27. The 1998 General Report (1999), para 1026, says that, in cases other than those where a majority vote is appropriate, the prospect of a qualified majority vote was sufficient to secure unanimity.
9 Rules of Procedure, supra, Art 11(2).
10 Note the incident of the farm prices, supra.

on the initiative of a member of the Council or of the Commission provided that a majority of the Council's members so decide.[11] Moreover the items on which votes are to be taken have to be specified on the agenda and brought to the notice of the members of the Council.[12] All these changes of the rules ought to improve efficiency and facilitate recourse to majority voting.

Despite this evident progress the Accords de Luxembourg remain alive. During the last phase of the Uruguay Round of negotiations within the GATT, France, quite successfully, brandished the threat of veto and the United Kingdom, hurt by seemingly disproportionate measures imposed by the Commission to solve the crisis in the beef industry,[13] announced its intention of blocking some 60 acts at various stages of enactment, until agreement on the matter had been reached.

E. Institutional interaction in Community legislation

(1) INSTITUTIONAL INVOLVEMENT

Legislation is a species of decision-making process in which the principal institutions are involved as regards the subject-matter and procedures laid down in the Treaties. The power 'to take decisions' is central to the concept of the Community and, vested in the Council, it accentuates the role of the Council in the institutional framework especially as regards its relations with the Commission. The term 'decision' has several meanings and, generally, connotes, internally, the Council's competences in the legislative process, implementation of the Treaty policies and the enactment of the Community budget, and, externally, the involvement in the foreign relations of the Community. Whilst it plays a decisive role in the life of the Community, the Council shares in various degrees with the other institutions its power of decision.

The Commission's initiative in policy-making and legislation which implements the latter is enhanced by the fact that in exercising its powers of decision under the Treaty the Council can in general act only upon a proposal from the Commission. The Commission's position in this process is further strengthened by the rules of voting in the Council.

The evolution of the legislative process has been marked by the ascendancy of the European Parliament which, mainly as a result of direct elections, has been aspiring to a role enjoyed by parliaments of the Member States. Thus, whilst originally there were two players in the game (the EP only on the side line where specifically empowered to be consulted) there are at present three players whose input into the process depends on their institutional functions in the Community. In the words of EC Article 249 (ex Art 189):

'In order to carry out their task and in accordance with the provisions of this Treaty, the European Parliament acting jointly with the Council, the Council and the Commission shall make regulations and issue directives, take decisions, make recommendations or deliver opinions'.

Whilst the principal role is assigned to the Council, the Commission is the initiator and the EP acts jointly with the Council where and how the Treaty so provides.

---

11   Rules of Procedure, Art 11(1).
12   Ibid, Art 3(2).
13   1996 General Report (1997) points 501 et seq.

(2)   INSTITUTIONS ACTING ALONE

The Treaty, in rare instances, enables the Commission to legislate without participation of the other institutions[14] by virtue of express provisions of the Treaty. The Commission may also legislate under express delegation of the Council implementing in detail more general provisions of Council decisions[15] or by virtue of EC Article 208 (ex Art 152) which provides that the Council may request the Commission to undertake any studies which the Council considers desirable for the attainment of the common objectives, and to submit to it any appropriate proposals. The Commission adopts its own Rules of Procedure.[16]

The EP has no power to enact general legislation though, as a master in its own house, it can regulate its own procedures[17] as an attribute of an institutional autonomy. The EP has no power to initiate legislation but by virtue of EC Article 192(2) (ex Art 138b(2)) it may request the Commission to submit any appropriate proposal on matters on which it considers that a Community act is required for the purpose of implementing the Treaty. The Commission is not legally bound to accede to the request and Parliament has no means of pursuing the matter but Parliament's proposal is a powerful signal to the Commission and the above Treaty provision may be regarded as a harbinger of future development in this respect.

The Council rarely legislates alone. It adopts its own Rules of Procedure[18] but has to approve the Rules of Procedure of the Court of Justice[19] and of the Court of the First Instance.[20] In a number of important areas the Council legislates on the basis of a proposal from the Commission but without the participation of the European Parliament though it may consult the latter within its own discretion.[1]

(3)   PARLIAMENT'S PARTICIPATION IN THE LEGISLATIVE PROCESS

Parliament's progress has been marked by the extension of its power to influence legislation in the Community. Originally the role of the EP was purely consultative. The SEA increased the instances in which it had to be consulted, introduced the 'assent procedure' and the 'co-operative procedure' and Maastricht added 'co-decision procedure', resulting in a truly byzantine law-making process.

(i)   The consultation procedure
Every legislative measure has to be proposed by the Commission. Under the consultative procedure the Commission's proposal has to be submitted to the EP before the Council takes the decision according to the relevant provisions of the Treaty. In practice the Council begins to consider the proposal without actually waiting for Parliament's opinion but the Council cannot proceed to its final

14   See supra, pp 240–241.
15   See supra, pp 241–244.
16   EC Art 218(2) (ex Art 162(2)).
17   See eg Case 230/81: *Luxembourg v European Parliament* [1983] ECR 255.
18   EC Art 207(3) (ex Art 151(3)).
19   EC Art 245(3) (ex Art 188(3)).
20   EC Art 225(4) (ex Art 168a(4)).
 1   See EC Art 26 (ex Art 28) – CCT; EC Art 45(2) (ex Art 55(2)) – exemption from the freedom of establishment; EC Art 49(2) (ex Art 59(2)) – extension of freedom to provide services to nationals of third counties; EC Art 55 (ex Art 66) – exemption from the freedom to provide services; EC Arts 60(2) (ex Art 73g(2)) – measures on the movement of capital as regards third countries; EC Art 96 (ex Art 101) – elimination of distortion of competition arising from national laws; EC Art 99(2) (ex Art 103(2)) – co-ordination of economic policies; EC Art 104(6) (ex Art 104c(6)) – control of excessive government deficits; EC Art 133(3) (ex Art 113(3)) – negotiation of trade agreements, and EC Art 301 (ex Art 228a) – economic sanctions.

decision until it has heard from the EP. The rationale of the parliamentary consultation has thus been explained by the Court of Justice:

> 'The consultations provided for in third sub-paragraph of Article 43(2) [now 37(2)], as in other similar provisions of the Treaty, is the means which allows parliament to play an actual part in the legislative process of the Community. Such power represents an essential factor in the institutional balance intended by the Treaty. Although limited, it reflects at Community level the fundamental democratic principle that the peoples should take part in the exercise of power through the intermediary of a representative assembly. Due consultation of the Parliament in cases provided for by the Treaty therefore constitutes an essential formality disregard of which means that the measure concerned is void'.[2]

In the instant case the applicant was successful in having a regulation repealed on the ground of infringement of an essential procedural requirement in so far as the Council had adopted it without receiving the Parliament's opinion. It is interesting to note that the Court rejected the argument that the Parliament was in default as it did not respond to the urgency of the situation.

The required consultation has to be substantial, not a mere formality. Thus Parliament has to be consulted a second time if the proposal on which it expressed its opinion is amended by the Commission or the Council.[3] A second opinion may not be necessary if the amendments are only technical or coincide with Parliament's wishes.[4]

The procedure still applies in certain areas, ie right to vote and stand in municipal elections,[5] and election to the EP;[6] agriculture;[7] implementation of competition rules;[8] state aids;[9] harmonization of indirect taxation;[10] approximation of laws for the establishment and functioning of the common market;[11] ESCB statute;[12] executive board of the ECB;[13] fiscal measures relating to the environment;[14] research programmes;[15] Community's own resources;[16] financial regulations[17] and international agreements.[18]

(ii)   The co-operation procedure
This procedure was introduced by the SEA, refined in the Maastricht Treaty and taken aboard by the Amsterdam Treaty.[19] In essence it is a more elaborate consultation procedure introducing a second reading of the proposal devised to

2   Case 138/79: *Roquette Frères v Council* [1980] ECR 3333 (3360).
3   Case C-388/92: *European Parliament v Council* [1994] ECR I–2067.
4   Case 41/69: *ACF Chemiefarma v Commission* [1970] ECR 661 (702); Case 1253/79: *Battaglia v Commission* [1982] ECR 297; Case 817/79: *Buyl v Commission* [1982] ECR 245; Case C–331/88: *R v Minister of Agriculture, ex p FEDESA* [1990] ECR I–4023; Case C–65/90: *European Parliament v Council* [1992] ECR I–4593.
5   EC Art 19(1) (ex Art 8b(1)).
6   EC Art 19(2) (ex Art 8b(2)).
7   EC Art 37(2) and (3) (ex Art 43(2) and (3)).
8   EC Art 83(1) (ex Art 87(1)).
9   EC Art 89 (ex Art 94).
10   EC Art 93 (ex Art 99).
11   EC Art 94 (ex Art 100).
12   EC Art 107(5) (ex Art 106(5)).
13   EC Art 112(2)(b) (ex Art 109a (2)(b)).
14   EC Art 175(2) (ex Art 130s(2)).
15   EC Art 172(1) (ex Art 130.o(1)).
16   EC Art 269 (ex Art 201).
17   EC Art 279 (ex Art 209).
18   EC Art 300(3) (ex Art 228(3)).
19   EC Art 252 (ex Art 189c).

speed up the completion of the internal market but, in constitutional terms, its effect is to up-grade the European Parliament.

Under this procedure:

(1) The Council, acting by a qualified majority on a proposal from the Commission, and after obtaining an opinion from the EP, adopts a common position which is communicated to the EP.

(2) The Council and the Commission are to inform the EP fully of the reasons which led the Council to adopt its common position and also of the Commission's position. If within three months the EP has either approved the common position or has not taken a decision within that period the Council shall definitively adopt the act in question in accordance with the common position.

(3) The EP may, within the period of three months, propose amendments by an absolute majority of its component members. Alternatively it may, by the same majority reject the Council's common position. If the EP rejects the Council's common position the Council can only adopt the act by unanimity.

(4) If, on the other hand, the EP proposes amendments the Commission shall within a month re-examine the original proposal in the light of these amendments. The Commission shall forward the re-examined proposal to the Council, together with the amendments of the EP which it has not accepted, and express its opinion on these amendments. The Council may accept these amendments by unanimity.

(5) The Council then, acting by qualified majority, shall adopt the proposal as re-examined by the Commission. Unanimity is required for the Council to amend the proposal as re-examined by the Commission.

(6) In the cases referred in points (c) (d) and (e), the Council is required to act within a period of three months. If no decision is taken within this period, the Commission proposal shall be deemed not to have been adopted.

(7) The periods referred to in points (b) and (f) may be extended by a maximum of one month by common accord by the Council and the EP.

In a technical sense this procedure has created two readings of the proposed act: the first when the EP gives an opinion on the proposal *before* the Council adopts its common position, as outlined in point (a) above; and the second *after* the Council has adopted its common position, as outlined in points (b) and (c).

Originally the procedure was applied to the completion of the common market, in particular the harmonization of the relevant aspects of national laws.[20] It was extended by the TEU to transport;[1] aspects of economic policy;[2] workers' health and safety;[3] implementation of decisions relating to the European Social Fund;[4] implementation of decisions relating to the European Regional Development Fund[5] and environmental policy.[6]

(iii)   The co-decision procedure

Yet another procedure grafted originally upon EC Article 189 (as it then was), designed to enhance the powers of the EC was introduced by the Maastricht

---

20   EC Art 94 (ex Art 100).
1   EC Art 71 (ex Art 75).
2   EC Art 102(2) (ex Art 104a(2)) and EC Art 103(2) (ex Art 104b(2)).
3   EC Art 137(2) (ex Art 118(2)).
4   EC Art 148 (ex Art 125).
5   EC Art 159 (ex Art 130b).
6   EC Art 175(1) (ex Art 130s(1)).

Treaty with a slight modification of the text by the Amsterdam Treaty. The object is to reach a joint decision of the Council and the EP or perhaps to avoid adopting a decision without the approval of both institutions. The procedure is intricate, to say the least and one wonders at 'the behind-the scenes negotiations' responsible for this product. The procedure outlined in EC Article 251 (ex Art 189b) applies wherever the Treaty so provides, ie measures concerning the movement of workers;[7] rules to prohibit discrimination on grounds of nationality;[8] the right to move and reside in a Member State;[9] directives implementing the freedom of establishment;[10] co-ordination of exemptions to free movement of workers;[11] directives on mutual recognition of diplomas;[12] co-ordination of provisions relating to self-employed persons;[13] harmonization of provisions relating to the internal market;[14] incentives for education, vocational training and youth;[15] incentive for the promotion of culture;[16] incentives for the protection of public health;[17] measures relating to consumer protection;[18] promotion of research and technological development[19] and the action programme for environment;[20] development co-operation;[1] principles applicable to transparency;[2] countering frauds affecting the financial interests of the Community;[3] statistics[4] and advisory authority on data protection.[5]

(1) The process of co-decision begins, as in the co-operation, with the submission of Commission proposals to the EP and the Council.
(2) The Council, having obtained the opinion of the EP, may, by a qualified majority do one of three things:
    (a) adopt the proposed act as amended by the EP; or
    (b) adopt the proposed act if the EP does not propose any amendment; or
    (c) adopt a common position and communicate it both to the EP and the Commission giving its reasons for the common position.
(3) Within three months of such communication the EP can do one of the following three things:
    (a) approve the common position or take no decision in which case the act in question shall be deemed to have been adopted in accordance with the common position; or
    (b) reject, by an absolute majority of its component members, the common position, in which case the proposal shall be deemed not to have been adopted; or

  7   EC Art 40 (ex Art 49).
  8   EC Art 12 (ex Art 6).
  9   EC Art 18(2) (ex Art 8a(2)).
 10   EC Art 44(1) (ex Art 54(1)).
 11   EC Art 46(2) (ex Art 52(2)).
 12   EC Art 47(1) (ex Art 57(1)).
 13   EC Art 47(2) (ex Art 57(2)).
 14   EC Art 95(1) (ex Art 100a(1)).
 15   EC Art 149(4) (ex Art 126(4)), and EC Art 130(4) (ex Art 127(4)).
 16   EC Art 151(5) (ex Art 128(5)).
 17   EC Art 152(4) (ex Art 129(4)).
 18   EC Art 153(4) (ex Art 129a(4)).
 19   EC Art 166(1) (ex Art 130i(1)).
 20   EC Art 175(1) (ex Art 130s(1)).
  1   EC Art 179 (ex Art 130w).
  2   EC Art 255(2) (ex Art 191a(2)).
  3   EC Art 280(4) (ex Art 209a(4)).
  4   EC Art 285 (ex Art 213a).
  5   EC Art 286(2) (ex Art 213b(2)).

(c) propose amendments to the common position by an absolute majority which shall be forwarded to the Council and the Commission which shall deliver an opinion on those amendments.

(4) If, within three months of the referral the Council approves by a qualified majority the amendments of the EP, the act in question shall be deemed to have been adopted in the form of the common position as amended; however, the Council shall act unanimously on the amendments on which the Commission had delivered a negative opinion. If the Council does not approve all the amendments, the President of the Council, in agreement with the President of the EP, shall within six weeks convene a meeting of the Conciliation Committee.

(5) If, within six weeks of its being convened, the Conciliation Committee approves a joint text, the EP, acting by an absolute majority of the votes cast and the Council, acting by a qualified majority, shall each have a period of six weeks from that approval in which to adopt the act in question in accordance with the joint text. If, however, either of the two institutions fails to approve the proposed act within that period, it shall be deemed not to have been adopted.

(6) Where the Conciliation Committee does not approve a joint text, the proposed act shall be deemed not to have been adopted.

(7) The Conciliation committee is composed of equal numbers of the Council and the EP. Its task is to endeavour to reach agreement on a joint text by a qualified majority of the Members of the Council and by a majority of the representatives of the EP. The Commission participates in the Committee's proceedings taking all the necessary initiatives with a view to reconciling the positions of the Council and the EP. In fulfilling this task the Conciliation Committee shall address the common position on the basis of the amendments proposed by the EP.

(iv)   The assent procedure

The assent procedure was introduced by Articles 8 and 9 of the SEA in respect of application for membership of the Community and in respect of certain international agreements. It simply means that, as under the conciliation procedure, a proposal from the Commission requires a formal approval of the Council and the EP in accordance with the respective Treaty provisions. Where assent is required, the Council may act only after it has obtained Parliament's approval.

The Maastricht Treaty extended the scope of the assent procedure. It now applies to the Membership of the Union;[6] association agreements;[7] ECB's supervision of credit and financial institutions;[8] the statute of the ESCB;[9] the organization of Structural Funds and the setting up of a Cohesion Fund;[10] direct election procedure[11] and sanctions in the event of a serious and persistent breach of fundamental rights by a Member States.[12]

Under this procedure the Council acts unanimously and the EP by an absolute majority of its component members.

---

6   TEU Art 49 (ex Art O).
7   EC Art 300(2) (ex Art 228(2)).
8   EC Art 103(5) (ex Art 105(5)).
9   EC Art 107(5) (ex Art 106(5)).
10   EC Art 161(1) (ex Art 130d(1)) and EC Art 161(2) (ex Art 130d(2)), respectively.
11   EC Art 198(4) (ex Art 138(4)).
12   TEU Art 7(1) (ex Art F 1(1)).

Chapter 10

The Court of Auditors and budgetary procedure

A. The Court of Auditors

The Court of Auditors, established in 1977 under the terms of the Financial Provisions Treaty 1975,[1] was promoted by the Maastricht Treaty to be one of the principal institutions of the Community. The Court of Auditors replaced the two former audit bodies of the Communities: the ECSC Auditor and the Audit Board which served the EEC and Euratom. The decision to set up this new body was linked with the decision to grant to the European Parliament the sole responsibility of discharging the Commission of its responsibility concerning the accounts of the Community. It was therefore felt that the new financial arrangements introduced by the 1975 Treaty 'should be accompanied by an intensification of control and audit and this could best be achieved by the creation of a new instrument, the Court of Auditors'.[2]

In some respects the rules governing the membership of the Court of Auditors are similar to those governing the Court of Justice.[3] At present the Court of Auditors is composed of fifteen members unanimously appointed by the Council in consultation with the European Parliament for renewable terms of six years. The Court elects a President from amongst its members for a renewable term of three years. Members of the Court are chosen from persons who have had relevant auditing experience. They must not only be independent, but must also act at all times in the interest of the Community. In the performance of their duties they must neither seek nor take instructions from any government or any other quarters. During the term of their office they may not engage in any other occupation whether gainful or not. When taking up their duties they make a solemn promise that, both during and after termination of their office, they will respect their obligations and, in particular, their duty of integrity and discretion

1 Financial Provisions Treaty 1975, Art 15, replacing EEC Treaty, Art 206. Also see Financial Regulation of 21 December 1977, Title VI (OJ 1977, L356).
2 Report of the Court of Auditors for the Financial Year 1977 (OJ 1978, C 313), at p 5, para 1.3.
3 EC Arts 246 and 247 (ex Arts 188a and 188b), replacing EC Art 206.

as regards the acceptance, after they have ceased to hold their position, of certain appointments and benefits.[4] They may be removed from office, but only if the Court of Justice is satisfied that the conditions and obligations of office are no longer being met. In such a case a member of the Court of Auditors may be deprived of his right to a pension or other benefits.[5] They enjoy the same privileges and immunities as members of the Court of Justice.

The Court of Auditors is charged with the responsibility of examining the accounts of all revenue and expenditure of the Community and of all bodies set up by the Community, unless exempted by their statutes, in a manner set out in EC Article 248 (ex Art 188c). It has to provide the EP and the Council with a statement of assurance as to the reliability of the accounts and the legality and regularity of the underlying transactions. In particular it has to probe whether all revenue has been received and all expenditure incurred in a lawful and regular manner.

It is also part of its task to examine financial management within the Community. In other words, it not only assesses the financial soundness of operations carried out, but also judges whether the means employed are the most economic and efficient. As regards management, in accordance with the Commission Decision of 1990[6] the Internal Financial Control conducts a financial audit of the Directorates-General and reports accordingly. This exercise may provide the Commission with information on financial frauds affecting the Community budget.

The audit is based on records and, if necessary, on the spot by means of visits in the institutions of the Community as well as on the premises of any body which manages revenue or expenditure on behalf of the Community and in the Member States, including on the premises of any person in receipt of payments from the budget.

In the Member States the audit is carried out in liaison with the relevant national authorities. The Court's access to information held by the European Investment Bank in respect of the Bank's activity in managing Community expenditure and revenue is subject to agreement between the Court, the Bank and the Commission.

The Court of Auditors draws up an annual report after the close of each financial year. This report, adopted by the majority of its members, is forwarded to the other institutions and must be published, together with the replies of these institutions, in the Official Journal. The institutions of the Community have the right to seek the opinion of the Court of Auditors on specific questions.[7]

The Court of Auditors assists the EP and the Council in exercising their powers of control over the implementation of the budget. The EP, in particular, regards this as a means of reinforcing its own authority over the Community resources and expenditure. The extent of its authority is perhaps best conveyed in the terms of its own first Annual Report:[8]

'The principal distinctions between the Court and its predecessors are that the Court enjoys a quasi-institutional status, its members are full-time, it has enhanced powers especially as regards the auditing of all Community income and expenditure (whether budgetized or not), it may start its work immediately

---

4   EC Art 247(5) (ex Art 188b(5)).
5   EC Art 247(7) (ex Art 188b(7)).
6   *Twenty-fourth General Report* point 1007.
7   EC Art 248(3) (ex Art 188c(3)).
8   OJ 1978, C 313, p 6, para 1.5.

expenditure has been committed, ie it need not wait until the accounts are closed, it is entitled to carry out on-the-spot audits in the Member States on its own initiative, it can make observations at any time on specific questions of its own choosing, it gives opinions on financial legislation and it publishes its reports in the Official Journal.'

The institutions of the Community have the right to seek the opinion of the Court of Auditors on specific questions. The European Parliament, in particular, regards this as a means of reinforcing its own authority over Community resources and expenditure. In a resolution on parliamentary control of Community finances which it adopted in 1976, it declared its intention 'to make use of the close and permanent assistance of the Court of Auditors'.

The personnel of the Court of Auditors comprised in 1998 412 permanent and 91 temporary posts.[9]

In accordance with the Financial Regulation the Court is obliged to forward its observation to the Commission and the other institutions and draw up an annual report which is published in the Official Journal.[10]

B.   Budgetary procedure

Since the parliamentary control of state finances is a key to the development of democratic government it is not surprising that the evolution of the European integration has been intrinsically linked with the ascendancy of the European Parliament.

The European Parliament has long had pretensions towards becoming a truly parliamentary body and it has been particularly insistent that its control not only over its own budget but also over the budget of the Communities as a whole should be increased.[11] In the first place it has always had the power to draft its own estimates and to debate the Community budgets. But apart from that the budgetary powers of the European Parliament differed originally as between the ECSC on the one hand and the EEC/Euratom on the other. In the case of the former, where funds were paid direct to the Community in the form of levies, the Parliament had virtually full power over its budget and had in practice (although not by virtue of any Treaty provision) acquired advisory rights over the whole of the ECSC budget. In the case of the EEC/Euratom, where finances used to derive from contributions from Member States, the European Parliament had no power at all and it was the Council which had a decisive voice over both the Parliament's budget and the Communities' budgets generally. Since the European Parliament received one-third of its budget from each Community this meant that it had no direct control over the allocation of two-thirds of its budget.

The question of enlarging the European Parliament's powers was discussed in 1964 in connection with the Merger Treaty, but no action was taken. It will also be recalled that a proposal that the Communities be financed independently out of their own resources instead of out of contributions from the Member States was part of the proposed package-deal which was the focus of the constitutional crisis of 1965. When the matter was considered by the Council prior to the crisis

---

9   1998 General Report (1999), para 1102.
10   See eg OJ 1996, C 340.
11   On this topic see *Les ressources propres aux Communautés européennes et les pouvoirs budgétaires du Parlement européen* (European Parliament, 1970).

there was a general consensus in favour of postponing the establishment of direct revenues until 1970 and all members except France were in favour of firmly linking the question of direct revenues with that of increasing the European Parliament's powers. After the crisis it was agreed to postpone these matters until the end of the Communities' transitional period.

Consideration was resumed at the Summit Meeting held at The Hague in December 1969. At that meeting it was agreed that with effect from 1 January 1971 the Communities would progressively draw a greater proportion of finance directly from the revenue of customs duties and levies on agricultural imports. From 1 January 1975 all such duties and levies had been paid direct to the Communities subject to a 10% rebate to cover allocation costs. The balance of the revenue necessary for the Communities is made up out of not more than 1.4% of a Value Added Tax which is in force in the Member States.[12] The system of own resources was amended in 1988. While revenues from customs duties, agricultural levies and the Value Added Tax remain (the last at a rate of 1% of the VAT assessment base as from 1999), a new fourth resource has been introduced based on the sum of all the Member States' gross national product at market prices defined in accordance with Community rules. As from 1999, the total amount of the own resources assigned to the Communities may not exceed 1.27% of the total GNPs of the Member States for payment appropriations.[13]

The Member States at The Hague Summit in 1969 also drew up the Budgetary Treaty which amended certain budgetary provisions of the founding Treaties. These included the conferment upon the European Parliament of increased budgetary powers over part of the Communities' budget, the so-called non-compulsory part, which deals with the functioning of the Communities; institutions. During the period 1971–74 the European Parliament's budgetary powers were strengthened by making it more difficult for the Council to reject amendments proposed by the Parliament. Since 1 January 1975 the European Parliament has had complete control over that part of the budget including the power to amend it.[14] The non-compulsory part of the budget amounts, in practice, to between 20 and 30%.[15] The political importance of this control may outreach the amount of money actually involved. Control over the non-compulsory part of the budget gives the European Parliament important powers in relation to the administrative costs of the institutions and such operational expenditure as the Social and Regional Funds.

As far as the remaining part of the budget is concerned the European Parliament has not been given the last word in this field. This is called the compulsory part of the budget in that it is the automatic consequence of the Community rules, most notably the cost of implementing the agricultural policy. In respect of this part of the budget the European Parliament may only propose modifications to the Council which has undertaken to give its reasons to the Parliament if it does not accept such modifications.[16]

---

12 See Council Decision 85/257/EEC, Euratom (OJ 1985, L128); repealing and replacing Council Decision 70/243.
13 The new system has been set up and is being implemented by Council Decisions 88/376 (OJ 1988, L185/24) and 94/728 (OJ 1994, L293/9) and Council Regs 1552/89 and 1553/89 (OJ 1989, L155/1 and 9). The rules for compiling the gross national product of the Member States are set out in Council Dir 89/130 (OJ 1989, L49/26). See now Regulation 1150/2000, OJ 2000, L130/11, and Decision 2000/597 (OJ 2000, L253/42).
14 Budgetary Treaty 1970, Arts 1–9.
15 See Noel, E, *Working Together: The Institutions of the European Communities* (1988), pp 33, 34.
16 Eg Budgetary Treaty 1970, Art 4.

At the time the Budgetary Treaty was signed in 1970 the Commission undertook to draft proposals to increase further the budgetary powers of the European Parliament.[17] After some delay, occasioned by the membership negotiations and the enlargement of the Community, the Commission eventually submitted its proposals in June 1973 in the form of a draft Treaty to amend further the budgetary provisions of the Community Treaties.[18] On the basis of those proposals, the governments of the Member States eventually agreed and accepted the Financial Provisions Treaty of 1975,[19] which came into force on 1 June 1977. The principal changes brought about by that Treaty were (i) to give the European Parliament the exclusive authority to adopt the annual budget and to give a discharge to the Commission in respect of its implementation; (ii) the creation of an independent Court of Auditors as a new Community institution to replace the Audit Board;[20] and (iii) that the so-called 'inverted majority rule' be applied to some proposed modifications to the compulsory part of the budget, ie that those proposals should be deemed to have been adopted unless expressly rejected by the Council. In order to promote co-operation on budgetary matters between the Council and the European Parliament a special conciliation procedure has been established under the terms of a Council Resolution of 22 April 1970.[1]

The role of the European Parliament in the budgetary procedure as amended by the Budgetary and Financial Provisions Treaties, may be described as follows.[2] The financial year of the Community is the calendar year. Each year, as a preliminary step, the Commission establishes by reference to such factors as gross national product and inflation the maximum rate by which expenditure in the coming year may be increased. Once that rate has been fixed it may be exceeded only by agreement between the Council (acting by qualified majority) and the European Parliament (acting by a majority of its members and three-fifths of the votes cast).[3] Within that framework, each institution draws up estimates of its expenditure and sends them to the Commission by 1 July. The Commission collates these estimates and forwards them to the Council by 1 September as a preliminary draft budget. This will be the subject of the so-called 'first reading' by the Council. On the basis of the preliminary draft and acting by a qualified majority[4] the Council will establish the draft budget. By 5 October the draft budget must be placed before the European Parliament for its 'first reading'. This gives the parliament the opportunity, during the ensuing 45 days, to adopt the budget or to make amendments by majority of its members and three-fifth of the votes cast to non-compulsory items and to propose modifications by an absolute majority to compulsory items.

If such amendments are made and/or modifications proposed, the draft budget thus revised is sent back to the Council for a 'second reading'. At this stage the Council, acting by a qualified majority, can in its turn modify any of the European

---

17 *Sixth General Report on the Activities of the European Communities* (1973), pp 5, 6.
18 See *Bulletin of the European Communities* (1973), Supplement 9/73.
19 OJ 1977, L359.
20 See Ch 10, infra.
1 For the text of the Resolution see *Treaties Establishing the European Communities* (1978 edn), at p 885. This conciliation procedure is quite distinct from that which was created in 1975 in connection with decision-making. Also see Council Decision 94/729 on budgetary discipline (OJ 1994, L293/14). That decision referred to an Interinstitutional Agreement of 29 October 1993 (OJ 1993, C 331/1) that was replaced by a further Agreement in 1999 (OJ 1999, C 172/1).
2 See EC Art 272 (ex Art 203), as amended, and Rules of Procedure of the European Parliament, Rule 66 and Annex IV and V.
3 EC Art 272(9) (ex Art 203(9)).
4 In accordance with EC Art 205(2) (ex Art 148(2)), as amended.

Parliament's amendments to non-compulsory items. As far as the Parliament's proposed modifications to compulsory items are concerned, the Council can accept or reject them by a qualified majority. But that basic rule is subject to important qualifications, depending whether the effect of the European Parliament's proposed modifications is simply to reallocate sums of expenditure within the total sum established in the draft budget, or whether it is to increase the size of that total sum. In the former case, the European Parliament's modifications will stand as accepted in the absence of a Council decision to reject them; in the latter case, the European Parliament's modifications will stand as rejected in the absence of a Council decision to accept them. If, at this stage, the Council should accept the modifications proposed and amendments made by the European Parliament, the draft budget is deemed to be adopted. If not, the draft budget will be returned for a 'second reading' by the European Parliament. At this final stage the Parliament has no further specific powers in respect of items of compulsory expenditure. The European Parliament does however have the last word on items of non-compulsory expenditure. The European Parliament can further amend these; for example it may reinstate its own 'first reading' amendments which may have been changed by the Council at its 'second reading'. For this purpose the Parliament must act by a majority of its members and three-fifths of the votes cast. A period of 15 days is allocated for this.

When this complex procedure has run its course, it is for the European Parliament formally to adopt the budget, ie to transform it from a draft to an operational budget for the coming year. But if there are, in the opinion of a majority of the members of the European Parliament and two-thirds of the votes cast, 'important reasons'[5] why the budget should not be adopted as it stands, the Parliament may reject it and ask for a new draft budget to be submitted to it. If, as a result of such a rejection, no budget has been adopted at the beginning of the next financial year, the Community is financed on the 'provisional twelfths' basis. Until a budget is adopted, an amount not exceeding one-twelfth of the previous year's budget may be spent during each month.[6]

The European Parliament has shown that it is prepared to reject a draft budget if it is not satisfied with it. During the consideration of the draft budget for 1980 the European Parliament made it clear that its adoption of the budget would depend, inter alia, on the Council's acceptance of increases in non-compulsory items and the implementation of measures to curb agricultural expenditure.[7] A lengthy use of the conciliation procedure[8] failed to secure the Council's agreement, particularly in relation to the latter point. The European Parliament therefore rejected the budget on 13 December 1979 because the conditions which it had set had not be satisfied.[9] The budget for 1980 was not finally agreed and adopted until 9 July 1980,[10] the date on which the Commission completed its preparation of the preliminary draft budget for 1981![11] Thus the European Parliament 'demonstrated its determination to exercise its budgetary powers to the full'.[12]

5　See EC Art 272(8) (ex Art 203(8)).
6　See EC Art 273 (ex Art 204).
7　See *Bulletin of the European Communities*, 1979–11, pp 86, 108.
8　See *Thirteenth General Report on the Activities of the European Communities* (1980), pp 46, 48.
9　See *Bulletin of the European Communities*, 1979–12, p 120.
10　See *Fourteenth General Report on the Activities of the European Communities* (1981), p 47.
11　Ibid, pp 47, 48.
12　See *Thirteenth General Report on the Activities of the European Communities* (1980), p 24. Also see Sopwith, Sir C, 'Legal Aspects of the Community Budget' (1980) 17 CML Rev 315 and Pipkorn, J, 'Legal Implications of the Absence of the Community Budget at the Beginning of a Financial Year' (1981) 18 CML Rev 141. The 1985 budget was also rejected; see European Parliament: *The Impact of the European Parliament on Community Policies* (Research and Documentation Papers, Action Taken Series No 3, 1988), at pp 16–17.

While the European Parliament now has real budgetary powers, they are clearly not without limitation. Although its President alone has the power to adopt the budget it is clear, as the European Court has pointed out,[13] that during the budgetary procedure the European Parliament must act in partnership with the Council under the terms laid down in the Treaty. In 1985 the Commission for the purposes of the 1986 budget fixed the maximum rate of increase for non-compulsory expenditure at 7.1%.[14] In establishing the draft budget for 1986 the Council provided for a 7.05% increase for non-compulsory expenditure. During the course of the budgetary procedure the European Parliament argued for a greater rate of increase. After recourse to conciliation the Council proposed a new maximum rate of 14.6%. The European Parliament did not agree and after further conciliation the Council proposed an increase of 17.02%, subject to acceptance by the European Parliament. Without making a direct response to that proposal the Parliament proceeded to resolve to increase non-compulsory expenditure by 19.5%. The Council thereupon withdrew its proposal, but the President of the Parliament nevertheless declared the budget to be adopted and so informed the Council. These events prompted actions in the European Court to annul the 1986 budget and/or its final adoption.[15] Following its own previous case law the Court had no hesitation in accepting the admissibility of the action.[16] On the merits the Court held that since the Treaty laid down no criteria for increasing the maximum rate fixed by the Commission but made it a matter for agreement between the Council and the Parliament, an agreement of such importance may not be inferred from the presumed intention of one or other of those institutions.[17] It therefore concluded that at the time the President purported to adopt the budget the budgetary procedure had not in fact been completed since there was no agreement on the maximum rate of increase. Therefore the adoption of the budget was vitiated by illegality.[18] In an interim order the Court had already authorized the implementation of the 1986 budget to the extent that its legality was not being challenged.[19] In its final judgment it did not order the budgetary procedure to be reopened from the beginning, but that it resume at the point at which the parliament adopted an excessive rate of increase.[20] Within one week of the judgment agreement was reached by Council and Parliament. The budget which was formally and legally adopted a week later ironically exceeded that which the Court had annulled.[1]

Against this background of repeated conflict and crisis which dates back to the early 1980s, it is encouraging to be able to report that the budgets for 1989 and 1990 were adopted on time and in compliance with the Inter-institutional Agreement between the Commission, the Council and the Parliament on budgetary

---

13   Case 34/86: *Council v European Parliament* [1986] ECR 2155, [1986] 3 CMLR 94.
14   The facts are conveniently sent out ibid, at 96–101.
15   Individual actions were first brought by Luxembourg, the Netherlands, France, Germany and the United Kingdom but it was agreed to proceed with the Council's action. See Case 23/86R: *United Kingdom v European Parliament* [1986] 3 CMLR 82 and Case 34/86: *Council v European Parliament* [1986] ECR 2155, [1986] 3 CMLR 94.
16   See Case 294/83: *Parti Ecologiste Les Verts v European Parliament* [1986] ECR 1339, [1987] 2 CMLR 343.
17   [1986] ECR 2155, para 34, [1986] 3 CMLR at p 149.
18   Ibid, at p 150.
19   Cited ibid, at pp 101–102.
20   Ibid, at pp 150–152.
 1   See *Twentieth General Report on the Activities of the European Communities* (1987), pp 54, 57 and Table 1 on p 55.

discipline and improvement of budgetary procedure of 1988.[2] That Agreement and its associated Council Decision,[3] which incorporate budget forecasts and a financial perspective for the period 1988 to 1992, had a positive and beneficial effect on the budgetary process.[4]

Under the financial framework laid down for 1993–99 at the Edinburgh Council[5] the own resources ceiling was to rise gradually from 1.20% of GNP in 1993 to 1.27% in 1999 and the structure of these resources would change. Thus between 1995 and 1999 the call-in rate for VAT gradually droped from 1.4% to 1.0% of the common base. For countries with per capita GNP of less than 90% of the Community average, the base to be taken into account for the VAT resource was reduced from 55% to 50% of GNP of the Member States concerned whilst for the others that change was to be implemented in stages during 1995–99.

Under a new Inter-institutional Agreement signed by the Council and Parliament[6] a conciliation procedure for compulsory expenditure was introduced and this secured some influence of the EP over a category of expenditure for which the Council is ultimately responsible. However, should the conciliation fail, the procedure laid down in EC Article 272 (ex Art 203) will apply.

As a result of the Edinburgh Council the Commission adopted proposals replacing Decision 88/377[7] concerning budgetary discipline, establishing a Guarantee Fund to cover the risks incurred under guarantees from the general budget amending the 1977 Financial Regulation[8] and amending Regulation 1552/89[9] on the system of own resources.

The preliminary draft budget for 1994 which was formally adopted by the Commission on 21 June 1993 was drawn up in accordance with the financial guidelines adopted at Edinburgh. The allocation for the Cohesion Fund was increased for research and technological development, the trans-European networks and other internal policies besides aid to developing countries, the Mediterranean countries, and the programmes for the East European countries. After some adjustments by the Commission and Parliament on the subsequent reading the budget for 1994, in an atmosphere of calm, was adopted in December 1993.[10]

The 1995 budget procedure was to be governed by the rules of the inter-institutional agreement on budgetary discipline and improvement of the budgetary procedure.[11] However protracted negotiations and delays impeded the process and eventually the President of the EP declared the budget as adopted. This, in turn, led the Council to challenge the President's decision[12] as premature bearing in mind that there was an unresolved disagreement on certain items, in particular, concerning compulsory expenditure. The Court of Justice ruled that Parliament's vote and the President's decision were in breach of the Treaty and of the inter-institutional agreement and

2 See *Twenty-second* and *Twenty-third General Reports on the Activities of the European Communities* (1989) and (1990), at pp 66–71 and 69 respectively.
3 OJ 1988, L185/24 and 33.
4 See European Parliament: *The Work of the European Parliament: July 1988–June 1989* (1989), at pp 19–23.
5 See *Twenty-sixth General Report* (1993), point 13 et seq.
6 OJ 1993, C 331 and EC Bull 10–1993, point 15.1.
7 OJ 1988, L185.
8 OJ 1977, L356.
9 OJ 1989, L155.
10 EC Bull 12—1993.
11 OJ 1993, C 331; *Twenty-seventh General Report*, point 1978.
12 Case C-41/95: *Council v Parliament* [1995] ECR I-4411, referred to in the 1994 General Report, point 1118.

annulled the act in question because the budgetary procedure was not completed. However, since the financial year was almost over the Court upheld the invalid budget until a new budget could be adopted, thus avoiding the application of the provisional twelfth arrangements.

The budgets for 1996[13] and for 1997[14] revealed the usual wrangling between the three *dramatis personae* of the budgetary exercise over the allocation expenditure. It is clear that the division of the budget into a compulsory and a non-compulsory part and the respective responsibility of the EP and the Council shall remain a source of friction in the future. At the time of writing, budgetary procedure is the subject of an Interinstitutional Agreement made in May 1999.[15]

The EC Treaty contains some new provisions concerning financial arrangements. In the first place[16] without prejudice to other revenue the budget shall be financed wholly from own resources but the Council, acting unanimously on a proposal from the Commission and after consulting the EP, shall lay down provisions relating to the system of own resources. The Council shall then submit its scheme to the Member States for adoption in accordance with their respective constitutions.

Secondly,[17] the administrative expenditure to be incurred by the institutions in respect of a common foreign and security policy and co-operation in the areas of justice and home affairs shall be charged to the budget.

To maintain the budgetary discipline[18] the Commission is precluded from making proposals for a Community act or for implementing measures which are likely to have appreciable implications for the budget without making sure that such a venture is capable of being financed within the Community's resources.

Finally, alarmed by the spread of fraud on the Community resources reported by the Member States[19] the EC Treaty[20] enjoins the Member States to take the same measures to combat fraud affecting the Community financial interests as they do to combat fraud which debilitates their own financial interests. To that end they ought to co-ordinate their action and, with the assistance of the Commission, organize close and regular co-operation between the competent departments of their administration.

Fraud on the Community financial interests remains a continuous concern.[1] To combat this phenomenon, which threatens the political credibility of the European Union,[2] the internal organization of the Commission departments responsible for the prevention of fraud has established a Unit for the Co-ordination of Fraud Prevention (UCLAF) and resorted to wider use of data-processing methods. In 1995 UCLAF had at its disposal 120 staff engaged mainly in investigative field operations.[3]

---

13 See 1996 General Report (1997) point 989 et seq.
14 Ibid, point 977 et seq. For the 1999 budgetary procedure, see the 1998 General Report (1999), para 985–992.
15 OJ 1999, C 172/1.
16 EC Art 269 (ex Art 201).
17 EC Art 268(2) (ex Art 199(2)).
18 EC Art 270 (ex Art 201a).
19 In 1992 ECU 152.1 million of Community resources and ECU 117.8 million of the EAGGF Guarantee Section relating mainly to olive oil, beef and milk powder was lost because of fraud; *Twenty-seventh General Report* (1984), p 392.
20 EC Art 280 (ex Art 209a).
 1 See 1995 General Report (1996), p 413 and 1996 General Report (1997), p 403.
 2 Bull 3–1996, point 1.6.12.
 3 See 1996 General Report, supra, point 1014.

In 1996 the Commission adopted a programme on fraud prevention[4] and the Council adopted regulation 2185/96[5] providing a legal basis for conducting inspections and on-the-spot checks carried out by Commission staff in the Member States. However the Amsterdam Treaty did little to improve the efficiency of the preventive system. It only exhorted the Council, after consulting the Court of Auditors, 'to adopt the necessary measures in the fields of the prevention of and fight against fraud ... with a view to affording effective and equivalent protection in the Member States'.[6] To this vacuous wording it added the proviso that 'these measures shall not concern the application of national criminal law and the national administration of justice'.[7] It is difficult to see how repressive measures envisaged by the Treaty can operate in isolation from national substantive law and procedure. The repeated concern about fraud led in 1999 to the creation of a new body, the European Anti-fraud Office (or OLAF), which has extensive powers of investigation, and to the adoption of further measures directed against fraud and internal corruption.[8]

---

4   COM(96) 17, Bull 1.2–1996, point 1.6.7.
5   OJ 1996, L292; Bull 11–96, point 1.6.8.
6   EC Art 280(4) (ex Art 209a(4)) (introduced by the Amsterdam Treaty).
7   EC Art 280(4) (ex Art 209a(4)).
8   See Commission Decision 1999/352, establishing OLAF; the Interinstitutional Agreement between the EP, the Council and the Commission concerning investigations by OLAF; and Regs 1073/1999 and 1074/1999 concerning those investigations (OJ 1999 L136, pages 20, 15, 1 and 8, respectively); and Council Decision 1999/394 and Commission Decision 1999/396, both concerning internal investigations in relation to the prevention of fraud, corruption and so forth (OJ 1999, L149, pp 36 and 57, respectively).

Chapter 11

Ancillary Community institutions

A. Introduction

In addition to the principal institutions already mentioned there are a number of ancillary institutions which either advise on or otherwise participate in the activities of the Communities. Some of these owe their origin to the Treaties themselves; others have been established in the light of experience.

B. Consultative bodies

(1)   THE ECSC CONSULTATIVE COMMITTEE

The Consultative Committee established under the ECSC Treaty[1] ought to consist of between 72 and 96 members made up of an equal number of producers, workers, consumers and dealers. At present the national representation appears as follows: Germany 19, the United Kingdom 18, France 13, Italy 9, Belgium and Spain eight each, the Netherlands, Sweden and Austria five each, Luxembourg four, and Denmark, Finland, Greece, Ireland and Portugal, three each. Members of the Committee are appointed for two years in their personal capacity by the Council from a list drawn up by organizations representing the above-mentioned interests. Generally the functions of the Committee are comparable with the functions of the Economic and Social Committee[2] but specifically it is concerned with economic and social problems of the coal and steel industry. For example, it was consulted on the market of solid fuels in 1992[3] and in 1993 and 1994;[4] on the European Energy Charter;[5] on trade agreements with East European Countries;[6] it adopted a resolution on social research;[7] it exchanged views with the Commission on co-operation with

1   Arts 18 and 19.
2   See below.
3   Bull 4 – 1992; see also Resolution on coal policy in the internal market (OJ 1992, C 94).
4   Bull 3 – 1994, point 1.2.82; Bull 10 – 1994, point 1.2.60.
5   Bull 10 – 1994, points 1.3.23–1.3.25.
6   1994 General Report (1995) p 429 and 1995 General Report (1996) p 451.
7   OJ 1995, C 206.

countries of Eastern Europe and the former Soviet Union on restructuring their steel industries;[8] adopted a memorandum on the social aspects connected with the expiry of the ECSC Treaty;[9] etc.

(2) THE SCIENTIFIC AND TECHNICAL COMMITTEE OF EURATOM

The Committee established under Article 134 of the EAEC Treaty, attached to the Commission, consists of 33 members appointed for five years in their personal capacity by the Council in consultation with the Commission. Its main task is to give the Commission advice before setting up the Joint Nuclear Research Centre and on the standards for the protection of the workers and general public from ionising radiations.[10]

(3) THE ECONOMIC AND SOCIAL COMMITTEE

The Economic and Social Committee, appointed under the terms of EC Articles 257 and 262 (ex Arts 193 and 198), EAEC Articles 165 and 169[11] and Article 5 of the Common Institutions Convention, consists of 222 persons representing producers, farmers, carriers, workers, dealers, craftsmen, professional occupations and the general public. The 222 members are allocated on a national basis as follows: France, Germany, Italy and the United Kingdom have 24 each, Spain has 21, Belgium, Greece, the Netherlands, Portugal Austria and Sweden have 12 each, Denmark Finland and Ireland have nine each and Luxembourg has six.

In the case of both Committees although the members are appointed for a renewable term of four years by the Council from lists provided by the Member States[12] they are appointed in their private capacity and are expressly forbidden to act on any mandate or instructions from the bodies nominating them. There is also an obligation on the Council to consult the Commission on appointments to the Economic and Social Committee and it may also obtain the opinion of European organizations representing particular economic and social sectors of interest. Subject to such considerations, the Council has a wide discretion. Given the limited number of places on the Economic and Social Committee, it is not possible for each category of activity to be represented by nationals of each Member State; the Committee's representative character is to be achieved at the Community level. It is the responsibility of the Council to ensure this.[13] The Committee itself is divided into three groups each representing a particular set of interests: Group I, the Employers' Group, is made up of representatives of employers' organizations and chambers of commerce; Group II, the Workers' Group, is made up of representatives of trade unions; and Group III, the Various Interests' Group, which includes representatives of small businesses, the co-operative movement, consumer and family organizations, the environmental lobby, the professions and local government.[14] It is the practice of the Committee, rather like that of the European

---

8 Bull 3 – 1995, point 1.10.25.
9 Bull 10 – 1996, point 1.10.28. See also the 1998 General Report on the activities of the EU, para 1114.
10 See eg Dir 84/467/Euratom, OJ 1984, L265, which amended Dir 80/836 (OJ 1980, L246(1).
11 As amended by the First Act of Accession, Art 21, the Second Act of Accession, Art 18, Third Act of Accession 1985, Art 21, Fourth Act of Accession 1995.
12 EC Art 259 (ex Art 195).
13 See Case 297/86: *Confederazione italiana dirigenta di azienda v Council* (C104) [1988] ECR 3531, at pp 3354–3355, [1989] 3 CMLR 851.
14 See EC Art 257 (ex Art 193); Economic and Social Committee *Annual Report* 1989 Ch IV.

Parliament and its political groups, for its members to vote by group and not by nationality. The members of the Committee may not be bound by any mandatory instructions. They are completely independent in the performance of their duties in the general interests of the Community.[15]

The Committee elects its own president from among its members for a term of two years and adopts its own Rules of Procedure.[16] The meetings of the Committee are convened by its president at the request of the Council or of the Commission.[17] The members of the Committee enjoy the privileges and immunities laid down in the Protocol to the Treaty.[18] The Committee must include specialised sections for the principal fields of activity covered by the Treaty. It currently comprises six sections: economic and monetary union and social cohesion; single market, production and consumption; transport, energy, infrastructure and the information society; employment, social affairs and citizenship; agriculture, rural development and the environment; and external relations.[19]

The Committee must be consulted by the Council or the Commission where the Treaty so provides and may be consulted by the EP.[20] Although the opinions of the Committee are not binding on the Council or the Commission the failure to consult where consultation is obligatory enables the Court of Justice to annul the final act of the Council on the ground of the infringement of an essential procedural requirement. The EC Treaty provides for consultation on a number of issues, notably the Common Agricultural Policy;[1] movement of persons;[2] right of establishment;[3] freedom of services;[4] transport policy;[5] harmonization of taxes;[6] approximation of laws;[7] employment policy;[8] working conditions;[9] equal pay,[10] the European Social Fund;[11] education, vocational training and youth;[12] public health;[13] consumer protection;[14] trans-european networks,[15] industry;[16] economic and social cohesion;[17] research and technology[18] and the environment.[19]

With only 135 permanent staff and 516 shared with the Committee of the Regions, the Economic and Social Committee adopted in 1998 192 opinions and

---

15 EC Art 258 (ex Art 194).
16 See EC Art 260 (ex Art 196). The Treaty refers to the president as the 'chairman' of the Committee. For the Rules of Procedure, see decision 96/235 (OJ 1996, L82/1).
17 EC Art 260 (ex Art 196).
18 Rules of Procedure, Rule 58(2).
19 Ibid, EC Art 261 (ex Art 197), Rules of Procedure, Rule 11.
20 EC Art 262 (ex Art 198).
 1 EC Art 37(2) (ex Art 43(2)).
 2 EC Art 40(1) (ex Art 49(1)).
 3 EC Art 44(1) (ex Art 54(1)).
 4 EC Art 52(1) (ex Art 63(1)).
 5 EC Art 71(2) (ex Art 75(2)) and Art 79 (ex Art 83).
 6 EC Art 93 (ex Art 99).
 7 EC Art 94 (ex Art 100).
 8 EC Art 128(2) (ex Art 109q).
 9 EC Art 137(2) (ex Art 118(2)).
10 EC Art 141(3) (ex Art 119(3)) and Art 143 (ex Art 120).
11 EC Art 148 (ex Art 125).
12 EC Art 149(4) (ex Art 126(4)) and Art 150(4) (ex Art 127(4)).
13 EC Art 152(4) (ex Art 129(4)).
14 EC Art 153(4) (ex Art 129a(4)).
15 EC Art 156 (ex Art 129d).
16 EC Art 157(3) (ex Art 130(3)).
17 EC Art 159 (ex Art 130b) and Art 161 (ex Art 130d).
18 EC Art 175 (ex Art 130i) and Art 172 (ex Art 130o).
19 EC Art 175 (ex Art 130s).

two information reports. Its opinion was requested on 71 occasions where it was compulsory and 89 times when it was optional.[20] It is clear that the Treaty allocated to the Committee an important advisory role in a substantial range of matters and that the institutions increasingly avail themselves of the expertise of the Committee.

(4)   THE COMMITTEE OF THE REGIONS

This Committee was established under the Maastricht Treaty[1] with advisory status on the same lines as the Economic and Social Committee. The members of the Committee are appointed for a renewable term of four years by the Council unanimously on proposals from the respective Member States and their numbers as per Member State are the same as numbers of the Economic and Social Committee. The Members of the Committee are completely independent in the performance of their duties in the general interests of the Community. They cannot be bound by any mandatory instructions and their appointment is incompatible with the membership of the European Parliament.[2]

The Committee of the Regions adopts its own Rules of Procedure,[3] elects its chairman (or president) and officers from among its members for a term of two years. It meets as convened by the chairman at the request of the Council or the Commission or on its own initiative. It is consulted by the Council or the Commission where provided by the Treaty and in all other cases, in particular those which concern cross-border co-operation.[4] It is informed of all requests for an opinion addressed to the Economic and Social Committee and where it considers that specific regional interests are involved the Committee of the Regions may issue opinions of its own initiative. It may also be consulted by the European Parliament. Its own remit comprises consultations in matters related to education;[5] the European Social Fund;[6] vocational training and youth;[7] culture;[8] public health;[9] trans-European networks;[10] economic and social cohesion[11] and the environment.[12] Many activities of the Committee are centred on the economic and social issues facing the border regions but impinge also on the formation of Community legislation and the integration process generally. Reflecting the aspirations of the citizens of Europe, the Committee, still in its infancy, has a substantial economic and political potential contributing to the elimination of political frontiers between Member States and direct co-operation between their people.

(5)   OTHER ADVISORY COMMITTEES

The Commission is surrounded by committees of experts[13] relating to specific areas of Community activity, eg economic policy, transport, customs, research

---

20   1998 General Report (1999), paras 1103 and 1107.
1   Amsterdam EC Art 263, (ex Art 198a).
2   Ibid.
3   See OJ 2000, L18/22.
4   EC Art 265, (ex Art 198c).
5   EC Art 137(3) (ex Art 118(3)).
6   EC Art 148 (ex Art 125).
7   EC Art 149(4) (ex Art 126(4)) and Art 150(4) (ex Art 127(4)).
8   EC Art 151(5) (ex Art 128(5)).
9   EC Art 152(4) (ex Art 129(4)).
10   EC Art 156 (ex Art 129d).
11   EC Art 159 (ex Art 130b).
12   EC Art 175 (ex Art 130s).
13   Some 235 in number, See Rideau, J, *Droit Institutionnel de l'Union et des Communeautés Européennes* (2nd edn, 1996), p 310.

and technology, agriculture, employment, European Social Funds, consumer policy, social security, hygiene and safety at work, public health, legal profession, procurement and contracts and the co-ordination of the internal market. The committees are composed of government and non-government experts, or of both. Perhaps the most important of these committees are:

(a) Economic and Financial Committee

A Monetary Committee was set up under the terms of EC Article 105 to keep the monetary and financial position of the Member States under review. Under the amended Treaty[14] a new Monetary Committee, consisting of two members from each Member State and two from the Commission was created to keep under review the monetary situation of the Member States and of the Community. At the start of the third stage of the Monetary Union it was to be dissolved and replaced by the Economic and Financial Committee. The latter shall deliver opinions at the request of the Council or the Commission or on its own initiative, keep under review the economic and financial situation of the Member States and of the Community and pave the way to the achieving of the Economic and Monetary Union.

The Member States, the Commission and the European Central Bank shall each appoint two members of the Committee.[15]

(b) Customs Code Committee

A Customs Committee was appointed by the Council under the terms of Article 111 of the EEC Treaty (now repealed) to assist the Commission in tariff negotiations with third countries and various technical committees to administer the Common Customs Tariff and the protective measures under the Common Commercial Policy. Under the Community Customs Code[16] which consolidated the Community Customs Law, the Customs Code Committee[17] supervises the administration of the various aspects of Customs law. It consists of the representatives of the Member States chaired by a representative of the Commission.

(c) Transport Committee

EC Article 79 (ex Art 83) provides for the establishment of an Advisory Committee, consisting of experts designated by the Member States, attached to the Commission. The Commission is free to consult the Committee on transport matters without prejudice to the powers of the Economic and Social Committee.

(d) Employment Committee

Alarmed by the level of unemployment in the Community the makers of the Amsterdam Treaty put the policy of employment high on the agenda.[18] Accordingly[19] the Council was charged with the establishment of an Employment Committee 'with advisory status to promote co-ordination between Member States on employment and labour market policies'. The Committee consists of two

---

14 EC Art 114(1) (ex Art 109c(1)).
15 EC Art 114(2) (ex Art 109c(2)). See Council Dec 98/743 on the composition of the Committee (OJ 1998, L358/109) and the Statutes of the Committee (OJ 1999, L5/72).
16 Reg 2913/92 (OJ 1992, L302/1).
17 Ibid, Arts 247–249.
18 EC Arts 125–130 (ex Arts 109m–109s).
19 EC Art 130 (ex Art 109s).

members from each State and the Commission. Its task is to monitor the employment situation and employment policies in the Member States and the Community, and to formulate opinions at the request of either the Council or the Commission or on its own initiative and to contribute to the preparation of the Council's guidelines in this area.

(e) The Functions of the Committees
Although the opinions of these consultative committees are in no way binding they are not without their influence. The suggestion has been made that they may be more influential than the opinions of the European Parliament since they are the informed views of those involved in activities likely to be affected by the policies of the Communities.[20] The Commission appears to treat their views with respect and the Economic Social Committee has certainly tended to support the Commission's proposals. The Council in the past adopted a more restrictive attitude.[1] More recently, the Committee has had some success in developing more systematic contacts with the Council. In 1987 for the first time the President-in-Office of the Council addressed the Committee on matters to be discussed at a forthcoming meeting of the European Council.[2] Indeed, since that time a pattern has developed of ministers from the Member State occupying the presidency addressing meetings of the Committee.[3] Steps have also been taken to improve co-operation between the two institutions, in particular by ensuring that the Committee's Opinions are received by the Member States as soon as they are issued and by monitoring that due account is taken of such Opinions.[4] Since 1972 the Committee's right to advise on its own initiative on all matters affecting the Community has been recognized and regular use has been made of this right.[5]

C. Management and regulatory committees

We have already seen that, with the development of the common policies of the Communities into new areas, particularly agriculture, the Council has delegated to the Commission considerable law-making powers. Under the terms of the Treaties the Commission is not in a subordinate position to the Council, and so if this delegation took the form of empowering the Commission to act independently it would remove such matters entirely from the control of the Council. Further, since these powers would have been transferred to the Commission by the Council upon the Commission's proposal, it is believed that the Commission could only be deprived of such powers by the same process, namely on the Commission's initiative. The member governments wished to avoid

---

20 See Torelli, M, *L'Individu et le Droit de la CEE* (1970), at p 58, and Zellentin, G, 'The Economic and Social Committee' (1962) I Journal of Common Market Studies 22. For a review of the influence of the Committee's Opinions, see *Annual Report 1988*, Table C, p 107 et seq.
1 See Palmer, M, et al, *European Unity* (1968), at p 186.
2 See *Annual Report 1987*, p 9.
3 See *Annual Reports 1987, 1988 and 1989*, at pp 9, 10 and 11–12 respectively.
4 See *Annual Reports 1988 and 1989*, at p 11 and Annex B respectively.
5 See *Sixth General Report on the Activities of the European Communities* (1973) at p 16; Economic and Social Committee: *The Right of Initiative of the Economic and Social Committee* (1977); and the Committee's Rules of Procedure, Decision 96/235 (OJ 1996, L82/1), in particular Rule C. The monthly *Bulletin* and the *Annual Report* of the Committee record this and other aspects of its activities.

these consequences of delegation which might prove disadvantageous to themselves. In addition, particularly in the field of agriculture, it was practically desirable that the process of implementing the common policies should be carried out in close consultation with the governments of the Member States. The system of Management Committees was devised to achieve those objectives.

The management committee procedure was introduced by Regulation 19 of 1962.[6] Article 25 of that Regulation established a Management Committee for Cereal Products made up of representatives of the Member States and presided over by a representative of the Commission. Similar management committees have since been set up for each of the main categories of agricultural products. The chairman of a management committee is a member of the staff of the Commission, usually the head of the Department which covers the products dealt with by the Committee. The chairman has no vote. The procedure is for the Commission to submit a draft implementing measure to the appropriate management committee for its opinion. The management committee employs the system of weighted voting used in the Council itself. The management committee's opinion is not binding on the Commission. The Commission may modify its draft in the light of the opinion or adhere to its original proposal. In either event the Commission's decision, after submission of its proposal to the management committee, will have the immediate force of law. But if there is a conflict between the views of the Commission and the opinion of the Committee and if that opinion has received the qualified majority of 62 votes, the matter must be referred to the Council which may within a period of one month reverse the Commission's decision. If, on the other hand, the Commission's draft is acceptable to the Committee or if the Committee is opposed to it but cannot muster the qualified majority or if the Committee fails to respond to the request for an opinion,[7] the Commission's decision is not subject to an appeal to the Council.

It is generally agreed that the management committee procedure works well in practice. In 1989 as a result of 318 meetings of management committees 1,449 favourable opinions were expressed, no opinion was expressed in 133 cases, and an unfavourable opinion was expressed in only one case.[8] This is a typical situation and it testifies to the degree of co-operation and mutual confidence between the Commission and the Member States which has been engendered by this procedure. When the Commission differs from a committee opinion given by a qualified majority, which happens infrequently, the procedure operates as an alarm mechanism and gives a clear indication of a serious problem which can be effectively resolved only by the Member States acting through the Council. The original intention was that this procedure should only be resorted to during the transitional period of the Community's development but because of its success it has been expressly continued in existence for an indefinite period.[9]

6   JO No 30 of 4 April 1962, p 933/62, since replaced by what is now Regulation 1766/92 (OJ 1992, L181/21) as amended.
7   See Case 35/78: *N G J Schouten BV v Hoofdproduktschap Voor Akkerbouwprodukten* [1978] ECR 2543 at 2558.
8   See *Twenty-third General Report on the Activities of the European Communities* (1990), Table 14, at p 258.
9   See Regulation 2602/69 (JO 1969, L324). See also Council Decision 1999/468, Art 4 (OJ 1999, L184/23) and the Declarations published in OJ 1999, C 203/1.

Another development has been the application of a similar procedure to areas of community activity other than the agricultural, with a result that committees of government representatives have been set up to assist in the implementation of the common customs tariff and in connection with the control of standards in relation to food and animal health.[10] These latter committees, whilst they are manifestations of the management committee procedure, are usually distinguished from the management committees properly so-called and are referred to as regulatory committees. In connection with these committees the powers delegated by the Council to the Commission are more circumscribed. The Commission's proposal only has immediate binding effect if it is approved by the committee. If the committee disapproves of a proposal by an opinion reached by the qualified majority, or if no opinion is forthcoming because of the committee's inability to reach the qualified majority, then the Commission must refer its proposal to the Council for acceptance by a qualified majority vote. There is a final rider to this procedure, however, and that is if the Council in such a case has failed to take a decision within three months then the Commission itself may adopt the proposed measure and it will thereby acquire the force of law. In Community jargon this is known as the 'net' or *'filet'* procedure. The management committee procedure is also incorporated into the machinery for administering structural funds such as the European Regional Development Fund.[11]

The constitutional validity of the management and rule-making committee procedures has been questioned in the past.[12] The crux of the question is the vagueness of the Treaty provisions relating to the delegation of powers by the Council to the Commission. EC Article 211 (ex Art 155) in its final provision states that the Commission shall 'exercise the powers conferred on it by the Council for the implementation of the rules laid down by the latter'. It has been argued that the force of that provision is to enable the Council to confer upon the Commission powers which are materially identical with the powers possessed by the Council itself. Thus, where under EC Article 37(2) (ex Art 43(2)) the Council has the power to adopt regulations for the implementation of the Common Agricultural Policy, if the Council purports to delegate that power to the Commission it may only do so absolutely and not conditionally. By imposing the management committee procedure upon the powers delegated it has been suggested that the Council is making an unlawful change in the decision-making powers of the Commission. In other words the suggestion is that the management committee procedure depends on political expediency within the Communities rather than on constitutional authority under the terms of the Treaty.

The view taken by both the Commission and Council in support of the management committee procedures is that they are perfectly compatible with the Treaties. The view of these institutions was clearly put by the Commission in its *Second General Report on the Activities of the Communities* (1968).[13] There

---

10   Eg the Committee on Origin, originally established by Reg 802/68 (OJ 1968, L148); the Standing Veterinary Committee established by Council Decision 68/361 (JO 1968, L255); and the Common Customs Tariff Nomenclature Committee established by Reg 97/69, (JO 1969, L14). The first and third Committees were effectively replaced by a single Customs Code Committee created by Reg 2913/92 (OJ 1992, L302/48).

11   See Regulation 4253/88 (OJ 1988, L 374/1), Arts 27–30.

12   Eg Schindler, P, 'The Problems of Decision-Making by way of Management Committee procedure in the EEC' (1971) 8 CMLRev 184.

13   Paras 639–42. Also see *Rapport sur les procédures communautaires d'exécution du droit communautaire dérivé* (European Parliament, Document de Séance, No 115/68).

it is pointed out that whilst EC Article 155 (now Art 211) does not prevent the Council from exercising its implementing powers itself, it is clear that any implementing powers not retained by the Council may only be delegated to the Commission. Further the Council is, in any event, bound to observe the institutional balance of the Communities.

As early as 1958 in the case of *Meroni & Co v High Authority*[14] the Court of Justice commented on the general concept of delegated powers in the Communities. In its judgment in that case the Court stressed the necessity of preserving the balance of powers which is a characteristic of the institutional structure of the Communities and concluded that any delegation of a discretionary power upon institutions different from those established by the Treaties would be invalid.[15] These principles laid down in the *Meroni* case underlie the judgment of the Court in three cases decided in December 1970 in which the validity of the management committee procedures was directly challenged.[16]

Part of the Community's agricultural policy takes the form of regulations to forestall unexpected movements of agricultural products which, if permitted, would threaten the common organization of markets in those products. To that end the Commission has made regulations providing for compulsory import and export certificates to be obtained by those who wish to make imports or exports of particular agricultural products. It is further required that such certificates should be supported by the payment of a security which will be forfeit if the imports or exports were not made during the period of the certificate's validity. In these cases the legality of this system of certificates was challenged on the ground, inter alia, that the management committee procedure which had been employed in the making of the regulations was contrary to the EC Treaty.

The arguments against the legality of the management committee procedure were that it permitted the management committees to interfere in the legislative activities of the Commission, that it gave to the Member States a right of appeal to the Council against a Commission regulation, thus derogating from the rôle of the Court, and that consequently it disturbed the institutional balance of the Community. The Council expressed the contrary view in terms which have already been outlined above. The Court supported the Council's view. It held that EC Article 155 (now Art 211) which authorizes the Council to delegate rule-implementing powers to the Commission must be understood as permitting the Council to lay down provisions and procedures whereby its own policy decisions may be implemented. The management committee procedure was held to come within the modalities upon which the Council is allowed to make such an authorization of the Commission dependent. Further, the allegation that the management committees interfere in the legislative activities of the Commission was not substantiated since the rôle of a management committee is merely to give opinions and it has no power to make decisions. Its views may influence the Commission but, subject to one proviso, the power of decision remains with the Commission. As far as the proviso is concerned, which involves the allegation that the management committee procedure gives a right of appeal to the Council from a decision of the Commission, this the Court also held to be unsubstantiated. The management committee procedure merely enables the Council to take action instead of the

14 Case 9/56: [1957–58] ECR 133.
15 Ibid at 150. Also see Case 23/75: *Rey Soda v Cassa Conguaglio Zucchero* [1975] ECR 1279 at 1300.
16 Case 25/70: *Einfuhr-und Vorratsstelle für Getreide und Füttermittel v Koster, Berodt & Co* [1970] ECR 1161, [1972] CMLR 255.

Commission where the committee hands down a negative opinion. Practice has shown these cases to be exceptional and in any event whether the final decision is made by the Commission or Council the powers of the Court to review such decisions are left unimpaired.

Finally, the Court said that there is no question of this procedure disturbing the institutional equilibrium of the Communities. The Council has in effect delegated powers to the Commission subject to the condition that the opinion of the appropriate management committee is sought. Regardless of the contents of that opinion the Commission has the power to make binding decisions. In the event of an adverse opinion the Commission is obliged to refer its decision to the Council which may then choose to substitute its own decision for that of the Commission. Thus the Council is merely reserving to itself the freedom to use its own rule-making power in circumstances in which there is a substantial difference of opinion between its delegate, the Commission, and the representatives of the Member States. Since the rôle of the management committees is essentially consultative and since, subject to the power to delegate, the rule-making powers are conferred by the Treaty upon the Council, the institutional order was held to be unaffected. It is submitted that these conclusions apply equally to rule-making committees.

There is general agreement that the management committee procedure works well. Not only has it been decided to retain it indefinitely but more use is likely to be made of it in future in view of the Council's decision to make wider use of its powers under the last paragraph of EC Article 211 (ex Art 155).[17] In delicate areas of Community policy which impinge on individual national interests the management committee procedure has made it possible for considerable progress to be made in the implementation of that policy. But for the introduction of management committee procedures which provide a means for close consultation between the Commission and the governments of the Member States, the Council would probably have been reluctant to transfer wide-ranging legislative powers to the Commission. As a result the Commission's authority within the EC has tended to be strengthened. Thus the political significance of the management committee procedures must not be overlooked. As one commentator has observed, it has enabled the wills of the Member States to be joined in common activity, thus achieving one of the basic aims of the Communities.[18]

The conferment on the Commission of power to implement rules laid down by the Council has been given a further boost and its utility given further recognition by an amendment introduced by the Single European Act 1986.[19] This new provision gives general authority to the Council to confer such powers on the Commission in accordance with principles and rules which are to be determined in advance. The Council is authorized to lay down procedures for this purpose on the basis of a Commission proposal and after obtaining the opinion of the European Parliament. At the Inter-governmental Conference which preceded the adoption of the Single European Act the discussion of possible procedures included not only the existing management and regulatory committee procedures but also an advisory committee procedure of an entirely consultative nature. The Conference also requested that for the purposes of completing the internal market priority should be given to

17 See *Bulletin of the European Communities* (1974), Part 6, p 122. Also see comments on the rôle of management committees in *Report on European Institutions* (1979) at pp 47, 48.
18 Bertram, C, 'Decision-making in the EEC: the Management Committee Procedure' (1967–68) 5 CML Rev 264.
19 Art 10, amending EEC Art 145 (now Art 202).

that latter procedure.[20] The Commission, with the general support of the European Parliament, drew up an appropriate proposal incorporating the three types of procedure and referring to the preferred use of advisory committees.[1] The decision which the Council took under these powers, known as the 'comitology' decision, departed significantly from those proposals.[2] It provided that implementing powers conferred on the Commission shall be exercised either independently, or by one of the advisory, management or regulatory committee procedures, or by a special emergency procedure in relation to safeguard measures.[3] There are in fact seven possible procedures since both the management and regulatory procedures are each subject to two variants. The Council, for reasons which it has not divulged, deliberately omitted to specify which form of procedure should be used for any given purpose.[4]

The 'comitology' decision has provoked criticism and challenge. Attention has been focused in particular on the variants in procedure, which effectively enable the Council to block implementing action, and the Council's express reservation of the right to exercise executive action itself. The Commission's criticisms were recorded in the minutes of the Council meeting which adopted the decision in terms that the decision would impose restraints on the Commission's freedom of action and that it contained no general guarantee of implementing action being taken.[5] Initial experience has tended to confirm such fears: the Council has not given priority to the advisory committee procedure; it has made increasing use of the variant of the regulatory committee procedure which allows it to block Commission proposals by a simple majority; and it has kept implementing powers to itself in some cases.[6] A request from the Commission to the Council to take steps to improve the situation has not so far elicited any response.[7] Attempts to challenge the legality of the 'comitology' decision and the Council's use of it have also been unsuccessful. An action by the European Parliament contending that the decision was unlawful was ruled to be inadmissible on the ground that the Parliament lacks the necessary *locus standi* to bring such an action.[8] An action by the Commission challenging recourse to the management committee procedure on a matter over which it claimed exclusive competence was dismissed on the merits.[9]

D. Monetary union institutions

Two new organisations, the European System of Central Banks (ESCB) and the European Central Bank (ECB) have been established by virtue of Article 4a of the Maastricht Treaty (Amsterdam Treaty Article 7) to launch the Monetary

---

20 See 'Declaration on the powers of implementation of the Commission' adopted by the Inter-governmental Conference and annexed to the Single European Act.
1   For the Commission's proposal, see COM(86) 35 final; for the opinion of the Parliament, see PE DOC A2–138/86.
2   Council Decision 87/373 (OJ 1987, L197/33).
3   Ibid, Arts 1–3. Art 4 made it clear that existing procedures for the exercise of conferred powers by the Commission remain in force until amended. See now Council Decision 1999/468 (OJ L184/23).
4   See *Thirty-fifth Review of the Council's Work* (1988), p 15.
5   See *Bulletin of the European Communities* (1987), Part 6, point 2.4.14.
6   See *Twenty-third General Report on the Activities of the European Communities* (1990), pp 31–32.
7   Ibid, p 32. The Council was required by Art 5 of the 'comitology' decision to review the procedures it provides on the basis of a Commission report before the end of 1990.
8   Case 302/87: *European Parliament v Council* [1988] ECR 5615.
9   Case 16/88: *Commission v Council* [1989] ECR 3457.

Union. These will be discussed below.[10] Their establishment made it possible to wind up the European Monetary Institute (EMI), an institution with a number of consultative functions, that was set up to prepare for stage II of EMU as from 1 January 1994.

E. European Investment Bank

The European Investment Bank is an independent institution, established by EC Article 266 (ex Art 198d)[11] and endowed with legal personality, and may have non-contractual liability, though not an institution of the Community.[12] The members of the Bank are the Member States of the Community. The task of the Bank, as set out in EC Article 267, is to contribute, by means of its own resources and access to the capital market, to the balanced and steady development of the Common Market. To that end the Bank, operating on a non-profit-making basis, is empowered to grant loans and to give guarantees to facilitate the financing of three types of project in all sectors of the economy: (i) projects for developing the less developed regions of the Community; (ii) projects for modernizing or converting undertakings or for developing fresh activities called for by the progressive establishment of the Common Market; and (iii) projects of common interest to several Member States. In the cases of the latter two types of project, the Bank's assistance is limited to projects which are of such a size or nature that they cannot be entirely financed by the various means available in the individual Member States. In carrying out its tasks the Bank facilitates the financing of investment programmes in conjunction with assistance from the Structural Funds and the Community financial instruments.

The organization, function and powers of the Bank are set out in detail in a separate Statute annexed to the EC Treaty. The Bank was originally set up with a capital of 1,000 million European Currency Units (ECU) subscribed by the Member States.[13] Over the years the total capital of the Bank has been increased. At the last accession the subscribed capital amounted to 62,013m. ECU divided as follows: Germany, France, Italy and the United Kingdom 19.766% each; Spain 6.53%; Belgium and The Netherlands 4.92% each; Sweden 3.26%; Denmark 2.49%; Austria 2.44%; Finland 1.40%; Greece 1.33%; Portugal 0.86%; Ireland 0.62% and Luxembourg 0.62%.[14] In 1998 the Board of Governors decided to increase the Bank's subscribed capital to EUR 100,000m as from 1 January 1999.[15]

The seat of the bank is in Luxembourg. The bank is directed and managed by a Board of Governors, a Board of Directors and a Management Committee.[16]

---

10 See Ch 24, infra.
11 Originally EC Arts 129 and 130, becoming EC Arts 198d and 198e as a result of the TEU before becoming EC Arts 266 and 267 as a result of the Amsterdam Treaty. See also the Protocol on the Statute of the EIB attached to the EC Treaty, as amended (the amendment made in 1993 is to be found in OJ 1994, L173/14 and 21, and is incorporated in the latest published versions of the Protocol.
12 See Case C-370/89: *SGEEH v EIB* [1992] ECR I-6211.
13 Statute of the Bank, Art 4(1). For the method of calculating the value of the European Currency Unit see Reg 1971/89 (OJ 1989, L189/1).
14 See Fourth Act of Accession 1995, Protocol 1, Art 2.
15 See OJ 1999, C 247/6.
16 Statute of the Bank, Art 8. Privileges and immunities are enjoyed by the members of the organs, the staff of the Bank and the national representatives of the bank under the terms of the Protocol on Privileges and Immunities 1965, Art 22.

The Board of Governors consists of the Ministers of Finance of the Member States. The essential role of the Board of Governors is to lay down directives for the credit policy of the Bank and to ensure that those directives are implemented.[17] The system of voting which is provided for the Council by EC Article 205 (ex Art 148) also applies to the board of Governors.[18] The Board of Directors consists of 25 directors with 13 alternates. They serve five year renewable terms and are appointed by the Board of Governors. Three directors are nominated by each of France, Germany, Italy and the United Kingdom; two directors are nominated by Spain; one director is nominated by each of the remaining Member States and the Commission. Germany, France, Italy and the United Kingdom nominate two alternates each; Spain and Portugal together, the Benelux Countries, Denmark, Greece and Ireland together, and Austria, Finland and Sweden together, by common accord nominate one alternate, as does the Commission.[19] It is the task of the Board of Directors to manage the Bank in accordance with the Treaty and Statute and the general directives laid down by the Board of Governors. It has the sole power to grant loans and guarantees and to raise loans and it fixes the interest rates and commission payable on loans and guarantees respectively.[20] The current business of the Bank is in the hands of the Management Committee consisting of a President and seven Vice-Presidents. These are appointed for six-year renewable terms by the Board of Governors upon a proposal from the board of Directors. The Management Committee acts under the authority of the President and the supervision of the Board of Directors. Its functions are to prepare the decisions of the Board of Directors on both the raising of loans and the granting of loans and guarantees and to ensure the implementation of those decisions.[1] The President, or in his absence one of the Vice-Presidents, acts as non-voting Chairman of the Board of Directors.[2]

The control of accounts is in the hands of a committee of three appointed by the Board of Governors from persons competent in the field of public accountancy. The committee controls the regularity of operations and the Bank's books in accordance with the principles of public accountancy. It is assisted by an organ of internal audit and an international organ of external audit. The Bank is divided into seven sections: administration, two sections concerned with financing within the Community, financing outside the Community, finances and treasury, research and legal affairs. The personnel of the Bank consists of some 800 persons. The EIB is not subject to the jurisdiction of the Court of Auditors though the latter may be involved in the course of its control of the Commission's financial activities.

The Bank obtains its funds primarily from loans floated on the capital markets of the world. The loans granted by the EIB totalled 26,203 million ECU in 1997 and 29,526 million ECU in 1998, including 4,410 million ECU within the framework of Community co-operation with non-member countries.[3]

Under the terms of EC Article 237 (ex Art 180) the Court of Justice of the Communities has jurisdiction over certain types of dispute concerning the Bank. In particular the Board of Directors enjoy the powers conferred on the Commission

17 Statute of the Bank, Art 9.
18 Ibid, Art 10.
19 See Third Act of Accession 1985, Protocol 1, Art 5, the Fourth Act of Accession and Council decision 95/1 (OJ 1995, L1.1).
20 Statute of the Bank, Arts 11 and 12.
 1 Ibid, Art 13.
 2 Ibid, Art 11(2).
 3 1998 General Report (1999), para 80.

by EC Article 226 (ex Art 169) in connection with the non-fulfilment by Member States of obligations under the Statute of the Bank; also under the terms of EC Article 230 (ex Art 173) any Member State, the Commission or the Board of Directors may challenge measures adopted by the Board of Governors and similarly any Member State or the Commission may challenge measures adopted by the Board of Directors.[4]

Article 29 of the Statute of the Bank provides that disputes between the Bank and its creditors and debtors shall be decided by the competent national courts unless jurisdiction has been conferred on the Court of the Justice of the Communities.

F.   European Bank for Reconstruction and Development

The Bank was established in 1990[5] by 41 parties who became its shareholders, ie 39 countries, the European Community and the European Investment Bank, with the object of fostering the transition towards open market-orientated economies and promoting private and entrepreneurial initiatives in Central and Eastern Europe. Its structure and *modus operandi* resemble that of the EIB. Though it is not, strictly, a Community institution, the Bank reflects the Community policy towards the former Soviet-controlled countries and the Community participation in the international initiative in this respect.

The bulk of the Bank's capital comes from the Community and the Member States, the balance from the USA, Canada and Japan.

In 1996 in Board of Governors decided to increase the Bank's capital to 20 billion ECU and, consequently, the Community decided to subscribe for new shares in the EBRD capital.[6]

---

4   Case 85/86R: *Commission v Board of Governors of the European Investment Bank* [1988] ECR 1281.
5   For the agreement establishing the EBRD, see OJ 1990, L372/4; for the decision adopting the agreement, see OJ 1990, L372/1; for the date of its application, see OJ 1991, L107/52.
6   See Council Dec 97/135 (OJ 1997, L52/15).

Chapter 12

The Court of Justice and the Court of First Instance

A. The Court of Justice

(1) COMPOSITION AND PROCEDURE

(a) Composition and organization[1]
The Court of Justice of the European Communities (ECJ), as we have seen, has its origins in the Court which was originally set up under the ECSC Treaty. In the words of the EC Treaty the role of the Court is to 'ensure that in the interpretation and application of [the] Treaty the law is observed'.[2] Since 1989 the jurisdiction of the ECJ over certain cases has been allocated to the Court of First Instance (CFI), discussed later in this chapter, with a right of appeal to the ECJ.

At present the ECJ is composed of 15 judges unanimously appointed by the Governments of the Member States. In practice each Member State has a judge of its nationality on the Court.[3] They hold office for six-year renewable terms. The Treaties provide that the judges must be chosen 'from persons whose independence is beyond doubt and who possess the qualifications required for appointment to the highest judicial offices in their respective countries or are jurisconsults of recognized competence'.[4] In practice the Bench has been made up of a mixture of professors of law, judges, lawyers in private practice and government legal advisers.

---

1   EC Arts 220–245 (ex Arts 164–188) (as amended by First Act of Accession 1972, Arts 17–19, Second Act of Accession 1979, Arts 16 and 135. Third Act of Accession 1985, Arts 17–19 and 384, Fourth Act of Accession 1995, and Single European Act, Arts 11 and 12) and Protocol on the Statute of the Court of Justice, Titles I and II, signed at Brussels on 17 April 1957, *Court of Justice of the European Communities*, 1993 edition.
2   EC Art 220 (ex Art 164); see also ECSC Art 31 and EAEC Art 136.
3   The present United Kingdom judge is David Edward, QC, Scottish Advocate, former Professor of European Institutions in the Europa Institute of the University of Edinburgh.
4   EC Art 223 (ex Art 167). Lasok, K P E, *The European Court of Justice: Practice and Procedure* (1994), pp 4 et seq; Lasok, K P E, and Millett, T, *The Court of Justice and the Court of First Instance*, in *Vaughan's Law of the European Communities* (1998), p 52 et seq.

The judges enjoy the usual guarantees of independence and impartiality. They enjoy immunity from suit and legal process during their tenure of office and they retain that status after ceasing to hold office in respect of acts done in the performance of their duties. This immunity may, however, be suspended by the Court itself in plenary session.[5] The judges also enjoy privileges and immunities in respect of taxation, currency and exchange regulations. They may not hold any office of an administrative or political nature nor engage in any occupation or profession paid or unpaid, although in the case of the latter in an exceptional case permission may be given by the Council.[6]

Judges may resign or be removed from office. To resign, a judge must inform the President of the Court who in turn notifies the President of the Council which latter act creates the vacancy. A judge may be removed from office if, in the unanimous opinion of his brethren, he no longer fulfils the conditions required or meets the obligations resulting from his office. The Court's decision to remove a judge must be communicated to the President of the European Parliament and the President of the Commission and must be notified to the President of the Council. The latter notification produces a vacancy.[7]

The President of the Court is appointed by the judges from among their own number by an absolute majority vote in a secret ballot. The President holds office for a three-year term which may be renewed. The Court may sit for certain purposes in chambers of which there are six (consisting of three, five or seven judges), each of which has a President. Certain judges preside over two chambers as Presidents of Chambers. Presidents of Chambers are elected for one-year renewable periods by the same process used to elect the President of the Court.[8] The Court of Justice shall sit in plenary session when a Member State or a Community institution that is a party to the proceedings so requests.[9] The number of judges may, at the request of the Court, be increased by a unanimous decision of the Council.[10] The arrangement into chambers, as a matter of organization, falls within the scope of the Court's automony.[11]

The judges of the Court are assisted at present by nine Advocates-General who must possess the same professional qualifications as the judges and eight of whom are appointed for a six-year renewable term by a unanimous decision of the Council.[12] Each of the five larger Member States has an Advocate-General of its nationality.[13] Three posts are held in rotation[14] by nationals of the remaining Member States and the ninth has been appointed for a term of office running from 1 January 1995 to 6 October 2000.[15] It is held by an Italian national who lost his rotating post in the Community of 12. One of their number is designated annually by the Court as First Advocate-General. The office of Advocate-General is one which has no precise parallel in the English legal system. The institution of Advocate-General, like

---

5   Protocol on the Statute of the Court, Art 3.
6   Ibid, Art 4.
7   Ibid, Arts 5 to 7.
8   Rules of Procedure of the Court, Arts 7, 9 and 10; current version of Rules Procedure (OJ 2001, C 34/1).
9   EC Art 221(3) (ex Art 165(3)).
10   EC Art 221(4) (ex Art 165(4)).
11   Case C-7/94: *Landesamt für Ausbildungsförderung Nordrhein – Westfalen v Lubor Gaal* [1995] ECR I-1031 (paras 13 & 14); Council Decision 95/1 (OJ 1995, L1).
12   EC Arts 222 and 223 (ex Arts 166 and 167). See Pavlopoulos, A J, *The Advocate General's Office* (1986).
13   The present British Advocate-General is Francis Jacobs QC, formerly Professor of European Law in the University of London.
14   Council Decision 95/1 (OJ 1995, L1).
15   EC Art 222, 2nd sentence.

much of the procedure of the Court itself, is largely derived from French law. The function of the Advocate-General is similar to that of the *Commissaire du Gouvernement* at the French *Conseil d'Etat*. It is the rôle of the *Commissaire du Gouvernement* to act as what has been called 'the embodied conscience of the Court'.[16] He is required to consider the issues in a case impartially and individually and to reach his own personal conclusion as to what in law and justice should be done. Before the *Conseil d'Etat* considers its judgment the *Commissaire*, orally and in public, states the facts and the law as he sees them and suggests the principles in accordance with which he thinks the case should be decided. The *Commissaire* does not participate in the giving of judgment, still less is he the representative of or subordinate to the government. His purpose is to act as an entirely uncommitted and fearless defender of the law and justice. Similarly, in the case of the Advocates-General of the Court of Justice of the Communities, the Treaties require them to 'acting with complete impartiality and independence to make, in open court, reasoned submissions', on cases before the Court.[17] Their task is a threefold one: to propose a solution to the case before the Court; to relate that proposed solution to the general pattern of existing case law; and, if possible, to outline the probable future development of the case law. The Advocates-General therefore represent neither the institutions of the Communities nor the public; they function only as the spokesmen of the law and justice in the context of the Treaties.

As in the case of the submissions of the French *Commissaires du Gouvernement* so the submissions of the Advocates-General are in no way binding on the Court. But their submissions are invariably published with the judgment of the Court and where, as often happens, the Court agrees with the Advocate-General, the Advocate-General's full consideration of the wider aspects of the case not only throws valuable light on the Court's judgments, but also acts as an indicator of the direction the jurisprudence of the Court is likely to take in the future. In this way the Advocates-General are in a position to influence the development of Community law.[18]

As has been said there is no precise parallel in the English legal system to the office of Advocate-General. The Attorney-General does have a rôle as guardian of the public interest or protector of public rights, eg as a party in civil proceedings for an injunction or declaration in cases of public nuisance and his appearance before public tribunals of inquiry as a spokesman for the public interest. Similarly, a court may also ask the Official Solicitor or, as the case may be, the Attorney General, to instruct counsel to ensure that all points of view on matters of law are fully before the court (an amicus curiae). But in these cases the rôles of the Attorney-General and the Official Solicitor are limited and special whereas that of the Advocates-General is unlimited and general.[19] The rôle of the Advocate-General is a hybrid in that it has both advocatory and judicial characteristics. As an independent advocate of the legal interests of the Community, he may be regarded as a sort of institutionalized *amicus curiae*. As a person appointed with the same qualifications and on the same conditions as the judges and whose views have a formative influence on the law, he may be regarded almost as a first instance judge whose opinions are never decisive but are always

---

16   Hamson, C, *Executive Discretion and Judicial Control* (1954), p 80.
17   Eg EC Art 222 (ex Art 166).
18   See Brown, L N, and Jacobs, F G, *The Court of Justice of the European Communities* (4th edn, 1994) ch 4.
19   See Edwards, J LlJ, *Law Officers of the Crown* (1964), ch 14; *Halsbury's Laws of England* (4th edn), vol 10, para 950.

considered by the Court.[20] Advocates-General may retire and be removed by the same procedure as in the case of judges and they enjoy similar privileges and immunities. The Treaties are silent on the nationality of the judges and Advocates-General but in practice they are always of the nationality of one of the Member States.

Articles 12-15 and 18 of the Protocol on Privileges and Immunities apply to the Members of the Court of Justice, the Court of First Instance and to the Court's Registrar.[1]

The seat of the Court is in Luxembourg and, subject to public holidays and the usual vacations, it is in permanent session. In case of urgency the President may convene the Court during vacations.

The day-to-day administration of the Court is in the hands of the Registrar and his staff. The Registrar is elected by the judges by majority vote after consultation with the Advocates-General (EC Article 224 (ex Art 168)). The Registrar's term of office is six years and he is eligible for re-election. The Court may dismiss him if he no longer complies with the obligations of his office.[2]

Each judge and Advocate-General is assisted by three legal secretaries. The legal secretaries are normally of the same nationality as their masters and are required to have legal training. Their main tasks are to prepare pre-trial studies on the legal questions involved in a case before the Court and to assist in the drafting of opinions and judgments. They thus provide a service similar to that of the Law Clerks to the Judges of the United States Supreme Court.[3] In 1998 there were altogether 727 permanent posts and 226 temporary posts in the Court of Justice and the Court of First Instance.[4]

In principle the Court sits in plenary session with a quorum of nine, but it is enabled to set up separate chambers of three, five or seven judges. The quorum for the first two is three judges; that for a seven judge chamber is five.[5] It is the function of these chambers, at the request of the Court, to undertake preliminary examinations of evidence in particular cases. They can also hear and decide references for preliminary rulings and any actions brought by natural or legal persons the nature or circumstances of which do not necessitate a hearing by the full Court. If a Member State or a Community institution is party to the latter type of action it can insist on a hearing by the full Court.[6] Each chamber is assisted by an Advocate-General.[7]

In 2000, 503 cases came before the Court of which 224 were references for preliminary rulings, 79 appeals and 200 others. Of the 273 judgments given by the Court of Justice, 152 were preliminary rulings, 37 were appeals and 84 were other cases. The Court of First Instance had 398 new cases and gave 116 judgments.[8]

---

20 Cf Warner, J-P, 'Some Aspects of the European Court of Justice' (1976) 14 JSPTL (NS) 17–19.
1   Protocol on the Statute of the Court, Art 3, as amended.
2   See Rules of Procedure of the Court, Title I, Chapter 3; Lasok, op cit, p 22.
3   For comment see Feld, W, *Court of the European Communities* (1964), p 27 and Brown and Jacobs, op cit, pp 17–18.
4   1998 General Report (1999), para 1097.
5   Protocol on the Statute of the Court, Art 15.
6   Rules of Procedure, Art 95.
7   See Rules of Procedure of the Court, Art 10.
8   Statistics supplied by the ECJ.

(b)   Practice and procedure

The practice and procedure of the Court are based on a code of Rules of Procedure drawn up by the Court.[9] The procedure of the Court is divided into three stages: a written stage; a preparatory inquiry stage; and an oral stage. As soon as a written application is filed with the Registrar, the President appoints one of the judges as judge-rapporteur. The task of the judge-rapporteur is to prepare a preliminary report on the case for the consideration of the Court. This is followed by the First Advocate-General assigning one of his colleagues to the case.[10]

The written stage takes the form of pleadings. The applicant in his application will set out his claim against the defendant and the grounds upon which it is made. The defendant will then be notified of the application and will be given a period of one month within which to prepare and submit to the Court a statement of defence. The applicant may make a written reply to the defence and the defendant may then also make a final rejoinder. This exchange of submissions comprises the written stage in the proceedings. It should be pointed out that these written submissions go far beyond the scope and purpose of English pleadings. The arguments of the parties are set out fully together with the nature of the evidence upon which reliance is placed. This form of documentary advocacy has the effect of stressing the written stage at the expense of the other two stages.

The judge-rapporteur then examines the pleadings and considers whether the case requires a preparatory inquiry,[11] ie a proof-taking stage which is a familiar part of continental legal procedure. The judge-rapporteur reports to the Court on whether a preparatory inquiry is necessary and after the Court has also heard the Advocate-General on this point it will decide whether to proceed to a preparatory inquiry. If the Court decides that a preparatory inquiry is necessary it can be held before the full Court, before one of the chambers of the Court or it may be entrusted to the judge-rapporteur himself. In any event, the preparatory inquiry may take the form of a personal appearance of the parties and their witnesses for oral examination, the production and inspection of documentary evidence, experts' reports or an inspection by the Court of the place or thing in question. This procedure of preparatory inquiry is principally conducted not by the lawyers representing the parties, but, following continental practice, by the Court, chamber or judge-rapporteur as the case may be. The Advocate-General may also participate in the preparatory inquiry. The representatives of the parties may only question witnesses 'subject to the control of the President'.[12] In addition to witnesses who are called at the request of the parties, the Court and the Advocate-General also have the power to summon witnesses. Evidence is given on oath sworn either in accordance with the laws of the state of the witness's nationality, or alternatively in the form set out in the Rules of Procedure. The Court has the power to exempt a witness from taking the oath.[13] At the end of the preparatory inquiry the Court may allow the parties to submit written observations on matters which have arisen in the course of the preparatory inquiry.

---

9   The Rules require the unanimous approval of the Council: EC Art 245 (ex Art 188). The Rules were approved on 26 November 1974 (see OJ 1974, L350) and have been amended on many occasions. A consolidated version of the Rules was published in OJ 2001, C 34.

10 See Rules of Procedure, Arts 9 and 10 and Title 2.

11 Rules of Procedure, Arts 44–46.

12 Rules of Procedure, Art 47(4).

13 Rules of Procedure, Art 47(5).

After the conclusion of the preparatory inquiry, or, if there has been no preparatory inquiry,[14] at the end of the written proceedings, the oral[15] stage takes place before the Court. Immediately prior to the oral stage the judge-rapporteur will issue his report for the hearing which will outline the case, summarize the arguments of the parties and make a statement on the facts of the case on the basis of the evidence presented during the written and preparatory inquiry stages. This will be followed by oral argument on behalf of the parties. There is no formal hearing of witnesses or oral examination at this stage. The parties must be legally represented during the oral stage.[16]

Members of the Court and the Advocate-General may put questions to agents and counsel during the oral proceedings. The Court may also at this stage order a further preparatory inquiry to be held either by a chamber or by the judge-rapporteur. At the conclusion of the case the parties' representatives make closing speeches to the Court: applicant first, followed by defendant. The Advocate-General, usually on another occasion, presents his opinion which brings the oral proceedings to a close. There is usually an adjournment between the speeches by counsel and the Advocate-General's delivery of his opinion.

The judges withdraw to deliberate in private without the participation of Advocates-General, legal secretaries or interpreters. In the course of their deliberations they may reopen the oral proceedings if they so wish. These deliberations finally result in the Court's judgment which is usually drafted by the judge-rapporteur. Judgment is delivered in open court. Again, following continental practice, the court renders a single collegiate judgment; separate or dissenting opinions are not permitted. Even if the judgment is based on a majority decision that fact, let alone the nature of the majority, is not disclosed.[17] It has already been pointed out that in the vast majority of cases the Court accepts the conclusions of the Advocate-General. But in those cases where the Court has not followed the Advocate-General, his opinion can in a sense be regarded as a dissenting judgment.

The languages of the Court are the official languages of the Communities, viz Danish, Dutch, English, Finnish, French, German, Greek, Italian, Portuguese, Spanish and Swedish. Irish may also be used although it is not an official language.[18] French has become the working language of the Court and it is the language in which the Court's deliberations are conducted. In principle, only one of the Community languages may be used as the procedural language in a given case. The basic rule is that the choice of procedural language is made by the applicant where one of the Communities' institutions is the defendant, on the basis that the representatives of the Communities are well versed in all the official languages. But where the defendant is one of the Member States or a court of a Member State is seeking a preliminary ruling then the procedural language must be the language of that state. The Court's judgments, together with the report for the hearing and the opinion of the Advocate-General, are published in each of the official languages;

14 As is usually the case. See Brown and Jacobs, op cit, p 255.
15 Rules of Procedure, Arts 55–62.
16 Member States and Community institutions must be represented by an agent who may be assisted by a lawyer entitled to practise before a court of a Member State or of the EEA. Corporate bodies and individuals may also have an agent but they must be represented by a lawyer entitled to practise before a court of a Member State or of the EEA. See Protocol on the Statute of the Court, Art 17; Lasok, op cit, p 124 et seq.
17 For comment on the practice of single collegiate judgments, see Bebr, op cit, p 24 and Feld, op cit, p 99.
18 Rules of Procedure, Art 29(1).

the copy in the procedural language of a given case being regarded as the authentic and definitive version.[19]

The Court's judgments have binding force from the date of their delivery.[20] As far as the enforcement of the Court's judgments is concerned the position varies depending on the outcome of the case and the identity of the defendant. If the Court gives judgment against a Member State under the ECSC Treaty enforcement is achieved by enabling the Commission, acting jointly with the Council, to impose sanctions on the defaulting member. This procedure was not reproduced in the Treaties of Rome which contained no enforcement measures for use against Member States. The Rome Treaties merely provided that the Member State in question was required to take the measures necessary to execute the Court's judgment bearing in mind that, in principle, the judgment was declaratory and Member States are law-abiding states. The TEU amended the Rome Treaties to include provision for the imposition of a fine or penalty payments if a Member State fails to take the measures neccessary to comply with a judgment of the Court.[1] Lastly, if the Court gives judgment against a corporate body or individual in the form of a fine, such judgment debts are enforceable without further formality by the national courts of the Member States.[2]

(c) Revision and interpretation of judgments
The decisions of the Court are final and are not subject to appeal; it is not open to a national court when called upon to enforce a judgment of the Community Court to challenge that judgment in any way. The only possible course of action open to an unsuccessful litigant is to request a revision of the Court's judgment.[3] Such a request may be made on the ground of the discovery of a fact likely to prove of decisive importance which, before judgment, was unknown both to the Court and to the party requesting revision. Two periods of limitation apply to requests for revision: the request must be made within ten years of the date of the judgment and within three months of the date on which the new fact became known to the applicant. If these conditions are satisfied, and without prejudice to the merits, the Court hears the Advocate-General and considers the parties' written submissions before deciding whether the alleged new fact does exist and whether it justifies revision. If the Court decides that the request is admissible then it proceeds to consider the merits of the case and this can, if necessary, involve a completely new trial. In *Acciaieria Ferriera di Roma v High Authority of the ECSC* (1960) the Court made it clear that the newly discovered fact must have been unknown both to the Court and to the party, and that knowledge of it prior to judgment by either Court or a party will make the request inadmissible.[4] In *Fonderie Acciaierie Giovanni Mandelli v Commission* (1971), the Court refused an application for revision in a similar case in which a relevant document could have been obtained by the applicant either at the time of the commencement of the original action or at the inquiry stage.[5] The Court regards the procedure for revision as an exception to the doctrine of *res judicata*. As such it interprets the

---

19 See Rules of Procedure, Arts 29, 30 and 31.
20 Rules of Procedure, Art 65.
 1 EC Art 228(2) (ex Art 171(2)); EAEC Art 143(2).
 2 EC Arts 244 and 256 (ex Arts 187, 192).
 3 See Protocol on the Statute of the Court, Art 38, and Rules of Procedure of the Court, Arts 98 to 100.
 4 Case 1/60: [1960] ECR 165.
 5 Case 56/70: [1971] ECR 1.

conditions for revision strictly and will not allow the procedure to be used for the purpose of bringing an appeal.[6]

A final point concerning the practice of the Court relates to the possibility in case of difficulty as to the meaning or scope of a judgment of asking the Court to interpret its judgment.[7] Such a request may be made by any of the parties to the case or by a Community institution which can show that it has an interest in the decision. The only part of a judgment which may be the subject of a request for interpretation is the operative part or what we would call the *ratio decidendi*. As the Court itself put it in *Assider v High Authority of the ECSC* (1955)[8] 'the only parts of a judgment which can be interpreted are those which express the judgment of the Court in the dispute which has been submitted for its final decision and those parts of the reasoning upon which this decision is based and which are, therefore, essential to it … the Court does not have to interpret those passages which are incidental and which complete or explain that basic reasoning'.

In the later case of *High Authority and European Court v Collitti* (1965)[9] the Court considered the nature of the 'difficulty' necessary to justify a request for an interpretation. In the *Assider* case the court had said that it was sufficient for the parties to give different meanings to the judgment. In the *Collitti* case the Court defined the nature of the difficulty more precisely. The Court held: 'In order to be admissible, an application for interpretation … must not raise the possible consequences of the judgment in question on cases other than the one decided, but only the obscurity and ambiguity of the meaning and scope of the judgment itself in relation to the case decided by the judgment in question.' An application for interpretation may concern the effect of the judgment on the legal relations of the parties to the case, but not the application of the judgment nor the consequences which flow from it.[10]

(2)   CONTENTIOUS JURISDICTION[11]

The Court is the creature of the Community Treaties and so its jurisdiction derives exclusively from those Treaties. It was enlarged by the Treaties of Maastricht and Amsterdam. Any attempt to attribute other jurisdiction to the Court will fail. In the case of *Schlieker v High Authority of the ECSC* (1963)[12] the plaintiff alleged that through the inactivity of the High Authority she had suffered loss. It was argued on behalf of the High Authority that the right to bring proceedings before the Court based on the inactivity of a Community institution was limited by the Treaty to Member States, other Community institutions and undertakings and associations. Frau Schlieker argued in reply, upon analogy with German municipal law, that the Court had a residual jurisdiction to enable it to protect the interests of individuals where the Treaty texts are silent. This view was rejected both by the Advocate-General and the Court. The Advocate-General observed that 'the Treaty system … does not in a general clause guarantee legal protection without any gaps. Reference to … the Basic Law (*Grundgesetz*) of the Federal Republic

---

6   Case 116/78 Rev: *Bellintani v Commission* [1980] ECR 23.
7   See Protocol on the Statute of the Court, Art 40, and Rules of Procedure of the Court, Art 102.
8   Case 5/55: [1954–56] ECR 135.
9   Case 70/63A *bis*: [1965] ECR 275.
10 Case 9/81: *Court of Auditors v Williams* [1983] ECR 2859.
11 The Court's jurisdiction to give preliminary rulings at the request of the courts of the Member States will be discussed later in connection with the relationship between Community law and municipal law; see Ch 13.
12 Case 12/63: [1963] ECR 85, [1963] CMLR 281.

of Germany cannot lead to any other solution, for the Court can define the limits of its supra-national legal protection only by using the text of the Treaty and not by following national law'.[13] The Court agreed with this submission and held that: 'Whatever may be the consequence of a factual situation of which the Court may not take cognizance, the Court may not depart from the judicial system set out in the Treaty'. Thus in interpreting the Treaties the Court is bound to adhere strictly to the provisions of the text, and, being the creature of the Treaty, it has no power other than that conferred by the Treaty.[14]

In other words the ECJ, like any other Community institution, operates within the scope of attributed powers. However, occasionally, the Court is confronted with a situation where, operating within the letter of the Treaties, it could be accused of a denial of justice. Given the wide scope of EC Article 220 (ex Art 164), the Court may feel justified in adopting a broad interpretation of attribution and behave like a supreme court of a federal state which occasionally has to make a political decision whilst interpreting the constitution. The question, in our view, is not whether the Court arrogates to itself 'inherent jurisdiction'[15] but whether it can logically justify its decision in the name of justice or fair and efficient working of the system. Such justification seems to have been shown in the Chernobyl[16] case where the Court sanctioned the European Parliament's action to seek annulment of a Council regulation adopted in disregard of the co-operation procedure. An example is the case of a Dutch investigating judge[17] who requested Commission's reports and the authority of questioning Commission officials in his investigation of alleged fraud in the application of Community fishery legislation. The Commission argued that the matter should have come to the ECJ via the procedure for a preliminary ruling but such argument had no substance because such procedure could not have been used since there was, at that stage, no case before a national court. The ECJ, following the logic of the Chernobyl decision,[18] ruled that, in the light of its mission under EC Article 220 (ex Art 164), it had to devise a remedy that would enable the Commission to co-operate with the national judicial authorities in the spirit of solidarity of EC Article 10 (ex Art 5).[19]

The jurisdictional provisions of the Treaties are somewhat complex; as one commentator has observed, 'No international tribunal has ever been equipped with so varied a jurisdictional competence as has the Court of the European Communities'.[20] The contentious jurisdiction conferred upon the Court by the Treaties falls under two main heads which will be treated in the following order:

(a) Actions against Member States; and
(b) Actions against Community institutions.

(a) Actions against Member States
Actions against Member States take two forms:

---

13 Unwritten rules of Community law for the protection of fundamental rights may, however, be derived from national law; see Ch 5, supra.
14 See Case 66/76: *CFDT v Council* [1977] ECR 305, [1977] 1 CMLR 589.
15 See Arnull, A, *Does the Court of Justice have Inherent Jurisdiction?* (1990) 27 CMLRev 683.
16 Case C-70/88, supra.
17 Case C-2/88 Imm: *J J Zwartveld* [1990] ECR I-3365, [1990] 3 CMLR 457.
18 Case C-70/88 at para 23.
19 Case C-2/88 at para 23.
20 Bowett, D W, *Law of International Institutions* (3rd edn, 1975), p 278.

(1) Actions by Member States against Member States.
(2) Actions by Community institutions against Member States.

(1) All the Treaties confer upon the Court a compulsory jurisdiction to decide disputes between Member States concerning the application of the terms of the Treaties and a permissive jurisdiction, based on the consent of the parties, over disputes between states related to the object and purpose of the Communities in general. Thus the EC Treaty provides first at EC Article 227 (ex Art 170), that 'A Member State which considers that another Member State has failed to fulfil an obligation under this Treaty may bring the matter before the Court of Justice'.[1] Secondly, the EC Treaty provides at EC Article 239 (ex Art 182), that 'The Court of Justice shall have jurisdiction in any dispute between Member States which relates to the subject matter of this Treaty, if the dispute is submitted to it under a special agreement between the parties'.[2] The Court's jurisdiction over both of these types of dispute is exclusive; recourse by Member States to other means of settlement is expressly forbidden by the Treaties. EC Article 292 (ex Art 219) provides that 'Member States undertake not to submit a dispute concerning the interpretation or application of this Treaty to any method of settlement other than those provided for therein'.[3] This insistence on referring inter-state disputes to the Court of Justice underlines one of the major purposes of the Court and that is to guarantee uniformity of interpretation and application of the law of the Communities.

Under the terms of EC Article 227 (ex Art 170), before one Member State brings another before the Court the matter must be referred to the Commission. This gives the Commission an opportunity to deliver a reasoned opinion on the alleged breach of Treaty in the light of observations made by the Member States in dispute. This procedure seems to be designed for the purpose of promoting the resolution of the dispute without resort to litigation. But whether or not the Commission delivers such an opinion, the Member State making the allegation can insist on proceeding with the action. In general, Member States prefer to resolve their disputes outside the courtroom; only one EC Article 227 (ex Art 170), action has so far been heard. In that case[4] France alleged that the United Kingdom's fishery conservation measures were contrary to Community law. The Commission delivered an opinion in support of the French view. The European Court agreed with that opinion and gave judgment against the United Kingdom.[5]

(2) By virtue of Article 88 of the ECSC Treaty the Commission is given the power to decide whether a Member State has failed to comply with its obligations under the Treaty. If it so decides in relation to a given Member State the Commission must invite that state to express its views on the matter. The Commission may then record the state's wrongdoing in a reasoned opinion and give the state a limited time within which to take steps to fulfil its obligations. The purpose of this process is to enable both the Commission and the Member State to exchange views in the hope that the issue may thereby be settled. If it is

---

1   Cf ECSC Art 89, and EAEC Art 141.
2   Cf ECSC Art 89, and EAEC Art 154.
3   Cf ECSC Art 87, and EAEC Art 193.
4   Case 141/78: *France v United Kingdom* [1979] ECR 2923, [1980] 1 CMLR 6.
5   Disputes between Member States may be at the root of litigation between the Commission and a Member State. See Case 232/78: *Commission v France* [1979] ECR 2729 where the dispute had earlier been the subject of an Art 170 (now Art 227) action brought by Ireland against France (Case 58/77: OJ 1977, C 142) which was later withdrawn (OJ 1978, C 76).

not, it is open to the Member State in question to bring proceedings before the Court challenging the Commission's decision. Although such litigation takes the form of a Member State bringing proceedings against the Commission, in substance the issue before the Court is an alleged breach of Treaty obligations by a Member State; the Treaty places the onus of challenging that allegation upon the Member State. In the EC Treaty by virtue of EC Article 226 (ex Art 169) a somewhat different procedure is followed.[6] There if the Commission considers that a Member State has failed to fulfil any of its obligations under the Treaties then it shall issue a reasoned opinion after giving the state concerned the opportunity to submit its comments. If the Member State does not comply with the terms of such opinion within the period laid down by the Commission the Commission may bring the matter before the Court of Justice. Thus, whilst in the ECSC the Commission has the power to determine finally a Member State's breach of obligations subject to the Member State's right to appeal to the Court, in the EC and EAEC the Commission can only provisionally determine the breach of obligation and it must apply to the Court for that determination to be confirmed. A similar right of action by the Commission against a Member State is given by EC Article 88(2) (ex Art 93(2)), in the context of the rules concerning state aid. If the Commission finds that financial aid granted by a Member State is incompatible with the Treaty it shall require that Member State to abolish or alter such aid. If the Member State does not comply within the prescribed period, the Commission may refer the matter to the Court direct.

Proceedings will lie against Member States not only for any acts on the part of a Member State but also for omissions, including administrative failures to implement Community law.[7] This reflects the dual duty of solidarity which EC Article 10 (ex Art 5), imposes on Member States: to take all appropriate measures to ensure the fulfilment of Treaty obligations and to abstain from any measure which could jeopardize the attainment of Treaty objectives. These actions not only serve the narrow purpose of enforcing the obligations of Member States in specific cases, but they also provide the Court with a vehicle for elaborating more broadly the nature of the Treaty obligations of Member States.

In one of the early cases, the Commission brought actions against Belgium and Luxembourg in which it alleged that a tax which those Member States were imposing on important licences for dairy products was contrary to the EC Treaty.[8] The defendant governments argued that a Council resolution of 1962 which had not yet been implemented would have justified the tax. They maintained that the Commission had no authority to require the abolition of a tax which but for the failure to implement the Council resolution would be part of Community policy. But the Court held that, except for cases expressly authorized by the Treaty, Member States are prohibited from taking justice into their own hands. Therefore a failure by the Council to carry out its obligations could not excuse the defendant Member States from carrying out theirs. Similarly, in a later case against Italy the Court rejected an attempted defence which was based on the fact that Member States other than Italy had also failed to carry out the obligation in question by the required date.[9]

In other cases in which a Member State has failed to fulfil its Treaty obligations the Court has not been moved by pleas that such failure is attributable

---

6   Also EAEC Art 141.
7   See Case 31/69: *Commission v Italy* [1970] ECR 25, [1970] CMLR 175.
8   Cases 90–91/63: *Commission v Luxembourg and Belgium* [1964] ECR 625, [1965] CMLR 58.
9   Case 52/75: *Commission v Italy* [1976] ECR 277, [1976] 2 CMLR 320.

to the special characteristics of the legal and constitutional order of a Member State or to prevailing political or economic conditions. Therefore, a political crisis in Italy which paralysed Italian legislative processes was not accepted as a defence to an EC Article 226 (ex Art 169), action.[10] In the same way the Court rejected a plea by the United Kingdom that its refusal to comply with a Community obligation was justified for economic and practical reasons including opposition by Trade Unions.[11] As the Court said in that latter case, 'practical difficulties which appear at the stage when a Community measure is put into effect cannot permit a Member State unilaterally to opt out of fulfilling its obligations'.[12] Partial and idiosyncratic implementation of Community obligations will not satisfy the Court.[13] Nor can a Member State avoid an EC Article 226 (ex Art 169), action by delaying taking implementing measures until the particular obligation has been revoked.[14] Community law must apply in each Member State independent of its unilateral will.

The case law on EC Article 226 (ex Art 169), also throws some light on the nature of the reasoned opinion which the Commission must make concerning the alleged breach of Treaty obligations. In *Commission v Italy* (1961)[15] the Commission wrote a letter to the Italian Government, after giving the Government an opportunity to make its observations, stating that a particular Italian decree was contrary to the Treaty. The Government was asked to end the alleged infringement within one month. This letter did not contain a full review of the situation of the Italian market nor whether that situation justified the decree. Italy did not comply with the Commission's request within the stated period and so the Commission instituted proceedings under EC Article 169 (now Art 226). Italy challenged the admissibility of these proceedings on the ground, inter alia, that the Commission's letter was not a reasoned opinion within the meaning of that Article. The Court rejected that argument and said that an opinion is considered to be reasoned 'when it contains, as in the present case, a coherent statement of the reasons which convinced the Commission that the state in question had failed to fulfil one of its obligations under the Treaty'. This was also the view expressed by the Advocate-General in his submissions where he said that 'no formalism is required ... because ... the reasoned opinion is not an administrative act, checked by the Court as far as its legal character is concerned. There is no question here of 'insufficient reasons' giving rise to a formal defect. The only purpose of the reasoned opinion is to specify the point of view of the Commission in order to inform the Government and, possibly, the Court.' Thus, if a purported reasoned opinion did not coherently express the Commission's viewpoint that would be a ground on which the Court might dismiss the Commission's case.[16]

In the case of Article 88 of the ECSC Treaty if the Member State does not appeal to the Court or if it loses its appeal, the Commission may, subject to a concurring two-thirds majority of the Council, impose on the Member State the

---

10   Case 30/72: *Commission v Italy* [1973] ECR 161.
11   Case 128/78: *Commission v United Kingdom* [1979] ECR 419, [1979] 2 CMLR 45.
12   Ibid at 429. Also see Case 102/79: *Commission v Belgium* [1980] ECR 1473 at 1487.
13   Case 39/72: *Commission v Italy* [1973] ECR 101, [1973] CMLR 439.
14   Ibid. In the context of EC Art 226 (ex Art 169), and EC Art 88(2) (ex Art 93(2)), actions, interim measures may be taken against a Member State in emergency situations; see Cases 31, 53/77R: *Commission v United Kingdom* [1977] ECR 921.
15   Case 7/61: [1961] ECR 317, [1962] CMLR 39.
16   Another essential part of the pre-litigation procedure under EC Art 226 (ex Art 169), is the giving to a Member State of an adequate and realistic opportunity to make observations on an alleged breach of treaty obligations; Case 31/69: *Commission v Italy* [1970] ECR 25, CMLR 175.

sanctions mentioned earlier. Thus in such cases the Court's judgments are essentially declaratory in nature indicating that it is sufficient to point out authoritatively the error into which the State fell and to show what has to be done to remain on the path of legality. The Member States have, in good faith, submitted to the Court of Justice and ought to implement its judgments in good faith. The concept of the Member States' 'delinquency' has not been explored but it is clear that as long as sovereignty remains a feature of the character of the membership of the Community/Union, they are not subject to physical execution of the judgments of the Court. Their obligation in this respect is of a legal nature since the Member States are not only governed by law but also because they demand obedience from their subjects. It is also of a moral nature since they set an example to their subjects and the fellow Member States. In the last analysis the success of the Community depends on the respect of the rule of law as an essential element of European integration.

An analysis of the breaches of obligations may allow one to guess a variety of causes ranging from erroneous interpretation of Community rules, inefficiency of the national system, political or economic problems facing the government and perhaps a cavalier attitude to accepted obligations. The Court does not censure the conduct of the Member States as irrespective of the cause it simply refers to 'breach' of the Treaties or of Community legislation, and endeavours to guide the State in question in the right direction, though the brevity of the judgment often speaks for itself.

In 1998 the Commission commenced 1,105 infringement procedures and issued 674 reasoned opinions. It referred 114 cases to the Court as follows: Belgium 19, Denmark none, Germany four, Greece 17, Spain five, France 22, Ireland ten, Italy 16, Luxembourg 11, Netherlands three, Austria two, Portugal five, Finland none, Sweden none and the United Kingdom none.[17] Although annual statistics are inconclusive it is a fact that over the years, certain countries accumulated a disproportionate number of breaches.

In monitoring the conduct of the Member States the Commission has another weapon in its armoury. According to EC Article 228 (ex Art 171) a failure to carry into effect a judgment constitutes an infringement of the Treaty. In such a case the Commission shall institute another procedure in a reasoned opinion specifying the points on which the Member State concerned has not complied with the judgment. If the State fails to take the necessary measures to comply with the judgment within the time limit laid down by the Commission, the latter may bring the case before the Court of Justice, which shall result in another declaration of the legal position. The Maastricht Treaty, responding to complaints of certain States, that obligations of the others are too often flaunted, added a rider to the effect that the Commission, bringing the second case 'shall specify the amount of the lump sum or penalty payment to be paid by the Member State concerned which it considers appropriate in the circumstances'. However such cases are relatively rare,[18] which proves that the enforcement procedure is quite effective. It is clear that Member States do not wish to be exposed as breakers of the legal order which they have created or joined as a going concern. As for the pecuniary sanction, it has been applied in Case C-387/97 *Commission v Greece*,[19] in which the ECJ held that the principal objective of the

---

17   1998 General Report (1999), para 1044.

18   Eg Case 48/71: *Commission v Italy* [1972] ECR 527, [1972] CMLR 699; Case 383/85: *Commission v Belgium* [1989] ECR 3069; Case C-266/89: *Commission v Italy* [1991] ECR I-2411; Case C-19/91: *Commission v Belgium* [1991] ECR I-5937; Case C-75/91: *Commission v Netherlands* [1992] ECR I-549; Case C-328/90: *Commission v Greece* [1992] ECR I-425; Case C-334/94: *Commission v France* [1996] ECR I-1307.

19   [2000] ECR I-5047.

sanction is to cause the Member State concerned to end the infringement as soon as possible. Accordingly, the sanction should be fixed by reference to the duration and gravity of the infringement and the State's ability to pay.

(b)   Actions against Community institutions
We have already seen that French law has exerted a strong influence on the procedure of the Court of Justice of the Communities. This is also true of the jurisdiction of the Court to exercise control over the acts of the institutions of the Communities. French administrative law traditionally recognizes two main categories of litigation: the *recours de la légalité* and the *recours de pleine juridiction*. The former is a kind of judicial review of the legality of administrative acts in which the Court is merely asked to annul, ie declare void, an administrative act on one of a number of specified grounds. In such a case if the Court finds that a given act is unlawful on one of those grounds it can merely give judgment to that effect; it cannot substitute its own decision on the merits for that of the institution whose act has been challenged, nor can it award any other remedy such as damages. In addition to *recours de la légalité* French administrative courts may also hear *recours de pleine juridiction*. In such cases those courts are not limited to controlling the legality of acts on specific grounds but they are free to pronounce on the actual merits of the parties' case and to substitute their own decision for that of the administrative authority. Such jurisdiction is *pleine*, ie full or plenary, in the sense that when exercising it the court has the complete powers of a civil court to award compensation for damage. These two types of administrative jurisdiction are possessed by the Court of Justice of the Communities and the following discussion will be in terms of that classification:

(i)   Actions concerning legality (recours de la légalité)
The acts of the institutions of the Communities take a variety of forms but not all of them are susceptible to challenge. Only those acts which are binding in law are susceptible to challenge. Under the ECSC Treaty the Commission may act in three forms: decisions, recommendations and opinions. Of these, decisions and recommendations are legally binding whilst opinions have no binding force; thus ECSC Article 33 gives the Court jurisdiction to hear actions for the annulment of such decisions and recommendations. Under the EC and EAEC Treaties, the acts of the Commission and the Council may take five forms: regulations, directives, decisions, recommendations and opinions; of these the first three are legally binding and are susceptible of an action for annulment. Thus the Court has declined to entertain an action for annulment in connection with any act which is not designed to produce binding legal effects. In *Sucrimex SA and Westzucker GmbH v Commission*[20] the Court rejected an action challenging the legality of a telex message from the Commission to the authorities of a Member State. In accordance with Community rules Sucrimex had exported a quantity of sugar to Westzucker. When the appropriate national authority was asked to pay the export refunds in respect of that transaction, payment in full was refused in accordance with the terms of the Commission's telex message. In dismissing the action, the Court held that under Community law the application of provisions concerning export refunds was a matter for the appropriate authorities of the Member States. In these matters the Commission had no power of decision, but it could express an opinion. This

20   Case 133/79: [1980] ECR 1299, [1981] 2 CMLR 479.

was confirmed by the contested telex message which did not disclose any intention to produce binding legal effects. The Court does, nevertheless, adopt a flexible approach to this issue. It will look to the substance of an act rather than to its form. Therefore, if an act is in the form normally used for non-binding acts, but in the view of the Court it does in fact create binding obligations, such an act would be actionable despite its apparent informality.[21] There is recent authority for the proposition that even a decision communicated orally during a conversation may be an act which is susceptible to an action for annulment.[1] It has also been held that certain acts of the European Parliament are open to challenge. Thus by invoking Article 38 of the ECSC Treaty which provides, inter alia, that on the application of either a Member State or the High Authority, an act of the European Parliament may be held void, the Court has claimed jurisdiction to review a decision of the European Parliament concerning its seat.[2] More generally the Court has held that acts of the European Parliament, at least in the budgetary field, which are intended to have legal effects on third parties are susceptible to an action for annulment under EC Article 230 (ex Art 173).[3]

Although the review of legality of Community acts takes place primarily in direct actions before the ECJ it is possible to challenge the validity of such acts in proceedings for a preliminary ruling commenced in national courts under EC Article 234 (ex Art 177).[4] However, since the latter have no competence in the matter, only the ECJ has the power to pronounce, exclusively, upon the validity of Community acts. The broad meaning of Community acts has been explained by the ECJ as acts which purport to have legal effect.[5]

EC Article 230 (ex Art 173) provides as follows:

'The Court of Justice shall review the legality of acts adopted jointly by the European Parliament and the Council, of acts of the Council, of the Commission and of the ECB, other than recommendations and opinions, and acts of the European Parliament intended to produce legal effects vis-à-vis third parties.

It shall for this purpose have jurisdiction in actions brought by a Member State, the Council or the Commission on grounds of lack of competence, infringement of an essential procedural requirement, infringement of this Treaty or of any rule of law relating to its application, or misuse of powers.

The Court shall have jurisdiction under the same conditions in actions brought by the European Parliament, by the Court of Auditors and by the ECB for the purpose of protecting their prerogatives.

Any natural or legal person may, under the same conditions, institute proceedings against a decision addressed to that person or a decision which, although in the form of a regulation or decision addressed to another person, is of direct and individual concern to the former.

The proceedings provided for in this Article shall be instituted within two months of the publication of the measure, or of its notification to the plaintiff,

---

21 See Case 22/70: *Commission v Council* [1971] ECR 263, [1971] CMLR 335.
1 See Cases 316/82 and 40/83: *Kohler v Court of Auditors* [1984] ECR 641.
2 See Cases 230/81 and 108/83: *Luxembourg v European Parliament* [1983] ECR 255 and [1984] ECR 1945.
3 See Case 34/86: *Council v European Parliament* [1986] 3 CMLR 94; and Case 294/83: *Parti Ecologist 'Les Verts' v European Parliament* [1987] 2 CMLR 343.
4 See eg Case 314/85: *Foto-Frost v HZA Lubeck-Ost* [1987] ECR 4199, [1988] 3 CMLR 57.
5 Case C-366/88: *France v Commission* [1990] ECR I-3571; Joined Cases 193 and 194/87; *Maurissen v Court of Auditors* [1989] ECR 1045, where an action against a measure adopted by the Court of Auditors was held admissible notwithstanding the absence, at that time, of that institution from Art 173.

or, in the absence thereof, of the day on which it came to the knowledge of the latter, as the case may be.'

The first three indents of EC Article 230 (ex Art 173), give effect to the new legislative procedures which have enhanced the position of the EP among the institutions and include the European Central Bank (ECB) created under the TEU. However it should be noted that actions of the EP and of the ECB are intended to serve only the 'protection of their prerogatives'.

(ii)   Procedural capacity

Actions may be brought not only by Member States and by Community institutions but also by private parties. In the first place, EC Article 230(1) (ex Art 173(1)), states that the legality of measures taken by the bodies referred to may be challenged in proceedings instituted by a Member State, the Council or the Commission[6] to which the TEU, in an amendment to EC Article 230 (ex Art 173), added the European Parliament and the European Central Bank but only for the purpose of protecting their prerogatives. As far as the EP is concerned the right of action for that purpose was conceded by the ECJ in the *Chernobyl* case ahead of the present amendment. The Commission's contention that it was able to protect the EP's position was dismissed. However the imbalance between the institutions, though mitigated, remains.

In general terms only a party which can show sufficient legal interest in a case can institute proceedings before the Court, but such is the nature of the Communities that all Member States are deemed to have an interest in the legality of all Community acts. Thus, for example, in *Netherlands v High Authority of the ECSC*[7] the Netherlands was permitted to challenge a decision of the High Authority which was in fact addressed to some German coal enterprises on the ground that it conflicted with the terms of the ECSC Treaty. The unfettered nature of the right of Member States to challenge Community acts is illustrated by a case in which Italy sought the annulment of a regulation for which it had voted in the Council. The Court rejected the Council's plea that the action was inadmissible. It held that every Member State has the right to challenge every Council regulation 'without the exercise of this right being conditional upon the position taken up by the ... Member States ... when the regulation in question was adopted'.[8]

It is clearly possible under the Treaties for one Community institution to challenge an act of another Community institution. To date this has not happened very often.[9] In his submissions in the first of those cases the Advocate-General referred to the novelty of the proceedings and attributed this to the fundamental harmony which reigns between the two institutions. Be that as it may, in that action the Commission challenged certain activities of the Council in the field of the external relations of the Communities. In March 1970 the Council discussed the attitude to be taken by the members of the Communities at a meeting to be held in April of that year to conclude negotiations for a European Road Transport Agreement (ERTA) under the auspices of the UN Economic Commission for Europe. At that April meeting the members of the Communities negotiated and

6   Cf ECSC Arts 33 and 38, and EAEC Art 146.
7   Case 66/63: [1964] ECR 533, [1964] CMLR 522.
8   Case 166/78: *Italy v Council* [1979] ECR 2575 at 2596.
9   See Case 22/70: *Commission v Council* [1971] ECR 263, [1971] CMLR 335; Case 81/72: *Commission v Council* [1973] ECR 575, [1973] CMLR 639, Case 70/74 *Commission v Council* [1975] ECR 795, [1975] 2 CMLR 287, and Case 218/82: *Commission v Council* [1983] ECR 4063, [1984] 2 CMLR 350.

concluded the Agreement in accordance with the terms of the Council's discussion. The Commission challenged the validity of that discussion on the ground that it involved violation of Treaty provisions, particularly since under EC Art 228 (now 300) the Commission is given the task of negotiating agreements between the Community and non-Member States subject to the approval of the Council. The Council challenged this action on the grounds of its admissibility and its merits. On the question of admissibility the Advocate-General submitted that, whilst in principle the action was admissible because the discussion in issue was an official discussion of the Council, upon analysis that discussion was not a legally binding act of the Council as defined by the Treaty and so was not susceptible to challenge. The Court disagreed with the Advocate-General on this point and held that the action was admissible. The Court pointed out that EC Article 173 (now Art 230) specifically excluded recommendations and opinions from review by the Court. Not only was this discussion neither a recommendation nor an opinion, it had definite legal effects on the Member States since during their negotiations on the ERTA they consistently acted in accordance with the conclusion of the Council discussion. But although the Court differed from the Advocate-General on the question of admissibility they both agreed that the action should be rejected on the merits.[10]

The question arose whether the European Parliament might challenge acts of the other institutions under EC Article 230 (ex Art 173), at a time when it was not named as a potential plaintiff. In 1987 the Parliament tested its claim by seeking the annulment of a Council decision on grounds that it had unlawfully failed to delegate authority to the Commission and had thereby deprived the Parliament of its prerogative of exercising political control over the Commission.[11] In response to the Council's plea that the action was inadmissible, the Parliament argued that given that the Treaty had been liberally interpreted to recognize the Parliament as a defendant under this Article[12] it should be similarly interpreted to recognize it as a plaintiff, particularly bearing in mind its Treaty right to challenge inaction.[13] The need for the Parliament to be able to protect its prerogatives was also stressed. The Court declared the action inadmissible.[14] It rejected the submission that there should be parallelism between the active and passive role of Parliament in proceedings under EC Article 173 (now Art 230), noting that that Article had not been amended by the Single European Act which, inter alia, was concerned with the Parliament's powers. Regarding any possible encroachment by the Council on the Parliament's prerogatives, the Court took the view that it was the responsibility of the Commission under EC Article 155 (now Art 211) to ensure that such prerogatives were respected.[15] This rebuff to the European Parliament's hopes was later partially redressed by the judgment in another case.[16] There it sought to challenge a Council regulation on the ground that it was based on a Commission proposal which failed to respond to the Parliament's disagreement with the legal base chosen for the regulation in the context of the

---

10 The merits of this case have already been discussed in connection with the external relations of the Communities; see p 74 supra.
11 Case 302/87: *European Parliament v Council* [1988] ECR 5615.
12 See p 303, supra.
13 See p 314, infra.
14 [1988] ECR, at pp 5636–5644.
15 As to EC Art 211 (ex Art 155), see Ch 7, supra.
16 Case C-70/88: *European Parliament v Council* [1990] ECR-I-2041. See also Case C-187/93: *European Parliament v Council* [1994] ECR I-2857.

co-operation procedure.[17] The Court agreed that in such a situation the Parliament clearly could not rely completely on the Commission to safeguard its prerogatives. In such circumstances the action by the Parliament was admissible. The position has been regularized by the Treaty of Maastricht which amended EC Article 173 (now Art 230) enabling the EP to bring an action 'for the purpose of protecting its prerogatives'.

Secondly, actions may be brought against acts of Community institutions by private parties, that is to say by individuals or corporate bodies.[18] The *locus standi* of private parties differs somewhat as between the ECSC on the one hand and the EC on the other. In the ECSC undertakings or associations of undertakings may challenge acts of Community institutions where either those acts apply to them individually or, although acts of a general nature, nevertheless involve a misuse of powers affecting them.[19] *Groupement des Industries Sidérurgiques Luxembourgeoises v High Authority*[20] is a clear illustration of this. The plaintiffs were manufacturers of steel and the main industrial consumers of coal in Luxembourg. They challenged the refusal of the High Authority to declare illegal a Luxembourg levy on coal for industrial use. The Luxembourg government intervened in the proceedings and argued that the plaintiffs' action was inadmissible on the ground that they were steel producers and the action was solely concerned with coal. But the Court held that the Treaty did not limit actions relating to coal undertakings and, since prima facie this levy was detrimental to the plaintiffs, their right of action could not be denied. In the EC, on the other hand, the right of action is not limited to undertakings but is available to any individual or corporate body against either a decision directed to him or it or a decision which, although in the form of a regulation or a decision addressed to someone else, is of direct and individual concern to him or it.[1]

Certain points of principle concerning the *locus standi* of private parties to challenge acts in the context of the EC are clear. The Treaty does not recognize an *actio popularis* but requires the party bringing the action to have sufficient legal interest in the issue.[2] This is comparable to the notion of standing (or sufficient interest) in English administrative law[3] and to the French maxim *pas d'intérêt, pas d'action*.[4] A right of action is admitted against three types of act: decisions addressed to the party bringing the action; decisions in the form of regulations addressed to other persons; and decisions addressed to other persons. In the last two cases the party bringing the action must be able to satisfy the Court that the decisions affect him directly and individually. Despite dicta in some cases in which a generous interpretation of these provisions has been suggested,[5] the Court has tended to interpret them restrictively and the resulting case law has not yet evolved an entirely consistent line of authority.

Least difficulty arises where the act challenged is a decision expressly addressed to the private party bringing the action, such as in connection with the Community's

17   As to this procedure, see Ch 9, supra.
18   The novelty of this right of audience is fully justified by the fact that Community law applies directly to private parties which EC Art 230 (ex Art 173), refers to as natural and legal persons.
19   Eg ECSC Arts 33(2) and 80.
20   Cases 7 and 9/54: [1954–56] ECR 175.
 1   EC Art 230(2) (ex 173(2)); see also EAEC Art 146(2).
 2   See Case C-298/89: *Government of Gibraltar v Council* [1993] ECR I-3605.
 3   Wade, H W R, and Forsyth, C F, *Administrative Law* (7th edn, 1994), pp 696 et seq.
 4   See Brown, L N, and Garner, J F, *French Administrative Law* (3rd edn, 1983), pp 102, 103.
 5   See Case 25/62: *Plaumann & Co v Commission* [1963] ECR 95 at 106, 107; and Case 69/69: *S A Alcan Aluminium Raeren v Commission* [1970] ECR 385 at 393.

rules on competition. In such cases there appears to be a conclusive presumption that the plaintiff has *locus standi*.[6] On the question whether a given act is a decision, particularly in the context of decisions in the form of regulations, the Court looks to the object and content of the act rather than to its form.[7] A distinction is drawn between acts which apply to a limited, identifiable number of destinees and acts of a normative character which apply to categories of persons envisaged in the abstract and as a whole; the former are decisions, the latter regulations.[8] Thus the Court has held that a regulation relating to the manufacture of a particular product by a limited number of producers is nevertheless a regulation because of its objective, normative character.[9] Whereas a regulation which was only concerned with import licences which had been sought before that regulation was made was, in fact, a bundle of individual decisions.[10]

This distinction between regulations and decisions also impinges on the requirement that decisions addressed to other persons[11] must be of both direct and individual concern to the party bringing the action. The Court has tended to reverse the order of these two conditions as they are set out in the Treaty on the ground that if the applicant is not individually concerned by the decision, it becomes unnecessary to inquire whether he is directly concerned.[12] In *Plaumann & Co v Commission* (1964) the Court defined individual concern in the following terms: 'Persons other than those to whom a decision is addressed may only claim to be individually concerned if that decision affects them by reason of certain attributes which are peculiar to them or by reason of circumstances in which they are differentiated from all other persons and by virtue of these factors distinguishes them individually just as in the case of the person addressed'.[13] In applying that definition the Court has declined to find individual concern where a decision is addressed to an abstractly defined category of persons even where in reality the decision only affects an ascertainable number of such persons.[14] Such a decision potentially affects an indeterminate number of persons. But where, on the other hand, at the time a decision is made the number of persons affected by it is already finitely determined, eg if the decision is

6   Eg Case 48/69: *ICI Ltd v Commission* [1972] ECR 619, [1972] CMLR 557; Case 6/72: *Europemballage Corpn and Continental Can Co Inc v Commission* [1973] ECR 215, [1973] CMLR 199, and Cases 6 and 7/73: *Istituto Chemioterapico Italiano SpA and Commercial Solvents Corpn v Commission* [1974] ECR 223, [1974] 1 CMLR 309.

7   Cases 16–17/62: *Confédération Nationale des Producteurs de Fruits et Légumes v Council* [1962] ECR 471 at 478. See also Case 117/86: *UFADE v Council and Commission* [1986] ECR 3255 para 12.

8   Ibid at 478, 479. See also Case T-12/96: *Areacova SA et al v Council and Commission* [1999] ECR II-2301, paras 24-70.

9   Case 6/68: *Zuckerfabrik Watenstedt GmbH v Council* [1968] ECR 409, [1969] CMLR 26. Also see Case 123/77: *UNICME v Council* [1978] ECR 845 and Case 101/76: *Koninklijke Scholten Honig NV v Council and Commission* [1977] ECR 797.

10 Cases 41–44/70: *N V International Fruit Co v Commission* [1971] ECR 411, [1975] 2 CMLR 515. Also see Case 138/79: *SA Roquette Frères v Council* [1980] ECR 3333.

11 'Other persons' includes Member States; see Case 25/62: *Plaumann & Co v Commission* [1963] ECR 95 and Case 730/79: *Philip Morris Holland BV v Commission* [1980] ECR 2671, [1981] 2 CMLR 321. It may also include other private parties; see Case 26/76: *Metro-SB-Grossmärkte GmbH & Co KG v Commission* [1977] ECR 1875, [1978] 2 CMLR 1.

12 Case 25/62: *Plaumann & Co v Commission* [1963] ECR 95 at 107.

13 Ibid.

14 Eg Case: 1/64: *Glucoséries Réunis v Commission* [1964] ECR 413; Case 38/64: *Getreide-Import Gesellschaft v Commission* [1965] ECR 203, [1965] CMLR 276; and Case 64/69: *Compagnie Française Commerciale et Financière SA v Commission* [1970] ECR 221, [1970] CMLR 369.

retroactive or if it refers to certain persons by name, then those persons are individually concerned.[15]

Thus, in order for a measure to be of individual concern to the persons to whom it applies, it must affect their situation which differentiates them from all other persons and distinguishes them individually in the same way as a person to whom it is addressed.[16]

The Court's approach to the question of direct concern appears to depend on whether the person to whom the decision was addressed had a discretion to implement it. If there was no discretion then, subject to the other criteria, the decision is of direct concern; if there was a discretion then it is not.[17] In *Alfred Toepfer v Commission* (1966) the plaintiff's application for a licence to import maize was rejected by the German authorities on 1 October 1963, because of protective measures which they were taking under the terms of EEC Regulation No 19. On the same day the German authorities notified the Commission of those measures which were subject to confirmation, amendment or rejection by the Commission within four days of notification. On 3 October the Commission made a decision authorizing the German authorities to maintain the protective measures in force between 1 to 4 October inclusive. The plaintiffs challenged that decision. The Court of Justice held that they had the necessary *locus standi*. The decision concerned them directly because it was immediately enforceable and left no discretion with the German authorities; it concerned them individually because the number and identity of the persons affected was determined before 3 October.

There is clearly a close relationship between the notion of a decision as an act which determines what is to happen in a limited number of particular cases and the notions of direct and individual concern. In one case the Court apparently assumed that if an act affects persons directly and individually then the act is a decision.[18] The Court adopted this approach expressly in *UNICME v Council* (1978)[19] in which the annulment of a regulation was sought. This is possible at the suit of a private party only if the act in question is a decision in the form of a regulation. But the Court observed: 'It is unnecessary to consider whether the contested measure may be regarded as a regulation and it is sufficient to establish whether it is in fact of direct and individual concern to the applicants.'[20] The Court has also accepted the possibility that a provision in a regulation may, at the same time, be both general and specific: general as far as most of those affected by it are concerned, but of direct and individual concern with respect to some. In such a situation the latter, but not of course the former, would have *locus standi* to challenge that provision.[1]

15 See Cases 106–107/63: *Alfred Toepfer and Getreide-Import Gesellschaft v Commission* [1965] ECR 405, [1966] CMLR 111; Case 62/70: *Bock v Commission* [1971] ECR 897, [1972] CMLR 160; and Cases 41–44/70: *NV International Fruit Co v Commission* [1971] ECR 411, [1975] 2 CMLR 515; Cases 113/77: *NTN v Council and Commission* [1979] ECR 1185, [1979] 2 CMLR 257.

16 Case 26/86: *Deutz and Geldemann v Council* [1987] ECR 941 at para 9, [1988] 1 CMLR 668.

17 See Case 69/69, supra, p 306, note 5 and Case 11/82: *Piraiki-Patraiki v Commission* [1985] ECR 207.

18 Case 100/74: *Société CAM SA v Commission* [1975] ECR 1393 at 1402, 1403.

19 Case 123/77: [1978] ECR 845.

20 Ibid, at 851.

1 See Cases 239, 275/82: *Allied Corpn v Commission* [1984] ECR 1005, [1985] 3 CMLR 572.

(iii)   Grounds of review

On the question of the grounds of action all three Community Treaties mention the same four grounds which are derived from French administrative law, viz:

(aa)   lack of competence, or
(bb)   infringement of an essential procedural requirement, or
(cc)   infringement of the Treaties or of any rules of law relating to their application, or
(dd)   misuse of powers.[2]

(aa) Lack of competence is broadly comparable to the English doctrine of substantive *ultra vires*. 'Each institution,' in the words of EC Article 7 (ex Art 4), 'shall act within the limits of the powers conferred upon it ...'. Therefore, if a Community institution acts without authority that act may be declared void on the ground of lack of powers. Lack of competence covers situations in which the Communities have no power, have power but invoke the wrong Treaty provision,[3] or in which the Communities have power but it has been exercised by the wrong body. Thus in *Meroni v High Authority* (1958)[4] the plaintiff challenged certain levies imposed by the High Authority on the basis of decisions taken by subordinate bodies to whom the High Authority had purported to delegate certain powers. The Court held that those subordinate bodies lacked the power to take such decisions since the Treaty did not authorize the High Authority to delegate its decision-making power. Other areas in which questions of lack of competence have arisen are where an institution has claimed implied powers or the authority to extend its jurisdiction beyond the territorial limits of the Community. While the Court has acknowledged the existence of implied powers in relation to the EC,[5] there are clearly limits to such powers. If those limits should not be respected, a plea of lack of competence could be raised.[6] In the context of the Community's rules on competition,[7] on several occasions the Commission has imposed penalties for breach on corporations based outside the Community. Pleas by such corporations that the Commission lacked competence to impose those penalties have so far failed. The Court has been satisfied that the penalties related to activities carried on within the Community.[8] But here again there is clearly a limit to the Commission's authority which if exceeded would justify a plea of lack of competence.[9]

(bb) Infringement of essential procedural requirements also has an equivalent in English law, viz procedural ultra vires. But, as in the case of both English and French administrative law, the Court of the Communities will not annul an act merely because some minor and unimportant procedural rule has not been

---

2   ECSC Art 33; EC Art 230 (ex Art 173); EAEC Art 146.
3   See Case 68/86: *United Kingdom v Council* [1988] ECR 855, [1988] 2 CMLR 543.
4   Case 9/56: [1957–58] ECR 133.
5   See Case 22/70: *Commission v Council* [1971] ECR 263, [1971] CMLR 335.
6   Cf Case 8/55: *Fédération Charbonnière de Belgique v High Authority* [1954–56] ECR 245.
7   EC Arts 81–89 (ex Arts 85–94).
8   Eg Case 48/69: *ICI v Commission* [1972] ECR 619, [1972] CMLR 447 and Cases 6–7/73: *Istituto Chemisterapico Italiano SpA and Commercial Solvents Corpn v Commission* [1974] ECR 223, [1974] 1 CMLR 309.
9   See Joined Cases 89, 104, 114, 116, 117 and 125 and 129/85: *A Åhlström Osakeyhtiö v Commission* [1988] ECR 5193.

observed; an action for annulment on this ground will only be granted when the procedural rule which has been infringed is an essential rule in the sense that it is substantial or basic. Such procedural requirements can be imposed either by the Treaties or by secondary legislation. An example of the former is provided by the case of *Germany v Commission* (1963).[10] Prior to the establishment of the EEC, Germany used to import cheap wines for the production of 'Brennwein'. In 1961 it asked the Commission for a tariff quota of 450,000 hectolitres of wine for this purpose. The Commission granted a quota of only 100,000 hectolitres. EC Article 190 (now 253) requires that the Commission's decisions shall 'state the reasons on which they are based'. Germany challenged the partial rejection of its request on the ground that that decision was insufficiently reasoned. The Commission had merely said that its decision was based on 'information that has been gathered' which indicated 'that the production of wines of this nature within the Community is amply sufficient'. The Court agreed with the Advocate-General that the Commission's decision should be annulled on the ground that it gave inadequate reasons and thus infringed an important procedural rule. The Court said 'In imposing upon the Commission the obligation to state reasons for its decisions, Article 190 is not taking mere formal considerations into account but seeks to give an opportunity to the parties of defending their rights, to the Court of exercising its supervisory functions and to Member States and to all interested nationals of ascertaining the circumstances in which the Commission has applied the Treaty. To attain these objectives, it is sufficient for the decision to set out, in a concise but clear and relevant manner, the principal issues of law and of fact upon which it is based and which are necessary in order that the reasoning which has led the Commission to its decision may be understood'.[11] This, the Court held, the Commission's vague statements failed to do.[12] In *Transocean Marine Paint Association v Commission* (1974)[13] the procedural requirement arose under a Regulation. In 1967 the plaintiff had been granted an exemption from applicability of the Community's rules on competition under the terms of EC Article 85(3) (now Art 81(3)). In 1972 the exemption came up for renewal. The Commission refused to renew it on the original terms and imposed additional conditions because of changes which had occurred in the competitive situation. The plaintiff found one of the additional conditions particularly onerous and sought its revocation on the ground that no notice was given of it nor any opportunity to comment. The Court held that the Regulation under which the Commission had acted incorporated 'the general rule that a person whose interests are perceptibly affected by a decision of a public authority must be given the opportunity to make his point of view known'.[14] That obligation had not been fulfilled in this case and so the Commission's Decision was, to that extent, annulled.[15]

---

10 Case 24/62: [1963] ECR 63, [1963] CMLR 347. Also see Case 73/74: *Groupement des Fabricants de Papiers Peints de Belgique v Commission* [1975] ECR 1491, [1976] 1 CMLR 589.
11 [1963] ECR at 69.
12 A failure to consult the European Parliament when required so to do by the Treaty is also a violation of an essential procedural requirement; see Case 138/79: *SA Roquette Frères v Council* [1980] ECR 3333.
13 Case 17/74: [1974] ECR 1063, [1974] 2 CMLR 459.
14 Ibid at 1080.
15 As to the consequences of a failure by the Council to follow its own rules of procedure, see Case 68/86: *United Kingdom v Council* [1988] ECR 855, [1988] 2 CMLR 543 and Case 131/86: *United Kingdom v Council*, ibid at 905.

(cc) Infringement of the Treaty or of any rule of law relating to its application is a ground broad enough to embrace the other three more specific grounds of challenge. Indeed, cases brought on any of those grounds could equally be brought under this. In practice however this general ground has by no means been superfluous. Its broad formulation has provided the juridical basis upon which the Court has developed the Community concept of legality beyond the terms of the Community Treaties and secondary legislation to general principles of law recognized by the Member States. An illustration is provided by *August Töpfer & Co GmbH v Commission* (1978).[16] The plaintiff held a number of export licences for sugar. In accordance with Community rules the amount of export refund he would receive in respect of such transactions was fixed in advance. In principle, if the value of such refunds changes as a result of currency fluctuations before the transaction is carried out, the licence holder may apply to have the licence cancelled. In this instance this basic scheme was varied by a Commission Regulation which withdrew the plaintiff's right of cancellation and substituted the payment of compensation. This was financially disadvantageous to the plaintiff and so he sought the annulment of the Regulation. He alleged that the Regulation breached a general principle of law, namely the principle of legitimate expectation. The plaintiff maintained that by the terms under which his export licences had been granted, he could expect either to receive the export refunds or be able to exercise his right of cancellation. Because of the Commission's intervention that expectation had not been realized. Although the Court dismissed the plaintiff's action on the merits, it did acknowledge expressly that the plaintiff's argument was one which it would entertain. 'The submission that there has been a breach of [the] principle [of legitimate expectation] is admissible in the context of proceedings instituted under Article 173 [now Art 230], since the principle in question forms part of the Community legal order with the result that any failure to comply with it is an "infringement of this Treaty or of any rule of law relating to its application" within the meaning of the Article quoted.'[17] It follows from this that the breach of any principle accepted by the Court as a general principle of Community law may be invoked as a ground for the annulment of a Community act. Such principles are regarded by the Court as forming an integral part of the legal order of the Community established by the Treaties.

(dd) Misuse of powers provides the basis of an action for annulment when it can be shown that a discretionary power has been used to achieve some object other than that for which the power was conferred. Thus proceedings for an action on this ground involve the Court in determining the object which the act in question was intended to achieve and then to decide whether that object comes within the purpose for which the power was conferred. As the Advocate-General put it in *Fédération Charbonnière de Belgique v High Authority*[18] 'It is a matter of discovering what was the object in fact pursued by the author of the act, when he took the decision, in order to be able to compare it with the object he ought to have pursued and which, unless the contrary is proved, he is deemed to have pursued'. The question is, therefore, whether the author of the act really had an illegal or legal object in view at the time he took the act. It is not necessary for an illegal objective to have been actually achieved, it is sufficient that the motive behind the act was illegal. Further, if an act achieves a legal object but also incidentally achieves other illegal objects that will not be a misuse of power, provided that the

16 Case 112/77: [1978] ECR 1019.
17 Ibid, at 1033.
18 Case 8/55: [1954–56] ECR 245.

legal object is the dominant object. In *France v High Authority* (1954),[19] for example, the High Authority, purporting to act under Article 60 of the ECSC Treaty, made a number of decisions authorizing steel enterprises to deviate from their published prices provided that such deviations did not constitute discrimination which is forbidden by the Treaty. The French Government challenged those decisions alleging that the High Authority had no power to achieve those particular aims under Article 60 but should have acted under Articles 61 and 65 for the real object of those decisions was to lower steel prices generally and prevent price agreement and this could only be done under those latter Articles. Therefore it was asserted that by issuing those decisions under Article 60 it had misused its powers. But the Court held that in fact there had been no misuse of powers, for even if those decisions had in fact been made to achieve an unjustified object the decisions would not be vitiated provided the essential object of the power was achieved. The Court held that was so in this case. Misuse of powers has a particular significance under the ECSC Treaty since it is the ground upon which coal and steel undertakings may challenge Community acts which are general in character.[20] In the other two Communities this ground has had little significance.[1]

(iv) Limitation

An action for annulment must be brought within limited periods of one month under the ECSC Treaty and two months under the EC and Euratom Treaties,[2] since the publication of the measure in question or of its notification to the plaintiff, or, in the absence thereof, on the day on which it came to the knowledge of the latter. These periods are necessarily short since the economic regime set up by the Treaties is a dynamic thing which it would be impossible to alter long after the event by actions against decisions taken. In the new version of EC Article 254 (ex Art 191) regulations, directives and decisions adopted jointly by the EP and the Council and directives adopted by the Council and Commission as well as directives of those institutions which are addressed to all Member States enter into force on the date specified in them or, in the absence thereof, on the twentieth day following that of their publication. Other directives and decisions shall be notified to those to whom they are addressed and shall take effect upon such notification.[3]

Detailed rules regarding limitation of actions under EC Article 230(3) (ex Art 173(3)), are contained in Articles 80 and 81 of the ECJ's Rules of Procedure. According to Article 81(2), extension of the prescribed time is allowed on account of the distance between the Court and the applicant's habitual residence. However, according to Article 42 of the Court's Statute, no right shall be prejudiced in consequence of the expiry of a time limit if the party concerned proves the existence of unforeseeable circumstances or of *force majeure*.[4]

---

19 Case 1/54: [1954–56] ECR 1.
20 ECSC Art 33(2).
1 But see Cases 18, 35/65: *Gutmann v EAEC Commission* [1966] ECR 103 and Case 105/75: *Guiffrida v Council* [1976] ECR 1395 concerned with the terms of appointment of Community officials.
2 ECSC Art 33; EC Art 230 (ex Art 176); EAEC Art 146.
3 See Case 6/72: *Europemballage Corpn and Continental Can Co Inc v Commission* [1973] ECR 215 at 241.
4 See eg Case C-59/91: *France v Commission* [1992] ECR I-525.

Even if the period laid down by EC Article 230(3) (ex Art 173(3)), has expired it is still possible to challenge the validity of a general Community act in other proceedings of the ECJ by raising the plea of illegality.[5]

(v)   Effect of annulment

In general the effect of an annulment is quite simply to declare the Community act in question to be void and this is the basic rule to be found in all three treaties.[6] The Court has no power to make any specific order regarding the implementation of the judgment.[7] In the ECSC the Commission is required to take steps to give effect to the annulment and to compensate for any loss suffered as a result of the annulled act. The EC and Euratom Treaties simply require the institution whose act has been annulled to take the necessary steps to comply with the Court's judgment. Thus, subject to compensation under the ECSC Treaty, which in any event is awarded by the Commission, annulment has essentially a negative effect but may generate the necessity for the institution whose act is annulled to take some action to stop to deal with the consequences of annulment. But the annulment may not affect the whole of the act against which an action has been brought. EC Article 231 (ex Art 174) enables the Court to confirm particular parts of a regulation which it has otherwise annulled. Thus in a case in which a regulation concerned with the price of fruit and vegetables was challenged, the Court declared void that part of the regulation which related to tomatoes.[8] The EC Treaty itself does not expressly extend this possibility of partial annulment to acts other than regulations, but nevertheless we find the Court in *Consten and Grundig v EC Commission* (1966)[9] annulling a decision in part. In that case Consten and Grundig entered into a contract whereby Consten became the sole agent for the distribution of Grundig products in France. Other firms selling Grundig products in France complained to the Commission that this contract was contrary to EC Article 85 (now Art 81), which controls restrictive practices. The Commission issued a decision which stated that the contract did violate EC Article 85. Consten and Grundig then brought these proceedings challenging the decision and the Court held that certain elements in the contract infringed the Treaty and certain others did not, therefore the decision was partially annulled and partially upheld. This is an example of the flexible approach which the Court adopts. Indeed there would seem to be no reason in principle why a process of partial annulment should not be applied generally in appropriate cases to acts other than regulations *stricto senso*.[10] The Court's willingness to do this is illustrated by *Council v European Parliament*[11] in which the decision to annul the declaration by the President of the European Parliament that the 1986 budget was adopted was expressly held not to affect the validity of payments already made and commitments already

---

5   See infra pp 316 et seq.
6   ECSC Art 33; EC Art 231 (ex Art 174); EAEC Art 147.
7   Eg Case 53/85: *AKZO Chemic BV and AKZO Chemic UK Ltd v Commission* [1986] ECR 1965, para 23.
8   Case 151/73: *Ireland v Council* [1974] ECR 285, [1974] 1 CMLR 429. In Case 138/79: *SA Roquette Frères v Council* [1980] ECR 3333 the Court declared an entire regulation void despite the fact that the private plaintiffs sought only its partial annulment and that they only had locus standi in respect of those parts of the regulation which concerned them directly and individually.
9   Cases 56 and 58/64: [1966] ECR 299, [1966] CMLR 418.
10 Also see Case 17/74: *Transocean Marine Paint Association v Commission* [1974] ECR 1063, [1974] 2 CMLR 459.
11 Case 34/86: [1986] 3 CMLR 94.

entered in implementation of the budget. Indeed, the Court held that the annulment was operative prospectively from the point in the budgetary procedure at which the illegality occurred. It also appears that in cases in which a regulation is declared to be void on the ground that it invoked the wrong Treaty provision or should have been more exacting, the Court will order that the effects of such regulation shall remain in force until new measures taken in compliance with its judgment have entered into force.[12]

In principle the declaration of nullity takes effect *erga omnes* and *ex tunc*, that is to say against the whole world and as from the adoption of the annulled act.[13] However, exceptionally, the effect may be declared to be prospective 'where the purpose to be achieved so demands and the legitimate expectations of those concerned are duly respected'.[14]

(vi)   Actions against inactivity
The second main category of actions concerning legality is the action against inactivity. Where the Treaties impose a duty to act on a particular institution and it fails to act then an action may be based on a violation of the Treaty through inactivity. The inactivity must first be brought to the attention of the institution concerned and if it has not taken satisfactory steps to remedy or justify its inactivity an action may be instituted.[15] Under the ECSC Treaty such actions may be brought against the Commission either by Member States, or by the Council or by undertakings or associations of undertakings. Under the EC and Treaties the Member States and the Community institutions (including the European Parliament) have a general competence to challenge the inactivity of either the Commission or the Council. The TEU adds the EP and the ECB to the institutions whose acts may be challenged. The latter may also bring such proceedings (against another institution) but only 'in the areas falling within [its] field of competence'.

The EP was originally omitted from EC Article 175 (now Art 232) but the ECJ held that acts of the European Parliament were subject to review[16] under EC Article 173 (now Art 230). Thus the position has been rectified and for good reason because of the enhanced role of the EP in the legislative process.

Individuals and corporate bodies may bring such proceedings if they can show that one of those institutions has failed to address an act (other than a recommendation or opinion)[17] to him or it.[18] An example of such an action under the ECSC Treaty is *Groupement des Industries Sidérurgiques Luxembourgeoises v High Authority* (1956).[19] The Luxembourg Government imposed a levy on coal intended

---

12   See Case 275/87: *Commission v Council* [1989] ECR 259; Case 264/82: *Timex v Council and Commission* [1985] ECR 849, para 32.
13   However, where a decision addressed to several persons is annulled at the suit of them, the judgment does not have the effect of annulling the decision, in so far as it applies to those addressees who did not challenge it, if, on it's true construction, the decision is to be regarded as a bundle of different decisions each of which is addressed to a different addressee: Cases T-305/94, T-306/94, T-307/94, T-313 to T-316/94, T-318/94, T-325/94, T-328/94, T-329/94 and T-335/94: *Limburgse Vinyl Maatschappij v Commission* [1999] ECR II-931, paras 167-174.
14   Case 108/81: *Amylum v Council* [1982] ECR 3107.
15   ECSC Art 35; EC Art 232 (ex Art 175); EAEC Art 148.
16   Case 294/83: *Parti Ecologiste La Verts v European Parliament* [1986] ECR 1339, [1987] 2 CMLR 343.
17   See Case 6/70: *Borromeo Arese v Commission* [1970] ECR 815, [1970] CMLR 436.
18   See Case 103/63: *Rhenania Schiffahrts- und Speditions-Gesellschaft mbH v Commission* [1964] ECR 425 per A-G Roemer at 431, 432.
19   Cases 7 and 9/54: [1954–56] ECR 175.

for industrial use for the purpose of subsidizing the price of household coal. The plaintiffs, who were the main users of industrial coal, alleged that this levy was contrary to the ECSC Treaty and requested the High Authority to use its powers to require the Luxembourg Government to abolish the levy. During the two months following this request the High Authority did nothing and the plaintiffs brought an action under ECSC Article 35 and the Court held that the action was admissible.

Cases brought by private parties under the EC Treaty show that action under EC Article 232 (ex Art 175) will fail if the act sought is one which cannot be properly addressed to the plaintiff or where an applicant requests a measure addressed to third parties rather than to himself.[20] In one case a complaint that the Commission had failed to issue a decision amending the rules concerning intra-Community trade was dismissed since the proper addressees of such a decision would have been the Member States.[1] Similarly, where a plaintiff's claim could only be met by making a regulation the action was dismissed since a regulation cannot be described 'by reason either of its form or of its nature' as an act which could be addressed to the plaintiff.[2] An EC Article 232 (ex Art 175) action will also fail if the allegedly defaulting institution has 'defined its position' within two months of being called upon to act. Thus in *Alfons Lütticke GmbH v Commission* (1966)[3] the action was held to be inadmissible since the Commission had declared its position and had made clear its attitude to the matter in question within that two-month period. This clearly falls far short of compelling the performance of a specific act. Similarly the action should fail if the applicant asks the Commission to adopt an act that would, in reality, constitute an opinion[4] or a recommendation since these are not binding acts within the meaning of EC Article 249 (ex Art 189).[5]

In Case C-25/91 an action under EC Article 175 (now Art 232) that the Commission failed to grant financial aid for the construction of a new fishing vessel in contravention of Regulation 4028/86 was dismissed. The ECJ found that the Commission had defined its position as it in fact rejected the application on the ground of insufficient funds being at its disposal. The Court reiterated that EC Article 175 (now Art 232) refers to failure to act or to define the position but not to a failure to adopt a measure to the satisfaction of the applicant.

The Court also distinguishes between a failure to act and a refusal to act. While the former prima facie comes within the scope of EC Article 232 (ex Art 175), the latter does not since it is regarded as constituting a negative decision. A refusal by the Commission to revoke an allegedly illegal act has been held not to be actionable under EC Article 232 (ex Art 175).[6] In the same way, if, when called upon to act, the Commission adopts a measure other than that sought by the plaintiff the action will fail.[7] In such cases the appropriate remedy is to seek the annulment of the action in question under the terms of EC Article 230 (ex Art 173). It is also clear that where the Council or Commission adopts the measure

---

20 Case 246/81: *Lord Bethell v Commission* [1982] ECR 2277, [1982] 3 CMLR 300.
1   Case 15/71: *Firma C Mackprang, Jr v Commission* [1971] ECR 797, [1972] CMLR 52.
2   Case 90/78: *Granaria BV v Council and Commission* [1979] ECR 1081 at 1093.
3   Case 48/65: [1966] ECR 19, [1966] CMLR 378.
4   See Case 15/70: *Chevally v Commission* [1970] ECR 975.
5   Case C-25/91: *Pesqueras Echebastar SA v Commission* [1993] ECR I-1755 following Joined Cases C-15/91 and C-108/91: *Buckl & Söhne OHG v Commission* [1992] ECR I-6061.
6   Cases 10 and 18/68: *Società 'Eridania' Zuccherifici Nazionali v Commission* [1969] ECR 459.
7   Case 8/71: *Deutscher Komponistenverband eV v Commission* [1971] ECR 705, [1973] CMLR 902.

requested after the action has been brought but before judgment has been given, the Court will take the view that the action no longer has any substance and a decision is therefore unnecessary.[8] One successful action to date under EC Article 232 (ex Art 175) is *European Parliament v Council*,[9] in which the Court condemned the Council's failure to introduce a common transport policy as required by EC Article 71 (ex Art 75). The Court held, notwithstanding the Parliament's omission to specify the measures which should have been taken, that the Council had failed to carry out, by the Treaty deadline, measures which were sufficiently precise so as to ensure the provision of services in the field of international transport and to fix conditions under which non-resident carriers might operate within a Member State.

The effect of a positive judgment of the Court is merely a declaration that the institution in question is in breach of a duty under the Treaty and consequently has to take the necessary measures to comply with the judgment of the Court as stipulated under EC Article 233 (ex Art 176). However the obligation implied therein shall not affect any obligation arising from the provisions of EC Article 288(2) (ex Art 215(2)), governing non-contractual liability of the Community.[10] In other words, the institution may still be liable in damages for the consequences of its inaction even if it complies properly with the judgment.

(vii)   The plea of illegality

We have seen that a restrictive period of limitation is applied to actions for annulment with the general result that if an act is not challenged within that period the act becomes unassailable. But a situation may arise in an action before the Court in which the illegality of an act forming the legal basis of the act whose annulment is sought in the meetings may be in issue. If the period of limitation were to be applied strictly such an issue could not be raised outside the period, but to overcome such a possible result all three Treaties make it possible for such a question of illegality to be raised in such proceedings;[11] this again is a form of procedure known to French law. Under the ECSC Treaty both types of binding act, namely decisions and recommendations, may be challenged by this procedure. But under the EC and Euratom Treaties only regulations are open to challenge. EC Article 241 (ex Art 184) has been extended to regulations adopted jointly by the EP and the Council and regulations of the Council, of the Commission and of the ECB. This provision can only be relied upon as a plea that can be raised in proceedings before the Court; it does not of itself give rise to an independent cause of action.[12] If such a plea of illegality is successfully invoked its technical effect will not be to declare the act in question illegal in terms of its general application but inapplicable in relation to the applicant (and therefore to the act whose annulment is sought, thus depriving it of its legal basis). This is made clear by the case law. In *Meroni & Co v High Authority* (1958)[13] the High Authority requested Meroni to pay a levy on the authority of earlier decisions of a general nature which it had taken. Meroni declined to pay and challenged the High Authority's request on the ground that the general decisions on which it was based were illegal. The High Authority argued

8   See Case 377/87: *European Parliament v Council* [1988] ECR 4017.
9   Case 13/83: [1985] ECR 1513, [1986] 1 CMLR 138.
10 EC Art 233(2) (ex Art 176(2)).
11 ECSC Art 36; EC Art 241 (ex Art 184); EAEC Art 156.
12 Cases 31 and 33/62: *Milchwerke Heinz Wöhrmann and Sohn KG v Commission* [1962] ECR 501, [1963] CMLR 152 and Joined Cases 275/80 and 24/81: *Krupp Stahl AG v Commission* [1981] ECR 2489.
13 Case 9/56: [1957–58] ECR 133.

that such a plea was inadmissible since the time limit for the challenge of those decisions had expired. The question therefore arose whether Meroni could rely on the defence of illegality. The Court held that it could and in its judgment considered the nature of this plea: 'An applicant's right, after the expiration of the period prescribed [for actions for annulment], ... to take advantage of the irregularity of general decisions or recommendations in support of proceedings against decisions or recommendations which are individual in character cannot lead to the annulment of the general decision, but only to the annulment of the individual decision which is based on it'.[14] In view of the limited right which individual and corporate bodies have to sue for the annulment of general decisions this plea of illegality is important since it widens the legal protection of such parties.

Since the remedy applies only to regulations the ECJ[15] ruled that a Member State is constrained from pleading 'the unlawfulness of a decision addressed to it as a defence in an action for a declaration that it had failed to fulfil its obligations arising out of its failure to implement that decision'. The Court however added a rider[16] to the effect that the position would be different 'only if the measure at issue contained such particularly serious and manifest defects that it could be deemed non-existent'.

It does not immediately appear from the wording of EC Article 241 (ex Art 184), in what precise context the illegality of a regulation may be pleaded. When attempts were made to use this procedure to challenge regulations directly and in isolation, the Court elaborated on the view which it had earlier expressed in the *Meroni* case[17] and made it clear that a regulation may only be challenged by virtue of EC Article 241 (ex Art 184) when it provides the legal basis of an act which is the primary objective of the action. For example, in *Italy v Council and Commission* (1966)[18] the primary objective of the action was to challenge a 1965 regulation. In addition the Italian Government invoked EC Article 184 (now Art 241) and asked that two 1962 regulations be declared inapplicable. The action was dismissed on the ground that the 1962 regulations did not provide the legal basis of the 1965 regulation, so that if the former were declared inapplicable they would in no way affect the authority of the latter. The Court said that the intention of EC Article 184 (now Art 241) 'is not to allow a party to contest at will the applicability of any regulation in support of an application. The regulation of which the legality is called in question must be applicable, directly or indirectly, to the issue with which the application is concerned'.[19] Another uncertainty concerns the meaning of 'regulation' in relation to EC Article 241 (ex Art 184): is the plea of illegality available in respect of a Community act which is not a regulation in form but is in substance a general act which determines rights and obligations objectively and in advance? Consistent with its approach to the distinction between general and individual acts, the Court has held that an act which is general in substance but not in form shall be treated as a regulation for the purposes of EC Article 241 (ex Art 184).[20]

EC Article 241 (ex Art 184) refers to 'any party' being able to invoke this plea and the question has been raised whether this expression includes Community institutions and Member States as well as individuals and corporate

14 Ibid, at 140.
15 Case 226/87: *Commission v Greece* [1988] ECR 3611, para 14, [1989] 3 CMLR 569.
16 Ibid para 16.
17 Case 9/56: [1957–58] ECR 133.
18 Case 32/65: [1966] ECR 389.
19 Ibid, at 409.
20 See Case 92/78: *Simmenthal SpA v Commission* [1979] ECR 777 at 800.

bodies. As far as Community institutions are concerned it is generally agreed that the plea is not available on both legal and practical grounds. In the first place the plea is designed to protect the private interests of a party which may be affected by an illegal general act, but a Community institution has no private interests only a share in the general interests of the Communities. Further, Community institutions have no restrictions on their right to challenge a general act and so, unlike the case of individuals and corporate bodies, there is no reason to extend the period of limitation in this way. Secondly, it is difficult to envisage in practice a situation in which, say, the Council would direct an individual decision to the Commission requiring it to respect a Council regulation. As far as Member States are concerned there are also reasons in principle why the plea should not be available. Member States, as in the case of institutions, have no restrictions on their competence to challenge acts provided they do so within the period of limitation and so in their case also there would appear to be no reason to make the defence of illegality available. Secondly, the Member States wield political influence over Community acts through the Council and this influence plus the general right of challenge should give ample protection to their interests.[1]

For some time it was believed that the Court supported the view that Member States could plead the plea of illegality. In *Italy v Council and Commission* (1966)[2] the Italian Government had relied on EC Article 184 (now Art 241) and although, as we have seen, the plea was dismissed the Court did not question its admissibility. But in the light of a more recent case, the better view probably is that EC Article 241 (ex Art 184) is only available to private parties. In an enforcement action brought by the Commission against Belgium under EC Article 93(2) (now Art 88(2)),[3] Belgium maintained that the decision which had been addressed to it under that Article had no legal basis. The legality of the decision had not been challenged under EC Art 173 (now 230), but on analogy with EC Article 184 (now Art 241) Belgium pleaded the illegality of that decision. The action could have been disposed of on the sole ground that the act in issue was an individual decision, but the Court considered the case on a broader basis. It referred to the right which Belgium had to challenge the decision under EC Article 173 (now Art 230) and to the period of limitation in that Article being intended to safeguard legal certainty. It then observed: 'It is impossible for a Member State which has allowed the strict time limit laid down ... in Article 173 to expire without contesting by the means available under that Article the legality of the Commission decision addressed to it, to be able to call in question that decision by means of Article 184 of the Treaty.'[4] While the Court addressed itself expressly to the individual decision in issue, its reasoning is equally applicable to any act, including a regulation, which a Member State could have challenged under EC Article 230 (ex Art 173). This would certainly be in keeping with the Court's own view that the purpose of EC Article 241 (ex Art 184) is 'to provide those persons who are precluded ... from instituting proceedings directly in respect of general acts, with the benefit of a judicial review of them at the time when they are affected by implementing decisions which are of direct and individual concern to them'.[5]

1 See Bebr, op cit, pp 141 et seq.
2 Case 32/65: [1966] ECR 389, [1969] CMLR 39.
3 Case 156/77: [1978] ECR 1881.
4 Ibid, at 1896.
5 Case 92/78: *Simmenthal SpA v Commission* [1979] ECR 777 at 800.

(viii)   Plenary jurisdiction
In addition to its jurisdiction to declare actions of Community institutions to be null and void the Court has a plenary jurisdiction in certain cases. This enables the Court in those instances to go into the merits of the parties' cases and to substitute its own judgments for those of the Communities' institutions. We have in fact already dealt with one example of this plenary jurisdiction in connection with violations of the Treaties by Member States. In addition there are three other instances of plenary jurisdiction.

In general the liability of the Communities in contract falls under the jurisdiction of municipal courts, unless in accordance with EC Article 238 (ex Art 181) the contracting parties agree to the contrary.[6] EC Article 240 (ex Art 183) provides that, subject to the powers of the Court of Justice, there is nothing to prevent a case to which the Community is a party from being determined by the domestic courts of the Member States.[7] But jurisdiction over non-contractual (tortious) liability on the other hand has been conferred upon the Court of the Communities. Under ECSC Art 34 an action for damages will lie where the Commission fails to comply within a reasonable time with a judgment declaring a decision or recommendation to be void. ECSC Art 40 provides for liability for wrongful administrative acts in terms that an action will lie in respect of damage resulting from acts or omissions on the part of the Community or its servants. The EC and EAEC Treaties do not expressly distinguish between legislative and administrative wrongdoing as grounds for seeking damages. EC Articles 235 and 288 (ex Arts 178, 215) and EAEC Art 151/188 respectively provide generally for non-contractual liability in the context of damage caused by the institutions or servants of the Communities in the performance of their duties in accordance with the general principles common to the laws of the Member States.

Under all three Treaties the extent of this non-contractual liability is in practice in terms of the distinction known to French law as that between *faute de service* and *faute personnelle*.[8] A *faute de service* occurs where damage results from the malfunctioning of Community institutions or Community servants; there is said to be a *faute personnelle* when the damage results from some personal wrongdoing on the part of a Community official which is in no way linked with his official position. In the case of a *faute de service* the Communities are liable; in the case of a *faute personnelle* the individual wrongdoer alone is personally liable. This distinction is comparable, although not identical, with the distinction well known to English law between a servant acting in the course of his employment and a servant on a frolic of his own. The non-contractual liability of the Community is that of a public authority. It is not liable for what may be termed ordinary torts committed in the course of Community activities, but only in respect of wrongs arising out of activities which form a necessary part of its official activities as defined in the Treaties, ie the legislative and administrative acts of the institutions and their officials. In accordance with this view, the Community was not held liable for injuries resulting from a road accident caused by a Euratom engineer who was driving his own car in the course of his work: 'the Community is only liable for those acts ... which ... are the necessary extension of the tasks entrusted to the institutions'.[9] Within those limits actual liability under the EC Treaty is in accordance with the general principles

---

6   EAEC Art 153 is to the same effect; see Case 23/76: *Pellegrini & C Sas v Commission* [1976] ECR 1807, [1977] 2 CMLR 77.
7   Also see ECSC Art 40(3) and EAEC Art 155.
8   See Brown, L N, and Garner, J F, op cit, pp 99 et seq.
9   Case 9/69: *Sayag v Leduc* [1969] ECR 329 at 336.

common to the laws of the Member States. This involves the Court in a comparative study of the relevant national laws in order to pick out the decisive elements which may reflect a trend. National law is not analysed in order to produce a principle acknowledged uniformly by all the Member States. Such an exercise would be unlikely to produce a workable legal principle. The aim is to identify trends generally, but not necessarily universally, recognized and to use them as the juridical basis for the development of particular rules of Community liability.[10]

The relationship between the action for damages and the actions for annulment and inactivity has caused the Court some difficulty. When first confronted with this question the Court expressed the view that the action for damages was quite distinct both by reason of its object and the grounds upon which it can be brought.[11] But when, later, an action for damages arose out of an allegedly unlawful act which had not been annulled, the Court changed its mind and held that 'An administrative measure which has not been annulled cannot of itself constitute a wrongful act on the part of the administration inflicting damage upon those whom it affects. The latter cannot therefore claim damages by reason of that measure'.[12] More recently, against the background of strong criticism,[13] the Court has reverted to its original view. In *Alfons Lütticke GmbH v Commission* (1971)[14] it observed that the action for damages is an independent action having its own special purpose and subject to conditions which were designed for that purpose. It would be contrary to the independence of this right of action if its exercise was made subject to other Treaty provisions designed for different purposes. This view has been reiterated in a series of subsequent cases which appears now to represent the *jurisprudence constante* of the Court.[15] Where an action for damages is brought in respect of a legislative act which involves choices of economic policy the Community will only be liable if the individual applicant can prove that there has been a sufficiently serious breach of a superior rule of law protecting him.[16] Such a rule could be either a rule in the Treaty such as the prohibition on discrimination[17] or one of the unwritten rules of Community law, such as the principle of legitimate expectation, which the Court draws from the laws of the Member States, which are designed to protect individual rights.[18] That the alleged breach of such a rule has to be sufficiently serious is in practice a very difficult condition to satisfy. The Court has taken the view that liability in these cases will not be incurred unless the defendant institution has manifestly and gravely disregarded the limits of its powers to such a degree that its conduct verges on the arbitrary.[19] The applicant in an

10   Ibid, at 340, per A-G Gand.
11   Cases 9 and 12/60: *Société Commerciale Antoine Vloeberghs SA v High Authority* [1961] ECR 197.
12   Case 25/62: *Plaumann & Co v Commission* [1963] ECR 95 at 108.
13   Eg A-G Roemer's submissions in Case 5/71: *Aktien-Zuckerfabrik Schöppenstedt v Council* [1971] ECR 975 at 990 et seq.
14   Case 4/69: [1971] ECR 325.
15   See Case 5/71: *Aktien-Zuckerfabrik Schöppenstedt v Council* [1971] ECR 975; Cases 9 and 11/71: *Compagnie d'Approvisionnement de Transport et de Crédit SA and Grands Moulins de Paris SA v Commission (No 2)* [1972] ECR 391, [1973] CMLR 529; Case 43/72: *Merkur-Aussenhandels GmbH v Commission* [1973] ECR 1055.
16   Eg Case 153/73: *Firma Holtz and Willemsen v Council and Commission* [1974] ECR 675 at 692 and Cases 83 and 94/76, 4, 15 and 40/77: *Bayerische HNL Vermehrungsbetriebe GmbH & Co KG v Council and Commission* [1978] ECR 1209 at 1224.
17   Eg Cases 44–51/77: *Groupement d'Intérêt Economique 'Union Malt' v Commission* [1978] ECR 57, [1978] 3 CMLR 702.
18   See eg Case 74/74: *Comptoir National Technique Agricole SA v Commission* [1975] ECR 533.
19   See, for example, Case 238/78: *Ireks-Arcady GmbH v Council and Commission* [1979] ECR 2955 and Cases 116, 124/77: *GR Amylum NV v Council and Commission* [1979] ECR 3497.

action for damages must, of course, establish a causal connection between the injury and the act or omission on the part of the Community and the quantum of damages must be ascertainable and not speculative.[20] Problems about the appropriate forum for claims for damages against the Community are likely to arise in some circumstances. Where the alleged wrong results from the act of a Community official acting in that capacity, the action will lie in the European Court.[1] But where, as is common, the act is that of an authority in a Member State, a complex body of case law has developed on the question whether in such cases the action should lie in the courts of the Member State, in the European Court, or in both. The precise nature of the claim is a crucial factor in such cases. If the claim is for a liquidated sum, such as for repayment of a sum paid to a national authority or for payment of a sum due from a national authority under Community law, the action will lie in the relevant national court.[2] But if the claim is for an unliquidated sum to compensate for harm caused by a national authority in implementing a Community act, the action may be brought in the European Court notwithstanding the concurrent availability of a national remedy.[3]

The Court's plenary jurisdiction also extends to the settlement of disputes between the Communities and their employees over contracts of employment. The terms of service are set out in the Communities' Staff Regulations, and EC Article 236 (ex Art 179), for example, provides that the Court shall be competent to adjudicate in any dispute between the Community and its servants within the limits and under the conditions laid down by their service regulations or conditions of employment. Actions concerning contracts of service cannot be lodged directly with the Court of Justice. Claims must first be made to the appointing body via an hierarchical administrative process. If the dispute is not resolved by this process then a right of action lies to the Court of First Instance which has the power to consider the dispute in its entirety and to settle it by its judgment. This is a fairly fertile source of litigation before the Court but it is somewhat specialist and it is neither appropriate nor practicable to discuss it in the present context.[4]

Lastly the Court has plenary jurisdiction to hear appeals against fines and other pecuniary penalties. The Court not only has jurisdiction to quash a penalty of this sort but it may also lower or increase this penalty when in the Court's view it is either unacceptable or inappropriate.[5] An example is provided by Article 17 of Regulation 17 which authorizes appeals against fines and periodic penalty payments imposed by the Commission for breaches of the Community's rules on competition.[6]

---

20 See Cases 5, 7 and 13–24/66: *Firma E Kampffmeyer v Commission* [1967] ECR 245 and Case 30/66: *Kurt A Becher v Commission* [1967] ECR 285, [1968] CMLR 169.
1 See Case 145/83: *Adams v Commission* [1985] ECR 3539, [1986] 1 CMLR 506.
2 See Case 132/77: *Société pour l'Exportation des Sucres SA v Commission* [1978] ECR 1061, and Case 133/79: *Sucrimex SA v Commission* [1980] ECR 1299. Where there is no national remedy available a claim will lie in the European Court: Cases 197–200, 243, 245, 247/80: *Ludwigshafener Walzmühle Erling KG v Council and Commission* [1981] ECR 3211.
3 See eg Cases 261, 262/78: *Interquell Stärke-Chemie GmbH & Co KG v Commission* [1979] ECR 3045.
4 See pp 62 et seq, supra. For further information, see Brown & Jacobs, op cit, ch 9. Since November 1989 these cases must initially be brought before the CFI subject to a limited right of appeal to the ECJ.
5 ECSC Art 36(2); EC Art 229 (ex Art 172); EAEC Art 144.
6 EG Case 41/69: *ACF Chemiefarma NV v Commission* [1970] ECR 661 and Case 7/72: *Boehringer Mannheim GmbH v Commission* [1972] ECR 1281, [1973] CMLR 864.

(ix)   Miscellaneous forms of jurisdiction

(1) EC Article 235 (ex Art 178):   jurisdiction in disputes relating to compensation for damage provided for in EC Art 288(2), ex Art 215(2).[7]

(2) EC Article 236:   jurisdiction in any dispute between the Community and its servants within the limits and under the conditions laid down in the Staff Regulations or the Conditions of Employment. Such disputes are within the competence of the CFI subject to appeal to the ECJ. The same applies to disputes between the European Central Bank and its servants[8] and between the European Monetary Institute and its servants[9] which will be heard before the CFI.[10]

(3) EC Article 237 (ex Art 180):   jurisdiction in disputes concerning the fulfilment by Member States of their obligations under the Statute of the European Investment Bank; measures adopted by the Board of Governors of the EIB; and measures adopted by the Board of Directors of the EIB;

Under EC Article 237(d) (ex Art 180(d)) the Court of Justice shall have jurisdiction in disputes concerning the fulfilment by national central banks of obligations under the Treaty and the Statute of the ESCB. In this context the powers of the Council of the ECB in respect of national banks shall be the same as enjoyed by the Commission in respect of the enforcement action against the Member States under EC Article 226 (ex Art 169). If the Court of Justice finds that a national central bank has failed to fulfil an obligation under the Treaty, that bank shall be required to take the necessary measures to comply with the judgment.

(4) EC Article 238 (ex Art 181):   jurisdiction to give judgment pursuant to any arbitration[11] clause contained in a contract concluded by or on behalf of the Community.

(5) EC Article 239 (ex Art 182):   jurisdiction in any dispute between Member States, in the context of the Treaty, submitted under a special agreement between the parties.

(6) EC Article 243 (ex Art 186):   jurisdiction to order interim relief but only in cases pending before the Court.[12] In case of urgency the President of the Court may act alone and he usually does so.[13]

(7) Agreement on the European Economic Area: jurisdiction arising from the provisions of the Agreement which came into force on 1 January 1994.[14]

(3)   NON-CONTENTIOUS JURISDICTION

(a)   References for preliminary rulings[15]

Although references for preliminary rulings have to arise from contentious proceedings in national jurisdictions the ECJ acts in an advisory capacity to the court or tribunal which refers the matter to the ECJ.

---

7   See pp 319 et seq, supra.

8   Statute of the European Systems of Central Bank and of the European Central Bank, Art 36(2).

9   Statute of the European Monetary Institute, Art 18(2).

10   Declaration on Disputes between the ECB and EMI and their servants annexed to the TEU.

11   Eg Case 23/81: *Commission v SA Royale Belge* [1983] ECR 2685; Case 426/85: *Commission v Zoubek* [1986] ECR 4057; Case C-330/88: *Alfredo Grifoni v EAEC* [1991] ECR I-1045.

12   See Lasok, KPE, op cit pp 230 et seq.

13   Rules of the Court, Art 85.

14   See p 88, supra.

15   See p 356, infra.

(b)   Opinions[16] on international agreements

Under EC Article 300(6) (ex Art 228(b)), as amended the Council, the Commission or a Member State may obtain an opinion of the Court of Justice as to whether an agreement to be negotiated on behalf of the Community is compatible with the provisions of the Treaty. Should the opinion of the ECJ be adverse, the agreement may enter into force only in accordance with TEU Article 48 (ex Art N).

B.   The Court of First Instance

Since the late 1970's, the ECJ has been faced with an ever-increasing workload.[17] Over the period 1980 to 1987 the annual number of new cases lodged with the Court increased from 279 to 395. In 1987 the Court and its Chambers combined delivered 422 judgments, while in the same year 208 cases were still pending before the Court and another 181 before its Chambers. The average length of proceedings before the Court had also steadily increased over the same period and in 1987 it was 20 months for direct actions and 18 months for preliminary rulings. Various factors have contributed to this situation. There has long been a general trend as the Community develops for more and more cases to be brought. This trend has been strongly reinforced by the doubling of the numbers of the Member States with all the resulting new opportunities for direct actions and requests for preliminary rulings. The Court has done its best to improve the situation by simplifying, improving and making more efficient its working methods; the steady increase in the number of judgments delivered annually testifies to this.[18] But the scale of the problem had become such as to call for more drastic measures in order to ensure the proper administration of justice.

In the past proposals for reform largely focused on the Court's jurisdiction over staff cases, ie disputes between the Community and its employees, which often involve complex issues of fact and occupy a disproportionate amount of the Court's time. In other international organizations, notably the United Nations, the International Labour Organizations, and other UN agencies, such disputes are referred to special Administrative Tribunals. In 1978 the Commission proposed the establishment of a similar body to deal with Community staff cases but no action was taken on it.[19] Then discussion centred on the establishment of a more general first instance tribunal to relieve the burden on the Court and its Chambers. This has borne fruit in that the Single

---

16   See pp 87, supra.

17   The statistics which follow have been taken from *Synopsis of the work of the Court of Justice of the European Communities in 1986 and 1987* (1988), Section I, 1, A.

18   Ibid, Graph No 4, at p 19. In 1993, 486 cases were brought (203 references for preliminary rulings, 17 staff cases and 266 others). Of the 272 judgments given by the ECJ, 163 were preliminary rulings, seven were in staff cases and 102 were other cases. The Court of First Instance dealt with 589 cases and delivered 76 judgments – see *Twenty-seventh General Report* (1984) p 365. More up-to-date statistics can be found in the evidence given to the House of Lords, Select Committee on the European Committees in 1999: See 13th Report, Session 1998-99, HL Paper 82, pages 37-39.

19   See Commission Proposal for a Council Regulation establishing an Administrative Tribunal for the European Communities (OJ 1978, C 222, at p 6). For a discussion of that proposal, see House of Lords, Select Committee on the European Communities, Session 1978/79, 17th Report.

European Act 1986 amended the EC Treaty[20] so as to authorize the Council, acting unanimously, at the request of the Court and after consulting the Commission and the European Parliament, to 'attach to the Court of Justice a court with jurisdiction to hear and determine at first instance, subject to a right of appeal to the Court of Justice on points of law only, ... certain classes of action or proceeding brought by natural or legal persons'. As a result of subsequent amendments, the Treaty provides that the CFI can be entrusted with jurisdiction at first instance over any class of action or proceeding with the sole exception of references for a preliminary ruling.[1]

In accordance with the above procedure, in November 1988 the Council took the decision to establish a Court of First Instance (CFI) which became operational on 1 November 1989.[2] The CFI consists now of 15 judges appointed by common accord by the governments of the Member States from persons of undoubted independence who possess the ability required for appointment to judicial office.[3] The judges are appointed for six-year terms and are eligible for reappointment. They elect their President from among their own number for a term of three years. No Advocates-General are appointed to the CFI but the judges of the CFI may themselves be called upon to act in that capacity, in which case their task is the same as that of Avocates General of the Court of Justice.[4] The CFI generally sits in chambers of five or three judges (for which the quorum is three), although it may provide for plenary sessions (for which the quorum is nine) in its Rules of Procedure and it may be constituted by a single judge.[5] Cases can be heard and determined by a single judge only if: (a) the case is a staff case, an action that raises only questions that have already been clarified by established case law, or an action over which the Court has jurisdiction pursuant to an arbitration clause; and (b) the case has been allocated by a chamber to a single judge on the ground that it is suitable to be determined in that way. A single judge cannot hear and determine certain types of case, such as those concerning the legality of an act of general application, competition cases, trade protection cases

---

20 Single European Act, Art 11 adding Art 168A to the EC Treaty (as then numbered) and making an addition to Art 188 (now Art 245). For the CFI generally, see Kennedy, T, 'The Essential Minimum: The Establishment of the Court of First Instance' (1989) 14 EL Rev 7 and Toth, A-G, 'The Court of First Instance of the European Communities', in White, R, and Smythe, B, (eds), *Current Issues in European and International Law* (1990), at 19; Millet, T, *The Court of First Instance of the European Communities* (1990): Lasok, K P E, *The European Court of Justice* (2nd edn, 1994).

1 EC Art 225(1) (ex Art 168A(1)).

2 Decision 88/591 (OJ 1988, L319/1) as corrected at OJ 1989, L241/4 and amended by a decision published on 17 June 1993. For background to this Decision see: the Proposal by the Court of Justice at [1988] 1 CMLR 185; House of Lords Select Committee on the European Communities, Session 1987/88, 5th Report; and European Parliament, Document A2–107/88. See also ruling of the President of the ECJ that the Court of First Instance had been constituted according to law (OJ 1989, L317/48).

3 Decision 88/591, Art 2 as amended by the Act of Accession (1994) Art 17(2) as amended by Council Decision 95/1, Art 10. In practice there is one judge of the nationality of each of the Member States. The United Kingdom judge is Nicholas Forwood QC, Member of English Bar.

4 See Case T-51/89: *Tetra Pak Rausing v Commission* [1990] ECR II-309.

5 The Rules of Procedure of the CFI came into force on 1 July 1991 but until then CFI used the Rules of the Court of Justice. The enabling Decision has added a new Title concerning the CFI to the EEC Statute of the Court of Justice, Art 46 of which governs procedure. The Rules of Procedure were published originally in OJ 1991, L136/1; [1991] 3 CMLR 795, and have been amended several times. A consolidated version is published in OJ 2001, C 34/39.

and intellectual property cases.[6] The jurisdiction of the CFI consists of categories of action which have been transferred to it from the Court of Justice by act of the Council from time to time. In such cases the jurisdiction of the CFI is exclusive, subject to a right of appeal to the Court of Justice on points of law. At the time of writing, the CFI's jurisdiction covered all actions capable of being brought by natural or legal persons, including disputes between the institutions and their employees (staff cases) and actions over which the Court has jurisdiction pursuant to an arbitration clause contained in a contract concluded by or on behalf of the Community after 1 August 1993.[7]

Matters currently excluded from the CFI are cases brought by Member States and institutions, all references for preliminary rulings from the courts and tribunals of the Member States. A reservation is made for acts setting up a body governed by Community law which may withhold jurisdiction from the CFI;[8] and cases brought under an arbitration clause in a Community contract in respect of contracts concluded before 1 August 1993 are currently excluded from the CFI's jurisdiction even if brought by a national or legal person.[9] At the time of writing there was a proposal further to extend the jurisdiction of the ECJ so as to cover all actions based on an arbitration clause and certain actions for annulment brought by Member States.[10] If new competence is added to the Court of Justice it automatically devolves upon the CFI within the limits of the Council decision which identifies the class of cases allocated to the CFI. A recent example is the jurisdiction of the ECJ over actions against the decisions of the Board of Appeal of the Community Trade Mark Office,[11] which is exercised at first instance by the CFI.[12]

As a result of the current division of jurisdiction between the ECJ and the CFI, it is possible for the same issue to be litigated simultaneously in both courts, such as where a Member State and a legal or natural person both seek the annulment of the same act.[13]

To deal with overlapping of jurisdictions Article 47 of the Statute of the Court makes a simple rule. Where the ECJ and the CFI are both seised with cases in which the same relief is sought, the same interpretation is raised or the validity of the same act is called into question: (a) the CFI may stay the proceedings before it until such time as the ECJ gives judgment; (b) the ECJ may stay the proceedings before it, in which case the CFI proceedings continue to judgment; or, where the parallel cases are actions to have the same act declared void, (c) the CFI may decline jurisdiction causing the action before it to transfer to the ECJ.[14] By contrast, where the CFI finds that it has no jurisdiction at all in a case falling within the competence of the ECJ it is required to remit it to the latter. And, vice versa, if

---

6 Rules of Procedure, art 14(2).
7 Decision 88/591, Art 3, as originally worded; The Decisions defining and extending the CFI's jurisdiction from time to time are: Council Decision 93/350 (OJ 1993, L144/21); Council Decision 94/149 (OJ 1994, L66/29). Council Decision 1999/291 (OJ 1999, L114/52), as implemented by the amendments made to the CFI's Rules of Procedure published in OJ 1999, L135/92. For the background to this Decision: House of Lords Select Committee on the European Committee, 25 Report Session 1997-98, HL Paper 114.
8 Council Decision 88/591, Art 3(1).
9 Council Decision 93/350, Art 3(2).
10 For the background to this proposal, see: House of Lords Select Committee on the European Committees 13th Report, Session 1998-99, HL Paper 82.
11 Council Reg 40/94, Art 63.
12 Eg Case T-163/98: *Procter & Gamble Co v Office for Harmonisation in the Internal Market (Trade Marks and Designs)* [1999] ECR II-2383.
13 Eg Cases C-68/94 and C-30/95: *France and others v Commission* [1998] ECR I-1375.
14 It is usual for both cases to be heard by the ECJ: eg Case T-42/91: *Koninklijke PTT Nederland NV and PTT Post BV v Commission* [1991] ECR II-273.

the ECJ finds that it has no competence it will refer the case to the CFI which may not decline jurisdiction.

C.   Appeals

Decisions of the CFI on both substantive and procedural issues are appealable to the Court of Justice on points of law within two months of the notification of the decision.[15] Since appeals are allowed only on points of law it is incumbent upon the CFI to establish the facts of the case but it is not easy in practice to disentangle neatly points of fact and points of law.[16] Advocate General Jacobs[17] thought that: 'in general it would be helpful if the Court of First Instance, when giving judgment on one ground in favour of an applicant, were to make the necessary findings of fact relevant to any other grounds on which the applicant has relied and on which, in the event of an appeal, he might seek to rely as respondent'. However this suggestion has not been taken up so far.

Three grounds of appeal are available: lack of competence of the CFI; a breach of procedure which adversely affects the interests of the applicant; and an infringement of Community law by the CFI.[18] In all except staff cases, Member States and institutions may lodge an appeal even where they were not interveners in the action before the CFI.[19] Procedure on appeal before the Court of Justice consists of written and oral stages, although the latter may be dispensed with.[20] If an appeal is allowed the decision of the CFI will be quashed. Final judgment may then either be given by the Court of Justice or the case may be referred back to the CFI; the latter is likely where complex facts need to be taken into consideration. Where there is a reference back, the CFI is bound by the judgment of the Court of Justice on points of law.[1] It may also be presumed that the CFI is under a general obligation to follow and apply the case law of the Court of Justice and that a failure to do so would justify an appeal on the ground of an infringement of Community law.

In the short term the CFI has been able to contribute to the easing of the problems which have confronted the Court of Justice in recent years. However, some doubts may be raised about its impact in the longer term. The range of cases transferred to the CFI is small and is in part counterbalanced by the additional appellate function conferred on the Court of Justice. Further, the number of Community actions has continued to increase. The advent of additional Member States and further additions to the jurisdictions of the ECJ and the CFI have added a further dimension to the rate of increase. As a result, further reforms to the judicial arrangements of the Community may prove to be necessary.[2]

---

15   Protocol on the Statute, Art 49, but appeals against a decision dismissing an application to intervene must be brought within two weeks.
16   See Case C-283/90P: *Vindránji v Commission* [1991] ECR I-4339; Case C-132/90 P: *Schwedler v Parliament* [1991] ECR I-5745; Case C-346/90P: *F v Commission* [1992] ECR I-2691; Case C-378/90P: *Pitrone v Commission,* [1992] ECR I-2375; NB letter P indicates judgment of the ECJ on appeal from the CFI.
17   Case C-185/90P *Commission v Gill* [1991] ECR I-4779.
18   Protocol on the Statute of the Court, Art 51.
19   Ibid, Art 49, para 3.
20   Ibid, Art 52.
 1   Ibid, Art 54.
 2   At the time of writing, there were further proposals before the Member States for more radical changes to the current judicial arrangements.

D. Enforcement of judgments

(1) JUDGMENTS AGAINST MEMBER STATES

There can be no physical enforcement of judgments against Member States. The Treaty simply relies on the provisions of EC Article 228 (ex Art 171), that states have an obligation to take the necessary measures to comply with the judgment. The Community follows the ethos of *Rechtsstaat*, ie the state governed by law and the ultimate sanction of the law which is an ethical one. Moreover it is common ground that the Community would collapse if the Member States were to flout the judicial authority which they established and to which they submitted themselves without reservation under EC Article 292 (ex Art 219).

(2) JUDGMENTS AND DECISIONS AGAINST PRIVATE PARTIES

EC Articles 244 and 256 (ex Arts 187 and 192), ECSC Articles 42 and 92, and EAEC Articles 159 and 164 impose a direct obligation upon the Member States to enforce the judgments of the ECJ (and the CFI) and decisions of the Council of Ministers and of the Commission of a pecuniary nature against individuals and corporations and indicate the procedure in this respect. Thus enforcement is governed by the rules of civil procedure in force in the state in whose territory the judgment or decision is to be carried out. Each state designates the national authority for this purpose and communicates its decision to the Commission and the Court of Justice as well as the Arbitration Committee set up under EAEC Article 18. The said authority will execute the decisions and judgments automatically, without any formality except verification of their authenticity.

There can be no appeal in national courts against the execution orders, which can be suspended only by a decision of the Court of Justice. However, national courts have jurisdiction over complaints that enforcement has been carried out in an irregular manner, ie in breach of the national procedures.

Part III

The relationship between Community law and the municipal law of the Member States

Chapter 13

Implementation of Community law in the legal systems of the Member States

A. Introduction

The most intricate and complex aspect of Community law is its relationship to
the municipal law of the Member States. Conceptually Community law, like
public international law, feeds upon the internal law of states, but once emancipated
and worked into a system, Community law emerges as a different, autonomous
body of law.

Volumes have been written on the subject from a theoretical and practical
point of view not only because the growth of Community law is symptomatic of
the growth of the Community but also because of the theoretical and practical
consequences of conflicts between Community law and the municipal law of
the Member States. At a theoretical level the starting point of a discussion on the
relationship between Community law and the municipal law of the Member States,
that is between an 'external' and an 'internal' system of law, is the doctrine of
sovereignty; at a practical level it is the Treaty obligation and the resulting status
of Community law in the territory of the Member States.

Sovereignty is a conceptual chameleon: it can be seen in different colours
and be described in different ways. In classic terms Jean Bodin (1530–96) wrote
that 'it is the distinguishing mark of the sovereign that he cannot in any way be
subject to the commands of another, for it is he who makes Law for the subject,
abrogates Law already made, and amends obsolete Law. No one who is subject
either to the Law or to some other person can do this. That is why it is laid down
in the civil Law that the prince is above the Law, for the word *Law* in Latin implies
command of him who is invested with sovereign power . . .'.[1] For the purpose of
our discussion sovereignty may be described in positive terms as the oneness of the
legal system within the territory of a state. Oneness does not exclude plurality of
laws within the system (as is, eg, the case in the United Kingdom or the USA)
but implies one supreme source of law embodied in the constitution of the state;

---

1   *Six Books of the Commonwealth*, Book 1, ch 8.

in other words the jurisdiction over the territory is in the hands of one authority (eg government in Parliament) which is supreme. In negative terms sovereignty means a system of law and administration of justice which is free from outside interference. Proceeding from the assumption of the oneness of the legal system, the Member States of the Community are not entirely sovereign for, by Treaty, they have delegated a portion of their law-making power to an external authority (the Community) and at the same time consented to abide by the law so made. In the field of the administration of justice they recognize the authority of the Community Court over matters and persons in their territory falling within the jurisdiction of that Court and also consent to their municipal courts taking judicial cognizance of Community law. In theory, therefore, as long as the state remains a member of the Community there should be no conflict between the municipal (internal) law of the Member States and the Community (external) law because the latter becomes part of the former. In fact, however, conflicts do arise and this raises the question of the supremacy of the one over the other. Reduced to a practical level sovereignty means the ultimate authority in respect of a particular matter and raises the question whether the Community or the state law governs a particular situation.

Another digression into the theory of relations between external and internal law leads us to consideration of two rival doctrines, dualism (parallelism) and monism,[2] which purport to explain the basis of legal obligation. According to the positivist philosophy of law, the relationship between the law of a sovereign state and the law of mankind, reflected in the law generated by agreements between states, has been expressed in the dualist (parallelist) doctrine. In simple terms this doctrine presupposes the existence of two separate systems of law: international and national, co-existing side by side as it were in watertight compartments. Though international law is the universal law of mankind it stops at the door of the sovereign state and remains outside unless admitted to the territory of the state. It means that international law binds states in their relations with each other but has, subject to few exceptions, no binding force in the territory of the state unless transformed or translated into rules of municipal law. This doctrine, favouring sovereignty, is still the reigning theory and the United Kingdom is among its adherents.

Monism is the rival doctrine propounding the existence of a single system of norms or legal rules binding states and individuals alike. States are, after all, nothing but forms of organization or legal fictions whilst the individual is the ultimate subject of law. Both international and municipal law are only parts of the same structure and their rules are interrelated. Consequently monism cuts across sovereignty, bringing the individual face to face with international law and relieving the state of that task of transforming it into rules of domestic law. The origins of monism can be traced to the medieval concept of the unity of law as natural law was considered to be a reflection of the wisdom of God through the reason of man. It ceased to be fashionable when the theory of natural law was superseded by the theory of positive law. The twentieth century revival of the monist doctrine in its positivist rather than naturalist garb is a reaction against the nineteenth century apotheosis of the sovereign state degenerating into nationalism, which saw international law solely as a product of the 'will' of states.

The legal concept of the European Community reflects a monist approach. Therefore, to understand the relationship between Community law and the law

---

2   Starke, J G, 'Monism and Dualism in the Theory of International Law' (1936) 17 BYBIL 66.

of the Member States it is unhelpful to think in terms of sovereignty (nationalism) versus collectivity (internationalism). We have to formulate instead a functional approach which in practical terms reconciles the needs of Community law with the aspiration of states to be supreme within their territories. Once this is appreciated the question of the supremacy of one system or the other resolves itself into a division of labour or functions of the respective bodies or rules within a unitary concept of law. Within its respective sphere each system is supreme as stated by the Community Court:[3]

'. . . The Community is founded on a common market, common objectives, and common institutions . . . Within the specific domain of the Community, ie for everything which relates to the pursuit of the common objectives within the common market the institutions [of the Community] are provided with exclusive authority . . . Outside the domain of the Community, the governments of the Member States retain their responsibilities in all sectors of economic policy . . . They remain masters of their social policy; the same undoubtedly holds true for large segments of their fiscal policy . . .'

Ten years later, in the ERTA case which was, inter alia, concerned with the treaty-making power of the Community and the Member States the Court held that

'. . . By the terms of Article 5 [now 10], the Member States are required on the one hand to take all appropriate steps to ensure the carrying out of the obligations arising out of the Treaty . . . and on the other hand to abstain from any steps likely to jeopardize the attainment of the purposes of the Treaty. If these two provisions are read in conjunction, it follows that to the extent that Community rules are promulgated for the attainment of the purposes of the Treaty, the Member States cannot, outside the framework of the Community institutions, assume obligations likely to affect such rules or alter their scope . . .'[4]

These two dicta delimit the respective spheres of the Community and the Member States both in the 'internal' and 'external' aspect of sovereignty.

Let us turn now to the founding Treaties, especially the EC Treaty, which is a unique treaty. It cannot be compared with traditional international treaties which set out the obligations of the parties and, in most cases, leave the implementation and enforcement of the obligations to the forces which make international law effective. It is a self-executing treaty. The EC is, by the will of the founding states, a separate legal entity, a new subject of law and, although it takes life from the agreement of states, it has a quasi-independent existence. Being a subject of law it enjoys the treaty-making power and the power of diplomatic representation but, above all, it has its own institutions and a law-making power. Community law is therefore an autonomous legal order binding not only the Member States but also their citizens directly and immediately.

The EC Treaty itself has a legal framework – actually two such frameworks – the constitutional framework which we have already analysed and the economic framework which we shall consider later on. What we must discuss now is the

---

3 Case 30/59: *De Gezamenlijke Steenkolenmijnen in Limburg v High Authority of the ECSC* [1961] ECR I at 23.
4 Case 22/70: *Commission v Council* [1971] ECR 263 at 273, [1971] CMLR 335 at 355; at paras 21 and 22; see also Opinion 1/75: *Re the OECD Understanding on a Local Cost Standard* [1975] ECR 1355, [1976] 1 CMLR 85.

impact of the Treaty and the Community legislation on the legal systems of the Member States. In doing so we should bear in mind[5] that ' . . . the Community constitutes a new legal order of international law, in favour of which the states within certain areas have limited their sovereign rights . . .' because it reflects the difficulties inherent in the 'dualist' thinking which has so far dominated the European legal scene. Indeed some of the constitutions of the Member States had to be amended in order to ease the process of assimilation of international obligations inherent in the Community Treaties into the law of the land. In this respect the United Kingdom is not in a unique position. However, with the continuing growth of Community law expanding into most areas legal sovereignty may soon become an outmoded concept relegated by political and economic integration into the historical museum of the European continent.

The Maastricht Treaty on European Union is based on the same principles as the EC Treaty. It simply takes aboard the contents of the EC Treaty, amends and enlarges its scope and extends the competences of the EC institutions and adds new institutions to administer the provisions applicable to the Economic and Monetary Union and, as an innovation, includes provisions (foreign and security policy and justice and home affairs) which are reserved to inter-governmental conference rather than EC institutions.

B. Constitutions of the Member States and Treaty obligations

The admission of external law to the territory of a state raises a constitutional problem of transmission, on the one hand, and supremacy in the case of a conflict with municipal law, on the other. A further problem, as far as the countries with written constitutions are concerned, arises from the internal relationship between the constitution and the ordinary law of the land. The constitution, as the basic law of the land, consists not only of the rules which organize the political framework of the state but also of the general principles on which rests the whole edifice of law and order. It follows that there is a hierarchy of legal norms or in Pound's rather inelegant phrase, 'authoritative starting points for legal reasoning'[6] which, in the event of a conflict with external law, raises the question whether external law is superior/subordinate to the law of the Constitution and the ordinary law of the land alike or whether the hierarchy of legal norms will affect the issue. In view of the diversity of the legal systems involved it seems necessary to investigate the position in each Member State.

(1) RATIFICATION OF THE EC TREATY AND OF THE TEU

According to the constitutions of the original six Member States treaties are made and ratified by the Head of State.[7] However in the case of especially important

---

5 Case 26/62: *Algemene Transport- en Expeditie Onderneming van Gend en Loos NV v Nedeerlandse Tariefcommissie* [1963] ECR 1 at 12, [1963] CMLR 105 at 129; see also Case 6/64: *Costa v ENEL* [1964] ECR 585 at 594, [1964] CMLR 425 at 456.
6 Pound, R, 'Hierarchy of Sources and Forms in Different Systems of Law' [1933] Tulane Law Rev 475 at 483.
7 Belgium, Art 68; France (Constitution of 1946 which was in force at that time), Art 31, Constitution of 1958, Art 52; Federal Republic of Germany, Art 59; Italy, Art 80; Luxembourg, Art 37; the Netherlands, Art 50 (in force at that time). See generally, Eisemann, PM (ed) *The Integration of International and European Community Law into the National Legal Order* (1996).

treaties these Constitutions require parliamentary approval in the form of either a resolution or a special law. In France, Italy, Germany and the Netherlands a special Act enabling the Head of State to ratify and thus commit the country internationally was necessary.[8] Accordingly these laws were passed during 1957.[9]

In Italy the Maastricht Treaty was approved by the Senate (by 176 votes to 16) on 17 September 1992 and by the Chamber of Deputies (by 403 votes to 46) on 29 October 1992 and ratified on 5 December 1992.

In the Netherlands the Maastricht Treaty was approved by the Chamber of Deputies (by 137 votes to 13) on 12 November 1992, and by the Senate unanimously on 15 December 1992 and ratified on 28 December 1992.

In France the Constitutional Court[10] decided on 9 April 1992 on the revision of the Constitution and the amendments of the Constitution were passed by the Congress (by 592 votes to 73) and the Treaty was approved by referendum on 20 September 1992 by 51.05% to 48.95% of votes cast. The treaty was ratified on 4 November 1992.

The last country to ratify was Germany. The Treaty was approved on 2 December 1992 by the Bundestag (by 543 votes to 17), and on 18 December 1992 by the Bundesrat unanimously. However before the deposition of the ratification instrument, which occurred on 12 October 1993, the Treaty had to be declared to be compatible with the Constitution by the Federal Constitutional Court. A positive decision was handed down on 12 October 1993.[11]

The position in Belgium and Luxembourg is somewhat different. The effect of the law passed by reference to Article 37(1) of the Constitution of Luxembourg, which enables the Grand Duke to conclude treaties, is to exercise parliamentary control over the acts of the executive.[12] The interpretation of the Belgian Constitution was subject to controversy as to the rôle of Parliament in this matter[13] but Parliament approved the Treaty by the Law of 22 December 1957 and so according to custom the Treaty may '*sortir son plein et entier effet*'.[14]

The Maastricht Treaty was approved on 17 July 1992 by the Belgian Chamber of Representatives (by 146 votes to 33); on 20 October 1992 by the Council of the French-speaking Community; on 22 October 1992 by the Council of the Flemish-speaking Community; on 4 November 1992 by the Senate (by 115 votes to 26), on 23 November by the Council of the German-speaking Community and on 10 December the instrument of ratification was deposited. The Luxembourg Chamber of Deputies approved the Maastricht Treaty by 51 votes to six on 2 July 1992 and it was ratified on 24 August 1992.

In the United Kingdom treaties are made and ratified by the Crown,[15] so much so that the battle about the membership of the Community was fought in the

---

8 France, Art 27; Italy, Art 80; Germany, Art 59(2); the Netherlands, Art 60 at the time of the signing of the Treaties.
9 France, 8 August 1957; Germany, 27 July 1957; Italy, 14 October 1957; the Netherlands, 5 December 1957.
10 Conseil Constitutionel [1993] 3 CMLR 345.
11 *Brunner v European Union Treaty* [1994] 1 CMLR 57.
12 Law of 30 November 1957; Pescatore, P, *Introduction à la Science du Droit* (1960), pp 170 and 175.
13 Constantinides-Mégret, C, *Le Droit de la Communauté Economique Européenne et l'Ordre Juridique des Etats Membres* (1967), pp 14-15.
14 Constantinides-Mégret, op cit, p 15.
15 *Blackburn v A-G* [1971] 1 WLR 1037 (see Lord Denning MR at 1040). See *R v Secretary of State for Foreign and Commonwealth Affairs, ex p Rees-Mogg (re Maastricht Treaty)* QBD, DC [1994] 1 All ER 457.

political arena of the House of Commons rather than the courts of law. Formally the Treaty obligations were implemented by the European Communities Act 1972, as subsequently amended, which has the effect of both a 'constitutional' and an 'ordinary' law.

The Maastricht Treaty was approved by the House of Commons (by 292 votes to 112) on 20 May 1993 and by the House of Lords (by 141 votes to 29) on 20 July 1993 and the ratification instrument was deposited on 2 August 1993.

In Ireland treaties are made by the government and ratified by Parliament.[16] Every treaty has to be laid before the lower house (Dáil Eireann) and if a charge on public funds is involved the terms must be approved by the Dáil. However, if the treaty is to be part of domestic law it can only be such as determined by the Oireachtas,[17] ie the body composed of the President of the Republic and both houses (ie the Dáil and the Senate). Such determination cannot take effect otherwise than by legislation.[18] However in order to enable the country to accede to the Communities a bill was passed by the Oireachtas in 1971 adding sub-section 3 to Article 29.4 of the Constitution and a referendum was held in 1972.

Constitutional problems arising in connection with ratification of the Single European Act 1986 were aired before the Irish High Court and the Supreme Court.[19] They decided that the Bill to ratify the Act was not unconstitutional. The amendments of the founding Treaties such as the changes in the voting system of the Council, the extension of the Community domain into the protection of the environment and the establishment of the Court of First Instance were held to be within the scope of the amendments of the Irish Constitution necessitated by the accession to the Community. However, Title III of the Single European Act (which is in reality a separate Treaty), which includes provisions on European Co-operation in the Sphere of Foreign Policy and thus impinges upon the freedom of the Member States in the conduct of their external affairs, was considered not ratifiable without a referendum and amendment of the Irish Constitution.

On 18 June 1992, by a national referendum an amendment of the Constitution, according to which 'the State may ratify the Treaty on European Union signed at Maastricht and may become a member of that Union' was approved by 69.05% to 30.95% of votes cast and the Treaty was ratified on 23 November 1992.

According to the Danish Constitution of 1953 (Article 19) the Monarch acts in international affairs on behalf of the Kingdom but without the consent of the Folketing cannot commit the country to any obligations of importance or for which parliamentary approval is necessary. Therefore in practice treaties are negotiated and ratified by the Executive subject to parliamentary approval. Accession to the Communities as approved by the Folketing and a referendum held in 1972. Attempts to have the procedures leading to the accession declared unconstitutional[20] and the 'signatures on the treasonable document declared void and unauthorized whereby our Queen may be saved from the biggest swindle in the history of

---

16 Constitution of 1937 (as amended in 1941, and 1972), Art 29, which deals with international relations, and Art 28 under which executive powers in this respect can be conferred upon the government.
17 Ibid, Art 29(6).
18 Kelly, J M, *The Irish Constitution* (1980), pp 155-156.
19 *Crotty v An Taoiseach* [1987] 2 CMLR 666.
20 *Tegen v Prime Minister of Denmark* [1973] CMLR 1.

Denmark'[1] were dismissed by the courts on the ground that the Head of State could not be held to account before her courts.

The Maastricht Treaty was originally approved by the Danish Parliament (by 130 votes to 25) on 12 May 1992 but on 2 June 1992 it was rejected by referendum (by 50.7% to 49.3% of the votes cast). After the renegotiations it was approved by Parliament (by 15 votes to 16) on 30 March 1993 and approved by referendum (by 56.7% to 43.3% of votes cast) and ratified on 17 June 1993. A challenge to the constitutionality of the EC Treaty, as framed by the TEU, was dismissed by the Danish Supreme Court in 1998.[2]

In Greece too treaties are negotiated by the Executive subject to parliamentary approval.[3]

The Maastricht Treaty was approved by the Greek Parliament (by 286 votes to eight) on 31 July 1992 and ratified on 3 November 1992.

Under the Spanish[4] Constitution of 1978 (Article 63(2)) the power to make international treaties belongs to the Crown, but since the King is a constitutional monarch the negotiations are in the hands of the government and the conclusion is subject to parliamentary control. Certain treaties require prior authorization of the national parliament (Cortes Generales). In this way the Cortes Generales gives authorization to the King to give his assent to the treaty negotiated by the government. The King signs the instrument of ratification.

Article 95(1) provides for prior constitutional amendment to enter into treaties which contain provisions contrary to the Constitution. Community treaties, limiting the sovereign power of the state, fall into that category. However the necessity of constitutional amendment can be overcome by virtue of an 'organic law' enacted by the Cortes Generales under Article 93 which provides that 'authorization may be granted for concluding treaties by which powers derived from the Constitution shall be vested in an international organization or institution'. Such authorization was granted by Organic Law 10/1985 of 2 August 1985.[5]

Following the decision of the Constitutional Court on 1 July 1992 requiring the revision of the Constitution the Congress of Deputies passed the amendment to the Constitution unanimously on 22 July 1992 and so did the Senate on 30 July 1992. Thereupon the Treaty was approved by the Congress of Deputies (by 314 votes to three) on 29 October 1992 and by the Senate (by 222 votes with three abstentions). The Treaty was ratified on 31 December 1992.

By virtue of Article 138(b) of the Constitution of Portugal of 1976 international treaties are negotiated by the Government and ratified by the President after having been duly approved by the appropriate body, ie the Government, the Constitutional Court or the National Assembly, depending on the type of treaty in question. Treaties involving participation in international organizations, treaties of peace and defence and those affecting the frontiers of the state as well as treaties submitted by the Government have to be approved by the National Assembly. The act of approval takes the form of a statute. Clearly Community Treaties fall into that category. Such a law was passed in 1982.

---

1   *Aggergren v Queen and Prime Mininster* [1973] CMLR 5.
2   *Carlsen v Rasmussen*, 6 April 1998 [1999] 3 CMLR 854.
3   Act No 945 (Official Gazette Part 1 No 170 of 27 July 1979), Roucounas, E, 'Pour le dialogue entre droit communautaire et droit grec' (1980) *Rev Hellénique de Droit International* 11 at 15
4   Aurrecoechea, J, 'Some Problems concerning the Constitutional Basis for Spain's Accession to the European Community' (1987) 1 ICLQ, 14 et seq.
5   Ibid, Art 22.

To ratify the Maastricht Treaty it was necessary to amend the Constitution and the amendments were carried on by the National Assembly (by 196 votes to 20) on 17 November 1992. Thereupon the Treaty was approved by the Assembly (by 200 votes to 21) and the Treaty was ratified on 16 February 1993.

(2)   INCORPORATION OF THE TREATY INTO MUNICIPAL LAW

The method of incorporation depends on whether a country follows the monist or the dualist doctrine. Among the original Six, France and Italy represent the two extremes: the former is monist, the latter is dualist, whilst the remaining four occupy a middle position with a distinct dualist leaning. Denmark, Ireland, Greece and the United Kingdom fall into the dualist category.

The French Republic started with a dualist posture but by Article 26 of the Constitution of 1946 reversed the tradition and turned monist. Article 26 provided that Treaties duly ratified by the Head of State and published have the force of law even if they are inconsistent with French law 'without there being any need of resorting to any legislative measures other than those necessary to secure ratification'. The Constitution of 1958, now in force, not only adopted the position but Article 55, as if to confirm the supremacy of Community law, provided that Treaties or Agreements ratified or approved 'have an authority superior to that of laws'. It follows that Treaties are not subject to transformation into the rules of French municipal law but take their place automatically by virtue of the Constitution in the internal legal order, subject to reciprocity and the sovereign will of the French people. However in the case of the EC Treaty the condition of reciprocity is satisfied in the light of Article 170 which contains Community remedies to enforce it.[6]

The Italian Constitution of 1948 contains no reference to the incorporation of treaties into Italian law. Article 11 permits a delegation of national sovereignty to international organizations but fails to deal with the problem of treaties. Accordingly a practice has been established in accordance with the hierarchy of legal rules: if the treaty affects a law the execution of the treaty takes the form of a law, if it affects merely administrative rules a decree of the Executive will take care of the situation. Reflecting this formula the law of ratification of the two Treaties of Rome passed on 14 October 1957 provided in Article 2 that 'the agreements specified in Article 1 will receive full and complete execution'. In this way the act of ratification became the act of execution or incorporation of the Treaties into Italian law. The consequences, as far as supremacy is concerned, are quite significant because, being equal to an internal legislative act, the Treaty, in principle, assumes no higher or lower rank than the corresponding piece of Italian legislation. Conflicts with domestic law are implicitly avoided in accordance with the principle that *lex posterior derogat priori*.[7] In practice, as we shall see later, difficulties arise.

In Germany, the general view is that the act of ratification signifies not only the approval of the Treaty but also incorporation.[8] Article 24 of the Federal

---

6   *Administration des Douanes v Société Cafés Jacques Vabre et J Weigel et Compagnie Sarl, Cour de Cassation* [1975] 2 CMLR 336, 13 CMLR Rev 128-32.
7   Cf the decision of the Italian Constitutional Court of 7 March 1964 in *Costa v ENEL* [1964] CMLR 425 at 456; *Frontini v Ministero delle Finanze* No 183/1973 [1974] 2 CMLR 372, Const Court Menis, C, *Traité CEE et Ordre Juridique Italien*, 2-3 (1983) CDE, 120 et seq.
8   Seidl-Hohenveldern, I, 'Transformation or Adoption of International into Municipal Law' (1963) 12 ICLQ, pp 101 et seq.

Constitution provides for the transfer of sovereign powers to inter-governmental institutions. Article 25, on the other hand, provides that the 'general rules of international law shall form part of federal law; they shall take precedence over the laws and create rights and duties directly applicable to the inhabitants of the territory of the federation'. This has been interpreted restrictively to include the general customary rules of international law but to exclude the conventional rules.[9] It follows that international treaties have the force of a federal law, that is, ordinary *law*, not constitutional law. Being no more than *law* in the hierarchy of legal rules they can derogate from a preceding federal law or the law of the *Länder* but cannot override a constitutional rule of the Federation of (presumably) the *Länder*. This was at the heart of the controversy over the alleged breach of the German *Grundgesetz* by Commission Regulations instituting a system of forfeitable export/import deposits. On that occasion[10] the Bundesverfassungsgericht held that: '. . . Article 24 does not actually give authority to transfer sovereign rights, but opens up the national legal system (within the limitations indicated) in such a way that the Federal Republic of Germany's exclusive claim to rule is taken back in the sphere of validity of the Constitution and room is given, within the state's sphere of rule, to the direct effect and applicability of law from another source'. Addressing itself specifically to the sensitive issue of conflicts between the guarantees of fundamental rights and the Community legislation the Federal Constitutional Court held that the reservation derived from Article 24 shall apply as long ('*so lange*') as the Community integration has not resulted in a directly elected legislative assembly and a charter of fundamental rights. However, while keeping an open mind to this particular reservation[11] the Bundesverfassungsgericht had no hesitation in recognizing the binding force of the ECJ's rulings under EC Article 177 (now Art 234).

According to a 1970 amendment of the Constitution of Belgium[12] Article 25 *bis* provides that 'the exercise of powers may be conferred by a Treaty or by Law on institutions of Public International Law'. This formula resembles the delegation of powers under the Italian Constitution and certainly confirms the dualist approach to treaties which are denied the authority of superior law. Amidst the discussions[13] on the relations between the constitution and treaty law the Belgian Cour de Cassation struck a valiant blow for the recognition of the supremacy of the treaty law in the judgment of 27 May 1971.[14] The Constitution of Luxembourg

---

9   Bebr, G, 'Law of the European Communities and Municipal Law' (1971) 34 MLR 481 at 487 quoting Mangeldt-Klein, *Das Bonner Grundgesetz* (1957) 675-677; Carstens, K, 'Der Rang europäischer Verordnungen gegenüber deutschen Rechtsnormen', *Festschrift für Otto Riese* (1964) 65, 75. See also Bundesverfassungsgericht, 14 May 1968 (Regel des Völkerrechts) BverfGe 23, 288 at 316.

10 Case 52/71: *Internationale Handelsgesellschaft mbH v Einfuhr- und Vorratsstelle für Getreide und Futtermittel* [1974] 2 CMLR 540 at 551-552. Majority decision of Federal Constitutional Court of 29 May, 1974.

11 See Bundesverfassungsgericht in *Steinike und Weinling v Ernährung und Forstwirtschaft* [1980] 2 CMLR 531 at para 12.

12 Law of 18 August 1970; Louis, J V, 'L'article 25 bis de la constitution belge' [1970] *Rev du Marché Commun* 136, 410-416.

13 Ganshof van der Meersch, W J, 'Le juge belge à l'heure du droit international et du droit communautaire' (1969), 84 *Journal des Tribunaux* 4671, 537-551; Waelbroeck, M in Donner, A M, et al, *Le juge devant le droit national et le droit communautaire* (1966) at pp 29 et seq.

14 *Etat Belge v S A Fromagerie Franco-Suisse le Ski* (1971) RTDE 494.

was amended in a similar way, Article 49 *bis* providing for a delegation of legislative and administrative powers to international organizations.[15]

The effect of the delegation of sovereignty in these three constitutions seems to provide room for the recognition of the binding force of the Community law enshrined in treaties whilst retaining at the same time the sovereignty of parliament. It now remains to be seen whether the formula is sufficiently wide to read into it the supremacy of Community law necessary for the functioning of the Community as a supranational organization.

To meet this situation the amendment of the Constitution of the Netherlands of 1956[16] provided that international treaties and agreements shall be the supreme law of the land (Article 68). The Constitution of 1983 further accentuates the monist approach. It provides in Article 92 that legislative, administrative and judicial powers may be conferred on international organizations by, or in virtue of, a treaty. Article 93 rules that provisions of treaties and of decisions of international organizations, the contents of which may be binding on anyone, shall have this binding effect as from the time of publication. This means that both precedent and subsequent national laws are overridden by international obligations as was already the position under the 1956 amendment. Article 120 also confirmed the principle that courts are not competent to judge the constitutionality of laws and international treaties.

According to Article 96(1) of the Spanish Constitution treaties once officially published form part of the internal legal order. This means that formal incorporation is required. They then rank as statutes.[17] By this device Spain adopted the Community Treaties and the existing volume of Community law but has not solved the problem of supremacy.

The three members admitted in 1973 proceed from a dualist position. In the United Kingdom it was necessary to pass the European Communities Act 1972[18] in order to transform the Treaty obligations into domestic law, to adopt the so-called 'enforceable Community rights' and to set up machinery for the implementation of the remaining rules of Community law. In Ireland, too, this object was achieved by the European Communities Act 1972, which provided, inter alia, that 'from the first day of January 1973, the Treaties governing the European Communities and the existing and future acts adopted by the institutions of those Communities shall be binding on the state and shall be part of the domestic law thereof under the conditions laid down in those Treaties'. In Denmark the law of 11 October 1972 expressly adopted the Treaties enumerated therein and make provisions for the delegation of sovereign powers to the Communities and for the adoption of Community acts directly applicable by virtue of Community law.

The Greek Constitution of 1975 enacted in anticipation[19] of admission to the Community provides (Article 28) for the limitation of the exercise of national sovereignty subject to safeguards of human rights, democratic government and the

---

15 Pescatore, P, 'L'autorité en droit interne des traits internationaux selon jurisprudence luxembourgeoise' (1962) 18 *Pasicrisie Luxembourgeoise* 99-115.
16 Van Panhuys, H F, 'The Netherlands Constitution and International Law' (1964) 58 AJIL 88-108; Van Dijk, P, 'The Implementation and Application of the Law of the European Communities within the Legal Order of the Netherlands' (1969) 6 CML Rev 283-308.
17 Judgment of Supreme Court of 12 December 1980, quoted by Aurrecoechea at 28, supra.
18 See Ch 15, infra.
19 Roucounas, op cit, p 13.

principle of equality and reciprocity with her partners. The same Article (28) guarantees incorporation and supremacy of international law and international conventions duly ratified under the condition of reciprocity. However Article 93(4) which governs the review of the constitutionality of laws states that courts are not bound to apply laws which are contrary to the constitution. This is a potential source of conflict with Community law.

In terms similar to Article 25 of the German Constitution the Constitution of Portugal (Article 8) provides that the principles of customary international law form part of the Portuguese legal order. There is no automatic reception of international conventional law. Moreover Articles 7 and 9 charge the state with the duty of safeguarding national independence and provide that Portugal must, in her international relations, always respect the Constitution . It means, in effect, that the Constitution overrides treaty obligations. Therefore it was necessary in 1982 to amend Article 8 of the Constitution which provides, in paragraph 4, that the rules enacted by the competent institutions of international organizations to which Portugal is a party are directly applicable in the international order as long as this is expressly provided for in the corresponding treaties. This has effectively dealt with the problem of Community treaties and the direct applicability of Community law but has left open the problem of supremacy.

This brief survey of the constitutional scene of the Member States shows not only a diverse approach to the status of the Treaties but also indicates a cautious commitment of the majority of these states to the Community rather than a formal and irrevocable abdication of their national sovereignty.

C. Incorporation of Community legislation

(1) RECEPTION OF COMMUNITY LAW

The logic of the acceptance of Treaty obligations demands an unconditional reception not only of the primary but also of the derivative rules of Community law. EC Article 10 (ex Art 5) reminds the Member States that they must 'take all appropriate measures, whether general or particular, to ensure fulfilment of the obligations arising out of this Treaty or resulting from action taken by the institutions of the Community. They shall facilitate the achievement of the Community's tasks. They shall abstain from any measure which could jeopardize the attainment of the objectives of this Treaty'. Moreover, as provided by EC Article 4(1) (ex Art 3a(1), which replaced a similar provision), 'For the purposes set out in Article 2 (ie purposes of the Community), the activities of the Member States and the Community shall include, as provided in this Treaty and in accordance with the timetable set out therein, the adoption of an economic policy which is based on the close co-ordination of Member States' economic policies, on the internal market and on the definition of common objectives, and conducted in accordance with the principle of an open market economy with free competition'. Since policies are enforced through the instrumentality of the law, the Member States must adapt and modify their laws in order to bring about harmony within the Community and, above all, remove the legal barriers to the creation and working of the Community. Since the EC is concerned with customs duties, movement of goods, persons, services and capital, agriculture and fisheries, transport, competition and restrictive practices, state aid to industry, taxation, and social security, and whilst the ECSC and Euratom are concerned with coal, steel and nuclear energy industries, the Member

States undertake a considerable number of specific obligations. These obligations are in many respects regulated by the Community legislation whose scope ranges from relatively trivial provisions like the calculation of the compensation for hatching eggs[20] to the most solemn historical provisions regarding the establishment of the Community.

In the case of the new members, the accumulated volume of Community law (often referred to as the 'acquis communitaire') became the object of a wholesale reception at the time of their accession. By Article 2 of the 1972 Act of Accession they became subject to 'the provisions of the original Treaties and the acts adopted by the institutions of the Communities' whilst by Article 149 they were considered 'as being addressees of and having notification of directives and decisions within the meaning of Article 189 of the EEC Treaty [now Art 249] and of Article 161 of the EAEC Treaty, and of recommendations and decisions within the meaning of Article 14 of the ECSC Treaty, provided that those directives, recommendations and decisions have been notified to all the original Member States'. The same principles govern the position of Greece, Portugal and Spain subject to specifically negotiated derogations.

The impact of Community law upon the laws of the Member States depends on two principles: the direct applicability and the supremacy of Community law. The former is relevant to the implementation, the latter to the enforcement of Community law.

(2)   DIRECTLY APPLICABLE RULES OF COMMUNITY LAW

Depending on their nature and function the rules of Community law are either 'directly' or 'indirectly' applicable. In this context a distinction should be made between rules which are 'directly applicable',[1] that is rules becoming automatically upon their enactment part of the *corpus juris* of the Member States, and rules 'directly enforceable', that is rules having a 'direct effect' as far as rights and obligations of the citizen are concerned.[2] In other words 'directly applicable' rules concern the state, whilst 'directly enforceable' rules concern the rights of individuals. The former imply state duties, the latter citizens' rights flowing from state duties to implement and enforce Community law.

Despite the subtle distinction between 'direct applicability' and 'direct effect', the ECJ has not been using these terms consistently. Thus, for example, it held that 'Article 52 of the Treaty [now 43] is a directly applicable provision'[3] and that 'in such a situation, at least, Article 119 [now Art 141] is directly applicable and may thus give rise to individual rights which the Courts must protect'.[4] In the *Van Gend* case,[5] on the other hand, it decreed that 'Article 12 [now Art 25] must be interpreted as producing direct effects and creating individual

---

20   Article 77(2) of the 1972 Act of Accession provides that 'the compensatory amount per hatching egg shall be calculated on the basis of the compensatory amount applicable to the quantity of feed grain required for the production in the Community of one hatching egg'.

1   'Enforcement Community rights' according to s 2(1) of the British European Communities Act 1972.

2   See Winter, J, 'Direct Applicability and Direct Effect – Two Distinct and Different Concepts in Community Law' [1972] CML Rev 425; Wyatt, D, 'Directly Applicable Provisions of EEC Law' [1975] 125 NLJ, pp 458, 575, 669, 793.

3   Case 2/74: *Reyners v Belgium* [1974] ECR 631, [1974] 2 CMLR 305.

4   Case 43/75: *Defrenne v SABENA* [1976] ECR 455, [1976] 2 CMLR 98.

5   Op cit [1963] ECR 1 at 13, [1963] CMLR 105 at 130, 131.

rights which Courts must protect' and on another occasion[6] stated that in 'applying the principle of co-operation laid down in Article 5 of the Treaty [now Art 10], it is the national courts which are entrusted with ensuring the legal protection which citizens derive from the direct effect of the provisions of Community law . . .'. However, despite this dictum, it should be borne in mind that EC Article 10 [ex Art 5] is addressed to the Member States alone, stating their general obligation to further the objectives of the Treaty. In that sense it is directly applicable to the states but not to individuals since it is incapable of generating subjective rights and thus cannot be said to have a direct effect as far as individuals are concerned.[7]

It seems accordingly that 'directly applicable' provisions take force in the territory of the Member States without further enactment whilst provisions having a 'direct effect' are capable of creating enforceable Community rights. The latter follows from the former. These rights are created either by the Treaty directly or, as stated by the ECJ[8] 'also by reason of obligations which the Treaty imposes in a clearly defined way upon individuals as well as upon the Member States and upon the institutions of the Community'.

The notion of 'direct applicability' is derived from the monist concept of international law and the self-executing nature of certain Treaties or Treaty provisions. It, therefore, enables the rules of Community law, despite their extraneous source, to become automatically part of the *corpus juris* of the Member States. The notion of 'direct effect', on the other hand, is derived from the judicial interpretation of the will of the legislator who decides whether a provision is merely programmatic[9] or constitutes a command to its subject,[10] or a right vested in an individual,[11] or an obligation imposed upon him.[12] Thus, whilst the distinction between 'direct applicability' and 'direct effect' appears of little significance in the eyes of the Community Court, its jurisprudence, through the instrumentality of the doctrine expressed by both terms, has advanced the rights of individuals grounded in Community law.

The doctrine of direct effect can be traced to certain leading cases. In the *Van Gend* case the ECJ held that there was an unconditional obligation on the part of the Member State to refrain from introducing new customs duties which, in turn, created a corresponding right in favour of the citizen. The alternative to the direct effect, through the Court, 'would remove all direct judicial protection of the individual rights'. In *Alfons Lütticke v Hauptzollamt Saarlouis*[13] the Court held that a Member State must not impose on the product of another Member State any internal tax in excess of that applicable to similar domestic products

---

6 Case 33/76: *Rewe-Zentralfinanz GmbH v Landwirtschaftskammer für das Saarland* [1976] ECR 1989, [1977] 1 CMLR 533.
7 See Case 9/73: *Schlüter v Hauptzollamt Lörrach* [1973] ECR 1135; Case 44/84: *Hurd v Jones* (HM Inspector of Taxes) [1986] ECR 29, [1986] 2 CMLR 1; Case C-333/88: *Tither v IRC* [1990] ECR I-1133, [1990] 2 CMLR 779.
8 *Van Gend*, supra at p 12.
9 Eg EC Art 70 (ex Art 74): 'The objectives of this Treaty shall, in matters governed by this Title, be pursued by Member States within the framework of a common transport policy.'
10 Eg EC Art 72 (now repealed): 'Member States shall keep the Commission informed of any movements of capital to and from third countries which come to their knowledge.'
11 Eg EC Art 232(3) (ex Art 175(3)): 'Any natural or legal person may . . . complain to the Court.'
12 Eg EC Art 82 (ex Art 86): 'Any abuse . . . of a dominant position within the common market . . . shall be prohibited.'
13 Case 57/65: [1966] ECR 205, [1971] CMLR 674; see also Case 28/67: *Mölkerei-Zentrale Westfalen/Lippe GmbH v Hauptzollamt Paderborn* [1968] ECR 143, [1968] CMLR 187.

and this safeguarded the importer's interests. In *Salgoil SpA v Italian Ministry of Foreign Trade*[14] the ECJ confirmed that a Member State had no discretion in the application of the Treaty provisions governing import quotas within the Community. In the *Van Duyn* case the freedom of movement was recognized as an enforceable right though, in the circumstances, it was curtailed by the application of a derogation clause. Both the right and the exception were held to be 'directly applicable'.[15] The right of establishment of a lawyer who, though not a national, was qualified according to the law of the host state, was deduced from EC Article 43 (ex Art 52)[16] and Italy was held to be in breach of the same article for having failed to remove a nationality qualification in respect of customs agents[17] and persons employed in tourism, journalism and retail pharmacies.[18] In the much criticized[19] *Defrenne* case a Belgian air hostess was able to vindicate her right to equal pay by virtue of EC Article 141 (ex Art 119), which (coupled with a directive) was held to have direct effect as from the end of the period of transition.

However the Community Court has stated the doctrine in a most forthright manner in the second *Simmenthal* case[20] emphasizing that a directly applicable Community rule takes precedence over the national legislation whether antecedent or subsequent to the relevant Treaty provision. Irrespective of the constitutional implications the national courts are bound to give effect to it. The message of the Community Court is that certain provisions of the EC Treaty are by their very nature and purpose directly enforceable in national courts. As they affect private interests they create Community rights which, as a corollary, correspond to Community obligations imposed upon the Member States. These, as confirmed by the Community Court, and national courts, include the following:

(1) EC Article 12 (ex Art 6) which prohibits discrimination on grounds of nationality;[1]
(2) EC Article 23 (ex Art 9) and former EC Article 11 (now repealed) on the customs union as from the end of the transitional period;[2]
(3) EC Article 25 (ex Art 12) which forbids new customs duties or similar charges;[3]

---

14 Case 13/68: [1968] ECR 453, [1969] CMLR 181.
15 Cf the opposite decision of the French Conseil d'Etat in the *Cohn-Bendit* case, Dalloz 1979, J155.
16 Case 2/74: *Reyners v Belgium* [1974] ECR 631, [1974] 2 CMLR 305; see also Case 71/76: *Thieffry v Conseil de l'Ordre des Avocats à la Cour de Paris* [1977] ECR 765, [1977] 2 CMLR 373.
17 Case 159/78: *Commission v Italy* [1979] ECR 3247 at 3264, [1980] 3 CMLR 446 at 463.
18 Case 168/85: *Commission v Italy* [1986] ECR 2945, [1988] 1 CMLR 580.
19 Hamson, C, 'Methods of Interpretation – a Critical Assessment of the Results', *Reports of the Judicial and Academic Conference Luxembourg* (1976).
20 Case 106/77: *Amministrazione delle Finanze dello Stato v Simmenthal SpA* [1978] ECR 629, [1978] 3 CMLR 263. See also Case 158/80: *Rewe Handelsgesellschaft v HZA Kiel (Re direct application of directive)* [1981] ECR 1805, [1982] 1 CMLR 449.
1 Case 1/78: *Kenny v National Insurance Comr, Liverpool* [1978] ECR 1489, [1978] 3 CMLR 651. Case 45/75: *Rewe-Zentrale v HZA Landau-Pfalz* [1976] ECR 181, at 198, [1976] 2 CMLR 1 at 25. Case 22/80: *Boussac v Gerstenmeier* [1980] ECR 3427, [1982] 1 CMLR 202.
2 Case 33/70: *SACE SpA v Italian Ministry of Finance* [1970] ECR 1213, [1971] CMLR 123. Case 18/71: *Eunomia di Porro & C v Italian Ministry of Education* [1971] ECR 811, [1972] CMLR 4; Case 251/78: *Denkavit v Minister für Ernährung* [1979] ECR 3369 at 3384, [1980] 3 CMLR 513.
3 Case 26/62: *Van Gend*, supra, p 342, note 5.

(4) former EC Article 13(2) (now repealed) on the abolition of charges having an equivalent effect to customs duties on imports;[4]

(5) former EC Article 16 (now incorporated in EC Art 25) on the abolition of customs duties on exports;[5]

(6) former EC Articles 30 and 31 (see now EC Art 28) which forbid quantitative restrictions and measures having equivalent effect;[6]

(7) former EC Article 32(1), (2) (now repealed) on the abolition of quotas in trade between Member States;[7]

(8) EC Article 30 (ex Art 36) as far as 'disguised restrictions on trade' are concerned;[8]

(9) EC Article 31(1) and (2) (ex Art 37(1) and (2)) which forbids measures likely to restrict the abolition of customs duties and quantitative restrictions between Member States or adjustment of state monopolies;[9]

(10) EC Article 39(2) (ex Art 48(2)), on discrimination between workers on the ground of nationality;[10]

(11) EC Article 39(3) (ex Art 48(3)); Regulations 15 and 38/64; Directive 64/221 on the restrictions of the freedom of movement;[11]

(12) EC Article 43 (ex Art 52), concerning the right of establishment;[12]

(13) former EC Article 53 (now repealed) which forbade new restrictions on the right of establishment;[13]

---

4   Case 77/72: *Capolongo v Azienda Agricolo Maya* [1973] ECR 611 at 622, [1974] 1 CMLR 230. Case 63/74: *W Cadsky SpA v Instituto Nazionale per il Commercio Estero* [1975] ECR 281, [1975] 2 CMLR 246; Case 94/75: *Süddeutsche Zucker v HZA Mannheim* [1976] ECR 153, [1976] 2 CMLR 54.

5   Case 48/71: *Commission v Italy* [1972] ECR 527, [1972] CMLR 699. Case 45/76: *Comet BV v Produktschap voor Siergewassen* [1976] ECR 2043, [1977] 1 CMLR 533.

6   Case 13/68: *Salgoil SpA v Italian Ministry of Foreign Trade* [1968] ECR 453, [1969] CMLR 181. Case 12/74: *Commission v Germany* [1975] ECR 181, [1975] 1 CMLR 340. Case 74/76: *Iannelli and Volpi SpA v Meroni* [1977] ECR 557, [1977] 2 CMLR 688; Case 251/78, supra; Case 124/81: *Commission v United Kingdom* [1983] ECR 203, [1983] 2 CMLR 1; Case 42/82: *Commission v France* [1983] ECR 1013, [1984] 1 CMLR 160; Case 16/83: *Re Prantl* [1984] ECR 1299; Case 207/83: *Commission v United Kingdom* [1985] 2 CMLR 259.

7   Case 13/68: *Salgoil*, supra.

8   Case 78/70: *Deutsche Grammophon GmbH v Metro-SB-Grössmärke BmbH & Co KG* [1971] ECR 487, [1971] CMLR 631. Case 192/73: *Van Zuylen Frères v Hag AG* [1974] ECR 731, [1974] 2 CMLR 127. Case 29/72: *Marimex SpA v Italian Finance Administration* [1972] ECR 1309, [1973] CMLR 486. Case 21/75: *Firma I Shröeder KG v Oberstadt-direktor der Stadt Köln* [1975] ECR 905, [1975] 2 CMLR 312.

9   Case 59/75: *Pubblico Ministero v Flavia Manghera* [1976] ECR 91, [1976] 1 CMLR 557; Case 148/77: *Hansen v HZA Flensburg* [1978] ECR 1787, [1979] 1 CMLR 604.

10   Case 167/73: *Commission v France* [1974] ECR 359, [1974] 2 CMLR 216. Case 41/74: *Van Duyn v Home Office* [1975] Ch 358, [1974] ECR 1337, [1975] 1 CMLR 1. Case 13/76: *Donà v Mantero* [1976] ECR 1333, [1976] 2 CMLR 578; Case 152/73: *Sotgiu v Deutsche Bundespost* [1974] ECR 153; Case 36/75: *Rutili v Ministère de l'Interior* [1975] ECR 1219, [1976] 1 CMLR 140.

11   Case 67/74: *Bonsignore v Oberstadtdirektor der Stadt Köln* [1975] ECR 297, [1975] CMLR 472. Case 41/74: *Van Duyn v Home Office*, supra; Case 36/75, supra; Case 48/75: *Re Royer* [1976] ECR 497, [1976] 2 CMLR 619; Case 118/75: *Re Watson and Belmann* [1976] ECR 1185, [1976] 2 CMLR 552.

12   Case 2/74: *Reyners v Belgium* [1974] ECR 631, [1974] 2 CMLR 305. Case 33/74: *Van Binsbergen v Bestuur van de Bedrijfsvereniging voor de Metaalnijverheid* [1974] ECR 1299, [1975] 1 CMLR 298. Case 11/77: *Patrick v Ministère des Affaires Culturelles* [1977] ECR 1199, [1977] 2 CMLR 523.

13   Case 6/64: *Costa v ENEL*, supra; Case 96/85: *Commission v France* [1986] ECR 1475, [1986] 3 CMLR 57.

(14) EC Article 49 (ex Art 59) and former EC Article 62 (now repealed) on the freedom to provide services;[14]

(15) EC Articles 81 and 82 (ex Arts 85 and 86), on competition;[15]

(16) EC Article 86(2) (ex Art 90(2)), on revenue-producing monopolies;[16]

(17) EC Article 88(2) (ex Art 93(2)), concerning aids by states;[17]

(18) EC Article 90(1) (ex Art 95(1)), which prohibits internal taxation of products of other Member States;[18]

(19) EC Article 141 (ex Art 119), on equal pay for men and women.[19]

It goes without saying that the majority of EC Articles 189-314 (ex Arts 137-248), representing the 'organizational law' of the EC are 'directly applicable' though by their nature and function they do not necessarily constitute rights enforceable by individuals.[20]

The list is by no means complete as certain provisions of the EC Treaty remain yet to be considered judicially. By way of contrast, provisions of the ECSC Treaty generally do not confer rights on individuals that can be invoked before national courts because the structure of that Treaty is very different from the structure of the EC Treaty: the primary mechanism for enforcement of the ECSC Treaty is action by the Commission rather than individual action before national courts.[1] As for the criterion of direct enforceability, the Community Court[2] held as follows:

'. . . The Treaty's objective of establishing a common market the functioning of which affects the subjects of Member States entails that the Treaty is

14 Case 33/74: *Van Binsbergen*, op cit; Case 36/74: *Walrave and Koch v Association Union Cycliste Internationale* [1974] ECR 1405, [1975] 1 CMLR 320; Case 39/75: *Coenen v Sociaal Economische Raad* [1975] ECR 1547, [1976] 1 CMLR 30; Cases 110 and 111/78: *Ministère Public and Chambre Syndicale des Agents Artistiques et Impresari de Belgique, ASBL v van Wesemael* [1979] ECR 35, [1979] 3 CMLR 87; Case 13/76: *Donà v Mantero* [1976] ECR 1333; Case 71/76: *Thieffry v Conseil de l'Ordre des Avocats à la Cour de Paris* [1977] ECR 765: Case 107/83: *Ordre des Avocats au Barreau de Paris v Klopp* [1984] ECR 2971, [1985] 1 CMLR 99; Case 90/76: *Van Ameyde v UCL* [1977] ECR 1091; Case 15/78: *Société Générale Alsacienne de Banque v Koestler* [1978] ECR 1971; Case 115/78: *Knoors v Secretary of State for Economic Affairs* [1979] ECR 399; Case 136/78: *Ministère Public v Auer* [1979] ECR 437, [1979] 2 CMLR 373; Case 271/82: *Auer v Ministère Public* [1983] ECR 2727, [1985] 1 CMLR 123; Case 52/79: *Procureur du Roi v Debauve* [1980] ECR 833.

15 Case 13/61: *Kledingverkoopbedriff de Geus en Uitdenbogerd v Robert Bosch BmbH* [1962] ECR 45, [1962] CMLR 1; Case 127/73: *BRT v SABAM* [1974] ECR 51 and 313, [1974] 2 CMLR 238; Case 37/79: *Marty v Lauder* [1980] ECR 2481, [1981] 2 CMLR 143 and subsequent cases.

16 Case 155/73: *Italy v Sacchi* [1974] ECR 409, [1974] 2 CMLR 177.

17 Case 120/73; *Lorenz v Germany* [1973] ECR 1471; Case 6/64, supra; Cases 91/83 and 127/83: *Heiniken v Inspecteur der Vennootschapselasting* [1984] ECR 3435, [1985] 1 CMLR 389.

18 Case 57/65: *Lütticke v HZA Saarlouis* [1966] ECR 205, [1971] CMLR 674; Case 28/67: *Mölkerei-Zentrale Westfalen/Lippe GmbH v Hauptzollamt Paderborn* [1968] ECR 143, [1968] CMLR 187; Case 216/81: *Compagnia Generale Interscambi SpA v Amministrazione delle Finanza dello Stato* [1982] ECR 2701, [1983] 1 CMLR 685.

19 Case 43/75: *Defrenne v SA SABENA* [1976] ECR 455, [1976] 2 CMLR 98 and ch 30, infra.

20 Eg Case C-282/90: *Vreugdenhil v Commission* [1992] ECR I-1937. For exceptions, see EC Arts 230, 241 and 288 (ex Arts 173, 184, 215).

 1 Case C-128/92: *H J Banks & Co Ltd v British Coal Corpn* [1994] ECR I-1209; Case C-18/94: *Hopkins v National Power and PowerGen* [1996] ECR I-2281.

 2 Case 28/67: *Mölkerei-Zentrale Westfalen/Lippe GmbH v Hauptzollamt Paderborn* [1968] ECR 143 at 152, [1968] CMLR 187 at 217.

something more than an agreement creating obligations between state parties alone. The Community is a new legal system, in support of which the Member States have limited their sovereign rights in certain fields, and the subjects of the new legal system are not only the Member States but their inhabitants as well. Community Law, being independent of the legislation passed by Member States, therefore, creates rights as well as duties for individual persons who are subject to the legal order of Member States. These rights and obligations arise not only when they are expressly provided for in the Treaty, but also as a result of the duties imposed by it in a clearly defined manner upon nationals of Member States themselves and the institutions of the Community . . .'

Advocate-General Mayras, quoting several precedents in the *Van Duyn* case,[3] thought that ' . . . the provision must impose on the Member State a clear and precise obligation; it must be unconditional, ie not accompanied by any reservation, . . . and the application of the Community rule must not be conditional on any subsequent legislation whether of the Community institutions or of the Member States; and must not lead to the latter having an effective power of discretionary judgment as to the application of the rule in question'.

The test of direct effect is, therefore, primarily the capacity of the text to produce rights and obligations which individuals may seek to enforce against the state. The national law should not bar the enforcement of such rights and obligations,[4] even though the enforcement may in the context of national law present considerable technical difficulties. However, as indicated by decisions arising from the application of EC Articles 81 and 82 (ex Arts 85 and 86), a text may, even indirectly, give rise to directly enforceable rights and obligations.[5] In this sense the nature of a specific provision may have to be inferred from its purpose and the intention of the authority which brought into being such a provision (ie whether the Treaty of Community legislation).

To what extent procedures prescribed by the Treaty may give rise to directly enforceable rights and obligations has changed over the years. Procedural law is, in many respects, the guarantor of substantive rights. Where the prescribed procedures are not observed, the individual may suffer and should, in justice, be entitled to relief.[6] This, among other things, seems to have been in the mind of the Giudice Conciliatore Fabbri in *Flaminio Costa v ENEL*[7] when he referred to the ECJ a complaint that the Italian decree nationalizing the electricity industry, passed in the absence of consultation with the Commission (EC Article 96 and 97 (ex Arts 101 and 102)), distorted the conditions of competition and infringed the rights of the individual. Although the Community Court held that EC Article 97 (ex Art 102), created no directly enforceable rights, the general question remained open.

To take another example: EC Article 234 (ex Art 177), is surely directly applicable but has no direct effect in so far as it does not create directly enforceable

---

3   Supra, ECR at p 1355; CMLR at p 8.
4   *Salgoil SpA*, supra.
5   Eg Case 48/72: *Brasserie de Haécht v Wilkin-Janssen* [1973] ECR 77, [1973] CMLR 287; Case 127/73: *BRT v SABAM* [1974] ECR 51, [1974] 2 CMLR 238.
6   Cf World Court in *The Free Zones Case* (1932) PCIJ Rep Ser A/B No 46; *Wimbledon Case* (1923) PCIJ Rep Ser A No 1; *German Settlers Case* (1923) PCIJ Rep Ser B No 6.
7   Case 6/64, supra.

rights. However it is also capable of creating an expectation in the minds of litigants that their case will be heard by the Community Court. However the procedure for the preliminary ruling is governed largely by the national systems[8] which may, through cumbersome procedures or appeals on the point whether or not to refer, frustrate that expectation. In the opinion of the ECJ a state policy to restrict the reference would amount to a breach of the Treaty[9] and so would procedural discrimination against a person endeavouring to assert a Community right.[10] Whilst the ECJ made it plain that '. . . in the absence of Community rules on this subject it is for the domestic legal system of each Member State to designate the courts having jurisdiction and to determine the procedural conditions governing actions at law intended to ensure the protection of the rights which citizens have from the direct effect of Community law'[11] it seemed at that stage a rather tenuous proposition that procedural safeguards implicit in the enforcement of Community rights do themselves constitute 'enforceable Community rights'. Since then, the ECJ has developed the clear principle that, while EC law relies on the domestic legal systems of each Member State for the substantive and procedural rules to be employed to protect and vindicate rights under EC law (unless EC law itself supplies those rules), domestic law applies subject to the EC law principles of equivalence and effectiveness, developed by the ECJ in its case law. The principle of equivalence requires the treatment of rights derived from EC law to be no less favourable than the treatment of similar rights under domestic law. The principle of effectiveness precludes the application of domestic rules that would in practice render the exercise of EC law rights excessively difficult or impossible.[12]

The principle of direct applicability of Treaty provisions defined by the Community Court applies also to secondary legislation. Regulations[13] fall into that category unless they give the Member States discretion in their implementation.[14] If they do not allow any discretion an action, as in the slaughtered cows case,[15] may be brought against the state by the individual whose Community right has been impaired through the deficiency of the national system. Moreover, in such a case, the state in default will be exposed to enforcement proceedings.[16]

---

 8 Eg Cases 36, 71/80: *Irish Creamery Milk Suppliers Association v Ireland* [1981] ECR 735, [1981] 2 CMLR 455.   Case 244/78: *Union Laitière Normande v French Dairy Farmers* [1979] ECR 2663, [1980] 1 CMLR 314.   Case 146/73: *Firma Rheinmühlen-Düsseldorf v Einfuhr-und Verratsstelle für Getreide und Futtermittel* [1974] ECR 139, [1974] 1 CMLR 523.
 9 Case 77/69: *Commission v Belgium* [1970] ECR 237.
10 Case 33/76: *Rewe-Zentralfinanz GmbH and Rewe Zentral AG v Landwirtschafskammer für das Saarland* [1976] ECR 1989, [1977] 1 CMLR 533 (limitation of actions).
11 Ibid.
12 See, for example, Case 199/82: *Amministrazione delle Finanze dello Stato v SpA San Giorgio* [1983] ECR 3595 and, more recently, Cases C-46/93 and C-48/93: *Brasserie du Pêcheur v Germany and R v Secretary of State for Transport, ex p Factortame* [1996] ECR I-1029, paras 67-74; and Case C-228/96: *Aprile v Amministrazione delle Finanze dello Stato* [1998] ECR I-7141, paras 18 ff.
13 See pp 133 et seq. See also Case 83/78: *Pigs Marketing Board v Redmond* [1978] ECR 2347, [1979] 1 CMLR 177.
14 Eg Reg 15/64/EEC (JO 573/64) concerning the import of cattle from Denmark to Germany; see also Case 31/74: *Re Galli* [1975] ECR 47, [1975] 1 CMLR 211.
15 Case 93/71: *Leonesio*, supra.
16 Case 39/72: *Commission v Italy* [1973] ECR 101, [1973] CMLR 439; Case 309/84: *Commission v Italy (Re Non-Payment of Premium for Renunciation of re-planting of Vines under Reg 56/80)* [1986] ECR 599.

Directives, as we have observed earlier,[17] may have direct effect creating thereby enforceable Community rights. However they have also another potential since '. . . the individual invokes a provision of a directive before a national court in order that the competent national authorities, in exercising the choice which is left to them as to the form and the methods for implementing the directive, have kept within the limits as to their decisions set out in the directive . . .'.[18]

(3) INDIRECTLY APPLICABLE RULES OF COMMUNITY LAW

In addition to provisions which contain rules of law directly applicable in the territory of the Member States the founding Treaties comprise a number of policies or general provisions which have to be implemented by state legislation. The former are cognisable by the national courts and for all intents and purposes are regarded as having a direct and immediate effect with regard to persons and things in the territory of the Member States. The latter consist of Treaty obligations which by virtue of the Treaty provisions have to be transformed into detailed rules of law. The ECJ expressly ruled that certain provisions of the EC Treaty have no direct effect. These include the Community 'solidarity principle' expressed in EC Article 10 (ex Art 5);[19] former (now repealed) EC Articles 32(2) and 33[20] concerning quotas in inter-state trade; former (now repealed) EC Articles 67 and 71[1] concerned with the movement of capital; EC Article 86(2) (ex Art 90(2))[2] permitting Member States to grant special or exclusive rights to public undertakings entrusted with the operation of services of general economic interest; EC Article 87(1) (ex Art 92(1))[3] which prohibits aids granted by states save in specific circumstances; former (now repealed) EC Article 97(1)[4] permitting Member States which levy a turnover tax to establish average rates; EC Article 97, (ex Art 102)[5] concerned with consultations between the Commission and any Member States regarding the approximation of laws; EC Article 108 (ex Art 107)[6] concerned with the rates of exchange; and EC Articles 136 and 137 (ex Arts 117 and 118) concerned with social policy.[7] To these we can add the decisions and directives of the Community organs addressed to one or several states which are of a general or mixed character and have to be further elaborated. The rules of

---

17 Case 51/76: *Verbond van Nederlandse Ondernemingen v Inspecteur der Invoerrechten en Accijnzen* [1977] ECR 113 at 127, [1977] 1 CMLR 413; See also Case 21/78: *Delkvist v Anklagemijndigheden* [1978] ECR 2327 at 2340.

18 Case 51/76: *Verbond von Nederlandse Ondernemingen v Inspecteur der Invoerrechter en Accijnzen* [1977] ECR 113 at 127, [1977] 1 CMLR 413; and, more recently, Case C-287/98: *Luxembourg v Linster*, 19 September 2000, paras 31-39 (and the cases cited there and in the Opinion of Advocate General Leger). See Cases C-6/90 and C-9/90: *Francovich v Italy* [1991] ECR I-5357, [1993] 2 CMLR 66.

19 Case 9/73: *Schlüter v HZA Lörrach* [1973] ECR 1135 at 1162; see also Cases 44/84 and C-333/88, supra (p 343, note 7). The solidarity principle may however produce rights that can be relied on before a national court when combined with another provision of EC law.

20 Case 13/68:*Salgoil SpA v Italian Ministry of Foreign Trade* [1968] ECR 453 at 461.

1 Case 203/80: *Re Casati* [1981] ECR 2595 at 2615-2616.

2 Case 10/71: *Ministère Public de Luxembourg v Müller* [1971] ECR 723 at 730.

3 Case 77/72: *Capolongo v Maya* [1973] ECR 611 at 621, [1974] 1 CMLR 230 at 244-245; Case 78/76: *Steinike und Weinig v Germany* [1977] ECR 595, [1977] 2 CMLR 688.

4 Case 28/67: *Mölkerei-Zentrale v HZA Paderborn* [1968] ECR 143 at 156, [1968] CMLR 187 at 221.

5 Case 6/64: *Costa v ENEL* [1964] ECR 585 at 595.

6 Case 9/73, supra, at 1161.

7 Case 126/86: *Giménez Zaera v Istituto Nacional de la Seguridade Social (Re Pensions of Spanish Civil Servants)* [1987] ECR 3697, [1989] 1 CMLR 827.

law indirectly applicable have this in common: that they have to be enacted by the Member States to become part of their municipal law and that the Member States have a considerable discretion in the choice of the methods. In most cases the Member States have merely to adapt their existing laws to the overall strategy of the founding Treaties, notably the Common Market in the EC. However the intensity of the adaptation and the degree of discretion accorded to Member States depend on the Treaty provisions. Thus according to the EC Treaty three such degrees can be discerned.[8]

First, the states may enjoy complete discretion in the implementation of their obligations. Two examples, discussed by a learned writer,[9] illustrate the point. To implement Regulation No 3 concerning the social security of migrant workers (reference to EC Article 42 (ex Art 51)) Italy set up a special pension for miners;[10] the Netherlands, on the other hand, considered that their existing law was inadequate and took the opportunity of remodelling the system and adapting it to the problems of migrant workers.[11] To implement the EC agricultural policy France passed a general statute (*loi d'orientation agricole*),[12] whilst Belgium decided to recast the whole system and so repealed the law of 1931 on import, export and transit of goods and substituted for it a new law on agriculture.[13]

Secondly, the states may have a choice of either implementing or not implementing the Community law, but in the exercise of their option they have to act within the scope of authority accorded to them. The following provisions of the EC Treaty are relevant in this respect:

(1) Former (now repealed) EC Article 25, which enabled the Council to grant to the Member States, on the recommendation of the Commission, tariff quotas at a reduced rate of duty or duty-free;[14]
(2) EC Article 134(1) (ex Art 115(1)), which enables the Commission to authorize the Member States to take protective measures in derogation from the general principles of the commercial policy of the Community;[15]
(3) Former (now repealed) EC Article 226, which enabled the Commission to authorize the Member States to take protective measure during the transitional period in derogation from the rules of the Treaty.[16]

Thirdly, there are measures which the Member States have to take in order to discharge their obligations. In this respect they act merely as agents of the Community instrumental in the execution of Community law. For example, to carry into effect the CAP Member States have to set up Agricultural Intervention Boards. These are national institutions founded upon Community law. They

---

8   Sohier, M, and Megret, C, 'Le role de l'exécutif national et du législateur national dans la mise en oeuvre de droit communautaire', *Semaine de Bruges* (1965), op cit, pp 108 et seq; Constantintinidès-Mégret, op cit, pp 132 et seq.
9   Constantinidès-Mégret, op cit, p 133.
10   Law of No 5, 3 January 1960, Gaz Uff, No 27, 1960.
11   Law of 13 January 1965; reference to Regulations 15 and 38/64 on the free movement of workers, EC Art 39 (ex Art 48).
12   Law of 8 August 1962, JORF, 10 August 1962.
13   Law of 11 September 1962; MB 26 October 1962, p 9491, and Law of 20 July 1962; MB 26 July 1962, p 6218.
14   Eg decisions of the Commission of 9 November 1964 (JO 1964, p 3259) and of 12 November 1964 (JO 1964, p 3549) quoted by Constantinidès-Mégret, op cit, p 134.
15   Eg decision of 21 September 1964 (JO 1964, p 2497, op cit, p 134).
16   Eg decisions of 20 December 1963 (JO 1964, p 145) and of 16 April (JO 1964, p 1162).

administer the Community system and collect, inter alia, charges levied by the authority of Community legislation. Should such charges be declared illegal because based upon an invalid regulation the repayment of these charges falls upon national law.[17]

(4) TECHNIQUES OF INCORPORATION

A study of the problems of state legislation turning the rules of Community law indirectly applicable into the municipal law of the Member States reveals not only a diversity of approach, but, above all, a slow progress. Parliaments are far from being eager to act and their procedures are lengthy and cumbersome. As guardians of national sovereignty they seem to resent the intrusion of extraneous law-making authority although they have accepted the Community Treaties. As legislators parliaments, no doubt, do not relish their subordinate position, or having their functions reduced to mere formality, in the matter of Community legislation. As parliament debates seem nugatory in view of clear Treaty obligations to execute Community law, the tendency is to leave the matter in the hands of the Excecutive.[18]

Should parliament turn perverse and pass a law inconsistent with the Treaty obligations, precious little can be done. Evidently the state concerned could be in breach of the Treaty which in turn would enable the Commission to act under EC Article 226 (ex Art 169). Should the state be recalcitrant in not heeding the 'reasoned opinion' of the Commission, the matter could be brought before the Community Court.[19] If the Community Court decides against the state, the state is bound to 'take the necessary measures to comply with the judgment' EC Article 228 (ex Art 171), which means the repeal of the offending legislation. However, in theory, the game could go on for ever if the government concerned were unable to influence its parliament. Although the Community would be in jeopardy, the Community Court could not strike down the municipal legislation it considers 'illegal' in the eyes of Community law, simply because the Court has no direct authority in the territory of the Member State. Rather than putting the Community at risk the Member States have evolved a practical, though individualistic, approach to the implementation of Community law. Their solution of the problem depends on the Constitution.

The French Constitution of 1958 sharply distinguishes between legislation by statute (*loi*) and legislation by decree (*décret*). Whatever is not listed in Article 34 as being subject to legislation by Parliament falls, by virtue of Article 37, into the Government's lap and becomes subject to *pouvoir réglementaire*. In addition the Government may be authorized to make ordinances by statute which is usually of a limited duration but may be renewed. Consequently the French Government appears well equipped constitutionally to deal with Community legislation,

---

17 Case 130/79: *Express Dairy Foods Ltd v Intervention Board for Agricultural Produce* [1980] ECR 1887, [1981] 1 CMLR 451; See also Case 68/79: *Hans Just I/S v Danish Ministry of Fiscal Affairs* [1980] ECR 501, [1981] 2 CMLR 714; Cases 66, 127 and 128/79: *Amministrazione delle Finanze v SrL Meridionale Industria Salumi* [1980] ECR 1237, [1981] 1 CMLR 1; Cases 205-215/82: *Deutsche Milchkontor GmbH v Germany* [1983] ECR 2633, [1984] 3 CMLR 586; Case 349/85: *Denmark v Commission (Re Export Refunds)* [1988] ECR 169.

18 Reports on Constitutional Laws in France (1964-65) by M de Grailly (The House of Deputies) and M Marcilhacy (Senate) quoted by Constantinidès-Mégret, op cit, p 145. See also Eisemann, P M (ed), *The Integration of International and European Community Law into the National Legal Order* (1996).

19 Cf Case 45/64: *Commission v of Italy* [1965] ECR 857 at 864, 865, [1966] CMLR 97 at 107-108.

assuming, of course, that politically this is acceptable to Parliament. However the government will, if necessary, refer to the *Conseil Constitutionnel* matters which may impinge upon the Constitution. Thus when certain budgetary provisions of the EEC Treaty were modified in 1970, the Government asked the Conseil Constitutionnel to consider whether the new Treaty included any provisions contrary to the Constitution or necessitating an amendment to the Constitution. The answer was in the negative.[20] More recently the Conseil was asked to rule whether the direct universal suffrage to the European Parliament[1] by the French electorate did affect the sovereignty of the French Parliament. Here too the answer was in the negative. In *Re Isoglucose*[2] (No 1 and No 2) the Conseil confirmed that Community taxation was directly enforceable in France though when included in the national Budget it had to be distinguished from the national revenue.

On 10 July 1966 the law 'relative to the application of certain treaties' authorized the Government to issue ordinances to ensure the implementation of EC directives. The government ordinances are made by the Council of Ministers after advice from the Conseil d'Etat. They come into force on publication but become void if the bill ratifying them is not submitted to Parliament before the date fixed by the enabling statute.[3] Parliament too makes statues to harmonize French law with Community law.[4] In France the Code of Customs Law enables the Government to take certain measures which have to be approved by Parliament. This method was used in order to carry out the Community customs regulations.[5] The result[6] is a very complex and diverse system of implementation based, in principle, on parliamentary delegation authorized by Article 38 of the Constitution and the Government's own power of legislation.

Countries in which the executive cannot rely on a direct constitutional authority in this respect, have evolved a system of delegation of powers. This implies parliamentary approval of the acts of the government which, in practice, is often ranted retrospectively, so much so that parliament appears to exercise a merely formal control.

Examples of this practice can be taken from the Benelux countries, notably in the field of customs law and agriculture.[7]

In Belgium the Customs and Excise Law of 2 May 1958, having authorized the King to take measures by decree subject to parliamentary approval, has adopted basically the French solution. A similar law was passed in the Netherlands on 25 June 1960 but it does not require parliamentary sanction for measure taken under the authority of the said law.

The execution of the agricultural policy of the Community in the Benelux countries reveals a more complex picture. Without going into details it may suffice to note that in Belgium under the law of 1962, which replaced the law of 1931 on import, export and transit of agricultural produce, powers were delegated

---

20   JCP 1970, II. 16510.
1   [1977] 1 CMLR 121.
2   [1978] 2 CMLR 361 and 364.
3   Eg 24 July 1966 on commercial companies; 3 July 1970 on monopoly over all explosives; 22 May 1971 on forestry reproductive materials; 8 July 1971 on customs bonded warehouses.
4   Eg 15 April 1970 on the nationality of public service concessionaries; 11 February 1971 on transport; 22 February 1971 on investments in the Community.
5   Eg the decision of the EEC Council of 4 April 1962 was incorporated in Art 19 of the French Customs Code by decree (JO 1962, p 999).
6   For a complete and up-to-date account, see Bailleux, A, *Techniques d'application du Droit Communautaire dans l'ordre juridique français*, unpublished doctoral thesis, Nice, 1975.
7   Constantinidès-Mégret, op cit, pp 150-154.

to the King to make decrees relevant to the Community agricultural policy. A similar law was passed in Luxembourg. In the Netherlands, where the agricultural system is quite unique and complex because it is based on a network of 'professional' organizations endowed with a great deal of autonomous power, authority, under the Agricultural Law, is delegated to the Queen to carry out the Community agricultural policy by decree. Summing up the position in the Benelux countries we can say that their governments put into effect Community law by virtue of a general delegation of power.

A system of general delegation can be said to exist also in Denmark by virtue of the Constituiton[8] (Article 20) and in Ireland and the United Kingdom by virtue of the European Communities Acts 1972, sections 2 and 2(2) respectively. In Ireland, dissatisfaction with the operation of the 1972 Act led to the enactment of the European Communities (Amendment) Act 1973. Under this Act ministerial regulations have statutory effect but the control over the exercise of this power is in the hands of a watchdog committee drawn from the Dáil and the Senate. Its function is to monitor all drafts prepared by the Commission and all acts of the Communities as well as all regulations issued by the Irish ministers as a result of the membership of the Communities. It can also make recommendations to Irish Parliament.

An authority for general delegation can be found in Article 78(5) of the Greek Constitution which provides for delegated legislation to carry out 'economic measures within the framework of international relations with economic organizations'. Community legislation prior to accession is to be implemented by presidential decrees on the proposal of competent ministers. Similar instruments are to be used to implement post-accession legislation under parliamentary supervision since, according to article 3 of the Act of Accession, the Government is obliged to submit annual reports on Community affairs. A parliamentary watchdog committee is likely to be established.[9]

A system of specific delegation of legislative power operate in Italy and the German Federal Republic.

Article 76 of the Italian Constitution provides that the exercise of the legislative power may be delegated to the Government for a specific purpose and only for a limited period. On this principle Article 4 of the act of ratification of 14 October 1957 authorizes the Government to promulgate by decree having the force of ordinary law, in accordance with the 'general principles enshrined in the EC Treaty', the necessary rules to:

(1)   ensure the execution of the obligations arising from Article 11 (now repealed);
(2)   carry out measures provided in EC Articles 37, 46, 70, 89, 91, 107, 108, 109, 115 and 226 (now EC Articles 31, 38, 85, 108, 109, 111, 134, the others being repealed);
(3)   carry out dispositions and principles comprised in Articles 95, 96, 97 and 98 of the EC Treaty (now EC Articles 90, 91 and 92, former Art 97 being repealed).

8   Sørensen, M, 'Compétences supranationales et pouvoirs constituionnels en droit danois', *Miscellanea W J Ganshof van der Meersch* (1972), Vol 2, pp 481 et seq. See also the decision of the Danish Supreme Court in *Carlsen v Rasmussen*, 6 April 1998 [1999] 3 CMLR 854.
9   Evrigenis, D, 'Legal Constitutional Implications of Greek Accession to the European Communities' (1980) 17 CMLR Rev, p 157 at 168.

The original delegation expired in 1961 but has been extended quinquennially. By virtue of this delegation several decrees have been passed. However, before taking any measure the Government has to seek advice of a Parliamentary Commission consisting of 15 Members of the House of Deputies and 15 Members of the Senate.

A technique of reproducing Community regulations into national law has caused some confusion between domestic and Community law, the identity of the latter being lost and the law enforcement authorities disregarding the directly applicable force of Community measures. The practice was condemned by the Community Court[10] as well as the Italian Constitutional Court[11] with the result that the normative power of the Community institutions was recognized and Community law assumed its correct position in the Italian legal system.

Article 80(1) of the Basic Law of the German Federal Republic of 1953 provides for the delegation of legislative power to the Executive by statute which has to determine the context, purpose and extent of the delegation. The law of ratification granted to the Federal Government the power to carry into effect EC Articles 14, 16, 17(1) and 23(2) (Customs Provisions) (now repealed) as well as certain provisions of the protocols on mineral oils and bananas. Such decrees could be made without approval of the Federal Parliament (Bundestag) unless the Parliament objected within three weeks from the date when draft decrees were laid before it. No approval of the decrees by the Federal Council (Bundesrat) was required though the Council had fourteen days to make comments on the draft decrees.

The Customs Law of 1957[12] made under the above rules was amended by the Law of 1961[13] which enlarged the powers of the Federal Government. Article 77 of the Law of 1961 is particularly relevant to the implementation of Community law. It concerns measures under EC Article 103 (now Art 99) (short-term economic policy) and, more generally, Community legislation. The former will be studied by the relevant parliamentary committee and submitted to the Bundestag which will accept or reject the decrees. The Bundestag cannot approve these by silence. They will also be submitted to the Bundesrat but merely for opinion. Drafts of decrees for the implementation of the Community legislation are laid before the Bundestag and the Bundesrat and the Bundestag is presumed to have approved the decrees if within three months from this submission they have not been formally abrogated by Parliament. The function of the Bundesrat is purely advisory. Customs laws have been modified on several occasions by this process. In the field of agriculture several laws have been passed. Of these the Law of 1964[14] conferred upon the Federal Government the power of legislating by decree in order to put into effect the regulations, decisions and directives of the Council and the Commission of the EEC governing the marketing of cereals, milk products and rice.

It is clear from this brief survey of the methods of implementing Community law that the Member States have retained a measure of parliamentary control in

---

10 See Case 39/72: *Commission v Italy* [1973] ECR 101, [1973] CMLR 439 and Case 34/73: *Variola SpA v Amminstrazione Italiana della Finanze* [1973] ECR 981.
11 Judgment No 183 of 27 December 1973 in *Re Frontini*, Foro Italiano, 1974, I/314; Judgment No 232 of 30 October 1975 in *Re Industrie Chimiche della Italia (ICIC)*, Foro Italiano, 1975, 2667-2668.
12 Law of 27 July 1957, BGBI II (1957), p 753.
13 Law of 14 June 1961, BGBI I (1961), p 758.
14 Law of 13 August 1964.

this matter. The problem is by no means simple and in the interests of the smooth running of the Community as well as the efficacy of the Community law in the territory of the Member States, it ought to be studied in depth with a view to formulating a common approach and a uniform procedure.

D. Incorporation through the Community Court

(1) THE ROLE OF THE ECJ

We have already considered the meaning and effect of Community legislation as a source of Community law; we should emphasize now the role of the Community Court in the process of the incorporation of Community legislation into the municipal laws. The Court has an indirect influence under EC Articles 230 and 234 (ex Arts 173 and 177). Under EC Article 230 (ex Art 173) the Court has the power of annulment and indeed, should the action for annulment be well founded, the Court will strike down the offending piece of Community legislation: EC Article 231 (ex Art 174). On the other hand whatever is uncontested or declared valid by the Court has the force of law in the territory of the Member States. It is important to note that the decisions of the Court in respect of the validity of the Community legislation have a universal application; they are enforceable *erga omnes*: EC Article 231 (ex Art 174).

However, perhaps more significant, from a practical point of view, is the Court's impact through its interpretation of Community law. Where the national court requests interpretation the impact is direct and instructive. It is equally instructive in other cases, though the impact has to be measured through the doctrine of judicial precedent. Here the British and Irish judges are out of step with their continental brethren as they lavishly cite the decisions of the Community Court as well as the judgments of national courts.[15] However a rigid application of the doctrine of *stare decisis* must be discounted simply because the Community Court is not bound by its own decisions and a slavish adherence to a precedent unrecognized on the Continent would lead to serious anomalies and distortions of Community law by British or Irish judges.

In spite of the merely persuasive authority of precedents in continental jurisprudence the decisions of the Community Court are gaining prestige in national jurisdiction. They are being cited[16] and some courts occasionally cite decisions of national courts.[17] They do so not in principle or out of habit but because they appreciate the authoritative exposition of Community law by the Community Court and of the relevant national law by national courts. As for the authority of the Community precedents there is as yet no uniform approach to this matter. Reports indicate that the French Cour de Cassation[18] considered that French courts are generally bound by the rulings of the Community Court

---

15   See eg *Bulmer v Bollinger*, infra.
16   *Fiorini v Société Nationale des Chemins de Fer Français* [1975] 1 CMLR 459; *Re Dry Shavers* [1975] CMLR 550; *Administration des Douanes v Société Cafés Jacques Vabres* [1975] 2 CMLR 336, Paris Court of Appeal.
17   85/71: *Francesco Cinzano & Cie GmbH v Java Kaffeegeschäfte GmbH* [1974] 2 CMLR 21, Bundesgerichtshof.
18   *Enterprises Garoche v Striker Boats (Nederland), Cour de Cassation* [1974] 1 CMLR 469; *Glinel Case* [1984] 2 CMLR 137 at 151; *Ministère Public v Cambournac* [1984] 2 CMLR 556 at 558 but not so the Conseil d'Etat, see *Cohn-Bendit*, supra.

and so did the Belgian[19] Cour de Cassation; the German Federal Supreme Court[20] felt that the decisions of the Community Court are binding 'beyond the instant case', whilst the Milan Court of Appeal applied[1] the Community Court's ruling in one case and considered it binding only inter partes, in another.[2] No doubt a trend towards recognition of Community precedents is gaining momentum.

(2)   TREATY PROVISIONS

EC Article 234 (ex Art 177) provides:

> 'The Court of Justice shall have jurisdiction to give preliminary rulings concerning:
> (a)   the interpretation of this Treaty;
> (b)   the validity and interpretation of acts of the Community and of the ECB;
> (c)   the interpretation of the statutes of bodies established by an act of the Council, where those statutes so provide.
> Where such a question is raised before any court or tribunal of a Member State, that court or tribunal may, if it considers that a decision on the question is necessary to enable it to give judgment, request the Court of Justice to give a ruling thereon.
> Where any such question is raised in a case pending before a court of tribunal of a Member State against whose decisions there is no judicial remedy under national law, that court or tribunal shall bring the matter before the Court of Justice.'

EC Article 234 (ex Art 177)[3] gives the Community Court the power of interpretation of the Treaty, of the acts of the Community organs and of the statutes of bodies[4] established by the Council in the form of a preliminary ruling. This means that non-Community Treaties of the Member States even though noted in EC regulations are not included in the interpretative competence of the Court.[5] The Treaty is silent as to the scope of a ruling: is it valid *erga omnes* or only *quoad casum*? Some writers[6] doubt the *erga omnes*

---

19   *Procureur du Roi v Debauve* [1984] 2 CMLR 204 at 208; see also Tribunal de Commerce, Liège which emphasized that the rule of precedent is inspired by the common law systems (*stare decisis et non quieta movere*) rather than the civil law principles of *res judicata: AGROTAB v Distrimis SA* [1985] 3 CMLR 294 at 301-302.
20   Case KZR 7/69: *Re Brewery Solus Agreement* [1975] 1 CMLR 611. Same as the *Bundesverwaltungsgericht: Rewe-Zentralfinanz GmbH v Landwirtschaftskammer für das Saarland* [1978] 2 CMLR 594 and the *Bundesverfassungsgericht:* Case IZR 114/73: *Terrapin (Overseas) Ltd v Terranova Industrie* [1978] 3 CMLR 102; *Hoffmann-La Roche v Centrafarm* [1984] 2 CMLR 561.
 1   *Sirena SRL v EDA SRL* [1975] 1 CMLR 409.
 2   *SAFA v Amministrazione delle Finanze* [1973] CMLR 152.
 3   ECSC, 41; EAEC, 150. On the interpretation of ECSC 41 see Case C-221/88: *ECSC v Busseni* [1990] ECR I-495.
 4   See Case 110/75: *Mills v European Investment Bank* [1976] ECR 955 (on admissibility), [1976] ECR 1613 (on merits) and Case 44/84: *Hurd v Jones (Re tax of English headmaster of a European School in England)* [1986] ECR 29, [1986] 2 CMLR 1.
 5   Case 28/68: *Caisse Régionale de Sécurité Sociale du Nord v Torrekens* [1969] ECR 125, [1969] CMLR 377.
 6   Eg Catalano, N, *Manuel de droit des Communautés Européennes* (1965) (French Translation), p 88.

effect, others[7] argue that it has this effect. Even though a national court may repeatedly request a preliminary ruling in similar circumstances and the Community Court, not being bound by its previous decisions, may change its mind, a preliminary ruling states the law as it is and always has been, and as it must be applied even to legal relationships arising before the date of the ruling, unless the Court exercises its power to limit the temporal effect of its judgment.[8] However, whatever the effect of the judgment, it is an instrument of integration of Community law with municipal law and of uniformity throughout the Community. Therefore preliminary rulings should have a universally biding effect despite the warning against the spectre of the 'government by judges'.[9] This effect can be inferred not only from the function of the Court but also from the procedure on reference which provides for the intervention of the Member States and the Commission, as well as the recent amendment of the rules which allows issues on which there is an established body of law to be decided by a chamber of three judges instead of the whole Court,[10] which indicates the general effect in other cases of earlier rulings.

It is common ground that, if greater attention were paid to precedents, many a reference for a preliminary ruling would be unnecessary.[11] In this context the reply given by the ECJ to the question[12] whether, following an earlier judgment[13] on the interpretation of Article 2(1) of the Sixth Council Directive on the harmonization of turnover taxes, no such tax should be levied on the supply of narcotic drugs within the territory of a Member State, is quite instructive. However the Court may avoid a question relating to its previous ruling and simply rule on the underlying point of law as if it were doing so anew, regarding the reference to precedent as being inadmissible, as it did on a previous occasion.[14]

EC Article 234 (ex Art 177) should be read together with Article 20 of the Protocol on the Statute of the Community Court, which provides for the procedure to be applied when a preliminary ruling is sought. When any court or tribunal of a Member State decides that it cannot proceed to judgment without the elucidation of a point of Community law relevant to the case the proceedings are suspended and the court or tribunal refers the matter to the Community Court. The decision to seek a ruling is notified by the Registrar of the Community Court to the parties, the Member States and to the Commission, and also to the Council if the act, the validity or interpretation of which is in dispute, originates from the Council. Within two months of this notification, the parties, the Member States, the

---

7   Eg Zuccala, 'Di una forma d'interpretazione guirisprudenziale autentica delle leggi', Guirisprudenzie Italiana (1959), IV, Coll 139-144; quoted by Constantinidès-Mégret, op cit, pp 39-40. Trabucchi, 'L'effect "erga omnes" des decisions préjudicielles rendues par la Cour de Justice des Communautés Européennes' (1974) RTDE 56 quoted with approval by A-G Warner in Case 112/76: *Manzoni v Fonds National de Retraite des Ouvriers Mineurs* [1977] ECR 1647 at 1661-1663, [1978] 2 CMLR 416 at 429-430.

8   Eg Case C-163/90: *Administration des Douanes et Droits Indirects v Legros* [1992] ECR I-4625, paras 28-36; Case C-228/92: *Roquette Fréres v Hauptzollamt Geldern* [1994] ECR I-1445, paras 17-30.

9   Lecourt, R, *Le juge devant le Marché Commun* (1970), p 57.

10 Rules of Procedure, Arts 95, 103 and 104; cf Case 120/75: *Riemer v Hauptzollamt Lübeck-West* [1976] ECR 1003.

11 See Case 283/81: *CILFIT v Minister of Health* [1982] ECR 3415 at para 13, 1 CMLR 472, the ECJ hinted that previous case law may obviate reference.

12 Case 289/86: *Vereniging Happy Family Rustenburgerstraat v Inspecteur der Omzetbelastingen* [1988] ECR 3655, [1989] 3 CMLR 743; and Case 269/86: *Mol v Inspecteur der Invoerrechten en Accijnzen* [1988] ECR 3627, [1989] 3 CMLR 729.

13 Case 294/82: *Einberger v HZA Freiburg (No 2)* [1984] ECR 1177, [1985] 1 CMLR 765.

14 Case 24/66 bis: *Getreidehandel v Commission* [1973] ECR 1599 at 1606.

Commission and, where appropriate, the Council, are entitled to make their submissions or observations to the Court. In this way the matter ceases to be of sole concern to the parties and the adjudicating court; it becomes of common concern to the whole Community. By giving the national judge access to the Community Court, whilst enabling all the Member States and the Community organs to make representations, the Treaty sets the stage for an understanding between the municipal courts and the Community Court and for a development towards a common law of the Community. At the same time the Treaty asserts the superiority or exclusive competence of the Community Court to interpret authoritatively Community law.

(3)   THE REFERENCE[15]

Many cases have been submitted for a preliminary ruling and the Court has developed a practice in this field and recently issued certain guidelines[16] to national courts. In the first case[17] under EC Article 234 (ex Art 177) the Court advised that the referring court is free to adopt a direct and simple form of reference which will enable the Community Court to rule strictly within the limits of its jurisdiction. Thus formalism was dispensed with but at the same time the Court implied that it would not be politic to decide the issue otherwise than in the terms of interpretation of Community law. Furthermore the Court stressed that whilst two different legal orders are involved (national and Community) the national court is about to administer Community law albeit under the guidance of the Community Court.

In the *Van Gend* case[18] the Court observed that the considerations which may guide the national court in the choice of its questions and their pertinence to the issue to be decided are outside the jurisdiction of the Community Court. In this case a Dutch Administrative Tribunal inquired whether EC Article 12 (as originally worked – now Art 25 but amended) 'entailed internal legal effects, that is whether or not an individual may directly derive rights which have to be protected by his national courts'. EC Article 12 provided that Member States shall refrain from introducing between themselves any new customs duties on imports or exports, or any charges having equivalent effect, and from increasing those which they already apply in their trade with each other. The question raised a constitutional issue, that is whether the Community Court was really interpreting Community law or whether it usurped the power to interpret the Dutch Constitution (ie the power to levy taxes). The Dutch Government was of the opinion that the Community Court had no jurisdiction in matters involving Dutch customs duties. However the Community Court firmly asserted its jurisdiction and the power to rule in the matter, as it pointed out that EC Article 12 came for

---

15   Lasok, K P E, *The European Court of Justice* (1994), pp 552-567; Anderson, D, *References to the European Court* (1995).

16   See [1999] 2 CMLR 799, which sets out both the guidance issued by the ECJ and the practice direction issued in consequence by the English High Court and Court of Appeal. The approach to the exercise by English courts of the discretion whether or not to make a reference is often said to be that laid down by Lord Denning MR in *Bulmer v Bollinger* [1974] Ch 401; but later cases have varied that approach – see, for example, *R v Stock Exchange, ex p Else* [1993] QB 534 and *BLP v Customs and Excise Comrs* [1994] STC 41.

17   Case 13/61 *Kleidingverkoopbedriff de Geus en Uitdenbogerd v Boschen Van Rijn* [1962] ECR 45, [1962] CMLR 1.

18   Case 26/62: supra (p 342, note 5); see also Case 56/65: *Société Technique Minière v Machinenbau Ulm GmbH* [1966] ECR 235, [1966] CMLR 357.

interpretation not for *application* according to Dutch law. In this delicate situation the Court refrained from ruling upon the conflict between Dutch and Community law but firmly declared that EC Article 12 had a direct effect though the mode of application was left to the internal process of the Netherlands.

Indeed, there must be a question[19] on a point of Community law the answer to which will determine the outcome of the case. In other words there must be a dispute involving aspects of Community law and the reference must be necessary to settle the issues. Thus, eg a national measure that only first-class passengers[20] may use express trains reveals no connection with Community law and, therefore, questions of discrimination and free movement will be inadmissible in the context of the dispute. As in that case, no Community law was involved in the case concerned with the FEOGA accounts[1] and, therefore, the case was not referable. Similarly there was no cause for reference in the matter of agreement between national bureaux of motor insurers.[2] Although the agreement was vital for the implementation and operation of Directive 72/166 on compulsory motor insurance the agreement was not a 'Community Act' within the terms of the first paragraph of EC Article 234 (ex Art 177), and therefore its interpretation was outside the scope of the ECJ's jurisdiction. Where there is a real dispute involving Community law reference will not be ousted simply because the Commission may embark upon an enforcement action[3] nor will a reference act as estoppel to an enforcement action under EC Article 226 (ex Art 169) of the Treaty even if the interpretation of Community law in the preliminary ruling has rendered such action unnecessary.[4]

However the relevance of the request is not for the ECJ to determine but for the referring court.[5]

In *Costa v ENEL* the Court held that it had power to select what was relevant from the list of questions imperfectly formulated by the referring court and in this way refused to be drawn into an internal conflict. 'Consequently,' held the Court, 'the decision should be given not upon the validity of an Italian law in relating to the Treaty but upon the interpretation of the above-mentioned articles in the context of the points of law stated by the *Guidice Conciliatore*.'[6]

In *Schwarze v Einfuhr-und Vorratsstelle für Getreide und Futtermittel*[7] the Court had to decide whether a badly drafted reference should be sent back whence it came as suggested by the French Government. The ECJ refused to do this and

---

19   Advocate-General Lagrange in Case 28-30/62: *Da Costa en Shaake v Nederlandse Belastingadministratie* [1963] ECR 31, [1963] CMLR 224.
20   Case 298/84: *Iorio v Azienda Autonoma delle Ferrovie dello Stato* [1986] ECR 247, [1986] 2 CMLR 665.
 1   Case 133/84: *United Kingdom v Commission* [1986] ECR 1259, [1987] 1 CMLR 294.
 2   Case 152/83: *Demouche v Fonds de Garantie Automobile* [1987] ECR 3833, [1989] 1 CMLR 544.
 3   Case 172/82: *Syndicat National des Fabricants Raffineurs d'Huile v Groupement d'Intérêt Economique Inter-Huiles* [1983] ECR 555, [1983] 3 CMLR 485.
 4   Case 231/78: *Commission v United Kingdom* [1979] ECR 1447, [1979] 2 CMLR 427 following the reference in Case 118/78: *Meijer v Department of Trade* [1979] ECR 1387, [1979] 2 CMLR 398; Case 124/81: *Commission v United Kingdom* [1983] ECR 203, [1983] 2 CMLR 1, following the reference in Case 244/78: *Union Laitière v French Dairy Farmers* [1979] ECR 2663, [1980] 1 CMLR 314.
 5   Case 232/82:*Baccini v Office National de l'Emploi* [1983] ECR 583, [1983] 3 CMLR 572. See also Cases C-299/88 and C-197/89: *Dzodzi v Belgium* [1990] ECR I-3763.
 6   Case 6/64: [1964] CMLR 425 at 455 [1964] ECR 585.
 7   Case 16/65: [1965] ECR 877 at 886, 887, [1966] CMLR 172 at 186-187. See Case 83/78: *Pigs Marketing Board (Northern Ireland) v Redmond* [1978] ECR 2347, [1979] 1 CMLR 177 and Case 28/85: *Deghillage v Caisse Primaire d'Assurance Maladic* [1986] ECR 991; Case C-221/89 *R v Secretary of Transport, ex p Factortame Ltd (No 3)* [1991] ECR I-3905, [1991] 3 CMLR 589.

held that 'when it appears that questions asked by a municipal court for the purpose of interpretation in reality concerned the validity of a Community act, it is for the Court of Justice to enlighten the national court immediately without insisting upon a formalism which would be purely dilatory and which would be incompatible with the true nature of the machinery established by' EC Article 234 (ex Art 177). Thus the ECJ will, in a helpful manner, assist the referring court in focusing its attention upon the relevant aspects of Community law and will, if necessary, reformulate the reference[8] provided, of course, it is reasonably possible to reformulate the questions.[9] This does not mean that the ECJ will decide[10] the issue for the referring court or become involved in a national controversy.[11]

However, no matter how helpful the Community Court is in the process of the elucidation of the points before it, there is a limit to its competence for the object of the reference is limited to answering questions on issues raised by the referring court.[12] Therefore it cannot be used to apply the Treaty to a particular situation or determine the validity of a national measure,[13] and thus do the work of the referring court.

Nevertheless the ECJ may be able to extract points of Community law from the reference and deal with these as if properly presented[14] or even to comment on a matter which was not raised by the national court.[15] Thus, in Case C-15/96: *Kalliope Schöning-Kougebetopoulau v Freie und Hansestadt Hamburg* the ECJ said: 'The Court has consistently held that, in the context of the application of [EC 234, ex 177] . . . it has no jurisdiction to decide whether a national provision is compatible with Community law. The Court may, however, extract from the wording of the questions formulated by the national court, having regard to the facts stated by it, those elements which concern the interpretation of Community law for the purpose of enabling that court to resolve the legal problem before it.'[16] The ECJ sees itself as having a duty to accept the reference without questioning the reasons for it or criticizing the referring court.[17] However it is incumbent upon the referring court to determine the facts of the case[18] and therefore reference will be rejected if the issue is merely 'academic' in the sense that it does not reveal any real dispute between the parties.[19] Presumably the national court of its own motion will refuse to refer

---

8   Eg Case 78/70: *Deutsche Grammophon GmbH v Metro-SB Grössmärke GmbH* [1971] ECR 487, [1971] CMLR 631.

9   See Case 14/86: *Pretore di Salo v X* [1987] ECR 2545, [1989] 1 CMLR 71.

10 *Van Gend*, supra, p 342, note 5.

11 *Costa v ENEL*, supra, p 359, note 6.

12 Case 5/72: *Fratelli Grassi v Amministrazione delle Finanze* [1972] ECR 443, [1973 CMLR 322.

13 Case 20/64: *SARL Albatros v SOPECO (Société de Pétroles et des Combustibles liquids)* [1965] ECR 29, [1965] CMLR 159; Case 100/63: *Kalsbeck v Sociale Verzekeringsbank* [1964] ECR 565 at 572.

14 Case 82/71: *Pubblico Ministero della Repubblica Italiana v SPA Società Agricolo Industria Latte* [1972] ECR 119, [1972] CMLR 723. See also Case 251/83: *Eberhard Haug-Adrion v Frankfurter Versecherungs AG* [1984] ECR 4277, [1985] 3 CMLR 266.

15 Case C-280/91: *Finanzamt Kassel-Goethestrasse v Viessmann KG* [1993] ECR I-971, [1993] 3 CMLR 153.

16 [1998] ECR I-47, para 9. See also Cases C-332/92, C-333/92 and C-335/92: *Eurico Italia* [1994] ECR I-711, para 19.

17 Case 10/69: *Portelange SA v SA Smith Corona Merchant International* [1969] ECR 309, [1974] 1 CMLR 397; Case 155/73: *Italy v Sacchi* [1974] ECR 409, [1974] 2 CMLR 177; Case 126/80: *Salonia v Poidomani and Baglieri* [1981] ECR 1563, [1982] 1 CMLR 64.

18 Case 222/78: *ICAP Distribution Srl v Beneventi* [1979] ECR 1163, [1979] 3 CMLR 475; *Lord Bethel v SABENA* (English Commercial Court) [1983] 3 CMLR 1.

19 Case 104/79: *Foglia v Novello* [1980] ECR 745, [1981] 1 CMLR 45. Case 244/80: *Foglia v Novello (No 2)* [1981] ECR 3045, [1982] 1 CMLR 585 but see Case C-150/88: *Eau de Cologne v Provide Srl* [1989] ECR 3891, [1991] 1 CMLR 715.

if facts have not been ascertained to its satisfaction[20] or if, despite the arguments to the contrary, it is clear that no point of Community law is involved.[1]

Thus the Court will not feel to be obliged to respond to a reference 'if it is quite obvious that the interpretation of Community law or the examination of the validity of a rule of Community law sought by that court bears no relation to the actual nature of the case or the subject matter of the main action'.[2] Similarly the Court will not allow itself to be used in a situation where there was no real dispute between the parties but the litigants managed to persuade an Italian court to make a reference with the object of obtaining a ruling on compatibility of French law with Community law.[3] Again the Court refused[4] to be drawn into an academic discussion on the compatibility of the German theory of disguised non-cash subscription of capital with the Second Company Law Directive.[5] However the prize for ingenuity goes to a court which posed the following highly speculative questions:[6]

'(1) The Court of Justice is requested to state whether, apart from the Community and Italian legal orders, there is today also a third legal order (Community-cum-Italian) which is accompanied by the Community-cum-English, Community-cum-German legal orders, and so forth, and which is characterized:
   (a) by the fact that the rules governing it are to be found primarily in the provisions of Community law and sub-primarily in the provisions of Italian law (the two categories of provisions – primary and sub-primary – merge to form a *unitary* legislative framework);
   (b) by the fact that it concerns substantial Community interests which are realized *also* through Italian instruments.
 (2) The Court of Justice is requested to state that the third paragraph of Article 189, and Articles 177 and 5 of the EEC Treaty [now EC 249, 234 and 10] must be interpreted as meaning that the Member States, when they give effect to the Community directives, must also provide for the relevant procedural instruments regarded as necessary for ensuring adequate judicial protection, which entails the obligation to alter *for the better* the judicial instruments already in existence and, in any event, the duty not to alter those instruments for *the worse*.
 (3) The Court of Justice is requested to state whether it *necessarily* follows from Articles 5 and 177 and the third paragraph of Article 189 of the EEC Treaty, read together, that there is a duty – on the part of the

---

20 *Church of Scientology of California v Customs and Excise Comrs* [1980] CMLR 114; on appeal [1981] 1 CMLR 48, CA. See Joined Cases 36 and 71/80: *Irish Creamery Milk Suppliers Association v Ireland* [1981] ECR 735 paras 6 and 7, [1981] 2 CMLR 455; and Case 72/83: *Campus Oil v Minister for Industry and Energy* [1984] ECR 2727, [1984] 3 CMLR 544.
1 *British Leyland Motor Corpn Ltd v TI Silencers Ltd* [1980] 1 CMLR 598; *Re Virdee* [1980] 1 CMLR 709, English High Court; *Re Budlong and Kember* [1980] 2 CMLR 125; *Surjit Kaur v Lord Advocate* [1980] 3 CMLR 79, Ct of Sess; but see Case 175/78: *R v Saunders* [1979] ECR 1129, [1979] 2 CMLR 216 (which should not have been referred).
2 Case 126/80: *Salonia v Poidomani* [1981] ECR 1563, [1982] 1 CMLR 64.
3 Case 104/79: *Foglia v Novello* [1980] ECR 745, [1981] 1 CMLR 45; Case 244/80: *Foglia v Novello (No 2)* [1981] ECR 3045, [1982] 1 CMLR 585.
4 Case C-83/91: *Meilicke v ADV/ORGA FA Meyer AG* [1992] ECR I-4871.
5 Dir 77/91 (OJ 1977, L26/1).
6 Case C-286/88: *Falciola Angelo SpA v Commune di Pavia* [1990] ECR I-191. Complex questions not relevant to the issues before the referring court were also referred in Case C-428/93: *Monin Automobiles – Maison du Deux-Roues* [1994] ECR I-1707.

Member States – to provide that disputes relating to matters governed by "Community-cum-Italian" law (and thus governed *primarily* by Community provisions and *sub-primarily* by Italian provisions) must be decided by national judges who, as regards the essence of the judicial function, are on the same footing as the Court of Justice (and accordingly are not "*less judicial*" than the Court).

(4) (In the alternative) the Court of Justice is requested to state whether it *necessarily* follows from Articles 5 and 177 and the third paragraph of Article 189 of the EEC Treaty, read together, that there is an obligation on the part of the Member States to provide, as regards the 'implementation of the Community directives', that disputes relating to matters governed by "Community-cum-Italian" law shall be decided by institutions vested with "real", and not "*apparent*", judicial power ("*utilis, non inutilis jurisdictio*").'

Such questions could not solve in any practical way the conundrum caused by the artificial classification of the law or perhaps the desirability of reforming the national adjudicative system which exercised the minds of the judges. Such problems were clearly outside the jurisdiction of the ECJ and the Court considered the questions to be 'manifestly irrelevant'.

Whatever the predicament of the national judge he is the judge of facts[7] and he is the one who seeks elucidation of points of law relevant to his decision. If he is unable to meet these two conditions of a reference he has to go back to the drawing board, as it were. This was the conclusion of the ECJ[8] in a dispute which was centred on the interpretation of the treaty competition rules and the Court was expected to establish whether the national system of distributing frequencies for television broadcasts was compatible with Community law. The ECJ refused to give a ruling because the reference lacked a statement of facts and of the law involved which would have made it possible to discern the purpose of the questions submitted and thereby to understand the meaning and scope of the problem.

While reference techniques have developed within the national practice the ECJ issued certain guidelines in this respect reiterating the principles involved.[9] Having to decide a dispute over the payment of a fixed health inspection levy on wool from outside the Community the Italian Supreme Court asked the ECJ whether, in the sense of the third paragraph of EC Article 234 (ex Art 177), the obligation to refer was subject to any conditions. The ECJ replied that the obligation to refer was based on co-operation between national courts and the Community Court. More particularly the third paragraph sought to prevent the occurrence within the Community of divergencies in judicial decisions on questions of Community law. However, EC Article 234 (ex Art 177), does not constitute a means of redress available to the parties. Therefore the court or tribunal concerned cannot be compelled to refer but may of its own motion do so. Furthermore courts of tribunals envisaged in the second and third paragraph of EC Article 234 (ex Art 177), 'have the same discretion' to ascertain whether a ruling on a question of Community law is necessary to enable them to give judgment. 'Accordingly, they are not obliged to refer a question concerning the interpretation of Community law raised before them if that question is not relevant, that is to say, if the answer . . . can in no way affect the outcome of the case.'

---

7 Case 14/86: *Pretore di Salò v X* [1987] ECR 2545, [1989] 1 CMLR 71.
8 Joined Cases C-320-322/90: *Telemarsicabruzzo SpA v Circostel* [1993] ECR I-393.
9 Case 283/81: *CILFIT v Ministry of Health* [1982] ECR 3415, paras 17-20.

Turning to the specific point raised by the Supreme Court the ECJ cited its early ruling[10] to the effect that although the third paragraph of EC Article 234 (ex Art 177), unreservedly requires court or tribunals mentioned therein to refer questions raised before them,

'... the authority of an interpretation under Article 177 already given by the Court may deprive the obligation of its purpose ... Such is the case especially when the question raised has already been the subject of a preliminary ruling in a similar cause.'

However, stressed the Court in the present ruling,

'... in such circumstances national courts and tribunals ... remain entirely at liberty to bring a matter before the Court of Justice if they consider it appropriate to do so.'

'Finally,' observed the ECJ,

'... the correct application of Community law may be so obvious as to leave no scope for any reasonable doubt as to the manner in which the question raised is to be resolved. Before it comes to the conclusion that such is the case, the national court or tribunal must be convinced that the matter is equally obvious to the courts of the other Member States and to the Court of Justice. Only if those conditions are satisfied may the national court or tribunal refrain from submitting the question to the Court of Justice and take upon itself the responsibility for resolving it ...'

The guidelines comprise three reasons why the court of the last instance need not refer, ie the question raised is irrelevant, there has already been a ruling of the ECJ on the subject and the position is so obvious as to leave no scope for any reasonable doubt.

(4) THE TIMING

The question arises as to when the reference should be made.[11] It goes without saying that a question of Community law must be raised before the national court and that the answer to it must be relevant to the issue, that is, necessary to enable the court to adjudicate. Community law does not determine either the timing or the degree of necessity. All this is left to national procedures. As far as references from the English High Court are concerned it is expressly provided[12] that such an order may be made at any stage of the proceedings. This is correct because the court controls the proceedings from the beginning to the end and the court alone is in the position of judging the timing and the necessity.

A subsidiary question regarding interlocutory proceedings has been raised and answered in the affirmative.[13] The position is covered by EC Article 234(2) (ex Art 177(2)), because a problem of Community law may occur at the initial or interlocutory stage of the proceedings and has to be settled by the court before proceeding further. The court may have to make a ruling which will determine

---

10 Joined Cases 28-30/62: *Da Costa v Netherlandse Belastingadministratie* [1963] ECR 31, [1963] CMLR 224.
11 See Jacobs, F, 'When to refer to the European Court' (1974) 90 LQR 486.
12 RSC Ord 114, r 2(1).
13 Case 107/76: *Hoffmann-La Roche v Centrafram Vertriebsgesellschaft Pharmazeutischer Erzeugnisse mbH* [1977] ECR 957, [1977] 2 CMLR 334; see Jacobs, F, [1977] 2 ELRev 354.

the subsequent course of the action or even dismiss it; but if the proceedings will continue and the point of Community law can be raised again, even a national court of last resort disposing of the interlocutory issue is not obliged to make a reference. The referring court may also grant some form of interim relief in order to preserve the positions between the parties pending the outcome of the reference, including the suspension of the operation of a natural measure implementing a provision of EC law whose lawfulness is in dispute (but not the EC provision itself).[14]

(5) MULTIPLE AND REPEATED REFERENCES

These are admissible[15] and even desirable to save time and expense. In the cited case such a multiple reference gave the ECJ an opportunity of ruling on turnover equalization tax in relation to various groups of products. Perhaps a more interesting variant of multiple reference was the *EMI v CBS*[16] case which was concerned with a trademark dispute between an English and an American company, the matter being litigated simultaneously in England, Denmark and Germany. Since the questions raised in all three countries were basically the same, it was possible to bring these within one reference and dispose of it accordingly, although in fact each national court made its own reference.

If dissatisfied with the response the referring court is free to try again since repeated references are not prohibited.[17]

(6) QUESTIONS OF CRIMINAL LAW

The enforcement of Community law is in the hands of national authorities. They dispose of coercive rules and of the machinery to apply these. Even in the limited area of direct Community coercion the fines and periodic penalties imposed by the Commission to enforce the rules of competition are, under EC Article 256 (ex Art 192), executed by the competent national authorities in accordance with national law and procedures.

Where a Community rule has to be supported by a criminal sanction the relevant legislative Community act can merely provide that such sanction will be enacted by the Member States. Failure to enact the sanction would not give rise to a reference to the Community Court so that it could be read a sanction into the national legislation in question but rather to an enforcement action as, eg, in the *Tachograph* case.[18] Therefore references involving questions of criminal law are likely to occur in cases where the defendant seeks the protection of Community law from the existence or severity of a national criminal sanction. Indeed such references are admissible.[19] In theory, where the national law is manifestly incompatible with Community law, the doctrine of supremacy should enable the court to disregard the offending national law but, in practice, it is more likely

---

14 Cases C-143/88 and C-92/89: *Zuckerfabrik Süderdithmarschen AG and Zuckerfabrik Soest GmbH v Hauptzollamt Itzehoe and Hauptzollamt Paderborn* [1991] ECR I-415; Case C-465/93: *Atlanta Fruchthandelgesellschaft mbH v Bundesamt für Ernährung und Forstwirtschaft* [1995] ECR I-3761.
15 Case 29/68: *Milch-Fett- und Eierkontor GmbH v Hauptzollamt Saarbrücken (No 2)* [1969] ECR 165, [1969] CMLR 390.
16 Case 51/75: *EMI Records Ltd v CBS (United Kingdom) Ltd* [1976] ECR 811, [1976] 2 CMLR 235.
17 See eg Case 244/80: *Foglia v Novello (No 2)*, supra; Case 14/86, supra (p 362, note 7).
18 See p 137, supra, note 8.
19 Case 82/71: *Pubblico Ministero v SPA Agricola Industria Latte* [1972] ECR 119, [1972] CMLR 723.

that a reference will be made. Indeed the position is not always clear. A few random samples illustrate the point.

A Dutch licensed victualler, prosecuted for selling liquor at prices below the minimum fixed by national law, successfully pleaded EC Article 28 (ex Art 30), (movement of goods) in his defence.[20] Similarly, in the *Northern Irish Pigs* case[1] a conviction under the Movement of Pigs Regulations (Northern Ireland) 1972 and forfeiture of the pigs in question were held contrary to Regulation 2759/75 governing the market in pig meat.

However a German baker[2] was unable to persuade the Court that the German bakery law which prohibits baking and deliveries of the product during certain hours at night was contrary to the provisions of EC Articles 12 (ex Art 6, ex Art 7) and 28-29 (ex Arts 30-34).

A migrant worker[3] was able to resist an expulsion order served by an administrative authority as an object lesson to other foreigners but not so a rapist.[4] Expulsion was held to be too severe a sanction for breach of a minor offence against immigration rules.[5] Requirements for a driving licence irrelevant to road safety could not be enforced by criminal sanctions.[6]

Importers of pornographic materials contrary to a national law had their convictions confirmed as falling within the derogation of public policy or public morality notwithstanding the fact that such materials were goods in free circulation in another Member State.[7] Pleas based on the Community principle of the freedom of movement of capital and goods were of no avail to persons convicted according to national rules for the illegal importation of Krugerrands and attempted exportation of silver alloy coins no longer in circulation.[8] Forfeiture of both gold and silver coins followed.[9]

Prosecutions arising from breaches of national sea fishery laws have led to references to the ECJ[10] and indeed to a head-on collision between two Member States, one suing the other on behalf of one of its citizens convicted of offences against the fishery law of the latter.[11] Whilst holding the defendant state guilty of a breach of Community law the ECJ lost no time in stressing that: 'Where criminal proceedings are brought by virtue of a national measure which is contrary to Community law a conviction in those proceedings is also incompatible with that law'.[12]

---

20 Case 82/77: *Openbaar Ministerie of the Netherlands v van Tiggele* [1978] ECR 25, [1978] 2 CMLR 528.
1 Case 83/78: *Pigs Marketing Board (Northern Ireland) v Redmond* [1978] ECR 2347, [1979] 1 CMLR 177.
2 Case 155/80: *Re Sergius Oebel* [1981] ECR 1993.
3 Case 67/74: *Bonsignore v Oberstadtsdirektor der Stadt Köln* [1975] ECR 297, [1975] 1 CMLR 472.
4 Case 131/79: *R v Secretary of State for Home Affairs, ex p Santillo* [1980] ECR 1585, [1980] 2 CMLR 308, ECJ; on appeal [1980] 3 CMLR 212; affd [1981] QB 778 [1981] 1 CMLR 569, CA.
5 Case 157/79: *R v Stanislaus Pieck* [1980] ECR 2171, [1980] 3 CMLR 220.
6 Case 16/78: *R v Michael Choquet* [1978] ECR 2293, [1979] 1 CMLR 535.
7 Case 34/79: *R v Henn and Darby* [1979] ECR 3795, [1980] 1 CMLR 246 but see Case 121/85: *Conegate v Customs and Excise Comrs* [1986] ECR 1007, [1986] 1 CMLR 739.
8 Case 7/78: *R v Thompson, Johnson and Woodiwiss* [1978] ECR 2247, [1979] 1 CMLR 47.
9 *Allgemeine Gold- und Silberschideanstalt v Customs and Excise Comrs* [1980] QB 390, [1980] 1 CMLR 488, CA.
10 Eg Cases, 3, 4, 6/76: *Officier van Justitie v Kramer* [1976] ECR 1279, [1976] 2 CMLR 440; Case 812/79: *A-G v Burgoa* [1980] ECR 2787, [1981] 2 CMLR 193; Case 269/80: *R v Tymen* [1981] 2 CMLR 544, CA; refd, [1981] ECR 3079 [1982] 2 CMLR 111.
11 Case 141/78: *France v United Kingdom, Re Fishing Net Mesh Sizes* [1979] ECR 2923, [1980] 1 CMLR 6. See also Case 63/83: *R v Kirk* [1984] ECR 2689, [1984] 3 CMLR 522.
12 Ibid.

These samples confirm that points of criminal law are referable to the Community Court for a preliminary ruling and illustrate the potential of further developments in this field.

The field was more recently widely opened through the prosecution of traders in England and Wales for breaches of the Shops Act 1950. The temptation to trade on Sunday had been sustained by the incongruities of the Act (which did not apply in Scotland), the rise of large diversified trading emporia which combine business with recreational facilities and the lacklustre enforcement of the law. Fines proved too low to deter the breaches of the Act while the unwillingness to guarantee costs in applications for injunctions encouraged both trading and defences against prosecutions. A defence on the ground of the freedom of movement of goods brought the controversy within the scope of the Community law.[13]

(7) THE RULING

In a sense the rulings of the ECJ under EC Article 234 (ex Art 177), may be regarded as abstract points of law because the Community Court, content with the definition of the law, leaves its application to the referring national court. This indeed is the message of the *Van Gend* case, reflecting a division of functions between the Community and the national jurisdictions. It is, therefore, necessary to distinguish between 'interpretation' and 'application', the former being the task of the ECJ, the latter of the national court involved.[14] Indeed when concluding, for example, that the national measure which is the subject matter of the reference is contrary to Community law, the ECJ contents itself with saying that it is 'incompatible' with the relevant provision of the Treaty. The obvious inference that it ought not to be applied because it is 'invalid' is left to the referring court. Similarly, when the prosecution and conviction founded upon national law are declared to be 'incompatible', the inference is that the conviction ought to be quashed by the national court. Sometimes, having stated the principle to be applied, the ECJ refers matters of fact back to the referring court: eg the question whether a national trade agreement[15] which restricts the supply of national but not of foreign newspapers to retailers does have an effect on inter-state trade was referred back with the reminder that it is for the referring court to decide, as a matter of fact, whether or not it does so.

It would be instructive to follow cases through to see how the preliminary ruling was applied, but few records are available in this respect. In the British references there has been no reluctance in applying the rulings.[16]

However in the *Santillo* case the Queen's Bench Divisional Court[17] appears to have misinterpreted the ruling but the apparent error was corrected by the Court

---

13   See the ambiguous ruling of the ECR in Case C-145/88: *Torfaen Borough Council v B & Q plc* [1989] ECR 3851, [1990] 2 QB 19, [1990] 1 CMLR 337, the purported interpretation of the ruling in *Council of the City of Stoke-on-Trent and Norwich City Council v B & Q plc* [1990] 2 CMLR 377, and the closing chapter – Case C-169/91: *Stoke-on-Trent City Council v B & Q* [1993] AC 900, [1992] ECR I-6635, [1993] 1 CMLR 426.

14   Case 183/73: *Osram GmbH v Oberfinanzdirektion Frankfurt* [1974] ECR 477 at 485, [1974] 2 CMLR 360 at 366; Case 228/87: *Pretura Unificata di Torino v Persons Unknown (Re Water Pollution)* [1988] ECR 5099, [1990] 1 CMLR 716.

15   Case 126/80: *Salonia v Poidomani and Baglieri* [1981] ECR 1563, [1982] 1 CMLR 64.

16   See Case 129/79: *Macarthys Ltd v Smith* [1980] ECR 1275, [1980] 2 CMLR 205; apld [1981] QB 180, [1980] 2 CMLR 217, CA. *R v Thompson, Johnson and Woodiwiss* supra; *R v Henn and Darby* [1979] 2 CMLR 495, HL; *R v Henn and Darby* [1980] AC 850, [1980] 2 CMLR 229, HL, *Pigs Marketing Board v Redmond* [1979] 3 CMLR 118, but see the problem of interpretation raised by the Sunday Trading cases.

17   *R v Secretary of State for Home Affairs, ex p Santillo* [1980] 3 CMLR 212.

of Appeal.[18] No difficulty arose in a social insurance case[19] where the National Insurance Commissioner, applying a ruling of the ECJ which he had requested, held that an Irishman claiming British benefits was not disqualified for the period of his imprisonment in Ireland although an Englishman imprisoned in the United Kingdom would be so disqualified.

(8)   COURTS AND TRIBUNALS

EC Article 234 (ex Art 177) is addressed to both the courts and tribunals 'against whose decision there is no judicial remedy under national law'[20] and 'any court or tribunal'.[1] The former include, prima facie, the Supreme Courts and the highest specialist courts of the Member States, ie the *Cour de Cassation* and the *Conseil d'Etat* in Belgium and France; the *Corte di Cassazione*, the *Consiglio di Stato* and *Corte Costituzionale* in Italy; the *Bundesgerichtshof*, the *Bundessozialgericht*, the *Bundesverwaltungsgericht*, the *Bundesdisziplinarhof* and the *Bundesfinanzhof* in Germany; the *Hoge Road*, the *Tariefcommissie* and the *College van Beroep* in the Netherlands; the Supreme Court in Ireland; the *Højesteret* in Denmark; the House of Lords and in some cases the English Court of Appeal, the Scottish Court of Session and the Northern Irish Court of Appeal in the United Kingdom. However, in *Costa v ENEL*[2] the Community Court considered that an Italian *Guidice Conciliatore* was a court against whose decisions there was no remedy on the ground that, because of the small claim involved in that case, the magistrate in question had sole jurisdiction under Italian law (in other cases, the magistrate would not have been a court of first and last instance). The Court's *dictum* that references can be made from any court whose decisions are final (*sans recours*) has broadened the basis of EC Article 234(3) (ex Art 177(3)) because it shows that the obligation to make a reference does not apply only to the highest courts in the judicial hierarchy of a Member State. The reference to 'any court or tribunal' (EC Article 234(2), (ex Art 177(2))) includes, apart from the inferior courts of law, any adjudicating body or institution which in the domestic jurisdiction exercises judicial functions,[3] including, of course, the English magistrates' court, but not a professional[4] body like the Paris Bar (unless it, or a committee of it, is exercising a judicial function),[5] private arbitrators,[6] a consultative body[7] or an administrative body.[8] A reference from the Deputy High Bailiff's Court of

---

18   Ibid [1981] QB 778, [198] 1 CMLR 569.

19   *Kenny v Insurance Officer* [1978] 1 CMLR 181; Case 1/78: *Kenny v Insurance Comr* [1978] ECR 1489, [1978] 3 CMLR 651; *Kenny v Insurance Officer* [1979] 1 CMLR 433.

20   Dont les decisions ne sont pas susceptibles d'un recours juridictionnel de droit interne; dessen Entscheidungen selbst nicht mehr mit Rechtsmitteln des innerstaatlichen Rechs angefochten wedern können; avverso le cui decisioni non possa proporsi un ricorso giurisdizionale di diritto interno.

1   Une juridicion; ein Gericht; una giurisdizione.

2   Case 6/64: [1964] ECR 585, [1964] CMLR 425.

3   See Case 61/65: *Vaassen-Göbbels v Beambtenfonds voor het Mijnbedrif* [1966] ECR 261, [1966] CMLR 508 and Case 246/80: *Broekmeulen v Committee for Registration of Medical Practitioners* [1982] 1 CMLR 91.

4   Case 138/80: *Re Jules Borker* [1980] ECR 1975, [1980] 3 CMLR 638.

5   Case 246/80: *Broekmeulen v Huisarts Registratie Commissie* [1981] ECR 2311.

6   Case 102/81: *Nordsee Deutsche Hochseefischerei GmbH v Reederei Mond an Reederei Friedrich*, [1982] ECR 1095.

7   Case 318/85: *Proceedings against Regina Greis Unterweger*, reference by Commissione Consultiva per le Infrazioni Volutarie, [1986] ECR 955.

8   Case C-24/92: *Corbiau v Administratin des Contributions* [1993] ECR I-1277; Case C-134/97: *Victoria Film A/S v Riks-skatteverket* [1998] ECR I-7023, [1999] 1 CMLR 279 (a national court exercising an administrative function).

Douglas, Isle of Man, despite the peculiar constitutional position of the Isle of Man, was accepted.[9]

The position of the National Insurance Commissioner in the British system has posed some questions[10] since his decisions are not subject to appeal though they may be quashed for error of law by the High Court. It seems that he has no obligation to refer[11] though a reference can be made by the High Court on an application for judicial review.[12] It can also be done by the Commissioner himself.[13] Whilst reference from the 'final court' is obligatory[14] it is only discretionary from the other courts or tribunals[15] that is, if the court considers it necessary to enable it to give judgment. However, obligatory reference does not mean that the Supreme Court must in every case involving Community law seek a ruling from Luxembourg. Should it be so the Community Court would become a kind of court of appeal from the national jurisdiction which it was never meant to be, for its jurisdiction under EC Article 234 (ex Art 177), is limited to interpretation of Community law in cases where such interpretation is requested by national courts. There is, therefore, no automatic reference but a judicial reference which implies uncertainty of the law in the opinion of the referring court and this, to use the expression of Advocate-General Lagrange,[16] embodies *une règle de bon sens et de sagesse*. The point has now been made by the Court itself[17] which emphasized the limited discretionary power of the courts of last instance as opposed to the compulsion which might be read into the verb 'shall bring' used in the third paragraph of EC Article 234 (ex Art 177).

In the same case the ECJ stressed the judicial nature of the reference and added that the national court may, if so inclined, refer of its own motion. This reflects an inquisitorial concept of the judicial process. In the adversarial system the judge may not be so inclined. Indeed, in the absence of a plea he may prefer to resolve the matter according to national law. Thus if neither party argues for reference or if both oppose it, it is unlikely that a reference would be made.[18]

Apart from arguing in court the parties cannot engineer a reference by inserting into their contract an 'Article 234 (ex Art 177) clause'[19] or contrive a situation in which there is an apparent conflict but, in fact, no litigious issue between them[20] or

9   Case C-355/89: *Department of Health and Social Security v Barr and Montrose Holdings Ltd* [1991] ECR I-3479, [1991] 3 CMLR 325.
10   Jacobs, F, 'Which Courts and Tribunals are bound to refer to the European Court?' (1977) 2 ELRev 119.
11   See *Re Holiday in Italy* [1975] 1 CMLR 184.
12   Case 41/77: *R v National Insurance Comr, ex p Warry* [1977] ECR 2085, [1977] 2 CMLR 783; Case 143/79: *Walsh v National Insurance Officer* [1980] ECR 1639, [1980] 3 CMLR 573.
13   *Kenny*, p 326, supra; Case 110/79: *Coonan v Insurance Officer* [1980] ECR 1445.
14   'That court shall; cette juridiction est tenue; dieses Gericht ist verpflichtet; tale giurisdizione è tenuta.'
15   'That court or tribunal may; cette juridiction peut; so kann; tale giurisdizione può.' National courts have 'the widest discretion in referring matters': see Case 166/73: *Rheinmühlen-Düsseldorf v Einfuhr- und Vorratstelle für Getreide und Futtermittel* [1974] ECR 33.
16   In Case 28-30/62: *Da Costa en Schaake v Nederlandse Administratie der Belastingen* [1963] ECR 31, [1963] CMLR 224 at 234; See also Lagrange, M, 'The Theory of the Acte Clair: A Bone of Contention or a Source of Unity?' (1971) 8 CMLRev 313.
17   Case 283/81: *CILFIT Srl v Minister for Health* [1982] ECR 3415, [1983] 1 CMLR 472. See also Case 107/76: *Hoffmann-La Roche v Centrafarm* [1977] ECR 957 at 973.
18   See *English-Speaking Union of the Commonwealth v Customs and Excise Comrs* [1981] 1 CMLR 581.
19   Case 93/78: *Mattheus v Doego Fruchtimport und Tiefkühlkost eG* [1978] ECR 2203, [1979] 1 CMLR 551.
20   Case 104/79: *Foglia v Novello* [1980] ECR 745, [1981] 1 CMLR 45; Case 244/80: *Foglia v Novello (No 2)* [1981] ECR 3045, [1982] 1 CMLR 585.

where the object of the reference is to obtain a ruling concerning the law of a Member State other than the state for which the question has been raised. In such cases the ECJ has no jurisdiction since the duty assigned to it by EC Article 234 (ex Art 177) is not that of delivering advisory opinions on general or hypothetical questions but of assisting in the administration of justice in the Member States.[1]

(9) *ACTE CLAIR*

This rule of common sense in exercising the powers to refer will differ, no doubt, according to the style of the national judiciary, their sense of independence and their Community orientation. Since reference under EC Article 234 (ex Art 177) involves interpretation, perhaps the most vital factor in the decision whether or not to refer is the confidence of the national court in the art of the interpretation of Community law. Indeed, if the court is certain of the position it need not, in accordance with the doctrine of *acte clair* or *sens clair*, seek the ruling of the Community Court. *Acte clair* implies that the legal rule in question is clear and, therefore, requires no interpretation in accordance with maxim *clara non sunt interpretanda*. However, *certainty* may mean literally certainty in an objective and undisputed sense. It may also mean *certainty* as a form of subterfuge applied to avoid the cumbersome machinery of preliminary ruling as remarked bluntly by a French *Avocat Général*[2] 'bien entendu, la théorie de l'acte clair intervient essentiellement pour metre un obstacle au renvoi pour interprétation'. Conscious of this tendency the ECJ reminded the national jurisdictions that the doctrine of *acte clair* ought to be resorted to only with utmost care.[3] On the other hand courts, being well versed in the art of interpretation, need not be reminded that reference to Luxembourg should be an exception rather than a rule and that it should be resorted to out of necessity and not out of habit.[4]

(10) APPEALS

The principle of *acte clair* applies to the inferior as much as to the final courts but in this context a practical question of appeals against the reference from the inferior courts arises. This basically is a matter for each individual country and there is no uniform practice among the Member States. In Germany, Denmark[5] and the Netherlands the reference goes forward to the Community Court whilst in Belgium, the United Kingdom[6] and France the appeal has first to be disposed of. Ireland, however, went further than any other Member State in clearing the way for references made by any court in so far as there is no appeal against the order. In so ruling the Supreme Court held that the constitutional right of appeal available in the domestic jurisdiction must give way to the supremacy of Community law

1 Case 261/81: *Walter Rau v De Smedt PubA* [1982] ECR 3961, [1983] 2 CMLR 496; Case 46/80: *Vinal SpA v Orbat SpA* [1981] ECR 77, [1981] 3 CMLR 524; Case 244/78: *Union Laitière Normande v French Dairy Farmers Ltd* [1979] ECR 2663, [1980] 1 CMLR 314.
2 Quoted by Pescatore, P, 'Interpretation of Community Law and the Doctrine of "Acte Clair"', *Legal Problems of an Enlarged European Community*, ed by Bathurst, M E, et al (1972), p 42.
3 Case 283/81: *CILFIT*, supra, at paras 16 and 17.
4 Cf Graham, J, in *Löwenbrau München v Grünhalle Lager International Ltd* [1974] 1 CMLR 1.
5 *Firma Hans Just I/S v Ministeriet for Skatter OG Afgifter* [1980] 1 CMLR 4; (Danish Supreme Court). Decided by ECJ: Case 68/79: *Hans Just I/S v Ministry for Fiscal Affairs* [1980] ECR 501, [1981] 2 CMLR 714.
6 Order 114(5); see Ch 15.

expressed in EC Article 234 (ex Art 177).[7] The Community Court, on the other hand, follows its own guidelines which are determined by its function in the Community. This was succinctly stated in the *Bosch* case:[8]

> 'In fact, just as the Treaty does not prohibit domestic supreme courts from receiving the appeal for annulment, but leaves the examination of its admissibility to domestic law and to the opinion of the domestic judge, the Treaty subjects the jurisdiction of the Court of Justice solely to the existence of a request within the meaning of Article 177, without requiring the Community judge to examine whether the decision of the domestic judge is appealable under the provisions of his domestic law.'

However, the spirit of non-intervention has not solved the problem as in two cases involving the same parties the Court was in effect asked to make a ruling on a conflict of opinion between German courts.[9] This conflict was, in the terms of the reference from the *Bundesfinanzhof*, reduced to the question whether an inferior court had an unfettered right of reference to the Community Court or whether EC Article 234 (ex Art 177) upheld the hierarchy of national courts with the effect that on points of law an inferior court is bound by the ruling of a superior court. The Community Court, addressing itself to the *Hessisches Finanzgericht*,[10] ruled that EC Article 234 (ex Art 177) did not preclude an inferior court making its reference to the Community Court whilst the Community Court had no choice but to attend to the questions put before it. Addressing itself to the *Bundesfinanzhof*[11] the Community Court ruled that the existence of a rule of domestic law whereby a court is bound on points of law by the rulings of the court superior to it cannot of itself take away the power provided for in EC Article 234 (ex Art 177) of referring cases to the Court. If inferior courts were bound without being able to refer matters to the Court, the jurisdiction of the latter to give preliminary rulings and the application of Community law at all levels of the judicial systems of the Member States would be compromised. It seems that the problem is basically a domestic one though for the sake of uniformity and in the spirit of the integration of judicial remedies within the Community a common solution should be found.

The relationship between the Community Court and the judiciary of the Member States is delicately poised between the recognition of the independence of the courts of sovereign states and the need for a uniform application of Community law throughout the Community. It is a problem which, one hopes, will solve itself in the course of time and as a result of the consolidation of the Community, though nuances between the styles of the national judiciaries are bound to remain.

---

7 *Campus Oil Ltd v Minister for Industry and Energy* [1984] 1 CMLR 479 (Irish Supreme Court).

8 Case 13/61: *Kledingverkoopbedriff De Geus en Uitdenbogerd v Bosch en Van Rijn* [1962] ECR 45 at 50, [1962] CMLR 1 at 26.

9 Case 166/73: *Rheinmühlen-Düsseldorf v Einfuhr- und Vorratstelle für Getreide und Füttermittel* [1974] ECR 33, [1974] 1 CMLR 523 and Case 146/73: [1974] ECR 139, [1974] 1 CMLR 523.

10 Case 146/73: [1974] ECR at 147.

11 Case 166/73: [1974] ECR at 38,39.

Chapter 14

Enforcement of Community law

A.   Enforcement of Treaty obligations

The enforcement of the Treaty is safeguarded by political, economic and legal means. The most important weapon, which in classic international law states may resort to in order to frustrate a treaty, is interpretation. This weapon has been taken away from the signatories of the EC Treaty and so they cannot resort to legal subterfuge. Though they can defy the Treaty by breaking it they cannot get round it or, under the guise of sovereignty, flout their obligations with impunity. Moreover they cannot claim, as Italy[1] did, the benefit of an 'international agreement' when the Treaty obligations have been further specified by a decision, ie decision 66/532 urging Italy to accelerate the reduction of the import rates on the basis of the continued protection of the Italian lead and zinc industry.

The interpretation of the Treaty has been entrusted to the Community Court (EC Articles 220 and 234 (ex Arts 164 and 177)) but there is a double check because by EC Article 292 (ex Art 219),[2] 'the Member States undertake not to submit a dispute concerning the interpretation or application of this Treaty to any method of settlement other than those provided for therein'. This, in addition to administrative action, establishes a judicial system of settling disputes, the Community Court having a monopolist position.

Restricted in their classic weaponry the Member States may be tempted to flout the Treaty overtly but this too was provided for. The Treaty provides for repressive measures, should this occur. The procedure of repression is gentle and well suited to the type of likely offender.

Member States can sue one another before the Community Court but before doing so they must bring their complaint before the Commission.[3] In practice

---

1   Case 38/69: *Customs Duties on Lead and Zinc, Commission v Italy* [1970] ECR 47 at 56, 57 [1970] CMLR 77 at 89-90.
2   ECSC, 87; EAEC 193.
3   EC Art 227 (ex Art 170); ECSC Art 89; EAEC Art 142.

371

the task of suing the defaulter is undertaken by the Commission[4] as the guardian of the Treaties.

The reluctance of states to sue each other is understandable: such actions are invidious and the plaintiff state of today may well be the defendant tomorrow. Moreover a suit by the Commission tends to be technical rather than vindictive and, from a Community point of view, the Commission has the title to represent the Community's objective interests. In the light of this procedure France[5] suing the United Kingdom directly over the arrest of a French trawler exhibited a deviation from the norm understandable perhaps in the atmosphere of the *guerre des moutons*.[6]

Each country[7] has been before the Community Courts on a number of charges which vary so much that it is quite impossible to determine the pattern of state delinquency. Technically we are concerned with failures to carry out the obligations arising from the membership of the Communities. The principal, if not the only, object of the enforcement action is to ensure that these obligations are carried out and thus vindicate the rule of law.

Should a state fail to execute the judgment of the Community Court it may once more be sued, this time for breach of EC Article 228 (ex Art 171). This procedure has in fact been applied but the Member State in question complied with the original judgment.[8] There is also a precedent that a Member State had refused to comply[9] with the judgment but this is rare.

The efficacy of the enforcement procedure has inherent limitations because a recalcitrant state cannot really be forced to abide by the judgment of the Court, though by virtue of ESCS Article 88(3) sanctions of a pecuniary nature and retaliatory measures by way of derogations from the provisions of Article 4 of that Treaty in order to correct infringements of Treaty obligations may be applied under the control of the Council of Ministers. Such sanctions have not been applied to date. The lack of sanctions under the EC and Euratom Treaties (which is in many respects the last vestige of state sovereignty) may be regarded as a weak point of the system though it has been, up to a point, remedied by the amendment of EC Article 228 (ex Art 171), so as to include the possibility of imposing on a recalcitrant state the obligation to pay a lump sum or a penalty payment.[10] Another, indirect, sanction for failure to comply with Community law is state liability in damages to persons who have suffered loss as a result.[11] In this respect the Community differs from a federal state which may have federal means at its disposal for the execution of the judgments of the federal court or the decisions of the federal executive. Therefore the ultimate sanction in the

---

4 EC Art 226 (ex Art 169); ECSC Art 88, EAEC Art 141.
5 Case 141/78: *France v United Kingdom (Re Fishing Net Mesh Sizes)* [1979] ECR 2923, [1980] 1 CMLR 6.
6 Case 232/78: *Commission v France, Re Restrictions on Imports of Lamb* [1979] ECR 2729, [1980] 1 CMLR 418.
7 Lasok, D, 'The United Kingdom before the Community Court' in *Rechtsvergleichung Europarecht und Staatemintegration, Gedächtnisschrift für Léontin-Jean Constantinesco* (ed by Luke, G, Ress, G, Will, M R) (1982), pp 439 et seq.
8 Case 7/68: *Commission v Italy (first art treasures case)* [1968] ECR 423, [1969] CMLR 1, and Case 48/71: *Commission v Italy (second art treasures case)* [1972] ECR 527, [1972] CMLR 688.
9 Cases 24, 97/80R: *Commission v France (second imports of lamb case)* [1980] ECR 1319.
10 As to which, see Case C-387/97: *Commission v Greece*, 4 July 2000, and Case C-197/98: *Commission v Greece*, pending.
11 See in particular Cases C-46/93 and C-48/93: *Brasserie du Pêcheur v Germany* [1996] ECR I-1029, [1996] 1 CMLR 889.

EC is political and economic. The former consists of the pressure of public opinion within the Community and persuasion by the fellow Member States. The economic sanction lies in the common interest inherent in the preservation and improvement of the Community, quite apart from any counter-measures which may be taken by the Member States individually or collectively or actions for compensation brought by private persons. Though the machinery of enforcement is far from perfect there is no reason to believe that states would wantonly act contrary to the accepted obligations. They are only too well aware that the smooth working of the Community depends on their co-operation and that the economic intertwining cannot be disentangled without self-inflicted hardship.

B. Enforcement of Community law at Community level

Away from the lofty stage of inter-state conflicts or internal Community disputes, the enforcement of Community law occurs in the more usual setting of disputes in which individuals, corporations and states are involved. Such disputes are decided either at Community or state level bearing in mind that Community law is *state law* and, therefore, subject to the judicial notice of municipal courts.

The underlying philosophy of the Community and, indeed, the practical assurance of the Community development in accordance with the Treaty and the Community legislation is the doctrine of the supremacy of Community law. It is still a theory because in spite of the constitutional adjustments of the Member States there is, generally, a certain amount of hesitation, if not reluctance, to accept that monist doctrine and by-pass national legislatures. At the root of this is not only distrust of the Brussels bureaucrats who are neither directly controlled by nor responsible to the Member States but, more importantly, an instinctive aversion to external laws and authorities invading, as it were, the sacred preserve of sovereign states. These states have a long and proud history and a strong sense of national identity coupled with an individualistic notion of national interest. Therefore psychological barriers have to be removed in order to make the legal obligations enshrined in Treaties and derivative legislation meaningful and acceptable. In the circumstances it is not surprising that the lead in the process of the enforcement of Community law had to come from the Community Court.

The main difficulty is that, apart from EC Article 249 (ex Art 189), the EC Treaty contains no formal and unequivocal assertion of the supremacy of Community law. Yet, it is common ground that the edifice of the Community would collapse if the Community were to degenerate into a legal Tower of Babel. Thus the Community Court in a number of cases formulated and reaffirmed the principle of supremacy. The Court, as the guardian of legality and instrument of cohesion within the Community has, from the start, been in a strong position to define the status of the Community law and to give it precedence when in conflict with the municipal law of the Member States. Most of these cases were brought under EC Article 234 (ex Art 177) and the Court did not hesitate to use its authority in furthering the aims of the Community.

Whilst the Community Court in its judicial capacity has no rival system of law to administer and is only remotely concerned with the political consequences of its decisions, the municipal courts have to face the juristic and practical problems arising from the conflict between domestic law and Community law forming part of their national system. The theory that Community law is part, albeit autonomous, of national law does not solve these problems.

Indeed municipal courts often have to face the fact that the legislature has not removed from the national statute book measures which have been declared by the ECJ 'incompatible with Community law'. Impliedly such measures are *invalid* but the ECJ has no power to strike them out. It can only expect that they will be either formally repealed by the legislature or disregarded by the municipal courts. At a Community level this is a matter of state responsibility for its legislature and, therefore, a state in default incurs the risk of enforcement action under EC Article 226 (ex Art 169). At a national level the problem remains unresolved. Therefore, as the Tribunal de Grande Instance once asked in Paris, 'Are these measure directly and immediately inapplicable?'[12]

The question arose from the prosecution of importers and advertisers of certain aperitifs for offences under the French 'Drinks Code'. Certain provisions of this Code, notwithstanding the health implications, were declared to have breached EC Article 28 (ex Art 30), and the ECJ[13] condemned France in the stereotyped terms of its judgments in comparable cases, ie: 'The Republic of France, regulating the advertising of alcoholic beverages in a discriminatory manner, thus maintaining obstacles to freedom of intra-Community trade, has neglected to fulfil the obligations imposed on it under Article 30 of the EEC Treaty.' However the Republic took no notice of this *dictum* and the public prosecutor continued his work. The trial court put its problem thus at a knife point: 'It seems that Community law, although possessing authority which is superior to that of French internal law, does not necessarily have to be directly and immediately applicable to the internal code of law. It must be determined then whether Community law such as it has been laid down . . . by the Court of Justice, renders directly and immediately inapplicable the Articles L1, L17, L18 and L21 of the Drinks Code and the measures against alcoholism in French national law.'[14]

In response[15] the ECJ recorded the failure of the French Government to remedy the infringements found in its earlier judgment and reiterated the obligation of the national legislature to amend the law in order to render effective the directly applicable provisions of Community law.

However, the fact that municipal courts are not only prepared to follow the Community Court but also to assert independently the supremacy of Community law is quite significant. It shows that they are prepared to follow the rule of law established by the Community Court and in doing so do not hesitate to disregard the possible claim of municipal law or of their national government to confine disputes involving Community matters to domestic jurisdiction and municipal law. The judge sworn to administer the law of his country has to overcome the temptation to give precedence to the law in which he has been trained over the law derived from an external source.

---

12   *Europe*, No 3287; 14 January 1982, p 12.
13   Case 152/78: *Commission v France, Re Advertising of Alcoholic Beverages* [1980] ECR 2299, [1981] 2 CMLR 743.
14   Quoted from Europe, op cit.
15   Cases 314-316/81 and 83/82: *Procureur de la République v Waterkeyn* [1982] ECR 4337, [1983] 2 CMLR 145.

C. Enforcement of Community law at national level

The corollary to the incorporation of the Treaties and Community legislation into municipal law is the judicial notice of Community law in the Member States. Community law, being part of the national legal structure, is applicable and enforceable by the municipal courts as the internal law of the states irrespective of its external origin. However, conflicts arise in practice and an analysis of decisions of the municipal courts shows, at least during the first decade of the operation of the EC Treaty, a great deal of confusion and erratic jurisprudence. National judges and lawyers had to settle down to the novel experience and assimilate the challenge of Community law. In this process, the doctrine of supremacy of Community law elaborated by the Community Court and the lessons drawn from preliminary rulings under EC Article 234 (ex Art 177) had a steadying effect. The recognition by national courts of the direct effect of certain rules of Community law and of its supremacy is therefore the most important factor in the process of enforcement of Community law at the Member State level.

We have already observed that, in some cases in which a preliminary ruling under EC Article 234 (ex Art 177) was requested, the national courts were involved in conflicts between Community law and national law. Moreover, conflicts were often made more acute when the Constitution, the highest law of the land, was said to be infringed. The Community Court refrained from entering the lists, confined itself to interpretation of the relevant rule of Community law, but, nevertheless, albeit indirectly, indicated that Community law had to prevail, irrespective of whether the conflict was with the Constitution or the ordinary law of the land.

It seems in the light of the experience of the founder members of the Community, that once the Treaties have been duly ratified and incorporated into their legal systems, allegations of unconstitutionality of these Treaties can hardly be made an issue of litigation. By the same token, the constitutionality of the Community legislation can *ex hypothesi* hardly be raised because, in order to be 'unconstitutional', the Community acts would have to be inconsistent with Community law and this is a matter for the Community Court.[16] In theory, the Community Court could, by upholding the validity of Community legislation, contribute to a constitutional crisis in a Member State, the outcome of which cannot be predicted. If the supremacy of Community law and the authority of the Community Court were to prevail, the state concerned would have to put its own house if order; if, on the other hand, the authority of the Community Court were to be questioned, the matter would develop into a political crisis within the Community which could be solved only by political means. Putting these highly conjectural questions aside, it seems that more typical is the conflict between Community law and the ordinary law of the Member States. Indeed, as far as the United Kingdom is concerned, it is from this type of conflict that lessons can be learned simply because we do not have an hierarchy of legal norms as our Acts of

---

16 Hence, where a provisions of EC law is impugned before a national court on the ground that it is incompatible with EC law itself, the national court is free to dismiss the claim if it is a bad one but, if it is arguable, the national court cannot pass judgment on the provision but must refer the matter to the ECJ for it to decide the point. The national court has no power to suspend the operation of the contested EC provision even as an interim measure pending final resolution of the dispute: see Cases C-143/88 and C-92/89: *Zuckerfabrik Süderdithmarschen v Hauptzollamt Itzehoe et al* [1991] ECR I-415.

Parliament have the same status whether they are concerned with the reform of the House of Lords or the reform of the law of illegitimacy.

Arising from Treaties the Community law, notwithstanding its incorporation into the legal systems of the Member States, presents certain problems of enforcement by municipal courts when in conflict with municipal law. According to the prevailing doctrine, international law takes priority over municipal law in the jurisprudence of the International Court of Justice[17] but there is no uniformity in state practice. France, the Netherlands and Luxembourg admit supremacy of international law over municipal law, but the other countries treat the rules of international law on an equal footing with the rules of municipal law. In the British[18] system a distinction is made between customary and conventional rules of international law. The former are incorporated through the doctrine of precedent, the latter through legislation. The Greek[19] Constitution recognizes supremacy of international conventional law over ordinary non-constitutional enactments but customary rules are on an equal footing with domestic law. However Community law, though generated by Treaties, is not, strictly speaking *international law* in the traditional sense of the term. Therefore the analogies with international law which are occasionally raised are not particularly helpful. Being a *sui generis* system it has to be treated as such and its enforcement has to be seen in the light of the practice evolving in the Member States. One starts with international law as far as the Treaties are concerned but secondary Community law raises specific Community problems. At the basic practical level these problems can be reduced to the application of Community law (including the doctrine of supremacy) and the readiness to seek preliminary rulings from the ECJ.

(1)   FRANCE

In the light of Article 55 of the French Constitution of 1958, Parliament must refrain from passing legislation inconsistent with the international obligations of France since 'a treaty duly ratified has, from the moment of its publication, an authority superior to that of statutes'.[20] Should a bill be presented to Parliament it could be declared unconstitutional by the *Conseil Constitutionnel* (Article 61).[1] The judiciary and public authorities have to conform. As confirmed by the *Conseil d'Etat* in the *Kirkwood* case[2] an individual may contest the validity of administrative acts of the state on the ground that they violate international obligations. Case law,[3] even under the previous Constitution, conforms to the rule that international obligations have to be honoured by the courts, and judges, through the instrumentality of interpretation, endeavour to avoid conflicts on the assumption that Parliament did not intend to violate international law.

---

17   *The Free Zones Case* (1932) PCIJ Rep Ser A/B No 46; *The Wimbledon Case* (1923) PCIJ Rep Ser A No 1; *German Settlers Case* (1923) PCIJ Rep Ser B No 6.
18   Lasok, D, 'Les traits internationaux dans le système juridique anglais' (1966) *Rev Gén de Droit Int Public*, p 1 (at 3).
19   Evrigenis, D, 'Legal and Constitutional Implications of Greek Accession to the European Communities' (1980) 17 CMLR Rev 157 at 166.
20   Per Commissaire du gouvernement Mme Questiaux in *Re Syndicat Général des Fabricants de Semoules Conseil d'Etat* [1970] CMLR 395, [1970] Dalloz 285.
 1   Eg *The Abortion Law* held constitutional (1975) II. JCP 180 30 (*Conseil Constitutionnel*) despite the argument that it contravened the European Human Rights Convention.
 2   Decided on 30 May 1952, quoted by Constantinidès-Mégret, op cit, at p 85.
 3   Cited by Constantinidès-Mégret, ibid, at p 86.

Relying on the principle of reciprocity the *Conseil Constitutionnel* ruled in 1971[4] that the budgetary treaty of 1970 and the decision of the Council of Ministers whereby the Community budget was to be financed by the Community's own resources conformed to the Constitution. It also confirmed that direct elections to the European Parliament[5] did not constitute an unconstitutional transfer of sovereignty. In the *Isoglucose*[6] case the *Conseil* endorsed the direct effect of the Community legislation stressing that their binding force is not subject to control of national authorities, notably the French Parliament and that, therefore, subsidies to producers were governed by the relevant regulation issued under EC Article 249 (ex Art 189). Finally it ruled that the discriminatory tax on alcoholic beverages, condemned previously by the Community Court[7] as contrary to EC Article 90 (ex Art 95), was inconsistent not only with the Treaty but also with the principle of reciprocity enshrined in the Constitution.[8]

The existence of the Community Court with its inherent jurisdiction gave rise to the theory that since the Community Court solely administers Community law, whilst the national courts administer both the municipal law and Community law, the latter is called upon to resolve conflicts between the two systems without reference to the former.[9] In practice initially French courts have experienced some difficulty, probably because 'traditionally French tribunals, at least in the past, regarded foreign legislation and pronouncements of foreign courts with some mistrust'.[10] Consequently they were rather reluctant to administer Community law. Thus in *Re Shell-Berre*[11] the *Conseil d'Etat*, applying the doctrine of *acte clair*, refused to refer to the Community Court the question whether a law of 1928 which enabled the government to exercise control over the import and distribution of oil was incompatible with what were then EC Articles 3, 7, 30, 35, 37, 59, 62, 85, 92 and 96 (now Arts 3, 12, 28, 31, 49, 81, 87 and 91). A similar attitude was shown by the first sub-section of the *Conseil d'Etat* in *Syndicat Général des Fabricants de Semoules*[12] which held that a French decree introducing an import levy on semolina inconsistent with Community regulations was to prevail. It could be said that the case was rather exceptional as it concerned imports from Algeria which, by virtue of French legislation, were to remain within the French customs frontiers but, in fact, the *Conseil d'Etat* preferred to apply French law to Community law. The breakthrough came in *Re Syndicat National du Commerce Extérieur*.[13] In that case a syndicate dealing in cereals requested the interpretation of the term 'any holder' (EEC Regulation 1028/68) to be referred to the Community Court as it considered itself to be prejudiced by the narrow interpretation of this term by the ONIC (ie the National Cereals Board). The *Conseil* agreed that the

4   Décision recources propres, RGDIP 1971, p 239.
5   Décision Assemblée Européenne, AFDI 1976, p 787.
6   Décision Isoglucose, RTDE 1979, p 142.
7   Case 168/78: *Commission v France* [1980] ECR 347, [1981] 2 CMLR 631.
8   Décision Alcools, RGDIP 1981, p 600, supra, p 374.
9   See *Riff v Société Grande Limonaderie Alsacienne*, decided by the Cour de Cassation (Chambre Criminelle), 19 February 1964, [1965] 1 Clunet 85-90; 2 CML Rev 448-449; *Etat Français v Nicolas and Société Brandt*, decided by the Cour d'Appel of Amiens, 9 May 1963; [1963] CMLR 239 at 245; [1964] Clunet 93; upheld on other grounds by the Cour de Cassation (Chambre Criminelle), 22 October 1964, [1965] Clunet 90; 2 CML Rev 449.
10 Simon, M, 'Enforcement by French Courts of European Community Law' (1974) 90 LQR 467 at 471.
11 [1964] CMLR 462, [1964] Clunet 794.
12 [1970] CMLR 395, [1968] Dalloz 285, 6 CML Rev 419.
13 [1971] Dalloz 576 and 645.

Community Court gave a wide interpretation which, in turn, enabled the *Conseil* to annul the decision of the ONIC in this respect.

Dealing with the individuals the *Conseil* acted in a rather individualistic manner. It set aside a Prefect's order to deport aliens who applied for a resident permit in order to establish a production co-operative to be known as a 'Pioneer European Village',[14] but denied admission to a person who in his youth, a decade earlier, achieved notoriety during the student troubles.[15] The latter case is remarkable because the *Conseil* ignored the relevant Community precedents, refused to make a reference to the Community Court and ruled that directives (in particular directive 64/221) cannot be invoked by individuals in national proceedings in order to challenge an administrative act. Its defiance was extended to the VAT Directive 77/388 which it considered to have no direct effect.[16]

The Civil Courts appear to be more favourably disposed towards Community law but they too had their difficulties. In the *Consten*[17] saga involving the validity of an exclusive distribution contract, the Paris Court of Appeal quashed the judgment of a Commercial Court (which effectively denied the application of EEC Regulation 17/1962 in this respect)[18] and stayed the action until the Commission had made its decision in the matter. Two years later a Court of First Instance dealing with the same problem[19] noted the Commission decision in the previous case and stayed the action to await the outcome of the proceedings before the Community Court. From that time on the French Civil Courts became quite prepared to resort to the proceedings under Article 177, a notable early example being the *Ulm* case.[20] Thus, the Paris Court of Appeal, applying the judgment of the Community Court in the *Beguelin* case,[1] held EC Article 81 (ex Art 85) and Regulations 10/1965 and 67/1967 directly applicable in France with the effect that a contract between a French and a Dutch firm, granting the former exclusive distribution rights, was declared invalid. The decision was confirmed by the *Cour de Cassation*.[2]

The Criminal Chamber of the *Cour de Cassation* also made its contribution. In *Administration des Contributions Indirectes, etc v Ramel*[3] the *Cour de Cassation* dismissed an appeal against the acquittal of the respondent on the charge of offering for sale inferior wine imported from Italy. The wine was admitted to France under the EEC regulations although its quality did not comply with French law. In *Republic v Von Saldern et al*[4] the *Cour de Cassation* dismissed an appeal against conviction for breach of exchange control regulations involved in the import of chemicals from the USA. The appeal was based on Community customs regulations concerning the valuation of imported goods which were issued after the alleged offence. Since these regulations were not retrospective the appeal had to fail and the question of conflict with national law did not arise. In the *Guerrini* case,[5] concerning a conviction for an offence under a 1939 law laying

---

14 *Re Hill and Holzappel* [1978] 2 CMLR 554.
15 *Minister of the Interior v Cohn-Bendit* [1980] 1 CMLR 543, [1979] Dalloz 155.
16 *Re la directive No 77/388* [1981] Dalloz I R 331.
17 Cases 56, 58/64: *Consten and Grundig v Commission* [1966] ECR 299, [1966] CMLR 418.
18 *Consten v UNEF* [1963] CMLR 176, [1963] Dalloz 189.
19 *Consten v Willy-Leissner, Rev Trim de Droit Européen* (1965) 487.
20 Case 56/65: *Société Technique Minière v Maschinenbau Ulm GmbH* [1966] ECR 235, [1966] CMLR 357.
 1 Case 22/71 *Béguelin Import Co v SAGL Import-Export* [1971] ECR 949, [1972] CMLR 81.
 2 *Entreprises Garoche v Société Striker Boats Nederland* [1974] 1 CMLR 469.
 3 [1971] CMLR 315, [1971] Dalloz 211.
 4 (1971) 10 CML Rev 223.
 5 *Guerrini Case*, 7 February 1972 (JCP 1972, II), (1971) 10 CML Rev 451.

down standards for the marketing of eggs, the Court of Appeal at Aix disregarded the relevant EEC regulations (122/67 and 1619/68) as it considered itself bound by the unrepealed statute. However the *Cour de Cassation* reversed that decision on the ground that the regulations had a direct effect repealing, as it were, the French legislation from the date on which the regulations came into force.

However, perhaps the most significant case is that of *Administration des Douanes v Société Cafés Jacques Vabre and J Weigel et Cie Sarl*.[6] The central point of that case was whether importers of instant coffee from Holland were legitimately charged with import duties which put them at a disadvantage as compared with French manufacturers of the produce and thus suffered discrimination contrary to EC Article 90 (ex Art 95). The French customs authorities claimed that Article 265 of the *Code de Douanes*, being enacted after the French accession to the Community, had to be applied, notwithstanding Article 55 of the Constitution. French courts had no jurisdiction in the matter of the constitutionality of the Code. In the court of first instance and the Paris Court of Appeal these arguments were rejected and finally the *Cour de Cassation* decided that the EEC Treaty established a separate legal order which prevails in France even over subsequent legislation. The requirement of reciprocity under Article 55 of the Constitution has been satisfied in the Treaty of Rome. It held:

> '. . . the treaty which by virtue of the above-mentioned article of the Constitution has an authority superior to that of statutes, established its own juridical order integrated with that of Member States, and by virtue of this special character the juridical system which it has created is directly applicable to the nationals of these states and is binding on their courts; and therefore . . . Article 95 of the Treaty [now Art 90] has to be applied . . . to the exclusion of Article 265 of the Customs Code, despite the fact that the latter is of a later date.'

Recognizing the supremacy of Community law (ie the right of establishment) the *Cour de Cassation* quashed the judgment of a court of appeal and ruled that a German was entitled to recover his farm from a French tenant on expiry of the lease despite the provision of the *Code Rural* which insists that aliens are not allowed to farm in France without a special permit to that effect. It held that 'the provisions of French international law which imposed the requirement of an administrative permit on those who wanted to farm in France have ceased to be applicable'.[7]

In a case concerned with French monetary compensatory amounts, the *Cour de Cassation*[8] quashed a decision of a court of appeal in which the latter decided that in its ruling in Case 145/79[9] the Community Court had exceeded its competence by encroaching upon the jurisdiction of the national judiciary in so far as it ruled upon the consequences of an annulled Commission regulation. Whilst it conceded that the court of appeal was not obliged to seek a preliminary ruling it held that the court of appeal indulged in the interpretation of the Treaty, which it had no power to do, and on that ground quashed the decision. In doing so the *Cour de Cassation* not only affirmed the principle of supremacy of

6 Court of Appeal, Paris, 7 July 1973, Dalloz (1974) 159, Cour de Cassation, 24 May 1975, Dalloz (1975) 497. [1975] 2 CMLR 336. Also see Simon, M, (1976) 92 LQR 85.
7 *Van Kempis v Geldof* [1976] 2 CMLR 152, Cour de Cass Civil Chamber, 15 December 1975, Dalloz (1976) 33.
8 Arret No 1096 P of 10 December 1985; See Schermers, H G, CMLRev (1986) 473 et seq.
9 Case 145/79: *Roquette Frères SA v France* [1980] ECR 2917.

Community law but also the binding force of a preliminary ruling. Moreover it stressed that the extent of the Community competence is a matter of Community law which ought to be defined by the Community Court.

A selection of more recent cases confirms that the French judiciary at all levels strives to uphold Community law. Thus, for example, a *Tribunal de Grande Instance*[10] ruled that, in the absence of a proof of lawful manufacture in the Member State of origin, the import of motor car spare parts produced in breach of an industrial property right (ie design) could be prohibited by virtue of EC Article 30 (ex Art 36). This was, no doubt, correct, bearing in mind the case[11] decided by the ECJ that French manufacturers of motor cars had the right to patent certain elements of the bodywork of their product and thus prohibit the manufacture, sale and export of these elements by certain specialists in imitating parts detached from the original model.

The *Cour d'Appel* of Aix-en-Provence, noting that the national law on minimum petrol prices had been declared illegal by the ECJ,[12] had no hesitation in applying Community law directly on the principle that it was inconsistent with EC Article 28 (ex Art 30).[13] The same court, following the ECJ,[14] considered the French domestic rule which prohibits lawyers from Marseille opening office in Paris and Conakry (Guinea) contrary to the right of establishment enshrined in EC Article 43 (ex Art 52) and, therefore, inapplicable.[15] In the same field the *Cour de Cassation* confirmed the principle, in another case, declaring that the French rule against multiple chambers (ie prohibiting a French lawyer to open chambers in Brussels unless he leaves the Nice Bar) was a breach of EC Article 43 (ex Art 52).[16]

A Paris *Cour d'Appel* referred a question arising from the application of the consumer protection directive on doorstep selling, ie whether the prohibition of such sales of educational[17] courses was incompatible with EC Article 28 (ex Art 30).

The *Conseil d'Etat* refused a residence permit to a German applicant who, though not qualified to practise medicine, wanted to establish himself in such practice.[18] Since he had no right to carry out self-employed activities he was considered not to be entitled to a resident permit. It seems that a reference for a preliminary ruling might have been more appropriate.

The *Conseil* ruled that the grant by statute of voting rights to non-European overseas French citizens in the election to the European Parliament was compatible with EC Article 299(1) (ex Art 227(1)) which defines the Community territory. The ruling was based on the principle that the Treaty and other international treaties prevail over subsequent French statutes.[19] The *Conseil* also considered the duty of the state to implement Community directives on VAT. It ruled that it was inappropriate to continue in force or enact national rules incompatible with the objectives of Community legislation. Such national law would be unlawful after

---

10 *Regie Nationale des Usines Renault v Thevenous*, Trib de Grande Instance, Roanne [1988] 3 CMLR 686.
11 Case 53/87: *CIRCA v Règie Renault* [1988] ECR 6039, [1990] 4 CMLR 265, para 11.
12 See also Cases 271-274/84 and 6-7/85: *Procureur de la République v Chiron* [1986] ECR 529, [1988] 1 CMLR 753.
13 *Aldis SA v Chabrand* [1987] 2 CMLR 396.
14 Case 107/83: *Ordre des Avocats au Barreau de Paris v Klopp* [1984] ECR 2971, [1985] 1 CMLR 99.
15 *Maitre Commarata v Conseil de l'Ordre de Avocats de Marseille* [1988] 1 CMLR 243.
16 *Conseil de l'Ordre des Avocats au Barreau de Nice v Raynel* [1990] 2 CMLR 190.
17 *Ministère Public v Buet and Educational Business Services Sarl* [1988] 3 CMLR 426.
18 *Re Joseph Weber* [1988] 2 CMLR 809.
19 *Re Nicolo* [1990] 1 CMLR 173.

the end of the implementation period of the relevant directive. It also annulled the refusal of the executive to legislate in order to repeal the offending national provisions.[20] Exercising its judicial control over executive legislation the *Conseil* annulled a ministerial order fixing the hunting season for water fowl as being incompatible with the Wild Birds Directive (79/409). In doing so it emphasized the need for national legislation to conform to the provisions of directives.[1]

The *Cour de Cassation*, following the judgment of the ECJ[2] in which the latter held invalid a special provision of Regulation 1408/71 applicable to France which denied children allowances to foreign workers temporarily out of France, held that such allowances had to be paid. Discrimination against migrant workers in France was thus brought to an end.[3] In two cases[4] the *Cour de Cassation* held, following the decisions of the ECJ,[5] that discriminatory taxes imposed on high-power cars manufactured in the Community but outside France were illegal and those already paid ought to be repaid.

(2) THE NETHERLANDS

Since the amendment of the Netherlands Constitution in 1953 and 1956, there seems to be no doubt that, in principle, Community law should be given precedence before Dutch law. We have already noted the *Van Gend en Loos* case[6] which, prior to coming before the Community Court for preliminary ruling, unfolded as a case involving a conflict between the Constitution and Community law. Similarly in *de Geus v Bosch*[7] the argument that only rules of international law of a 'universal application' take precedence over national law failed. These decisions had, undoubtedly, a profound effect upon the practice of Dutch courts.

Of later cases *Centrafarm*[8] calls for special mention. In that case the *Hoge Raad*, applying the preliminary rulings of the Community Court, refused an injunction to a trademark holder and a patentee which would restrain the marketing in Holland of protected pharmaceutical products originating from the United Kingdom.

In *Officer Van Justitie v Adriaan de Peijper, Managing Director of Centrafarm BV*, the *Kantongerecht*[9] at Rotterdam pronounced upon the freedom of movement and parallel imports of pharmaceutical products but left a question open as to whether certain rules of national law regarding the authentication and certification of such products, imposed by another Member State, were contrary to the EEC principles of the freedom of movement of goods. Applying the ruling of the ECJ[10] the *Kantongerecht* acquitted the importer of drugs therapeutically indistinguishable from approved national products from a charge arising under national drug control

---

20 *Re Alitalia Cie* [1990] 1 CMLR 248.
1   *Re Rassemblement des Opposants à la Chasse* [1990] 2 CMLR 831.
2   Case 41/84: *Pinna v Caisse d'Allocations Familiales de la Savvie* [1986] ECR 1, [1988] 1 CMLR 350.
3   *Pinna v Caisse d'Allocations Familiales de la Savoie* [1990] 2 CMLR 366.
4   *Directeur General des Impôts v Dubois* [1990] 2 CMLR 823 and *Directeur General des Impôts v Feldain* [1990] 2 CMLR 827.
5   Case 112/84: *Humblot v Directeur des Services Fiscaux* [1985] ECR 1367, [1986] 2 CMLR 338 and Cases 76, 86-89 and 149/87: *Seguela v Administration des Impôts* [1988] ECR 2397, [1989] 3 CMLR 823.
6   Case 26/62: [1963] ECR 1, [1963] CMLR 105.
7   Case 13/61: [1962] ECR 45, [1962] CMLR 1.
8   Case No 10. 712: *Centrafarm BV and De Peijper v Sterling Drug Inc* [1976] 1 CMLR 1.
9   [1976] 1 CMLR 19.
10 Case 104/75: *Re De Peijer* [1976] ECR 613, [1976] 2 CMLR 271.

legislation which requires certain documentation which could not be procured because the drugs in question were imported.[11]

In the *Ruigrok* case[12] the Supreme Court upheld the conviction for cultivating hyacinth bulbs commercially without a licence. Thus the convicted cultivator had to pay the fine notwithstanding the fact that the relevant Dutch law was inconsistent with Community law as previously decreed by the Community Court. Whilst accepting the ruling of the ECJ as binding (and resulting in the quashing of the conviction in the cited case) the Supreme Court distinguished the present case in so far as it concerned an application to set aside a judgment which had become absolute and this, according to Dutch law, was inadmissible. The conviction was a result of an error of law and not of facts unknown to the court at the time of the conviction and sentence and, therefore, could not be set aside.

Dealing with aliens, the *Raad van State*, without referring the matter to the ECJ, held that a British subject continuously wilfully unemployed was not entitled to have his residence permit renewed.[13] However another,[14] though in irregular employment and guilty of petty offences, was allowed to stay in Holland. More recently the question whether a British wife of a South African citizen[15] was entitled to the status of 'favoured EC citizen' for the purpose of residence despite the fact that her earnings were below the national subsistence level, was referred to the ECJ. At stake was her status as 'worker'. Advocate-General Sir Gordon Slynn thought that the principal test was not the number of hours worked but whether 'work' was the 'genuine and substantial purpose of the application to reside'. The ECJ concurred. Less fortunate was a Turkish worker who, on reference to the ECJ, was held ineligible for extension of a residence permit by virtue of the EEC-Turkey Association Agreement.[16]

The *Raad van State* held inadmissible the appeal against the refusal of the Government to bring before the ECJ an action for annulment of a Council regulation which imposed a levy for the production of isoglucose. Such a Government decision was not subject to judicial review in accordance with Dutch administrative law and, therefore, a citizen could not force the Government to bring an action in this respect.[17]

(3)   LUXEMBOURG

The Constitution of Luxembourg contains no provision regarding the relationship between international law and municipal law, but the judiciary, in the course of time, has evolved the principle of supremacy of international law.[18] In this process a judgment of the *Conseil d'Etat* of 1950 and a judgment of the Superior Court of 1954 have a special significance as they established the principle that a rule of international law will prevail over a rule of national law even if the latter is subsequent to the former.[19]

---

11   *Officer Van Jusitie v De Peijper* [1977] 1 CMLR 321.
12   [1977] 1 CMLR 306.
13   *Williams v Secretary of State for Justice* [1977] 1 CMLR 669.
14   *Simbula v Secretary of State for Justice* [1978] 2 CMLR 74.
15   Case 53/81: *Levin v Staatssecretaris van Justitie* [1982] ECR 1035, [1981] 3 CMLR 663.
16   Case C-192/89: *Sevince v Staatssecretaris van Jusitie* [1990] ECR I-3461.
17   *Koninklijke Scholten-Honig NV v Minister of Agriculture and Fisheries* [1978] 3 CMLR 251.
18   Pescatore, P, 'Prééminence des traits sur la loi interne: la jurisprudence luxembourgeoise', *Journal des Tribunaux* (1953) p 445; see also Constantinidès-Mégret, op cit, p 88,89.
19   Cases cited in *Les Novelles: Droit des Communautés Européennes* (1969), p 67.

(4)   BELGIUM

The Belgian Constitution of 1831 has been revised, mainly to accommodate Belgian membership of the European Community. Accordingly Article 25(b) provides that the exercise of certain state powers may be delegated by treaty or by statute to institutions set up under international law. Since 1925 Belgian courts gave precedence to international law over national law if the latter was inconsistent with a treaty.[20] This rule was broadened by the *Cour de Cassation* in 1964.[1] The court distinguished between treaties binding the state and treaties creating rights and obligations directly enforceable by individuals. Only the latter, by their very nature, can be in conflict with Belgian domestic law and if they are in conflict they must have precedence over municipal law. This ruling was complemented by a decision of the *Conseil d'Etat* made a month before the decision of the *Cour de Cassation*.[2] In a case brought against the Belgian Ministry of Agriculture, the Treaty of 1953 between Belgium and France concerning the protection of birds was construed as an obligation binding the state alone and having no direct effect upon the rights and obligations of citizens. It would appear, accordingly, that depending on their classification (ie whether binding the citizen or merely the state) some provisions of the EC Treaty are directly enforceable by Belgian courts, whereas others are not so enforceable. Following this philosophy the *Tribunal de Commerce de Bruxelles* considered EC Article 81(1) (ex Art 85(1)) directly applicable.[3] Being directly applicable, the Treaty may render void a contract valid when made.[4]

No doubt the process of accommodating Belgian traditions to the problem of Community law enforcement was influenced by the two famous cases *Costa v ENEL* and *Van Gend en Loos* which had a considerable impact within the Community. Their influence can be seen in the decision of the Magistrates' Court of Antwerp[5] which, having lavishly cited authorities and juristic opinion, concluded that, should there be a conflict between the EC Treaty and subsequent Belgian legislation, the former would prevail.[6] The Belgian Government too agreed that the Treaty should be given precedence over any subsequent legislation inconsistent with the Treaty.[7]

In the field of social legislation the District Court of Tongeren has held that Article 12 of Council Regulation 3 prevailed over Belgian legislation on industrial accidents in accordance with the principle that *lex posterior derogat priori*.[8]

In the *Corveleyn*[9] case the *Conseil d'Etat* applied the Community directive 64/221 of 25 February 1964 in order to quash a deportation order. But the high water mark of the evolution towards the recognition of the supremacy of Community law was reached in the decision of the *Cour de Cassation* in *Minister*

20   Ibid, p 63.
 1   Ibid, p 63.
 2   Ibid, p 64.
 3   *Van Heuvermeiren v Buitoni* [1967] CMLR 241 at 245, (1966) 1 CDE, 317.
 4   *Association Générale des Fabricants de Ciment Portland Artificiel v SA Carrière Dufour* [1965] CMLR 193 at 207-208.
 5   *Sociaal Fonds voor de Diamantarbeiders v Ch Brachfeld & Sons SA and Cougal Diamond Co* [1969] CMLR 335 at 320-323.
 6   The Community Court in another context (effects of the introduction of the common external tariff) involving the same parties, implied the same result; Cases 2-3/69: [1969] ECR 211 at 221-224, [1969] CMLR 335 at 349-353.
 7   *SPRL Corn and Food Trading Co v Etat Belge* (1968) CDE 550 at 554.
 8   *NV Essimex v J Jans* [1972] CMLR 48.
 9   *Corveleyn v Belgium*, 7 October 1968, (1969) CDE 343 at 345-346.

for Economic Affairs v SA Fromagerie Franco-Suisse 'Le Ski'.[10]   This case, concerning recovery of customs duties paid by mistake on the ground that, by reason of what was then EC Article 12 (now EC Art 25 but amended), the duties in question did not apply to the products imported from Member States of the Community, gave the Procureur-Général Ganshof van der Meersch an opportunity to discuss the nature of the self-executing provisions of the Treaty, the binding force of Community law, sovereignty and the relationship between Community law and the law of Belgium.   In his erudite submissions, he reviewed a host of learned writings and 48 cases decided by the Community Court, the Belgian courts and the court of Luxembourg and Germany.[11]   Quoting *Van Gend en Loos* and *Costa v ENEL* he submitted that:

> 'Community law is integrated in the law of Member States.   From its very nature, it follows that a subsequent measure of state legislation cannot be set against it . . . As Professor Pescatore has said: "One is entitled to think that the fundamental argument is to be found in this last passage: the very existence of the Community is called in question if the Community legal system cannot be established with identical effects and with uniform effectiveness over the whole geographical areas of the Community . . ."[12]

> The primacy of the rules of Community law is doubly justified on legal grounds. First by their agreement on the transfer of their rights and obligations under the Treaty to the Community legal system, the states definitely limited their "sovereign rights", or to put it more accurately, "the exercise of their sovereign powers".   The Community system implies some surrender of sovereignty and Community law is a specific law which gives effect to this surrender.   The integration aim of the Treaties of Paris and of Rome is attained by handing over to the Community institutions powers having as their object and effect the determination of a corresponding limitation of the powers of Member States . . .

> Thus was created for these states a duty to abstain from action in the fields regulated by the Treaty and a duty to take all complementary steps needed to enforce Community legislation.

> Secondly, Community law is a specific and autonomous law which is binding on the courts of the Member States and makes it impossible to set against it any domestic law whatsoever. The very nature of the legal system instituted by the Treaties of Rome confers that primacy on its own foundation, independently of the constitutional provisions in states.[13]   The specific character of Community law stems from the objectives of the Treaty which are the establishment of a new legal system to which are subject not only states, but also the nationals of those states.   It also stems from the fact that the Treaty has set up institutions having their own powers and especially that of creating new sources of law.   From their very structures, these institutions reflect the will of the authors of the Treaty to go beyond the state framework and to impose obligations directly on individual persons and to confer rights directly on them[14] . . . If the Community system is not recognized as superior, rules would not

---

10   [1972] 2 CMLR 330.
11   See, in particular, ibid, pp 351-358.
12   Pescatore, P, *Droit communautaire et droit national* (1969), p 183, quoting from *Costa v ENEL* [1964] CMLR 425 at 455, 456.
13   Quoting Tallon, D, *le droit communautaire* (1966) 1 *Cahiers de Droit Eurpéen* 571.
14   Quoting his own writings, 'Le droit communautaire et ses rapports avec les droits des Etats membres', in *Droit des Communautés européennes* (1969), Nos 138-139.

be the same within each Member State, and the consequences would be that such a situation would necessarily give rise to forms of discrimination proscribed by the treaties, that obligations would not bear equally on everybody and that not everyone would derive equal benefit from the rights derived from the Treaties . . .'

This long passage represents the quintessence of the Belgian and Community *doctrine* and reflects, it seems, the mood within the Community. The Court, on the other hand, in its terse judgment ruled:

'Even if assent to a treaty as required by Article 68(2) of the Constitution, is given in the form of a statute, the legislative power, by giving this assent, is not carrying out a normative function. The conflict which exists between a legal norm established by an international treaty and a norm established by a subsequent statute, is not a conflict between two statutes.

The rule that a statute repeals a previous statute in so far as there is conflict between the two, does not apply in the case of a conflict between a treaty and a statute.

In the event of a conflict between a norm of domestic law and a norm of international law which produces direct effects in the internal system, the rule established by the treaty shall prevail. The primacy of the treaty results from the very nature of international treaty law. This is a fortiori the case when a conflict exists, as in the present case, between a norm of internal law and a norm of Community law.

The reason is that the treaties which have created Community law have instituted a new legal system in whose favour the Member States restricted the exercise of their sovereign powers in the areas determined by those treaties.

Article 12 of the Treaty [now Art 25] . . . is immediately effective and confers on individual persons rights which national courts are bound to uphold.

It follows from all these considerations that it was the duty of the judge to set aside the application of provisions of domestic law that are contrary to this Treaty provision . . .'[15]

Belgian courts, from the lowest to the highest, are not inhibited either procedurally or psychologically from making references under EC Article 234 (now ex Art 177), the first one occurring in 1967.[16] More recently a problem of the position of road transport services came to light. According to Belgian law a carrier, in order to qualify for a road transport licence, must be established in Belgium. Thus questions regarding the status of a company with a real base in the Netherlands but operating from an unmanned and locked-up caravan were raised. The licence was refused on the assumption that the refusal did not breach the Treaty provisions on the right of establishment. However the *Conseil d'Etat*[17] was troubled with the uncertainty regarding services and referred the matter to the ECJ which ruled that licence had to be granted. The tendency[18] is to accord the judgments of the Community Court *l'autorité de la chose jugée* and to consider violations of Community law equivalent to violations of a Belgian statute.

15 [1972] CMLR at 372, 373.
16 Case 6/67: *Pace (née Guerra)* [1967] ECR 219.
17 *Lambregts Transportbedrijf PVBA v Belgium* [1989] 2 CMLR 987, Case 4/88: [1989] ECR 2583, [1991] 1 CMLR 351.
18 Lenaerts, K, *The Application of Community Law in Belgium* (1986) 23 CML Rev 253 at 282. See also Wytink, P, 'The Application of Community Law in Belgium (1986-1992), (1993) 30 CML Rev 982.

(5)   GERMANY

The starting point of the German practice is the strong dualist tradition of which Triepel[19] was perhaps the most influential exponent. According to this doctrine a rule of international law becomes enforceable only if expressly incorporated into the municipal law. Having been so incorporated, it ranks in the hierarchy of legal norms among the ordinary rules of internal law (statutes) and is subject to the principle *lex posterior derogat priori*. However, in this context, Community law was soon recognized as having a special status being a *sui generis* law though the courts have, for a while, followed an erratic course.

Learned writers, especially Ophüls,[20] Ipsen[1] and Wohlfart,[2] advocated a departure from the tradition arguing the Community law ought to have precedence over national law. The courts, on the other hand, had to deduce the rule of supremacy from the provisions of the Federal Constitution which, by Article 24(1), enables the Federal State to transfer sovereign powers to international institutions and, in Article 25, proclaims that the general rules of International Law form an integral part of the federal system. Ipsen[3] called Article 24 the *Integrationshebel* (lever of integration) and Vogel[4] argued that the legislature must contribute towards European integration. The judges must follow the legislature and give precedence to Community law inconsistent with internal law.[5] The prevailing juristic opinion favoured supremacy of Community law but courts were faced with arguments that Community law was 'unconstitutional' in so far as it contravenes 'fundamental rights'. Under a written constitution which guarantees 'fundamental rights' with little ingenuity any question can be raised to a constitutional issue.

The following are the landmarks on the road to the supremacy rule.

In *Re Tax on Malt Barley*[6] the Federal Constitutional Court (*Bundesverfassungsgericht*) clarified the position of the EEC Treaty Ratification Law and the Community agricultural regulations whose constitutionality was doubted by the *Finanzgericht* of Rheinland-Pfalz. It held:[7]

'Section one of the EEC Treaty Act is based upon the power contained in Article 24(1) of the Constitution, and is within the limits imposed on the transfer of sovereign rights to international authorities by Article 79(3) of the Constitution. A balanced system for the co-operation of the Community's Council, Commission and Parliament guarantees a control of power which is institutionally preserved as effective as the traditional separation of powers. It satisfies the most stringent demands of "the rule of law" . . .'

---

19   Triepel, H, *Völkerrecht und Landesrecht* (1899); *Rec, de Cours de l'Académie de la Haye,* 'Les rapports entre le droit interne et le droit international', 1923, Vol 1, pp 76 et seq.
20   Ophüls, C F, 'Zwischen Völkerrecht und staatlichem Recht, Grundfragen des europäischen Rechts', *Juristen-Jahrbuch,* Vol 4 (1963-64), pp 137-162.
 1   Ipsen, H P, 'Rapport du droit des Communautés Européennes avec le droitnational', *Le Droit et les Affaries* (1964), No 47.
 2   Wohlfart, E, 'Europäisches Recht, Von der Befugnis der Organe der europäischn Wirtschaftsgemeinschaft zur Rechtsetzung', *Jahrbuch für Internazionales Recht,* Vol 9, pp 12-32.
 3   Ipsen, op cit, p 26.
 4   Vogel, K, *Die Verfassungsentscheidung des Grundsetzes für eine internationale Zusammenarbeit* (1964), p 46.
 5   Fuss, E W, 'Rechtsschutz gagen deutsche Hoheitsakte zur Ausführung des Europäischen Gemeinschaftsrechts', *Neue Juristische Wocheinschrift* (1966), p 1782.
 6   Case III 77/63 [1964] CMLR 130.
 7   2 BvL 29/63: *Re Tax on Malt Barley* [1967] CMLR 302 at 311, 316.

Turning to the regulation issued under the EC Article 249 (ex Art 189), the Court declared:

'. . . Article 189 is of great importance in the framework of the whole Treaty. But it would be wrong to conclude from this that the whole Treaty would be purposeless if Article 189 and the regulations passed thereunder were not immediately binding in the Federal Republic. In the Court's opinion, the nullity of one provision does not in principle entail the validity of the whole act or law. The whole law would only be void in such a case if on its true construction, the remaining provisions had no significance on their own or if the unconstitutional provisions are part of a self-contained set of regulations which would have no sense of efficacy if one of their constituent parts is taken away.

These provisions apply to Treaty law too. The effect of their application to section one of the EEC Treaty Act is that, even if this provision were to be held unconstitutional in so far as it relates to Article 189 of the Treaty, the EEC Treaty Act would still not become totally invalid; the effectiveness of the remaining provisions in the German Federal Republic would not be disturbed . . .'

As a result, a substantial body of case law has confirmed the view that EC Article 249 (ex Art 189) and the Treaty are directly applicable in Germany.[8]

On the question of Community law being inconsistent with previous German Law the *Finanzgericht* of Münster held:[9]

'. . . the organs of the Community were given powers of legislation in matters pertaining to the Community and that legislation is binding on the Member States. If those powers are to mean anything Community legislation must have the effect, within its sphere of competence, of amending or repealing, by implication, national legislation which is repugnant to it . . .'

The Courts went further because in a number of cases[10] they held that Community law superseded subsequent German legislation.

On the specific question of direct application of the EEC Treaty (then EC Article 95(1) (now EC Art 90 but amended)) two cases should be specially noted. In the *Mölkerei* case[11] the Court held that the rate of compensatory tax imposed on an imported agricultural product from another state violated the non-discrimination principle. The Court arrived at this conclusion because '. . . in so far as the court finds that there is a contravention of that rule of Community law it must take account of the *precedence* of Community law. That is the only way in which the immediate effectiveness accorded to Article 95 [now Art 90] by the European Court[12] can be interpreted and a corresponding judicial protection be given to the individual subjects of the Member States of the Community . . .'. In *Re Imported Thai Sand Flower*[13] the *Finanzgericht* of Bremen held that imported products had to be classified for the purpose of customs duties according to the EEC regulations governing the common organization of the

---

8 See cases listed by Campbell, op cit, Vol 1, 1.83 and Supplement No 2, p 15.
9 In Case IVc 20-21/63: *Re Import of Pork* [1966] CMLR 491 at 498-499.
10 See cases listed by Campbell, op cit, Vol 1, 1.103, and Supplement No 2, p 16, Supp 1975, p 43.
11 VII 156/65: *Mölkerei-Zentrale Westfalen/Lippe GmbH v Hauptzollamt Paderborn* [1969] CMLR 300 at 312.
12 In Case 48/65: *Lütticke v Commission* [1966] ECR 19, [1966] CMLR 378.
13 [1971] CMLR 521 at 523.

market for cereals rather than German rules. The Court ruled that '. . . to the extent that the Member States have assigned legislative powers in levying tariff matters to the Community in order to ensure the proper operation of the common market for cereals, they no longer have the power to make legislative provisions in this field'. More recently the Federal Supreme Fiscal Court ruled that the increased excise duty rates based on annual total production of source brewery did not infringe what was then EC Article 95(1) (now EC Art 90 but amended) because the same treatment was applied to foreign and national breweries.[14]

However, in a case[15] involving the validity of export deposits said to be in violation of the German Constitution, the Administrative Court in Frankfurt am Main held that Community law enjoyed only a limited superiority over national law.

The Court reviewed a substantial body of juristic opinion representing inter alia the view that Community law can be scrutinized against the provisions of the Federal Constitution which the Federal legislature has no power to abrogate or restrict. The Court held that Article 12(3) of Regulation 120/67 of the EEC Council of 13 June 1967 and Article 9 of Regulation 473/67 of the EEC Commission of 21 August 1967, which require export deposits, constituted an infringement of the Federal Constitution because they infringed the 'freedom of development, economic freedom and the principle of proportionality' and were, therefore, unconstitutional. The Court considered that 'these regulations are not German statutes but legal provisions of the European Economic Community which constitute neither public international law nor national law of the Member States' and concluded that like statutes (*Gesetze*) operating in Germany they are subject to scrutiny against the fundamental principles of the Constitution. However it referred the matter for a preliminary ruling to the Community Court, which rejected its argument, holding that:[16]

'The validity of acts of the Community institutions may be assessed only by reference to Community law since national legal provisions . . . cannot have priority over the law created by the Treaty . . . unless its character as Community law is to be denied and the legal basis of the Community itself questioned. The validity of a Community act and its applicability to a Member State cannot therefore be affected by the claim that fundamental rights . . . or the principles of its constitution have been infringed . . .'

The Administrative Court, not satisfied with the ruling, submitted the case to the Federal Constitutional Court[17] which considered that the contested ruling on deposits did not offend the fundamental rights guaranteed by the German Constitution but affirmed its determination to scrutinize the secondary Community law in the light of the *Grundgesetz*. It also expressed the hope that complete integration of the Community and the development of a Community Parliament should bring about a Community Charter of Fundamental Rights. Until this has occurred conflicts between Community law and German Fundamental Rights are not excluded and in such conflicts the German law may claim priority.[18]

---

14 *Re Taxation of Imported Beer* [1988] 1 CMLR 482.
15 *Internationale Handelsgesellschaft mbH v Einfuhr- und Vorratsstelle für Getreide und Futtermittel* [1970] CMLR 294.
16 Case 11/70: *International Handelsgesellschaft v Einfuhr- und Vorratsstelle für Getreide und Futtermittel* [1970] ECR 1125, [1972] CMLR 255.
17 [1972] CMLR 177.
18 Note to European Parliament, PE 37.907, p 7. Also see [1974] CMLR 540.

The many references to the ECJ noted in the preceding pages demonstrate a liberal application of EC Article 234 (ex Art 177) by the German courts. However the cases to be especially noted are those involving constitutional issues. Another interesting feature of the German case law is the willingness to acknowledge the persuasive authority of the judgments of the European Court.

Recognizing the implications of the European Convention on Human Rights and the strength of the Community case law in this field the Federal Constitutional Court has dropped its reservations about the ECJ handling of German human rights cases. It also acknowledged the supremacy of Community law in this delicate area as well as the *erga omnes* effect of the ECJ's rulings under EC Article 234 (ex Art 177).[19] Thus the ghost of the *Handelsgesellschaft* case has been finally laid to rest. Thus the Supreme Federal Administrative Court,[20] citing several EC precedents, saw no contravention of the constitutional guarantee of property rights in the refusal of the National Agricultural Intervention Agency to buy agricultural produce under the CAP system. It also ruled that a retrospective national regulation issued by virtue of a Commission direction restricting subsidies in respect of home-produced wheat was not unconstitutional since the German Constitution does not prohibit legislation having a retrospective effect.

The same court held that a time-barred[1] action could not be revived after the ruling of the ECJ in favour of the appellant.[2] Thus an applicant, who waited until the ECJ had decided in his favour, was unable to obtain reimbursement of illegally levied phythosanitary inspection fees on apples imported from France. The national limitation statute was applied.

The *Verwaltungsgericht* in Frankfurt am Main,[3] interpreting the CAP rules regarding milk quotas, awarded damages to a former tenant farmer on the ground of maladministration. On surrendering his quota the applicant applied for milk cessation payments but these were refused. No landowner's permission was required and the fact that the reversioner could not claim the quota was irrelevant. Since the tenancy ended before the surrender of the quota and the authorities had not accepted the surrender in time the applicant was a victim of maladministration and, therefore, was entitled to compensation to the extent of the cessation payments which, otherwise, would have been due to him.

The Federal Supreme Court[4] expressly recognized the persuasive authority of a Community precedent[5] in so far as the existence of such a precedent absolved the Supreme Court from the obligation of making a reference under EC Article 234 (ex Art 177). Following precedents and the *acte clair* doctrine the Federal Supreme Court ordered the repayment of a state aid granted by a government agency and refused to make reference for a preliminary ruling.[6]

---

19 *Re the Application of Wünsche* [1987] 3 CMLR 225. Cf *Steinike* case p 339, note 11, supra and p 390, note 10, infra.

20 *Re Intervention Buying* [1978] 2 CMLR 644.

1 Case 71/74: *Nederlandse Vereniging voor Fruit en Groentenimporthandel v Commission* [1975] ECR 563, [1975] 2 CMLR 123.

2 In Case 33/76: *Rewe-Zentralfinanz RG and Rewe Zentral AG v Landswirtschaftskammer für das Saarland* [1976] ECR 1989, [1977] 1 CMLR 533.

3 *Re the Küchenhof Farm* [1990] 2 CMLR 289.

4 *Terrapin (Overseas) Ltd v Terranova Industrie CA Kapferer & Co* [1978] 3 CMLR 102. See also *Re Skimmed Milk Powder for Animal Feed* [1988] 1 CMLR 265 and *Re the 'KLINT' (Trade Marks)* [1988] 1 CMLR 340.

5 Case 119/75: *Terrapin (Overseas) Ltd v Terranova Industrie CA Kapferer & Co* [1976] ECR 1039, [1976] CMLR 482.

6 *Re Skimmed Milk Powder for Animal Feeds* [1988] 1 CMLR 265.

The Federal Supreme Court also considered 'reverse discrimination' in relation to the right of establishment of a lawyer to be quite in order since, in this context, inequality of treatment was neither unconstitutional nor prevented by Community law. Citing the *CILFIT* case it refused to make a reference to the ECJ on the basis of *acte clair*.[7] In another case,[8] concerning the position of an East German lawyer, it ruled that the matter was purely internal, ie his right to practise in West Germany was subject to German law rather than Community law since the German Democratic Republic was not part of the Community and, therefore, he could not claim the right of a Community citizen. Therefore the Community rules on establishment did not apply, nor did the Protocol on internal German trade since the latter was concerned solely with the movement of goods.

Ruling in the matter of direct elections to the European Parliament the Federal Constitutional[9] Court held that the European Parliament had functions similar to national parliaments. In European elections the principles of the German electoral law were applicable.

The same court, upholding, no doubt, the principle of the separation of functions between the Community institutions and the national institutions, ruled that the validity of Community legislation applicable in the Member States cannot be reviewed by German courts.[10]

Decisions of inferior courts are also reflective of the general mood of compliance. The Kammergericht[11] of Berlin confirmed that Community law prevails in the field of competition where a breach of the national law is justified by a decision of the Commission made by virtue of a binding Council regulation. In such a case the trader is protected even though he is not a direct addressee of the decision in question. If in such a case an interlocutory injunction is called for a reference to the ECJ is either unnecessary or inappropriate.

A Provincial Court of Appeal in Hamburg[12] granted an injunction to a German patent holder to enable him to restrain the importation of a product from an American licensee of an American patent. The product was imported into Belgium where no parallel patent existed and thence to Germany where, however, a parallel patent did exist. There was thus no exhaustion of the patent right and the German patent holder was able to protect his rights.

Also in the field of intellectural property the *Hanseatische Oberlandesgericht*,[13] dealing with a trade mark, simply followed the *Coffee HAG* saga[14] and applied a Community precedent,[15] declining to refer the matter to ECJ in accordance with the *acte clair* principle. Thus the German HAG was able to resist the importation into Germany of the Belgian HAG coffee since, following the break in the chain of ownership of the mark through post-war expropriation, the principle of exhaustion governed the issue. Reference to ECJ was refused.

The Court of Appeal in Hamburg,[16] banning the advertising of a Dutch product in Germany, acted in conformity with German law on misleading

---

7   *Re a German Advocate* [1990] 1 CMLR 254; Case 283/81: *CILFIT Sarl v Ministry of Health* [1982] ECR 3415, [1983] 1 CMLR 472.

8   *Re an East German Lawyer* [1990] 2 CMLR 185.

9   *Re the European Elections Act* [1980] 1 CMLR 497.

10   *Firma Steinike und Weinlig v Bundesamt für Ernährung und Forstwirtschaft* [1980] 2 CMLR 531.

11   *Verband Sozialer Wettbewerb eV v F Berlin KG* [1987] 3 CMLR 418.

12   *Re Patented Bandaging Material* [1988] 2 CMLR 359.

13   *Re HAG Coffee* [1989] 3 CMLR 154.

14   Case 192/73: *Van Zuylen Frères v HAG AG* [1974] ECR 731, [1974] 2 CMLR 127.

15   Case 19/84: *Pharmon BV v Hoechst AG* [1985] ECR 2281, [1985] 3 CMLR 775.

16   *Re Advertising of Dutch Slimming Tea* [1989] 3 CMLR 373.

advertising which it considered, in turn, conformed to the relevant Community directive. The ensuing restriction was held justified on health grounds by virtue of EC Article 30 (ex Art 36) since attributing health properties to foodstuffs was considered misleading. No reference to ECJ.

Similarly the Court of Appeal in Cologne[17] issued, on the ground of consumer protection, an injunction against the use of German language on labels which concealed the Dutch origin of the product. The injunction did not restrict imports but merely the type of get-up which was considered misleading. No reference to the ECJ was made, judging that no breach of EC Articles 28 and 30 (ex Arts 30 and 36) was involved.

One can also cite an example of non-conformity. We have noted earlier the problem of direct applicability of the VAT directive 77/388 which was considered by the *Bundesfinanzhof*[18] to be of no direct effect but orthodoxy seemed to have been restored when in the *Becker*[19] case the ECJ, on reference from a lower finance court, following well-established case law, ruled that direct effect of directives could arise in appropriate conditions. However the controversy flared up again. In a similar case[20] a lower finance court asked whether the same directive was applicable prior to the time relevant in the *Becker* case, to which the ECJ gave an affirmative answer. The referring court duly proceeded to confirm the claimant's exemption from the VAT[1] but the tax office appealed and the *Bundesfinanzhof*[2] annulled the decision of the finance court. In both cases the *Bundesfinanzhof* held the directive inapplicable on the ground that it had not been implemented by legislation. Elaborating its judgment in the latter case the *Bundesfinanzhof* questioned whether the referring court examined correctly the constitutional position, ie whether a sufficient degree of sovereignty was delegated by Article 24 of the Constitution to the Community in this respect. It then proceeded to interpret EC Article 249(3) (ex Art 189(3)) concluding that, whilst the ECJ had competence to interpret the Community law, it had no competence to interpret its effects in the national systems. Thus the *Bundesfinanzhof* deviated from the German line of authorities including the decision of the Federal Constitutional Court[3] relevant in this area. This baffling controversy came before the Federal Constitutional Court[4] which decreed that the *Bundesfinanzhof* was wrong in denying the direct effect of the directive since such a power is vested in the ECJ only. In doubt the national court had to ask the ECJ for a preliminary ruling. However, the rulings of the ECJ are binding upon the German courts and the national law implementing Community directives has to be interpreted in accordance with ECJ's interpretation of the directives. The principle of supremacy of Community law

17 *Re Labelling of Dutch Poultry* [1990] 2 CMLR 104.
18 Case VB 51/80, 16 July 1981 *Re VAT Directives* [1982] 1 CMLR 527.
19 Case 8/81: *Becker v Finanzamt Münster-Innenstadt* [1982] ECR 53, [1982] 1 CMLR 499 at paras 21-25; see also Case 255/81: *Grendel GmbH v Finanzamt für Körperschaften, Hamburg* [1982] ECR 2301, [1983] 1 CMLR 379.
20 Case 70/83: *Kloppenburg v Finanzamt Leer* [1984] ECR 1075, [1985] 1 CMLR 205.
 1 Niedersächsisches Finanzgericht, judgment of 11 May 1984, RIW 85, 234.
 2 Judgment of 25 April 1985, EuR 1985 p 191.
 3 *Re Lütticke*, BverfGE 31, 145; 9 June 1971; AWD 1971, pp 418-420; Europarecht, 1972, p 51.
 4 For the reaction of German writers see: Schmidt, G, 'Die Durchführung des Europäischen Gemeinschaftsrechts in der BRD und anderen EG-Mitglid-staaten' 4/84, *Integration*, pp 205 et seq; Scheuing, D H, 'Rechts-probleme bei der Durchsetzung des Gemeinschaftsrechts in der Bundesrepublik Deutschland', EuR 1985, pp 229 et seq; Tomuschat, C, 'Nein, und abermals nein!' Zum Urteil des BFH vom 25 April 1985', EuR 1985, pp 346 et seq.

applies here. Recognizing the binding force of Community precedents the *Bundesfinanzhof* paid a compliment to the ECJ for being in tune with the common European traditions and using the case law method in developing the Community law in conformity with practice in the common law and civil law systems.[5]

The saga ends with the statement of the *Bundesfinanzhof* that, irrespective of the rulings of the ECJ, the VAT directive applies notwithstanding the lack of its implementation in Germany.[6]

In a case involving the refusal of the Supreme Federal Court to make a reference to the ECJ the Federal Constitutional Court dismissed the complaint for a constitutional review. It recognized the status of the ECJ as a 'statutory court' under the German Constitution. Therefore an arbitrary refusal to make a reference under EC Article 234 (ex Art 177) would amount to a breach of Article 101(1) of the German Constitution. However the Federal Constitutional Court is not competent to review errors though a deliberate failure to make a reference would amount to an error and would expose the German Republic to an enforcement action at the hands of the European Commission. Since in the case under review there was no arbitrary refusal to proceed with the action, the refusal to refer was not arbitrary.[7] The litigation arose from the importation into Germany of feeding stuffs from the Netherlands which contained additives patented in Germany, though not in the Netherlands which was, apparently, deliberate. The court below found for the German patentee and the Supreme Court refused to do so and in the eyes of the Constitutional Court there was no breach of the Constitution.

In a rather intriguing case the Federal Constitutional Court declared German tobacco companies to have no *locus standi* in their attempt to obtain a judicial review of the constitutionality of the voting of the German Minister in the Council of Ministers.[8] Leading to an injunction to muzzle him they wished to influence his decision in the adoption of the common position on the draft directive on the labelling of cigarettes which carried a health warning. They argued, albeit unsuccessfully, that the directive, if adopted, would be in conflict with fundamental rights guaranteed by the German Constitution, ie the freedom of expression, commerce and property rights.

(6) ITALY

In Italy's practice the dualist doctrine, represented by Judge Anzilotti,[9] has left a deep imprint on the relationship between Community law and Italian law. The dualist tradition coupled with a rigid Constitution put the Italian judge in a position which is more difficult than that of the judge in any other country of the EC. The relevant provisions of the Constitution (Articles 10 and 11) state that the Italian legal order conforms to the generally recognized rules of international law and that Italy will agree, on equal terms with other states, to the limitation of sovereignty necessary to establish a lasting peace and justice among nations. This is hardly conducive to the courts being Community-minded when confronted with the compelling challenge to obey the Constitution.

---

5 In *Re Application of Frau Kloppenburg* [1988] 3 CMLR 1.
6 123/84: *Kloppenburg v Finanzamt Leer* [1989] 1 CMLR 873.
7 *Re Patented Feedingstuffs* [1989] 2 CMLR 902.
8 *Bayerische Staatsregirung v Bundesregierung* [1990] 1 CMLR 649.
9 Anzilotti, D, *Corso di Diritto Internazionale*, Vol 1 (3rd edn, 1928), pp 51 et seq.

Italy's problem is well reflected in the *Costa v ENEL* case which, parallel to its career in the Community, had a full run at home. The Constitutional Court, as we have seen, was called upon to decide whether or not the decree nationalizing the electricity industry and establishing a monopoly in the shape of the ENEL as well as certain provisions of the EEC Treaty were contrary to the Constitution. According to the Constitution, the Constitutional Court has the power to review legislation and declare 'illegitimate' Acts of Parliament and subordinate legislation which do not conform to the Constitution (Article 136(1)). Community law was brought into the contest as it was alleged that what were then EC Articles 37(2), 53, 93(2) and 102 (now Arts 31(2), 88(2) and 97), which were relevant to this case, infringed Article 11 of the Constitution. In terms of the conflict of legislations, the nationalization decree of 1962 was said to have repealed an earlier (Community) law.

The Court dealt with the problem in a classic dualist fashion: infringement of the Treaty would entail international responsibility of the state of Italy, but would not necessarily affect the validity of the law enacted in contravention of Treaty. In this way, the Court, in accordance with the dualist doctrine, accorded to the Treaty no higher rank than that of the ordinary legislation. The problem was reduced to a conflict between two 'internal' laws where the principle *lex posterior derogat priori* should apply. It appears that the position would have been different[10] if the Treaty had been promulgated as a *constitutional law* in accordance with Article 138 of the Constitution in which case the nationalization decree would have to be tested in the light of the Treaty. However, Article 11 of the Constitution enabled the State of Italy to surrender by treaty some of its sovereign powers to an international institution and this indeed occurred when the EEC Treaty was ratified. The Court recognized this, but concluded that it did not have to discuss the nature of the EEC or the consequences of the ratification of the Treaty, or, indeed, decide whether or not the decree infringed the Treaty.[11]

The decision of the Constitutional Court stimulated the jurists and the lively discussions which followed produced a trend in favour of the supremacy of Community law which was in conflict with Italian law. This has been deduced by Quadri[12] and others from Article 10 of the Constitution. They reasoned in their dualist fashion that, transformed into Italian law, a rule of international law is binding: *pacta recepta sunt servanda*.

The second support for the doctrine of supremacy is derived from Article 11 of the Constitution. The most plausible is the argument of the former judge of the Community Court, Catalano[13] who sees two effects of Article 11: a permissive effect which enables the Italian state to delegate its sovereignty and a dispositive effect which limits the powers of the constitutional organs of the state. He argues further that, although the measure which, in effect, limits sovereignty may take the form of an ordinary law, it differs nevertheless from ordinary law because it has a constitutional effect. If, therefore, a treaty limits the legislative power of the Italian law-making bodies within certain areas, the legislature, acting within the scope of its authority, can no longer exercise its power in these areas.

---

10   Neri, S, 'Le juge italien et le droit communautaire', *Le juge national et le droit communautaire* (1966), p 81.
11   24 February-7 March 1964, *Foro Italiano* (1964), I, 465.
12   Quadri, R, *Diritto Internazionale Pubblico* (1963), pp 59 et seq.
13   Catalano, N, 'La position du droit communautaire dans le droit des Etats membres', *Droit communautaire et droit national* (Bruges 1965), p 61 et seq.

In *Società Acciaierie San Michele v High Authority of the ECSC*[14] the Constitutional Court recognized the 'permissive' effect of Article 11. In this case the appellant, a steel company, contested the constitutionality of a fine imposed by the High Authority of the ECSC for failure to produce invoices relating to the consumption of electricity by the appellant. The Court, in dismissing the appeal held: '. . . in recognizing the Community order the state was endeavouring not so much to insert the same in its own system, but rather to make way within such system for the international co-operation which the state has as its aim . . . the organs of our internal jurisdiction are not qualified to criticize acts by organs of the ECSC because the latter are not subject to the sovereign power of the Member States of the Community, and cannot be found within the framework of any such state. Therefore, their acts can only be subject to a legislative qualification on the part of individual Member States albeit within the limits where there may exist an obligation not to refuse to acknowledge their effect . . .'

Recognizing the 'right of the individual to his jurisdictional protection' the Court acknowledged the power of the Community Court to exercise its jurisdiction and of the Italian subject to plead Community law where appropriate.

The principle of supremacy of Community law was thus accepted, but it fell to a body of jurists assembled in Rome in February 1966 to affirm supremacy not only in respect of previous but also in respect of subsequent Italian legislation. An important exception to the rule *lex posterior derogat priori* was conceded in favour of Community law. But, at the same time, the jurists affirmed the power of the Italian judiciary, especially the Constitutional Court, to scrutinize Community acts and determine whether or not they conform to the Italian Constitution.[15]

Developments in the post-*San Michele* period testify to general compliance with the principle. In *Salgoil SpA v Ministry for Foreign Trade*[16] the Rome Court of Appeal, following the ruling of the Community Court in the same case,[17] held that what was then Article 31 of the EEC Treaty (now repealed) gave rise to individual rights which can be enforced by national courts, though such rights have to be regarded as rights within the national system of law. The Italian attitude is conveniently summarized in *Frontini v Ministero delle Finanze*.[18] On a reference from the *Tribunale* of Turin the *Corte Costituzionale* confirmed the constitutionality of the Italian EEC Treaty Ratification Act and upheld the supremacy of Community regulations. By the same token the supremacy of the EEC Treaty itself was implicitly recognized. The *Corte Costituzionale* made a significant reservation in connection with human rights. It recognized that the European Court was the guarantor of the rights and interests of individuals in fields of law concerned with economic relations. But, if ever the legislative power of the EEC were to be used to violate the fundamental principles of the Italian Constitution or the inalienable rights of man, then the *Corte Costituzionale* would reserve the right to control the continuing compatibility of the EEC Treaty with such principles and rights.[19]

The question whether all Italian courts have to refuse to apply national law when inconsistent with Community law or whether this is a matter reserved

14 Case 98/65: [1967] CMLR 160, 4 CML Rev 81, [1965] *I Foro Italiano* 569.
15 French text of the Jurists' Resolution, Neri, S, 'Le droit communautaire et l'ordre constitutionnel italien' (1966), CDE 363 at 376, 377.
16 [1970] CMLR 314 at 335-336.
17 Case 13/68: [1968] ECR 453 at 462, 463, [1969] CMLR 181 at 196.
18 [1974] 2 CMLR 372. Cf the attitude of the German Constitutional Court discussed above.
19 Cf German Federal Constitutional Court in the *Handelsgesellschaft* case [1974] 2 CMLR 551-552, supra.

exclusively for the Constitutional Court (left open in the *Frontini* case) was considered in the *ICIC* case.[20] Whilst the Italian and the Community texts concerning the application of the import licensing system for cereals were identical there was the technical question whether the Italian text, being the *lex posterior* to the relevant Community regulation, was the governing text to be applied by the courts. There was also a problem of divergent interpretation as between the ECJ and Italian courts. The *Corte Costituzionale* declared the national text unconstitutional, saying that: 'There was no reason . . . to reproduce the regulations . . . in national laws. The adoption of the corresponding Italian law violates the principles of . . . the Treaty, whose constitutionality has been accepted . . .'. However on the practical point of direct application of the Community law the Court held that: 'the existing legal order does not attribute to the Italian judge any power to refuse the application of subsequent internal rules . . . on the ground of the general priority of Community law over national law . . . Therefore the judge is bound to raise the question of the constitutionality of legislative rules which reproduce directly applicable Community regulations and transform them into internal law . . .'

This attitude was in strong terms condemned unequivocally by the Community Court in the *Simmenthal (No 2)* case[1] where it held that:

'. . . every national court must . . . apply Community law in its entirety and protect rights which the latter confers on individuals and must accordingly set aside any provision of national law which may conflict with it, whether prior or subsequent to the Community rule.

Accordingly any provision of a national legal system . . . which might impair the effectiveness of Community law by withholding from the national court . . . the power to do everything necessary at the moment of its application to set aside national legislative provisions which might prevent Community rules from having full force and effect are incompatible with those requirements which are the very essence of Community law . . .'

In the *ICIC* case the *Corte Costituzionale* hinted at the need of legislation to solve the problem and this seemed to be the only way out of the impasse. However in the absence of such legislation the matter came once more before the courts[2] when an Italian importer claimed restitution of charges for sanitary inspection of poultry levied in accordance with Italian law but contrary to Community law. The question of supremacy was referred by the Milan court to the *Corte Costituzionale* which by then had the benefit of the ECJ's decision in the *Second Simmenthal* case. The Milan court wanted to know whether to follow the Community or the Italian case law. This was, in effect, an invitation to re-examination the latter. Since the relevant Italian statute was already abrogated the Constitutional Court held that there was no reason why this repeal should not have a retrospective effect in the light of the delegation of sovereignty to the Community by virtue of Article 11 of the Constitution. It also confirmed that the relevant Community regulations had the effect of a *lex posteriori* which,

20 *Industrie Chimiche della Italia v Minister of Foreign Trade*, Constitutional Court, 20, 30 October 1975, No 232 CC III, 1975, 319-327; (1976) RTDE 396-403. Quotations taken from Brinkhorst, L J, and Schermers, H G, *Judicial Remedies in the European Communities* (2nd edn, 1977), pp 217-220.
1 Case 106/77: *Amministrazione dell Finanze dello Stato v Simmenthal SpA* [1978] ECR 629, [1978] 3 CMLR 263, at paras 21 and 22.
2 Case *Società Comavicola v Ministry of Finance*, Corte Costituzionale, 26 October 1981, No 176, GU 4.11.1981, No 304.

in conformity with the Italian Constitution, abrogated the preceding Italian law. In this way supremacy of Community law was put into effect, albeit in a manner inconsistent with the doctrine established by the Community Court. Thus the problem lingers on unless judges of first instance are accorded the authority of disregarding national *subsequent* law in conflict with Community law.[3]

(7) DENMARK

In Denmark in an action for infringement of a trademark in which Community law was introduced at a late stage, the court decided to hear the arguments and give judgment on the points of Danish law first. Points of Community law were deferred with the possibility of reference to the Community Court.[4]

(8) IRELAND

Direct applicability and supremacy of Community law was recognized by the Irish Supreme Court[5] and the references for preliminary rulings, once accepted,[6] present no procedural problem.[7]

. During recent years the Irish judiciary became more involved. The High Court had several sex discrimination problems to resolve. Having to interpret a national implementing statute[8] it had to consider the relevance of work of 'less value' to 'work of equal value'; it referred the matter to the ECJ, it seems rather grudgingly. It thought in this context that Community law would be irrelevant unless there is ambiguity in the wording of the statute. The question was answered by the ECJ[9] which said, *in casu*, that a comparator's work was of less value than that of the complainant but stressed that EC Article 141 (ex Art 119) applied just the same. The High Court,[10] applying the ruling it had requested, stressed the supremacy of Community law where conflict with national law has to be resolved.

Still in the field of employment the High Court considered the complaint of discrimination against married women who, on their marriage, were forced to resign from the Irish Airlines. The Court found such employment condition equivalent to sex discrimination and ruled that Directive 76/207 was applicable, the procedures and remedies available under Irish law being in tune with the directive.[11] However, the Court dismissed the complaint of discrimination against men[12] when it ruled that marriage gratuity for female bank staff (but not for men) paid on the basis of seniority not on basis of sex did not infringe the Anti-Discrimination (Pay) Act 1974 but in fact reflected accurately EC Article 141 (ex Art 119) and the relevant ECJ case law.

Sex discrimination in the field of social security[13] was brought before the High Court after the ECJ found[14] that there was unlawful discrimination, contrary to

---

3 Menis, C, 'Traité CEE et Ordre Juridique Italien', 2-3 (1983) CDE, p 320 at 344.
4 *EMI Records Ltd v CBS Grammofon A/S* [1975] 1 CMLR 572.
5 *Pigs and Bacon Commission v McCarren* (Irish Supreme Court) [1981] 3 CMLR 408.
6 Case 812/79: *A-G v Burgoa* [1980] ECR 2787, [1981] 2 CMLR 193; Case 36, 71/80: *Irish Creamery Milk Supplies Association v Ireland* [1981] ECR 735, [1981] 2 CMLR 455.
7 *Campus Oil Ltd v Minister for Industry and Energy* (Irish Supreme Court) [1984] 1 CMLR 479.
8 *Murphy v Bord Telecom Eireann* [1987] 1 CMLR 559.
9 Case 157/86, supra [1988] ECR 673, [1988] 1 CMLR 879.
10 *Murphy*, supra [1988] 2 CMLR 753.
11 *Aer Lingus Teoranta v Labour Court* [1989] 1 CMLR 857.
12 *Governor and Company of the Bank of Ireland v Kavanagh* [1990] 1 CMLR 87.
13 *Cotter v Minister for Social Welfare* [1990] 2 CMLR 141.
14 Case 286/85: *McDermott and Cotter v Minister for Social Welfare* [1987] ECR 1453, [1987] 2 CMLR 607.

Directive 79/7, because married women received lesser unemployment benefit than men or single women. The complaint this time was brought on behalf of mothers of dependent children. According to Irish law such mothers were entitled to a special benefit only in the absence of a resident father. This was not a breach of Directive 79/7. A wife is automatically considered to be a dependent adult which enables the husband to claim a special benefit. A husband is not dependent unless he is physically or mentally handicapped. This is discrimination contrary to Directive 79/7. There is, however, no benefit where a husband is not financially dependent on his wife, but there is no remedy in such a case because, in the opinion of the Court, it would be unjust and inequitable for the taxpayer to carry the burden. The Court found Directive 79/7 directly effective in Ireland from the time it came into force, ie since December 1984, but a remedy became available only after the judgment of the ECJ in Case 286/85.[15]

Legislation implementing agricultural regulations concerning milk[16] quotas came before the High Court as a constitutional issue involving the guarantee of property rights. The Court ruled that such legislation was necessary in view of the obligations arising from the membership of the Community and, therefore, covered by the Constitution. However, it would have to be applied even if contrary to the Constitution. Ruling on merits the Court held that the transfer of milk quotas *pro rata* with the transfer of farmland did not constitute a retrospective abridgement of property rights and upheld the validity of the quota reduction arising from the sale of a part of the holding involved.

The High Court acknowledged the twin objective of Directive 75/268 on hill farming[17] as conservation and security of farm incomes, when considering the Irish implementing law. It ruled, however, that while a means test and inclusion of a spouse's off-farm income was permissible for the calculation of the subsidy under the directive of the provision regarding her inclusion of a spouse's off-farm income was contrary to the Irish Constitution. As it constituted a threat to the institution of marriage the implementing legislation had to be, to that extent, declared invalid.

The High Court made a reference for a preliminary ruling[18] on the proportionality of penalty of the forfeiture of an export deposit where the exporter was unable to carry out the contract because of the theft of the product while in England en route to its continental destination. The ECJ[19] considered that the theft of the consignment from the exporter's depot was not caused by *force majeure* and that, therefore, there was no lawful excuse for saving the deposit. Since exportation was the exporter's principal obligation the forfeiture of the whole security was not disproportionate.

Concerning the Spanish crews on board Irish fishing boats in an Irish-Spanish joint venture, the High Court enquired of the ECJ whether the requirement of the Irish law that the crews must be at least 75% Irish nationals was compatible with Community law.[20] The ECJ,[1] surprisingly, ruled that this was not a case of discrimination contrary to EC Article 12 (ex Art 6, ex Art 7). Following this

---

15 Supra.
16 *Lawlor v Minister for Agriculture* [1988] 3 CMLR 22.
17 *Greene v Minister for Agriculture* [1989] 3 CMLR 830.
18 *Anthony McNicholl Ltd v Ministry for Agriculture* [1987] 1 CMLR 847.
19 Case 296/86: *Anthony McNicholl Ltd v Ministry for Agriculture* [1988] ECR 1491, [1988] 2 CMLR 275.
20 *Pesca Valentia Ltd v Minister for Fisheries & Forestry* [1987] 1 CMLR 856.
 1 Case 223/86: *Pesca Valentia Ltd v Minister for Fisheries & Forestry* [1988] ECR 83, [1988] 1 CMLR 888.

ruling the Irish High Court[2] discharged the interlocutory injunction granted on reference to the ECJ. The ruling of the ECJ is surprising as it sharply contradicts the precedent laid down in Case 167/73[3] where it held that a mere threat of discrimination contained in the maritime law which required that captains, certain officers and a proportion of the crew of French merchant vessels had to be French nationals was incompatible with Community law.

A delicate, controversial issue impinging upon the Irish Constitution came before the Supreme Court when it had to rule on the freedom to receive services, *in casu*, abortion services lawful in the United Kingdom and available generally while the principle of the sanctity of life enshrined in the Irish Constitution prohibits such services.[4] The question was whether, in the light of Community law on the movement of persons and the freedom to provide and receive services, information about abortion services available in the United Kingdom can be legitimately prohibited. The Supreme Court answered the question in the affirmative. The matter came once more before the High Court and the Supreme Court[5] which made a reference to the ECJ refusing an appeal against the reference. Ireland is the last bastion against the rising tide of demands for abortion and the powerful industry which has been thriving on the relaxation of the moral code and on the theory which, for social convenience, denies humanity to the unborn. Unless there is a change in the Irish Constitution the moral dilemma will continue and with it the question how the economic freedom of the Common Market can outweigh the traditional approach to the sanctity of human life.

(9)   CONCLUSION

We can say, in the light of this limited review of practice in the members of the Community, that Community law is enforced as 'Community law', or the 'internal law' and that, in the case of conflict with municipal law, whether previous or subsequent, the Community rule prevails. This situation has not come about without difficulty or heart-searching as the dualist tradition entrenched in the national systems of law had to succumb to the challenge of the Community. In this process, the Community Court acted as the pacemaker and, as we have noted, some of its decisions not only settled matters for the given Member State, but also set a trend within the Community. The Community Court acted as an agent of cohesion and uniformity. However, without the stimulating contribution of jurists the message of Luxembourg would not have been as effective and successful as it was. Here the *doctrine* came into its own as a factor contributing to integration if not an auxiliary source of law. Its power and authority should not be underestimated.

---

2   *Pesca Valentia Ltd v Minister for Fisheries & Forestry* [1990] 1 CMLR 707.
3   Case 167/73: *Commission v France* [1974] ECR 359, [1974] 2 CMLR 216.
4   *A-G v Open Door Counselling Ltd* [1988] 2 CMLR 443.
5   *Society for the Protection of Unborn Children (Ireland) Ltd v Grogan* [1990] 1 CMLR 689. See Case C-159/90 [1991] ECR I-4685, [1991]3 CMLR 849. Protocol 17 annexed to the TEU and the Treaties establishing the EC provides that those Treaties and any Treaties or acts modifying or supplementing them shall not affect the application in Ireland of Art 40.3.3 of the Irish Constitution, which embodies the right to life and prohibits abortion.

Chapter 15

Community law in the United Kingdom[1]

A. Ratification of the Treaties

By the constitutional law of the United Kingdom treaty-making power is a prerogative power vested in the Sovereign and customarily exercised on her behalf either by her Ministers or by duly authorized plenipotentiaries. Ratification is the formal act whereby the Crown confirms and finally agrees to be bound by the terms of a Treaty. Under the terms of Article 2 of the First Treaty of Accession the High Contracting Parties undertook to ratify the Treaty in accordance with their respective constitutional requirements and to deposit their instruments of ratification with the Italian Government by 31 December 1972 at the latest. In the event three of the four applicant states complied with that obligation and the Treaty entered into force on 1 January 1973.[2] By the act of ratification the United Kingdom acceded to the three European Communities. Article 2 of the Act annexed to the First Treaty of Accession thus provides that 'from the date of accession, the provisions of the original Treaties [as defined in Article 1] and the acts adopted by the institutions of the Communities shall be binding on the new Member States and shall apply in those States under the conditions laid down in those Treaties and in this Act'.

In the United Kingdom, the Courts, and for that matter Parliament, have no rôle to play in the negotiation and ratification of treaties. In a case concerning a treaty of 1842 between the Crown and the Emperor of China Lord Coleridge CJ stated that the Queen had 'acted throughout the making of the treaty and in relation to each and every of its stipulations in her sovereign character, and by her own inherent authority; and, as in making the treaty, so in performing the treaty, she is beyond the control of municipal law and her acts are not to be examined in

---

1 For a more detailed treatment of this topic, see Collins, L, *European Community Law in the United Kingdom* (5th edn, 1999).
2 As a result of Norway's decision not to ratify, the Council used its authority under the Treaty of Accession, Art 2, para 3 to make the necessary adjustments; see Adaptation Decision of 1 January 1973 (OJ 1973, L2).

her own Courts'.[3] Thus when in 1971 a Mr Blackburn applied for declarations to the effect that by signing the Treaty of Rome Her Majesty's Government would be irrevocably surrendering part of the sovereignty of the Queen in Parliament and by doing so would be acting contrary to law his statements of claim were struck out as disclosing no reasonable causes of action. The Court of Appeal unanimously upheld Eveleigh J's dismissal of the plaintiff's appeal against the Master's order. The court applied the dicta of Lord Coleridge CJ cited above. In the words of Lord Denning: 'The treaty-making power of this country rests not in the courts, but in the Crown; that is, Her Majesty acting upon the advice of her Ministers. When her Ministers negotiate and sign a treaty, even a treaty of such paramount importance as this proposed one, they act on behalf of the country as a whole. They exercise the prerogative of the Crown. Their action in so doing cannot be challenged or questioned in these courts.'[4]

B.   Maastricht

The ratification of the Maastricht Treaty became possible by virtue of the European Communities (Amendment) Act 1993[5] which made 'provision consequential on the Treaty on European Union signed at Maastricht on 7th February 1992'. In section 1(1) the Act amends the European Communities Act 1972 (Section 1(1)) by providing that those parts of the TEU which relate to the European Communities are included among the 'Community Treaties' listed in that section of the Act except the Protocol on Social Policy.

For the purpose of section 6 of the European Parliamentary Elections Act 1978, Section 1(2) approves the treaties which increase the powers of the European Parliament as detailed in the TEU.

S.2 records the United Kingdom's decision not to move to the third stage of the Economic and Monetary Union leading to a single currency and single monetary policy without prior approval by Act of Parliament. However section 3 requires the Government and the Governor of the Bank of England to submit an annual report to Parliament in matters of economic and monetary union in implementation of EC Article 109 (ex Art 108). In accordance with EC Article 99(3) (ex Art 103(3)), the United Kingdom shall submit to the Commission relevant information relating to performance on economic growth, industrial investment, employment and balance of trade together with comparisons with those items of performance from other Member States (Section 4). Section 5 provides that, before submitting the information required by EC Article 99(3) (ex Art 103(3)) on the assessment of the medium-term economic and budgetary position in relation to public investment expenditure and to social, economic and environmental goals as detailed in EC Article 2, as amended, the Government shall seek the approval of the Parliament of its report in this respect which then will form the basis of its submissions to the Council and Commission as required by EC Articles 99 and 104 (ex Arts 103 and 104c).

Section 6, regarding the composition of the Committee of the Regions, provides that any persons proposed to serve as member or alternative member for the UK must be at the time of the proposal an elected member of a local authority.

3   *Rustomjee v R* (1876) 2 QBD 69 at 74.
4   *Blackburn v A-G* [1971] 1 WLR 1037 at 1040; Salmon and Stamp LJJ to the same effect at 1041.
5   1993 c.32.

Finally the coming into force of the Act was postponed until each House of Parliament had resolved the question of the adoption of the Protocol on Social Policy (Section 7) which occurred on 23 June 1993 when the House of Commons reached its resolution,[6] the House of Lords having done likewise on 23 June 1993.[7]

Ratification of the TEU was challenged by means of an application for judicial review[8] which revived the old controversy over the membership of the European Community.[9] The applicant contended that the United Kingdom could not lawfully ratify the Treaty on three grounds, ie that by ratifying the Protocol on Social Policy, which would increase the powers of the European Parliament, the Government would be in breach of section 6 of the 1978 Act; that the Government would alter the content of the Community law under the EEC Treaty without approval by an Act of Parliament; and that by ratifying Title V of the Treaty which established a common foreign and security policy the Government would be transferring part of the royal prerogative to Community institutions without statutory authority. All three objections were easily disposed of.

The Court (per Lloyd LJ) held that:

(1) Ratification of the Protocol on Social Policy would not increase the powers of the EP since the protocols were ancillary or incidental or supplementary to the Treaty and, therefore, ratification of the Treaty means ratification of the whole Treaty.
(2) By ratifying the Protocol on Social Policy the government would not be altering domestic law since the Protocol was not a 'treaty' for the purpose of section 2(1) of the 1993 Act. Moreover, if Parliament had intended to curtail the Crown's treaty-making power it would have done so *expressis verbis*, not by implication. There is not sufficient ground to hold that it had.
(3) With regard to Title V of the TEU, which the applicant claimed to be a transfer of the Crown's prerogative without parliamentary authority, there was a simple answer since the matters comprised therein were not justifiable in the English courts and therefore the applicant's concern was without foundation. Within the term of the Treaty matters of foreign policy, security and ultimately, defence remained subject to 'inter-governmental conference' rather than 'institutional decision' of the Union. Therefore the Crown's prerogative was not affected. In other words Title V did not entail an abandonment or transfer of prerogative powers but an exercise of those powers under control of HM Government.

C. Incorporation of the Treaties into the law of the United Kingdom

Although, at least since the time of Blackstone, the customary rules of international law have been regarded as part and parcel of the common law and directly enforceable by English judges, the United Kingdom adopts a distinctly

---

6   229 HC Official Report (6th series) col 627.
7   548 HL Official Report (5th series) col 797.
8   *R v Secretary of State for Foreign and Commonwealth Affairs, ex p Rees-Mogg* [1994] 1 All ER 457, QB.
9   *Blackburn v A-G* [1971] 2 All ER 1380, [1971] 1 WLR 1037, CA; see also *Maclaine Watson v Department of Trade and Industry* [1984] 3 All ER 523, CA, sub nom *J H Rayner v Department of Trade and Industry* [1990] 2 AC 418, [1989] 3 WLR 969, HL.

dualist approach to treaties. A treaty to which the United Kingdom is a party is, as we have seen, the result of an exercise of the prerogative and as such is not self-executing in the sense that the provisions of such a treaty do not automatically have the force of law in the United Kingdom. The intervention of Parliament is necessary in order to enable the provisions of such a treaty to be enforced in British courts. The classic statement of this doctrine is contained in an opinion of the Judicial Committee of the Privy Council in 1937:

'It will be essential to keep in mind the distinction between (1) the formation, and (2) the performance, of the obligations constituted by a treaty, using that word as comprising any agreement between two or more sovereign states. Within the British Empire there is a well established rule that the making of a treaty is an executive act, while the performance of its obligations, if they entail alternation of the existing domestic law, requires legislative action. Unlike some other countries, the stipulations of a treaty duly ratified do not within the Empire, by virtue of the treaty alone, have the force of law. If the national executive, the government of the day, decide to incur the obligations of a treaty which involve alternation of law they have to run the risk of obtaining the assent of Parliament to the necessary statute or statutes. To make themselves as secure as possible they will often in such cases before final ratification seek to obtain from Parliament an expression of approval. But it has never been suggested, and is not the law, that such an expression of approval operates as law, or that in law it precludes the assenting Parliament, or any subsequent Parliament, from refusing to give its sanction to any legislative proposals that may subsequently be brought before it. Parliament, no doubt ... has a constitutional control over the executive: but it cannot be disputed that the creation of the obligations undertaken in treaties and the assent to their form and quality are the function of the executive alone. Once they are created, while they bind the state as against the other contracting parties, Parliament may refuse to perform them and so leave the state in default. In a unitary state whose legislature possesses unlimited powers the problem is simple. Parliament will either fulfil or not treaty obligations imposed upon the state by its executive. The nature of the obligations does not affect the complete authority of the legislature to make them law if it so chooses.'[10]

This doctrine applies equally to the Community Treaties so that the mere accession of the United Kingdom to those Treaties did not give them the force of law within the United Kingdom. Legislation was necessary to achieve that result and in the absence of such legislation, as the Court of Appeal has pointed out, the Community Treaties would fall outside the cognizance of British Courts.[11] Thus one of the aims of the European Communities Act 1972 is to give the force of law to those provisions of the Treaties which are intended to take direct effect within the Member States. Section 2(1) of the Act provides that:

---

10   *A-G for Canada v A-G of Ontario* [1937] AC 326 at 347, 348, per Lord Atkin. A similar statement was made in *Legal and Constitutional Implications of United Kingdom Membership of the European Communities* (1967) (Cmnd 3301), at para 22. Section 6 of the European Parliamentary Elections Act 1978 has introduced a constitutional innovation in that British ratification of any treaty which increases the powers of the European Parliament is subject to the prior approval of the United Kingdom Parliament. For an instance of recourse to that provision see s 3(4) of the European Communities (Amendment) Act 1986.

11   *McWhirter v A-G* [1972] CMLR 882 at 886, per Lord Denning MR and at 887, per Phillimore LJ.

'All such rights, powers, liabilities, obligations and restrictions from time to time created or arising by or under the Treaties, and all such remedies and procedures from time to time provided for by or under the Treaties, as in accordance with the Treaties are without further enactment to be given legal effect or used in the United Kingdom shall be recognized and available in law, and be enforced, allowed and followed accordingly; and the expression "enforceable Community right" and similar expressions shall be read as referring to one to which this sub-section applies.'

Therefore, what the Act terms 'enforceable Community rights' are to be given direct effect in the United Kingdom. This provision is strengthened by section 3(2) which provides inter alia that United Kingdom courts shall take judicial notice of Community Treaties, which term is defined by section 1.

D. Implementation of Community secondary legislation in the United Kingdom

It has already been pointed out in earlier chapters that Community secondary legislation falls into two categories: that which is and that which is not directly applicable in the Member States. As far as the former is concerned, viz, ECSC decisions and EC and Euratom regulations, whilst within the Community legal system they will be binding on the United Kingdom as soon as they are made, they need statutory authority to give them the force of law within the United Kingdom, just as in the case of the provisions of the Treaties themselves. Section 2(1) of the European Communities Act 1972 applies to them also and without further enactment they are to be given legal effect within our domestic legal systems. Thus the entire body of ECSC decisions and EEC and Euratom regulations in force at the commencement of British membership automatically became part of the law of the United Kingdom on 1 January 1973. Similarly all such decisions and regulations made after the commencement of British membership will also automatically become part of the law of the United Kingdom as soon as they are made. In addition those provisions of Community secondary legislation which have direct effect in the legal systems of the Member States constitute 'enforceable Community rights' under section 2(1) of the European Communities Act 1972 and as such are enforceable in the courts of the United Kingdom.

An important issue in connection with directly applicable Community secondary legislation made after British entry is the rôle of the United Kingdom Parliament. Whilst the actual making of such secondary legislation will be in the hands of the Council or Commission and outside the direct control of Parliament, in the absence of effective democratic control within the Communities themselves it is vital that Parliament should have an opportunity to consider such legislation. By the time, say, an EC regulation has been made it will be too late for comment for such a regulation will already be part of United Kingdom law. In order to enable Parliament to examine and comment upon proposed Community legislation and thus express views for the guidance of the British representatives on the Council of the Communities, each House has established a select committee to scrutinize Community secondary legislation: the House of Commons Committee on European Secondary Legislation and the House of Commons Committee on the European Communities. Both Committees are concerned with draft Community legislation which has been proposed by the Commission to the Council, but there are differences in approach and in terms of reference. The reports of the Commons Committee express opinions whether the proposed legislation raises questions of legal or political importance and how it may affect matters of principle or policy. The Lords Committee, which is organized into specialist sub-committees, not only reports on matters of policy and principle but also on the merits of the proposed legislation. The Committees are able to confer together. Each is assisted by a legal advisor. Debates are held in each House on the recommendation of its Committee. The procedure is a useful one but there are practical difficulties in timing and of a congested parliamentary timetable.[12]

In the case of Community secondary legislation which is not directly applicable, such as ECSC recommendations and EC and Euratom directives, but leaves the choice of the means of their implementation to the individual Member States,[13] there are two possible courses of action. Such Community legislation could be implemented in the United Kingdom either by statute or by subordinate legislation. Whilst the European Communities Act does not expressly rule out the use of statutes for such purposes its emphasis is on the use of delegated legislation. Thus section 2(2) of the Act confers extensive authority upon Her Majesty in Council and upon Ministers and Government Departments to make subordinate legislation:

'(a) for the purpose of implementing any Community obligation of the United Kingdom, or enabling any such obligation to be implemented, or of enabling any rights enjoyed or to be enjoyed by the United Kingdom under or by virtue of the Treaties to be exercised; or

(b) for the purpose of dealing with matters arising out of or related to any such obligation or rights or the coming into force, or the operation from time to time, of sub-section (1) above.'

The wide extent of these delegated law-making powers is confirmed by section 2(3) which lays down that a provision made under sub-section (2) includes 'any such provision (of any such extent) as might be made by Act of Parliament'. In other words the subordinate legislation made under section 2(2) to implement Community obligations can by used to repeal or amend any past or future Act of Parliament the provisions of which are incompatible with Community law.

But these powers of making subordinate legislation are not entirely without limitation and are subject to Schedule 2 to the Act. That Schedule provides that the powers conferred by section 2(2) shall not include the power:

'(a) to make any provision imposing or increasing taxation; or

(b) to make any provision taking effect from a date earlier than that of the making of the instrument containing the provision; or

(c) to confer any power to legislate by means of orders, rules, regulations or other subordinate instrument, other than rules of procedure for any court or tribunal; or

---

12 See Erskine May's *Parliamentary Practice*. For an account of the work of the Scrutiny Committees, see Bates, T St JN, 'The Scrutiny of European Secondary Legislation at Westminster' (1975-76) 1 European Law Rev 195 and Fraser, Lord, 'Scrutiny of Community legislation in the UK Parliament', in Bates, St J, (ed) *In Memoriam J D B Mitchell* (1983) at 29. The reports of the House of Lords Committee are particularly valuable sources of information and comment on Community affairs.

13 See Ch 5, supra.

(*d*) to create any new criminal offence punishable with imprisonment for more than two years or punishable on summary conviction with imprisonment for more than three months or with a fine of more than level 5 on the standard scale (if not calculated on a daily basis) or with a fine of more than £100 a day.'

These limitations are also given a measure of entrenchment since section 2(4) states that they shall remain in force unless and until amended or repealed by a subsequent statute. As far as the form and procedure of such subordinate legislation is concerned Schedule 2 states that the power to make regulations shall be exercisable by statutory instrument and that wherever the power is exercised without a draft having been approved by resolution of each House of Parliament, then it shall be subject to annulment in pursuance of a resolution of either House.[14] This gives the Government a choice as to the procedure to be adopted and that choice will no doubt be exercised in the light of the subject matter of the legislation.[15]

Thus under the provisions of section 2 of the Act ample provision appears to have been made for the implementation of Community secondary legislation in the United Kingdom subject to the important constitutional safeguards in Schedule 2. Community law is having an immediate and a continuing impact on the law of the United Kingdom and whilst that impact should not be underestimated it also should not be exaggerated. In the words of the White Paper reporting on the negotiations 'the English and Scottish legal systems will remain intact. Certain provisions of the treaties and instruments made under them, concerned with economic, commercial and closely related matters, will be included in our law. The common law will remain the basis of our legal system and our courts will continue to operate as they do at present . . . All the essential features of our law will remain, including the safeguards for individual freedom such as trial by jury and habeas corpus and the principle that a man is innocent until proved guilty as well as the law of contract and tort (and its Scottish equivalent) the law of landlord and tenant, family law, nationality law[16] and land law'.[17]

E. Enforcement through the Community Court

The enforcement of Community law through the agency of the European Court is achieved by direct and indirect means. The direct means takes the form of actions against Member States who fail to fulfil their obligations under the Treaties.[18] By mean of such actions the Court can directly influence the enforcement of Community law in the national legal orders of the Member States. Thus if the United Kingdom either legislates contrary to Community law or fails to legislate as required by Community law that would amount to a failure to fulfil Treaty obligations and the Commission or another Member State would be able to bring proceedings against

---

14 Statutory Instruments made to implement Community obligations are conveniently reproduced in Sweet & Maxwell's *Encyclopedia of European Community Law* Secondary Legislation.
15 Sch 2, para 2.
16 But on the question of immigration, see Vaughan, D (ed), *Law of the European Communities*, part 15.
17 *The United Kingdom and the European Communities* (Cmnd 4715), para 31.
18 See Ch 12, *supra*.

the United Kingdom in the European Court.[19] If judgment were given against the United Kingdom there would arise an obligation to take steps necessary to comply with the judgment.[20] Actions have been brought against the United Kingdom both by the Commission under the terms of EC Article 226 (ex Art 169) and by a fellow Member State under the terms of EC Article 227 (ex Art 170). Two cases decided in 1979 will serve as illustrations.

The first case concerned potatoes,[1] which are included among the agricultural products which come with the Common Agricultural Policy of the Community. The United Kingdom operated a system for regulating the market in potatoes which included controls on their import and export. In December 1977 the United Kingdom Government imposed a ban on the import of potatoes until further notice. In the view of the Commission such a ban was contrary to the United Kingdom's obligations under the EC Treaty. An EC Article 226 (ex Art 169) action resulted in which the Court gave judgment against the United Kingdom. It held that the import ban was contrary to the Community's freedom of movement of goods between the Member States.[2] The second case concerned measures to conserve fisheries.[3] The Community has authority over all questions relating to the protection of fishing grounds and the conservation of the resources of the sea. In pursuance of that authority the Community resolved that the Member States should not take any unilateral conservation measures without first consulting and seeking the approval of the Commission. In April 1977 the United Kingdom Government, without referring to the Commission, made an order prohibiting the use in British waters of certain small mesh nets. The master of a French trawler was subsequently fined for infringing that order. France (supported by the Commission) complained that this United Kingdom order did not comply with Community policy. In the resulting EC Article 227 (ex Art 170) action the Court gave judgment against the United Kingdom because of the failure to consult and seek the approval of the Commission.

The European Court also influences the enforcement of Community law indirectly by means of its competence to give preliminary rulings on points of Community law at the request of national courts and tribunals. The provision of the Treaties which give the rights, and in some cases impose the duty, to request preliminary rulings became part of the laws of the United Kingdom by virtue of section 2(1) of the European Communities Act 1972 which specifically refers to 'remedies and procedures' provided for, by or under the Treaties. This right/duty applies not only to the ordinary courts, from lay magistrates up to the House of Lords, but also to tribunals. Thus, all courts and tribunals in the United Kingdom have been able to request preliminary rulings in appropriate cases since 1 January 1973 when the European Communities Act came into force. The unfamiliarity of such a procedure in the United Kingdom prompted the drawing up of special rules of procedure for some, but not all, courts. As far as the English courts are cocnerned[4] rules have been made for the High Court and

---

19   Eg under the terms of EC Arts 226, 227 (ex Arts 169, 170).
20   Eg by virtue of EC Art 228 (ex Art 171).
1   Case 231/78: *Commission v United Kingdom* [1979] ECR 1447, [1979] 2 CMLR 427.
2   In particular EC Article 28 (ex Art 30) which prohibits quantitative restrictions on imports between Member States. For further examples of such actions against the United Kingdom see Cases 128/78: [1979] ECR 419, [1979] 2 CMLR 45; 170/78: [1980] ECR 417, [1980] 1 CMLR 716 and 32/79: [1980] ECR 2403. Also see Collins, L, op cit.
3   Case 141/78: *France v United Kingdom* [1979] ECR 2923, [1980] 1 CMLR 6.
4   For Scottish Courts, see SI 1972 No 1981, and SI 1973 Nos 450 and 543. For Northern Irish Courts, see SR & O 1972, Nos 317, 354 and 380.

Court of Appeal, Civil Division;[5] the Court of Appeal, Criminal Division;[6] the County Court;[7] and the Crown Court.[8] No changes have been made to the Judicial Standing Orders of the House of Lords and it is believed that when requesting preliminary rulings the House makes use of the procedure adopted by the Supreme Court.[9] The rules of magistrates' courts have not been changed, but the attention of magistrates' clerks has been drawn to the possibility of seeking a preliminary ruling by a Home Office Circular.[10] In connection with tribunals, consultation with the responsible government departments led to the conclusion that adequate procedural machinery exists to deal with references to the European Court.[11]

The Rules which have been made for English courts all follow a particular pattern. Orders referring questions to the European Court may be made before, or at any stage during, the trial or hearing of a cause or matter. Such Orders shall be made by the Court requesting the preliminary ruling and shall normally have the effect of staying proceedings pending the ruling. In cases before the English High Court and Court of Appeal the transmission of an Order requesting a preliminary ruling to the Registrar of the European Court is undertaken by the Senior Master of the Supreme Court (Queen's Bench Division). Where such an Order is open to appeal the Senior Master must not forward it to the European Court until the time for appealing has expired, or, if an appeal is brought, until the appeal has been settled. It has been argued by some commentators that both the use of the Senior Master as an intermediary between English courts and tribunals and the European Court, and making Orders requesting a preliminary ruling subject to appeal are incompatible with Community law.[12] As far as the transmission of the request for a preliminary ruling is concerned it is the practice of continental courts to deal directly with the European Court, which does, for this purpose, form an integral part of the legal systems of the Member States. On the question of a request for a preliminary ruling being subject to appeal it has already been pointed out that continental practice is not uniform[13] nor has the question been decided conclusively by the European Court.[14] The English rules on appeals may certainly be questioned to the extent that they have the effect of interposing an obstacle between the English courts and the European Court. The use of the

---

5 Rules for the Supreme Court (Amendment No 3) 1972 (SI 1972 No 1898 L27) which added Order 114 to the Rules of the Supreme Court. See now the Civil Procedure Rules, Sch 1, sc 114.
6 Criminal Appeal (References to the European Court) Rules 1972 (SI 1972 No 1786 (L25)).
7 The County Court (Amendment No 2) Rules 1973 (SI 1973 No 847 (L13)). See now the Civil Procedure Rules (above).
8 Crown Court (References to the European Court) Rules 1972 (SI 1972 No 1787 (L26)). See now the Crown Court Rules (SI 1982 No 1109), rule 29.
9 This statement is based on information kindly supplied by the Judicial Office of the House of Lords.
10 Circular No 149/1973 (CS 18/1973), dated 4 September 1973.
11 This statement is based on information kindly supplied by the Council on Tribunals and the Lord Chancellor's Office.
12 See Jacobs, F G, and Durand, A, *References to the European Court: Practice and Procedure* (1975), at pp 164, 165, 171, 172 and Advocate-General Warner in Case 166/73: *Rheinmühlen-Düsseldorf v Einfuhr-und Vorretstelle für Getreide und Futtermittel* [1974] ECR 33 at 47. For a contrary opinion, see Collins, L, op cit. In order to avoid the delays caused by deferring sending the request until the time for appealing has expired, it is common practice to include in the order making the reference a provision that it be forwarded to the European Court forthwith.
13 See Ch 13, supra.
14 See the case and literature cited in note 12, supra.

Senior Master and the possibility of appeal may also cause unjustifiable delays in the reference procedure.[15]

It has already been pointed out that while courts and tribunals which are not of last instance have a discretion whether to seek a preliminary ruling, courts and tribunals of final instance are under an obligation to do so. Some doubts exist in the United Kingdom concerning which courts and tribunals are those 'against whose decisions there is no judicial remedy under national law'.[16] The position of the House of Lords is clear; subject to the relevant Treaty provisions it will be obliged to request preliminary rulings. The House of Lords has indeed recognized its obligations to refer issues concerning the applicability and interpretation of Community law to the European Court.[17] But the position of the Court of Appeal is not so clear. The Court of Appeal may be a court of final instance in two situations. The Court of Appeal may be declared by statute to be the final court of appeal.[18] If a question of the validity or interpretation of Community law came before the Court of Appeal in such a situation then it would clearly be obliged to seek a preliminary ruling from the Community Court. But rather more problematic may be the commoner situation in which despite the possibility of an appeal to the House of Lords the Court of Appeal may be, and indeed usually is, the final court of appeal. Since appeal to the House of Lords is only by leave that leave may either not be sought or may be sought and refused. In such situations it is suggested that the Court of Appeal should be obliged to seek a preliminary ruling in an appropriate case since, although it is not the supreme appellate court, there is no judicial remedy against its decisions in those situations.[19] A similar problem arises in connection with tribunals. Is a tribunal from whose decision there is no appeal but which is open to review by certiorari obliged to seek a preliminary ruling? Certiorari is a form of judicial remedy under national law. But, it is a discretionary and highly technical remedy and in most cases the decision of such a tribunal would be final. It is therefore suggested that, as in the case of the Court of Appeal, such a tribunal should regard itself as under the obligation to request a preliminary ruling.[20] Thus in terms of the dispute in continental legal circles between the 'concrete' and 'abstract' theories of the last paragraph of EC Article 234 (ex Art 177) the 'concrete' theory is thought to be preferable.[1]

The initial reaction of English courts and tribunals to this question did not, however, reflect this attitude. In the Court of Appeal no general view has yet

---

15 These factors may have contributed to the inordinate delay in transmitting to the European Court the first United Kingdom request for a preliminary ruling in *Van Duyn v Home Office*. The Order requesting a preliminary ruling was dated 1 March 1974 (see [1974] 1 WLR at 1118) and it was lodged at the European Court on 13 June 1974 (see [1975] 1 CMLR at 14).

16 This expression replaces 'from whose decisions there is no possibility of appeal under internal law' which was used in the earlier unofficial Foreign Office translation. The new translation certainly seems to be closer to the French 'dont les decisions ne sont pas susceptibles d'un recours juridictionnel de droit interne'.

17 See *R v Henn and Darby* [1979] 2 CMLR 495; *Garland v British Rail Engineering* [1981] 2 CMLR 542.

18 Eg County Courts Act 1984, s 82.

19 See *Chiron v Murex Corpn* [1995] All ER (EC) 88 and the comment in *Practitioners' Handbook of EC Law*, para 7.6.2.1

20 Cf Jacobs, F G, and Durand, A, op cit at p 163. Also see Freeman, Elizabeth, 'References to the Court of Justice under Article 177' (1975) 28 Current Legal Problems 176 at 184-186.

1   See Donner, A M, 'Les rapports entre le competence de la Cour de Justice des Communautés Européennes et les tribunaux internes', 115 *Recueil des Cours de la Haye* (1965) at pp 42 et seq.

emerged. In *Bulmer v Bollinger* Lord Denning expressed the opinion that 'short of the House of Lords no other English Court is bound to refer a question to the European Court at Luxembourg'.[2] But in the same case Stamp and Stephenson LJJ refused to commit themselves on that point in the absence of further argument.[3] More recently, conflicting views have been expressed by differently constituted Courts of Appeal. In one case support for a variant of the 'concrete' theory was given in terms that the ultimate court of appeal in England is either the Court of Appeal (if leave to appeal to the House of Lords is unobtainable) or the House of Lords.[4] In another case it was unanimously declared that a court or tribunal below the House of Lords can only be subject to the obligation to seek a preliminary ruling 'where there is no *possibility* of further appeal from it'.[5] What appears to be common ground between these two views is that in cases where leave to appeal to the House of Lords is not granted the Court of Appeal thereby becomes obliged to seek a ruling. But such a suggestion is clearly fraught with procedural difficulties. Once the Court of Appeal has given judgment in a case it is functus officio and if leave to appeal to the House of Lords is not then granted the matter cannot be revived before the Court of Appeal.[6] Nor does this cope with the more typical situation in which leave to appeal from the Court of Appeal is not sought. Similar uncertainty exists regarding tribunals. Lord Denning's view has been echoed in a decision of the National Insurance Commissioner (now the Social Security Commissioner). He held that since his decision may be set aside by certiorari, he did not 'constitute a tribunal against whose decision there is no judicial remedy under national law, even though an order of certiorari cannot be made without the leave of the High Court'.[7] As far as the Court of Appeal is concerned, a practical solution could take the form of that Court being obliged to give leave to appeal to the House of Lords in a case in which a point of Community law is in issue but the Court of Appeal does not itself seek a preliminary ruling.[8] A simpler solution, and one fully in keeping with the spirit and objectives of EC Article 234 (ex Art 177), would be for the obligation to refer to arise with regard to courts or tribunals at the point from which a further judicial remedy becomes discretionary.

---

2 [1974] Ch 401 at 420.
3 Ibid, at pp 427, 430.
4 *Hagen v Fratelli D and G Moretti SNC* [1980] 3 CMLR 253.
5 *R v Pharmaceutical Society of Great Britain, ex p Association of Pharmaceutical Importers* [1987] 3 CMLR 951 at 969, emphasis added.
6 Cf *Magnavision NVSA v General Optical Council* [1987] 1 CMLR 887. Strictly speaking, an English court is functus officio when its order is perfected. Between the delivery of the reasons supporting its judgment and the perfection of the order, the court retains jurisdiction to alter its decision. However, for the purposes of a reference to the ECJ, a court is functus once it has delivered the reasons supporting the judgment because, at that stage (and not at the later stage of the perfection of the order), the court has reached a conclusion on the issue of Community law before it without (ex hypothesi) finding it necessary to make a reference to the ECJ. The court's state of mind could, of course, be disturbed by an intervening factor (such as a decision of another court or of the ECJ itself) occurring before the perfection of the order and after the delivery of the reasons supporting the judgment.
7 *Re a Holiday in Italy* [1975] 1 CMLR 184 at 188.
8 See Jacobs, F, 'Which courts and tribunals are bound to refer to the European Court?' (1977) 2 EL Rev 119.

F.   The question of supremacy[9]

It has been repeatedly laid down by the Community Court and is in general accepted by the original six Member States that the Community Treaties have established a new and distinct system of law, the rules of which have to prevail over the rules of the municipal laws of the Member States. Thus from the commencement and for the duration of British membership the municipal law of the United Kingdom must yield in cases of conflict to the superior Community law. To the generations of British lawyers schooled in the Diceyan orthodoxy such a prospect is no doubt unthinkable if not impossible; but nevertheless it is one of the obligations of membership. The implications were clearly summarized in the 1967 White Paper:

> 'The Community law having direct internal effect is designed to take precedence over the domestic law of the Member States. From this it follows that the legislation of the Parliament of the United Kingdom giving effect to that law would have to do so in such a way as to override existing national law so far as it is inconsistent with it. This result need not be left to implication, and it would be open to Parliament to enact from time to time any necessary consequential amendments or repeals. It would also follow that within the fields occupied by the Community law Parliament would have to refrain from passing fresh legislation inconsistent with that law as for the time being in force. This would not however involve any constitutional innovation. Many of our treaty obligations already impose such restraints – for example, the Charter of the United Nations, the European Convention on Human Rights and GATT.'[10]

As far as the body of Community law in force on the eve of British membership was concerned no difficulty was experienced. That law, as we have seen, was given legal force in the United Kingdom by section 2(1) of the European Communities Act 1972 and will have precedence over prior British law by the simple operation of the rule *lex posterior derogat priori*.[11] Certain difficulties may arise, however, in avoiding and resolving conflicts between Community law and statutes passed after the commencement of United Kingdom membership. The 1967 White Paper stated that Parliament will have to refrain from passing fresh legislation inconsistent with Community law and remarked

---

9   The literature on this topic from the British standpoint includes the following: Martin, A, 'The Accession of the United Kingdom to the European Communities: Jurisdictional Problems' (1968-69) 6 CML Rev 7; Hunnings, N M, 'Constitutional Implications of joining the Common Market', ibid, 50; de Smith, S A, 'The Constitution and the Common Market: a tentative appraisal' (1971) 34 MLR 597; Wade, H W R, 'Sovereignty and the European Communities' (1972) 88 LQR 1; Mitchell, J D B, et al, 'Constitutional aspects of the Treaty and Legislation relating to British membership' (1972) 9 CMLR Rev 134; Trinidade, F A, 'Parliamentary Sovereignty and the Primacy of European Community Law' (1972) 35 MLR 375; Winterton, G, 'The British Grundnorm: Parliamentary Supremacy Re-examined' (1976) 92 LQR 591; Bridge, J W, 'Abstract Law and Political Reality in the Post-European-Accession British Constitution', [1987] Denning LJ 23; and Bradley, A W, 'The sovereignty of Parliament-in perpetuity?' in Jowell, J and Oliver, D (eds), *The Changing Constitution* (2nd edn, 1989), p 25.

10   *Legal and Constitutional Implications of United Kingdom Membership of the European Communities* (Cmnd 3301), para 23.

11   Certain express amendments are in fact made by Part II of the European Communities Act 1972.

this was by no means an innovation because of existing restraints under other treaties. But the critical question is whether our doctrine of Parliamentary sovereignty means that such restraints must always be voluntarily imposed by Parliament or whether they can be compulsorily guaranteed.

The application of the orthodox doctrine of the absolute sovereignty of Parliament to statutes designed to implement treaty provisions into United Kingdom law has meant that such statutes have been regarded as in no way different from ordinary statutes and may be either expressly or impliedly amended or repealed by subsequent inconsistent statutes. It is true that there is a legal presumption that Parliament does not intend to derogate from international law, but such a presumption cannot prevail in the face of an expressly inconsistent subsequent enactment.[12] If this doctrine were to be applied to Community law it would hardly satisfy the Communities since there would be no legal guarantee of Parliament's good behaviour.

There are a variety of possible solutions to this problem. Some are suggested in the writings of those contemporary constitutional lawyers who challenge the orthodoxy of Dicey and his followers. Professor Mitchell has argued that the Act of Union with Scotland 1707 is fundamental law which imposes legal restraints on the United Kingdom Parliament and just as a new legal order was established in 1707 so there is no reason why another new legal order in the context of the Communities should not be created in 1972.[13] Professor Heuston, whilst not denying that Parliament is sovereign in terms of the area of its power, maintains that limitations may be imposed on the manner and form by which that power is exercised.[14] Applied to the matter in hand that thesis would involve the imposition of procedural restrictions on Parliament's freedom to legislate inconsistently with Community law which would not absolutely prevent such legislation but would make it more difficult. But not all of the possible solutions are of such a fundamental nature. It has been suggested that a formal clause be inserted in all statutes,[15] or that the enacting formula of all statutes should be amended,[16] to include a statement that the statute is to be construed as not conflicting with Community law. Another commentator has drawn on the experience of the Canadian Bill of Rights and has suggested that a strongly worded presumption against anything other than an express derogation from Community law should be written into the enabling act.[17] Yet others have suggested that reliance should be placed on the gradual emergence of a constitutional convention by which it would be recognized that Parliament could not legislate contrary to Community law.[18]

In dealing with the problem of the supremacy of Community law the European Communities Act adopts a subtle approach which does not incorporate any of the fundamentalist or procedural solutions described above nor is it content to rely on the uncertain emergence of conventional limitations. The Act avoids

---

12   See *Collco Dealings Ltd v IRC* [1962] AC 1, [1961] 1 All ER 762.
13   See Mitchell, J D B, 'What Happened to the Constitution on 1st January 1973?' (1980) II *Cambrian Law Review* 69. For an even more drastic solution, see Hood Phillips, O, *Reform of the Constitution* (1970), ch 7.
14   See Heuston, R F V, *Essays in Constitutional Law* (2nd edn), ch 1.
15   See Hunnings, N M, loc cit in note 9, supra.
16   See Wade, H W R, loc cit in note 9, supra, and Wade, H W R, *Constitutional Fundamentals* (1980), ch 3.
17   See de Smith, S A, loc cit in note 9, supra, and *R v Drybones* (1970) 9 DLR (3d) 473.
18   See Martin, A, loc cit in note 9, supra, and cf Lloyd, Lord, *The Idea of Law* (1966) at pp 169, 170.

any outright statement of the supremacy of Community law. It was probably thought that this was unnecessary in view of the practice of the original six Member States. It would also be contrary to the main stream of British constitutional practice and it would in any event have been politically dangerous to have adopted such an approach. The supremacy of Community law in the United Kingdom is effectively guaranteed by the combined operation of the provisions of sections 2 and 3 of the Act. As we have seen section 2(1) gives present and future Community law legal force in the United Kingdom and creates the concept of enforceable Community rights. Thus since the doctrine of the supremacy of Community law is part of that law section 2(1) makes that doctrine part of the law of the United Kingdom. The effectiveness of that doctrine is guaranteed by two further provisions. First, section 2(4) provides that, subject only to the limitations specified in Schedule 2, 'any enactment passed or to be passed, other than one contained in this Part of this Act, shall be construed and have effect subject to the foregoing provisions of this section', in other words, subject to the rule of the supremacy of Community law which is an enforceable Community right.[19] Secondly, section 3(1) provides that:

'For the purposes of all legal proceedings any question as to the meaning or effect of any of the Treaties, or as to the validity, meaning or effect of any Community instrument, shall be treated as a question of law (and, if not referred to the European Court, be for determination as such in accordance with the principles laid down by and any relevant decision of the European Court or any court attached thereto).'

Thus in all matters of Community law the courts and tribunals[20] of the United Kingdom are to defer to the relevant decisions of the Community Court whether or not such matters have been actually referred to the Community Court. This is a very important factor since the doctrine of supremacy has been developed by the Community Court.

The European Communities Act does not therefore seek to guarantee the supremacy of Community law by forbidding Parliament to enact conflicting legislation. Instead the guarantee is proved by denying effectiveness to such legislation within the legal systems of the United Kingdom to the extent that it conflicts with Community law. Thus the ultimate sanction remains an extra-legal one. There is nothing to prevent a future Parliament from repealing the European Communities Act in its entirety. If it chose to do so it would indicate that the political will that the United Kingdom should remain a member of the Communities was lacking and in the last analysis there is nothing which any mere rule of law can do in such a situation. In other words it must be assumed that as long as the United Kingdom is a member of the Communities she will honour the legal and constitutional obligations of membership. The legal guarantees of good faith contained in the Act are adequate, subject to the political will of the Member States that the Community system shall succeed.[1]

The question of supremacy has received some attention from the judiciary. In the pre-accession case of *Blackburn v A-G* Lord Denning observed 'we have all

---

19   See the statement by the Lord Chancellor, Lord Hailsham, when introducing the Bill in the Lords, *Parliamentary Debates, House of Lords*, Vol 333, No 111, 25 July 1972, col 1230.
20   See *Shields v E Coomes (Holdings) Ltd* [1979] 1 All ER 456 per Lord Denning MR; *Worringham and Humphreys v Lloyds Bank Ltd* at 461, 462 [1980] 1 CMLR 293 at 300, per Kilner Brown J; *R v Goldstein* [1983] 1 CMLR 252.
 1   Cf Warner, J-P, 'The Relationship between European Community Law and the National Laws of the Member States' (1977) 93 LQR 349 at 364, 365.

been brought up to believe that, in legal theory, one Parliament cannot bind another and that no Act is irreversible. But legal theory does not always march alongside political reality'.[2] After referring to the practical impossibility that Parliament would legislate contrary to the statutes emancipating the Dominions and Colonies he added, 'Legal theory must give way to practical politics'.[3] He then went on to say that if and when Parliament legislated contrary to Community law 'we will then say whether Parliament can lawfully do it or not'.[4] Since the accession, there has clearly been an awareness of the implications of the doctrine of the supremacy of Community law. In *Esso Petroleum v Kingswood Motors Ltd* Bridge J observed that where Community law 'is in conflict with our domestic law the effect of the [European Communities] Act of 1972 is to require that the Community law shall prevail'.[5] Similarly in *Aero Zipp Fasteners v YKK Fasteners*, Graham J said that the European Communities Act 1972 'enacted that relevant Common Market law should be applied in this country and should, where there is a conflict, override English law'.[6] In *R v Secchi* a Metropolitan magistrate has remarked that the effect of making Community law part of English law 'is to make English law, both statue and common law, subject to Community law, in those fields in which Community laws have been passed'.[7] More recently, Hoffmann J has declared that 'The Treaty of Rome is the supreme law of this country, taking precedence over Acts of Parliament'.[8]

For some time the House of Lords has recognized the force of Community law.[9] In *R v Secretary of State for Transport, ex p Factortame* it was faced with the constitutional issues involving the supremacy of Community law. The case arose as a result of changes introduced by the Merchant Shipping Act 1988 whereby the registration of fishing vessels as British was forbidden if the shareholders of the companies which owned them were not British. As a result, fishing vessels owned by British companies with Spanish shareholders did not qualify for registration. They instituted proceedings alleging that the new UK rules on registration contravened Community law, in particular the Common Fisheries Policy. They also sought interim relief in the form of the suspension of the new rules pending a final determination of the action. The Divisional Court of the Queen's Bench Division, by way of interim relief, ordered that the new rules be disapplied to the applicants pending final judgment.[10] The Court of Appeal reversed that decision on the ground that under the UK constitution the courts had no power to disapply Acts of Parliament.[11] On further appeal, the House of Lords confirmed that there was a presumption that an Act of Parliament was compatible with Community law unless and until it was declared to be incompatible but it held that as a matter of English law there was no jurisdiction to grant the interim relief requested. The House acknowledged, however, that if there was an overriding principle of

2 [1971] 1 WLR 1037 at 1040.
3 Ibid.
4 Ibid.
5 [1974] QB 142 at 151.
6 [1973] CMLR 819 at 820.
7 [1975] 1 CMLR 383 at 386.
8 *Stoke-on-Trent City Council v B & Q plc* [1990] 3 CMLR 31 at 34.
9 *R v Henn and Darby* [1979] ECR 3795, [1980] 2 CMLR 229.
10 [1989] 2 CMLR 353. The Divisional Court also sought a preliminary ruling on the substantive questions of Community law: Case C-221/89 (No 3) [1991] ECR I-3905, [1991] 3 CMLR 589. The Commission also brought proceedings against the United Kingdom arising out of the same issue: Case C-246/89 [1991] ECR I-4585, [1991] 3 CMLR 706. For an interim order in that case, see [1989] ECR 3125, [1989] 3 CMLR 601.
11 [1989] 3 CMLR 1.

Community law which required national courts, irrespective of the position under national law, to grant interim relief to protect alleged rights under Community law, then it was under a duty to devise such a remedy. It sought a preliminary ruling on that point.[12] The European Court, invoking its previous case law that no law of the Member States should compromise the full effectiveness of Community law, ruled that 'a national court which, in a case before it concerning Community law, considers that the sole obstacle which precludes it from granting interim relief is a rule of national law must set aside that rule'.[13] In the light of that ruling the House of Lords unanimously granted the relief sought.[14] On the issue of supremacy, in the words of Lord Bridge, 'under the terms of the [European Communities Act] 1972 it has always been clear that it was the duty of a United Kingdom court, when delivering final judgment, to override any rule of national law found to be in conflict with any directly enforceable rule of Community law . . . Thus . . . to insist that, in the protection of rights under Community law, national courts must not be inhibited by rules of national law from granting interim relief in appropriate cases is no more than a logical recognition of that supremacy'.[15]

Another related issue which has come before English courts concerns the response, in terms of interpretation, which should be made in the face of incompatibilities between English law and Community law. An approach advocated by Lord Denning has received a measure of support from the House of Lords.[16] That suggests that a distinction should be made between mere inconsistencies on the one hand and deliberate derogations on the other. In the former category of cases, where the incompatibility may be assumed to be inadvertent, it is suggested that the courts are under a duty to apply Community law on the presumption that Parliament intended to fulfil the Treaty obligations of the United Kingdom. But should the incompatibility be deliberate and clearly intended by Parliament, then the courts would be under a duty to apply English law.[17] More recently the House of Lords has been able to examine this issue, taking into consideration the presumption in favour of Community law contained in the European Communities Act 1972.[18] In *Duke v GEC Reliance Ltd*[19] the female plaintiff alleged sex discrimination contrary to Community law in that she had been required to retire at 60 while comparable male colleagues retired at 65. English law in force at the material time did not extend equality between the sexes to retirement ages. In earlier litigation the European Court had held such inequality contrary to Community law and had declared that the consequent right to equal treatment had direct effect but only against the state and its agencies.[20] Since the plaintiff could not rely on direct effect, she argued that the incompatible English law should be interpreted in a non-discriminatory way. The House of Lords rejected that argument on the grounds that the presumption of interpretation only applied to statutes which intended to enforce Community law and where the

---

12 [1990] 2 AC 85.
13 Case C-213/89: [1990] ECR I-2433, para 23, [1990] 3 CMLR 1 at 30.
14 [1990] 3 CMLR 375.
15 [1990] 3 CMLR 375 at 380.
16 See *Garland v British Rail Engineering Ltd* [1983] 2 AC 751 at 771.
17 See *Macarthy's Ltd v Smith* [1979] 3 All ER 325, [1979] 3 CMLR 44 at 47; *Shields v E Coomes (Holdings) Ltd* [1979] 1 All ER 456 at 460.
18 Section 2(4).
19 [1988] AC 618.
20 See Case 152/84: *Marshall v Southampton and South West Hampshire Area Health Authority* [1986] ECR 723, [1986] 1 CMLR 688.

Community right in question had direct effect.[1] In later cases involving sex discrimination the House of Lords has adopted a similar approach. Thus where there has been a conflict between UK regulations intended to implement Community law and the Community law in question, there has been a willingness to interpret such regulations contrary to their literal meaning in the interests of achieving compatibility with Community law.[2] Although this goes a long way towards overcoming inconsistencies by means of interpretative techniques, it must nevertheless be doubted whether the factor of the intention of Parliament may be legitimately taken into account as a matter of Community law. In a recent ruling, the European Court has held that national courts must always interpret national law in the light of the wording and purpose of Community law whatever the date of the national law in question.[3]

G.   Community law before United Kingdom courts and tribunals

Since the commencement of British membership the courts, tribunals and lawyers of the United Kingdom have been confronted with the 'incoming tide' of Community law.[4] They have been faced with the unprecedented challenge of participating in a novel and unique system of law based on unfamiliar continental legal principles. During this time, points of Community law, of varying degrees of significance, have arisen in numerous reported British cases. All levels of the judicial hierarchy have been involved: Value Added Tax tribunals, industrial tribunals, the Social Security Commissioner, the Special Commissioners for Income Tax, the Employment Appeal Tribunal, magistrates, county courts, crown courts, judges of the High Court, the Queen's Bench Divisional Court, both Divisions of the Court of Appeal and the House of Lords.[5] Earlier in this chapter reference has been made to the light which these cases throw on the questions of the supremacy of Community law and the identity of those courts and tribunals which are under the obligation to request preliminary rulings from the European Court. In addition the cases reveal the nature and extent of judicial understanding and assimilation of Community law in the United Kingdom at present.

The first and obvious question concerns the extent to which the rules of Community law have become part of the corpus of law which the courts and tribunals of the United Kingdom themselves apply. There is clearly a general acceptance that Community law can now form part of the law of the United Kingdom.[6] As far as the EC Treaty is concerned there was initially a mistaken impression that every provision of the Treaty must now be given legal effect by United Kingdom courts and tribunals. Lord Denning was a proponent of that

---

1   [1988] AC at 630, 639-640, per Lord Templeman with the concurrence of the other law lords.
2   See *Pickstone v Freemans plc* [1989] AC 66, [1988] 2 All ER 803; *Litster v Forth Dry Dock and Engineering Co* [1990] 1 AC 546, [1989] 1 All ER 1134.
3   See Case C-106/89: *Marleasing SA v La Commercial de Alimentation SA* [1990] ECR I-4135, followed by the House of Lords in *Webb v Emo Air Cargo Ltd* [1993] 1 WLR 49 at 59F-60G.
4   Cf Lord Denning in *H P Bulmer v J Bollinger SA* [1974] Ch 401 at 418.
5   For example see the cases cited in Collins, op cit.
6   Eg *Lerose Ltd v Hawick Jersey International Ltd* [1973] CMLR 83 at 95, per Whitford J; *Minnesota Mining Co v Geerpres Europe Ltd* [1973] CMLR 259, at 264, 265, per Graham J; *Dymond v G B Britton (Holdings) Ltd* [1976] 1 CMLR 133 at 135, per Oliver J.

view.[7] His judgments contain such statements as 'the Treaty is part of our law. It is equal in force to any statute. It must be applied by our courts'[8] and the Treaty of Rome 'is by statute part of the law of England'.[9] But the heresy that all Treaty provisions are part of the law of England and enforceable by its courts has now been abandoned in favour of the established view that only those provisions which satisfy the conditions for direct effect have that status.[10] In the context of the secondary legislation of the Community there appears to be a general recognition that regulations are directly applicable in the United Kingdom. As far as the direct effect of the secondary legislation of the Community is concerned, after some initial wavering,[11] there now seems to be a general appreciation of the circumstances in which this applies. For example, under the influence of Vice-Chancellor Pennycuick's judgment in *Van Duyn v Home Office*[12] and the European Court's ruling in that case,[13] it is now accepted that directives can confer rights on individuals which are enforceable by them in English courts and which those courts must protect.[14] The consequences for domestic remedies of directly enforceable Community rights have also been acknowledged. The House of Lords has held that where such rights have been created in favour of individuals, their breach constitutes a breach of a statutory duty which gives rise to liability in damages.[15] Accordingly, a breach of a Treaty provision which confers rights and duties on individuals and Member States respectively is actionable against the State not only by way of an application for judicial review but also by way of liability in damages (where the conditions for such liability have been established) even if the common law tort of misfeasance in public office has not been committed.[16]

Another matter which emerges from the reported cases is the mode of interpretation of Community law. The unfamiliarity of the style and format of the EC Treaty and Community secondary legislation have provoked judicial comment. The Treaty 'lays down general principles. It expresses its aims and purposes, all in sentences of moderate length and commendable style. But it lacks precision. It uses words and phrases without defining what they mean. An English lawyer

7   Also see *Esso Petroleum Co Ltd v Kingswood Motors Ltd* [1974] QB 142 at 151, per Bridge J.
8   *Application des Gaz SA v Falks Veritas Ltd* [1974] Ch 381 at 393.
9   *Schorsch Meir GmbH v Hennin* [1974] 3 WLR 823 at 830. Also see *H P Bulmer Ltd v J Bollinger SA* [1974] Ch 401 at 418-419 and *Re Westinghouse Electric Corpn Uranium Contract* [1978] AC 547 at 564. For an early case in which the significance of Treaty provisions was clearly appreciated see *Van Duyn v Home Office* [1974] 1 WLR 1107 at 1116, per Pennycuick VC.
10 See, for example, Lord Denning's exposition of the 'direct applicability' of Treaty provisions in *Shields v Coomes (Holdings) Ltd* [1979] 1 All ER 456 at 461.
11 Compare *H P Bulmer Ltd v J Bollinger SA* [1974] Ch 401 at 418, 419 with *Processed Vegetable Growers Association Ltd v Customs and Excise Comrs* [1974] 1 CMLR 113 at 127, 128.
12 [1974] 1 WLR 1107 at 1037, 1040.
13 Case 41/74: [1974] ECR 1337 at 1348, 1349.
14 *Shields v E Coomes (Holdings) Ltd* [1979] 1 All ER 456 at 462, per Lord Denning MR.
15 *Garden Cottage Foods Ltd v Milk Marketing Board* [1984] AC 130, [1983] 2 All ER 770.
16 See *R v Secretary of State for Transport, ex p Factortame* [2000] 1 AC 524. It is generally considered that the correct defendant in an action for damages based on the Community law principle of State liability for breach of Community law is the Attorney-General: see *R v Secretary of State for Employment, ex p Equal Opportunities Commission* [1995] 1 AC 1 at 32. In *Bourgoin SA v Ministry of Agriculture, Fisheries and Food* [1986] QB 716, [1985] 3 All ER 585 (the claim was settled pending appeal to the House of Lords [1987] 1 CMLR 169), it was held that liability in damages would arise only if the tort of misfeasance in public office were committed. That has effectively been overruled by the *Factortame* cases. For the current position regarding misfeasance in public office and the interaction with Community law, see *Three Rivers District Council v Bank of England (No 3)* [2000] 3 All ER 1.

would look for an interpretation clause, but he would look in vain. There is none. All the way through the Treaty there are gaps and lacunae'.[17] The ultimate authority of the European Court on the interpretation of Community law has been acknowleged,[18] as has the necessity of uniform interpretation of that law in all the Member States.[19] As aids to interpretation the case law of the European Court and of the national courts of the Member States has been invoked and some use has been made of the texts of Community instruments other than those in English.[20] But the generality and apparent incompleteness of the texts of Community law have led some English judges to claim the right to play a creative rôle in interpreting Community law so as to fill gaps in its formal fabric. English courts have been exhorted to 'divine the spirit of the Treaty and gain inspiration from it. If they find a gap, they must fill it as best they can. They must do what the framers of the instrument would have done if they had though about it'.[1] This is indeed what the European Court does and what national courts guided by the European Court may do. But if that approach is adopted without seeking guidance from the European Court then the integrity and uniformity of Community law may be put at risk. This is particularly so in the case of a Member State whose legal traditions differ in many ways from the continental legal traditions upon which the Community legal order is founded.

At the time of British accession there was an influential body of judicial opinion in England which held that difficulties over the interpretation of Community law will not often arise; in the majority of cases lower courts and tribunals should have no difficulty in interpretation Community law; courts and tribunals should not be too ready to request preliminary rulings from the European Court because of the burden that would place on the Court and because of the increased costs and delay for the litigants.[2] The judgment of Lord Denning in *Bulmer v Bollinger* represents the high water mark of this approach.[3] Stress was placed on the complete discretion of all courts other than the House of Lords to decide when a preliminary ruling is necessary. Drawing largely upon the national case law of the six original Member States, Lord Denning purported to lay down 'guidelines' to assist English courts in deciding whether a reference is necessary and in exercising their discretion. Quite apart from the fact that the practice of national courts on preliminary rulings is not necessarily an accurate representation of Community law on preliminary rulings, a number of questionable recommendations are contained in the 'guidelines', without qualification. These include recourse to the *acte clair* doctrine; that the facts of a case should always be decided before a decision is taken to request a preliminary ruling; that judges' discretion should

17 *H P Bulmer Ltd v J Bollinger SA* [1974] Ch 401 at 425, per Lord Denning. Also see *Application des Gaz SA v Falks Veritas Ltd* [1974] Ch 381 at 393, 394.

18 *H P Bulmer Ltd v J Bollinger SA* [1974] Ch 401 at 419, per Lord Denning.

19 Ibid, at 425. Also see *EMI Records v CBS Ltd* [1975] 1 CMLR 285 at 297, per Graham J.

20 *Re a Holiday in Italy* [1975] 1 CMLR 184 at 190. Where recourse is had to other language versions of a provision of EC law, the correct translation of those other versions should either be agreed between the parties or else substantiated by evidence from qualified translators: see *R v Customs and Excise Comrs, ex p EMU Tabac Sarl* [1997] EuLR 153, Schiemann LJ.

1 *H P Bulmer Ltd v J Bollinger SA* [1974] Ch 401 at 426, per Lord Denning.

2 See Lord Diplock, 'The Common Market and the Common Law' (1972), 6 JALT 3 at 13, 14; Lord Denning in *The Times, Forward into Europe*, Part 1, 2 January 1973 at 11; Lord Hailsham in an extract from a speech to magistrates appended to Home Office Circular No 149/1973 (CS 18/1973).

3 [1974] Ch 401 at 420-425, particularly.

be influenced by such factors as time, the burden on the European Court, the nature and importance of the question in issue, expense and the wishes of the parties. All of these 'guidelines' are subject to serious reservations.[4] Lord Denning's assumption that the importance of a question of Community law is directly related to the position in the national judicial hierarchy of the court in which the question arises[5] is not borne out by the experience of the European Court. Questions of fundamental importance to Community law and its development have not infrequently come before the European Court in the form of references from lowly national courts and tribunals.[6] Whenever there is a risk of divergent views on Community law it is in everyone's interest, not least that of actual and potential litigants, to seek a ruling from the European Court at the earliest opportunity.[7]

The threat of the uniformity of Community law posed by national courts and tribunals, when interpreting that law, going on voyages of discovery of their own without taking advantage of the navigational aids provided by the European Court is clearly illustrated by one of the early cases which came before the Court of Appeal. In *Schorsch Meier GmbH v Hennin*[8] the defendant was indebted to the plaintiffs in a sum of German Marks. The debt was not paid and as a result of a fall in the value of sterling the plaintiffs brought an action in the County Court claiming payment in German Marks. The judge rejected the plaintiff's argument based on what was then EC Article 106 (now repealed) on the ground that the article had no bearing on English law, and a request that that matter be referred to the European Court was refused. The plaintiffs appealed against both of those rulings. In connection with the first, on the assumption that the EC Treaty has the status of an Act of Parliament, the Court of Appeal unanimously held EC Article 106 to be a rule of law for English courts to apply. No consideration was given to the case law of the European Court concerning the direct effect of Treaty provisions. In the absence of any European or national case law on the direct effect of EC Article 106, no reference was made to scholarly commentaries on the subject.[9] When interpreting EC Article 106 the Court of Appeal took the lead of Lord Denning who said, 'There is no need to refer the interpretation to the court at Luxembourg. We can do it ourselves'.[10] The Court of Appeal then attempted to divine the purpose and intent of the article. Since it was concerned, inter alia, with the obligation of Member States to authorize payments connected with the movement of goods in the currency of the Member State in which the creditor resides, the Court of Appeal held that the German plaintiffs were entitled

---

4 For critical comments, see Mitchell, J B D, 'Sed Quis Custodiet Ipsos Custodes?' (1974) 11 CMLR Rev 351; Jacobs, F G, 'When to Refer to the European Court' (1974) 90 LQR 486; Freeman, Elizabeth, 'References to the Court of Justice under Article 177' (1975) 28 Current Legal Problems 176.
5 [1974] Ch 401 at 421.
6 Eg Case 6/64: *Costa v ENEL* [1964] ECR 585; Case 61/65: *Voor Het Vasen (née Göbbels) v Beambtenfounds Mijnbedrijf* [1966] ECR 261, [1966] CMLR 508; Case 33/70: *SpA SACE v Italian Ministry for Finance* [1970] ECR 1213, [1971] CMLR 123.
7 Cf Case 190/73: *Officer van Jusitie v J W J van Haaster* [1974] ECR 1123, at 1136, per A-G Mayras.
8 [1975] QB 416, [1975] 1 All ER 1520.
9 Eg at that time *Les Novelles: Droit des Communautés européennes*, chapter VI; Campbell, A, *Common Market Law*, Vol 3, paras 15.99 to 15.103; Kapteyn, P J G and Verloren van Themaat, P, *Introduction to the Law of the European Communities* (1973), pp 222.
10 [1975] QB 416 at 426.

to payment in German currency.[11] Beyond that no genuine attempt was made to interpret the article as a whole nor to place it properly in the context of the Treaty. The case raised entirely novel points of some importance and a preliminary ruling from the European Court was manifestly necessary.

Lord Denning's 'guidelines', as might be expected, have exercised some influence on judicial attitudes towards preliminary rulings, particularly in the case of tribunals and the lower courts. A metropolitan magistrate, for example, has observed that Lord Denning has supplied 'the essential guidelines which English courts must follow'.[12] A Value Added Tax Tribunal,[13] the Employment Appeal Tribunal[14] and a High Court Judge sitting in the crown court[15] have all accepted the authority of the 'guidelines'. Under their influence preliminary rulings have not been sought apparently on the simple ground that the parties believed that it would be contrary to their interests.[16] On the other hand, such guidelines cannot fetter the exercise of a judicial discretion[17] and therefore can only be regarded as indicative.[18] The reported cases also show that English judges and others exercising judicial powers acknowledge the significance and importance of preliminary rulings and demonstrate their willingness to seek the guidance of the European Court. There has been a steady and increasing flow of references on such diverse questions as: the scope of the Community's equal pay provisions;[19] the direct effect of directives;[20] uncertainty concerning Community rules on intellectual property;[1] the authority of the United Kingdom to introduce fish conservation measures;[2] the meaning and effect of the free trade agreement with Portugal;[3] whether a self-employed person is a worker for the purpose of the social security provisions of the Community;[4] and the validity and meaning of a regulation concerned with the financial structure of the Common Agricultural Policy.[5] The House of Lords has even obtained a preliminary ruling for the purpose of giving the Criminal Division of the Court of Appeal an elementary lesson in Community law.[6]

11 Since Art 106 appeared in the part of the Treaty concerned with economic policy and balance of payments it was probably of public law rather than private law significance, that is, concerned with exchange control rather than the currency in which debts may be paid. The relevance of Art 106 to judgment debts was questioned obiter in the House of Lords; *Miliangos v George Frank (Textiles) Ltd* [1975] 2 CMLR 585 at 596, per Lord Wilberforce.
12 *R v Secchi* [1975] 1 CMLR 383 at 386.
13 *English-Speaking Union of the Commonwealth v Customs and Excise Comrs* [1981] 1 CMLR 581 at 599.
14 *Burton v British Railways Board* [1981] 3 CMLR 100 at 102.
15 *R v Tymen* [1980] 3 CMLR 101 at 107.
16 *Extrude Hone Corpn v Heathway Machine Sales Ltd* [1981] 3 CMLR 379 at 399 and *English-Speaking Union of the Commonwealth v Customs and Excise Comrs* [1981] 1 CMLR 581 at 599.
17 *Lord Bethell v SABENA* [1983] 3 CMLR 1.
18 As pointed out above (see supra, pp 358–364), the ECJ considers that national courts have 'the widest discretion' and the approach of English courts to the exercise of their discretion has varied over the years.
19 *Macarthys Ltd v Smith* [1979] 3 All ER 325, [1979] 3 CMLR 44.
20 *Burton v British Railways Board* [1981] 3 CMLR 100.
1 *EMI Records Ltd v CBS United Kingdom Ltd* [1975] 1 CMLR 285.
2 *R v Tymen* [1981] 2 CMLR 544.
3 *Polydor Ltd v Harlequin Records Shops Ltd* [1980] 2 CMLR 413.
4 Case 21/5: *Re an illness in France* [1976] 1 CMLR 243.
5 Case 146/77: *British Beef Co Ltd v Intervention Board for Agricultural Produce* [1978] 2 CMLR 83.
6 *R v Henn and Darby* [1980] 2 CMLR 229 at 234, per Lord Diplock.

After an understandably hesitant start United Kingdom cases reveal no reluctance to consider and apply Community law.[7] United Kingdom courts and tribunals are now, on the whole, adopting a positive and constructive approach to the challenge of this novel body of law. The reasons for this promising outcome lie partly in the clearly observable differences between English and Community law.[8] It is becoming increasingly acknowledged that Community law demands a different approach and this should help to promote a fruitful relationship between the law of the United Kingdom and the law of the Community. The Commission, in a review of the attitudes of national courts to Community law, had expressed general satisfaction with the practice of UK courts both in regard to upholding the primacy of Community law and to frequent use of the preliminary ruling procedure.[9]

7 The Court of Appeal has even been restrained by the House of Lords for over-enthusiasm. See *James Buchanan & Co Ltd v Babco Forwarding and Shipping (UK) Ltd* [1978] 1 CMLR 156 at 164, per Viscount Dilhorne and *The Siskina* [1978] 1 CMLR 190 at 220, per Lord Diplock.
8 See Bridge, J W, 'National Legal Tradition and Community Law: Legislative Drafting and Judicial Interpretation in England and the European Community' (1981) 19 Journal of Common Market Studies 351.
9 See *Sixth Annual Report to the European Parliament on Commission Monitoring of the Application of Community Law*, COM (89) 411 final, Appendix, pp 31-34.

Part IV

The Law of the Economy

Chapter 16

The Law of the Economy: concept and scope

A. What is in a name?

Like the modern constitutions of Germany or Italy, the European Community legal system reflected in the EC Treaty consists of a political and socio-economic charter. The former comprises the 'Organizational' or 'Constitutional Law', the latter the 'Law of the Economy'. As we have seen in the preceding chapters the Constitutional Law of the EC and of the European Union comprises both substantive and procedural rules. The Law of the Economy, which certain writers (erroneously) call the 'Substantive Law', too consists of substantive and procedural rules. Substantive (or material) rules reflect the rights and obligations of the Member States and individuals whilst procedural (or formal, or adjective) rules serve to implement and enforce the former. Thus, for example, EC Articles 81 and 82 (ex Arts 85 and 86) comprise the substantive rules of competition applicable to undertakings, whilst most of the procedural rules can be found in Regulation 17 of 1962.[1]

The expression 'Economic Law' was coined by one of the early French socialists, Pierre J Proudhon[2] who regarded it as a solution for the social problems of his day. To resolve the contradiction in society he advocated a new system of law which would even oust the differences between the rich and the poor and bring about a *conciliation universelle*. He hoped to achieve this through an equitable division of land and property: an emancipation of workers from the power of their employers, a reorganization of industry according to a division of labour, individual and collective responsibility, suppression of idleness and relief of poverty. Because it did not fit into the rigid classification of the French legal

---

1   OJ 1959-1962, Sp Ed 87.
2   *De la capacité des classes ouvrières* (1865).

system into the public and private law, Proudhon had to invent a new branch of the law: *un droit économique, complement et corollaire du droit politique et du droit civil*. His theory remained a theory but focused attention on the relationship between law and the economy.

Much work was done in Germany[3] but, understandably, there is in this respect no unanimity among the jurists.[4] Quite apart from its scope and philosophy, the main controversy revolves around the question whether or not the Law of the Economy is an autonomous branch of the law. The majority view is that it is not and considers *Wirtschaftsrecht* to be a sub-division of Administrative Law.[5]

Although there is no unanimity on the exact meaning and scope of the *Wirtschaftsrecht* there is a broad understanding that it reflects the power of the state authorities to organize and direct the national economy. More precisely these authorities organize certain sectors of the economy (eg agriculture or transport) and intervene in the management of nationalized industries and external trade and lay down rules for subsidies, trading standards, monopolies and restrictive practices. In exercising their substantive powers they have to follow the due process of the law.

French scholarship in this field was influenced by German writers[6] but, as in Germany, has not produced a uniform concept of Economic Law.[7] Views extend from a narrow one contending that Economic Law comprises the *mesures autoritaires d'organisation économique*[8] to a broad one of a *droit de la concentration ou de la collectivisation des biens de la production et de l'organisation de l'économie pour des pouvoirs privés ou public*.[9]

A review of scholarship in this field[10] emphasizes government involvement as an essential aspect of the law of the economy.[11] Thus the regulatory function is expressed in rules and regulations affecting both micro- and macro-economies.

In the field of micro-economies the law purports to regulate the operation of the market starting with the definition of property. In the system of market economy an object has no economic value unless it represents an enforceable right. Thus property, ie things and claims which represent a money value and rights in respect of property (ie ownership or use), forms the basis of market exchange. Things and services are put into circulation as they are offered for sale, barter, hire and use and the relations between the parties involved in such transactions are defined and controlled by the law. From an economic point of view the subject matter of these transactions represents a utility value to which the market attaches a price. From a legal point of view the transactions have to be carried out in an orderly fashion and vested rights ought to be protected by means of civil and criminal sanctions.

---

3   Piepenbrock, R, *Der Gedanke eines Wirtschaftsrechts in der nouzeitlichen Literatur bis zum ersten Weltkrieg* (1964).
4   See Rinck, G, *Wirtschaftsrecht* (3rd edn, 1972).
5   Rinck, ibid, p 3; Huber, H, *Wirtschaftsverwaltungsrecht* (1953).
6   Cf Kiraly, de F, *Le droit économique, branche indépendente de la science juridique, Recueil d'études sur les sources du droit, en honneur de F Geny* (1935) vol 3, pp 111 et seq.
7   Svoboda, K, *La notion de droit économique, Etude sur les conceptions récentes du droit économique en France et dans les pays socialistes* (1966).
8   Houin, K, *Le droit commercial et les décrets de 1953* Droit Social (1954).
9   Farjat, G, *Droit Economique* (1971) p 14; see also Champaud, C, *Contribution à la définition du droit économique*, Dalloz (1967), Chron. Pp 215 et seq.
10 For a summary see Lasok, D, *The Law of the Economy in the European Communities,* (1980) pp 2-25; VerLoren van Themaat, P, *The Changing Structure of International Economic Law* (1981).
11 Cf Schmitthoff, C M, *The Concept of Economic Law in England* (1966) pp 309 et seq.

In the capitalist system of private enterprise and initiative the freedom of contract and the abundant supply of property (ie goods and services which have an economic value) form the basis of economic exchanges or market activities. However, in modern society these freedoms are not without restrictions as society through its laws controls the use of property and of economic power. It also provides the basic needs for those who cannot provide for themselves. In other words the laws which govern the economy have also a social dimension since a society which claims to be just cannot afford to be controlled entirely by the market forces of supply and demand or by the market power exercised by the concentration of either capital or organized labour. Thus to ensure fair competition and check abuses of the freedom of contract monopolies and restrictive practices have to be brought under the law.

In the world of advanced technology and credit facilities the law has to protect from the freedom of contract not only the ignorant and the gullible but also those of reasonable discernment. At a minimum it has to prescribe that the seller and the manufacturer provide the essential information about the products they put on the market and to assume liability for defective goods. Credit sales and hire-purchase agreements have to be subject to legal controls.

In such a sophisticated and complex market situation, corporate structures and financial institutions have developed. These too have to be regulated by law since unregulated they can become instruments of fraud and abuse of the freedom of contract and of the freedom to trade. In this respect the agents of the market economy, be they individuals or corporate bodies, have to operate within the framework of the law which defines their capacity, powers and spheres of activity.

In the macro-economic context the state plays a dominant role and, since the direction of the economy depends upon the political complexion of governments, the government brings internal politics and economics together. Historically the state's involvement in the economy has progressed from indifference (*laissez-faire*) through remote supervision (*état-gendarme*) to the present position of direct participation (*état commerçant*). Through the intervention of the state the capitalist economy has undergone a fundamental change. It has become a 'mixed economy', that is a system in which public and private enterprise co-exist and in which the state lays down economic policy, on the one hand, and plays the rôle of manufacturer, merchant, purveyor of services and money lender, on the other. This is, in essence, the stage of 'directed economy' (*l'économie dirigée*), the state acting through the mechanism of public administration on the basis of parliamentary legislation and ministerial decrees. The body of the law at the disposal of the state relevant to the direction of the national economy is the Law of the Economy.

B.   The Law of the Economy in the Member States

Although there is no uniformity among the Member States of the Community they all have a mixed economy and they all subscribe to the concept of directed economy. The systems differ in details. Thus it was possible for the purpose of a survey of the national systems commissioned by the Commission to agree that the Law of the Economy comprised 'the whole body of legal regulations promulgated to serve economic policy'.[12] Within that definition the experts also agreed that no fewer than eight types of the Law of the Economy could be identified.[13]

---

12   Verloren van Themaat, *Economic Law of the Member States of the European Communities in an Economic and Monetary Union* (1973) p 9.
13   Ibid pp 9-11.

(1) Legal regulation of economic forecasting based on assumptions regarding the economic policy which is to be pursued;
(2) Short- and medium-term economic planning supplemented by means to attain the objectives of the plans adopted;
(3) Forms of national financial assistance designed to further the economic policy which is to be pursued;
(4) Contractual agreements between state authorities and business whereby the latter undertake to carry out a particular programme within the framework of the agreed policy;
(5) All other mandatory rules of law which have economic purposes and objectives;
(6) Special rules of law within the confines of a general economic policy but concerned with particular sectors of economic activity;
(7) Rules designed to ensure the enforcement of the Law of the Economy; and
(8) Judicial protection of enterprises and individuals against the action of public authorities in relation to the Law of the Economy.

C.   The EC Law of the Economy

The European Union reflects certain common features of the national systems without actually being manifestly modelled upon any one of these systems. However, as we shall see later, it endeavours to link economies with social concerns. Another feature of the EU is a dynamism built into its institutions which ought to work towards progressive integration of the economic and political life of the Member States. Economic integration ought to bring about political integration but, as experienced with the Treaty of Maastricht 1992, fundamental economic decisions can be made only if there is political will to do so.

In a legal sense the EU is founded upon the three Communities: Coal and Steel (or ECSC), Euratom (or EAEC) and the European Community (the EC).[14] Each of these reflects an economic programme and an institutional framework for its execution. The former two are concerned with specific sectors of the economy; the EC is one of a general and (due to its dynamism) a universal nature. In this context, the Law of the Economy is not, in any real sense, an 'EU' Law of the Economy because it is derived from the three Communities and, more particularly, from the EC.

(1)   COAL AND STEEL COMMUNITY

The main function of the ECSC is to establish a Common Market for Coal and Steel (ECSC Article 2). To that end the Treaty has set up appropriate institutions and in Article 3 provided that they must ensure:

(1) an orderly supply to the common market;
(2) equal access to comparably placed customers;
(3) the lowest prices whilst allowing necessary amortization and normal return on invested capital;
(4) the conditions encouraging the expansion and improvement of production and the rational use of natural resources;
(5) improved working conditions and an improved standard of living for the workers in the industries involved in the Community;

---

14   TEU Art 1 (ex Art A).

(6) the promotion of international trade and equitable export pricing;
(7) the promotion of orderly expansion and modernization of production and the improvement of quality.

Article 4 has prohibited the following as being incompatible with the Common Market for coal and steel:

(1) import and export duties or charges having equivalent effect and quantitative restrictions on the movement of products;
(2) discriminatory measures and practices affecting producers, purchasers and consumers especially as regards prices, delivery terms, transport rates and conditions as well as the purchaser's free choice of supplier;
(3) subsidies or aids granted by states, or special charges in any form whatsoever imposed by the states;
(4) restrictive practices with the object of sharing or exploiting of markets.

Article 5 provides guidelines for the Community institutions stressing the demarcation lines traced by the Treaty and the policy of 'limited intervention'. Thus the Community has to provide guidance and assistance to the parties concerned, place financial resources at the disposal of undertakings, ensure conditions for fair competition and take the necessary measures for the implementation of the Treaty whilst giving reasons for the action taken.

The economic and social provisions of the Treaty impose upon the High Authority (ie the Commission under the EAEC, EC and the Merger Treaties) the duty of consulting the governments of the Member States as well as the undertakings, workers, consumers and dealers in connection with the execution of its tasks, in particular, in its study of market and price trends; in the making of forecasts and drawing up programmes of action; in considering modernization and long-term planning of production; in dealing with problems arising from technical changes and market situations regarding the deployment of workers, their working conditions and living standards (Article 46).

In order to be able to carry out the administration and to discharge the tasks involving financial expenditure the Community is empowered to raise loans and impose levies on the production of coal and steel (Article 49). Funds raised on money markets may be used only for the purpose of granting loans to the industries (Article 51(1)) but the Community's own resources may be employed to finance the various schemes and activities in support of the Common Market such as investments and financial aids. The concern for the well-being of workers is shown in the power of using the funds for their benefits, particularly, where the change of market conditions or production methods results in hardship to the workers and their employers.

In the field of production the Treaty prefers indirect means of action, singling out co-operation with governments to regularize or influence general consumption and intervention in regard to prices and commercial policy (Article 57). The Treaty contains a fairly detailed regime of pricing and conditions of sale, giving considerable power to the Commission in this field. Subject to the general supervisory power of the Commission the Member States may pursue their commercial policy, though the minimum and maximum rates of customs duties on coal and steel in trade with third countries may be fixed by the Council of Ministers. Import and export licences for trade with third countries are in the hands of Member States but the Commission has the power of supervising the issue and verification of these licences.

As in the case of the EC, the Common Market for Coal and Steel is buttressed by provisions with regard to competition (Articles 65-67) and transport (Article 70) but these are in a number of respects less sophisticated than the rules which have evolved under EC practice.

Finally, the social aspect of the Common Market for Coal and Steel reappears once more in the provisions governing wages and the movement of workers. The freedom of movement of workers is complemented by the principle of non-discrimination on the ground of nationality (Article 69) whilst the level of wages and social security benefits remains the domain of the Member States. However both form an important ingredient of the Common Market as indeed is the case of the EC.

(2) EURATOM

The function of the European Atomic Energy Community is to promote the conditions necessary for the establishment and development of nuclear industries and thus lead to the setting up of a Nuclear Common Market. In particular the Community (Article 2) shall:

(1) promote research and ensure the dissemination of technical information;
(2) establish uniform safety standards to protect the health of workers and of the general public;
(3) facilitate investment necessary to develop a nuclear energy industry;
(4) ensure that all users receive a regular and equitable supply of ores and nuclear fuels;
(5) ensure that nuclear materials are not diverted to improper use;
(6) exercise the right of ownership conferred upon it with respect to special fissile materials;
(7) ensure wide commercial outlets and access to the best technical facilities by the creation of a Common Market in specialized materials and equipment, by the free movement of capital for investments in the field of nuclear energy and by freedom of employment for specialists within the Community;
(8) establish with other countries and international organizations relations to foster progress in the peaceful uses of nuclear energy.

Point (7) above is of a particular relevance to the Nuclear Common Market which, in a technical sense, has been expounded in Articles 92-100. The Common Market concentrates on the movement of goods and products specified in the lists attached to the Treaty. Accordingly Member States must abolish between themselves all customs duties on imports and exports as well as charges having equivalent effect and all quantitative restrictions on imports and exports in respect of the listed materials (Article 93). However these rules do not apply to non-European territories of a Member State which may continue to levy import and export duties or equivalent charges if such are of an exclusively fiscal nature and are applied without discrimination between that State and another Member State of the Community.

The Treaty provides for a common customs tariff for trade with third countries, the rates of duty being determined according to the classification of the products in the lists mentioned above (Article 94).

Subject to limitations on the grounds of public policy, public security and public health the Member States must abolished restrictions based on nationality affecting the right of the citizens of any Member State to take skilled employment in the field of nuclear energy (Article 96).

The principle of non-discrimination applies also to individuals and corporations wishing to embark on the construction of nuclear installations of a scientific or industrial nature (Article 97).

Movements of capital intended to finance activities listed in Annex II to the Treaty and transfers of currency to pay for goods, services and earnings are to be liberalized (Articles 99 and 100). Insurance facilities to cover nuclear risks are to be extended with the co-operation of the Member States involved (Article 98).

The Treaty makes provisions in respect of the 'external relations' of Euratom which, in some respects, correspond broadly to the 'commercial policy' envisaged by the ECSC and EC Treaties. It refers to 'agreements or contracts' with a third state, an international organization or a national of a third state within the scope of the Treaty (Article 101). Such agreements or contracts shall be negotiated and concluded according to the procedure laid down in the Treaty. If such agreements or contracts include, besides the Community, one or more Member States, they will not enter into force until the Commission has been notified by all the Member States concerned that those agreements or contracts have become enforceable within their respective national legal systems (Article 102).

(3)   EUROPEAN COMMUNITY

The EC, as the angular stone of European integration, transcends the economic objectives of the two other Communities. Originally, the European *Economic* Community, the EC is now the European Community, a change that reflects the broadening of its role and functions. In an economic sense, it uses a Common Market (which is not limited to a particular sector of the economy but applies generally, with the exception of matters covered by the ESCS and EAEC),[15] an economic and monetary union, and certain common policies or activities to achieve specified objectives of an economic or a socio-political nature: a harmonious and balanced and sustainable development of economic activities, a high level of employment, sustainable and non-inflationary growth, a high degree of competitiveness and convergence of economic performance, the raising of the standard of living and economic cohesion between Member States (economic); a high level of social protection, equality between men and women, a high level of protection and improvement of the quality of the environment, the raising of the quality of life, social cohesion and solidarity among Member States (socio-political).[16]

Articles 3 and 4 (ex Arts 3 and 3a) further elaborate these generalities by listing the activities of the EC that are intended to achieve those purposes. These activities include:

(1)   the prohibition, as between Member States, of customs duties and quantitative restrictions on imports and exports, and of all other measures having equivalent effect;

(2)   a common commercial policy;

---

15   EC Art 305 (ex Art 232). See Case 328/85: *Deutsche Babcock Handel GmbH v Hauptzollamt Lubeck-Ost* [1987] ECR 5119; Case C-18/94: *Hopkins v National Power and PowerGen* [1996] ECR I-2281.

16   EC Art 2 (ex Art 2) in its present form. Originally it provided for more limited economic objectives and the political objective of 'closer relations' between the Member States, to be achieved by a Common Market and the progressive approximation of the economic policies of the Member States.

(3) an internal market characterised by the abolition, as between Member States, of obstacles to the free movement of goods, persons, services and capital;

(4) measures concerning the entry and movement of persons into and through the EC;

(5) a common policy in the sphere of agriculture and fisheries;

(6) a common policy in the sphere of transport;

(7) a system ensuring that competition in the internal market is not distorted;

(8) the approximation of the laws of Member States to the extent required for the functioning of the Common Market;

(9) the promotion of co-ordination between employment policies of the Member States with a view to enhancing their effectiveness by developing a co-ordinated strategy for employment;

(10) a policy in the social sphere comprising a European Social Fund;

(11) the strengthening of economic and social cohesion;

(12) a policy in the sphere of the environment;

(13) the strengthening of the competitiveness of Community industry;

(14) the promotion of research and technological development;

(15) encouragement for the establishment and development of trans-European networks;

(16) a contribution to the attainment of a high level of health protection;

(17) a contribution to education and training of quality and to the flowering of the cultures of the Member States;

(18) a policy in the sphere of development co-operation;

(19) the association of overseas countries and territories in order to increase trade and promote jointly economic and social development;

(20) a contribution to the strengthening of consumer protection;

(21) measures in the spheres of energy, civil protection and tourism;

(22) the adoption of an economic policy, conducted in accordance with the principles of an open market economy with free competition and based on close co-ordination of Member States' economic policies, on the internal market, and on the definition of common objectives;

(23) the introduction of a single currency and the definition and conduct of a single monetary and exchange rate policy.

All but the last two activities must be conducted with the object of eliminating inequalities, and promoting equality, between men and women. The last two activities must be conducted on the basis of compliance with the following principles: stable prices, sound public finances and monetary conditions and a sustainable balance of payments. In practical terms the Treaty objectives are to be attained by means of common policies which are listed in the Treaty. However, these policies are not listed exhaustively. New policies, as children of necessity, have emerged. These are policies consequential upon the development of the Community devised within the broad spectrum of the Treaty. Some of those policies, and several new ones, were incorporated into the Treaty when it was amended by the Maastricht and Amsterdam Treaties. The evolution is not necessarily at an end.

A Community policy consists of a defined objective, the means of its achievement and the machinery of implementation and enforcement. Though the objective is primarily economic the remaining elements emanate from the legal process which involves implementing legislation and enforcement both at the Community and national level. It has to be so because the Treaty, like a Constitution, provides merely a legal framework within which the Community develops and within which the

Member States carry out their obligations. A Community policy is, therefore, an enforceable legal obligation common to all the Member States, extending over their territories and creating rights and duties applicable to the states and individuals.

Elaboration and definition of Community policies entails intensive collaboration between the Community institutions in which the Commission makes the proposals and, subject to the participation of the European Parliament as well as of the Economic and Social Committee, the Council of Ministers takes decisions. Indeed, within the complex legislative process, it is the function of the Council of Ministers to 'ensure co-ordination of the general economic policies of the Member States [and] . . . to take decisions'.[17] The Member States' input into the process is effected through the various technical committees and, ultimately, through the Council of Ministers. On the ground, as it were, the implementation and enforcement of Community policies falls within the responsibility of the Member States.

The Community system is conceived upon a federal pattern without, however, adopting any particular model. It presupposes, though, a division of functions between the Community and the Member States[18] and a progressive diminution of sovereign powers of the Member States as the exclusive Community competence (termed the 'occupied field') expands. There is, therefore, a correlation between the development of Community policies and the diminution of state power inasmuch as the existence of a common policy commits the Member States to carry it into effect.[19]

D. Towards an Economic and Monetary Union

The Economic Law of the Community is based on the concept of the Common Market as expounded in the founding Treaties and implemented in practice. Its development reflects the development of the Community by stages.

The Common Market is a single 'internal' market embracing several sovereign states, ie autonomous economic territories. The Common Market territory[20] is marked out by the political frontiers of the Member States subject to special provisions regarding certain overseas and European territories for which the Member States are responsible.[1] It also includes the territorial waters and the air space of the Member States.[2] The single 'internal' market projects the Community on the world market as a single trading unit with its own customs barrier consisting of the Common Customs Tariff and the Common Commercial Policy.

However, the Common Market is not confined to trade in goods. In fact it consists of an internal market comprising four freedoms, ie the freedom of movement of goods, persons, services and capital[3] to which can be added the two

---

17 EC Art 202 (ex Art 145); ECSC Art 26; EAEC Art 115.
18 See Case 30/59: *De Gezamenlijke Steen-Kolenmijnen in Limburg v High Authority* [1961] ECR 1 at 23, supra, p 285.
19 See eg Case 804/79: *Commission v UK* [1981] ECR 1045 at para 17; *R v Ministry of Agriculture, Fisheries and Food, ex p First City Trading Ltd* [1997] 1 CMLR 250.
20 EC Art 299, (ex Art 227); Case 199/84: *Procuratore della Repubblica v Migliorini* [1985] ECR 3317, [1987] 2 CMLR 941.
1 See Case 148/77: *Hansen v HZA Flensburg* [1978] ECR 1787, [1979] 1 CMLR 604.
2 Reg 2151/84 (OJ, 1984, L192/1).
3 EC Art 14(2) (ex Art 7a(2)).

principal policies, ie the Common Agricultural Policy and the Competition Policy as the most advanced ones of the economic policies of the Community to which may now be added the policies supporting the single currency. The object of the four freedoms is to break down barriers, the object of the policies is to create a uniform body of law in areas essential to the Community.

The Treaty enjoining the Community to create the Common Market provided a blueprint of economic policies which, however, did not develop uniformly. The Treaty, as originally worded, envisaged that its primary objectives would be achieved within a transitional period that came to an end on 31 December 1969. That did not prove to be the case. After 30 years of its existence the Community, faced with the agitation for a new constitution[4] was shown to be deficient in the completion of the tasks laid down in the Treaty.

Spurred by the Commission White Paper[5] presented to the Council of Ministers (which detailed the unaccomplished objectives of the Treaty and indicated the course of action) the inter-governmental conference produced the Single European Act 1986[6] laying down a timetable for the completion of the internal market by the end of 1992. The completion of the internal market confirms the Community concept of Economic Law as laid down in the founding Treaties but the TEU has expanded the concept of the Law of the Economy and of the Community itself which has become an 'Economic and Monetary Union'. Eleven Member States were found by the Council to have fulfilled the necessary conditions for the adoption of the single currency (the Euro) with effect from 1 January 1999.[7] As a result, legislation was adopted setting out the legal framework for the introduction of the euro; and the conversion rates between the currencies of the Member States participating in the euro were fixed irrevocably with effect from 1 January 1999.[8]

---

4   Draft Treaty establishing the European Union adopted by the European Parliament in 1984.
5   COM(85) 310 Final (1985).
6   European Communities No 12 (1986) Cmnd 9758.
7   Council Decision 98/317 (OJ 1998, L139).
8   See in particular Council Regs No 974/98 and No 975/98 (OJ 1998, L139/1 and 6) and No 2866/98 (OJ 1998, L359/1), the last as amended by Reg No 1478/2000 (OJ 2000, L167/1).

Chapter 17

EC trade law: external market

A. Introduction

The Community's external trade is regulated by the twin principles of the Common Customs Tariff (CCT) and the Common Commercial Policy (CCP). The former is a code of law based on the Treaty[1] implemented in 1968 and consolidated in the present version of Regulation 2913/92, the Customs Code,[2] which has repealed and amended some thirty pieces of Community legislation. However it is not an entirely new law. Therefore references to previous Community acts and case law shall remain relevant to its interpretation and application. Moreover, in view of the nature of external trade, the rules are likely to be continuously updated, such changes to be communicated to the Member States via TARIC, ie the Integrated Tariff of the European Community which is a data bank for the use of the national customs authorities.[3]

Community customs law is administered by the national customs authorities. Disputes and appeals are governed by procedures determined by the Member States[4] subject to the recourse to the ECJ via EC Article 234 (ex Art 177).

Overall supervision of the system is in the hands of the Customs Code Committee[5] consisting of representatives of Member States chaired by a representative of the Commission. As an expression of close co-operation between national customs authorities Article 250 provides that the various actions and documents issued by the authorities of one Member State shall have the same legal effect in the other Member States.

---

1 EC Arts 23 and 26-27 (ex Arts 9 and 18-20).
2 OJ 1992, L302/1. The Customs Code is supplemented by Commission Regulation No 2454/93 (OJ 1993, L253/1), which expands on a number of its provisions and has frequently been amended.
3 OJ 1992, C 170.
4 Reg 2913/92, supra, Art 245.
5 Reg 2913/92, Arts 247-249.

The CCP,[6] on the other hand, together with the Community External Treaties, the Economic Policy[7] and Monetary Policy[8] as well as the protective legislation, forms an integral part of the Community's overall Economic Policy.

B. The Common Customs Tariff

In order to regulate the flow of goods into the Community, which may be affected or even prevented by the imposition of customs duties (designed to raise revenue or to protect Community products), or by quotas or other measures reducing the volume of goods that may be imported, it is necessary to have rules that not only indicate which administrative procedures are to be followed but also classify goods, enable their country of origin to be determined, lay down how their value is to be determined, and so forth. Such rules must be applied uniformly throughout the Community. Otherwise, traders would soon learn where the laxest import regimes were and direct their imports through those regimes, thus taking trade out of its normal pattern and disrupting the system. Those matters are covered by the Customs Code and the EC legislation implementing it. The Common Customs Tariff comprises a nomenclature, or classification of goods, known as the Combined Nomenclature, other nomenclatures devised for applying tariff measures, rates of customs duties, agricultural levies and other charges applicable to goods, preferential tariff arrangements contained in agreements made with third countries or adopted unilaterally by the Community, measures providing for a reduction in or relief from import duties, and other Community tariff measures.[9]

(1)   THE CCT NOMENCLATURE

As from 1 January 1988 the CCT applies the new version of the Combined Nomenclature (CN) which is based on the internationally agreed Harmonized Commodity Description and Coding System[10] drafted under the auspices of the Customs Co-operation Council established in Brussels.

The CCT (CN) is divided into 21 sections consisting of 99 chapters. The first 24 of these cover agricultural products and the remaining 75 cover industrial products. It consists of four columns showing the CN code numbers, the description of goods and two rates of duties. One column represents 'autonomous' duties which are the original CCT rates and 'conventional' duties which are negotiated in GATT (or the WTO) and apply to members of GATT (or the WTO) and countries to which the EC grants the most favoured nation treatment.[11]

Although the EC lays down the rules[12] the system is administered by the national authorities which apply the CCT and collect duties which have to be passed on to the EC as the Community's own resources (subject to a deduction of 10% to defray administrative expenses). Since the adoption of the CCT the

---

6   EC Arts 131-135 (ex Arts 110-116).
7   EC Arts 98-104 (ex Arts 102a-104c).
8   EC Arts 105-111 (ex Arts 105-109).
9   Reg 2913/92, Art 20(3).
10   Convention (OJ 1987, L37); Protocol (OJ 1987, L198/11); Council Decision 87/369 (OJ 1987, L198/1).
11   See Reg 2658/87 (OJ 1987, L256/1), the annex of which, containing the CN itself, is published annually (eg Reg 2261/98, OJ 1998, L292/1).
12   Uniform Application of CN, see OJ 1993, C 142/3. For the explanatory notes to the CN, see OJ 2000, C199/1.

Member States can no longer enact autonomous provisons[13] but are bound by the nomenclature as well as the explanatory notes and notices issued by the EC Customs Co-operation Council.[14]

However the authorities of one Member State cannot challenge the classification of the product in another Member State in order to levy additional customs duties in customs clearance, though challenge for other purposes is permitted.[15]

Moreover, since the EC Official Journal is the only authoritative source of information (and everyone is deemed to know the law) an outdated national manual of customs tariff cannot be binding. However the outdated manual was not considered to be equivalent to misleading information since the trader is deemed to know the appropriate rate of duty. Therefore post-clearance recovery duty was in order.[16]

The conditions under which information on the classification of goods may be obtained by customs authorities are now laid down in Articles 11-12 of the Customs Code.

In spite of the periodic updating and revision of the tariff problems of interpretation arise and these have eventually to be solved by the Court of Justice. In the 'turkey tails' case[17] the ECJ laid down certain guidelines in this respect saying that 'products which are not covered by any tariff heading must be classified under the heading for the products to which they are most analogous' and this classification 'should be decided on the basis not only on their physical characteristics but also their use and commercial value'. Subsequent case law includes the definition of tapioca;[18] maizegroats;[19] diet-mayonnaise;[20] sausage[1] (which, *in casu*, was a revolting article manufactured from fat and low-grade meat offal); glass reflectors;[2] ice cream;[3] laughing devices;[4] work of art;[5] books for children;[6] chocolate;[7] game[8] (which in the instant case was concerned with caribou

13 Case 74/69: *HZA Bremen-Freihafen v Waren-Import Gesellschaft Krohn & Co* [1970] ECR 451 at 463, [1970] CMLR 466.
14 Case 14/70: *Deutsche Bakels GmbH v Oberfinanzdirektion München* [1970] ECR 1001, [1971] CMLR 188; Case C-233/88: *Gijs van de Kolk v Inspecteur der Invoerrechten* [1990] ECR I-265.
15 Case C-384/89: *Ministère Public v Tomatis and Fulchiron* [1991] ECR I-127.
16 Case C-80/89: *Erwin Behn v HZA Itzehoe* [1990] ECR I-2659, [1992] 1 CMLR 517.
17 40/69: *HZA Hamburg-Oberelbe v Bollmann* [1970] ECR 69 at 81, [1970] CMLR 141; see also Case 153-157/88: *Ministère Public v Fauque, Re tents and accessories* [1990] ECR I-649, [1991] 3 CMLR 101.
18 Case 72/69: *HZA Bremen v Bremen Handelsgesellschaft* [1970] ECR 427, [1970] CMLR 466; Case 74/69 supra.
19 Case 13/71: *Henck v HZA Emmerich* [1971] ECR 767.
20 Case 30/71: *Siemers v HZA Bad Reichenhall* [1971] ECR 919, [1972] CMLR 121.
1   Case 12/73: *Muras v HZA Hamburg-Jonas* [1973] ECR 963.
2   Case 183/73: *Osram GmbH v Oberfinanzdirektion Frankfurt am Main* [1974] ECR 477, [1974] 2 CMLR 360.
3   Case 53/75: *Belgium v Vandertaelen and Maes* [1975] ECR 1645.
4   Case 22/76: *Import Gadgets Sarl v LAMP Spa, Re the Japanese doll* [1976] ECR 1371.
5   Case 23/77: *Westfälischer Kunsterverein v HZA Münster* [1977] ECR 1985, [1978] 1 CMLR 373; Case 155/84: *Onnasch v HZA Berlin-Packhof* [1987] ECR 1449, [1986] 2 CMLR 456.
6   Case 62/77: *Carlsen Verlag GmbH v Oberfinanz-Direktion Köln* [1977] ECR 2343, [1978] 3 CMLR 14.
7   Case 77/71: *Gervais-Danone AG v HZA München-Scwanthalerstrasse* [1971] ECR 1127, [1973] CMLR 415.
8   See also Case 28/70: *Witt v HZA Lüneburg, Re Rock Cornish Game Hens* [1970] ECR 1021, [1971] CMLR 163.

meat), the classification into 'wild' or 'domestic' product depending upon the country of origin since these animals roam freely in Greenland but are domesticated in Norway;[9] artificial stone;[10] sports shoes;[11] sailing boards;[12] lithographs;[13] rosé wine;[14] animal waste;[15] tobacco waste;[16] medicinal products;[17] 'programmable calculators';[18] photographs (ie whether 'artistic works');[19] semi-conductors;[20] artistic objects (ie whether an artistic paperweight is a 'sculpture' or 'glassware');[1] 'kikis' (ie figurines resembling partly humans, partly animals);[2] apricot purée;[3] a product composed orange juice and sugar[4] and another composite product;[5] and motor vehicles.[6]

(2) ORIGIN OF GOODS

(a) Introduction
The declaration of the origin of goods is vital to determine whether or not the goods originate from the Community or from a third country and, therefore, whether or not they are subject to free movement or the CCT or the CCP. If they come from outside the Community they may benefit from some beneficial import arrangement (such as a referred rate of customs duty) depending on their country of origin. They become goods in free circulation by virtue of EC Article 24 (ex Art 10) when the customs formalities have been complied with and the import duty (if any) has been paid.[7]

The Community rules on origin are now contained in Articles 22-27 of the Customs Code.[8] They differentiate between the rules applicable to the 'non-preferential origin of goods' and those applicable to the 'preferential origin of goods'. The former apply to goods that are subject to the normal customs rules. The latter apply to goods that benefit from some beneficial import arrangement. The Community rules are, and always have been, based on

---

9 Case 149/73: *Witt v HZA Hamburg-Ericus* [1973] ECR 1587.
10 Case 234/81: *E I Du Pont v Customs and Excise Comrs* [1982] ECR 3515.
11 Case 298/82: *Gustav Schickendanz KG v Oberfinanzdirektion Frankfurt am Main* [1984] ECR 1829.
12 Case 32/84: *Van Gend v Inspecteur Inverrechten en Accijnzen, Enschede* [1985] ECR 779.
13 Case 291/87: *Huber v HZA Frankfurt am Main-Flughafen* [1988] ECR 6449, [1990] 2 CMLR 159.
14 Case 89/84: *Fédération Nationale des Producteurs de Vins de Table et Vins de Pays v Ramel* [1985] ECR 1385, [1986] 2 CMLR 526.
15 Case 90/83: *Paterson v W Weddel & Co Ltd* [1984] ECR 1567, [1984] 2 CMLR 540.
16 Case 141/86: *R v H M Customs and Excise, ex p Imperial Tobacco Ltd* [1988] ECR 57, [1988] 2 CMLR 43.
17 Case 35/85: *Procureur de la République v Tissier* [1986] ECR 1207, [1987] 1 CMLR 551.
18 Case 234/87: *Casio Computer Co GmbH Deutschland v Oberfinanzdirektion München* [1989] ECR 63.
19 Case C-1/89: *Raab v HZA Berline-Packhof* [1989] ECR 4423, [1991] 2 CMLR 239.
20 Case C-66/89: *Directeur Général des Douanes v Powerex Europe* [1990] ECR I-1959 [1991] 2 CMLR 529.
 1 Case C-228/89: *Farfalla Flemming v HZA München-West* [1990] ECR I-3387, [1992] 1 CMLR 133.
 2 Case 38/85: *Bienengräber v HZA Hamburg-Jonas* [1986] ECR 815.
 3 Case C-324/89: *Nordegetränke GmbH & Co KG v HZA Hamburg-Ericus* [1991] ECR I-1927.
 4 Case C-219/89: *Westergold GmbH & Co KG v Oberfinanzdirektion München* [1991] ECR I-1895.
 5 Case C-120/90: *Post v Oberfinanzdirektion München* [1991] ECR I-2391.
 6 Case C-384/89: *Ministère Public v Tomatis and Fulchiron* [1991] ECR I-127.
 7 Reg 2913/92, Art 79.
 8 Reg, 2913/92, as supplemented by Arts 35-140 of Reg 2454/93.

international agreements.[9] Although the current rules date only from 1992, the earlier case law remains useful in practice.

(b) Non-preferential origin of goods
The common (or 'non-preferential') definition of the origin of goods applies to internal trade as well as to non-preferential trade with third countries. Goods produced or obtained in one country are regarded as originating in that country,[10] which includes that country's territorial sea, whilst goods produced in two or more countries are regarded as originating in the country in which the last substantial process or operation that is economically justified was performed.[11] Thus, for example, in Case 100/84[12] the origin of fish caught was determined in accordance with the part played in a joint operation between British and Polish fishermen. The British cast and raised their nets but the Polish boats did the trawling. Therefore the origin of the fish was attributed to the boats which trapped them in their nets.

However, any processing or working with the object of circumventing the provisions applicable in the Community to goods from a specific country shall not be deemed to confer on the goods thus produced the origin of the country where it is carried out.[13]

Case law on the origin of goods includes cases of poultry products from Poland;[14] synthetic textile fabrics from the Middle East in circulation in Belgium but imported into France;[15] Spanish grapes dispatched from Italy to France[16] and millboard sails from Hong Kong made with Japanese cloth.[17]

The phrase 'the last substantial process or operation' was considered in Case 49/75.[18] Having stated that the determination of the origin of goods must be based on an objective distinction between raw material and processed product but not simply in differences in tariff classification, the ECJ held that a process or operation is only 'substantial' if the 'product resulting therefrom has its own properties and a composition of its own, which it did not possess before the process or operation'. There must have been a 'significant qualitative change' of the product. Consequently, ruled the Court, the cleaning and grinding of a raw material (*in casu*, raw casein), together with the grading and packaging of the product obtained, could not confer a new status on that product.

---

  9   Originally on the 1950 Brussels Convention that was enshrined in Reg 802/68 (OJ 1968, L148/1). The Community also adopted the 1973 Kyoto Convention on Simplification and Harmonisation of Customs Procedures: Council Decision 77/415 (OJ 1977, L166/1) and Commission Decision 87/204 (OJ 1985, L87/8).
 10   Reg 2913/92, Art 23. See also Reg 2454/93, Arts 35-65.
 11   Reg 2913/92, Art 24.
 12   100/84: *Commission v United Kingdom, Re Anglo-Polish Fishing* [1985] ECR 1169, [1985] 2 CMLR 199.
 13   Reg 2913/92, Art 25.
 14   Case 9/72: *Firma Georg Brunner v HZA Hof* [1972] ECR 961, [1985] 2 CMLR 931.
 15   Case 41/76: *Criel (née Donckerwolke) v Porcureur de la République* [1976] ECR 1921, [1977] 2 CMLR 535.
 16   Case 52/77: *Cayrol v Rivoira* [1977] ECR 2261, [1978] 2 CMLR 253; see also Case 179/78: *Procureur de la République v Rivoira, Re penalty for false declaration* [1979] ECR 1147, [1979] 3 CMLR 456.
 17   Case 385/85: *SR Industries v Administration des Douanes* [1986] ECR 2929, [1988] 1 CMLR 378 at para 7.
 18   49/76: *Gesellschaft für Übersehandel mbH v Handelskammer Hamburg* [1977] ECR 41.

In the *Yoshida* cases[19] the Court had to determine the origin of slide fasteners consisting essentially of 'two parallel tapes, scoops or other inter-locking elements, slides and end pieces'. The Court had to interpret Commission Regulation 2077/77[20] which defined the working or processing that conferred the status or originating products on slide fasteners. The cases arose from the manufacture in Germany and in the Netherlands, by the German and Dutch subsidiaries of the Japanese Yoshida group, of slide fasteners containing sliders made in Japan. The Court found that six principal operations were carried out in the production, ie weaving, binding and dyeing the tapes; pressing metal scoops, or the manufacture of nylon inter-locking spirals to the tapes, and joining the tapes together; fixing the stops at top and bottom; the insertion and, where necessary, dyeing of the sliders; and drying and cleaning the fasteners, and cutting them into separate slide fasteners. The Court concluded that the last four of these operations taken together should be regarded as the 'last substantial process or operation' whilst the slider was only one element in the whole assembly and manufactured in Japan. The Court repeating its conclusion in the *Uberseehandel* case ruled that the inclusion of the slider in the definition of the operations conferring the originating status on slide fasteners would go beyond the last substantial process or operation.[1]

The *Brother* case,[2] reflects a variation of the theme. Here Brother imported electronic typewriters from Taiwan into Germany, declaring their Taiwanese origin where they were assembled out of parts some of which came from Japan. The German authorities concluded that the product originated from Japan and imposed anti-dumping duties. The Commission supported the German authorities, contending that the mere assembly of previously manufactured parts should not be regarded as a substantial process or operation within the meaning of Article 5 of the Regulation where in view of the work involved and the expenditure on materials on the one hand and the value added on the other, the operation is clearly less important than other processes or operations carried out in another country or countries. In the ECJ's opinion, complex operations involving the consideration of technical criteria may not be decisive in determining the origin of goods and in such cases it is necessary to take into account the value added by the assembly as an ancillary criterion. However the assembly operations as a whole must involve an appreciable increase in the commercial value of the finished product at the ex-factory stage.

The Court also dealt with the question whether the transfer of the assembly from the country of manufacture of the component parts of a country where the use if made of already existing factories in itself justified the presumption that the sole object of the transfer was to circumvent the applicable provisions and, in particular, the application of anti-dumping duties, within the meaning of Article 6 of the Regulation. It considered that the use of the existing factories did not in itself justify the presumption but the manufacturer must prove that there were reasonable grounds other than avoiding the consequences of the operations in the country from which the goods were exported. In conclusion, it seems that

---

19 Case 34/78: *Yoshida Nederland v Kamer* [1979] ECR 115; Case 114/78: *Yoshida GmbH v Industrie-Handelskammer Kassel* [1979] ECR 151; see also Case 93/83: *Zentralgenossenschaft des Fleischgewerbes v HZA Bochum* [1984] ECR 1095; and Case 162/82: *Directeur des Douanes v Cousin* [1983] ECR 1101, [1984] 2 CMLR 780.
20 OJ 1977, L242/5.
1 Case 34/78, supra at 221.
2 Case C-26/88: *Brother International GmbH v HZA Geissen* [1989] ECR 4253, [1990] 3 CMLR 658.

the Court has shifted the emphasis from technical aspects of the operation or process to a value added by the assembly thereby, the burden of proof remaining with the trader.

The *Brother* case reminds one of the problems of the so-called 'screwdriver assembly' technique. Using this technique, it is alleged, foreign companies established in the Community import components which are assembled in the Community with the minimum of effort and present the end-product as a Community product. The practice was subject to a complaint before the GATT panel.[3]

(c) Preferential origin of goods

In addition to the general principles regarding origin there are special rules which may be laid down for the purpose of identifying the origin of goods for which the benefit of preferential tariff measures is claimed. Such rules are either laid down in the particular agreement, concluded with a third country, that defines the preferential measures or, where the preferential measures are granted by the Community unilaterally to a particular third country, the rules are determined by the Commission on the advice of the Customs Code Committee (formerly the Committee on Origin).[4] The Commission regulations emanating from this process are subject to judicial review.[5]

(d) Evidence of the origin

The burden of proving the origin of goods is imposed upon the importer since he alone knows or can be reasonably expected to know it. The failure to disclose is an offence governed by national law but the prosecuting authorities have to bear in mind the administrative nature of the offence and moderate the sanction accordingly.[6] In principle they have to accept the declaration of the origin unless they have a reason to believe that it is false.[7]

(3) VALUATION OF GOODS

(a) General principles

Customs valuation is based on the Brussels Valuation Convention 1950 adopted by Regulation 803/68[8] substantially amended by Regulation 1224/80[9] which adopted the provisions of the GATT Customs Valuation Code of 1979 concluded within the Tokyo Round.[10] The rules applicable at present are contained in the Customs Code.[11]

The application of the valuation rules is supervised by the Customs Code Committee (formerly the Customs Valuation Committee).

---

3 *Japan v European Economic Community (Re Screwdriver Assembly, GATT Economic Panel)* [1990] 2 CMLR 639. See Case C-179/87: *Sharp Corpn v Council* [1992] ECR I-1635, [1992] 2 CMLR 415.
4 Reg 2913/92, Art 27. See also Reg 2454/93, Arts 66-104.
5 See Case 162/82: *Directeur des Douanes v Cousin* [1983] ECR 1101, [1984] 2 CMLR 780.
6 See Cases 41/76 and 52/77, supra, p 437, notes 15 and 16.
7 Case C-83/89: *Openbaar Ministerie v Houben* [1990] ECR I-1161, [1991] 2 CMLR 321.
8 OJ, Sp Ed 1968 II.436.
9 OJ 1980, L134/1.
10 Text OJ 1980, L71/3 and Council Decision 80/271.
11 Reg 2913/92, supra, Arts 28-36. See also Reg 2454/93, Arts 141-181.

In principle the value of the imported goods ought to be declared[12] according to their actual value at the time of export to the Community or at the time the goods are being valued.[13]

The customs value is, in principle, expressed in the currency of the Member State in which the valuation has occurred; in other cases the foreign currency is converted according to the appropriate rates of conversion.[14]

Under the Community rules there are five valuation methods[15] which have to be successfully applied until the appropriate method has been ascertained. These are:

(b)   Transaction value or 'normal price'
The first method applies: (a) where there are no restrictions as to the disposition or use of the goods other than those which (i) are imposed or required by law or by the public authorities in the country of importation or (ii) limit the geographical area in which the goods may be resold, or (iii) do not substantially affect the value of the goods; (b) the sale or price is not subject to any conditions or consideration for which a value cannot be determined with respect to the goods being valued (such as an obligation to buy other goods); and (c) no part of the proceeds of any subsequent resale, disposal or use of the goods by the buyer will accrue directly or indirectly to the seller, unless an appropriate adjustment can be made. The buyer and the seller are to be independent and, where they are related, the declared transaction value will be accepted unless the price has been affected by the relationship.[16]

Article 32 of the Regulation lists certain categories of costs which must be included in transaction value (eg the cost of containers) and Article 33 provides that certain charges are excluded. Where software is embodied in the goods the cost of acquiring that 'intangible property' (software as such is not 'goods' and, therefore, is not subject to the CCT) must be regarded as an integral part of the price paid or payable for the goods, hence of the transaction value.[17]

Since the value has to be calculated according to the conditions of actual sale the cost of weighing of goods on their arrival may not be included,[18] neither can the transport within the Community.[19]

(c)   Transaction value of identical and similar goods
The second method refers to the transaction value of 'identical goods', ie goods produced in the same country which are the same in all respects, including physical characteristics, quality and reputation.

The third method refers to the transaction value of 'similar goods', ie goods produced in the same country which, though not alike in all respects, have like characteristics and like component materials which enable them to perform the same functions and to be commercially interchangeable. The customs value is

---

12   Reg 2454/93, Art 178.
13   Reg 2913/92, Arts 29(1) and 30(2)(a), (b).
14   Reg 2913/92, Art 35.
15   Reg 2913/92, Art 30(1).
16   Reg 2913/92, Art 29(1) and (2).
17   See Case C-79/89: *Brown Boveri v HZA Mannheim* [1991] ECR I-1853, [1993] 1 CMLR 814.
18   Case 65/85: *HZA Hamburg-Ericus v Van Houten* [1986] ECR 447, [1988] 2 CMLR 941.
19   Case 290/84: *HZA Schweinfurt v Mainfrucht Obstverwertung GmbH* [1985] ECR 3909, [1987] 1 CMLR 684; Case C-17/89: *HZA Frankfurt v Deutsche Olivetti GmbH* [1990] ECR I-2301, [1992] 2 CMLR 859.

based on the price at which the identical or similar imported goods are sold for export to the Community in substantially the same quantities as the goods being valued.[20]

(d)   Unit price of identical or similar goods
The fourth method is based on the unit price of identical or similar imported goods sold in the Community in the greatest aggregate quantity to persons not related to the sellers.[1]

(e)   Computed value
If the test of similarity is not applicable a 'computed' value will be calculated.
    The computed value consists of the sum of (i) the cost or value of materials and manufacture or other processing employed in the production of the imported goods; (ii) an amount of profit and general expenses equivalent to that usually reflected in sales of goods of the same class or kind as the goods being valued which are made by producers in the country of exportation for export to the Community, and (iii) the cost or value of the items which have to be added in accordance with Article 32(1).[2]

(f)   The reasonable test
Where the customs value cannot be determined by applying the five main methods it should be determined using reasonable means, consistent with principles and general provisions of the Code and of Article VII of GATT, and on the basis of data available in the Community.[3] However, certain methods have been explicitly ruled out[4] ie, (i) the selling price in the Community of goods produced in the Community; (ii) acceptance of the higher of two alternative values; (iii) the price of goods on the domestic market of the country of exportation; (iv) the cost of production, other than computed values which have been determined for identical or similar goods; (v) prices for export to countries not forming part of the customs territory of the Community; (vi) minimum customs values; and (vii) arbitrary or fictitious values.

(g)   Case law
Cases decided before the present valuation rules were adopted in 1992 are still relevant; although they must now be read subject to the rules as they now stand. Cases decided by the ECJ include, inter alia, the valuation of spare parts imported into Belgium by the Belgian branch of the Swiss subsidiary of the American Caterpillar Tractor Company;[5] the pricing of pharmaceutical raw materials imported into France (at a price which suggested a capital transfer) by a French subsidiary of a Swiss company;[6] the question whether warehousing charges should be included in the declared value;[7] valuation of pharmaceutical products where

---

20   Reg 2913/92 Art 30(2)(a) and (b); Reg 2454/93, Arts 142(1)(c) and (d), 150 and 151.
 1   Reg 2913/92, Art 30(2)(c); Reg 2454/93, Art 152.
 2   Reg 2913/92, Art 30(2)(d); Reg 2454/93, Art 153.
 3   Reg 2913/92, Art 31.
 4   Reg 2913/92, Art 31(2).
 5   Case 111/79: *Suisse Caterpillar Overseas SA v Belgium* [1980] ECR 773, [1980] 3 CMLR 597.
 6   Case 65/79: *Procureur de la République v Chatain* [1980] ECR 1345.
 7   Case 38/77: *Enka BV v Inspecteur der Invoerrechten en Accijnzen, Arnhem* [1977] ECR 2203, [1978] 2 CMLR 212.

the buyer and the seller were 'persons associated in business';[8] the question whether 'know-how' (being an intangible property) is part of the 'normal price' of a machine;[9] whether transport costs within the Community[10] or the combined transport costs within the Community and overseas ought to be included in the valuation;[11] licence fees payable by the buyer of seeds to the plant breeder for his services performed in the Community had to be included in the transaction value;[12] but not so commission fees paid to an agent to the importer[13] or charges for extended credit.[14]

Two cases are particularly interesting, ie the Caterpillar case[15] and the prosecution of Chatain,[16] the former involving an undervaluation and the latter an overvaluation of imported goods. In the former case the price at which the spare parts were purchased had been arrived at by adding to Caterpillar Tractor's expenses and overhead costs 50% of the consolidated profit obtained by Caterpillar Tractor and its Belgian branch on the sale and resale of the spare parts to independent buyers. Caterpillar claimed that this purchase price, together with the delivery costs, constituted the value of the spare parts for customs purposes, while the Belgian authorities contended that this value should be increased by approximately 20% by deducting from the price charged by the Belgian branch the costs of delivery, warehousing and processing the products on the Community customs territory. The Court held that the aim of the relevant Regulation was to avoid arbitrary or fictitious valuations and to base the customs value on the real value of the imported goods. Thus the recognition of the price paid or payable was merely one method of calculating the normal price and it was only taken into account to the extent that it effectively corresponded to the normal price. In the circumstances it is permissible to re-value upward the declared value.

In the *Chatain* case, by contrast, the question of possible re-valuation downwards was considered. In that case a director of a French subsidiary of a Swiss company was prosecuted for having submitted a false declaration as to the value of products as well as unlawfully transferring capital abroad. He submitted invoices showing high prices of the goods which the French customs authorities, on the basis of an analysis of the prices of comparable products, would have reduced substantially. In other words the French subsidiary had paid excessive prices in order to transfer its profits to its Swiss parent company and thus avoid paying French tax. The Court explained that the object of Regulation 803/68 was to prevent goods from being undervalued and that adjustments allowed thereunder were intended to avoid undervaluation. The Court also cited Regulation 375/69[17] on the particulars relating to the value of goods which only

8   Case 82/76: *Farbwerke Hoechst AG v HZA Frankfurt-am-Main* [1977] ECR 335, [1977] 1 CMLR 565.

9   Case 1/77: *Robert Bosch GmbH v HZA Hildesheim* [1977] ECR 1473, [1977] 2 CMLR 563.

10 Case 290/84: *HZA Schweinfurt v Mainfrucht Obstverwertung GmbH* [1985] ECR 3909, [1987] 1 CMLR 684. See also Case C-11/89: *Unifert Handelsgesellschaft GmbH v HZA Münster* [1990] ECR I-2275 [1992] 3 CMLR 304.

11 Case C-17/89: *HZA Frankfurt am Main-Ost v Deutsche Olivetti GmbH* [1990] ECR I-2301, [1992] 2 CMLR 859.

12 Case C-116/89: *BayWa v HZA Weiden* [1991] ECR I-1095, [1992] 3 CMLR 685.

13 Case C-299/90: *HZA Karlsruhe v Gebr Hepp GmbH* [1990] ECR I-4301, [1993] 3 CMLR 328.

14 Case C-21/91: *Wünsche Handelsgesellschaft International GmbH v HZA Hamburg-Jonas* [1992] ECR I-3647, [1992] 3 CMLR 208.

15 Supra.

16 Supra.

17 OJ 1969, L52/1.

provided for the invoice price to be adjusted upwards. Thus, ruled the Court, the invoice price may only be increased. The result may appear illogical but the conclusion is sound for the declarant may not be prevented from paying customs duties he considered just even if they appear to be high. In a subsequent case[18] the ECJ confirmed the 'immutability' of invoice prices by ruling that even excessive invoice prices cannot be lowered by EC customs.

(4) CUSTOMS PROCEDURES

(a) Entry of goods
Goods brought into the EC customs territory are subject to customs supervision[19] until they are assigned to a customs-approved treatment or use. Customs-approved treatment or use comprise the placing of goods under a customs procedure, their entry into a free zone or free warehouse,[20] their re-exportation from the customs territory of the Community, their destruction and their abandonment to the Exchequer.[1] When goods are released for free circulation (one of the customs procedures), they have conferred upon them the customs status of Community goods, any customs duties and other legally due charges must be paid, and any commercial policy measures applicable to imports into the Community are applied.[2] If goods are not released for free circulation, they may be entered for one of the other procedures referred to below.

(b) External transit
The external transit procedure allows the movement of goods from one point to another within the Community of (1) non-Community goods, without such goods being subject to import duties and other charges or to commercial policy measures; and (2) Community goods which are subject to a Community measure applied to their export to third countries and customs formalities for export. Such movement shall take place:

(a) under the external Community transit procedure; or
(b) under the cover of a TIR carnet[3] provided that such movement (i) began or is to end outside of the Community; or relates to consignments of goods which must be unloaded in the Community and which are conveyed with goods to be unloaded in a third country; or (ii) is effected between two points in the Community through the territory of a third country;
(c) under cover of an ATA carnet (ATA Convention) used as a transit document;
(d) under cover of the Rhine Manifest (of the Rhine Convention);
(e) under cover of the NATO convention;
(f) by post[4]

---

18   Case 54/80: *Procureur de la République v Wilner* [1980] ECR 3673.
19   Reg 2913/92, Art 37 et seq.
20   Free zones and free warehouses are areas within the customs territory of the Community in which goods are considered as being outside the Community's customs territory: Reg 2913/92, Art 166.
 1   Goods are abandoned to the Exchequer where national legislation so provides: Reg 2913/92, Art 182(1).
 2   Reg 2913/92, Art 79. The commercial policy measures in question include such things as anti-dumping duties.
 3   Cf, the Convention on a common transit procedure (OJ 1987, L226/2), as amended.
 4   Reg 2913/92 Art 91.

The detailed rules for the operation of the procedure and the exemptions are to be determined in accordance with the committee procedure.[5] However in the context of the implemented Community measures the Member States shall be allowed to lay down simplified procedures.[6]

The external procedure shall end when the goods and the corresponding documents are produced at the customs office of destination.[7]

(c)   Internal transit

The internal transit procedure allows the movement of Community goods within the Community and also through the territory of a third country without any change in their customs status and follows substantially the same pattern as external transit.[8] The transit with the EFTA countries is governed by the Convention on a Common Transit Procedure[9] as amended.

(d)   Customs warehousing

Customs warehousing is a procedure whereby goods are stored without being subject to import or export duties or commercial policy measures. A customs warehouse is any place approved by, or under the supervision of the customs authorities for storage under those conditions. While being stored, the goods may be subjected only to a limited number of operations intended to preserve them, improve appearance or marketable quality or prepare them for distribution or resale. When taken out of the warehouse, import or export duties (as the case may be) must be paid unless the goods are then placed under some other procedure.[10]

(e)   Inward processing

Inward processing is a procedure whereby goods (whether non-Community goods or goods which have been released for free circulation) may be used in the customs territory of the Community for one or more processing operations and then exported from the Community in the form of a different product.[11]

(f)   Processing under customs control

Processing under customs control is a procedure whereby non-Community goods are used in the customs territory of the Community for operations that change their nature or state. The imposition of import duties and commercial policy measures is deferred until the goods have been altered and are applied to the goods in their altered state.[12]

(g)   Temporary admission

The temporary admission procedure permits non-Community goods intended for re-export to be used in the customs territory of the Community with total or partial relief from customs duties and without imposition of commercial policy measures.[13]

---

5   Reg 2913/92, Art 97(1).
6   Reg 2913/92, Art 97(2).
7   Reg 2913/92, Art 92.
8   Reg 2913/92, Art 163.
9   OJ 1987, L226/2; see Case 340/87: *Commission v Italy* [1989] ECR 1483, [1991] 1 CMLR 437.
10   Reg 2913/92, Arts 98-113.
11   Reg 2913/92, Arts 114-129.
12   Reg 2913/92, Arts 130-136.
13   Reg 2913/92, Arts 137-144.

(h)   Outward processing
Outward processing is a procedure permitting Community goods to be exported temporarily from the customs territory of the Community so that they can be processed and the products resulting from the processing imported into the Community with total or partial relief from import duties.[14]

(i)   Export procedure
The export procedure allows Community goods to leave the customs territory of the Community. It entails the application of exit formalities including commercial policy measures and, where appropriate, export duties.[15]

(j)   Community Customs Code and Customs Committee
As from 1 January 1994 the Community Customs Code established by Regulation 2913/92 has come into effect, repealing and consolidating the plethora of Community legislation. The advantage of codification is obvious. As the customs rules have to be updated and adapted to market conditions the Community system remains subject to continuing supervision of the Customs Code Committee consisting of the Member States' civil servants chaired by non-voting representatives of the Commission which shall make recommendations to the Commission resulting, as appropriate, either in Council or autonomous Commission legislation. This Committee shall cover as hitherto the specialist committees, ie Nomenclature, Origin and Valuation, Movement of Goods, Customs Procedures, Common Warehouses and Free Zones Committees.

(k)   Rules applicable to specific sectors
EC Article 32 (ex Art 38) provides that the rules laid down for the establishment of the Common Market (including the CCT) apply to agricultural products, except as otherwise provided in EC Articles 33–38 (ex Arts 39–46). These special rules emanate from the organization of markets in cereals, rice, sugar, olive oil and milk products; eggs, poultrymeat and pigmeat; beef and veal; fruit and vegetables and wine; oils and oilseeds, and fisheries.

Special regimes also apply to Euratom products and coal and steel. Whilst certain Euratom products are subject to the CCT, others are not and remain subject to negotiation between the Member States.[16] The CCT does not apply to ECSC products, though the Member States and tend to apply it in practice.[17]

C.   Common Commercial Policy

Whilst the CCT forms the external customs barrier the CCP is meant to integrate the Member States' trade with the outside world into a Community system. Therefore the CCP has to be seen in the broader context of the Community external relations policy dictated not only by economic but also by political considerations.[18]

---

14   Reg 2913/92, Arts 145-160.
15   Reg 2913/92, Art 161-162 and Art 183.
16   Lasok, *The Trade and Customs Law of the European Union* (3rd edn, 1998), pp 343-344.
17   Ibid p 344.
18   Ibid pp 363 et seq and Ch 3, supra.

(1) COMMUNITY TRADE CONVENTIONAL ARRANGEMENTS

The positive aspects of the CCP are reflected in the exercise of the Community treaty-making power. Thus Accession Agreements, though primarily concerned with the building of the Common Market (and under the Maastricht Treaty of the Economic Union) perforce affect external trade. The new Member States are bound by common rules but may negotiate temporary derogations. By virtue of EC Article 307 (ex Art 234) the existing trade agreements to which the Member States are parties remain valid but have to be adjusted to their obligations within the Community. Agreements between the Member States made before the entry into force of the EC Treaty cannot justify restrictions on intra-Community trade.[19]

Association agreements and trade agreements[20] in various forms and proportions reflect a network of conventional arrangements. In this process the treaty-making power of the EC is used extensively, thus replacing the traditional role of sovereign states and projecting the Community as the sole trade unit. However it is essential to distinguish between (i) the Community's sole competence to act on behalf of the collective and (ii) joint competence where the Community becomes involved in 'mixed agreements', ie international treaties in which the contracting parties comprise the EC and one or more Member States on the one side and one or more non-Community parties on the other.[1] Such treaties are not expressly provided for in the EC Treaty but are provided for in Article 102 of the Euratom Treaty. The EC competence in the context of trade agreements governed by EC Article 133 (ex Art 113) has been the subject of substantial case law.[2]

Bilateral agreements (whether within the sole or joint EC competence) represent one aspect of trade pattern, multilateral (the so-called 'commodity agreements' made within the framework of the UNCTAD) another. A special feature of EC multilateralism is the trade relations on a regional basis and in relation to groups of countries and other 'Communities'. However, perhaps more portentous to the development of Europe is the European Economic Area (EEA), ie the EC-EFTA Agreement negotiated in 1991. Since the EC External Treaties form 'an integral part of the Community law'[3] they are not only subject to judicial control but are also a source of legal obligations affecting the Community, the Member States and private parties. Thus, apart from being instruments of Community policy in international trade, they are part of the Community normative system.

In this context one has to observe the position of Member States not only in the formation and execution of Treaties[4] but also in their partnership in GATT and, latterly, WTO negotiations. The EC in its own right and on behalf of the Member States takes part in the negotiations in GATT and the WTO. However, in view of the bicephalous nature of the Community external relations, the agreements reached in GATT and the WTO have to be ratified by the Member States. Thus the intransigence of one Member State may not only protract

19 See Cases T-69/89: *Radio Telefis Eireann v Commission;* T-70/89: *BBC and BBC Enterprises Ltd v Commission;* T-76/89: *Independent Television Publications Ltd v Commission* [1991] ECR II-485; II-535; II-575. On appeal: Cases C-241/91P and C-242/91P: *RTE and ITP v Commission* [1995] ECR I-743, paras 83-87.
20 See pp 80–85, supra.
1   Eg Opinion 1/78: *Re International Agreement on Natural Rubber* [1979] ECR 2871.
2   See p 76, supra, notes 3–4.
3   Opinion 1/78, supra.
4   See pp 75, et seq, supra.

negotiations but also jeopardize the achievement of a world-wide agreement, as testified by the endless wrangles of the Uruguay Round.

(2)   COMMUNITY PROTECTIVE MEASURES

Measures to protect the interests of the Community represent the negative aspects of the CCP in the context of world trade. Whilst proclaiming the virtue of liberalized trade the EC pursues a selfish policy. In this respect the 'Fortress Europe' resembles another economic giant, the USA.

Community measures can be divided into technical rules and instruments of policy.

(a)   Anti-dumping

Article 91 of the EEC Treaty (now repealed) applied to the phenomenon of 'dumping' where it occurred within the Community during the transitional period and before the establishment of the customs union and free movement of goods between Member States. It lost its significance after the end of the transitional period, at which point dumping would contradict the principle of the single domestic market and would ordinarily be dealt with under the competition rules. On the other hand, special anti-dumping rules apply to goods originating from third countries imported into the Community.[5] These rules are based on EC Article 133(1) (ex Art 113(1)) and the GATT anti-dumping code and are at present comprised in Regulation 384/96.[6]

The Regulation covers all products, both agricultural and industrial, except those coming within the scope of the ECSC Treaty, which are dealt with separately by Commission Decision 2277/96.[7] Services as such are not included. In order to invoke the Regulation there must be actual dumping in the Community, a resulting 'injury' or threat of injury to Community industry, and the Community interest must call for intervention.

(i)   Dumping

Both the GATT code and the Regulation consider a product to be dumped where its export price to the Community is lower than[8] a comparable price for the like product, in the ordinary course of trade, as established for the exporting country (a concept that is usually referred as to as 'normal value'). The regulations provide for a number of different ways of computing the normal value of the product. Normal value is 'normally' based on the price paid or payable, in the ordinary course of trade, by independent customers in the exporting country; but there may be many reasons why that price would be an unreliable guide. For example, if sales to independent customers in the exporting country are very small (conventionally put at less than 5% of sales to the Community) they may not be

---

5   Eg Case 9/72: *Georg Brunner v HZA Hof, Re ducks from Poland* [1972] ECR 961, [1972] CMLR 931.
6   OJ 1996, L56/1; amended by Reg 2331/96 (OJ 1996, L317/1), Reg 905/98 (OJ 1998, L128/18) and Reg 2238/2000 (OJ 2000, L257/2). The current GATT Anti-dumping Code is contained in the Agreement on Implementation of Article VI of the General Agreement on Tariffs and Trade 1994, which is included in Annex 1A to the Agreement establishing the WTO. The Community legislation must be interpreted in the light of the GATT Code: Cases T-33/98 and T-34/98: *Petrotub SA and Republica SA v Council* [1999] ECR II-3837, para 105.
7   OJ 1996, L308/11; amended by Decision 1000/99 (OJ 1999, L122/35).
8   Reg 384/96, Art 1. For details see Lasok, *The Trade and Customs Law of the European Union* (3rd edn, 1998), pp 401 et seq.

regarded as representative. In such circumstances the normal value may be what is often referred to as the 'computed or constructed value', that is, a value determined on the basis of the cost of production of the goods, plus a reasonable amount for selling, general and administrative costs and for profits, or on the basis of representative export prices to an appropriate third country. Special rules apply to imports from non-market economies and there are variations to those rules for Russia and China because some firms in those countries may operate under normal market conditions.[9]

The export price is the price actually paid or payable for the product when sold for export to the Community. Where there is no export price in that sense (such as where the third country manufacturer is itself the importer and seller in the Community) or when the export price is unreliable (such as where the goods are sold by the exporter to a subsidiary in the Community), the export price can be 'constructed' by working backwards from the price at which the goods are first resold to an independent buyer in the Community, or on any reasonable basis.[10]

Once the normal value and the export price have been determined, they must be compared 'fairly'. In order to do so, it may be necessary to adjust one or other of them so as to ensure that the comparison is made at the same level of trade, at as nearly as possible the same time and with due account being made for other factors affecting price comparability.[11] If the normal value exceeds the export price, there is a finding of dumping; and the difference between the two is known as 'the dumping margin'. The dumping margin must normally be established on the basis of a comparison between a weighted average normal value and a weighted average export price or by a comparison between individual normal values and individual export prices on a transaction-by-transaction basis. The dumping margin can also be determined by comparing the export price for a particular sale not with a normal value of a comparable sale but with a figure representing the average of a number of different normal sales.[12] The dumping margin is usually expressed as a percentage of the c.i.f. price of the product for export to the Community.

(ii)   Injury

Anti-dumping measures may be imposed only if the dumping practice causes or threatens to cause material injury to an established Community industry or materially retards the setting up of planned Community industry.[13]

An examination of injury takes into consideration the value of dumped imports, the prices of such imports and the consequent impact on the industry concerned.[14]

---

9   Reg 384/96, Art 2(1)-(7), as amended by Reg 905/98. It would seem that the different methods of determining normal value must be considered following the order in which they are set out in the Regulation: Case T-48/96 *Acme Industry v Council* [1999] ECR II-3089, para 36 (which was concerned with a predecessor to the present regulation).
10   Reg 384/96, Art 2(8)-(9).
11   Reg 384/96, Art 2(10), as amended by Reg 2331/96.
12   Reg 384/96, Art 2(11)-(12). See Cases 240/84: *NTN Toyo Bearing Co v Council*; Case 255/84: *Nachi Fujkoshi Corpn v Council*; Case 256/84: *Koyo Seiko Co Ltd v Council*; Case 258/84: *Nippon Seiko v Council*; and Case 260/84: *Minebea Co v Council* [1987] ECR 1809, 1861, 1899, 1923, 1975 and [1989] 2 CMLR 76.
13   Reg 382/96, Art 3(1).
14   Reg 382/96, Art 3(2); See Cases 113/77: *NTN Toyo Bearing Co v Council* [1979] ECR 1185; *Acrylic Fibres* from the USA Case (OJ, 1979, L308/11); Case T-171/97: *Swedish Match Philippines Inc v Council* [1999] ECR II-3241, paras 61-76.

The term 'Community industry' is interpreted broadly, covering the producers as a whole of the like products or those of them whose collective output constitutes a major proportion of the total Community production.[15] Normally the Community producers are protected but the consumer may also be considered where for example the Commission thought that certain photo albums were not produced in sufficient volume in the Community and, therefore, there might be a shortage if the protective measures were imposed.[16]

(iii) Anti-dumping procedure

The anti-dumping procedure starts with a complaint on a model complaint form to the Commission or a Member State of a person or body acting on behalf of a Community industry which considers itself injured or threatened. The complaint must be substantiated. Where, in the absence of a formal complaint, a Member State is in possession of sufficient evidence it must advise the Commission accordingly.[17]

The Regulation provides for consultations within an Advisory Committee which consists of representatives of the Member States with a representative of the Commission in the chair. Consultations are held on request of a Member State or on the initiative of the Commission.[18] Their object is to cover the existence of dumping, the extent of the injury and the link between the dumped imports and the injury and the measures which would be appropriate to remedy the position.

Where, after the consultation, there appears to be a prima facie case the Commission will investigate the dumping practice and the injury,[19] giving the parties an opportunity to make their representations. The procedure is inquisitorial and the Commission is not prevented from reaching preliminary determinations or from applying provisional measures expeditiously. Preliminary, or even final, findings may be made in the light of the available facts if any interested party or a third country refuses or fails to provide information or significantly hinders the investigations.[20]

(iv) Sanctions and judicial reviews

During the investigations undertakings may be offered by the parties concerned or suggested by the Commission. If such an offer is accepted by the Commission the investigations may be terminated without the imposition of provisional or definitive anti-dumping duties.[1] Such undertakings are signed by the exporter, though not by the Commission, and constitute a unilateral promise to remedy the position, ie to revise the prices or cease exports until the Commission is satisfied that either the dumping margin or the injury is removed. The undertakings shall lapse if at the time of the proceedings the Commission determines that no injury exists.

Where the preliminary investigations show that there is sufficient evidence of dumping and injury to Community industry, and the Community interest calls

---

15 Reg 382/96, Art 4(1).
16 Com Decision, *Re photo albums from South Korea and Hong Kong* (OJ 1990, L138/48).
17 Reg 384/96, Art 5.
18 Reg 384/96, Arts 5(9), 9(4) and 15.
19 Reg 384/96, Art 5.
20 Reg 384/96, Art 18.
 1 Reg 384/96, Art 8.

for intervention, the Commission shall impose a provisional duty.[2] Provisional duties last for six months and may be extended. They are not collected but the exporter must provide an appropriate security.

Finally the Council acting by qualified majority on a proposal of the Commission and after consultation with the Advisory Committee will impose a definitive duty.[3] Provisional or definitive anti-dumping duties are imposed by a regulation which must specify the amount and type of duty, the product covered, the country of origin or export, the name of the supplier and the reasons on which it is based.[4] An anti-dumping duty may be no greater than the dumping margin and should be less if a lesser amount would be adequate to remove the injury to Community industry.[5] The anti-dumping duties are collected by the Member States independently of any customs duties, taxes and other charges normally imposed on imports in accordance with regulations applicable to customs debts.[6] These duties shall be neither imposed nor increased with retrospective effect except where there is history of dumping or the injury has caused massive dumped imports in a relatively short period or where an undertaking has been violated.[7]

A measure imposing anti-dumping duties remains in force only to the extent necessary to counteract the dumping and a measure imposing a definitive duty expires automatically after five years. In the meantime, an administrative review may be held either at the request of a Member State or on the initiative of the Commission or the request of an interested party. However the latter (ie the complainants, exporter and importer) must submit evidence of changed circumstances sufficient to justify the need of review, provided one year has elapsed since the conclusion of the investigations. Their requests shall be addressed to the Commission which shall inform the Member States.[8]

The grounds upon which requests for review have been granted include: renewed or increased dumping;[9] absence of dumping;[10] absence of injury;[11] replacement of duty with undertaking;[12] and violation of undertaking.[13]

The ECJ has admitted applications for judicial review of an anti-dumping measure imposed by the Council which, though legislative in nature, may be of a direct and individual concern to the exporters concerned[14] or to a company

---

2   Reg 384/96, Art 7. On Community interest see Art 21 and, for example, Com Reg 2140/89, OJ 1989, L205/5, paras 131-138.
3   Reg 384/96, Art 9(4).
4   Reg 384/96, Art 14(2).
5   Reg 384/96, Art 9(4). A failure to consider whether or not a lesser amount would suffice may lead to the annulment of the duty: Case 53/83: *Allied Corpn v Council* [1985] ECR 1621.
6   Reg 384/96, Art 14(1).
7   Reg 384/96, Art 10(4)-(5).
8   Reg 384/96, Art 11.
9   Eg Lithium Hydroxide (USA, USSR) OJ 1980, L158/5 and OJ 1983, L294/3; Hercide (Romania) OJ 1982, L218/17; Copper Sulphate (Yugoslavia) supra; Copper Sulphate (Czechoslovakia) OJ 1984, L225/22; Ball Bearings (Japan) OJ 1984, L340/41; Kraft Liner (Austria, Canada, Finland, Portugal, Sweden, USA, USSR) OJ 1983, L64/25; Ferro-Chyromium (S Africa, Sweden) OJ, 1983, L161/17.
10 Eg Louvre Doors (Taiwan) OJ 1981, L158/5; Polyester Yarn (USA) OJ 1982, L50/1 and OJ 1984, C 257/3.
11 Eg Saccharin and Salts (China, S Korea, USA) OJ 1983, L352/50; Acrylic Fibres (USA) OJ 1984, L209/1.
12 Eg Standardized Multi-Phase Electric Motors (USSR) OJ 1984, L123/22.
13 Eg Sodium Carbonate (Bulgaria) OJ 1981, L337/5; Hardboard (Czechoslovakia, Poland, Sweden) OJ 1983, L361/7; Hardboard (USSR) OJ 1984, L170/68.
14 Eg Case 240/84: *NTN Toyo Bearing Co Ltd v Council* [1987] ECR 1809, paras 5-7.

comprising the Community industry affected by the dumping[15] but has refused to regard as admissible actions brought by importers[16] and has refused the review of provisional duties where definitive duties were already in force.[17]

The importer may claim reimbursement of the duty collected if the duty exceeds the actual dumping margin.[18]

(b) Countervailing measures

(i) Meaning and scope

The object of countervailing measures, ie anti-subsidy measures, authorised by Article VI of GATT, is to neutralize the injurious effects of subsidized exports. Countervailing measures were the subject of a code adopted under the auspices of GATT but are now the subject of an agreement annexed to the Agreement establishing the WTO.

In the EC anti-subsidy measures used to be linked with anti-dumping duties but are now governed by separate legislation: Council Regulation 2026/97, in respect of products generally, and Commission Decision 1889/98, in respect of products covered by the ECSC Treaty.[19] Countervailing measure take the form of the imposition of a 'countervailing duty' on imports of the subsidised goods with the Community. The amount of the duty must not exceed the amount of the subsidy from which the exporter has benefited and should be less if a lesser amount would be adequate to remove the injury to Community industry.[20]

(ii) Conditions of imposition of duties

'A countervailing duty may be imposed for the purpose of off-setting any subsidy granted, directly or indirectly, for the manufacture, production, export or transport of any product whose release for free circulation in the Community causes injury.'[1] As in the case of dumping, four conditions have to be present, ie the existence of a subsidy, the existence of injury to Community interests, a causal link between these elements, and the Community interest must call for intervention. A subsidy is deemed to exist if (a) there is a financial contribution by a government in the country of origin or export of the products in question or some form of income or price support and (b) a benefit is thereby conferred on the manufacture, production, export or transport of the product.[2] A subsidy may give rise to the imposition of a countervailing duty if it is specific to an enterprise or an industry or to a group of enterprises or industries; and certain subsidies are stated to be immune from countervailing measures.[3]

---

15 Case 264/82: *Timex Corpn v Council and Commission* [1985] ECR 849, [1985] 3 CMLR 550.
16 Eg Case 279/86: *Sermes v Commission* [1987] ECR 3109.
17 Case 294/86 and 77/87: *Technointorg v Commission and Council* [1988] ECR 6077, [1989] 1 CMLR 281 at para 12.
18 Reg 384/96, Art 11(8). Cases 239/82 and 275/82: *Allied Corpn v Commission* [1984] ECR 1005, [1985] 3 CMLR 572; Case 312/84: *Continentale Produkten v Commission* [1987] ECR 841, [1988] 2 CMLR 453; see Reimbursement of Anti-Dumping Duties, Commission Practice Notes [1986] 3 CMLR 633.
19 OJ 1997, L288/1 and 1998, L245/3, respectively.
20 Reg 2026/97, Art 15(1).
 1 Reg 2026/97, Art 1(1).
 2 Reg 2026/97, Art 2. Annex 1 to the Regulation sets out an illustrative list of subsidies.
 3 Reg 2026/97, Arts 3-4.

(iii) Valuation of subsidy

The valuation of the subsidy is carried out for the purpose of determining the maximum extent of the duty that can be imposed. The amount of the subsidy is to be calculated in terms of the benefit conferred on the recipient. Certain rules apply to the calculation of the benefit. For example, a provision of equity capital by the government of a third country is not considered to confer any benefit at all unless the investment is inconsistent with the usual investment practice of a private investor. The amount of the subsidy is determined per unit of the subsidised product exported to the Community, subject to various permitted deductions and, where appropriate, the allocation of the amount of the subsidy over the total level of production, sales or exports during the relevant period.[4]

(iv) Determination of injury

As in the case of anti-dumping measures, the injury justifying a countervailing duty is material injury, or a threat of material injury, to Community industry, or the material retarding of the establishment of Community industry. A determination of injury must be based on positive evidence and involves an objective examination of the volume of the subsidised imports, their effect on prices for like products in the Community, and the consequent impact on Community industry.[5]

(v) Procedure and sanctions

Anti-dumping and anti-subsidy proceedings are broadly the same.[6] Anti-subsidy, like anti-dumping measures are subject to administrative[7] and judicial review.[8] In the *FEDIOL* case the complainants were accorded the right to put before the Commission any matter that would facilitate the review of the Commission's decision but ultimately failed in substance.

As in the case of anti-dumping measures there are two types of anti-subsidy measures, ie countervailing duties and undertakings. In both cases provisional and definitive duties may be applied if the Community interest so requires.[9] Neither can be imposed with a retrospective effect save in exceptional situations.[10]

In practice countervailing duties take the form of a flat rate applicable collectively to all imports of the product in question originating in a particular third country. By contrast, anti-dumping duties are applied individually. The flat rates applied have consisted of a percentage of the export price at port of export or frontier;[11] an amount of ECU per 1,000 kilograms net[12] and a percentage of the net price per tonne, free at the Community frontier.[13]

The rules applicable to undertakings in anti-dumping proceedings correspond to anti-subsidy proceedings, ie undertakings may be accepted where the subsidy is eliminated or measures concerning its injurious effects taken, by the government of the origin of export; or prices are revised or exports cease to the satisfaction of

---

4 Reg 2026/97, Arts 5-7.
5 Reg 2026/97, Art 8. For the definition of Community industry, see Art 9.
6 Compare Reg 384/96, Arts 5-20 with Reg 2026/97, Arts 10-30.
7 See, eg Seamless tubes of non-alloy steel from Spain, OJ 1983, L116/7.
8 Case 191/82: *FEDIOL (Seed Crushers and Oil Processors Federation) v Commission* [1983] ECR 2913, [1984] 3 CMLR 244; Case 70/87: *(No 2)* [1989] ECR 1781.
9 Reg 2026/97, Arts 12(1)(d) and 15(1). As to the Community interest, see Art 31.
10 Reg 2026/97, Art 16.
11 OJ 1980, L196/34.
12 Sheet and plates of iron and steel from Brazil, OJ 1983, L45/11; Steel plates from Brazil, OJ 1993, L209/29.
13 Tube and pipe fittings and malleable cast iron from Spain, OJ 1984, L74/74.

the Commission. The consent of the third country involved must be obtained. Thus, for example, in the case of women's shoes[14] the Brazilian government informed the Commission that it would impose a tax on exports of the product which should equalize the subsidy and that it did not intend to adopt any fiscal or other measures to compensate the exporter. On the basis of such undertaking the Commission terminated the countervailing measure.

Where the importer can show that the duty collected exceeds the amount of the subsidy the excess shall be reimbursed.[15]

(c)   Injurious pricing of vessels

Experience showed that it was impractical to apply anti-dumping or countervailing duties to the sale of ships below their normal value. A special code dealing with the situation was drawn up under the auspices of the WTO and has been implemented in the Community by Council Regulation 385/96.[16] That regulation provides for the imposition of an injurious pricing charge on the builder of any injuriously priced vessel whose sale to a buyer other than a buyer in the country in which the vessel originates causes injury. A vessel is injuriously priced if it is sold for less than a comparable price for a like vessel when sold in the ordinary course of trade to a buyer in the exporting country. The concept of an injurious pricing charge is therefore similar to that of an anti-dumping duty; and the regime applied is broadly similar to that applicable to dumping. The charge is imposed on the ship builder (not, as in the case of an anti-dumping duty, on the ship). If it is not paid, the Commission will adopt a decision denying the ship loading and unloading rights in the Community. It will not, therefore, be possible to use the ship for commercial purposes in trade to or from the Community.

(d)   Protective measures

(i)   Import restrictions

Certain protective measures reflect the escape clause of Article XIX of the GATT, which enables a party to the Agreement to impose quantitative restrictions on imports of products incoming in such increased quantities and such conditions as to cause or threaten serious injury to domestic producers of like or directly competitive products and has effectively been preserved after the foundation of the WTO. The Agreement on safeguards, which forms part of the bundle of agreements annexed to the Agreement establishing the WTO, was specifically concerned to reinforce Article XIX of GATT. Its requirements are reflected in Regulation 3285/94[17] which lays down justified exceptions to the principle of free trade.

The Regulation contains provision for the provision of information, consultations, and investigations by the Community for the purpose of determining whether or not the circumstances justify either surveillance or safeguard measures.[18] Surveillance measures may be imposed where import trends threaten to cause injury to Community producers and where the Community interest so requires. Products under surveillance may be imported only on production of an import

---

14   OJ 1981, L327/29.
15   Reg 384/96, Art 21.
16   OJ 1996, L56/21.
17   OJ 1994, L349/53; amended by Reg 139/96 (OJ 1996, L21/7) and Reg 2315/96 (OJ 1996, L314/1).
18   Arts 2-10.

document and the importer may be required to produce additional information about them. The information so obtained is passed on by the Member States and the Commission to enable it to decide whether or not safeguard measures are justified.[19] Safeguard measures may be adopted where a product is being imported into the Community in such greatly increased quantities and/or in such terms or conditions as to cause, or threaten and cause serious injury to Community producers. The measures that can be taken comprise limiting the period of validity of import documents and altering the import rules for the product in question so as to make its release for free circulation conditional on production of an import authorisation. Where the latter measures involve the establishment of a quota, account must be taken of a number of factors, such as the desirability of maintaining traditional trade flows as far as possible. More generally, account must also be taken of the Community's obligations regarding members of the WTO.[20] Common procedures for the administration of quotas are subject to Regulation 520/94.[1]

Regulation 3258/94 does not apply to imports from state trading countries or to textiles which are subject to extensive Community legislation.[2] Common rules for imports from state trading countries are laid down in Regulation 519/94.[3] That regulation provides for an importation regime for products from state trading countries that reflects the general interest of the Community as a whole rather than the interest of particular Member States.[4] Those rules do not apply to countries with which the Community has an association agreement or free trade agreement.

(ii) Export restrictions
In principle exports of Community goods to third countries are free of quantitative restrictions.[5] However certain sensitive products are exempted either to counter shortages where essential materials are concerned or to fulfil international obligations[6] or to ease tensions in various parts of the world caused by certain countries developing sophisticated weaponry and using high technology for military purposes.[7] In such a case a Member State may resort to EC Article 30 (ex Art 36).[8]

(iii) Review
The measures envisaged in Regulation 3285/94 are subject to administrative and, ultimately, judicial review. The Community institutions and the Member States

---

19   Ibid, Arts 11-15.
20   Ibid, Arts 16-22.
1   OJ 1994, L66/1, amended by Reg 138/96 (OJ 1996, L21/6) and implemented by Commission Reg 738/94 (OJ 1994, L87/47) and No 657/95 (OJ 1995, L69/13), as amended.
2   See Reg 3030/93 (OJ 1993, L275/1), which concerns textile imports from countries with which the Community has some form of trade agreement, or which are members of the WTO, and Reg 517/94 (OJ 1994, L67/1), which concerns textile imports from all other countries (both regulations have been extensively amended).
3   OJ, 1994, L67/89; amended by Reg 839/95 (OJ 1995, L85/9), Reg 139/96 (OJ 1996, L21/7), Reg 168/96 (OJ 1996, L25/2), Reg 1138/98 (OJ 1998, L159/1).
4   Case C-150/94: *United Kingdom v Council* [1998] ECR I-7235; Case C-284/94: *Spain v Council* [1998] ECR I-7309.
5   Reg 2603/69 OJ 1969, L324/25, last amended by Reg 3918/91 (OJ 1991, L372/31).
6   See eg Case 174/84: *Bulk Oil (Zug) AG v Sun International Ltd (No 2) (Re export of oil to Israel)* [1986] ECR 559, [1986] 2 CMLR 732.
7   See Reg 3381/94 (OJ 1994, L367/1), amended by Reg 837/95 (OJ 1995, L90/1), which repealed Reg 428/89 (OJ 1989, L50/1) and instituted a system of export controls for dual purpose goods (that is, goods used for military and for pacific purposes); Case C-70/94: *Fritz Werner Industrie v Germany* [1995] ECR I-3189, Case C-83/94: *Leifer* [1995] ECR I-3231.
8   See Case C-367/89, *Criminal Proceedings against Richardt, Re export shipment of military technology* [1991] ECR I-4621, sub nom *Ministre des Finances v Richardt* [1992] 1 CMLR 6.

are competent to request a judicial review under EC Article 230 (ex Art 173). Private parties, whether importers or exporters, ordinarily have no such right, though they may challenge such measures indirectly through the machinery of EC Article 234 (ex Art 177), eg an importer seeking redress before a national court against the refusal to grant him a licence by a competent national authority.[9]

(iv)   Informal arrangements
These arrangements are known as 'voluntary export restraints', 'voluntary restraints agreements' or 'orderly marketing arrangements'. The voluntary nature of these arrangements can be questioned because they are not explicitly sanctioned by the GATT and, in practice, they are usually the result of pressure from the importing country. However they have become a feature of the regulation of trade because, as far as the exporting countries are concerned, they are preferred to mandatory restrictions which the EC favours because they can be implemented informally and can be applied to individual countries. Such was the position in the Stoneware case[10] where the Commission, having instituted protective measures against South Korea, decide to replace these by a system of automatic authorization negotiated with the South Korean government. Despite Germany's objection on the ground that the Commission had no such power the Council confirmed the arrangements.[11] In principle, such arrangements must be eliminated pursuant to the rules adopted under the aegis of the WTO.

(e)   Derogations under EC Article 134 (ex Art 115) and other restrictions

(i)   Article 134
EC Article 134 (ex Art 115) (as amended), provides the derogations from the principle of free movement of goods. It authorizes the Commission to allow protective measures to be taken by the Member States in two situations: where commercial policy measures taken by any Member State in accordance with the Treaty would be obstructed by deflection of trade;[12] or where differences between the commercial policy measures taken by Member States in accordance with the Treaty lead to economic difficulties in one or more Member States. In such situations, the first step is for the Commission to recommend methods of co-operation between the Member States concerned; failing which the Commission may authorise protective measures, the conditions and details of which are determined by the Commission. In cases of urgency, a Member State cannot take action unilaterally but must request the Commission's authorisation to take the necessary measures. The Commission must make its decision on such a request as soon as possible. If it permits measures to be taken, it may at any time decide that the Member State concerned should amend or abolish them. In the selection of measures taken under EC Article 134 (ex Art 115) priority must be given to measures that cause the least disruption to the functioning of the Common Market. Being in the nature of a derogation EC Article 134 (ex Art 115) has to be interpreted restrictively[13] and, consequently, the requirement of an import

---

 9   Case 112/80: *Dürbeck v HZA Frankfurt* [1981] ECR 1095, [1982] 3 CMLR 314; Case 126/81: *Wünsche v Germany* [1982] ECR 1479.
10   *Stoneware* (OJ 1983, L96/8).
11   OJ 1983, L200/43.
12   Eg where traders seek to avoid a commercial policy measure applicable in a particular Member State by importing the goods in question into another Member State and then taking them into the first Member State through the territory of the Community.
13   Case 41/76: *Criel (née Donckerwolcke) v Procureur de la République* [1976] ECR 1921 para 29.

licence for goods in free circulation in another Member State is incompatible with the Treaty.[14]

In that sense Commission Decision 87/433[15] applies to products which are not covered by uniform conditions of importation under the CCP.[16] If such imports threaten to create economic difficulties surveillance should take place, but protective measures are to be applied where the importers have actually created such difficulties. Measures are not to be disproportionate to the risk of economic difficulties and are to be authorized by the Commission only for a limited period.

(ii)   Other restrictions on imports

Other restrictions may be imposed for the protection of health, for example in respect of hormone-treated beef;[17] chlorofluorocarbons;[18] ivory[19] and counterfeit goods.[20]

(f)   Protection against unlawful trade practices

Following the example of the US Trade Agreements Act 1979 (which gave the President the power to respond to foreign import restrictions or export subsidies) the Community enacted Regulation 2641/84[1] (also known as the New Commercial Policy Instrument) for the purpose of 'strengthening the Common Commercial Policy with regard to protection from illicit practices'. That regulation was repealed and replaced by Regulation 3286/94[2] which is intended to improve upon the regime established by Regulation 2641/84. Regulation 3286/94 does not apply in cases covered by other existing CCP rules (notably those concerning dumping and subsidies) and complements the rules applicable to the common organization of agricultural markets and goods processed from agricultural products.[3]

Regulation 3286/94 sets out procedures designed to ensure the effective exercise of the Community's rights under international trade rules. It is aimed at obstacles to trade, applied outside the Community, that have an effect on the market in the Community or in a third country. Where the effect is on the Community market, the objective is to remove the injury (felt in the Community or by Community industry). Where the effect is on the market of a third country, the objective is to remove the adverse trade effects (that is, to secure appropriate access to that third country market for goods or services originating in the Community).[4] The obstacles to trade against which the regulation is directed are those trade practices in respect of which international trade rules (in particular those established under the auspices of the WTO) establish a right of action in the sense that they are either prohibited by those rules or give another trading party affected by them a right to seek elimination of the effect of the trade practice in question.[5] Provision is made for investigation by the Commission into alleged

---

14   Ibid at para 39.
15   OJ 1987, L238/26.
16   See Case 59/84: *Tezi Textiel v Commission* and 242/84: *Tezi Textiel v Minister for Economic Affairs* [1986] ECR 887 and 933, [1987] 3 CMLR 64.
17   Dir 85/649 (OJ 1985, L382/228); see Case 68/86: *United Kingdom v Council* [1988] ECR 855, [1988] 2 CMLR 543; Case C-331/88: *R v Minister of Agriculture, ex p Federation Européenne de la Sante Animale* [1990] ECR I-4023, [1991] 1 CMLR 507.
18   Com Decision 89/149 (OJ 1989, L192/37).
19   Com Reg 2497/89 (OJ 1989, L240/7).
20   Council Reg 3842/86 (OJ 1986, L357/1).
 1   OJ 1984, L252/1.
 2   OJ 1994, L349/71, amended by Reg 356/95 (OJ 1995, L41/3).
 3   Reg 3286/94, Art 15.
 4   Reg 3286/94, Art 1.
 5   Reg 3286/94, Art 2(1).

unlawful trade practices at the request of Community industry, particular Community enterprises or Member States.[6]

Like all the Regulations concerned with protective measures Regulation 3286/94 sets up an Advisory Committee which must be consulted.

The Regulation provides for the adoption of retaliatory measures which comprise:

(1) the suspension or withdrawal of any concessions resulting from commercial policy negotiations;
(2) the raising of existing customs duties or the introduction of any other charges on imports;
(3) the introduction of quantitative restrictions or any other measures modifying import or export conditions or otherwise affecting trade with the third country concerned.[7]

By analogy to the *FEDIOL*[8] case a disappointed complainant may seek review in the ECJ or in appropriate cases by an action before national authority with a possibility of a preliminary reference under EC Article 234 (ex Art 177).

(g)   Protection against the effects of extra-territorial application of third country legislation

Regulation 2271/96[9] provides for measures to be taken to protect natural persons within the Community and legal persons incorporated within the Community, who engage in international trade and/or the movement of capital and related commercial activities between the Community and third countries, from the effects of the extra-territorial application of the laws and other actions of third countries.[10] The laws and other actions in question are specified in the annex to the regulation, which may be amended from time to time. Where the economic and/or financial interests of a protected person are affected, directly or indirectly, by such laws or actions, certain consequences follow: judicial or administrative measures adopted outside the Community and giving effect to such laws or actions shall not be recognised or enforced in any manner within the Community; protected persons are obliged not to comply with any measure based on or resulting from the laws or actions in question (unless authorised to do so by the Commission); a protected person may recover any damages caused to that person by the application of the laws or actions in question; Member States must impose effective, proportional and dissuasive sanctions for breach of any relevant provision of the regulation.[11]

---

6   Reg 3286/94, Arts 3-6.
7   For examples of the operation of Reg 3286/94, see Commission Decision 98/354 (OJ 1998, L159/65) concerning obstacles to trade represented by Japanese practices in respect of imports of leather; Commission Decision 98/618 (OJ 1998, L295/46) concerning measures maintained by Argentina on the export of bovine hides and the import of finished leather; Commission Decision 98/731 (OJ 1998, L346/60) concerning obstacles arising under US copyright law; and Commission Decision 1999/234 (OJ 1999, L86/22) concerning the import licensing system in Brazil.
8   Supra p 452, note 8.
9   OJ 1996, L309/1.
10   Reg 2271/96, Art 1. For a fuller description of the classes of protected person see Art 11.
11   Reg 2271/96, Arts 2, 4-6 and 9.

(h) Trade sanctions

The Community may also impose trade sanctions in order to obtain a political objective, ie a change of policy of the countries subjected to sanctions. The tendency is to give support to United Nations resolutions but the EC acts not so much on the basis of EC Article 133 (ex Art 113) as in the context of European Political Co-operation (EPC).

EC sanctions were imposed to back up the UN resolutions in the 1960s and 1970s to pave the way for a black majority government in Rhodesia (now Zimbabwe), to disapprove of the Soviet invasion of Afghanistan and of the suppression of the Solidarity movement in Poland in 1981-82. Imports from Argentina were suspended following the invasion of the Falkland Islands in 1982[12] though Italy and Ireland refused to implement this measure. In 1990 the Community imposed an embargo on trade with Iraq (except for certain foodstuffs and medical products) in order to end Iraq's occupation of Kuwait[13] and in 1991 certain measures were taken to bring about a negotiated settlement to the civil war in Yugoslavia.[14]

Apart from doubts about the effectiveness of economic sanctions in general it is clear that EC Article 133 (ex Art 113) is inadequate as a legal authority for the EC flexing its economic muscle. The better view is to rely on the EPC as has already been intimated in the preambles to regulations imposing sanctions on Iraq and Yugoslavia. However it must be borne in mind that the EPC reflects a bicephalous approach to EC External Policy which is still in its infancy.

EC Article 301 (ex Art 228a) provides that the Council, acting by a qualified majority on a proposal from the Commission, shall implement economic measures envisaged in a common position or a joint action adopted in the context of the common foreign and security policy.[15] Moreover, following the action contemplated in EC Article 301 (ex Art 228a), the Council may take additional urgent measures affecting the movement of capital and payments as regards the third countries concerned.[16] Similar action may be taken unilaterally by individual Member States for serious political reasons and on grounds of urgency if the council has not yet acted, though ultimately such unilateral measures may be abolished or amended by a decision of the Council taken by a qualified majority on a proposal from the Commission.[17]

---

12 Sanctions imposed by Council Reg 877/82 (OJ 1982, L102/1) and lifted by Council Reg 1577/82 (OJ 1982, L177/1).
13 Council Reg 2340/90 (OJ 1990, L213/1).
14 Council Reg 3300/91 (OJ 1991, L315/1) (suspending trade concessions); Reg 3302/91 (OJ 1991, L315/46) (suspending the benefits of the GSP); Council Decision 91/602 (OJ 1991, L325/23) (denouncing the EC-Yugoslavia Co-operation Agreement); Reg 3567/91 (OJ 1991, L342/1) (extending trade concessions to Bosnia-Herzegovena, Croatia, Macedonia and Slovenia).
15 See, for example, Council Reg 926/98 (OJ 1998, L130/1), which provides for the 'reduction' of certain economic relations with Yugoslavia, in the form of a prohibition on the supply of certain military equipment to Yugoslavia and a prohibition on the provision of financial and related assistance to Serbia. The regulation gave effect to a common position defined by the Council (see OJ 1998, L95/1).
16 EC Art 60(1) (ex Art 73g(1)).
17 EC Art 60(2) (ex Art 73g(2)). The abilities of a Member State to take such unilateral measures is without prejudice to the obligation of Member States under EC Art 297 (ex Art 224) to consult each other with a view to taking together the steps necessary to prevent the functioning of the Common Market from being affected by measures which a Member State may be called upon to take in the event of serious internal disturbances, war, a threat of war, or obligation accepted for the purpose of maintaining peace and international security.

Chapter 18

The free movement of goods within the customs union

A. General principles

The EC Treaty envisages the Community based on a customs union.[1] EC Article 23 (ex Art 9) enumerates the basic elements necessary to achieve a customs union: the internal aspects comprise the removal of all customs duties and other charges from goods moving across national frontiers within the territory of the customs union; the external aspects comprise the establishment of a common customs regime governing the importation, into the territory of the customs union, of goods from outside it. The removal of customs duties on internal trade and the establishment of a uniform regime affecting external trade are effected by what are now EC Articles 25 to 27 (ex Arts 12 to 29). The reduction of the number of relevant provisions to three is explained by the removal of transitional provisions that were relevant at the beginning of the Community. The removal of customs duties on internal trade is supplemented by EC Articles 90 to 93 (ex Arts 95 to 99), which deal with indirect taxes (that is, taxes on goods). The customs union would be incomplete without the removal of non-pecuniary barriers to internal trade, which is effected by EC Articles 28 to 31 (ex Arts 30 to 37). The external trade aspects are covered by the Common Commercial Policy: EC Articles 131 to 134 (ex Arts 110 to 116).

There is no Treaty definition of 'goods' or 'products' but these terms are used interchangeably.[2] In the first art treasure case[3] the ECJ defined 'goods' as products which can be valued in money and which are capable, as such, of forming the subject of commercial transactions. The nature or the value of products is

---

1 Cases 2 and 3/62: *Commission v Luxembourg and Belgium, Re Gingerbread* [1962] ECR 425, [1963] CMLR 199: see also Cases 2-3/69: *Sociaal Fonds voor de Diamantarbeiders v S A Brachfeld* [1969] ECR 211, [1969] CMLR 335.
2 See generally Oliver, P, *Free Movement of Goods in the EEC* (3rd edn, 1995).
3 Case 7/68: *Commission v Italy* [1968] ECR 423 at 428, [1969] CMLR 1 at 8.

immaterial for even 'waste'[4] remains a product for the purpose of the movement of goods. The importance of the product to the national economy is also immaterial.[5] However, broadcasting or television signals,[6] other cable transmissions,[7] and rights, such as fishing rights, even when evidenced by a thing such as a licence,[8] though capable of being subject to commercial transactions, are not 'goods' or 'products' in this context. Means of payment[9] are different from goods. Thus in the White Paper[10] the Commission spoke of a 'financial product' which ought to be in free circulation in consequence of the liberalization of financial services, not the free movement of goods. Advertising material that is distributed to promote the supply of goods is 'goods' but not where it is used to promote the supply of services.[11]

Goods benefiting from the right to free movement are the products originating from the Member States and products coming from non-Member States ('third countries') that are in 'free circulation' in Member States (EC Article 23(2) (ex Art 9(2)). Products coming from non-Member States are deemed to be in free circulation in a Member State if the import formalities have been complied with and any customs duties or charges having equivalent effect have been levied in the state of entry (EC Article 24 (ex Art 10(1)).[12]

Free movement of goods was to have been attained progressively during a transitional period. Through three stages and two accelerations in 1960 and 1962 respectively, the Council of Ministers considered the *désarmement douanier* to be completed ahead of the Treaty schedule by 1 July 1968.[13] However, as demonstrated by case law and the 1985 Commission White Paper the process was by no means complete. When a new Member State accedes to the Community, any transitional period will be defined in the Act of Accession.

In a technical sense the customs union has, as a corollary to the elimination of internal barriers to trade, a uniform regulation of external trade. Here the EC differs from the Free Trade Area. The external barrier round the Community customs territory has been erected by the Common Customs Tariff and the Common Commercial Policy.

B. Elimination of customs duties between Member States (EC Articles 23-25 (ex Arts 9-17))

By 'customs duties' the Treaty means duties (ie pecuniary charges irrespective of the terminology) levied not only on imported goods but also on exports.

---

4 Case 172/82: *Syndicat National des Fabricants Raffineurs d'Huile de Grassage v Groupement d'Intérêt Economique Inter-Huiles* [1983] ECR 555, [1983] 3 CMLR 485.
5 See Case 72/83: *Campus Oil Ltd v Ministry for Industry and Energy* [1984] ECR 2727 at 2747, [1984] 3 CMLR 544 at 566.
6 Case 155/73: *Italy v Saachi* [1974] ECR 409, [1974] 2 CMLR 177.
7 Case 52/79: *Procureur du Roi v Debauve* [1980] ECR 833, [1981] 2 CMLR 362.
8 Case C-97/98: *Jägerskiöld v Gustafsson* [1999] ECR I-7319, paras 30-39.
9 Case 7/78: *R v Thompson, Johnson and Woodiwiss* [1978] ECR 2247 at 2247, [1979] 1 CMLR 47 at 70; Cases C-358 and C-416/93: *Bordessa* [1995] ECR I-361.
10 COM (85) 310 Final para 102.
11 Case C-362/88: *GB-INNO* [1990] ECR I-667; Case C-275/92: *Commissioners of Customs and Excise v Schindler* [1994] ECR I-1039.
12 See Case 2-3/69, supra, note 1; see Case C-117/88: *Trend-Moden v HZA Emmerich* [1990] ECR I-631, [1991] 1 CMLR 113; Case C-83/89: *Openbaar Ministrie v Houben, re burden of proof* [1990] ECR I-1161, [1991] 2 CMLR 321.
13 Reg of 28 June 1968 (OJ 1968, L167).

Neither the level nor the designation or objective of the charge, ie whether it is designed to benefit the state or to protect competing national products matter, but what does matter is the fact that the charge is imposed on goods crossing the frontier of a state.[14] EC Article 10(2) (now repealed) charged the Commission with the task of laying down the appropriate implementing measures whilst EC Article 11 (now repealed) imposed upon the Member States an obligation to carry out the corresponding duties resulting from those implementing measures. Article 12 (as originally worded) imposed a 'stand-still' duty upon the Member States, prohibiting the introduction of any new national measures in this field or any increase in existing duties, thus affording a Dutch importer protection from national law imposing on a product coming from a fellow Member State its own classification of goods and a duty in excess of the Community rate.[15] Articles 13 and 16, respectively, as originally worded, provided for the progressive removal of customs duties and charges having equivalent effect on imports and exports during the transitional period. At the end of that period, the prohibition on duties and charges became fully effective. The prohibition has now been consolidated into a single provision, EC Article 25, which also applies to customs duties of a fiscal nature. Because the obligation to eliminate these duties is absolute any exception must be clear and unambiguous and has to be interpreted strictly.[16] Moreover derogation of a non-economic nature authorized under EC Article 30 (ex Art 36) cannot be pleaded to justify duties on the export of goods.[17] The principle was reiterated in the Second Italian Art Treasure case.[18]

It is important to note that, though the duty to eliminate customs duty has been imposed upon the Member States, private parties may, as stated in the celebrated *Van Gend* case,[19] benefit from the principle of direct applicability of Community law as well as its supremacy in case of conflict with national rules.

In the *Radio Valves* case[20] Italy unsuccessfully claimed exception from the first tariff reduction on the ground of prior international agreement sanctioned by EC Article 307 (ex Art 234). The ECJ disposed of the argument ruling that 'rights and obligations' safeguarded by EC Article 307, (ex Art 234), applied to relations with third countries whilst, as between the Member States, these rights and obligations were superseded by subsequent rights and obligations arising from the EC Treaty.

Similarly unsuccessful was the defence of a charge imposed by Belgium and Luxembourg on the issue of import licences for milk products. In an enforcement action[1] the two countries claimed that, in the absence of a Community organization of the relevant market, in accordance with what were then Articles 43 and 45 (now EC Article 37, Article 45 being repealed), the national market organizations were allowed to continue, thereby justifying the charge in question. The ECJ ruled that any possible exception to such a fundamental provision as Article 12 (now EC Art 25) must be expressly laid down and interpreted strictly whilst Article 13 (now repealed) providing for progressive abolition of customs duties

14   Cases 2-3/69, supra.
15   Case 26/62: *Van Gend en Loos v Nederlandse Administratie der Belastingen* [1963] ECR 1, [1963] CMLR 105.
16   Cases 52 and 55/65: *Germany v Commission, Re Import duty on mutton* [1966] ECR 159, [1967] CMLR 22 at 43.
17   Case 7/68, *First art treasure case*, supra.
18   Case 18/71: *Eunomia v Italian Ministry of Education* [1971] ECR 811, [1972] 4 CMLR.
19   Case 26/62, supra.
20   Case 10/61: *Commission v Italy* [1962] ECR 1.
 1   Cases 90 and 91/63: *Commission v Luxembourg and Belgium* [1964] ECR 625 at 633, [1965] CMLR 58.

contained nothing from which any exception to Article 12 could be inferred. It is clear from this case that the obligation to eliminate customs duties would be enforced by virtue of EC Article 226 (ex Art 169) whilst at the national level private parties may have their objections referred to the ECJ under EC Article 234 (ex Art 177).

C.   Elimination of charges equivalent to customs duties

The Treaty does not define these charges, it simply prohibits their imposition on both imports and exports between Member States: EC Articles 23(1) and 25 (ex Arts 9(1) and 12). It fell to the ECJ to define these charges as 'duties whatever their description or technique, imposed unilaterally, which apply specifically to a product imported by a Member State but not to a similar national product and which by altering the price, have the same effect upon the free movement of goods as a customs duty'.[2] The same applies where the charge is applied to exports and even if the charge is not imposed for the profit of the State.[3]

'The justification for this prohibition is based on the fact that any pecuniary charge, however small, imposed on goods by reason of the fact that they cross a frontier constitutes an obstacle to the movement of such goods.'[4]

Cases involving 'equivalent charges' exhibit a certain ingenuity characteristic of revenue experts but carry little favour with the Court. Thus, for example, a statistical levy on imported or exported goods[5] and on cardboard egg containers[6] were both held to be prohibited by the Treaty.

By charging at 0.50% *ad valorem* duty for 'administrative services' in respect of goods imported from another Member State, Italy was found guilty of a failure to fulfil an obligation under the Treaty.[7] In a similar situation the Court held, on reference from Italy, such charges to be illegal.[8] A combination of *ad valorem* duty and a statistical levy on the import of pork products into Italy was also condemned.[9]

More plausible charges for phyto-sanitation of fruit[10] and public health inspection of meat[11] are also prohibited unless authorized under mandatory provisions of Community Law and applied accordingly.

---

2   Cases 2 and 3/62, supra [1962] ECR 425 at 432.
3   Cases C-441/98 and C-442/98: *Kapniki Michailidis AE v Idryma Koinonikon Asfaliseon* 21 September 2000, paras 13-17.
4   Case 24/68: *Commission v Italy, Re Levy on exports to finance the compilation of statistical data* [1969] ECR 193 at para 7, [1971] CMLR 611;
5   Ibid.
6   Case 77/72: *Capolonga v Azienda Agricolo Maya* [1973] ECR 611, [1974] 1 CMLR 230; Case 94/74: *Industria Comma v Ente Nazionale per la Cellulose* [1975] ECR 699, [1976] 2 CMLR 37.
7   Case 8/70: *Commission v Italy* [1970] ECR 961.
8   Case 33/70: *SACE SpA v Ministry of Finance* [1970] ECR 1213, [1971] CMLR 123, at para 15.
9   Case 43/71: *Politi SAS v Ministry of Finance* [1971] ECR 1039, [1973] CMLR 60.
10   Case 39/73: *Rewe-Zentralfinanz GmbH v Direktor der Landwirtschaftskammer Westfalen-Lippe* [1973] ECR 1039 at paras 3-5; Case 4/75: *Rewe-Zentralfinanz GmbH v Landwirtschaftskammer* [1975] ECR 843, [1977] 1 CMLR 599.
11   Case 29/72: *Marimex SpA v Italian Finance Administration* [1972] ECR 1309, [1973] CMLR 486 at para 7; a similar ruling was given in Case 87/75: *Bresciani v Amministrazione Italiana delle Finanze, Re inspection of raw cowhides* [1976] ECR 129, [1976] 2 CMLR 62.

However, even where Community legislation enables the Member States to levy duties, this does not necessarily mean compliance with the Treaty provision prohibiting the charge. Such was the ruling of the Court in Cases 80 and 80/77[12] where the disputed charge was levied under Council Regulation 816/70 which enabled the Member States to take measures limiting imports of wine to avoid disturbance of their wine market. The Court clarified the relationship between EC Articles 12-17 and 38-46 relating to agriculture (now EC Articles 25 and 32-38, respectively) and concluded that in order to be valid the disputed charge would have to be authorized by the Treaty. Since EC Article 40(3) (now 34(2)) stipulates that the organization of the market shall exclude any discrimination between producers and consumers and since EC Article 44 (now repealed) provided that, in certain circumstances, the Member States may apply a system of minimum prices in a non-discriminatory manner, the Regulation was incompatible with what were then EC Articles 13(2) and 38-46.

Where a Dutch cattle dealer claimed a refund of fees paid for veterinary and public health inspection of exported cattle the government argued that these charges did not exceed the actual cost of the inspection which the Netherlands had imposed in accordance with Council Directive 64/432. The Court ruled that the inspection introduced by the Directive, far from hindering trade, actually promoted the free movement of goods by rendering superfluous any public health inspection that might be justified by EC Article 30 (ex Art 36). Regarding fees for inspection of animals other than those covered by the Directive, the Court ruled that, although EC Article 30 (ex Art 36) does not prevent restrictions which take the form of public health inspections, it does not permit the collection of duties on the inspected goods.[13]

A similar problem arose in a case involving a fee charged for phyto-sanitary inspection on the export of plants where the Commission claimed these charges to be incompatible with Community law. The Court observed that the fees were imposed in compliance with the International Plant Protection Convention 1951 to which the Member States were parties and that the purpose of the Convention was to encourage free import of plants into the country of destination by carrying out inspections in the country of origin of the plants concerned. As in the previous case the Court, dissenting from the Advocate-General, ruled that such measures actually assisted the free movement of goods and, *in casu*, were not incompatible with Community law.[14]

In Case 32/80[15] a Dutchman was prosecuted for trading in pharmaceutical products without prior registration as required by Dutch law. The ECJ held that charges of the type required in this case, which were imposed on a parallel importer of pharmaceutical products either in the form of a single fee on registration of the products or in the form of an annual fee charged in order to meet the costs of producers incurred in checking whether the products subsequently marketed are identical with the registered products, did not contravene Community law if they formed part of a general system charged in accordance with criteria identical or comparable to the criteria employed in determining the fees on domestic products.

In the *Irish Creamery* case[16] a duty was applied to certain agricultural products at the time of delivery for processing, storage and export but it was inapplicable

---

12 Case 80/77: *Société les Commissiares Réunis Sàrl v Réceveur des Douanes* [1978] ECR 927.
13 Case 46/76: *Bauhuis v Netherlands* [1977] ECR 5 at paras 27-36.
14 Case 89/76: *Commission v Netherlands* [1977] ECR 1355 at 1370.
15 Case 32/80: *Officier van Jusitie v Kortmann* [1981] ECR 251.
16 Cases 36 and 71/80: *Irish Creamery Milk Suppliers' Association v Ireland* [1981] ECR 735.

to importers. The Court ruled that, in so far as it could be established that it fell more heavily on sales for exports than on domestic sales, the duty had an effect equivalent to a customs duty on exports and as such would be incompatible with Community law. However it would not be so (as was the case here) if the duty were applied systematically and according to uniform criteria to animals at the point of withdrawal from the national herd for export or for slaughter.

In Germany the Länder charged fees on the importation and transit of live animals to cover the inspection costs in the context of Directive 81/389. This was disputed.[17] The ECJ having recited the definition of equivalent charges, proceeded to define the position on the basis of its case law.[18] Thus: 'the Court has held that such a charge escapes that classification if it relates to a general system of internal duties applied systematically and in accordance with the same criteria to domestic products and imported products alike,[19] if it constitutes payment for a service in fact rendered to the economic operator of a sum in proportion to the service,[20] or again, subject to certain conditions, if it attaches to inspections carried out to fulfil obligations imposed by Community law'.[1]

The contested fee, which was payable on importation and transit, cannot be regarded as relating to a general system of internal duties. Nor did it constitute payment for a service rendered to the operator because this condition was satisfied only if the operator in question obtained a definite specific benefit,[2] which was not the case if the inspection served to guarantee, in the public interest, the health and life of animals in international transport.[3]

Since the contested fee was charged in connection with inspections carried out pursuant to a Community provision, it should be noted that according to the case law of the Court[4] such fees may not be classified as charges having an effect equivalent to a customs duty if the following conditions are satisfied:

'(a) they do not exceed the actual costs of the inspections in connection with which they are charged;

(b) the inspections in question are obligatory and uniform for all the products concerned in the Community;

(c) they are prescribed by Community Law in the general interest of the Community;

(d) they promote the free movement of goods, in particular by neutralizing obstacles which could arise from unilateral measures of inspection adopted in accordance with Article 36 of the Treaty [now EC Art 30].'

In this instance these conditions were satisfied by the contested fee. In particular, it was not contested that it did not exceed the real costs of the inspections in connection with which it was charged.

The ruling of the Court appears pretty conclusive but this may not be the last we have heard of charges equivalent to customs duties.[5]

---

17   Case 18/87: *Commission v Germany* [1988] ECR 5427.
18   Ibid, paras 6-9.
19   Case 132/78: *Denkavit v France* [1979] ECR 1923.
20   Case 158/82: *Commission v Denmark* [1983] ECR 3573.
 1   Case 46/76: supra, p 463, note 13.
 2   Case 24/68: *Commission v Italy* [1969] ECR 193.
 3   Case 314/82: *Commission v Belgium* [1984] ECR 1543.
 4   Case 46/76 cited above; Case 89/76: *Commission v Netherlands* [1977] ECR 1355; Case 1/83: *IFG v Freistaat Bayern* [1984] ECR 349.
 5   Case 77/72: *Capolongo v Maya* [1973] ECR 611 at 621, [1974] 1 CMLR 230 at 244-5.

D.   Charges for services rendered

The inspection cases, in particular, call for a distinction between the prohibited charges and charges legitimately imposed for services rendered in connection with the movement of goods. The point of distinction is that the charge for services must be genuine and it must be levied by 'an agency governed by public law'.

Case law reveals a narrow interpretation of services rendered. Thus, eg 'a frontier charge' for enquiry whether certain goods could be admitted to Germany was considered illegal[6] and so were charges for administrative duties carried out by customs officials[7] even in respect of overtime when the Community imposed a ten-hour working day.[8] Similarly, despite the convenience to the parties concerned, a special charge for customs clearance in a customs warehouse was held to be equivalent to a customs duty.

In the light of the then existing case law charges for customs clearance levied by postal services[9] were also ruled to be out of order though the ECJ, as if in a *post scriptum*, observed that VAT did not constitute a charge equivalent to a customs duty.

A point of genuine service was raised in Case 266/81[10] where port charges were levied on oil in transit from Italy to Germany and Austria. The ECJ ruled that, although the freedom of transit was a corollary to the free movement of goods, it was legitimate to charge the cost of the operation connected with transit which included the use of harbour water and facilities maintained by the public port authority.

It would seem that most of the problems arose from the uncertainty of Community law as revealed in the inspection cases which should have been taken care of by more extensive and more precise Community legislation. In the absence of uniform Community rules the Member States are tempted to use their residual powers and thus resort to unilateral action. However, with the abolition of the frontier posts and frontier controls as from 1 January 1993 most of the case law on this topic will be relegated to history though problems will not disappear altogether since goods can be controlled and inspected anywhere in the territories of the Member States by means of 'mobile customs posts'.

E.   Elimination of quantitative restrictions (EC Articles 28-29 (ex Arts 30-35))

Having abolished customs duties the Treaty purports to eliminate quotas by prohibiting quantitative restrictions on imports (EC Article 28 (ex Art 30)) and exports (EC Article 29 (ex Art 34)) as well as all measures having equivalent effect. The standstill provisions and those dealing with the gradual removal of quantitative restrictions and measures having equivalent effect (EC Articles 31-33, 34(2) and 35) have now been repealed.

---

6   Joined Cases 52 and 55/65: *Germany v Commission* [1966] ECR 159 at 169-170, [1967] CMLR 22 at 43.
7   Case 8/70: *Commission v Italy* [1970] ECR 961.
8   Case 340/87: *Commission v Italy, re Italian customs posts* [1989] ECR 1483 [1991] 1 CMLR 437.
9   Case 39/82: *Donner v Netherlands* [1983] ECR 19, [1983] 1 CMLR 711.
10   266/81: *SIOT v Ministry of Finance* [1983] ECR 731, [1984] 2 CMLR 231.

Quantitative restrictions were defined by the ECJ[11] as any measure which amounts to a total or partial restraint of, according to circumstances, imports, exports or goods in transit. Because the prohibition is absolute the principle *de minimis* does not apply here.[12]

A handful of judgments explain the position. In the first case the Commission succeeded, notwithstanding the defence of necessity, in an enforcement action against Italy for temporary suspension of the import of pork products. The ECJ ruled that the standstill obligation then contained in the Treaty was absolute and permitted no exception.[13] In another case[14] a private party succeeded against Italy in a case involving refusal to grant an import licence for a quantity of fuller's earth impregnated with fatty substances. The ECJ again emphasized the unconditional nature of the standstill clause. Other examples include the British ban on the import of Dutch potatoes[15] which could have been sustained had it not been extended beyond the expiry of the period of transition;[16] the French refusal to accept sheepmeat from the United Kingdom;[17] the British refusal to accept French UHT milk products after the expiry of a derogation clause of a Directive introducing the metric system[18] and poultry products.[19]

In the sheepmeat case the ECJ disposed of three arguments submitted by France, ie that the product in question was not of British origin, that there was no Community market organization for sheepmeat and that the British exports caused no injury to French farmers. None was relevant. Even if the product had been imported from a third country it would have been in free circulation by virtue of EC Article 24 (ex Art 10); the absence of a market regulation as decided earlier[20] cannot justify unilateral national measures restricting the free movement of goods and the complaints of producers of unfair competition are irrelevant. Lifting the restrictions the French government managed to obtain Community support for sheepfarmers. However, despite the official absence of restrictions, 'private activities' (ie violence to transporters and destruction of the product) continued sporadically, the authorities turning a blind eye to the events. As the ECJ refused to make an interim order[1] the question of the enforceability of the judgment remained open inasmuch as the responsibility of the government for mob activities was an issue. That issue was only resolved in Case C-265/95: *Commission v France*,[2] in which the ECJ held that EC Article 30 (now Art 28) applies where a Member State abstains from adopting the measures necessary to deal with obstacles to free movement.

Whilst the illegality of a national ban on imports may be raised within the national jurisdiction leading to a reference for a preliminary ruling under

---

11   Case 2/73: *Geddo v Ente Nazionale Risi* [1974] ECR 865 at para 7 [1974] 1 CMLR 13.
12   Case 103/84: *Commission v Italy* [1986] ECR 1759 [1987] 2 CMLR 825.
13   Case 7/61: *Commission v Italy* [1961] ECR 317 at 328-9, [1962] CMLR 39.
14   Case 13/68: *Salgoil SpA v Italy* [1968] ECR 453 at 460-1.
15   Case 118/78: *Meijer BV v Department of Trade* [1979] ECR 1387, [1979] 2 CMLR 398.
16   Case 231/78: *Commission v United Kingdom* [1979] ECR 1447, [1979] 2 CMLR 427 following the reference in Case 118/78.
17   Case 232/78: *Commission v France* [1979] ECR 2729, [1980] 1 CMLR 418.
18   Case 124/81: *Commission v United Kingdom* [1983] ECR 203, [1983] 2 CMLR 1.
19   Case 40/82: *Commission v United Kingdom* [1982] ECR 2793, [1982] 3 CMLR 497.
20   Case 48/74: *Charmasson v Minister of Economic Affairs and Finance* [1974] ECR 1383, [1975] 2 CMLR 208.
 1   Case 171/83R: *Commission v France* [1983] ECR 2621.
 2   [1997] ECR I-6959. Cf *R v Chief Constable of Sussex, ex p International Trader's Ferry Ltd* [1999] 1 CMLR 1320.

EC Article 234 (ex Art 177) the Commission will, as a rule, enforce the duties of States according to the procedure of EC Article 226 (ex Art 169).[3]

Regarding quantitative restrictions the ECJ found French rules requiring a certificate of quality standard as a pre-condition of an export licence contrary to EC Article 29 (ex Art 34). It stressed that such rules, irrespective of their objective, were incompatible with Community law. Moreover the distinction between goods for exports, to which the quality rules applied, and those for domestic use, to which the rules did not apply, is likely to lead to arbitrary discrimination between these two classes of products and this constitutes an obstacle to intra-Community trade.[4] However differences in manufacturing standards, especially in food trade, continue to cause problems in inter-state trade.[5]

The risk of discrimination between exports and domestic market was highlighted in the horsemeat[6] and the bakery prosecution[7] cases. The scope of EC Article 29 (ex Art 34) was thus explained in the latter case:

'Article 34 concerns national measures which have as their specific object or effect the restriction on patterns of exports and thereby the establishment of a difference in treatment between the domestic trade of a Member State and its export trade, in such a way as to provide a particular advantage for national production or for the domestic market of the state in question.'

However the seizure of goods subject to cross-border instalment sales cannot be pleaded as an obstacle to trade or a breach of EC Article 28 (ex Art 30).[8]

F. Elimination of measures equivalent to quantitative restrictions

The Commission issued a number of directives establishing procedures and a timetable for the removal of such measures, which were described as not only instruments having legislative effect but also administrative practices,[9] eg customs delays[10] which, though not legally binding, were de facto in place. The guilty parties were not only the government departments but also 'bodies established or approved by an official authority'.[11]

A much broader description of measures having equivalent effect to quantitative restrictions came out of the ECJ in the first *Scotch Whisky* case[12] where traders were prosecuted for not providing authentic certificates of the origin of the product

---

3 See also Case 288/83: *Commission v Ireland* [1985] ECR 1761, [1985] 3 CMLR 152.
4 Case 53/76: *Procureur de la République v Bouhelier* [1977] ECR 197 at 205.
5 See Case 52/88: *Commission v Belgium, re edible gelatine in meat* [1989] ECR 1137, [1991] 1 CMLR 755; Case 76/86: *Commission v Germany, re milk substitutes* [1989] ECR 1021 [1991] 1 CMLR 741.
6 Case 15/79: *Goenveld v Produktschap voor Vee en Vlees* [1979] ECR 3409, [1981] 1 CMLR 207. See also Case 52/88: supra.
7 Case 155/80: *Sergius Oebel* [1981] ECR 1993 at 2009, [1983] 1 CMLR 390; see also Case 172/82: *Syndicat National des Fabricants Faffineurs d'Huile de Graisse v Groupemenmt d'Intérêt Economique* [1983] ECR 555.
8 Case C-69/88: *H Krantz-GmbH v Ontvanger der Directe Belastingen* [1990] ECR I-583, [1991] 2 CMLR 677.
9 Preamble to Dir 70/50 (OJ 1970, Sp ed I p 17).
10 Case 42/82: *Commission v France* [1983] ECR 1013, [1984] 1 CMLR 160 and 42/82R: [1982] ECR 841.
11 Case 94/79: *Re Pieter Vriend* [1980] ECR 327 at 340, [1980] 3 CMLR 473; see also Case 249/81: *Commission v Ireland, Re Buy Irish Campaign* [1982] ECR 4005, [1983] 2 CMLR 104.
12 Case 8/74: *Procureur du Roi v Dassonville* [1974] ECR 837, [1974] 2 CMLR 436.

which was in free circulation in France, as required by Belgian law. The Court ruled that 'all trading rules enacted by Member States which are capable of hindering, directly or indirectly, actually or potentially, intra-Community trade are to be considered as measures having an effect equivalent to quantitative restrictions'. That definition applies not just to 'rules' in the strict sense but to any form of conduct attributable to the State, including practices (such as acquiescing to violent protests)[13] and court orders.[14] However this extreme stance had to be modified because the Belgian government would not give up its claim to a modicum of control. Therefore, in the second *Scotch Whisky* case[15] the ECJ conceded that the authenticity of the product could be guaranteed by appropriate certificates which, however, could be obtained not only from the producer state but also from an intermediate state as might have been the position in the first case. A further modification of the definition employed in the first Scotch Whisky case was introduced after that definition had been subject to considerable strain in the Sunday trading cases.[16] That modification applies to one particular class of measures affecting the movement of goods: measures that apply directly to the manner in which goods are marketed. Such measures can be divided into two categories.[17] The first comprises rules laying down requirements to be met by the goods such as rules concerning designation, form, size, weight, composition, presentation, labelling and packaging. Such measures are caught by the prohibition in EC Articles 28 and 29 (ex Arts 30 and 34), even if they apply in the same way both to domestic products and to imports. The prohibition will be disapplied only by virtue of EC Article 30 (ex Art 36), or by some public interest justification taking precedence over the free movement of goods (as to which, see below). The second category comprises rules restricting or prohibiting certain selling arrangements (such as restrictions on the days or hours on which shops may open,[18] prohibitions on sales at a loss or at a low profit,[19] and bans on advertising in particular places or particular ways).[20] Such rules are not prohibited as long as they apply to all relevant traders operating within the national territory and as long as they affect in the same manner, in law and in fact, the marketing of domestic products and of those from other Member States.

Examples of measures having equivalent effect are legion, as if (in the case of the more obvious ones) the Member States deliberately set out to evade their Treaty obligations. These include: territorially restrictive marketing systems;[1] excessive checking or inspection of imported goods;[2] advertising designed to champion or protect domestic products at the expense of competing imported

---

13   Case C-265/95: *Commission v France* [1997] ECR I-6959. See also Case C-5/94: *R v Ministry of Agriculture, Fisheries and Food, ex p Hedley Lomas (Ireland) Ltd* [1996] ECR I-2553, where conduct amounting to more than acquiescence was involved.

14   Eg Case 6/81: *Industrie Diensten Groep v Beele* [1982] ECR 707, para 7.

15   Case 2/78: *Commission v Belgium* [1979] ECR 1761.

16   In particular, Case C-145/88: *Torfaen Borough Council v B & Q plc* [1989] ECR 3851.

17   Cases C-267/91 and C-268/91: *Keck and Mithouard* [1993] ECR I-6097, paras 15-16.

18   Case C-69/93: *Punto Casa and PPV* [1994] ECR I-2355.

19   Keck (supra); Case C-63/94: *Belapore v ITM and Vocarex* [1995] ECR I-2467.

20   Case C-292/92: *Hünermund v Landesapothekerkammer Baden-Württenberg* [1993] ECR I-6787; Case C-412/93: *Lederc-Siplec v TFI Publicité* [1995] ECR I-179.

 1   83/78: *Pigs Marketing Board (Northern Ireland) v Redmond* [1978] ECR 2347, [1979] 1 CMLR 177.

 2   Case 272/80: *Frans-Nederlandse Maatchaapij voor Biologische Produkten BV* [1981] ECR 3277, [1982] 2 CMLR 497; Case 42/82: *Commission v France* [1983] ECR 1013, [1984] 1 CMLR 160; Case 124/81: *Commission v United Kingdom* [1983] ECR 203, [1983] 2 CMLR 1.

products;[3] pricing systems discriminating against imported goods;[4] marketing rules prescribing a particular description of goods;[5] or shape of a container (bottle in case);[6] or alcoholic strength;[7] purity of beer;[8] fat content of cheese;[9] roadworthiness tests of vehicles;[10] marks of origin;[11] refusal of imported postal franking machines;[12] compulsory lodging of security for payment of imported goods;[13] a requirement to obtain prior authorisation for the purchase of spectacles from another Member State in order to have the cost reimbursed from a Social Security fund;[14] and a requirement to obtain an exemption or derogation from a domestic restriction,[15] etc.

Certain measures, eg licences, coupled with quality controls[16] or declarations to be issued by domestic marketing boards[17] as a condition of exportation are also equivalent to quantitative restrictions contrary to EC Article 29 (ex Art 34). Dealing with a restriction on the importation of a product from outside the Community the ECJ stressed the general principle that EC Articles 28 and 29 (ex Arts 30 and 34(1)) preclude the application in intra-Community trade of national provisions which require, even as a pure formality, import or export licences.[18]

Among the many cases which illustrate the operation of the principles are the Simmenthal cases[19] which reflect a convergence of prohibited measures since the ECJ found that the practice of excessive sanitary inspection of meat was equivalent to a quantitative restriction whereas the fee for the operation was equivalent to a customs duty.

The word 'discrimination' does not form part of the wording of EC Articles 28 and 29 (ex Arts 30 and 34). Many cases involve discrimination against imported products in various forms, sometimes as subtle as ostensibly treating domestic and imported products on the same footing but, in fact, putting goods imported from or exported to a fellow Member State into a disadvantageous position.[20] Discrimination

---

3 Case 249/81: *Commission v Ireland* [1982] ECR 4005, [1983] 2 CMLR 104 and Case 113/80: *Commission v Ireland Re indication of Origin of Goods* [1981] ECR 1625, [1983] 1 CMLR 706; see also Case 222/82: *Apple and Pear Development Council v KJ Ltd Lewis* [1983] ECR 4083, [1984] 3 CMLR 733.
4 Case 65/75: *Tasca* [1976] ECR 291, [1977] 2 CMLR 183; Case 229/83: *Association des Centres Distributeurs Edouard Leclerc v Au Blé Vert Sarl* [1985] ECR 1, [1985] 2 CMLR 286.
5 Case 12/74: *Commission v Germany* [1975] ECR 181, [1975] 1 CMLR 340. See also Case C-366/98: *Criminal proceedings against Geffroy* [2001] All ER (EC) 222 (use of a particular language).
6 Case 179/85: *Commission v Germany* [1986] ECR 3879, [1988] 1 CMLR 135.
7 Case 182/84: *Miro BV* [1985] ECR 3731, [1986] 3 CMLR 545; Case 120/78: *Rewe-Zentral AG v Bundesmonopolverwaltung für Branntwein, Re Cassis de Dijon* [1979] ECR 649, [1979] 3 CMLR 494.
8 Case 178/84: *Commission v Germany* [1987] ECR 1227, [1988] 1 CMLR 780.
9 Case 286/86: *Ministère Public v Déserbais* [1988] ECR 4907, [1989] 1 CMLR 516.
10 Case 50/85: *Schloh v Auto Contrôle Technique* [1986] ECR 1855, [1987] 1 CMLR 450.
11 Case 113/80, note 3, supra, Case 207/83: *Commission v United Kingdom* [1985] ECR 1201, [1985] 2 CMLR 259.
12 Case 21/84: *Commission v France* [1985] ECR 1355.
13 Case 95/81: *Commission v Italy* [1982] ECR 2187.
14 Case C-120/95: *Decker* [1998] ECR I-1831.
15 Case C-473/98: *Kemikalieinspektionen v Toolex Alpha AB*, 11 July 2000, para 37.
16 Case 53/76, p 467, note 4, supra.
17 Case 68/76: *Commission v France* [1977] ECR 515 at 530-31.
18 Cases 51-54/71: *International Fruit Co NV v Prodktschaap voor Groenten en Fruit* [1971] ECR 1107 at 1116.
19 Case 35/76: *Simmenthal SpA v Ministero delle Finanze* [1976] ECR 1871; Case 106/77: (No 2) [1978] ECR 629; Case 70/77: *(No 3)* [1978] ECR 1453.
20 See eg Case 152/78: *Commission v France, Re advertising of alcoholic beverages* [1980] ECR 2299, [1981] 2 CMLR 743.

apart, the question at issue is whether the national measure interferes with the freedom of movement of goods and thus hinders intra-Community trade. If it does, the measure will be prohibited, despite its non-discriminatory nature, unless it has an overriding public interest justification or benefits from the exemption in EC Article 30 (ex Art 36).[1] In this respect 'reverse' discrimination, ie discrimination against national products, is not prohibited unless it is also disadvantageous in some respect to imports. As explained by the ECJ, when dealing with differential pricing of bread, ie imported bread being permitted to be sold below the minimum selling price of domestically produced bread, the purpose of EC Article 28 (ex Art 30) is to eliminate obstacles to the importation of goods and not to ensure equal treatment for goods of national origin and imported ones.[2] The same conclusion was reached in a Belgian case involving labelling products which required that the processor of butter produced in Belgium was identified. Since butter produced abroad need not be identified the labelling of domestic butter did not cause any obstacle to imports of the product.

G. Derogations from the prohibitions of quantitative restrictions and measures having equivalent effect

(1) THE *CASSIS DE DIJON* RULE[3]

The ECJ has developed the principle that a measure affecting the free movement of goods will escape prohibition if: (a) it applies to domestic products and to imports from other Member States without distinction; and (b) is justified by a public interest concern that overrides the free movement of goods. Discriminatory measures do not benefit from this principle.[4] The burden lies on the person invoking the principle to demonstrate that it applies.[5] The public interest justifications that the ECJ has accepted are: effectiveness of fiscal supervision; fairness of commercial transactions;[6] protection of the consumer;[7] protection of the environment;[8] improvement of working conditions;[9] the promotion of creative works;[10] maintenance of pluralism of the press.[11] A measure will not be so justified, and will not escape prohibition, unless it is both necessary and proportionate for the protection of the interest in question.[12]

---

1   Eg Case 120/78: *Rewe-Zentral v Bundesmonopolverwaltung für Branntwein* [1979] ECR 649.
2   Cases 80 and 159/85: *Nederlandse Bakkerij Stichting v Edah BV* [1986] ECR 3359, [1988] 2 CMLR 113; See also Case 355/85: *Ministère Public v Cognet* [1986] ECR 3231, [1987] 3 CMLR 942.
3   See the *Cassis de Dijon* case: [1979] ECR 649.
4   Eg Case 113/80: *Commission v Ireland* [1981] ECR 1625.
5   Case 788/79: *Gilli and Andres* [1980] ECR 2071.
6   Case 6/81: *Industrie Diensten Groep v Beele* [1982] ECR 707 (passing off).
7   Eg Case 207/83: *Commission v United Kingdom* [1985] ECR 1201 (prohibition of false indications of origin).
8   Case 302/86: *Commission v Denmark* [1988] ECR 4607.
9   Case 155/80: *Oebel* [1981] ECR 1993.
10   Cases 60 and 61/84: *Cinéthèque v Federation Nationale des Cinemas Francais* [1985] ECR 2605.
11   Case C-368/95: *Vereinigte Familiapress v H Bauer Verlag* [1997] ECR I-36 89.
12   Eg Case 182/84: *Miro* [1985] ECR 3731 (adequate labelling sufficient to protect consumers); Case C-470/93: *Vereingegen Unwesen in Handel and Geurerbe Köln v Mars* [1995] ECR I-1923 (consumers not confused by publicity markings).

(2)   EC ARTICLE 30 (EX ART 36)

EC Article 30 (ex Art 36) allows the Member States to derogate from the prohibitions in EC Articles 28 and 29 (ex Arts 30 and 34) on several grounds provided such derogations do not constitute 'a means of arbitrary discrimination or a disguised restriction on trade'. To avoid being an 'arbitrary' or 'disguised' restriction' the national measure in question[13] ought to satisfy the requirement of proportionality.

Derogation is a permissive rule addressed to the Member States which enables them to protect certain values of society from the unwelcome intrusion of free trade. Being in the nature of an exception to the general rule a derogation has to be pleaded specifically and proved on the grounds expressly listed in the Treaty.[14] Thus the Treaty has to be interpreted restrictively and the restrictive measure justified by the state.[15] In practice the scope of EC Article 30 (ex Art 36) has been narrowed down by Community legislation[16] as well as under the impact of the *Cassis de Dijon* case.[17] Thus, in accordance with the doctrine of the 'occupied field' derogations under EC Article 30 (ex Art 36) cannot be pleaded[18] unless, of course, the specific Community measure allows a derogation in which case the latter can be relied on. It follows that EC Article 30 (ex Art 36) operates in the 'unoccupied' field.[19] The grounds, said to be of non-economic character, are as follows:

(a)   Public morality
The leading case[20] involved the British prohibition of imported pornographic material freely available in certain Member States. On reference from the House of Lords the ECJ held that it was for each Member State to determine the requirement of public morality in accordance with its own scale of values. Thus the UK was within its rights to prohibit importation of 'hard pornography' and to prosecute those who, in contravention of British law, attempted to import the offensive material. The fact that other Member States have adopted a more liberal attitude was irrelevant. In the words of the ECJ 'In principle, it is for each Member State to determine in accordance with its own scale of values and the form selected by its requirements of public morality in its territory'.

---

13   Cases 2-4/82: *Delhaize Frères Le Lion SA v Belgium* [1983] ECR 2973 at para 12: Case 42/82: *Commission v France* [1983] ECR 1013 at paras 51-57.   Case 272/80: *Frans-Nederlandse Maatschappij voor Biologische Producten* [1981] ECR 3277, [1982] 2 CMLR 497.
14   Case 46/76: Case 113/80 note 4 supra; Case 95/81 p 469, note 13, supra at para 27.
15   Case 227/82: *Leendert van Bennskom* [1983] ECR 3883 at para 40.
16   Case C-235/91: *Commission v Ireland, re imports of animal semen* [1992] ECR I-5917, [1993] 1 CMLR 325.
17   Supra, Case 120/78; see also Case C-347/89: *Freistaat Bayern v Eurim-Pharm GmbH* [1991] ECR I-1747.
18   Case 148/78: *Pubblico Ministero v Ratti* [1979] ECR 1629, [1980] 1 CMLR 96; Case C-1/96: *R v Ministry of Agriculture, Fisheries and Food ex p Compassion in World Farming Ltd* [1998] ECR I-1251, [1998] 2 CMLR 661.
19   Case 5/77: *Tedeschi v Denkavit Commerciale srl* [1977] ECR 1555, [1978] 1 CMLR 1; Case 174/82: *Officier van Justitie v Sandoz BV* [1983] ECR 2445, [1984] 3 CMLR 43. See also Case 76/86: *Commission v Germany, re milk substitutes* [1989] ECR 1021, [1991] 1 CMLR 741; Case C-39/90: *Denkavit Futtermittel GmbH v Land Baden-Würtemberg* [1991] ECR I-3069 [1994] 1 CMLR 595; and Case C-473/98: *Kemikalieinspeltionen v Toolex Alpha AB*, 11 July 2000, paras 25-26.
20   Case 34/79: *R v Henn and Darby* [1979] ECR 3795, [1980] 1 CMLR 246.

In another British reference[1] the interpretation of EC Article 30 (ex Art 36) was completed as the ECJ held that the UK could not rely on the derogation in order to prohibit the importation of inflatable rubber dolls (allegedly used for certain sexual practices) because such products were also produced and freely marketed in the UK. To allow derogation in the circumstances would have been equivalent to an arbitrary discrimination or a disguised restriction on intra-Community trade.

Whilst the licensing of the so-called 'sex shops' does not constitute a hindrance to imports in the sense of EC Article 28 (ex Art 30), the import of particular objects may be covered by derogation under EC Article 30 (ex Art 36).[2]

(b)   Public policy

'Public policy' reflects the interests of the state to maintain a standard of behaviour commensurate to common good and public order. The concept defies precise definition for it reflects, on the one hand, legislative policy and judicial discretion, on the other. A lack of legislative policy, as we have seen in the Sunday trading saga, lands a Member State in difficulty.

It is not surprising that pleas of public policy have made little impact upon the ECJ. Thus the plea that the reservation of the appellation 'Sekt' and 'Weinbrand' exclusively for German wines in order to protect the German producers from unfair competition and the German consumers from deception did not impress the Court as it ruled that derogations from EC Articles 28 and 29 (ex Arts 30 and 34) were permissible only if it was necessary to protect the producer and the consumer from fraudulent commercial practices. In this way the argument was directed to aspects of proportionality.[3] Similarly, in criminal proceedings[4] arising from the use of the 'Bocksbeutel' wine bottle by the importer of Italian wine into Germany on the ground that the particularly shaped bottle was used traditionally and, therefore, was reserved for wine producers in Franconia and Baden, the argument of public policy was dismissed. Such a bottle was also, traditionally, used in the Bolzano area of northern Italy and was unlikely to confuse consumers. A criminal sanction was not necessarily tantamount to public policy but it hindered the movement of goods in a manner incompatible with the Treaty.

Certain Italian cases show also a vain recourse to public policy. Thus the requirement of advance payments for imports in the interests of the state solicitous of protecting the national currency was not considered to be a matter of public policy since, as observed by the ECJ, the derogation on that ground 'refers to matters of a non-economic nature'.[5] Similarly an attempt to justify on the ground of public policy a national measure requiring an inspection and registration of imported second-hand buses failed, the ECJ holding that, though legitimate on the ground of road safety, the measure, *in casu*, was disproportionate and discriminatory as being directed to imports. Another Italian measure requiring a new registration document for vehicles imported into Italy which were already registered in the Community as a condition of importation failed the test of public policy despite the argument that this was a precaution against registration of vehicles stolen abroad.[6]

1   Cases 121/85: *Conegate Ltd v Customs and Excise Comrs* [1986] ECR 1007, [1986] 1 CMLR 739 see also *R v Bow Street Metropolitan Stipendiary Magistrate, ex p Noncyp Ltd* [1988] 3 CMLR 84.
2   Case C-350/89: *Sheptonhurst Ltd v Newham Borough Council* [1991] ECR I-2387, [1991] 3 CMLR 463.
3   Case 12/74: *Commission v Germany* [1975] ECR 181 at 199, [1975] 1 CMLR 340.
4   Case 16/83: *Re Prantl* [1984] ECR 1299 at 1329, [1985] 2 CMLR 238.
5   Case 95/81: *Commission v Italy* [1982] ECR 2187 at 2204.
6   Case 154/85: *Commission v Italy* [1987] ECR 2717, [1988] 2 CMLR 951.

The plea of public policy was successful in the *Krugerrand*[7] case, where certain Britons were prosecuted for attempting to import into the UK South African gold coins and export to Germany silver alloy coins minted in the UK but no longer in circulation. The defendants argued that British legislation involved was contrary to the principle of free movement of capital (EC Articles 67-73 now repealed: see instead EC Arts 56-60) and could not be justified under EC Article 30 (ex Art 36). The ECJ defined capital as a 'means of payment' and, therefore, silver alloy coins which have been legal tender in the past and as such protected from destruction, could no longer be regarded as a means of payment. These coins have now become goods and, consequently, came within the scope of EC Articles 28-30 (ex Arts 30-36). A ban on exporting such coins in order to prevent their being melted down or destroyed in another Member State was justified on the ground of public policy because such ban stemmed from the need to protect the right to mint coinage which traditionally falls within the prerogative of the state. As for the gold coins there was as yet no Community rule preventing a Member State from dealing with such imports under its own legislation.

(c) Public security

It is common ground that the importation of implements of crime or materials likely to be used by terrorists can be restricted on the ground of public security since the maintenance of law and order is the prime responsibility of the state.[8]

The position is different in cases of imports of products which do not ostensibly threaten public security, though it is apposite to mention in this context that, as from 1 January 1993, the acquisition and possession of weapons have become subject to common rules based on a Community list of authorized weapons.[9] Presumably the importation of unauthorized weapons shall remain subject to national measures, ie public security.

We noted above Case 95/81[10] where the Italian government unsuccessfully defended a system of advance payments for imports on the ground of public policy. In the same case the defence of public security was also, albeit unsuccessfully, raised, the defendant arguing that public security consisted in safeguarding the fundamental interests of the state and the defence of its currency. The plea was rejected by the ECJ.

More successful was the Irish government[11] defending the measure which provided that Irish oil importers had to purchase a percentage of their supply from the national oil refinery. The ECJ acknowledged that the security of supplies of oil vital to the national economy and the essential services was involved and, therefore, a restriction on imports on that ground was justified.

(d) Protection of national treasures

EC Article 30 (ex Art 36) provides for a derogation for 'the protection of national treasures possessing artistic, historic or archaeological value' but there is no Treaty definition of such objects. An opportunity to define 'works of art' occurred for

---

7   Case 7/78: *R v Thompson, Johnson and Woodiwiss* [1978] ECR 2247 at 2275, [1979] 1 CMLR 47.

8   See British cases: *McAffee v Smyth and Quigley (radios which could be used by terrorists)* [1981] CMLR 410 (Belfast Magistrates' Court); *R v Goldstein ('citizen's radios' and similar equipment used by security forces)* [1983] 1 CMLR 252, HL.

9   Dir 91/447 (OJ 1991, L256/51).

10   P 469, note 13, supra.

11   Case 72/83: *Campus Oil Ltd v Minister for Industry and Energy* [1984] ECR 2727, [1984] 3 CMLR 544.

the purpose of customs classification in a case involving the work of a well known artist.[12] The ECJ ruled that a wall relief made from cardboard glued to expanded polystyrene was a work of sculpture rather than 'an article made of artificial resins and plastic material'. However it is doubtful whether the object *in casu* can be regarded as a 'national treasure' within the meaning of EC Article 30 (ex Art 36). It seems that EC Article 30 (ex Art 36), though unclear, contemplates only objects of national piety or historical sentiment which the states intend to keep at home. Once such objects have become commercialised they may no longer be regarded as a protected species. This can be inferred from the two Italian 'art treasure' cases[13] where Italy was unable to rely on EC Article 30 (ex Art 36) in order to justify a special tax on the export of objects of art.

The need of Community legislation in this field became urgent in the wake of the completion of the internal market.[14] Thus Regulation 3911/92[15] on export of cultural goods purports to ensure that exports of such goods are subject to uniform controls at the external borders of the Community. Exports can be effected only by a licence valid throughout the Community which is issued by the competent authorities of the Member State in which the cultural object is located. Export licences may be refused 'where the cultural goods in question are covered by legislation protecting national treasures of artistic, historical or archaeological value in the Member State concerned' (Article 2(2)). The Annex to the Regulation lists the categories of objects covered.

To complete the aforesaid, Directive 93/7,[16] in its Annex, lists further categories of protected cultural goods. The preamble to the Directive confirms that 'within the limits of Article 36 of the Treaty [now EC Art 30], the Member States will, after 1992, retain the right to define their national treasures and to take the necessary measures to protect them, though they will, on the other hand, no longer be able to apply checks of formalities at the Community's internal frontiers to ensure the effectiveness of those measures'.

The Directive provides for a guarantee for the return of the national treasures unlawfully removed from the national control and for co-operation between national authorities in this respect (Article 5). There is also provision for compensation to a bona fide acquirer to be ordered by the courts if the cultural goods are returned to the country where they belong (Article 10).

(e)   Protection of health of humans, animals and plants
Considerations of public health have come to light in the context of charges having effect equivalent to customs duties and measures having effect equivalent to quantitative restrictions. They will resurface in the discussions on fiscal barriers to trade. They have a particular meaning and purpose in the context of EC Article 30 (ex Art 36) where the protection of public health constitutes a derogation from the free movement of goods. The protection of the health and life of humans is the most important aspect of EC Article 30 (ex Art 36).[17]

---

12   Case 155/84: *Omnasch v HZA Berlin-Packhof* [1987] ECR 1449, [1986] 2 CMLR 456.
13   Case 7/68: *Commission v Italy* [1968] ECR 423, [1969] CMLR 1; and Case 18/71: *Eunomia di Porro v Italian Ministry of Education* [1971] ECR 811, [1972] CMLR 4.
14   EC Bull Supp 4/87 p 10; COM (89) 594.
15   OJ 1992, L395/1. Further implementing provisions are to be found in Reg No 752/93 (OJ 1993, L77/24), as amended.
16   OJ 1993, L74/1.
17   Case C-473/98: *Kemikalieinspektionen v Toolex Alpha AB*, 11 July 2000, para 38.

In Case 153/78[18] Germany defended her Inspector of Meat Act which prohibited the import of meat products unless such products were prepared in establishments processing for export in the exporting country in which the animals were slaughtered, such establishment being approved by the Federal Ministry, and the consignment is accompanied by a certificate of fitness for consumption issued by an official veterinarian. The plea of the protection of public health was rejected because there was a directive establishing a Community procedure in this respect and the risk of meat becoming unwholesome is not affected by the mere fact of crossing a frontier.

In another German case[19] the ECJ considered the defence of animal health under the *Viehseuchenverordnung* which purported to control salmonellae in feeding-stuffs imported into Germany. Such products may only be imported if accompanied by an official certificate from the exporting country confirming that they have been subjected to a specific treatment and inspected. Since this matter was not, at that time, covered by Community legislation, the ECJ applied its judgment in Case 104/75.[20] Like in the *Dassonville*[1] case a parallel importer was unable to satisfy the national requirements regarding the documentary certification of the imported products (ie pharmaceuticals, *in casu*). The ECJ ruled that, although it was legitimate for the national authorities to ascertain whether medicinal products imported in parallel are identical with those about which they were already informed, it was a matter of co-ordination between the Member States involved to exchange the requisite documents. Thus the Dutch rules were not justified by virtue of EC Article 30 (ex Art 36) unless it was proved that any other rules or practices were beyond the wit of reasonable administration. In its judgment in Case 251/78 the ECJ added that national rules or practices do not fall within EC Article 30 (ex Art 36), if public health can be effectively protected by measures which do not restrict intra-Community trade and that EC Article 30 (ex Art 36), in particular, cannot be relied on to justify administrative convenience, or reduce public expenditure.

In Case 788/79[2] importers of apple vinegar from Germany containing acetic acid were prosecuted under Italian law which permitted only vinegar derived from the acetic fermentation of wine. On reference, the ECJ pointed out that apple vinegar contained no substances injurious to health and that, anyway, the receptacles containing the product were sufficiently well labelled, thus avoiding confusion between the two kinds of vinegar.

By French law there were restrictions on advertising alcoholic drinks which clearly discriminated against imported drinks, in particular natural sweet wines, liqueur wines and grain spirits such as whisky and geneva, as representing a health hazard. In particular the French government claimed that the legislation in question was based on the distinction between drinks which are habitually consumed as an 'aperitif' or as 'digestive', the former (imported) being more dangerous to health than the latter. Such distinction could not be defended under EC Article 30 (ex Art 36).[3]

---

18 *Commission v Germany, re health control of imported meat* [1979] ECR 2555 at 2563-2567; see also Case 274/87: *Commission v Germany, re quality of sausage* [1989] ECR 229, [1989] 2 CMLR 733.
19 Case 251/78: *Denkavit Futtermittel GmbH v Minister für Ernährung* [1979] ECR 3369, [1980] 3 CMLR 513.
20 *Officer van Justitie v De Peiper* [1976] ECR 613, [1976] 2 CMLR 271.
1 P 467, note 12, supra.
2 *Gilli and Andres* [1980] ECR 2071 at 2078; followed by Case 193/80: *Commission v Italy* [1981] ECR 3019.
3 Case 152/78: *Commission v France* [1980] ECR 2299 at paras 17–18; See also Cases 314-316/81 and 83/82: *Procureur de la République v Waterkeyn* [1982] ECR 4337 [1983] 2 CMLR 145.

Certain Dutch cases also reveal a conflict between Community law and national legislation which in the judgment of the ECJ could not be justified by EC Article 30 (ex Art 36). For example Case 27/80[4] on the labelling of alcoholic beverages; Case 130/80[5] on the ingredients, size and shape of bread; and Case 174/82[6] on vitamin additives in muesli bars lawfully marketable in Germany and Belgium. It should be noted that EC Article 30 (ex Art 36), does not preclude reverse discrimination. In Case 53/80[7] the ECJ held that national legislation prohibiting the use of nisin as a preservative in processed cheese intended for the domestic market alone was included among measures which EC Article 30 (ex Art 36) permits Member States to adopt for the protection of the health of humans. Since products intended for export were not included the measure did not constitute a 'means of arbitrary discrimination or disguised restriction on trade between Member States' in the context of EC Article 30 (ex Art 36).

In the field of protection the UK unsuccessfully pleaded the risk of the spread of Newcastle disease in order to justify a ban on the import of poultrymeat and eggs from other Member States save Denmark and Ireland.[8] The ban, which appears to be a clumsy retaliation in the *guerre des moutons* with France,[9] proved rather expensive to the British taxpayer as, after protracted litigation, the government agreed to pay compensation to the French poultry farmers involved.[10]

Following the German control of imported meat case[11] there was little point in prohibiting the import of French UHT milk products into the UK on similar grounds.[12]

In Case 4/75[13] the German authorities faced with the charge of breach of EC Article 28 (ex Art 30) arising from the phyto-sanitary inspection of imported apples (which was not required for the domestic product) pleaded unsuccessfully the health of plants derogation. In view of the existence of a Community directive[14] in this matter the ECJ confirmed the legality of the inspection but struck out the defence because of the discrimination against the imported product.

Pending the enactment of Community legislation the ECJ held that national tests of plant protection products imported from a fellow Member State where the products have been approved and lawfully marketed may be justified but 'the authorities of the importing state are, however, not entitled unnecessarily to require technical or chemical analysis or laboratory tests when the same analyses and tests have already been carried out in another Member State and their results are available to those authorities or may at their request be placed at their disposal'.[15]

In Case 190/87[16] the ECJ ruled that 'where . . . Community directives provide for the harmonization of the measures necessary to ensure inter alia the protection

4   *Fietje* [1980] ECR 3839, [1981] 3 CMLR 722.
5   *Fabriek voor Hoogwaardige Vaedingsprodukten Kelderman* [1981] ECR 527.
6   *Officer van Justite v Sandoz BV* [1983] ECR 2445, [1984] 3 CMLR 43.
7   *Officier van Justitie v Koninklijke Kaasfabrick Eyseen BV* [1981] ECR 409.
8   Case 40/82: *Commission v UK* [1982] ECR 2793, [1982] 3 CMLR 497.
9   See Case 232/78: *Commission v France* [1979] ECR 2729, [1980] 1 CMLR 418
10 *Bourgoin SA v Ministry of Agriculture, Fisheries and Food* [1986] QB 716 [1985] 3 All ER 585, followed by settlement before the case reached the House of Lords, [1987] 1 CMLR 169.
11 Case 153/78: *Commission v Germany* [1979] ECR 2555 at 2563-2567.
12 Case 124/81: *Commission v United Kingdom* [1983] ECR 203, [1983] 2 CMLR 1.
13 *Rewe-Zentralfinanz GmbH v Landwirtschaftskammer* [1975] ECR 843, [1975] 1 CMLR 599. See also Case C-128/89: *Commission v Italy, Re imports of grapefruit* [1990] ECR I-3239, [1991] 3 CMLR 720.
14 69/466 (OJ 1969, L323/5).
15 Case 272/80: *Frans-Nederlandse Maatschapij voor Biologische Producten* [1981] ECR 3277, [1982] 2 CMLR 497 at para 16.
16 *Oberkreisdirektor des Kreises Borken v Moormann* [1988] ECR 4689, [1990] 1 CMLR 656 at para 10.

of animal and human health and establish Community procedures to check that they are observed, recourse to Article 36 [now Art 30] is no longer justified and the appropriate checks must be carried out and protective measures adopted within the framework outlined by the harmonization directive'.[17]

The object of harmonization is to remove the technical barriers to trade[18] and thus facilitate free movement of goods whilst protecting certain national characteristics of the product, especially in the light of the eating habits which otherwise might provoke a defensive national reaction.[19]

It is clear that the membership of a specified trade organization as required by national practice cannot be a condition of engaging in export or import trade.[20]

(f)   Protection of intellectual property

Since intellectual property rights (ie patents, trade marks, copyrights and related rights) rooted in national law may be used in order to restrict the movement of goods or competition[1] by private parties we observe their erosion under the impact of the paramount principles of the Common Market. Notwithstanding the provision of EC Article 295 (ex Art 222) (which, in the opinion of Advocate-General Römer,[2] was 'solely to guarantee in a general manner the freedom of the Member States to organize their system of property') the ECJ contributed to their limitation. Recognizing that such rights represent 'one aspect of the regulation of trade'[3] the Court, in a series of cases, distinguished between the 'subject matter' and 'exercise' of intellectual property rights. The former is 'untouched' by the Treaty, the latter is 'completely subject to Community law'.[4] It would go beyond the purpose of the protection of rights if the holder were permitted to control further marketing since the right to prevent re-imports (*in casu*) 'does not form part of the essence of the industrial and commercial property mentioned in Article 36 [now Art 30]'.[5]

(3)   OTHER DEROGATIONS

Attempts, albeit unsuccessful; were made to extend the scope of EC Article 30 (ex Art 36) on the ground of the protection of the environment[6] by insisting that all containers for beer and soft drinks must be returnable. In an earlier case[7] the Court confirmed that the protection of the environment is 'one of the Community's essential objectives' but the measures adopted for this purpose must not 'go beyond the inevitable restrictions which are justified for . . . environmental protection'.

---

17   See also Case 5/77: *Tedeschi v Denkavit* [1977] ECR 1555; Case 148/78: *Pubblico Ministero v Ratli* [1979] ECR 1629; Case 251/78: *Denkavit* [1979] ECR 3369; Joined Cases 2-4/82: *Delhaize Frères Le Lion v Belgium* [1983] ECR 2973, [1985] 1 CMLR 561.

18   See p 479 et seq, infra.

19   See Case 304/84: *Ministère Public v Müller* [1986] ECR 1511 at para 21; Case 174/82 supra; Case 247/84: *Re Motte* [1985] ECR 3887, [1987] 1 CMLR 663.

20   Case 43/88: *Commission v Netherlands, retraders in seeds and bulbs* [1989] ECR 1649 [1991] 1 CMLR 734.

1   See infra Ch 31.

2   In Cases 56 and 58/64: *Consten and Grundig v Commission* [1966] ECR 299 at 366, [1966] CMLR 418.

3   A-G Trabucchi in Case 8/74, *Dassonville*, supra.

4   Per A-G Römer in Case 78/70: *Deutsche Grammophon GmbH v Metro* [1971] ECR 487, [1971] CMLR 631.

5   Ibid.

6   Case 302/86: *Commission v Denmark* [1988] ECR 4607, [1989] 1 CMLR 619; Case 380/87: *Enichem Basev Comune di Dinisello Balsamo* [1989] ECR 2491 [1991] 1 CMLR 313.

7   Case 240/83: *Procureur de la République v Association de défense des brûlers d'hules usages* [1985] ECR 531.

Similarly unsuccessful were the attempts to rely on EC Article 30 (ex Art 36) under the guise of consumer protection[8] but in such cases the ECJ tends to give credit to the intelligence of consumers and, generally, counsels the labelling of the product rather than restriction on imports. If the description of a product is inaccurate EC Article 30 (ex Art 36) may be invoked on health grounds, subject to the principle of proportionality but the importer may plead defence from prosecution if he relied on foreign official certification.[9]

EC Article 134 (ex Art 115) provides for derogation from the principle of free movement of goods in order to safeguard the execution of the Common Commercial Policy where there is deflection of trade caused by imports of goods from outside the Community or where differences between measures taken in accordance with the CCP lead to difficulties in one or more Member States. In such cases the Commission has power to authorize protective measures to be taken by the Member States concerned. By Decision 80/47[10] the Commission set up a system of intra-Community surveillance where there is a danger that imports of certain products may give rise to economic difficulties. A policy adopted in this respect in 1987[11] resulted in a reduction of instances where EC Article 134 (ex Art 115), has been invoked. The products concerned included motor vehicles, shoes and bananas. It was expected that complaints regarding the latter will disappear when the proposed common organization of the market in bananas has been set up.[12]

EC Article 297 (ex Art 224) allows for derogations in the event of serious internal disturbances affecting the maintenance of law and order, in the event of war or international tension constituting a threat of war, or in order to carry out obligations for the purpose of maintaining peace and international security. EC Article 296 (ex Art 223), on the other hand, permits the Member States to withhold information which they consider essential to their security and take such measures as they deem necessary for the protection of the essential interests of their security connected with the production of or trade in arms, munitions and war materials, but such measures must not affect adversely competition in the Common Market regarding products which are not intended for specifically military purposes.

Both articles have to be interpreted restrictively[13] since they could lead to unilateral action evading the duties imposed upon the Member States by the exigencies of the Common Market. It is interesting to note that no attempt has been made to rely on EC Article 297 (ex Art 224), where the movement of goods was disturbed by angry mobs resorting to violence.[14] Evidently, as stated

8   Case 261/81: *Rau v De Smedt PubA, re marketing of margarine* [1982] ECR 3961, [1983] 2 CMLR 46; Cases 341/82 and 189/83: *Commission v Belgium, re packaging of margarine* [1985] 1 CMLR 120 (the cases were withdrawn after the delivery of the advocate general's opinion); Case 176/84: *Commission v Greece re beer purity standards* [1987] ECR 1193 [1988] 1 CMLR 813; Case 179/85: *Commission v Germany, re use of champagne-type bottles* [1986] ECR 3879 [1988] 1 CMLR 135; Case 178/84: *Commission v Germany, re purity of beer* [1987] ECR 1227, [1988] 1 CMLR 780; Case 286/86: *Ministère Public v Déserbais, re marketing of cheese* [1988] ECR 4907, [1989] 1 CMLR 516.
9   Case 25/88: *Bouchara (née Wurmser) and Norlaine SA* [1989] ECR 1105, [1991] 1 CMLR 173.
10 OJ 1980, L16/14.
11 XXI General Report on the Activities of the European Communities, point 196.
12 XXVI General Report on the Activities of the European Communities point 525; See Reg 404/93 (OJ 1993, L47/25).
13 See Case 13/68: *Salgoil SpA v Italian Ministry of Foreign Trade* [1968] ECR 453 at 463, [1969] CMLR 181.
14 See Case 42/82: *Commission v France, re imports of sheepmeat* [1983] ECR 1013, [1984] 1 CMLR 160.

by A-G Verloren van Themaat,[15] local disturbances do not seem to justify measures affecting the freedom of imports or exports unless they are so serious as to necessitate a large-scale intervention of security forces. However, individuals exposed to mob rule (as, for example, experienced by the British carriers of lambs and sheepmeat in France during the summer of 1990 or fishermen in 1993) would take a different view and would expect that Member States ensure a free flow of trade in peacetime.[16]

H. Removal of technical barriers to trade

Derogations from the freedom of movement of goods reflect the residual power of the Member States which, however, tends to shrink in the face of economic integration. Thus, for example, the harmonizing directives for the protection of human and animal health, which lay down standards and procedures for inspection, place the responsibility upon the authorities of the exporting state and relieve the authorities of the importing state which shall not subject the product to systematic inspection though they may resort to spot checking to ensure compliance with Community rules.[17]

Technical barriers consist of national legislation which lays down market rules and often also standards for products as well as testing and verification procedures. The divergences between the national regulations and standards challenge the unity of the single market. In dealing with this problem the Community at first adopted a one-dimensional approach, laying down rules for individual products (the 'recipe' method), for example, certain foodstuffs, industrial products, pharmaceutical and agricultural products. This was a slow and laborious process. The new approach, outlined in the 1985 White Paper, is a multi-dimensional strategy based on two principles: selective harmonization and mutual recognition. Accordingly, a distinction is made between what is essential to harmonize and what may be left to mutual recognition of national standards. Therefore the Community action is to be restricted to those sectors in which it is essential to create a uniform market, ie establishing minimum health and safety regulations as a result of which manufacturers who conform to these regulations will have the access to the markets of the other Member States.

The principle of mutual recognition in non-essential fields is based on the *Cassis de Dijon* formula[18] which means that the Member States must accept each other's products 'which have been lawfully produced and marketed' though they may be different in some detail but which, essentially, respond to the same demand. Regarding manufactured goods it means that the Member States must accept products from the others which, though manufactured to a different design, nevertheless perform the same function as those manufactured specially to national standards.

---

15 In Case 231/83: *Cullet v Centre Leclerc* [1985] ECR 305, [1985] 2 CMLR 524 at 534.
16 Relying on Case C-265/95: *Commission v France* [1997] ECR I-6959.
17 Case 251/78: *Denkavit Futtermittel GmbH v Minister for Food* [1979] ECR 3369 at para 14; Case 227/78: *Dansk v Van Beenekom* [1983] ECR 3883, [1985] 2 CMLR 692, at para 35; Case 29/87: *ApS Denkavit* [1988] ECR 2965; Case 190/87: *Oberkreisdirektor des Kreises Borken v Handelsondernem Ing Moorman BV* [1988] ECR 4689, [1990] 1 CMLR 656; Case C-304/88: *Commission v Belgium* [1990] ECR I-2801.
18 Case 120/78: *Rewe-Zentral AG v Bundesmonopolverwaltung für Branntwein (Re Cassis de Dijon)* [1979] ECR 649, [1979] 3 CMLR 494 at para 14.

In order to prevent the Member States from continuing to lay down their own national product standards different from the Community, Council Directive 83/189[19] obliged them to notify the Commission in advance of any newly proposed regulations and technical standards. Implementation of such proposals is deferred so that the Commission can ascertain whether or not they create any new barriers to intra-Community trade. There is an extensive body of EC legislation setting standards for a wide range of products.

I.   Removal of physical barriers to trade

The physical barriers consist of the national frontiers with the whole apparatus of frontier controls. They are the visible obstacle to the free movement of goods and persons and in a 'People's Europe' constitute an anachronism. The object is not merely to simplify the existing procedures but to eliminate completely internal frontier controls. This, however, does not prevent the Member States from instituting spot checking anywhere in their territories by means of 'mobile customs posts'.

Health, veterinary and plant controls have been harmonized in considerable detail, thus rendering frontier checks redundant. Legislation has been adopted to facilitate the physical inspection and administrative formalities in respect of the carriage of goods between Member States;[20] eliminate frontier controls in the field of road and inland waterway transport;[1] eliminate controls and formalities applicable to the cabin and hold baggage of persons taking an intra-Community flight or sea-crossing;[2] and on controls carried out within the Community in the field of road and inland waterway transport in respect of means of transport registered or put into circulation in a third country.[3]

Export controls of sensitive goods and technologies (because of their dual civilian and military nature and potential) are the subject of a specific regime.[4]

Hitherto the operation of the CAP involved a number of controls and formalities at the national frontiers. These have been removed by the MCAs as the latter were replaced by a new agri-monetary system based on exchange[5] rates. Other controls consequent upon the common organization of markets for certain products (ie milk, cereals and sugar) will be adjusted.

J.   Administrative co-operation and fraud control

In order to apply uniformly the common rules through the EC the Commission has set up a programme of exchange of information and mutual assistance between the national customs authorities and the Commission departments.

---

19 OJ 1983, L109/8. See now Dir 98/34 (OJ 1998, L204/37). As to the effect of a failure to notify, see for example: Case C-194/94: *CIA Security International v Signalson and another* [1996] ECR I-2201 and Cases C-425/97 to C-427/97: *Albers Van den Berkmortel and Nuchelmans* [1999] ECR I-2947.
20 Dir 83/463 (OJ 1983, L359/8) as amended.
 1 Reg No 4060/89 (OJ 1989, L390/18), as amended.
 2 Reg No 3925/91 (OJ 1991, L374/4).
 3 Reg No 3912/92 (OJ 1992, L395/6).
 4 See Regulation 3381/94 (OJ 1994, L367/1), as amended.
 5 OJ 1992, L387.

Directive 77/799[6] was applied to direct taxation. Regulation No 218/92[7] was applied to indirect taxation, essentially Value Added Tax and set up procedures for the exchange of VAT information on intra-Community trade by electronic means (VIES). Regulation 3330/91[8] and Commission Regulation 3590/92[9] established a system of statistics (INTRASTAT) on trade between Member States. Combined with the common VAT identification number system designed by Directive 91/680[10] these measures enable the monitoring of intra-Community transactions to replace the controls hitherto carried out at frontiers. Computerization of Community customs legislation will further strengthen cohesion of the internal market in goods.

It is evident that the abolition of frontier controls has contributed to the incidents of fraud, illegal drug traffic and illegal immigration and, consequently, accentuated the Community responsibility in this respect. As a result, the Council is committed to adopting measures to strengthen customs co-operation between the Member States and between them and the Commission.[11]

K. Removal of fiscal barriers (EC Articles 90-93 (ex Arts 95-99))

(1)   DISCRIMINATORY TAXES

EC Articles 90 and 91 (ex Arts 95and 96) assume the application of the 'destination principle' in intra-Community trade whereby goods exported from a Member State are not subject to internal taxation but are, in turn, subject to internal taxation of the country of their destination. The purpose of EC Article 90 (ex Art 95) is to prevent a heavier burden being placed on imported than domestic goods and of EC Article 91 (ex Art 96) to ensure that where goods are exported to a Member State any repayment of internal taxes shall not exceed the internal taxes imposed whether directly or indirectly. Those provisions are complemented by EC Article 92 (ex Art 98), which prohibits any remission or repayment of tax by the exporting Member State and the imposition of any countervailing charge (purportedly to equalise the tax burden lying on the import with the burden on domestic products) by the importing State. If any such measure is to be imposed, it must first be approved by the Council, acting by a qualified majority, and may be applied only for a limited period of time. The prohibition in EC Article 92 (ex Art 98), does not apply to turnover taxes, excise duties and other forms of indirect taxation; but that is because those duties and taxes are subject to EC Articles 90 and 91 (ex Arts 95 and 96).

EC Article 90(1) (ex Art 95(1)), which the ECJ has held to be enforceable in the Member States,[12] prohibits the imposition on the products of other Member

---

 6   OJ 1977, L336.
 7   OJ 1992, L24/1.
 8   OJ 1991, L316/1.
 9   OJ 1992, L364/32.
10   OJ 1991, L376.
11   EC Art 135 (ex Art 116). The following measures have already been taken: Dir 91/308 on prevention of the use of the financial system for the purpose of money laundering (OJ 1991, L166/77); Reg No 2988/95 on the protection of the European Communities' financial interests (OJ 1995, L312/1); Reg No 2185/96 concerning on-the-spot checks and inspections in order to protect those interests against fraud and other irregularities (OJ 1996, L292/2).
12   Case 28/67: *Mölkerei-Zentrale v HZA Paderborn* [1968] ECR 143 at 155, [1968] CMLR 187 at 155; Case 57/65: *Lütticke GmbH v HZA Saarlouis* [1966] ECR 205, [1971] CMLR 674.

States of internal taxation of any kind in excess of the tax imposed upon similar domestic products.

EC Article 90(2) (Ex Art 95(2)) prohibits any internal taxation intended to afford protection to domestic products. The principle has been demonstrated in the enforcement actions against certain Member States[13] charging discriminating indirect taxes on imported alcoholic beverages with a clear intention of protecting similar national products. The principle has been applied to exports.[14]

Whether or not a tax is discriminatory will depend not only on the rate of charges but also on a comparison between the products involved. In this respect EC Article 90 (ex Art 95) lays down a double test. Not only must there be equality of fiscal treatment between similar imported and domestic products but the internal taxation must also be such as to avoid indirect protection to other competing products.[15] The ECJ ruled further that not only the rate of direct and indirect internal taxation on domestic and imported products, but also the basis of assessment and rules for levying the tax must be taken into consideration.[16]

Though relevant to the movement of goods EC Article 90 (ex Art 95) does not purport to regulate both fiscal policy and customs laws. Thus discriminatory taxes are not equivalent to customs duties.[17] They fall into different and distinct categories of rules.

The principle was further explained in the case concerning tax on sales of photocopying and other reproductive machines as well as a levy on books with the object of raising a fund to subsidize the publication of quality works and purchase of French and foreign books by libraries. The ECJ held that even a charge on a product from another Member State where there is no equivalent domestic charge, cannot be regarded as a charge equivalent to a customs duty but has to be considered as internal tax subject to EC Article 90 (ex Art 95) 'if it relates to a general system of internal dues applied systematically to categories of products in accordance with objective criteria irrespective of the origin of the products'.[18]

Dealing with Danish tax on alcoholic drinks the ECJ held that fruit wine and grape wine were similar products but the former was a domestic product whereas the latter was imported. Therefore a tax discriminating between these products was contrary to EC Article 90 (ex Art 95).[19] However, fortified fruit wine and whisky were not similar products and, here again, the former was a domestic product whereas the latter was not. The Danish tax system covered a variety of domestic and imported drinks and, where the products were different, irrespective of their origin, the rate of tax was also different. There was, therefore, no discrimination contrary to EC Article 90 (ex Art 95).[20]

---

13 Case 168/78: *Commission v France* [1980] ECR 347, [1981] 2 CMLR 631; Case 169/78: *Commission v Italy* [1980] ECR 385, [1981] 2 CMLR 673; Case 171/78: *Commission v Denmark* [1980] ECR 447, [1981] 2 CMLR 688; see also Cases 106/84: *Commission v Denmark, Re Taxation of Wine* [1986] ECR 833, [1987] 2 CMLR 278; Case 170/78: *Commission v United Kingdom* [1980] ECR 417, [1980] 1 CMLR 716; Case No 2: [1983] ECR 2265, [1983] 3 CMLR 512.

14 Case 51/74: *Van der Hulst's Zonen v Produkschap voor Siergewassen* [1975] ECR 79, [1975] 1 CMLR 236.

15 Case 27/67: *Fink-Frucht GmbH v HZA München-Landsbergerstrasse* [1968] ECR 223 at 234, [1968] CMLR 187.

16 Case 74/76: *Iannelli v Meroni* [1977] ECR 557 at 579-580, [1977] 2 CMLR 688.

17 Case 25/67: *Milch-Fett-und Eierkontier v HZA Saarbrücken* [1968] ECR 207; Case 32/80: *Officier van Justitie v Kortmann* [1981] ECR 251.

18 Case 90/79: *Commission v France* [1981] ECR 283 at 301, [1981] 3 CMLR 1 at 19.

19 Case 106/84, note 13, supra.

20 Case 243/84: *John Walker v Ministeriet for Skatter* [1986] ECR 833, [1987] 2 CMLR 275.

The conclusion to be drawn from the case law is that, while Member States may legitimately distinguish between various alcoholic drinks, they may not use that distinction to justify tax discrimination or to allow tax advantages or confer tax protection to domestic products.[1]

Further examples include the Irish excise duty payable to importers immediately on import whilst allowing domestic traders time to pay,[2] tax rebates to the disadvantage of competing national products;[3] tax on imported drinks to support a national spirits monopoly[4] and taxes on foreign cars.[5] The principle applies to all products.

The duty to avoid discrimination rests upon the Member States absolutely and cannot be shifted from the executive to any other branch of the government. The ECJ declared that 'the obligation arising from Article 95 [now Art 90] devolved upon states as such and the liability a Member State incurs under Article 169 [now Art 226] arises whatever the agencies of the state whose action or inaction is the cause of the failure to fulfil its obligations, even in the case of a constitutional independent insitution'[6] (ie the Parliament which failed to enact the appropriate legislation).

EC Article 90 (ex Art 95) is complemented by EC Article 91 (ex Art 96) which provides that any repayment of internal taxation in respect of exported goods shall not exceed 'the internal tax imposed upon them whether directly or indirectly'. 'Direct taxes' are taxes charged upon finished products; 'indirect taxes' are charged upon the product at the various stages of production. EC Article 91 (ex Art 96) covers, therefore, both eventualities. However, from a practical point of view, a line has to be drawn between taxes affecting the undertakings and those which fall upon the product. The ECJ has held that a refund of taxes which are charged to the undertaking as a taxable entity to encourage exports was inconsistent with EC Article 91 (ex Art 96).[7] Should this not be so, the undertaking would enjoy an advantage over another exporter and this, in turn, would affect competition and trade in the Common Market.

Discriminatory taxes, like charges equivalent to customs duties illegally collected by Member States, have to be refunded.[8] However, the repayment is subject to national rules for the recovery of national taxes unduly collected provided the national rules do not treat claims based on Community law less favourably than domestic claims and that the procedural rules do not render the

---

1 Cases 68/79: *Hans Just I/S v Danish Ministry for Fiscal Affairs* [1980] ECR 501, [1981] 2 CMLR 714; 46/80: *Vinal SpA v Orbut SpA* [1981] ECR 77, [1981] 3 CMLR 524; 216/81: *Cogis v Amministrazione delle Finanze dello Stato* [1982] ECR 2701, [1983] 1 CMLR 685; 277/83: *Commission v Italy, Re Marsala Liqueur Wine* [1985] ECR 2049 [1987] 3 CMLR 324.
2 Case 55/79: *Commission v Ireland* [1980] ECR 481, [1980] 1 CMLR 734; see also Case 26/80: *Schneider – Import GmbH & Co KG v HZA Mainz* [1980] ECR 3469, [1981] 3 CMLR 562.
3 Case 277/83: *Commission v Italy, Re Marsala Liqueur Wine* [1985] ECR 2049, [1987] 3 CMLR 324.
4 Case 253/83: *Sektkellerei CA Kupferberg Cie KG v HZA Mainz* [1985] ECR 157, [1987] 1 CMLR 36.
5 Case 112/84: *Humblot v Directeur des Services Fiscaux* [1985] ECR 1367, [1986] 2 CMLR 338; Cases 76, 86-89 and 149/87: *Seguela v Administration des Impots* [1988] ECR 2397, [1989] 3 CMLR 225.
6 Case 77/69: *Commission v Belgium, Re duty on timber* [1970] ECR 237, [1974] 1 CMLR 203.
7 Case 45/64: *Commission v Italy* [1965] ECR 857, [1966] CMLR 97.
8 Case 199/82: *Amministrazione delle Finanze dello Stato v San Giorgio SpA* [1983] ECR 3595, [1985] 2 CMLR 658.

exercise of the Community right based on the Treaty nugatory.[9] Thus, for example, the Italian presumption that the burden of tax had been passed on to the consumer and, therefore, the claimant had to provide documentary evidence to the contrary was incompatible with EC Article 90 (ex Art 95),[10] and so was the French legislation which imposed a special limit on the claims for repayment of the tax.[11]

If, however, the tax element, being incorporated in the price, has been passed to the purchasers the taxpayer may be prevented from recovering it[12] since to permit recovery would result in the unjust enrichment of the claimant.

(2) TAX OFFENCES, AVOIDANCE AND EVASION

Tax offences are subject to national laws. However, the sanctions which can be imposed by national authorities may be mitigated by the Community principle of proportionality,[13] the ECJ ruling that penalties for non-payment or evasion of tax would be contrary to EC Article 90 (ex Art 95) if they were more severe in cases involving imported goods.

Tax avoidance or tax evasion is subject to Directive 77/799[14] which provides that the national authorities shall exchange information to enable them to assess correctly the tax on income and on capital. They may seek assistance in specific cases where they have reason to believe that there may be tax avoidance or evasion.

(3) TAX HARMONIZATION

EC Article 93 (ex Art 99, as amended by the SEA) is the basis for the harmonization of turnover taxes, excise duties and other forms of indirect taxation. The Council, 'acting unanimously on a proposal from the Commission and after consulting the European Parliament, shall adopt provisions for the harmonization of legislation concerning turnover taxes, excise duties and other forms of indirect taxation to the extent that such harmonization is necessary to ensure the

---

9   Case 68/79: *Hans Just I/S v Danish Ministry for Fiscal Affairs* [1980] ECR 501 at 523, [1981] 2 CMLR 714 following Cases 33/76; *Rewe-Zentralfinanz GmbH v Landwirtschaftskammer für Saarland* [1976] ECR 1989, [1977] 1 CMLR 533; 45/76: *Comet BV v Produktschap voor Siergewassen* [1976] ECR 2043, [1977] 1 CMLR 533; 61/79: *Amministrazione delle Finanze dello Stato v Denkavit* [1980] ECR 1205, [1981] 3 CMLR 694; 811/79: *Amministrazione delle Finanze dello Stato v Ariete SpA* [1980] ECR 2545 [1981] 1 CMLR 316; 826/79: *Amministrazione delle Finanze dello Stato v MIRECO* [1980] ECR 2559; Case C-175/88: *Biehl v Administration des Contributions du Grand-Duché de Luxembourg* [1990] ECR I-1779, [1990] 3 CMLR 143; and later cases such as Case C-231/96: *Edilizia Industriale Siderurgica v Ministero delle Finanze* [1998] ECR I-4951; Case C-260/96: *Ministero delle Finanze v Spac SpA* [1998] ECR I-4997 and Cases C-279/96, C-280/96 and C-281/96: *Ansaldo Energia SpA and GMB Srl v Amministrazione delle Finanze dello Stato* [1998] ECR I-5025. This case law influenced the House of Lords in *Woolwich Equitable Building Society v IRC* [1993] AC 70, [1992] STC 657.
10   Case 104/86: *Commission v Italy* [1988] ECR 1799, [1989] 3 CMLR 25; see also Case 199/82: supra and Cases 331, 376, 378/85: *Les Fils de Jules Bianco v Directeur Général des Douanes* [1988] ECR 1099, [1989] 3 CMLR 36.
11   Case 240/87: *Deville v Administration des Impôts* [1988] ECR 3513.
12   Case 61/79 note 9 supra; Cases 142, 143/80 *Amministrazione delle Finanze dello Stato v Essevi and Salengo* [1981] ECR 1413; Case 68/79 note 1 supra and Case 199/82 note 8 supra; Cases C-192/95 to C-218/95: *Comateb v Directeur General des Douanes et Droits Indirects* [1997] ECR I-165; Cases C-441/98 and C-442/98: *Kapniki Micheilidis v Idryma Koinonikon Asfaliseon*, 21 September 2000, paras 30-42.
13   Case 299/86: *Criminal proceedings against Drexl* [1988] ECR 1213, p 402 [1989] 2 CMLR 240.
14   Supra, sub nom *Italy v Drexl*.

establishment and functioning of the internal market within the limits laid down in Article 14'.

Harmonization does not mean uniformity, but a tolerable state of affairs which permits diversity within the ideal of the Common Market. In this context the principle of subsidiarity, enshrined in the Maastricht Treaty, may well prove to be a brake upon the enthusiasm of the Community legislator.[15] Moreover, in relation to EC Article 90 (ex Art 95) which is fundamental in the tax field, directives adopted under EC Article 93 (ex Art 99) cannot create derogations from the principles embodied in it.[16]

Some progress has been made in the harmonization of excise duties[17] affecting tobacco,[18] alcoholic beverages[19] and mineral oils,[20] direct taxation[1] and, through the Arbitration Convention 1990,[2] double taxation. Of the numerous directives issued by the Council, by far the most important and most numerous are the directives intended to introduce a common system of turnover tax known as Value Added Tax.

The First and Second VAT Directives[3] set out a general outline of the principles, the definition of the VAT and the timetable according to which it should become part of a reformed tax system of the Member States and went some way towards establishing a uniform basis of assessment. The principal measure is now the Sixth VAT Directive, as amended. Under that Directive, as amended in particular by the Twenty-First Directive,[4] VAT is a Community-wide tax (whereas excise duties remain to a far greater extent national taxes) part of the yield from which (calculated by reference to the tax base in each Member State) forms part of the Community's 'own resources'.[5]

VAT is a tax on the consumption of goods and services. It is borne by the final consumer. The tax is collected from so-called 'taxable persons' (that is, traders) in instalments by reference to the value that each taxable person adds to the value ultimately passed on to, and consumed by, the final consumer. Until the goods or services reach the final consumer, VAT is therefore chargeable on each transaction by which the goods or services in question are passed on, subject to deduction of the VAT already borne by the goods or services.[6] Thus, suppose

15 See eg Guidelines on Company Taxation, DOE SEC (90) 601 final; see EC Bull 4/91. For details, see Easson, A J, *Taxation in the European Community* (1993).
16 See Case 21/79: *Commission v Italy* [1980] ECR 1, [1980] 2 CMLR 613; Case 15/81: *Gaston Schul Expediteur BV v Inspecteur der Invoerrechten en Accijnzen* [1982] ECR 1409 at 1434, [1982] 3 CMLR 229 at 253.
17 See, in particular, Dir 92/12 (OJ 1992, L76/1), amended by Dir 92/108 (OJ 1992, L390/1) Dir 74/94 (OJ 1994, L365/46) and Dir 99/96 (OJ 1997, L8/12), whose implementation in the United Kingdom has caused some difficulties: see, for example, *Hodgson v Commissioners of Customs and Excise* [1997] 3 CMLR 1082. Other aspects are discussed in *R v HM Treasury, Customs and Excise Comrs and A-G, ex p Shepherd Neame Ltd* [1999] Eu LR 522.
18 92/79 (OJ 1992, L316/8); 92/80 (OJ 1992, L316/10); 95/59 (OJ 1995, L291/40).
19 Dirs 92/83 (OJ 1992, L316/21), and 92/84 (OJ 1992, L316/29).
20 Dir 92/81 (OJ 1992, L316/12), 92/82 (OJ 1992, L316/19), 74/94 (OJ 1994, L365/46), 97/425 (OJ 1997, L182/22), 255/99 (OJ 1999, L99/26).
 1 Dirs 90/434 and 90/435 (OJ 1990, L225 and L225).
 2 OJ 1990, L436.
 3 67/227 (OJ 1167, 1301); OJ 1967, 14 and 67/228 (OJ 1967, 1303); OJ 1967, 16 replaced by Dir 77/388 (OJ 1997, L145/1) (the Sixth VAT Directive).
 4 86/247 (OJ 1986, L2/164/27).
 5 Council Decision 70/243 (OJ 1970, L94/19) and Council Decision 85/257 (OJ 1985, L128/15); Reg 2892/77 (OJ 1977, L336), replaced by Reg 1553/89 (OJ 1989, L155).
 6 Case C-317/94: *Elida Gibbs v Customs and Excise Comrs* [1996] ECR I-5339, para 19–24.

that a bicycle manufacturer buys in the component parts of a finished bicycle from various suppliers (the wheels, brake components, gears and so forth), manufactures bicycles from those parts, sells the finished bicycle to a wholesaler who sells them to various retailers who then sell the bicycles to members of the public who wish to use them for their own enjoyment. The suppliers of the parts to the manufacturer will charge the manufacturer VAT at the appropriate rate (a percentage of the price of the part). The manufacturer will in turn charge the wholesaler VAT on the price of the finished bicycle (say, 17½% of £200). But the manufacturer will pay to the competent national tax authorities the amount of tax on the finished product less the tax already paid on the parts. Suppose that the wholesaler sells the finished bicycle to retailers for £250. The retailers will be charged the prevailing rate of VAT (in this example, 17½% of £250) by way of VAT but the wholesaler will pay to the competent national tax authorities the amount of tax due on the price of the bicycle (17½% of £250) less the amount already paid to them (17½% of £200). The retailer will do likewise when it sells the bicycle to the final consumer (at a price of, say £300 plus VAT at 17½%). The result is that the final consumer will pay £300 plus 17½% of that amount by way of VAT; and the national tax authorities will have received the correct amount of VAT in instalments from each of the 'taxable persons' in the chain of transactions leading from the production and sale of the component parts of the bicycle to the sale of the finished product to the final consumer. In principle, none of the taxable persons in the chain will have actually borne the economic burden of the tax because they will have passed the burden on to the next person in the chain until it finally comes to rest on the shoulders of the final consumer.

VAT is applied to the supply of goods or services for consideration within the territory of the country by a taxable person and the importation of goods.[7] As from January 1993[8] the expression 'importation' refers only to importation of goods from non-Community countries. 'Goods received from another Member State' means 'intra-Community acquisition' of those goods. Thus goods in Community trade are not 'imported' but merely 'acquired'. Directive 91/680 also subjects to VAT 'intra-Community acquisition of goods for consideration within the territory of the country by a taxable person (and, in certain cases, by a non-taxable person) and intra-Community acquisition of new means of transport'.

'Taxable persons' include persons or bodies who carry out 'independently', ie otherwise than employed persons, certain economic activities.[9] State, regional and local government authorities and other bodies governed by public law are not regarded as taxable in respect of the activities within their public competence.[10]

'Taxable transactions' include all activities of producers, traders, suppliers of services including agricultural, mining and professional activities as well as the exploitation of property for continuous income.[11]

Member States enjoy a very limited measure of discretion as regards the granting of exemptions from VAT because the Community rules in this respect

---

7 Sixth Dir Art 2.
8 Dir 91/680 (OJ 1991, L376); Art 1(2) and 22.
9 Art 5(4)(b)(c).
10 Art 4(5).
11 Art 4(2); see Case 89/81: *Staatssecratis van Finanzien v Hong Kong Trade Development Council* [1982] ECR 1277, [1983] 1 CMLR 73; Case 230/87: *Naturally Yours Cosmetics Ltd v Customs and Excise Comrs, Re taxation of free gifts to hostesses* [1988] ECR 6365, [1989] 1 CMLR 797.

are mandatory and taxpayers are entitled to protection[12] whilst Member States may face infringement proceedings.[13] Exemptions cover activities of public interest, eg medical and dental care, postal services, educational, charitable, religious and other non-profit activities, cultural goods and services and non-commercial radio and television, welfare services and goods and services associated with the protection of children and young persons.[14] In the other category fall certain transactions concerned mainly with banking, financial insurances and transactions connected with land and buildings.[15]

No VAT is chargeable on illegally imported narcotics[16] or counterfeit currency[17] for such transactions are outside the commercial circuit. Drugs imported for strictly medical purposes are in a different category but they are not subject to VAT.

Member States have a certain latitude as regards rates of VAT. Even in the event of the completion of the internal market it was not possible to impose uniform rates. The Sixth Directive, as amended,[18] merely prescribes a minimum standard rate of 15 per cent and permits one or two reduced rates for a wide range of goods and services provided that the reduced rates may not be lower than five per cent. Member States, however, continued to rely on certain derogations to apply zero or reduced rates below the five per cent threshold.[19] Member States are prohibited from maintaining or introducing any form of turnover tax other than VAT.[20]

L.   State monopolies (EC Article 31 (ex Art 37))

EC Article 31(1) (ex Art 37(1)) provided that state monopolies of a 'commercial character shall be progressively adjusted' in order to eliminate discrimination in the conditions under which goods are procured and marketed between nationals of Member States. This adjustment should have occurred by the end of the

12   See Cases 8/81: *Becker v Finanzamt Münster-Innestadt* [1982] ECR 53, [1982] 1 CMLR 499 at 512; 39/82: *Donner v Netherlands* [1983] ECR 19, [1983] 1 CMLR 711; 207/87: *Weissgerber v Finanzamt Neustadt* [1988] ECR 4433; 173/88: *Skatteministeriet v Henricksen* [1989] ECR 2763.

13   Cases 107/84: *Commission v Germany* [1985] ECR 2655; 353/85 *Commission v United Kingdom* [1988] ECR 817; 122/87: *Commission v Italy* (unlike medical services, veterinary services are not exempted) [1988] ECR 2685, [1989] 3 CMLR 844: C-35/90: *Commission v Spain* [1991] ECR I-5073.

14   Sixth Dir Art 13.

15   Ibid Art 13A.

16   Case 221/81: *Wolf v HZA Düsseldorf* [1982] ECR 3681; Case 240/81: *Einberger v HZA Freiburg* [1982] ECR 3699; Case 294/82: *Einberger (No 2)* [1984] ECR 1177; Case 269/86: *Mol v Inspecteur der Invoerrechten en Accijnzen* [1988] ECR 3627, [1989] 3 CMLR 729; Case 289/86: *Vereniging Happy Family v Inspecteur der Omzetbelasting* [1988] ECR 3655, [1989] 3 CMLR 743.

17   Case C-343/89: *Witzemann v HZA München-Mitte* [1990] ECR 4477.

18   Sixth Dir, Art 11, as amended by Dir 92/77 (OJ 1992, L316/11), 92/111 (OJ 1992, L384/47), 94/5 (OJ 1994, L60/16), 96/42 (OJ 1996, L170/34), 96/95 (OJ 1996, L338/89).

19   Sixth Dir Art 28(2); Case 415/85: *Commission v Ireland* [1988] ECR 3097, [1988] 3 CMLR 189; Case 416/85: *Commission v United Kingdom* [1988] ECR 3127, [1988] 3 CMLR 169; Case 203/87: *Commission v Italy, Zero-rating for earthquake victims* [1989] ECR 371, [1989] 2 CMLR 461.

20   Sixth Directive, Art 33(1). See eg Case C-318/96: *SPAR Osterreichische Warenhandels v Finanzlandsdirektion fur Salzburg* [1998] ECR I-785.

transitional period of the EC.[1] In its present form, Member States are obliged by EC Article 31(1) to adjust any State monopolies of a commercial character, without that obligation being made subject to any time limit for its completed performance.

A prohibition on introducing new measures was of direct effect as from the inception of the EC.[2] However state monopolies of a commercial nature are still with us despite numerous enforcement actions.[3] It seems that the near permissive formulation of EC Article 31 (ex Art 37) and the close involvement of those monopolies in the national economy have a great deal to answer for.

In essence these monopolies tend to occupy a dominant position in the market but in the legal sense they enjoy the exclusive right, or privilege, to produce and market goods. The possibility of EC Article 31 (ex Art 37), applying to a monopoly in services has been noted by the ECJ[4] in so far as it may have an effect on trade in goods. Otherwise services as such are not subject to EC Article 31 (ex Art 37), eg television commercial advertising for which licence from the state was not incompatible with EC Article 31 (ex Art 37).[5]

The article assumes that these monopolies are run by the state directly or by bodies supervised by the state or operating as 'delegated monopolies',[6] ie private parties under state control. An example of the latter are certain French enterprises which exercise the state's oil monopoly expressly by virtue of the *Service des Carburants*.

State commercial monopolies are, in principle, incompatible with EC Article 31 (ex Art 37) in so far as they cause discrimination among goods procured and marketed between nationals of Member States. However the ECJ has expanded the scope of the provision. Thus the application of EC Article 31 (ex Art 37) was not confined to imports or exports directly subject to the monopoly but covered all measures which corresponded to the prohibitions laid down in EC Article 90(2) (ex Art 95(2)). Thus it was contrary to EC Article 31(1) (ex Art 37(1)), to extract from the imported product a contribution to the monopoly[7] or a special price equalization charge.[8] In the first *Peureux* case[9] a 'cash adjustment' charge which French producers of a certain type of alcohol were required to pay in order to exempt that product from the national marketing monopoly of ethyl alcohol was held compatible with EC Article 31 (ex Art 37) since the charge, in the circumstances, 'constitutes a reverse discrimination'.[10] In other words, Community law is concerned with 'discrimination against goods produced or

---

1 Case 59/75: *Pubblico Ministero v Manghera* [1976] ECR 91, [1976] 1 CMLR 557; See Case C-306/91: *Commission v Italy, Re Pricing of manufactured tobacco* [1993] ECR I-2133.
2 Case 6/64: *Costa v ENEL* [1964] ECR 585, [1964] CMLR 425; Case 45/75: *Rewe-Zentrale v HZA Landau-Pfalz* [1976] ECR 181, [1976] 2 CMLR 1.
3 Eg Case 90/82: *Commission v France* [1983] ECR 2011, [1984] 2 CMLR 516; Case 78/82: *Commission v Italy re tobacco margins* [1983] ECR 1955; Case 161/82: *Commission v France* [1983] ECR 2079, [1984] 2 CMLR 296.
4 Case 161/82: *Commission v France* [1983] ECR 2079, [1984] 2 CMLR 296; Case 271/81: *Société d'Insémination Artificielle* [1983] ECR 2057.
5 Case 155/73: *Italy v Sacchi* [1974] ECR 409, [1974] 2 CMLR 177; see also Case 52/79: *Procureur du Roi v Debauve* [1980] ECR 833 [1981] 2 CMLR 362; Case 62/79: *Coditel v Cine Vog Films* [1980] ECR 881, [1981] 2 CMLR 362.
6 Eg the *Bundesmonopolverwaltung fur Branntwein* in Germany; see Case 120/78 *Rewe-Zentral AG v Bundesmonopolverwaltung* [1979] ECR 649, [1979] 3 CMLR 494.
7 Case 45/75: *Rewe-Zentral des Lebensmittel-Grosshandels GmbH v HZA Landau* [1976] ECR 181.
8 Case 91/75: *HZA v Miritz* [1976] ECR 217.
9 86/78: *Grandes Distilleries Peureux v Services Fiscaux de la Haute-Saône* [1979] ECR 897.
10 Ibid at 921.

marketed by nationals of other Member States'. In the second *Peureux* case[11] the French local tax administration contested the plaintiff's right to distil oranges steeped in alcohol imported from Italy on the ground that the monopoly prohibited the distillation of all imported raw material except certain types of fresh fruit. Turning to EC Article 31 (ex Art 37) the ECJ ruled that 'the rules contained in Article 37(1) and (2) [now Art 31(1) and (2)] concern only activities intrinsically connected with the specific business of the monopoly and are irrelevant to national provisions which have no connection with the specific business of the monopoly and are irrelevant to national provisions which have no connection with such specific business'. Such connection consisted in the fact that the French producers were obliged to sell their alcohol to the monopoly. The Court concluded that the French provisions not only infringed EC Article 28 (ex Art 30) but also constituted discrimination prohibited by EC Article 31(1) (ex Art 37(1)) because they treated nationally-produced alcohol differently according to whether it had been obtained from domestic or from imported raw material.

The power of a national monopoly to set retail prices at different levels for importers and domestic producers infringes both EC Articles 28 and 31 (ex Arts 30 and 37).[12]

---

11   Case 119/78: *Grandes Distilleries Peureux v Services Fiscaux* [1979] ECR 975.
12   Case 90/82: *Commission v France, Re tobacco prices* [1983] ECR 2011, [1984] 2 CMLR 516.

Chapter 19

The free movement of workers
(EC Articles 39-42 (ex Articles 48-51))

A. General principles

As originally conceived the object of the free movement of workers was to create a Common Market in manpower. Therefore the Treaty provisions were correlated to the movement of goods,[1] the right of establishment,[2] the provision of services[3] and movement of capital[4] – the basic freedoms essential to the mobility of the human factor in the economy. However economic objectives had to be complemented by social objectives. Thus 'the freedom of movement constitutes a fundamental right of workers and their families; mobility of labour within the Community must be one of the means by which the worker is guaranteed the possibility of improving his living and working conditions and promoting his social advancement, while helping to satisfy the requirements of the economy of the Member States'.[5]

The political objective is to create a greater cohesion of the peoples of the Community through the elimination of barriers to migration and the promotion of a citizenship of the Union.[6] Two groups of provisions deal with the freedom of movement of workers who are citizens or nationals of the Member States: the provisions concerning citizenship of the Union;[7] and the provisions concerning free movement of workers (the subject of this chapter).

EC Article 39 (ex Art 48) and Regulation 1612/68 are the key provisions concerning the free movement of workers. Together with EC Articles 12 and

1   EC Arts 28-29 (ex Arts 30-35).
2   EC Arts 42-48 (ex Arts 52-58).
3   EC Arts 49-55 (ex Arts 59-66).
4   EC Arts 56-60 (which replaced EEC Arts 67-73).
5   Preamble to Reg 1612 (OJ 1968, L257/2).
6   EC Arts 17-22 (ex Arts 8-8(e)).
7   EC Arts 17-22 (ex Arts 8-8(e)).

136-143 (ex Arts 6 and 117-120), their objective is to guarantee non-discriminatory treatment on the labour market in the Community.[8] EC Article 39 (ex Art 48), applies just as much to discriminatory treatment resulting from the conduct of private persons as it does to discriminatory treatment originating in State action.[9] It provides that:

(1) Freedom of movement for workers shall be secured within the Community by the end of the transitional period at the least.

(2) Such freedom of movement shall entail the abolition of any discrimination based on nationality between workers of the Member States as regards employment, remuneration and other conditions of work and employment.

(3) It entails the right, subject to limitations justified on grounds of public policy, public security or public health:

(a) to accept offers of employment actually made;

(b) to move freely within the territory of Member States for this purpose;

(c) to stay in a Member State for the purpose of employment in accordance with the provisions governing the employment of nationals of that state laid down by law, regulation or administrative action;

(d) to remain in the territory of a Member State after having been employed in that state, subject to conditions which shall be embodied in implementing regulations to be drawn up by the Commission.

(4) The provisions of this article shall not apply to employment in the public service.

The general effect of the Treaty is to facilitate the exercise by Community nationals of economic activities, of whatever sort,[10] anywhere in the Community, and to prohibit measures that could disadvantage Community nationals when they wish to do so. The Treaty applies at all stages at which a person may be discouraged from exercising the right of free movement: the point at which he considers leaving his State of origin for another Member State in which to carry out, or seek, an employed activity; his access to employment and the conditions under which he is employed; the cessation of employment, whether by retirement, ill-health or otherwise; and, where applicable, his return to his State of origin.[11] Regulation 1612/618 amplifies the workers' rights as regards eligibility for employment, equality of treatment and protection of workers' families.

The right of free movement, and all that it entails, can be invoked on the basis of EC Article 39 (ex Art 48), as against obstacles attributable to State action (or inaction) and as against obstacles attributable to private persons (whether those obstacles arise from the employment relationship between an employer and an employee or from arrangements made between employers that affect their actual or prospective employees).[12]

---

8 Case C-281/98: *Angonese v Cassa di Risparmio di Bolzano* [2000] All ER (EC) 577.

9 The *Angonese* case (above), paras 29–36.

10 Including sporting activities, where they constitute an economic activity (that is, an activity conducted in the course of gainful employment or by way of the provision of services for remuneration): Case C-415/93: *Union Royale Belge v Bosman* [1995] ECR I-4921, para 73.

11 Eg Case C-18/95: *Terhoevre v Inspecteur van de Belastingdienst Particulieren/Ondernemingen buitenland* [1999] ECR I-345, para 36-40. Not all disadvantages imposed on a worker are prohibited: see Case C-190/98: *Graf v Filzmoser Maschinenbau* [2000] All ER (EC) 170.

12 See the *Bosman* case (supra), paras 74-75 and 82-87; Case C-176/96: *Lehtonen v Federation Royale Belge des Societètes de Basket-Ball* [2001] All ER (EC) 97.

B.   The meaning of 'worker'

In the absence of a Treaty definition, the meaning of 'worker' as a concept of Community law[13] had to be defined by the ECJ. Broadly speaking, a 'worker' is a citizen of a Member State actually or potentially engaged in an economic activity for wages. His right to movement in the Community is guaranteed by the directly applicable provisions of the Treaty except in situations temporarily covered by any applicable transitional provisions in the case of a new Member State and subject to derogations under EC Article 39(3) (ex Art 48(3)), and the public service exception EC Article 39(4) (ex Art 48(4)). However, the guarantee does not extend to situations wholly internal to a Member State such as those involving a national of a Member State who has never resided or worked in another Member State, for example where such a person is bound over by a court order to reside in a part of a Member State's territory[14] or where the use of a certain means of transport is prescribed by national law.[15] Being a 'potential worker' has to be qualified by the behaviour of the person concerned in so far as he has to exercise or seek to exercise his right.[16] A possibility that he may take advantage of it some time in the future will not suffice.[17] Thus the barring of a communist from a teacher training course was held to be wholly internal to the Member State because the purely hypothetical prospect of employment in another Member State after qualification did not establish a sufficient connection with Community law.

The term 'worker' must be construed broadly and is related to employment[18] in the sense of activity carried out for remuneration under the direction of another person, which itself is regarded as genuine, and not marginal or incidental, work.[19] The meaning of 'worker' is not however to be defined by reference to natural concepts of what a worker, or an employment relationship, is. Thus Spanish fishermen employed on British boasts were classified as workers even if paid on a 'share of catch' basis.[20] A person whose income is supplemented from public funds may qualify as a worker[1] and so may a member of a religious order if his membership entails an economic activity.[2] However work which does not entail an economic activity but merely an activity leading to rehabilitation or re-integration into normal employment, for example in the case of a drug addict,[3] may not qualify. Further, a director of a company, who also happens to be its sole shareholder, cannot be said to be under the direction

---

13   See Case 75/63: *Hoekstra (née Unger) v Bestuur Bedrijfsvereniging* [1964] ECR 177.
14   Case 175/78: *R v Saunders* [1979] ECR 1129, [1979] 2 CMLR 216; but see Case 36/75: *Rutili v Ministère de l'Interieur* [1975] ECR 1219, [1976] 1 CMLR 140.
15   Case 298/84: *Iorio v Azienda Autonoma delle Ferrovie dello Stato* [1986] ECR 247.
16   Cases 35, 36/82: *Morson v Netherlands* [1982] ECR 3723, [1983] 2 CMLR 221.
17   Case 180/83: *Moser v Land Baden-Württemberg* [1984] ECR 2539.
18   See decisions of national courts in *Re a Belgian Prostitute*, Queen of the Netherlands in Council [1976] 2 CMLR 527; *R v Secchi, re 'international drifter'* [1975] 1 CMLR 383.
19   Case 53/81: *Levin v Staatssecrestaris van Justitie* [1982] ECR 1035, [1982] 2 CMLR 454; Case C-337/97: *Meeusen v Hoofddirektie van der Informatie Beheer Groep* [1999] ECR I-3289, para 13, and the cases cited there.
20   Case C-3/87: *R v Fishing Department of the Ministry of Agriculture, ex p Agegate Ltd* [1990] 1 CMLR 366; see also Case 9/88: *Lopes da Veiga v Staatssecretaris van Justitie* [1989] ECR 2989, [1991] 1 CMLR 217.
1   Case 139/85: *Kempf v Staatssecrestaris van Justitie, re part-time music teacher* [1986] ECR 1741, [1987] 1 CMLR 764.
2   Case 196/87: *Steymann v Staatssecretaris van Justitie* [1988] ECR 6159, [1989] 1 CMLR 449.
3   Case 344/87: *Bettray v Staatssecretaris von Justitie* [1989] ECR 1621.

of his 'employer' and is not therefore a worker.[4] On the other hand, it does not follow that the spouse of a director and sole shareholder of a company, who is employed by the company, is not under the direction of her employer merely because of the matrimonial relationship.[5]

The term 'worker' applies also to Community nationals who are employed by an undertaking of another Member State even during a period in which the employee temporarily works outside the Community;[6] and to frontier workers, who have their residence in one Member State but work in another.[7]

A grant awarded for maintenance to pursue a further education scheme is a 'social advantage' rather than remuneration for work.[8]

For the practical purpose of issuing a residence permit the exact classification of the economic activity (ie whether as employment or self-employment) does not matter[9] but a person whose activity is of a self-employed nature alone cannot rely on rights which pertain to the status of 'worker'.[10]

In principle only the citizens of the Member States are entitled to move freely within the Community[11] but each Member State defines according to its own law who its citizens are and how citizenship is acquired and lost. However the privilege has been extended to certain categories of persons, ie spouses and members of workers' families,[12] stateless persons,[13] refugees,[14] inhabitants of certain dependent and associated territories[15] and citizens of third countries with which the Community has made an agreement providing for freedom of movement.[16]

---

4   Case C-107/94: *Asscher* [1996] ECR I-3089, para 26.

5   The *Meeusen* case, supra, paras 15-17.

6   Case 237/83: *Prodest Sàrl v Caisse Primarire d'Assurance Maladie de Paris* [1984] ECR 3153.

7   Eg, Case C-35/97: *Commission v France* [1998] ECR I-5325; Case C-337/97: *Meeusen v Hoofddirektie van de Informatie Beheer Groep* [1999] ECR I-3289, paras 18-25.

8   See Cases 389 and 390/87: *Echternach v Netherlands Minister for Education* [1989] ECR 723.

9   See Case C-363/89: *Roux v Belgium* [1991] ECR I-273, [1993] 1 CMLR 3.

10 See Case C-15/90: *Middleburgh v Chief Adjudication Officer* [1991] ECR I-4655, [1992] 1 CMLR 353.

11 See Case 2A 72/72: *Residence Permit for an Egyptian National* (Admin Court of Appeal, Rheinland) [1975] 2 CMLR 402; *R v Secretary of State for Home Affairs, ex p Tombofa, Re deportation of a Nigerian* [1988] 2 CMLR 609; *R v Secretary of State for the Home Department, ex p Narin, re deportation of a Turkish national* [1990] 1 CMLR 682; *R v Home Secretary, ex p Colak, re return to a refugee* [1993] 3 CMLR 201; *R v Home Secretary, ex p Sheikh Mohammed Nasser Al-Sabah* [1992] 2 CMLR 676; Case C-147/91: *Ferrer Laderer* [1992] ECR I-4097, para 7; Case C-230/97: *Awoyemi* [1998] ECR I-6781, para 29. See cases involving Turkish nationals under the Ankara Agreement: Case 12/86: *Demirel v Stadt Schwäbisch Gmünd* [1987] ECR 3719, [1989] 1 CMLR 421; Case C-192/89: *Sevince v Staatssecretaris van Justitie* [1990] ECR I-3461, [1992] 2 CMLR 57; but see C-237/91: *Kus v Landeshauptstadt Wiesbaden, Re renewal of work permit after lawful residence* [1992] ECR I-6781, [1993] 2 CMLR 887.

12 See p 497 infra.

13 As defined by the New York Convention of 1954 relating to the Status of Stateless Persons, TS 41 (1960); Cmnd 1098, Art 1.

14 Geneva Convention of 1951 to the Status of Refugees, TS 39 (1954); Cmnd 9171, Art 1.

15 Eg Channel Islanders and Manxmen; see Case C-355/89: *Department of Health and Social Security (Isle of Man) v Barr* [1991] ECR I-3479, [1991] 3 CMLR 325.

16 The rights of such persons are defined by the terms of the agreement: see, for example, Case C-1/97 *Birden v Stadtgemeinde Bremen* [1998] ECR I-7747; Case C-210/97 *Akman v Oberkreisdirektor des Rheinisch-Bergischen-Kreises* [1998] ECR I-7519; Case C-416/96 *El-Yassini v Secretary for the Home Department*, [1999] ECR I-1209. On the definition of citizen or national, see Case C-192/99: *R v Secretary of State for the Home Department, ex p Kaur* [2001] All ER (EC) 250.

C.   The public service exception

Freedom of movement does not apply to 'employment in the public service' and therefore gives no right of access to such employment; but, when so employed, the worker is protected from discrimination on the ground of his nationality.[17]

In clarifying the ambiguous term 'public service' the ECJ held that EC Article 39(4) (ex Art 48(4)) 'removed a series of posts which involve direct or indirect participation in the exercise of powers confirmed by public law and duties designed to safeguard the general interests of the state or of other public authorities'. Such posts, in fact, 'presume on the part of those occupying them the existence of a special relationship of allegiance to the state and reciprocity of rights and duties which form the foundation of the bond of nationality'.[18] However this abstract formulation of the principle had to be further qualified.[19] The issue arose from the advertisement of various vacancies in the service of the Belgian National Railways, suburban railways, the City of Brussels and the town of Auderghem and of the Municipalities of Brussels and Auderghem, the jobs ranging from managerial, responsible posts, to unimportant, lowly ones. All were in the 'public service'. The case exposed the absurdity of the general label 'public service' which, if literally applied, would have imposed restrictions on foreign manpower beyond what is reasonably necessary to safeguard the vital interests of the state. The posts involved trainee locomotive drivers, unskilled workers, loaders, plate-layers to be employed on the railways and hospital nurses, children's nurses, night watchmen, architects, plumbers, carpenters, electricians and various semi-skilled workmen.

In the first judgment the ECJ did not decide the case on its merits but purported to define the scope of 'public service'. It reiterated the stand taken in the *Sotgiu* case as regards the restrictive interpretation of the exception clause and its limitations.[20] It thought that the provision of public service removed from the scope of EC Article 39 (ex Art 48) posts which involve direct or indirect participation in the exercise of powers conferred by public law and duties designed to safeguard the interests of the state or of other public authorities.

It is not surprising that in the second case[1] the Court found the list of posts reserved for Belgian nationals excessive but, reaching for a compromise, held that posts other than those of head technical officer, supervisor, principal supervisor, work supervisor, stock controller and night watchman with the municipalities of Brussels and Auderghem could not be exempted. Whilst exempting posts of managerial responsibility the Court implicitly identified them with the exercise of the power of the state but hardly examined their intrinsic relationship to the sensitive area of sovereignty or functions exercised by the State *jure imperii* rather than *jure gestionis*.

This casuistic interpretation has not established a precedent of universal application. Therefore particular questions arise as certain Member States have a broad concept of public service. So far the Court has ruled that the exception does not apply to nurses in state hospitals;[2] a trainee teacher;[3] foreign language

---

17   Case 152/73: *Sotgiu v Deutsche Bundespost* [1974] ECR 153; Case 225/85: *Commission v Italy* [1987] ECR 2625 and Cases 389 and 390/87: *Echternach* [1989] ECR 723. The protection afforded to a Member State by the public service exception is therefore lost as soon as a state accepts persons from other Member States into its public service, or into those branches for which the protection of the exception is later claimed: Sotgiu, para 4.

18   Case 149/79: *Commission v Belgium (No 1)* [1980] ECR 3881, [1981] 2 CMLR 413.

19   Case 149/79: *Commission v Belgium (No 2)* [1982] ECR 1845, [1982] 3 CMLR 539.

20   Case 149/79 (No 1) at para 10.

1   Case 149/79 (No 2), ECR at 1847–1848.

2   Case 307/84: *Commission v France* [1986] ECR 1725, [1987] 3 CMLR 555.

3   Case 66/85: *Lawrie-Blum v Land Baden-Würtenberg* [1986] ECR 2121.

assistant at a public university;[4] employees of a National Research Council;[5] customs agents, journalists, pharmacists and tourist guides in Italy[6] and secondary school teachers in the French educational system[7] or Luxembourg trade union officials acting as government advisers on legislation.[8]

However in purely domestic situations the Community rules on public service do not apply. Thus a German national, who was refused admission to a teacher training college because of his affiliation to the Communist Party, could not take advantage of the provisions of EC Article 39(2) (ex Art 48(2)) (reverse discrimination).[9] Had he been a foreigner, presumably, the derogation on the ground of public policy would have applied in view of the State's even-handed policy.

D. Right of entry and residence

The right of movement necessarily implies the right of unrestricted entry and residence in another Member State, which itself presupposes the right to leave a Member State in order to enter another Member State and reside there in order to pursue an economic activity.[10] Whilst these rights are derived directly from the Treaty, details are listed in implementing legislation which also extends the protection to the worker's spouse and family.

However, a person being prima facie a worker cannot stay unemployed indefinitely after entry in another Member State 'unless he provides evidence that he is continuing to seek employment and that he has genuine chances of being engaged'.[11] Under the British system, a person in that position is entitled to exercise his Treaty right of entry and seeking employment for up to six months. The ECJ upheld the British rule *in casu*, but held that the time allowed in the circumstances ought to be 'reasonable'.

Regulation 1612/68[12] amplifies EC Article 39(2) (ex Art 48(2)), and Directive 68/360[13] purports to abolish restrictions on movement and residence within the Community for workers and their families. Thus Member States shall grant to Community nationals 'the right to leave their territory in order to take up activities as employed persons and to pursue such activities in the territory of another State'. Such rights shall be exercised simply on production of a valid identity card or passport.[14] The immigration authorities have no longer the right to inquire about the purpose of the visit or the visitor's means where the visit entails the receipt of a service.

---

4   Case 33/88: *Allué v Università Degli Studi di Venezia* [1989] ECR 1591, [1991] 1 CMLR 283; see also Case C-272/92: *Spotti v Freistaat Bayern* [1993] ECR I-5185.

5   Case 225/85: *Commission v Italy* [1987] ECR 2625, [1988] 3 CMLR 635.

6   Case 168/85: *Commission v Italy* [1986] ECR 2945, [1988] 1 CMLR 580.

7   Case C-4/91: *Bleis v Ministère de L'Education Nationale* [1991] ECR I-5627.

8   Case C-213/90: *Association de Soutien aux Travailleurs Immigres* [1991] ECR I-3507, [1993] 3 CMLR 621.

9   Case 180/83: *Moser v Land Baden-Württemberg* [1984] ECR 2539.

10   The *Bosman* case, supra, paras 95-104.

11   Case C-292/89: *R v Immigration Appeal Tribunal, ex p Antonissen* [1991] ECR I-745, [1991] 2 CMLR 373.

12   Supra.

13   OJ 1968, (Sp Ed) (II) 485.

14   Dir 68/360, Art 2(1); Art 3(1); Case C-68/89: *Commission v Netherlands* [1991] ECR I-2637, [1993] 2 CMLR 389. The requirement to hold and produce a valid identity card or passport will not disappear until there has been complete harmonization of national laws concerning immigration into the Community, the grant of visas, asylum and so forth: see Case C-378/97: *Wijsenbeck* [1999] ECR I-6207, paras 39-45.

The right of residence shall be granted on the production of an identity card or passport and no visa or equivalent document may be demanded save from members of the family who are not Community nationals.[15] The worker has the right to enter into a Member State and reside there for the purposes intended by the Treaty[16] but the Member State is entitled to check the passports or identity cards[17] and require that the nationals of the other Member States report their presence to the competent authorities of the host states.[18] According to Italian law[19] foreigners had to register their presence within three days of their entry. This was held unreasonable and to be contrary to Community law.[20] The ECJ also held that a host state cannot impose the obligation of registering with a prescribed social security agency as a condition for obtaining a residence permit nor deport a worker who falsely claims to be self-employed.[1]

In order to obtain a residence permit the migrant worker has to produce a document with which he entered the territory and a confirmation of engagement from the employer or a certificate of employment.[2]

The migrant worker is entitled to a residence permit which is valid for five years for the whole territory of the host state and which is automatically renewable, though failure to attend to the formalities is subject to sanctions 'comparable to those attaching to minor offence by nationals . . . though . . . not . . . so disproportionate to the gravity of the infringement that it becomes an obstacle to the free movement of persons'. This would be so in the case of imprisonment or deportation.[3]

The residence documents shall be issued and renewed free of charge or on payment of an amount not exceeding the dues and tax charges for the issue of identity cards to nationals.[4] A valid residence permit may not be withdrawn from a worker solely on the grounds that he is no longer in employment, or he is temporarily incapable of work as a result of illness or accident, or because he is involuntarily unemployed. When the permit is renewed for the first time, the period of residence may be restricted, but not to less than 12 months, where the worker has been involuntarily unemployed in the Member State for more than 12 consecutive months.[5] Voluntary unemployment or prolonged absence apart, the host state may terminate a valid residence permit only on the grounds stated in EC Article 39(5) (ex Art 48(5)), ie public policy, public security or public health.

The Directive also regulates temporary residence permits, the position of frontier workers and seasonal workers, breaks in residence and absence on military service. Breaks in residence not exceeding six consecutive months and absence on military service does not affect the validity of resident permits[6] but this provision implies that non-residence in excess of six months would be prejudicial to the right of residence.

15 Ibid Art 3(2) and Art 4(1).
16 See Case 48/75: *Re Royer* [1976] ECR 497, sub nom *State v Royar* [1976] 2 CMLR 619.
17 Case 321/87: *Commission v Belgium* [1989] ECR 997.
18 Dir 68/360, Art 8(2); Case 48/75, supra; Case 118/75: *Re Watson and Belmann* [1976] ECR 1185, sub nom *State v Watson and Belmann* [1976] 2 CMLR 552.
19 See Case 118/75, ibid.
20 See Case C-265/88: *Re Messner* [1989] ECR 4209, [1991] 2 CMLR 545.
 1 See Case C-363/89: *Roux v Belgium* [1991] ECR I-273, [1993] 1 CMLR 3.
 2 Dir 68/360, Art 4(3).
 3 Case 157/79: *R v Pieck* [1980] ECR 2171, [1980] 3 CMLR 220, at paras 18 and 19; following Case 8/77: *Sagulo, Brenca and Bakhouche* [1977] ECR 1495.
 4 Dir 68/360, Art 9.
 5 Ibid Art 7.
 6 Art 6(2). See also Reg 1251/70, Art 6(2).

E. Residence of spouse and family member

Regulation 1612/68[7] extends the worker's right of residence of his spouse and their descendants, who are under the age of 21 years or are dependants, and dependent relatives in the ascending line of the worker and his spouse. Such persons, irrespective of their nationality, have the right to install themselves with a worker who is a national of one Member State and who is employed in the territory of another Member State. The Regulation endeavours to preserve the family unit beyond the limit of the nuclear family.

The reference to 'spouse' implies a relationship based on marriage[8] but the ECJ ruled that, according to the principle of non-discrimination, cohabiting foreigners have to be treated as cohabiting citizens. In other words the unmarried companion of a British worker, who resided in the Netherlands, was entitled to a residence permit as if she had been a Dutch citizen living together with a Dutchman.[9] Presumably the right would be lost if the couple separated and ceased to live together.

In the case of a married couple the Regulation does not require the spouse of a migrant worker to live with him in order to renew her residence permit. So ruled the ECJ[10] in the case of a Senegalese national married to a Frenchman who resided and worked in Berlin. The couple separated, the wife intended to obtain a divorce but, in fact, their marriage was not dissolved. The Court held that 'the marital relationship cannot be regarded as dissolved so long as it has not been terminated by the competent authority'[11] and consequently Mrs Diatta was entitled to the benefit of her status.

Regulation 1612/68[12] enables the worker's spouse and those of the children who are under 21 years or dependent on him to take up an activity as an employed person throughout the territory of the same state, even if they are not nationals of any Member State. Thus, the ECJ[13] ruled that a Cypriot doctor was entitled to a residence permit as a spouse of a British national working as a hairdresser in Germany. Whether he could be employed in his profession was, of course, a matter for the competent German authorities who would verify his qualifications.

Although family dependency of descendants is limited by age the ECJ held that a 25 year-old-daughter of a French worker resident in Belgium was entitled to social welfare assistance since, being disabled, she was incapable of self-support. Her right to assistance constituted a 'social advantage' for the migrant worker in terms of Regulation 1612/68.[14] As long as she was 'dependent' she was entitled to a right of residence.

Member States shall 'facilitate the admission of dependent relatives in the ascending lines, ie the parents and grandparents of the worker or his spouse living under his roof in the country whence he comes, on the condition that the worker

---

7   Art 10. Since there is an objective difference between the position of persons established in a Member State and the position of workers from another Member State, there are legitimate grounds for treating the spouses and dependants of both groups of persons in different ways: cf Case C-356/98: *Kaba v Secretary of State for the Home Department* [2000] All ER (EC) 537.
8   Case 9/79: *Wörsdörfer (née Koschniske) v Raad van Arbeid* [1979] ECR 2717, [1980] 1 CMLR 87.
9   Case 59/85: *Netherlands v Ann Florence Reed* [1986] ECR 1283, [1987] 2 CMLR 448.
10 Case 267/83: *Diatta v Land Berlin* [1985] ECR 567.
11 Ibid at 590.
12 Reg 1612/68, supra, Art 11.
13 Case 131/85: *Gül v Regierungspräsident Düsseldorf* [1986] ECR 1573.
14 Case 316/85: *Centre Public d'Aide Sociale Courcelles v Lebon* [1987] ECR 2811.

provides adequate housing in the area where he is employed.[15] However this provision does not apply to the relatives of a worker who is the national of the host state and, of course, does not claim the right of free movement in his own country.[16] It applies, though, where a worker of a Member State who was employed in another returns to the country of his origin.[17]

In the case of a worker's spouse and children under the age of 21 the right of residence is obtained upon production of the document with which they entered the host state and a document issued by the competent authority of the state of origin or the state whence they came, proving their relationship.[18] Dependent children over the age of 21 years and other dependent relatives in the ascending line of the worker and the worker's spouse are required, in addition, to prove their dependence by the state of their origin or the state whence they came.[19]

Dependent relatives other than children or those in the ascending line are not entitled to enter or residence merely on ground of their relationship to the worker but Member States are obliged to 'facilitate their admission' to the worker's host country. The worker has to prove that they are dependent, were living under his roof and that he is able to provide accommodation for them which is 'normal' in the region where the worker is employed.[20] If accommodation is 'normal' at the time of entry of such relatives and the family has been brought together, the renewal of the residence permit cannot be refused if the housing position has subsequently deteriorated.[1] The proviso of the 'normal' accommodation serves to avoid discrimination between the migrant worker's family and the indigenous population but cannot be enforced literally all the time.

F.   Residence after retirement and incapacity

Regulation 1251/70[2] extended the right of residence to two categories of workers after the termination of their employment either through retirement or incapacity. The former qualify when they have reached the age laid down by the host state for an old-age pension, the latter when they have been employed in the host state for at least twelve months and have resided continuously in the host state for at least three years.[3]

The period of residence for a worker who ceases being employed through permanent incapacity has been reduced to two years. However, if the permanent incapacity is due to an accident at work or an occupational disease entitling him to a pension in the host state, he may remain irrespective of the duration of his previous residence.[4] There is also a concession to workers who live in one state and work in another. Thus a worker who, after three years' continuous employment

---

15 Reg 1612/68, Art 10(2)(3).
16 See Cases 35 and 36/82: *Morson v Netherlands, Re Surinamese parents of a Dutch national* [1982] ECR 3723, [1983] 2 CMLR 221.
17 Case C-370/90: *R v Immigration Appeal Tribunal and Surindr Singh* [1992] ECR I-4265, [1992] 3 CMLR 358.
18 Dir 68/360, Art 4(3)(c)(d); Case C-376/89: *Panagiotis Giagounidis* [1991] ECR I-1069, [1993] 1 CMLR 537.
19 Ibid Art 4(3)(e).
20 Reg 1612/68, Art 10(2)(3).
 1 Case 249/86: *Commission v Germany* [1989] ECR 1263.
 2 OJ 1970, Sp Ed p 402.
 3 Art 2(1)(a).
 4 Art 2(1)(b).

and residence in one state, works in another state whilst retaining his residence in the former to which he returns, as a rule, each day or at least once a week, is entitled to retain his right of residence in the former State in the event of retirement or incapacity.[5]

Temporary absence up to three months per year, or longer if due to military service, does not affect the entitlement to residence[6] nor does involuntary unemployment or absence due to accident or illness.[7]

However the conditions regarding the residence and employment outlined above do not apply if the retired or incapacitated worker's spouse is a national of the Member State concerned or has lost that nationality by marriage to the worker.[8]

A worker entitled to the right of residence by virtue of Regulation 1251/70 is allowed to decide within two years whether or not to take advantage of his right. During that period he is free to leave the territory of the Member State concerned without prejudice to his right which he can exercise without any formality.[9]

Members of the family of a retired or incapacitated worker who has the right of residence of a Member State are also entitled to remain in the host state after his death.[10] However, even if a worker dies during his working life the members of his family are entitled to remain in the host state continuously for at least two years or if his death resulted from an accident at work or an occupational disease or if the surviving spouse is a national of the state of residence or lost the nationality of that state by marriage of that worker.[11]

G.   Re-admission of retired and incapacitated workers

The Member States are enjoined to 'facilitate' readmission of workers who have left their territories after having resided there permanently for a long period and have been employed there and who wish to return there when they have reached retirement age or are permanently incapacitated for work.[12] To 'facilitate' does not imply a binding obligation but merely a benevolent exercise of discretion in favour of those workers who have, in the past, contributed to the economy of the countries in which they have worked.

H.   Residence rights of other groups

Three Directives extend the right of residence to persons other than workers or their families.

Directive 90/364[13] extends the right of residence to nationals of other Member States who do not enjoy it under any other provisions of Community law and Directive 90/365[14] to former employed and self-employed persons who have ceased

---

5   Art 2(1)(c).
6   Art 4(1).
7   Art 4(2).
8   Art 2(2).
9   Art 5.
10   Art 3(1).
11   Art 3(2).
12   Art 8(2).
13   OJ 1990, L180/26.
14   OJ 1990, L180/28.

their occupational activity as a result of retirement or incapacity. Both Directives contain important qualifications. The former provides that only those persons who have 'sufficient resources to avoid becoming a burden on the social assistance system of the host Member States during their period of residence' and who have comprehensive health insurance, are eligible. The latter provides that the retired or disabled person must be in receipt of either a retirement or old-age pension or an invalidity pension 'sufficient to avoid becoming a burden on the social security system of the host state' and also have a comprehensive health insurance. 'Sufficient resources' is defined in both Directives as an amount above the level at which the nationals of the host state may obtain state social assistance. Directive 93/96 provides a right of residence for students enrolled on vocational courses.[15]

I. Derogations from the freedom of movement

Whilst the freedom of movement is guaranteed by the Treaty to certain categories of persons (ie workers, self-employed persons and providers of services) the Member States may derogate from their duty in this respect on the grounds of public policy, public security and public health.[16] Private parties may also rely on those grounds of justification.[17] Though the object of the derogations is identical the wording of the relevant provisions of the Treaty or implementation legislation[18] is not uniform. Directive 64/221,[19] which purports to regulate the application of the derogations expressly states that it applies to the aforementioned three categories of persons as well as their spouses and the members of their families, had to be amended by Directive 72/194[20] and supplemented by Directive 75/35[1] in order to cover all aspects of the right of movement.

Being akin to exceptions, the derogations have to be interpreted strictly,[2] the burden of proving the application of a ground of derogation resting on the national authorities who wish to curtail the rights safeguarded by the Treaty.[3] Yet, though a concept of Community law, there is no uniform national definition of the grounds of the derogations, so much so that the national authorities have, within the limits of their Treaty obligations, a certain discretion in their application. This is evident not only because of the nuances in the national systems but also because of the differing perceptions of national values and of the sanctions to protect such values. The problem is well illustrated by cases involving criminal drug abuses and trade in obscene materials since there is no uniform approach to

---

15 OJ 1993, L317/59, the directive replaces Dir 90/366, which was annulled at the suit of the European Parliament on the ground that EC Art 308 (ex Art 235), did not provide the appropriate legal basis for its adoption: see Case C-295/90: *Parliament v Council* [1992] ECR I-4193, [1992] 3 CMLR 281.
16 EC Art 39(3) (ex Art 48(3)) – workers; EC Art 46(1) (ex Art 56(1)) – self-employed; EC Art 55 (ex Art 66) – providers of services.
17 Case C-415/93: *Union Royale Belge des Sociétés de Football Association v Bosman* [1995] ECR I-4921, para 86.
18 Dir 68/360, Art 10; Dir 73/148, Art 8; Dir 75/34, Art 9.
19 OJ 1964, 850, Art 1.
20 OJ 1972, L121/32 – workers.
 1 OJ 1975, L14/14 – self-employed.
 2 Case 41/74: *Van Duyn v Home Office (No 2)* [1974] ECR 1337, [1975] 1 CMLR 1 at paras 9–15; Case 36/75: *Rutili v Ministère de l'Intérieur* [1975] ECR 1219, [1976] 1 CMLR 140 at paras 15–20, 27.
 3 Case 36/75, at para 39.

these matters either as regards the appreciation of the risk to society or the sanctions for the breaches of the law.

Directive 64/221 does not define the grounds of the derogation but merely states the circumstances in which they can be invoked and the procedural safeguards.

(1) PUBLIC POLICY

The derogation on the ground of public policy, though translated from *ordre public* in the original texts,[4] is not in substance identical with its French equivalent. Therefore the ECJ[5] thought that, when arriving at the interpretation, one must proceed from the national concepts and allow for a certain degree of discretion. Indeed, in the national systems, 'public policy' implies a judicial discretion to correct a legal position in accordance with contemporary moves or trends in society.

However, despite the attempt of Advocate-General Warner[6] to clarify the concept of public policy in the case of a person convicted of minor drug offences, it remains a general concept that can be invoked against a real and sufficiently serious threat to a fundamental interest of society. As stated the ECJ[7] in the *Rutili* case concerning the legality of an exclusion order served upon a trade union agitator, Member States continue to be free to determine the requirements of public policy in the light of national needs.

(2) PUBLIC SECURITY

Derogation on the ground of public security implies a restriction on free movement justified in the interests of the safety of the state and its inhabitants in face of violence, disturbances and threats whether from within or without the country. It also applies as an additional sanction after conviction of a criminal act sufficiently serious to constitute a menace to society. Political, ideological or trade union agitators, though a public nuisance in the eyes of the authorities, unless entailing a serious criminal activity, do not come within the derogation. However convictions for crimes do not per se constitute a reason for invoking the derogation.[8]

(3) PUBLIC HEALTH

The state has a responsibility to take precautions or remedial action to safeguard the health of the nation. Directive 64/221[9] lists diseases subject to quarantine in accordance with the International Health Regulation No 2 of the World Health Organization of 25 May 1951: tuberculosis, syphilis and other infectious diseases and disabilities such as drug addiction and profound mental disturbance; manifest conditions of psychotic disturbance with agitation, delirium, hallucinations or confusion. Diseases and disabilities listed above would justify refusal of entry into another Member State but would not justify expulsion if occurring after the grant of residence.

---

4   *Offentliche Ordnung, openbare orde, ordinere pubblico.*
5   *City of Wiesbaden v Barulli re an 'idle layabout'* [1968] CMLR 239 at 245.
6   Case 30/77: *R v Bouchereau* [1977] ECR 1999, [1977] 2 CMLR 800, see in particular para 35 of the judgment.
7   Case 36/75, *supra* at para 26.
8   Dir 64/221, Art 3(2).
9   Annex.

Although the Directive distinguishes between three grounds of derogation it seems that the wide notion of public policy encompasses all three.

(4)   PERSONAL CONDUCT AND CRIMINAL CONVICTION

Directive 64/221[10] provides that measures taken on the grounds of public policy, public security and public health must be based 'exclusively on the personal conduct of the individual concerned' and 'shall not be invoked to serve economic ends'.[11] It follows that measures must be applied to voluntary behaviour manifested by individuals and exposing their character and activities detrimental to the host country. A Member State cannot prevent entry or order mass expulsion to safeguard jobs for its nationals or to protect them from foreign competition.

The difficulties inherent in the notion of 'personal conduct' have been highlighted in the *Van Duyn* case[12] where the British Government refused entry to the UK of a Dutch citizen on the ground that it would be contrary to public policy to allow her to take up employment with an organization known as the Church of Scientology. The organization, though not illegal in the UK, was previously denounced by the British Government as 'socially harmful' and foreigners were warned not to work for it. The ECJ held that Miss Van Duyn's membership of the organization constituted 'personal conduct' within the scope of the Directive and that, in view of the Government's declared policy, the UK was justified to derogate. The Court also rejected the argument that the measure was discriminatory and ruled that a Member State, on the ground of public policy, may refuse a national of another Member State the benefit of the Treaty in cases where its own nationals are not subject to any restrictions regarding employment.[13]

The Court was more lenient in the case concerning the expulsion of prostitutes (described as 'waitresses in a bar').[14] Whilst prostitution as such is not prohibited in Belgium certain aspects, ie living on immoral earnings by third parties, constitute a criminal offence. The Belgian authorities, 'anxious to remove from the territory prostitutes because they could promote criminal activities' would have to adopt 'with respect to the same conduct on the part of their own nationals repressive measures or other genuine and effective measures intended to combat such conduct'.[15] Whilst the connection with the trade and underworld would, in specific cases, come within the concept of public policy a mere suspicion would not suffice. Indeed, personal conduct within the meaning of Article 3 of Directive 64/221 must be 'personal' in order to be regarded as 'socially harmful' and the state may not discriminate between its own nationals and others in this respect. The distinction between these cases and *Van Duyn* is very subtle indeed.

Previous criminal convictions[16] are not per se grounds for resorting to derogations. It follows that a previous conviction of a crime does not automatically justify refusal of entry or deportation[17] even if it were to act as a deterrent. The national authorities have to evaluate in individual cases the danger

10   Art 3(1).
11   Art 2(2).
12   Case 41/74, supra.
13   Judgment paras 22 and 23.
14   Cases 115 and 116/81: *Rezguia Adoni and Dominique Cornuaille v Belgium* [1982] ECR 1665, [1982] 3 CMLR 361.
15   At paras 10 and 9.
16   Dir 64/221, Art 3(2).
17   *Proll v Entry Clearance Officer Re a former member of a terrorist group* [1988] 2 CMLR 387; Case C-348/96: *Calfa* [1999] ECR I-11, paras 24-25.

to society as a whole and the sense of revulsion or retribution which a particular crime is likely to provoke. Whilst the national sanction must fit the crime the national authority ought to consider the likely future conduct of the offender and avoid discrimination. Thus, following the preliminary ruling of the ECJ;[18] the national judge considered that a small fine was appropriate where the state originally argued for deportation since in his opinion the conduct of the offender did not cause the deep public revulsion that would be required to justify his departure. Where deportation (in cases for life) follows automatically by operation of law, without taking into account the person concerned's personal conduct, it cannot be justified.[19]

As the Community case law imports 'proportionality' into national sanctions to safeguard the State's right against offending migrants it is worth considering contrasting cases. In Case 67/74[20] the ECJ held that the sanction of deportation (teaching a lesson and to discourage criminal activities of foreign workers) was far too harsh to be imposed on a first offender who accidentally shot his younger brother, was acquitted of homicide but was convicted of illegal possession of a fire-arm. It was clearly different in the case of a convicted rapist whose long prison term seems to have failed to reform him.[1] The absence or otherwise of a 'deep public revulsion' is a decisive factor in such cases. Incidentally the decision to deport, in the case of a person sentenced to imprisonment, should not be taken at the time of his conviction but sufficiently closely to his departure in order to take into consideration any factors which affect his position. However a long prison sentence for drug offences may justify deportation on conviction notwithstanding Directive 64/221 without reference to the ECJ.[2]

Expiry of the identity card or passport used by the person concerned to enter the host country and to obtain a residence permit shall not justify expulsion from the territory.[3]

(5) CONTROL OF ALIENS AND PROCEDURAL SAFEGUARDS

The Member States control the movement of people and enforce their immigration laws within the duties imposed by the Treaty. The provisions of the Treaty and the relevant Community legislation have direct affect. In this context the contention that Directive 64/221[4] has no direct affect advanced by the French Conseil d'Etat has to be considered as a maverick decision. On the whole the Member States have retained certain residual rights and where national measures do not constitute an abridgment of Treaty rights their application ought not to amount to discrimination on the ground of nationality.[5]

It goes without saying that aliens have to identify themselves and to that end have to produce at the point of entry a valid passport or identity card and acquire a residence permit. However these requirements need not be rigorously enforced

---

18 Case 30/77, supra at para 35.
19 Case C-348/96: *Calfa* [1999] ECR I-11, paras 26-30.
20 Case 67/74: *Bonsignore v Oberstadtdirektor der Stadt Köln* [1975] ECR 297, [1975] 1 CMLR 472.
 1 Case 131/79: *R v Secretary of State for Home Affairs, ex p Santillo* [1980] ECR 1585, [1980] 2 CMLR 308: but contrast the decision of the *Immigration Tribunal in Monteil v Secretary of State* [1984] 1 CMLR 264 – reformed criminal.
 2 Case 131/79, supra para 17; and see also *Santillo* [1981] 2 All ER 897, CA.
 3 Dir 64/221, Art 3(3); Case 157/79: *R v Pieck* [1980] ECR 2171, [1980] 3 CMLR 220.
 4 See Case *Cohn-Bendit* (1979) Dalloz 155, [1980] 1 CMLR 543.
 5 See Case 118/75: *Watson and Belmann* [1976] ECR 1185 at paras 17-18 and 22.

since spot checks are sufficient.[6] This is important in 'the Europe without frontiers'. The state which issued the identity card or passport must allow the holder of such document to re-enter its territory without any formality even if the document is no longer valid or the nationality of the holder is in dispute.[7] A valid identity card implies the recognition of the right of residence in another Member State even if the card does not allow the holder to leave the territory of the state in which it was issued.[8]

A decision to grant or refuse a first residence permit must be taken as soon as possible and in any event not later than six months from the date of application. In the meantime the applicant must be allowed to remain temporarily in the territory.[9]

In order to reach a decision the host country may request the Member State of origin of the applicant and, if need be other states, to provide information regarding the police record of the applicant but such inquiry must not be made as a matter of routine.[10]

When a decision on the ground of public policy, public security or public health has been made the person concerned must be informed accordingly unless this is contrary to the interests of the security of the state involved.[11] Moreover such a person must be officially notified of any decision to refuse the issue or renewal of a residence permit or to expel him from the territory. The period allowed for leaving the territory shall be stated in this notification. Save in cases of urgency, this period shall not be less than fifteen days if the person concerned has not yet been granted a residence permit and not less than one month in all other cases.[12] Such a person must have the same remedies as are available to nationals of the host state in respect of acts of the administration.[13] In order to provide minimal guarantees of protection where there is no right of appeal to a court, or where an appeal is limited to the legal validity of the decision appealed against, or where an appeal does not have suspensive effect, a decision refusing renewal of a residence permit or ordering the expulsion of a person from the territory of a Member State cannot taken before the person concerned has been given an opportunity to exercise the rights of the defence.[14]

It is clear that decisions adverse to Community nationals must not be executed summarily though such persons may be kept in custody according to the law of the host state because the Community has not as yet imposed any specific obligations on the Member States in this regard.[15]

---

6   Case 321/87: *Commission v Belgium, Re Belgium Passport Controls* [1989] ECR 997, [1990] 2 CMLR 492.
7   Dir 64/221, Art 3(4).
8   Case C-376/89: *Giagounidis v City of Reutlingen* [1991] ECR I-1069, [1993] 1 CMLR 537.
9   Art 5(1)(2).
10   Art 5(3).
11   Art 6.
12   Art 7.
13   Art 8.
14   Art 9. These minimum guarantees do not apply in the case of decisions refusing entry into a Member State unless such a decision is made after the person concerned has been permitted physically to enter the State (in which case the refusal of entry is effectively a decision to expel even if, by a legal fiction, it is still regarded in the State concerned as a refusal of entry: Case C-357/98: *R v Secretary of State for the Home Department, ex p Yiadom* [2001] All ER (EC) 267).
15   Case 48/75: *Re Royer* [1976] ECR 497, sub nom *State v Royer* [1976] 2 CMLR 619.

In *Watson and Belmann*,[16] *Royer*[17] and *Peick*[18] the ECJ had ruled on the application of national immigration control laws. In the first case there was a failure to report and register presence; in the second a clandestine entry with the object of visiting his wife of a person allegedly with a criminal record; and the third a failure to obtain extension of the residence permit. In all these cases the Court confirmed that the right of entry and residence was an enforceable Community right which was necessarily forfeited by breaches of the law of the host country. However the ECJ also confirmed the state's right to control immigration and to impose criminal sanctions though it held that failure to comply with the formalities required by national law did not justify expulsion.[19] In other words the sanctions ought not to be disproportionate to the gravity of the offence. In this respect the ECJ considered that it would be contrary to Community law to impose upon a Community citizen, whose passport, travel documentation or identity card was not in order, a sanction more severe than the penalty imposed on a German citizen whose identity card has expired.[20] The ECJ observed that punishment must not be so severe as to constitute an impediment to the freedom of movement and neither deportation nor custodial sentence with a view to deportation were sanctions that can be imposed in such circumstances.[1] In the light of these cases a judgment of the English Court of Appeal[2] merits attention. That Court confirmed the deportation order of a national of India and Portugal who came to England in 1975 and from 1981 was a consultant psychiatrist for the National Health Service. In 1986 he was convicted of serious drug trafficking offences and sentenced to 14 years. His sentence was reduced to 11 years but on release he was to be deported. Though he had no propensity to commit further crimes his appeal was dismissed since the Court had to consider the seriousness of the offence and whether that itself merited deportation. The offence itself was an affront to the requirements of public policy and involved disregard of the basic tenets of society.

Whilst exercising their right of control and imposing sanctions the national authority must also respect the due process of law such as fair hearing and right of appeal. The procedure in comparable administrative cases of a domestic nature and the dignity of the offender ought also to be respected.[3]

J. Basic rights

EC Article 39(2) (ex Art 48(2)) provides that the freedom of movement shall entail the abolition of any discrimination based on nationality between workers of the Member States as regards employment, remuneration and other conditions

---

16 Case 48/75, supra.
17 Case 157/79, supra.
18 Case 157/79 at paras 20-21 and Case 48/75 at paras 38-43.
19 See also Case 8/77: *Sagulo, Brenca and Bakhouche v Public Ministry Amtsgericht Reutlingen* [1977] ECR 1445, [1977] 2 CMLR 585.
20 See Case 48/75 supra at paras 42-43 and Case 118/75 supra at paras 20-21.
  1 Case 131/79: *R v Secretary of State, ex p Santillo* [1980] ECR 1585 at para 15, [1980] 2 CMLR 308.
  2 *R v Secretary of State for Home Department, ex p Marchon* [1993] 1 CMLR 207; deportation upheld by CA [1993] 2 CMLR 132.
  3 Case 98/79: *Pecastaing v Belgium* [1980] ECR 691, [1982] 3 CMLR 361; and Cases 115 and 116/81, supra.

of work and employment. EC Article 39 (ex Art 48) also prohibits national rules that are applicable irrespective of the nationality of the workers concerned but that nonetheless impeded their freedom of movement.[4]

This basic right is further elaborated by Directive 68/360[5] which ensures abolition of restriction on movement and residence within the Community for workers of Member States and their families and Regulation 1612/68[6] which covers eligibility for employment and equality of treatment for workers and their families.[7]

(1) ELIGIBILITY FOR EMPLOYMENT

'Any national of a Member State shall, irrespective of his place of residence, have the right to take up an activity within the territory of another Member State in accordance with the provisions laid down by law, regulation or administrative action governing the employment of national of that state'[8] and in that respect he shall have "the same priority" as the nationals of the host state.

National provisions and practices which limit the right to seek or pursue employment or which impose conditions not applicable to their own nationals are inapplicable except as regards linguistic requirements necessitated by the nature of the position involved.[9] In the case of a teacher in Ireland,[10] the knowledge of Gaelic was not relevant to the duties implied in the post, but the ECJ nevertheless held that the linguistic knowledge required for a permanent full-time post in a public vocational institution was justified provided that the requirement was imposed as a part of a policy for the promotion of the national language and that it was applied in a proportional and non-discriminatory manner.

The Regulation also deals with ancillary matters such as recruitment, advertising of vacancies, assistance offered by state employment offices and prohibits the restriction of foreign nationals by number or percentage. The latter was specifically condemned by the ECJ as it ruled on the French Maritime Code which preserved for French citizens senior posts and a proportion of the crew on board merchant ships.[11]

(2) EMPLOYMENT AND EQUAL TREATMENT

The Treaty prohibition of any discrimination based on nationality between workers of the Member States as regards employment, remuneration and other conditions of work and employment[12] has been amplified by the provisions of Regulation 1612/68.[13] Not only must discrimination be eliminated but foreign

4 Eg, Case C-190/98: *Graf v Filzmoser Maschinenbau GmbH* [2000] All ER (EC) 170.
5 OJ 1968, Sp Ed (II) p 485.
6 Supra.
7 Supra.
8 Reg 1612/68, supra, Art 1.
9 Art 3. For example, it is legitimate to restrict access to a particular employed post to persons possessing a qualification indicating that they are capable of discharging the functions involved in that post; but the selection of the appropriate qualification and the process of deciding whether or not there are equivalent qualifications in other Member States, must be consistent with Community law: eg, Case C-234/97: *Bobadilla v Museo Nacional del Prado* [1999] ECR I-4773.
10 Case 379/87: *Groener v Minister for Education* [1989] ECR 3967, [1990] 1 CMLR 401.
11 Case 167/73: *Commission v France* [1974] ECR 359; Case 334/94: *Commission v France* [1996] ECR I-1307.
12 EC Art 39(2) (ex Art 48(2)).
13 Arts 7-9.

workers must also be accorded the same social and tax advantages as national workers; they must be given access to training in vocational school and training centres; they must not be disadvantaged by collective or individual labour agreements; they must be eligible for membership of trade unions (though they may be excluded from taking part in the management of bodies governed by public law and from holding an office governed by public law);[14] and they ought to have the same rights and benefits accorded to national workers in matters of housing, including ownership of housing.

Article 7 of Regulation 1612/68 applies to all relationships within the Community[15] either because of the place where they have arisen or because of the place where they take effect. The relationships which have given rise to litigation are mainly concerned with social security.[16] In this section they will reflect the rights defined as above.

Equality of treatment has been infringed by Luxembourg[17] simply by the state excluding from practice medical practitioners, dentists and veterinary surgeons who were Community nationals but continued their practice in other states. In that case Luxembourg was held to be in breach of its obligations embodied in EC Article 39 (ex Art 48). The same conclusion was reached in respect of discriminatory taxation since its effect was incompatible with the freedom of movement of workers[18] and also in respect of the British requirement that 75% of Spanish fishermen employed on British boats be resident in the United Kingdom.[19]

The prohibition of discrimination on the ground of nationality applies not only to overt discrimination practised deliberately against foreign workers but also to all kinds of covert discrimination, that is, where the ostensibly equal treatment in fact benefits only the state's own nationals.[20] The former is illustrated by the case of a Dutch citizen employed in Germany, who having become incapacitated in consequence of an accident at work was dismissed by his employer. Under German legislation seriously disabled workers were protected from dismissal but this protection was not afforded to non-German nationals. The ECJ upheld the principle of equal treatment of German and foreign workers alike.[1]

Examples of covert discrimination include the case of an Italian who was employed in Germany and who had to perform national military service in his country. Had he been a German citizen the period in military service would have been taken into consideration for the purpose of seniority in his employment in Germany. There was no provision in German law in respect of foreigners in a similar situation but the ECJ ruled that the Italian citizen was to be treated in the same way as a German one as far as his military service had to be recognized for seniority in his employment.[2] The principle was applied to an Italian worker

14 Case C-213/90: *Association de Soutien aux Travailleurs Immigrés* [1991] ECR I-3507, [1993] 3 CMLR 621.
15 Case 237/83: *Prodest Sàrl v Caise Primaire d'Assurance Maladie de Paris* [1984] ECR 3153.
16 See Ch 21 infra.
17 Case C-351/90: *Commission v Luxembourg* [1992] ECR I-3945, [1992] 3 CMLR 124.
18 Case C-175/88: *Biehl v Administration des Contributions du Grand-Duché de Luxembourg* [1990] ECR I-1779, [1990] 3 CMLR 143.
19 Case C-3/87: *R v Ministry of Agriculture, ex p Agegate Ltd* [1989] ECR 4459, [1990] 1 CMLR 366.
20 Eg Case C-35/97: *Commission v France* [1998] ECR I-5325, para 37, and the cases cited there; Case C-195/98: *Osterreichischer Gewerkschaftsbund v Republik Osterreich* 30 November 2000, paras 39-40.
1 Case 44/72: *Marsman v Rosskamp* [1972] ECR 1243, [1973] CMLR 501.
2 Case 15/69: *Württembergische Milchverwertung-Sudmilch AG v Ugliola* [1969] ECR 363, [1970] CMLR 194.

who, at the beginning of his employment in Germany received a separation allowance like any other German worker in his situation but when the allowance was increased he was denied the increase. The Government circular which provided that the increased allowance was payable to workers residing in Germany at the time of their recruitment but not to those (German as well as foreign) who were residing abroad at that time of their recruitment, was held to be discriminatory since the discrimination on the ground of residence could have effect as discrimination on grounds of nationality.[3]

The provisions of a contract of employment may also infringe the basic right under the Treaty. A provision withdrawing a right to compensation on termination of employment where the contract is terminated by the worker in order to allow him to take up employment in another Member State, is not contrary to the Treaty because the entitlement to compensation is based on the occurrence of an event that is too uncertain and indirect a possibility to hinder free movement.[4]

The concept of 'social advantage'[5] has a wide meaning but it does not include social security benefits to which migrant workers are entitled.[6] However it includes advantages based not only on the law but also on discretionary powers. It is based on non-discrimination. Fiscal advantages include the joint tax treatment of spouses.[7]

Such advantages are granted generally to national workers because they are workers, or they are resident on the national territory, and are extended to workers of other Member States since this would facilitate the free movement of workers in the Community.[8] On this principle the ECJ[9] considered that the concession to ex-servicemen to receive early pension at full rate was properly reserved to nationals of the awarding Member State and could not be extended to others. Conversely the ECJ held that interest-free loans on childbirth to foreign workers to help with their young families was a social advantage to which they were entitled even if the grant was discretionary but emanated from a credit institution set up under public law.[10] The restriction of a funeral payment (a means-tested social benefit intended to cover costs incurred by the claimant or a member of his family on the occasion of a death in the family) to situations where the funeral takes place on the territory of the state granting the payment was held to be indirectly discriminatory because it was more likely to affect a person who had exercised the right of free movement than a person who had not.[11] These examples include assistance to use one's own language in judicial proceedings;[12] minimum subsistence allowance;[13] a special unemployment benefit for young job-seekers not covered by Regulation 1408/71;[14] old-age pension falling outside the scope of the national social security rules[15] and a minimum income for senior citizens.[16]

---

3 Case 152/73: *Sotgiu v Deutsche Bundespost* [1974] ECR 153 at 164.
4 Case C-190/98: *Graf v Filzmosen Maschinenbaur GmbH* [2000] All ER (EC) 170.
5 Reg 1612/68, Art 7(2). Eg Case C-35/97: *Commission v France* [1998] ECR I-5325.
6 Case 1/72: *Frilli v Belgium* [1972] ECR 457 at 464, [1973] CMLR 386 at 406.
7 Case C-87/99: *Zurstrassen v Administration des Contributions directes*, 16 May 2000.
8 Case 207/78: *Ministère Public v Evan* [1979] ECR 2019, [1980] 2 CMLR 71.
9 Ibid.
10 Case 65/81: *Reina v Landeskreditbank Baden-Württemburg* [1982] ECR 33, [1982] 1 CMLR 744.
11 Case C-237/94: *O'Flynn v Adjudication Officer* [1996] ECR I-2617.
12 Case 137/84: *Ministère Public v Mutsch* [1985] ECR 2681, [1986] 1 CMLR 648.
13 Case 249/83: *Hoeckx v Openbaar Centrum voor Maatschappelijk Welzijn, Kalmhout* [1985] ECR 973.
14 Case 94/84: *Office National de l'Emploi v Deak* [1985] ECR 1873.
15 Case 157/84: *Frascogna v Caisse des Dépôts* [1985] ECR 1739.
16 Case 261/83: *Castelli v Office National des Pensions* (ONPTS) [1984] ECR 3199.

Social advantages embrace also the workers' families. Such was the ruling of the ECJ in the case involving reduced fares on the French national railways for French large families even after the death of the foreign worker.[17]

(3) WORKERS' FAMILIES

The right of the worker's family to 'install themselves' with the worker in the host state[18] comprises equal access to housing, employment and educational facilities for his children. If his children are residing in the territory they are entitled to be admitted to the state's 'general educational, apprenticeship and vocational training courses on the same conditions as the nationals of that state'.[19]

The principle was generously interpreted in favour of the mentally handicapped son of a deceased Italian worker in Belgium.[20] Though the Court warned that Article 7 of the Regulation protected workers but not their family it nevertheless ruled that protection could be inferred from Article 12 supported by the Preamble which referred to 'the conditions for the integration of (the worker's) family into the host country'. That interpretation demanded that the handicapped child ought to be accorded the same treatment as available to the state's nationals in a similar position.

Following this interpretation the ECJ held that the daughter of an Italian worker could not be refused entry to a French teachers' training college and had to be treated like any other French applicant provided she fulfilled the requisite academic conditions of admission.[1] Similarly, in an earlier case[2] the child of a deceased Italian was held entitled to an educational grant on the same conditions as a Bavarian student.

In applying Article 12 the ECJ held that any form of education, including University or Technical College, is covered.[3] The problem of discrimination in vocational training[4] and funding[5] has now become part of a wider issue concerning the mobility of students.[6]

K.   Towards a common citizenship

EC Article 17 (ex Art 8) confers citizenship of the Union on every person holding the nationality of a Member State. The citizenship of the Union complements but does not replace national citizenship. It entails the right to move freely and reside freely within the territory of the Member States, the right to vote and to

---

17   Case 32/75: *Fiorinin (Christini) v Société Nationale des Chemins de Fer Français* [1975] ECR 1085, [1976] 1 CMLR 573.
18   Supra.
19   Reg 1612/68, Art 12.
20   Case 76/72: *Michel S v Fonds National de Reclassement Social des Handicapés* [1973] ECR 457 at 463. See also Cases 63/76: *Inzirillo v Caisse d'Allocations Familiales* [1976] ECR 2057, [1978] 3 CMLR 596. Social advantages benefiting a member of the worker's family may nonetheless fall within Art 7 where the former is supported by the worker: see Case C3/90: *Bernini* [1992] ECR I-1071, para 24; Case C-337/97: *Meeusen v Hoofddirectie van de Informatie Beheer Groep* [1999] ECR I-3289, paras 18-25.
1   Case 68/74: *Alaimo v Préfét du Rhône* [1975] ECR 109, [1975] 1 CMLR 262.
2   Case 9/74: *Casagrande v Landeshauptstadt München* [1974] ECR 773, [1974] 2 CMLR 423.
3   Cases 389 and 390/87: *Echternacht and Moritz* [1989] ECR 723, [1990] 2 CMLR 305.
4   Eg Case 293/83: *Gravier v City of Liège* [1985] ECR 593, [1985] 3 CMLR 1.
5   Eg Case C-3/90: *Bernini v Netherlandse Ministry of Education* [1992] ECR I-1071.
6   See infra.

stand as a candidate at municipal elections[7] as well as the right to vote and stand as a candidate in elections to the European Parliament in the country where the citizen resides.[8] However these rights are subject to implementation by the Council acting unanimously on a proposal from the Commission after having obtained the assent of the European Parliament. The Treaty does not envisage as yet a right (active or passive) to participate in national general elections.[9]

Whilst in a third country, every citizen of the Union shall be entitled to diplomatic and consular protection of any Member State on the same conditions as the nationals of that state (if the citizen's own Member State is not represented in that country). In order to implement this objective the Member States must establish themselves the necessary rules and to secure this protection by means of appropriate international negotiations.[10]

We have already noted three important Directives[11] extending residence rights to Community citizens[12] and Directive 68/360[13] on the abolition of restrictions on movement and residence or workers. The ECJ ruled against systematic checking at borders but allowed spot checking of passports or identity cards as well as of residence permits.[14] It also held illegal the enquiries about the purpose and duration of the journey as well as the financial means of Community nationals coming to the Netherlands.[15] However, control at the external frontiers of the Member States of the Community is subject to national rules until there is harmonization of national immigration policies, visas, and the right of asylum.[16]

To facilitate travel within the Community two Directives governing driving licences have been adopted. Directive 80/1263[17] introduced a Community model of such licences laying down the minimum requirements for drivers' tests and medical standards. It was repealed with effect from July 1996 by Directive 91/439,[18] which required that licences issued by one Member State be recognized by all others. Directive 91/439 like Directive 80/1263 before it, may be relied upon irrespective of the nationality of the holder of the driving licence; but, where an offence has been committed, the principle of proportionality may moderate the sanction to be imposed only when the person concerned's right of free movement would be affected.[19] Council Regulation 3925/91[20] prohibited all systematic controls of checked and cabin baggage in intra-Community air and

---

7   See Council Dir 94/80 (OJ 1994, L368/38), amended by Dir 96/30 (OJ 1996, L122/14), which lays down detailed arrangements for the exercise of that right.

8   See Council Dir 93/109 (OJ 1993, L329/34), which lays down detailed arrangements for the exercise of that right.

9   EC Arts 18 and 19 (ex Arts 8a and 8b).

10   EC Art 20 (ex Art 8c). See Decision 95/553 of the representatives of the Governments of the Member States regarding protection for citizens of the EU by diplomatic and consular representatives (OJ 1995, L314/73).

11   Dir 90/364; 90/365 and 93/96.

12   Supra.

13   Supra.

14   Case 321/87: *Commission v Belgium* [1989] ECR 997, [1990] 2 CMLR 492; Case C-378/97 *Wijsenbeck* [1999] ECR I-6207.

15   Case C-68/89: *Commission v Netherlands* [1991] ECR I-2637, [1993] 2 CMLR 389.

16   See further section L below and the Convention on examination of applications for asylum lodged in one of the Member States of the EC (Dublin 15 June 1990) signed by all Member States.

17   OJ 1980, L375/1.

18   OJ 1991, L237/1, amended by Dir 94/72 (OJ 1994, L337/86), 96/47 (OJ 1996, L235/1) and 97/26 (OJ 1997, L150/41).

19   Case 16/78: *Choquet* [1978] ECR 2293; Case C-193/94: *Skanavi and Chryssanthakopoulos* [1996] ECR I-929; Case C-230/97: *Awoyemi* [1998] ECR I-6781.

20   OJ 1991, L374/4.

sea travel, subject, of course, to security. Directive 91/477[1] harmonized national rules for the acquisition and possession of weapons. Accordingly Member States are obliged to prohibit the acquisition or possession of weapons without authorization which is to be granted only 'for good cause' to persons 'not likely to be a danger to themselves or to public safety'.[2] Dealers in weapons are subject to licence and they have to keep registers which ought to identify the weapon and the purchaser.[3] The Directive also lays down conditions for the intra-Community trade in weapons[4] and for importation of weapons from outside the Community.[5]

Certain measures have only a symbolic value, such as the introduction of a Community passport in 1985 which is meant to replace the national passport in due course,[6] the Community flag in 1986 (a circle of twelve gold stars on a blue background) which ought to be exhibited in front of buildings housing the Community institutions, and a Community anthem.

L.   Visas, asylum, immigration and other policies related to the free movement of persons

Under EC Title IV (ex Title IIIa), in order to establish the Community progressively as an area of freedom, security and justice, the Council is obliged to adopt various measures,[7] namely: (i) measures aimed at ensuring the free movement of persons in accordance with the concept of the internal market, in conjunction with directly related measures relating to external border controls, asylum and immigration and with measures to prevent and combat crime;[8] (ii) other measures in the fields of asylum, immigration and safeguarding the rights of nationals of third countries;[9] (iii) measures in the field of judicial co-operation in civil matters

---

1   OJ 1991, L256/51. See also the Commission Recommendations of 25 February 1993 and 12 January 1996 on the European firearms pass (OJ 1993, L93/39 and OJ 1996, L30/47).
2   Art 3.
3   Art 4.
4   Arts 11-14.
5   Art 15.
6   See the Resolutions of 23 June 1981, 30 June 1982, 14 July 1986 and 10 July 1995 (OJ 1981, C 241/1; OJ 1982, C 179/1; OJ 1986, C 185/1; OJ 1995, C 200/1). See also in this connexion Decision 96/409 on the establishment of an emergency travel document (OJ 1996, L168/4).
7   EC Art 61 (ex Art 73i). Procedures determining how the Council must exercise its powers are set out in EC Art 67 (ex Art 73o); but they appear to apply only where express reference to that provision is made. Express provision to that effect is to be found in EC Arts 62, 63, 65 and 66 (ex Arts 73j, 73k, 73m and 73n) but not in EC Art 61 (ex Art 73i).
8   These measures are to be adopted within five years of the entry into force of the Amsterdam Treaty. EC Art 62 (ex Art 73j) sets out a related obligation to adopt the following measures: measures to ensure the absence of controls on persons (irrespective of their nationality) when crossing internal borders; measures on the crossing of the external borders of the Member States that establish standards and procedures in carrying out checks on persons at such borders and rules on visas for extended stays of no more than three months; and measures setting out the conditions under which nationals of third countries shall have the freedom to travel within the territory of the Member States during a period of no more than three months.
9   Some of these measures, but not all, must also be adopted within five years of the entry into force of the Amsterdam Treaty: see EC Art 63 (ex Art 73k) (in particular the first and last sentences). EC Art 63 obliges the Council to adopt the following measures: measures on asylum in accordance with the Geneva Convention of 28 July 1951 and the Protocol of 31 January 1967 relating to the status of refugees and other relevant treaties in relation to the

having cross-border implications, insofar as is necessary for the proper functioning of the internal market;[10] (iv) appropriate measures to encourage and strengthen administrative co-operation between the Member States in relation to visas, asylum, immigration and related policies;[11] and (v) measures in the field of police and judicial co-operation in criminal matters aimed at a high level of security by preventing and combating crime within the Union in accordance with the TEU.

Such measures do not affect the exercise by Member States of their responsibilities for securing maintenance of law and order and internal security. If a Member State is confronted with an emergency situation characterised by a sudden inflow of third country nationals, the Council may adopt provisional measures of a duration not exceeding six months for the benefit of the Member States concerned.[12]

The operation of the Council's powers under Title IV of the Treaty is subject to more specific provisions concerning Denmark, Ireland and the United Kingdom contained in protocols attached to the Treaty.[13] In particular, the United Kingdom (including territories for whose external relations the United Kingdom is responsible) is empowered, notwithstanding any other provision of Community law, to exercise at its frontiers with other Member States such controls on persons seeking to enter the United Kingdom as it may consider necessary for the purposes of: (a) verifying the person concerned's right to enter the United Kingdom under the Agreement on the European Economic Area and any other agreement to which the United Kingdom is bound; and (b) determining whether or not to grant other persons permission to enter the United Kingdom.[14] The United Kingdom and Ireland are also authorised to continue to make arrangements between themselves relating to the free movement of persons between their territories, while fully respecting the rights of persons under the Agreement on the European Economic Area and other agreements binding the United Kingdom.[15] Similarly, the other Member States are entitled to impose,

criteria and mechanisms for determining which Member State is responsible for considering an application for asylum, minimum standards on the reception of asylum seekers, minimum standards on the qualification of third country nationals as refugees, and minimum standards for granting or withholding refugee status; measures on refugees and displaced persons concerning minimum standards of temporary protection for displaced persons and other persons needing international protection, and concerning the balance of responsibility between the Member States for receiving refugees and displaced persons and bearing the consequences of their reception; measures on immigration policy concerning conditions of entry and residence, standards on procedures for the issue of long term visas and residence permits, illegal immigration and illegal residence (including repatriation); and measures defining the rights and conditions under which third country nationals who are legally resident in one Member State may reside in another.

10   See also EC Art 65 (ex Art 73m), which provides that such measures shall include: measures improving and simplifying the system of cross-border service of judicial and extrajudicial documents, co-operation in the taking of evidence and the recognition and enforcement of decisions in civil and commercial cases, including decisions in extrajudicial cases; measures promoting the compatibility of the rules applicable in the Member States concerning the conflict of laws and jurisdiction; and measures eliminating obstacles to the good functioning of civil proceedings, if necessary by promoting the compatibility of the rules on civil procedure applicable in the Member States.

11   See also EC Art 66 (ex Art 73n).

12   EC Art 64 (ex Art 73l). The Council acts by qualified majority on a proposal from the Commission.

13   EC Art 69 (ex Art 73q).

14   Protocol on the application of certain aspects of Art 14 of the Treaty establishing the European Community to United Kingdom and Ireland, Art 1.

15   Ibid, Art 2.

at their frontiers or at any point of entry into their territories, controls having the same purpose on persons seeking to enter their territory from the United Kingdom (or territories for whose external relations it is responsible) and Ireland.[16]

Denmark, Ireland and the United Kingdom may not take part in the adoption by the Council of measures pursuant to Title IV of the Treaty unless they have first given written notice to the President of the Council that they wish to do so. Notice must be given within three months of the presentation of the proposal or initiative to the Council. Appropriate variations have been made to the rules for adopting such measures to take account of the participation, or non-participation, of those States in the adoption procedures. If any of those States does not participate, the measure in question (together with any consequential measure and any judgment of the ECJ interpreting the measure) has no effect within that State. It is also important to note that Title IV measures that are not accepted by all Member States do not affect the '*acquis communautaire*', that is the accumulated body of Community law that is accepted by all Member States, both existing and new, and do not form part of Community law applicable in the non-accepting State. Denmark, Ireland and the United Kingdom may at any time after the adoption of a Title IV measure indicate that it wishes to accept the measure. In that event, the Commission gives an opinion on the matter to the Council and thereafter decides on it and on such specific arrangements related to the acceptance of the measure that it deems necessary.[17]

The provisions of EC Title IV, and the measures adopted on the basis of those provisions (that is, Title IV measures themselves), are subject to consideration by the ECJ on a basis that is different from other provisions of the Treaty: the ECJ may entertain references for a preliminary ruling concerning the interpretation of these Treaty provisions, or the interpretation or validity of the measures based on them, only where the reference is made by a national court against whose decisions there is no judicial remedy under national law; the ECJ has no jurisdiction to rule on any measure or act taken pursuant to EC Article 62(1) (ex Art 73j(1)), relating to the maintenance of law and order and the safeguarding of internal security; and the Council, the Commission and the Member States each have a general right to request the ECJ to rule on the interpretation of these Treaty provisions, or acts of the Community institutions based on them, although the ruling so given may not apply to any judgment of a national court that has become *res judicata* by the time when the ECJ's ruling is delivered[18] (implicitly, therefore, the ECJ's ruling can be applied to a pending case).

The principal measures that have been adopted to date are summarised below.

(1) *Visas.* Council Regulation 1683/95[19] provides for a uniform format for visas. Council Regulation 574/1999[20] determines the third countries whose nationals

---

16 Ibid, Art 3.
17 Protocol on the position of the United Kingdom and Ireland; Protocol on the position of Denmark; EC Art 11(3). The position of Denmark is slightly different from that of Ireland and the United Kingdom. In particular, Denmark's anomalous position as regards the other Member States does not extend to measures determining the third counties whose nationals must be in possession of a visa when crossing the external borders of the Member States, and measures relating to a uniform format for visas; and Denmark has an option whether or not to accept a Title IV measure that builds upon the Schengen *Acquis* (as to which, see p 44, supra). Provision is made for Denmark and Ireland to abandon their special positions under the protocols.
18 EC Art 68 (ex Art 73p).
19 OJ 1995, L164/1.
20 OJ 1999, L72/2.

must be in possession of visas when crossing the external borders of the Member States.

(2) *Asylum.* In 1990, in Dublin, the Member States agreed a Convention determining the State responsible for examining asylum applications lodged in one of the Member States.[1] In 1995, the Council adopted a resolution on minimum guarantees for asylum procedures.[2]

(3) *Rights of refugees and displaced persons not eligible for asylum.* In 1995, the Council adopted a resolution on burden sharing with regard to the admission and residence of displaced persons on a temporary basis[3] and an alert and emergency procedure for identifying and dealing with crisis situations was adopted in 1996.[4] In the same year, the Council adopted a joint position on the meaning of 'refugee'.[5] In 1999, joint action was taken to support projects and measures providing practical support for persons who had fled from Kosovo.[6]

(4) *Immigration from third countries.* In 1994, the Council adopted various resolutions concerning the admission of third country nationals into the Member States for the purposes of employment, self-employed activities and study.[7] In 1995, the Council adopted recommendations on harmonizing the means of combating illegal immigration and illegal employment, and improving means of control, and expulsion measures.[8] A resolution on the status of third country nationals who are long-term residents in the Member States and a recommendation on combating the illegal employment of third country nationals were adopted in 1996.[9] In 1997, the Council adopted a decision on the exchange of information concerning assistance for the voluntary repatriation of third country nationals and resolutions on unaccompanied minors who are third country nationals and on measures to combat marriages of convenience.[10]

(5) *Extradition.* A Convention relation to extradition between the Member States was signed in 1996.[11]

1   OJ 1997, C254/1. Various decisions have been taken pursuant to the Convention, in particular, Decision 1/97 (OJ 1997, L281/1) and Decision 1/98 (OJ 1998, L196/49), both concerning provisions for the implementation of the Convention.
2   OJ 1995, C 274/13.
3   OJ 1995, C 262/1.
4   Decision 96/198 (OJ 1996, L63/10).
5   OJ 1996, L63/2.
6   OJ 1999, L114/2.
7   OJ 1996, C 274/3, 7 and 10.
8   OJ 1996, C 5/1 and 3.
9   OJ 1996, C 80/2 and C304/1.
10   OJ 1997, L147/3 (Decision 97/340), C221/23 and C382/1.
11   OJ 1996, C313/11.

Chapter 20

The right of establishment (EC Articles 43-48 (ex Articles 52-58)[1]

A. General principles

In addition to 'workers' (who are salaried) EC Article 43 (ex Art 52) contemplates a group of people who, in principle, pursue activities as self-employed persons or set up and manage companies or firms within the meaning of EC Article 48 (ex Art 58). Such persons very often belong to recognized professions whose status and membership is regulated by law, or to professional bodies themselves operating within the scope of national rules. Hence the need of harmonizing the national rules and regulations to facilitate their mobility within the Community and, in the first place, to remove restrictions on the ground of nationality and other peculiar national practices established by the professions themselves.

The right of establishment is the right of a person to enter a Member State and establish himself or herself there for the purpose of carrying on economic activities in that State otherwise than under a contract of employment.[2] Since there is no precise definition of the persons entitled to the right of establishment the status of certain fringe professional activities, including sport activities, had to be judicially considered. In *Walrave and Koch v Association Union Cyclistes Internationales*[3] professional pacemakers for track cyclists challenged the rules of the World Cycling Federation which provided that, in championships, a pacemaker had to be of the same nationality as the cyclist. On reference from a Dutch court the ECJ ruled that the practice of sport was subject to Community law if it constituted an economic activity within the scope of EC Article 2. However, the prohibition of discrimination on the ground of nationality did not affect the

---

1 Lasok, K P E, and Thompson, R, in *Law of the European Communities* (Butterworth, ed D Vaughan), Part 16.
2 Eg Case C-107/94: *Asscher v Staatsecretaris van Financien* [1996] ECR I-3089, paras 25-26.
3 Case 36/74: [1974] ECR 1405, [1975] 1 CMLR 320. See also Case C-415/93: *Union Royale Belge des Sociétés de Football Association v Bosman* [1995] ECR I-4921.

composition of sports teams whose function was not economic. It was a matter for the national court to determine, as a fact, whether in the activity in question the pacemaker and cyclist constituted such a team. The Court also ruled that the rules of an international sporting body had to be disregarded if their effect would be to neutralize the abolition of barriers based on discrimination on the ground of nationality.[4]

In *Donà v Mantero*,[5] Donà was engaged by Mantero, the chairman of an Italian football club, to recruit new players. To that end, Donà placed an advertisement in Belgium to attract football players. Mantero refused to consider the applications arising from the advertisement and to refund Donà's expenses arguing that, under the rules of the Italian Football Federation, only Italian nationals could take part in domestic league matches. In the reference to it, the ECJ pointed out that EC Articles 48-51 and 59-66 (now EC Arts 39-42 and 49-55) as well as the implementing Community legislation sought to abolish all discrimination based on nationality of Community citizens as regards their employment, establishment and the provision of services. It reiterated its ruling in the *Walrave* case as regards the economic nature of sporting activities as well as restrictive rules emanating not only from public authorities but also any other body, for example a national football federation. However amateur sporting activities remain outside the Community rules. The principle was followed in the case of a professional trainer.[6]

To determine the nature of an establishment certain criteria have been suggested, such as a centre from which a particular activity is carried out;[7] a prolonged residence in a Member State coupled with the intention of setting up in business on a permanent basis;[8] a permanent, habitual or actual residence in a Member State;[9] a permanent presence or installation in a Member State;[10] the performance of self-employed activities from an installation set up for an indeterminate duration[11] and a permanent integration into the host state's economy.[12] In the cases, involvement in the economic life of a Member State on a stable and continuous basis is sufficient to constitute establishment; but establishment does not necessarily require the physical presence of the person concerned in the Member State in question since an establishment can be created by setting up a company.[13] The exercise of the right of establishment need not be confined to a single country[14] and there is in principle no limitation on the number of places in which a person may be established. Indeed the wording of EC Article 43(2) (ex Art 52(2)) is permissive in so far as it refers to 'activities of self-employed persons' and the 'setting-up and management of undertakings'

---

4   Ibid at 1419.
5   Case 13/76: [1976] ECR 1333, [1976] 2 CMLR 578.
6   Case 222/86: *Union Nationale des Entraîneurs et Cadres Techniques Professionels du Football v Georges Heylens* [1987] ECR 4097, [1989] 1 CMLR 901.
7   Everling, U, *The Right of Establishment in the Common Market* (1964) 205.
8   Maestripieri, *Freedom of Establishment and Freedom to Supply Services*, 10 CMLRev (1973) 150-51.
9   A G Mayras in Case 33/74; *Van Binsbergen v Bestuur van de Bedrijfsverening voor de Metaalnijverheid* [1974] ECR 1299 at 1315 [1975] 1 CMLR 298 at 303.
10 Cerexhe, C, *Le Droit Européen: La Libre Circulation des Personnes et des Entreprises*, (1982) 13; Kapteyn, P J G and Verloren van Themaat, P, *Introduction to the Law of the European Communities* (3rd edn, 1998), p 731.
11 Goldman, B and Lyon-Caen, A, *Droit Commercial Européen* (5th edn, 1994), p 330.
12 Wyatt and Dashwood's, *European Union Law* (4th edn, 2000), p 429.
13 Eg, Case C-70/95: *Sodemare v Regione Lombardia* [1997] ECR I-3395, paras 23–24.
14 Case 107/83: *Ordre des Avocats au Barreau de Paris v Klopp* [1984] ECR 2971 at 2976, [1985] 1 CMLR 99 at 109.

within the scope of EC Article 48(1) (ex Art 58(1)). This suggests the possibility of a principal and secondary establishment for someone who has a permanent residence and a main office in one Member State but also an office in another for sporadic or ancillary activities; though the latter may well be classified as a performance of services rather than the exercise of the right of establishment. For a practical purpose the function of EC Article 43 (ex Art 52), is to guarantee the right of exercising a profession throughout the Community and thus enable an individual to choose the place where he prefers to act.[15]

To be meaningful the right of establishment had to be backed up not only by abolition of restrictions on the ground of nationality but also by rules governing entry and residence as well as social security, in analogy to rights of workers, and finally by a harmonization of the national laws applicable to self-employed persons, ie members of the professions.

B.   Entry, residence and right to remain

Directive 73/184,[16] which superseded Decision 64/220 and closely followed Directive 68/360,[17] brought the rules governing the entry and residence of self-employed persons into line with the rules applicable to workers.
Directive 73/184 applies to both self-employed persons and the providers of services. It covers:[18]

'(a)   nationals of a Member State who are established or who wish to establish themselves in another Member State in order to pursue activities as self-employed persons, or who wish to provide services in that state;
(b)   nationals of Member States wishing to go to another Member State as recipients of services;
(c)   the spouse and the children under 21 years of age of such nationals, irrespective of their nationality;[19]
(d)   the relatives of the ascending and descending lines of such nationals and of the spouse of such nationals, which relatives are dependent on them, irrespective of their nationality.'

Moreover, the above persons are entitled to be allowed to leave national territory and to be issued with an identity card or passport[20] and to enter the territory of the Member States merely on production of a valid identity card or passport.[1] They are entitled to a residence permit which must be valid for not less than five years and be automatically renewable.[2]

Directive 75/34[3] on the right of self-employed persons to remain in Member States repeats the provision of Regulation 1251/70[4] applicable to workers.

---

15   See Case 143/87: *Stanton v INASTI* [1988] ECR 3877 [1989] 3 CMLR 761. Cases 154 and 155/87: *Rijksinstituut voor de Sociale Verzekering du Zelfstandigen v Wolf* [1988] ECR 3897.
16   OJ 1973, L172/14.
17   See p 495, supra.
18   Art 1(1).
19   See Case C-370/90: *R v Immigration Appeal Tribunal, ex p Singh* [1992] ECR I-4265.
20   Art 2.
 1   Art 3. See Case 157/79: *R v Pieck* [1980] ECR 2171, [1980] 2 CMLR 220; Case 321/87: *Commission v Belgium* [1989] ECR 997; Case C-369/90: *Micheletti v Delegacion del Govierno* [1992] ECR I-4239; Case C-9/92: *Commission v Greece* [1993] ECR I-4467.
 2   Art 4(1).
 3   OJ 1975, L14/10.
 4   Supra, p 498.

Directive 90/364[5] extends the right of residence to persons who do not enjoy it under any other provisions of Community Law and Directive 90/365[6] to former employed as well as self-employed persons who have ceased their professional activity as a result of retirement or incapacity.

Regulation 1408/71[7] on social security protection of workers is extended to the self-employed by virtue of Regulation 3795/81.[8]

The case law governing workers and dependants applies *mutatis mutandis* to self-employed persons.

C.   Exceptions and derogations

EC Article 45 (ex Art 55), provides that the Council may, acting on a proposal from the Commission, decide, by a qualified majority, that the Treaty provisions shall not apply to 'certain activities' in the field of establishment and services. That power applies also in the context of the freedom to provide services: see EC Article 55 (ex Art 66). The power has never been exercised.

EC Article 45(1) (ex Art 55(1)), applying both to establishment and services, provides that the Treaty rights shall not apply as far as any given Member State is concerned, to activities which in that State are connected, even occasionally, with the exercise of 'official authority'. In the absence of a definition of this exception the corresponding provision of EC Article 39(4) (ex Art 48(4)) applicable to workers and case law govern the position.[9] 'Official authority' has been interpreted restrictively by the ECJ in a number of cases involving members of the teaching profession;[10] managements of private schools;[11] employees of Italian banks;[12] employees of a National Research Council;[13] customs agents, journalists, pharmacists and tourist guides;[14] nurses in state hospitals;[15] and data processing activities carried on for the benefit of a public authority.[16]

The argument of 'public service' was also raised, albeit unsuccessfully, in relation to the legal profession[17] where a Dutch national who became qualified as a lawyer in Belgium was refused admission to the Belgian Bar on the ground that under a Belgian Royal Decree only Belgian citizens were allowed to practise law. Considering the functions of an advocate the ECJ stated that the professional legal activities involving even regular and organic contacts with the administration of justice did not constitute the exercise of 'official authority'.[18] Even if the performance of activities such as consultation and legal assistance,

---

5   Supra, p 499.
6   Supra, p 499.
7   See infra, p 541.
8   See OJ 1981, L378/1.
9   See Case 152/73: *Sotgiu v Deutsche Bundespost* [1974] ECR 153 at 156 and Case 149/79 (No 1) and (No 2): *Commission v Belgium* [1980] ECR 3881, [1980] 2 CMLR 413 and [1982] ECR 1845, [1982] 3 CMLR 539.
10   Case 33/88: *Allué v Universitá Degli Studi di Venezia* [1989] ECR 1591, [1991] 1 CMLR 283.
11   Case 147/86: *Commission v Greece* [1988] ECR 1637, [1987] 2 CMLR 845.
12   Case 166/85: *Bullo and Bonivento* [1987] ECR 1583, [1988] 1 CMLR 832; Case 422/85: *Mattiazzo* [1987] ECR 5413, [1989] 2 CMLR 482.
13   Case 225/85: *Commission v Italy* [1987] ECR 2625, [1988] 3 CMLR 635.
14   Case 168/85: *Commission v Italy* [1986] ECR 2945, [1988] 1 CMLR 580.
15   Case 307/84: *Commission v France* [1986] ECR 1725, [1987] 3 CMLR 555.
16   Case C-42/92: *Thijssen v Control dienst voor de Verzekeringen* [1993] ECR I-4047.
17   Case 2/74: *Reyners v Belgium* [1974] ECR 631 at 654-5, [1974] 2 CMLR 305.
18   Ibid at 633, 658.

or the representation and defence of parties in judicial proceedings, is compulsory or subject to professional monopoly, it cannot be construed as the exercise of 'official authority'.[19] The Court concluded that the objective of the exception is satisfied when the exclusion of foreign nationals is limited to those activities which, taken on their own, constitute a direct and specific connection with the exercise of official authority and the exception cannot be extended any further or to embrace the legal profession as a whole.[20] Needless to say this ruling is of a greater practical importance especially in so far as senior advocates in private practice (especially in the United Kingdom) often sit as judges.

Derogations can be invoked in respect of the professions and services[1] in analogy to the derogations from the movement of persons on grounds of public policy, public security and public health.[2] Although the wording differs in so far as EC Article 46(1) (ex Art 56(1)) adds a rider referring to 'provisions laid down by law, regulation or administrative action providing for special treatment for foreign nationals', the grounds are the same. Therefore the case law[3] governing workers applies, *mutatis mutandis*, to the members of the professions as well as the providers of services.

D. Abolition of restrictions

EC Article 43 (ex Art 52) prohibits restrictions on the freedom of establishment 'within the framework of the provisions set out below' (that is, within the framework of EC Articles 43-48 (ex Arts 52-58)). The Treaty provisions recognized that the freedom of establishment could not be achieved simply by abolishing provisions or practices in the Member States that hindered establishment by persons from other Member States; positive steps also needed to be taken in order to make the freedom of establishment a reality.

In order to carry out its mandate the Council adopted, in 1962, two General Programmes for the Abolition of Restrictions on Freedom to Provide Services and Freedom of Establishment, respectively.[4] The Programmes defined the beneficiaries of the drive against discrimination on the ground of nationality, laid down a framework for their mobility and established both a list of restrictions to be abolished and a timetable within which these objectives were to be accomplished. In addition the Programme for the right of establishment provided for co-ordination of safeguards required for the protection of Member States' interests as well as for the prohibition of State regulation which might distort the conditions of establishment. The Programmes gave rise to numerous directives[5] aiming to abolish the restrictions listed in Title III of the Programmes and to introduce into national systems detailed provisions designed to facilitate the effective exercise of the right of establishment and the freedom to provide services. Taking Directive 64/224[6] on the Freedom of Establishment and Services as an example, the

---

19   Ibid at 653.
20   Ibid at 654.
 1   EC Arts 46(1) and 55 (ex Arts 56(1) and 66), respectively.
 2   EC Art 39(3) (ex Art 48(3)), see p 500, supra.
 3   See pp 502 et seq, supra.
 4   No 32/62, JO 1992, p 2 and No 36/62, JO 1962, p 7.
 5   Lasok, D, *The Professions and Services in the European Economic Community* (1986), pp 105-32; Lasok, K P E, and Thompson, R, op cit.
 6   JO 1964, 869.

legislation envisaged activities to be liberalized according to ISIC classification;[7] restrictions to be removed (as identified in certain countries), the right to joint professional and trade organizations; prohibition of state aids to their nationals for the purpose of pursuing any activity defined in the Directive; proof of financial standing, and the oath or solemn promise made upon the taking up of professional activities.

The Programmes provided for transitional measures to facilitate the taking up and pursuit of activities of self-employed persons pending the enactment of the Directive on Recognition of Diplomas and Professional Qualifications and the co-ordination of national and administrative rules governing the exercise of self-employed activities. However, as recorded in the Commission White Paper[8] the results as of 1985 were unsatisfactory and the Commission threatened to take enforcement action against Member States in default.

Member States' sluggishness apart, certain imperfections of the Treaty contributed to the delay in the liberation of the professions. EC Article 43(2) (ex Art 52(2)) implicitly enabled the Member States to lay down the conditions for the exercise of the professions as long as the conditions were applied without discrimination between their citizens and the other Community nationals. However the prohibition of having more than one place of activity inhibited their own citizens from establishing themselves abroad, for example by excluding a director of a company registered in another country from the benefit of national security schemes,[9] and would in effect restrict their mobility. Moreover rules affecting the mobility of members of professions and their families (ie entry, residence and remaining in another Member State) and social security had to be brought into line with the rules applicable to workers in the same way as general facilities affecting the access to social housing[10] and reduced mortgage rates or acquisition of immovable property had to be.[11]

The abolition of restrictions on the freedom of establishment has therefore been conducted on two fronts: through judicial interpretation of the Treaty provisions; and through legislation designed to modify national laws and practices.

E. The case law

Through its case law, the ECJ has established that the Treaty prohibits directly: discrimination on grounds of nationality;[12] discrimination based on the State in which a company has its registered office;[13] discrimination based on the State in which a qualification has been obtained;[14] and both discriminatory and non-discriminatory restrictions on the freedom to establish oneself in another Member State.[15] The prohibition in the Treaty applies both to measures

---

7 International Standard Industrial Classification of Economic Activities published by the Statistical Office of the United Nations, Series M, No 4, Rev 1, UN (1958) 58 xvii. 7; see Cases 110 and 111/78: *Ministère Public v Van Wesemael* [1979] ECR 35, [1979] 3 CMLR 87.
8 COM (1985) 310 Final, in particular paras 54,55, 58, 81-83, 87, 89-91, 94-95, 152-154.
9 See Case 79/85: *Segers v Bestur van de Bedrijfsvereninging* [1986] ECR 2375 at para 11.
10 See Case 63/86: *Commission v Italy* [1988] ECR 29 at para 12.
11 Case 305/87: *Commission v Greece* [1989] ECR 1461 at para 23.
12 Eg Case C-375/92: *Commission v Spain* [1994] ECR I-923, paras 5-10.
13 Case C-311/97: *Bank of Scotland v Elliniko Dimosio* [1999] ECR I-2651, para 23.
14 Eg Case C-375/92: *Commission v Spain*, supra, paras 12-19.
15 Eg Case C-200/98: *X AB and Y AB v Riksskatteverket* [1999] ECR I-8261, paras 26-29.

imposed by or in the Member State to which the person concerned wishes to come [16] and to measures imposed by or in the Member State *from* which the person concerned comes.[17] A few concrete examples will be given to illustrate the point. In the *Reyners*[18] case, the ECJ held that a Dutch national resident in Belgium with the appropriate Belgian qualifications to practise law in Belgium could not be debarred from his professional activity on the ground that, according to Belgian law, a lawyer must be a Belgian national.

In *Thieffry v Conseil de l'Ordre des Avocats de Paris*[19] a Belgian lawyer, holding a Belgian degree of doctor of laws was recognized by the University of Paris I as having a qualification equivalent to a first degree in law of a French university and, on that basis, he took a course of study in Paris and obtained a qualifying certificate for the profession of *avocat* from the Institute of Judicial Studies of the University of Paris II. However the Paris Bar Council refused to register him for a course or practical training on the ground that he submitted no evidence of having obtained qualifications equivalent to a French first degree or a French doctorate in law as required by French law of 1971. On reference, the ECJ held that such a refusal was tantamount to indirect discrimination prohibited by EC Article 43 (ex Art 52).

In *Patrick v Ministère des Affaires Culturelles*[20] a British holder of a diploma from the UK Architectural Association applied for authorization to practise as an architect in France by virtue of a French law which enabled foreign nationals to practise, on the condition of reciprocity, on production of a certificate equivalent to that required for French architects. On reference from a Paris administrative tribunal, the ECJ, following the *Reyners* decision, held that a Member State could not make the right of establishment subject to an exceptional authorization if a national of another Member State fulfils the conditions laid down for its own nationals. The same principle was applied to a Dutch motor insurance claims investigator in Italy.[1]

In this context the judgment of the ECJ in the *Klopp* case complements that of the *Reyners* case. Klopp, a German lawyer, qualified as a lawyer both in Germany and France and wished to open an office in Paris whilst continuing his practice in Nuremberg, but the Paris Bar, on the basis of French practice that an *avocat* cannot practise simultaneously in more than one area of the *Cour d'Appel*, refused his application. The Court ruled in favour of Klopp.[2] This enabled the Courts of Appeal in Aix-en-Provence[3] and the *Cour de Cassation*,[4] respectively, to overrule the rule of practice prohibiting multiple chambers whether in France or in France and overseas. The ruling was also applied to doctors and dentists overseas[5] and persons with more than one place of business.[6]

16 Eg Case C-307/97: *Compagnie de Saint-Gobain v Finanzamt Aachen-Innenstadt* [1999] ECR I-6161.
17 Eg *X AB v Y AB*, supra; Case C-251/98: *Baass v Inspecteur der Belastingin Particulieren/ Ondernemingen Gorinchem* 13 April 2000.
18 Supra, p 518, note 17.
19 Case 71/76: [1977] ECR 765, [1977] 2 CMLR 373.
20 Case 11/77: [1977] ECR 1199, [1977] 2 CMLR 523.
 1 Case 90/76: *Van Ameyde v UCL* [1977] ECR 1091, [1977] 2 CMLR 478.
 2 Case 107/83: *Ordre des Avocats au Barreau de Paris v Klopp* [1984] ECR 2971, [1985] 1 CMLR 99.
 3 *Maître Cammarata v Conseil de l'Ordre des Avocats au Barreau de Marseille* [1988] 1 CMLR 243.
 4 *Conseil de l'Ordre des Avocats au Barreau de Nice v Raynel* [1990] 2 CMLR 190.
 5 Case 96/85: *Commission v France, Re Registration of Foreign Doctors* [1986] ECR 1475, [1986] 3 CMLR 57.
 6 Cases 143/87 and 154 and 155/87, p 517, note 15, supra.

In an earlier case[7] the ECJ thus dealt with the inhibition to the exercise of the right of establishment of a central heating contractor arising from the provision of EC Article 52 (now Art 43) which enables the Member States to regulate the position internally:

> 'Although it is true that the provision of services cannot be applied to situations which are purely internal to a Member State, the position nevertheless remains that the reference in Article 52 [now Art 43] to "nationals of a Member State" who wish to establish themselves "in the territory of another Member State" cannot be interpreted in such a way as to exclude from the benefit of Community law a given Member State's own nationals when the latter, owing to the fact that they have lawfully resided on the territory of another Member State and have there lawfully acquired a trade qualification which is recognized by the provisions of Community law, are, with regard to their State of origin, in a situation which may be assimilated to that of any other persons enjoying the rights and liberties guaranteed by the Treaty.'[8]

Under the case law, there are two qualifications to the rights and prohibitions derived from the Treaty. The first is that Community law cannot be relied on for abusive or fraudulent ends. The second is a more general qualification on the extent of the prohibitions contained in the Treaty.

A person may be denied the benefit of a provision of Community law if there is objective evidence to support the conclusion that he or she is relying upon the provision for some abusive or fraudulent end.[9] A typical example of the use of Community law for such an illegitimate end is its invocation in order to avoid the application to the person concerned of rules of national law that would otherwise be applicable to him or her. However, care needs to be taken when applying that principle to the facts of any particular case.

For example, in Case C-61/89: *Bouchoucha*,[10] a French national had obtained a qualification as an osteopath in the United Kingdom and attempted to practise as such in France on the strength of that qualification. In France, the profession of osteopath was regulated and only qualified doctors were entitled to practise as such. Mr Bouchoucha was not a qualified doctor. He was prosecuted by the French authorities and relied on Community law, saying that he should be allowed to practise as an osteopath in France on the strength of his United Kingdom qualification and that the French requirement that osteopaths be qualified doctors was disproportionate. The Court accepted that the Treaty did not preclude the application of the French rules governing the exercise of the profession of osteopath and said that Member States had a legitimate interest in preventing certain of their nationals from evading domestic legal requirements by means of facilities created under the Treaty. For that reason, the *Bouchoucha* case is occasionally cited as an illustration of the rule that Community law cannot be relied upon in order to achieve an abusive or fraudulent end. However, the

---

7 Case 115/78: *Knoors v Secretary of State for Economic Affairs* [1979] ECR 399 at para 24.
8 On situations purely internal to a Member State, see for example Case C-108/98: *RISAN Srl v Commune di Ischia* [1999] ECR I-5219. In such situations, reverse discrimination (that is, discrimination against a national of the State concerned) does not offend Community law: eg Case 24/89: *Re a German Advocate, German Federal Supreme Court* [1990] 1 CMLR 254.
9 Eg Case C-212/97: *Centros v Erhvervs-og Selskabsstyrelsen* [1999] ECR I-1459, paras 24-25.
10 [1990] ECR I-3551.

Bouchoucha case was one in which there was no system for recognizing the qualifications of osteopaths in the Community. Each Member State was in principle entitled to set its own standards regarding access to and the practice of that profession. In that sense, and in that alone, could it be said Mr Bouchoucha's reliance upon Community law was abusive or illegitimate?[11] The position would have been completely different had there been mutual recognition of qualifications (as there is in relation to other branches of medicine). In that event, the fact that Mr Bouchoucha had chosen to obtain his qualification in a Member State other than France would not have been sufficient to conclude that he had used Community law for an abusive or fraudulent end.

In consequence, before concluding that a provision of Community law is being invoked for an abusive or fraudulent end, such as the avoidance of the application of domestic law, it is necessary to identify the purpose of the provision of Community law: its purpose may in fact be to permit a person to avoid the application of national law. Thus, in the *Centros* case,[12] a Danish married couple resident in Denmark formed a company under the laws of England and Wales ('Centros') and then sought to set up a branch in Denmark. Under Danish law, foreign companies were entitled to do so but the Danish authorities refused to register the Centros branch on the ground that Centros did not trade in the United Kingdom and its creation was simply a device to get around a particular rule of Danish company law concerning the minimum paid up capital of limited liability companies. It was not denied that Centros had been set up in order to avoid the Danish rule. However, the Court rejected the argument that Community law could not be relied upon because the specific purpose of the right of establishment enshrined in the Treaty is to enable people to form companies under the laws of a Member State and use such companies to do business throughout the Community. Accordingly, the fact that a national of a Member State had chosen to form a company in the Member State whose company law was the least restrictive could not be regarded as an abuse of the right of establishment. In order to deal satisfactorily with the problem in the *Centros* case, the Court then turned to consider the second qualification to the rights and prohibitions in the Treaty referred to above.

When developing its views about the direct effect of the Treaty provisions, it soon became apparent to the Court that the right of establishment could not be regarded as an unfettered right based on the Treaty alone. In particular, there were situations in which the Member States had a legitimate interest in restricting the right of establishment in order to maintain such things as training standards and rules of professional conduct that were justified in the public interest. The Court therefore developed a limit on the scope of the Treaty rules that is best regarded as forming part of the definition of what may constitute a prohibited restriction on the right of establishment instead of being a derogation from or exception to that right.

The principal can today be formulated as follows – national measures that are liable to hinder or make less attractive the exercise of fundamental freedoms

---

11   It is therefore doubtful that the *Bouchoucha* case is a true example of reliance on Community law for an abusive or fraudulent end. It is in fact more often the case that abuse arises in the context of the freedom to provide services than the right of establishment. It has also arisen in the context of the Community legislation adopted in order to give effect to the right of establishment: see eg Case C-367/96: *Kefalas v Elliniko Dimosio* [1998] ECR I-2843.

12   Supra.

guaranteed by the Treaty (here the right of establishment; but the same applies to the freedom to provide services) are prohibited, subject to express provision otherwise in the Treaty, unless they satisfy the following four conditions: (i) they must apply in a non-discriminatory manner; (ii) they must be justified by imperative requirements in the general interest; (iii) they must be suitable for attaining the objective which they pursue; and (iv) they must not go beyond what is necessary in order to attain it.[13]

The first, third and fourth conditions are self-explanatory.[14] The second condition refers to 'imperative requirements in the general interest'. These are mandatory requirements. If their application is merely optional or facultative, they are not important enough to override a Treaty right. Not all mandatory requirements satisfy the second condition: to do so, they must be justified in the general interest. As that has been explained in the case law, that means that they may not serve an economic aim[15] but may concern: professional rules intended to protect recipients of services or consumers; protection of intellectual property; protection of workers; conservation of the national historic and artistic heritage; turning to account the archaeological, historical and artistic heritage of a country and the widest possible dissemination of knowledge of the artistic and cultural heritage of a country; the maintenance of pluralism in the media;[16] the maintenance of order in society;[17] road safety;[18] maintaining the good reputation of the financial sector;[19] and the effectiveness of fiscal supervision.[20] In addition to the guidance to be drawn from the case law, the Commission has in various areas attempted to summarise the principles governing the exercise of a particular professional or business activity.[1]

F. Harmonization of the professions

To make the right of establishment effective the Community, on the authority of EC Article 47(1)(2) (ex Art 57(1)(2)), embarked on a harmonization process which, according to the General Programme[2] would ensure access to professional activities on the evidence of 'actual and legitimate exercise of the activity in the country of origin'. In the *Thieffry*[3] case the ECJ thought that the objective of EC Article 47 (ex Art 57) was to reconcile the freedom of establishment with the application of the national professional rules justified by the general good

---

13 See eg the *Centros* case, supra, para 34.
14 Illustrations of how they are applied can be seen in the cases cited here. For example, in relation to the third and fourth conditions, see the *Centros* case, supra, paras 35-39.
15 Eg Case C-398/95: *Syndesmos ton en Elladi Touristikon kai Taxidiotikon Grafeion* [1997] ECR I-3091, paras 22-25.
16 See Case C-288/89: *Stichting Collectieve Antenne voorziening Gouda v Commissariat voor de Media* [1991] ECR I-4007, paras 14 (and the cases cited there) and 23. More recent cases include Case C-222/95: *Parodi v Banque Albert de Bary* [1997] ECR I-3899, paras 21-22.
17 Case C-275/92: *H M Customs & Excise v Schindler* [1994] ECR I-1039, para 58.
18 Case C-55/93: *van Schaik* [1994] ECR I-4837, para 19.
19 Case C-384/93: *Alpine Investments BV v Minister van Financien* [1995] ECR I-1141, para 44.
20 Case C-250/95: *Futura Participations SA v Administration des Contributions* [1997] ECR I-2471, para 31.
1 See eg the Commission's Interpretative Communication concerning the insurance sector: OJ 2000, C 43/5.
2 OJ 1974, Sp Ed Second Series IX, Title IV p 10.
3 Supra p 521, note 19.

and, in particular, to enact rules relating to organization, qualifications, professional ethics, supervision and responsibility for professional misconduct without discrimination on the ground of nationality.

The resulting Directives (repetitive in substance) purport to ensure the elimination of restrictions imposed upon non-nationals and to provide rules for the recognition of the relevant professional qualifications and standards of moral character and financial standing. They include measures for the exercise of the right of establishment in agriculture; horticulture; forestry; fishing; financial services; the film industry; mining and quarrying; electrical, gas, water and sanitary services; food and beverage manufacturing; manufacturing and processing industries; wholesale trade; retail trade; itinerant activities including hawkers and peddlers; trade in toxic products; intermediaries in commerce and industry; real estate and business services; restaurants and hotels; and other assorted activities, including astrology and fortune telling.

The second phase saw the attempt to harmonize the classical professions, in which the rules governing the formation and exercise of the medical professions have become the example to follow.[4] These Directives were followed by measures in respect of nursing;[5] dentistry;[6] midwives;[7] and veterinary[8] professions as well as exercise of the professions of architect[9] and pharmacist.[10]

The Directives on the medical professions reflect the pattern of legislation by professions or sectors. Under Directive 93/16 and in relation to what can be described as primary or basic qualifications as a medical practitioner, each Member State is obliged to recognize certain specific qualifications in medicine granted by the other Member States and to give to those qualifications the same effect in its territory as the comparable qualification awarded by that state.[11] In order to underpin the system of mutual recognition of qualifications, the Member States are also obliged to ensure that persons wishing to take up and pursue a medical profession have a qualification that meets certain minimum standards laid down in the Directive. Thus, each Member State can be confident that any person holding one of the specified qualifications granted in another Member State has been trained up to the same basic standards required within its own territory; and each Member State can be confident that no person is able to practise as a medical practitioner within any of the Member States unless he or she has those basic standards. In the case of qualifications in specialised medicine (such as thoracic surgery or tropical medicine), the position is more varied. Not all the Member States have the same specialised qualifications. It is only to the extent

---

4   Dir 93/16 (OJ 1993, L165/1), as amended. That Directive replaced: Dir 75/362 (OJ 1975, L167/1) (recognition of qualifications); Dir 75/363 (OJ 1975, L167/14) (medical training); 75/364 (OJ 1975, L167/17) (advisory committee on medical training); Council Decision 75/365 (OJ 1975, L167/19) (advisory committee of senior public health officials); Dir 86/457 (OJ 1986, L267/26) (special training for general medical practitioners).
5   Dir 77/4520 (OJ 1977, L176/1) and 77/453 (OJ 1977, L176/8), as amended.
6   Dir 78/686 (OJ 1978, L233/1) and 78/687 (OJ 1978, L233/10), as amended.
7   Dir 80/154 (OJ 1980, L33/1) and 80/155 (OJ 1980, L33/8); Decisions 80/156 (OJ 1980, L33/13) and 80/157 (OJ 1980, L33/15), as amended.
8   Dir 78/1026 (OJ 1978, L362/1); 78/1027 (OJ 1978, L362/7); 78/1028 (OJ 1978, L362/10), as amended.
9   Dir 85/384 (OJ 1985, L223/15).
10 Dir 85/432 (OJ 1985, L253/34) (qualification in pharmacy); Dec 85/433, OJ 1985, L253/37 (recognition of diplomas in pharmacy); Dec 85/434 (OJ 1985, L253/37), as amended.
11 On the obligation to recognize qualifications, see Case 271/82: *Auer v Ministère Public* [1983] ECR 2727.

that a Member State has a qualification in a particular speciality that it is obliged to recognize and give effect to the comparable qualification in another Member State. The specialities in question and the Member States that offer qualifications in them are listed in the Directive. As in the case of primary or basic qualifications, the Directive lays down minimum standards for the training that must be completed in order to obtain a qualification in a particular specialization.[12] The Directive also provides for the recognition by a Member State of periods of training completed in other Member States so that a person who has not yet obtained a particular qualification can move from one Member State to another without having to start his or her training again from the very beginning. The Directive also contains provisions on such things as the use of professional and academic titles, ethical standards and the recognition of qualifications under national social security schemes.

Piecemeal legislation, such as that originally applied to the medical professions proved slow and cumbersome; and was abandoned in favour of a global scheme by Directive 89/48[13] on 'a general system for the recognition of high education diplomas awarded on completion of professional education and training of at least three years' duration', which came into effect on 11 January 1989. It implies a comparability of educational standards in the Community and applies to professions regulated by national laws except those (for example the medical professions and others) already governed by Community legislation. It introduces a general system unrelated as hitherto to any specific profession relying on comparability of university and similar courses. It is limited to the recognition of foreign qualifications necessary for the exercise of the right of establishment, leaving to the Member States the details of implementation. It reserves to the Member States the right to regulate and to ensure respect for the rules of personal conduct and etiquette of the members of the professions. It also provides for the documentation and proof of good character or good repute, etc. Member States may impose in addition an adoption, or aptitude test but not both cumulatively. This is to ensure that paper qualifications are confirmed by practical experience.

Directive 89/48 has been limited to professions based on higher education of university type. Where the professions require a lower educational standard Decision 92/51[14] has instituted a harmonization scheme based on secondary and post-secondary education. The underlying principles are the same as in Directive 89/48. However, it covers two levels of education and training involving occupations, the pursuit of which depends upon the possession of professional or vocational education and training qualifications of secondary level and generally requires manual skills. The Directive also provides for the recognition of such qualifications even if they have been acquired solely through occupational experience in a Member State which does not regulate such occupation by law.

Even in the absence of harmonizing Directives enacted under EC Article 47 (ex Art 57), recognition of diplomas may be required under EC Article 43 (ex Art 52) on the basis that EC Article 43 (ex Art 52) 'is a manifestation of the principle of equal treatment under Article 7 of the Treaty'.[15] This was already

---

12   Cf Case 306/84: *Commission v Belgium* [1987] ECR 675.
13   OJ 1989, L19/16.
14   OJ 1992, L209, as amended.
15   Case 63/86: *Commission v Italy* [1988] ECR 29; Case 305/87: *Commission v Greece* [1989] ECR 1461.
16   Title III (B) p 8.

part of the General Programme[16] and the Community jurisprudence reflected in the *Thieffry*[17] case where the ECJ considered that the refusal of the Paris Bar to allow practical training despite a Belgian academic qualification and a French qualifying certificate because there was no French equivalence, amounted to indirect discrimination. The Court subsequently held[18] that, when dealing with applications for authorization to practise a profession regulated by the national law, the authorities are obliged to consider qualifications acquired in another Member State and compare skills evidenced by foreign diplomas with the skills required by national rules. Such comparison must be carried out according to a procedure that would ensure the protection of rights conferred by the Treaty on nationals of Member States. Moreover the authorities must give the reasons for their decisions and the procedure must enable the applicants to rely on a judicial review in which the legality of national decisions can be tested under Community law.

However, it has to be conceded that legislation is a more powerful instrument of legal certainty than case law. Harmonization of the professions serves, clearly, the purpose of a People's Europe quite apart from the economic integration.

G. Establishment of companies

EC Article 48 (ex Art 58) provides:

> 'Companies or firms formed in accordance with the law of a Member State and having their registered office, central administration or principal place of business within the Community shall, for the purposes of this Chapter, be treated in the same way as natural persons who are nationals of Member States.'

However, though treated like 'natural persons', companies (ie artificial legal persons) do not enjoy exactly the same right to mobility so as to establish themselves in the Community. Referring to the provisions of EC Articles 43 and 48 (ex Arts 52 and 58) the ECJ held:

> 'Even though those provisions are directed mainly to ensuring that foreign nationals and companies are treated in the host Member State in the same way as nationals of that State, they also prohibit the Member State of origin from hindering the establishment in another Member State of one of its nationals or of a company incorporated under its legislation which comes within the definition contained in Article 58 [now Art 48].'[19]

According to EC Article 48(2) (ex Art 58(2)), 'companies or firms' means:

> 'companies or firms constituted under civil or commercial law, including co-operative societies, and other legal persons governed by public or private law, save those which are non-profit-making'.

Thus EC Article 48 (ex Art 58) contemplates a wide range of beneficiaries[20] though reference to 'other legal persons' implies legal personality, ie the capacity of entering transactions within the terms of the instruments of incorporation as well as the power to sue and be sued in its own name and on its own account.

---

17 See supra, p 521, note 19.
18 Case 222/86: *UNECTEF v George Heylens, Re a Football Trainer* [1987] ECR 4097, [1989] 1 CMLR 901; Case C-340/89: *Vlassopoulou v Ministerium für Justiz, Re a Lawyer* [1991] ECR I-2357, [1993] 2 CMLR 221.
19 Case 81/87: *Ex p Daily Mail and General Trust plc* [1988] ECR 5483 at para 16.
20 Everling, op cit, p 69.

Non-profit-making bodies corporate are exempt because the Treaty has economic objectives but there may be situations where a religious or charitable organization becomes engaged in commercial or other economic activities.[1]

A company or firm formed in accordance with the law of a Member State is entitled to establish itself anywhere in the Community as long as it has a registered office, a central administration or a principal place of business in the Community. Therefore a state would be in breach of the Treaty if it treated a company differently solely because its registered office were in another Member State.[2] Moreover, a different tax treatment, specially, would be inconsistent with the Treaty because, as ruled the Court:

'The second sentence of the first paragraph of Article 52 [now Art 43] expressly leaves traders to choose the appropriate legal form in which to pursue their activities in another Member State and that freedom of choice must not be limited by discriminatory tax provisions.'[3]

The principle of equal treatment in taxation was applied to a company incorporated under German law whose registered office was situated in Germany[4] but which did not qualify, under British law, for repayment of overpaid tax because it was not, for tax purposes, a company resident in the United Kingdom. The ECJ, following its previous judgments,[5] held that 'Articles 52 and 58 [now Arts 43 and 48] . . . prevent the legislation of a Member State from granting repayment supplement on overpaid tax to companies which are resident for tax purposes in that state whilst refusing the supplement to companies which are resident for tax purposes in another Member State. The fact that the latter would not have been exempt from tax if they had been resident in that state is of no relevance in that regard.'[6]

In the case of a company, the right of establishment is generally exercised by the setting up of agencies, branches or subsidiaries as is expressly provided in the second paragraph of EC Article 43 (ex Art 52).[7]

However a company registered in one Member State which maintains a permanent presence in another Member State 'comes within the scope of the Treaty . . . even if that presence does not take the form of a branch or agency but consists merely of an office managed by the undertaking's own staff or by a person who is independent as would be the case with an agency'.[8]

For practical purposes a company set up in a Member State (primary establishment) where it has its registered office or its principal place of business, will establish a secondary establishment in the form of a branch, a subsidiary or simply a permanent presence. The place of the primary establishment serves as the connecting factor with the legal system of a Member State in the same way as nationality in the case of a natural person; and the different forms of secondary establishment amount to an exercise of the right of establishment guaranteed by the Treaty.[9]

---

1 See eg Case 196/87: *Steymann* [1988] ECR 6159.
2 Case 79/85: *Segers* [1986] ECR 2375, [1987] 2 CMLR 247.
3 Case 270/83: *Commission v France* [1986] ECR 273 at para 22, [1987] 1 CMLR 401.
4 Case C-330/91: *R v IRC, ex p Commerzbank AG* [1993] ECR I-4017, [1993] 4 All ER 37.
5 Case 270/83, supra and Case 152/73: *Sotgiu v Deutsche Bundespost* [1974] ECR 153.
6 Case 330/91, supra, paras 18-20.
7 Case 81/87, supra, at para 17.
8 Case 205/84: *Commission v Germany* [1986] ECR 3755 at para 21, [1987] 2 CMLR.
9 Case 79/85: supra, note 2, paras 12-14; and, more recently, Case C-141/99: *Algemene Maatschappij voor Investering en Dienstverlening v Belgium* 14 December 2000.

A change of primary establishment may have an inhibiting effect if the result would be the loss of the corporate capacity in the state of incorporation or a necessity of setting up anew in the host state. The answer to this problem lies in harmonization of company law[10] into a coherent Community system[11] which yet remains to be accomplished seeing that the 1968 Convention on the Mutual Recognition of Companies and Bodies Corporate has not been ratified.

However the ECJ recognized that an undertaking established in a Member State providing services in the construction and public works sector in another Member State may move with its own labour force which it brings from the former for the duration of the works in question.[12]

EC Article 44(3)(f) (ex Art 54(3)(f)) purports to remove restrictions on the transfer of senior personnel involved in the management of companies. If such persons enjoy the freedom of movement the provision appears superfluous but, if, as often happens, they are nationals of third countries the problem may have to be resolved through international agreements in accordance with EC Article 49(2) (ex Art 59(2)) which, as yet, have not materialized.

H. Harmonization of company law[13]

Whilst the Member States are bound to abolish existing restrictions on the right of establishment and refrain from introducing any new ones, the Community must co-ordinate the safeguards for the protection of the interests of members and others, which are applied by the Member States to companies and firms, with a view to making such safeguards equivalent throughout the Community.[14]

In order to promote the mobility of the corporate providers of services and to facilitate their establishment a Convention under EC Article 293 (ex Art 220), on the Mutual Recognition of Companies and Bodies Corporate was signed in 1968 but it still awaits ratification. The failure of this measure made the harmonization of company law imperative.

The complexity of the subject and the diversity of national laws have forced the Community to adopt a piecemeal approach to company legislation. This has been achieved so far by the following:

(1) The First Directive[15] deals with the duty of disclosure, the filing of accounts and other documents relevant to the formation of the company and the protection of the public as well as the obligations of company's officers;

(2) The Second Directive[16] concerns the formation of public companies and the maintenance of capital;

(3) The Third Directive[17] lays down the conditions required for the mergers of public companies registered in the same Member State;

(4) The Fourth Directive[18] deals with the annual accounts of limited liability companies, other than banks and insurance companies;

10 See Case 81/87, supra, at para 23.
11 See Ch 36, pp 837 et seq.
12 Case C-113/89: *Rush Portugesa Lda v Office nationale d'immigration* [1990] ECR I-1417.
13 For details see Maitland-Walker, S, *Guide to European Company Laws* (2nd edn, 1997).
14 EEC Art 54(3)(g).
15 68/151 (OJ 1968, 41).
16 77/91 (OJ 1977, L26/1).
17 78/855 (OJ 1978, L295/36).
18 78/660 (OJ 1978, L222/11).

(5) The Sixth Directive[19] deals with divisions of public companies and complements the Directive on mergers;

(6) The Seventh Directive[20] regulates consolidated annual accounts of companies, other than banks and insurance companies;

(7) The Eighth Directive[1] standardizes the auditing of companies most commonly involved in business in the EC;

(8) The Eleventh Directive[2] deals with disclosures and the accounts of branches of companies established in another Member State or in a non-Community country;

(9) The Twelfth Directive[3] regulates the formation of private limited liability companies by individuals.

In additional to the nine directives on the statute book there is a regulation[4] on the European Economic Interest Grouping with the object of facilitating, or developing, the economic activities of enterprises across the national frontiers without losing their independence but without making profits for the grouping itself and a draft regulation[5] providing for a European Company (Societas Europea) statute. It contains a complete code of law with the object of creating a European alternative to national company law. Such a company would be formed by the merger of companies from two or more Member States, though individuals may become its shareholders on transfer of shares or an increase of capital. It could be created anywhere in the EC and would have the status of a public company registered at the Court of Justice. It would be managed broadly on the lines envisaged by the Draft Fifth Directive.

There are still on the table the following proposals:

(1) The highly controversial Fifth Directive which deals with the composition of the boards of public companies, the compulsory workers' participation in management, the annual general meeting, annual audit and the appointment of independent auditors;

(2) The Ninth Directive on the conduct of groups of companies and the protection of employees, creditors and the minority interests in a dependent company;

(3) The Tenth Directive concerning mergers between public companies registered in different Member States;

(4) The Thirteenth Directive on take-overs purporting to establish minimum rules for such operations;

(5) The Partnership Directive purporting to extend the provision of the Fourth and Seventh Directives to partnerships;

(6) The Directive to amend the Fourth Directive to extend its application to small and medium-sized companies and to make its provisions less stringent;

(7) The Significant Shareholding Directive laying down minimum rules for the disclosure of changes in shareholdings of listed companies.

---

19 82/891 (OJ 1982, L378/47).
20 83/349 (OJ 1983, L193/1).
 1 84/253 (OJ 1984, L126/20).
 2 88/627 (OJ 1988, L348/62).
 3 OJ 1989, L395/36.
 4 2137/85 (OJ 1985, L199/1).
 5 OJ 1989, C 263/69.

Chapter 21

Freedom to provide services (EC Articles 49-55 (ex Articles 59-66))

A. General principles

According to EC Article 50 (ex Art 60), 'services' means services that are 'normally provided for remuneration', particularly activities of an industrial or commercial character, or craftsmanship and professional activities. The concept is broad and general while the descriptive definition is non-exhaustive. However, the vagueness of the concept necessitated the ECJ to resolve the doubt whether certain activities such as televised commercial advertising;[1] stock exchange operations carried out by a bank on a client's instructions;[2] commercial agency;[3] employment agency;[4] tourism;[5] and lottery activities[6] fell within the concept of services. By implication services rendered gratis are outside the Treaty.[7] The freedom to provide services encompasses the right to supply and to receive the benefit of economic activities performed outside the context of an employment relationship. It covers situations in which the provider and the recipient of the service are in different Member

---

1   Case 155/73: *Italy v Sacchi* [1974] ECR 409, [1974] 2 CMLR 177.
2   Case 15/78: *Société Générale Alsacienne de Banque v Koestler* [1978] ECR 1971, [1979] 1 CMLR 89.
3   Cases 110, 111/78: *Ministère Public and ASBL v Van Wesemael and Poupaert* [1979] ECR 35, [1979] 3 CMLR 87.
4   Case 279/80: *Re Alfred John Webb* [1982] 1 CMLR 719.
5   Cases 286/82 and 26/83: *Luisi and Carbone v Ministero del Tesoro* [1984] ECR 377, [1985] 3 CMLR 52.
6   Case C-275/92: *Customs and Excise Comrs v Schindler* [1994] ECR I-1039, Case C-124/97: *Läärä v Kihlakunnansjyttäjä* [1999] ECR I-6067.
7   See A-G Warner in Cases 52/79: *Procureur du Roi v Debauve* [1980] ECR 833 and 62/79: *Coditel v Ciné vog Films* [1980] ECR 881, Opinion at 876; [1981] 2 CMLR 362. Both cases are relevant to television advertising: Case 352/85: *Bond van Averteerders* [1988] ECR 2085 at paras 31-39. Sporting activities may or may not be economic activities, depending upon the circumstances: see, for example, Cases C-51/96 and C-191/97: *Deliège v Ligue francophone de judo et disciplines associées*, 11 April 2000.

States and situations in which both the provider and the recipient are in the same Member State but the provision of the service requires one of them to go to another Member State or effect the supply across an internal Community frontier.[8] The beneficiaries of the freedom to provide services are not only the persons who provide the services but also the persons who receive them.[9]

Provision of a service is often connected with the exercise of a profession and it is in this respect complementary to the right of establishment. However the freedom to provide services is intended to cover the transnational conduct of economic activities by means that fall short of the creation of an establishment in a different Member State. The provision of services should be separated from the movement of goods. As explained by the ECJ, for example, copyright imports are covered by the free movement of goods rules of the Treaty whereas performing rights constitute services, not goods and are, therefore, outside the scope of those rules.[10]

B.   Abolition of restrictions on the freedom of services

EC Article 49 (ex Art 59) provides for progressive abolition of restrictions on freedom to provide services in respect of nationals of Member States who are established in a state of the Community other than that of the person for whom the services are intended. In the light of judicial interpretation:[11]

EC Articles 49 and 50 (ex Arts 59 and 60):

> 'preclude a Member State from prohibiting a person providing services established in another Member State moving freely on its territory with all his staff and preclude that Member State from making the movement of staff in question subject to restriction such as a condition as to engagement *in situ* or an obligation to obtain a work permit. To impose such conditions on the person providing services established in another Member State discriminates against that person in relation to his competitors established in the host country who are able to use their own staff without restrictions, and moreover affects his ability to provide the service.'

In Case 205/84[12] the Court considered that the requirement of a permanent establishment in another Member State was 'the very negation' of freedom to provide insurance services if it was a condition of doing business in that state.

On the other hand, when dealing with a restriction based on residential qualification of a properly qualified professional person the ECJ[13] ruled that:

---

8   For example: a broadcasting company in State A supplies television broadcasts to a customer in State B; a plumber in State A goes to State B to install central heating in the holiday home of a customer resident in State A; a tourist resident in State A goes to State B in order to receive services provided in State B by persons resident there; a violin virtuoso resident in State A goes to State B in order to participate in a concert held there.

9   Eg the *Luisi* and *Carbone* cases, supra – tourists; Case C-294/97: *Eurowings Luftverkehrs AG v Finanzamt Dortmund-Unna* [1999] ECR I-7447, para 34.

10   Case 262/81: *Coditel v Ciné Vog Films SA (No 2)* [1982] ECR 3381, [1983] 1 CMLR 49; See also Case 352/85, supra.

11   Case C-113/89: *Rush Portuguesa Lda v Office Nationale d'Immigration* [1990] ECR I-1417: at para 12.

12   *Commission v Germany Re Co-Insurance* [1986] ECR 3755 para 52; [1987] 2 CMLR 69.

13   Case 33/74: *Van Binsbergen v Bedrijfverening voor de Metaalnijverheid* [1974] ECR 1299 at para 13, [1975] 1 CMLR 298.

'. . . a Member State cannot be denied the right to take measures to prevent the exercise by a person providing services whose activity is entirely or principally directed towards its territory of the freedom guaranteed by Article 59 [now Art 49] for the purpose of avoiding the professional rules of conduct which would be applicable to him if he were established in that state; such a situation may be subject to judicial control under the provisions of the chapter relating to the right of establishment and not that on the provision of services.'

In another case[14] the Court applied EC Article 49, (ex Art 59), to a Dutch national resident in Belgium who ran an insurance agency in the Netherlands since the object of the Article was to abolish restrictions on freedom to provide services imposed on persons 'who do not reside in the State where the service is to be performed'. Although many of the decided cases concern restrictions that are discriminatory in nature, any restriction that is liable to prohibit, impede or render less advantageous the activities of a provider of services in another Member State is prohibited even if it is not discriminatory in nature. However, as in the case of the right of establishment,[15] the freedom to provide services may be restricted by rules that are justified by overriding requirements relating to the public interest.[16]

In Case 76/81[17] the ECJ interpreted Directive 71/305 as precluding a Member State from requiring a tenderer for a public works contract, established in another state, to furnish proof by any means, for example, by an establishment permit, other than those prescribed in Articles 23-26 of that Directive that he satisfied the criteria laid down in those provisions and relating to his good standing and qualifications. However, the State is free to require explanation of an obviously abnormally low tender.

Restrictions on the freedom of services must be removed as regards both the providers and the recipients of services. Thus in the first place, the recipient of a service has a primary right to remain in the Member State of which he is not a national for the purpose of receiving the service in question.[18] In *Luisi* and *Carbone*[19] the ECJ held that individuals who were recipients of services were free to go to another state for medical treatment and tourism, the two activities involving services.

In a rather extreme situation a British tourist, injured by unidentified assailants in the Paris metro, was awarded the right to compensation available to victims of crime which was originally denied to him by the French authorities on the ground that the scheme was not available to non-nationals. The ECJ, citing *Luisi* and *Carbone*,[20] thus summarized the protection to which the tourist was entitled under Community law:[1]

'When Community law guarantees a natural person the freedom to go to another Member State the protection of that person from harm in the Member

14 Case 39/75: *Coenen v Sociaal-Economische Raad* [1975] ECR 1547, [1976] 1 CMLR 30.
15 See pp 523–524, supra.
16 Eg Cases C-369/96 and C-376/96: *Arblade v Leloup* [1999] ECR I-8453, in particular paras 33-39.
17 *Transporoute et Travaux SA v Minister of Public Works* [1982] ECR 417.
18 See Case 118/75: *Watson and Belmann* [1976] ECR 1185 at para 16, sub nom *The State v Watson and Belmann* [1976] 2 CMLR 552.
19 Cases 286/82 and 26/83: [1984] ECR 377, [1985] 3 CMLR 52.
20 Supra, at para 9.
1 Case 186/87: *Cowan v Trésor Public* [1989] ECR 195 at para 17, [1990] 2 CMLR 613.

State in question, on the same basis as that of nationals and persons residing there, is a corollary of that freedom of movement. It follows that the prohibition of discrimination is applicable to recipients of services within the meaning of the Treaty as regards protection against the risk of assault and the right to obtain financial compensation provided for by national law when that risk materializes.'

The Court also emphasized[2] the function of incompatibility with EC Article 12 (ex Art 6, ex ex Art 7) in affording the protection of the tourist, on the ground of non-discrimination.[3]

The case law keeps on recording instances of incompatibility with EC Article 49 (ex Art 59) such as for example the Dutch prohibition of cable network operators from relaying programmes received via satellite from broadcasts in other Member States which contained advertisements aimed directly at the audience in the Netherlands;[4] and national rules which prohibited a company established in one Member State from providing a patent monitoring service in another Member State on the ground that such service in that state was reserved to experts holding special professional qualifications.[5] The Court objected not only to discrimination on the ground of nationality of the provider of the service but also on the ground that services lawfully provided in another Member State were restricted.

However the Court will not object to discrimination which is objectively justified. Thus, for example, an insurance scheme whereby no-claim bonuses were denied to owners of vehicles carrying customs registration plates was held to be compatible with EC Articles 12 and 49 (then Arts 7 and 59) since it was based on objective actuarial criteria and the fact of registration under customs plates. The scheme, though concerning mainly the nationals of other Member States, was also able to affect the citizens of the German Federal Republic.[6]

EC Article 52 (ex Art 63), like EC Article 44 (ex Art 54) on establishment, provided for a General Programme for the abolition of restrictions in the field of services[7] which was analogous to the General Programme for the abolition of restrictions on the right of establishment. The Programme also provides for transitional measures in these fields. However in the light of the ever expanding case law (especially the application of EC Article 12 (ex Art 6, ex ex Art 7) to EC Articles 43 and 49 (ex Arts 52 and 59)) legislation to eliminate restrictions seems to have become superfluous in a number of respects.

C. Exceptions and derogations

Like the right of establishment, the freedom to provide services is constrained by exceptions and derogations. EC Article 45 (ex Art 55), which is applicable to both establishment and services, refers to the exercise of official authority.

2 At paras 14 and 15.
3 See also Case 63/86: *Commission v Italy* [1988] ECR 29, [1989] 2 CMLR 601; Case 305/87: *Commission v Greece* [1989] ECR 1461, [1991] 1 CMLR 611.
4 Case 352/85: *Bond van Averteerders v Netherlands* [1988] ECR 2085, [1989] CMLR 113. Cf Case C-6/98: *Arbeitsgemeinschaft Deutscher Rundfunkan-stallt v PRO Seben Media AG* [1999] ECR I-7599.
5 Case C-76/90: *Säger v Dennemeyer & Co Ltd* [1991] ECR I-4221 at para 12.
6 Case 251/83: *Eberhard Haug-Adrion v Frankfurther Versicherungs-AG* [1984] ECR 4277, [1985] 3 CMLR 266.
7 36/62 (OJ 1962, p 7).

The case law explaining employment on public service under EC Article 39(4) (ex Art 48(4)) is relevant to EC Article 45 (ex Art 55).[8]

Derogations regarding the professions[9] and services can be invoked by Member States by analogy to derogations from the freedom of movement of persons on grounds of public policy, public security and public health.[10] Although the wording differs in so far as EC Article 46(1) (ex Art 56(1)), adds a rider regarding special treatment for foreign nationals by law, regulation or administrative action, the effect is the same. Therefore, the case law generated by the derogation regarding the movement of persons applies, where appropriate, to members of the professions and providers of services.

The ECJ reiterated the principle that derogations have to be interpreted restrictively and the grounds thereof expressly stated in the Treaty have to be justified by the state.[11] Moreover, any measures taken under authority of EC Articles 46 or 55 (ex Arts 56 or 66) must not be disproportionate to the objective the state purports to achieve.[12]

In Case 15/78[13] the ECJ had to interpret the meaning of service and to decide whether, in the circumstances, the national law could derogate from the freedom of the service performed in another Member State. Mr Koestler, when resident in France, made arrangements with a French bank whereby the bank would buy and sell shares on his behalf and credit or debit his account. The transaction was legal in France but Mr Koestler became indebted to the bank and was unable to meet his obligation. The bank endeavoured to recover in Germany where the debtor had returned without having paid his debts. The Court ruled the transaction was in the nature of a service but the bank was unable to recover because, according to German law, it was classified as a wager and, as such, it was unrecoverable.[14]

In Case C-159/90[15] the Court had to consider the provision of abortion as a service available in other Member States, notably in the United Kingdom, but permitted only in exceptional circumstances in Ireland.

The question arose in an action for an injunction brought by the Society for the Protection of Unborn Children (SPUC) against representatives of students' organizations engaged in the distribution of information relating to the identity and location of abortion clinics in the United Kingdom. The Irish court referred to the ECJ three questions, ie:

(1) whether the medical termination of pregnancy comes within the definition of 'services' governed by the EC Treaty;
(2) whether in the absence of uniformity of national laws in this regard, a Member State A (Ireland) can prohibit the distribution of information on the facilities for legal abortion in another Member State B (the UK);
(3) whether under EC law a person in State A has a right to distribute such information where abortion is prohibited both under the constitution and the criminal law whilst it is lawful in State B.

---

8   See supra, p 494.
9   See supra, p 500.
10 EC Arts 46 and 55 (ex Arts 56 and 66).
11 Case 352/85, supra at paras 32-34.
12 Ibid at para 36.
13 *Societé Générale Alsacienne de Banque SA v Koestler* [1978] ECR 1971, [1979] 1 CMLR 89.
14 Ibid at para 5.
15 *Society for the Protection of Unborn Children Ireland Ltd (SPUC) v Stephen Grogan* [1991] ECR I-4685, [1991] 3 CMLR 849.

The ECJ answered the first question in the affirmative holding that the provision of abortion is a service within the meaning of EC Article 50 (ex Art 60), which defines 'services' as services normally provided for remuneration including, in particular, activities of an industrial and commercial character and activities of craftsmen and of the professions, but did not attempt to relate abortion to any of the categories of services listed above. It staved off the moral question saying that 'it is not for the Court to substitute its assessment for that of the legislature in those Member States where the activities in question are practised legally'.[16]

Considering the second and third questions the ECJ had to determine whether Ireland had, within EC law, the right to restrict dissemination of information about the facilities available in the UK and the students had the right to disseminate such information. The Court distinguished the present case from Case C-362/88[17] in which it held that a prohibition on advertising goods was capable of constituting a barrier to free movement of goods and, therefore, had to be seen in that context. Since, in the present case, the defendants were not engaged in a commercial activity but merely indulged in expressing their views and disseminating information which was independent of the economic activity carried on by the abortion clinics, an analogy to the free movement of goods could not be maintained. Consequently the matter fell under EC Article 52 (ex Art 63) which forbade the Member States introducing any new restrictions on the freedom to provide services since the entry into force of the Treaty. Prohibition to disseminate information on activities which contravened the Irish constitution and Irish criminal law could not be classified as 'new restrictions'. However, the ECJ, perhaps gratuitously, raised the question of commercial advertising. If the students have been engaged in commercial advertising their activities might have been considered a 'service' but, in such a hypothesis, the argument would have shifted in the area of derogation on the ground of public policy. The answer, it is submitted, should not be different.

The Court dismissed the argument that, by curbing the defendants' activities, Ireland infringed Article 10(1) of the Human Rights Convention as it considered that it was not required to apply the Convention to matters outside the domain covered by the Treaty.

Advocate-General Van Gerven considered inter alia 'the imperative requirements of public interest' entrenched in national law which may justify limitations on the freedom to provide services provided they are applied without discrimination and subject to proportionality. Citing Cases 15/78[18] and 52/79[19] he concluded that it is for each Member State to define these concepts in accordance with 'its scale of values'.

As the list of 'public interests' is not closed the case law tends to expand, thus justifying restrictions on the provisions of services to protect, for example, historical, artistic and archaeological treasures[20] or cultural interests.[1]

---

16   Ibid at para 20.
17   *GB-INNO-BM v Confédération du Commerce Luxembourgeoise Asbl* [1990] ECR I-667.
18   Supra, p 535, note 13.
19   Supra, p 531, note 7.
20   Case C-154/89: *Commission v France* [1991] ECR I-659.
 1   Case 353/89: *Commission v Netherlands* [1991] ECR I-4069. See further pp 523–524, supra.

D. Harmonization legislation

EC Articles 41 and 55 (ex Arts 50 and 66) provide for legislation for the mutual recognition of diplomas, certificates and other proof of formal qualifications in the services sector. The resulting harmonizing process of professions applies *mutatis mutandis* to the providers of services.[2] Moreover EC Article 51 (ex Art 61) provides that the harmonization of services in certain sectors shall be carried out in context of specific Treaty provisions, ie transport policy[3] and banking and insurance 'in step with the progressive liberalization of movements of capital'.

The harmonizing legislation that has so far been adopted tends to deal both with the right of establishment and with the function to provide services because the basic concerns are the same. In particular areas, of which financial services is a good example, the provisions dealing with the freedom to provide services can be highly complex.[4]

---

2 See Ch 20, supra.
3 See infra EC Art 61.
4 See, for example, Dir 73/239 (OJ 1973, L228/3), as amended, on direct non-life insurance, and the more diffuse banking legislation. So far as the freedom to provide services is concerned, the main measures in these areas are Dir 92/49 (OJ 1992, L228/1) – insurance – and Dir 89/646 (OJ 1989, L386/1) – banking.

Chapter 22

Social security (EC Article 42 (ex Article 51))

A. General principles

EC Article 42 (ex Art 51) charges the Council to enact such measures 'in the field of social security as are necessary to provide freedom of movement for workers' and to that end 'make arrangements to secure for migrant workers and their dependants' aggregation of benefits and payment of benefits to persons resident in the territories of Member States. The principles had to be extended to other groups of persons to take account of developments in the field of establishment and services.

There is, as yet, no uniform Community social security system and the Member States retain competence to determine the conditions for the grant of social security benefits (as long as those conditions do not involve discrimination between Community workers,[1] or otherwise infringe the right of citizens of the Union to move around and reside in the territory of the Member States).[2] However the diversity of the national systems is so great that the Community legislation cannot achieve more than a co-ordination of national rules along certain common principles. The essential purpose of that co-ordination is to achieve freedom of movement throughout the Community. Other EC legislation affects social security systems for the purpose, in particular, of securing equal treatment between men and women; but such legislation is considered in Chapter 32. Basic principles distinguish between social security, social assistance and social advantage.

Social security benefits are available as of right in consequence of either a comprehensive national scheme of universal application or affiliation to a variety of arrangements coming within the concept of the national system; but social assistance benefits depend on the needs of the individual claimant and are in the nature of discretionary grants awarded out of the public purse. Since there is no

---

1 Eg Case C-320/95: *Alvite v Inem and INSS* [1999] ECR I-951, para 23.
2 Case C-135/99: *Elsen v Bundesversicherungs-anstalt fur Angestellte* 23 November 2000, para 33.

universality in the Community in this respect each Member State has to make a declaration explaining the nature of benefits available under its system.[3] The ECJ held on certain occasions that these declarations were inconclusive since the two categories of benefits overlapped and in such cases found at first for the claimants[4] but later stated that a declaration must be accepted as proof that the particular benefits granted on the basis of that law are social security benefits.[5] Even if the national law fails to classify the benefit (for example compensation for victims of Nazi persecution in Germany) it does not necessarily follow that it does not fall within the scope of the Regulation.[6] The problems of classification have receded due to the amendment of Regulation 1408/71 by Regulation 1247/92[7] which has extended the range of benefits as of right.

In the *Newton* case[8] the ECJ considered whether a mobility allowance to a handicapped person payable in the United Kingdom is also payable where such a person resides in another Member State. If such benefit were to be classified as a social security benefit it would not be restricted by the national residence rule.[9] The Court thought that the mobility allowance had a twofold function, ie to ensure a minimum income to a handicapped person who is embraced by the social security system and also to provide a supplementary income to recipients of social security benefits who suffer from physical disability. Where a disabled person is covered by virtue of his previous occupational activity, the mobility allowance provided under the British system is to be classified as a social security benefit.

In the *Hughes*[10] case the Court held that a family credit, ie a weekly non-contributory cash benefit available for families of limited means, is subject to Article 4(1) of the Regulation. It has to be classified as a social security benefit, not a social welfare benefit because it is granted on the basis of a statutory provision without any individual or discretionary assessment of personal needs.

Social advantage is available on the principle of non-discrimination under Regulation 1612/68.[11] Though it is not related to social security its application may raise the question of classification between social security and social assistance. Thus in Cases 379-381/85 and 93/86[12] the 'topping-up' of low income to the minimum wage level was considered to be available to a worker as of right but it was not so where the applicant was not yet a worker[13] for such benefit could not be claimed through a father as a social advantage available to a worker. The only right the applicant had was the right to equal treatment regarding the access to employment. Similarly the 'topping-up' of

3   Reg 1408/71 (OJ 1971, 149/1), Arts 5 and 97.
4   See Case 24/74: *Caisse Régionale d'Assurance Maladie de Paris v Biason* [1974] ECR 999, [1975] 1 CMLR 59; Case 79/76: *Fossi v Bundesknappschaft* [1977] ECR 667.
5   See Case 35/77: *Beerens v Rijksdienst voor Arbeidsvoorziening* [1977] ECR 2249, [1978] 2 CMLR 320; Case 237/78: *Little Caisse Régionale d'Assurance Maladie v Palermo* [1979] ECR 2645, [1980] 2 CMLR 31.
6   See eg Case 70/80: *Vigier v Bundesversicherungsanstalt für Angelstallte* [1981] ECR 229, [1982] 2 CMLR 709.
7   OJ 1992, L136/1.
8   Case C-356/89: *RS Newton v Chief Adjudication Officer* [1991] ECR I-3017.
9   Reg 1408/71, Art 10.
10   Case C-78/91: *R Hughes v Chief Adjudication Officer, Belfast* [1992] ECR I-4839.
11   See pp 495 et seq, supra.
12   *Caisse Régionale d'Assurance Maladie Rhone-Alpes v Giletti* [1987] ECR 955, [1988] 1 CMLR 740.
13   Case 316/85: *Centre Public d'Aide Sociale, Courcelles v Lebon* [1987] ECR 2811, [1989] 1 CMLR 337.

a pension[14] was classified as social assistance. However, *in casu*, the Algerian-born husband of a French wife was not eligible because of his nationality. He had an invalidity pension in his own right but could not claim a supplementary pension as a member of his wife's family because his wife had never been employed, was not a Community worker and, therefore, the husband could not claim 'social advantage' by virtue of Regulation 1612/68.

Social security provisions are corollary to immigration rules or rather to the right to nationality but, in the case of change of nationality, the time of the completion of the relevant insurance period is the determining factor rather than nationality at the time when the claim is made. Therefore the benefits, like vested rights, belong to the individual who has earned them even if he lost his nationality thereafter.[15]

The cardinal principle of Community law, ie non-discrimination on the ground of nationality, is also enshrined in the social security system. Thus Regulation 1408/71 (Article 3(1)) provides that persons contemplated in the Regulation 'shall be subject to the same obligations and enjoy the same benefits under the legislation of any Member States as the nationals of that state'. In Community case law it means workers of other Member States cannot be excluded from the national security systems;[16] exemption from the payment of social security contributions or taxes applicable to the national of the host state must be available to non-nationals;[17] social contributions of employers in respect of trainee workers must be calculated according to the same criteria for the nationals and non-nationals within the national education system;[18] differentiation between the claimant's children according to their nationality cannot be tolerated;[19] and the same conditions regarding the payment of benefits must apply as regards beneficiaries within the territory of the state concerned and those outside it.[20]

Some doubt arose as to whether the system allows reverse discrimination. The problem was exposed in the *Kenny* case[1] where an Irish national claimed sickness benefit in the United Kingdom for a period during which he was in prison in Ireland. Under the British rules he would be disqualified if he served a prison sentence in the United Kingdom. The British authorities denied his claim contending that this would, in effect, discriminate against the British nationals. The ECJ[2] reiterated the principle that the various national laws 'must affect all persons subject to them in accordance with objective criteria and without regard to their nationality'. However this abstract formula has not resolved the doubt, though it seems that if the claimant was entitled under the system where his benefit was earned, the fact that he was in prison in another country should not have deprived him of his right.

---

14 Case 147/87: *Zaoui v Caisse Régionale d'Assurance Maladie de l'Ile de France* [1987] ECR 5511 [1989] 2 CMLR 646.
15 Case 10/78: *Belbouabe v Bundesknappschaft* [1978] ECR 1915, [1979] 2 CMLR 23.
16 Case 33/88: *Allué and Coonan v Università degli Studi di Venezia* [1989] ECR 1591, [1991] 1 CMLR 283.
17 Case 143/87: *Stanton v INASTI* [1988] ECR 3877, [1989] 3 CMLR 761; Case C-204/90: *Bachmann v Belgium* [1992] ECR I-249; Case C-300/90: *Commission v Belgium* [1992] ECR I-305, [1993] 1 CMLR 785.
18 Case C-27/91: *Urstaff v Société Hostellerie Le Manoi* [1991] ECR I-5531.
19 Case 237/78: *Caisse Régionale d'Assurance Maladie Palermo* [1979] ECR 2645, [1980] 2 CMLR 31 – children allowances granted to French but denied to Italian children of the same mother.
20 Case C-124/99: *Borawitz v Landesversichesungsanstalt Westfalen* 21 September 2000.
1 Case 1/78: *Kenny v National Insurance Comr, Liverpool* [1978] ECR 1489, [1978] 3 CMLR 651.
2 At para 18.

Application of Article 73(2) of Regulation 1408/71 revealed discrimination in the *Pinna* cases[3] which was eventually removed by Regulation 3427/89.[4] The ECJ held Article 73(2) invalid because the special rules for France allowed discrimination against migrant workers to the extent that French residence for family allowances was required and this denied protection to the family which left the country while the head of the family continued to live and work in France.

Apart from the foregoing, the Community system is based on the classification of benefits corresponding to branches of insurances, competent law, aggregation, apportioning and overlapping of benefits; subrogation and reimbursement between the Member States.

B. Beneficiaries of Community legislation

The original beneficiaries were workers[5] referred to as 'employed persons' by Regulation 1408/71[6] which constituted the core of the system. Regulation 1408/71 (Article 2(1)) now applies to 'employed or self-employed persons and students who are or have been subject to the legislation of one or more Member States and who are nationals of one of the Member States . . . as well as to the members of their families and their survivors'. It also applies to refugees and stateless persons within the meaning of the 1951 Geneva Convention on Status of Refugees and the 1954 New York Convention on the Status of Stateless Persons, respectively and to the members of their families and their survivors.[7]

In the case law the concept of 'worker' is given a broad definition. It includes, among 'wage-earners and comparable workers', a Dutch worker who fell ill during her visit to her parents in Germany;[8] an Italian self-employed artisan in Germany being regarded as 'comparable worker';[9] a German miner killed on holiday in France in a road traffic accident when his motorcycle was in collision with another vehicle;[10] a Belgian injured in the Netherlands while on his way to work;[11] a self-employed person who formerly was employed;[12] a person who was not paying (and was not obliged to pay) insurance contributions at the relevant time;[13] a missionary priest in the former Belgian Congo who was considered to be 'self-employed' as he was maintained by his congregation[14] but not an au pair girl who was never insured.[15]

---

3 Case 41/84: *Pinna v Caisse d'Allocations Familiales de la Savoie* [1986] ECR 1, [1988] 1 CMLR 350; Case 359/87: *Pinna (No 2) (explanatory judgment)* [1989] ECR 585, [1990] 2 CMLR 561.
4 OJ 1989, L331.
5 Reg 3 (OJ 1958, 561); implemented by Reg 4 (OJ 1958, 597).
6 OJ 1971, L149/1, implemented by Reg 574/72 (OJ 1972, L74/1); updated and consolidated by Reg 118/97 (OJ 1997, L28/1), but amended several times thereafter.
7 Reg 1408/71, Art 1(d), (e).
8 Case 75/63: *Hoekstra (née Unger) v Bestuur der Bedrifsvereniging voor Detailhandel en Ambachten* [1964] ECR 177, [1964] CMLR 319.
9 Case 19/68: *De Cicco v LVA Schwaben* [1968] ECR 473, [1969] CMLR 67.
10 Case 44/65: *Hessiche Knappschaft v Singer* [1965] ECR 965, [1966] CMLR 82.
11 Case 31/64: *De Sociale Voorzorg Mutual Insurance Fund v Bertholet* [1965] ECR 81.
12 Case 17/76: *Brack v Insurance Officer* [1976] ECR 1429.
13 Case 143/79: *Walsh v National Insurance Officer* [1980] ECR 1639.
14 Case 300/84: *Van Roosemalen v Bestuur van der Bedrifsverenigng voor de Gezondheit Goestelijke en Maatschappelijke Belangen* [1986] ECR 3097, [1988] 3 CMLR 471.
15 Case 84/77: *Caisse Primaire d'Assurance v Tessier (née Recq)* [1978] ECR 7, [1979] 1 CMLR 249.

The status of 'worker' was particularly crucial before the Regulation was extended to the self-employed, members of workers' families and survivors of employed or self-employed persons. A 'member of the family' is a person recognized as such by the legislation under which social security is provided[16] but persons in this class can only claim benefits derived from the relevant national law.[17] A 'survivor' is a person defined as such by the legislation under which the benefits are provided[18] which includes persons living under the roof of the deceased and dependent on him. In order to come within cover of the Regulation a person must fulfil the conditions of one of the following cases:

(1) compulsory or optional continued insurance of one or more of the contingencies covered by the branches of a social security scheme for employed or self-employed persons;

(2) compulsory insurance for one or more of the contingencies covered by the branches of social security listed in Article 4 of Regulation 1408/71 applicable to all residents or the whole working population;

(3) compulsory insurance for several of the contingencies covered by the Regulation under a 'standard social security scheme for the whole rural population' as per Annex I;

(4) voluntary insurance for one or more of the contingencies covered by the branches of the Regulation under a social security scheme for employed or self-employed persons or for all residents or for certain categories of residents.[19]

The system is not comprehensive but, as we have noted earlier,[20] it is complemented by the notion of 'social advantage' under Regulation 1612/68.

However, ultimately the beneficiaries are determined according to the national rules which means that a person may enjoy the status of worker when drawing a pension[1] or even when uninsured provided he complies with the conditions laid down by the relevant social security scheme.[2]

In the *Walsh* case[3] the lady in question was employed in the United Kingdom from 1967 but between 1973 and 1974 she worked in Ireland and paid contributions to the Irish scheme. Then she returned to the United Kingdom where she was employed from January to October 1974, at which time she ceased work and went back to Ireland. She was still in Ireland when she gave birth to a child in July 1975 but the following month she returned to England and, in October, claimed maternity benefit. She could have claimed the benefit in Ireland but did not claim it there. In the United Kingdom she was entitled to the benefit at a reduced rate on account of her contribution to the British scheme. At the time of the birth of her child she neither paid nor was she obliged to pay contributions to the British scheme. Article 8 of Regulation 574/72 (which

---

16   Reg 1408/71, Art 1(f).
17   See Case 40/76: *Kermaschek v Bundesanstalt für Arbeit* [1976] ECR 1669; Case 94/84: *Official de l'emploi v Deak* [1985] ECR 1873; Case 157/84: *Franscogna v Caisse des dépots et consignations* [1985] ECR 1739; Case C-243/91: *Belgium v Taghavi* [1992] ECR I-4401.
18   Reg 1408/71, Art 1(g).
19   Art 1(a).
20   See supra, p 539.
1   Case 182/78: *Bestuur v Pierik* [1979] ECR 1977, [1980] 2 CMLR 88.
2   Case 39/76: *Bestuur v Mouthaan* [1976] ECR 1901.
3   143/79, p 541, note 13, supra.

implemented Regulation 1408/71) provide that, where a person is entitled to a maternity benefit in two or more Member States, the benefit is payable under the legislation of the Member State in which the confinement occurred. The ECJ held that, though not employed and not contributing in the United Kingdom she retained the status of 'worker' and was covered by insurance based on previous contributions.

The concept of 'worker' was further defined in *Galinsky's* case.[4] Galinsky had been covered by the British compulsory national insurance scheme as a self-employed person until 1964 when he moved to the Netherlands where he was compulsorily insured under the Dutch scheme as an employed person but he continued to pay voluntary contributions to the British scheme as a 'non-employed' person until he reached the retirement age of 65 according to British law. In this way he continued his contributions entitling him to a British retirement pension at the full rate without taking into consideration any insurance periods completed in the Netherlands. He also made voluntary contributions under the Dutch scheme to cover part of the period before 1964 so as to increase his insurance record there. At that time there was in force a bilateral Convention between the United Kingdom and the Netherlands on Social Security[5] which gave the nationals of either contracting party a choice: either to opt for a pension obtained by aggregating and apportioning insurance periods completed under the legislation of both parties[6] or to choose to receive separate pensions under the legislation of each contracting party without regard to insurance periods completed under the legislation of the other party.[7] The option was to be exercised at the time where the right to receive pension was 'established'. Galinsky seems to have taken the second option. In 1970 he reached the age of 65 and was awarded a partial Dutch retirement pension (as he did not have a full insurance record under Dutch law) and he had decided to obtain a separate pension under the Convention rather than one calculated by aggregation and apportionment. He did not, however, receive a United Kingdom retirement pension at this time because he was still working.[8] In 1975, when he was 70, Galinsky was deemed, by English law[9] to have retired and was, therefore, entitled to a United Kingdom retirement pension.

In the meantime the United Kingdom became a member of the Community and, consequently, the Hague Convention was replaced by Regulation 1408/71 and Galinsky was caught in a situation where his case fell partly within and partly without the system. The Insurance Officer applied Chapter 3 of the Regulation in order to calculate his pension. However Galinsky was also entitled to a pension increase in respect of his children. Had the Convention been in force the increase would have been paid despite the United Kingdom law requiring the children to be resident in the United Kingdom because the Convention would have restriction of the United Kingdom national law. However Galinsky (and his children) were living in the Netherlands. Article 3(1) of the Regulation prohibits residence requirements for the receipt of benefits but Article 77(2)(b) specifically provides for the payment of benefits in respect of children (including pension increases)

4 99/80, [1981] ECR 941, [1981] 3 CMLR 361.
5 The Hague Convention 1954 which was incorporated into the National Insurance and Industrial Injuries (Netherlands) Order 1955 (SI 1955, No 874).
6 Art 19.
7 Art 22.
8 S 30(1)(a) of the National Insurance Act 1965, then s 28(1)(a) of the Social Security Act 1975.
9 S 30(4) of 1965 Act and s 27(5) of the 1975 Act.

in the Member State in which the pensioner resides. Therefore the Insurance Officer concluded that Galinsky could not be granted a pension increase in respect of his children

The ECJ held[10] that a person who has been compulsorily insured as a self-employed person in one Member State and as an employed person in another must be considered a worker throughout the Community by virtue of Articles 1(a) and 2(1) (as originally worded) of Regulation 1408/71. Although Galinsky was covered by the Regulation by virtue of his insurance in the Netherlands the Court held, on the authority of case law laid down under Regulation 3, which was followed by Regulation 1408/71, that the expression 'pensions for old-age' in Article 77 of Regulation 1408/71 does not cover benefits granted in a Member State to a person insured under a social security scheme applicable to self-employed persons where they are based on the legislation of that Member State alone. Thus in the Netherlands, where Galinsky was a 'worker', the Dutch authorities could not rely on the Regulation to take into account any rights Galinsky may have acquired in the United Kingdom[11] but they would apply Article 77(2)(a) of the Regulation (which applies to a case of a pensioner who draws a pension under the legislation of one Member State alone) in so far as his right under Dutch law to benefits in respect of his dependent children was concerned.

In the United Kingdom, where Galinsky was not a 'worker', but where the Regulation applied because he is a person covered by it,[12] the British authorities had to take into consideration the rights acquired by Galinsky in the Netherlands as a 'worker' within the Regulation. On the other hand his right to a United Kingdom pension increase fell outside the scope of the Regulation which, to that extent, replaced the United Kingdom-Netherlands Convention. Therefore the British authorities had to apply the Convention and not Article 77 of the Regulation.

The *Mouthaan* case[13] shows that formal affiliation to a social security system mentioned in Article 1(a) of Regulation 1408/71 is not necessary provided the person complies with the conditions of affiliation laid down by national law, even if he is not, as a result, insured under that system. Mouthaan worked first in the Netherlands, where he was insured and, thereafter, in Germany. His employer failed to have him insured, as he was obliged to by German law. When he lost his job Mouthaan registered as unemployed in the Netherlands and was granted an unemployment benefit. The Dutch authorities claimed thereafter repayment of the benefit under Article 13(2)(a).[14] The ECJ ruled that the status of the worker is acquired if the person concerned complies with the substantive conditions for affiliation to the social security scheme applicable to him even if, in fact, the necessary steps to join the scheme have not been taken and, in consequence, he was not insured.

Affiliation to a social security scheme in one Member State does not entitle a worker to be affiliated to the scheme of another Member State unless the conditions of affiliation in the latter allow it. In *Brunori*[15] the worker had completed insurance periods in Italy as a worker but then came to Germany where he worked first as an employed person and than as a self-employed craftsman. Under German

10   At para 9.
11   See Case 19/68, p 541, note 9, supra.
12   See Case 23/71: *Janssen v Alliance Nationale des Mutualités Chrétienner* [1971] ECR 859.
13   Supra, p 542, note 2.
14   See infra, p 545.
15   Case 266/78: *Brunori v LVA Rheinprovinz* [1979] ECR 2705.

law craftsmen who have not made a minimum number of contributions are subject to compulsory affiliation to the old-age insurance scheme for employed persons. In order to avoid compulsory affiliation Brunori claimed credit for the insurance periods he had completed in Italy. The ECJ held that affiliation to a national scheme is a matter for national law alone. A similar case[16] arose where Coonan claimed to be entitled to be affiliated to the United Kingdom scheme by virtue of insurance periods completed in Ireland. Here too the ECJ held that Regulation 1408/71 does not oblige a Member State to take into account periods completed in another Member State for affiliation purposes though they are relevant for aggregation.

C. The competent law

In order to avoid a conflict of laws Article 13(1) of the Regulation has imposed the law of the workplace (*lex loci laboris*) as the principal connecting factor to ensure the application of the legislation of a single Member State only. Thus an employed person is subject to the law of his workplace,[17] even if he resides in another state or if the registered office or place of business of his employer is situated in another Member State.[18] Similarly, a person self-employed in one Member State is subject to the law of that state even if he resides in another state.[19] A person employed on board a ship flying the flag of a Member State is subject to the law of the flag state. Civil servants[20] are governed by the law of the state which they serve, while persons called up or recalled for military or civilian service retain their connection with the law of the workplace[1] for the purpose of the periods of insurance and social security rights in the Community.

However there are exceptions to the principle.[2] Thus a person (other than a mariner) who is employed in one state by an undertaking to which he is normally attached, and who is posted by his employer to another Member State, remains subject to the legislation of the former if the anticipated duration of his posting does not exceed 12 months and he is not sent to replace another person who has completed his term of posting.[3] If the duration of the work to be done, owing to unforeseen circumstances, extends beyond the period originally planned and exceeds 12 months, the law of the first state continues to apply until the completion of such work, subject to the consent of the competent authority of the state to which the person has been posted and provided that the extension does not itself exceed 12 months.[4]

Where a person is normally employed (or operates on his own account) in two or more Member States by an international transport undertaking, he is usually subject to the law of the state in which the undertaking has its registered office or

16 Case 110/79: *Coonan v Insurance Officer* [1980] ECR 1445.
17 See Case 73/72: *Bentzinger v Steinbruchs – Berufsgenossenschaft* [1973] ECR 283.
18 Case C-2/89: *Bestuur van de Sociale Verzekringbank v Kits van Heijningen* [1990] ECR 1753.
19 See Case 13/73: *Anciens ELS d'Angenieux fils ainé v Hakenberg* [1973] ECR 935.
20 Case C-245/88: *Daalmeijer v Bestuur der Sociale Verzekeringsbank* [1991] ECR I-555.
 1 See Case 15/69: *Württembergische Milchverwertung-Sudmilch AG v Ugliola* [1969] ECR 363, [1970] CMLR 194.
 2 Reg 1408/71, Arts 14-17A.
 3 See Case 35/70: *Manpower Sàrl v Caisse d'Assurance Strasbourg* [1970] ECR 1251, [1971] CMLR 222; Case C-202/97: *Fitzwilliam Executive Search Ltd v Bestuur van het Landelijk instituut sociale verzekeringen* [2000] QB 906n; Case C-404/98: *Plum v Allgemeine Ortskrankenkasse Rheinland* [2000] All ER (EC) 240.
 4 See Cases 73/72 and 13/73: note 17 and 19, supra.

place of business. But if the employer has a branch or permanent representation in another Member State, a person employed by such branch or permanent representation is subject to the legislation of the state where the branch or representation is situated. Where a person is employed principally in the Member State in which he resides, he is subject to the law of that State even if the employer has no place of business there. Similarly, a person who is normally employed in two or more Member States is subject to the law of the state in which he resides, if he works partly in that state or if he is attached to several undertakings or several employers[5] who have their registered offices or places of business in different Member States. If the person does not reside in the territory of any of the Member States where he pursues his activity, he is subject to the legislation of the Member State in whose territory is situated the registered office or place of business of his employer.

A person who is employed in the territory of one Member State by an undertaking which has its registered office or place of business in the territory of another state with a common frontier is subject to the law of the Member State in whose territory the undertaking has its registered office or place of business.

A person normally self-employed in the territory of a Member State who performs work in another state is subject to the same rules as a worker in a comparable situation.[6] However, a person normally self-employed in the territory of two or more Member States is subject to the legislation of the country of his residence if he pursues any part of his activity there. Otherwise he is subject to the legislation of the Member State in whose territory he pursues his main activity. However, if the legislation to which he should be subject in accordance with the preceding rules does not enable him, even on a voluntary basis, to join a pension scheme, he becomes subject to the legislation of the other Member State which would apply apart from these particular provisions; and should the legislation of two or more Member States apply, the question of the governing law is to be decided by agreement between the Member States involved or their competent authorities.

More detailed provisions apply to persons employed on board vessels, by way of exception to the basic rule referring to the flag state. Thus a person who is normally employed by an undertaking in one Member State or on board a ship flying the flag of a Member State, and who is posed on board a ship flying the flag of another Member State in order to carry out work there, and a self-employed person in a similar position, remain subject to the law of the place of normal employment. Thus a Belgian seaman employed by a Belgian company on board a British ship remains subject to Belgian law.[7] A person who, without being normally employed at sea, performs work in the territorial waters or in a port of a Member State on a vessel flying the flag of another Member State, but is not a member of its crew, is subject to the law of the place of the actual work. And a person who is employed on board a ship flying the flag of one Member State but receives his pay from an employer whose registered office or place of business is in another Member State in which he himself is resident is subject to the law of the state of the registered office or place of business and the residence.

A person who is employed simultaneously in the territory of one Member State and self-employed in another is subject to the legislation of the state in which he

---

5   See Case 73/72, supra. The rule applies also to commercial travellers; see Case 13/73, supra.
6   Art 14A. The 'work' in question can be any activity, whether employed or self-employed: see Case C-178/97: *Banks v Théâtre de la Monnaie* [2000] QB 865.
7   See Case C-196/90: *Fonds voor Arbedisongevallen v De Paep* [1991] ECR I-4815, [1993] 3 CMLR 593.

is engaged in paid employment, except as regards occupations listed in Annex VII to Regulation 1408/71, where he is simultaneously subject to the legislation of two Member States.[8]

Special provisions apply to service personnel of diplomatic missions as well as the personal service to officials of such missions. In principle the place of employment determines the competent law but such persons may opt for their *lex patriae*. A wider option is available to auxiliary staff of the European Communities.[9]

Two further points have to be considered in the context of the competent law. Next to the *lex loci laboris*, the Regulation designates the law of the country of residence as another connecting factor. It defines 'residence' as 'habitual residence'[10] without any further refinement, distinguishing it from 'stay', defined as 'temporary residence'. Both concepts reflect a factual situation or a degree of physical attachment to a place of abode, ie factors other than those connected with work. In the case of an international commercial traveller, 'habitual residence' was defined by the European Court as 'the permanent centre of his interests to which he returns in the intervals between his tours'.[11]

The other point concerns the contents of the competent law. Article 4 of Regulation 1408/71 refers to benefits under national 'legislation'. This means[12] all laws, regulations and other provisions and all other present or future implementing measures of each Member State relating to the sectors of social security and schemes for social security covered by Article 4.

The ECJ, deciding under Regulation 3,[13] gave a broad interpretation of the term to include private arrangements integrated into the national insurance system, where intended to supplement or replace the existing statutes. It also held[14] that national measures may include provisions regarding territories enjoying a special relationship with a Member State. It has also warned that the phrase, 'present or future', must not be construed so as to exclude measures which were previously in force but had ceased to be operative when the Community regulations were adopted.[15]

However the term excludes provisions of existing or future industrial agreements, whether or not they have been made compulsory or extended in scope, though the limitation on the term may be lifted by the Member State concerned, so as to bring such an agreement within the Community Regulation. The term also excludes provisions governing special voluntary schemes for self-employed persons set up by their own initiative or which apply only to a part of the territory of a Member State, irrespective of whether or not they have been made compulsory.[16]

National legislation which makes admission to voluntary or optional continued insurance schemes conditional upon residence within the territory of the state is made inapplicable to persons resident in another Member State, provided that at some time in their past working life they were subject to the legislation of the

---

8   Reg 1408/71, Art 14C.
9   Art 16. See Case C-360/97: *Nijhuis v Bestuur van het Landelijk instituut sociale verzekeringen* [1999] ECR I-1919; Case C-211/97: *Rivero v Bundesanstalt fur Arbeit* [1999] ECR I-3219.
10 *Sejour habituel.*
11 Case 13/73, supra at 951. See also Case C-90/97: *Swaddling v Adjudication Officer* [1999] ECR I-1075.
12 Art 1(j).
13 See Case 61/65: supra, and Case 33/65: *Dekker v Bundesversicherungsanstalt für Angestellte* [1965] ECR 901.
14 Case 87/76: *Bozzone v Office de Securité Sociale d'Outre-Mer* [1977] ECR 687.
15 Case 109/76: *Blottner v Bestuur* [1977] ECR 1141.
16 Reg 1408/71, Annex II, as amended.

first state as employed or self-employed persons. Where admission to voluntary or optional continued insurance is conditional upon completion of periods of insurance, the periods of insurance or residence completed under the legislation of another Member State have to be taken into account to the extent required as if they were completed under the legislation of the first state.[17] Interpreting this provision, the ECJ held[18] that where national legislation allows periods of study to be assimilated to periods of employment, it means that such periods have to be counted as being part of 'voluntary or optional insurance'. However, since Member States themselves determine the conditions of admission to their own schemes, they are not obliged to take into account periods completed in another state if the claimant has not paid in that state the contributions necessary to confirm his status as an insured person in the state where he claims a benefit.[19]

D. Community benefits

Under Regulation 1408/71 (Article 4(1)) certain benefits can be claimed as of right in all the Member States as 'Community' benefits. These include: sickness and maternity, invalidity, old-age, unemployment, accidents at work and occupational diseases, death grants, and family benefits which include family allowances and supplementary or special allowances for orphans. All these benefits arise from national legislation, ie statutes, regulations and other provisions as well as implementing measures. 'Benefits' comprise all payments out of public funds as well as all revalorization increases and supplementary allowances.[20]

Regulation 1408/71[1] applies to all general and special social security schemes irrespective of their contributory or non-contributory nature. The latter cover benefits which are not included in Article 4(1) where such benefits constitute a supplement or substitute for the social security benefits covered by the Regulation; or are intended solely for the protection of the disabled, or are intended to guarantee a minimum income.

Into that group fall cases involving handicapped persons;[2] family credit;[3] preventive health measures against tuberculosis;[4] widows' remarriage gratuity;[5] and a legal aid scheme which covers the cost of reference to the Court of Justice and is available to British citizens and foreigners alike.[6]

---

17   Reg 1408/71, Art 9.

18   Case 93/76: *Liégois v Office National des Pensions pour Travailleurs Salariés* [1977] ECR 543.

19   See Case 70/80: *Vigier v Bundesversicherungsanstalt für Angestellte* [1981] ECR 229.

20   Ibid Art 1(t).

1   Ibid Art 4(2).

2   Case 1/72: *Frilli v Belgium* [1972] ECR 457, [1973] CMLR 386; Case 187/73: *Callemeyn v Belgium* [1974] ECR 553 at 561; Case 39/74: *Costa v Belgium* [1974] ECR 1251 at 1260-1261; Case 7/75: *F v Belgium* [1975] ECR 679, [1975] 2 CMLR 442; Case 63/76: *Inzirillo v Caisse d'Allocations* [1976] ECR 2057, [1978] 3 CMLR 596; Case C-356/89: supra.

3   Case C-78/91, supra.

4   Case 14/72: *Heinze v Landesversicherungsantalt Rheinprovinz* [1972] ECR 1105 at 1114 and 1115; Case 15/72: *Land Niedersachsen v Landesversicherungsanstalt Hannover* [1972] ECR 1127 at 1137; Case 16/72: *Allgemeine Ortskrankenkasse Hamburg v Landesversicherungsanstalt Schleswig-Holstein* [1972] ECR 1141 at 1151 and 1152.

5   Case 130/73: *Vandeweghe v Berufsgenossenschaft für die Chemische Industrie* [1973] ECR 1329, [1974] 1 CMLR 449.

6   Case 30/77: *R v Bouchereau* [1978] QB 732, [1977] ECR 1999, [1977] 2 CMLR 800.

Regulation 1408/71 (Article 4(4)) expressly excludes benefits for victims of war[7] and social and medical assistance.

The Community benefits, as categorized by Regulation 1408/71 and the implementing Regulation 574/72,[8] have to be considered in the light of their specific rules, ie:

(1) SICKNESS AND MATERNITY BENEFITS (ARTICLES 18-36)

Article 19 provides for benefits in kind and in cash. Cash benefits aim to compensate for the loss of earnings resulting from sickness or child-bearing[9] and in that respect have to be distinguished from invalidity benefits.[10] The calculation of cash benefits is governed by Article 23 and takes into account insurance periods completed under the legislation of other Member States and, where applicable, members of the employed or self-employed person's family resident in other Member States.

Benefits in kind include reimbursement of medical and pharmaceutical expenses[11] but do not include a supplementary pension to finance the beneficiary's sickness insurance.[12]

Sickness and maternity benefits are almost always claimed in the country of residence[13] even if this is not the 'competent' state, ie the state where the 'competent institution', ie the institution with which the person concerned is insured at the time of the application for the benefit, or the institution designated by the Member State concerned,[14] is situated. This principle was applied to a worker who was once employed in the United Kingdom but then settled in Ireland without continuing in employment there.[15]

Articles 19-22 cover the persons concerned during their stay abroad. The position was clarified in the *Hoekstra*[16] case which, incidentally, contributed to the definition of the term 'worker'. A Dutch citizen, whilst visiting her parents in Germany, fell ill, required treatment immediately and became, subsequently, unable to carry on any gainful occupation. Back in the Netherlands she successfully claimed disability benefits under Dutch law but her claim in respect of medical treatment in Germany was disallowed on the ground that Article 11(2)(a) of Regulation 3 (then in force) allowed such a benefit only to persons who were 'workers' at the relevant time. Moreover, if they went abroad for treatment, a prior authorization would be required. On reference, the ECJ defined 'worker' as a Community concept which included the claimant (a wife of a worker). Workers included persons covered by different national systems of social security.

---

7   See 93/75: *Alderblum v Caisse Nationale d'Assurance Vieillesse des Travailleurs Salariés de Paris* [1975] ECR 2147, [1976] 1 CMLR 236; Case 144/78: *Tinelli v Berufsgenossenschaft der Chemische Industrie* [1979] ECR 757, [1979] 2 CMLR 735; Case 9/78: *Dirécteur Régional de la Sécurité Sociale de Nancy v Gillard* [1978] ECR 1661, [1978] 3 CMLR 554.
8   OJ 1973, L230/6, as amended.
9   Case 61/65: *Vaassen (née Göbbels) v Beambtenfonds voor het Mijinbedriff* [1966] ECR 261, [1966] CMLR 508.
10 Case 69/79: *Jordens-Vosters* [1980] ECR 75, [1980] 3 CMLR 412.
11 Case 61/65, supra.
12 Case 33/65: *Dekker v Bundesversicherungsanstalt für Angestellte* [1965] ECR 901, [1966] CMLR 503.
13 Case 23/71, supra.
14 For a list of competent institutions of each of the Member States see Reg 574/72, Art 4(1); Annex I, as amended.
15 Case C-215/90: *Chief Adjudication Officer v Twomey* [1992] ECR I-1823.
16 Case 75/63: supra; see also Case 117/77: *Bestuur v Pierik* [1978] ECR 825, [1978] 3 CMLR 343.

If temporarily abroad such persons remained workers if they enjoyed the status of workers at home. Therefore the claimant was a worker when she fell ill in Germany. As she did not go there specially for treatment no prior authorization was called for.

If a worker takes a holiday abroad on medical advice, then falls ill and receives immediate medical attention, his claim for sickness benefit covering the period abroad cannot be rejected on the ground of absence from home as would be the case under national legislation.[17]

Medical treatment must involve an application of medical skill. Consequently going abroad even on medical advice, merely for a 'change of air' was not regarded in the United Kingdom as 'treatment' justifying the payment of sickness benefit.[18]

(2)   INVALIDITY BENEFITS (ARTICLES 37-43)

'Invalidity' is permanent incapacity (partial or total) to work in consequence of an accident or sickness. The degree of invalidity is a matter of fact to be determined by the competent authority in accordance with the national law concerned and has to be recognized by the institutions of any other Member State provided that they have mutually acknowledged concordance between them on degrees of invalidity.[19]

Benefits are granted on the basis of a qualifying period during which the claimant has contributed to the relevant insurance scheme designated by national legislation. Problems arise in cases where such period has not been completed in the country in which benefit is claimed; Article 38 of Regulation 1408/71 purports to solve the problem through the principle of aggregation which was illustrated in the *Janssen* case[20] in connection with the maternity benefit. Another problem is that of the apportionment of the 'overlapping' benefits governed by Article 12.[1]

A national law which does not allow credit for contributions made abroad would be incompatible with Community law.[2] However contributions have to be made in the Community since, as held by the ECJ,[3] an Italian who worked in Austria (then a third country) could not aggregate his rights earned in Austria to those credited to him in the Community. Such a problem can be solved by bilateral treaties between Member States and a third country.

The position is different in the case of a person who contributed to an insurance scheme whilst working in what used to be a dependent territory of a Member State, eg the Belgian Congo before it became Zaire. In such a case, held the ECJ,[4] aggregation applies and the claimant (living in Italy) was entitled to social security benefits under Belgian law as if living in Belgium. The change of nationality seems immaterial.[5] However, a person who, until 1960 was a British citizen but thereafter was a Nigerian citizen and worked in Zaire, was not covered

17   Case 17/76: *Brack v Insurance Officer* [1976] ECR 1429, [1976] 2 CMLR 592.
18   *Re Convalescence in Germany* [1979] 1 CMLR 390.
19   Art 40(4) and Annex V; Case 79/81: *Baccini v Office National de l'Emploi* [1982] ECR 1063, [1984] 2 CMLR 640; Case 232/82: *Baccini v Office National de l'Emploi* [1983] ECR 583, [1983] 3 CMLR 572.
20   Supra, p 544, note 12.
1   See infra, pp 559 et seq.
2   Cf Case CS 7/76: *Re Absence in Ireland* [1977] 1 CMLR 5.
3   Case 75/76: *Kaucic v Institut National d'Assurance Maladie-Invalidité* [1977] ECR 495, [1977] 2 CMLR 259.
4   Case 87/76: *Bozzone v Office de Sécurité Sociale d'Outre-Mer* [1977] ECR 687, [1977] 2 CMLR 604.
5   Cf Case 10/78: *Belbouab v Bundesknappschaft* [1978] ECR 1915, [1979] 2 CMLR 23.

because neither the state where he worked nor the state of his citizenship were Member States of the Community.

Where periods of unemployment are involved in the consideration of entitlement to a disability pension[6] reference must be made to the national legislation under which such periods were completed.[7] If such periods are assimilated to periods of work they will count towards the entitlement.

In the case of aggravation of invalidity, Article 41 applies.

Invalidity benefits are converted into old-age benefits under the conditions laid down in the legislation under which they were granted and according to the Community rules governing old-age pensions.[8]

Invalidity benefits depend upon entitlement to sickness benefit and the latter, in turn, upon the completion of insurance periods. The entitlement to a sickness benefit in another Member State will be taken into account and so will the insurance periods completed in that country as if they had been completed in the competent state.[9]

(3)   OLD-AGE AND SURVIVORS' PENSIONS (ARTICLES 44-51A)

The age at which there is an entitlement to an old-age pension differs from country to country and has not been harmonized by EC legislation. Upon the death of a person, his or her 'survivors' may be entitled to a pension or benefit.

'Survivor' means any person defined or recognized as such by the legislation under which the benefits are granted. Where, however, the said legislation regards as a survivor only a person who was living under the same roof as the deceased, this condition shall be considered satisfied if such person was mainly dependent on the deceased.[10] Thus survivors can claim only rights derived from the status of a member of the family of the deceased and are entitled only to benefits specifically provided for them.[11] Old-age and survivors' pensions are subject to the same rules.

(a)   Aggregation

Where the acquisition, retention or recovery of a right to benefit is dependent upon the completion of periods of insurance or residence, account must be taken of periods completed under the legislation of other Member States.[12] Article 46(1) provides that the competent institution of the relevant state shall first calculate the amount payable under its own national legislation in relation to the total length of the periods of insurance or residence to be taken into account in pursuance of such legislation. If necessary the rules laid down in paragraph (2)(a) and (b) will apply. Thus the institution shall calculate the theoretical amount that the beneficiary could claim if all the periods of insurance or residence completed under the legislation of the Member States to which the beneficiary has been subject

---

 6 Case C-105/89: *Haji v INASTI* [1990] ECR I-4211.
 7 Case 2/72: *Murru v Caisse Régionale d'Assurance Maladie de Paris* [1972] ECR 333, [1972] CMLR 888.
 8 Art 43(1); See Case 180/78: *Brouwer-Kaune v Bestuur* [1979] ECR 2111, [1980] 2 CMLR 145; Case 4/80: *D'Amico v Office Nationale des Pensions pour Travailleurs Salariés* [1980] ECR 2951.
 9 Case 41/77: *R v National Insurance Comr, ex p Warry* [1977] ECR 2085, [1977] 2 CMLR 783; see also [1981] 1 All ER 229.
10 Reg 1408/71, Art 1(g).
11 Case 40/76: *Kermaschek v Bundesanstalt für Arbeit* [1976] ECR 1669; see also Case 63/76: *Inzirillo v Caisse d'Allocations Familiales de l'Arrondissement de Lyon* [1976] ECR 2057, [1978] 3 CMLR 596.
12 Art 45(1).

had been completed in the Member State in question. If, under that legislation, the amount of the benefit does not depend on the length of the periods completed then that amount shall be taken as the theoretical amount. The institution then shall establish the actual amount of the benefit on the basis of the theoretical amount, and in the ratio of the length of the period of insurance or residence completed to the total length of the periods of insurance or residence completed in all the Member States concerned.

Article 46(2) refers to pro rata benefits, that is, benefits calculated in relation to insurance credits earned in various Member States. The *De Moor* case,[13] decided under Regulation 3, illustrates the point. A commercial traveller, operating in Germany, Belgium and Luxembourg, had contributed to old-age pension schemes in all three countries and claimed that, in order to calculate his entitlement, his contributions in all three countries should be aggregated. He qualified under the Luxembourg scheme but, when granted a pension related to his contributions in that country alone, argued that the Community principle of aggregation ought to be superimposed upon the national system. The ECJ ruled that: 'The first object of Article 51 of the Treaty [now Art 42] is not to ensure a balance of benefits between social security institutions, but to offer any worker in danger of losing the benefit of a qualifying period insufficient in itself to entitle him to a pension the possibility of avoiding this loss by adding together the qualifying periods.'[14]

Thus the beneficiary is entitled to the total sum of the pension calculated in the countries concerned within the highest theoretical amount.[15] Where this limit is exceeded the calculation by the competent institution applying its own law must be adjusted by an amount corresponding to the proportion which the amount of the benefit concerned bears to the total of the benefits.[16] Difficulties have arisen in the application of the above as there would be the tendency to reduce the benefits accumulated in different jurisdictions. However the ECJ decreed, in the first place, that there can be no apportionment of the obligation to pay benefits if aggregation of periods has not been necessary in order to determine the entitlement, that is to say, if in each country involved the benefit has accrued independently.[17] It is only in the case where apportionment is necessary to secure benefits under national legislation that the obligation to pay benefits can be apportioned pro rata between the Member States involved.[18]

Under Article 46(3) the claim may be adjusted in proportion to the benefits earned under the national systems involved. This could lead the paying institution to scale it down with the result that the benefit resulting from aggregation may be lower than the benefit accorded under one national system alone. Should this be the result of the calculation the object of the Community legislation would be defeated. Thus the ECJ ruled that Article 46(3) of the Regulation is incompatible with EC Article 42 (ex Art 51) if it permits a reduction of a benefit through aggregation and apportionment between the Member States involved to a level falling below the entitlement earned in one country alone.[19] A number of decisions

---

13   Case 2/67: *De Moor v Caisse de Pension des Employés Privés* [1967] ECR 197, [1967] CMLR 223.
14   CMLR p 230.
15   Art 46(2)(a)(b) and 46(3) (1st para).
16   Art 46(3) (2nd para).
17   Case 34/69: *Caisse d'Assurance Vieillesse des travailleurs salariés de Paris v Duffy* [1969] ECR 597, [1971] CMLR 391; Case 191/73: *Niemann v Bundesversicherunganstalt für Angestellte* [1974] ECR 571.
18   Art 46(2).
19   Case 24/75: *Petroni and Silvana Amarelli v Office National des Pensions pour Travailleurs Salariés* [1975] ECR 1149.

followed suit resulting in the conclusion that, in that respect, Article 46(3) would be invalid.[20] The case law as it stands now leads to the conclusion that, whilst the Regulation does not prevent the application of national law, including the rules against overlapping benefits, it will prevail to ensure that the worker obtains a higher pension than otherwise awarded under national law.[1]

All the relevant periods under the law of the competent state have to be taken into account even if the claimant is also entitled to a pension under another Member State.[2]

(b) Supplementation and revalorization
Should the amount calculated according to Article 46(3) be lower than the statutory minimum provided by the law of the state where the beneficiary resides, a supplementary benefit would be awarded under Article 50. However supplementation depends on the law of the state where the benefit is payable and, therefore, there is no claim for supplement if such is not provided for in the law of the state concerned.[3]

Article 51 provides for revalorization[4] of benefits taking into account any increase in the cost of living or wages or salaries in the state concerned and for recalculation should the methods of determining or the rules of calculation be altered. Recalculation because of change of status (eg single pensioner's marriage) has to be effected according to Article 46.[5]

Revalorization can be carried out only in the light of changed circumstances but not in the light of 'the general evolution of the economic and social situation'.[6]

(4) UNEMPLOYMENT BENEFIT (ARTICLES 67-71A)

Unemployment benefits are relevant to the concept of 'worker' particularly since Articles 69 and 70 provide that unemployed workers or self-employed persons in search of employment in another Member State are entitled to retain their unemployment benefits. Benefit is payable for a maximum period of three months from the time the person concerned ceased to be available to the employment services of the state which he left, provided that the total duration of the benefits does not exceed the period of benefits he was entitled to under the legislation of that state.[7] However such persons must register with the relevant employment office. Failure to register may be fatal to the claim in respect of the period of absence from the competent country.[8] However this need not be so if the claimant travels abroad in search of work but returns home within

---

20 Eg Case 62/76: *Strehl v National Pensioenfonds voor Mijnwerkers* [1977] ECR 211, [1977] 2 CMLR 743.
 1 Case C-108/89: *Pian v ONP* [1990] ECR I-1599; see also Case C-109/90 ibid.
 2 Case C-342/88: *Rijksdienst voor Pensionen v Spits* [1990] ECR I-2259.
 3 Case 64/77: *Torri v Office National des Pensions pour Travaillerus Salariés* [1977] ECR 2299, [1978] 2 CMLR 711; see also Case 22/81: *R v Social Security Comr, ex p Browning* [1981] ECR 3357, [1982] 1 CMLR 427.
 4 Case 7/81: *Sinatra v Fonds National* [1982] ECR 137, [1982] 3 CMLR 77; see also Case 104/83: *Cincuolo v Union Nationale des Fédérations Mutualistes Neutres* [1984] ECR 1285.
 5 Case 83/87: *Viva v Fonds National de Retraite des Ouvriers Mineurs* [1988] ECR 2521, [1990] 1 CMLR 220.
 6 Case C-141/88: *CNAVTS v Jordan* [1989] ECR 2387; Case C-199/88: *Cabras v INAMI* [1990] ECR I-1023; Case C-85/89: *Ravida v ONP* [1990] ECR I-1063; Case C-93/90: *Cassamali v ONP* [1991] ECR I-1401.
 7 Art 69(1)(c).
 8 Case CU 4/78: *Re Absence in Germany (UK National Insurance Comr)* [1978] 2 CMLR 603.

three months.[9] The right is not accorded to a person who has never been employed and not been treated as an unemployed person under the competent national law.[10]

(a) Aggregation

According to Article 67(1) where the competent law accords benefits on the condition of the completion of insurance periods, the competent institution shall take into account periods of insurance or employment completed under the law of any other Member State, as though they were periods of insurance completed under the legislation it administers, provided, however, that the periods of employment would have been counted as periods of insurance had they been completed in the competent state.

Where the benefits are accorded on the condition of the completion of periods of employment the competent institution shall take into account periods of insurance or employment completed as an employed person under the legislation of any Member State, as though they were periods of employment completed in the competent state (Article 67(2)).

In a case concerning an Italian worker in Belgium[11] the ECJ ruled that periods of insurance may be aggregated 'only if they would have counted as insurance periods had they been completed under the legislation of the competent state (ie Belgium)'. Relying on a precedent[12] the Court held that the claimant did not qualify for the benefit. She was a domestic worker in Italy where she was affiliated to an insurance scheme. In Belgium she worked for a while in that capacity but was not insured against unemployment because domestic workers in Belgium were not eligible to be insured. She changed her job and then became insured but the two periods in Italy and Belgium did not qualify for aggregation.

However, despite the ruling that rights under Regulation 1408/71 should be consistent with the protection afforded by EC Articles 39-42 (ex Arts 48 to 51),[13] the ECJ held, in the *Testa*[14] case, that Article 69(2) was not inconsistent with the Treaty. The circumstances justify the conclusion. Workers in receipt of unemployment benefit in Germany went to Italy in search of employment but returned after the expiry of the three-month period stipulated in the Regulation. The Court ruled that (at para 15):

'. . . As part of a special system of rules which give rights to workers which they would not otherwise have, Article 69(2) cannot, therefore, be equated with the provisions held invalid by the Court in . . . *Petroni* . . . to which their effect was to cause workers to lose advantages in the field of social security guaranteed to them in any event by the legislation of a single Member State . . .'

---

9 Art 69(2), Case CU 251/1978: *Re a Farm Manager* [1979] 1 CMLR 445; Case CU 13/77: *Re Search for Work in Ireland* [1978] 2 CMLR 174; see also Case 139/78: *Coccioli v Bundesanstalt für Arbeit* [1979] ECR 991, [1979] 3 CMLR 144.

10 Case 66/77: *Kuyken v Rijksdienst voor Arbeidsvooriening* [1977] ECR 2311, [1978] 3 CMLR 304.

11 Case 126/77: *Frangiamore v National Employment Office* [1978] ECR 725, [1978] 3 CMLR 166.

12 Case 2/72, p 551, note 7, supra.

13 Case 24/75: *Petroni*, p 552, note 19, supra.

14 Cases 41, 121 and 796/79: *Testa, Maggio and Vitale v Bundesanstalt für Arbeit* [1980] ECR 1979, [1981] 2 CMLR 552. See also Cases C-62/91: *G Sinclair Gray v Adjudication Officer* [1992] ECR I-2737, [1992] 2 CMLR 584 and Case C-272/90: *Jan van Noorden v ASSEDIC* [1991] ECR I-2543.

In somewhat different circumstances the Court did not disqualify the claim.[15] The lady in question was employed in Belgium where she received unemployment benefit. She then moved to Germany where she received benefit by virtue of Article 69(1) for a period of three months. Thereafter she worked in Germany but later returned to Belgium where she claimed unemployment benefit. The ECJ held that she was entitled for the remaining period under Belgian law.

Earlier the Court ruled that the national courts ought to determine the circumstances under which a worker has his residence outside the State where he is employed.[16]

If a wholly unemployed worker resident in a Member State other than the competent state remains available to the employment services in the competent state he is entitled to receive unemployment benefit in accordance with its law, as though he were resident there.[17] If, on the other hand, he makes himself available in the state where he resides, he is entitled to the benefit in accordance with the law of that state, as though he had last been employed there.[18] The worker has an option in this respect but cannot claim benefit in the competent state by virtue of registration for work in the state of residence.[19] Entitled in the state of residence the unemployed worker cannot claim in the state where he was last employed because Article 69 applies only to persons moving to a Member State other than the competent state, since the state of last employment is in this situation the competent state.[20]

The option in favour of the state of residence, being an exception to the general rule, has to be construed strictly. The place of residence must not be of a casual interest but must be where the claimant 'habitually continues to reside and where the habitual centre of his interests is also situated'.[1] Thus an Italian who lived with her parents in Belgium and, having completed her education there, went to England to work in order to perfect her English, was unsuccessful in trying to aggregate her periods of education in Belgium with that of employment in England.

Frontier workers, ie workers who reside in one state and work in another, are entitled to receive benefits in accordance with the law of the state of their residence as if they had been subject to that law whilst last employed.[2]

(b) Calculation of benefits

If the law of a Member State provides that benefits should be calculated on the basis of the worker's previous earnings, such earnings shall take into account exclusively the wage or salary received in respect of his last employment in that state. If he has been employed for less than four weeks, the benefits shall be calculated on the basis of the normal wage or salary corresponding, in the place of residence, to an equivalent or similar employment to his last employment in

15 Case 192/87: *Vanhaeren v Rijksdienst voor Arbeidsvoorziening* [1988] ECR 2411.
16 Case C-216/89: *Reate Reibold v Bundesanstalt für Arbeit* [1990] ECR I-4163; See also Case C-163/89: *Office National de l'Emploi v Di Conti* [1990] ECR I-1829.
17 Art 71(1)(b)(i).
18 Art 71(1)(b)(ii).
19 Case 227/81: *Aubin v Union Nationale Interprofessionnelle pour l'Emploi dans l'Industrie et le Commerce* [1982] ECR 1991.
20 Case 145/84: *Cochet v Bestuur van de Bedrijfsvereniging voor de Gezondheid Geestelijke en Maatschappelijke Belangen* [1985] ECR 801.
 1 Case 76/76: *Di Paulo v Office National de l'Emploi* [1977] ECR 315, [1977] 2 CMLR 59.
 2 Art 71(1)(a)(ii).

another Member State.[3] However, in the case of a frontier worker the competent authority should take into account the earnings in the Member State where he was last employed.[4]

Where the law of a Member State provides that the amount of benefits should vary with the number of members of the family, the competent authority must take into account also members of the family of the person concerned who are residing in another Member State, as though they were residing in the competent state. However this provision does not apply if, in the country of residence of the members of the family, another person is entitled to unemployment benefits in respect of the same members of the family.[5]

(5)   ACCIDENTS AT WORK AND OCCUPATIONAL DISEASES (ARTICLES 52-63A)

Benefits (both in kind and in cash) under this heading are normally payable to the claimants residing[6] in the competent state but the Regulation makes several provisions departing from this principle so as to ensure protection of the worker who suffers an accident at work or contracts an occupational disease elsewhere. Thus, the United Kingdom National Insurance Commissioners held that injury caused to the claimant in a road traffic accident in West Berlin, while he was travelling in the course of his employment, entitled him to injury benefit as if the accident had occurred in the United Kingdom, ie the competent state.[7]

However, where consecutive injuries occur in two different states, the competent authorities dealing with the claims arising from the earlier injuries need not take into consideration the later injuries suffered in another state.[8]

Article 57(1) makes a special provision in respect of occupational diseases in so far as, where a person who has contracted an occupational disease in two or more Member States was involved in an activity likely to cause that disease, the benefits that he or his survivors may claim are awarded exclusively under the law of the last of those States.

(6)   DEATH GRANTS (ARTICLES 64-66A)

Death grants, ie once-and-for-all payments, are awarded in the case of death of a worker, a pensioner, or a pension claimant or a member of his family who dies either in a competent state or elsewhere in the Community.

The competent institution of the state whose law provides for death grants subject to the completion of periods of insurance or residence must take account, where necessary, of such periods completed under the laws of any other Member State as though they had been completed under the legislation it administers.[9]

Where death occurs in a Member State, only the right of a death grant under its law is effective since the right acquired in any other Member State lapses.[10]

---

3   Art 68(1); Case 268/78: *Pennartz v Caisse Primaire d'Assurances Maladie des Alpes-Maritimes* [1979] ECR 2411, [1980] 1 CMLR 682.
4   Case 67/79: *Fellinger v Bundesanstalt für Arbeit, Nuremberg* [1980] ECR 535, [1981] 1 CMLR 471.
5   Art 68(2).
6   Or 'staying', see Decision DI 202/1977, *Re the Key Gibraltar Oil-Drilling Rig* [1979] 1 CMLR 362.
7   Decision DI 487/1974, *Re Car Accident in West Berlin* [1979] 2 CMLR 42.
8   Case 173, 174/78: *Villano v Nordwestliche-Eisen-und Stahl-Berufsgenossen-schaft* [1979] ECR 1851, [1980] 1 CMLR 613.
9   Art 64.
10   Reg 574/72, Art 9(1), as substituted.

Where such a right has been acquired in two or more Member States only the right acquired in the state to which the deceased person was last subject can be claimed.[11]

Where the person concerned dies in the Member State other than the competent state the death is deemed to have occurred in the competent state and the competent institution must award the grants payable under its own law even if the persons entitled reside outside the competent state.[12]

(7) FAMILY BENEFITS (ARTICLES 72-79)

'Family benefits' means all benefits in kind or in cash intended to meet family expenses.[13] They include family allowances and supplementary or special allowances for orphans. Provision is made for aggregation[14] of periods of insurance or employment completed in any Member State by the worker or self-employed person.

However difficulties in the classification of the benefit may arise. It was held, for example, that the Belgian annual holiday allowance was to be distinguished from the regular monthly family allowance and, therefore, it could not be equated with the dependent children allowance. Consequently the holiday allowance should not be deducted from the salary of an employee of the Commission.[15] In another case[16] the widow of an Italian worker who was killed in a Belgian pit disaster returned with her children to Italy but continued to draw the Belgian pension and children's allowances. When the children reached the age specified by Belgian legislation the allowances were stopped on the ground that family allowances were payable as long as the children were entitled to benefits awarded to orphans of victims of industrial accidents. However the ECJ ruled that children's allowances were not linked to orphans' benefits and, as they were available in Belgium, they were payable abroad.

In the *Hughes* case[17] the ECJ not only clarified the meaning of 'family credit', holding it to be within the ambit of social insurance, but also that to qualify for the entitlement it is not necessary that both parents live in the competent state. The Regulation has to take into account the family situation and the economic conditions today. Thus the Court held that the competent state must provide family benefits not only to workers employed in the competent state for children who are unemployed in the competent state but also for children who are residing in another Member State while unemployed. The denial of the benefit in such a situation would hamper the free movement of juvenile workers.[18]

In the *Dammer*[19] case the family was resident in the Netherlands but the father was in Belgium and the mother in Germany. The mother was in receipt of family benefits in Germany but the father's application for the benefits in Belgium was rejected because the mother was entitled to receive the same in Germany. The Court considered that in the light of Article 76 there was no definite solution of the problem of the child residing in a third state because the Article applied only if the children reside in one of the two states where the parents

---

11 Ibid Art 9(2), as substituted.
12 Reg 1408/71, Art 65(1) and Art 65(3), as substituted.
13 Art 4(1)(h).
14 Art 72.
15 Case 106/76: *Francine Gelders-Doeboeck v Commission* [1977] ECR 1623, [1978] 2 CMLR 627.
16 Case 100/63: *Kalsbeck-Van der Veen v Bestuur der Sociale Verzekeringsbank* [1964] ECR 565, [1964] CMLR 548.
17 Supra, p 539, note 10.
18 Case 228/88: *Bronzino* [1990] ECR I-531; see also Case 12/89: *Gatto* [1990] ECR I-557.
19 Case C-168/88: *Dammer* [1989] ECR 4553.

were working. Therefore one has to have recourse to a general principle to be found in the *Petroni* case.[20] Thus if the benefit is higher in the second state than in the first state the parent in the second state is entitled to the benefit but this can be reduced to the level payable under the law of the first state.

Entitlement to family benefits or allowances due under the law of a Member State is suspended when they are due under the relevant Community provisions during the same period and for the same members of the family.[1]

Entitlement is also suspended if, by reason of an economic activity (ie professional or trade activity) family benefits or allowances are also payable by virtue of the law of the Member State in which the members of the family are residing.[2] However the suspension does not apply when the father works abroad in a Member State but the mother is employed in another country but has no right to the benefits either because only the father is accorded the status of the head of the household or because the necessary conditions for awarding the right to payment have not been fulfilled.[3]

Family benefits are provided, in the case of an employed person, by the state to which he is subject but, in the case of an unemployed person, by the state where he is receiving unemployment benefits.[4]

Persons in receipt of pensions for old-age, invalidity, accidents at work or occupational disease are entitled to family benefits in respect of their children[5] irrespective of where the pensioner or the children are residing, in accordance with the rules laid down in Article 77.[6]

Orphans receive benefits in accordance with rules laid down in Article 78[7] irrespective of where the orphans or the natural parents or persons actually maintaining them are residing.

Benefits are provided according to the legislation of the competent state but where there are several competent states benefits are to be paid in accordance with the legislation of the state to which the pensioner or the deceased was last subject.[8]

The right to orphans' benefits is suspended if the children become entitled to family benefits or family allowances under the law of a Member State by virtue of the pursuit of an economic activity.[9] The ECJ explained that the effect of suspension is relevant to the economic activity.[10] In such a case the children are regarded as members of the family of an employed or self-employed person.[11]

---

20 P 552, note 19, supra.
 1 Reg 574/72, Art 10(1).
 2 Reg 1408/71, Art 76 as substituted.
 3 Case 134/77: *Raggazoni v Caisse de Compensation pour Allocations Familiales 'Assubel'* [1978] ECR 963, [1979] 3 CMLR 67.
 4 Reg 1408/71, Art 75(1) as substituted.
 5 See Case 17/75: *Anselmetti v Caisse de Compensation des Allocations Familiales de l'Industrie Charbonnière* [1975] ECR 781, [1976] 2 CMLR 350; Case 99/80: *Galinsky*, supra.
 6 As substituted.
 7 As substituted; see Case 3/70: *Caisse de Compensation pour Allocations des Charbonnages du Couchant de Mons v Beninator* [1970] ECR 415, [1970] CMLR 232.
 8 Art 79, as substituted.
 9 Art 79(3), as substituted; see Case 100/78: *Rossi v Caisse de Compensation pour Allocations Familiales des Régions de Charleroi et Namur* [1979] ECR 831, [1979] 3 CMLR 544 (following Case 134/77, supra).
10 Case 733/79: *Caisse de Compensation des Allocations Familiales des Régions de Charleroi et Namur v Laterza* [1980] ECR 1915, [1981] 1 CMLR 158; Case 807/79: *Gravina v Landesversicherungsanstalt Schwaben* [1980] ECR 2205, [1981] 1 CMLR 529; Case 320/82: *D'Amario v Landesversicherungsanstalt Schwaben* [1983] ECR 3811.
11 See Case 9/79: *Wörsdorfer (née Koschniske) v Raad van Arbeid* [1979] ECR 2717, [1980] 1 CMLR 87.

E. Aggregation and appointment

The Community nature of the social insurance co-ordination rules is reflected in the principle of aggregation which requires the competent authorities of a Member State to take into account rights earned in another Member State when computing certain benefits guaranteed by the Regulation. This means that the competent authority of a Member State, whose legislation makes the acquisition, retention or recovery of the rights to benefits conditional upon the completion of periods of insurance, employment or residence, must, to the extent necessary, take account of such periods completed in another Member State as if they were periods completed under its own legislation. The result is the verification of the entitlement to the given benefit.

Corollary to the principle of aggregation is the principle of reimbursement between the Member States involved whereby the state paying the benefit will recoup itself from the other state(s) pro rata, ie in proportion to the relevant periods completed in each state. The object is to verify the amount of the benefit payable.

F. Cumulation and overlapping of benefits

Whilst the principle of aggregation purports to secure protection of the beneficiary, the provisions against cumulation and overlapping are meant to secure equality of treatment between nationals of the host state and migrant workers. The prevention of overlapping serves further to check abuse of the Community system which might result in fictitious claims and duplication of benefits payable under different national laws.[12]

Article 12(1) of Regulation 1408/71 provides that:

'This Regulation can neither confer nor maintain the right to several benefits of the same kind for one and the same period of compulsory insurance. However this provision shall not apply to benefits in respect of invalidity, old-age, death (pensions) or occupational disease which are awarded by the institutions of two or more Member States in accordance with the provisions of Articles 41, 43(2) and (3), 46, 50 and 51 or Article 60(1)(b).'

The second paragraph of Article 12 enables the Member State to reduce, suspend or withdraw benefits which overlap with other social security benefits or other income if these were derived from the legislation of another Member State.

The third paragraph of Article 12 enables the Member States to apply the restrictions of the preceding paragraph in respect of persons in receipt of invalidity benefits or anticipatory old-age benefits pursuing a professional or trade activity even if that activity were executed in another Member State. However provisions against overlapping do not apply to benefits obtained under voluntary or private schemes operating outside the scope of the compulsory national insurance scheme.

Dealing with the problem of overlapping benefit the ECJ ruled that social security benefits available under two or more national systems cannot be reduced if the benefits are secured independently of the Regulation, that is, without the aid of aggregation of periods of insurance under different national systems in order to qualify for the benefit.[13]

---

12 Cf Case 12/67: *Guissart v Belgium* [1967] ECR 425.
13 Case 34/69: *Caisse d'Assurance Vieillesse des travailleurs salariés de Paris v Duffy* [1969] ECR 597, [1971] CMLR 391. See also Case C-153/97: *Rodriguez v INSS and IGSS* [1998] ECR I-8645.

If the claimant is entitled in two different countries the benefits may not be apportioned unless, in order to establish the right to benefit, it is necessary first to aggregate the periods completed under different national laws. However no such apportionment can be made if the effect would be to reduce the benefits to which the claimant is entitled, under the law of a single state.[14] As put in other cases[15] entitlement under national law alone may not be reduced by Community law. However, where the periods of insurance do not legally coincide because one is compulsory and the other voluntary, they cannot be aggregated.[16]

Dealing with a variety of overlaps[17] the Court ruled that:

'... so long as a worker is receiving a pension by virtue of national legislation alone, the provisions of Regulation 1408/71 do not prevent the national legislation, including the national rules against the overlapping of benefits, from being applied to him in its entirety, provided that if the application of such national legislation proves less favourable than the application of the rules regarding aggregation and apportionment, those rules must, by virtue of Article 46(1) of Regulation 1408/71 be applied ...'[18]

Where benefits overlap (eg invalidity and old-age) the beneficiary may opt for the more advantageous one.[19]

Cumulation of benefits of the same kind is not allowed. Thus family allowances for orphan children in one country are not payable if the children in question live with their mother in another country and whose step-father is in receipt of such benefits in respect of these children in the latter country.[20]

The ECJ has also ruled on the question of double protection and thus double contribution.[1] When a Dutchman, who previously worked in the Belgian mines, moved to the Netherlands he was required to pay contributions under the Dutch general social security scheme. He refused since he was already a pensioner in Belgium and was also entitled to child benefits and sickness benefits. The Court held Article 13 applicable since Belgian law was the governing law as the law of the competent state in which he was employed during his working life.

---

14 Case 26/78: *Institut National D'Assurance Maladie-Invalidité v Viola* [1978] ECR 1771, [1979] 1 CMLR 635, and cases cited in the Report.

15 Case 112/76: *Manzoni v Fonds National de Retraite des Ouvriers Mineurs* [1977] ECR 1647, [1978] 2 CMLR 416; Case 22/77: *Fonds National de Retraite des Ouvriers Mineurs v Muru* [1977] ECR 1699, [1978] 2 CMLR 416; Case 32/77: *Giuliani v Landesversicherungsantalt Schwaben* [1977] ECR 1857, [1978] 2 CMLR 416; Case 37/77: *Greco v Fonds National de Retraite des ouvriers Mineurs* [1977] ECR 1711, [1978] 2 CMLR 416.

16 Case 176/78: *Schaap v Bestuur van de Bedrijfs-vereniging voor Bank en Veizekeringswezen (No 2)* [1979] ECR 1673, [1980] 2 CMLR 13.

17 Case 83/77: *Naselli v Caisse Auxilaire d'Assurance* – invalidity pension in Italy and Belgium [1978] ECR 683, [1979] 1 CMLR 270; Case 98/77: *Schaap v Bestuur van de Bedrijfs vereniging voor Bank en Verzekeringswezen (No 1)* – invalidity pension under Dutch and German law [1978] ECR 707, [1979] 1 CMLR 270; Case 105/77: *Bestuur der Sociale Verzekeringsbank v Boerboom-Kersjes* – widow's pension under Dutch law and survivor's benefit under German law [1978] ECR 717, [1979] 1 CMLR 270.

18 See the *Schaap* case, supra, para 10.

19 Case 180/78, p 551, note 8 supra.

20 Case 115/77: *Laumann v Landesversicherungsanstalt Rheinprovinz* [1978] ECR 805, [1978] 3 CMLR 201.

1 Case C-140/88: *Noij v Staatsecratris van Financie* [1991] ECR I-387.

G. Subrogation

In accordance with the principle of insurance, where a person receives social security benefits under the legislation of one Member State in respect of an injury suffered in another Member State for which the wrongdoer is liable to pay compensation, Article 93 requires all Member States to recognize a right of recovery by the competent institution from the responsible party, by way of subrogation or direct action provided that such a right is conferred in the institution by the legislation it administers.[2]

In a case[3] decided under Regulation 3 the ECJ accorded the right of recovery to a national institution in subrogation to the claim of the dependants of a worker killed whilst on holiday abroad. However the obligation of the third party to pay compensation is governed by the private international law relating to torts; the *lex loci delicti*.[4]

The right of subrogation 'covers only the compensation to which the victim or his legal successors are entitled under the legislation of the state in the territory of which the injury occurred which corresponds to the benefits paid by the institution liable to pay benefits and not compensation granted for non-material damage or in respect of other items of damage of a personal nature'.[5]

---

2 Case 31/64: *Caisse Comune d'assurances la preroyance sociale v Bertholet* [1965] ECR 81, [1966] CMLR 191; Case 27/69: *Caisse de Maladie des CFL Entráide médicale v Co Belge d'Assurances Générales sur la Vie et contre les accidents* [1969] ECR 405, [1970] CMLR 243.
3 Case 44/65: *Hessische Knappschaft v Maison Singer et Fils* [1965] ECR 965, [1966] CMLR 82.
4 See Case 78/72: *L'Etoile Syndicat Général v De Waal* [1973] ECR 499; Case 72/76: *Landesversicherungsanstalt Rheinland-Pflaz v Topfer* [1977] ECR 271, [1977] 2 CMLR 121; Case C-397/96: *Caisse de pension des employés privés v Kordel* [1999] ECR I-5959, para 15-17.
5 Case 72/76, supra, note 4 at para 19.

Chapter 23

Freedom of movement of capital and payments (EC Articles 56-60 (ex Articles 67-73 and 104-109)[1]

A. Introduction

The economic freedoms on which the common market and, now, the European Union are founded would be largely illusory without the corresponding liberalization of money flows and financial operations between the Member States. Without such liberalization, cross-frontier payments for work and services provided by a person from another Member State would be in doubt; and persons wishing to establish themselves in another Member State would encounter difficulties in moving the capital required to do so. In addition, the services associated with the transfer of funds, whether as means of payment or as capital, could not be performed or would be performed only with difficulty and, hence, in an inefficient manner. The Treaty deals in different ways with transfers of money that constitutes the means of paying for goods or services (often referred to as 'current payments') and transfers that amount to the movement of capital.

The Treaty provisions concerned with the free movement of goods contain no reference to the liberalization of money flows required to pay for goods supplied from one Member State to another. The provisions concerned with the free movement of workers also contain no reference to the liberalization of money flows, whether taking the form of remuneration for the worker or the transfer of the worker's capital to, for example, his state of origin or to the place where he or she wishes to retire. In the case of the freedom to provide services, the exercise of that freedom would not ordinarily involve the transfer of capital. Instead, it tends to involve transfers of money to be used as the means of paying for the provision of a service.[2] Like the Treaty provisions concerned with the free

1 For a fuller account see Vaughan, op cit, Part 17 (J Handoll and Lord Kingsland).
2 Eg Cases 286/82 and 26/83: *Luisi & Carboni v Ministero del Tesoro* [1984] ECR 377.

movement of workers, those concerned with the freedom to provide services contain no general reference to the liberalization of money flows, save that EC Article 51(2) (ex Art 61(2)), provides that the liberalization of banking and insurance services is to be effected in step with the liberalization of movement of capital. That provision means that, where a banking or insurance service involves the transfer of capital (as in the case of the grant of a loan or the making of an investment in the context of a life assurance contract), the performance of that service is subject to the rules governing the movement of capital. It does not follow that all payments made in connection with the performance of the service are subject to those rules: payments made in consideration for the provision of the service (such as the payment of commission in return for the provision of the service) are distinct from the capital transfer that is the subject matter of the service; and such payments are not subject to the rules governing the movement of capital. Further, the application of the Treaty provisions governing the freedom to provide services is excluded in the case of banking and insurance services only to the extent that there remain restrictions on the free movement of capital that are compatible with the Treaty and that affect the movement in question.[3] In the case of the right of establishment, the position is different again. Exercise of the right of establishment typically involves a transfer of capital, if it involves transfer of resources at all, because the money transferred will be used in order to provide funds for the creation and continuance of an establishment in the state concerned and any non-monetary capital assets will be transferred for the same purpose: there will be no corresponding transfer of value back to the capital exporting state, as there would be if (for example) the money transfer were used in order to pay for the acquisition of goods or services. The right of establishment was therefore made subject to the Treaty rules governing capital movements.[4] As in the case of the freedom to provide services, that meant only that, if the exercise of the right of establishment involved a movement of capital, the Treaty provisions governing the right of establishment did not prevail over any restrictions on the movement of capital that were compatible with EC law and that were applicable to the movement in question. The Treaty provisions concerned with the free movement of capital also drew a distinction between capital movements themselves and payments connected with such movements, which were to have been liberalized by the end of the first stage of the transitional period at the latest.[5]

Although the Treaty provisions governing the free movement of goods and of workers, the freedom to provide services and the right of establishment do not contain provisions liberalizing payments made in return for the supply of goods or services effected pursuant to those Treaty rights, the Member States undertook elsewhere in the Treaty to authorize any payments connected with the movement of goods, services and capital, to the extent that the underlying movement of goods, services, capital and persons between Member States had been liberalized pursuant to the Treaty.[6] Insofar as movements of goods, services and capital were limited only by restrictions on payments connected with them, those restrictions were to be abolished progressively by applying, *mutatis mutandis*, the Treaty provisions relating to the free movement of goods, the liberalization of services and the free movement of capital.[7] The object of

---

3 Case C-222/95: *Societe Civile Immobiliere Parodi v Banque Albert de Bary* [1997] ECR I-3899, para 10.
4 EC Art 43 (ex Art 52), last sentence.
5 EC Art 67(2) (now repealed).
6 EC Art 106(1), as originally worded (now repealed).
7 EC Art 106(2), as originally worded (now repealed).

those provisions was to ensure free movement by authorizing all necessary transfers of currency.[8]

The result was that the liberalization of payments made in return for the supply of goods, labour, services or capital was effected in step with the liberalization of the basic freedom whose exercise gave rise to the payment. That liberalization applied where payment was made in a currency of one of the Member States but not where the currency of a third country was used.[9]

Where a money transfer (whatever its form, whether as a credit or in the physical form of banknotes or coins) or a transfer of some other form of capital (such as securities) is or would be made otherwise than in return for a corresponding transfer of value (such as the provision of goods or services), the transfer is not remuneration and, accordingly, it does not fall within the rules liberalizing payments.[10] Instead, it is a capital movement. Capital movements were originally the subject of EC Arts 67–73 (now repealed) and were gradually liberalized by means of secondary legislation.[11]

The freedom to transfer funds and capital generally from one Member State to another was a sensitive issue for a number of reasons connected with exchange rate movements, balance of payments, the stability of capital markets and the credit system, and economic and monetary policy generally. However, all the Treaty provisions concerned with such movement were revised radically by the TEU in the context of the move towards economic and monetary union and in the light of the degree of liberalization that had been achieved by the time of the making of the TEU. This chapter summarizes the effect of the current Treaty rules and describes the secondary legislation on which they are based.

B. The Treaty rules

EC Article 56 (ex Art 73b) prohibits restrictions on both the movement of capital and on payments in relation not only to movements and payments between Member States but also to movements and payments between Member States and third countries. The secondary legislation adopted before the insertion of EC 56 into the Treaty remains relevant for the purpose of determining what is a movement of capital.[12] The prohibition applies not only to measures that effectively prevent a person from having recourse to a currency other than that of the state in question[13] but also to measures of a less stringent nature, such as a requirement to obtain prior authorization.[14] The prohibition operates within the framework of the provisions set out in Chapter 4 of Title III of Part 3 of the EC Treaty. The qualifications imposed on the prohibition by those provisions

---

8   Case 203/80: *Casati* [1981] ECR 2595, para 24; Case 95/81: *Commission v Italy* [1982] ECR 2187, paras 21-25.
9   See EC Art 106(1) itself and the *Luisi & Carboni* cases, supra, para 28.
10 *Luisi & Carboni*, supra, paras 20-22; cf *Casati*, supra, paras 24-25.
11 See further below.
12 Case C-222/97: *Trummer and Mayer* [1999] ECR I-1661, para 21.
13 Eg *Trummer and Mayer*, supra; Case C-464/98: *Westdeutsche Landesbank Girozentrale v Stefan* 11 January 2001.
14 Cases C-163/94, C-165/94 and C-250/94: *Sanz de Lera* [1995] ECR I-4821, paras 24-25; Case C-54/99: *Association Eglise de Scientologie de Paris v Prime Minister*, 14 March 2000, para 14 (and see, under the earlier legislation, Cases C-358/93 and C-416/93: *Bordessa* [1995] ECR I-361). In contrast, the requirement of a prior declaration is acceptable where it is imposed in order to verify the nature, reality and purpose of a movement: eg the *Sanz de Lera* case, supra, paras 37-38.

are relatively limited and are set out below. To the extent that none of those qualifications is relevant, the prohibition can be relied upon in proceedings before a national court; and, to the extent that they are potentially applicable, their application is subject to judicial review.[15]

Restrictions in existence on 31 December 1993 under national or Community law may be applied to third countries to the extent that they affect the movement of capital to or from third countries involving direct investment (including investment in real estate), establishment, the provisions of financial services or the admission of securities to capital markets.[16] The Council may adopt measures in relation to the same movements by a qualified majority but must act unanimously if its measures would constitute a step back in Community law as regards the degree of liberalization already reached in the movement of capital to or from third countries.[17]

The prohibition on restrictions on the movement of capital and on payments is also without prejudice to the right of Member States to: (a) apply domestic tax laws distinguishing between taxpayers who are not in the same situation regarding their place of residence or the place where their capital is invested; and (b) take all requisite measures to prevent infringements of national laws and regulations (particularly in the fields of taxation and the prudential supervision of financial institutions) or to lay down procedures for the declaration of capital movements for the purpose of administrative or statistical information, or to take measures justified on the grounds of public policy or public security.[18] The Member States are in principle free to determine the requirements of public policy and public security in the light of their national needs but the following limitations apply to their reliance upon those concepts: first, they must be strictly construed so that their scope cannot be determined unilaterally by the Member States; secondly, they can be relied upon only if there is a genuine and sufficiently serious threat to a fundamental interest of society; thirdly, they cannot be used to serve purely economic ends; fourthly, there must be access to effective legal redress against any such measure; finally, a measure can be justified on the grounds of public policy or public security only if it is necessary for the protection of the interests in question and only in so far as those objectives cannot be attained by less restrictive measures.[19] That right of the Member States to restrict capital movements and payments may be exercised in such a way as to result in restrictions on the right of establishment as long as such restrictions are otherwise compatible with the Treaty;[20] it may not be exercised in such a way as to constitute a means of arbitrary discrimination or a disguised restriction on the free movement of capital and payments.[1]

---

15   See the *Sanz de Lera* case, supra, paras 41-48.
16   EC Art 57(1) (ex Art 73c(1)). That provision does not apply to the physical transfer of means of payment: see the *Sanz de Lera* case, supra, para 33.
17   EC Art 57(2) (ex Art 73c(2)).
18   EC Art 58(1) (ex Art 73d(1)). Under this provision, measures may be taken to combat illegal activities such as tax evasion, money laundering, drug trafficking or terrorism: see the *Sanz de Lera* case, supra, para 22.
19   The *Association Eglise de Scientologie de Paris* case (supra), paras 17-18. In that case, the measure was defective because it did not explain what was the threat to public policy or public security that justified it: see paras 20-23.
20   EC Art 58(2) (ex Art 73d(2)). There is already a considerable body of case law concerning the extent to which fiscal legislation is consistent with the Treaty: see, for example, Case C-141/99: *Algemene Maatschappij voor Investering en Dienstverlening v Belgium* 14 December 2000.
1   EC Art 58(3) (ex Art 73d(3)). The phrases 'arbitrary discrimination' and 'disguised restriction' are to be read in the same way as the similar phrases appearing in EC Art 30 (ex Art 36) (see p 471, supra). For an illustration of their application, see the *Sanz de Lera* case, supra, paras 21-30.

The Council may take safeguard measures with regard to third countries where, in exceptional circumstances, movements of capital to or from third countries cause, or threaten to cause, serious difficulties for the operation of economic and monetary union. Any such measures must be limited to a period not exceeding six months and must be strictly necessary.[2] There is no provision for similar measures to be taken in relation to movements of capital between Member States.

Where the Community interrupts or reduces its economic relations with one or more third countries,[3] the Council may also take the necessary urgent measures on the movement of capital and on payments as regards the third countries concerned.[4] Where the Council has not taken any such measures, and without prejudice to any discussions on the subject between the Member States under EC Article 297 (ex Art 224), a Member State may itself take unilateral measures against a third country in regard to capital movements and payments if it has serious political reasons for doing so and if there are sufficient grounds to justify urgent unilateral action of that sort.[5]

C. Liberalization directives

The combined effect of the first and second Directives[6] was the elimination of exchange controls in respect of current transactions, transfer of personal funds, investments of real estate and transfers in connection with the movement of goods and the provision of services. However the ECJ, propounding on the effects of current transactions, found the Directive inapplicable to stock exchange dealings. Thus Irish purchasers of shares in Irish companies listed on the London Stock Exchange had to obtain Irish exchange control permits. These transactions were not liberalized but remained subject to Irish law.[7]

The third Directive[8] standardized the measures to be taken by the Member States to rectify disturbances of the capital flows and minimize the detrimental effects of these measures upon domestic liquidity. Coupled with these problems was the effort to harmonize the services of banks and other financial institutions in order to remove restrictions imposed on their activities by national legislation.

The real impetus for legislation came from the Commission's 1985 White Paper[9] which urged greater liberalization of capital movements in the Community, restriction on the use by the Member States of the protective clauses under what

---

2 EC Art 59 (ex Art 73f). The measures in question are adopted by the Council by a qualified majority on a proposal from the Commission and after consulting the ECB.
3 See EC Art 301 (ex Art 228a).
4 EC Art 60(1) (ex Art 73g(1)). The Council follows the same procedure as that laid down in EC Art 301 (ex Art 228a). By way of example, see Council Reg 1607/98 (OJ 1998, L209/16), which prohibited the transfer of funds or other financial assets to Yugoslavia and Serbia.
5 EC Art 60(2) (ex Art 73g(2)). The Commission and other Member States must be informed of the measures taken by the date of their entry into force at the latest. The Council has power to require the Member State concerned to amend or abolish the measures that it has taken.
6 JO 1960, 921; OJ (Sp edn 1959-62) p 49 and JO 1963, 63; OJ (Sp edn 1963-64) p 5.
7 Case 143/86: *East (t/a Margetts and Addenbrooke) v Cuddy* [1988] ECR 625 [1988] 2 CMLR 1.
8 72/156 (JO 1972, L91/13; OJ 1972, 296).
9 Ibid paras 95-107.

were then EC 73 and 108(3) and the creation of a 'financial product' through the harmonization of laws governing financial services. Thus:

(1) Directive 85/583[10] completed the liberalization of capital operations necessary for the proper functioning of the Common Market and for the integration of domestic capital markets. It imposed an obligation upon the Member States to grant authorization and exchange facilities for transactions related to long-term commercial credits, acquisition of securities (shares, bonds and units) which were not dealt with on a stock exchange and admission (ie introduction, issue and placing) of securities to the capital markets.[11]
(2) Directive 88/361[12] removed the remaining restrictions on capital movements between the Member States as part of the completion of the internal market. It imposed an obligation upon the Member States to abolish restrictions on the movement of capital between persons resident in the Community and to ensure that capital transfers were made at the same rate of exchange as those applying to current transactions. It also laid down procedures under which the Member States might take protective measures restricting certain capital movements. These were permitted when foreign exchange markets were under the strain of short-term capital movements of exceptional magnitude which might lead to serious disturbances in Member States' monetary and exchange rate policies.

The EC Treaty was then amended by the TEU so as to reflect the degree of liberalization that had been achieved by the secondary legislation. After the amendment of the EC Treaty by the TEU, the legislative programme moved on to more positive measures designed to implement and facilitate economic and monetary union: Directive 97/5 lays down provisions for facilitating cross-border credit transfers;[13] Directive 97/9 deals with investor-compensation schemes;[14] and Directive 98/26 deals with settlement finality in payment and securities settlement systems.[15]

---

10 OJ 1985, L372, amending the first Directive.
11 See Case 157/85: *Brugnoni v Cassa di Risparmio de Genoa, Re ECSC Bonds purchased in Germany* [1986] ECR 2013, [1988] 1 CMLR 440.
12 OJ 1988, L178.
13 OJ 1997, L43/25.
14 OJ 1997, L84/22.
15 OJ 1998, L166/45.

Part V

The Law of the Economy: Community Policies

Chapter 24

Economic and monetary union

Originally, the EC Treaty envisaged only the co-ordination of the economic policies of the Member States and remedial measures designed to remove disequilibria in their balances of payment. The provisions of the Treaty dealing with economic policy dealt with three matters: short term economic (or conjectural) policy; balance of payments; and the common commercial policy (that is, the policy regarding trade with third countries). In relation to the first, the Member States merely committed themselves to treating their short term economic policy as a matter of common concern and to consultations between themselves and the Commission. There was a very limited power of action on the part of the Community institutions. In relation to balance of payments, the Member States committed themselves to pursuing economic policies that would ensure equilibrium in their overall balance of payments and maintain confidence in their currency. Provision was made for the co-ordination of economic policies to that end and for action to be taken at Community level if a Member State got into difficulties.[1] As early as 1958[2] a Monetary Committee to review the monetary and financial situation of the Member States had been established. In 1971, the Council and the representatives of the governments of the six original Member States issued a resolution on the attainment of economic and monetary union by stages;[3] and in 1974[4] the Council set up an Economic Policy Committee to link up financial and economic matters. However the most significant development in this field resulted in the European Monetary System (EMS), which became the first stage of the Economic and Monetary Union (EMU).

A. The EMS

The work on the monetary union began in 1970[5] and resulted in the Werner Report[6] which contained a number of recommendations. It proceeded from the

1 EC 3(g) and 103-116, as originally worded and originally numbered.
2 JO 1958, 390; OJ 1952-58, 60.
3 OJ 1971, C 28/1. See also the resolution made the following year (OJ 1972, C 38/3).
4 Decision 74/122 (OJ 1974, L63/21).
5 Council decision to set up a working party chaired by Professor Werner, the Luxembourg Minister of Finance (JO 1970, L59/44).
6 JO 1970, C 136/2.

premise that monetary policy cannot be treated in isolation and that its implementation would require new powers and new institutions. It should include a strengthening of consultation procedures, the conduct of the budgetary policies of the Member States, a measure of fiscal harmonization, co-ordination of monetary and credit policies and integration of the capital markets. The proposed European Monetary Union (EMU), as seen through the Werner Report, would display certain characteristics, ie total and irreversible reciprocal currency convertibility without fluctuations in the rates of exchange with immutable parity ratios, or, preferably, a single Community currency; the creation of liquidity in the Community and the centralization of monetary and credit policy; a common monetary policy vis-à-vis the rest of the world; the unification of national policies with regard to capital markets; the control at the Community level of the national budgets, regional and structural policies; and a continuous dialogue between the two sides of the industry conducted systematically at the Community level. The consequences would go far beyond the technical aspects of capital management.[7]

The Council endorsed the main elements of the Werner Report[8] but failed to implement it though it took three Decisions in the spirit of the Report, ie Decision 71/141[9] to improve the co-ordination of national short-term economic policies; Decision 71/142[10] to strengthen the co-operation between the central banks of the Member States; and Decision 71/143[11] to establish a short-term and medium-term monetary support mechanism to enable any Member State facing balance of payment difficulties to apply for and to be granted by the Council temporary financial assistance. Accordingly each participating central bank was assigned a debtor quota and a creditor quota in accordance with a distribution scale appropriate to each Member State.[12] The highest quotas, ie of 22.03% each, were allocated to the Central Banks of Germany, France and the UK, the lowest quota, ie of 1.27%, to the Central Bank of Ireland.

A further Resolution of the Council in 1972[13] envisaged further consultations and exchange of information relative to short- and medium-term financial policies as well as guidelines to be elaborated by an Economic Policy Group attached to the Council and consisting of a special representative of the relevant Minister of each Member State and a representative of the Commission, co-operating with the COREPER.

The Resolution also proposed to set up a Regional Development Fund and recommended that the European Agricultural Guidance and Guarantee Fund (EAGGF) should be used in order to foster regional development.

Following the Paris Summit of October 1972 the Council established a European Monetary Co-operation Fund[14] which was to become a positive step towards the Economic and Monetary Union characterized by the Werner Report. The Fund, having a distinct legal personality, was to promote:

---

7   Compendium of Community Monetary Texts, issued by the Monetary Committee, 1979, pp 17 et seq.
8   Resolution 22 March 1971, Compendium, supra, pp 25 et seq.
9   JO 1971, L73/12.
10   OJ 1971, L73/14.
11   OJ 1971, L73/15.
12   See amended Art 29 of the First Act of Accession and Decision 75/85 (OJ 1975, L330/50); 78/49 (OJ 1978, L14/14); 78/1041 (OJ 1978, L379/3).
13   JO 1972, C 38/3.
14   Reg 907/73, JO 1973, L89/2.

'(a) the proper functioning of the progressive narrowing of the margin of fluctuation of the Community currencies against each other;

(b) interventions in Community currencies on the exchange markets, and settlements between central banks leading to a concerted policy on reserves.'

The Annex to the Regulation contained the statute of the Fund and the provisional rules of procedure.[15]

However, whilst in the late 1960s the economic and monetary situation, culminating in a monetary crisis during 1969, brought home the need of a concerted economic and monetary policy, the dollar flow continued to affect the currency margins as well as the balance of payments of certain Member States, inflation continued unabated, the fuel crisis loomed large, and the Member States, facing the problem of economic stagnation and rising unemployment, became introspective. Maybe some were apprehensive of the common currency and the central direction of the national economy by the Community by the end of the decade.

Despite the set-back to the monetary policy certain measures taken during 1974 and 1975 were encouraging. These included:

(1) Council Directive 74/120[16] on the attainment of a high degree of convergence of the economic policies of the Member States;
(2) Directive 74/121[17] on the stability, economic growth and full employment; and
(3) the Resolution[18] on short-term monetary support.

Moreover, Regulation 397/75[19] governing Community loans authorized the Community to raise funds either directly from third countries and financial institutions, or on the capital markets, for the purpose of re-lending those funds to the Member States experiencing balance of payment difficulties caused by the increase in the prices of petroleum products. However the effects of these measures on the development of the monetary policy were negligible.

In order to revive the drooping spirit of the Community the Summits of Copenhagen, Bremen and Brussels, in April, July and December 1978 urged action to resume the work, this time, on a narrower concept of monetary co-operation resulting in the European Monetary System (EMS).

The EMS was launched by the Resolution of the Brussels Summit[20] on the following lines:

(1) In the centre of the EMS was the European Currency Unit (ECU) initially identical in value with the European Unit of Account (EUA).
(2) The ECU would be used:
(a) as the denominator for the exchange rate mechanism;
(b) as the basis for a divergence indicator;
(c) as the denominator for operations in both the intervention and the credit mechanism; and

---

15 Compendium, supra p 46 et seq.
16 JO 1974, C 20/1.
17 JO 1974, L63/19.
18 JO 1974, C 20/1.
19 JO 1975, L46/1 implemented by Reg 298/75 (JO 1975 L46/3).
20 Text, Compendium, supra, p 40 et seq.

(d)   as a means of settlement between monetary authorities of the Community.

(3) (a)   Each national currency would have an ECU-related central rate used to establish a grid of bilateral exchange rates.

    (b)   Fluctuation margins of ± 2.25% would be established around these exchange rates but countries with floating currencies might opt for a margin up to ± 6% on the understanding that these margins would be reduced gradually.

(4)   Adjustments of central rates would be subject to mutual agreement between the participating countries.

(5) (a)   In principle intervention would be made in participating currencies;

    (b)   It would be compulsory when the intervention points defined by the fluctuation margins had been reached.

(6) (a)   An ECU basket formula would be used as an indicator of divergencies between national currencies;

    (b)   A 'threshold of divergence' would be fixed at 75% of the maximum spread of divergence for each currency;

    (c)   When a currency crossed its 'threshold of divergence' the authorities concerned had to correct the situation by any of the following measures:

        (I)   diversified intervention;

        (II)   measures of domestic monetary policy;

        (III) changes in central rates;

        (IV) other measures of economic policy.

(7)   To serve as a means of settlement, an initial supply of ECU was provided by the European Monetary Co-operation Fund (EMCF) established in 1973 against the deposit of 20% of gold and 20% of dollar reserves currently held by Central Banks.

(8)   Initially the existing credit mechanisms would be maintained but these would be consolidated into a single fund in the final phase of the EMS.

(9)   In the international context the EMS would require co-ordination of exchange policies vis-à-vis non-participating countries.

(10) European countries would participate in the exchange rate based on agreements between Central Banks.

The United Kingdom was the last Member State to join the EMS in 1990 and was forced out of it in September 1992.

B.   The Maastricht scheme

(1)   GENERAL PRINCIPLES

Much of the preparatory work for the EMU was done by a committee of the governors of the national Central Banks and independent experts chaired by the President of the Commission. In April 1989 the committee proposed a three-stage process, albeit without a definite timetable. In spite of British opposition the work continued and negotiations were carried out at various levels thus preparing the ground for the Maastricht Summit in December 1991. The Maastricht Treaty endorsed the three-stage development but a special Protocol enabled the United Kingdom to opt out of the third stage. It means that the United Kingdom is not legally bound to move to the final stage without a separate decision of the British Government and Parliament. With or without the United Kingdom the scheme reflects a logical extension of the Common Market and a significant step towards the conversion of the EC into a Political and Economic Union.

In order to achieve the objectives of the Union the Member States and the EC shall adopt an economic policy based on a close co-operation of national policies, the internal market and common objectives defined in accordance with open market economy and free competition.[1] Concurrently with these principles there shall be irrevocable fixing of exchange rates leading to the introduction of a single currency (now the Euro) and the definition and conduct of a single monetary policy and exchange rate policy. The primary objective of the single monetary policy and exchange rate policy is to maintain price stability. Without prejudice to that primary objective, their other objective is to support the general economic policies of the Community. Both the Community and the Member States shall apply stable prices, sound public finances and monetary conditions and a sustainable balance of payments as their guiding principles.[2]

The Treaty envisages that economic and monetary union will be achieved in three stages. The first had no specific commencement date. During that stage, the Member States were to have implemented the single internal market and, more particularly, removed restrictions on the free movement of capital and introduced multiannual programmes intended to ensure the lasting convergence necessary for the achievement of economic and monetary union.[3] The second stage began on 1 January 1994. During it, the Member States were to endeavour to avoid excessive government deficits and, where appropriate, start the process leading to the independence of their Central Banks. Various provisions dealing essentially with budgetary discipline came into effect and preparatory steps were taken paving the way for the third stage.[4] The third stage was to start with the adoption of a single currency and, accordingly, could not commence before that was possible. The Treaty specified that the third stage should start on 1 January 1999 if it was not possible to commence it before then.[5] In the event, the conditions required for the commencement of the third stage were satisfied by that date and the third stage duly commenced.

(2) ECONOMIC POLICY

New provisions complement and extend the EC framework of economic policy. The Member States are now committed to conducting their economic policies with a view to contributing to the achievement of the objectives of the Community and in the context of broad guidelines adopted by the Council on a recommendation made by the Commission and after the European Council has discussed and reached a conclusion on the guidelines in draft form. Both the Member States and the Community must act in accordance with the principles of an open market economy with free competition, favouring an efficient allocation of resources and in compliance with the principles set out in EC Article 4 (ex Art 3a).[6] Further, the Member States must regard their own economic policies as a matter of common concern and co-ordinate these within the Council[7] and, in this context, the Community institutions are granted new powers. Thus the Council, acting by a

1 EC Art 4(1) (ex Art 3a(1)).
2 EC Art 4(2) and (3) (ex Art 3a(2), (3)).
3 Cf EC Art 116(2) (ex Art 109e(2)).
4 EC Art 116-117 (ex Art 109e-109f).
5 EC Art 121(4) (ex Art 109j(4)).
6 EC Art 98 and 99(2) (ex Art 102a and 103(2)).
7 EC Art 99(1) (ex Art 103(1)).

qualified majority on a recommendation from the Commission, shall draft proposals for guidelines of the economic policies of the Member States and the Communities and submit these to the European Council. On the basis of the European Council's conclusions the Council shall, by a qualified majority, direct a recommendation to the Member States informing the European Parliament accordingly.[8]

The Member States ought to inform the Commission of the important measures regarding economic policies taken by them, and the Council, on the basis of that information, shall monitor the progress as well as the application of the guidelines in this field. Where national economic policies are found to be inconsistent with the guidelines or putting the system at risk, the Council by a qualified majority may direct appropriate recommendations to the country concerned.[9] The Council may, on a proposal from the Commission, make the necessary recommendations to the state concerned and decide to make these recommendations public (no doubt to justify its action before public opinion). The President of the Council and the Commission shall report to the European Parliament on the result of multilateral surveillance.[10] The President of the Council may be invited to appear before the competent Committee of the European Parliament if the Council has made its recommendations public. The Council may adopt detailed rules for the multilateral surveillance procedure.[11]

The Council may decide upon measures appropriate to the economic situation, in particular where severe difficulties arise in the supply of certain products. A Member State facing severe economic difficulties caused by exceptional circumstances beyond its control may, on a proposal from the Commission, receive financial assistance which the Council will grant by a unanimous decision. If such difficulties arise from a natural disaster the decision to grant assistance shall be taken by a qualified majority.[12]

The Treaty prohibits overdraft facilities and any other type of credit facility with the European Central Bank (ECB) or with the national Central Banks in favour of Community institutions, Member States' central government or regional organizations or to public authorities and public undertakings; and any measure granting the Community institutions or bodies and similar national bodies, public authorities and undertakings privileged access to financial institutions.[13] Without prejudice to mutual financial guarantees for the joint execution of a specific project, the Community shall not be liable for or assume the commitments of national governments (whether central or regional) or other national public authorities, bodies and undertakings; and the same applies as between Member States.[14]

---

8 EC Art 99(2) (ex Art 103(2)). See Council Recommendation 99/570 (OJ 1999, L217/34) (for earlier guidelines, see OJ 1994, L7/9 and L200/38; OJ 1995, L191/24; OJ 1996, L179/46; OJ 1997, L209/12; OJ 1998, L200/34).

9 EC Art 99(2)-(3) (ex Art 103(3)(4)). See also Council Reg 1466/97 (OJ 1997, L209/1), which provided for the strengthening of the surveillance of budgetary positions and economic policies. Economic accounts use a standardized methodology set out in Council Reg 2223/96 (OJ 1996, L310/1), as amended, which was implemented by Reg 1500/2000 (OJ 2000, L172/3).

10 EC Art 99(4) (ex Art 103(4)).

11 EC Art 99(5) (ex Art 103(5)).

12 EC Art 100 (ex Art 103a).

13 EC Arts 101 and 102 (ex Arts 104 and 104a). The prohibition on the grant of overdraft and credit facilities does not apply to publicly-owned credit institutions. So far as concerns the supply of reserves by Central Banks, such institutions are to be given the same treatment by national Central Banks and by the ECB as that given to private credit institutions. Definitions for the application of these prohibitions were laid down in Council Regs 3603/93 and 3604/93 (OJ 1993, L332/1 and 4).

14 EC Art 103 (ex Art 104b). See Reg 3603/93, supra.

Member States must avoid excessive budget deficits subject to the detailed provisions of EC Art 104 (ex Art 104c), which govern the intervention of the Community institutions in this respect. In this context the Commission shall monitor government debts and examine the budgetary discipline. If there is a risk of excessive deficit the Commission shall inform the Council which can make recommendations to the state concerned with a view to bringing the situation under control. If there is no response the Council may make its recommendation public. Where the state persists in failing to put these into practice the Council may give notice that within a specified time limit the deficit reduction must be achieved. Whilst the enforcement actions under EC Arts 226 and 227 (ex Arts 169 and 170) are expressly excluded in such situations it is provided that the Council may resort to certain prophylactic measures. Thus it may require further information, invite the EIB to reconsider its lending policy towards the Member State concerned and require the Member State to make a non-interest-bearing deposit with the Community until the excessive deficit has been corrected. Ultimately it may impose fines and inform the European Parliament of its decision, which have to be taken on a proposal from the Commission by a majority of two-thirds of the weighted votes excluding the votes of the state concerned. Further provisions relating to the implementation of the rules described above are set out in the Protocol on the excessive deficit procedure annexed to the Treaty.[15]

(3)   MONETARY POLICY

The primary objective of the European System of Central Banks (ESCB), consisting of the European Central Bank (ECB) and the national Central Banks, is to maintain price stability. Subject to that, the ESCB's function is to support the Community's general economic policies. To that end the ESCB shall define and implement the monetary policy of the Community; conduct foreign exchange operations; hold and manage the official foreign reserves of the Member States and promote the smooth operation of payments systems. It shall also contribute to the supervision of credit institutions by the competent authorities and to the stability of the financial system.[16]

The ECB has the exclusive right to authorize the issue of banknotes in the Community both by the ECB and the national Central Banks. Such banknotes alone shall have the status of legal tender in the Community. However Member States will be able to issue coins subject to ECB approval. The Council shall enact measures to harmonize denominations and technical specifications of coins.[17] Thus national currencies shall be replaced by a common Community currency and from the start of the third stage the value of the common currency 'shall be irrevocably fixed'.[18] At that stage the Council acting with unanimity and without derogation shall, on a proposal from the Commission and after consulting the ECB, adopt the conversion rates at which the Member States' currencies shall be irrevocably fixed and at which the common Community currency shall be

---

15   See also Council Reg 3605/93 (OJ 1993, L332/7), on the application of the Protocol; Council Reg 1467/97 (OJ 1997, L209/6), which speeded up and clarified the procedure; and Commission Decision 95/501 (OJ 1998, L225/29).
16   EC Art 105(1) and (2) (ex Art 105(1) and (2)). The ESCB's task of holding and managing the official foreign reserves of the Member States is without prejudice to the holding and management of foreign exchange working balances by the Member States: see ibid Art 105(3) (ex Art 105(3)). The ECB has issued guidelines on the management of foreign reserves: see OJ 2000, L207/24.
17   EC Art 106 (ex Art 105a). See Council Reg 975/98 (OJ 1998, L139/6), as amended.
18   EC Art 118 (ex Art 109g).

substituted for these currencies. The common Community currency shall be a currency in its own right. Its external value (that is, its value as against the currencies of third countries) will not be modified by the internal fixing of the conversion rate as between it and the currencies of the Member States.[19] The Treaty calls the common Community currency the 'ECU'. It was decided at the Madrid summit that that was a generic name. The name actually given to the common currency is the Euro.

The Council, unanimously determined, shall, on a recommendation from the ECB or the Commission, after consulting the European Parliament, conclude formal agreements on an exchange rate system for the ECU vis-à-vis non-Community countries. However, acting by a qualified majority on a recommendation from the ECB or the Commission and consulting the ECB, the Council may adopt, adjust or abandon the central rates of the ECU within the exchange rate system. The European Parliament ought to be informed accordingly.[20]

In derogation from the exercise of the treaty-making power regulated by EC Art 300 (ex Art 228), international agreements concerning monetary or foreign exchange regime matters between the Community and non-Community States or international organizations, shall be negotiated and concluded according to arrangements laid down by the Council acting by a qualified majority on a recommendation from the Commission. These arrangements shall ensure that the Community speaks with one voice on such occasions. Agreements concluded according to such arrangements shall be binding on the ECB, the Community institutions and the Member States.[1]

However outside the Community competence and Community Agreements regarding the Economic and Monetary Union, the Member States are free to negotiate in their own right in international bodies and conclude international agreements.[2]

(4)   INSTITUTIONAL FRAMEWORK OF THE EMU

The development towards the EMU has necessitated an adjustment of the functions of the existing Community institutions and the creation of new ones. At the head of the EMU power structure is the European Council which is involved in the major EMU decisions. In its deliberations it is assisted by the Ministers of Finance and Economy.

(1) The Commission, as always responsible for initiating Community action, is charged with additional duties of proposing policies to the Council of Ministers, assisting the Council in the surveillance of economic activities and monitoring implementation of the EMU measures. It participates in the Economic and Financial Committee (which consists of two members representing each Member State and the Commission)[3] in an advisory capacity and a member of the Commission participates, without voting, in the Governing Council of the ECB.[4]

(2) The European Parliament has to be informed and consulted on economic policy surveillance and certain aspects of monetary policy. Its assent is required for institutional adjustments.

---

19   Ibid Art 123(4) (ex Art 109l(4)).   See Council Reg 2866/98 (OJ 1998, L359/1).
20   EC Art 111(1)-(2) (ex Art 109(1)-(2)).
 1   EC Art 111(3) (ex Art 109(3)).
 2   EC Art 111(5) (ex Art 109(5)).
 3   EC Art 114(2) (ex Art 109c(2)).
 4   EC Art 113(1) (ex Art 109b(1)).

(3) The Council of Ministers as the chief executive body plays a central role in the EMU. It reports to the European Council on major issues and informs the European Parliament as required. It takes decisions either by a unanimous or qualified majority vote and together with the Commission enforces the obligations arising under the system. The President of the Council, like a Member of the Commission, has a non-voting participation in the Governing Council of the ECB.[5]

(4) The Treaty set up a Monetary Committee[6] consisting of two members from each Member State and the Commission. Its function was advisory. It kept under review the monetary and financial situation of the Member States and the Community and reported to the Commission and the Council during the first and second stages of economic and monetary union.

When the Union reached the third stage, the Monetary Committee was dissolved and replaced by the Economic and Financial Committee.[7] In addition to representatives of the Member States and the Commission, that Committee comprises no more than two appointees of the ECB. The Council of Ministers, on the proposal from the Commission, after consulting the ECB and the Committee itself, is responsible for laying down detailed provisions for its composition and functioning. In principle it continues the work of its predecessor on a wider scale, including the review of the monetary and financial situation and the general payments system of the Member States which have obtained derogations from the EMU system. It shall report to the Commission and the Council and assist the latter in the preparation of measures to implement the system.

(5) The European System of Central Banks (ESCB) is composed of the European Central Bank (ECB) and of the Central Banks of the Member States.[8] The ESCB and the ECB were established on 1 June 1998.[9] The ESCB is similar to the German central banking system where the state banks form part of the Bundesbank. It is governed by the decision-making bodies of the ECB which are the Governing Council and the Executive Board.[10] The Protocol attached to the Treaty lays down the statute of the ESCB and the ECB and defines their respective functions. During the second stage, the development of EMU through the co-ordination of monetary policies, preparing for the introduction of a single currency, monitoring EMS and facilitating the use of the ECU were the main tasks of the European Monetary Institute, a body having legal personality and directed and managed by a Council consisting of a President, a Vice-President, and the Governors of the Central Banks of the Member States.[11] When it was established, the ECB took over the tasks of the EMI, which was then liquidated.[12]

The ECB has legal personality[13] and enjoys in each of the Member States the most extensive legal capacity accorded to legal persons under their laws.[14] In particular it may acquire and dispose of movable and immovable property and may be a party to legal proceedings. It is an independent institution[15] and

5 EC Art 113(1) (ex Art 109b(1)).
6 EC Art 114(1) (ex Art 109c(1)).
7 EC Art 114(2) (ex Art 109c(2)). For its Statutes see OJ 1999, L5/72 (adopted by Decision 99/8 (OJ 1999, L5/72)).
8 EC Arts 8 and 107(1) (ex Arts 4a and 106(1)), and Protocol Art 1.1.
9 Bulletin 6-1998, para 1.3.4.
10 EC Art 113(1) (ex Art 106(3)), and Protocol Art 1.2.
11 EC Art 117 (ex Art 109f). The Statute of the EMI was laid down in a Protocol annexed to the Treaty.
12 EC Art 123(2) (ex Art 109L(2)).
13 EC Art 107(2) (ex Art 106(2)).
14 Protocol Art 9.
15 EC Art 108 (ex Art 107), and Protocol Art 7.

as such it may not seek or take instructions from Community institutions, from any government of a Member State or any other body. Correspondingly, the above-mentioned entities must not seek to influence the members of the decision-making bodies of the ECB. The same principle of independence applies to the national Central Banks, which must neither seek instruction nor be subjected to influence from Community institutions or the governments or any other bodies.

The Governing Council of the ECB[16] comprising the members of the Executive Board and the governors of the national central banks takes decisions by a simple majority, in the event of a tie the President having a casting vote. Each member has one vote unless otherwise provided in the Statute. A quorum of two-thirds is required. In principle only those present may vote but, exceptionally, votes may be cast by means of teleconferencing.

In certain matters (the capital of the ECB, transfer of foreign reserve assets to the ECB, allocation of monetary income of national Central Banks and allocation of net profits and losses of the ECB) decisions will be taken by a qualified majority according to the national Central Banks' shares in the subscribed capital of the ECB.

The Governing Council formulates the monetary policy of the Community including decisions relating to intermediate monetary objectives, key interest rates and the supply of reserves in the ECB and establishes the necessary guidelines for their implementation.

The Governing Council meets at least ten times a year. The President of the Council of Ministers and a member of the Commission may participate in these meetings without the right to vote. Whilst the Council may submit a motion for the deliberations of the Governing Council, the President of the ECB shall be invited to participate in-Council meetings when discussing matters relating to the ESCB.

The ECB makes an annual report on the activities of the ESCB and on the monetary policy to the European Council, the Commission, the Council of Ministers and the European Parliament. This report is presented by the President of the ECB in person to the Council of Ministers and the European Parliament. The latter may hold a general debate on it. Moreover the President of the ECB and members of the Executive Board may, at the request of the European Parliament, or on their own initiative, be heard by the competent committees of the European Parliament.

The Executive Board,[17] responsible for the day-to-day conduct of the business of the ECB, consists of the President, the Vice-President and four other members. Unlike the members of the Governing Council, all are full-time employees of the ECB appointed by the European Council for a non-renewable eight-year term of office. They have to be nationals of the Member States and persons of recognized standing and professional experience in monetary and banking matters. The terms and conditions of their employment are subject to a contract fixed by the Governing Council on a proposal of a Committee comprising three members appointed by the Governing Council and three members appointed by the Council of Ministers. A member of the Board who fails to carry out his duty or is guilty of serious misconduct shall be dismissed by the decision of the Court of Justice on application by the Governing Council or the Executive Board.

16 Protocol Art 10.
17 Protocol Art 11.

The Executive Board implements monetary policy in accordance with the guidelines and decisions laid down by the Governing Council and carries out duties delegated to it.[18] It gives the necessary instructions to the national Central Banks. The meetings[19] of the Governing Council and of the Executive Board are chaired by the President or one of the Vice-Presidents. The President or his nominee shall represent the ECB externally, but the ECB shall decide how the ESCB shall be represented in the field of international co-operation.

In order to align its system with the ESCB each Member State must ensure that its legislation concerning the national Central Bank is compatible with the Treaty and Protocol.[20] In particular the term of office of a governor of the national Central Bank must be no less than five years and a governor may be relieved from office only on the grounds of serious misconduct or failure to perform his duties. A decision to this effect may be referred to the Court of Justice by the governor concerned or the Governing Council.[1]

Because they are an integral part of the ESCB the national Central Banks must act in accordance with the guidelines and instructions of the ECB.[2] Compliance shall be ensured by the Governing Council.

National Central Banks may perform functions other than those specified in the Protocol unless the Governing Council decides by a majority of two-thirds of votes cast that they interfere with the objectives and tasks of the ESCB.[3] Such functions cannot be attributed to the ESCB and any responsibility or liability in this respect shall fall upon the national Central Banks.

Monetary functions and operations of the ESCB are regulated by the Protocol.[4] These include provisions on the accounts with the ECB and the national central banks; open market and credit operations; minimum reserves;[5] instruments on monetary control; operations with public entities; clearing and payment systems and external operations. In the latter context the ECB and the national Central Banks may establish relations with central banks and financial institutions in other countries and with international organizations; acquire and sell (spot and forward) all types of foreign exchange assets, which include securities and all other assets in currency of any country or units of account; and conduct all types of banking transactions in relations with third countries and international organizations, including borrowing and lending operations.

The ECB may offer advice and be consulted by the Council of Ministers, the Commission and the Member States on the scope and implementation of Community legislation relating to the prudential supervision of credit institutions and to the stability of the financial system.[6]

The financial year[7] of the ECB and the national Central Banks begins on 1 January and ends on 31 December. The annual accounts of the ECB drawn up by the Executive Board shall be published after being approved by the Governing

---

18 Protocol Art 12.
19 Protocol Art 13.
20 EC Art 109 (ex Art 108) and Protocol Art 14. Provision is made for the consultation of the ECB on draft legislative provisions by Council Decision 98/415 (OJ 1998, L189/42).
1 Protocol Art 14.2.
2 Protocol Art 14.3.
3 Ibid Art 14.4.
4 Ibid Art 17 et seq.
5 As to which see Council Regs 2531/98 (OJ 1998, L318/1), and 2818/98 (OJ L356/1 (as amended by Reg 1921/2000 (OJ 2000, L229/34))).
6 Ibid Art 25.
7 Ibid Art 26.

Council. These as well as the accounts of the national central banks must be audited by independent external auditors recommended by the Governing Council and approved by the Council of Ministers.[8]

The ECB has an operational capital[9] of at least ECU 5,000 million provided by the national Central Banks which shall be its sole subscribers and holders. These subscriptions shall be made in a key[10] which determines the weighting of the voting power according to the size of the population and the share in the gross domestic product. Thus each national Central Bank shall be assigned a weighting equal to the sum of: 50% of the share of its country in the population of the Community: and 50% of the share of its country in the gross domestic product at market prices of the Community.

These weightings shall be adjusted every five years after the establishment of the ESCB.

The ECB shall be provided by national Central Banks with foreign reserve assets other than Member States' currencies, ECUs, IMF reserve positions and DSRs up to an amount equivalent to ECU 50,000 million. The subscriptions to be called up shall be determined by the Governing Council and the contributions of each national Central Bank shall be fixed in proportion to its share in the subscribed capital of the ECB.[11]

Whilst the national Central Banks are allowed to perform transactions in accordance with their obligations towards international organizations, all other operations in foreign reserve assets shall be subject to approval by the ECB in order to ensure consistency with the exchange rate and monetary policy of the Community.[12]

The income accruing to the national Central Banks in the execution of the ESCB's monetary policy shall be equal to their annual income derived from their assets held against notes in circulation and deposit liabilities vis-à-vis credit institutions.[13] An amount of the ECB's net profit not exceeding 20% shall be transferred to the general reserve fund and the remainder distributed to the shareholders of the ECB in proportion to their subscribed shares. Should the ECB incur a loss the shortfall may be offset against its general reserve fund or, if necessary, following a decision of the Governing Council, against the monetary income of the relevant financial year in proportion to the amounts received from the allocation of the monetary income.[14]

In order to carry out its duties the ECB shall have the power to issue recommendations and opinions, take decisions and adopt regulations within the scope of its functions. Whilst the recommendations and opinions shall have no binding force, decisions shall be binding in their entirety upon those to whom they are addressed and regulations shall have general application in all the Member

---

8   Ibid Art 27.
9   Ibid Art 28. The subscriptions of the Member States participating in the single currency were to be paid in full by 1 June 1998: ECB Decision 1999/2 (OJ 1999, L8/33). The amounts due from non-participating Member States by that date were limited to 5% of their subscription to the ECB's capital: ECB Decision 1998/14 (OJ 1998, L110/33). The capital of the ECB may be increased by an additional amount of up to Eur 5,000 million: see Council Reg 109/2000 (OJ 2000, L115/1).
10   Protocol Art 29. See also Council Decision 98/382 (OJ 1998, L171/33) and ECB Decision 1999/331 (OJ 1999, L125/33).
11   Protocol Art 30.
12   Ibid Art 31. The ECB has published guidelines on monetary policy instruments and on the Eurosystem procedure (OJ 2000, L310/1).
13   Ibid Art 32.
14   Ibid Art 33.

States. Moreover, under the conditions laid down by the Council of Ministers, acting by a qualified majority on a proposal from the Commission and after consulting the ECB, or, acting on a recommendation from the ECB and after consulting the Commission and the European Parliament, the ECB shall be able to impose fines and periodic penalties on undertakings for failures to comply with the ECB regulations and decisions.[15]

Those Member States that do not participate in the single currency (at the time of writing, Denmark, Sweden and the United Kingdom) do not participate in decisions concerning the monetary policy to be adopted with regard to the single currency and their Central Banks retain their powers under domestic law in relation to monetary policy.[16] The Central Banks of non-participating states nonetheless remain members of the ESCB. The result is that there are in fact two parallel systems within the ESCB: the ESCB comprising the ECB and all the Central Banks of the Member States, whose functions are essentially consultative; and what is known as 'the Eurosystem', which comprises the ECB and the Central Banks of those Member States participating in the single currency, and which performs all the functions of the ESCB. The operational framework of the Eurosystem comprises three types of activity: (1) conducting open market operations designed to steer interest rates, manage liquidity and signal the Eurosystem's stance on monetary policy;[17] (2) offering standing facilities which aim to provide and absorb overnight liquidity, indicate the general monetary policy stance of the Eurosystem and affect overnight market interest rates; and (3) requiring credit institutions to hold minimum reserves on account with national Central Banks within the euro area (this is intended to assist the stabilising of money market interest rates, create or enlarge a structural liquidity shortage and possibly to contribute to control of monetary expansion).

(5) JUDICIAL CONTROL

The Court of Justice has to ensure the conformity of the EMU with the Treaty. Whilst it is not concerned with the technicalities of the EMU it has to exercise judicial control over its implementation. Thus it may be called upon to adjudicate upon the exercise of the powers granted to the Community institutions, the conduct of the Member States in the performance of their duties and the constitutional issues arising from the creation of the new institutions. It may also have to adjudicate upon the exercise of the Community external relations corollary to the EMU.[18]

More specifically the Court of First Instance has jurisdiction in any dispute between the ECB and its servants (and, so afar as is relevant, between the EMI and its servants) in matters concerning their employment and, more generally, in any action brought against them by a legal or natural person.

The acts or omissions of the ECB are subject to judicial review or interpretation like the acts or omissions of Community institutions. Conversely the ECB is able, within its field of competence, to institute proceedings in accordance with

---

15 Ibid Art 34. On the power to impose sanctions see Council Reg 2532/98 (OJ 1998, L318/4), and ECB Reg 2157/1999 (OJ 1999, L264/21).
16 See EC Art 122(3) (ex Art 109k(3)) and Art 43 of the Protocol on the Statute of the ESCB and the ECB.
17 Five types of instruments are used: reserve transactions, outright transactions, issue of debt certificates, foreign exchange swaps and collection of fixed term deposits.
18 See EC Arts 230, 232, 233, 234, 237, 241 (ex Arts 173, 175, 176, 177, 180, 184); and Protocol on ESCB, Art 35; Protocol on EMI, Art 19.

EC Articles 230-235 and 241 (ex Arts 173 to 178 and 184). The ECJ and CFI also have jurisdiction to hear cases pursuant to any arbitration clause contained in a contract concluded by or on behalf of the ECB irrespective of whether the contract in question is governed by public or private law.[19] Since both the ECB and the EMI are subject to non-contractual liability in accordance with EC Article 288 (ex Art 215) cases in that category too would be heard by the ECJ or CFI, as the case may be.

The duties of the national Central Banks under the EMU are enforceable by the ECB in a manner analogous to the enforcement action of the Commission under EC Article 226 (ex Art 169). Accordingly, if the ECB considers that a national Central Bank has failed to fulfil an obligation under the statute of the ESCB it shall deliver a reasoned opinion giving time to reply and to comply and, in the event of non-compliance, may bring the matter before the ECJ.[20] A decision of the ECB to bring an action before the ECJ shall be taken by the Governing Council.

Lastly, decisions regarding compulsory retirement of the President and of the Members of the Executive Board of the ECB are within the jurisdiction of the ECJ.[1]

However disputes between the ECB and its creditors, debtors or any other persons, fall within the jurisdiction of the competent national courts unless jurisdiction in such cases has been specifically conferred upon the ECJ.[2] The national Central Banks shall be liable according to their respective national laws.[3]

(6) IMPLEMENTATION OF THE EMU

As noted above, the Treaty laid down a timetable for the implementation of EMU in three stages. The first stage proceeded under the existing Treaty provisions leading to the completion of the internal market, a further co-ordination of Member States' economic and fiscal policies and the single financial area with (it was envisaged) all the Member States in the European Monetary System. The second stage began when the TEU came into force and, more specifically, on 1 January 1994 with the establishment of the EMI.

During the second stage, the Commission and the EMI were to report on the progress achieved by the Member States towards the convergence of their economic and monetary policies.[4] If the majority of the Member States (ie seven or six without the UK) met four convergence criteria,[5] ie price stability (a rate of inflation no more than 1.5% above the average of the three best performing countries); government deficit not exceeding 3% of the GDP and public debt not exceeding 60% of the GDP; stable exchange rates within the EMS; and interest rates no more than 2% above three best-performing countries over the previous 12 months; the Council would, by a qualified majority decision, move to stage three on 31 December 1996. If no date had been fixed by the end of 1997 the ESCB had to be established by 1 July 1998 and stage three would begin on 1 January 1999. The Council was to determine, by a qualified majority, which Member States were able to participate. Those which were not would be

---

19 Protocol on ESCB, Art 35.4.
20 Protocol on ESCB, Art 35.6.
 1 Ibid, Art 11.4.
 2 Ibid Art 35.2.
 3 Ibid Art 35.3.
 4 EC Art 121 (ex Art 109j).
 5 EC Art 121 (ex Art 109j). Protocol on the Excessive Deficit Procedure, Art 1; Protocol on the Convergence Criteria, Arts 1-4.

subject to derogation. At that point the participating states would agree the conversion rates at which their currencies would be irrevocably fixed and would be exchanged for ECUs. The ECU would then become the single currency. In the event, the third stage commenced on 1 January 1999. The transition to the third stage is 'irreversible'.[6]

(7)   THE BRITISH PROTOCOL

Under a special Protocol, the United Kingdom negotiated the right to opt out of stage three of the EMU without a positive decision of the government and Parliament. The United Kingdom had to notify the European Council by 31 December 1996 whether it intended to move to stage three or by 1 January 1998 if no decision had yet been taken by the Council. In the event, the United Kingdom gave notice to the Council on 30 October 1997 that it did not intend to move to the third stage.

As a result of its decision not to move to the third stage, the United Kingdom retains control of its monetary and exchange rate policy and, therefore, is not subject to EC discipline. However, having accepted stage two, it is bound not to run into an excessive public deficit.

During its absence from the third stage, the weighted vote of the United Kingdom shall be inapplicable when computing the qualified majority for EMU decisions. Moreover the United Kingdom shall not participate in the appointment of the Executive Board of the ECB; the ECB statutes will not apply to the United Kingdom and references to the Community or the Member States will not include the United Kingdom. References to national Central Banks will not include the Bank of England. However the Bank of England must pay its subscription to the capital of the ECB as a contribution to its operational costs on the same basis as national banks of Member States with a derogation.

However the United Kingdom is free to change its mind and move to stage three if it satisfies the four criteria of convergence and complies with the consequential obligations.

(8)   TEETHING PROBLEMS

The convergence of economic and monetary policies advances the idea of central control at the expense of national sovereignty and, in a sense, confirms the theory that economic integration will further political integration. However, as a result of political setbacks reflected in the British Protocol, the initial rejection of the whole Maastricht Treaty by the first Danish referendum and the reluctant endorsement by the French referendum, the Economic and Monetary Union had a bad start.

Debates in the British Parliament during the summer of 1993, on the ratification of the Maastricht Treaty following the second Danish referendum which turned the slender negative vote into a slender positive majority, the German ratification of the Treaty (after a positive judgment albeit weakened by reservations of the Federal Constitutional Court) in October 1993, not only delayed the coming into force of the Treaty for one year but also darkened the prospects of the Union.

By 1992 only three countries (ie France, Luxembourg and the United Kingdom) had measured up to all the criteria of convergence though the last,

---

6   See the Protocol on the transition to the third stage of Economic and Monetary Union.

unable to withstand the pressures of currency depreciation, had to leave the ERM. As regards the other countries, Denmark and Ireland failed in terms of public debt, Belgium in both public debt and budget deficit, Germany in inflation, budget deficit and public debt, Greece, Italy and Portugal measured up to none of the criteria while Spain succeeded only in the field of public debt. At the end of 1992, Denmark notified the Council that it would not participate in the third stage, thus bringing into effect Protocol 12 of the EC Treaty and applying to Denmark the derogations from EMU provided for in the Treaty.

On the monetary side the British pound and the Italian lira had to leave the Exchange Rates Mechanism of the EMS (the ERM), the French franc barely survived only thanks to the support of the Bundesbank, the Portuguese and Spanish currencies had to be devalued while the ERM had to be relaxed by widening the fluctuation bands from 2.5% to 6% and to 15% for the weaker currencies. Thus the Finance Ministers' decision of 31 July-1 August 1993 effectively declared the ERM suspended. However, with the hope of the recession receding, the future of the Economic and Monetary Union appeared brighter.

In the flush of optimism, the Brussels Summit of December 1993 declared the development of the Economic and Monetary Union of course, designated Frankfurt as the site of the European Central Bank and appointed Mr Lamfalussy as the President of the EMI for a three-year period starting on 1 January 1994.[7]

During the course of the third stage, it became apparent that, although the early start date for the third stage could not realistically be met, the later date of 1 January 1999 was feasible. Therefore, at the Madrid summit in 1995, the European Council selected that as the date for the commencement of the third stage.[8] The following year, in Dublin, the European Council reached agreement on the main elements of a Stability and Growth Pact that, when finally elaborated in 1997, comprised a Resolution of the European Council,[9] a Council Regulation on the strengthening of the surveillance of budgetary positions and the surveillance and co-ordination of economic policies,[10] and a Council Regulation on speeding up and clarifying the implementation of the excess deficit procedure (that is, the procedure set out in EC Article 104 (ex Art 104c)).[11] The Stability and Growth Pact arose from the fact that monetary union would be affected by prevailing economic circumstances. However, economic policies (and wage determination) remained national responsibilities and were constrained only by the Treaty provisions concerning government deficits. The Pact was therefore based on the objective of achieving sound government finances as a means of strengthening the conditions for price stability and for strong sustainable growth conducive to employment creation.[12] In that way, a sound economic basis would be created for the adoption of a single currency. At the same time, it was agreed that, at the start of the third stage, the EMS would be replaced by an exchange rate mechanism (ERM II) linking the currencies of Member States outside the Euro to the Euro.[13]

By 1998, the Council was able to conclude that the following Member States had achieved a high degree of sustainable convergence and therefore fulfilled the necessary conditions for the adoption of the single currency: Belgium, Germany,

---

7 On the progress of the Monetary Union, see *Twenty-seventh General Report* [1994] p 10 and subsequent General Reports.
8 Bulletin, 12-1995, para 1.3.1.
9 OJ 1997, C 236/1.
10 Reg 1466/97 (OJ 1997, L209/1).
11 Reg 1467/97 (OJ 1997, L209/6).
12 Ibid, recital (2).
13 See the European Council resolution of 16 June 1997 (OJ 1997, C 236/5).

Spain, France, Ireland, Italy, Luxembourg, the Netherlands, Austria, Portugal and Finland.[14] Greece had not fulfilled any of the four convergence criteria. Sweden had not fulfilled the third criterion. No assessment was made of the United Kingdom and Denmark because they had excluded themselves from the third stage. It was therefore decided in May 1998 that only 11 Member States would proceed to adopt the single currency with effect from 1 January 1999.[15] At the same time, various other decisions were taken concerning, in particular, the introduction of the single currency (to be called the Euro).[16] After some degree of political manoeuvring, a Dutch banker, Mr Wim Duisenberg, was appointed President of the ECB, which was formally established on 1 June 1998. The final part of the legislative jigsaw was the fixing of the conversion rates between the Euro and the currencies of those Member States adopting the Euro, which was effected on 31 December 1998, using the then prevailing bilateral central rates within the ERM.[17]

In October 1998, the Governing Council of the ECB set out the stability-oriented monetary policy strategy adopted by the Eurosystem. It has three main elements: a quantitative definition of price stability[18] supported by two 'pillars', a prominent role for money (indicated by the announcement of a quantitative reference value for the growth rate of a broad monetary aggregate) and a broadly based assessment of the outlook for price developments and risks to price stability in the Euro area as a whole.

As from 1 January 1999, the currency of the Member States participating in the single currency has been, in principle, the Euro, which was substituted for the currency of each of those Member States at the conversion rate fixed at the end of 1998. However, for a transitional period, the Euro was to be divided into national currency units in accordance with that conversion rate. Hence, within the participating states, the Euro has been from 1 January 1999 both their currency and a unit of account but, during the transitional period, the Euro has taken the physical form of the coins and banknotes that changed hands in the participating states before the move to a single currency. The fact that the

---

14   In the case of Italy and Finland, sufficient stability had been reached in relation to the third criterion only in the previous two years.

15   Council Decision 98/317 (OJ 1998, L139/30). See also the recommendation that preceded it and the contemporaneous Council declaration (OJ 1998, L139/21 and 28).

16   Council Reg 974/98 (OJ 1998, L139/1) (amended by Reg 2596/2000 (OJ 2000, L300/2)). See also: the Commission recommendations of 23 April 1998 on banking charges for conversion to the Euro, dual display of prices and facilitating the introduction of the Euro (OJ 1998, C 130/22, 26 and 29); Council Reg 975/98 on the denominations and technical characteristics of Euro coins and banknotes (OJ 1998, L139/6); ECB Decision 99/33 on the denominations, specifications, reproduction, exchange and withdrawal of Euro banknotes (OJ 1999, L8/36); ECB Recommendation of 7 July 1998 on measures to enhance the legal protection of Euro banknotes and coins (OJ 1999, C 11/13); the ECB guidelines on certain provisions regarding the Euro banknotes, as amended (OJ 1999, L258/32); the agreement of 1 September 1998 between the ECB and the Central Banks of the non-participating Member States laying down operating procedures for an exchange rate mechanism (OJ 1998, C 345/6); and, more recently, ECB Decisions 2000/9 and 2000/17 on the volume of coin issuance in 2000 and 2001 (OJ 2000, L4/18 and L336/118); the Council framework decision on increasing protection against the counterfeiting of the Euro (OJ 2000, L140/1).

17   Council Reg 2866/98 (OJ 1998, L359/1). A fuller account of events in 1998 can be found in the 1998 General Report on the activities of the European Union, paras 40 and following.

18   Inflation below 2% measured by reference to harmonized indices of consumer prices (or HICP, as to which see Council Reg 2494/95 (OJ 1995, L257/1), implemented in particular by Commission Regs 2454/97 and 2646/98 (OJ 1997, L340/24 and OJ 1998, L335/30, respectively)).

different national currencies in the participating states represent the Euro in physical form at the relevant conversion rate does not render them legal tender throughout the participating states.[19]

In the course of 2000, the single currency took a step forward in that Greece met the convergence criteria and became a participating state as from 1 January 2001.[20] On the other hand, Denmark voted against the adoption of the Euro in a referendum, the British Government's sympathies moved against joining the single currency, and Sweden's position did not alter. Further, since its introduction, the Euro has declined on the international money markets, leading to concerted intervention by the G7 countries in support of the Euro in September 2000. Various explanations have been given for the decline: that, as a newly introduced currency, the Euro was bound to be the victim of speculators; that its parities were fixed too high for political reasons; that there were reasonable doubts about the ability of the participating states to maintain a consistent level of economic performance to underpin the value of the Euro. The ECB has taken the view that the exchange rate of the Euro has been out of line with economic fundamentals for a prolonged period of time but it is accepted that Government deficits have tended to deteriorate rather than improve after the introduction of the Euro. Interest rate measures were taken by the ECB in the last few months of 2000 in order to contain the emergence of inflationary expectations and convince social partners, and the general public, that price stability in the Euro area would be maintained.

---

19   Reg 974/98 (OJ 1998, L139/1), Arts 5-9.
20   See Decision 2000/427 (OJ 2000, L167/19).

Chapter 25

Common Agricultural and Fisheries Policies

A. Treaty policies

(1) GENERAL PRINCIPLES (EC ARTICLES 32-38 (EX ARTS 38-47))[1]

In his report to the Messina Conference which paved the way for the creation of the EC the Belgian statesman, Henri Spaak, wrote:

'On ne peut concevoir l'établissement d'un marché commun général en Europe sans que l'agriculture s'y trouve incluse. C'est l'un des secteurs où le progress de productivité qui résulteront du marché commun, c'est-à-dire de la specialisation progressive des productions et de l'élargissement des debouches, peuvent avoir les effets les plus importants sur le niveau de vie des producteurs aussi bien que des consommateurs. En outre, cette inclusion de l'agriculture dans le marché commun est une condition d'équilibre des échanges entre les différentes economies des États membres . . .'[2]

Agriculture, as an absolutely essential sector of the economy, had to be included in the concept of the Common Market together with industry and commerce. Moreover, because of its nature and rôle in the economy of the Member States, agriculture had to be singled out for a special regime. In view of the conflicting interests of the Member States, the problem of agriculture in the Community has proved to be not only special, but also the most difficult to solve.

Having been recognized as 'a sector closely linked with the economy as a whole' (EC Article 33(2)(c) (ex Art 39(2)(c))) and given its 'particular nature'

---

1 For a fuller account see Law of the European Communities (Butterworths, ed D Vaughan), Parts 13 (B Atwood) and 14 (R Sturt); and Usher, J A, *Legal Aspects of Agriculture in the European Community* (1988).
2 Quoted by Olim, G, 'L'Agriculture', *Les Nouvellees*, op cit, p 680.

(EC Article 33(2)(a) (ex Art 39(2)(a))[3] the agricultural regime of the Community rests on its own philosophy. This philosophy can be reduced to two principles enshrined in EC Article 32 (ex Art 38), ie that the rules governing agriculture derogate from the rules which establish the Common Market (EC Article 32(2) (ex Art 38(2)) and that the operation and development of the Common Market for agricultural products[4] must be accompanied by a Common Agricultural Policy (EC Article 32(4) (ex Art 38(4))).

It follows that there can be no common market for agricultural products without a Common Agricultural Policy. Whilst there is no definition of the agricultural policy in the Treaty, EC Article 33 (ex Art 39) enumerates the objectives of this policy and EC Article 37 (ex Art 43) gives considerable powers to the organs of the Community, authorizing them to devise and enforce the Common Agricultural Policy. It follows that there is no question of the co-ordination at the Community level of the various national policies but there is one policy for the whole Community.

As for the basic principles of the Common Market in Agriculture, EC Article 36 (ex Art 42) provides that 'the rules on competition shall apply to the production of and trade in agricultural products only to the extent determined by the Council'. The relevant Common Agricultural Policy Regulation 26,[5] Article 2, issued in 1962, excludes the operation of EC Article 81 (ex Art 85)[6] (prohibition of agreements between undertakings which may affect trade between Member States and are designed to stultify free competition) in relation to agreements, decisions or concerted practices that are necessary for the attainment of the objectives set out in EC Article 33 (ex Art 39), and agreements, decisions or concerted practices involving farmers, farmer's associations or such associations belonging to a single Member State which concern the production or sale of agricultural products or the case of joint facilities for the storage, treatment or processing of agricultural products (as long as the parties are not obliged to charge identical prices). In relation to the second group of agreements, decisions or concerted practices, the Commission can intervene but only if competition is wholly excluded or the objectives of EC Article 33 (ex Art 39), are being jeopardized.[7] EC Article 82 (ex Art 86)[8] of the Treaty (prohibition of the abuse of a dominant position by one or more undertakings), however, does apply by virtue of Art 1 of Regulation 26. Furthermore EC Articles 87 and 88(2) (ex Arts 92 and 93(2)) do not apply to agriculture. EC Article 87 (ex Art 92) declares state aids incompatible with the Common Market and EC Article 88 (ex Art 93) governs the procedure to be followed by the Commission in cases involving alleged breaches of EC Article 87 (ex Art 92). It follows that state aids to agriculture are not ruled out as a matter or principle, but, in practice, specific Regulations[9] expressly provide

---

3   This particular nature 'results from the social structure of agriculture and from structural and natural disparities between the various agricultural regions': EC Art 33(2)(a) (ex Art 39(2)(a)).

4   Agricultural products comprise the products of the soil, of stock-farming, of fisheries and products of first-stage processing directly related to the foregoing (EC Art 32(1) (ex Art 38(1))). For a list of these see EEC Treaty, Annexe II.

5   JO/993/62 (S Edn 1959-62).

6   See pp 647 et seq, infra; Case 71/74: *Frubo v Commission* [1975] ECR 563, [1975] 2 CMLR 123 and Cases 40-48/73, etc: *Co-operative Vereniging 'Suiker Unie' UA v Commission* [1975] ECR 1663, [1976] 1 CMLR 295.

7   See, for example, Cases C-319/93, C-40/94 and C-224/94: *Dijkstra v Friesland (Frico Domo) Co-operative* [1995] ECR I-4471.

8   See Ch 29, infra.

9   Eg the legislation at issue in Case 177/78: *Pigs and Bacon Commission v McCarren* [1979] ECR 2161 and Case 169/82: *Commission v Italy* [1984] ECR 1603.

that EC Articles 87-89 (ex Arts 92-94) shall not be derogated from unless stipulated to the contrary.

B.   Common Agricultural Policy

EC Article 33(1) (ex Art 39(1)) sets out the objectives of the Common Agricultural Policy as follows:

'(a) to increase agricultural productivity by promoting technical progress and by ensuring the rational development of agricultural production and the optimum utilization of the factors of production, in particular labour;

(b) thus to ensure a fair standard of living for the agricultural community, in particular by increasing the individual earnings of persons engaged in agriculture;

(c) to stabilize markets;

(d) to assure the availability of supplies; and

(e) to ensure that supplies reach consumers at reasonable prices.'

In order to achieve the objectives of the policy the Member States must adopt a Common Organization of Agricultural Markets (EC Article 34(1) (ex Art 40(2)).

(1)   COMMON ORGANIZATION OF AGRICULTURAL MARKETS

The Common Organization of Agricultural Markets has not been defined in the Treaty, but EC Article 34(1) (ex Art 40(2)) provides that it should take one of the following forms depending on the product concerned:

(1)   common rules as regards competition;

(2)   compulsory co-ordination of the various national marketing organizations;

(3)   a European organization of the market.

In practice (c), the 'European market organization' model, has invariably been followed. This involves the replacement of individual national marketing arrangements for an agricultural product by a single, Community-wide marketing structure for that product. That task has been entrusted to the Community Institutions and in the terms of EC Article 37(2) (ex Art 43(2)): 'The Council shall, on a proposal of the Commission and after consulting the European Parliament acting by a qualified majority make regulations, issue directives, or take decisions, without prejudice to any recommendations it may also make.' The Commission's proposals emerged from a conference held in July 1958 at Stresa, which defined the guidelines of the Common Agricultural Policy.[10] In June 1960, the Commission, after consulting the Economic and Social Committee, submitted its proposals to the Council in respect of four main considerations: structural, market, commercial and social.[11] Having had the benefit of the views of the Special Committee for Agriculture created in 1960 the Council adopted certain guidelines which were to form the future Common Agricultural Policy, viz free movement of agricultural products within the Community, a joint commercial and agricultural policy, a common price level for agricultural

10   See *First General Report*, 1958, ss 97-101.
11   See *Third General Report*, 1960, s 230 and *Fourth General Report*, 1961, s 103.

products within the Community and co-ordination of national structural reform. These guidelines added practically nothing to the existing provisions of the Treaty, but reaffirmed the role to tackle the Community agricultural problem and in some respects interpreted the Treaty provisions. The importance of the problem is well reflected in the machinery of Community legislation which involved the co-operation of the Commission, the European Parliament and the Council.

The first regulation issued by the Council concerned the market organization in cereals[12] and applied during the transitional period to wheat, rye, barley, oats, maize, buckwheat, millet, hardwheat, meal and groats of wheat and rye and processed grain products. The current basic rules concerning the market in cereals are now contained in a consolidating regulation made in 1992 which shall be used here as illustrative of the general shape taken by the common organizations applicable to other agricultural products.[13] This regulation sets up a single Community market based on a common price system within the Community and regulates trade and third countries. The price system comprises a target price, an intervention price and a threshold price.

The *target price* is determined annually by the Council acting on a proposal of the Commission after consulting the Parliament (EC Article 37(2) (ex Art 43(2))). This is not a fixed price, but a price intended to enable the producers to plan their production for the following year; it provides an expectation of the price the product should fetch during the next marketing year (1 July to 30 June). The target price is also designed, inter alia, to encourage trade in cereals from Community surplus areas to community deficit areas. The target price therefore reflects the transport costs involved in such trade.

The *intervention* or *guarantee price*, determined according to the same procedure as the target price, is the price at which the national authorities must buy in cereals offered to them by producers who are unable to sell their product on the market at prices higher than the intervention price. It forms a guarantee to farmers. However, whilst the target price is uniform within the Community, the intervention price varies as from area to area according to the circumstances of the area. The intervention price is lower than the target price. The basic intervention price has been fixed by the Council in relation to the market conditions in the area of the Community having the greatest surplus for all cereals.

The *threshold price* is the price fixed by the Community for cereals imported from third countries. It is fixed in respect of the same standard quality as the target price. It is calculated in relation to cereals, notionally imported through Rotterdam to be sold in the area of the Community having the greatest deficit for all cereals. The aim is that cereals thus imported should eventually sell at or above the target price. In other words, the threshold price is the target price less the cost of transport from Rotterdam to the area of greatest deficit.

The threshold price is determined by the Council in accordance with the procedure outlined above every year. It is fixed in relation to a system of levies imposed on imported cereals, these levies being equal to the difference between the threshold price and the c.i.f. price at Rotterdam. The levies are fixed by the Commission whilst the c.i.f. prices for Rotterdam are calculated on the basis of the most favourable purchasing possibilities on the world market. It follows that the threshold prices are lower than the Community prices.

---

12 Reg of 14 January 1962, No 19 (JO 933/62).
13 Reg 1766/92 (OJ 1992, L181/21), as amended.

Whilst the price system is designed to ensure production within the Community and to guarantee a fair return to Community producers, the system of levies on imports is designed to protect Community producers against competition from third countries. In a sense, this is a Community preference and an example of the economic barrier round the Community. However, the Regulation requires strict control of the quality of the product to preserve not only a high standard of the market, but also an equitable basis of competition.

Intervention prices and threshold prices are reviewed monthly to take into account the cost of interest and stockpiling. These reviews result in price increases spread out over the marketing year.

In order to encourage exports, the Regulation provides for refunds to exporters from the Community to third countries. These refunds constitute a form of subsidy which is the same for the whole Community, but varies according to the destination of the products and the use to which they are to be put. The refunds are calculated in relation to the difference between the world and Community prices for the given product. This is necessary since world prices are usually lower than Community prices and there is a policy against the accumulation of surpluses within the Community. Exports and imports are under control by means of appropriate certificates.

At the Community level, the system is supervised by a Management Committee set up under the Regulation and consisting of representatives of the Member States presided over by a representative of the Commission. The Chairman refers matters to the Committee either on his own initiative or at the request of the representative of a Member State. The decisions are implemented by the Commission. If there is a difference of opinion between the Committee and the Commission, the latter must submit the matter to the Council which may adopt a different decision from that proposed by the Commission.[14] In conjunction with the basic rules dealing with prices, intervention, imports and exports, the Community provides a support system for producers of certain cereals. This takes the form of payments made to producers in return for them taking all or part of their land out of production ('set aside').[15]

In addition to the Regulation for cereals, the Community has adopted Regulations in respect of other essential sectors of agriculture, notably pigmeat,[16] eggs,[17] poultry meat,[18] fruit and vegetables,[19] wine,[20] milk and milk products,[1] beef and veal,[2] rice,[3] vegetable oils, fats, oil seeds and olives,[4] sugar,[5] dried fodder[6] tobacco,[7] sheepmeat and goatmeat,[8] bananas,[9] processed fruit and vegetable

14   See Ch 11, p 280 supra.
15   Council Regulation 1765/92 (OJ 1992, L181/12), as amended.
16   Reg 2759/75 (OJ 1975, L282/1), as amended.
17   Reg 2771/75, ibid p 49, as amended.
18   Reg 2777/75, ibid, p 77, as amended.
19   Reg 2200/96 (OJ 1996, L297/1), as amended.
20   Reg 822/87 (OJ 1987, L84/1), as amended.
 1   Reg 1255/1999 (OJ 1999, L160/48), as amended.
 2   Reg 805/68 (JO 1968, L148/24 (Sp edn 1968(1) p 187)), as amended.
 3   Reg 3072/95 (OJ L329/18), as amended.
 4   Reg 136/66 (JO 1966 (Sp edn 1965-66), as amended.
 5   Reg 2038/1999 (OJ 1999, L252/1).
 6   Reg 603/95 (OJ 1995, L63/1), as amended.
 7   Reg 2075/92 (OJ 1992, L215/70), as amended.
 8   Reg 2467/98 (OJ 1998, L312/1).
 9   Reg 404/93 (OJ 1993, L47/1), as amended.

products,[10] hops,[11] seeds,[12] flax and hemp,[13] flowers, bulbs and live plants,[14] certain other agricultural products[15] and fisheries.[16]

As a result of these Regulations, several essential sectors of agriculture have become subject to Community rules. The organization of these markets differs from sector to sector, but, broadly speaking, the pattern of the Regulation for Cereals, which we have considered as an example of a Community Market Organization, has been followed.

Alongside the market organizations the Community postulates a structural reorganization of agriculture. The problem is by no means simple and has, over the years, focused the attention of the Community. In order to solve it, the Commission in 1968 submitted to the Council a 'Memorandum on the Reform of Agriculture in the European Economic Community' (Agriculture 1989)[17] and, in 1971, the Council adopted a resolution[18] based on this Memorandum. The Commission analysed and made recommendations in respect of several aspects of the structural reform of agriculture. In particular it considered the problem of the manpower engaged in agriculture, the size of farms and production methods.

On the first problem, the Commission concluded that in view of high productivity and overproduction fewer people will be needed in the farming industry of the future. This creates a social problem which the Community must alleviate by helping those who wish to leave the land, by assisting farmers over fifty-five years of age who wish to give up their occupation and by providing schemes for retaining and placement of those who wish to find another occupation.

On the second problem, the Commission found that the average farm within the Community was too small to engage in profitable industrial farming and recommended a definite policy for the increase of the size of farms in accordance with the type of production.

On the third problem, the Commission felt that the production methods were not modern enough and that, coupled with the lack of flexibility, this contributed to the relatively low incomes of farmers in the Community. It proposed the modernization of production methods, greater adaptability to market needs and better marketing.

The Commission costed its recommendation estimating the relative contribution of the Community and the Member States to the cost of the reform programme.

The Memorandum and the ensuing discussions in the European Parliament and the Economic and Social Committee led to the above-mentioned Council Resolution on the subject which, in turn, paved the way for a new set of proposals

---

10   Reg 2201/96 (OJ 1996, L297/29), as amended.
11   Reg 1696/71 (OJ 1971, L175/1 (Sp edn 1971(II))) p 634.
12   Reg 2538/71 (OJ 1971, L246/1 (Sp edn 1971(II))) p 894, as amended.
13   Reg 1308/70 (JO 1970, L146 (Sp edn 1970(II))), as amended.
14   Reg 234/68 (JO 1968, L55 (Sp edn 1968(I))), as amended.
15   Reg 827/68 (JO 1968, L151/16 (Sp edn 1968(I) p 209)), as amended.
16   Reg 3796/81 (OJ 1981, L379).
17   See *Second General Report*, 1968.
18   JO 1971, C 52.

by the Commission.[19] These proposals resulted in the issuing of directives on 17 April 1972 on the modernization[20] of the farming industry, assistance to farmers leaving the land[1] and professional training and advice.[2] A further directive concerned with the special problems of farming in less favoured areas was issued in 1975.[3] Taken together with the Council Resolution, the emerging picture of agriculture is one of a modernized industry, manned by well-qualified and efficient farmers, organized into a competitive market and catering for the social and human problems involved in the movements of the farming population. In this set-up, state aids and subsidies authorized under EC Articles 87 and 88 (ex Arts 92 and 93) will have to go as the principles of a Common Market in agriculture will be implemented. However implementation has been delayed and problems continue to arise. To deal with these problems various reforms have been introduced from time to time. In particular, major new initiatives were taken in 1985, 1992 and 1999 to improve and reform the CAP. At the time of writing, the principal measure dealing with rural development (which includes provisions facilitating the establishment of young farmers, vocational training, early retirement, support for less-favoured areas, agri-environmental measures, the improvement of the processing and marketing of agricultural products, and the control of state aids for rural development) is Regulation 1257/1999.[4]

(3) FINANCE AND IMPLEMENTATION

In connection with agriculture, two further points have to be mentioned: finance and the machinery for implementing the Community Agricultural Policy.

The financing of the Common Agricultural Policy, although germane to agricultural problems, is really part of the Community budget. Indeed, agriculture figures prominently in the budget, representing about one half of the whole.[5] The underlying philosophy of the financing of the agricultural policy is the principle that, since there is a common policy and a common price system, the financial responsibility must be undertaken by the Community. Accordingly, on the basis of EC Article 34(3) (ex Art 40(4)), the European Agricultural Guidance and Guarantee Fund[6] was set up and an elaborate system of Community agricultural finance was established.

As for the machinery to implement the Community Agricultural Policy, we have already observed that, at the Community level, the crucial decisions have to be taken by the Council after consulting the Parliament, whilst the background work and the administrative actions stem from the Commission. Agriculture has the constant attention of the highest Community organs. At the national level, the execution of the decisions of the Council has been left to the machinery of the Member States. In particular the Member States assume responsibility for the purchase of the agricultural product at the intervention

---

19 [1971] JO C 75.
20 72/159 (JO 1972, L96 (Sp edn 1972 II)), as amended.
1 72/160, ibid, as amended.
2 72/161, ibid, as amended.
3 75/268 (OJ 1975, L128). See now Reg 1257/1999 (OJ 1999, L160/80).
4 OJ 1999, L160/80, implemented by Reg 1750/1999 (OJ 1999, L214/31).
5 See General Report on the Activities of the European Union (1998), Tables 19 and 21 (part of the sums attributable to structural operations must be added to the line dealing with CAP expenditure in order to provide a full picture of the position).
6 By Reg No 25 (JO 991/62); the present definitive scheme is laid down by Reg 1258/1999 (OJ 1999, L160/103).

price determined by the Council. They also operate the system of import and export certificates, collect levies and pay out refunds. Their financial liability to the Community forms part of their contribution towards the Community budget.

The states who became members of the Community in 1973 and later had to accept the Common Agricultural Policy as a condition of their accession. They were, therefore, committed to a process of adaptation and integration during a transition period as set out in the Act annexed to the relevant Treaty of Accession.[7] For the United Kingdom, this meant a radical change in the system. To implement the Community Policy an Intervention Board for Agricultural Produce was set up with provision for such consequential changes as appear necessary.[8]

The implementation of the Common Agricultural Policy requires a uniform body of Community law. Competence to act in relation to agriculture has been transferred to the Community. The Member States have no competence to act in the areas transferred to the Community.[9] If, within the area transferred to it, the Community has failed to act, the Member States may fill the gap but can do so, on a temporary and provisional basis, only by means of measures that are compatible with the aims and principles of the common organization of the market.[10] Where Member States retain competence to act, they may not exercise that competence in such a way as to undermine or create exceptions to the Community regime, they may not interfere with the proper functioning of the common organization of the market, and they must act consistently with the mechanisms and principles governing the common organization of the market.[11]

(4)   REFORM OF THE CAP

It can be said that the CAP is a victim of its own success. It has raised the standard of living of farmers but increased the price of food; it has resulted in an unprecedented rise of production but caused surpluses and costly storage problems. It has made the Community self-sufficient in food supplies and a major food exporter but has not been able to relieve certain overpopulated Third World countries of famine and starvation. For political reasons the CAP has become the bone of contention between agricultural and non-agricultural countries, a hungry sacred cow eating up a disproportionate part of the Community budget, leaving little for the development of other well-deserving policies. Within the GATT it became a subject of dissension and a stumbling block to the completion of the Uruguay Round. It is evident that, having fulfilled its original function, it is in need of reform but the problem is, politics apart, how to reconcile the contention that the Community is both an economic and social organization. The other problem is that the CAP has become a complex mass of rules and regulations

---

7   Eg First Act of Accession, 1972, Arts 50 et seq; Second Act of Accession 1979, Arts 57 et seq; and Third Act of Accession 1985, Arts 67 et seq and 233 et seq.
8   See European Communities Act 1972, s 6 and the orders and regulations made thereunder.
9   Eg Case 68/76: *Commission v France* [1977] ECR 515 (in particular para 23); Case 231/78: *Commission v United Kingdom* [1979] ECR 1447, para 30.
10   Eg Cases 47 and 48/83: *Pluimveeslachterjen Midden-Nederland* [1984] ECR 1721, paras 21-25.
11   Eg Case 148/85: *Director Général des Impôts v Forest* [1986] ECR 3449, para 14; Case 218/85: *Cerafer v Le Campion* [1986] ECR 3513, para 13; Case C-27/96: *Danisco Sugar v Allmänna Ombudert* [1997] ECR I-6653, para 24.

which, because of their complexity, challenge a would-be reformer with a Herculean task.

Since a root and branch reform was for a long time not on the agenda various palliatives have been adopted. These, apart from export incentives which extend the Community protectionism to the world market, include production disincentives and measures for the protection of the environment put at risk through intensive farming.

The reform package adopted in 1992[12] was put into operation for a three year cycle in 1993.

Monetary compensatory amounts were abolished in 1992 and replaced by the new agrimonetary arrangements using the ECU as the unit of account for fixing agricultural prices and amounts. In that operation the conversions between the ECU and the national currencies were carried out according to the rules within the framework of the European Monetary System but the monetary disturbances experienced in 1992 and 1993 resulted in the realignments in the EMS and major movements by most of the floating currencies and, finally, in the decision to increase the fluctuation margins of the EMS exchange-rate mechanism[13] to 15%. Thus the agrimonetary rules applicable to the floating currencies were applied to all the Community currencies.[14] In July 1997, the Commission published 'Agenda 2000', which mapped out how the EU and its policies should be developed beyond 2000, in particular in the light of the accession of more countries to the EU.[15] Agenda 2000 envisaged the continuation of the reforms launched in 1992 but also marked a significant shift in emphasis in the CAP. As eventually adopted and implemented, the main feature of the new policy guiding the CAP is a transition from the historically high prices for agricultural products within the EU to prices at the same level as world prices, thus benefiting consumers, reducing he risk of there being expensive and unsaleable surpluses, making it easier to integrate new Member States, and avoiding difficulties within the WTO. However, such a transition is feasible only in conjunction with direct income aid to producers, whence the adoption of a more comprehensive policy regarding rural development.[16]

C.   Common Fisheries Policy (CFP)

(1)   ESTABLISHMENT OF THE CFP

The EC Treaty provides the basis for a CFP within the framework of the CAP: EC Article 32(1) (ex Art 38(1)), defines fisheries and products thereof as 'agricultural products'. Indeed, originally, the CFP was regarded as an aspect of the CAP and the first two Council regulations[17] providing respectively for a common structural policy for the fishing industry and a common organization of the market in fishery products, followed the pattern of the CAP legislation.

---

12   *Twenty-sixth General Report*, point 506.
13   OJ 1992, L387.
14   Reg 3528/93 (OJ 1993, L320).
15   See 1997 General Report, Ch II.
16   See Reg 1257/1999, supra.
17   Reg 2141/70 (OJ 1970, L236/1) and Reg 2142/70 (OJ 1970, L236/5). It was only by the Maastricht Treaty that EC Art 3(e) (ex Art 3(d)), was amended so as specifically to refer to a Common Fisheries Policy.

Conflict of interest of the Member States exacerbated by the first enlargement of the Community delayed the establishment of the CFP. The first Act of Accession accorded certain concessions to the new members as they were allowed, until the end of 1982, to restrict fishing in a six nautical mile sea belt to fishermen exercising traditional rights in those waters and to their fishing zones in certain areas to 12 miles.[18] However, the Act[19] gave the Council power to legislate on the management of the fishing industry, and the conservation of sea resources. Pending such enactments the Member States retained their competence to regulate fisheries[20] subject to certain guidelines laid down in the Hague Resolutions of 1976.[1] Eventually, in 1983, a CFP, as a set of regulations, emerged.

A decade later the Community embarked on a reform of the system and announced a new CFP[2] based on monitoring arrangements for fishing activities and a more effective implementation of the policy and setting up a fishing licence scheme and integrating the structural aspects in a revised Structure Fund scheme.[3] The CFP does not apply to fishing vessels flying the flag of a third country even if they are present within the territory of a Member State.[4]

(2)   ELEMENTS OF THE CFP

(a)   Equal access
In view of the mobile nature of fish no national ownership of them can be claimed. Therefore the CFP accords to Community fishermen equal access to the 'Community pond' delimited by the national limits of 200 nautical miles or a median line. They can fish there without discrimination subject, however, to the constraints imposed by the conservation policy.[5]

(b)   Conservation
The conservation and management of fish stocks are controlled by the total allowable catches (TACs) fixed annually. The volume of catches available to the Community are distributed between the Member States.[6] Quotas are exchangeable between the Member States in respect of a species of groups of species allocated to them but these have to be caught in specified fishing zones.[7]

Council Regulation 3690/93[8] established a Community system of fishing licenses as envisaged by Regulation 3760/92[9] which reformed the policy for fisheries and agriculture. In pursuance of the latter the Council adopted Decision 94/15

---

18   Act of Accession 1972, Arts 100 and 101.
19   Ibid, Arts 102 and 103.
20   See Cases 3, 4, 6/76: *Officier van Justitie v Kramer* [1976] ECR 1279, [1976] 2 CMLR 440.
  1   EC Bull 10/1976, item 1502 et seq. See Case 61/77: *Commission v Ireland* [1978] ECR 417, [1978] 2 CMLR 466; Case 88/77: *Minister of Fisheries v Schonenberg* [1978] ECR 473, [1978] 2 CMLR 419; Cases 185-204/78: *J van Dam en Zonen* [1979] ECR 2345, [1980] 1 CMLR 350; Case 124/80: *Officier van Justitie v Van Dam* [1981] ECR 1447, [1982] 2 CMLR 93; Case 32/79: *Commission v United Kingdom* [1980] ECR 2403, [1981] 1 CMLR 219; Case 804/79: *Commission v United Kingdom* [1981] ECR 1045, [1982] 1 CMLR 543; Case 63/83: *R v Kirk* [1984] ECR 2689, [1984] 3 CMLR 522.
  2   *Twenty-sixth General Report* (1993) point 559.
  3   *Twenty-seventh General Report* (1994) point 394.
  4   Case C-286/90: *Poulsen and Diva Corpn* [1992] ECR I-6019, paras 12-28.
  5   Reg 101/76, Art 2(1) (OJ 1976, L20/19).
  6   See Commission communication on access to fishing quotas [1990] 2 CMLR 97.
  7   Reg 3760/92, Art 9(1) (OJ 1992, L389/1).
  8   OJ 1993, L341.
  9   OJ 1992, L388.

containing detailed rules for restructuring the fishery sector on the basis of a programme laid down in 1992.[10]

By Regulation 2847/93[11] the Council established monitoring and control arrangements covering all fishing activities in Community waters and Community vessels fishing in third country waters and on the high seas. However the monitoring remains the responsibility of the Member States subject to the Commission's supervision.

The Commission monitors compliance with TACs and the quotas as well as with the conservation measures and with the international agreements. Where a quota or a TAC is exhausted the Commission will take action and, where appropriate, imitate infringement procedure for over-fishing.

The setting up and monitoring of TACs presents a continuing problem, so much so that during 1993 a Regulation[12] fixing TACs and quotas was amended three times.[13]

(c) Structural reform

The extension of the fishing rights and extensive over-fishing resulted in surplus fishing capacity which had to be reduced within the restructuring of the industry. The basis for action was originally provided by Regulation 2141/70 and the subsidies by the European Agricultural Guidance and Guarantee Fund. The two main aspects of structural reform are the reduction in the size of national fishing fleets[14] and limits placed on national 'fishing efforts', that is, fishing capacity as measured by the capacity of a fishing vessel and the time that it can spend in active fishing.[15]

By Regulation 2080/93[16] the Council established a financial instrument for fisheries guidance (FIFG) to gather together the financial resources allocated to structural measures in the fisheries sector which were originally within the CFP or the CAP. By Regulation 3699/93[17] the Council provided structural assistance in the fisheries and aquaculture sector and the processing and marketing of the fishery products with the object of integrating the structural aspects of the CFP into Structural Funds.

(d) Marketing organization

The common organization of fishery markets was set up by Regulation 3759/92[18] with the object of rationalizing the development of fisheries, securing a fair deal for fishermen, stabilizing the markets in order to bring supplies of good products to the consumer at reasonable prices. The market organization consists of producers' associations, common marketing standards and a price support system financed by the European Agricultural Guidance and Guarantee Fund.

---

10   OJ 1992, L401.
11   OJ 1993, L261.
12   Reg 3919/92 (OJ 1992, L397).
13   OJ 1993, L96; OJ L285; OJ L310.
14   Eg Decision 97/413 (OJ 1997, L175/27), and Decision 98/124 (OJ 1998, L39/32).
15   For the definition of fishing effort, see Reg 3760/92, Art 3(f). The rules for limiting fishing efforts are in Reg 2847/93.
16   OJ 1993, L193.
17   OJ 1993, L346.
18   OJ 1992, L388/1, as amended. It replaced Reg 2142/70, as amended by Reg 100/76 (OJ 1976, L20/1) and revised by Reg 3796/81 (OJ 1981, L379/1).

(3) INTERNATIONAL ASPECTS

International aspects of the CFP are now within the competence of the Community.[19] In this capacity the Community has entered into agreements with certain countries (eg Norway, Sweden, Canada and the USA) and international organizations (ie the North Atlantic Fisheries Organization, the North Atlantic Convention on Salmon Conservation and the Convention on Living Resources in the Antarctic).

These activities have been intensified[20] both in the form of bilateral and multilateral arrangements and cover various parts of the world. However Member States have no longer competence to enter into autonomous and unilateral agreements with third countries or international organizations.

Fishery products are subject to the Common Customs Tariff and external trade agreements within the Common Commercial Policy.

---

19 Sturt, R H B, *Fisheries*, Halsbury's Laws of England, op cit, pp 407 et seq.
20 *Twenty-seventh General Report* (1994) items 571-580.

Chapter 26

Common Transport Policy

A. General principles (EC Articles 70-80 (ex Articles 74-84))

Integrated transport appears to be an indispensable element of the Common Market. Yet devising the Transport Policy heralded in EC Article 3(f), (ex Art 3(c)), has proved to be a difficult task. It should be borne in mind that transport, including transport under the ECSC Treaty (Article 70), impinges upon many aspects of economic life,[1] and has, in the Community setting, a distinct international character.[2] It is also relevant to several Community policies, notably the movement of goods, state aids, taxation, competition, the right of establishment and the freedom to provide services. The fact is that the transport system developed in each Member State individually and was designed to serve the national needs (often military) rather than a wider territorial unit. Hence the problem of integration.

According to EC Article 71(1) (ex Art 75(1)) the Transport Policy includes:

(a) common rules applicable to international transport to or from the territory of a Member State or passing across the territory of one or more Member States;
(b) the conditions under which non-resident carriers may operate transport services within a Member State;
(c) measures to improve transport safety;[3] and
(d) any other appropriate provisions.

EC Article 80 (ex Art 84) refers only to 'transport by rail, road and inland waterway' but the Council may extend the policy to transport by air and sea.

---

1   For a detailed consideration see Close, G, *Transport*, in Halbsury's Laws of England, op cit, pp 667 et seq and Greaves, R, *Transport Law of the European Community* (1991).
2   See in particular the *ERTA* case [1971] ECR 263, [1971] CMLR 335, and Opinion 1/76: *Re Draft Agreement establishing a European Laying-up Fund for Inland Waterways Vessels* [1977] ECR 741, [1977] 2 CMLR 279.
3   (c) was added by the Maastricht Treaty.

However, irrespective of the implementation of the policy the ECJ held that job discrimination on board merchant vessels on the ground of nationality could not be maintained.[4]

Legislative measures have to be enacted in accordance with the co-decision procedure laid down in EC Article 251 (ex Art 189b), after consulting the Economic and Social Committee and the Committee of the Regions. Where the application of the principles of the regulatory system for transport would be liable to have a serious effect on the standard of living and on employment in certain areas and on the operation of transport facilities, the Council must act unanimously on a proposal from the Commission, after consulting the Parliament and the Economic and Social Committee; and the Council must take into account the need for adaptation to the economic development that will result from establishing the Common Market.[5]

B. Initial implementation

In an attempt to implement the policy the Commission proposed in 1961[6] to establish a 'Common Market in Transport organized according to Community rules, able to respond to the needs of transport in the Community and ensuring elimination of discrimination based on nationality'. This was to be achieved through a uniform approach to the modes of transport, carriers and users; financial independence of carriers; operational freedom; co-ordination of investments and the users' freedom of choice between the modes of transport and carriers. Furthermore,[7] the policy was to embrace the principle of sound competition between the various modes of transport and between the carriers. Later[8] further elements reflecting the anxieties of our technological age have been added: regional needs, problems of urbanization, pollution and energy.[9]

However, the lack of tangible progress prompted the Parliament to censure the Council by applying to the Court of Justice for a declaration that the Council had failed to adopt a Common Transport Policy in accordance with EC Article 71(1) (ex Art 75(1)).[10] The Parliament made its point but achieved little since the ECJ, whilst confirming that the Council was remiss, also held that the Parliament failed to indicate what specific measures ought to have been taken.

Subsequently the Commission 1985 White Paper[11] listed the failures in this field and singled out priorities but also warned the Council that if no action were taken regarding the application of competition rules to air and sea transport, the Commission would record the existing infringements and authorize Member States to take measures as determined by the Commission according to EC Article 85 (ex Art 89), which defines the powers of the Commission relevant to the enforcement of the Community Competition Policy.

The first steps in the implementation of the Common Transport Policy consisted of attempts to regulate operational, technical and social aspects of transport.

The operational harmonization consisted of tariff and non-tariff measures. The former consisted of maximum and minimum charges bilaterally agreed

4   Case 167/73: *Commission v France* [1974] ECR 359, [1974] 2 CMLR 216.
5   EC Art 71(1) and (2) (ex Art 75(1) and (3)).
6   Memorandum of 10 April 1961, see also *Ninth General Report*, 1966, item 207 et seq.
7   Council Decision 67/790, JO 1967, 322/4; OJ 174 (2nd) IV, 23.
8   Commission Memorandum of 24 October 1973, COM (73) 1725 final.
9   See Bull 12/1978; *Twelfth General Report* (1978), 199; *Thirteenth General Report* (1979), 177.
10 Case 13/83: *European Parliament v Council* [1985] ECR 1513, [1986] 1 CMLR 138.
11 Supra, p 432 at paras 108-112.

between Member States (hence 'bracket tariffs') applicable to transport by rail, road and inland waterways. It was introduced experimentally in 1967[12] for a three-year period, extended until 31 December 1982 and replaced by what is now Regulation 4058/89.[13]

Non-tariff measures comprise the rules of competition and the various conditions for the operation of the transport service. Above all it is intended to liberalize transport from national control and to reorganize the service in response to market forces of supply and demand.

The operation of the service is linked with insurance[14] against civil liability arising from the use of motor vehicles on the road. The exercise of the profession of transport operator, on the other hand, is subject to freedom of the provision of services and the right of establishment of the operator. Council directives[15] lay down rules regarding the professional formation of road haulage and road passenger transport operators as well as the recognition of professional qualifications. However a Member State may refuse the operator's licence to a person with a criminal record.[16] The directives purport to establish an integrated profession resulting from formal training but allow the Member States to grant licences to persons with adequate practical experience.[17]

Technical harmonization is concerned with the rules governing technical standards of equipment, safety and comfort as well as the control of pollution. Directive 70/156[18] on the approximation of national laws relating to the type-approval of motor vehicles and trailers and Directive 74/150[19] on agricultural and forestry tractors provide a model of legislation in this respect.

Social harmonization consists of Council regulations[20] setting out to establish common standards for working conditions in internal and inter-state transport. These standards apply to drivers irrespective of whether or not they are employees or independent traders;[1] the resting periods laid down by the Regulation apply not only to drivers but also to employers when driving[2] and the penal sanctions cannot be flouted.[3] The Member States[4] are bound to see that the use of certain

---

12 Reg 1174/68 (JO 1969, L194/1; OJ 1968, L411).

13 OJ 1989, L390/1, preceded by Reg 3568/83 (OJ 1983, L359/1), and Reg 2831/77 (OJ 1977, L334/22); see Commission arbitration award (OJ 1980, L4/14); [1980] 1 CMLR 699. See Case 12/82: *Ministère Public v Trinon* [1982] ECR 4089, [1983] 3 CMLR 85.

14 See Dir 72/166 (OJ 1972, L360); Dir 72/430 (OJ 1972, L77); Dir 84/5 (OJ 1984, L8/17); Dir 90/232 (OJ 1990, L129/33).

15 Dir 96/26 (OJ 1996, L124/1), as amended. See Cases 28/81 and 29/81: *Commission v Italy* [1981] ECR 2577 and [1981] ECR 2585 (which concerned the predecessor to Dir 96/26).

16 Case 21/78: *Delkvist v Anklagemyndigheden* [1978] ECR 2327, [1979] 1 CMLR 372.

17 Cf Case 145/78: *Augustijn v Staatssecretaris van Verkeer en Waterstaat* [1979] ECR 1025, [1979] 3 CMLR 516; Case 146/78: *Wattenberg v Staatssecretaris van Verkeer en Waterstaat* [1979] ECR 1041, [1979] 3 CMLR 516.

18 JO 1970, L42/1; OJ 1970, L96 as amended.

19 OJ 1974, L84/10, as amended.

20 Reg 3820/85 (OJ 1985, L370/1).

1 Cf Case 65/76: *Re Deryke* [1977] ECR 29, [1977] 1 CMLR 449.

2 Cf Case 76/77: *Auditeur du Travail v Dufour* [1977] ECR 2485, [1978] 1 CMLR 265.

3 Cf Case 97/78: *Re Schumalla* [1978] ECR 2311, [1979] 2 CMLR 176; Case C-193/99 *Hume* [2000] All ER (EC) 852.

4 Cf Case 128/78: *Commission v United Kingdom (Tachograph)* [1979] ECR 419, [1979] 2 CMLR 45; see also *Concorde Express Transport Ltd v Traffic Examiner Metropolitan Area* [1980] 2 CMLR 221 (Crown Court, Kingston-upon-Thames). Case 90/83: *Paterson v W Weddell* [1984] ECR 1567, [1984] 2 CMLR 540; Case 133/83: *R v Thomas Scott & Sons* [1984] ECR 2863, [1985] 1 CMLR 188; Case C-387/96: *Sjöberg* [1998] ECR I-1225; Case C-47/97: *E Clarke & Sons (Coaches) Ltd & D J Ferne* [1998] ECR I-2147; Case C-297/99: *Skills Motor Coaches Ltd v Denman* [2001] All ER (EC) 289.

road transport vehicles both in domestic and inter-state traffic is controlled by means of the recording equipment prescribed by Council Regulation 3821/85.[5]

C.   Towards the completion of the policy

(1)   GENERAL STRATEGY

The Commission's White Paper on the future development of the Common Transport Policy,[6] which outlined the general strategy in this area, was endorsed by the European Parliament, the Economic and Social Committee and the Council which particularly welcomed the Commission's integrated approach, which encompassed economic, social and environmental aspects as well as infrastructure and research.[7] That was followed by the adoption of an action programme in 1995, updated in 1998, intended to cover the period to 2004.[8] However whenever a new strategy is proposed several previous initiatives are either overtaken by events or simply become relegated to historical experience.

The Maastricht Treaty in furtherance of the objectives of the internal market and economic and social cohesion[9] postulated that citizens of the Union, economic operators and regional and local communities should derive full benefit from the setting up of an area without internal frontiers, and that 'the Community shall contribute to the establishment and development of trans-European networks in the areas of transport, telecommunications and energy infrastructures'.[10] In order to achieve these objectives the Community shall establish the necessary guidelines, implement the measures involved and support the financial efforts made by the Member States for projects of common interest.[11]

The Member States,[12] on the other hand, shall, in liaison with the Commission, co-ordinate among themselves policies pursued at national level which may have a significant impact on the objectives of the Community Transport Policy.

The Community[13] may decide to co-operate with third countries to promote projects of mutual interest and to ensure the inter-operability of networks.

In anticipation of Maastricht the Council had already approved the high-speed rail network master plan[14] and adopted three decisions[15] on combined transport, road and inland waterways. The Commission began working a multi-model strategy combining all the master plans for the port, airport and conventional rail networks.[16]

(2)   INLAND TRANSPORT

Measures common to road, rail and inland waterways transport cover such matters as public service taxation, state intervention and state aids[17] and competition.[18]

5   OJ 1985, L370/8, as amended.
6   *Twenty-sixth General Report*, point 643; Supp 3-93, Bull EC.
7   *Twenty-seventh General Report*, point 303.
8   1995 General Report, para 385; 1998 General Report, para 429.
9   EC Art 14 and 158 (ex Art 7a and 130a).
10   EC Art 154(1) (ex Art 129b(1)). See Dec 1692/96 (OJ 1996, L228/1).
11   EC Art 155(1) (ex Art 129c(1)).
12   EC Art 155(2) (ex Art 129c(2)).
13   EC Art 155(3) (ex Art 129c(3)).
14   *Twenty-fourth General Report*, point 562.
15   Decisions 93/628, 93/629, 93/630.
16   COM(93) 701; Bull EC 12-1993.
17   Reg 1191/69 (OJ 1969, L156/1) and Reg 1107/70 (OJ 1970, L130/1), both as amended. Cf Case C-412/96: *Kainuun Liikenne Oy* [1998] ECR I-5141.
18   Reg 1017/68 (OJ 1968, L175/1).

Measures regulating road transport specifically include provisions for: a Community driving licence;[19] physical inspections and administrative formalities in respect of the carriage of goods between Member States;[20] the approximation of national laws relating to insurance against civil liability in respect of the use of motor vehicles;[1] the use of vehicles hired without drivers for the carriage of goods;[2] social legislation relating to road transport;[3] the weights, dimensions and other technical characteristics of certain road vehicles;[4] standard procedures for the implementation of Regulation 3820/85;[5] the fixing of rates for the carriage of goods between Member States;[6] admission to the occupation of road haulage or road passenger transport operator in national and international transport operations;[7] the conditions under which non-resident carriers may operate national road haulage services within a Member State;[8] the elimination of controls of road and inland water transport at the frontiers of Member States;[9] the harmonization of national laws relating to the tread depths of tyres of certain categories of vehicles and trailers;[10] the control of documents for shuttle services with accommodation and for occasional international coach and bus services;[11] taxes on certain vehicles and for the carriage of goods by road and tolls and charges for the use of certain types of infrastructure requiring heavy goods vehicles to contribute towards the costs of the infrastructure in question;[12] the conditions under which non-resident carriers may operate national road passenger transport services;[13] the installation and use of speed limitation devices for certain vehicles;[14] recognition of distinguishing signs of the Member State in which vehicles and trailers are registered;[15] transport of dangerous goods by road.[16]

(3)   RAILWAY TRANSPORT

Rail transport has attracted little Community legislation concerning mainly matters of accounting;[17] uniform costing principles for railway undertakings;[18] rates for the international carriage of goods by rail;[19] the commercial independence of the railways in the management of their international passenger

---

19   Dir 91/439 (OJ 1991, L237/1), as amended.
20   Dir 83/643 (OJ 1983, L359/8).
 1   Dir 84/5 (OJ 1984, L8/17) and 90/232 (OJ 1990, L129/33).
 2   Dir 84/647 (OJ 1984, L335/72).
 3   Reg 3820/85 (OJ 1985, L370/1).
 4   Dir 96/53 (OJ 1996, L235/59).
 5   Dir 88/599 (OJ 1988, L325/55).
 6   Reg 4058/89 (OJ 1989, L390/1).
 7   Dir 96/26 (OJ 1996, L124/1).
 8   Reg 3118/93 (OJ 1993, L279/1), as amended, and Reg 792/94 (OJ 1994, L92/13).
 9   Reg 4060/89 (OJ 1989, L390/18).
10   Dir 89/459 (OJ 1989, L226/4).
11   Council Reg 684/92 (OJ 1992, L74/1); Commission Reg 1839/92 (OJ 1992, L187) amended by Com Reg 2944/93 (OJ 1993, L266).
12   Dir 1999/62 (OJ 1999, L187/42). Cf Case C-193/98: *Pfennigmann* [1999] ECR I-7747 on the preceding Directive.
13   Reg 12/98 (OJ 1998, L4/10).
14   Dir 92/6 (OJ 1992, L57/27).
15   Reg 2411/98 (OJ 1998, L299/1).
16   Dir 94/55 (OJ 1994, L319/7).
17   Reg 1192/69 (OJ 1969, L156/8, Sp Ed 69(1) p 283), as amended; Reg 1108/70 (OJ 1970, L180/4, Sp Ed 70(II) p 363), as amended; Reg 2830/77 (OJ 1977, L334/13).
18   Reg 2183/78 (OJ 1978, L258/1).
19   Dec 82/529 (OJ 1982, L239/5).

and luggage traffic;[20] public service obligations;[1] and the carriage of dangerous goods.[2]

Directive 91/440[3] ensures the right of access to railway infrastructure. It has been followed by a Directive[4] on the licensing of railway undertakings and by another one[5] on the allocation of railway infrastructure capacity and the charging of infrastructure fees.

(4) INLAND WATERWAYS

Legislation on inland waterway transport includes provisions for: reciprocal recognition of navigability licences for vessels;[6] technical requirements for inland waterway vessels;[7] the conditions for access to the arrangements under the revised Convention for the navigation of the Rhine;[8] access to the occupation of carrier of goods by inland waterway and the mutual recognition of professional qualifications;[9] structural improvements in inland waterway transport;[10] a fleet capacity policy to promote inland waterway transport;[11] reciprocal recognition of national boatmasters' certificates for the carriage of goods and passengers;[12] conditions under which non-resident carriers may transport goods or passengers;[13] chartering and pricing systems.[14]

(5) MARITIME TRANSPORT

The Council set up a consultation procedure on relations between Member States and third countries in shipping matters and on action relating to such matters in international organizations[15] and issued a regulation concerning the ratification by the Member States of, or their accession to, the UN Convention and a Code of Conduct for Liner Conferences.[16]

Specific legislation includes provisions for: the freedom to provide services in maritime transport between Member States and third countries;[17] freedom to provide services by way of maritime cabotage;[18] the application of the competition

20   Dec 83/529 (OJ 1983, L237/33).
 1   Reg 1191/69 (OJ 1969, L156/1, Sp Ed 69(1) p 276).
 2   Dir 96/49 (OJ 1996, L235/25), as amended.
 3   OJ 1991, L237.
 4   Dir 95/18 (OJ 1995, L143/70).
 5   Dir 95/19 (OJ 1995, L143/75).
 6   Dir 76/135 (OJ 1976, L21/10).
 7   Dir 82/714 (OJ 1982, L301/1).
 8   Reg 2919/85 (OJ 1985, L280/5).
 9   Dir 87/540 (OJ 1987, L322/20).
10   Reg 1101/89 (OJ 1989, L116/25). Cf Case T-155/97: *Natural van Dam AG v Commission* [1998] ECR II-3921; Case T-63/98: *Transpo Maastricht BV v Commission* 1 February 2000.
11   Reg 718/1999 (OJ 1999, L90/1); Reg 805/1999 (OJ 1989, L102/64).
12   Dir 91/672 (OJ 1991, L373/29).
13   Reg 3921/91 (OJ 1991, L373/1).
14   Dir 96/15 (OJ 1996, L304/12).
15   Dec 77/587 (OJ 1977, L239/23).
16   Reg 954/79 (OJ 1979, L121/1).
17   Reg 4055/86 (OJ 1986, L378/1). Cf Cases C-176/97 and C-177/97: *Commission v Belgium and Luxembourg* [1998] ECR I-3557; Case C-170/98: *Commission v Belgium* [1999] ECR I-5493; Cases C-171/98, C-201/98 and C-202/98: *Commission v Belgium and Luxembourg* [1999] ECR I-5517; Case C-62/98: *Commission v Portugal,* 4 July 2000; Case C-84/98: *Commission v Portugal* 4 July 2000.
18   Reg 3577/92 (OJ 1992, L364/7).

rules of EC Articles 81 and 82 (ex Arts 85 and 86) to maritime transport;[19] unfair pricing practices in maritime transport;[20] free access to cargoes in ocean trades;[1] minimum requirements for vessels bound for or leaving Community ports and carrying dangerous or polluting goods;[2] transfer of ships from one register to another in the Community;[3] pilotage of vessels in the North Sea and English Channel;[4] minimum training for seafarers;[5] safety rules and standards.[6]

(6) AIR TRANSPORT

A rather late start of Community regulation of air transport commenced with the setting up of a consultation procedure on relations between Member States and third countries as well as international organizations in this field.[7] Further legislation includes measures concerning: the procedure for the application of competition rules;[8] the application of EC Article 81(3) (ex Art 85(3)) to certain categories of agreements and concerted practices in the air transport sector;[9] fares and rates for scheduled air services between Member States;[10] the sharing of passenger capacity between air carriers on scheduled services between Member States and the access for air carriers to scheduled service routes between Member States;[11] the application of EC Article 81(3) (ex Art 85(3)) to certain categories of agreements between undertakings, decisions of associations of undertakings and concerted practices concerning joint planning and co-ordination of capacity, sharing of revenue and consultation on tariffs on scheduled services and slot allocations at airports;[12] a code of conduct for computerized reservation systems[13] and air traffic management equipment and systems;[14] access to the ground handling market at Community airports;[15] operation of air cargo services between Member States;[16] licensing of air carriers;[17] access to intra-Community routes;[18] allocation of slots at Community airports;[19] air carrier liability in the event of accidents.[20]

---

19 Reg 4056/86 (OJ 1986, L378/4); Reg 2842/98 (OJ 1998, L354/18). See also Reg 479/92 (OJ 1992, L55/3), and Reg 870/95 (OJ 1995, L89/7), on exemptions under EC Art 81(3) (ex Art 85(3)).
20 Reg 4057/86 (OJ 1986, L378/14).
1 Reg 4058/86 (OJ 1986, L378/21).
2 Dir 93/75 (OJ 1993, L247/19).
3 Reg 613/91 (OJ 1991, L68/1).
4 Dir 79/115 (OJ 1979, L33/32).
5 Dir 94/58 (OJ 1994, L319/28), as amended.
6 Reg 3051/95 (OJ 1995, L320/14) (ro-ro ferries); Dir 98/18 (OJ 1998, L144/1) (passenger ships).
7 Dec 80/50 (OJ 1980, L18/24).
8 Reg 3975/87 (OJ 1987, L374/1).
9 Reg 3976/87 (OJ 1987, L374/9).
10 Reg 2409/92 (OJ 1992, L240/15).
11 Reg 2343/90 (OJ 1990, L217/8).
12 Reg 1617/93 (OJ 1993, L155/18).
13 Reg 2299/89 (OJ 1989, L220/1), as amended.
14 Dir 93/65 (OJ 1993, L187).
15 Dir 96/67 (OJ 1996, L272/36).
16 Reg 294/91 (OJ 1991, L36/1).
17 Reg 2407/92 (OJ 1992, L240/1).
18 Reg 2408/92 (OJ 1992, L240/8).
19 Reg 95/93 (OJ 1993, L14(1)).
20 Reg 2027/97 (OJ 1997, L285/1).

Chapter 27

Competition: general principles

A. Introduction

In the Western type of economy, competition is regarded not only as an essential element of capitalist efficiency but also as a safeguard against the abuse of economic power; a healthy rivalry between firms is good for the economy as a whole and for the consumer. Despite considerable European experience in the field of competition law, particularly in Germany, much in Community competition law is owed to the United States, which has long had a sophisticated system for dealing with anti-competitive activities.[1] However, the two systems, US and Community competition law, have sometimes developed different solutions to similar problems.

Competition law is based on economic considerations. The principal theory behind competition law is that market structure determines the conduct of businesses in the market and their conduct, in turn, determines how the market performs. It is in the interests of society that markets perform efficiently. Therefore, the object of competition law is to achieve that end (so far as is possible). That involves the law influencing, or checking developments in the market such as changes in the number and size of the businesses operating in the market and arrangements made between businesses which affect how the market performs. Competition theory is not an exact science and in many respects the predictions of different theories of competition are not always borne out in practice. That inevitably affects competition law. Although the problems that competition law is called on to rectify in different jurisdictions are similar, the answers that different jurisdictions come to are not always the same: they may depend upon the nature of the economy in which the law is to be applied; they will depend upon underlying policy considerations, such as the ultimate aims of competition and prevailing

---

1   For historical reasons, US competition law is known as 'anti-trust law': in the 19th century, trusts were the legal device favoured by commerce and industry in the USA as a vehicle for anti-competitive conduct.

views of how the competitive process works or of what constitutes a distortion of competition that merits the imposition of legal sanctions.[2]

Some understanding of the policy behind the law is therefore necessary in order to appreciate how it is applied. Before considering what the competition policy of the Community is, it may be useful to explain certain basic features of the competitive process.

B. The competitive process

The participants in the competitive process can, broadly speaking, be divided into two groups: suppliers (of goods or services) and customers. Customers acquire what the suppliers provide. The relationship between those two groups is often termed a 'vertical' relationship. The different stages in that vertical relationship, by which goods (or services) are brought into existence and supplied to a customer, can be complex. In broad terms, the first stage is innovation: the invention of a new product or improvement of an existing product. Next, there is manufacture, which may involve the acquisition of raw materials (that is, products such as coal or timber that are available in nature), or of products which have themselves been invented and manufactured, and the subjection of such raw materials or other products to a process resulting in the creation of a different product. After being manufactured, the product must be distributed. That stage may involve a number of separate stages: supply to a wholesaler, from him to a retailer and from the retailer to a person who uses the product (the consumer). In some cases, a customer will himself be a supplier, as where he buys a raw material or a manufactured product from a supplier for manufacture into another product and sale to someone else.

Competition is nothing more than rivalry. But persons who operate at different stages in the process described above are not (generally) rivals. A person who does nothing but manufacture a particular product is not (normally) a rival of a person who does nothing but sell that product to the general public: although both those persons are in the business of supplying the same product, they supply it to different people (wholesalers, or perhaps retailers, in the case of the manufacturer; the general public in the case of the retailer) and therefore they are not in competition with one another for potential buyers. Competition takes place between different persons operating at the same level: between manufacturers, or between wholesalers, or between retailers. The relationship between persons operating at the same level is often termed a 'horizontal relationship'. Competition law is therefore concerned mainly with such relationships. Vertical relationships are of less concern because the relationship is between persons who are not competitors.

There are, however, situations where a vertical relationship is of concern, such as where it has horizontal effects. For example, where a manufacturer makes an agreement with three wholesalers that they shall distribute his products but not the products of any competitor of the manufacturer, the vertical relationship between that manufacturer and the wholesalers concerned may have horizontal effects at the

---

2   The classic example of how a shift in economic theory may affect competition law is the change that has taken place in US competition law over the last 30 years under the influence of the 'Chicago School'. Another example is the significant shift in the attitude of the Commission to so-called 'vertical agreements', that is, agreements between persons operating at different levels in the production and distribution chains: see in particular the Commission's communication published in OJ 1999, C 270/7; the guidelines in OJ 2000, C 291/1; and Lever, J, QC, and Neubauer, S, 'Vertical Restraints, their motivation and justification' [2000] ECLR 7.

level of manufacture or at the level of wholesale distribution. The effect at the level of manufacture may be to limit the ability of other manufacturers to distribute their products (if there are only three wholesalers in existence, the other manufacturers may have no way of distributing their products or may have to use another, possibly more expensive or less efficient, method of distribution). At the level of wholesale distribution, the effect may be to reduce or eliminate competition between the three wholesalers: they will now be obtaining the same products from the same manufacturer at (possibly) the same price so that, from the viewpoint of the retailer, there may be little or no difference between them. Accordingly, when analysing a particular situation for the purpose of assessing the effects (if any) on competition, it is usually necessary to examine all the commercial relationships of and between the persons involved. For example, analysis of a particular agreement between two persons at the same level in the competitive process requires an examination of the effect on competition between them, the effect on any vertical relationship between those persons and others (where a vertical relationship is between one person and another operating at a previous stage in the process, such as the relationship between a distributor and a manufacturer, it is occasionally described as an 'upstream' relationship; where it is between one person and another operating at a later stage in the process, such as a relationship between a wholesaler and a retailer, it is occasionally described as a 'downstream' relationship), and the effect on any horizontal relationship involving persons who have only a vertical relationship with the parties to the agreement.

There are various ways in which competition between persons at the same level is possible. Probably the most important basis for competition is price: in general, a supplier is more competitive if he offers his products at a lower price than his competitors because, if given the choice, customers are more likely to buy a lower-priced product than a higher-priced product. Price is not the only basis for competition: quality, reliability, security of supply (in the case of goods that are required frequently or in significant volume) are others. In some instances, a supplier may deliberately set out to emphasize characteristics of his product other than the price in order to make it more competitive: examples are perfumes, which are often marketed with a luxury image that implies a high price. The intrinsic value of the product may be no greater than that of a much cheaper product but, to the buyer, the image justifies payment of a higher price. The degree to which there can be competition between similar products by reference to a particular feature of those products varies. Some products are particularly sensitive to movements in price: if the price goes up, customers buy less; but if the price goes down, they buy more. In the case of other products, the customer may well be prepared to pay a higher price if the quality is better. In all cases, the customer's ability to make a choice by reference to variances in the characteristics of similar products depends on the knowledge of those characteristics available to the customer. For example, in some cases, differences in quality are not an effective basis for competition because the customer lacks the technical knowledge to identify such differences or evaluate them and compare them with other factors (such as price) in order to make a decision between the products offered by competition suppliers.[3] 'Transparency' is the term

---

3 For example, an ordinary person who is faced with the need to undergo an operation is unable to choose between different surgeons because he does not know who are the surgeons who perform that particular operation and he lacks the technical knowledge and experience to judge whether one of those surgeons is better than another. In such cases, the role of intermediaries in the market (such as the general practitioner who knows how to find out the identity of competent surgeons) can be of particular importance because they enable there to be competition on the basis of quality.

that is often used to describe the existence in a particular market of knowledge about the factors that determine the degree of competition between different products.

So far, attention has been paid to the persons who compete and the respects in which they may compete but not to the products that they compete with or the geographical areas in which they compete. It is obvious that suppliers of the same type of product (such as nails of a certain length or, in the case of services, employment agencies) are in principle in competition with each other in relation to that product. However, if they are located in different parts of the world, the distance between them may preclude any degree of competition between them. Taking the product aspect first, it is easy to see that products of the same or similar characteristics and uses are in competition with one another (say, six-inch nails); and that products that are completely different in characteristics and uses do not compete with each other (say, six-inch nails and bananas). Between those two extremes, there are situations where it is not at all obvious whether one product is in competition with another. In general, the test to be applied is whether the products in question are 'substitutable' for one another. The test of substitutability is not, however, an exact yardstick: in many instances there may be a greater or lesser degree of substitutability between different products, depending upon the surrounding circumstances, and a judgment must be made as to whether or not the degree of substitutability (if any) found to exist is sufficient to justify the conclusion that the products in question are in competition with one another. Thus, in one case, bananas were found to be in a market that was sufficiently differentiated from the market for other fruit to be considered a separate market;[4] in another case, wine and beer were regarded as competing products despite their different characteristics.[5]

So far as the geographical aspect is concerned, suppliers who supply competing products to customers within the same area are in competition with each other even if they themselves are located in different geographical areas. Where the consumers of the products are located in different geographical areas, the question may arise as to whether or not the suppliers are in competition with one another. As in the case of the definition of competing products, the question of whether two or more different areas form part of the same geographical market is often a question of judgment and of degree. In essence, the question is whether or not the products of the suppliers in question *could* be sold in the same area.[6] For example, if the product in question deteriorates over time and cannot be preserved in the course of transit, the product cannot be sold at more than a certain distance from the place where it is manufactured. In consequence, if the suppliers in question are so far apart that the product would have become unsaleable through deterioration by the time that it was transported to the area in which one of the suppliers actually sells or could sell the product to consumers, then that supplier is not in competition with the remaining suppliers.

There are various ways in which rivalry between suppliers (or between customers) may be restricted, eliminated or distorted. The first distinction to make is that between private and public interventions in the competitive process. Both are of concern to Community competition law but they are dealt with in different ways. The former arise from the actions of legal or natural persons in

---

4 Case 27/76: *United Brands v Commission* [1978] ECR 207, paras 12-35.
5 Case 170/78: *Commission v United Kingdom* [1980] ECR 417, paras 12-14.
6 They may not actually be sold in the same geographical area because the suppliers have decided to keep to their own territories and not compete with each other. For that reason, the test is one of potential competition.

their private or personal capacity; the latter arise from the actions of a Member State, the different constitutional organs of a state or legal or natural persons that have been entrusted by the state with special rights or powers.

So far as private interventions are concerned, a broad distinction can be drawn between co-operative forms of behaviour involving two or more persons and unilateral action by one person. Co-operative forms of behaviour are the classic examples of private distortions of competition. The most important are agreements between competitors that restrict or remove the freedom of action of the parties to the agreement; agreements to charge the same prices or impose the same contractual terms and conditions; or agreements dividing the market up between them. Such arrangements are often called 'cartels' or 'horizontal agreements'. 'Vertical agreements', that is, agreements between persons at different levels in the competitive process, may also distort competition: for example, an agreement between a manufacturer and a distributor whereby the latter agrees to distribute the manufacturer's products and not to distribute products of the same type made by any other manufacturer.

Unilateral action is not, in general, regarded as a cause for concern unless the author of the action enjoys significant economic power. The most extreme example is that of a monopoly. A lesser degree of economic power may be enough: in the parlance of EC Article 82 (ex Art 86), a 'dominant position'. Another phenomenon that may give rise for concern is 'concentration'. In broad terms, a concentration is a rearrangement in the structure of one or more participants in the market, such as a merger between two companies or the sale by one company of a business to another company. An agreement is often the means, or one of the means, by which a concentration is effected. In contrast to cartel-type agreements, an agreement giving rise to a concentration does not result in continued co-operation between two or more independent trading entities. Once the concentration has been effected, either one party to the agreement (if there is one) has been swallowed up (as in the case of a take-over) by or merged with the other or the parties continue to operate independently of one another (as in the case of a sale of a business or assets). The problem of concentrations is twofold: the accumulation of economic power may result in the creation of a dominant position or monopoly; even if it does not do so, the accumulation of economic power implies a reduction in the number of independent suppliers (or customers) in the market and the emergence of a few large suppliers (or customers). Where the number of suppliers (or customers) in the market grows smaller or the market becomes dominated by a small number of large suppliers (or customers), the risk of collusion between them increases and so does the risk that the market may become an oligopoly in which, even without collusion, competition becomes impossible because each competitor is constantly looking over its shoulder at what the others are doing.

Public interventions in the competitive process range from the general (such as interest rate policy, legislative measures affecting the way in which businesses can operate, such as by prohibiting or restricting particular sales techniques – doorstep and pyramid selling and the offer of free gifts are examples of techniques which have at different times received the attentions of the legislature in different countries – and the definition of the scope of protection afforded by the state to intellectual property rights) to the particular (such as the grant of financial or other assistance by the state or an emanation of the state to a particular business – this is known as a 'state aid' – or the creation of a monopoly of a business activity in favour of a particular business). As a result of the vast range and different types of, and the reasons for, public intervention in the competitive process, a flexible approach to the control of such intervention is called for. For example, the policy considerations determining a state's interest rate policy are of a completely different order from those which determine the decision whether or not to sell a plot of publicly-owned land to a business for development at a price which is less than the open market price of the land (a form of state aid). Accordingly, only certain forms of public intervention in the competitive process are dealt with by the competition rules in the Treaty.

In theory, most distortions of competition of a private nature can be eliminated simply by the operation of market forces. For example, if a number of manufacturers agree to charge the same (high) price to all customers, that creates the opportunity for another manufacturer to undercut them and take away their business. As customers switch to the low-priced manufacturer, the price-fixing agreement will become unworkable. Accordingly, competition law is very much concerned with the facts that may enable market forces to rectify a distortion of competition or, on the contrary, that prevent market forces from doing so. In particular, competition law is very much concerned with what is known as 'potential competition'. Thus far, the description given of competition as rivalry between different persons at the same level of business has implied that competition takes place between existing players in the market. That is referred to as 'actual competition'. Potential competition refers to the possibility of new competitors entering the market. They may be attracted by the existence of a distortion of competition that (for example), by increasing prices, creates a marketing opportunity; or they may be able to enter the market and pose a new challenge to the incumbent players because of a technological or commercial development. The expression 'contestable markets' is used to denote markets in which the costs incurred in entering the market are the same as the costs incurred by a dominant firm in operating in the market. Accordingly, in theory at least, a dominant firm cannot keep out new entrants; and the threat that new competitors may enter the market is in itself (according to theory) enough to ensure that the market will remain fully competitive. Thus, competitive forces are able to rectify distortions of competition. 'Entry barriers' is the expression often used to denote factors (such as the need to incur costs in setting up a manufacturing or distribution facility; the need to acquire intellectual property rights; the loyalty of consumer to well-known products – 'brand loyalty' – and the resultant difficulty to break well-entrenched habits of consumers and persuade them to buy a new product) which may render markets less easy, or impossible, for new competitors to enter and less 'contestable' or not 'contestable' at all.

In reality, market forces (including potential competition) are often unable to restore conditions of undistorted competition or are able to do so only after a lengthy period of time. In the example given at the beginning of the preceding paragraph, manufacturers who are not parties to the price-fixing agreement may decide to align their prices to those fixed in the agreement rather than attempt to undercut them; or the price level fixed in the agreement may not be high enough to make it worthwhile for someone else to make the necessary investment in order to enter the market as a manufacturer. Sometimes, a lack of transparency in the market makes it possible for suppliers to distort competition with impunity because customers do not have sufficient information to identify competitive offers. In some cases, the absence of undistorted competition is not the result of the behaviour of competitors but of the structure of the market. The significance of a distortion of competition, and the need for action under the competitor rules to remove it, therefore depends on whether or not, having regard to the surrounding circumstances, market forces are able to deal with the problem in sufficient time.

In contrast, public interventions in the competitive process are not generally vulnerable to market forces (save that in the case, for example, of interest rate policy, the effect on exchange rates – that is, the effect on competition between different currencies – may well influence movements in interest rates) because the originator of the intervention (typically central or local government) is motivated by political considerations which may well run in a contrary direction to market forces.

Hitherto, the main emphasis has been on distortions of competition effected by suppliers. It should not be forgotten that customers, too, may distort competition by taking the same type of action as suppliers, such as agreements to pay only a certain price for a given product and so forth. Such action is occasionally referred to as 'demand-side' distortions of competition (in contrast to 'supply-side' distortions of competition effected by suppliers). In practice, anti-competitive behaviour on the part of customers is rarely encountered or, at least, is rarely regarded as giving rise to problems under the competition rules. One of the reasons for that is that the main emphasis in competition theory is on the factors that enable suppliers to charge customers prices for products which exceed the cost of producing the product, the theory being that undistorted competition should lead to the supply of products at a price equal to their cost of production. Demand-side distortions of competition lead in theory to the same result as undistorted competition in that their effect is to pressurize suppliers into supplying more economically albeit (for obvious reasons) not usually at prices below the costs of production. They therefore counterbalance any supply-side distortions of competition or other imperfections in the market. Another relevant factor is that, typically (although not invariably), the number of *customers* at the different stages in the competitive process is greater than the number of *suppliers* with the consequence that negotiating power (often described as 'market' power) on the demand side is much less strong than on the supply side: the smaller number of suppliers are in a better position to 'divide and rule'. Thus, demand-side distortions of competition are less likely to have a material effect on the market than supply-side distortions of competition. Having said that, there is no general principle or assumption that demand-side distortions of competition can never be a matter of concern. In some markets, market power is concentrated into fewer hands on the demand side than on the supply side.[7] In addition, anti-competitive arrangements on the demand side may provoke the creation or reinforcement of anti-competitive arrangements on the supply side, thus affecting adversely the performance of the market.

C. Principles of Community competition law

One of the activities of the Community is the institution of a system ensuring that competition in the internal (formerly the common) market is not distorted;[8] it is therefore a fundamental principle of the Treaty that competition in the

---

7 For example, the milk market in the United Kingdom has a very large number of relatively small milk producers. The number of dairies, who purchase by far the greater part of the milk produced, is very much smaller. The number of supermarket chains, which account for a substantial amount of the milk sold for consumption in liquid form, is very much smaller again. The number of consumers is, of course, very much greater than the number of producers. The result is that (in the absence of co-operative or other arrangements between producers), dairies exercise market power over producers while the supermarket chains exercise market power over dairies and are not subject to any countervailing market power exercised by consumers.

8 See EC Art 3(g) (ex Art 3(f)). The main works on EC competition law are: Bellamy & Child, *Common Market Law of Competition* (5th edn, 2001), Faull & Nikpay, *The EC Law of Competition* (1999); Ritter, Braun & Rawlinson, *EC Competition Law* (2nd edn, 2000).

Community should not be distorted. That principle underpins many Treaty provisions[9] and is implemented specifically by the competition rules of the Treaty.[10] The Treaty does not define what is meant by a system of undistorted competition or what undistorted competition is.

Completely undistorted competition, in a literal sense, is not necessarily advantageous; it does not necessarily promote economic efficiency or increase the welfare of society. There are occasions where some 'distortion' of competition is necessary or desirable in order to satisfy some prevailing consideration of public policy or in order to make the market more competitive and therefore more able to ensure the fulfilment of the objectives of the Community. One example is intellectual property. Patents and similar rights distort competition by giving the holder of the right a temporary monopoly. The justification for this is that, without a temporary monopoly guaranteeing a return to the holder of the right, people would be deterred from investing in research and development or from communicating knowledge of their innovations to others. The distortion of competition at the level of production and supply that arises from an intellectual property right is therefore the price paid for encouraging competition at the level of innovation.

The ECJ has called the form of competition envisaged in the Treaty 'effective'[11] or 'workable'[12] competition, which it has defined as 'the degree of competition necessary to ensure the observance of the basic requirements and the attainment of the objectives of the Treaty, in particular the creation of a single market achieving conditions similar to those of a domestic market'.[13] Effective competition accepts some distortions of competition, but only those that are desirable for the purpose of achieving the objectives of the Treaty.

In theory, a system of effective competition has two requirements: (1) the maintenance of a satisfactory market structure, that is, the combination of factors characterizing the market (including in particular the number of participants in the market, both buyers and sellers, and their size) that will generate conditions conducive to economic efficiency; and (2) behaviour on the part of the undertakings operating in the market that is conducive to economic efficiency, in other words, that undertakings act so as to take full advantage of the opportunities that the structure of the market gives them.

Competition law is therefore concerned with both the structure of the market and the behaviour of undertakings. However, while it is relatively easy to distinguish between conduct that favours competition and economic efficiency and conduct that does not, the maintenance of a satisfactory market structure is much more difficult. It depends upon a correct assessment of a variety of changing factors, such as whether the market for a particular product or group of products (whether goods or services) is in a stage of development, has reached maturity, is stagnating or is in decline, and the extent to which the market is accessible to new participants. There is no single optimum market structure and therefore no specific target for competition law to aim at. On the other hand, there are certain rough and ready rules, such as the general rule that the more concentrated a market

---

9   See, eg, Case C-202/88: *France v Commission* [1991] ECR I-1223, [1992] 5 CMLR 552, para 41, for the relationship between EC Art 28 et seq (ex Art 30 et seq) and EC Art 3(f), as it then was.
10   EC Arts 81-89 (ex Arts 85-96).
11   Case 6/72: *Europemballage Corpn and Continental Can Co Inc v Commission* [1973] ECR 215, para 25.
12   Case 26/76: *Metro v Commission* [1977] ECR 1875, para 20.
13   Ibid.

becomes (that is, the smaller in number and greater in size the suppliers or, as the case may be, the customers, become), the less competitive it is likely to be. That rule does not apply in all cases. For example, in a stagnating or declining market, concentration may increase the level of competition by rationalizing the industry.

Apart from maintaining a system of effective competition, the Community's competition rules have two other main concerns. One is the creation of a single market out of the different national markets of the Member States. The Community authorities are particularly sensitive about business practices that tend to partition the common market; but they are more receptive to certain forms of co-operation between undertakings, where they involve undertakings in different Member States, because such arrangements tend to promote the integration of national markets. The second concern of note is the protection of fair competition. The preamble to the EC Treaty refers expressly to the maintenance of fair competition. Although there is no further reference to fair competition in the body of the Treaty, the Commission has referred to it as one of the objectives of the Community's competition policy[14] and it is certainly one of the considerations that has influenced the ECJ in several decided cases.

A particular concern of EC competition law in recent years has been state intervention in the competitive process. The EC Treaty singles out certain forms of state involvement for specific treatment: state monopolies of a commercial character (EC Article 31 (ex Art 37)); public undertakings (EC Article 86 (ex Art 90)); state aids (EC Article 87 to 89 (ex Art 92-94)). Certain general principles have now emerged in the ECJ's case law and can be summarized as follows.

The Member States are bound by the prohibition of discrimination on grounds of nationality enshrined in EC Article 6 (now Art 12, formerly Art 7). This means that, for example, national competition law must be applied without discrimination based on the nationality or country of origin of the undertakings concerned and must affect all legal and natural persons subject to it in accordance with objective criteria and without regard to nationality; disparities in treatment resulting from divergences between the competition laws of the Member States are not, however, prohibited by Article 6.[15] EC Article 10 (ex Art 5) imposes on Member States a general duty to co-operate and assist in the attainment of the objectives of the Treaty. The actual content of that general duty in a specific case is to be determined by examining EC Article 10 (ex Art 5) in the light of other Treaty provisions or provisions of secondary legislation (including provisions such as EC Articles 81 and 82 (ex Arts 85 and 86) which are directed at persons other than Member States) or rules which can be derived from the general scheme of the Treaty, its principles, aims and objectives, and the system adopted for their attainment.[16] Accordingly, national competition law cannot be applied in such a way as to prejudice the full and uniform application of EC competition law or the effects of measures taken or to be taken in implementation of EC competition law, such as measures enabling private undertakings to escape from the constraints imposed on them by the competition rules.[17] In general terms, therefore, state

---

14 See eg the Ninth Report on Competition Policy (Brussels-Luxembourg, 1980), p 10.
15 Case 14/68: *Walt Wilhelm v Bundeskartellamt* [1969] ECR 1, para 13.
16 Case 78/70: *Deutsche Grammophon GmbH v Metro-SB Grossmärkte GmbH & Co KG* [1971] ECR 487, para 5.
17 The *Walt Wilhelm* case, supra, para 5-9; Case 13/77: *GB-Inno-BM NV v ATAB* [1977] ECR 2115, paras 31 and 33; Case 229/83: *Association des Centres Distributeurs Edouard Leclerc v Au Blé Vert Sàrl* [1985] ECR 1, [1985] 2 CMLR 286, para 14; Case 231/83: *Cullet v Centre Leclerc, Toulouse* [1985] ECR 305, [1985] 2 CMLR 524, para 16.

action which brings about a distortion of competition directly, such as by compelling an undertaking or group of undertakings to carry out what would be a breach of the competition rules if it was done by them voluntarily, or by rendering any restriction or elimination of competition by undertakings themselves unnecessary (eg government price fixing), is prohibited by the Treaty. State action which encourages, facilitates, authorizes or approves, but does not cause by direct means, a distortion of competition effected by one or more undertakings (such as where state action provides the opportunity for undertakings to distort competition, of which the undertakings concerned then take advantage) is not necessarily prohibited (much turns on the precise extent to which the state can be held to be responsible for the resulting distortion of competition) but the undertakings concerned are responsible for their own actions taken in response to the acts of the state.[18] The state may be responsible where it reinforces the effects of unlawful arrangements between undertakings or entrusts to undertakings the taking of decisions affecting the economic sphere.[19]

D. The legal framework

(1) THE BASIC TREATY PROVISIONS

The competition rules in the EC Treaty are now divided into two sections. They can be further sub-divided into provisions dealing with the substantive law, provisions setting out procedures to be followed and provisions empowering the adoption of implementing legislation. The Treaty provisions and the implementing legislation are to be construed in the light of the aims of the Treaty and the principles set out in its preamble.[20]

The first section (EC Articles 81-86 (ex Arts 85-90)) covers the rules applicable to 'undertakings'. An 'undertaking' is an economic unit, comprising one or more legal or natural persons, that carries on an economic activity, whether or not it is profit-making.[1] In brief, EC Article 81(1) (ex Art 85(1)) prohibits certain agreements between undertakings, decisions of associations of undertakings and concerted practices. EC Article 81(2) (ex Art 85(2)) declares that prohibited agreements or decisions are automatically void. EC Article 81(3) (ex Art 85(3)) allows prohibited arrangements to be exempted from prohibition under certain conditions. EC Article 82 (ex Art 86) prohibits the abuse of a dominant position. There is no provision for obtaining an exemption from prohibition. EC Article 83 (ex Art 87) authorizes the adoption of implementing legislation. EC Articles 84 and 85 (ex Arts 88 and 89) set out rules of a procedural nature that are largely of historic interest. EC Article 86 (ex Art 90) deals with the position of public and other undertakings that require special treatment because of their relationship with the state.

---

18 See eg Cases 240-242, 261, 262, 268 and 269/82: *SSI v Commission* [1985] ECR 3831, [1987] 3 CMLR 661, para 30.
19 See eg Case 267/86: *Van Eycke v ASPA NV* [1988] ECR 4769, [1990] 4 CMLR 330, para 16; Case C-2/91: *Meng* [1993] ECR I-5751, para 14. See generally Case T-387/94: *Asia Motor France v Commission* [1996] ECR II-961, paras 60-61.
20 Case 32/65: *Italy v Council and Commission* [1966] ECR 389 at 405.
 1 Case 170/83: *Hydrotherm Gerätebau GmbH v Compact de Dott Ing Mario Andreli & CSAS* [1984] ECR 2999, para 11; Commission Decision 85/615: *Protection and Indemnity Clubs Agreement* (OJ 1985, L376/2, recitals 1 and 2). See further p 648, infra.

The second section (EC Articles 87 to 89, (ex Arts 92-94)) covers state aids. EC Article 87(1) (ex Art 92(1)) declares certain state aids to be incompatible with the common market. EC Article 87(2) and (3) (ex Art 92(2) and (3)) provides for exceptions to that principle. EC Article 88 (ex Art 93) deals with procedural matters. EC Article 89 (ex Art 94) provides for the adoption of implementing legislation. Before the amendment of the EC Treaty by the Amsterdam Treaty, there was another section comprising a single article (former Article 91) covering dumping within the Community. It was of historic interest and has now been deleted.[2]

Those Treaty provisions lay down the major part of the substantive law. Other Treaty provisions deal with competition but are not in formal terms part of 'the competition rules': for example, EC Articles 28-30 (ex Arts 30-36) cover the free movement of goods and are of particular relevance to the exercise of intellectual property rights; EC Article 90 (ex Art 95) covers discriminative and protective taxation; EC Articles 96-97 (ex Arts 101 and 102) deal with the situation where a difference between the provisions laid down by law, regulation or administrative action in the Member States leads to distortion in the conditions of competition in the common market.

The substantive rules apply generally to all goods and services other than those covered by the ECSC Treaty but the agricultural sector is covered by special rules (special rules of an essentially procedural, not substantive, nature apply in the transport sector and are discussed below).

EC Article 36 (ex Art 42) provides that the competition rules shall apply to the production of and trade in agricultural products only to the extent determined by the Council within the framework of EC Articles 37(2) and (3) (ex Arts 43(2) and (3)), account being taken of the objectives of the Common Agricultural Policy set out in EC Article 33 (ex Art 39). It also provides specifically that the Council may authorize the grant of aids '(a) for the protection of enterprises handicapped by structural or natural conditions; (b) within the framework of economic development programmes'. In 1962, the Council exercised its power under EC Article 36 (ex Art 42) and adopted Regulation 26[3] which provides, in essence, that EC Articles 81-86 (ex Arts 85 to 90) and any implementing provisions apply to the production of and trade in agricultural products. Article 2 of the Regulation gives limited exemption from EC Article 81(1) (ex Art 85(1)) to restrictive practices which form an integral part of a national market organization or which are necessary for the attainment of the objectives of the Treaty, in particular, those concerning 'farmers, farmers' associations or associations of such associations belonging to a single Member State which concern the production or sale of agricultural products or the use of joint facilities for the storage, treatment or processing of agricultural products, and under which there is no obligation to charge identical prices, unless the Commission finds that competition is thereby excluded or that the objectives of EC Article 33 (ex Art 39) of the Treaty are

---

2   It is not considered to be possible for dumping to take place in trade between Member States that are fully integrated into the Community's Customs Union. If it did take place, the phenomenon could be dealt with under the first section of the competition rules and does not require special provision. In practice, dumping in trade between a new member of the Community and the other Member States is covered by the Act governing the accession of the former to the Community or is the subject of special legislation (in the case of Spain and Portugal, Reg No 812/86 (OJ 1986, L78/1)). Dumping of goods in the Community (including a new Member State) from countries outside the Community is dealt with as part of the Community's external trade policy.

3   OJ 1962/993.

jeopardized'. As far as the rules relating to state aids are concerned, Article 4 of the Regulation provides that only EC Article 93(1) (now Art 88(1)) and the first sentence of EC Article 88(3) (ex Art 93(3)) shall apply to agricultural products.

(2) THE BASIC SECONDARY LEGISLATION

Under EC Articles 83 and 89 (ex Arts 87 and 94), the Council is entrusted with the principal legislative power; the Commission is, for the most part, only the administrative authority responsible for applying the competition rules in the Treaty and any implementing legislation. However, EC Article 86(3) (ex Art 90(3)) confers on the Commission power to adopt directives as well as decisions; and certain of the Council legislation implementing the competition rules confers on the Commission power to adopt regulations within parameters defined by the Council.

The implementing legislation falls essentially into three parts: legislation of a general procedural nature; block exemption regulations, that is, legislation exempting categories of agreements from the prohibition in EC Article 81(1) (ex Art 85(1)) and defining the conditions under which such exemption applies; and directives adopted by the Commission under EC Article 86(3) (ex Art 90(3)). Of a slightly different character is Council Regulation 4064/89,[4] which deals with the control of concentrations between undertakings. That regulation goes further than simply implementing the competition rules in the Treaty because the Treaty lacks any provision for the control of concentrations. The regulation therefore contains a mixture of substantive and procedural provisions.

(3) PROCEDURAL LEGISLATION

The most important procedural measures are Council Regulations 17, 3385/94 and 2842/98,[5] as amended. In brief, the first sets out the procedure for notifying restrictive practices to the Commission and for granting exemptions under EC Article 81(3) (ex Art 85(3)); the Commission's powers of investigation and measures that it can take against undertakings found to have infringed the competition rules; and the basic procedural elements of inquiries into alleged infringements of the competition rules. Regulation 3385/94 sets out in greater detail the procedure to be followed and the form to be used for applying to the Commission for a negative clearance (that is, a decision finding that a particular practice is not prohibited by the competition rules) or for an exemption from prohibition under EC Article 81(3) (ex Art 85(3)). Regulation 2842/98 deals with hearings before the Commission. Finally, Regulation 2988/74[6] sets out limitation periods in proceedings for the enforcement of sanctions.

Regulation 141 of 1962[7] excluded transport from the procedural rules set out in Regulation 17. It was replaced by Regulation 1017/68[8] in so far as it concerned transport by rail, road and inland waterway. It continued in force in relation to sea and air transport until 1986 for the former and 1987 for the latter. In that time, the basic Treaty provisions applied alone. That created a complex

---

4   See further Ch 29.
5   OJ 1959-1962/87, OJ 1994, L377/28 and OJ 1998, L354/18, respectively. Reg 3385/94 replaced Reg 27 (OJ 1959-1962/132). Reg 2842/98 replaced Reg 99/63 (OJ 1963-1964/47) with effect from 1 February 1999.
6   OJ 1974, L319/1.
7   JO 1962/2751 (OJ 1959-1962/291).
8   JO 1968, L175/1 (OJ 1968/302).

situation in which the competent national authorities had certain powers derived from EC Article 84 (ex Art 88) and the Commission could act under EC Article 85 (ex Art 89).[9] At present, the procedural rules for the enforcement of the Treaty provisions in relation to transport by rail, road and inland waterway are still contained in Regulation 1017/68, supplemented by Regulation 2843/98,[10] which concerns the formalities for making complaints and applying for exemptions and so forth, and Regulation 2842/98,[11] which concerns hearings before the Commission. Sea transport is covered by Regulation 4056/86,[12] supplemented by Regulation 2843/98,[13] which covers the same ground as Regulation 2842/98. Air transport is covered by Regulation 3975/87,[14] supplemented by Regulation 2843/98.

(4) EXEMPTING LEGISLATION

EC Article 81(3) (ex Art 85(3)) provides that EC Article 81(1) (ex Art 85(1)) may be declared inapplicable in respect of any particular arrangement (whether it be an agreement, decision of an association of undertakings or concerted practice) or category of arrangements falling within the scope of Article 85(1). The exemption of individual arrangements is effected by an administrative decision of the Commission relating to that particular arrangement alone. The exemption of an entire category of arrangements is affected by regulation (known as a 'block exemption').

The Council has granted certain block exemptions in the procedural regulations adopted by it, namely, block exemptions for groups of small and medium-sized undertakings in the rail, road and inland waterway transport sectors,[15] arrangements between carriers concerning the operation of scheduled maritime transport services (liner conferences) and between liner conferences and users.[16] By virtue of powers conferred on it by the Council,[17] the Commission has adopted block exemption regulations dealing with certain types of vertical arrangement (that is, arrangements between two or more undertakings operating at different levels in the production or distribution process),[18] technology transfer

---

9 For the position concerning air transport, see Case 66/86: *Ahmed Saeed Flugreisen and Silver Line Reisebüro GmbH v Zentrale zur Bekämpfung Unlauteren Wettbewerbs* [1989] ECR 803.
10 OJ 1998, L354/22. Reg 2843/98 replaced Reg 1629/69 (OJ 1969, L209/1) with effect from 1 February 1999.
11 Reg 2842/98 (see note 5, supra) replaced Reg 1630/69 (OJ 1969, L209/11) with effect from 1 February 1999.
12 OJ 1986, L378/4.
13 OJ 1998, L354/22. Reg 2843/98 replaced Regs 4260/88 and 4261/88 (OJ 1988, L376/1 and 10).
14 OJ 1987, L374/1, as amended.
15 Reg 1017/68, art 4.
16 Reg 4056/86, arts 3-7.
17 See Council Reg 19/65 (OJ 1965/533) on exclusive supply and purchasing agreements and agreements relating to industrial property rights, amended by Council Reg 1215/1999 (OJ 1999, L148/1); Council Reg 2821/71 (OJ 1971, L285/46) on standardization, research and development and specialization agreements; in the case of air transport, Council Reg 3976/87 (OJ 1987, L374/9), amended by Council Reg 2411/92 (OJ 1992, L240/19); Council Reg 1534/91 (OJ 1991, L143/1) on agreements in the insurance sector; Council Reg 479/92 (OJ 1992, L55/3) on agreements between liner shipping companies.
18 Council Reg 2190/1999 (OJ 1999, L336/21), which replaced the block exemption Regulations dealing with exclusive distribution arrangements (Reg 1983/83, as amended by Reg 1582/97 (OJ 1983, L173/1 and OJ 1997, L214/27, respectively)), exclusive purchasing arrangements (Reg 1984/83 (OJ 1983, L173/5), as amended by Reg 1582/97) and franchising arrangements (Reg 4087/88, OJ 1988, L359/46).

agreements (essentially patent and know-how licensing arrangements),[19] motor vehicle distribution and servicing arrangements,[20] specialization arrangements,[1] research and development arrangements,[2] arrangements in the insurance sector concerning the establishment of common risk-premium tariffs, the establishment of standard policy conditions, the common coverage of certain types of risk and the establishment of common rules on the testing and acceptance of security devices;[3] in the air transport sector, arrangements concerning computer reservation systems,[4] joint planning and co-ordination of capacity, consultations on tariffs and slot allocation at airports;[5] in the sea transport sector, arrangements between liner shipping companies (consortia).[6] Each block exemption granted by the Commission is granted for a specified period of time and is therefore subject to periodic review.

(5) DIRECTIVES ADOPTED UNDER EC ARTICLE 86(3) (EX ART 90(3))

Under EC Article 86(3) (ex Art 90(3)) the Commission has the power to adopt directives addressed to the Member States, as well as decisions, in order to ensure the application of the provisions of EC Article 86 (ex Art 90). The exercise of that power has always been and continues to be a matter of some controversy. The first directive adopted by the Commission concerned the transparency of financial relations between Member States and public undertakings.[7] The lawfulness of the directive was disputed by several Member States but the ECJ found in favour of the Commission.[8] Later directives adopted by the Commission applied to the telecommunications sector and their lawfulness has been upheld in part only.[9]

(6) OTHER ACTS

The Commission adopts from time to time notices that indicate its present views on a particular aspect of competition law or policy. Such notices have no legal

---

19 Reg 240/96 (OJ 1996, L31/2). This Regulation replaced Reg 2349/84 (OJ 1984, L219/15 and Reg 556/89 (OJ 1989, L61/1).
20 Reg 1475/95 (OJ 1995, L145/25). This Regulation replaced Reg 123/85 (OJ 1985, L15/16).
1 Reg 2658/2000 (OJ 2000, L304/3).
2 Reg 2659/2000 (OJ 2000, L304/7).
3 Reg 3932/92 (OJ 1992, L398/7).
4 Reg 3652/93 (OJ 1993, L333/37). This Regulation has now expired and, at the time of writing, had not been replaced.
5 Reg 1617/93 (OJ 1993, L155/18) as amended by Reg 1523/96 (OJ 1996, L190/11). At the time of writing, Reg 1617/93 had expired but the Commission had expressed an intention to re-enact parts at least of it. In respect of slot allocation, see also Council Reg 95/93 (OJ 1993, L14/1). Reg 82/91 (OJ 1991, L10/7) exempted certain arrangements concerning ground handling services but, at the time of writing, had expired and had not been replaced. Access to the ground handling market at Community airports is covered by Dir 96/67 (OJ 1996, L272/36).
6 Reg 823/2000 (OJ 2000, L100/24, which replaced Reg 870/95 (OJ 1995, L89/7).
7 Dir 80/723 (OJ 1980, L195/35), as amended.
8 Cases 188-190/80: *France, Italy and United Kingdom v Commission* [1982] ECR 2545, [1982] 3 CMLR 144.
9 Dir 88/301 (OJ 1988, L131/73), challenged in Case C-202/88: *France v Commission* [1991] ECR I-1223, [1992] 5 CMLR 552; Dir 90/388 (OJ 1990, L192/10), challenged in Case C-271/90: *Spain v Commission* [1992] ECR I-5833. Both Directives have been amended several times.

effect other than, perhaps, to preclude the Commission from altering its position as set out in such a notice without first withdrawing or amending the notice.[10] As at the time of writing, the Commission had published notices on exclusive dealing contracts with commercial agents,[11] co-operation between undertakings,[12] Japanese imports,[13] sub-contracting agreements,[14] the block exemptions for exclusive distribution and exclusive purchasing agreements,[15] the block exemption for motor vehicle distribution agreements,[16] agreements of minor importance,[17] ancillary restraints (in connexion with mergers),[18] the distinction between merger-type and co-operative operations,[19] state aids to public undertakings in the manufacturing sector,[20] clarification of the activities of motor vehicle intermediaries,[1] co-operation between the national courts and the Commission,[2] the assessment of co-operative joint ventures pursuant to EC Article 81 (ex Art 85),[3] the definition of relevant market,[4] the concept of full-function joint ventures,[5] the concept of concentrations,[6] the concept of 'undertakings concerned' for the purposes of merger control,[7] the calculation of turnover for the purposes of merger control,[8] the alignment of procedures for processing mergers under the ECSC and EC Treaties,[9] information on the assessment of full-function joint ventures pursuant to the EC competition rules[10] guidelines on the setting of fines;[11] and guidelines on vertical restraints.[12]

The Commission has power to adopt decisions. Such measures are administrative, not legislative, in nature. Although they are often used by the Commission to create 'case law', they are not binding on persons other than those to whom they are addressed (and, through the addressees, on national courts where the decision is relied on as against an addressee and where the Commission has exclusive jurisdiction over the matters covered by the decision)[13] and go no further

---

10   The most important such notice is the notice on agreements of minor importance (see now OJ 1997, C 372/13), which sets out the Commission's views regarding the application of the *de minimis* rule in competition cases. The Commission has also issued notices explaining some block exemption regulations.
11   OJ 1962/2921.
12   OJ 2001, C 3/2.
13   OJ 1972, C 111/13.
14   OJ 1979, C 1/2.
15   OJ 1984, C 101/2.
16   This replaced an earlier notice concerning Reg 123/85 (OJ 1985, C 17/4).
17   OJ 1997, C 372/13.
18   OJ 1990, C 203/5.
19   OJ 1994, C 385/1.
20   OJ 1991, C 273/2.
 1   OJ 1991, C 329/20.
 2   OJ 1993, C 39/6.
 3   OJ 1993, C 43/2. See now OJ 2000, C 3/2
 4   OJ 1997, C 372/5.
 5   OJ 1998, C 66/1.
 6   OJ 1998, C 66/5.
 7   OJ 1998, C 66/14.
 8   OJ 1998, C 66/25.
 9   OJ 1998, C 66/36.
10   OJ 1998, C 66/38.
11   OJ 1998, C 9/3.
12   OJ 2000, C 291/1.
13   Case C-128/92: *H J Banks & Co Ltd v British Coal Corpn* [1994] ECR I-1209, para 23. See also *Iberian UK Ltd v BPB Industries plc* [1996] 2 CMLR 601; Cases T-125/97 and T-127/97: *Coca Cola v Commission* 22 March 2000; Case C-344/98: *Masterfoods Ltd v HB Ice Cream Ltd* [2001] All ER (EC) 130.

than indicate a decisional practice, or possible decisional practice, that the Commission is free to alter. Decisions of the ECJ and CFI in competition matters override decisions of the Commission and are binding on national courts where they explain the true meaning and effect of a provision of Community law.

E. Enforcement of the competition rules

The Community competition rules represent a uniform system superimposed upon the national legal systems. The two systems co-exist and are applied concurrently subject to the principles of autonomy, direct applicability and supremacy of EC law and the principle of subsidiarity. The competition rules are enforced in two ways: by the action of the competent administrative bodies; and by private right of action before national courts. The competent administrative bodies are the Commission and the competition authorities in the Member States.[14]

(1) ENFORCEMENT BY THE COMMISSION

Decisions of the Commission are, in principle, made by the college of Commissioners after consultation with an Advisory Committee comprising representatives of the Member States.[15] The power to make some decisions of a procedural nature has been delegated to the Commissioner responsible for competition matters.[16] In practice, decisions of the Commission are prepared by the Competition Directorate General (formerly Directorate-General IV) of the Commission's services, as advised by the Commission's Legal Service. On occasion, in specialist areas such as agriculture and telecommunications, the Competition Directorate-General may act in consultation with another Directorate-General responsible for that particular area. The Competition Directorate-General consists of six Directorates. Directorate A is concerned with general competition policy and co-ordination. Directorate B is the Merger Task Force and deals with merger cases falling within Regulation 4064/89. The remaining Directorates are responsible for investigating infringements of the competition rules by undertakings in the different industrial sectors assigned to them. Directorate C covers information, communication and multimedia industries. Directorate D covers financial services, transport, trade and other services. Directorate E covers cartels, basic industries and energy. Directorate F covers capital and consumer goods industries. The Competition Directorate-General has limited resources in terms of manpower and is unable to deal with every case that comes to its attention. In consequence, it concentrates on cases of importance whether by reason of their economic significance or the points of

---

14 In 1999, the Commission published a White Paper proposing significant changes in the rules implementing EC Arts 81 and 82 (ex Arts 85 and 86): See OJ 1999, C 132. That was followed up by a proposal for a regulation replacing Reg 17 and introducing a decentralised system for administering EC competition law: See COM (2000) 582 final (27 September 2000).

15 On the role of the Advisory Committee, see Reg 17, art 10; Case T-69/89: *RTE v Commission* [1991] ECR II-485, paras 21-27; Case T-19/91: *Vichy v Commission* [1992] ECR II-415, para 39; Case T-9/89: *Hüls AG v Commission* [1992] ECR II-499, para 77.

16 The general principle is that measures that create rights or obligations for persons must be deliberated on by the members of the Commission acting together whereas accessory measures of management may be taken pursuant to a delegation of authority: Case T-275/94: *Groupement des Cartes Bancaires v Commission* [1995] ECR II-2169, para 70.

principle raised by them. The Commission has the power to prohibit practices found to be contrary to the competition rules (and, thus, to order the undertaking(s) concerned to cease and desist from such practices whether by final or by interim[17] order) and to impose fines upon undertakings. Decisions imposing fines on undertakings are enforceable in the Member States in accordance with the rules of civil procedure of the state in which enforcement is sought.[18] The Commission does not have the power to award damages or some other form of compensation to persons injured by a prohibited practice. The procedure before the Commission is considered below.

(2) ENFORCEMENT BY THE NATIONAL COMPETITION AUTHORITIES

The national competition authorities were empowered to apply EC Article 81 and 82 (ex Arts 85 and 86) (but not other provisions of the competition rules) by EC Article 84 (ex Art 88) and that power was preserved by Regulation 17, subject to two qualifications: the national authorities cannot declare EC Article 81(1) (ex Art 85(1)) inapplicable pursuant to EC Article 81(3) (ex Art 85(3)) (the Commission is alone able to apply EC Article 85(3)); and they cease to remain competent to apply EC Article 81(1) and 82 (ex Arts 85(1) or 86) should the Commission initiate a procedure under Regulation 17.[19] The position regarding the control of mergers is more complex and is discussed further below. The powers of the national authorities to take action against practices found to contravene the competition rules are determined by national law: Community law only lays down substantive rules of law that the national authorities may apply.[20] Evidence of an infringement of the competition rules which has been obtained in the course of the proceedings before a national court may not be used by the Commission for the purposes of any procedure which it intends to commence or has commenced. Hence, the risk that disclosure of evidence in the course of national proceedings may tend to incriminate an undertaking cannot be relied on, as a matter of Community law, to justify withholding such evidence in those proceedings.[1]

(3) ENFORCEMENT BY NATIONAL COURTS

Enforcement of the competition rules by private right of action is limited to those parts of the competition rules that have direct effect and that can be relied on by individuals before national courts. The prohibitions in EC Articles 81(1) and 82 (ex Art 85(1) and 86) have direct effect, as do EC Articles 86(1) and 88(3) (ex Arts 90(1) and 93(3)) (the latter in the case of the unlawful implementation of a new state aid scheme). A private right of action may also arise where a provision of the competition rules is applied by Commission decision to a specific state of affairs, thus defining in a concrete way how the competition rules affect that state of affairs.[2] One example is a Commission decision finding that an existing state aid scheme is incompatible with the common market and cannot be exempted from prohibition. Even in cases where a provision of the competition rules (such

17 Case 792/79R: *Camera Care Ltd v Commission* [1980] ECR 119; Reg 3975/87, art 4a.
18 EC Art 192 (now Art 256).
19 Art 9(1) and (3) of Reg 17.
20 Case C-67/91: *Dirección General de Defensa de la Competencia v Asociación Espanola de Banca Privada* [1992] ECR I-4785, paras 31-32.
1 Case C-60/92: *Otto v Postbank* [1993] ECR I-5683. Contrast *Rio Tinto Zinc Corpn v Westinghouse Electric Corpn* [1978] AC 547, [1978] 1 CMLR 100.
2 This is one interpretation of Case C-128/92: *H J Banks & Co Ltd v Commission* [1994] ECR I-1209, para 23.

as EC Article 81(1) (ex Art 85(1)) can already be relied on in respect of a particular practice, the existence of a Commission decision applying that provision to that practice may be of assistance in seeking relief from a national court.[3] The procedures to be followed and the relief available are determined by national law. In England and Wales, the right of action based on infringement of a directly effective provision of the competition rules is akin to an action for breach of statutory duty. Damages or injunctions may be awarded by the court.[4] It has been held that, as an infringement of EC Article 81 (ex Art 85) (and also EC Article 82 (ex Art 86)) carries with it liability to penalties and to fines imposed by the Commission, the standard of proof of such an infringement which must be satisfied in proceedings before an English court (in which the relief sought could be only damages or injunctive relief) is a high degree of probability exceeding the normal standard of proof (proof on a balance of probabilities) in civil proceedings.[5]

F. The relationship between Community and national competition law and between the Commission and national enforcement agencies

The Community competition rules and national competition law do not necessarily duplicate one another for two reasons: national competition law is concerned with the situation on the domestic market whereas Community competition law is concerned with competition in the common market as a whole; the principles and public policy considerations defining the pre-occupations of the authorities responsible for administering national and Community competition law and determining the manner in which the rules are to be applied may, and often do, differ. The two systems therefore co-exist, subject to the doctrines of the autonomy, direct applicability and supremacy of Community law. There is a degree of co-ordination between the two systems in the sense that the Member States are informed of proceedings before the Commission and must be consulted before the Commission makes certain decisions. Consultation is effected through Advisory Committees comprising representatives of national authorities.[6] Further, there is an overlap in the means of enforcing Community competition law since a competition case may be commenced and disposed of either before the Commission or before the national competition authorities or even by private right of action before a national court. That state of affairs gives rise to the possibility of two sorts of conflict: a conflict between Community and national competition rules; and a conflict between the different agencies responsible for the application of Community law to a given case.

---

3   See *Iberian UK Ltd v BPB Industries plc* [1996] 2 CMLR 601.
4   *Garden Cottage Foods v Milk Marketing Board* [1984] AC 130. A party to an unlawful agreement cannot sue for damages: *Trent Taverns v Sykes* [1998] Eu LR 571 (but see Case C-453/99: *Courage v Crehan*, pending). For the position in Germany, see *British Telecommunications plc v Deutsche Telekom* [1998] 2 CMLR 95 and 114.
5   *Shearson Lehman Hutton v Maclaine Watson & Co Ltd* [1989] 3 CMLR 429. The matter is not free from doubt. The usual practice of English Courts is to apply the normal standard of proof in civil proceedings, or a standard at the higher end of the normal civil scale: see *Society of Lloyd's v Clementson* [1996] CLC 1590 at 1598.
6   The Advisory Committee on Restrictive Practices and Monopolies (see Art 10 of Reg 17) and the Advisory Committee on Concentrations (Article 19 of Reg 4064/89).

(1) CONFLICTS BETWEEN COMMUNITY AND NATIONAL COMPETITION LAW

The first type of conflict arose in the *Walt Wilhelm* case.[7] There, the German competition authority, the *Bundeskartellamt*, had imposed fines on the plaintiffs for breaches of German cartel law because they had agreed, inter alia, to raise between themselves and other manufacturers of dyestuffs from other Member States and non-member countries the price of aniline. In the meantime, the Commission, of its own initiative, commenced proceedings against the plaintiffs as it considered, inter alia, that the price-fixing in question was a 'concerted practice' within the meaning of EC Article 85(1) (now Art 81(1)). The plaintiffs raised the question whether the German authorities were competent to pursue the proceedings concurrently. On a reference from the Berlin *Kammergericht*, the ECJ ruled that the parallel application of national and Community competition law is possible as long as it does not prejudice the uniform application of Community law and the full effect of any measures adopted in implementation of the Community rules. Where both national and Community competition law prohibit the conduct in question, the risk of a double sanction may be avoided by taking into account any earlier sanction imposed by another authority. Thus, if the Commission finds an infringement of the Community competition rules after a national authority has imposed a penalty on the same person in respect of the same conduct but in accordance with national competition law, the Commission should take that into account when deciding the amount of any fine or other penalty that it may impose in respect of the breach of Community law, and vice versa.

That deals with the situation where national and Community competition law come to the same conclusion. Where they come to conflicting conclusions, the conflict is resolved by applying the principle of the supremacy of Community law; and, where the conflict is only potential, because the national authority wishes to apply national law to conduct that is currently under investigation by the Commission but the Commission has not yet made its decision, it is for the national authority to take appropriate measures if it appears possible that its decision may conflict with the Commission's decision.[8] In cases where the conflict is potential because the outcome of the procedure is not known, the national authority may postpone making its decision until the Commission has reached a conclusion or, if the circumstances do not permit postponement, liaise with the Commission before acting. It does not follow from the supremacy of Community law that national authorities cannot apply national competition law at all but, where national law permits certain conduct and Community law prohibits it, the permission under the former cannot prevent the application of the prohibition under the latter. On the other hand, where Community law applies to certain conduct and is not merely permissive but positively approves of it, in the form of a formal exemption from prohibition granted by the Commission, the national authorities must limit the effect of any prohibition of such conduct in national competition law.

Thus, in Cases 253/78 and 1-3/79: *Procureur de la République v Giry and Guerlain*,[9] the Commission had sent letters to the persons concerned saying that, in its opinion, there was no need to take action under EC Article 85(1) (ex Art 81(1)) and that the files on the case would be closed. It was argued in subsequent national proceedings that the letters were informal decisions exempting the agreements in question from prohibition. The ECJ held that the letters simply

---

7 Case 14/68: *Walt Wilhelm v Bundeskartellamt* [1969] ECR 1, [1969] CMLR 100.
8 Ibid, pp 14-15.
9 [1980] ECR 2327, in particular para 18.

closed the files on the case and did not preclude the national authorities from applying national competition law: 'The fact that a practice has been held by the Commission not to fall within the ambit of the prohibition contained in [EC Articles 81(1) and (2) (ex Arts 85(1) and (2))], the scope of which is limited to agreements capable of affecting trade between Member States, in no way prevents that practice from being considered by the national authorities from the point of view of the restrictive effects which it may produce nationally.' If the conduct is caught by the Community competition rules but benefits from an exemption granted formally by the Commission, it seems that the national authorities must respect that exemption when deciding whether or not to invoke national competition law.

(2) CONFLICTS IN THE APPLICATION OF COMMUNITY COMPETITION LAW

Passing now to conflicts involving the application of Community competition law to the same conduct at the same time by different bodies, Article 9 of Regulation 17 regulates the situation where the Commission and the national competition authorities are involved: in effect, the national competition authorities are competent to apply the Community rules unless and until the Commission initiates formal proceedings that will result in the grant or refusal of a negative clearance relating to EC Articles 81 and 82 (ex Arts 85 or 86),[10] a finding that those Articles have (or have not) been infringed, or the grant or refusal of an exemption under EC Article 81(3) (ex Art 85(3)). Since the Commission has limited manpower, it encourages recourse to the national competition authorities even for the purpose of the application of the Community rules. The Commission is not likely to take a case over from a national authority unless the case gives rise to serious problems, such as a question of competition law in relation to which the policy of the Community has not been settled, or conduct that affects more than one Member State and may therefore be of concern to several national competition authorities (in such a case, the risk of divergent decisions from those authorities justifies the matter being placed within the hands of a single authority, the Commission). Where either the Commission or a national authority has terminated an investigation under the Community competition rules before the other has commenced proceedings, the principle of *non bis in idem* applies and a further sanction cannot be applied in respect of the same conduct. That principle would also preclude the Commission from reassessing conduct that a national competition authority has already considered in the light of the Community rules.

Article 9 of Regulation 17 deals only with the relationship between national competition authorities and the Commission. It does not apply to national courts because it cannot override the direct effect of the prohibitions in EC Articles 81(1) and 82 (ex Arts 85(1) and 86) that confer on individual rights that national courts must protect.[11] In the same way, national courts are competent to determine whether or not a block exemption regulation applies, although they are not competent to grant an individual exemption under EC Article 81(3) (ex Art 85(3)) because that involves an exercise of discretion (and not the mere application of a provision of Community law) which falls within the remit of the Commission.[12] Hence,

---

10 A negative clearance is a declaration that the conduct in question does not infringe EC Art 85 or, as the case may be, Art 86.
11 Case 127/73: *BRT v SABAM* [1974] ECR 51.
12 Case 63/75: *Fonderies Roubaix-Wattrelos SA v Société nouvelle des Fonderies A Roux* [1976] ECR 111, para 11.

national courts remain competent to apply the prohibitions in EC Articles 81(1) and 82 (ex Arts 85(1) and 86) even where the Commission has already commenced proceedings for negative clearance, the finding of an infringement or grant of an exemption; nonetheless, it is open to a national court to delay making a decision until the Commission has concluded its proceedings with a formal decision, if the national court thinks it appropriate for reasons of legal certainty.[13] In practice, a national court is very likely to stay the proceedings before it if the same conduct is under investigation by the Commission unless, as often happens where an exemption has been applied for, the proceedings appear to be dormant. It is open to a national court to ask the Commission to inform it of the stage which any pending procedure has reached. Where the Commission has made a decision on the application of EC Articles 81 or 82 (ex Arts 85 and 86) to a particular case, and the decision has not been annulled by the CFI or the ECJ, national courts are precluded from coming to a different conclusion on the same matter.[14]

Where there are no proceedings pending before the Commission, the national court is entitled to pass judgment on the conduct at issue in the litigation before it where the conditions for applying the prohibition in EC Articles 81(1) and 82 (ex Arts 85(1) and 86) have clearly not been satisfied (in which case the allegation that the competition rules have been infringed is dismissed) or where there is no doubt that those conditions have been satisfied (in which case the national court finds that there has been an infringement); and where, in the case of conduct falling under EC Article 81(1) (ex Art 85(1)), it can in no way benefit from exemption either by individual decision under EC Article 81(3) (ex Art 85(3)) or by block exemption (in which case, again, a finding that there has been an infringement may be made). On the other hand, if the national court concludes that, having regard to the relevant legislation and the decisional practice of the Commission, the conduct might possibly benefit from exemption, it may stay the proceedings or adopt appropriate interim measures.[15] The purpose of staying the proceedings or ordering some other interim measure is to enable a reference to the ECJ under EC Article 234 (ex Art 177) or, if national procedural rules permit it, consultation of the Commission itself. The ECJ considers that, subject to national procedural rules, a national court is entitled not only to ask the Commission about the stage reached in any proceedings before it and on the probability of it making a final decision, but also to obtain from it any economic and legal information that may be of use where the application of EC Articles 81(1) and 82 (ex Arts 85(1) and 86) by the national court creates special difficulties.[16] The extent to which expressions of opinion or assertions of fact made by the Commission in that way would be admissible in or relevant to proceedings before English courts is as yet unclear.

Where the Commission's investigations end not with a formal decision but with a letter telling the undertakings concerned that their conduct is 'not capable of being affected' by the EC competition rules, such a letter does not prevent a national court, before which the alleged incompatibility of the conduct with the competition rules has been raised, from reaching a different finding on the basis of the information available to it; whilst it does not bind the national court, the opinion of the Commission contained in the letter is still a factor that the national

---

13 Case 37/79: *Anne Marty SA v Estée Lauder SA* [1980] ECR 2481, paras 13-14.
14 Case C-344/98: *Masterfoods Ltd v HB Ice Cream Ltd* [2001] All ER (EC) 130.
15 Case C-234/89: *Delimitis v Henninger Bräu AG* [1991] ECR I-935, paras 47-52; Case C-250/92: *Gottrup-Klim v Dansk Landbrugs Grovvareselskab* [1994] ECR I-5641, paras 58-60, cf *HTV Europe v BMG Record (UK) Ltd* [1997] 1 CMLR 867.
16 *Delimitis*, para 53.

court may take into account when reaching its decision.[17] It cannot be excluded that the facts on which the Commission reached its conclusion may be different from those put to or proved before the national court.

G. Determination of infringements at Community level

At the Community level, the powers of investigation and determination of infringements of the competition rules are vested in the Commission,[18] whose decisions are subject to judicial review by the CFI with an appeal on points of law only to the ECJ. The Commission is an administrative body, not a judicial body or tribunal within the meaning of the Human Rights Convention.[19] It therefore benefits from an administrative discretion when deciding when and how to exercise its powers; whereas a court cannot refuse to accept a case which falls within its jurisdiction and is obliged to bring the proceedings to a close (unless they are terminated beforehand by the parties). Accordingly, the Commission is not obliged to investigate and make a decision in respect of any and every possible infringement of the competition rules brought to its attention; and, where it does find that there has been an infringement, it retains a discretion as to what action (if any) to be taken against the undertakings involved.[20] A person dissatisfied with the Commission's action or inaction can challenge it only on the basis that the Commission exercised its discretion wrongly, such as where the Commission has not properly directed its mind to the issues in the case in order to make a correct appraisal of its importance or has made an error concerning some factor relevant to the exercise of its discretion (such as the availability of relief before the national courts).[1] The Commission is obliged to make a decision only in respect of matters which fall within its exclusive jurisdiction (that is, outside the state aids sector, the grant or refusal of an individual exemption under EC Article 81(3) (ex Art 85(3)).[2] In the conduct of investigations, the Commission is obliged to observe the same kind of rules of impartiality as a court must.

Although the Commission's procedure is laid down in different procedural regulations depending upon the sector concerned, the format of the procedure is the same and, for the purposes of exposition, reference will be made to Regulation 17, which applies to investigations into the conduct of undertakings

---

17 *Anne Marty SA v Estée Lauder SA* (above), para 10. See also Case 99/79: *Lancôme SA v Etos BV* [1980] ECR 2511 and the *Giry and Guerlain* case (supra, p 626, note 9), at paras 10 and 13, respectively.

18 See generally Kerse, C, *EEC Antitrust Procedure* (4th edn, 1998): Smith, M, *Competition Law: Enforcement and Procedure* (2001).

19 Cases 209-215/78 and 218/78: *Van Landewyck v Commission* [1980] ECR 3125, para 81, followed in Case T-11/89: *Shell International Chemical Co Ltd v Commission* [1992] ECR II-757, para 9. Judgment in the *Van Landewyck* case was given before the decisions of the Human Rights Commission in *Société Stenuit v France* (1992) 14 EHRR 509 and *Niemitz v Germany* (1992) 16 EHRR 97.

20 Case T-24/90: *Automec Srl v Commission* [1992] ECR II-2223; Case T-16/91: *Rendo NV v Commission* [1992] ECR II-2417, paras 98-99; Case T-32/93: *Ladbroke v Commission* [1994] ECR II-1015, paras 34-45 (EC Art 86 (ex Art 90)); Case T-387/94: *Asia Motor France v Commission* [1996] ECR II-961, para 46; Case C-107/95P: *Bundesverband des Bilanzbuchhalter v Commission* [1997] ECR I-947, paras 23-30 (EC Art 86 (ex Art 90)).

1 See the *Automec* and *Asia Motor France* cases; Case T-114/92: *BEMIM v Commission* [1995] ECR II-147, para 72.

2 *Automec*, supra; *Rendo*, supra.

in all sectors save transport. In relation to investigations by the Commission into state-induced distortions of competition, different rules apply.[3]

(1) OUTLINE OF THE COMMISSION'S PROCEDURE

The Commission is informed of the existence of possible infringements of the competition rules in the following ways: (1) by notification to it of an arrangement for a negative clearance (that is, a declaration that the arrangement does not infringe the competition rules) or exemption under EC Article 81(3) (ex Art 85(3)); (2) by complaint by a person who has been adversely affected by the arrangement; (3) by inquiries into sectors of the economy;[4] (4) by other means, such as information provided by the authorities of the Member States, press reports, consumer associations and so forth. The proceedings commenced by a notification are essentially 'friendly' in the sense that the persons making the notification are seeking from the Commission a decision which is favourable to the arrangements which have been notified. Naturally, it may well be that the proceedings turn out to be distinctly 'unfriendly' if the Commission is not willing to grant a negative clearance or exemption. Proceedings commenced by any of the other ways indicated above are 'hostile' in the sense that they involve an attack on the arrangements in question even though, at the end of the day, the Commission may conclude that there has not been an infringement of the competition rules. The difference in character between those different ways in which a possible infringement may come to the attention of the Commission is reflected in the subsequent procedure.

Strictly speaking, where the matter is brought to the Commission's attention by notification, proceedings are commenced formally upon receipt by the Commission of the notification. The Commission will then carry out any necessary inquiries. If it considers that the arrangement is eligible for a negative clearance or exemption, it will publish a notice to that effect in the Official Journal inviting comments from interested parties.[5] Depending upon the content of those comments, the Commission will then either adopt a formal decision granting a negative clearance or exemption or issue a comfort letter. Formal decisions are relatively infrequent. In the course of the procedure, the Commission may well require the parties to the arrangement to alter it if it contains some provision which the Commission finds unacceptable. If the Commission is of the view that the notified arrangement is not eligible for a negative clearance or an exemption, it will usually inform the parties and give them an opportunity to amend the arrangement (if that is possible). Otherwise, the Commission may give formal notice withdrawing the immunity from the imposition of a fine that attaches when a notification is made,[6] which is a necessary step if the Commission wishes eventually to impose a fine. The Commission may also issue a cease and desist order requiring the parties to terminate the arrangement.

In all cases in which a matter is brought to the Commission's attention save by way of a notification, the procedure does not start when the Commission is first informed of the alleged infringement. The Commission may, in order to

---

3   In relation to state aids, the procedure to be followed is that laid down in EC Art 88 (ex Art 93) and Reg 659/1999 (OJ 1999, L83/1).
4   Under art 12 of Reg 17, the Commission may of its own motion conduct a general inquiry into a sector of the economy if there are circumstances which suggest that competition in the common market is being restricted or distorted.
5   Reg 17, art 19(3).
6   Reg 17, art 15(6).

decide whether or not a particular case merits investigation, make a formal or informal request for information or documents directed at an interested party or carry out an investigation on the premises of an undertaking. In all cases in which a complaint has been made, there may be extensive and long-running exchanges between the complainant, the Commission and the undertaking against whom the complaint has been made before proceedings are formally commenced. Such requests for information, investigations and exchanges are often misconstrued as indicating that the Commission has initiated a formal procedure whereas they are nothing more than preliminary steps designed to put the Commission in a position to make an informed decision as to whether or not to initiate a procedure. The formal commencement of proceedings is effected by an internal decision of the Commission (in practice, the Commissioner responsible for competition on the advice of his services) and the fact that proceedings have been formally commenced will be revealed to the undertaking under investigation by service of a document called a 'Statement of Objections' (or 'SO') which sets out the Commission's case against that undertaking.

At that point, the Commission may also consider adopting interim measures in order to preserve the position until its final decision is made. If interim measures are envisaged, a separate SO is issued. There have been cases where an interim measures SO has been issued before the main SO. Equally, the Commission is not obliged to issue an interim measures SO at the outset of the proceedings but may do so at any time before the making of the final decision terminating the proceedings, should the circumstances justify it.

The undertaking under investigation is given a period of time within which to respond in writing to the SO (unless, in the case of an interim measures SO, the degree of urgency precludes that step). There is then a hearing before the Commission. Finally, the Commission makes its decision.

(2) NOTIFICATIONS

An arrangement (whether an agreement, decision or concerted practice) is notified to the Commission in writing using a form supplied by the Commission known as 'Form A/B'.[7] As its name suggests, the form is a combination of two different forms: one for exemption and another for a negative clearance (that is, a declaration that the arrangement is not prohibited by the competition rules). For the sake of convenience, both are dealt with in a single form and it is usual to request both forms of relief in the alternative. The notification must be made in one of the official languages of the Community and must be accompanied by all relevant documents. It is submitted by one or more of the undertakings involved in the arrangement. In the case of a standard form agreement to be used on a number of different occasions, only one notification need be made.[8] If a false or misleading statement is made by the person effecting the notification, a fine may be imposed.[9] Any changes in the notified arrangement or its economic or commercial context should also be brought to the attention of the Commission.

---

7 The account given here applies to the generality of agreements. Slightly different considerations apply to the dwindling class of what is known as 'old agreements', that is, agreements already in existence when the competition rules and the procedures for notification and obtaining exemption came into effect.
8 Case 1/70: *Parfums Marcel Rochas Vertriebs-GmbH v Bitsch* [1970] ECR 515, [1971] CMLR 104.
9 Reg 17, art 15(1)(a).

The making of the notification is an essential step for obtaining an exemption under EC Article 81(3) (ex Art 85(3))[10] save in the case of those categories of agreement which do not require notification under the procedural regulations[11] and those agreements which are covered by a block exemption and which are therefore exempted automatically.[12] Where notification is a condition of obtaining an exemption, the exemption, if granted, will usually be backdated to the date of notification but cannot have effect as from an earlier date.[13] Notification also confers protection from the imposition of a fine by the Commission if it eventually decides that the competition rules have been infringed but that an exemption is not possible; the Commission may remove the protection from fines by decision in the course of the procedure.[14]

When a notification is made, the Commission acknowledges receipt and informs the maker of the notification of the number given to the case for the Commission's internal purposes. Due to a lack of resources, it is not every notification that is followed up by the Commission. In many instances, the Commission may be able to tell at once that the arrangement is not entitled either to a negative clearance or to an exemption. In such cases, the parties may be so informed informally and given an opportunity to remedy the situation; the Commission may even contemplate opening a procedure against them which may lead to the imposition of a fine. In other cases, if the Commission considers that the arrangement may merit negative clearance or exemption, a notice to that effect will be published in the Official Journal and interested parties will be given an opportunity to submit observations to the Commission. In the light of those observations, there may then be a process of negotiation between the Commission and the parties to the arrangement before the arrangement is put in acceptable form. In principle, a negative clearance or exemption, if granted, should take the form of a formal Commission decision.[15] The administrative burden of taking a formal decision is such that few formal decisions are adopted in every year. The Commission tends to reserve its decision-making power to important cases which establish a point of principle or indicate Commission policy. Cases are more often dealt with by 'comfort letter', that is, by a letter from the Commission indicating informally that the Commission sees no need to take action under EC Articles 81(1) or 82 (ex Arts 85(1) and 86) or else that the conditions required for granting an exemption under EC Article 81(3) (ex Art 85(3)) have been satisfied. Comfort letters are of doubtful utility since they do not bind national courts and are merely of 'persuasive' authority.[16]

---

10 Reg 17, art 4(1).

11 See eg Reg 17, art 4(2).

12 Some block exemption regulations provide for what is known as an 'opposition' procedure under which an agreement which is not exactly within the scope of the block exemption may nonetheless be exempted if it has been notified to the Commission and the Commission has not indicated any objection to it within a fixed period: see, eg Reg 240/96, art 4.

13 Reg 17, art 6(1). The exception is, again, agreements which may be exempted without notification: see art 6(2).

14 Reg 17, art 15(5) and (6). For the circumstances in which the Commission may remove the protection from fines, see Case T-19/91: *Vichy v Commission* [1992] ECR II-415, paras 111-121.

15 Eg Case 37/79: *Anne Marty SA v Estée Lauder SA* [1980] ECR 2481, para 9.

16 Cases 253/78 and 1-3/79: *Procureur de la République v Giry and Guerlain* [1980] ECR 2327, para 13, [1981] 2 CMLR 99.

(3) COMPLAINTS

A complaint is made in writing to the Commission by a person with a 'legitimate interest'.[17] The complaint should indicate the nature of the alleged infringement of the competition rules, the identity of the persons perpetrating the infringement and the complainant's interest. A person has sufficient interest to be a complainant if it is a party to the alleged infringement, a victim of it or a consumer or group of consumers affected by the alleged infringement. Since the Commission has a discretion in deciding which complaints to follow up, the complainant should also explain why the Commission should take action. Normally, if the interests of the complainant would be adequately protected by an action brought before the national courts, the Commission will not feel it necessary to commence a procedure.

The submission of a complaint to the Commission does not commence a procedure against the undertakings accused of infringing or having infringed the competition rules. At this point, the function of the Commission is to examine the complaint and make any necessary further inquiries for the purpose of deciding whether or not the subject matter of the complaint is sufficiently important to justify taking matters further. The Commission may therefore exercise its powers to request information or examine the books and records or enter the premises of the undertakings concerned in order to obtain the information necessary to determine how its discretion is to be exercised. In the course of reaching its conclusion, the Commission may initiate what is in effect an (informal) exchange of views between the complainant and the undertakings against whom the complaint is directed with the latter responding to the complaint and the former replying to the latter's response. Those investigations and exchanges may take several months before the Commission is in a position either to reject the complaint (in which case no formal procedure ever commences) or to initiate a procedure. Nonetheless, the Commission must take some form of action within a reasonable time of receiving the complaint.[18]

(4) INTERIM RELIEF

Such may be the length of time between the submission of the complaint and the decision of the Commission whether or not to initiate a procedure that the question of interim relief to preserve the position may arise. Strictly speaking, however, the grant of interim relief presupposes that the complaint merits investigation and, normally, interim relief is adopted in order to preserve the position pending the making of a formal decision at the end of a procedure which the Commission has decided to initiate; it is not usually contemplated when the Commission is merely considering whether or not to initiate a procedure.

The Commission's power to adopt interim relief is intended to prevent the effectiveness of the Commission's final decision from being prejudiced by the passage of time. There must be sufficient evidence to suggest that there may be an infringement of the competition rules and sufficient evidence of such a threat to the status quo as would bring into question the effectiveness of the final decision if the Commission were not to act. Since the nature of that final decision is unknown at the outset of the procedure, any decision ordering some form of interim

---

17   Reg 17, art 3(2)(b). No form need be used. A special form for complaints ('Form C') exists but is rarely used.
18   Case T-127/98: *UPS Europe SA v Commission* [1999] ECR II-2633.

relief must be designed just as much to preserve the position in the event that an infringement is found to exist as to preserve it in the event that the complaint is rejected and the undertakings concerned exonerated. Therefore, the relief must not have permanent effects.[19]

(5) REQUESTS FOR INFORMATION AND INVESTIGATIONS

Where the Commission needs to obtain more information about an arrangement which has been brought to its notice, whether before or after the formal initiation of a procedure, it can make a request for information[20] or carry out an investigation into the undertaking.[1]

The Commission makes extensive use of requests for information. The request is made in writing and must state the legal basis for it, the purpose of the request and the penalties for supplying incorrect information. It may be addressed to an undertaking whose conduct is under investigation or to another undertaking which appears to be in a position to assist the Commission even if it is not itself involved in the matters under consideration by the Commission. If the addressee of the request fails to supply the information requested within the time limit fixed by the Commission or supplies incorrect information, the Commission adopts a decision requiring the information to be supplied. This decision specifies the information required, fixes a time limit within which it is to be supplied and indicates both the penalties for non-compliance and the addressee's rights of redress before the CFI. The period fixed for answering requests and complying with decisions varies between three weeks and two months depending upon the case. In the case of requests, the Commission will usually agree to an extension of time if the undertaking so requests and gives good reason for it. If the addressee of a decision (but not a mere request) refuses to supply the information or supplies incorrect information, he may be fined any amount between ECU 100 and ECU 5,000 (the same amounts in euros), whether the failure to comply with the decision is intentional or negligent.[2] The Commission may also impose a periodic penalty payment of between ECU 50 and ECU 1,000 per day until the decision is properly complied with.[3]

Although a request for information must not be so onerous as to be disproportionate to the Commission's real need for additional information,[4] it is in principle for the Commission to decide whether or not a request is to be made and what the request is to cover.[5] Nonetheless, the scope of the request is limited by the scope of the procedure to which it relates.[6] The Commission may request factual information but cannot put a question whose answer is not limited to a

19 See generally Case 792/79R: *Camera Care Ltd v Commission* [1980] ECR 119, [1980] 1 CMLR 334; Cases 228-229/82: *Ford v Commission* [1984] ECR 1129, [1984] 1 CMLR 649; Case T-23/90: *Peugeot v Commission* [1991] ECR II-653; Case T-44/90: *La Cinq SA v Commission* [1992] ECR II-1.
20 Reg 17, art 11. See generally Case T-46/92: *Scottish Football Association v Commission* [1994] ECR II-1039, paras 29-40, and Case T-34/93: *Société Générale v Commission* [1995] ECR II-545, para 37 et seq.
1 Ibid, art 14.
2 Ibid, art 15(1)(b).
3 Ibid, art 16(1)(c).
4 Case T-39/90: *SEP v Commission* [1991] ECR II-1497, para 25, [1992] 5 CMLR 33.
5 Case 374/87: *Orkem v Commission* [1989] ECR 3283, para 15, [1991] 4 CMLR 502.
6 Case T-39/90: *SEP v Commission* [1991] ECR II-1497, paras 25 and 29, on appeal, Case C-36/92P: *SEP v Commission* [1994] ECR I-1911.

matter of pure fact if the answer might tend to incriminate the undertaking concerned.[7] A private law duty not to disclose information or a public law duty to the same effect which is imposed by the law of a third country are neither of them grounds for refusing to answer a request for information.[8]

Commission officials carrying out an investigation are empowered to: examine the books and other records of the undertaking; take copies of or extracts from the books and other records; ask for oral explanations on the spot; enter any premises, land and means of transport of undertakings.[9] An investigation can be carried out in two ways: upon production of an authorization in writing;[10] or by decision.[11] Where the Commission proceeds by authorization in writing, the Commission officials carrying out the investigation exercise their powers on the basis of a written authorization, often known as a 'mandate', specifying the subject matter and purpose of the investigation and the penalties provided for if production of the required books or other business records is incomplete. The authorization, and a note attached to it which explains the Commission's power, is shown to the representatives of the undertaking under investigation and the inspectors prove their identity. If the undertaking refuses to submit to the investigation, the inspectors record the refusal. They do not have power to force an entry but a formal decision ordering the undertaking to submit to the investigation is then prepared.

An investigation by decision may be resorted to not only because the undertaking has refused to submit to an investigation upon production of a written authorization but also where the Commission suspects that there has been a serious infringement of the competition rules and is concerned that documents or other evidence may be spirited away. The decision specifies the subject matter and purpose of the investigation, sets out the date on which it is to begin, indicates the penalties for a failure to comply and the addressee's rights of redress before the CFI. A certified copy of the decision is handed to the representative for the undertaking. If the undertaking still refuses to submit to the investigation, two things happen. First, the Commission officials call on the authorities of the Member State in which the investigation is being carried out for the necessary assistance to enable them to carry out the investigation. The national authorities are obliged to provide assistance. In the United Kingdom, it would take the form of a court order and, if necessary, the police would be called to assist. Secondly, the undertaking is liable to a fine of anything between ECU 100 to ECU 5,000 and to periodic penalty payments of between ECU 50 and ECU 1,000 per day.[12]

A report drawn up by the Commission after an investigation is not an act capable of being the subject of an action for annulment.[13]

---

7   The *Orkem* case, supra; the *Société Generale* case (above), paras 71-79.
8   See the Commission decision in *CSV* (OJ 1976, L192/27) and *Fides* (OJ 1979, L57/33, [1979] 1 CMLR 650).
9   Reg 17, art 14(1).
10   Ibid, art 14(2).
11   Ibid, art 14(3).
12   Ibid, arts 15(1)(c) and 16(1)(d). For the general position regarding inspections by decision, see: Case 136/79: *National Panasonic (UK) Ltd v Commission* [1980] ECR 2033, [1980] 3 CMLR 169; Case 5/85: *AKZO v Commission* [1986] ECR 2585, [1987] 3 CMLR 716; Case 46/87: *Hoechst AG v Commission* [1989] ECR 2859, [1991] 4 CMLR 410; Case 85/87: *Dow Benelux NV v Commission* [1989] ECR 3137, [1991] 4 CMLR 410.
13   Case T-9/97: *Elf Atochem v Commission* [1997] ECR II-909.

(6) RIGHTS OF THE DEFENCE

Respect for the rights of the defence is a fundamental principle of Community law and applies to competition investigations conducted by the Commission.[14] By virtue of that principle, an undertaking must, in general terms, (1) be informed in good time of the case against it; (2) be given a reasonable opportunity to examine the evidence on which the case against it is based; (3) be given a reasonable opportunity to make its point of view known; (4) be allowed, if it wishes, legal representation;[15] and (5) be accorded immunity from disclosure in relation to communications between itself and its lawyers.[16] An undertaking accused of having infringed the competition rules benefits from the presumption of innocence, which means that the case against it must be proved by relevant and cogent evidence.[17] Those aspects of the rights of the defence also apply *mutatis mutandis* to persons who are involved in the Commission proceedings not as persons against whom a decision may be made but as persons who are interested in the result of the proceedings, as complainants[18] or as persons whose position will be affected by the outcome of the proceedings.[19] The procedural rights of complainants and others must, in the event of any conflict with the rights of the person immediately implicated in the proceedings, cede to the rights of those persons;[20] and, save in regard to those immediately implicated in the proceedings and complainants (whose interest is manifest), a person must demonstrate a direct and concrete interest in the outcome of the proceedings in order to benefit from procedural rights (a subjective or indirect interest is not enough).[1]

A person's right to be informed in good time of the case against him is safeguarded by the principle that the case which he must answer must be set out in the SO.[2] The objections raised by the Commission in the SO must be sufficiently clear to give the addressee(s) of the SO a proper opportunity to prepare a defence.[3] The right to a reasonable opportunity to examine the evidence on which the case against him is based is safeguarded by the principle that the evidence on which the Commission relies, or wishes to rely, in support of its case against the person concerned must be disclosed to that person (disclosure is effected either by attaching relevant documents to the SO or else by providing copies to the persons concerned in the course of the procedure), the Commission being disbarred from relying on further material which it has

---

14   See eg Case 322/81: *Michelin v Commission* [1983] ECR 3461, para 7.
15   See eg Cases 100-103/80: *Musique Diffusion Française v Commission* [1983] ECR 1825, paras 10, 14 and 36.
16   Case 155/79: *AM & S v Commission* [1982] ECR 1575, [1982] 2 CMLR 264.
17   Eg Case C-199/92P: *Hüls AG v Commission* [1999] ECR I-4287, [1999] 5 CMLR 1016, paras 149-155.
18   Cases 142 and 156/84: *British American Tobacco Co Ltd and R J Reynolds Industries Inc v Commission* [1987] ECR 4487, para 20.
19   Eg the recipient of a state aid: see Case C-294/90: *British Aerospace plc and Rover Group Holdings plc v Commission* [1992] ECR I-493, [1992] 1 CMLR 853.
20   The *BAT* case (above).
1   See eg Case C-170/89: *BEUC v Commission* [1991] ECR I-5709. Note also Case T-17/93: *Matra Hachette v Commission* [1994] ECR II-595 paras 34-37.
2   However, an undertaking is not obliged to respond to the SO if it does not wish to do so: Case T-30/89: *Hilti v Commission* [1991] ECR II-1439, paras 37-38.
3   Cases 89, 104, 114, 116, 117 and 125-129/85 etc. *A Ahlstrom Oy v Commission* [1993] ECR I-1307, [1993] 4 CMLR 407.

not disclosed before the making of its final decision in the case.[4] There is no general right to inspect the Commission's files but the Commission has accepted that it should give the undertakings concerned access to its files in order to see any additional incriminatory or exculpatory material; and that duty will be enforced by the CFI and the ECJ.[5] The Commission is not entitled to decide on its own whether documents in its possession are capable of exonerating an undertaking. Its obligation is therefore to draw up a sufficiently detailed list of the documents not annexed to the SO so that the undertaking concerned may request access to specific documents that it considers may be likely to assist its defence.[6] The right to a reasonable opportunity to make one's views known is safeguarded by the right to reply in writing in response to the SO and the right to an oral hearing before any final decision is made. If, for example, the SO is supplemented by another SO which makes a material alteration in the case originally made against he undertakings concerned, the latter must be given a proper opportunity to respond to the supplementary SO; otherwise, the final decision is unlawful in so far as it is based on the new matters raised in the supplementary SO.[7] The rights of the defence do not include any right to comment on the report of the Commission's hearing officer, who presides at Commission hearings.[8]

(7) CONFIDENTIALITY

EC Article 287 (ex Art 214) (repeated in substance in Article 20 of Regulation 17) forbids all agents and officials of the Community to 'disclose information of the kind covered by the obligation of professional secrecy, in particular information about undertakings, their business relations or their cost components' which has been obtained in an official capacity. Articles 19-21 of Regulation 17 further protect the confidentiality of information supplied to the Commission in that, when the Commission publishes notices and decisions, it is enjoined to 'have regard to the legitimate interest of undertakings in the protection of their business secrets'.

The Commission, when publishing its decision, respects the wishes of the parties and, in certain cases, has omitted figures from the text. Despite the sensitivity of the parties, information which they have published themselves or which is readily available to any inquirer, cannot be regarded as a 'business secret'. It is more difficult to distinguish between 'secret' and 'public' information and know-how as well as financial and turnover data in specialized lines of business. Moreover the interests of the parties have to be balanced against the legitimate interests of the adversaries as well as the public interest in the enforcement of the competition rules. Finally, there is the objective interest of the law which requires

---

4 See eg Case C-62/86: *AKZO Chemie BV v Commission* [1991] ECR I-3359, paras 16 and 18-24; Case T-9/89: *Hüls AG v Commission* [1992] ECR II-499, para 38. If the Commission has relied upon documents which have not been disclosed to the undertaking concerned, it is usually said that the defect in procedure can be remedied either by allowing the undertaking concerned an adequate opportunity to deal with the undisclosed evidence in any subsequent proceedings before the CFI or ECJ or by excluding the undisclosed evidence from consideration in such subsequent proceedings and examining the sufficiency of the Commission's findings in its absence: Case 85/76: *Hoffmann-La Roche & Co AG v Commission* [1979] ECR 461, paras 9-19.

5 See eg Case T-9/89: *Hüls AG v Commission* [1992] ECR II-499, paras 47-49.

6 See eg Case T-175/95: *BASF Coating AG v Commission* [1999] ECR II-1581, paras 45-59, and the authorities cited there.

7 Cases T-39 and T-40/92: *Groupement des Cartes Bancaires v Commission* [1994] ECR II-49, paras 46-62.

8 See eg Case T-4/89: *BASF AG v Commission* [1992] ECR II-1523, paras 51-52.

that the decisions, being Community 'acts' within the terms of EC Article 249 (ex Art 189) have to be substantiated. It is unavoidable, therefore, that a certain amount of information has to be disclosed. There is no obligation on the part of the Commission to publicize, or refrain from publicizing, the imposition of a sanction on an undertaking; but the Commission will normally publicize it as a form of deterrent, a practice approved by the ECJ.[9] The Commission has invoked the obligation of confidentiality to justify refusing to disclose to undertakings information which the Commission has obtained in the exercise of its powers and which may be useful to the defence of such undertakings.[10] That reliance on the obligation of confidentiality appears to be misconceived to the extent that it gives priority to the confidentiality of one undertaking's commercial secrets (which may in any event be protected adequately by means other than their total non-disclosure) over the proper administration of the competition rules.

The obligation to maintain the confidentiality of information obtained by the Commission in the performance of its functions and the exercise of its powers does not prevent the Commission from discharging its duty to communicate information to the Member States in the context of the consultation of the Member States that is required by the procedural regulations governing the Commission's procedures. Nonetheless, where such information comes into the hands of the authorities of the Member States by virtue of the process of consultation, it must not be divulged by the national authorities and it may not even be communicated to public bodies or parts of the public administration other than those involved in the consultation process. In particular, it may not be used by a national competition authority for the purpose of enforcing national competition rules, although it may be used to justify the commencement of an investigation by the national authorities.[11] On the other hand, Article 20 of Regulation 17 does not inhibit the Commission in responding to requests from national courts (as opposed to national competition authorities) for information relevant to proceedings before them concerning alleged infringements of the EC competition rules.[12] Further, neither Article 20 of Regulation 17 nor EC Article 281 prevents a person who has received documents or information from the Commission, in the course of the administrative proceedings before the Commission, from using them in proceedings before national courts concerning the EC competition rules; although the Commission is obliged to take appropriate steps to protect confidential information or business secrets.[13]

(8) FINAL DECISIONS

The Commission has the power at the end of the proceedings either to exonerate the undertaking(s) under investigation or else, as the case may be, to refuse to grant an exemption,[14] make a declaration that there has been an infringement of

---

9 Case 41/69: *ACF Chemiefarma v Commission* [1970] ECR 661.
10 See Ehlermann, C D, in EC Competition Policy Newsletter (1994) vol I pp 3-4.
11 Case T-39/90: *SEP v Commission* [1991] ECR II-1497, paras 51 and 55-56; Case C-67/91: *Dirección Général de Defensa de la Competencia v Asociación Espanola de Banca Privada* [1992] ECR I-4785, paras 33-35; Case C-36/92P: *SEP v Commission* [1994] ECR I-1911, paras 25 et seq.
12 Case T-353/94: *Postbank v Commission* [1996] ECR II-921. If the information requested from the Commission includes confidential information and business secrets, the national court is obliged to guarantee the protection of their confidentiality: ibid, para 69.
13 The *Postbank* case, paras 89 et seq.
14 Reg 17, art 9(1).

the competition rules,[15] order the undertaking(s) concerned to cease and desist from the infringement[16] and, where the infringement has been intentional or negligent, order the payment of a fine of between ECU 1,000 and ECU 1 million or of a sum in excess but not exceeding 10% of the turnover of the undertaking(s).[17] Periodic penalty payments of between ECU 50 and ECU 1,000 per day may also be imposed in order to compel the undertaking(s) concerned to put an end to the infringement.[18] The decision must cover the matters at issue identified in the SO; the Commission cannot make a finding adverse to the undertaking(s) concerned which does not relate to something raised in the SO.[19] The decision may deal with a range of different infringements of the competition rules committed by different undertakings.[20] A cease and desist order may not require the undertaking(s) concerned to do something which is in other respects contrary to national law;[1] and it may not require the undertaking(s) concerned to enter into a contract with another person (at least where there are alternative ways of terminating the infringement).[2]

Any fine imposed is not criminal in nature.[3] When fixing the level of the fine, the Commission exercises a discretion and may take into account various factors including the seriousness and duration of the infringement, the legal and economic background, the number and size of the undertakings concerned, the deterrent effect of a high fine, and the fact that the undertaking concerned has infringed before.[4] An infringement is intentional if the undertaking(s) concerned could not have been unaware of the anti-competitive object or effect of the conduct in question; it is not necessary for the undertaking(s) concerned to have known that the competition rules were being infringed.[5] Where the infringement was merely negligent, a lower fine should be imposed. The Commission may exercise its discretion not to impose a fine where the infringement in question is 'relatively novel'.[6] A fine cannot be imposed if the conduct in question was notified to the

---

15　Reg 17, art 9(2).

16　Reg 17, art 3(1). See eg Case T-69/89: *RTE v Commission* [1991] ECR II-485, para 97.

17　Reg 17, art 15(2). An undertaking responsible for an infringement committed by another undertaking may be made jointly liable for payment of the fine: Cases T-339/94, T-340/94, T-341/94 and T-342/94 *Metsä-Serla Oy v Commission* [1998] ECR II-1727. The power to impose a fine includes the power to determine the rate and period of running of default interest in the event that the fine is not paid on the due date: Case T-275/94: *Groupement des Cartes Bancaires v Commission* [1995] ECR II-2169, para 47.

18　Reg 17, art 16(1).

19　Case T-2/89: *Petrofina SA v Commission* [1991] ECR II-1087, para 39. That does not mean that the decision, if adverse, must be a copy of the SO. The Commission is entitled to reject some points, accept others and modify others again; what it cannot do is to take a point not raised in the SO (see Case T-9/89: *Hüls AG v Commission* [1992] ECR II-499, para 59).

20　See eg Case T-1/89: *Rhône-Poulenc SA v Commission* [1991] ECR II-867, para 131.

1　Case T-16/91: *Rendo v Commission* [1992] ECR II-2417, paras 102-107.

2　Case T-24/90: *Automec Srl v Commission* [1992] ECR II-2223, paras 50-52.

3　Reg 17, art 15(4).

4　See eg Cases 40-48, 50, 54-56, 111, 113 and 114/73: *Suiker Unie v Commission* [1975] ECR 1663, p 2022; Case T-6/89: *Enichem Zinc SpA v Commission* [1991] ECR II-1623, para 295; Case T-11/89: *Shell International Chemical Co v Commission* [1992] ECR II-757, para 369; Case T-12/89: *Solvay et Cie SA v Commission* [1992] ECR II-907, para 309; Case C-137/95P: *SPO v Commission* [1996] ECR I-1611, para 54.

5　See eg Case T-61/89: *Dansk Pelsdyravlerforening v Commission* [1992] ECR II-1931, para 157.

6　*Re Tetra Pak I (BTG Licence)*, OJ 1988, L272/27, [1990] 4 CMLR 47; see also Case C-62/86: *AKZO v Commission* [1991] ECR I-3359, where the ECJ reduced a fine imposed by the Commission because the law relating to the infringement was not settled at the time when the infringement was committed.

Commission (the immunity from fines running from the date of the notification) unless, at some time during the procedure, the Commission has by decision informed the undertaking(s) concerned that EC Article 81(1) (ex Art 85(1)) applies and an exemption is not justified.[7] A fine or periodic penalty payment also may not be imposed in respect of conduct which has taken place (and, in the case of continuous or repeated infringements, ceased to take place) more than five years beforehand (three years in the case of procedural infringements).[8]

Final decisions may be challenged in an action for annulment brought in the first instance before the CFI (with an appeal on points of law to the ECJ). Decisions other than final decisions cannot ordinarily be challenged. Their unlawfulness can be taken into account only in so far as it impugns the lawfulness of the final decision.[9] Some procedural decision made before the final decision can be attacked independently of the final decision if they have final and irreversible effects which cannot be altered by the final decision (such as decisions rejecting a complaint, which are in practice final; and decisions disclosing confidential information to a person not entitled to receive such information).[10] A decision may be attacked on the usual grounds, such as procedural defects[11] and errors of law or fact.[12] In relation to fines, the CFI (and the ECJ) have unlimited jurisdiction and may make their own assessment of the appropriate level of fine.[13]

H. Intertemporal law

Since the Community competition rules have been imposed upon the existing national systems without expressly abrogating the latter, some questions of intertemporal law have arisen in practice. The EC and EAEC Treaties were concluded for an indefinite period and the ECSC Treaty for a period of 50 years. Whilst each Treaty envisages a transitional period for the implementation of its provisions, neither considers the impact of its 'new legal order' upon the relationships which have existed before its inception.

In the field of competition, the problem of intertemporal law was thus solved by the ECJ: '. . . if the agreements have been concluded before the entry into force of the Treaty it is necessary and sufficient that their effects continue after

---

7   Reg 17, arts 15(5) and (6). See eg Case T-19/91: *Vichy v Commission* [1992] ECR II-415, paras 111-117.

8   Council Reg 2988/74 (OJ 1974, L319/1). Provision is also made in the Regulation for the interruption and suspension of the limitation period while proceedings are pending.

9   Case 60/81: *IBM Corpn v Commission* [1981] ECR 2639, [1981] 3 CMLR 635; Cases T-10 to T-12 and T-15/92: *Cimenteries CBR SA v Commission* [1992] ECR II-2667.

10 See eg Case 53/85: *AKZO Chemie BV v Commission* [1986] ECR 1965, [1987] 1 CMLR 231; Case T-37/92: *BEUC v Commission* [1994] ECR II-285, paras 27-39; Case C-36/92P: *SEP v Commission* [1994] ECR I-1911.

11 See eg Cases T-79, T-84 to T-86, T-89, T-91, T-92, T-94, T-96, T-98, T-102 and T-104/89: *BASF v Commission* [1992] ECR II-315, on appeal, Case C-137/92P: *Commission v BASF* [1994] ECR I-2555; Case T-38/92: *All Weather Sports Benelux BV v Commission* [1994] ECR II-211.

12 See eg Cases T-68, T-77 and T-78/89: *SIV v Commission* [1992] ECR II-1403, paras 319-320.

13 Reg 17, art 17. Where the court reduces or increases a fine set by the Commission, it merely alters that fine and does not impose a distinct fine; hence default interest (if any) will still run from the date fixed originally by the Commission for the payment of the fine (save in respect of any increase in the fine made by the court): Case T-275/94: *Groupement des Cartes Bancaires v Commission* [1995] ECR II-2169, paras 58-65.

this date' for the Treaty to apply.[14] Incidentally, the contract in question was made in 1937.

In the *Bosch* case,[15] involving also a contract made well before the advent of the Community, the ECJ had to define the relationship between EC Article 81 (ex Art 85) and the implementing Regulation 17. The ECJ held that 'until the entry into force of the Regulation envisaged by EC Article 83 (ex Art 87) together with Article 85(3) of the Treaty, Article 85(2) is applicable only to those agreements and decisions which the authorities of the Member States, acting under EC Article 84 (ex Art 88), have expressly declared to come within Article 85(1) and to be eligible for exemption under Article 85(3), or to those agreements which the Commission by decision under EC Article 85(2) (ex Art 89(2)), has held to be contrary to Article 85'.

For new Member States, the operative date, corresponding to the entry into force of the Treaty in the original six Member States, is the entry into force of the Treaty of Accession. However, in the light of the judgment in the *Sirena* case, the actual inception of the prohibited practice appears to be immaterial as long as the effects continue after the Treaty has come into effect in the Member State concerned. Moreover, in proceedings commenced before the entry into force of the Treaty, the parties ought to be able to amend their pleadings in order to give effect to the relevant provisions of Community law.[16]

A problem of intertemporal law has come to light, inter alia, in the *Sirdar/Phildar* case.[17] A British firm made an agreement in 1964 with a French firm to the effect that the former would not market its knitting yarns in France under its Sirdar trademark while the latter would not do likewise in the United Kingdom under its Phildar trademark. The agreement was notified to the Commission in 1973. However, following the British accession to the Community, the French firm came to the conclusion that the agreement was void under EC Article 81(1) (ex Art 85(1)) and began marketing yarns in the United Kingdom under its Phildar name. Sirdar's application for an interim injunction to restrain the French firm from using its trademark in the United Kingdom,[18] based, inter alia, on the 1964 agreement, was dismissed by the High Court. The Court also decided that there was no confusing similarity between the marks. However, Sirdar continued its action opposing the French firm's application to register its trademark Phildar in the United Kingdom and failed on the ground stated above. The Commission, for its part, opened a formal procedure against the two firms and concluded that the 1964 agreement was void under EC Article 85(1). This ruling was accepted with approval by the British High Court Judge. An appeal to the ECJ from the Commission's decision on the ground that the parties had not been given an oral hearing was withdrawn.

In Case C-39/92: *Petróleos de Portugal – Petrogal SA v Correia, Simoes & Co Lda*,[19] the question arose as to whether or not an exclusive agreement concerning

---

14 Case 40/70: *Sirena Srl v Eda Srl* [1971] ECR 69, [1971] CMLR 260. See Cases 97-99/87: *Dow Chemical Ibéria v Commission* [1989] ECR 3165, [1991] 4 CMLR 410, for an example of the exercise of the Commission's power to request information in relation to an undertaking based in a new Member State and concerning conduct prior to the accession of that state to the Community.

15 Case 13/61: *Kledingverhoopbedriff de Geus en Utidenbogerd v Robert Bosch GmbH* [1962] ECR 45, [1962] CMLR 1.

16 Eg *H P Bulmer Ltd v J Bollinger* [1974] Ch 401.

17 Case 75/297: *Re Agreement of Sirdar Ltd* [1975] 1 CMLR D93; *Re Sirdar and Phildar Trade Marks* (Commission Statement) [1976] 1 CMLR D93.

18 *Sirdar Ltd v Les Fils de Louis Mulliez* [1975] 1 CMLR 378, para 7.

19 [1993] ECR I-5659.

the supply of petrol to a service station in Portugal benefited from the block exemption in Regulation 1984/83 even though it had been concluded before Portugal joined the Community. The block exemption did not apply to agreements concluded for an indefinite period or for more than ten years; the agreement in question was such an agreement. However, under the transitional arrangements introduced at the time of the accession of Spain and Portugal to the Community, such an agreement did benefit from exemption until either its expiry or the expiry of the block exemption, as long as the agreement was brought into conformity with the block exemption (in regard to respects other than its duration) before 1 January 1989.

I. Extra-territorial enforcement

The Community competition rules apply to practices that affect trade and competition within the common market, that is, within the territory of the Union. On the one hand, that excludes from their scope activities whose effects are limited to the territory of one Member State and which are therefore purely local; on the other hand, it excludes from their scope activities whose effects are felt entirely outside the common market. The extra-territorial enforcement of the Community competition rules therefore concerns persons located outside the territory of the Union whose activities affect trade and competition within it. Two main problems arise in connection with the application of the competition rules to such persons. The first concerns the practical question of how to apply the competition rules to persons physically located outside the jurisdiction of the Community institutions and the Member States; the second concerns the question of the degree of effect in the common market that is, or should be, required to bring conduct involving person located outside the Union within the sphere of application of the Community rules. Such questions are of great sensitivity in part because of the very idea that the rules of the Union (or of any state) may be applicable to persons outside its jurisdiction and in part because the application of the Community's competition rules to persons located outside the Union risks bringing about a clash between the Union's competition policy and the competition policy of states outside the Union.[20]

As a general rule, the fact that a party to an agreement (or practice) is physically located outside the Union does not put that party or the agreement (or practice) beyond the reach of Community competition law: in Case 22/71: *Béguelin Import v GL Import Export*,[1] a Japanese manufacturer entered into an exclusive distribution agreement with a Belgian company whereby the latter was granted the exclusive right to distribute the former's products in France and Belgium; the ECJ held that the fact that one party to the agreement was subject to Japanese law was irrelevant; the question determining the application of the competition rules was whether the agreement was 'operative' on the territory of the Community.[2]

---

20 For the approach in the United States, see *US v ICI* 10 F Supp 504 (1951) (SDNY) 152; *US v Watchmakers of Switzerland, Information Center Inc* Trade Cases, 70, 60 (1963) (SDNY) and same case Trade Cases 71, 352 (1965).

1 [1971] ECR 949, para 11.

2 In the same way, the ECJ held in Case 36/74: *Walrave and Koch v AUCI* [1974] ECR 1405, para 28, in the context of the prohibition of discrimination in the EC Treaty, that it applies in judging all relationships in so far as these relationships, by reason either of the place where they are entered into or of the place where they take effect, are located within the territory of the Community.

If there was any doubt as to the jurisdiction of the EC institutions in respect of 'foreign' undertakings operating in the Community, that doubt was resolved in the *Dyestuffs* case. That case (or series of cases) concerned a price cartel operated by some sixty companies in the common market and abroad. The Commission found that the concerted practices, consisting inter alia in fixing the rates of price increases of dyestuffs and conditions of application of such increases, constituted an infringement of EC Article 81 (ex Art 85) since practically all the undertakings selling dyestuffs in the Community were involved. It imposed fines upon four German, one French, one Italian, three Swiss and one British company (ICI), the last being the ringleader.[3] Most of the undertakings involved appealed but the ECJ upheld the Commission's decision (though it reduced slightly the fine imposed upon one of the undertakings).[4] The companies established outside the Community (which included ICI because the United Kingdom was not a member of the Community at the time of the acts in question) challenged the jurisdiction of the EC institutions. In particular, ICI contended that contracts to supply its subsidiaries within the Community were governed by English law and that, therefore, the activities in which ICI was involved were carried out in the United Kingdom, ie outside the territorial jurisdiction of the Community. Those arguments were rejected as unfounded by both the Advocate-General and the ECJ.

The Advocate-General suggested three conditions as the test of the applicability of EC law, viz the imposition of direct and immediate restrictions on the common market by agreement or concerted practice; the reasonably foreseeable character of the effect; and the substantial nature of the effect produced in the Community. He concluded that 'Article 85 gives as the sole criterion the anti-competitive effect in the common market, without taking into account either nationality or the locality of the headquarters, of the undertakings responsible for the breaches of competition'. The question of jurisdiction did not trouble the ECJ once it had been established that the concerted practice in question fell under the rubric of EC Article 81 (ex Art 85), ie that it was of a type prohibited by the Treaty and that it took effect in the Community. It follows, therefore, that the Community, being a legal entity of a federal type and operating a federal type of law, is in a position analogous to that of a state. If a state's law has a long arm, so does that of the Community.

In *Geigy and Sandoz v Commission*,[5] where a Swiss undertaking complained of being incorrectly charged by the Commission with a breach of EC Article 81(1) (ex Art 85(1)), the ECJ dismissed the plea that the Commission had no jurisdiction. It reiterated its reasoning in the *ICI* case and concluded that 'such jurisdiction is not based merely on the effects of action committed outside the Community, but on activities attributable to the claimant within the common market area'. The ECJ also dismissed the argument that the Commission notified the applicant in a manner which did not comply with the law of Switzerland, holding that it was sufficient to observe the procedure laid down by Community law. Thus, it seems, a foreign undertaking cannot insist that the Commission communicates with it through diplomatic channels or according to its national procedures.

The Commission also assumed jurisdiction in respect of the *Franco-Japanese Ballbearings Agreement*[6] involving French and Japanese manufacturers and declared

---

3 Decision in Case 69/243: *Re Dyestuffs Cartel* [1969] CMLR D23.
4 See Case 48/69: *ICI Ltd v Commission* [1972] ECR 619, [1972] CMLR 557.
5 Cases 52 and 53/69: [1972] ECR 787 and 845, [1972] CMLR 557 and 637 respectively.
6 Case 74/634: [1975] 1 CMLR D8.

their Agreement affecting trade between Member States to be illegal. Similarly, in relation to the *Franco-Taiwanese Mushroom Agreement*,[7] the Commission held the practices in which the parties were engaged as being contrary to EC Article 81(1) (ex Art 85(1)). It imposed substantial fines upon the French undertakings but none upon their Taiwanese partners because the latter were unaware of the Commission Notice[8] relevant to the case. The Commission specifically emphasized its jurisdiction based on the effects of the Agreement in the common market. In the *Hoffmann-La Roche* case,[9] both the Commission and the ECJ had no hesitation in assuming jurisdiction in respect of a Swiss multinational company with subsidiaries in the Community which, by operating a system of fidelity rebates, was held to have abused its dominant position.

The most recent analysis of what may constitute the degree of effect in the common market that is, or should be, required to bring conduct involving persons located outside the Union within the sphere of application of the Community rules is contained in the ECJ's judgment in the *Woodpulp* case.[10] There, various undertakings established outside the territory of the Community were accused of having engaged in a concerted practice affecting the selling price of woodpulp to purchasers established in the Community. The ECJ held that infringements of EC Article 81 (ex Art 85) consist of conduct comprising two elements: the formation of an agreement, decision or concerted practice; and its implementation. For the purpose of determining the applicability of the prohibition in EC Article 81 (ex Art 85), the decisive factor is the place where the agreement, decision or concerted practice is implemented, not the place where it is formed. An agreement, decision or concerted practice is implemented where it has effects on the competitive behaviour of the undertakings party to it. Where producers established outside the Community sell directly to purchasers established within the Community and engage in price competition in order to win orders from the latter, that constitutes competition by the former within the common market; and where they have entered into an agreement, decision or concerted practice (albeit outside the Community) and put it into effect in relation to their dealings with those purchasers, they take part in conduct whose object and effect is the restriction of competition within the common market. It is immaterial whether or not the producers concerned had recourse to subsidiaries, agents, sub-agents or branches within the Community in order to make their contacts with purchasers within the Community.

In a case concerning the merger of mining operations in South Africa, it was held that the Community had jurisdiction and that its jurisdiction was justified under public international law because it was foreseeable that the merger would have an immediate and substantial effect in the Community: the mining operations were significant sources of supply to buyers in the Community. It was also held that the Community's assertion of jurisdiction did not violate a principle of noninterference in the affairs of another state and did not infringe the principle of proportionality.[11]

The questions of double jeopardy and double sanction arising from parallel proceedings, concerning the same anti-competitive conduct, potentially arise just

7   [1975] 1 CMLR D83.
8   OJ 1972, C 111/13.
9   Case 76/642 [1976] 2 CMLR D25; before the ECJ, Case 85/76: [1979] ECR 461, [1979] 3 CMLR 211.
10   Cases 89, 104, 114, 116, 117 and 125-129/85: *A Ahlström Osakeyhtiö v Commission* [1988] ECR 5193, [1988] 4 CMLR 901.
11   Case T-102/96: *Gencor v Commission* [1999] ECR II-753, [1999] 4 CMLR 971, paras 89-111.

as much in relation to proceedings in different jurisdictions within and outside the Community as they do in relation to proceedings in different jurisdictions within the Community.[12] The international aspect was considered in the two *Boehringer* cases. Following the first case,[13] in which a fine imposed by the Commission in respect of the activities of the Quinine Cartel was reduced by the ECJ, the Commission was requested for a further reduction of the fine in order to take into consideration the fine imposed on the applicant by the US District Court of New York in consequence of a violation of US Anti-trust Law. The Commission refused to do so and stated its reasons (the ECJ had reduced the fine slightly but without taking into account the US fine). Subsequently, the Commission once more[14] refused the request, reiterating its reasons, namely that the Treaty and its implementing regulations did not provide for the other sanctions being taken into consideration and that, in any case, the laws of the Member States did not require their courts to take into account penalties imposed in the fellow Member States. This applied a fortiori in cases where a third country was involved. Moreover, in the opinion of the Commission, the grounds upon which the applicant had been fined in the USA and the Community were not identical. In further proceedings, the second *Boehringer* case,[15] the ECJ conceded that, in order to make out a case, the applicant would have to show that the acts alleged were identical and this the ECJ found not to be the case. Whilst at pains to explain why it reduced the original fine imposed by the Commission, the ECJ nevertheless concurred with the Commission on the issue of double jeopardy and upheld its decision.

The position is not entirely satisfactory but cannot be considered in isolation from the practice of the enforcement agencies outside the Community, notably in the USA. On the one hand, it can be said that a wrongdoer chooses at his own risk to offend more than one system of law; on the other hand, it seems harsh to be punished twice for the same conduct (even though it gives rise to virtually the same offence in more than one jurisdiction). The problem has to be solved first in the Community, since the implications of the *Walt Wilhelm* case[16] are far from conclusive. As regards the relations between the Community and non-Member States, considerations of international comity as much as the desire to ensure the effective enforcement of the Treaty rules has led to the inclusion in certain trade agreements made by the Community with third countries of 'competition clauses' which set out procedures for the reciprocal enforcement of the competition rules of the contracting parties.[17] The competition clauses are silent on the questions of double jeopardy and double sanction and, to that extent, require further elaboration. Practically nothing can be done outside those trade agreements for there is no basis for reciprocity on which questions of double jeopardy and double sanction could be considered.

In 1991, the Commission made an agreement with the US government concerning the application by both parties of their respective competition legislation in regard to behaviour of mutual concern.[18] The agreement broke

---

12 As to the latter, see above and the *Walt Wilhelm* case.
13 Case 45/69: *Boehringer Mannheim v Commission* [1970] ECR 769.
14 OJ 1971, L282/46, [1972] CMLR D121.
15 Case 7/72: *Boehringer Mannheim v Commission* [1972] ECR 1281, [1973] CMLR 864.
16 Above.
17 See, in particular, the summary given by Rouam, Jakob and Suni in EC Competition Policy Newsletter (1994) vol 1, p 7.
18 [1991] 4 CMLR 823.

new ground in terms of international co-operation.[19] Co-operation between the EC and the USA is now governed by an agreement made in 1998[20] and a similar agreement was made with Canada in 1999.[1] The other international agreements of relevance here are the trade agreements referred to above. The most important (so important that it is difficult to characterize it as a simple trade agreement) is the Agreement on the European Economic Area ('the EEA') which contains basic competition rules derived from the EC Treaty[2] and whose territorial application covers both the Member States of the Union and the member countries of EFTA. There are two authorities competent to enforce those rules: the Commission and the EFTA Surveillance Authority, each subject to the jurisdiction of the relevant court (the CFI and ECJ in the case of the Commission and the EFTA Court in the case of the EFTA Surveillance Authority). In principle, infringements are investigated by one of the competent authorities alone and its decision is enforceable throughout the EEA. Each competent authority has jurisdiction over matters arising or taking effect solely within its part of the EEA. Where a restrictive practice has effect in both parts of the EEA (the Union and EFTA), special rules apply for determining which authority is responsible. Less complex arrangements apply in the context of other trade agreements.[3]

19 The lawfulness of the agreement was challenged by France and it was annulled: Case C-327/91: *France v Commission* [1994] ECR I-3641. The agreement was then effectively remade as an agreement between the EC and the government of the USA: see OJ 1995, L95/45 (corrigendum OJ 1995, L131/38).
20 OJ 1998, L173/26 and 28; [1999] 4 CMLR 502.
1 OJ 1999, L175/49 and 50; [1999] 5 CMLR 713.
2 See eg Decision 3/94 of the EFTA Surveillance Authority (OJ 1994, L153/1).
3 See Rouam, Jakob and Suni, op cit. For the position under the previous Free Trade Agreements with the EFTA countries see, for example, Case 53/84: *Adams v Commission* [1985] ECR 3539, [1986] 1 CMLR 506; and the *Woodpulp* case, supra, paras 29-33.

Chapter 28

Competition: practices contrary to Article 81 (ex Article 85)

A. Introduction

EC Article 81 (ex Art 85) comprises three paragraphs. The first defines a prohibition; the second specifies certain civil law consequences of the prohibition; the third sets out an exemption from the prohibition. EC Article 81 (ex Art 85) also refers to various concepts which appear in other Treaty provisions, notably EC Articles 82, 86 and 87 (ex Arts 86, 90 and 92): in particular 'undertakings', the concept of an effect on trade between Member States and the 'prevention, restriction and distortion of competition within the common market'. The explanation of those concepts given in this chapter applies equally in relation to the other Treaty provisions in which those concepts appear; and therefore in some instances the explanation given is more expansive than would otherwise have been the case if it had been limited to EC Article 81 (ex Art 85) in isolation.

B. The prohibition

EC Article 81(1) (ex Art 85(1)) provides:

'. . . the following shall be prohibited as incompatible with the common market: all *agreements* between *undertakings, decisions* by associations of undertakings and, *concerted practices* which *may affect trade between Member States* and which have as their *object* or *effect* the *prevention, restriction or distortion of competition* within the common market, and *in particular* those which:

(a) directly or indirectly fix purchase or selling prices or any other trading conditions;
(b) limit or control production, markets, technical development, or investment;
(c) share markets or sources of supply;
(d) apply dissimilar conditions to equivalent transactions with other trading parties, thereby placing them at a competitive disadvantage;

(e) make the conclusion of contracts subject to acceptance by the other parties of supplementary obligations which, by their nature or according to commercial usage, have no connection with the subject of the contracts'.

As can be seen, the text consists of a general principle followed by specific illustrations. The list of illustrations is by no means exhaustive. Practices which have not been specifically listed may be caught if they exhibit characteristics which bring them within the scope of the principle. In this way the legislator gives a certain margin of discretion to the enforcement authorities as long as they operate within the framework of EC Article 81 (ex Art 85) and, in the course of time, EC Article 81(1) (ex Art 85(1)) has been the subject of considerable exegesis in the cases. Before considering the various practices caught by EC Article 85(1), we have to understand the basic concepts determining the scope of the prohibition.

(1) UNDERTAKINGS

(a) General
EC Articles 81 to 85 (ex Arts 85 to 89) apply generally to all undertakings whereas EC Article 86 (ex Art 90) contains particular rules applying to four particular types of undertaking. All four types are here referred to for the sake of brevity as 'public undertakings'. There is no definition in the EC Treaty of 'undertaking'.[1] The concept of an 'undertaking' is not defined by reference to the legal status or form of an entity under public or private law,[2] as can be seen from the fact that EC Articles 81 and 82 (ex Arts 85 and 86) refer in general terms to 'undertakings' without qualification, whereas EC Article 86 (ex Art 90) refers to four particular types of undertaking identified by reference to their relationship to the State, thus indicating that the concept of an undertaking is not defined by reference to the existence or absence of some connexion with the state. Accordingly, EC Article 87 (ex Art 92), which refers to undertakings without qualification, applies to all undertakings, whether public or private.[3] Since 'undertaking' is used in a generic sense, it is not necessary to define the particular characteristics of what could loosely be described as 'private undertakings', that is, undertakings operating in the private sector of the economy. It is sufficient to give an indication of the general meaning attributed to 'undertaking' and then to describe those particular types of undertaking falling within that general meaning which are referred to in EC Article 86 (ex Art 90) and dealt with under the competition rules in a slightly different way from other undertakings.

The most obvious meanings to be attributed to the term 'undertaking' are 'company or firm', 'business' or 'enterprise'. In the context of 'establishment', EC Article 48 (ex Art 58) defines 'companies or firms' as 'companies or firms constituted under civil or commercial law, including co-operative societies, and other legal persons governed by public or private law, save for those which are non-profit-making'. These, as a rule, are the types of entity likely to be involved in competition but they are not an exhaustive list of such entities. As various Commission decisions show, the concept of an 'undertaking' includes individuals

---

1 Unternehmen; enterprise; impresa.
2 See Case T-61/89: *Dansk Pelsdyravlerforening v Commission* [1992] ECR II-1931, para 50 (a co-operative).
3 Case C-387/92: *Banco de Crédito Industrial v Ayuntamiento de Valencia* [1994] ECR I-877, para 11.

engaged in economic activity by themselves,[4] through firms they control,[5] and associations of undertakings acting through a chairman and delegates of firms,[6] or even associations without a formal constitution,[7] if they are engaged in economic activities. The ECJ has had occasion to define 'undertaking' in the context of the ECSC Treaty[8] and has held that the concept 'is constituted by a unitary organization combining personal, material and immaterial elements attached to an autonomous juristic subject and pursuing permanently a definite economic objective'.[9] This indicates that an undertaking has to have an autonomous legal existence and personality, an economic autonomy and, above all, it has to be involved in the trade, manufacture or distribution of goods or services. The last may include the exercise of a liberal profession as envisaged in EC Article 50 (ex Art 60) excluding however, purely personal or cultural pursuits. The subjective intention of the undertaking (or those managing it) regarding the purpose served by the economic activities in which the undertaking engages (such as whether they are profit-making, non-profit-making or charitable in intention) has no bearing on the question of whether or not the undertaking is an undertaking.[10]

On the other hand, not all activities (whether or not profit-making) can be described as economic or commercial activities. Where a person carries on activities that are typically those of a governmental body, it cannot be said to be an undertaking even if it charges for the services that it provides.[11] It is sometimes difficult to decide whether or not the activities carried on by a person are economic or commercial or governmental. For example, in Case C-41/90 *Höfner and Elser v Macrotron GmbH*,[12] the ECJ held that a public employment exchange was an undertaking for the purposes of the Treaty because, so far as competition law is concerned, an undertaking comprises any entity performing an economic activity, whatever its legal status and means of financing; and acting as an employment agency or exchange is the performance of an economic activity. Even so, it would appear that, in Germany, the public employment exchange was regarded as a typical example of a government agency, not an undertaking.

A number of persons who, from the strictly legal point of view, are distinct entities in law will nonetheless constitute one undertaking if they form a single economic unit. Thus, where one of the parties to an agreement comprises two companies with an identical interest which are controlled by the same natural person, who is also a party to the agreement, there is and can be no competition between all three persons and they are to be regarded as constituting a single undertaking.[13] Thus, a person who is employed by another forms part of the same

---

4   Case 76/29: *Re AOIP/Beyrard* [1976] 1 CMLR D14.

5   Case 76/743: *Re Reuter/BASF AG* [1976] 2 CMLR D44.

6   Case 76/684: *Pabst and Richarz/Bureau National Interprofessionnel de l'Armagnac* [1976] 2 CMLR D63.

7   Case 74/431: *Re Groupement des Fabricants de Papiers Peints de Belgique* [1974] 2 CMLR D102; see also Case 80/234: *Re Rennet* [1980] 2 CMLR 402 (a co-operative).

8   See eg Cases 42 and 49/59: *SNUPAT v High Authority* [1961] ECR 53, [1963] CMLR 60; Cases 17-20/61: *Klöckner-Werke AG v High Authority* [1962] ECR 325.

9   Case 19/61: *Mannesman AG v High Authority* [1962] ECR 357. The same approach to the definition of an undertaking was followed in Case T-11/89: *Shell International Chemical Co Ltd v Commission* [1992] ECR II-757, paras 311 and 315.

10 Cf Case C-244/94: *Fédération Française des Sociétés d'Assurance v Ministère de l'Agriculture et de la Peche* [1995] ECR I-4013.

11 Case C-364/92: *SAT Fluggesellschaft mbH v Eurocontrol* [1994] ECR I-43; Case C-343/95: *Cali & Figli Srl v Servizi Ecologici Porto di Genova SpA* [1997] ECR I-1547.

12 [1991] ECR I-1979.

13 Case 170/83: *Hydrotherm Gerätebau GmbH v Compact de Dott Ing Mario Andreoli & CSAS* [1984] ECR 2999, paras 11-12.

undertaking as that other person. By the same token, where a subsidiary of another company, although possessing in law separate legal personality from its parent, does not decide independently upon its own conduct in the market but carries out the instructions given to it by the parent, the two companies form a single economic unit and, hence, one undertaking. Accordingly, any agreements or practices to which those companies alone are a party fall outside the scope of EC Article 81 (ex Art 85) because they do not involve more than one undertaking.[14] For two or more persons to form a single undertaking, it is nonetheless necessary for that single grouping to perform economic activities in some way. Organizations created by national law that group together undertakings or the representatives or undertakings but that do not themselves perform economic activities are not undertakings.[15]

In theory, two or more persons who are controlled by the same person may constitute different undertakings if they are so organized that each acts independently of the other. In practice, the existence of common control leads normally to the conclusion that they form a single undertaking; and, hence, to the conclusion that an agreement between persons subject to common control falls outside EC Article 81(1) (ex Art 85(1)) because it does not involve more than one 'undertaking'. The nature of the control, exercised by one person over another, which is sufficient to indicate that both form a single undertaking can be expressed in various ways. At one extreme, where one person (whether legal or natural) owns all the shares in a company, the degree of control is absolute and the almost inevitable inference will be that the two form a single undertaking. The same conclusion may be drawn where the degree of control falls far short of the absolute, such as where one person (whether legal or natural) holds only a bare majority of the shares in a company (at least where a bare majority suffices to influence in a determinative manner the commercial decision-making of the company). On the other hand, if a person (whether legal or natural) only has sufficient influence over a company to block certain types of decision, that would not ordinarily be regarded as sufficient to render the two persons a single undertaking. There are also circumstances where two persons are regarded as a single undertaking even though one does not own the other: employer and employee provide one example;[16] another example may be where a creditor (such as a bank) has effective control over a person's commercial activities in order to ensure that the latter's debts will eventually be repaid.

However, where commercial arrangements or, indeed, the bargaining power of a supplier over a purchaser (or vice versa) confer on one person the power to exercise a determining influence over another, it is not usually said that the two persons form a single undertaking: if that were so, many forms of anti-competitive behaviour would fall outside the scope of the competition rules. In order for two or more persons to constitute a single undertaking the relationship between them must generally be of an 'institutional' rather than a 'commercial' nature. In other words, there must be some formal power of control exercised by one person over another instead of some de facto form of control resulting from a commercial or trading relationship.

---

14 Case 48/69: *ICI Ltd v Commission* [1972] ECR 619, paras 133-134. See also Case 69/165: *Re Christiani and Nielson* [1969] CMLR D36; Case 70/332: *Re Kodak* [1970] CMLR D19; Case 22/71: *Béguelin Import Co v GL Import/Export SA* [1971] ECR 949, [1972] CMLR 81.
15 Case 123/83: *BNIC v Clair* [1985] ECR 391.
16 Case C-22/98: *Becu* [1999] ECR I-5665, paras 25-26. Employees taken collectively are not an undertaking: see ibid, para 27-29.

Due to the definition of an undertaking as a combination of personal, material and immaterial elements attached to an autonomous person (whether legal or natural), the responsibility for an infringement of the competition rules may pass from person to person where, after the infringement has taken place, the person responsible for exploiting the undertaking in question has ceased to exist and the elements comprising that undertaking have passed to another person.[17]

(b) Public undertakings

The Member States of the Union practise a 'mixed economy' in which the state participates alongside the private interest. The state's involvement in trade and industry is expressed through legislative and administrative measures which may affect parts of or the whole national economy. At the operational level, the state controls the 'public sector' in which it operates through public undertakings of different types. The structures, the forms and the degree of government control of these bodies differ from country to country[18] and so does the field of their activity. They exhibit, however, a common tendency towards monopolies and in that sense enjoy by law a 'dominant position' which the Union purports to contain within the concept of the Common Market. Since they are there to stay (although trends regarding the extent of their role in the modern economy fluctuate),[19] the Treaty had to come to terms with their existence. For the sake of the liberalization of trade, the Treaty set out to limit their monopolist position by a 'progressive adjustment of state monopolies' (EC Article 31 (ex Art 37)) and by bringing public undertakings within the EC competition policy (EC Article 86 (ex Art 90)).

However, as we have seen earlier, the process of adjustment (not abolition) of state monopolies has been painfully slow. The attempt to bring the public sector within the Community competition system succeeded on paper but the full realization of the effect of the Treaty provisions was not felt until relatively recently; in many respects, the text of the Treaty proved ineffective against the political and economic reality and it was not until prevailing opinion concerning the desirability of limiting state involvement in the competitive process altered that the full implications of the Treaty were appreciated and acted upon.

EC Article 86 (ex Art 90) covers the application of the competition rules to the following classes of undertakings[20] in which Member States have an interest or through which they may affect the structure of competition in the Union:

Public undertakings are undertakings controlled directly or indirectly by the state. The Commission has defined such undertakings as 'any undertaking over which the public authorities may exercise directly or indirectly a dominant influence by virtue of their ownership of it, their financial participation therein, or the rules which govern it'.[1] A public undertaking may be a body distinct from

---

17 Case T-6/89: *Enichem Anic SpA v Commission* [1991] ECR II-1623, paras 235-237.
18 See generally, Friedmann W (ed), *Public and Private Enterprises in Mixed Economies* (1974).
19 For example, for many years after the Second World War the tendency was for the rôle of public undertakings to increase rather than diminish; whereas, since the beginning of the 1980s, there has been a tendency to diminish state involvement in the economy through public undertakings.
20 For the purpose of determining the scope of Art 86 (ex Art 90), the same definition of 'undertaking' is used as in the case of Arts 81 and 82 (ex Arts 85 and 86): see Case C-41/90: *Höfner and Elser v Macrotron GmbH* [1991] ECR I-1979, para 20.
1   Commission Dir 80/723 of 25 June 1980 (OJ 1980, L195/35), Art 2. A dominant influence is to be presumed when the public authorities (ie the state or regional or local authorities) hold the major part of the undertaking's subscribed capital or control the majority of the votes attaching to shares issued by it or can appoint more than half of its administrative, managerial or supervisory bodies.

the state or an integral part of the state administration; its legal form is not relevant.[2] The basis for distinguishing between a public undertaking and other persons or bodies performing state functions lies in the nature of the activities carried on rather than in the status, within the administrative organs of the state, of the person or body carrying them on. Identifying a public undertaking by reference to the activities carried on by it rather than by reference to its form or status raises difficult questions at a time when the accepted frontiers between the public and the entrepreneurial functions of the state are in flux. For example, an employment exchange has been characterized as an undertaking because finding people jobs is an economic activity; and the fact that such an activity is normally entrusted to a public service does not affect the economic nature of the activity since it is not always and not necessarily carried on by a public body.[3]

Undertakings to which Member States grant special or exclusive rights are defined by reference to the rights granted to them by the state and not by reference to the persons who own or control them. Thus, an undertaking entirely owned and controlled by private sector interests may still be an undertaking of this type. A special right is a right from which persons do not ordinarily benefit: for example, an easement over property is a typical right which the general law confers without the requirement for special provision, whereas a compulsory power to enter someone else's property in order to carry out works there (such as repair work carried out by a water, gas or electricity utility) is not a right which everyone possesses.[4] An exclusive right normally comprises a national, regional or local monopoly. Undertakings having special or exclusive rights include a limited company set up by a number of insurance companies and recognized by the government of a Member State as the sole body competent to settle certain insurance claims;[5] an undertaking to whom the exclusive right to provide certain funeral services in a particular locality has been granted;[6] an airline granted the right to operate on a particular air route either alone or in company with one or two other airlines;[7] a port operator and the bodies providing the services of dockworkers who have been given the sole right to operate in a particular port;[8] a person on whom a Member State has conferred the sole right to collect, transport and deliver post;[9] and a body granted the exclusive right to offer pilotage services in a particular port.[10] The treaty does not prevent Member States from removing certain economic *activities* from the field of competition for reason of a non-economic nature connected with the public interest; they may do this by conferring on an undertaking an exclusive right to conduct the activities in question;[11] but the *undertaking* concerned is not excluded from the ambit of the competition rules.

---

2   Case 118/85: *Commission v Italy* [1987] ECR 2599.
3   *Höfner and Elser v Macrotron*, above, paras 20-23. Contrast the *Eurocontrol* case, above.
4   But see Case C-302/94: *R v Secretary of State for Trade and Industry, ex p British Telecommunications* [1996] ECR I-6417. The meaning given in that case to 'exclusive or special rights' was, however, determined by the legislative context, which was not the same as that of EC Article 86 (ex Art 90).
5   Case 90/76: *van Ameyde v UCI* [1977] ECR 1091.
6   Case 30/87: *Bodson v Pompes Funèbres* [1988] ECR 2479.
7   Case 66/86: *Ahmed Saeed Flugreisen and Silver Line Reisebüro GmbH v Zentrale fur Bekampfung unlauteren Wettbewerbs* [1989] ECR 803, para 50.
8   Case C-179/90: *Merci Convenzionali Porto di Genova SpA v Siderurgica Gabrielli SpA* [1991] ECR I-5889, para 9.
9   Case C-320/91: *Corbeau* [1993] ECR I-2533, para 8.
10   Case C-18/93: *Corsica Ferries Italia v Corpo dei Piloti del Genova* [1994] ECR I-1783.
11   Case 155/73: *Italy State v Sacchi* [1974] ECR 409, para 14. But see Case C-353/89: *Commission v Netherlands* [1991] ECR I-4069.

Undertakings entrusted with the operation of services of general economic interest (which may include undertakings within the preceding categories)[12] include a company set up to create and develop a river port and given certain privileges for that purpose[13] (but not merely operating a port);[14] a public body (*in casu* a public employment exchange) entrusted with the function of implementing a general legislative object for the purpose of which the carrying on of a particular economic activity is entrusted to it;[15] a person entrusted with a telecommunications monopoly;[16] a person entrusted with a postal monopoly;[17] and a person entrusted with the supply of electricity.[18] A private undertaking may fall within this class as long as it has been entrusted with the operation of services of general economic interest by an act of public authority and as long as it does not manage purely private interests.[19] Legislation which simply defines the rules applicable to undertakings that carry on a particular activity does not constitute a public authority act which entrusts the undertaking concerned with the performance of the activity for these purposes.[20]

Undertakings having the character of a revenue-producing monopoly are undertakings to which the state has granted monopolistic powers in order to secure the profits from trade; the legal form of the undertaking is irrelevant so long as it possesses a monopoly and all its profits go to benefit the state. However, such monopolies are to be distinguished from the monopolies of a commercial character covered by EC Article 31 (ex Art 37).

Public undertakings and undertakings granted special or exclusive rights[1] benefit from a strong presumption of their legality.[2] In other words, their mere existence, far from being put in question, is tacitly approved by the Treaty. However, they remain subject to the Treaty positions, in particular the competition rules, and Member States are specifically prohibited from further sheltering them from competition, or facilitating any anti-competitive acts that they may indulge in, by enacting or maintaining in force any measure contrary to the Treaty.[3] Thus, such undertakings may be brought to account under EC Article 81 and 82 (ex Arts 85 and 86) (where applicable) in respect of action taken by them of their own initiative; the Member State concerned may also be brought to account if it places the undertaking in question in a situation in which a distortion of competition is inevitable (and is not dependent upon some act taken by the undertaking of it own initiative),[4] such as where a Member State creates a system under which apparatus can be sold or used only if approved by a particular person and that person is itself a competing supplier of such apparatus.[5]

12 Cf Case C-320/91: *Corbeau* [1993] ECR I-2533, para 14.
13 Case 10/71: *Ministère Public of Luxembourg v Muller* [1971] ECR 723, para 11.
14 The *Porto di Genova* case, supra, paras 26-28.
15 *Hofner & Elser v Macrotron*, supra, para 24.
16 Case C-18/88: *Régie des Télégraphes et des Téléphones v GB-Inno-BM SA* [1991] ECR I-5941, para 16.
17 The *Corbeau* case, supra, para 15.
18 Case C-393/92: *Commune d'Almelo v Energiebedrijf Ijsselmij* [1994] ECR I-1477, paras 47-48.
19 Case 127/73: *BRT v SABAM* [1974] ECR 313, paras 20 and 23; Case 172/80: *Züchner v Bayerische Vereinsbank AG* [1981] ECR 2021, para 7.
20 Case 7/82: *GVL v Commission* [1983] ECR 483, para 31.
 1 The same classification is to be found in article XVII of the GATT.
 2 Case C-202/88: *France v Commission* [1991] ECR I-1223, per Advocate-General Tesauro (para 29 of his Opinion). However, note para 22 of the judgment.
 3 EC Art 86(1) (ex Art 90(1)).
 4 Cf the *Macrotron* case, supra; Case C-260/89: *ERT v DEP* [1991] ECR I-2925; the *Corsica Ferries* case, supra, paras 42-45.
 5 See eg Case C-18/88: *RTT v GB-Inno-BM* [1991] ECR I-5941; Case C-69/91: *Decoster* [1993] ECR I-5335; Case C-92/91: *Taillandier* [1993] ECR I-5383.

Undertakings entrusted with the operation of services of general economic interest and undertakings having the character of a revenue-producing monopoly remain, as a general rule, subject to the Treaty (in particular the competition rules) but there is an exception to that general rule from which they benefit: the competition rules (and the other Treaty provisions) apply only in so far as their application 'does not obstruct the performance, in law or in fact, of the particular tasks assigned to them', to which there is added the proviso that 'the development of trade must not be affected to such an extent as would be contrary to the interests of the Community'.[6] The general rule and the exception to it operate in the following manner: the general rule applies (and the undertakings in question remain subject to the competition rules and the other Treaty provisions) to the extent that it has not been established that the application of those rules is incompatible with the performance of the particular task assigned to the undertaking concerned; where the matter is raised in national proceedings, it is for the national court to assess the compatibility of the conduct of the undertaking with the Treaty and to determine whether or not that conduct, if contrary to the Treaty, is justified by the exigencies of the task assigned to the undertaking.[7]

The effect of EC Article 86 (ex Art 90) is to bring both the undertaking in question and the Member State concerned under scrutiny. Where, for example, state action creates an undertaking falling within one of the categories covered by EC Article 86 (ex Art 90), the subsequent behaviour of the undertaking is caught by the Treaty rules (save where the limited exception referred to above applies). However, where the action of the state not only creates such an undertaking but also places it in a situation where its behaviour necessarily infringes the Treaty (such as where a monopoly is conferred on an undertaking which lacks the resources to meet demand),[8] it is the action of the state in creating such a situation that infringes the Treaty as much as any action of the undertaking. EC Article 86(3) (ex Art 90(3)) confers on the Commission power to adopt general rules (in the form of directives) or specific measures (in the form of decisions) giving further precision to the obligations flowing from the Treaty and concerning the undertakings referred to in EC Article 86(1) and (2) (ex Art 90(1) and (2)). Measures adopted under EC Article 86(3) (ex Art 90(3)) are legally binding and do not carry a mere 'moral' weight.[9] In principle, they are directed at the Member States themselves, the conduct of the undertakings in question being dealt with, as the case may be, under EC Articles 81 and 82 (ex Arts 85 or 86).[10]

---

6 EC Art 86(2) (ex Art 90(2)).
7 Case C-260/89: *Elliniki Radiophonia Tilerorassi AS v Cimotiki Etairia Pliroforissis* [1991] ECR I-2925, paras 33-34. For a more detailed discussion of the application of EC Art 86(2) (ex Art 90(2)) see the *Corbeau* case (above), paras 15-21; the *Commune d'Almelo* case (above), paras 48-49; Case T-260/94: *Air Inter SA v Commission* [1997] ECR II-997, paras 134-141.
8 The *Macrotron* case (above). See also, in this connection, Case C-323/93: *Centre d'Insemination de la Crespelle v Cooperative de la Mayenne* [1994] ECR I-5077, paras 18-22; Case C-242/95: *GT-Link v DSB* [1997] ECR I-4349, paras 33-34; Case C-163/96: *Salvano Raso* [1998] ECR I-533, paras 27-32.
9 Case 226/87: *Commission v Greece* [1988] ECR 3611, paras 10-12.
10 Case C-202/88: *France v Commission* [1991] ECR I-1223, paras 53-57; Cases C-48 and C-66/90: *Netherlands and PTT Nederland v Commission* [1992] ECR I-565, paras 25-35; Cases C-271, C-281 and C-289/90: *Spain v Commission* [1992] ECR I-5833, paras 23-27.

(2) AGREEMENTS BETWEEN UNDERTAKINGS

We have noted in the preceding chapter that the rules are addressed to 'undertakings'[11] and that the word has to be interpreted broadly to cover various kinds of entities and their associations.

There must be 'agreements', 'decisions' or 'concerted practices' between the undertakings. Agreements include not only contracts in the accepted sense but also broader understandings of a contractual type such as a 'gentlemen's agreement',[12] a mere meeting of minds[13] or the emergence of a common intention.[14] Conduct which merely forms part of an agreement – because it is envisaged or provided for in a provision of an agreement or because it arises in the context of the operation of a commercial arrangement (such as a selective distribution system) based on an agreement – falls within EC Article 81 (ex Art 85) even if, strictly speaking, the conduct was that of one undertaking only.[15] An agreement within the meaning of EC Article 81 (ex Art 85) may come into existence even if a party has adhered to it involuntarily.[16]

(3) DECISIONS

Decisions include resolutions by or recommendations of a trade association to its members irrespective of whether or not they are binding and whether or not the association has a legal personality. The very constitution of a trade association and any rules made thereunder may be regarded as decisions. Thus it was held that the following were decisions for the purpose of EC Article 81(1) (ex Art 85(1)): fixing of discounts by an association of undertakings;[17] making rules for exhibitions;[18] recommending prices and restrictive contract clauses to protect interests of dealers;[19] and collective boycott of a member of a Belgian association of manufacturers.[20] In the *Van Landewyck* case,[1] an association of cigarette and tobacco dealers in Belgium and Luxembourg made a number of decisions and drew up a recommendation for its members concerning such things as the grouping of wholesalers and retailers, maintenance of resale prices, restrictions on resales, and so forth. These measures were binding on the members of the association according to its rules. The fact that one (at least) of its members did not accept the restrictions did not exonerate it from responsibility for

---

11 See eg *Anne Marty SA v Estée Lauder SA* (Trib de Commerce, Paris), [1979] 3 CMLR 58.
12 In Case 69/240: *Re Quinine Cartel* [1969] CMLR D41; Case 74/634: *Re Franco-Japanese Ballbearings Agreement* [1975] 1 CMLR D8; Case 74/433: *Re FRUBO* [1974] 2 CMLR D89.
13 Case T-1/89: *Rhône-Poulenc v Commission* [1991] ECR II-867, para 120; Case T9/89: *Hüls v Commission* [1992] ECR II-499, para 291.
14 Eg Case T-141/94: *Thyssen Stahl AG v Commission* [1999] ECR II-347, para 262.
15 Case 107/82: *AEG v Commission* [1983] ECR 3151, [1984] 3 CMLR 325; Cases 25-26/84: *Ford v Commission* [1985] ECR 2725, [1985] 3 CMLR 528.
16 Cases 32/78 & 36-82/78: *BMW v Commission* [1979] ECR 2435, [1980] 1 CMLR 370, where the dealers concerned had little choice but to accept BMW's demands.
17 In Case 71/23: *Re German Ceramic Tiles discount Agreement* [1971] CMLR D6.
18 In Case 71/337: *Re CEMATEX* [1973] CMLR D135; see also in Case 79/37: *Re CECIMO* [1979] 1 CMLR 419.
19 Case 8/72: *Vereeniging van Cementhandelaren v Commission* [1972] ECR 977, [1973] CMLR 7 following Commission Decision; Case 72/22: [1973] CMLR D16.
20 In Case 74/431: *Re Groupement des Fabricants de Papiers Peints de Belgique* Commission Decision, [1974] CMLR D102.
1 Cases 209-215 and 218/78: *Van Landewyck v Commission* [1980] ECR 3125, [1981] 3 CMLR 134.

infringing Article 85 (now 81). The fact that the association was a non-profit-making organization without a commercial rôle of its own had no bearing on the case.[2] Decisions or recommendations of an association of associations of undertakings may also fall within the scope of EC Article 81(1) (ex Art 85(1)).[3]

(4) CONCERTED PRACTICES

A concerted practice was defined by the ECJ as 'a form of co-ordination between enterprises that has not yet reached the point where there is a contract in the true sense of the word but which, in practice, consciously substitutes a practical co-operation for the risks of competition . . .'.[4] In the *Sugar Cartel*[5] cases the Court amplified the concept of concerted practices, saying 'Although it is correct to say that this requirement of independence does not deprive economic operators of the right to adapt themselves intelligently to the existing and anticipated conduct of their competitors, it does however strictly preclude any direct or indirect contact between such operators the object or effect whereof is either to influence the conduct on the market of an actual or potential competitor or to disclose to such a competitor the course of conduct which they themselves have decided to adopt or contemplate adopting . . .'. It would seem that in order to constitute a concerted practice there must be a conscious effort on the part of the undertakings to act in a collective manner. Thus members of the Vegetable Parchment Association[6] were held to have engaged in a concerted practice in assisting their British member to retain control of the UK and Irish markets. The existence of a concerted practice is typically determined by reference to the behaviour of the alleged parties to the concerted practice; but, for that reason, a high standard of proof is required. A concerted practice may normally be inferred where there is proof of direct or indirect contact between the undertakings concerned, followed by parallel conduct, and there is no explanation of such parallel conduct other than the existence of concertation between them.[7] A particular form of conduct may be described as an agreement and a concerted practice without it being necessary to prove that it features the characteristics of both types of conduct.[8]

(5) AFFECTING TRADE

The agreements, decisions and concerted practices must be further tainted with the double vice of adversely affecting trade and distorting competition. The two characteristics are not alternative, they are cumulative. The requirement of an effect on trade between Member States is generally expressed as follows: 'it must be possible to foresee with a sufficient degree of probability on the basis of a set of objective factors of law or fact that it [the agreement, decision or concerted practice in question] may have an influence, direct or indirect, actual or potential,

2 Ibid, para 87-91.
3 Case 123/83: *BNIC v Clair* [1985] ECR 391, [1985] 2 CMLR 430.
4 Case 48/69: *ICI Ltd v Commission* [1972] ECR 619, [1972] CMLR 557.
5 Cases 40-48/73: [1975] ECR 1663, [1976] 1 CMLR 295.
6 Case 78/252: *The Community v Members of the Genuine Vegetable Parchment Association*, OJ 1978, 70/54, [1978] 1 CMLR 534. See also Commission Decisions: *Re Pioneer Hi-Fi Equipment* [1980] 1 CMLR 457 (hindrance of parallel imports) and 80/182: *Re Floral Düngemittelverkaufsgesellschaft* [1980] 2 CMLR 285 (use of joint subsidiary).
7 Cases T-1/89-T-4/89, T-6/89-T-15/89: *Rhône-Poulenc v Commission* [1991] ECR II-867, paras 121-123; Case T-9/89: *Hüls v Commission* [1992] ECR II-499, paras 293-295; Case C-199/92P: *Hüls v Commission* [1999] ECR I-4287, [1999] 5 CMLR 1016, paras 158-168.
8 Ibid, paras 127 and 299, respectively.

on the pattern of trade between Member States, such as might prejudice the realisation of the aim of a single market in all the Member States'.[9] The requirement of an effect on trade is a jurisdictional requirement; it is not intended to narrow down the type of industrial or commercial activity to which the competition rules apply.[10] It separates matters of Community concern from matters of concern to the domestic competition authorities of the Member States and from matters of concern to the competition authorities of states outside the Union.

Some difficulty arose early in connection with the interpretation of the word 'affect' (in the phrase used in the Treaty: 'affect trade between Member States') which revealed linguistic and conceptual nuances between the official languages of the Community and led Advocate-General Lagrange to suggest that the problem has to be considered in the spirit rather than the letter of the law.[11] 'Affect' means having a detrimental effect on the freedom of trade between the Member States by analogy to the inter-state commerce of the USA. In the context of the Common Market it means to undermine the unity of the market irrespective of whether the activity actually increases or decreases the volume of trade.[12] The effect is determined by reference to the operation of the agreement, decision or concerted practice as a whole, not by reference to any particular provision of it,[13] and by reference to the behaviour of all the parties, not any one of them.[14]

The 'trade' referred to is not any particular commercial activity, such as manufacture or distribution, involving the movement of goods or services across an internal Community frontier, but any form of economic activity which is capable of having a dimension going beyond a purely domestic context.[15] The most obvious form of effect on trade between Member States arises where the restrictive practice in question involves undertakings from more than one Member State which are in competition with each other in one or the other's domestic market, or in a market encompassing several Member States, or in the Community as a whole; or which trade with each other across an internal Community frontier. For example, in a case involving an exclusive dealer agreement between a German and a French company, the ECJ held[16] 'In the present case the contract . . . on the one hand by preventing undertakings other than Consten importing Grundig products into France, and on the other hand by prohibiting Consten from re-exporting those products to other countries of the Common Market, indisputably affects trade between Member States. These limitations on the freedom of trade, as well as those which might follow for third parties, from the registration in France . . . of the GINT trade mark, which Grundig places on all its products, suffice to satisfy the condition under discussion . . .'. At the other extreme are restrictive practices that are confined to the territory of one particular Member State. However, caution must be exercised before jumping to the conclusion that such arrangements do not involve an effect on trade between Member States. An agreement or practice which covers the entire territory of a Member State but which does not purport to extend

---

9   Eg Case C-250/92: *Gottrup-Klim v Dansk Landbrugs Grovvareselskab AmbA* [1994] ECR I-5641, para 54.

10 Cases 6 and 7/73: *Commercial Solvents v Commission* [1974] ECR 223, para 31.

11 Case 13/61: *Kledingverkoopbadrijf de Geus v Société Robert Bosch GmbH* [1962] ECR 45 [1962] CMLR 1.

12 Case 22/78: *Hugin v Commission* [1979] ECR 1869, [1979] 3 CMLR 345, para 17.

13 Case 193/83: *Windsurfing International Inc v Commission* [1986] ECR 611, [1986] 3 CMLR 489.

14 Case T-2/89: *Petrofina v Commission* [1991] ECR II-1087, paras 226-227.

15 Cf Case T-66/92: *Herlitz v Commission* [1994] ECR II-531 paras 31-33.

16 Cases 56 and 58/64: *Etablissements Consten SARL and Grundig-Verkaufs-GmbH v Commission* [1966] ECR 299, [1966] CMLR 418.

beyond it may well hold up the economic interpenetration which the Treaty is designed to bring about and thus affect trade between Member States.[17]

In the Dutch cement[18] cartel case the ECJ confirmed the Commission refusal to grant an exemption under Article 85(3). In doing so it disposed of the argument that the cartel, founded in 1928 with the object of making agreements and defending the interests of its members on the Dutch cement market, did not affect trade between Member States. The Court held: 'An agreement which extends to the whole of the territory of a Member State has, by its very nature, the effect of consolidating a national partitioning, thus hindering the economic interpenetration to which the Treaty is directed and ensuring a protection for the national production . . .'. That will be so because an arrangement covering the entire territory of a Member State affects the conditions of competition throughout that Member State and therefore the opportunities that undertakings from other Member States may have of competing in the State concerned. Trade may also be affected where the arrangement alters the structure of competition in the Community such as by causing the removal of an undertaking from a market.[19] The mere fact that the consequence, or a possible consequence, of an anti-competitive arrangement is to drive an undertaking, however small, out of a particular market or out of business altogether, is not necessarily a sufficient indication of an effect on trade between Member States. There must be some other factor, such as: the scale of the victim's presence in inter-state trade or the effect of its disappearance on that trade; or, if the victim does not engage at all in inter-state trade, its significance in the economy of the Member State in which it is (or was) active and the opportunities that its disappearance may give to competitors (particularly undertakings in other Member States); or the fact that the anti-competitive arrangement in question will prevent or deter other undertakings from entering the market. In that connexion, it is important to note that the required effect on trade between Member States is not limited to an effect on trade flows between Member States but encompasses effects on the ability of undertakings to enter into a market in another Member State whether by supplying goods or services to a purchaser in that Member State or by establishing themselves in that State.[20] In Case 45/85: *Verband der Sachversicherer v Commission*[1] the ECJ held that an arrangement fixing fire insurance premiums in Germany affected inter-state trade because it was capable of making it more difficult for foreign insurers to enter the German market.[2] An

---

17 Case 8/72: *Vereeninging van Cementhandelaren v Commission* [1972] ECR 977, paras 29-30, [1973] CMLR 7; Case 61/80: *Cooperature Stremsel-en v Commission* [1981] ECR 851, [1982] 1 CMLR 240; Case T-66/89: *Publishers Association v Commission (No 2)* [1992] ECR II-1995, paras 55-57.

18 Case 8/72, note 17, supra.

19 Cases 6 and 7/73: *Commercial Solvents Corpn v Commission* [1974] ECR 223, [1974] 1 CMLR 309, para 31.

20 Eg Cases C-215/96 and C-216/96: *Bagnasco v Banco Populare di Novava et al* [1999] ECR I-135, para 51.

1 [1987] ECR 405, see paras 15 to 19 of the Advocate-General's Opinion and paras 44-50 of the judgment.

2 Para 48 of the judgment is occasionally cited as authority for the proposition that an effect on the financial relationship between a subsidiary in one Member State and its parent company in another Member State (such as an effect on the subsidiary's profits or on the dividends passed to its parents) is an effect on inter-state trade. The better view is that the judgment does not go that far. The situation in that case was that contracts of insurance entered into by the German branch of a foreign insurer would have an immediate impact on the financial situation of the latter, which would have to meet claims made on the policies issued by the branch. The foreign insurer would finance the payment of claims out of its reserves and its premium income. The fixing of premiums in Germany would therefore effect the foreign insurer's competitive position.

effect on trade between Member States may arise not only where the arrangement covers an entire Member State but also where it takes the form of a single agreement, or a network of similar agreements, or even a series of networks of similar agreements, that tie up a significant part of the market in a Member State and thereby render access to that market uneconomic or very difficult, or make it impossible for a competitor already in the market to increase its market share. Two examples of that situation are beer supply (or tied house) agreements and exclusive agreements for the retail sale of ice cream. The former typically involve the grant by a brewery of a tenancy of premises owned by the brewery on terms that the premises will be used as a retail outlet for the sale of beverages to be consumed on the premises. The tenant agrees to obtain all or a part of the beverages to be sold on the premises from the brewer (or a supplier nominated by the brewer). The ice cream supply agreements were agreements entered into by a manufacturer or distributor of certain ice cream products with individual retailers whereby the latter agreed to sell the products of the former and no similar products supplied by a competitor of the former. As an inducement, the manufacturer or distributor of the ice cream might offer the retailer a freezer on generous terms subject to the condition that the freezer would not be used to contain the products of a competitor. Taken individually, both types of agreement could not have any effect on trade between Member States because it is highly unlikely that a competitor based in another Member State would be prevented or deterred in any way from competing in the Member State concerned merely by reason of the fact that one particular public house or one particular retail outlet, somewhere in that Member State, has been signed up by a competitor. However, where such agreements form part of a network of similar agreements made by the same brewer or, as the case may be, manufacturer or distributor of ice cream, or where other brewers or manufacturers or distributors of ice cream adopt the same policy of making such agreements, their effect is magnified and they may then affect inter-state trade.[3] Even so, an effect on trade between Member States may be avoided if the agreement gives the retailer a real opportunity to sell competing products.[4]

Two further aspects of the effect on inter-state trade must be considered before dealing with the question whether or not the effect must be significant: the effect may be 'direct or indirect' and 'actual or potential'.

A direct effect on inter-state trade arises where the anti-competitive arrangement has an immediate impact upon such trade. In such a case, the arrangement operates in the context of a market in which inter-state trade is possible or actually exists. However, it is well-established that the required effect on inter-state trade need not appear in the market for the products to which the anti-competitive arrangement applies. The usual illustrations of that proposition are cases concerning anti-competitive conduct in relation to a product that is not itself the subject of inter-state trade but that is incorporated in or transformed into a product that is the subject of inter-state trade. For example, in Case 123/83: *BNIC v Clair*,[5] the arrangement in question affected the price of a semi-finished product (spirits used for blending) which was not traded between Member States

---

3   See Case C-234/89: *Delimitis v Henninger Brau* [1991] ECR I-935, in particular paras 27, 31 and 33, and the earlier cases, like Case 23/67: *Brasserie de Haecht v Wilkin and Wilkin* [1967] ECR 407, [1968] CMLR 26 and Case 43/69: *Bilger Fehle* [1970] ECR 127, [1974] 1 CMLR 382, for beer supply agreements; and Case T-7/93: *Langnese-Iglo GmbH v Commission* [1995] ECR II-1553, paras 119-123 (upheld on appeal in Case C-279/95P: *Langrese-Iglo GmbH v Commission* [1998] ECR I-5609) for ice cream agreements.

4   The *Delimitis* case, supra.

5   [1985] ECR 391, [1985] 2 CMLR 430, paras 28-30.

but which was used for the production of another product (cognac) that was traded between Member States. The arrangement was therefore capable of affecting trade between Member States. The case-law goes as far as establishing that an effect in the market for the product (or products) to which the anti-competitive arrangement applies and any contiguous product market (essentially, that for any product in, or into, which the former product is incorporated or transformed directly) is sufficient. By the same process of reasoning, there seems to be no difficulty of principle in accepting that it is sufficient if the anti-competitive arrangement affects a product derived from a raw material that is the subject of inter-state trade. The case-law does not establish with any degree of clarity whether or not a looser connexion with other markets may also be sufficient, such as a market for a product that incorporates an intermediate product that itself incorporates the product to which the anti-competitive arrangement relates. The case-law also sheds little light on the question whether or not there is an effect on trade between Member States where, for example, an anti-competitive arrangement in one product market (in relation to which there is no conceivable effect on inter-state trade) may affect a completely unrelated market (from the viewpoint of the products involved) because an undertaking affected by the arrangement has a presence in that other market and, by being made richer or poorer in the first market, will alter its competitive performance in the second market and thereby affect inter-state trade.

It is occasionally said that the question whether or not the conditions for applying the competition rules have been satisfied depends upon complex economic assessments.[6] Largely for that reason, the Treaty does not require evidence of an actual effect on inter-state trade; a 'potential' effect will suffice. In order to decide whether or not there is a 'potential' effect, it is sufficient to ask if the anti-competitive arrangement is capable of having the required effect.

However, the effect, actual or potential, must not be insignificant. In *Völk v Vervaecke*[7] the ECJ, pronouncing upon the validity of a contract to sell German washing machines in Belgium and Luxembourg, held that: 'to be capable of affecting trade between Member States, the agreement must, on the basis of a collection of objective legal or factual factors, permit a reasonable expectation that it could exercise an influence, direct or indirect, actual or potential, on the trade trends between Member States in a direction which would harm the attainment of the objectives of a single market between States . . .'. Therefore, an agreement escapes the prohibition of EC Article 81 (ex Art 85) when it only affects the market insignificantly, account being taken of 'the weak position held by the parties on the market in the product in question . . .'. The significant or insignificant effect of an arrangement is usually gauged by reference to the size in absolute terms (that is, by reference to turnover) or relative terms (market share) of the parties to the arrangement. In order to fall outside the scope of EC Article 81 (ex Art 85), an arrangement must be insignificant by reference to both measures, not just any one of them. The test of significance focuses on the size of the participants in the arrangement and not by reference to the concrete effects of the arrangement for two main reasons: first, any behaviour involving an undertaking with a significant presence in the market can properly be regarded as significant (if it were not significant, a relatively large undertaking would

6 Eg, the *Bagnasco* case (supra, p 658, note 20) para 50.
7 Case 5/69: [1969] ECR 295, [1969] CMLR 273; see also Case 1/71: *Cadillon v Höss* [1971] ECR 351, [1971] CMLR 420 and Case 22/71: *Belguelin Import v GL Import/Export SA*, ibid 949.

presumably not bother to engage in it); secondly it is easier to gauge significance by reference to the size of the undertakings involved because, as a result of the complexity of commercial and economic life, it is often very difficult to get a firm idea of the effect in practice of a particular form of behaviour.[8] However, the mere fact an anti-competitive arrangement can be described as significant by reason of the position of the parties, whether stated in absolute or relative terms, is not always a sure indication that there is a significant affect on inter-state trade. For example, in Case T-77/94: *Vereniging van Groothandelaren in Bloemkwekerijproduklen v Commission*,[9] the undertakings involved sold to wholesalers whereas the agreements at issue concerned retailers. Accordingly, the CFI was unwilling to conclude, without further investigation, that the size of the undertakings (at wholesale level) was a sufficient indication of a significant effect on inter-state trade at the retail level.

Some assistance on the question of the significance of effect on inter-state trade (and on competition) is provided by the Commission's notice on agreements of minor importance.[10] In a notice published in 1986, an arrangement was usually said to lack significance if the aggregate size of the participating undertakings was less than ECU 200 million in terms of turnover (ECU 300 million from 1994) *and* if their aggregate market share was less than 5%. Those figures were to be taken as indicators and not as expressing a uniform rule.[11] The current notice is also indicative only but is based on market share and not turnover. An arrangement is regarded as outside the prohibition in EC Article 81(1) (ex Art 85(1)) if the aggregate market shares of the participating undertakings in all relevant markets does not exceed 5% (in the case of horizontal arrangements, that is, those between undertakings operating at the same level of production or marketing), 10% (in the case of vertical arrangements, that is, those between undertakings operating at different economic levels) or 5% (in the case of mixed horizontal/vertical arrangements or those which it is difficult to classify). At first sight, the notice excludes reference to markets in which the parties to the arrangement have no market share at all. For example, suppose that there is a price-fixing cartel of electricity distributors in a Member State without an electricity interconnector with another Member State (or an interconnector with very low capacity) and suppose that the distributors have no other commercial interests. On that hypothesis, there is no possibility of any or any significant trade between Member States in electricity; and the members of the cartel have no market share in any other market. Does that mean that the price-fixing cartel must be regarded as significant, and therefore outside the prohibition in EC Article 81(1) (ex Art 85(1)) even though the distributors can, by charging very high prices for electricity, seriously distort competition between industrial users of electricity and thereby seriously affect inter-state trade in the goods that they produce? Intuitively, the answer is in the negative. The notice must therefore be treated with some caution.

Finally we should note that the concept of inter-state trade does not confine the scope of the competition rules to arrangements that are wholly limited to the

---

8   Case 99/79: *Lancôme SA and Cosparfrance Nederland BV v Etos BV and Albert Heijn Supermart BV* [1980] ECR 2511, [1981] 2 CMLR 164, para 24.

9   [1997] ECR II-759, para 139.

10 OJ 1997, C 372/13. That notice replaced an earlier notice published in OJ 1986, C 231/2, as amended by OJ 1994, C 368/20.

11 For example, the ECJ accepted that, in relative terms, activities of the order of 5% were significant in Case 19/77: *Miller v Commission* [1978] ECR 131, [1978] 2 CMLR 334; in Cases 100-103/80: *Musique Diffusion Française v Commission* [1983] ECR 1825, [1983] 3 CMLR 221, lower figures were regarded as significant.

geographical area of the Common Market. This inference can be drawn from the *Grossfillex-Fillisdorf Agreement*[12] where a French firm granted a Swiss firm exclusive selling rights in Switzerland in respect of goods produced in the Common Market. Therefore the object was not to affect trade within the Common Market. However, the agreement prohibited the Swiss firm from selling in the Common Market not only products covered therein but also any other products likely to compete with them irrespective of the origin of the competing products. The Commission granted negative clearance because there was ample competition in the market for household and sanitary plastic goods covered by the agreement. Moreover, should the products delivered in Switzerland return to the Common Market they would cross a new customs frontier and, therefore, would be unlikely to compete with the same goods delivered directly in the territory of the Common Market. However, this case sounded a warning against agreements by which distributors outside the Community would prohibit export of goods back into the Common Market. A similar conclusion was reached in Case C-306/96: *Javico International v Yves Saint Laurent Parfums SA*.[13] As stated by the ECJ in another context[14] 'The Community authorities must . . . consider all the consequences of the conduct complained of for the competitive structure of the Common Market without distinguishing between production intended for sale within the market and that intended for export . . .'.

(6) RESTRAINTS ON COMPETITION

The object or effect of the offending practice must be the 'prevention, restriction or distortion of competition'. How this occurs will be demonstrated by examples from practice for the study of the competition rules is in reality a study of case law. Clearly the existence and the severity of the actual or potential threat to the free market is a matter of fact in each case though, as far as the Court is concerned, the legal rather than economic analysis of the relevant factors will take precedence. The Commission assisted by its experts should give precedence to economic argument. In this way the two institutions contribute, in their specific areas, to a pragmatic development of the law.

'Prevention, restriction and distortion' seem to indicate a descending order of restraint on competition. To prevent competition means to stop it occurring or eliminating it. To restrict competition means to blunt the edges of rivalry or limit competition quantitatively or geographically, whilst to distort competition means to put it out of shape, thus placing the parties into an unequal position. All three key words imply a manipulation of the market in a manner which is improper or unlawful. It seems, however, that all three could have been adequately

---

12   JO 1964, [1964] CMLR 237.
13   [1998] ECR I-1983, which concerned an agreement made between two undertakings within the EC about the distribution of goods outside the EC, the agreement containing a prohibition on the sale of the goods within the EC. The ECJ held that such an agreement could be caught by EC Art 85(1) (now Art 81(1)) if there was a real possibility that the goods could and would otherwise be sold in the EC (such as if the market in the EC were oligopolistic, there were an appreciable price difference between the price for the goods inside and outside the EC, and if the volumes sold outside the EC, and capable of being sold in the EC, were appreciable). See also *Re SABA* JO 1975, C 28/19, [1976] 1 CMLR D61, where the Commission granted an exemption to a distribution contract having noted that the principal had undertaken to remove a prohibition on exports to non-member countries. It seems that a total ban on export out of or import into the Common Market would contravene the competition rules.
14   Case 6-7/73: *Commercial Solvents Corpn v Commission* [1974] ECR 223, [1974] CMLR 309.

represented by one, ie 'restraint' on competition (as is, for example, the position in Germany),[15] without adverse effect on the sharpness of the law. Another point of difference, which characterizes EC law as compared with German law, is that whilst under the latter a prohibited practice has to contain a legal obligation to restrain competition ('control theory'), the former is concerned with the 'object or effect' of a practice upon competition ('result theory'). Moreover, as indicated by the word 'may' in EC Article 81 (ex Art 85) it is sufficient, in the EC system, that there is a potential threat to competition.[16] Parties may, therefore, be in breach of EC Article 81 (ex Art 85) even if they have not executed their designs,[17] and if the arrangement is merely 'capable' of being anti-competition.[18]

If an arrangement is shown to have an anti-competitive 'object', there is no need to prove that it also has such an 'effect'; conversely, if there is no evidence of an intent to harm competition, the effect of the arrangement must then be considered.[19] The distinction between 'object' and 'effect' should not, however, be regarded as nothing more than a distinction between 'intention' and 'effect'. Object is not the same as intention. The distinction between object and effect has been explained as differentiating between arrangements which, viewed objectively and in the abstract, have no other function than to restrict freedom of competition between the parties or between them and third parties (such arrangements being anti-competitive by reason of their 'object') and arrangements that are capable of performing a more complex function (such arrangements being anti-competitive by reason of their 'effect', if at all).[20] The distinction is perhaps best explained as reflecting a temporal problem rather than an attempt to classify anti-competitive arrangements into what could be described as 'bare' restrictions of competition and 'more complex' arrangements: in many instances, particularly where an arrangement has been notified to the Commission at an early stage for the purpose of obtaining a negative clearance or an exemption, it may not be possible to determine the effect of the arrangement in practice. Thus, in many respects (but not all) examination of an agreement by reference to its 'object' is akin to examination *ex ante* (before it takes effect) whereas examination by reference to its effect is examination *ex post* (after it has taken effect). Examination by reference to its 'object' is therefore examination by reference to its anticipated effect rather than its actual effect. Apart from the temporal reason for such an approach, there are many instances in which examination by reference to actual effect would be difficult or impossible or yield uncertain results because of the complexity of economic and commercial life. Examination by reference to object, or anticipated effect, is therefore a useful device. It has, however, the disadvantage that it may produce theoretical results which may not be borne out in practice. On the other hand, it is often a matter of complaint that the competition authorities have condemned an arrangement because of some factor resulting from its practical effects which was not or could not have been envisaged when the arrangement was entered into (and thus which fell outside its 'object'). That, however, is a point that may be relevant to the treatment of the parties to the

---

15 Deringer, A, 'Inhalt and Auswerkungen der ersten Kartellverordnung der europäischen Wirtschaftsgemeinschaft', GRUR, AIT, 1962, p 292.
17 Eg *Re WEA-Filigacchi Music SA, Commission Decision* [1973] CMLR D43.
18 Case C-219/95P: *Ferriere Nord v Commission* [1997] ECR I-4411, para 19.
19 Cases 56 and 58/64: *Etablissements Consten and Grundig v Commission* [1966] ECR 299 at 342; the *Cooperatieve Stremsel* case, supra, paras 12-13; Case 56/65: *Société Technique Minière v Maschinenbau Ulm* [1966] ECR 235 at 249, [1966] CMLR 357.
20 Case C-250/92: *Gottrup-Kilm v Dansk Landbrugs Grovvareselskab* [1994] ECR I-5641, Advocate-General's Opinion para 16.

arrangement as to the past (such as whether they should be fined or required to pay damages to injured third parties); it may not be sufficient to prevent the termination, as to the future, of what has proved to be an anti-competitive arrangement.

In broad terms, a restriction of competition can be expressed as a fettering of the commercial freedom of an undertaking,[1] and the provisions of an arrangement can, for the purpose of determining its compatibility with EC Article 81 (ex Art 85), profitably be analysed by simply identifying those terms which fetter the freedom of a party to the agreement or a third party. Having said that, however, things do not rest there. In certain situations, arrangements which involve a fettering of the commercial freedom of an undertaking have been regarded as falling outside the scope of EC Article 81(1) (ex Art 85(1)) because the overall effect of the arrangement was to enhance competition in the market. Thus, a provision in an agreement for the sale of a business, which restricts the vendor from competing with the purchaser for a reasonable period of time after the sale, does not cause the agreement to fall within EC Article 81(1) (ex Art 85(1)) because it is an essential part of such a transaction and the sale of a business is not intrinsically anti-competitive;[2] so-called 'simple' selective distribution systems fall outside the scope of EC Article 81(1) (ex Art 85(1)) because, although they distort competition by limiting the number of outlets through which goods are sold, the resultant limitation of competition as between sellers of the goods in question ('intra-brand competition') is outweighed by the beneficial effect on competition between those goods and competing products (inter-brand competition);[3] and, where a restriction of a person's freedom of action is a necessary counterpart of receiving some benefit enabling that person to compete (as in the case of an agreement for the letting of retail premises for the purpose of selling the lessor's goods), the pro-competitive effects of the benefit may be sufficient to prevent the arrangement as a whole from falling within the scope of EC Article 81(1) (ex Art 85(1)).[4] Further some forms of behaviour are regarded as anti-competitive not so much because they fetter the commercial freedom of another undertaking as because they are simply damaging to the other undertaking's business (as in the case of state aids) or to the interests of consumers.

In the *Consten-Grundig* case the applicant argued that EC Article 81(1) (ex Art 85(1)) applied only to 'horizontal agreements', ie between parties operating at the same economic level, and the Italian government suggested that sole distributorship contracts 'do not constitute agreements between undertakings' as envisaged by EC Article 81(1) (ex Art 85(1)) concluding that the freedom of

---

1 'Restriction' is commonly used in a more general sense. In Case C-7/95P: *John Deere Ltd v Commission* [1998] ECR I-3111, paras 85-91, the ECJ upheld the view that the exchange of information between certain suppliers in the market was a 'restriction' of competition not because it fettered any commercial freedom of the undertakings concerned but because it reduced the degree of uncertainty in the market regarding the behaviour of competitors.

2 Case 42/84: *Remia BV v Commission* [1985] ECR 2545, [1981] 1 CMLR 1. However, the sale of a business may be anti-competitive if it results in an unacceptable degree of concentration in the market and, in such circumstances, a restriction on competition from the vendor could fall within the scope of EC Art 85(1) (now 81(1)).

3 Case 107/82: *AEG v Commission* [1983] ECR 3151, [1984] 3 CMLR 325, paras 40-43. For a description of 'simple' selective distribution systems, see p 683, infra.

4 Case C-234/89: *Delimitis v Henninger Bräu* [1991] ECR I-935, paras 10 et seq: it is therefore necessary to examine the economic context of the agreement in order to determine whether or not it is anti-competitive; the presence of a restriction in the agreement is not enough to conclude that it is anti-competitive.

competition in that field was protected by EC Article 82 (ex Art 86). However, the ECJ would have none of this and held[5] . . . 'Neither the wording of Article 85 nor that of Article 86 gives any ground for holding that distinct areas of application are to be assigned to each of the two articles according to the level in the economy at which the contracting parties operate. Article 85 refers in a general way to all agreements which distort competition with the Common Market and does not lay down any distinction between those agreements based on whether they are made between competitors operating at the same level in the economic process or between non-competing persons operating at different levels.' It follows that, as confirmed by the Court in the *Ulm*[6] case, a contract granting an exclusive right of sale may be caught by EC Article 81(1) (ex Art 85(1)) irrespective or whether it is 'horizontal' or 'vertical'. In the latter case the parties are at a different level in the economic process, eg supplier and customer or patent holder and licensee.

C. Examples of prohibited practices

(1) PRICE FIXING AND TRADING CONDITIONS (EC ARTICLE 81(1)(A) (EX ART 85(1)(A))

Where one undertaking sells goods or services to another and, in the contract of sale, the price of the goods or services to be supplied is stipulated, the result is that the price has been fixed by an agreement between undertakings. That form of activity is not generally of concern to the EC competition rules to the extent that its immediate effects are felt only as between the purchaser and seller of the goods or services in question. The position is different where two or more undertakings agree on the price at which each shall supply its own goods or services to one or more third parties; or, where one undertaking agrees with another the price at which the latter shall supply goods or services to third parties (whether or not they have been obtained from the former). In this context, agreements on certain aspects of the price of goods or services, such as discounts and rebates, are as much of concern as agreements affecting directly and immediately the price of goods or services. By the same token, where one undertaking sells goods or services to another and, in the context of sale, stipulates terms of sale (other than price, such as place of delivery), relating only to the supply of the goods or services in question to the purchaser, that form of activity is not of concern to the EC competition rules. The position is different where the agreed terms of sale purport to regulate the future supply of the goods, or services, by the purchasers, to other persons, or where the agreement fetters the freedom of each undertaking to settle its own terms of sale with third parties. In all of the situations described, EC competition law applies either because the undertakings in question have effectively agreed as between themselves not to compete with each other on price (or other terms of sale) or have agreed how the goods or services in question shall compete in a downstream market, ignoring the operation of market forces. The same reasoning applies where the fixing of prices or trading conditions relates to the purchase of goods or services.[7]

---

5 P 663, note 19; CMLR at 434.
6 P 663, note 19; see also Decisions in Case 77/66: *Re application of Gerofabrik NV* [1977] 1 CMLR D35 and in Case 77/129: *Theal NV and Cecil Watts* [1977] 1 CMLR D44; and Case 28/77: *TEPEA v Commission* [1978] 3 CMLR 392.
7 See eg *Re Aluminium Imports from Eastern Europe*, OJ 1985, L9211, [1987] 3 CMLR 813, para 40.

In the *Quinine Cartel*[8] case a number of undertakings were involved in the division of national markets in Germany and the Netherlands as well as the fixing of prices and quotas for the export of quinine and quinidine to all other countries of the Common Market. Following an inquiry by the German *Bundeskartellamt* they concluded a new agreement providing for the fixing of prices and rebates applicable to exports; the allocation of export quotas and the reservation of certain markets outside the Community; the retention of the clause making the agreement inapplicable to exports in the Common Market; a system of compensatory quantities in the event of export quotas being exceeded or unfulfilled; and the prohibition of collaboration outside the Common Market with undertakings which were not parties to the agreement. Further agreements followed relating to the joint purchase of raw materials, a general price increase and the purchase of reserves from the American stockpile. The Commission, having carried out an investigation and having discussed the position with the parties, withdrew some of its objections (ie to the stockpile agreement) but imposed fines upon certain undertakings against which they appealed to the ECJ.

The ECJ[9] dismissed the appeal against the decision but annulled a part of it and reduced the fines and ordered the applicants to pay the costs of the proceedings. In particular the ECJ found the following to be in contravention of EC Article 81 (ex Art 85): sharing out of domestic markets, fixing of common prices, determination of sale quotas and prohibition against manufacturing synthetic quinidine. A less complex system of price fixing, but affecting the position in different Member States, was condemned in the *Imperial Chemical Industries Ltd*[10] case.

In *Bulloch & Co v Distillers*[11] the Commission condemned a dual pricing system and conditions of sale under which British dealers had to forego discounts on whisky sold for export.

Even direct influence on pricing policy may be prohibited as indicated by the Commission in *Re IFTRA*[12] where the rules of a producers' association were treated as an 'agreement'. In that case the parties agreed not to sell below their published prices and agreed to exchange information regarding the prices charged.

An agreement to fix maximum buying prices appears also to be prohibited as suggested in *Re Industrial Timber*[13] where, following the Commission's investigation, the parties abandoned the practice.

The fact that several undertakings apply the same or similar prices is not necessarily indicative of an agreement or concerted practice between them to fix prices: at least in markets where there are only a few competitors producing homogeneous products, a similarity in pricing may well result from the structure of the market instead of from an agreement or practice between the undertakings concerned. In such cases, further evidence (such as meetings between the undertakings or the exchange of information concerning prices) will be required before it can be concluded that EC Article 81(1) (ex Art 85(1)) has been

---

8   Commission Decision 69/240: [1969] CMLR D41.
9   Case 45/69: *Boehringer Mannheim v Commission* [1970] ECR 769.
10 P 656, note 4.
11 Decision 78/163: [1978] 1 CMLR 400; upheld by the ECJ in Case 30/78: *Distillers Co v Commission* [1980] ECR 2229, [1980] 3 CMLR 121; see also Decision 78/697: *Re the Notification by William Teacher & Sons Ltd* [1978] 3 CMLR 290; see also *Re Agreements of the Distillers Co* [1980] 1 CMLR 541.
12 *Rules for Producers of Virgin Aluminium* OJ 1975, L228/3, Case 75/497: [1975] 2 CMLR D20.
13 [1976] 1 CMLR D11.

infringed.[14] In a number of markets, the ability of undertakings to compete on price may be limited in some way by state action (such as price control legislation). Where such action completely precludes price competition between undertakings, the remedy is action against the state itself; where competition is not prevented, any attempt by undertakings to reduce further the play of competition by agreement, decision or concerted practice is prohibited by EC Article 81(1) (ex Art 85(1)).[15]

The extent to which agreements to exchange information on prices may restrain competition was also considered in *Re IFTRA*.[16] Whilst in accordance with the 1968 Notice on Co-operation Agreements,[17] the exchange of statistical data is permitted, the exchange of information regarding the competitors' prices may not be so. The reason seems to be that if these prices are known there is no incentive for price reduction. The position was clarified in *Re COBELPA*[18] where the Commission raised no objection to a general exchange of statistical data regarding the industry's production and sales provided by the national association provided that individual firms remained anonymous and could not be identified. The condition of anonymity would be breached if invoices were sent on an individual basis thus bringing the firms into the open in an exercise unnecessary for the preparation of trade statistics.[19] The giving of information to competitors relating to 'trade secrets' would amount to a prohibited concerted practice.

The fixing of trading conditions other than price does not invariably result in an infringement of EC Article 81(1) (ex Art 85(1)). The concern arises in respect of those trading conditions relating to the price paid for the goods or services provided (credit terms, interest charges) or to the nature or quality of what is to be supplied by the undertakings concerned (agreements on the guarantees to be provided or on the type or standard of product to be supplied).[20] Agreements relating to certain aspects of business, such as bank opening hours, may cause no difficulty because of their minimal effect on competition.[1]

(2) LIMITATION OF PRODUCTION, MARKETS, TECHNICAL DEVELOPMENTS OR INVESTMENT (EC ARTICLE 81(1)(B) (EX ART 85(1)(B)))

The effect of the above is to restrict, by agreement, both industrial expansion and competition, typically through agreed limits on the quantities produced or

---

14 See eg *Re Zinc Producer Group*, OJ 1984, L220/27, [1985] 2 CMLR 108; Cases 29-30/83: *CRAM and Rheinzink v Commission* [1984] ECR 1679, [1985] 1 CMLR 688.

15 Cases 209-215 and 218/78: *Van Landewyck v Commission* [1980] ECR 3125, [1981] 3 CMLR 134, paras 130-134.

16 P 666, note 12.

17 See now OJ 2000, C 3/2.

18 Decisions 77/592: *Vereeninging van Nederlandsche Papierfabrikanten (VNP) and the association des fabricants de pates, papiers et cartons de Belgique (COBELPA)* [1977] 2 CMLR D28; see also Case 79/90: *Community v Associated Lead Manufacturers Ltd* [1979] 1 CMLR 464 (exchange of information incompatible with EC Art 81(1) (ex Art 85(1))).

19 Commission Decision in Case 78/252: *Community v Genuine Vegetable Parchment* OJ 1978, L70/54, [1978] 1 CMLR 534.

20 See eg *Re Video Cassette Records*, OJ 1978, L47/42, [1978] 2 CMLR 160; Case 246/86: *Belasco v Commission* [1989] ECR 2117, paras 29-30. Agreements on the development of standards may, however, be beneficial and can be exempted from prohibition: see eg *The X/Open Group*, OJ 1987, L35/36, [1988] 4 CMLR 542.

1 *Re Irish Banks Standing Committee*, OJ 1986, L295/28, [1987] 2 CMLR 601. See Cases C-215/96 and C-216/96: *Bagnesco v Banca Popolare di Novara et al* [1999] ECR I-135, paras 35-37, for other examples.

supplied by undertakings (quotas) and agreements to limit investment whether in new plant or research and development. Limitations of production were considered in the *Quinine Cartel*[2] and *ACF-Chemiefarma*[3] cases. Even where there is no express agreement setting quotas, the fact that the undertakings concerned have agreed to exchange sales information between themselves may be regarded as anti-competitive because it makes it possible for each undertaking to react to its competitors' intentions in good time and may therefore result in a de facto quota arrangement.[4]

Such arrangements are occasionally made in order to cope with an excess of production capacity over demand in the market. Where over-capacity reflects a structural problem in the market and not the fact that the economic cycle has reached a particular (low) point, there may be a case for obtaining an exemption from prohibition.[5] The reason is that, if production capacity exceeds demand merely because the market is in recession, the problem is in principle temporary and market forces should be allowed to take effect. Those undertakings which are basically healthy will survive and, when the economic cycle moves on, conditions for new entry will be more propitious. On the other hand, if the problem is structural, it results from the fact that the industry in question is in decline: the fall in demand is permanent, not temporary, because the need for the product in question has diminished and will never reach its former levels whatever point is reached in the economic cycle.[6]

In this context the problem of limitation of production in pursuance of a specialization scheme arises. If the objective is genuine the decision may qualify for individual[7] exemption or for a group exemption.[8] In the absence of a ground for exemption the agreement would constitute a restraint.

Agreements to limit technical developments or investments have a similar effect but these too may qualify for exemption. As for the 'limitation of markets'[9] there seems to be no good reason for this particular label since it seems to overlap with the category discussed below.

(3) SHARING MARKETS OR SOURCES OF SUPPLY (EC ARTICLE 81(1)(C) (EX ART 85(1)(C)))

In this category fall both horizontal and vertical restraints. The former cover geographical cartels extending even beyond the boundaries of the Community in so far as they affect exports from and imports into the Community.[10] Vertical

---

2   P 666, note 8.
3   Case 41/69: [1970] ECR 661.
4   See *Re White Lead*, OJ 1979, L21/16, [1979] 1 CMLR 464. See also *Re VNP and Cobelpa*, OJ 1977, L242/10, [1977] 2 CMLR D28; *Re Fatty Acids*, OJ 1987, L3/17, [1989] 4 CMLR 445.
5   See eg *Re Synthetic Fibres Agreement (No 2)*, OJ 1984, L207/17, [1985] 1 CMLR 787.
6   Eg the introduction of metal tools in prehistoric times had a devastating impact on the production of flint implements from which the flint-producing industry in places such as Grimes' Graves in England never recovered.
7   Eg Decisions 69/241: *Re Clima/Chappée's Agreement* [1970] CMLR D7; *Papier mince* JO 1972, L182/24; 69/242: *Re Jaz SA's Agreement* JO 1968, C 75/3, [1970] CMLR 129; 78/194: *Re Jaz Peter Uhren Agreement* [1978] 2 CMLR 186.
8   Reg 2658/2000 (OJ 2000, L304/3).
9   Eg *Consten and Grundig* p 663, note 19; Decision 70/488: *Re Omega Watches* [1970] CMLR D49.
10 Eg *Quinine Cartel*, p 666, note 8, p 214; Case 41/69: *ACF Chemiefarma v Commission* [1970] ECR 661; Case 44/69: *Bucher v Commission* [1970] ECR 733 at 735, and 758-9; *Boehringer*, p 666, note 9; Cases C-89, C-104, C-114, C-116, C-117 and C-125-129/85: *A Ahlström Osakeyhtio v Commission* [1993] ECR I-1307, para 176.

restraints comprise exclusive distribution agreements where for example the manufacturer imposes upon the distributor a ban on exporting the product outside the designated area;[11] exclusive agency agreements;[12] restraints imposed by a patent or trademark holder upon the licensee.[13] Certain types of vertical agreements are exempted.[14] But, in principle, such agreements are prohibited. In addition to export bans and the like set out in agreements between undertakings, the sharing of markets may be affected by conduct whereby undertakings refrain from penetrating each other's markets[15] and by agreements or practices whereby undertakings raise barriers to entry.[16] Market sharing may be effected not only on a geographical basis but also by reference to particular distribution channels or different classes of customer. In some instances, the question whether or not the parties to an agreement have agreed to share markets or sources of supply turns on the true meaning of a particular clause of the agreement. When answering that question, account must be taken of the wording of the clause, the factual and legal context and, where appropriate, the manner in which the agreement has been applied by the parties.[17]

(4) DISSIMILAR CONDITIONS TO EQUIVALENT TRANSACTIONS (EC ARTICLE 81(1)(D) (EX ART 85(1)(D)))

Under this rubric fall practices leading to discrimination not against competitors but against customers or suppliers. Such discrimination, through applying different conditions to equivalent transactions, may be individual or collective, but in either case it is prohibited if it places the persons against whom it is directed at a competitive disadvantage. Thus in the *Distillers*[18] case a system of dual pricing as well as the export ban which it replaced was held by the Commission to be unlawful. Similarly, in *Re CIMBEL*[19] as regards subsidies of exports of cement at the expense of domestic sales. Another form of discrimination prohibited by EC Article 81(1) (ex Art 85(1)) is discrimination in the organization of trade fairs.[20]

In *Re Groupement des Fabricants Papier Peints de Belgique*[1] the Commission had to consider, inter alia, the effect of a collective boycott. It found that the Association of Belgian manufacturers of wallpaper set up a comprehensive

---

11 *Consten and Grundig*, p 663, note 11; *Ulm*, ibid.
12 Eg Case 72/403: *Re Pittsburg Corning Europe* [1973] CMLR D2; *Sugar Cartel* cases, p 656, note 5.
13 Eg Case 193/83 *Windsurfing International Inc v Commission* [1986] ECR 611, [1986] 3 CMLR 489.
14 See pp 620–621. The general approach to vertical agreements is now set out in the Commission's guidelines on vertical restraints: OJ 2000, C 291/1.
15 There may be a good reason why an undertaking refrains from entering another undertaking's market (such as insufficient commercial incentives, lack of initiative, lack of knowledge of local peculiarities, the existence of anti-competitive practices operated by other undertakings). As a result, in addition to establishing the existence of an agreement or concerted practice, it must also be demonstrated that there is no explanation for the failure to enter the market other than the agreement or practice in question: Cases 29-30/83: *CRAM and Rheinzink v Commission* [1984] ECR 1679, [1985] 1 CMLR 688, paras 10-23.
16 Where undertakings by agreement offer aggregated rebates to their customers, they may protect their markets from each other just as effectively as if they had expressly agreed not to compete with each other.
17 Case T-175/95: *BASF Coatings AG v Commission* [1999] ECR II-1581, paras 80-120.
18 P 666, note 11.
19 Decision 72/47: [1973] CMLR D167.
20 See eg *Re British Dental Trade Association*, OJ 1988, L233/15.
 1 Decision 74/341: [1974] 2 CMLR D102; Case 73/74: *Groupement des Fabricants de Papiers Peints de Belgique v Commission* [1975] ECR 1491, [1976] 1 CMLR 589.

marketing organization which included collective sales price fixing and the imposition of retail prices on dealers together with selling conditions, rebates etc. It also prevented members from obtaining advantages of their own advertising and services to customers. The agreement covered not only wallpaper produced by the members but also imported wall-paper sold in Belgium by them. In order to eliminate from business a member who did not toe the line and supplied wallpaper to self-service stores which retailed it below the fixed retail price, the Association imposed upon him a collective boycott. The Commission disapproved of the practice and imposed heavy fines upon the undertakings involved. The ECJ held on appeal that the control of the market exercised by the Association through price control and penalties was contrary to EC Article 81 (ex Art 85) but annulled the fines on the ground that the Commission failed to state precisely the reasons as required by EC Article 253 (ex Art 190). The latter conclusion was, no doubt, influenced by the severity of the fines and the fact that the Association did not challenge the Commission as regards its practices and promised to amend them accordingly.

In *Govers and Zonen v FRUBO*[2] an Association, grouping virtually all the Dutch fruit wholesaler importers, set up a system of auction sales in Rotterdam (the 'Europort'), for, mainly, citrus fruit imported into the Netherlands. In order to participate in these auctions the retail dealers had to comply with the conditions of the agreement which, apart from the technical aspects of the organization of the auction sales, imposed an obligation to market citrus fruit grown in non-member countries, only through the Rotterdam auction sales. Moreover the original agreement embraced not only citrus fruit grown in the Community but also restricted the participation in the auctions to Dutch importers only. As a result of the complaints to the Commission the original restrictions were removed but the main restrictions together with a compulsory additional trading stage (the customs clearance had to be obtained by another party) were retained. The Commission ruled this to be contrary to EC Article 81(1) (ex Art 85(1)) and stressed that the agreement being concluded between associations of undertakings came under the rubric of prohibited agreements. The Association appealed against the decision, denying that the agreement was 'an agreement between undertakings' within the meaning of EC Article 81(1) (ex Art 85(1)) as it was not directly enforceable between the parties. However the Court rejected this contention holding that 'Article 85(1) applies to associations in so far as their own activities or of those of the undertakings belonging to them are calculated to produce the results to which it refers'. Evidently in this case the practice was conducive to such results.

Most forms of discrimination involve treating the same situations, or trading partners in the same situation, in a different way. It is also discrimination to treat different situations, or persons in different situations, in the same way. That form of discrimination may arise where, for example, competitors agree to charge the same prices irrespective of the location of customers.[3]

(5) COLLATERAL OBLIGATIONS (EC ARTICLE 81(1)(E) (EX ART 85(1)(E)))

Collateral obligations or 'tying' clauses which, in a classic situation, compel purchasers to buy, as part of the transaction, products which are neither related

---

2   Decision 74/433: [1974] 2 CMLR D89; Case 71/74: *FRUBO v Commission* [1975] ECR 563, [1975] 2 CMLR 123.
3   Re *IFTRA Glass*, OJ 1974, L160/1, [1974] 2 CMLR D50.

to the transaction nor wanted by the purchaser, are prohibited. In the contemplation of EC Article 81(1)(e) (ex Art 85(1)(e)) it is not the tying or the tied transaction as such that is prohibited, but the agreement to insert a tying clause in contracts with third parties. Such clauses came to light in the *IFTRA*[4] case.

Akin to tying up clauses are clauses requiring a party to a contract to enter into a collateral obligation, the non-observance of which would be regarded by the other party as a breach of the contract. In the same category would be an obligation to purchase unpatented supplies for use in a patented process or in connection with a patented product.[5] Not all forms of tying are prohibited. When a brewery makes available a public house that it owns to a tenant for the purpose of exploiting it as such, it is acceptable for the brewery to tie the granting of a lease over the public house to obligations by the tenant to sell the brewery's beers in the public house.[6]

D. Negative clearance

Article 2 of Regulation 17[7] provides that the Commission may certify that 'on the basis of the facts in its possession, there are no grounds under Article 85(1) or EC Articles 81(1) and 82 (ex Art 86) . . . for action on its part . . .'. Hence 'negative clearance'. This is not an exemption but merely a statement of opinion in the form of a decision. Therefore it may be withdrawn should the circumstances change or should new facts come to light. In effect the Commission merely declares that it will not challenge the practice if continued according to the information received.

Unlike a notification for exemption under EC Article 81(3) (ex Art 85(3)), application for negative clearance secures no protection from sanctions provided for the infringement of competition rules, though it may be pleaded in mitigation. A copy of the application is sent to the competent authorities of the Member States.

Some applications have helped to clarify the law. Thus for example *Re Christiani and Nielsen*[8] contributed to the interpretation of the term 'undertaking'; *Re DECA's NV Rules*[9] helped to identify the territorial scope and *Re SOCEMAS*,[10] the quantitative effect of a restrictive practice upon trade.

In *Re Kodak*[11] the Commission was given an opportunity of considering whether European subsidiaries of an American company could have been in competition with it and whether the organization of sales it ran in the Common Market was compatible with EC Article 81(1) (ex Art 85(1)). The Kodak Group adopted a uniform sales code for its operations in Europe but, on the Commission's recommendation, amended it by removing a clause by which the European subsidiaries had to forbid their customers to export the product. The sales code operated on the basis of selective distribution as to quality, service and display. Amended as above the code was acceptable to the Commission.

---

4   Supra note 3.
5   Decision 79/86: *Re Vaessen v Moris* [1979] 1 CMLR 511; Case 193/83: *Windsurfing International Inc v Commission* [1986] ECR 611, [1986] 3 CMLR 489, paras 54-59.
6   Case C-234/59: *Delimitis v Henniger Bräu* [1991] ECR I-935.
7   JO 1962.
8   Decision 69/195: [1969] CMLR D36.
9   [1965] CMLR 50.
10 Case 68/138: [1968] CMLR D28.
11 Decision 70/332: [1970] CMLR D19.

The *Christiani* and *Kodak* cases suggest that, while a parent company and its subsidiaries wholly controlled by it cannot be in competition with each other, the practice itself may be in breach of the competition rules since, as shown in the latter case, a restrictive condition of sale may be imposed by the parent company through its subsidiaries upon undertakings dealing directly with the subsidiaries.

Another instructive example of negative clearance is a translantic joint venture[12] case. The application was made by Chevron Oil Europe Inc., incorporated in the State of Delaware but operating from New York and Brussels, and SHV, a Dutch company in respect of activities involving these two and their several European subsidiaries. Under their co-operation agreement Chevron and SHV set up, through a joint holding company incorporated under Dutch law jointly and equally owned subsidiaries to sell petroleum products covered by the agreement in certain Common Market countries and vested in these subsidiaries their distribution networks and relevant assets. As a result the distribution line of Chevron's and SHV's business had become integrated into a new trading structure of the subsidiaries forming a concentration between the two principal companies and their subsidiaries. The principal companies agreed not to compete in respect of petroleum products not distributed by the subsidiaries but, on the Commission's recommendation, deleted the relevant clause from their co-operation agreement. As regards distribution of the products covered by the agreement the principal companies agreed not to compete with each other without their prior consent but, in the circumstances, this clause was not regarded as restricting competition. Furthermore competition in areas other than those covered by the subsidiaries was not restricted by their agreement. The Commission, having analyzed the relationship between Chevron and SHV and their subsidiaries, granted a negative clearance and considered that in view of their share of the relevant market there was no question of either company occupying a dominant position in contravention of EC Article 81 (ex Art 85).

E. Civil consequences of the prohibition

EC Article 81(2) (ex Art 85(2)), provides: 'Any agreements or decisions prohibited pursuant to this Article shall be automatically void.'

Although EC Article 81(2) (ex Art 85(2)) specifies that prohibited *agreements* and *decisions* are void, the effect of EC Article 81(2) (ex art 85(2)) is to avoid only those *parts* of the agreement or decision which are incompatible with EC Article 81(1) (ex Art 85(1)). The consequences of the voidness of those parts, so far as the rest of the agreement or decision is concerned and so far as the validity and enforceability of other contracts made on the strength of the agreement or decision are concerned, are matters of national law, not Community law.[13] In the same way, although EC Article 81 (ex Art 85) prohibits the abuse of a dominant position, the effect of the unlawfulness of a prohibited abuse on the legal position of third parties and on contracts or provisions of contracts, are matters for the

---

12   Decision 75/95: *Re SHV and Chevron's Application* [1975] 1 CMLR D68.
13   Case 56/65: *Technique Minière v Maschinenbau Ulm* [1966] ECR 235, [1966] CMLR 357; Case 319/82: *Société de Vente de Ciments et Betons v Kerpen and Kerpen* [1983] ECR 4173, [1985] 1 CMLR 511, paras 10-12; Case 10/86: *VAG France v Magne* [1986] ECR 4071, [1988] 4 CMLR 98, para 16; Case C-234/89: *Delimitis v Henninger Bräu* [1991] ECR I-935, para 40.

national courts to determine.[14] It is therefore for national law to determine to what extent the voidness of particular clauses impugns other clauses or the contract as a whole.[15] 'Automatically void' means that the provision in question has no legal effect at all, or any colour or legality, and has had no such effect since its inception and without the need for any decision of the Commission or a national court finding that it is incompatible with EC Article 81(1) (ex Art 85(1)).[16] EC Article 81(2) (ex Art 85(2)) refers to agreements and decisions but not to concerted practices because the last, by their nature, are not such as to give rise to any legal effects and accordingly do not call for a declaration of their nullity.

F. Exemption from the prohibition

(1) EC ARTICLE 81(3) (EX ART 85(3))

EC Article 81(3) (ex Art 85(3)) provides for exemptions from the rigour of EC Article 81(1) (ex Art 85(1)) as it enables the Commission to declare it 'inapplicable' in specific cases where the agreement, decision or practice 'contributes to improving the production or distribution of goods or to promoting technical or economic progress, while allowing consumers a fair share of the resulting benefit, and which does not:

(a) impose on the undertakings concerned restrictions which are not indispensable to the attainment of these objectives;
(b) afford such undertakings the possibility of eliminating competition in respect of a substantial part of the products in question'.

It follows that even if a practice cannot be given negative clearance it is still possible that it may qualify for exemption. However, in order to meet the requirements of EC Article 81(3) (ex Art 85(3)) four conditions must be satisfied. The two positive conditions are that the practice in question is beneficial to the economy and the consumer whilst the two negative conditions require that it does not impose upon the undertakings restrictions which would negate the above objectives and render them unable to compete in the area covered by the products involved. These four conditions are not alternative but cumulative and, since exemption has to be expressly granted, they have to be proved by the applicant.[17] Thus exemption could not be granted where the applicant was capable of demonstrating advantages to the economy but the control of supply and demand was an indispensable condition of the working of the system and demand was an indispensable condition of the working of the system proposed.[18] In principle, any distortion of competition may benefit from exemption as long as the agreement, decision or practice in question has been notified and the conditions of EC Article 81(3) (ex Art 85(3)) have been satisfied.[19]

---

14 Case 127/73: *BAT v SABAM* [1974] ECR 313, [1974] 2 CMLR 238, para 14.
15 For the position in England, see *Chemidus Wavin v TERI* [1978] 3 CMLR 514; *Passmore v Morland* [1999] 1 CMLR 1129.
16 Case 22/71: *Béguelin Import Co v GL Import Export* [1971] ECR 949, [1972] CMLR 81, para 29; Reg 17, art 1.
17 Cases 43 and 63/82: *VBVB v VBBB* [1984] ECR 19, [1985] 1 CMLR 27, para 52.
18 Decision 74/433: *Re FRUBO* [1974] 2 CMLR D89.
19 Case T-17/93: *Matra Hachette v Commission* [1994] ECR II-595 paras 85-86.

Furtherance of economic progress was the ground for exemption in two cases concerning the organization of exhibitions, *Re CECIMO*[20] involving machine tools, and *Re CEMATEX*,[1] a case involving textile machinery.

'Consumers' (a somewhat doubtful rendering of the French 'utilisateurs') include not only 'customers' but also users and traders as the case may be. In the case of an agreement on technical co-operation and research for the purpose of developing and marketing an electrically driven bus the 'consumers' were bus companies and tour operators, not tourists or commuters.[2] In the *Blondel*[3] case, on the other hand, the agreement between a French distributor and a Dutch manufacturer to reduce prices and to alter the design of the goods to please the French market, was held to benefit the customers, ie not only ultimate consumers but also firms and industries supplied by the parties.

The applicant has to prove that the proposed arrangement will not eliminate competition in the field. This is a quantitative matter as shown in the *MAN/SAVIEM*[4] case where exemption was refused because the specialization agreement involved two manufacturers of industrial vehicles who, in the league of vehicle manufacturers in the Community, ranked sixth out of eleven and produced nearly 7% of all vehicles. It is also a quantitative matter whether or not the restraint on competition is 'indispensable'. It was held to be so in the *Consten and Grundig*[5] case.

There is no automatic exemption under EC Article 81(3) (ex Art 85(3)). Moreover exemption may be granted only by the Commission (not by national authorities) in accordance with the requisite procedure. It takes the form of a decision in the sense of EC Article 249 (ex Art 189) and, as such, has to be substantiated as provided in EC Article 253 (ex Art 190). It has to be notified to the parties concerned (EC Article 254(2) (ex Art 191(2))) and, according to the established practice, it is published in the Official Journal, though such publication is not mandatory. It is subject to judicial review and may be quashed if not adequately substantiated.[6] Since the decision whether or not to grant an exemption requires the Commission to make an assessment of complex economic facts, that assessment can be challenged only on the basis of manifest error.[7]

There are two types of exemption: individual and for categories of agreements, decisions and concerted practices (so-called block exemption).

(2) INDIVIDUAL EXEMPTION

(a) Notification
In order to be granted an exemption the practice in question must first be notified to the Commission in the proper manner. Documents and data supplied to the Commission in response to its own inquiries will not constitute such notification.[8]

Regulation 17 distinguishes between 'existing' and 'new' agreements. As far as the original Member States are concerned existing agreements are those

---

20 Case 69/90: [1969] CMLR D1.
1   Case 71/337: [1973] CMLR D135.
2   Decision 68/319: *Re Agreement ACEC and Berliet* [1968] CMLR D35.
3   Decision 65/366: *Koninklijke Fabrieken Diepenbrock Reigers NV, Blondel SA* OJ 1965, 2194, [1965] CMLR 180.
4   JO 1972, L31/29. See also *SNPE and Leafields Engineering Ltd* [1978] 2 CMLR 758.
5   P 663, note 19.
6   Cases 19 and 20/74: *Kali and Salz A-G and Dli-Chemie v Commission* [1975] ECR 499, [1975] 2 CMLR 154.
7   Case T-17/93: *Matra Hachette v Commission* [1994] ECR II-595, para 104.
8   *GB-INNO-BM SA v Fédétab* [1978] 3 CMLR 524.

which were in operation when Regulation 17 came into force, ie 13 March 1962. For the new Member States the date of accession provides the dividing line between 'existing' and 'new' agreements. As regards the Six, existing agreements were to be notified by 1 November 1962 (or 1 February 1963 in the case of bilateral agreements) and within six months from the date of accession as regards the new Member States unless the practice had already been caught by the rules independently of accession. New agreements have to be notified when they come into force but in doubtful cases it is advisable to consult the Commission before entering into agreement.

There are certain advantages of notification. To begin with, agreements or decisions contrary to EC Article 81(1) (ex Art 85(1)), unless exempted, are 'automatically void' (EC Article 81(2) (ex Art 85(2))) and the parties thereto are exposed to sanctions. There is no duty to notify but there is an incentive to do so either to secure peace of mind in case the practice is within the rules or to obtain exemption, quite apart from the immunity from sanctions.

Even if no exemption has been granted sanctions may be applied only in respect of the period during which the practice was operated prior to notification. However the sanction will not normally be applied in respect of practices occurring between the notification and the decision,[9] though the Commission has the power to impose sanctions despite notification. This is reserved for flagrant breaches of the rules. An 'old' agreement which has been notified within the time limit for doing so remains valid until the Commission has declared otherwise.[10] In the case of other agreements, the mere fact that they have been notified does not mean that they fall within the prohibition in EC Article 81(1) (ex Art 85(1)) and must therefore be regarded as void unless and until the Commission has granted an exemption: the application of EC Article 81(1) (ex Art 85(1)) must first be ascertained.[11] Contrary to the impression given in some early cases,[12] that does not mean that agreements other than 'old' agreements must be treated as valid, and enforced, while the application for an exemption is pending before the Commission. In principle, the arrangement is prohibited unless and until it is exempted from prohibition but, in order to avoid inconsistent decisions and the resulting legal uncertainty, national courts should not come to a final decision against the lawfulness of the arrangement unless it is clear that it cannot benefit from an exemption either because it has not been notified or because it clearly does not meet the requirements for being exempted.[13] The Commission may also limit the sanctions.[14] However any temporary or de facto validity as well as the protection from sanctions is lost if the Commission refuses to grant exemption. To cover such a risk during the period between the notification and the decision the parties would be advised to make the agreement subject to a favourable decision of the Commission resulting either in negative clearance or exemption.[15]

The obvious disadvantage is that the Commission obtains full knowledge of relevant facts without any effort on its part and that the notifying undertaking

---

9 Reg 17, art 15(5).
10 Case 13/61: *De Geus v Bosch* [1962] ECR 45, [1962] CMLR 1.
11 Case 10/69: *Portelange SA v Smith Corona International SA* [1969] ECR 309, [1974] 1 CMLR 397.
12 Notably the *Portelange* case, supra.
13 Case 37/79: *Anne Márty SA v Estée Lauder SA* [1980] ECR 2481, [1981] 2 CMLR 143, paras 13-14; Case C-234/89: *Delimitis v Henninger Bräu AG* [1991] ECR I-935, paras 47-54.
14 *CEMATEX*, p 674, note 1.
15 Cf decision in *Re Henkel/Colgate* JO 1972, L14/14.

may have to adjust its position in conformity with the Commission's directions. However, on balance, the risk of being caught out must outweigh the disadvantage.

(b) Dispensation from notification
Article 4(2) of Regulation 17[16] provides that certain practices are exempt from the notification requirements. These comprise agreements, decisions or concerted practices where:

(1) all the parties belong to one Member State and the agreement etc relates neither to imports nor exports between Member States;

(2) the parties to the agreements etc each operate, for the purposes of the agreement, at a different level of the production or distribution chain and the agreement etc relates to the conditions under which the parties may purchase, sell or resell certain goods or services;

(3) no more than two parties are involved in the agreement etc and it imposes restrictions only on the exercise of rights by (i) an assignee or user of industrial property rights (in particular patents, utility models, designs or trade marks) or (ii) the person entitled under a contract to the assignment or grant of the right to use a method of manufacture or knowledge relating to the use and to the application of industrial processes;

(4) irrespective of the number of parties the sole object is the development or uniform application of standards or types;

(5) irrespective of the number of parties the sole object is joint research and development;

(6) irrespective of the number of parties the agreement etc is concerned solely with specialization in the manufacture of products which do not exceed 15% of the particular market and the parties' turnover does not exceed ECU 200 million.

Some of these provisions have now become subject to judicial ruling. In *Bilger v Jehle*[17] and in *Roubaix v Roux*[18] the ECJ clarified the meaning of agreements which do not relate either to imports or exports between Member States. In *Parfums Marcel Rochas Vertriebs GmbH v Bitsch*[19] agreements involving 'no more than two parties' were explained. In the *European Sugar Cartel* case[20] the Commission regarded the agreements as being outside Article 4(2) because they controlled imports and exports. 'Joint research' was considered by the Commission in *Re Eurogypsum*[1] and specialization agreements were subject to several decisions.[2] In *Brasserie de Haecht v Wilkin-Janssen*[3] the ECJ confirmed that dispensation does not afford a foolproof protection but constitutes merely an indication that the practice in question is presumed to merit exemption.

---

16 As amended by Reg 2822/71 (JO 1971, L285/49; OJ 1971, 1035); and Reg 1216/1999 (OJ 1999, L148/5).
17 Case 43/69: [1970] ECR 127, [1974] 1 CMLR 382.
18 Case 63/75: [1976] ECR 111, [1976] 1 CMLR 538.
19 Case 1/70: [1970] ECR 515, [1971] CMLR 104.
20 OJ 1973, L140/17, [1973] CMLR D65; Cases 40-48, 50, 54-56, 111, 113 and 114/73: *Suiker Unie (Cooperative Vereniging) UA et al v Commission* [1975] ECR 1663, [1976] 1 CMLR 295.
 1 Case 68/128: [1968] CMLR D1.
 2 Eg *Jaz*; Case 72/24: *Re SOPELEM and Langen* [1972] CMLR D77; *MAN/SAVIEM*, p 674, note 4; Case 76/172: *Re Bayer and Gist-Brocades* [1976] 1 CMLR D98.
 3 Case 48/72: [1973] ECR 77, [1973] CMLR 287.

(c) Procedure
An application for exemption (and, incidentally, for negative clearance) has to be made on form A/B obtainable from the Commission or the Information Service of the European Communities. It requires the applicant to state the facts upon which exemption or negative clearance is requested. It also requires the applicant to state the reasons why in his view EC Article 81(1) (ex Art 85(1)) does not apply and/or that the application falls under EC Article 81(3) (ex Art 85(3)).

The applicant is entitled to a hearing which is governed by Commission Regulation 2842/98[4] and a summary of each application is published in the Official Journal. This publication serves as a notice to interested third parties who may submit comments to the Commission.[5]

The Commission is not bound by the terms of the application and may institute an investigation in accordance with Articles 13 and 14 of Regulation 17. In such a case it will inform the competent authority of the relevant Member State whose assistance may be sought.

A decision in application of EC Article 81(3) (ex Art 85(3)), may be issued for a specified period and may be subject to conditions.[6] It may be renewed if the conditions remain unchanged. It may also be amended or revoked if:

(1) the situation has changed with regard to a factor essential to granting the decision;
(2) those concerned infringe a condition attached to the decision;
(3) the decision is based on inaccurate information or has been obtained by deceit;
(4) those concerned abuse the exemption from EC Article 81(1) (ex Art 85(1)) granted by the decision (Regulation 17, Article 8).

(d) Block exemptions
In order to reduce the number of individual notifications under Regulation 17 the Council gave the Commission power to grant 'block' exemptions in respect of certain categories of agreements, decisions and concerted practices.[7]

The fact that a particular arrangement falls within the scope of a block exemption regulation does not necessarily mean that it must be taken to be otherwise within the scope of the prohibition in EC Article 81(1) (ex Art 85(1)) or that arrangements which do not comply with the terms of the block exemption must necessarily be prohibited.[8] However, while in some cases the preamble to a block exemption regulation may allow that agreements falling within its scope may not infringe EC Article 81(1) (ex Art 85(1)), in other cases the preamble is more specific in characterizing an arrangement as being prohibited.[9] Where the

---

4 OJ 1998, L354/18. This Regulation replaced Reg 99/63 (JO 1963, 2268; OJ 1963-64, 47).
5 See Decision 74/16: *Re Transocean Marine Paint Association (No 2)* [1974] 1 CMLR D11, Case 75/649: [1975] 2 CMLR D75; Case 17/74: *Transocean Marine Paint Association v Commission* [1974] ECR 1063, [1974] 2 CMLR 459.
6 Eg *Henkel/Colgate* p 675, note 15; *Transocean Marine Paint*, supra.
7 See p 620, supra.
8 Case 32/65: *Italy v Council and Commission* [1966] ECR 389, [1969] CMLR 39.
9 Contrast recital 3 of Reg 1984/83 ('exclusive purchasing agreements of the categories defined in this Regulation may fall within the prohibition contained in Art 85(1) of the Treaty') with recital 2 of Reg 1475/95 ('. . . the obligations listed in Arts 1, 2 and 3 normally have as their object or effect the prevention, restriction or distortion of competition within the common market and are normally liable to affect trade between Member States').

arrangement falls within the scope of a block exemption, it is normally idle to speculate whether or not it would otherwise have been prohibited by EC Article 81(1) (ex Art 85(1)): the effect of the block exemption is to give the same degree of protection to the arrangement as if it had been the subject of an individual exemption.[10] In order to receive the benefit of that protection, the arrangement must comply strictly with every term and condition of the block exemption. That does not mean that the arrangement must be identical in every respect to the block exemption by, for example, containing every type of term referred to in the block exemption. It does mean that the arrangement must not contain any restriction of competition other than those permitted by the block exemption. If it does contain an additional restriction, however unimportant, the entire arrangement falls outside the scope of the block exemption and is not protected. Further, as the block exemption is an exception to the general rule set out in EC Article 81(1) (ex Art 85(1)), it must be given a narrow construction; and, hence, any ambiguity in its terms is not to be construed in favour of widening the scope of the exemption. Any extension of the scope of a block exemption is a matter for the Commission, not the courts.[11] Block exemptions do not impose any obligation on undertakings to amend their agreements, they simply provide a measure of protection which undertakings are free to make use of or not, as they choose, subject to the condition that, if they wish to obtain the protection offered, they must comply with the terms of the block exemption.[12] It falls outside the scope of this work to analyse in detail the block exemptions which are currently available.

G. Common types of arrangement

(1) CO-OPERATION AGREEMENTS

In its Notice on Horizontal Co-operation Agreements[13] the Commission points out that horizontal co-operation can lead to substantial economic benefits: it can be a means of sharing risk, saving costs, pooling know-how and advancing innovation; and it can enable small and medium-sized undertakings to adapt to change.

In particular, co-operation agreements are considered to be outside EC Article 81(1) (ex Art 85(1)) if they involve co-operation between non-competitors, co-operation between competitors who cannot independently carry our the project or activity in question, and co-operation concerning an activity that does not influence the parameters of competition. Co-operation agreements that normally fall within EC Article 81(1) (ex Art 85(1)) are those whose object is the restriction of competition by means of price fixing, output limitation or

---

10   An agreement falling within the scope of a block exemption is exempted without the need to be notified to the Commission: Case 1/71: *Cadillon v Höss Maschinenbau* [1971] ECR 351, [1971] CMLR 420. Some block exemptions provide for an 'opposition procedure' under which agreements which do not fall exactly within the scope of the block exemption may nonetheless be covered by it if they have been notified to the Commission and the Commission has not raised an objection within a specified period of time.

11   Case C-234/89: *Delimitis v Henninger Bräu* [1991] ECR I-935, paras 34-42 and 46.

12   Case 10/86: *VAG France SA v Magne* [1986] ECR 4071, [1988] 4 CMLR 98.

13   OJ 2001, C 3/2.

sharing of markets or customers. Between those two classes of co-operation agreements is a third comprising agreements that may or may not fall within EC Article 81(1) (ex Art 85(1)), depending upon the conclusions to be drawn from market-related criteria such as the market position of the parties and other structural factors. Particular types of co-operation agreements that have been the subject of detailed consideration include: joint research or development projects;[14] joint selling arrangments;[15] joint advertising;[16] joint use of quality labels.[17] However, as we have noted earlier, a Notice has no binding effect and, therefore, it should be seen only as an expression of the Commission's intention and an aid to interpretation of EC Article 81(1) (ex Art 85(1)) and ECSC 65(1). In doubt negative clearance ought to be sought. The Notice on Co-operation Agreements has been supplemented by the Notice on Sub-Contracting Agreements.[18]

(2) SPECIALIZATION AGREEMENTS

Specialization agreements tend to infringe EC Article 81(1) (ex Art 85(1)) because they result in a reduction of competition in the area of specialization (generally production or sale).[19] However, such agreements usually allow an improvement in production or distribution because the parties to the agreement can concentrate on one particular activity, such as the manufacture of certain products. In consequence, they can operate more efficiently and supply the products more cheaply. As long as there is effective competition in the relevant market, consumers will receive a fair share of the resulting benefit. The block exemption regulation for specialization agreements covers unilateral specialisation agreements, by which one party agrees to cease or refrain from production and obtain the products in question from the other party, reciprocal specialisation agreements, by which two or more parties agree to cease or refrain from production of different products and to obtain them from the other parties, and joint production agreements by which the parties agree to produce certain products jointly.[20] The regulation applies only if the combined market share of the participating undertakings does not represent more than 20% of the market.[1]

(3) JOINT PURCHASING AND SELLING

Joint purchasing and selling arrangements limit competition by reducing the number of independent buyers and sellers in the market. The participants in the

14 Now covered by Reg 2659/2000. See Decision 68/128: *Re Eurogypsum* [1968] CMLR D1; Decision 68/319: *Re the Agreement of ACEC and Berliet* [1968] CMLR D35; *Re Research and Development* [1971] CMLR D31; *Re Transocean Marine Paint Association*, p 677, note 5; but note exemption was refused in *Re Henkel/Colgate*, p 675, note 15, and in Decision 79/298: *Beecham Parke Davis Agreement* [1979] 2 CMLR 157.

15 Decision 68/377: *Re the Comptoir Français de l'Azote* [1968] CMLR D57; Decision 71/22: *Re Supexie's Agreement* [1971] CMLR D1; *Re Wild and Leitz* [1972] CMLR D36; Case 72/23: *SAFCO Export* [1972] CMLR D83; but note exemption was refused in Case 75/76: *Re SOPELEM-Rank Agreements* [1975] 1 CMLR D72.

16 Decision 70/346: *Association pour la promotion du tube d'acier etc* [1970] CMLR D31; *Re Wild-Leitz* note 15, supra; *Re Henkel/Colgate*, p 675, note 15.

17 *Tube d'acier*, supra.

18 OJ 1979, C 1/2, [1979] 1 CMLR 264.

19 Eg Case T-141/89: *Tréfileurope Sales v Commission* [1995] ECR II-791.

20 Reg 2658/2000, art 1.

1 Ibid, arts 4 and 6.

arrangement cease to compete with one another in order to obtain better terms from their suppliers/purchasers and their jointly held market power may enable them to dominate their suppliers/purchasers. On the other hand, the aggregate market power of the undertakings involved in the arrangement may improve their bargaining position where individually they are of small size by comparison with their normal contracting parties. In the case of joint purchasing arrangements, this may lead to a reduction in prices. The beneficial effects of a joint purchasing or selling arrangement may therefore justify its exemption from prohibition.[2] The anti-competitive effects of joint selling agreements are slightly different from and more substantial than those arising from joint purchasing agreements because they affect the quantities, prices, means of distribution, quality and development prospects of the goods in question. The absence of competition in those areas, which does not apply in the case of joint purchasing, since it primarily affects buying power, can be very serious. In consequence, the Commission's view has been that, save possibly where small and medium-sized undertakings are concerned, joint selling arrangements are prohibited and are not likely to be exempted.[3]

(4) JOINT VENTURES

A joint venture may be defined as an undertaking which is jointly controlled by two or more economically independent firms and which performs all the functions of a business undertaking or is at least engaged in the production of goods or the provision of services.[4] While specialization agreements purport to divide the work and make the results available to the parties, joint ventures aim to combine the forces of different undertakings in order to obtain results through united or complementary effort. Structurally joint ventures may take various legal forms, such as a partnership or a separate company or organization, but this need not be so. It is perfectly possible to embark on a joint venture without any structural formation, for example by committing resources to a particular project or entering into a long-term supply contract. Depending upon the circumstances, joint ventures may fall under either EC Article 81 (ex Art 85) or EC Article 82 (ex Art 86). Joint ventures falling within EC Article 81 (ex Art 85) are those which are predominantly co-operative in character; joint ventures falling within EC Article 82 (ex Art 86) are those which involve a merger or partial merger of the business in the parent undertakings.[5] In complex cases, both EC Articles 81 and 82 (ex Arts 85 and 86) may be applicable.[6] In its published decisions, the Commission has almost invariably found that joint ventures which are predominantly co-operative in character fall within the prohibition in EC Article 81(1) (ex Art 85(1)).[7] On the other hand, it is generally favourable to granting an exemption under EC Article 81(3) (ex Art 85(3)), particularly where the joint venture involves major

2 See eg *Re National Sulphuric Acid Association Ltd*, OJ 1980, L260/24, [1980] 3 CMLR 429.
3 See the First Report on Competition Policy (Brussels-Luxembourg), paras 11-18.
4 *Re GEC Ltd and Weir Group Ltd Agreement*, OJ 1977, L327/26, [1978] 1 CMLR D42. The Commission took the view that the fact that a joint venture is not a distinct incorporated company, but is created solely by contract, is not a difference of substance, but one of legal form only.
5 *SHV and Chevron Oil Europe Inc*, OJ 1975, L38/14, [1975] 1 CMLR D68; Sixth Report on Competition Policy (Brussels Luxembourg, 1977), para 55.
6 Sixth Report on Competition Policy, para 53.
7 In *Re Optical Fibres*, OJ 1986, L236/30, the Commission found that EC Art 81(1) (ex Art 85(1)), was infringed because there were several interlinking joint ventures. It would appear that, taken individually, they did not infringe EC Art 81(1) (ex Art 85(1)).

new investment, transfer of technology from outside the Community, the introduction of improved products or processes or the opening up of new markets.

There is no block exemption for joint venture agreements. Therefore, each agreement has to be justified individually unless, in view of its nature, it belongs to an exempted category. Indeed some arrangements which we have considered elsewhere exhibit characteristics of a joint venture. Thus buying and selling arrangements, including price fixing and territorial demarcations, may be structured as joint ventures though they are more likely to resemble horizontal agreements. Such agreements, unless insignificant, would be incompatible with EC Article 81(1) (ex Art 85(1)). Such, for example, was the position of the *Dutch Fertilizers Organization*[8] where even sales outside the EEC territory were regarded as irrelevant. Early examples include the *Henkel and Colgate*[9] venture in which certain manufacturers of detergents combined forces in order to create a joint research and development company. In *Re SHV and Chevron*[10] a transatlantic arrangement to create joint subsidiaries for the purpose of marketing fuel oils was treated by the Commission as a merger which offended neither EC Article 82 (ex Art 86) nor EC Article 81(1) (ex Art 85(1)). However, in the *GEC/Weir*[11] Agreement the Commission insisted on various amendments to limit the scope of the co-operation and this curtailed its restrictive effect. Structurally the joint venture consisted of a committee composed of the representatives of the parties who were to manage the combined resources by unanimous decision. The object was to develop sodium circulators to cool atomic plants, in itself a sophisticated technological project to which GEC contributed information regarding nuclear reactors and Weir the technology relating to pumps and hydraulics. At the end of the agreement the parties were to resume an independent competitive position and each was to receive licences from the other.

In another case[12] the Commission ordered the parties to divest themselves of their joint interests in subsidiaries manufacturing safety glass for vehicles in France and Germany. The parties were the largest glass manufacturers in Western Europe and as such had little competition.

In its decision on the *Bayer and Gist-Brocades Agreement*[13] the Commission approved a long-term research and development project relating to penicillin production between a German and a Dutch company. In the *Transocean Marine Paint Association* case[14] it approved agreements for joint advertising, use of quality labels and standardization. In *CEMATEX*[15] it approved the rationalization of fairs and exhibitions run by an association of seven national federations grouping together the majority of the textile industry in the Common Market.

In *Re Vacuum Interrupters*[16] the Commission exempted a joint venture agreement between two companies to establish a joint subsidiary, though neither company at the time of the agreement was making vacuum interrupters. The

---

8   *Re Centraal Stikstof Verkoopkantoor NV* OJ 1978, L242/15, [1979] 1 CMLR 11.
9   P 675, note 15.
10 P 672, note 12.
11 Case 77/781: *Re GEC Ltd and Weir Group Ltd Agreement* [1978] 1 CMLR D42; cf concentration through interlocking directorships authorized subject to conditions: Case 78/538: *Re Takeover by ARBED*, OJ 1978, L164/14, [1978] 2 CMLR 767.
12 *St Gobain Pont à Mousson and BSN Gervais-Danone*, Fourth Report on Competition Policy, 1975, para 79.
13 P 676, note 2.
14 P 677, note 5.
15 P 674, note 1.
16 Case 77/160: *Re Vacuum Interrupters Ltd* [1977] 1 CMLR D67.

agreement could restrain competition between them and was capable of affecting trade between Member States.

It seems that joint ventures involving technological development are more likely to find favour with the Commission than arrangements affecting marketing, distribution and pricing. However each case has to be considered on its merits and, because of the variety of the agreements and practices in the field, common criteria for block exemptions seem hard to define.

In *Re SOPELEM*[17] a joint venture for the research, development and marketing of microscopes was granted exemption subject to the parties reporting on the modification of the arrangement and their progress to the Commission. The offending provisions included the technical co-operation and exchange of expertise which would eliminate competition between the parties in research and development; standardization of parts and specialization in production affecting their capacity to remain active; and the distribution agreement whereby one party became the sole distributor in the United Kingdom and Ireland and the joint subsidiary for both in the remainder of the EEC.

However in *Re Wano*[18] the Commission refused exemption to a joint venture between two rival manufacturers of blackpowder since the arrangement would eliminate competition for the manufacture and marketing of the product.

(5) EXCLUSIVE DISTRIBUTION

The general approach to exclusive distribution agreements has been that, if the effect of the agreement is to isolate a particular geographical area in the Community completely ('absolute territorial protection'), the agreement infringes EC Article 81(1) (ex Art 85(1)) and is not eligible for exemption under EC Article 81(3) (ex Art 85(3)); on the other hand, if the degree of exclusivity is partial only (such as where the distributor allocated to the territory is prohibited from selling actively outside the territory but may respond to offers made to him within the territory by persons established outside it), the agreement may be eligible for exemption.[19] Exclusive agreements between two undertakings for the resale of goods were covered by one of two block exemptions covering exclusive distribution and exclusive purchasing agreements.[20] The difference between them was that, in exclusive distribution agreements, the supplier of the goods allots a defined sales territory to the distributor of the goods and undertakes not to supply any other distributor in that territory; in exclusive purchasing agreements, the distributor agrees to purchase supplies only from the other contracting party whereas the latter is not committed to supply only that distributor in the sales area in question. The Regulations stated in detail the type of clauses which were permitted and those which were prohibited. Neither block exemption applied to competing manufacturers. There were special provisions for beer supply and service station agreements. Exclusive distribution arrangements are now covered by Regulation 2790/1999, which deals generally with vertical arrangements entered into by persons who are not competitors and where the market share of the supplier (and by undertakings connected with it) or, in the case of exclusive supply obligations, the market share of the buyer (and by undertakings connected with it) does not exceed 30%.[1]

17 Case 78/251: *Re Agreement between SOPELEM and Vickers Ltd* [1978] 2 CMLR 146.
18 Case 78/921: *Re Wano Schwarzpulver GmbH* [1979] 1 CMLR 403.
19 For the general position as it was, see Cases 56 and 58/64: *Etablissements Consten and Grundig v Commission* [1966] ECR 299, [1966] CMLR 418.
20 Reg 1983/83 and Reg 1984/83, respectively.
 1 OJ 1999, L336/21.

(6) SELECTIVE DISTRIBUTION

Selective distribution systems are networks of agreements whereby a supplier of goods distributes his products through distributors who meet certain standards fixed by the supplier. Such systems tend to result in a limitation of price competition as between the distributors of the product in question ('intra-brand competition') not only because the number of those distributors is limited by the supplier but also because the standards fixed by the supplier, which must be met by all his approved distributors, generally increase the costs of the distributors and their ability to compete between each other on price is reduced. Accordingly, consumer prices are higher than would otherwise be the case. On the other hand, selective distribution systems may enhance competition between similar products produced by different suppliers ('intra-brand competition') in regard to matters other than price, such as quality of after-sales service. Provided that resellers are selected on the basis of objective criteria of a qualitative nature relating to the technical qualifications of the reseller and his staff and the suitability of his premises, and provided that such criteria are laid down uniformly for all potential resellers and are not applied in a discriminative fashion, the selection of resellers is not generally regarded as infringing EC Article 81(1) (ex Art 85(1)).[2] Such systems are occasionally described as 'simple selective distribution systems'. Even such systems may fall foul of EC Article 81(1) (ex Art 85(1)), if they are so prevalent that the market can be said to be saturated with them.

Selection on the basis of quantitative criteria, such as by limiting the number of resellers in a given area by reference to the presumed purchasing power of consumers, does give rise to a breach of EC Article 81(1) (ex Art 85(1)). When assessing selective distribution systems, attention must be paid not only to the existence of other restrictions, such as obligations on the resellers not to compete with one another, but also to the general level of inter-brand competition. If the market in the product concerned were characterized by a high level of distribution through selective distribution systems, the resulting structural rigidity would raise doubts as to the compatibility of selective distribution with EC Article 81 (ex Art 85) in that market. Due to the nature of selective distribution systems, action taken by the supplier in operating the system is regarded as forming part of the contractual relations between the supplier and the approved resellers and is therefore caught by EC Article 81 (ex Art 85).[3]

In the motor vehicle sector, selective distribution systems covering motor vehicle distribution and servicing which typically include elements of exclusivity, are covered by a block exemption.[4] The Commission has not adopted a block exemption for selective distribution systems in other sectors but has adopted decisions which indicate its general policy towards such systems[5] and has included them in the general block exemption for vertical agreements.[6]

---

2 Case 26/76: *Metro – SB – Grossmärkte GmbH & Co KG v Commission* [1977] ECR 1875, [1978] 2 CMLR 1; Case 75/84: *Metro – SB – Grossmärkte GmbH & Co KG v Commission* [1986] ECR 3021, [1987] 1 CMLR 118.
3 Case 107/82: *AEG-Telefunken AG v Commission* [1983] ECR 3151, [1984] 3 CMLR 325, paras 31-39; Cases 25-26/84: *Ford v Commission* [1985] ECR 2725, [1985] 3 CMLR 528, paras 14-26.
4 Reg 1475/95.
5 See eg *Re Yves St Laurent*, OJ 1992, L12/24, [1993] 4 CMLR 120.
6 Reg 2790/1999 (OJ 1999, L336/21); see para 184 of the Commission's Guidelines on Vertical Restraints.

(7) FRANCHISING

There are, broadly speaking, three types of franchise agreements: (1) service franchises, in which the franchisee offers a service under the business name or symbol and sometimes the trademark of the franchisor, in accordance with the franchisor's instructions; (2) production franchises, in which the franchisee manufactures products according to the instructions of the franchisor and sells them under the franchisor's trademark; and (3) distribution franchises, in which the franchisee sells certain products in a shop which bears the franchisor's business name or symbol. In many respects, such arrangements are a means whereby an undertaking can build up a network of outlets in a relatively short period of time and without investing large sums of money in order to do so. In effect, the franchisor's business is the exploitation of his expertise by allowing others to use it in their business (and at their risk) in return for a payment. Franchises also give persons who would not otherwise be able to do so the opportunity to enter a market and build up their own business while benefiting from the franchisor's reputation and experience. In general terms, as a result of the nature of the relationship between the franchisor and the franchisee, a franchise agreement may, without risk of infringing EC Article 81(1) (ex Art 85(1)), contain clauses which are essential to enable the former to communicate his know-how to the latter and provide them with the necessary assistance in order to enable them to apply his methods without running the risk that competitors might learn of and benefit from the franchisor's know-how and assistance. The general position regarding distribution franchises is set out in Case 161/84: *Pronuptia de Paris GmbH v Pronuptia de Paris Irmgard Schillgalis*;[7] and franchise agreements are covered in part by the general block exemption for vertical agreements.[8]

---

7   [1986] ECR 353, [1986] 1 CMLR 414. See also *Re Yves Rocher*, OJ 1987, L8/49, [1988] 4 CMLR 592; *Re Pronuptia*, OJ 1987, L13/39, [1989] 4 CMLR 355; *Re Computerland*, OJ 1987, L222/12, [1989] 4 CMLR 259; *Re Charles Jourdan*, OJ 1989, L35/31, [1989] 4 CMLR 591; *Re ServiceMaster*, OJ 1988, L332/38, [1989] 4 CMLR 581.
8   Reg 2790/1999 (see para 199 of the Commission's Guidelines on Vertical Restraints). Previously, franchise agreements fell within Reg 4087/88.

Chapter 29

Competition: abuse of a dominant position and mergers

A. Introduction

EC Article 82 (ex Art 86) prohibits the abuse of a dominant position, that is, the anti-competitive behaviour of undertakings which, for various reasons but typically by reason of their size, occupy such a position on the market that they are immune, or largely immune, from the competitive forces which would otherwise prevent them from engaging in such behaviour.

EC Articles 81 and 82 (ex Arts 85 and 86) complement each other because 'they are intended to achieve the same aim on different levels'.[1] The aim is the same, ie to secure fair competition by curbing restraints on trade. The levels differ in so far as EC Article 81 (ex Art 85) is concerned with the effect on trade of various restrictive practices involving in most cases two or more undertakings whilst EC Article 82 (ex Art 86) is concerned primarily with what a layman would consider to be a monopolist situation in which, in most cases, a single undertaking dictates its terms to the trade. EC Article 82 (ex Art 86), like EC Article 81 (ex Art 85), is concerned with the 'abuse' rather than the 'existence' of economic power. In the case of EC Article 82 (ex Art 86), the required degree of economic power is greater than that required by EC Article 81 (ex Art 85).

The different forms of the abuse of a dominant position are generally regarded as falling into three categories: (1) exploitative abuses, that is, behaviour by which the dominant undertaking reaps benefits which it would not have reaped if there were normal and effective competition in the market;[2] such forms of abuse are typically practised by the dominant undertaking against its trading partners and are therefore to be seen in 'vertical' commercial relationships (that is, relationships between the dominant undertaking and undertakings operating at a different level in the market or consumers); (2) anti-competitive or exclusionary abuses, that

---

1 Cases 56 and 58/64: *Etablissements Consten and Grundig v Commission* [1966] ECR 299, [1966] CMLR 418, para 25.
2 Cf Case 27/76: *United Brands v Commission* [1978] ECR 207, [1978] 1 CMLR 429, para 249. An example is unfairly high prices.

is, behaviour by which the dominant undertaking damages a competitor; such forms of abuse are usually to be seen in 'horizontal' commercial relationships but often arise in the first instance in vertical relationships between the dominant undertaking and its trading partners because of the 'knock-on' effect on the position of the dominant undertaking's competitors;[3] and (3) structural abuses, that is, behaviour which affects the structure of the market such as a merger, take-over or the acquisition of the business or assets of another undertaking.[4] Structural abuses form a distinct category and are subject to special rules laid down in the Community's Merger Control Regulation.[5] They are therefore considered after the scope of EC Article 82 (ex Art 86) has been explained.

B. EC Article 82 (ex Art 86)

EC Article 82 (ex Art 86) provides that:

> 'Any *abuse* by *one or more* undertakings of a *dominant position within the Common Market* or *in a substantial part* of it shall be prohibited as incompatible with the Common Market in so far as it may affect trade between Member States. Such abuse may *in particular*, consist in:
>
> (a) directly or indirectly imposing unfair purchase or selling prices or other unfair trading conditions;
>
> (b) limiting production, markets or technical development to the prejudice of consumers;
>
> (c) applying dissimilar conditions to equivalent transactions with other trading parties, thereby placing them at a competitive disadvantage;
>
> (d) making the conclusion of contracts subject to acceptance by the other parties of supplementary obligations which, by their nature or according to commercial usage, have no connection with the subject of such contracts.'

Thus a 'dominant position' as such is not prohibited but its 'abuse' is. The incidents of abuse are not listed exhaustively in EC Article 82 (ex Art 86); they are enumerated by way of examples.[6] EC Article 82 (ex Art 86) sets out a prohibition only. There is no provision for the grant of any exemption from the prohibition (as in the case of EC Article 81 (ex Art 85)) and therefore no exemption is possible (save, in certain cases, pursuant to EC Article 86 (ex Art 90) in the case of public undertakings).[7] In order to apply EC Article 82 (ex Art 86) certain conditions must be present:

(1) there must be a 'dominant position',
(2) which is 'abused'; such abuse
(3) taking effect in the Common Market or a substantial part of it; and
(4) the abuse must be capable of 'affecting' trade between Member States.

---

3 Cf Cases 6 and 7/73: *Commercial Solvents Corpn v Commission* [1974] ECR 223, [1974] 1 CMLR 309, para 25 (a case where the relationship between the dominant undertaking and its competitor was vertical).

4 Case 6/72: *Europemballage Corpn and Continental Can Co Inc v Commission* [1973] ECR 215, [1973] CMLR 199, paras 25-26.

5 Reg 4064/89, (as amended) see the corrected version published in OJ 1990, L257/14.

6 The *Continental Can* case, supra.

7 See Ch 28, pp 653–654.

The prohibition is addressed to 'undertakings'[8] in the same sense used in the context of EC Article 81 (ex Art 85). The concept of 'undertaking' is not limited to bodies corporate set up under the laws of the Member States but includes also undertakings set up outside the Community and operating, as it were, from a foreign base.[9]

Moreover, the concept of 'undertaking' is broad enough to include a 'performing rights' society[10] set up to control authors, composers and music publishers. In the *Continental Can*[11] case and the *Commercial Solvents*[12] case the conduct of the subsidiaries was attributed to the parent companies, thus confirming the doctrine of imputabiltiy discussed by the ECJ in the *ICI*[13] cases. For the sake of exposition, this chapter will deal first with 'dominant position' and then with the 'relevant market' before exploring the concept of 'abuse'. In relation to the effect on trade between Member States, reference may be made to the parallel requirement in EC Article 81 (ex Art 85).[14]

C. Dominant position

A dominant position is 'a position of economic strength enjoyed by an undertaking which enables it to prevent effective competition being maintained on the relevant market by affording it the power to behave to an appreciable extent independently of its competitors, its customers and ultimately of the consumers. Such a position does not preclude some competition, which it does where there is a monopoly or a quasi-monopoly, but enables the undertaking which profits by it, if not to determine, at least to have an appreciable influence on, the conditions under which that competition will develop, and in any case to act largely in disregard of it so long as such conduct does not operate to its detriment'.[15] A finding that an undertaking occupies a dominant position is not in itself a criticism of the undertaking; it simply means that the undertaking lies under a special duty not to allow its conduct to affect adversely competition on the market.[16]

The most extreme example of a dominant position is a monopoly.[17] As stated succinctly by the Commission: 'GEMA[18] occupies a dominant position in the

---

8 See pp 648 et seq.
9 Eg Case 6/72: *Europemballage Corpn and Continental Can Co Inc v Commission* [1973] ECR 215 [1973] CMLR 199; Cases 6-7/73: *Commercial Solvents Corpn v Commission* [1974] ECR 223, [1974] 1 CMLR 309; Case 27/76: *United Brands v Commission* [1978] ECR 207, [1978] 1 CMLR 429; Case 85/76: *Hoffmann-La Roche & Co v Commission* [1979] ECR 461, [1979] 3 CMLR 211.
10 Commission decision in Case 71/224: *Re GEMA* [1971] CMLR D35; see also Case 22/79: *Greenwich Film Production, Paris v SACEM* [1979] ECR 3275, [1980] 1 CMLR 629.
11 Note 9, supra.
12 Ibid, note 9, supra.
13 Cases 48/69: *ICI Ltd v Commission* [1972] ECR 619; [1972] CMLR 557 at 601.
14 Ch 28, p 656. See eg Case T-69/89: *RTE v Commission* [1991] ECR II-485, para 76; Case T-65/89: *BPB Industries plc v Commission*, [1993] ECR II-389, paras 134-139.
15 Case 85/76: *Hoffmann-La Roche & Co AG v Commission* [1979] ECR 461, [1979] 3 CMLR 211, paras 38-39. See also Case 27/76: *United Brands v Commission* [1978] ECR 207, [1978] 1 CMLR 429, para 65.
16 Case 322/81: *Michelin v Commission* [1983] ECR 3461, [1985] 1 CMLR 282, para 57.
17 Eg Case C-115/97 to C-117/97 *Brentjens' Handelsonderneming BV v Stichting Bedrijfspensioenfonds voor de Handel in Bouwmaterialen* [1999] ECR I-6025, paras 90-92, where affiliation to a particular pension fund in a particular sector of industry was compulsory, thus giving the fund a legal monopoly in the supply of pensions.
18 Note 10, supra.

Federal Republic of Germany, which constitutes a substantial part of the Common Market. In fact it has no competitor there . . .'. This, in fact, was the first occasion on which EC Article 82 (ex Art 86), was applied. GEMA, being a society controlling the authors' rights with regard to musical works, was prohibited from restricting the economic freedom of authors, composers and music publishers. The practices in which GEMA was engaged were numerous and complex but their sum total was a rigid and virtually absolute control of general performing rights; broadcasting and transmission rights; film performance and film production; mechanical reproduction and diffusion of musical works; production, reproduction, diffusion and transmission of optical sound bases; and the exploitation rights resulting from the technical developments or from a future change of law.

The first attempt at a judicial definition of 'dominant position' had to wait until the *Sirena*[19] case although suggestions were made earlier by the Italian[20] government to apply EC Article 82 (ex Art 86) in cases where EC Article 81 (ex Art 85) was applied. This in turn enabled the ECJ to circumscribe the respective application of the two articles.[1] However, in the *Sirena* case the Court held that an undertaking does not necessarily occupy a dominant position by the sole fact of being able to prevent 'third parties from selling in the territory of a Member State products bearing the same trademark; moreover since Article 86 requires that this position covers at least a substantial part of the Common Market, it is necessary that it has the power of preventing effective competition within an important part of the market, considering also the possible existence and the position of producers or distributors of similar or substitute products . . .'.

This dictum was substantially reproduced in *Deutsche Grammophon GmbH v Metro*[2] where the ECJ held that a price maintenance scheme operating in Germany in respect of gramophone records produced in France and Germany but bearing the same trademark coupled with the control of supplies constituted an infringement of EC Article 82 (ex Art 86).

In *Re Continental Can Inc*[3] the Commission considered that 'undertakings are in a dominant position when they have the power to behave independently, which puts them in a position to act without taking into account their competitors, purchasers or suppliers'.

In *Re European Sugar Cartel*[4] the Commission held that: 'The RT has a dominant position on the Belgian and Luxembourg sugar markets which make up an important part of the Common Market. It controls the greater part of sugar production in Belgium and Luxembourg and has a large amount of surplus sugar at its disposal there. It holds at least 50% of the capital of the NV Suikerfabrieken van Vlaanderen . . . and of the SA Raffinerie Notre Dame . . . which gives it the opportunity to control those undertakings.'

In the *Commercial Solvents*[5] case the ECJ accepted the Commission's finding that the appellant 'has a dominant position in the Common Market for a raw material

---

19   Case 40/70: *Sirena Srl v Eda Srl* [1971] ECR 69, [1971] CMLR 260.
20   In *Consten and Grundig v Commission*, p 685, note 1, supra; and Case 32/65: *Italy v Council and Commission* [1969] CMLR 39.
1   *Italy*, supra.
2   Case 78/70: *Deutsche Grammophon GmbH v Metro-SB-Grossmärkte GmbH & Co KG* [1971] ECR 487 at 501, [1971] CMLR 631 at 658.
3   Commission Decision, JO 1972, L7/25; Case 72/21: [1972] CMLR D11; repeated in Commission decision in *Re United Brands Co* [1976] 1 CMLR D28.
4   Commission Decision [1973] CMLR D65; Cases 40-48, 50, 54-56, 111, 113, 114/73 [1975] ECR 1663, [1976] 1 CMLR 295.
5   Cases 6-7/73: *Istituto Chemioterapico Italiano SpA and Commercial Solvents Corpn v Commission* [1974] ECR 223, [1974] CMLR 309.

necessary for the manufacture of ethambutol, on the basis that it has a world monopoly in the production and sale of nitropropane and aminobutanol . . .'.

In the *General Motors*[6] case the ECJ thought that the 'legal monopoly, combined with the freedom of the manufacturer or sole authorized agent to fix the price for its service, leads to the creation of a dominant position within the meaning of Article 86 as, for any given make, the approval procedure can only be carried out in Belgium by the manufacturer or officially appointed authorized agent under conditions fixed unilaterally by the party', but in view of a change in the factual situation, ie reduction of charges to the level of the real cost and reimbursement of the complainants, it annulled the decision of the Commission.

In *Hoffmann-La Roche*[7] a Swiss multi-national company was held to be in a dominant position which it exercised by concluding agreements which contained an obligation upon purchasers, or by the grant of fidelity rebates offered them an incentive, to buy all or most of their requirements exclusively, or principally, from it. The extent of its activity was marked by the fact that it concluded agreements with 22 named undertakings engaged in the production and/or sale of vitamins in the Common Market for use either in the pharmaceutical industry (25%) or for food (15%) or as an additive in animal feeds (60%).

In the light of the above the existence of a dominant position is a matter of fact determined by the relevant market factors. How exactly the dominant undertaking achieved dominance, whether by means of intellectual property rights, state action or its own conduct, is irrelevant. Save in exceptional circumstances, market share is generally a reliable indicator of whether or not an undertaking occupies a dominant position: market shares of about 40% and above are usually sufficient to indicate the existence of a dominant position but it may be necessary to consider the stability of the market share, the market shares of competitors and other factors of competition.[8] An undertaking's ability to ignore competitive forces may also be indicative of the existence of a dominant position.[9]

In most cases, a dominant position is held by only one undertaking. From the fact that EC Article 82 (ex Art 86), refers to 'any abuse by one or more undertakings of a dominant position' it has been inferred that several undertakings may together occupy a dominant position ('joint or shared dominance'); although it may be that those words point to the somewhat different concept of 'joint abuse'. The ECJ has held that Article 86 may apply where a single group of undertakings holds a dominant position.[10] Two or more independent undertakings may, however, together occupy a dominant position where they are linked economically (such as by common possession of a technological advance which enables them to act independently of their competitors, customers and consumers).[11] The links between the undertakings must be such as to cause them to adopt the same conduct

6 Commission Decision 75/75: [1975] 1 CMLR D20; Case 26/75: *General Motors Continental v Commission* [1975] ECR 1367, [1976] 1 CMLR 95; para 7.

7 P 687, note 15.

8 The *Hoffmann-La Roche* case, supra, para 41; Case C-62/86: *AKZO Chemie BV v Commission* [1991] ECR I-3359, para 60; Case T-30/89: *Hilti v Commission* [1991] ECR II-1439, paras 90-92.

9 The *United Brands* case (p 687, note 9, supra), para 68.

10 See Case 30/87: *Bodson v Pompes Funèbres des Régions Libérées SA* [1988] ECR 2479, [1989] 4 CMLR 984, paras 21 and 26-27; Case 66/86: *Ahmed Saeed v Zentrale zur Bekämpfung unlauteren Wettbewerbs* [1989] ECR 803, [1990] 4 CMLR 102, para 35.

11 Cases T-68, T-77 and T-78/89: *SIV v Commission* [1992] ECR II-1403, para 357 et seq.

in the market.[12] But, in order to establish such a situation, it is not enough merely to recycle arguments appropriate to EC Article 81 (ex Art 85).[13] In particular, joint dominance does not arise merely because the situation on the relevant market is oligopolistic.[14]

In all cases, the existence or otherwise of a dominant person can be established only once the relevant market has been defined. The conditions on which EC Article 82 (ex Art 86) does or does not apply are assessed on the basis of the circumstances prevailing at the relevant time (that is, either contemporaneously or at the time when the conduct complained of occurred) and not on the basis of developments that could take place at some unspecified time in the future.[15]

(1) RELEVANT MARKET

According to Advocate-General Warner,[16] a position can only be 'dominant' within the meaning of Article 86 'if it is dominant in a relevant market'. This, in the light of decided cases, relates to product and territory.

(a) The product market
The product market comprises all the products which, with respect to their characteristics, are particularly suitable for satisfying constant needs and are only to a limited extent interchangeable with other products.[17] That test is directed to what is known as 'demand substitutability', that is, the extent to which buyers or consumers regard different products as interchangeable. Demand substitutability can be tested by comparing the physical characteristics and use of different products. It may also be tested by reference to what is known as 'cross-elasticity of demand', that is, the extent to which the demand for one product is affected by a change in the price of another product. Another aspect of substitutability is 'supply substitutability', that is, the extent to which producers of one product are able to switch production capacity to another product. Supply substitutability exists where the products in question are similar in terms of physical characteristics (in the sense that the production methods are similar) and the economic conditions (availability of spare production capacity, price and so forth) create a sufficient incentive for production to shift from one product to another. Supply substitutability is mainly useful as a means of cross-checking the conclusions drawn

---

12 Case C-393/92: *Municipality of Almelo v Energiebedrijf ljsselmij* [1994] ECR I-1477, paras 41-43; Case C-96/94: *Centro Servizi Spediporto v Spedizioni Marittima del Golfo* [1995] ECR I-2883, paras 32-34; Cases C-140/94 to C-142/94: *DIP v Commune di Bassano del Grappa et al* [1995] ECR I-3257, paras 25-27; Cases T-24/93 and T-28/93: *Compagnie Maritime Belge Transports v Commission* [1996] ECR II-1201, paras 60-67; Cases C-68/94 and C-30/95: *France v Commission* [1998] ECR I-1375, para 221; Case T-102/96: *Gencor v Commission* [1999] 4 CMLR 971, paras 273-277; Cases C-395/96P and C-396/96P *Campagnie Maritime Belge Transports v Commission* [2000] All ER (EC) 385, [2000] 4 CMLR 1076. Nonetheless, undertakings occupying a joint dominant position may abuse it either individually or jointly; Case T-228/97: *Irish Sugar v Commission* [1999] 5 CMLR 1300, para 60.
13 Cases C-215/96 to C-219/96: *Bagnasco v Banca Populare di Novara* [1999] ECR I-135, [1999] 4 CMLR 624, paras 47-48 of the Opinion of the Advocate-General.
14 Cf Case 85/76: *Hoffmann-La Roche v Commission* [1979] ECR 461, para 39.
15 Commission Decision 97/181: *GSM radio-telephony services in Spain*, OJ 1998, L76/19, recital 14. The fact that an undertaking is not currently in a dominant position is not proof that it never was in a dominant position: Commission Decision 1999/243: *Transatlantic Conference Agreement*, OJ 1999, L95/1, [1999] 4 CMLR 1415, recital 533.
16 *Commercial Solvents*, p 688, note 5.
17 Case C-62/86: *AKZO Chemie BV v Commission* [1991] ECR I-3359, para 51.

from the demand substitutability test. Its other main function is to indicate the existence or otherwise of potential competition, which may affect the conclusion that an undertaking does or does not occupy a dominant position on the relevant market; but, in that context, supply substitutability is not being used to assist in the definition of the relevant market.

The definition of the relevant product market can be a complex exercise. Perhaps the most instructive case to date is the banana case.

The *United Brands* case provides an insight into the world banana market and the way it was operated in the Community by a company incorporated in New York. It transpired that the company controlled the production, packaging, shipping, ripening, distribution, sales promotion, etc, of bananas on a world scale and imposed certain marketing and pricing practices in the Common Market refusing, inter alia, supplies to one distributor who had to be punished because he once advertised a rival brand. In a very detailed analysis of these practices the Commission concluded that they constituted an abuse of a dominant position.[18]

In order to condemn United Brands it was necessary to determine the extent to which the banana market was distinct from the market for fresh fruit. The ECJ upheld the Commission's findings saying that '. . . for the banana to be regarded as forming a market which is sufficiently differentiated from the other fruit markets it must be possible for it to be singled out by such special factors distinguishing it from other fruit that it is only to a limited extent interchangeable with them and is only exposed to their competition in a way that is hardly perceptible . . .'[19] The Court agreed that oranges are not interchangeable with bananas, and interchangeable only to a limited extent with apples and other domestic fruits in season. Consequently there was no 'significant long-term elasticity', nor was there any 'seasonal substitutability' between the bananas and all the seasonal fruits. The banana market was quite distinct.

In the *General Motors Continental NV*[20] case, a service of a kind relating to a particular product was involved. According to Belgian law every motor vehicle put on the road must have a certificate that it satisfies the requisite technical standard to be issued by the manufacturers or their agents. General Motors was authorized to issue such certificates for all vehicles in its group including vehicles imported privately. When new scales of charges, discriminating against the parallel importer, were introduced the exercise of General Motors' power was put under scrutiny. Both the Commission and the Court agreed that the service in question did affect the relevant market as being related to a product, but disagreed on the point whether or not there was a breach of EC Article 82 (ex Art 86).

A similar conclusion was reached by the Commission and the Court in the cash registers[1] case. Although Hugin, a Swedish manufacturer, did not enjoy a dominant position in the cash registers market it had one in the market for spare parts which were not obtainable elsewhere and which were not interchangeable. This was the relevant market because Hugin's own spare parts could be used only for repairs and reconditioning services of Hugin's products.

In the *Commercial Solvents* case, the Commercial Solvents Corporation, a company incorporated in the State of Maryland, had an almost global monopoly

18 *Re United Brands Co Decision* OJ 1976, L95/1, [1976] 1 CMLR D28.
19 *United Brands v Commission* para 22, p 687, note 9.
20 P 689, note 6.
1 Case 78/68: *Liptons Cash Registers and Business Equipment Ltd v Hugin Kassaregister AB* [1978] 1 CMLR D19; Case 22/78: *Hugin Kassaregister AB v Commission* [1979] ECR 1869 [1979] 3 CMLR 345.

of the manufacture of a certain drug used in the production of anti-tuberculosis medicines. It acquired an Italian company which acted as a reseller of the product in Italy and, through this intermediary, denied the supply of the product to Zoja, another Italian company, a customer of the former, who was unable to obtain the product on the world market and, therefore, was to be put out of business. It was clear that Zoja was totally dependent upon the supply and could not find a substitute. The Commission[2] upheld Zoja's complaint and ordered a limited supply. The ECJ,[3] in turn, upheld the Commission's decisions as it felt that behind the refusal to supply there was a scheme to eliminate competition and brushed aside the argument that the Commission's decision went outside the EEC territory and that the parent company was not responsible for its Italian subsidiary.

In *Hoffmann-La Roche*[4] product substitution figured prominently in the judgment of the ECJ. The product markets consisted, in this case, of seven groups of vitamins. Since, however, each group had 'specific metabolic functions' the groups were non-interchangeable. The Court held that: 'the concept of the relevant market implies that there can be effective competition between the products which form part of it and this presupposes that there is sufficient degree of interchangeability between all the products forming part of the same market in so far as a specific use of such products is concerned . . .'.

In *Re Continental Can Co Inc*[5] the problem of product substitution and the inability on the part of the Commission to define the relevant market in that respect led to the annulment of the Commission's decision.[6] The Commission considered three relevant product markets consisting of light metal closures for food products excluding crown corks, but, in its decision, failed to give sufficient weight to the possibility of product substitution. The Court ruled that: 'the definition of the relevant market is of essential significance, for the possibility of competition can only be judged in relation to those characteristics of the products in question by virtue of which those products are particularly apt to satisfy an inelastic need and are only to a limited extent interchangeable with other products' (para 32). Other illustrations of the definition of the relevant market concern weekly television programme information, whether offered as weekly listings or in the form of television magazines, which was regarded as forming a sub-market of the market for television programme information in general;[7] and the debate in the *Hilti* case over the question whether there was a distinct market for powder-actuated fastening systems comprising guns, cartridge strips and nails or separate markets for each component of such systems.[8]

(b)   The geographical or territorial market

The geographical or territorial localization of the relevant market is important in two respects. First, under EC Article 82 (ex Art 86), there must be an abuse of a dominant position 'within the common market or in a substantial part of it'. Secondly, the geographical definition of the market determines how many other competitors must be taken into account and this affects the assessment to be made

2   Decision 73/457, in *Re Zoja v Commercial Solvents Corpn* [1973] CMLR D50.
3   P 688, note 5.
4   P 690, note 14, para 28.
5   P 687, note 9.
6   Case 72/21: [1972] CMLR D11.
7   Case T-69/89: *RTE v Commission* [1991] ECR II-485, para 62.
8   Case T-30/89: *Hilti v Commission* [1991] ECR II-1439, paras 64–78, on appeal, Case C-53/92P: *Hilti v Commission* [1994] ECR I-667.

of the economic power wielded by the undertaking concerned. In general, the more extensive the market, the more diluted is the undertaking's economic power and the less likely it is that the undertaking will be found to be dominant. In principle, the geographical or territorial market is that area in which the objective conditions of competition applying to the product(s) in question are the same for all.[9] The objective conditions of competition may alter from one region to another for various reasons: state action, consumer preferences, transport costs, the characteristics of the product. For example, a perishable product can be transported only over a limited instance or period of time before it becomes unmarketable. That determines the relevant geographical market for that product. Depending upon the facts, the relevant market may be world-wide for certain products and narrowly localized for others. However the abuse of the dominant position must take effect in the Common Market or a substantial part of it.

In the *Bayer and Gist-Brocades Agreement*[10] the Commission considered the shares of the participants in the supply of penicillin practically in all four corners of the world except the Soviet and East European corner for which no information was available. In the *United Brands* case the trade in the Common Market was considered in the context of the world banana market though in view of their special market arrangements, three Community countries were excluded.

It is not quite clear how 'substantial' the part of the Common Market ought to be in order to be within the range of EC Article 82 (ex Art 86). In the Sugar Cartel[11] case the ECJ thought that in order to determine this factor '. . . the pattern and volume of production and consumption of the said products as well as the habits and economic opportunities of vendors and purchasers must be considered . . .'. It follows that the size of the geographical area is not the sole criterion. The business volume too has to be considered. Whilst the effect must take as its threshold a *de minimis* rule it is relative to the product and the situation in hand. This was indicated by Advocate-General Warner when he suggested that, though the customers of an oil company in the Netherlands took less than 0.5% of the motor spirit supplied in the Common Market, they might nevertheless constitute a 'substantial' part of the Common Market.[12] A port can be a substantial part of the Common Market if it is (for example) the leading port in the Mediterranean for container traffic and plays an important role in the intra-community trade.[13] In its decision in the *Finnish Airports* case[14] the Commission found that the Finnish Civil Aviation Authority, which provided airlines with access services to civil airport facilities in Finland in return for a fee, held a dominant position in the market for landing and take-off services in each of the five Finnish airports with international traffic; and that, taken together, the airports constituted a substantial part of the Common Market, as in cases involving contiguous monopolies.

(2) ABUSE OF A DOMINANT POSITION

The word 'abuse' sounds pejorative. The concept of 'abuse' is not. It is usually defined as 'an objective concept relating to the behaviour of an undertaking in a

---

9   Case 27/76: *United Brands v Commission* [1978] ECR 207, [1978] 1 CMLR 429, paras 44 and 53.
10 Case 76/172: [1976] 1 CMLR D98.
11 P 688, note 4.
12 Case 77/77: *Benzine en Petroleum Handels-maatschappij BV v Commission* [1978] ECR 1513, [1978] 3 CMLR 174.
13 Case C-163/96: *Silvano Raso* [1998] ECR I-533, paras 25-26.
14 Decision 1999/198 (OJ 1999, L69/24, [1999] 5 CMLR 90), recitals 34-36.

dominant position which is such as to influence the structure of a market where, as a result of the very presence of the undertaking in question, the degree of competition is weakened and which, through recourse to methods different from those which condition normal competition in products or services on the basis of the transactions of commercial operators, has the effect of hindering the maintenance of the degree of competition still existing in the market or the growth of that competition'.[15] That definition is particularly apt for exclusionary or anti-competitive abuses and less apt as a definition of exploitative abuses, which typically concern less the distortion of competition and rather more the reaping by the dominant undertaking of a benefit that it could not obtain by recourse to methods which condition normal competition (such as charging excessively high prices). In many respects, the key element of the concept of 'abuse' is the recourse to business methods which are not typical of behaviour under undistorted conditions of competition or which the dominant undertaking would not be able to indulge in if it were subjected to the full force of competition. Thus, a dominant undertaking may properly compete by offering a better-quality product or service or a better price; but it may not attempt to enhance its position by using methods other than those which come within the scope of competition on the basis of quality[16] or, more generally, on the basis of the intrinsic merits of what it has to offer, such as by using intellectual property rights to fetter the activities of its competitors.[17] The recourse to atypical business methods does not offer a complete picture of what is meant by 'abuse' because there are situations where recourse to 'typical' commercial behaviour is an abuse and unlawful even though it is not unlawful when perpetrated by a non-dominant undertaking.[18] Accordingly, it is often better to use the expressions 'objective justification' or 'objective business reason' to describe the circumstances that may be advanced in order to excuse conduct that is said to be abusive.[19] An abuse need not take place on the same markets as that in which the dominant position is held;[20] but there should be a

---

15 Case 85/76: *Hoffmann-La Roche v Commission* [1979] ECR 461, [1979] 3 CMLR 211, para 91; Case C-62/86: *AKZO Chemie BV v Commission* [1991] ECR I-3359, para 69; Case T-228/97: *Irish Sugar v Commission* [1999] ECR II-2969 [1999] 5 CMLR 1300, paras 111-112.

16 Case T-229/94: *Deutsche Bahn v Commission* [1997] ECR II-1689, para 78.

17 Case T-69/89: *RTE v Commission* [1991] ECR II-485, para 65 et seq; Cases C-241/91P and C-242/91P: *RTE and ITP v Commission* [1995] ECR I-743.

18 Examples are take-overs by non-dominant undertakings and price-cutting. The latter is often used by undertakings as a means of entering a new market and is not regarded as objectionable. Care may have to be taken when assessing whether or not a particular business method is 'typical' under conditions of normal competition because businessmen often regard as perfectly acceptable and normal behaviour which competition authorities regard as profoundly wicked.

19 Various circumstances may provide an objective justification for allegedly abusive conduct. For example, in Commission Decision 98/190: *Frankfurt Airport* (OJ 1998, L72/30, recital 83 and Art 1), Frankfurt Airport denied potential third-party handlers access to the ramp and airport users the right to 'self-handle'. The Commission found that that was an abuse save in respect of part of the airport, where the presence of more than one handler would result in major problems as a result of the configuration of the airport. In Cases C-215/96 to C-219/96: *Bagnasco v Banca Populare di Novara* [1999] ECR I-135, [1999] 4 CMLR 624, para 59, a change in interest rates offered by banks was not regarded as an abuse if it merely reflected changes in objective factors such as movements in the money markets. In Case T-229/94: *Deutsche Bahn v Commission* [1997] ECR II-1689, paras 87-93, an allegation of discrimination in the fixing of freight tariffs was met with the argument that the price differences were due to cost differences and differences in the degree of competition affecting the services in position. However, whatever the merits of that argument as a matter of principle, it was found to be unsustainable on the facts.

20 Case 311/84: *CBEM v CLT* [1985] ECR 3261, [1986] 2 CMLR 558.

link between the dominant position and the alleged abuse and, therefore, between the two markets concerned unless special circumstances dictate otherwise.[1]

Abuses expressly prohibited by EC Article 82 (ex Art 86) are, with the exception of sharing markets or sources of supply, the same as the practices prohibited by EC Article 81(1) (ex Art 85(1)). This reflects the complementary function of these two articles.

(a) Unfair prices or unfair trading conditions (EC Article 82(a) (ex Art 86(a)))
In this category fall the decisions in *General Motors* and *United Brands*. The former revealed a discriminately charge on parallel imports, the latter excessive prices allowing for a large profit margin. The difficulty, which will have to be resolved, is: who, and according to what criteria, is competent to determine the 'fair' price of a product or service?

The ECJ gave a general indication of the approach to be followed in the *United Brands* case.[2] In *Akzo*,[3] it held that not all competition by a dominant undertaking based on price is legitimate and that prices below average variable costs must be regarded as abusive. Prices below average total costs are abusive if they are determined as part of a plan for eliminating a competitor. That deals with unfairly low pricing, also known as 'predatory pricing'. Prices may also be unfairly high if they have no reasonable relation to the economic value of the goods or services supplied.[4]

A question of unfair trading conditions arose in *Re Eurofirma*[5] where a buyer of railway rolling-stock insisted on inserting in development contracts a condition to the effect that it would receive gratis unlimited patent licences (including a right to sub-license patents to third parties) resulting from these contracts. The Commission conceded that the technical co-operation between Eurofirma and its contractors justified the patent exploitation for its own needs but considered the claim to grant licences to third parties without additional compensation to be an abuse of a dominant position. However no formal decision was reached because the condition was removed from Eurofirma's contracts.

The concept of unfair trading seems broad enough to include restrictions on the exercise of copyrights and kindred rights by members and associate members of a 'Society of Authors, Composers and Publishers'.[6]

(b) Limitation of production, markets etc (EC Article 82(b) (ex Art 86(b)))
In order to come within the prohibition, the 'limitation of production, distribution or technical development' by the dominant undertaking must be to the detriment of consumers. Should it be otherwise no undertaking could embark on a reorganization or rationalization programme.

In the *Sugar* cases the dominant undertaking was held to have placed itself in an abusive position by prohibiting its distributors from exporting to Member

---

1   Case C-333/94P: *Tetra-Pak v Commission* [1996] ECR I-5951, para 27; Case T-228/97: *Irish Sugar v Commission* [1999] ECR II-2969, [1999] 5 CMLR 1300, paras 166-167.
2   [1978] ECR 207, paras 235-268.
3   [1991] ECR I-3359, paras 70-72. See also Case T-83/91: *Tetra-Pak v Commission* [1994] ECR II-755 and Case C-333/94P: *Tetra-Pak v Commission* [1996] ECR I-5951, [1997] 4 CMLR 662.
4   Case C-242/95: *GT-Link v DSB* [1997] ECR I-4449, para 39.
5   [1973] CMLR D217.
6   Case 127/73: *BRT v SABAM* [1974] ECR 51, [1974] 2 CMLR 238; see also Decision in Case 71/224: *Re GEMA* [1971] CMLR D35 and Case 72/268: *No 2* [1972] CMLR D115; and *Greenwich Film Production*, p 687, note 10.

States or bringing pressure upon its dealers to channel exports to particular distributors. Moreover by threatening to withhold supplies so as to oblige the dealer to resell the product to certain clients and for certain uses the dominant undertaking was said to be 'limiting the market'.

In a sense a refusal of supplies[7] can be construed as a limitation of the market. At least, that is the inference from the judgment of the ECJ which ruled that '. . . the refusal to sell would limit markets to the prejudice of customers and would amount to discrimination which might in the end eliminate a trading party from the relevant market . . .'.

(c) Dissimilar conditions in equivalent transactions (EC Article 82(c) (ex Art 86(c)))

The practices condemned in *GEMA* included discrimination by the Society against authors from other Member States in so far as they could not become ordinary members of the Society.

In the *United Brands* case price discrimination led to the conclusion that customers were not treated equally and this, no doubt, affected their competitive position. The dominant undertaking set prices for bananas already at sea in response to offers from the distributors and ripeners. At that stage the supply for the subsequent week was fixed, priority depending on demand. United Brands claimed that the different prices charged by it reflected the different conditions of supply and demand in different parts of the Community. The different prices were therefore justified. The ECJ disapproved of this practice. It pointed out that the various factors affecting price culminated in different selling prices at retail level; but United Brands did not sell its bananas at that level. It sold bananas to ripeners/distributors and they, not United Brands, bore the risks of the consumers' market. In contrast, United Brands was relatively isolated from what was happening at retail level. Accordingly, the interplay of supply and demand at retail level could not justify price differences at a different level of trade, where the interplay of supply and demand was different.[8] Discriminative pricing may arise where: (1) an undertaking charges others for supplying particular goods or services but provides the same goods or services in-house (or intra-group) without charge; or (2) where the undertaking charges different trading partners a different price for the same goods or services. In the former case, the discrimination may be avoided if there appears in the undertaking's accounts (or those for the group) an internal (or intra-group) charge for the supply that is commensurate with the price paid by an external purchaser. In the latter case, an undertaking may charge trading partners different prices (or may waive payment from particular trading partners) if there is some objective business reason for doing so, such as where two undertakings supplying each other reciprocally waive payment *and* the payments balance out (if they do not, one of the undertakings is getting something for nothing and there is accordingly discrimination).[9] In addition to there being discrimination, the discrimination must also lead to the creation of dissimilar conditions for equivalent transactions that places some trading parties at a competitive disadvantage in relation to others.[10]

---

7 *Commercial Solvents*, p 688, note 5.
8 [1978] ECR 207, paras 227-234.
9 Case C-242/95: *GT-Link v DSB* [1997] ECR I-4349, paras 41-43.
10 See in particular Commission Decision 98/513: *Alpha Flight Services/Aeroports de Paris*, OJ 1998, L230/10, recitals 83-127.

(d) Collateral obligations (EC Article 82(d) (ex Art 86(d)))

In the *Sugar* cases one of the German producers is reported to have tied its customers by a loyalty rebate which meant in effect that they were punished in various ways if they failed to perform according to the agreement imposed upon them by the dominant party.

The Court distinguished between a quantity rebate and a loyalty rebate, the former being permissible but not the latter. It held: 'the rebate is not to be treated as a quantity rebate exclusively linked with the volume of purchases from the producers concerned but has been rightly classified by the Commission as a 'loyalty' rebate designed through the grant of a financial advantage, to prevent customers obtaining their supplies from competing producers . . .' (para 18).

The problem was considered further in *Hoffmann-La Roche*,[11] where 'fidelity agreements' were condemned by both the Commission and the Court. In that case the dominant party either obliged its customers to purchase all or most of their requirements from it, or provided that it would make a periodic rebate to customers based on their overall purchases. The contracts also had a clause, the so-called 'English clause', where Hoffmann-La Roche ('HLR') undertook to bring prices down to any lower prices charged by manufacturers or, failing that, allowed customers to buy from such manufacturers without forfeiting fidelity rebates.

The Commission held that there was an abuse of a dominant position. The ECJ upheld the Commission's decision. It ruled that exclusive supply arrangements tying the purchaser to obtain all or a large proportion of its requirements were abusive irrespective of whether or not they were related to rebates. Fidelity rebates, conditional upon the customer obtaining all or most of its supplies from the undertaking in a dominant position, were also abusive because they prevented the customer from purchasing elsewhere. Moreover they were discriminatory since they distinguished between 'loyal' and 'disloyal' customers. The 'English clause', thought the Court, was incapable of mitigating the abuse because HLR had a discretion whether or not to allow the customer to take recourse to it.

In the *Hilti* case,[12] a supplier of nail guns and the consumables (nails, cartridge strips) used with them infringed EC Article 82 (ex Art 86) by tying the purchase of nails to the purchase of the cartridge strips in an attempt to exclude from the market competing manufacturers of nails.

(e) Refusal to supply

A refusal to supply can take the form of a straightforward refusal to supply or an indirect, or constructive, refusal, such as where the dominant undertaking is prepared to supply the goods or services in question but only on terms as to price or other conditions that are unacceptable to the customer or otherwise objectionable on competition grounds.[13] On that basis, the Commission has assimilated the practice of imposing restrictions on the availability of service controls to a refusal to supply, although it may also be characterized as the imposition of unfair trading conditions or a limitation on production or markets etc.[14]

In the *Tiercé Ladbroke* case,[15] the CFI declined to hold that a refusal to supply sound and pictures of French horse-racing to a large turf accountant operating in

---

11 P 694, note 15.
12 Case T-30/89: *Hilti v Commission* [1991] ECR II-1439.
13 The Commission put it in a slightly different way in Decision 1999/243: *Transatlantic Conference Agreement* (OJ 1999, L95/1, [1999] 4 CMLR 1415), recital 553.
14 Ibid.
15 Case T-504/93: *Tiercé Ladbroke v Commission* [1997] ECR II-923, paras 123-134.

Belgium was an abuse. The relevant market was found to be Belgium and the sole supplier of the sound and pictures was not supplying anyone in Belgium but did supply undertakings in other Member States. Even the apparent arbitrary nature of the refusal to supply was not regarded as sufficient to characterize it as an abuse. The conclusion might have been otherwise if the supplier had been supplying some undertakings in Belgium but not others or had been present in that market (in which case, the supplier might have been accused of having acted in a discriminative manner or in such a way as to keep a competitive advantage of itself). However, even if the supplier had been present in the relevant market and had been keeping a competitive advantage for itself, that would not have been an abuse, so the CFI held, unless: (1) the product or service supplied by the supplier was essential for the exercise of an economic activity (in the sense that there was no real or potential substitute for it); or (2) was a new product whose introduction on the market might be prevented, despite specific, constant and regular demand from consumers.

In *Philips Electronics v Ingman Ltd*,[16] refusal to supply was invoked by way of defence to a patent infringement action. The contention was that, as the patent barred access to the market (the manufacture of compact discs), a licence of the patent was essential for manufacture of compact discs (an 'essential facility') and it was abusive to refuse to grant a licence of the patent. Accordingly, the defendant was entitled to manufacture compact discs without a patent licence. That argument was rejected. It implied that any refusal to grant a licence (at least on fair and reasonable terms) would be unlawful, even though the existing case law clearly shows that the holder of a patent is perfectly entitled to work the patent himself/herself and not grant a licence to anyone.

The essential facilities doctrine came under scrutiny before the ECJ in Case C-7/97: *Oscar Bronner GmbH & Co KG v Mediaprint Zeitungs- und Zeitschriftenverlag GmbH & Co KG*.[17] There, the question was whether or not it was an abuse of a dominant position for a press undertaking ('Mediaprint') holding a very large share of the national market for daily newspapers and operating the only nationwide newspaper home-delivery system, to refuse to give a smaller rival newspaper publisher ('Bronner') access to the delivery system even though the latter was prepared to pay appropriate remuneration.

The Advocate General reviewed the case law and concluded that it showed that 'a dominant undertaking commits an abuse where, without justification, it cuts off supplies of good or services to an existing customer or eliminates competition on a related market by tying separate goods and services'; and that 'an abuse may consist in mere refusal to license where that prevents a new product from coming on a neighbouring market in competition with the dominant undertaking's own product on that market'.[18]

On the other hand, the Advocate-General also considered that any incursion on the right of an undertaking to choose its own trading partner requires careful justification and a careful balancing of conflicting considerations. As he put it, 'the mere fact that by retaining a facility for its own use a dominant undertaking retains an advantage over a competitor cannot justify requiring access to it'. Moreover, he emphasized that 'the primary purpose of Article 86 [now Art 82] is to prevent distortion of competition – and in particular to safeguard the interests of consumers – rather than to protect the position of

16   [1998] 2 CMLR 839.
17   [1998] ECR I-7791, [1999] 4 CMLR 112.
18   Para 43 of his Opinion.

particular competitors'.[19] That train of reasoning led the Advocate-General to conclude that the essential facilities doctrine has little or no application to the ordinary exercise of intellectual property rights even by a dominant undertaking.[20]

The upshot was that, in the view of the Advocate-General, a refusal of access to a facility is potentially abusive only if, as a result of the refusal, it would be extremely difficult, not only for the undertaking demanding access but also for any other undertaking, to compete. In the result, Mediaprint's refusal to give Bronner access to its network was not abusive because Bronner had alternative possibilities open to it to compete, even if those alternatives might be less convenient and require some investment.[1]

The first point made by the ECJ was that the relevant market had to be the market for the distribution and delivery of daily newspapers; and that it was for the referring court to decide on the facts how that market was to be defined and whether or not there was a separate market for home delivery systems.[2] If the referring court found that Mediaprint held a dominant position in that market, the question whether or not it had abused its dominant position would then arise. The ECJ considered that three criteria were to be applied: (1) would the refusal of access to the system be likely to eliminate all competition in the downstream market (that is, the market for daily newspapers); (2) would the refusal be incapable of objective justification; and (3) would the service provided by the system be indispensable to carrying on the business of the person seeking access (in other words, is there no actual or potential substitute in existence)?[3]

The ECJ went on to state that those criteria would not be satisfied where (as in the *Bronner* case): there are other methods of distribution, albeit less advantageous ones; it is not impossible or even unreasonably difficult for a newspaper publisher to set up a rival home-delivery scheme either alone or in combination with others; or where the person seeking access is merely too small or has too small a circulation to render setting up a rival system economically viable – the test is whether or not it is economically viable to set up a rival system for the distribution of daily newspapers having a circulation comparable to that of the owner of the existing system.[4]

(f) Other

The threat or actual commencement of legal proceedings can be an abuse in very exceptional circumstances, such as where the aim of the litigation is not to vindicate rights that the claimant could reasonably believe that it had and where the litigation forms part of a plan to eliminate competition.[5] The making of a contract or the acquisition of a right,[6] exercising a contractual right or a position of advantage resulting from an agreement in an anti-competition manner[7] and breaking a contract, or acting inconsistently with a contractual provision,[8] may also be abusive.

---

19 Ibid, paras 56-58.
20 Ibid, paras 62-64. A similar approach was followed by Laddie J in *Philips Electronics v Ingman* (supra, note 16).
1 Ibid, paras 65-70.
2 Ibid, paras 34-36 of the judgment.
3 Ibid, para 41.
4 Ibid, paras 42-46.
5 Case T-111/96 *ITT Promedia v Commission* [1998] ECR II-2937, paras 60-61, 72-73 and 117.
6 The *ITT* Case, supra, para 139.
7 Case T-229/94: *Deutsche Bahn v Commission* [1997] ECR II-1689, paras 80-83.
8 Commission Decision 98/538: *Amministrazione Autonoma del Monopoli di State* (OJ 1998, L252/47), recitals, 49, 52 and 54.

A demand that another party to an agreement should perform its part of the agreement may be an abuse if (in particular): (1) it goes beyond what the parties could reasonably infer from the agreement; or (2) the circumstances prevailing at the making of the agreement had not altered in the meantime.[9] A dominant undertaking may abuse its dominant position if it extends to its customers an inducement that, if accepted by them, will result in the dominant undertaking obtaining an exclusive commercial relationship with the customer, thus excluding competing suppliers (at least for a significant period of time).[10]

D. Determination of infringements and sanctions

EC Article 82 (ex Art 86), in contrast with EC Article 81 (ex Art 85), provides for neither nullity of the prohibited practice, nor for exemption. However there is a certain amount of overlap between the two articles in so far as conduct falling within EC Article 82 (ex Art 86) may also offend EC Article 81 (ex Art 85). Article 2 of Regulation 17 provides for negative clearance in respect of EC Article 82 (ex Art 86) which, if granted, would consist of a declaration that the applicant is not abusing its dominant position.

Infringements of EC Article 82 (ex Art 86) are dealt with by the Commission in the same way as infringements of EC Article 81 (ex Art 85).[11] They may also be dealt with by the national authorities. If proved they are subject to orders to 'cease and desist' or injunctions[12] reinforced by fines and periodical penalties (Articles 15 and 16 of Regulation 17).

E. Mergers

In the *Continental Can* case,[13] the Commission considered that the acquisition of European companies, manufacturing various kinds of containers and metal lids for glass jars, by an American company and its European subsidiary was an abuse of a dominant position. The ECJ annulled the decision as being 'tainted by fundamental uncertainty' but accepted the principle that mergers could be controlled by means of EC Article 82 (ex Art 86). However, EC Article 82 (ex Art 86) operates only after the event, that is, the Commission's powers come into operation when an abuse has taken place. EC Article 82 (ex Art 86) does not enable pre-emptive action to be taken to prevent an abuse from taking place. In many instances of abuse, that does not matter because the *status quo* can be restored. In the case of takeovers and mergers the position is different because it is less easy, and sometimes impossible, to unscramble the situation. Even though some form of divestment may be ordered, what emerges may not be the same as what originally existed before the take-over or merger took place: for example,

---

9 The *ITT* case, supra, para 140.
10 Eg Commission Decision 98/531: *Van den Bergh Foods Ltd* (OJ 1998, L246/1, recitals 262-270), which concerned an offer to supply freezer cabinets to retailers, and to maintain them, at no direct charge to the retailer, on the basis that the cabinets would be used only for the stocking and sale of the supplier's products.
11 See pp 629 et seq.
12 See eg *United Brands; Commercial Solvents*, supra.
13 Case 6/72: *Europemballage Corpn and Continental Can Co Inc v Commission* [1973] ECR 215, [1973] CMLR 199.

in order to remove the perceived abuse, it may be sufficient if the undertaking effecting the take-over simply divests itself of part of its pre-existing business or carves out of the new undertaking resulting from the take-over a separate business combining different elements of the pre-existing undertakings; in either event, the operation of EC Article 82 (ex Art 86) would not lead to *restitutio ad integrum*. In order to get over the particular problems presented by the application of EC Article 82 (ex Art 86) to take-overs and mergers, the Council adopted Regulation No 4064/89.[14] Under the scheme of that regulation, one regime applies to take-overs and mergers which have a 'Community dimension' and another to take-overs and mergers which lack such a dimension. The regulation uses the term 'concentration' to describe the take-overs, mergers and acquisitions which it covers and that term will be used here.[15]

F. Concentrations having Community dimension

(1) CONCENTRATION

A concentration is defined as arising where two or more previously independent undertakings merge or where direct or indirect control of all or part of one or more undertakings is acquired by (1) one or more *persons* already controlling at least one other undertaking or (2) one or more other *undertakings*.[16] Joint control may arise where, for example, two undertakings between them own all the shares in a company and, while one of them has more nominees on the Board of Directors of the company than the other, it is agreed between them that major decisions of the Board of Directors must be supported by at least one of the nominees of both parents.[17]

The means used to acquire control, whether it be by purchase of assets, purchase of shares or some other means, is not relevant. Control is defined as the possibility of exercising decisive influence on an undertaking in particular by (i) ownership or the right to use all or part of the assets of an undertaking and (ii) rights or contracts which confer decisive influence on the composition, voting or decisions of the organs of an undertaking.[18] For example, a minority shareholder in a company might be entitled to only one seat on the Board of Directors and, as a result of the size of its shareholding and its one representative on the Board, would ordinarily have little or no chance of determining the decisions of the Board and, thus, of exercising decisive influence. On the other hand, if that shareholder owned assets necessary for the carrying on of the company's business (such as aircraft leased to the company in order to enable it to carry on business as an airline) or had made a significant loan to the company under terms enabling the shareholder to call back the loan at short notice, the shareholder's

---

14 See the corrected version of the Regulation published in OJ 1990, L257/13; amended by Council Reg 1310/97 (OJ 1997, L180/1), which was also the subject of a corrigendum (OJ 1998, L40/17).
15 The major works on the subject are *Weinberg & Blank on Take-overs and Mergers*, Part IIIA, ch 2 (2000); Bos, P V F, Stuyck, J and Wytinck, P, *Concentration Control in the European Economic Community* (1992); Cook, J, and Kerse, C, *EC Merger Control* (1999); Jones, C and Gonzalez-Diaz, E, *The EEC Merger Regulation* (1992).
16 Reg 4064/89, Art 3(1).
17 See eg Case T-2/93: *Air France v Commission* [1994] ECR II-323.
18 Reg 4064/89, Art 3(3).

economic position in relation to the company might well enable it to exercise decisive influence over the Board.

A concentration is not deemed to arise where credit or other financial institutions or insurance companies acquire control of other undertakings essentially for the purpose of investment; where control is acquired by a liquidator or receiver in the context of a liquidation or winding up and so forth; and where a change of control is effected by a financial holding company which is not involved in the management of the undertaking in question but simply manages its own portfolio of shares and investments.[19]

(2) COMMUNITY DIMENSION

A concentration has a Community dimension where (1) the combined aggregate worldwide turnover of all the undertakings involved is more than ECU 5,000 million; and (2) the aggregate turnover within the Community of each of at least two of the undertakings involved is more than ECU 250 million; unless (3) each of the undertakings involved achieves more than two-thirds of its aggregate turnover in the Community within one and the same Member State.[20] A concentration may also have a Community dimension where: (a) the combined aggregate worldwide turnover of the undertakings involved is more than ECU 2,500 million; (b) in each of at least three Member States, the combined aggregate turnover is more than ECU 100 million; (c) in each of at least the same three Member States, the aggregate turnover of at least two of the undertakings involved is more than ECU 250 million; and (d) the aggregate community-wide turnover of each of at least two of the undertakings involved is more than ECU 100 million; unless (e) each of the undertakings involved achieves more than two-thirds of its aggregate Community-wide turnover is one and the same Member State.[1] When calculating the relevant turnover, account must be taken not only of the turnover of the undertakings directly involved in the concentration but also of the turnover of undertakings related to them.[2]

(3) APPRAISAL

In principle, a concentration having Community dimension will be declared incompatible with the common market and will therefore be prohibited if it (1) creates or strengthens a dominant position[3] and (2) as a result, effective competition would be significantly impeded in the common market or a substantial part of it.[4] The criteria for determining whether or not that is so are essentially competition law criteria similar to those employed in the context of EC Article 82 (ex Art 86).[5] The Commission is entrusted with appraising the compatibility of a concentration with the common market. The Member States are prohibited from applying their national competition law to concentrations having a Community dimension unless the Commission has, on request, referred the matter to the competent authority of a Member State. The Commission may do that if

---

19 Reg 4064/89, Art 3(5).
20 Reg 4064/89, Art 1(2).
1 Ibid, Art 1(3).
2 Ibid, Art 5(4).
3 The dominant position may be held either individually or jointly: see Cases C-68/94 and C-30/95: *France v Commission* [1998] ECR I-1375; Case T-102/96: *Gencor v Commission* [1999] ECR II-753, [1999] 4 CMLR 971.
4 Reg 4064/89, Art 2.
5 See eg Case M053: *Aérospatiale – Alenia/De Havilland*, OJ 1991, L334/42, [1992] 4 CMLR M2.

it finds that there is a market within the Member State concerned that presents all the characteristics of a distinct market and the concentration threatens to create or strengthen a dominant position within that market.[6]

The Member States may, however, take appropriate measures to protect legitimate interests relating to public security, plurality of the media, prudential rules and other interests recognized by the Commission as being compatible with Community law.[7]

(4) PROCEDURE

All concentrations having a Community dimension must be notified to the Commission before they are effected.[8] The implementation of the concentration is then suspended automatically (subject to a power on the part of the Commission to lift the suspension) until it has been declared to be compatible with the common market or is deemed to have been declared compatible.[9] The Commission makes an initial assessment of the concentration, the result of which is either the clearance of the concentration or the initiation of proceedings involving an appraisal of the concentration by the Commission or, if the matter is referred to a Member State, by the competition authorities of that state.[10] Where the Commission deals with the case, the concentration may then be approved or, if it is found to be incompatible with the common market, prohibited or permitted to be implemented subject to conditions; the Commission may also find that the concentration is not in truth a concentration or not a concentration having Community dimension. Where a Member State deals with the case, the relevant national legislation applies. The Commission has similar powers to request information and enter premises and impose fines to those it possess under Regulation 17.[11] The Commission is required to give the persons and undertakings concerned an opportunity to be heard before making certain decisions and is obliged to maintain the confidentiality of information acquired by it in the exercise of its powers.[12] The detailed procedural rules for the implementation of Regulation 4064/89 are laid down in Regulation 447/98.[13] Decisions of the Commission are subject to judicial review by the CFI and, by appeal on a point of law only, the ECJ.[14]

G. Concentrations lacking Community dimension

Recital 29 of Regulation 4064/89 states that concentrations not covered by the Regulation (which is presumed to mean concentrations lacking Community dimension) come in principle within the jurisdiction of the Member States. Article 22(2) excludes the application of the procedural regulations implementing EC Articles 81 and 82 (ex Arts 85 and 86) so far as such concentrations are concerned; and Article 22(3) provides that the Commission may appraise such

6 Reg 4064/89, Art 9. See Case M180: *Steetley/Tarmac*, 12 February 1992.
7 Reg 4064/89, Art 21(3).
8 Reg 4064/89, Art 4(1).
9 Ibid, Art 7.
10 Ibid, Arts 6, 9 and 10.
11 Reg 4064/89, Arts 11, 13, 14, 15.
12 Ibid, Arts 17 and 18.
13 OJ 1998, L61/1.
14 Reg 4064/89, Arts 10(5), 16 and 20(1).

concentrations if so requested by a Member State. It would therefore appear that concentrations lacking Community dimension are to be dealt with solely under national law unless the authorities of a Member State make a request under Article 22(3) for the Commission to deal with the matter. However, the position is unclear because the exclusion of the application of the procedural rules implementing EC Articles 81 and 82 (ex Arts 85 and 86) is not generally regarded as sufficient in law to prevent the application of those articles of the EC Treaty: at most, they limit the powers of the national competition authorities and the Commission to those set out in EC Articles 84 and 85 (ex Arts 88 and 89) and do not prevent the application of EC Article 82 (ex Art 86) by way of civil action.[15]

---

15 For a more detailed explanation of the position where there are no procedural rules implementing Arts 85 and 86, see Cases 209-213/84: *Ministère Public v Asjes* [1986] ECR 1425, [1986] 3 CMLR 173; Case 66/86: *Ahmed Saeed Flugreisen and Silver Line Reisebüro GmbH v Zentrale zur Bekampfung unlauteren Wettbewerbs* [1989] ECR 803, [1990] 4 CMLR 102. In the context of Art 22(3) of Reg 4064/89, the required effect on trade between Member States is the same as that required by EC Arts 81 and 82 (ex Arts 85 and 86): Case T-22/97: *Kesko Oy v Commission* [1999] ECR II-3775, paras 103-107.

Chapter 30

State aid (EC Articles 87–89 (ex Articles 92–94))

A. State aids and the Common Market

In principle State intervention in commerce and industry interferes in the operation of a market economy and, where it is practised in individual Member States of the Community, it can distort competition and create an unfair advantage for domestic producers or exporters. In brief, state aids undermine the philosophy of the Common Market.

However, state intervention, even in a market economy, does take place as governments regard it as their duty to intervene by employing public resources for the well-being of the country, particularly to combat the evil of economic decline with all its social consequences; to invest in the development of under-developed areas; to bale out and revive ailing industries; to encourage the development of new industries, relying on advanced technology and research and sophisticated equipment. Economic recession, particularly, reminds governments of their responsibilities to their electorates who look to the government's leadership for a solution to the country's problems.

The Treaty provisions for state aids reflect the reality of the economic situation, taking into account the political sensibility of existing aids whilst endeavouring to create a regime of state aids under the supervision of the Community institutions.

B. Aids incompatible with the Common Market (EC Article 87(1) (ex Art 92(1)))

EC Article 87(1) (ex Art 92(1)) provides:

> 'Save as otherwise provided in this Treaty, any aid granted by a Member State or through State resources in any form whatsoever which distorts or threatens to distort competition by favouring certain undertakings or the production of certain goods shall, in so far as it affects trade between Member States, be incompatible with the common market.'

Aids that are 'incompatible' are in fact prohibited.[1]

In general terms EC Article 87(1) (ex Art 92(1)) 'refers to the decision of Member States by which the latter, in pursuit of their own economic and social objectives, give, by unilateral and autonomous decisions, undertakings or other persons resources or procure for them advantages intended to encourage the attainment of the economic or social objectives sought'.[2]

The form or the purpose of the aid is immaterial: 'Article 92 [now Art 87] does not distinguish between the measures of State intervention concerned by reference to their cause or aims but defines them in relation to their effects . . .'.[3] Hence Italian legislation providing for a reduction, for three years, of the contributions payable by employers in the textile industry to cover their contributions in respect of their workers' family allowances was held to be a prohibited state aid notwithstanding the argument that it merely constituted a tax concession and that it was a measure within the state's social policy. However, it does not follow that all policy justifications for a measure must be ignored when considering whether or not it is a State aid. A measure benefiting some undertakings but not others may not be a State aid where the benefit is objectively justified by economic reasons[4] or is simply inherent in a particular scheme for legal or social reasons.[5]

In the absence of specific examples in the Treaty the Commission compiled a list of aids comprising: direct subsidies; exemptions from duties and taxes; exemption from parafiscal charges; preferential interests; guarantees of loans on especially favourable terms; making land or buildings available either gratuitously or on especially favourable terms; provision of goods or services on preferential terms; indemnities against operating losses; or any other measures of equivalent effect.[6] The list was further extended to include: reimbursement of costs in the event of success; state guarantees, whether direct or indirect, to credit operations; preferential rediscount rates; dividend guarantees; preferential public ordering; and deferred collection of fiscal or social contributions.[7] The list is not exhaustive.

The concept of an aid encompasses not only positive benefits, such as the payment of a subsidy to an undertaking, but also measures which mitigate the charges which are normally included in the budget of an undertaking.[8] Where the undertaking receives a positive benefit, the state (or some state body) is taking some positive action to give that undertaking an advantage. The advantage can take all kinds of forms, such as investment in the capital of the undertaking;[9] giving a guarantee; or purchasing goods or services from the favoured undertaking in the absence of any, or any sufficient, demand for them or at an overvalue.[10] When

---

1   Cases 6, 11/69: *Commission v France* [1969] ECR 523, Case 78/76: *Firma Steinike und Weinlig v Germany* [1977] ECR 595, [1977] 2 CMLR 688.
2   61/79: *Amministrazione delle Finanze dello State v Denkavit Italiana Srl* [1980] ECR 1205 at para 31, [1981] 3 CMLR 694.
3   Case 173/73: *Italy v Commission* [1974] ECR 709 at 718-719, [1974] 2 CMLR 593; Case T-14/96: *Bretagne Angleterre Irlande v Commission* [1999] ECR II-139, para 81.
4   Eg Cases 67,68 and 70/85: *Van der Kooy v Commission* [1988] ECR 219, para 30; Case C-251/97: *France v Commission* [1999] ECR I-6639 (where the justification was not grounded on the facts).
5   Eg Case C-200/97: *Ecotrade v Altiforni e Ferriere di Servola* [1998] ECR I-7907, para 36; and see Cases C-52/97 and C-54/97: *Viscido v Ente Poste Italiano* [1998] ECR I-2629, in particular the Opinion of A-G Jacobs, para 16.
6   JO 1963, 2235.
7   Doc 20.502/IV.68 (1968).
8   Eg Case C-200/97: *Ecotrade v Altiforni e Ferriere di Servola* [1998] ECR I-7907, paras 34-35.
9   Eg Case C-142/87: *Belgium v Commission* [1990] ECR I-959, paras 25-26.
10 Cf Case T-14/96: *Bretagne Angleterre Irlande v Commission* [1999] ECR II-139, paras 71-76.

an undertaking's charges are mitigated, it is being relieved of all or part of an obligation itself to pay money or allocate its own resources in some other way for the benefit of someone else, for example: a reduction in social charges to be paid by the undertaking[11] or a tax concession or tax exemption that reduces the undertaking's liability towards the State.[12] Whether the aid is a positive benefit or mitigates a charge, it is in the nature of the aid that the advantage conferred must be gratuitous, ie without a quid pro quo of the recipient, though the ECJ held that a measure remains gratuitous even if it is wholly or partially financed from contributions imposed upon the undertakings concerned.[13] It has also been said that, in order to determine whether a State measure constitutes aid, it is necessary to establish whether the recipient undertaking receives an economic advantage which it would not have obtained under normal market conditions.[14] That principle, often referred to as 'the private investor test', is designed to preserve the ability of States and State bodies to enter into ordinary commercial transactions. If a private sector operator would not have entered into the transaction in question at all (for example, because of the perilous state of the recipient undertaking) or would have done so only on less favourable terms, it is reasonable to infer that the recipient is getting something from the State that it would not otherwise have got.[15]

According to EC Article 87(1) (ex Art 92(1)) aid must be granted by a Member State or through state resources. What matters here is not the machinery of the aid but the source. Thus grants may be made either by the central or the regional or local government and they may be administered directly or indirectly by the government or by a public or private agency.[16]

In the words of EC Article 87(1) (ex Art 92(1)) there must be a causal connection between the aid and its effect manifested by distortion or threatened distortion of competition by favouring certain undertakings or the production of certain goods.[17] Moreover, trade between Member States must be affected. In this context the measure must be particular, ie targeting the specific undertakings or industries rather than generally affecting the state as a whole. Thus, eg devaluation of the national currency, though beneficial to national exporters, would not be regarded as aid, but a preferential discount rate for exports, even applied across the board to all national products, would be in the nature of an aid because the provision of credit at a reduced rate in order to stimulate exports should be of direct benefit

---

11 Eg Case C-251/97: *France v Commission* [1999] ECR I-6639, para 35.
12 Eg Case C-387/92: *Banco de Crédito Industrial v Ayuntamiento de Valencia* [1994] ECR I-877, paras 13-14; Case T-106/95: *FFSA v Commission* [1997] ECR II-229. The position regarding taxation is particularly complex: see the Commission Notice on the application of the state aid rules to measures relating to direct business taxation (OJ 1998, C 384/3).
13 Case 78/76: supra, p 706, note 1.
14 Eg Case C-39/94: *SFEI v La Poste* [1996] ECR I-3547, para 60.
15 For an example of consideration of the private investor test see Cases T-129/95, T-2/96 and T-97/96: *Neue Maxhütte Stahlwerke v Commission* [1999] ECR II-17, paras 104-140.
16 Case 78/76: supra; see also Case 173/73: supra; Case 290/83: *Commission v France* [1985] ECR 439, [1986] 2 CMLR 546; Case 67, 68 and 70/85: *Kwerkerij Gebroeders van der Kooy BV v Commission* [1988] ECR 219, [1989] 2 CMLR 804; Case 57/86: *Commission v Greece* [1988] ECR 2855, [1990] 1 CMLR 65; the *Viscido* case, supra, paras 12-16; the *Ecotrade* case, supra, para 43.
17 See Case 40/75: *Société des Produits Bertrand SA v Commission* [1976] 1 CMLR 220. Favouring 'certain undertakings' or the production of 'certain goods' (also referred to as the requirement of 'selectivity') is one of the defining features of an aid: see the *Ecotrade* case, supra, para 40.

to individual national exporters and give them an advantage in the Common Market.[18] The analysis of the consequences of a state aid must take account of foreseeable changes in competitive conditions and can alter over time.[19]

The granting of aid to private undertakings is often difficult enough to discover;[20] the injection of state resources into public undertakings is usually even more obscure. To clarify the position Directive 80/723[1] laid down rules for the transparency of financial relationship between the Member States and their public undertakings, so much so that any aid which fails the test of transparency ought to be terminated by the Member State within a given period. In this context falls having to supply the requested information on financial relations with public undertakings in the sectors of motor manufacture, shipbuilding, synthetic fibres, textile machinery and manufactured tobacco. Italy complied to a certain extent but it did not consider itself bound to supply the annual accounts relating to the tobacco sector. The Court, citing its own judgment in Joined Cases 188-190/80[2] to the effect that the essential purpose of Directive 80/723 'is to promote the effective application to public undertakings of the provisions contained in' EC Articles 87 and 88 (ex Arts 92 and 93), found Italy to be in breach of the said Directive.[3]

C. Aids compatible with the Common Market (EC Article 87(2) (ex Art 92(2)))

EC Article 87(2) (ex Art 92(2)) declares the following to be compatible with the common market:

(1) 'aid having a social character, granted to individual consumers, provided that such aid is granted without discrimination related to the origin of the products concerned';
(2) 'aid to make good the damage caused by natural disasters or exceptional occurrences';
(3) 'aid granted to the economy of certain areas of the Federal Republic of Germany affected by the division of Germany, in so far as such aid is required in order to compensate for the economic disadvantage caused by that division'.

The effect of (1) was explained by the ECJ,[4] where it held that the re-selling at a considerably lower price of wheat bought with state funds at the intervention price could not be considered an aid of a social character because it did not subsidize consumers directly, but instead gave an advantage to the milling business involved, in spite of reducing the price of bread. It follows that price subsidies

---

18 Cases 6 and 11/69: *Commission v France* [1969] ECR 523.
19 Cases T-132/96 and T-143/96: *Freistaat Sachsen v Commission* [1999] ECR II-3663, paras 211-218.
20 Eg Case C-294/90: *British Aerospace and Rover v Commission* [1992] ECR I-493.
1 OJ 1980, L195/35, as amended by Dir 85/413 (OJ 1985, L229), and by Dir 93/84 (OJ 1993, L254/16).
2 *France, Italy and United Kingdom v Commission* [1982] ECR 2545.
3 Case 118/85: *Commission v Italy, re Amministrazione Antonoma dei Monopoli di Stato* [1987] ECR 2599, [1988] 3 CMLR 255.
4 Case 52/76: *Benedetti v Munari Fratelli SAS* [1977] ECR 163 at 190.

of products to benefit the entire population would not be justified. However, a subsidy to a particularly deprived section of the population would be justified.

Examples of legitimate aids to alleviate hardship arising from natural disasters are furnished by the Italian state assistance to repair the damage caused by floods in 1977 in Liguria and the subsidies and low interest loans for the reconstruction of industrial plant destroyed by earthquake in northern Italy in 1976.[5] However, as shown by the aid granted in consequence of the earthquake which devastated parts of Southern Italy in 1981, the object has to be reconstruction rather than general development, hence the Commission's partial approval of the scheme and objection to the extension of the territorial scope and the increase of the level of investments comprised in the aid.[6]

Although the reunification of Germany has not removed the justification for the special treatment of certain areas of Germany affected by the division of that country,[7] aid to the economy of those areas is justified only to the extent that they have suffered from the existence of the former frontier between the Federal Republic and the Democratic Republic, such as through geographical isolation, the interruption of communications or the loss of access to markets.[8]

D. Discretionary exceptions (EC Article 87(3) (ex Art 92(3)))

To emphasize the institutional supervision of state aids the Treaty gives the Commission a wide discretion which, however, is limited to the objectives defined in EC Article 87(3) (ex Art 92(3)). In the Court's view the exercise of this discretion 'involves economic and social assessments which must be made in a Community context'.[9] In the Commission's view approval of any project for which a Member State intends to grant aid 'must contain a compensatory justification which takes the form of a contribution by the beneficiary of aid over and above the effects of a normal play of market forces to the achievement of Community objectives as contained in derogations of Article 92(3) . . .'.[10]

In the words of the Treaty (as amended) the following may be considered to be compatible with the Common Market:

(1) 'aid to promote the economic development of areas where the standard of living is abnormally low or where there is serious under-employment';
(2) 'aid to promote the execution of an important project of common European interest or to remedy serious disturbances in the economy of a Member State';
(3) 'aid to facilitate the development of certain economic activities or of certain economic areas, where such aid does not adversely affect trading conditions to an extent contrary to the common interest';

---

5 Comp Report 1978 point 164.
6 Case C-364/90: *Italy v Commission, re Aid for Certain Areas of Mezzo-Giorno* [1993] ECR I-2097.
7 Case T-132/96 and T-143/96: *Freistaat Sachsen v Commission* [1999] ECR I-3663, paras 129-131 (contrary to what the Commission had thought: see Comp Rep 1990, point 178).
8 Cases T-132/96 and T-143/96: *Freistaat Sachsen v Commission* [1999] ECR II-3663, paras 134-137.
9 Case 730/79: *Phillip Morris Holland BV v Commission* [1980] ECR 2671 at 2701, [1981] 2 CMLR 321.
10 Comp Rep 1980 point 213.

(4) 'aid to promote culture and heritage conservation where such aid does not affect trading conditions and competition in the Community to an extent that is contrary to the common interest';
(5) 'such other categories of aid as may be specified by decision of the Council acting by a qualified majority on a proposal from the Commission'.

(1) The application of EC Article 87(3)(a) (ex Art 92(3)(a)) was tested in the *Phillip Morris* case[11] where the government of the Netherlands was keen to support a reorganization of a cigarette manufacturer contending that two factories would be closed but one expanded, thus creating 475 new jobs. The Commission estimated that only five jobs would be created. The company was a subsidiary of the Phillip Morris International Group of Companies, the second largest group of tobacco manufacturers in the world but which came to Europe rather recently. The economic factor was important because in 1977 the Netherlands had a trade surplus of ECU 30 million in Community trade.

The Court rejected the economic argument since the subsidy would strengthen the position of Phillip Morris vis-à-vis its competitors in the relevant market at the expense of the taxpayer. Moreover the Court concluded that neither the social criteria (especially employment) nor economic criteria, such as disturbance in the Dutch economy or the relevancy of the project to be of 'common European interest' could be met.

(2) The second category of discretionary aid envisages two different types of aid: one to take remedial measures concerning a disturbance encompassing the entire national economy of a Member State[12] and the other to promote a project of European dimension. Measures taken in consequence of the oil crisis (1973-74) which caused world-wide havoc fit well within the first part of the rubric[13] but the manufacture of cigarettes would hardly fit.

As for the projects which promote a European interest, that interest cannot be implied in eg research and development but has to be shown to be likely to benefit the Common Market as a whole. That was made plain by the ECJ saying that a project (investment in glass industry, *in casu*) does not qualify

'unless it forms part of a transnational European programme supported jointly by a number of Governments of the Member States, or arises from concerted action by a number of Member States to combat a common threat such as environmental pollution'.[14]

Examples of the latter include the support for the European airbus project;[15] aid to develop a common standard for high-definition colour television[16] and to deal with environmental problems.[17] Whether or not a project deserves aid on account of its European dimension is a matter for the Commission to decide.[18]

---

11 Supra.
12 Case T-132/96 and T-143/96: *Freistaat Sachsen v Commission* [1999] ECR I-3663, paras 167-168.
13 Comp Rep 1975, point 133.
14 Joint Cases 62/87 and 72/87: *Exécutif Regional Wallon and Glaverbel v Commission* [1988] ECR 1573 at para 22, [1989] 2 CMLR 771.
15 EC Bull 4/74, point 2112.
16 Comp Rep 1989, point 151.
17 See Cases 62/87 and 72/87, supra.
18 For Commission's guidelines see Comp Rep 1987; see also Case 310/85: *Deufil GmbH & Co KG v Commission* [1987] ECR 901 [1988] 1 CMLR 533.

(3) Whilst category (2) aids are meant to benefit the Community or a country as a whole, category (3) aids can be applied to individual regions of a Member State or specific economic sectors. In the latter context the Commission singled out sectors in contemplation of an aids policy, ie energy, ship-building and ship-repair; textiles and clothing; synthetic fibres; industrial investment; car and spare parts industries; information technologies and consumer electronics; household appliances; primary aluminium and semi-finished aluminium products; ceramics, glass, paper, wood and rubber.[19] However the Commission's discretion is qualified by the notion of 'development' and the condition that aid 'must not adversely affect trading conditions to an extent contrary to the common interest'.

'Development' implied progress or improvement in economic performance and industrial technology. Thus aid merely to save a bankrupt or moribund enterprise or to preserve jobs will not qualify.[20] As for adverse effect of aid on trading conditions, the Commission has to be vigilant that by giving its approval it does not undermine fair trade and fair competition in the Common Market.

It has to be borne in mind that in the area of concern national interests should be balanced with objective Community criteria. In its own words[1] the Commission claims that it 'has established a system which takes account of national regional problems and places them in a Community context'. Thus the aid system is not designed to rescue individual undertakings but to help sectors of industry or regions. In this spirit the Court held[2] that:

'. . . In the case of an aid programme the Commission may confine itself to examining the characteristics of the programme in question in order to determine whether, by reason of the high amounts or percentage of aid, the nature of the investments for which aid is granted or other terms of the programme, it gives an appreciable advantage to recipients in relation to their competitors and is likely to benefit in particular undertakings engaged in trade between Member States . . .'.[3]

Examples include the approval of the various measures taken by the Italian government for the promotion of artisanship in Sicily,[4] the island being an economically depressed area without large employers but having a traditional handicraft industry; the development of the machine-tools sector in the United Kingdom[5] on the condition that there will be no stockpiling of the product: and the Dutch energy policy favouring the Dutch ammonia industry.[6] However the Commission objected to a Belgian project in aid of the production of tractors by the Ford company[7] because it meant, in effect, subsidizing a multi-national company operating in Belgium; to French aids to the textile industry to be financed by a special tax imposed on domestic and imported products;[8] to a Dutch subsidy to cigarette manufacturers;[9] to Dutch horticultural industry to provide preferential low

---

19 Comp Rep 1985, points 182-217.
20 See Case 84/82: *Germany v Commission, re Belgian Textile Aid* [1984] ECR 1451; Opinion AG Sir Gordon Slynn at p 1505.
1   Comp Rep 1989, point 147.
2   Case 248/84: *Germany v Commission* [1987] ECR 4013.
3   At para 18.
4   *Les Novelles*, p 865.
5   Europe No 1946 (22-23 March 1976) p 7.
6   Case C-169/84: *Société CdF Chimie Azote et Fertilisants SA (COFAZ) v Commission* [1992] 1 CMLR 177.
7   Case 64/651: *re Subsidies to Ford Tractor (Belgium) Ltd* [1965] CMLR 32.
8   Case 47/69: *France v Commission* [1970] ECR 487, [1970] CMLR 351.
9   Case 730/79, supra.

prices for heating;[10] to preferential rediscount rate for export granted to French exporters;[11] to easy-term loans and special interest rebates for Greek exporters;[12] and parafiscal taxes to support the French textile industry;[13] to the government assisting financially an ailing enterprise eg by buying the company's shares in a situation where a private investor would not risk his money;[14] to cover debts of a Greek state agency trading in grain;[15] to the increase of a company's capital by the public administrator;[16] to interest-free loans to be converted into equity capital[17] etc.

Focusing attention on possible adverse effects on trading conditions the Court confirmed the Commission's decision to oppose a French scheme of financing an aid by a parafiscal charge levied on domestic and imported textiles.[18] The charge was designed to aid research and the restructuring of textile undertakings, and in that sense seemed to comply with EC Article 87(3)(c) (ex Art 92(3)(c)). However the aid was provided specifically from a parafiscal charge which hit not only the French manufacturers but also imports (ie their foreign competitors). The amount of aid would increase with the increase of the revenue in that sector. Consequently the more the Community exporters earned from their sales in France the more they would contribute to their, perhaps less efficient, French competitors. This scheme raised the question as to what extent the method of financing of the aid was relevant to the assessment of its compatibility with the Common Market. Since it was capable of upsetting the trading conditions it was also contrary to the objectives of the Common Market. In conclusion the Court accepted the Commission's objections to the aid 'whilst acknowledging both the useful nature of the aid properly so called and the fact that it conformed with "common interest", if the method whereby it was financed could be modified'.[19]

The notion of 'common interest' raises the question of the degree of anti-competitive impact of an aid on the trading conditions. Any aid has an anti-competitive element but that element has to be weighed against its beneficial effect in the sector. The Commission has to assess to what extent common interest is put at risk. In *Intermills SA v Commission*[20] the ECJ ruled that 'the settlement of an undertaking's existing debts in order to ensure its survival does not necessarily adversely affect trading conditions to an extent contrary to the common interest, as provided in Article 92(3) [now Art 87(3)], where such an operation is, for example, accompanied by a restructuring plan'. Consequently, the Commission decision, prohibiting aid granted by the Belgian government to a paper-manufacturing undertaking, was annulled by the Court.

10   Cases 67-68/85 and 70/85, supra.
11   Cases 6/69 and 11/69, supra.
12   Case 57/86, supra.
13   Case 259/85: *France v Commission* [1987] ECR 4393, [1989] 2 CMLR 30.
14   Case 40/85: *Belgium v Commission, re Aid to Bosch SA* [1986] ECR 2321, [1988] 2 CMLR 301; Case 234/84: *Belgium v Commission re Aid to Meura* [1986] ECR 2263, [1988] 2 CMLR 331; Case C-142/87: *Belgium v Commission, re Tubemeuse* [1990] ECR I-959 [1991] 3 CMLR 213; Case C-303/88: *Italy v Commission, re Aid to ENI-Lanerossi* [1993] 2 CMLR 1; Case C-305/89: *Italy v Commission* [1991] ECR I-1603 at paras 18 and 19.
15   Case C-35/88: *Commission v Greece Re KYDEP* [1992] 1 CMLR 548.
16   Case C-134-135/91: *Karafina v Greece* [1993] 2 CMLR 277.
17   Case C-261/89: *Italy v Commission, re Aid to State-owned undertakings in the Aluminium Sector* [1991] ECR I-4437.
18   Case 47/69: *France v Commission* [1970] ECR 487, [1970] CMLR 351.
19   Ibid [1970] ECR at 496.
20   Case 323/82: *Re Aid for the Conversion of a Paper-Manufacturing Undertaking* [1984] ECR 3809 at para 39, [1986] 1 CMLR 614.

A similar conclusion was reached in Cases 296 and 318/82[1] though in the instant case the Commission failed to give sufficient reasons for its decision.

(4) Discretionary aids to promote culture and heritage conservation have to be seen in the context of the policy on culture.[2]

(5) Examples of aids approved by the Council on the proposal of the Commission can be seen in the shipbuilding industry.[3] Council Regulation 994/98[4] empowers the Commission to declare by regulation that the following categories of aid are compatible with the common market under conditions that the Commission defines: aid in favour of small and medium-sized enterprises, research and development, environmental protection or employment and training; and aid that complies with the map approved by the Commission for each Member State for the grant of regional aid.

E. Institutional supervision (EC Articles 88 and 89 (ex Arts 93 and 94))

EC Article 88 (ex Art 93) contains rudimentary procedural rules for supervising and dealing with state aids. Those rules were intended to be fleshed out by more detailed rules adopted by the Council under EC Article 89 (ex Art 94), which empowers the Council to make appropriate regulations for the application of EC Articles 87 and 88 (ex Arts 92 and 93) and in particular to determine the conditions under which EC Article 88(3) (ex Art 93(3)) would apply and the categories of aid exempted from this procedure. Detailed rules for the application of EC Article 88 (ex Art 93) were not laid down until 1999, by which time the various gaps in EC Article 88 (ex Art 93) had been partially filled in by the case law of the ECJ. The new procedural rules, contained in Council Regulation 659/1999,[5] reflect the case law.

(1) REVIEW OF EXISTING AIDS

The Treaty distinguishes between 'existing aids' which are subject to review and 'new aids' which, being plans to institute or alter aids, have to be scrutinized before they are put into effect. Existing aids are, in general terms, those aids already in effect in a Member State when the Treaty came into force in regard to that State and all aids that have at some time been authorized by the Commission or the Council or are deemed to be existing aid for one reason or another.[6] In relation to existing aids EC Article 88(1) (ex Art 93(1)) provides:

'The Commission shall, in co-operation with Member states, keep under constant review all systems of aid existing in those States. It shall propose to the latter any appropriate measure required by the progressive development or by the functioning of the common market.'

---

1 *Netherlands and Leeuwarder Papierwarenfabriek v Commission* [1985] ECR 809, [1985] 3 CMLR 380.
2 See infra Ch 35.
3 Eg Council Reg 1540/98 (OJ 1998, L202/1).
4 OJ 1998, L142/1. See also Reg 68/2001 on training aid, 69/2001 on de minimis aid and 70/2001 on aid to small and medium-sized enterprises (OJ 2001, L10/20, 30 and 33, respectively).
5 OJ 1999, L83/1.
6 Reg 659/1999, Art 1(6).

The task of supervising the state aids regimes has been entrusted to the Commission whose critical review may result in recommendations to the state concerned. If a recommendation is not heeded the Commission may resort to the enforcement procedure.[7] In cases of the misuse of an existing aid, the Commission may resort forthwith to the enforcement procedure.[8]

(2) ENFORCEMENT PROCEDURE

EC Article 88(2) (ex Art 93(2)) provides:

'If, after giving notice to the parties concerned to submit their comments, the Commission finds that aid granted by a State or through State resources is not compatible with the common market having regard to Article 87 [ex Art 92], or that such aid is being misused, it shall decide that the State concerned shall abolish or alter such aid within a period of time to be determined by the Commission.

If the State concerned does not comply with this decision within the prescribed time, the Commission or any other interested State may, in derogation from the provisions of EC Articles 226 and 227 [ex Arts 169 and 170], refer the matter to the Court of Justice direct . . .'

The procedure outlined above reflects the Commission's powers of supervision and a simplified version of enforcement action against Member States in breach of Treaty provisions.

The proceedings begin with a formal notice inviting comments from the parties concerned which is published in the Official Journal. As the subject matter of the notice concerns the government the undertakings benefiting from the aid are not entitled to individual notices but may, of course, defend their position.[9]

As a result of the dialogue the Commission may drop the case if it is convinced that the aid in question conforms to the Treaty, approve the aid subject to substantial modifications effected by the government, or adopt a 'negative decision' finding the aid to be unlawful.

If the Commission comes to the conclusion that the aid is either incompatible with the Treaty or is being misused, it will adopt a decision requiring either abolition of the aid or alteration within a specified time. If the government fails to comply with the decision, the Commission or any interested Member State may bring the case directly to the ECJ, thus bypassing the administrative stage prescribed by EC Articles 226 and 227 (ex Arts 169 and 170). In the event the dialogue serves the same purpose as the administrative stage as it safeguards the right to be heard. The burden of proof rests on the Commission and the intervening states.

Where the Commission concludes that the aid is unlawful it will issue an order to cease and desist but will allow the state concerned a time limit within which to advise the Commission of the measures undertaken to bring the illegality to an end. Failure to discontinue the aid within the timetable or inform the Commission will constitute a breach of the Treaty.[10] The duty of the Member States to respect the Commission's decision is illustrated in Cases 31/77 and 53/77R.[11]

---

7   Reg 659/1999, Arts 17-19.
8   Ibid, Art 16.
9   Case 323/82, supra, p 712, note 20. Reg 659/1999, Arts 4(4), 6–9, 19(2) and 26(2).
10 See Case 213/85: *Commission v Netherlands, Re Cheap Gaz for Dutch Horticulture* [1988] ECR 281, [1988] 2 CMLR 287.
11 *Commission v United Kingdom* [1977] ECR 921, [1977] 2 CMLR 359.

In that case the British government notified its intention to provide a temporary aid to pig producers in the form of a subsidy per kilogram deadweight. The Commission considered it incompatible and advised the United Kingdom accordingly. In response the United Kingdom applied to the Council for derogation under EC Article 88(2) (ex Art 93(2)) sub-paras 3 and 4. The Commission in turn ordered the United Kingdom to terminate the aid but the latter ignored the decision. Therefore the Commission brought an enforcement action,[12] whilst the United Kingdom requested the ECJ to annul the Commission's decision on the ground that the Commission either had no jurisdiction or misused its powers. The Court held against the United Kingdom as it considered that a Member State should not disregard the procedural requirements. Having found that the aid was incompatible with the Treaty the British government ceased paying the subsidy.

The decision of the Commission may be challenged in fact and law on the grounds of procedure and substance like any other institutional act in accordance with EC Article 230 (ex Art 173). If it satisfies the conditions of Art 173 the action shall be admissible in the case of the direct beneficiary of the aid,[13] the beneficiary's competitors who, in response to the Commission's invitation to make comments, have submitted evidence substantiating their contention,[14] trade associations representing the interests of the industry affected by the aid,[15] the State to whom the decision is addressed and, in certain circumstances, the State body granting the aid or required by the decision to take steps to recover it.[16] Where the Commission failed to consult the interested parties and, indeed, failed to conduct the necessary economic analysis, the decision was annulled at the instance of a competitor in the relevant sector.[17] The procedure under Article 88(2) (ex Art 93(2)) applies to both existing and new aids.

(3) AUTHORIZATION OF AID BY COUNCIL

An aspect of the institutional supervision is reflected in the Council's power to authorize an aid in 'exceptional circumstances' as provided by the third and fourth sub-paragraphs of EC Article 88(2) (ex Art 93(2)), ie:

'. . . On application by a Member State, the Council may, acting unanimously, decide that aid which that state is granting or intends to grant shall be considered to be compatible with the common market, in derogation from the provisions of Article 87 [ex Art 92] or from the regulations provided for in Article 89 [ex Art 94], if such a decision is justified in exceptional circumstances. If, as regards the aid in question, the Commission has already initiated the procedure provided for in the first sub-paragraph of this paragraph [that is, the enforcement procedure referred to above], the fact that the State concerned has made its application to the Council shall have the effect of suspending that procedure until the Council has made its attitude known.

---

12 Case 31/77, supra.
13 Case 730/79, supra and Case 323/82, supra.
14 Case 169/84: *COFAZ et al v Commission* [1986] ECR 391, [1986] 3 CMLR 385.
15 Cases 67/85 and 70/85: *Van der Kooy v Commission* [1988] ECR 219, paras 21–24; Cases T-447/93, T-448/93 and T-449/93: *AITEC v Commission* [1995] ECR II-1971, paras 53 and 62.
16 Case T-288/97: *Regione Autonoma Friuli-Venezia Giulia v Commission* [1999] ECR II-1871; Cases T-132/96 and T-143/96: *Freistaat Sachsen v Commission* [1999] ECR I-3663, paras 81-94.
17 Case C-198/91: *William Cook v Commission* [1993] ECR I-2487, [1993] 3 CMLR 206.

If, however, the Council has not made its attitude known within three months of the said application being made, the Commission shall give its decision on the case.'

The Treaty does not define the 'exceptional circumstances' which would justify the Council to step into what has to be considered to be a primary responsibility of the Commission. However, given the requirement of unanimity, the practical effects of the Council's powers, in this respect, must be regarded as negligible. Theoretically, if the Commission disapproved of such a decision of the Council, it could bring proceedings for its annulment before the ECJ; but there are no precedents to indicate what might happen in practice.

(4) NEW AIDS

EC Article 88(3) (ex Art 93(3)) lays down a procedure for prior control with the object of preventing the introduction of new aids incompatible with the Treaty. It provides:

'The Commission shall be informed, in sufficient time to enable it to submit its comments, of any plans to grant or alter aid. If it considers that any such plan is not compatible with the common market . . . it shall without delay initiate the procedure provided for in paragraph 2. The Member State concerned shall not put its proposed measures into effect until this procedure has resulted in a final decision.'

In order to forestall any unilateral action on the part of the Member States the Commission is entitled to receive a notification of a Member State's intention to grant new aid, or alter an existing aid, in sufficient time before the intention is to be put into effect.[18] Failure to inform the Commission constitutes a breach of duty.[19] However, if a new aid or an alteration to an existing aid is put into effect without having been notified, it does not follow that the aid is incompatible with the common market and therefore prohibited by EC Article 87(1) (ex Art 92(1)). Instead, the aid has been introduced in breach of the obligation of prior notification. That means that the aid is liable to be clawed back from the recipient by court order made by a national court at the suit of an interested party.[20] Under EC Article 88(3) (ex Art 93(3)) the Commission has no such power. It can order the aid to be recovered from the recipient only once it has decided that the aid is incompatible with the common market; although it may order that further payments of the aid be suspended until it has reached a final decision on compatibility.[1] However, since 1999, the Commission has been vested with the power to order the provisional recovery of aid that has been granted without first having been notified to the Commission.[2]

Having received a notification of the intended aid the Commission ought to examine it expeditiously and inform the Member State concerned of its findings.

18 Reg 659/1999, Art 2.
19 See Case 120/73: *Lorenz GmbH v Germany* [1973] ECR 1471, Case 169/82: *Commission v Italy* [1984] ECR 1603, [1985] 3 CMLR 30.
20 Case C-354/90: *Fédération Nationale du Commerce Exterieur v French State* [1991] ECR I-5505, paras 12-17.
1 Case C-301/87: *France v Commission* [1990] ECR I-307, paras 9 and 18-22; Case C-142/87: *Belgium v Commission* [1990] ECR I-959; Case C-39/94: *SFEI v La Poste* [1996] ECR I-3547, paras 43-45.
2 Reg 659/1999, art 11 (note that according to art 1(f), 'unlawful aid' means aid put into effect in breach of EC Art 88(3) (ex Art 93(3)) not aid that is incompatible with the common market and prohibited by EC Art 87(1) (ex Art 92(1))).

If it approves the plan within two months the aid will be deemed to be authorized by the Commission and will be dealt with as an 'existing aid' in the terms of the Treaty; and as such it will be subject to 'constant review' in the spirit of EC Article 87(1) (ex Art 93(1)).[3]

If the Commission has doubts as to the compatibility of the aid it must initiate a formal investigation that involves hearing the views of the notifying state, other Member States and interested parties such as representatives of the relevant industry.[4] Failure to observe this requirement will be fatal to the Commission's decision.[5]

Until the Commission decision has been reached the notifying state is precluded from implementing the proposed aid.[6]

If the state, having notified the Commission, alters the proposal the latter has to be informed of the proposed alteration unless such alteration has formed part of the consultations arising from the original notification.[7] If the Member State does not co-operate in providing all necessary information, the Commission is entitled to complete the assessment of compatibility in the light of the information in its possession and, where appropriate, order the repayment of the aid received.[8] Under Article 5(3) of Regulation 659/1999, the notification is deemed to be withdrawn where the Member State fails to provide information requested by the Commission. In that event, the aid cannot be put into effect.

At the end of the formal investigation, the Commission may decide that the notified measure does not constitute an aid after all or that it is compatible with the common market. The Commission may attach conditions to a decision finding the aid to be compatible with the common market. The Commission may also decide that the aid is incompatible with the common market, in which case it cannot be put into effect and any aid that has already been granted may have to be recovered from the recipient.[9]

F. Recovery of unlawful aids

Aid may be unlawful and subject to recovery from the recipient for two very different reasons: because it was granted without first having been notified to the Commission, contrary to EC Article 88(3) (ex Art 93(3)); or because it is incompatible with the common market and therefore prohibited by EC Article 87(1) (ex Art 92(1)). As noted above, where the first ground of illegality arises, recovery may be ordered by a national court on the basis of EC Article 88(3) (ex Art 93(3)), or by the Commission, on a provisional basis, under Article 11(2) of Regulation 659/1999. Only the Commission has power to decide whether or not the second ground of illegality applies. If the Commission

---

3 Reg 659/1999, art 4.
4 Reg 659/1999, arts 4(4), 6 and 20.
5 Case 84/82: *Germany v Commission, Re Belgian Textile Aid* [1984] ECR 1451 at 1488-1490 [1985] 1 CMLR 153/ Case C-294/90: *British Aerospace and Rover v Commission* [1992] ECR I-493.
6 Case 120/73: *Lorenz GmbH v Germany* [1973] ECR 1471 at 1483, Case 84/82: ibid; Reg 659/1999, art 3.
7 Joined Cases 91 and 127/83: *Heineken Brouwerijen BV v Inspecteur der Vennootschapsbelasting* [1984] ECR 3435, [1985] 1 CMLR 389.
8 Case 301/87, at paras 21 and 22.
9 Reg 659/1999, arts 7 and 14.

so decides in the case of a new aid (including an alteration to an existing aid), the aid may be the subject of recovery pursuant to a Commission decision.[10] If the Commission so decides in the case of an existing aid, its decision has prospective effect only[11] and therefore recovery is possible only in respect of aid granted after the decision finding it to be incompatible with the common market has been made.[12]

Where aid is ordered to be recovered by a national court, the person so ordered could conceivably be either the grantor of the aid or its recipient, depending upon which of them is the defendant in the national proceedings. The usual limitation period under national law applies. Otherwise, unlawful aids have to be repaid as ordered by the Commission[13] and recovery is subject to a ten-year limitation period.[14] Private recipients of state aids have been warned by the Commission[15] that they might have to refund it since no one is entitled to enrich himself by illegality. The responsibility to secure recovery rests with the state concerned as the addressee of the Commission's decision; but the devolution of power to a region in a quasi-federal constitution will not absolve the state from its obligation.

Failure to obey a repayment decision or to take the necessary measures to recover the payment and advise the Commission accordingly amounts to a breach of the Treaty.[16] A Member State may not plead provisions or practices in its legal system in order to justify a failure to comply with obligations resulting from Community law.

The Court has emphasized that the obligation to recover an unlawful aid is a strict one[17] even if the beneficiary might suffer financial difficulties resulting from the decision[18] or setback of legitimate expectation.[19]

In the present state of Community law the recovery of aids unduly paid is governed by national law and procedure subject to the proviso that national rules may not be applied in such a way as to make recovery, as required by Community law, practically impossible.[20] In that connexion, the ECJ observed:[1]

---

10 Reg 659/1999, art 14(1), which suggests that a decision requiring recovery must be made unless it would be contrary to a general principle of Community law. The case law had suggested that the adoption of a decision ordering recovery was a matter of discretion: eg Case C-75/97: *Belgium v Commission* [1999] ECR I-3671, para 66.

11 Case 173/73: *Italy v Commission* [1974] ECR 709 at 723; Case 177/78: *Pigs & Bacon Commission v McCarren* [1979] ECR 2161 at 2206 (AG Warner).

12 Cf Case 70/72: *Commission v Germany* [1973] ECR 813 (which, among other things, holds that the publication of a notice indicating that the Commission has started a formal investigation into an aid does not affect the rights of individuals in the period from publication to the adoption of the final decision).

13 Case C-74/89: *Commission v Belgium, re a State Shareholding in Synthetic Fibres* [1990] ECR I-491, [1990] 2 CMLR 393. A recovery decision must provide for interest to be paid on the aid at an appropriate rate: Reg 659/1999, art 14(2).

14 Reg 659/1999, art 15.

15 OJ 1983, C 318/3.

16 Case 5/86: *Commission v Belgium, Re Aid for Polypropylene* [1987] ECR 1773, [1988] 2 CMLR 258.

17 Case 310/85, supra.

18 See Case 63/87: *Commission v Greece, Re State Aid to Exports* [1988] ECR 2875, [1989] 3 CMLR 677.

19 See Case 52/83: *Commission v France* [1983] ECR 3707.

20 Case C-142/87: *Belgium v Commission* [1990] ECR I-959 at para 61; Case C-5/89: *Commission v Germany* [1990] ECR I-3437 at para 12; Reg 659/1999, art 14(3). The national authorities may, for example, take tax paid by the recipient of the aid into account when ordering recovery: Case T-459/93: *Siemens v Commission* [1995] ECR II-1675, paras 83-84.

 1 Cases 205-215/82: *Deutsche Milchkontor v Germany, Re Recovery of Aids Unduly Paid* [1983] ECR 2633, para 33.

'. . . Community law does not prevent national law from having regard, in excluding the recovery of unduly-paid aids, to such considerations as the protection of legitimate expectation, the loss of unjustified enrichment, the passing of a time limit or the fact that the administration knew, or was unaware owing to gross negligence on its part, that it was wrong in granting the aids in question, provided however that the conditions laid down are the same as for the recovery of purely national financial benefits and the interests of the Community are taken fully into account.'

However, Member States themselves may not invoke the legitimate expectations of the recipients of the aid in order to justify failing to comply with a recovery order[2] and the possibilities open to the recipients themselves to rely upon legitimate expectations are limited. The ECJ has pointed out that:

'. . . in view of the mandatory nature of the supervision of State aid by the Commission under Article 93 of the Treaty [now EC 88], undertakings to which an aid has been granted may not, in principle, entertain a legitimate expectation that the aid is lawful unless it has been granted in compliance with the procedure laid down in that article. A diligent businessman should normally be able to determine whether that procedure has been followed . . .'[3]

The ECJ went on to say:

'. . . a recipient of illegally granted aid is not precluded from relying on exceptional circumstances on the basis of which it had legitimately assumed the aid to be lawful and thus declining to refund that aid. If such a case is brought before a national court, it is for that court to assess the material circumstances, if necessary after obtaining a preliminary ruling on interpretation from the Court of Justice.'[4]

Further, in the view of the ECJ:

'. . . recovery of unlawful aid is the logical consequence of finding that it is unlawful. Consequently, the recovery of state aid unlawfully granted for the purpose of re-establishing the previously existing situation cannot in principle be regarded as disproportionate to the objectives of the Treaty . . .'[5]

The refund has to be made by the recipients of an unlawful aid and it is the duty of the government to secure recovery. In Case C-303/88,[6] the aids, consisting of injections of capital to a state holding company to sustain a group of its

---

2 Case C-5/89: *Commission v Germany* [1990] ECR I-3437, [1992] 1 CMLR 117, para 17.
3 Case C-5/89: *Commission v Germany, Re State Aid to Bug-Alutechnik* [1990] ECR I-3437, [1992] 1 CMLR 117, at para 14; see also Case C-94/87: *Commission v Germany* [1989] ECR 175, [1989] 2 CMLR 425.
4 Case 5/89: *Commission v Germany, Re State Aid to Bug-Alutechnik* [1990] ECR I-3437, [1992] 1 CMLR 117. Accordingly, in Case T-459/93: *Siemens v Commission* [1995] ECR II-1675, para 105, the CFI said that legitimate expectations could be relied on by way of defence to national proceedings for recovery of the aid but not in order to attack the legality of the recovery order itself.
5 Case C-142/87: *Belgium v Commission, Re Tubemeuse* [1990] ECR I-959, [1991] 3 CMLR 213, at para 66 – citing Case 310/85, *supra*.
6 *Italy v Commission Re Aid to ENI-Lanerossi* [1991] ECR I-1433, [1993] 2 CMLR 1, paras 57-60; followed by Case C-305/89: *Italy v Commission, Re Aid granted to Alfa Romeo* [1991] ECR I-1603.

subsidiaries, were incompatible with EC Article 87 (ex Art 92). Indeed, the reconstruction of the undertakings was unsuccessful and they continued to be run at a loss. It was contended by the government that the aids could not be recovered because the recipients of the aid had been sold off and the conditions of sale did not provide for the recovery of the aid. The ECJ rejected that argument, holding that the inability to recover under the contracts of sale 'cannot stand in the way of the full application of Community law and can therefore have no effect on the obligation to recover the aid in question'. Should, however, the government encounter unforeseen difficulties in implementing the order of recovery it ought to work together in good faith with the Commission with a view to overcoming the difficulties.

If the recovery proves to be impossible the beneficiary has to be wound up.[7] In such an event, assuming that the creditors cannot be satisfied in full, the repayment ought to be discharged from the assets generally available to creditors in accordance with bankruptcy rules.

Finally, the question arises whether the decision of the Commission ordering recovery of a state aid can be challenged by a recipient of the aid before the national courts. Since the recipient can bring an action for annulment directly before the CFI under EC Article 230 (ex Art 173) a failure by it to do so within the period for bringing such an action will preclude it from contesting the lawfulness of the decision in national proceedings.[8]

---

7   Case 52/84: *Commission v Belgium, Re State Equity Holding* [1986] ECR 89, [1987] 1 CMLR 710.
8   Case C-188/92: *TWD Textilweke Deggendorf GmbH v Bundesrepublik Deutschalnd* [1994] ECR I-833.

Chapter 31

Intellectual property rights

A. Common Market v intellectual property

The impact of the Common Market on intellectual property rights has had a twofold effect. On the one hand there is an erosion of these rights and on the other an effort to create a Community system of intellectual property. The main reason for the former is that, being rooted in the national systems of law and being essentially territorial, the exercise of intellectual property rights tends to maintain the division of the national markets which the Community, by virtue of its very existence, has to mould into one. Therefore, since they may be in collision with the paramount principles of the Common Market, they have to be sacrificed. The main reason for the creation of a European system of intellectual property rights is that it has become essential, if not indispensable, to industry and trade.

The EC Treaty expressly mentions intellectual property under the title of 'industrial' and 'commercial' property in EC Article 30 (ex Art 36) in the context of 'prohibitions or restrictions on imports, exports or goods in transit' as a justifiable exception to the principle of the freedom of movement of goods. It also alludes to it by implication in EC Article 295 (ex Art 222), stating that 'this Treaty shall in no way prejudice the rules in Member States governing the system of property ownership'.

Since the Treaty reference to 'industrial and commercial' property does not embrace all the relevant categories some writers[1] prefer to use the compendious expression 'intellectual rights'. The latter conveys the idea more felicitously.

It was thought by early commentators[2] that EC Articles 295 and 30 (ex Arts 222 and 36) combined constituted a general exception from the control of Community law and that their effect was to guarantee inviolability of property rights rooted in national laws. However this position was untenable. Advocate-General Römer[3]

---

1 Eg Harris, B, 'The Application of Article 36 to Intellectual Property' (1976) 1 ELR 5.5; Cornish, W R, Intellectual Property (2nd edn, 1989) p 3.
2 Eg Mann, F A, 'Industrial Property and the EEC Treaty' (1975) 24 1 CLQR 31 (at 34).
3 A-G Römer in Cases 56 and 58/64: *Etablissements Consten and Grundig v Commission* [1966] ECR 299 at 366.

put the matter into perspective. He thought that the object of EC Article 295 (ex Art 222) was 'solely to guarantee in a general manner the freedom of the Member States to organize their own system of property but not to provide a guarantee that the Community institutions may not in any way intervene in subjective rights of property'. Putting it into the context of the relationship between Community law and national law it means that intellectual property rights can exist and fulfil an economic function but they cannot be used to override the fundamental principles of the Common Market which are uniform and common to all Member States. Moreover intellectual property represents private, subjective rights whilst the free movement of goods and the rules on competition reflect objective trading rules, on the one hand, and rules of conduct in the market, on the other.

More recently the EC[4] ruled that, in principle, copyright like any other form of intellectual property necessarily falls within the scope of the Treaty and, consequently, any discrimination on grounds of nationality in national laws governing the existence or exercise of such rights is prohibited by virtue of EC Article 12 (ex Art 6 (ex Art 7)).

However, the importance of the existence and protection of intellectual property in our modern technological age cannot be denied and the European Community, which thrives on human genius and technology, has to find a compromise which means, on the one hand, accommodating intellectual property into the scheme of the Common Market and legislating for a new Community regime for intellectual property, on the other.

B. The general principles

The erosion of intellectual property occurred in a series of judgments in which the ECJ was requested to rule whether or not the holder of a patent or trademark could exercise his subjective right derived from national law in order to prohibit 'parallel imports' of a product protected by that right in another Member State where the product was lawfully marketed or whether or not the intellectual rights could be used in contravention of the Community competition rules comprised in EC Articles 81 and 82 (ex Arts 85 and 86). Thus the problem oscillated between these two paramount principles of the Common Market and, depending on where the effect of intellectual property was manifest, the Court decided either under one or the other principle.

In general terms the exclusive right of a proprietor of a patent or trademark is, in the eyes of Community law, exhausted in consequence of putting products into circulation within the Common Market. As remarked by the ECJ:

'. . . the proprietor of an industrial or commercial property right protected by the legislation of a Member State may not rely on that legislation in order to oppose the importation of a product which has lawfully been marketed in another Member State by, or with the consent of, the proprietor of the right himself or a person legally or economically dependent on him'.[5]

---

4   Joined Cases C-92/92 and C-326/92: *Phil Collins v Imtrat Handelsgesellschaft mbH and Patricia Im-und Export Varwaltungsgesellschaft v EMI Electroloa mbH* [1993] ECR I-5145 [1993] 3 CMLR 773.
5   Case 144/81: *Keurkoop BV v Nancy Kean Gifts BV* [1982] ECR 2853 at 2873, [1983] 2 CMLR 47.

Consten and Grundig [6] was the first case in which a claim to absolute protection of an intellectual property right was made and failed. In that case a sole distributorship agreement in favour of Consten was coupled with the grant of the Grundig trademark GINT which was registered in Germany and other EC countries. Consten, which was authorized to use it in its own name, registered it in France but undertook to transfer it back to Grundig if ceasing to be Grundig's sole representative and distributor. When Consten's territory was invaded by another enterprise, importing Grundig products and selling them in France, Consent brought two actions, one of which was to stop the infringement of the trademark. As the case was stayed by the French court the Commission decided, inter alia, that the agreement on the registration and use of the GINT trademark was an infringement of EC Article 81 (ex Art 85).

Both Consten and Grundig sought to have the Commission decision annulled on the ground that the guarantee of property rights mentioned in EC Article 295 (ex Art 222) was applicable to intellectual property rights and that this was confirmed by EC Article 30 (ex Art 36) which implied that such rights justified prohibitions on exporting and importing. The Commission argued that EC Article 30 (ex Art 36) was only concerned with measures taken by the Member States within the scope of EC Articles 28-29 (ex Arts 30-34) and did not govern the relationship between intellectual property and other provisions of the Treaty. Moreover, it contended, its decision was not directed against the elimination of prohibitions imposed by states but 'against private restrictions on importation'. Both the Advocate-General and the Court held that EC Article 30 (ex Art 36) was applicable only to the rules on the liberalization of trade and so could not affect the application of EC Article 81 (ex Art 85).

Several conclusions can be drawn from this case but the one that concerns us most is that neither EC Article 295 nor EC Article 30 (ex Arts 222 and 36) controls the exercise of rights or activities of undertakings and, therefore, offers no absolute protection to holders of such rights. Another conclusion is that neither article impedes the application of competition rules.

In *Parke, Davis & Co v Centrafarm* [7] the defendant companies marketed in the Netherlands a patented drug produced in Italy without the patent holder's permission. An action for infringement of the patent was met with the plea that the patent holder was acting in breach of EC Articles 81 and 82 (ex Arts 85 and 86) in using his Dutch patent to prevent the import of the drug manufactured and sold freely in Italy, Italian patent law excluding patent protection for all medicaments and processes for their preparation.

The ECJ thought that the differences between the national laws governing industrial property are 'liable to create obstacles both to the free circulation of the patented products and to competition within the Common Market'. In relation to EC Article 30 (ex Art 36) the Court admitted that the article justified prohibitions and restrictions on imports for the sake of protection of industrial property but narrowed down this opinion by saying: 'subject to the express qualification that they "shall not amount to a means of arbitrary discrimination nor to a disguised restriction on trade between Member States".' It added: 'For similar reasons, the exercise of the rights flowing from a patent granted under the laws of a Member State does not, of itself, involve a breach of the rules of competition.'

6 Cases 56 and 58/64: *Etablissements Consten and Grundig v Commission* [1966] ECR 299 at 366, [1966] CMLR 418.
7 Case 24/67: [1968] ECR 55, [1968] CMLR 47.

Having distinguished free movement of goods from competition the Court addressed itself to the protection of intellectual rights suggesting that it was subject to the same philosophy as that underlying the competition rules, ie that only acts contrary to the objectives of the Common Market were prohibited. It concluded that the existence of patent rights was not affected by the anti-trust rules and that their exercise would be prohibited only if inconsistent with the rules enshrined in EC Articles 81 and 82 (ex Arts 85 and 86).

Sirena Srl v Eda Srl [8] followed the doctrine of *Parke, Davis*. In that case an American company, which owned the trademark 'Prep' in certain toilet products in Italy and Germany, sold the Italian mark to Sirena and the German mark to a German company. Some years later the latter began marketing the 'Prep' products in Italy through Novimpex at prices lower than the prices charged by Sirena for the same products. Sirena brought an action for infringement of its trademark and the Italian court referred the matter to the ECJ. The question asked by the Italian court was whether EC Articles 81 and 82 (ex Arts 85 and 86) should be interpreted so as to prevent the holder of a trademark registered in one Member State from exercising his rights to prohibit the importation of the branded product from another Member State.

In the opinion of Advocate-General Dutheillet de Lamothe (echoed by the Court) interests protected by patent legislation were 'economically and humanely more respectable' than those protected by the law of trademark but he reiterated the proposition that 'the existence of rights granted by national legislation is not affected, although their exercise may be restricted by the provisions of the Treaty of Rome.' Referring specifically to EC Articles 81 and 82 (ex Arts 85 and 86) he held that the exercise of intellectual rights is in order unless it constitutes 'an improper exercise'.

The Court held that, whilst the Treaty failed to establish a relationship between the competition rules and the national law governing intellectual property rights, disparities between national industrial property laws might cause 'the national nature' of the protection afforded by these laws to 'create obstacles for the free movement of the branded products and for the competition system of the Community'.

Thus it began to dawn that there was a distinction between the 'existence' of rights and their 'exercise' and that, by analogy, the philosophy underlying the competition rules affected the relationship between intellectual property rights created by the laws of the Member States and fundamental principles of the Common Market. Inasmuch as restrictive practices are not prohibited per se but become so if inconsistent with the Common Market ideas of fair competition and the free movement of goods, intellectual property rights enjoy the protection of their national systems of law and of the Treaty as long as their exercise remains within the scope of fair competition and free movement of goods.

Moreover, by alluding to quantitative restrictions the Court set the stage for a deviation from the competition line. The turning point was reached in the *Deutsche Grammophon* case.[9] Deutsche Grammophon sold its records in Germany under a rigid price maintenance system and sought to prevent the importation into Germany of its own records from France, claiming that this 'infringed its rights over sound recordings' which, by analogy to copyright, were created by a German statute. The imported records were marketed by a French subsidiary of Deutsche Grammophon and they came into the hands of Metro-SB-Grossmärkte

---

8 Case 40/70: [1971] ECR 69, [1971] CMLR 260.
9 Case 78/70: [1971] ECR 487, [1971] CMLR 631.

which offered them on the German market below the retail price set by Deutsche Grammophon. It had been argued before the German court on behalf of Metro that Deutsche Grammophon had exhausted its right in the product when it was delivered to its French subsidiary and that, anyhow, the price maintenance system was prohibited by EC Articles 81 and 82 (ex Arts 85 and 86).

Faced with the uncertainty whether Deutsche Grammophon's rights had been exhausted the German court addressed to the ECJ questions which caused some difficulty as they were framed for the purpose of interpreting German rather than European Community law. However the European judges obligingly redrafted them and in their version the first question was whether:

> 'Community Law is infringed if the exclusive right conferred on a manufacturer of recordings by national legislation to distribute the protected products can be used to prohibit the domestic marketing of products that have been brought on to the market in the territory of another Member State by this manufacturer or with his consent.'

Advocate-General Römer thought that the principle of the *Parke, Davis* case, which was applicable here, was that:

> '. . . although the Treaty leaves the existence of and substance of industrial property rights untouched their exercise is completely subject to Community law'.

He then proceeded to discuss the now familiar theme of the existence and the exercise of rights and concluded that:

> '. . . the purpose of the protection of industrial rights was fulfilled when the goods were first marketed . . . it would undoubtedly go beyond the purpose of the protection of rights . . . if the holder was permitted to control further marketing'.

Summing-up, he said that the right to prevent re-imports: 'does not form part of the essence of the industrial and commercial property mentioned in Article 36' [now Art 30].

The ECJ held that if the exercise of a right did not fall within EC Article 81 (ex Art 85) it must further be decided whether the exercise of the right in issue conflicted with other provisions of the Treaty, in particular those relating to the free movement of goods.

The Court thought that EC Article 30 (ex Art 36) authorized prohibitions or restrictions on the free movement of goods if such were justified for the protection of industrial and commercial property, but only as far as they protected 'the rights which constitute the specific subject-matter of such property'. The proposition was further elaborated in the judgment with the conclusion that it would conflict with the provisions regarding the free movement of goods in the Common Market if a manufacturer of recordings exercised the exclusive right guaranteed to him by legislation of a Member State, in the manner in which Deutsche Grammophon had acted.

The Court has refined the interpretation of EC Article 30 (ex Art 36) by saying that 'although the Treaty does not affect the existence of the industrial property rights conferred by national legislation of a Member State, the exercise of these rights may come within the prohibition of the Treaty'. Reading this into the wording of the article one can see that, whilst the exception protects the existence of those rights, the qualification of the exception prohibits certain exercises of those rights. This in turn reconciles the distinction between 'existence and exercise' with the Court's conclusion that the exercise of a right can conflict with 'the provisions regarding the free movement of goods'.

The *Deutsche Grammophon* case was followed by the *Hag*[10] case. A German company producing decaffeinated coffee under the HAG trademark and registered the mark in Belgium and Luxembourg where the product was marketed through a subsidiary. As a result of a post-war sequestration the subsidiary and the mark it owned were sold and eventually the mark came into the hands of Van Zuylen Frères. When the German company began selling its coffee under the HAG mark in Luxembourg Van Zuylen brought an action to prevent this on the ground of a trademark infringement. The German company pleaded free movement of goods and the Luxembourg court asked the ECJ whether competition rules or the principle of the free movement of goods prevented the holder of a trademark from stopping the import of goods legally bearing the same mark in another Member State where originally the two trademarks belonged to the same holder but there was now 'no legal, financial, technical or economic link' between the present holders.

Advocate-General Mayras, drawing his interpretation of EC Article 30 (ex Art 36) from the *Deutsche Grammophon* case, submitted that Van Zuylen's 'power' to prevent Hag imports in defiance of its trademark did not 'form part of the very existence of the right of industrial and commercial property within the meaning of Article 36' but it constituted 'an exercise of a trademark right which conflicts with the fundamental principles of the Treaty arising from the provisions relating to the movement of goods'.

The Court decided the case on the basis of EC Articles 28-30 (ex Arts 30-36), simply because there was no element, factual or legal, which would bring the competition rules into play. It reiterated in essence the formula regarding the 'existence' and 'exercise' of intellectual property rights, adopted in the *Deutsche Grammophon* case, but defined more closely the circumstances in which an exercise of rights may be prohibited by the Treaty, ie when an exercise constitutes an arbitrary discrimination or a disguised restriction of the free movement of goods.

The Court ruled:

'. . . one cannot allow the holder of a trademark to rely on the exclusiveness of a trademark right – which may be the consequence of the territorial limitation of national legislations – with a view to prohibiting the marketing in a Member State of goods legally produced in another Member State under an identical trademark having the same origin. Such a prohibition would legitimize the isolation of national markets, would collide with one of the essential objects of the Treaty, which is to unite national markets in a single market. Whilst in such a market the identification of origin of a product covered by a trademark is useful, information to consumers on this point may be ensured by means other than such as would affect the free movement of goods.'[11]

Sandwiched between the patent and trademark cases is the *Dassonville*[12] case concerned with the 'designation of origin'. Dassonville Brothers bought Scotch whisky from the French distributors and sold it in Belgium at a price lower than that charged by the Belgian exclusive dealers. They labelled their bottled 'British customs certificate of origin' with the number and date of the French excise bond and in that form offered the product to the public. Under Belgian law it was a criminal offence to sell spirits bearing a designation of origin without official certification. French law, on the other hand, required an excise bond but no

10   Case 192/73: *Van Zuylen Frères SA v Hag AG* [1974] ECR 731, [1974] 2 CMLR 127.
11   Ibid [1974] ECR at 744.
12   Case 8/74: *Procureur du Roi v Dassonville* [1974] ECR 837, [1974] 3 CMLR 436.

official certification of designation of origin to accompany the products. Dassonville Brothers were prosecuted for contravening the law and also for the forgery of the official certificate of origin. The Belgian exclusive importers and distributors also made a claim for damages in respect of the loss suffered as a result of the illegal imports. The Belgian court asked the ECJ whether the Belgian law was, in the light of EC Articles 28-30 (ex Arts 30-34 and 36) a quantitative restriction or a measure having an equivalent effect.

The case is interesting because it raises the question whether the designation of origin is a species of intellectual property and also because a government, not a private holder of an intellectual property right, claimed the exception of EC Article 30 (ex Art 36). The former question was answered in the affirmative. Advocate-General Trabucchi thought that the designation of origin can be subject to ownership and does, in fact, fulfil the same function as a trademark. The Court did not dispute that but side-stepped the issue of intellectual property rights.

As regards the nature of the measures involved the Advocate-General said that 'the restriction on freedom of movement and on competition . . . derives objectively and necessarily from the law itself which applies without the need for any initiative on the part of the interested private parties'. Turning to the issue raised by the Belgian court, he thought that 'A trade rule enacted by a state which is unlike a quota but which . . . is capable of seriously hindering intra-Community trade in certain categories of goods must be regarded in principle as a measure having an effect equivalent to a quantitative restriction'.

The Court held that 'All trading rules enacted by Member States which are capable of hindering, directly or indirectly, actually or potentially intra-Community trade are to be considered as measures having an effect equivalent to quantitative restrictions'.

The breadth of this statement is quite staggering for it extends the concept of measures having an equivalent effect to quantitative restrictions beyond all recognition but it was toned down in the subsequent case where the Court held that the prohibition on marketing the product without documentary proof that it was genuine did not per se constitute an infringement of the Treaty.[13]

Dassonville was followed by the two *Centrafarm*[14] cases, in which infringement proceedings were taken against persons who held no rights in the patent and trademark respectively but claimed a right to trade in the products concerned. Centrafarm, a Dutch company, which had already been involved in the *Parke, Davis* case and was again to appear in the *De Peijper*[15] case, bought certain drugs from the subsidiaries of Sterling Drug Inc (a company incorporated in the State of New York) in the United Kingdom and Germany, where they were manufactured according to processes patented by Sterling. Sterling also had the Dutch patent, and its Dutch subsidiary Winthrop had the trademark right. Centrafarm imported the drugs into the Netherlands and sold them there, taking advantage of the higher prices charged for these drugs by Sterling in the Netherlands. In order to put an end to this practice Sterling attempted to enforce its patent rights and its Dutch subsidiary's trademark rights.

Advocate-General Trabucchi, having referred to *Sirena* and *Hag*, thought that 'a prohibition of parallel imports, linked on the basis of national law with

13 Case 2/78: *Commission v Belgium, Re Import of Spiritous Drinks* [1979] ECR 1761, [1980] 1 CMLR 216.
14 Case 15/74: *Centrafarm BV v Sterling Drug Inc* [1974] ECR 1147, [1974] 2 CMLR 480; Case 16/74: *Centrafarm BV v Winthrop BV* [1974] ECR 1183, [1974] 2 CMLR 480.
15 Case 104/75: *Officier van Justitie v Adriaan De Pijper* [1976] ECR 613, [1976] 2 CMLR 271.

the protection enjoyed by the patent holder, is contrary to Articles 30 and 32(2) [now EC Art 28]'. In his view it did not matter whether the obstacle to the movement of goods was caused by the conduct of Sterling Drug or the legislation in the Netherlands of which Sterling Drug wished to take advantage.

The Court went on to define the 'specific subject matter' of the patent and trademark holding, as in *Hag*, that the restrictions permitted by EC Article 30 (ex Art 36) were only allowed in so far as they protected the 'specific subject matter' of these rights. This was convenient in the two cases as one dealt with patents and the other with trademarks but the latter also offered an opportunity of refining the *Hag* ruling.

In the matter of definition the Court held that as regards patents, 'the specific subject matter of the industrial property is the guarantee that the patentee, to reward the creative effort of the inventor, has the exclusive right to use an invention with a view to manufacturing industrial products putting them into circulation for the first time, either directly or by the grant of licences to third parties, as well as the right to oppose infringement'. In relation to trademarks the Court thought that their object is 'the guarantee that the owner of the trademark has the exclusive right to use that trademark, for the purpose of putting products protected by the trademark into circulation for the first time, and is therefore intended to protect him against competitors wishing to take advantage of the status and reputation of the trademark by selling goods illegally bearing that trademark'.

Having thus defined the rights in question the Court addressed itself to the problem of their infringement or rather the question whether there is an infringement by a third party who markets the patented or branded goods (once these goods have been placed on the market by the owner of the patent or trademark or by another with his consent) in the territory claimed to himself by the owner of the relevant trademark or patent. In *Centrafarm v Sterling*[16] the Court held that: 'an obstacle to the free movement of goods may arise out of the existence, within a national legislation industrial and commercial property, of provisions laying down that a patentee's right is not exhausted when the product protected by the patent is marketed in another Member State, with the result that the patentee can prevent importation of the product into his own Member State when it has been marketed in another State'. In *Centrafarm v Winthrop*[17] the Court repeated the same formula in relation to trademarks adding: 'Such an obstacle is not justified when the product has been put on to the market in a legal manner in the Member State from which it has been imported, by the trademark owner himself or with his consent, so that there can be no question of abuse or infringement of the trademark'.

An ancillary question of considerable practical importance worried the Dutch court, ie whether the holder of a patent is authorized to exercise his rights under the patent, notwithstanding the Community rules on the free movement of goods, for the purpose of controlling the distribution of a pharmaceutical product with a view to protecting the public against the risks arising from the defects in the product.

The ECJ expressed its sympathy with this concern and remarked that EC Article 30 (ex Art 36) authorizes the Member State to derogate from the rules concerning the free movement of goods on grounds of the protection of human and animal health and life. 'However', said the Court, 'the measures necessary to achieve this must be such as may properly be adopted in the field of public health control and must not constitute a misuse of the rules concerning industrial and commercial property.'

16 *Centrafarm v Sterling* op cit note 14, supra, para 10.
17 *Centrafarm v Winthrop* op cit note 14, supra, at para 10.

The *De Peijper* [18] case echoed *Dassonville* but, being concerned with the parallel import of pharmaceutical products, it raised, inter alia, the question of the validity of national control of such products.

Centrafarm was engaged in parallel imports of branded medicines from the United Kingdom and marketed these in its own packages under new labels. In doing so it was not only undercutting the exclusive distributor but also infringing Dutch law on the control of pharmaceutical products which required, both for national and foreign products, an official permission and appropriate documentation. Mr de Peijper, a director of Centrafarm, was prosecuted because the company marketed the products without having previously obtained the consent of the Chief Public Health Inspector, and did not have the documents or requisite records of the products available for official inspection. In his defence Me de Peijper admitted that his company was technically in breach of the law but was unable to produce the requisite documents which were in the hands of the manufacturer and, therefore, available to the exclusive distributor but not the parallel importer. He argued that in the circumstances the Dutch law constituted a measure having an equivalent effect to quantitative restrictions prohibited by EC Article 26 (ex Art 30). Even if such a measure were justified 'on grounds of protection of health' it would be a 'means of discrimination or disguised restriction on trade between Member States' and, therefore, could not benefit from the exemption under EC Article 30 (ex Art 36).

The Dutch court referred to the ECJ two questions the gist of which was whether the Dutch law was contrary to EC Article 28 (ex Art 30) and whether it could be justified as an exception under EC Article 30 (ex Art 36). Advocate-General Mayras, following *Dassonville*, thought that it was contrary to EC Article 28 (ex Art 30) and could not be justified under EC Article 30 (ex Art 36). The Court held that:

> 'National rules or practices which result in imports being channelled in such a way that only certain traders can effect these imports, whereas others are prevented from doing so, constitute a measure having an equivalent effect to a quantitative restriction . . . [N]ational rules or practices which make possible for a manufacturer of the pharmaceutical product in question and his duly appointed representatives, simply by refusing to produce the documents . . . to enjoy a monopoly of the importing and marketing of the product must be regarded as being unnecessarily restrictive and cannot, therefore, come within the exceptions specified in [EC Article 30 (ex art 36)].'

A question of the meaning of intellectual property was raised in the *Re German Sparkling Wines and Brandies EC Commission v Germany*[19] case. The Commission brought an action against Germany claiming that German legislation, by reserving certain descriptions of alcoholic beverages to those of a German origin, impeded imports and contravened the Treaty provisions against quantitative restrictions. In defence, the German government relied on EC Article 30 (ex Art 36) but the Court held:

> '. . . Although the Treaty does not restrict the power of each Member State to legislate in matters of indications of origin, they are nevertheless prohibited by the second sentence of Article 36 [now Art 30] from introducing new measures of an arbitrary and unjustified nature whose effects are, for this reason, equivalent to quantitative restrictions.'

---

18 Op cit note 15, supra, at 640.
19 Case 12/74: *Commission v Germany* [1975] ECR 181, [1975] 1 CMLR 340, para 16.

Consequently, names like *Weinbrand, Sekt* and *Prädikatsekt,* though protected by German law, do not enjoy any protection in the Community. Moreover, since, in the opinion of the ECJ, these names are not true designations of origin, they cannot aspire to the status of 'intellectual property'.

Finally, it should be noted that the approach to intellectual property rights outlined above applies solely to trade within the EC (or EEA). Despite the fact that the EEC-Portugal Agreement (which was in force before Portugal joined the Community) contained clauses identical in wording to EC Articles 28 and 30 (ex Arts 30 and 36), the ECJ ruled that they could not be construed to the same effect because the requirements of the common market have no equivalent in the Community's external trade relations.[20]

With those remarks in mind, we can turn now to consider specific intellectual property rights.

C. Patents

(1) PATENTS AND FREE MOVEMENT

The specific subject matter of a patent is the guarantee that, in order to reward the creative effort of the inventor, the patentee has the exclusive right to (1) use an invention with a view to manufacturing a product and putting it into circulation for the first time, either directly or by the grant of licences to third parties, and (2) oppose infringements.[1] That guarantee relates to the exclusive or monopoly right of exploitation that is the means of obtaining the reward due for the inventor's creative efforts; there is no guarantee that a reward will be obtained in all circumstances.[2] A patent right may be exercised against a product coming from another Member State where: (a) it was manufactured under a patent originally held by a person legally and economically independent of the original proprietor of the patent in the importing state;[3] (b) it was unpatentable in the country of origin and was manufactured by third parties without the consent of the holder of the patent in the importing state,[4] or (c) it was manufactured in the country of origin under a compulsory patent licence granted to a third party, the patent being held by the patent holder in the importing state or having a common origin with his patent.[5] In the last case, the grant of the compulsory licence in the exporting state effectively deprives the patent holder of his exclusive right to prohibit the manufacturing and marketing of the product without his consent and it is therefore justified to allow the patent holder to oppose the importation and marketing of products manufactured under the compulsory licence in order to protect the substance of the patent granted in the importing state.[6]

---

20 Case 270/80: *Polydor Ltd v Harlequin Record Shops* [1982] ECR 329, [1982] 1 CMLR 677. The same approach was carried over into the Community's trademark legislation: see Case C-355/96: *Silhouette International v Hartlauer Handelsgesellschaft* [1998] ECR I-4799, [1998] 2 CMLR 953.

1 Case 15/74: *Centrafarm v Sterling Drug* [1974] ECR 1147, para 9; Case 187/80: *Merck v Stephar* [1981] ECR 2063, para 9; Case 19/84: *Pharmon v Hoechst* [1985] ECR 2281, para 26.

2 *Merck v Stephar,* supra, para 10.

3 *Centrafarm v Sterling Drug,* supra, para 11.

4 Ibid.

5 *Pharmon v Hoechst,* supra.

6 Ibid.

The basic rule is that a patent right may not be exercised so as to prevent the importation of goods produced anywhere in the Community under the patent by the patent holder or with his consent. A patent right may not be used to prevent the reimportation, into the state of manufacture or first marketing, of goods produced under the patent and since exported to another Member State; nor may it be used to prevent the importation of goods first marketed in another Member State under a parallel patent, that is, a patent right held by the proprietor of the patent granted in the importing state or by a person connected with him legally or economically.[7] This applies whether the goods were first marketed in the exporting state directly by the holder of the patent in the importing state or under a licence voluntarily granted by him.[8] The same also applies where the goods originate in a Member State where they are not patentable if they have been manufactured or marketed there for the first time by the patent holder or with his consent. The reason is that the patent holder is free to choose how he will exercise his exclusive right and, if he decides to market or allow the marketing of otherwise patentable goods for the first time in a Member State where there is no patent protection, he must take the consequences; the imposition of a prohibition or restriction on the importation of such goods into the state where the patent is held is in these circumstances excessive and unjustified, given that the patent holder could have protected his exclusive right by refusing to market or to allow the marketing of the goods in the exporting state.[9]

(2) PATENTS AND COMPETITION

There is nothing anti-competitive in being industrious enough or creative enough to develop a patentable invention even if the result is to confer upon the patent holder a monopoly within the territorial area covered by the patent, as may be the case where the goods produced by working the patent form a distinct product market. The legislation defining the rights derived by a patent holder from his patent, and the duration of those rights, also defines the balance that is to be drawn between the public interest in fostering innovation and the public interest in disseminating the fruits of innovation. Competition law intervenes in regard to the exercise of the patent holder's legal rights. The first thing that a patent holder must decide is ether to exploit his patent rights himself or enable others to exploit them through the grant of a patent licence. A patent holder is within his rights to decline to grant licences and, therefore, to remain the only person able to work the patent during the duration of the patent. If that is the choice made by the patent holder, the case law concerning copyright (described below) indicates that competition law will intervene only if the conduct of the patent holder in the market(s) for the product(s) produced by working the patent is anti-competitive. If, on the other hand, the patent holder decides to grant licences of the patent, the case law indicates that competition law will intervene to the extent that either the policy pursued in granting licences or the terms of the licences granted generate anti-competitive consequences on the market(s) for the product(s) produced by working the patent.

For example, a patent holder is perfectly entitled to work the patent himself but, if he then charges unfairly high prices for the products produced by working

---

7   The identity of the protected invention is the essential element in determining whether or not patents are parallel; divergences between national patent legislation are irrelevant: see *Centrafarm v Sterling Drug*, supra, paras 13-14.
8   Ibid, paras 10-11; *Pharmon v Hoechst*, supra, para 22.
9   *Centrafarm v Sterling Drug*, supra, para 11; *Merck v Stephar*, supra, paras 11-12.

the patent (which he may well be able to do because there will be no competing supplier of those products), he may (depending upon the circumstances) be accused of abusing a dominant position contrary to EC Article 82 (ex Art 86). If, on the other hand, he grants licences to third parties, he will by that means introduce competitors into the market who will, in the ordinary course, through competition, constrain the patent holder's ability to charge unfairly high prices. If the patent holder grants licences sparingly with the design of limiting such competition or includes in the licences terms that are intended to fetter price competition between licensees, he moves into the area in which competition law prevails and outside the area protected by his intellectual property right.

The competition law aspects of patent rights must be viewed not only from the perspective of the patent holder but also from the perspective of licensees. Licensees may themselves enter into anti-competitive agreements, in which case, the patent rights licensed to them provide the context for their anti-competitive activities but not any justification for such activities. Further, the acquisition of a patent licence by a dominant undertaking may itself be an abuse contrary to EC Article 82 (ex Art 86), where it strengthens that undertaking's dominant position and prevents or delays considerably the entry of new competitors into the market.[10]

D. Trademarks

(1) TRADEMARKS AND FREE MOVEMENT

The specific subject matter of a trademark is: (i) to guarantee to the proprietor of the trademark that he has the exclusive use of it for the purpose of putting products protected by the trademark into circulation for the first time and therefore to protect him against competitors wishing to take advantage of the status and reputation of the mark by selling products bearing it illegally; and (ii) to prevent any use of the trademark which is likely to impair its essential function of guaranteeing the identity of origin of the trademarked goods to the consumer or ultimate user, by enabling the latter to distinguish that product from products having another origin. The guarantee of origin means that the consumer or ultimate user can be certain that the trademarked product sold to him has not been the subject at a previous marketing stage to interference by third parties, without the authorization of the proprietor of the trademark, which is such as to affect the original condition of the product.[11] The case law has thrown up four types of situation in which the exercise of trademarks can (potentially at least) come into conflict with the requirements of the common market: (1) the problem posed by the importation into one Member State of goods bearing the trademark of the proprietor where that trademark was lawfully placed upon those goods in another Member State by the proprietor or by someone associated with the proprietor; (2) the problem posed by goods bearing a trademark that is different from the proprietor's trademark but could be confused with it; (3) the problem that arises where the same trademark comes into different hands; and (4) the problem posed by the importation of goods bearing the proprietor's trademark

---

10   Case T-51/89: *Tetra Park v Commission* [1990] ECR II-309, [1991] 2 CMLR 409, para 23.
11   Case 16/74: *Centrafarm v Winthrop* [1974] ECR 1183, [1974] 2 CMLR 480, para 8; Case 102/77: *Hoffmann-La Roche v Centrafarm* [1978] ECR 1139, [1978] 3 CMLR 217, para 7.

which have been tampered with by a third party. In relation to the last situation, it should be borne in mind that undertakings may alter the get-up of goods sold in different Member States with the object of getting consumers used to buying products with a particular look about them as well as a particular trademark. Intermediaries who obtain the same goods from the same undertaking, but in a Member State in which the price is particularly low, may find it necessary to alter the get-up of the goods in order to sell them in another Member State, where the price is higher, because of that practice. That, in turn, usually elicits the response that there has been unauthorized tampering with the goods.

The *EMI v CBS*[12] cases have the distinction of involving products coming from a non-Member State under a trademark identical with a trademark registered in all Member States except France. EMI held all trademarks including or consisting of the word 'Columbia' with regard to gramophone records. CBS, on the other hand, owned the 'Columbia' marks in North America, South America and other parts of the world. Originally all the 'Columbia' marks had been held by one company. EMI considered that the importation and marketing of CBS records bearing the 'Columbia' mark in the Community constituted an infringement of its trademark rights and requested the courts in the United Kingdom, Demark and Germany to order CBS to cease this activity. All these courts asked the ECJ for preliminary rulings on the question of whether the EC Treaty prevented EMI from enforcing its rights in order to prohibit the sale in the Community of the branded product manufactured by CBS outside the Community where the trademark is legitimately used, or the manufacture by CBS in the Community of the product bearing the 'Columbia' mark.

In relation to the free movement of goods CBS argued that once the imported product has been cleared by customs it was entitled to free movement in the Community and the protection against quantitative restrictions and similar measures. Relying on *Hag*, CBS claimed that, though the case was not confined to trade between Member States, the *Hag* ruling should be applied by analogy because the marks in question had a common origin.

Advocate-General Warner rejected both arguments. He pointed out that EC Articles 28-30 (ex Arts 30-36), only concerned restrictions on trade between Member States of the Community, not trade between the Community and third countries. As far as the analogy to the *Hag* case was concerned he thought that the whole basis of the decision was that 'industrial and commercial property rights, and in particular trademarks, may not be used as artificially to split up the Common Market'. The Court ruled that:

> '. . . the exercise of a trademark right in order to prevent the marketing of products coming from a third country under an identical mark, even if this constitutes a measure having an effect equivalent to a quantitative restriction, does not affect the free movement of goods between Member States and thus does not come under the prohibitions set out in Articles 30 et seq [now Arts 28-30]'.

As far as non-Community countries are concerned, benefit of free trade can only be acquired by a particular treaty between the Community and the contracting country but cannot be created by a bilateral treaty between a Member State of the Community and a non-Community country. The Court made this clear by pointing

---

12   Case 51/75: *EMI Records Ltd v CBS (United Kingdom) Ltd* and Case 86/75: *EMI Records Ltd v CBS Grammofon A/S* and Case 96/75: *EMI Records Ltd v CBS Schallplatten GmbH* [1976] ECR 811, 871, 913, [1976] 2 CMLR 235.

out that even Regulation 1439/74 of 4 June 1974, which introduced common rules for imports to be adopted by all Member States, relates only to quantitative restrictions but not to measures having equivalent effect. The Court concluded:

> 'It follows that neither the rules of the Treaty on the free movement of goods nor those on the putting into free circulation of products coming from third countries nor, finally, the principles governing the common commercial policy, prohibit the proprietor of a mark in all the Member States of the Community from exercising his right in order to prevent the importation of similar products bearing the same mark and coming from a third country.'

The same rule applies to the manufacturing and marketing of products within the Community either by the outside competitor himself or through his subsidiaries established in the Community. The Court dealt with this possibility, saying:

> '[T]he protection of industrial and commercial property . . . would be rendered meaningless if an undertaking other than the proprietor of a mark in the Member States could be allowed there to manufacture and market products bearing the same mark since such conduct would amount to an actual infringement of the protected mark.'

Where the proprietor of the trademark has permitted goods bearing the mark to come into the hand of a reseller, the proprietor is not only prevented from using the trademark rights to prohibit the use of the trademark by the reseller for the purpose of reselling the goods; he is also prevented from using his trademark rights to prohibit the reseller from using the trademark in other ways customary in the reseller's sector of business for the purpose of bringing the commercialization of the goods to the public's attention – unless that use of the trademark were to damage seriously the reputation of the trademark.[13]

The opportunity of considering a conflict of trademark rights of a diverse origin arose in the case of *Terrapin v Terranova*.[14] Terrapin, a British manufacturer and distributor of prefabricated building units, using the 'Terrapin' trademark, applied in 1961 to have the mark registered in Germany. Despite the opposition by Terranova, a German company producing and distributing building materials, the mark was registered in 1962 but in 1967 the *Bundespatentgericht* annulled the decision to register and prohibited the registration of the trademark 'Terrapin' on the ground that there would be confusion between it and 'Terranova'. After several years of litigation between Terrapin and Terranova the *Bundesgerichtshof* addressed a question to the Community Court asking whether 'an undertaking established in Member State A, by using its commercial name and trademark rights existing there, should prevent the import of similar goods of an undertaking established in Member State B if these goods have been lawfully given a distinguishing name which may be confused with the commercial name and trademark which are protected in State A for the undertaking established there . . .'.

With his eyes on the *Hag* and *Deutsche Grammophon* case Advocate-General Mayras discussed the nature of intellectual property rights, referring to the 'specific subject matter' of such rights (which seem now to have replaced the consideration of the 'exercise' of such rights). 'Specific subject matter' comes to be distinguished from 'incidental functions' of such rights and, if one follows this line of thinking, only the former deserves protection.

---

13 Case C-337/95: *Parfums Christian Dior v Evora* [1997] ECR I-6013, in particular para 54.
14 Case 119/75: *Terrapin (Overseas) Ltd v Terranova Industrie CA Kapferer & Co* [1976] ECR 1039, [1976] 2 CMLR 482.

The Court held that it would be compatible with the provisions of the EC Treaty to prevent the importation of products of an undertaking established in another Member State and bearing a name giving rise to confusion with the trademark and commercial name of the opposing party, provided that there are no agreements restricting competition and no legal or economic ties between the undertakings and that their respective rights have arisen independently of one another.

Thus, dealing with the situation where marks of separate origin have displayed a remarkable similarity (as distinguished from *Hag*, where there was a common origin of the mark) the Court held that:

'. . . in the present state of Community law an industrial or commercial property right legally acquired in a Member State may legally be used to prevent under the first sentence of article 36 of the Treaty [now EC Art 30] the import of products marketed under a name giving rise to confusion where the rights in question have been acquired by different and independent proprietors under different national laws. If in such a case the principle of the free movement of goods were to prevail over the protection given by the respective national laws, the specific objective of industrial and commercial property rights would be undermined. In the particular situation the requirements of the free movement of goods and the safeguarding of industrial and commercial property rights must be so reconciled that protection is ensured for the legitimate use of the rights conferred by national laws, coming within the prohibitions on imports "justified" within the meaning of Article 36 of the Treaty [now EC Art 30], but denied on the other hand in respect of any improper exercise of the same rights of such a nature as to maintain or effect artificial partitions within the common market.'[15]

This reasoning seems to flow from the much-repeated distinction between the existence of rights recognized by the Member States and their exercise within the limits of Community law. These limits have been circumscribed by the philosophy of the Common Market in general and the exception within EC Article 30 (ex Art 36) in particular.

With hindsight the moral of the story seems to be that Terrapin instead of fighting legal battles should have perhaps changed its trademark for the German territory and applied for registration, but this is no comfort to a company which has established a reputation under a mark. The risk of confusion between different trademarks was confirmed in later cases as providing a justification for opposing the importation of goods bearing the confusing mark.[16]

The doctrine of 'common origin' (ie that the trademark originally belonged to one and the same proprietor) attributed to the *Hag* case, already undermined by the sub-division of the original right, has been laid to rest in another *Hag* case.[17] In 1979 the firm Van Zuylen Frères was acquired by a Swiss company and transformed into a subsidiary of the latter. The subsidiary began to market decaffeinated coffee under the HAG trademark in Germany. Hag AG applied for an injunction, thus raising the question whether Hag AG could lawfully sell the product under the HAG mark in Belgium and Luxembourg whilst the subsidiary of the Swiss company could not lawfully sell it in Germany. The latter,

15   Ibid [1976] ECR 1039 at 1061-1062.
16   Case C-10/89: *HAG GF* [1990] ECR I-3711; Case C-317/91: *Deutsche Renault v Audi* [1993] ECR I-6227; Case C-9/93: *IHT Internationale Heiztechnik v Ideal Standard* [1994] ECR I-2789.
17   Case C-10/89: *SA CNL-Sucal NV v HAG GF AG* [1990] ECR I-3711, [1990] 3 CMLR 571.

relying on the first *Hag* case, argued that holders of identical marks of common origin could not oppose the marketing of the product bearing the mark affixed by another proprietor of the mark.

The Court thought that the *Hag* doctrine had to be reconsidered and effectively set it aside. It ruled:

> 'From the date of expropriation and notwithstanding their common origin, each of the marks independently fulfilled its function, within its own territorial field of application, of guaranteeing that the marked products originated from one single source.
>
> It follows from the foregoing that in a situation such as the present case, in which the mark originally had one sole proprietor and the single ownership was broken as a result of expropriation, each of the trademark proprietors must be able to oppose the marketing, in the Member State in which the trade mark belongs to him, of goods originating from the other proprietor, in so far as they are similar products bearing an identical mark or one which is liable to lead to confusion.'[18]

The ruling in *Hag* was later extended to the voluntary separation of trademark rights. The principle that emerges from the cases is that a trademark in the importing state cannot be used against goods bearing the same or a similar mark which have been marketed in another state by the proprietor of the trademark in the importing state or by a separate person economically linked to the proprietor. The economic links in question may take the form of a licence of the right, a parent-subsidiary relationship or an exclusive distribution agreement. The essential point is that the imported goods must at the point of manufacture be under the same control of their quality as the goods bearing the trademark that actually originate in the importing state. It is not necessary for that control actually to be exercised because the proprietor of a trademark may for its own reason be willing to launch in different Member States products of varying quality but bearing the same trademark.[19]

Lastly, there is the problem posed by tampering with trademarked goods. In *Hoffmann-La Roche & Co AG v Centrafarm*[20] a party purchased valium in the United Kingdom and sold it in Germany after repacking the product in smaller quantities but retaining the original marks and putting Centrafarm's marks on the packing. The ECJ upheld, in this case, the mark's holders' rights to protection under EC Article 30 (ex Art 36) since they claimed legitimate use of the marks against competitors abusing the reputation established by the mark.

The Court ruled that:

> 'The proprietor of a trademark right which is protected in two Member States at the same time is justified pursuant to the first sentence of Article 36 [now EC Art 30] . . . in preventing a product to which the trademark has lawfully been applied in one of those States from being marketed in the other Member State after it has been repacked in new packaging to which the trademark has been affixed by a third party.'[1]

This decision was followed in *Centrafarm BV v American Home Products Corpn*[2] where the repacking exercise involved different marks. The product consisted of

18   Ibid at paras 18 and 19.
19   Case 9/93: *IHT Internationale Heiztechnik v Ideal Standard* [1994] ECR I-2789, [1994] 3 CMLR 857, paras 34-39.
20   Case 102/77: [1978] ECR 1139, [1978] 3 CMLR 217.
 1   Ibid [1978] ECR at 1167.
 2   Case 3/78: [1978] ECR 1823, [1978] 2 CMLR 63.

pharmaceutically identical pills, though of a different taste. The manufacturer held slightly different trademarks in the United Kingdom and the Netherlands. Centrafarm bought pills bearing the UK mark, Seranid, and repacked them under the Dutch mark, Seresta. Centrafarm claimed to be entitled to place on the market in the Netherlands under the Seresta mark the corporation's products lawfully distributed in other countries of the Common Market. The Corporation disputed this liberty. On reference from a Dutch court the ECJ held that only the trademark holder had the right to decide to which products he would affix each mark and to prevent altering them without his permission provided, of course, he did this for his protection and not for the division of the market.

However, packaging which would expose the marks and give relevant information including the names and addresses of the manufacturer and the importer and indicating that the importer is responsible for the packaging, should not prevent the sale of the imported product. In such circumstances the protection under EC Article 30 (ex Art 36) afforded to the proprietor of the mark would not apply.[3]

The effect of the case law is that trademark rights can be used legitimately not only to prevent the risk of confusion between the goods sold by the proprietor of the mark and other goods but also to prevent other steps from being taken that might damage the reputation of the mark and of the goods bearing it.[4] On the other hand, there must be a genuine and real reason for relying upon trademark rights. If the underlying reason is to secure an artificial partitioning of the market resulting from the particular marketing system adopted by the proprietor of the right, the exercise of the trademark rights may be prohibited under the free movement of goods rules in the Treaty.[5]

(2) TRADEMARKS AND COMPETITION

Trademarks are in themselves pro-competitive because they enhance inter-brand competition by enabling the proprietor of the mark to develop in the mind of consumers a recognizable identity and reputation for his products that distinguish them from the products offered by competitors. Trademarks can also be used in an anti-competitive way. For example, the risk of confusion between different marks can create a degree of uncertainty and provide the opportunity for one undertaking to seek to control the operations of another.[6] In order to protect a particular trademark, an undertaking may register as trademarks a wide range of similar trademarks so as to keep other persons further away from the protected mark than is really justified.[7] Trademarks may also be assigned or otherwise disposed of in order to achieve a partitioning of the market. In that event, the trademarks are used as the means to achieve an objective determined by an underlying anti-competitive agreement. If that underlying agreement is prohibited by EC Article 81 (ex Art 85) (or, conceivably, by EC Article 82 (ex Art 86)), the assignments of the trademarks (or the other agreements concerning the trademarks) that are used to give effect to that underlying agreement, are themselves void.[8]

---

3   Case 1/81: *Pfizer Inc v Eurim-Pharm GmbH* [1981] ECR 2913, [1982] 1 CMLR 406.
4   Eg Cases C-427/93, C-429/93, C-436/93: *Bristol Myers-Squibb v Paranova* [1996] ECR I-3457; Case C-337/95: *Parfums Christian Dior v Evora* [1997] ECR I-6013.
5   Eg Case C-379/97: *Pharmacia & Upjohn v Paranova* [1999] ECR I-6927, paras 17 and 22.
6   Eg Case 35/83: *BAT v Commission* [1985] ECR 363, [1985] 2 CMLR 470. The risk of confusion is now regulated by Community legislation.
7   Protective trademarks can usually be revoked for non-use.
8   Eg Case C-9/93: *IHT Internationale Heiztechnik v Ideal Standard* [1994] ECR I-2789, [1994] 3 CMLR 857, para 59.

E. Copyright

Copyright covers not only the right to reproduce works (physical objects) subject to the right but also, in certain instances, the right to perform a protected work. Accordingly, issues concerning copyright have arisen not only in connection with the movement of goods but also in connection with the freedom to provide services.

(1) COPYRIGHT AND MOVEMENT OF GOODS

Copyrights, where forming part of imported goods, fall, of course, within the scope of Article 36 as has been demonstrated in such cases as the *Deutsche Grammophon*[9] case (entailing a right akin to copyright), the *EMI v CBS*[10] case and the *Polydor v Harlequin*[11] case but copyrights per se have achieved prominence rather late.

Ten years after the *Deutsche Grammophon* case a question of royalties on reproduced copyright came before the ECJ.[12] In the background of the case was an agreement between GEMA, a German member of the international organization BIEM[13] and another organization IFPI[14] grouping the manufacturers of sound recordings. Relations between these two organizations were governed by a network of agreements, on the basis of which licences to produce and sell records are granted. These agreements enabled the manufacturers to record any work of their choice and to export all or part of their output. On the question of royalties, the standard contracts for BIEM members require the manufacturer to pay (1) for records sold on the continent of Europe: 8% of the retail price of the record in the country of destination; and (2) for records sold in the United Kingdom and the Republic of Ireland, the royalties in force in these countries, which are lower than the royalties on the Continent. The BIEM agreements allow records to move from one Member State to another but only through the mechanism established by these agreements, which means that in moving from a low-royalty country (eg the UK) to a high-royalty country (eg Germany), records are subject to a higher charge in the country of destination.

Membran imported records into Germany, some of these coming from the UK, where they had been produced and marketed under a licence granted by the English copyright protection society MCPS. GEMA subsequently brought an action against two importers for having infringed German copyright law, in order to obtain payment of the difference between the royalties payable in both countries. The ECJ held that the existence of a disparity between national laws, which is capable of distorting competition in the Common Market, cannot justify the maintenance or introduction by a Member State of rules which are incompatible with the free movement of goods.

The Court stated that in a Common Market an author, acting directly or through his publisher, is free to choose the place, in any of the Member States, in which to put his work into circulation. He may make the choice according to

---

9　Case 78/70: *Deutsche Grammophon v Metro* [1971] ECR 487.
10　Cases 51/75: *EMI Records Ltd v CBS United Kingdom Ltd* [1976] ECR 811; 86/75: *EMI Records Ltd v CBS Grammophon A/S* [1976] ECR 871; 96/75: *EMI Records Ltd v CBS Schallplatten GmbH* [1976] ECR 913.
11　Case 270/80: *Polydor Ltd v Harlequin Record Shops* [1982] ECR 329.
12　Cases 55 and 57/80: *Musik-Vertrieb Membran GmbH v GEMA* [1981] ECR 147.
13　Bureau International des Sociètés Gérant les Droits d'Enregistrement et de Réproduction Mechanique.
14　International Federation of the Phonographic Industry.

his best interests, which involve not only the level of remuneration provided in the Member State in question but also other factors such as, for example, the opportunities for distributing his work and the marketing facilities. In those circumstances a copyright management society may not be permitted to claim, on the importation of sound recordings into another Member State, payment of additional fees based on the difference in the rates of remuneration existing in the various Member States.

This was the first case in which the European Court stated expressly that its case law on 'industrial and commercial policy' is also to be applied to real copyright as distinct from the record producers' right related to copyright which was involved in the *Deutsche Grammophon* case. This view was confirmed in the subsequent case[15] in which the French government intervened and contended that copyright was not comparable to other industrial and commercial property rights such as patents or trademarks because of the moral rights which are inherent in the copyright. The ECJ replied that copyright comprises various rights, one of which is that of commercial exploitation. Therefore, whatever the precise denomination of these various rights might be, they should be subject to the same principle according to which Article 36 of the EEC Treaty only admits of derogations from the free movement of goods where such derogations are justified for the purpose of safeguarding rights which constitute the specific subject matter of the property involved.

Considering the claim for additional fees[16] arising from the reproduction of a musical work publicly performed in France the Court ruled that even if such a claim had a restrictive effect on imports, it would not fall into the category of measures having an equivalent effect to quantitative restrictions prohibited by the Treaty because such fees have to be regarded as a normal exploitation of a copyright provided they do not constitute an arbitrary discrimination or a disguised restriction on intra-Community trade.

Concerning the marketing[17] of video cassettes the Court had to decide whether it was compatible with the Treaty provisions for a national law to permit the copyright proprietor to control reproduction after he had already put them into circulation in another Member State, whose legislation provided that the proprietor could control the first sales but afterwards had no authority to prevent reproduction. The Court observed that the commercialization of video cassettes is effected not only by the sales but also, increasingly, by the reproduction by those who possess the necessary equipment. Hence the importance of being able to determine where they should be sold. Having come to the conclusion that the legislation in question caused no arbitrary discrimination in trade between the Member States, the Court ruled that fees received by copyright holders only on the occasion of the first sale or hire of video cassettes do not provide for the makers of films a remuneration corresponding to the number of reproductions that can be made or secure a satisfactory part of the reproduction market. Therefore the laws which provide specifically for the protection of the right of reproduction appear to be justified on the ground of protection of intellectual property rights within the meaning of EC Article 30 (ex Art 36).

These two cases are interesting because the ECJ, defining the specific subject matter of copyrights, recognized in this concept the right of normal exploitation as well as the right to just remuneration.

---

15   Case 58/80: *Dansk Supermarked A/S v IMERCO A/S* [1981] ECR 181.
16   Case 402/85: *Basset v SACEM* [1987] ECR 1747, at para 16.
17   Case 158/86: *Warner Bros Inc v Christiansen* [1988] ECR 2605, at paras 15 and 16.

Copyrights come into prominence in the field of manufactured goods where they are concerned with the protection of industrial design. Such a situation arose in connection with the importation of handbags from Taiwan.[18] Nancy Kean Gifts registered the design of a handbag imported by them into the Netherlands and then brought an action against Keurkoop who were importing handbags of the same design. The question to be decided was whether the provisions of EC Article 30 (ex Art 36) allowed the application of a national law which, like the Uniform Benelux Law on Designs, gives an exclusive right to a person who files the design first. The second question was whether such a person could oppose the importation of products whose appearance was identical to the design which has been filed, from one of the Member States where their marketing did not infringe any right of the owner to an exclusive right in the country of importation.

The ECJ replied that in the absence of Community standardization or harmonization of national laws, protection of designs is a matter of national rules which, in the Benelux situation, are common rules for the three countries.

Answering the second question the Court said that, in principle, the position is similar to that arising under EC Article 30 (ex Art 36). It means that the restriction on the importation of goods in breach of the right arising from the filing of the design must be justified and cannot constitute an improper exercise of such a right so as to maintain or establish artificial partitions of the Common Market. Thus Nancy Kean Gifts, who registered the design of a handbag imported by them from Taiwan, could prevent Keurkoop from importing handbags of the same design into the Netherlands.

In another case[19] the ECJ had to decide on the protection of models used in the production of motor cars. The question was whether the manufacturers of motor cars, in this case the French company Renault, had the right to a protective right over certain elements of the bodywork of their cars and thus prohibit the manufacture, sales and exportation of these elements by certain, presumably Italian, specialists in imitating parts detached from the original model.

The imitators contended that only the complete model of the car could be subject to such a right whilst the parts of the body taken separately had no aesthetic value. Renault and the French government, on the other hand, claimed that the elements of the bodywork ought to be capable of being protected and that the proprietor of such a right ought to have the exclusive right of putting these products first on the market and also the right to protect himself from other manufacturers who wish to copy and sell these parts.

The Court stated that, in the present state of the Community law and in the absence of uniformity or harmonization of national laws, the conditions of protecting such rights depend on national laws.

(2) COPYRIGHT AND COMPETITION

It was stated in the handbags case that: 'Although a right to a design, as a legal entity, does not as such fall within the class of agreements or concerted practices prohibited by Article 85(1) of the EEC Treaty [now EC Art 81(1)], the exercise of that right may be subject to the prohibitions contained in the Treaty when it is the purpose, the means or the result of an agreement, decision or concerted practice.'[20]

---

18   Case 144/81: *Keurkoop BV v Nancy Kean Gifts BV* [1982] ECR 2853, [1983] 2 CMLR 47.
19   Case 53/87: *CIRCA and Maxicar v Renault* [1988] ECR 6039 at para 11. See also Case 238/87: *Volvo v Erik Veng (UK) Ltd* [1988] ECR 6211.
20   Case 144/81, supra.

In practice, however, copyrights fall more readily within the orbit of the prohibition of abuse of a dominant position envisaged by EC Article 82 (ex Art 86) than within the categories of restrictive practices prohibited by EC Article 81(1) (ex Art 85(1)). Moreover, unlike EC Article 81(3) (ex Art 85(3)), EC Article 82 (ex Art 86) gives no authority to the Commission to grant individual or block exemptions.

The first investigation conducted by the Commission was into the activities of a German Collecting Society GEMA concerned with both physical and performing rights in musical works.[1] The Commission found no difficulty in condemning GEMA for abusing its dominant position since it exploited its controlling power by: discriminating against nationals of the other Member States; binding its members by obligations which were not necessary; preventing, through its system, the establishment of a single market in the supply of services by music publishers; extending copyright through contractual means to non-copyright works; discriminating against independent importers of gramophone records as compared with manufacturers of records; and discriminating against the importers of tape records and optical sound records as compared with German manufacturers of such records.

GEMA Decision No 2 (amending Decision No 1) also established that a collecting society must not insist on receiving an assignment from its members of rights for countries in which the society does not carry out direct administration but authorizes a foreign society to act as its agent. Concerning countries where the society carries out direct administration it must permit its members to choose whether to assign to the society all the rights which the society is willing to administer or only one or more such rights, eg to assign the general performing right, but not broadcasting or recording rights. However the society may, as regards the categories of rights assigned, insist that all existing and future works of the author in the given category be included. The freedom of a member to withdraw any category of rights from the society on a three years' notice must be safeguarded.

In another case[2] the Commission ruled that it is an abuse for a collecting society administering performer's rights in a Member State to refuse to conclude management agreements with artistes who are neither nationals of nor resident in the state in which the collecting society is established, but are nationals of or residents in other Member States.

The Commission has certainly curtailed these activities by applying the competition rules to GEMA, and provided detailed guidance how to operate such a society within the law. The ECJ in *Belgische Radio en Televisie v SABAM*[3] dealt with the complaints of certain proprietors of copyrights against a Belgian collecting society that, in order to exercise their profession, they were compelled to assign their rights to the society.

The Court confirmed that account must be taken of the function of a collecting society to protect its members, especially against major users of their works, such as broadcasters and record manufacturers and that abuse depends on whether the relevant practices go beyond what is necessary to enable the society effectively to fulfil its function, but in this case compulsory assignment of rights constituted that abuse.

The GEMA decisions also establish that it is an abuse for a collecting society to charge royalties in respect of works of which it does not hold the copyright

---

1   *Re GEMA* [1971] CMLR D35; *Re Gema (No 2)* [1972] CMLR D115.
2   *Re GVL* [1982] 1 CMLR 221.
3   Case 127/73: [1974] ECR 313.

either because the copyright has expired or because it had not been assigned to the society.

In view of the conflicting interests of authors and users of copyright works the Commission ruled, in *GEMA (No 1)*, that persons associated with users of a collecting society's copyrights could not be excluded from membership of the society but their voting rights could be restricted. In reviewing GEMA's constitution the Commission[4] permitted GEMA to amend it so as to require that the assignments made to it by its members should prohibit the member from sharing his royalties with a user (eg a broadcaster) who has an agreement with the society in order to induce the user to favour the member's works. Such a royalty sharing would undermine the collective scheme of the Society.

(3) COPYRIGHT AND THE PROVISION OF SERVICES

At first sight there seems to be no connection between copyrights and the provision of services but developments in communications technology and transmissions of television programmes begin to make this connection. After all, sound and radio waves do not recognize national frontiers and territorial copyrights make little sense when in Europe a television programme can be heard and seen simultaneously in several countries of the Common Market.

European Community case law puts television advertising in the category of services. Thus an operator of a private television relay station was not considered to be in the business of selling goods and, therefore, could not complain that the state in which he operated either discriminated against him or was exercising a monopoly prohibited by the Common Market rules by prosecuting him for working his station without a licence required by national law. He simply had to comply with the national licensing system[5] and could not rely on the freedom to provide services in order to avoid this obligation. Following this judgment the ECJ held[6] that transmission of advertisements by cable television was a service and in the absence of any harmonization of the relevant national laws by the Community, could be regulated, restricted or even totally prohibited by a Member State despite the Treaty provisions regarding the freedom to provide services.

More specifically the question of services and copyright arose in cases involving cable television. In the *Coditel* case[7] a Belgian cinematographic film distribution company sued a French company and three Belgian cable television diffusion companies for damages caused by the reception in Belgium of a broadcast by German television of a film for which the Belgian Ciné Vog obtained exclusive distribution rights in Belgium. In 1969 the French company, acting as the owner of all the proprietary rights in the film called *Le Boucher*, gave Ciné Vog the 'exclusive right' to distribute the film in Belgium for seven years. The film was shown in cinemas in Belgium starting in 1970. However in 1971 German television broadcast a German version of the film and this broadcast prejudiced the commercial future of the film in Belgium. On that ground Ciné Vog complained to the French company, which had the rights in the film, for not having honoured the exclusive rights which it had transferred to Ciné Vog, and against the three companies for having relayed the German broadcast over their cable diffusion networks.

---

4   *Re GEMA* [1982] 2 CMLR 482.
5   Case 155/73: *Italy v Sacchi* [1974] ECR 409, [1974] 2 CMLR 177.
6   Case 52/79: *Procureur du Roi v Debauve* [1980] ECR 833.
7   Case 62/79: *Coditel SA v Ciné Vog Films SA* [1980] ECR 881, [1981] 2 CMLR 362; Case 262/81: *Coditel SA v Ciné Vog Films SA* [1982] ECR 3381, [1983] 1 CMLR 49.

The Belgian court considered that these companies made a 'communication to the public' of the film and concluded that the authorization given by the copyright owner (ie the French company) to German television to broadcast the film did *not* include the authority to relay the film over cable diffusion networks outside Germany, or at least those in Belgium.

It also examined the defence argument that any prohibition on the transmission of the film, the copyright in which had been assigned by the producer to a distribution company covering the whole of Belgium, was contrary to the provisions of the EEC Treaty, in particular EC Article 81 (ex Art 85) which prohibits restraints on competition and EC Articles 49 and 50 (ex Arts 59 and 60) which govern the freedom to provide services. The Court rejected the argument based on competition rules and referred to the ECJ questions arising from the freedom to provide services.

The ECJ considered that a cinematographic film belongs to the category of literary and artistic work made available to the public by performances which may be infinitely repeated. In this respect the problems involved in the observance of copyright in relation to the requirements of the EC Treaty are not the same as those which arise in connection with literary and artistic works, the placing of which at the disposal of the public is inseparable from the circulation of the material form of the works, as is the case of books or records. The Court ruled:

> 'In these circumstances the owner of the copyright in a field and his assigns have a legitimate interest in calculating the fees due in respect of the authorization to exhibit the film on the basis of the actual or probable number of performances and in authorizing a television broadcast of the film only after it has been exhibited in cinemas for a certain period of time.'[8]

The contract between the French company and Ciné Vog stipulated that the exclusive right which was assigned included the right to exhibit the film publicly in Belgium by way of projection in cinemas and on television but that the right to have the film diffused by Belgian television could not be exercised until 40 months after the first showing of the film in Belgium. Considering in this context the question whether an assignment of copyright limited to the territory of a Member State is capable of restricting the freedom to provide services the Court held:

> 'Whilst Article 59 of the Treaty [now EC Art 49] prohibits restrictions upon freedom to provide services, it does not thereby encompass limits upon the exercise of certain economic activities which have their origin in the application of national legislation for the protection of intellectual property, save where such application constitutes a means of arbitrary discrimination or a disguised restriction on trade between Member States. Such would be the case if that application enabled parties to an assignment of copyright to create artificial barriers to trade between Member States.'[9]

> 'The effect of this is that, whilst copyright entails the right to demand fees for any showing or performance, the rules of the Treaty cannot in principle constitute an obstacle to the geographical limits which the parties to a contract of assignment have agreed upon in order to protect the author and his assigns in this regard. The mere fact that those geographical limits may coincide with national frontiers does not point to a different solution in a situation where television is organized in the Member States largely on the basis of legal

8   Case 62/79, at para 13.
9   Ibid at para 15.

broadcasting monopolies, which indicates that a limitation other than the geographical field of application of an assignment is often impracticable.'[10]

The Court concluded that: 'The exclusive assignee of the performing right in a film for the whole of a Member State may therefore rely upon his right against cable television diffusion companies which have transmitted that film on their diffusion network having received it from a television broadcasting station established in another Member State, without thereby infringing Community law.'[11]

F. Accommodating intellectual property to the exigencies of the Common Market

(1) COMPETITION LAW

Exemptions from the rigour of EC Article 81(1) (ex Art 85(1)) may be granted by the Commission either by an individual decision under Articles 6-9 of Regulation 17/62[12] or by a general regulation covering a category of agreements.

By virtue of Council Regulation 19/65[13] the Commission adopted Regulation 240/96[14] on the application of Article 85(3) of the EEC Treaty (now EC Art 81(3)) to certain categories of technology transfer agreements, that is, pure patent or pure know-how licensing agreements and mixed patent and know-how licensing agreements (including agreements containing ancillary provisions relating to intellectual property rights other than patents). As required by Regulation 19/65 both Regulations are limited to agreements to which only two undertakings are party but this is only a formal condition because they may form part of a network of similar licences between the same licensor and various licensees.

For the purpose of the Regulation the following are deemed to be patents: patent applications; utility models; applications for registration of utility models; topographies of semiconductor products; certificats d'utilité and certificats d'addition under French law and applications for the same; supplementary protection certificates for medicinal products or other products for which such supplementary protection certificates may be obtained; and plant breeder's certificates.[15]

'Know-how' is defined[16] as a body of technical information which is secret, substantial and identitied in an appropriate form.

Perhaps the most important feature of the patent and know-how licences exempted from prohibition by the regulation is their exclusivity, ie they may contain provisions to guarantee the licensees exclusive rights of manufacturing and selling the licensed product in the allotted territory and to reserve similar exclusive rights to the licensor or his other licensees in other territories.[17]

---

10   Ibid at para 16.
11   Ibid at para 17.
12   OJ, Sp Ed 1959-62 p 87.
13   OJ, Sp Ed 1965-66, p 35.
14   OJ 1996, L31/2. It replaced Reg 2349/84, on patent licensing agreements (OJ 1984, L219/15) and Reg 556/90, on know-how licensing agreements (OJ 1989, L61/1).
15   Art 8(1).
16   Art 10.
17   Art 1(1).

At first the Commission[18] considered exclusivity and related clauses to constitute an infringement of EC Article 81(1) (ex Art 85(1)), even if the exclusive rights were limited to manufacturing, the parties being free to sell throughout the Common Market; but the ECJ, whilst confirming that view,[19] created an escape from EC Article 81(1) (ex Art 85(1)) through the so-called 'open exclusive licences', which may be justified in order to encourage innovation and the introduction of new technology.

The Regulation contains two lists of obligations: those which are permissible ('white list') and those which are so noxious that their inclusion in a licensing agreement disqualifies the agreement from the benefit of the exemption offered by the Regulation ('black list'). Where a licence contains restrictive clauses which are not otherwise mentioned in the Regulation, Article 4 offers a simplified procedure for gaining an individual exemption, under which an agreement notified to the Commission benefits from an exemption unless the Commission objects to it within four months.

The Regulation permits the licensor to require the licensee to co-operate with him in suppressing infringements of the licensed patents by third parties.[20] The licensee must be free to challenge the validity or secrecy of the licensed patents or know-how but the licensor may reserve the right to terminate the licence in that event.[1]

Non-challenge clauses (which preclude a licensee from disputing the validity of the licensed right) are often used in practice and raise the question of their standing under EC Article 81(1) (ex Art 85(1)). The judgment of the ECJ in Case 65/86[2] clarifies the position. The case involved cross-licences between German companies in respect of patents granted or applied for in Germany and other Member States in connection with polyurothane. The cross-licensing agreement was made in 1968 as a compromise of litigation which was pending in Germany between the parties. However the compromise was not embodied in a court order. In the course of subsequent litigation the matter came before the ECJ, which ruled that a non-challenge clause contained in a licensing agreement may, in appropriate legal and economic circumstances, amount to a restriction on competition prohibited by EC Article 81(1) (ex Art 85(1)). Moreover, that Article applies even if the agreement is designed to settle pending litigation but it left open the question if such agreement has been sanctioned by the order of a national court.

The Court explained, however, that there is no restrictive effect (contrary to EC Article 81(1) (ex Art 85(1)) in the case of a royalty-free licence, because such a licence does not prejudice the competitive position of a licensee. Equally, there would be no anti-competitive effect if the licence, although subject to royalties, related to a technology which had already become obsolete and, therefore, had no further use to the licensee.

In an earlier case[3] the ECJ ruled on a number of points arising from patent licences granted by an American holder of patents registered in the United

---

18 See eg Commission Decisions: *Raymond/Nagoya* [1972] CMLR D45; *Davidson Rubber Co* [1972] CMLR D52; *AOIP/Beyrard* [1976] 1 CMLR D14; *Eisele/INRA* [1978] 3 CMLR 434.
19 Cases 258/78: *Nungesser KG and Kurt Eisele v Commission* [1982] ECR 2015, [1983] 1 CMLR 278.
20 Art 2(1)(6).
1 Art 2(1)(15).
2 *Bayer AG and Maschinenfabrik Henneche GmbH v Süllhöfer* [1988] ECR 5249.
3 Case 193/83: *Windsurfing International Inc v Commission* [1986] ECR 611, [1986] 3 CMLR 489.

Kingdom and Germany. The product consisted of a board and a rig essentially used for windsurfing but the rig can also be used for ice yachts, sand yachts, surfboards, canoes, rowing boats and small sailing boats. However the licensing agreement in question defined the licensed product as a complete sailboard with clearly specified characteristics. Any modification required approval of the licensor.

Further clauses imposed obligations on the licensees, viz to sell the components covered by the German patent as completed sailboards though the patent was confined to rigs; to pay royalties on sales of components calculated on the basis of net selling price for the product; to affix to the boards manufactured and marketed in Germany a notice as if they were licensed by the licensor; to acknowledge the words 'Windsurfer' and 'Wind-surfing' as well as a design mark or 'logo' as a valid trademark and restricting production to a specific plant in Germany which enabled the licensor to terminate the agreement should the licensees change the location and finally not to challenge the validity of the licensed patents.

The Court ruled that all clauses were invalid except part of the clause stipulating the obligation to pay royalties on components on the net selling price of the product in so far as it applied to rigs.[4]

(2) PATENT LAW

(a) Patent Conventions

The Community patent law consists of a complex system of two inter-locked conventions, ie the Munich Convention for the Grant of European Patents of 1973 (ECP)[5] and the Luxembourg Convention for the European Patent for the Common Market (CMP) of 1975.[6] Both have been signed but only the first one is in force at present. The object of the former is to enable the European Patent Office in Munich to grant patents in accordance with a uniform procedure and a uniform substantive law in as many European counties as may join in. The object of the latter is to lay down a uniform legal regime applicable to patents in the whole of the Common Market as one patent territory. The result of the two Conventions is a single patent for the Member States of the Community and a European 'package patent' which may, but need not, embrace one or several or all the Member States of the Community together with non-Member States. In other words the Common Market patent is a 'non-national' patent, whilst the European patent is both a 'European' and, subject to certain exceptions, a 'national' patent.

The system does not exclude purely national patents governed by national legislation and granted for the national territory only but it has to conform to Community law.

European patents, unless otherwise provided in the ECP Convention, have, in each of the contracting states for which they are granted, the status of a 'national patent for that state'. They may be granted for one or more of the contracting states.

Common Market patents, on the other hand, have a 'unitary character'. They have equal effect within the territories covered by the CMP Convention and may only be granted, transferred, revoked or allowed to lapse in respect of the whole of such territories.

---

4   Ibid para 102.
5   International Legal Materials vol XIII (1974) p 270.
6   OJ 1976, L17/1.

(b) Patentability

Patentability covers inventions which are susceptible of industrial application, which are new and which involve an inventive step. An invention is considered new if it does not form part of the state of the art which comprises everything made available to the public by means of written or oral description, by use, or any other way before the filing of the application. It is considered as involving an inventive step if, having regard to the state of the art, it is not obvious to a person skilled in the art.

Excluded from the range of inventions are: discoveries; scientific theories, and mathematical methods; aesthetic creations, schemes, rules and methods of performing mental acts; playing games or doing business and programmes for computers; and presentation of the information. Similarly, methods for treatment of the human or animal body by surgery or therapy and diagnostic methods practised on the human or animal body are excluded although products for use in any of these methods are patentable. Patents also cannot be granted in respect of plants and animal varieties or essentially biological processes for the production of plants or animals.

(c) Patent protection

The European patent runs for 20 years from the date of filing of the application and the rights granted are the same in each contracting state as conferred by a national patent in that state. Any infringements of these rights are subject to the procedures and remedies available under national law.

In principle the Convention reflects the traditional approach as it enables the patent holder to prohibit certain activities adversely affecting his rights. However a distinction is made between the protection of a product and the protection of a process. Accordingly, the patent holder may, by injunction, prohibit 'direct use' of his invention, ie the manufacture of the product without his consent, the offering of the product for sale, lease or use and, finally, the marketing of the infringing product, subject to the exhaustion rule.

An infringement of the protection of a process will be committed if the patented process is offered for use in the territories of the contracting states and the offeree knows, or it is obvious in the circumstances, that the use of the process is prohibited without the consent of the patent holder. Whilst it is clear that the protection does not extend outside the patent territory it is also clear that the patent holder should be able to enforce his rights in respect of products manufactured through the use of his process outside, but subsequently imported into, the patent territory. Thus he has the same protection as a patent holder in respect of a product because he can prohibit the offering, marketing or using of a product resulting directly from the use of the patented process as well as the importation or stocking for these purposes of such a product.

'Indirect use', which means supplying or offering to supply any person, other than a party entitled to exploit the patented invention, with the means capable of putting a patented invention into effect, is also prohibited.

(d) Limitation of patent protection

Certain acts do not constitute infringements and, therefore, there is no corresponding protection of the patent holder. These include acts done privately and for non-commercial purposes; acts done for experimental purposes and in the service of science; the preparation of medicines according to a medical prescription for immediate use by individual patients but not for sale or keeping; the use of the invention on board ships, land vehicles and aircraft which venture into the territory of the contracting states accidentally or temporarily.

(e) Exhaustion of patent rights

Then there is the exhaustion of patent rights reflecting the paramount principle of the Common Market expressed in the freedom of movement of goods. Therefore, as soon as products are put on the market in one of the contracting states by the patent holder or another person with his consent, the patent holder's rights are exhausted. This means that he is prohibited from opposing the marketing of such products within the Common Market. This rule is derived from the jurisprudence of the ECJ and it applies to national patents as well.

(f) Licensing

The Community patent is susceptible to be dealt with according to its nature as an object of property. It has to be registered and as a piece of property it can be assigned subject to the formalities prescribed by the Convention. However from a business point of view licensing is perhaps the most important transaction. The Convention distinguishes between contractual licensing, licensing as of right and compulsory licensing.

A Community patent may be licensed by contract in whole or in part of the patent territory. A licence may be exclusive or non-exclusive and the rights conferred by the Community patent may be invoked against a licensee who contravenes any restriction imposed by his licence. However, whilst contractual rights are primarily governed by the relevant national law they must not be in conflict with Community law because in such a case Community law will prevail.

Licensing as of right occurs simply by the fact that, in consideration of a reduced renewal fee, a patent holder may file a statement with the Patent Office to the effect that he is prepared to allow any person to use his invention as a licensee in return for appropriate compensation. As a result any person shall be entitled to use the invention as of right in analogy to contractual licence.

Compulsory licences are governed by national laws of the contracting states. Such licences are applicable to Community patents but their effects are restricted to the territory of the state concerned.

(g) Rights arising from patent applications

The Convention reflects a unified system for granting and contesting patents by providing a set of rules and a machinery to create and to oppose the creation of patents. The grounds for annulment or revocation are the same as the grounds for opposition and these are considered in uniform proceedings by the relevant departments of the European Patent Office.

(h) Enforcement of patent rights

However, the enforcement of patent rights and the infringement proceedings are by no means uniform for they fall into the domain of national jurisdictions. Thus the national courts have the power to adjudicate upon patent disputes and grant remedies for infringements.

Actions for infringements may be heard before the courts of the contracting state in which the defendant has his residence, or if not so resident, his place of business. If he has neither residence nor place of business in one of the contracting states the action may, by derogation from the Convention on Jurisdiction and Enforcement of Judgments, be heard before the courts of the contracting state in which the plaintiff has his residence, or if he is not so resident, his place of business. Failing these qualifications, ultimately, the action can take place in the Federal Republic of Germany. However, wherever the action occurs, the court will have jurisdiction in respect of infringements anywhere within the whole patent territory.

The ECJ has no jurisdiction except in the matter of interpretation of the Convention when asked by a national court in a reference under the procedure for preliminary rulings.

(i) The Community Patent Convention (1975, revised 1989)
A Community Patent Convention was signed by the EC Member States at Luxembourg on 15 December 1975, but did not enter into force.[7] Subsequently, an Agreement relating to Community Patents was signed by the twelve EC Member States at Luxembourg on 15 December 1989.[8] The Agreement substitutes a revised version of the CPC, and supplements it with a Protocol on Litigation.

The Agreement will not enter into force until the first day of the third month following ratification by all twelve of the signatory states. A Protocol, also signed by the Member States, on a Possible Modification of the Conditions of Entry into Force of the Agreement, envisaged that, if the Agreement had not entered into force by the end of 1991, a Conference should be convened by the President of the Community Council with a view to amending the Agreement so as to enable it to enter into force with fewer ratifications. However the Protocol explicitly recognized that such an amendment would require unanimity, and a conference was held as envisaged but failed to reach agreement. The Agreement has not been ratified by all the Member States.

The Community Patent Convention, in both its original and its revised version, is designed to supplement the European Patent Convention (1973). The object of the Community Patent Convention is to create a unitary patent for the entire territory of the European Community, which will be known as a 'Community patent'. Such a patent will be governed by the provisions of the European Patent Convention (eg as to patentability) and the Community Patent Convention (eg as to revocation and infringement), largely to the exclusion of national law, and will be capable of transfer, revocation or lapse only in respect of the entire territory of the Community.

A Community patent will be granted by the European Patent Office to a successful applicant who has designated any Member State of the Community among the countries for which patents are sought.[9] The grant may 'bundle' the Community patent with patents for non-Member States, such as Switzerland, which have acceded to the EPC and which are designated in the application. But the Community Patent Convention will not prevent the Member States from granting purely national patents.[10]

(j) The revision of the CPC
The original version of the Community Patent Convention never came into operation, because of dissatisfaction by the Member States with the compromise

---

7   See OJ 1976, L17.
8   See OJ 1989, L401/1. The implementing regulations are at OJ 1989, L401/28.
9   However, for a transitional period, to be terminated by a decision of the Community Council, an applicant to the European Patent Office may, by filing an appropriate request with the Office, obtain quasi-national patents for various Community countries, instead of a Community patent. Conversely where an application seeking from the European Patent Office a bundle of patents for all the Member States is pending at the commencement of the Community Patent Convention, the applicant may amend his application to request instead a Community patent.
10 Where a national patent granted in a Member State and a Community patent relate to the same invention, and have been granted to the same inventor or his successor in title, and with the same priority date, the national patent will be ineffective to the extent of the overlap.

provisions, contained in its Articles 76 and 90, as to the possibility for an alleged infringer to challenge the validity of a Community patent in proceedings before a national court. These required a national court to treat a Community patent as valid, subject to an exception permitting a Member State to make a reservation enabling its court, when dealing with infringement, to determine validity also, but only for its own territory, only with the consent of the parties, and only for a period of ten years from the commencement of the Convention. Otherwise the validity of a Community patent could be challenged, after its grant, only by opposition or revocation proceedings in the European Patent Office.

Hence the main feature of the new Agreement, whereby it differs from the original version of the Convention, lies in the solution of this problem. The new provisions permit a challenge to the validity of a Community patent to be made by way of an application for revocation of the patent to a national court in which an infringement action is pending. On the other hand they also create at Community level a Common Appeal Court, to which a national court of second instance must refer, for decision of both facts and law, cases involving the validity or effects of a Community patent. The Common Appeal Court will also hear appeals from decisions of the Revocation and the Patent Administration Divisions of the European Patent Office.

The Protocol on Litigation, annexed to the new Agreement, requires each Member State to designate a limited number of its courts of first and second instance as 'Community patent courts', to perform in its territory the functions assigned by the Protocol. The judges of these courts must be persons experienced in patent law. For the United Kingdom the Annex to the Protocol specifies the English Patent Court (within the Chancery Division), the Outer House of the Scottish Court of Session, and the Northern Irish High Court, as Community patent courts of first instance; and the English and Northern Irish Courts of Appeal, and the Inner House of the Scottish Court of Session, as Community patent courts of second instance. The Community patent courts must apply the Community Patent Agreement, and on matters no covered by the Agreement, their national law (including its private international law). They must apply the same procedures in dealing with Community patents as in similar cases involving national patents, and must record in writing at least the essentials of their oral proceedings.

The Community patent courts of first instance are given exclusive jurisdiction over the following types of proceeding in respect of a Community patent: actions for infringement, threatened infringement, or a declaration of non-infringement; actions for compensation for use of the invention between the publication of the application and the grant of the patent; and counter-claims for revocation. Other types of proceeding involving a Community patent (including proceedings concerning ownership; compulsory licences; or compensation for Crown use) are subject to the jurisdiction of the ordinary courts and authorities of the Member States, rather than the Community patent courts.

The Protocol permits a defendant in an infringement action before a Community patent court of first instance to attack the validity of the patent by means of a counter-claim for revocation. The grounds for revocation are the same as in an application to the Revocation Division of the European Patent Office: unpatentable subject matter, inadequate disclosure, improper amendment, wrong ownership, or prior national rights. Where a counter-claim for revocation is filed, the court must inform the European Patent Office of the fact and the date of the counter-claim, and the Office will then record them in the Register of Community Patents. A counter-claim for revocation will lead to a decision by the court either ordering revocation of the patent, or rejecting the application for revocation, or ordering that the patent be maintained as amended. When the decision has become final, the court will send to the European Patent Office a copy of the judgment, and, where the decision was to maintain the patent as amended, the text of the amended specification. In the latter event the Office will proceed to publish the amended specification.

As regards remedies where actual or threatened infringement is established, the Protocol requires the grant of an injunction unless there are special reasons for its refusal, and also the grant of ancillary relief in support of the injunction (such as the delivery up for destruction of infringing goods) in accordance with the national law of the court seised. However other remedies, such as damages or accounting for profits are, rather surprisingly, remitted to the law of the Member State in which the infringement was committed. In each Member State any criminal sanctions for infringement of national patents will be extended to Community patents.

More radically, the Protocol provides for the establishment at Community level of a 'Common Appeal Court', to perform the functions assigned by the Protocol. From a judgment of a Community patent court of first instance, appeal lies to a Community patent court of second instance in the same Member State, in accordance with the law of that state. If, however, the appeal involves questions as to the effect of the Community patent under Articles 25-33 of the Community Patent Convention (other than questions remitted to national law), or as to the validity of the Community patent, the court of second instance must refer the case to the Common Appeal Court for decision of such questions. While the reference is pending, the proceedings in the court of second instance must be stayed, except in so far as their continuance (otherwise than to final judgment) could not possibly prejudice the eventual decision of the Common Appeal Court.

On the reference the Common Appeal Court will consider and determine the questions of validity or effect referred, and give a ruling on both facts and law, applying the provisions of the Community Patent Agreement. Its decision will be binding in the further proceedings in the case: ie in the court of second instance to which the case will revert for disposal of the appeal, and in a national court of further appeal to which an appeal from the decision of the court of second instance may be brought, in accordance with national law, on questions not referable to the Common Appeal Court.

In addition to its role in receiving references from a Community patent court of second instance on questions as to the validity or effect of a Community patent, the Common Appeal Court has two other functions. Firstly, it will hear appeals from the Revocation or Patent Administration Divisions of the European Patent Office. Secondly, it will give preliminary rulings, at the request of courts of Member States, on the interpretation of the Community Patent Agreement in respects not relating to the validity or effects of a Community patent (which it hears under the procedure already explained) nor to the allocation of jurisdiction between the courts of the various Member States (where references will be made to the ECJ) and also on the interpretation or validity of Community legislation implementing the Community Patent Agreement. The making of such a request will lie within the discretion of the relevant national court, unless it is a court of last resort, in which case a reference will be more or less obligatory.

In connection with Community patents the role of the main Community Court will be very limited, in view of the creation of the Common Appeal Court. However the Agreement specifies that it is to operate subject to the EC Treaty, and requires the Common Appeal Court to request a preliminary ruling from the

ECJ where there is a risk of an interpretation of the Agreement being inconsistent with the Treaty. Moreover such inconsistency will enable the Commission or a Member State to bring proceedings before the ECJ. In addition, references from national courts concerning the allocation of jurisdiction over actions relating to Community patents between the courts of the various Member States will be made to the ECJ, and not to the Common Appeal Court.

(3) TRADEMARK LAW

Work on a Trademark Convention began some twenty years ago but was abandoned in favour of a Directive proposed in 1985[11] and enacted three years later[12] to take effect by the end of 1992. That directive approximates the trademark laws of the Member States. It was followed five years later by Council Regulation 40/94, which provides for a Community trademark.[13] Thus, there are two parallel trademark regimes in the Community: the national regimes which, as adjusted in accordance with Community legislation and the case law of the ECJ, offer trademarks limited in their territorial extent to the Member States granting the trademark; and a separate Community regime that offers a trademark benefiting from uniform recognition and protection throughout the Community.

(a) The approximation of national trademark law
Directive 89/104 attempts merely to harmonize those national rules which directly affect the free movement of goods and services in the Community. It avoids a total harmonization. Consequently the Member States are not deprived of their right of continuing to protect trademarks registered under their laws provided, of course, they do not contravene the rules of the Common Market. The Directive takes this into account but indicates the advantages of a Community-wide system.

Since only partial harmonization has been attempted the protection of trademarks, such as it is, under EC Article 30 (ex Art 36) remains unaffected. However the advantage of the Directive is that registered trademarks shall enjoy uniform protection under the Member States' legal system. The object of such protection is to guarantee the trademark's function as an indicator of origin. However, as already observed, the protection must not exceed the limits laid down in Community law in relation to goods and services. National laws, which do not conform to these limits, must be amended accordingly.

The Directive applies to every trademark in respect of goods and services which is the subject of registration or of an application for registration as an individual trademark, a collective trademark or a guarantee mark, or which is subject of an international registration having effect in a Member State.

Registration shall be refused if the proposed trademark consists of signs which, under the law of the Member State concerned, cannot constitute a trademark or if such signs are devoid of distinctive character in that Member State[14] such as being merely descriptive of the kind of quality or value of the goods or services in question; or if they are solely signs of indications which are customarily used to designate goods or services. Registration shall also be refused or invalidated

11 OJ 1985, C 351/4.
12 Dir 89/104, OJ 1988, L40/1.
13 OJ 1994, L11/1. Implementing measures are to be found in Commission Reg 2868/95, OJ 1995, L303/1.
14 Cf Case T-19/99: *DKV Deutsche Krankenversicherung v Office for Harmonisation in the Internal Market (Trademarks and Designs)* [2000] All ER (EC) 193, a case on the parallel provision in Reg 40/94 (as to which, see, infra).

if the marks consist of a shape determined by the nature of the goods or which are liable to mislead the public or are repugnant to public policy, or to accepted principles of morality or which have been refused registration pursuant to the Paris Convention for the Protection of Industrial Property.[15]

Moreover a trademark may be refused registration if it is identical with an earlier mark or with an earlier right if the goods or services are similar and there is a likelihood of confusion.[16] Earlier rights mean Community trademarks, trademarks registered in the Member States and trademarks registered under international arrangements having effect in the Member State or if they are 'well known' in the Member State.[17] 'Earlier rights' also mean any signs used in the business world before the application for registration which under the law of the Member State governing them confer upon the proprietor the right to prohibit the use of subsequent trademarks; and any signs containing the name of a third person where the use of this name in relation to goods or services is liable to cause serious detriment to the honour, reputation or credit of that person; a portrait of a third person; a work of a third person protected by copyright or by an industrial model or design.

The registered trademark confers upon its proprietor exclusive rights in the mark. Thus he is entitled to prohibit any third party from using in the course of trade, except with his consent, any sign which is identical with the trademark he registered; any sign which is similar where, because of the similarity of the goods or services, there is likely to be confusion on the part of the public. In particular the following types of use are prohibited:

(1) affixing the sign to the goods or to their packaging;
(2) putting the goods on the market under that sign or supplying services thereunder;
(3) using the trademark where it is necessary to indicate the intended purpose of a product or service.

The proprietor of a trademark is not entitled to prohibit its use in relation to goods which have been put on the market in the Community under the trademark by himself or with his consent.[18]

The trademark protection shall be ineffective if the proprietor of a registered mark or an 'earlier right' as outlined above has knowingly acquiesced in the use of the mark or earlier right for a period of three successive years.

A trademark shall be invalidated if within an uninterrupted period of five years it has not been put to genuine use, unless there are legitimate grounds for non-use. However it shall not be invalidated where after the expiry of that period and before its validity is contested, the use has been started or resumed in good faith. A mark shall also be invalidated if after its registration it has, in consequence of inactivity of the proprietor, become the common name in trade for a product or service for which it is registered.

15 See Cases C-108/97 and C-109/97: *Windsurfing Chiemsee Prodcutions-und Vertzieler GmbH v Boots-und Segelzubelior Walter Huber* [1999] ECR I-2779.

16 See Case C-251/95: *Sabel v Puma* [1997] ECR I-6191; Case C-39/97: *Canon Kabushiki Kaisha v Metro-Goldwyn-Mayer* [1998] ECR I-5507; Case C-342/97: *Lloyd Schuhfabrik Meyer & Co v Klijsen Handel* [1999] ECR I-3819.

17 Ie in the sense of art 6(b) of the Paris Convention.

18 See in particular Cases C-427/93, C-429/93 and C-436/93: *Bristol-Myers Squibb v Paranova* [1996] ECR I-3457; Case C-337/95: *Parfums Christian Dior v Evora* [1997] ECR I-6013; Case C-63/97: *BMW v Deenik* [1999] ECR I-905; Case C-173/98: *Sebago v G-B Unic* [1999] ECR I-4103.

All the procedural aspects of trademarks such as registration, objections, invalidation and disputes are subject to the national law of the Member State concerned.

(b)   The Community trademark
The Community trademark does not replace trademarks registered under the laws of the Member States. It has equal effect throughout the Community and cannot be registered, transferred, surrendered, revoked, declared invalid or its use prohibited otherwise than in respect of the whole Community and in accordance with the Community legislation creating it. A Community trademark can consist of the same signs as a national trademark.[19] It is obtained by registration by the Office for Harmonisation in the Internal Market ('the Office'). The grounds for refusing to register a Community trademark, the rights conferred by a Community trademark, and other matters are essentially the same as in the case of national trademarks obtained under national law, as approximated in accordance with Directive 89/104.[20] In general, and subject to special provisions in Regulation 40/94, a Community trademark is dealt with as an object of property as if it were a national trademark registered in the Member State in which the proprietor has his seat, domicile or an establishment.[1] Decisions of the Office may be appealed to the CFI.[2]

(c)   Copyright, related rights and other rights
Only piecemeal attempts have been made to iron out the potential conflicts between the requirements of the common market and domestic intellectual property law outside the areas of patent law and trademark law.

Council Directive 92/100 goes some way towards harmonizing the legal protection afforded to copyright works and to the subject matter of related rights in regard to rental and lending. It includes provisions for certain performing rights.[3] Council Directive 93/83 provides a similar degree of protection for copyright and related rights applicable to satellite broadcasting and cable retransmission.[4] In similar vein, Council Directive 91/250 and Council and European Parliament Directive 96/9 deal respectively with protection for computer programs and databases.[5] For some years now there has been more specific legislation providing for legal protection of the topographies of semiconductors.[6] In 1998 legislation harmonizing the legal protection afforded by national laws to designs was adopted.[7]

Council Regulation 2100/94 provides for a system of Community plant variety rights that is intended to be the sole and exclusive form of Community industrial

---

19   Compare Art 4 of Reg 40/94 with Art 2 of Dir 89/104.
20   Compare Arts 7-8 of the Regulation with Arts 3-4 of the Directive, Art 9 with Art 5, and so forth.
1   Arts 16-24.
2   Eg Case T-163/98: *Proctor & Gamble Co v Office of Harmonisation in the Internal Market* [1999] ECR I-2383.
3   OJ 1992, L346/61. See also in this connection the Council Resolution of 14 May 1992 on increased protection for copyright and related rights (OJ 1992, C 138/1). Council Dir 93/98 (OJ 1993, L290/9) deals with the term of protection: see Case C-60/98: *Butterfly Music v CEMED* [1999] ECR I-3939.
4   OJ 1993, L248/15.
5   OJ 1991, L122/42 and OJ 1996, L77/20.
6   See Council Dir 87/54 (OJ 1987, L24/36; Council Decision 93/16 (OJ 1993, L11/20); Council Decision 94/700 (OJ 1994, L284/61); Council Decision 94/284 (OJ 1994, L349/201); and Council Decision 96/644 (OJ 1996, L293/18).
7   European Parliament and Council Dir 98/71 (OJ 1998, L289/28).

property rights for plant varieties, albeit that it operates in parallel with domestic industrial property regimes for plant varieties.[8] European Parliament and Council Directive 98/44 provides for the protection of biotechnological inventions through national patent laws, as adjusted to meet the requirements of the directive.[9] Community legislation also provides for supplementary protection for medicinal products and plant protection products in the form of certificates whose practical effect is to extend the duration of the protection afforded to such products under national law.[10]

8 OJ 1994, L227/1. See also Commission Reg 1768/95 (OJ 1995, L173/14), amended by Reg 2605/98 (OJ 1998, L328/6), which implements rules on the agricultural exemption provided for in Reg 2100/94. Cf Council Reg 2470/96 (OJ 1996, L335/10), which provided for extending the terms of a Community plant protection variety right for potatoes.

9 OJ 1998, L213/13.

10 Council Reg 1768/92 (OJ 1992, L182/1) – medicinal products (see Case C-110/95: *Yamanouchi Pharmaceutical Co v Comptroller-General of Patents* [1997] ECR I-3251; Case C-392/97: *Farmitalia Carlo Erba Srl* [1999] ECR I-5553); European Parliament and Council Reg 1610/96 (OJ 1996, 198/30) – plant protection products.

Chapter 32

Social policy

A. Social provisions (EC Articles 136-148 (ex Arts 117-125))

The blueprint of the Community postulates a close connection between economics and social problems embraced in the general principles of the EC Treaty[1] and specific 'social provisions'.[2]

EC Article 136 (ex Art 117) as originally worded, merely expressed an agreement between the Member States 'upon the need to promote improved working conditions and an improved standard of living for workers' and their belief that 'such a development will ensue not only from the functioning of the Common Market, which will favour the harmonization of the social systems, but also from the procedures provided for in this Treaty and from the approximation of provisions laid down by law, regulation or administrative action'. In its amended form, EC Article 136 (ex Art 117) expresses an obligation on the part of the Community and the Member States to have as their objectives 'the promotion of employment, improved living and working conditions, so as to make possible their harmonization while the improvement is being maintained, proper social protection, dialogue between management and labour, the development of human resources with a view to lasting high employment and the combating of exclusion'. In accepting that obligation, the Community and the Member States have in mind fundamental social rights such as those in the European Social Charter of 1961 and the 1989 Community Charter of the Fundamental Social Rights of Workers.

The Treaty provisions supporting that basic obligation envisage the following: action by the Community to support and complement the activities of the Member States;[3] action by the Commission to promote the consultation of management and labour at Community level and to facilitate their dialogue;[4] action to facilitate

1 EC Arts 2 and 3(1)(j) (ex Arts 2 and 3(1)).
2 EC Arts 136-148 (ex Arts 117-126). However, social policy remains an area in which the Member States retain a broad margin of appreciation: see, for example, Case C-322/98: *Kachelmann v Bankhaus Hermann Lampe KG* [2001] IRLR 49.
3 EC Art 137 (ex Art 118).
4 EC Art 138 (ex Art 118a).

agreements at Community level between management and labour;[5] action by the Commission to encourage co-operation between the Member States and facilitate the co-ordination of their action in all social policy fields;[6] application of the principle of equal treatment between men and women;[7] action by the Member States to endeavour to maintain the existing equivalence between paid holiday schemes;[8] and the drawing up of reports, a matter which is of little practical concern here.[9] In addition, the Council may assign to the Commission tasks in connection with the implementation of common social policy measures, particularly as regards social security for migrant workers.[10] Although the primary focus of such actions is their social effects, EC Article 136 (ex Art 117), specifically enjoins 'the Community and the Member States' to implement measure that 'take account of the diverse forms of national practices, in particular in the field of contractual relations, and the need to maintain the competitiveness of the Community economy'. Hence, social policy measures must be adjusted to the social context in which they come to be applied in the Member States; and, perhaps even more importantly, they may not go so far as to override the competitiveness of the Community economy (which would in fact lead to the weakening or even destruction of the economic foundation on which effective social policy measures of the sort envisaged can alone be based).

The areas in which the Community's supportive and complementary action is to take effect can be divided in two classes by reference to the procedure to be followed by the Community institutions when determining the action to take. Both classes exclude the following matters: pay; the right of association; the right to strike; and the right to impose lock-outs.[11] The measures taken in regard to matters falling within either class do not preclude the Member States from maintaining or introducing more stringent protective measures that are compatible with the Treaty.[12] Hence the social policy measures here in question can only amount to minimum requirements. Where the Community acts by way of directive, Member States may entrust to management and labour the task of implementing the directive in question if the latter so request and as long as management and labour introduce the necessary implementing measures by agreement within the time specified for the implementation of the directive. The generality of the language used in this connection indicates that the implementation of a directive in this way is possible only through collective agreements between management and labour and not (for example) through a single agreement between the management and the workforce of one company only. When this method of implementation is used, the Member State must have in force the measures necessary to enable it at any time to be in a position to guarantee the results required by the directive.[13]

In the first class of areas in which the Community may act lies action in relation to: the improvement in particular of the working environment to protect workers' health and safety; working conditions; information and consultation of workers; integration of persons excluded from the labour market (without prejudice to the Community's vocational training policy); equality between men and women with

5   EC Art 139 (ex Art 118b).
6   EC Art 140 (ex Art 118c).
7   EC Art 141 (ex Art 119).
8   EC Art 142 (ex Art 119a).
9   EC Arts 143 and 145 (ex Arts 120 and 122).
10   EC Art 144 (ex Art 121). The Council acts unanimously and after consulting the Economic and Social Committee.
11   EC Art 137(6).
12   EC Art 137(5).
13   EC Art 137(4).

regard to labour market opportunities and treatment at work; and encouragement of co-operation between Member States through initiatives aimed at improving knowledge, developing exchanges of information and best practices, promoting innovative approaches and evaluating experiences in order to combat social exclusion.[14] In relation to those areas, the Council acts in accordance with the procedure referred to in EC Article 251 (ex Art 189b),[15] and after consulting the Economic and Social Committee and the Committee of the Regions. The measures taken by the Council need not take any particular form. However, the Council is specifically empowered to adopt directives laying down minimum requirements for gradual implementation, having regard to the conditions and technical rules obtaining in each of the Member States; but such directives must avoid imposing administrative, financial and legal constraints in such a way as to hold back the creation and development of small and medium-sized undertakings.[16]

The second class of areas in which the Community may act comprises: social security and social protection of workers; protection of workers where their employment contract is terminated; representation and collective defence of the interests of workers and employers, including co-determination; conditions of employment for third country nationals lawfully resident in the Community; and financial contributions for promotion of employment and job-creation (without prejudice to the Social Fund). In relation to those areas, the Council acts unanimously on a proposal from the Commission, after consulting the European Parliament, the Economic and Social Committee and Committee of the Regions.[17] The forms that the Council's action may take are not specified but include directives.

The Commission's task of promoting the consultation of management and labour at Community level and facilitating their dialogue is expressed in very general terms. So far as the latter is concerned, the Commission is to act 'by ensuring balanced support for the parties', which appears to mean nothing more than that the Commission should be even handed.[18] As part of its task, the Commission must consult management and labour on the possible direction of Community action before submitting proposals in the social policy field.[19] If, after such consultation, the Commission considers that Community action is advisable, management and labour must be consulted on the context of the Commission's proposal and must forward to the Commission an opinion on it or, where appropriate, a recommendation.[20]

In the course of the consultation referred to above, management and labour may inform the Commission that they wish the dialogue between them at Community level to proceed to contractual relations. In that event, the Commission must give them nine months in which to reach agreement, although the period can be extended jointly by management, labour and the Commission.[1]

By virtue of EC Article 146 (ex Art 123) the European Social Fund has been established. The Fund is administered by the Commission, which is assisted by a Committee composed of representatives of governments, trade unions and

---

14 EC Art 137(1) and (2), 3rd sub-para.
15 The co-decision procedure described on pp 262-264, supra.
16 EC Art 137(2), 1st sub-para.
17 EC Art 137(3).
18 EC Art 138(1).
19 EC Art 138(2).
20 EC Art 138(3).
 1 EC Art 138(4).

employers' organizations (EC Article 147 (ex Art 124)).[2] The Council is charged with the adoption of implementing decisions relating to the Fund (EC Article 148 (ex Art 125)).

The Fund, as originally constituted, was reformed in 1971[3] and in 1983.[4] Its aim is 'to render the employment of workers easier and to increase their geographical and occupational mobility within the Community, and to facilitate their adaptation to industrial changes and to changes in production systems in particular through vocational training and retraining'.[5]

It is evident that the Treaty reflects a programme of action the success of which depends on the efficacy of legislation and budgetary provision.

B. Legislation and case law

Originally the implementing legislation focused attention on workers' rights of free movement, equal treatment and social advantage[6] and social security[7] and engendered a wealth of case law. However the battles of a Belgian stewardess for equal rights on the basis of EC Article 141 (ex Art 119) called for legislation which, in turn, provide to be in need of interpretation. In Case 43/75[8] the ECJ considered that EC Article 141 (ex Art 119) pursued a double aim:

'First, in the light of the different stages of the development of social legislation in the various Member States, the aim of Article 119 [now Art 141] is to avoid a situation in which undertakings established in States which have actually implemented the principle of equal pay suffer a competitive disadvantage in intra-Community competition as compared with undertakings established in States which have not yet eliminated discrimination against women workers as regards pay.

Secondly, this provision forms part of the social objectives of the Community, which is not merely an economic union, but is at the same time intended, by common action, to ensure social progress and seek the constant improvement of the living and working conditions of their peoples, as is emphasized by the Preamble to the Treaty . . .'

One can say that on these two premises rest the implementing legislation and the Court's willingness to extend the scope of the principle of non-discrimination between the sexes. However, the economic aim now takes second place to the social aim because the right of equal treatment is a fundamental human right.[9]

The TEU marked a new stage in the process of creating a closer union between the peoples of Europe and, in particular, reinforced the emphasis placed on the right to equality before the law and protection against all forms of discrimination.

---

2 The management of the Fund is dealt with by Commission Decision 83/673 (OJ 1983, L377/1).

3 JO 1971, L28.

4 Decision 83/516 (OJ 1983, L289/38), amended by Decision 85/568 (OJ 1985, L370/40).

5 See Dir 76/207 and p 743, infra.

6 Reg 1612/68 (JO, 1968, L257/2).

7 Regs 3 and 4 (JO, 1958, 561 and 597), superseded by Reg 1408/71 (JO 1971, L149) and subsequent amendments.

8 *Defrenne v SABENA*, [1976] ECR 455, [1976] 2 CMLR 98, at paras 9 and 10.

9 Case C-50/96: *Schröder v Deutsche Telekom* [2000] IRLR 353.

Discrimination based on racial or ethnic origin was also regarded as capable of undermining the attainment of a high level of employment and of social protection within the Community. In consequence, the Council adopted Directive 2000/43.[10] The purpose of that Directive is to lay down a framework for combating discrimination on the grounds of racial or ethnic origin, with a view to putting into effect the principle of equal treatment (Article 1). The Directive prohibits both direct and indirect discrimination based on racial or ethnic origin and includes within the definition of discrimination both harassment and instructions to discriminate (Article 2).[11] It does not apply to differences of treatment that are based on nationality (Article 3(2)). The Directive is intended to be implemented so as to impose the prohibition of such discrimination on all persons and as regards both the public and private sectors. However, its scope is limited to the following matters: (a) conditions for access to employment, self-employment and to occupation (including selection criteria and recruitment conditions) whatever the branch of activity and at all levels of the professional hierarchy, including promotion; (b) access to all types and levels of vocational guidance, vocational training, advanced vocational training and retraining and practical work experience; (c) employment and working conditions, including dismissal and pay; (d) membership of, involvement in, and the benefits provided by, workers' or employers' organizations and professional bodies; (e) social protection, including social security and healthcare; (f) social advantages; (g) education; (h) access to and supply of goods and services which are available to the public, including housing. It does not cover provisions and conditions relating to entry into Member States and residence therein of third country nationals and stateless persons and any treatment arising from their legal status (Article 3).[12]

The requirement of equal treatment in the Directive is not absolute. Member States may provide that a difference of treatment based on a characteristic related to racial or ethnic origin is not discrimination where it is a genuine and determining occupational requirement. A requirement will have that character if it is objectively justified having regard to the nature of the particular occupational activity in question or to the context in which the activity is carried on and if the requirement is proportionate (Article 4). The Directive does not preclude positive action designed to prevent or to compensate for disadvantages linked to racial or ethnic origin (Article 5) or provisions that are more favourable to the protection of the principle of equal treatment: the Directive is prescriptive only as to the minimum level of protection to be afforded to persons and does not even permit

---

10   OJ 2000, L180/22. The Directive is to be implemented by the Member States by 19 July 2003: Article 16. However, the Member States may entrust management and labour with the implementation of the Directive in relation to provisions falling within the scope of collective agreements. In that event, the necessary measures must be introduced by agreement between management and labour by the same date. Directive 2000/78 (OJ 2000, L303/16) sets out a general framework for equal treatment in employment and occupations; and an action programme to combat discrimination was adopted in Decision 2000/750 (OJ 2000, L303/23).

11   Art 2(2) defines what is meant by direct and indirect discrimination, the definitions following those to be gleaned from the earlier legislation and case law on sex discrimination. In the case of harassment, it should be noted that the concept of harassment is to be defined by reference to national law and practice and shall be deemed to be discrimination when unwanted conduct related to racial or ethnic origin takes place with the purpose or effect of violating the dignity of a person and of creating an intimidating, hostile, degrading, humiliating or offensive environment: Art 2(3). In the result, therefore, harassment amounting to discrimination is the product of a combination of national law and EC law.

12   The Directive does not define a number of the concepts that it employs, such as what is meant by 'conditions for access to employment' and 'pay'. However, there is a considerable body of case law on the meaning of such terms in the context of the sex discrimination legislation (see below); and it seems likely that that case law will provide useful guidance to the meaning to be given to the Directive.

Member States to lower existing standards of protection that they possess to the minimum levels in the Directive (Article 6). The Directive also provides that the Member States must put in place appropriate judicial or administrative procedures and sanctions for dealing with breaches of the principle of equal treatment (Articles 7-9 and 15), promote social dialogue between the two sides of industry and with non-governmental organizations (Articles 11-12), and designate one or more bodies to promote equal treatment (Article 13).

The bulk of the legislation and the case law in this area focuses on sex discrimination and protection of employees.

C. Sex discrimination

(1) DIRECTIVE 75/117:[13] EQUAL PAY FOR WORK OF EQUAL VALUE

The Directive amplifies the provisions of EC Article 141 (ex Art 119) as it provides that the principle of equal pay means 'for the same work or for work to which equal value is attributed, the elimination of all discrimination on grounds of sex with regard to all aspects and conditions of remuneration'. Moreover, 'in particular, where a job classification system is used for determining pay, it must be based on the same criteria for both men and women and so drawn up as to exclude any discrimination on grounds of sex' (Article 1).

The Directive imposes a duty on Member States not only to abolish discrimination in the pay structure and the contractual (whether collective or individual) arrangements[14] but also to introduce into their national systems an effective machinery for dealing with the complaints of employees 'who consider themselves wronged by failure to apply the principle of equal pay' and to 'protect employees against dismissal by the employer as a reaction' to complaints.[15] Member States must also ensure that employees are informed of their rights at their place of employment. The legislation applies to discrimination based on sex or gender but not to discrimination based on sexual orientation.[16] On the other hand, transsexuals are treated on the same basis as if they were originally of the same gender as that to which they have converted.[17]

Given the background of the traditional rôle of women in society and the treatment of women at the workplace as unequal factors of production it is not surprising that, as a result of the Community legislation, attitudes had to change but the change had to be brought about by national legislation and fought for in the courts.

The *Defrenne* cases, though crucial to the problem, marked only a modest beginning. Mlle Defrenne's complaints included a reduced pay packet, a lower

---

13 OJ 1975, L45/19.
14 The principle of equal treatment also applies where the elements of the pay are determined by collective bargaining or by negotiation at local level: Case C-400/93: *Specialarbejderforbundet i Danmark v Dansk Industri* [1995] ECR I-1275, paras 45-47; Case C-281/97: *Krüger v Kreiskrankenhaur Ebersberg* [1999] ECR I-5127.
15 Cf Case C-326/96: *Levez v T H Jennings (Harlow Pools) Ltd* [1998] ECR I-7835. Note also Case C-167/97: *R v Secretary of State for Employment, ex p Seymour-Smith* [1999] ECR I-623, where it was held that damages for unlawful dismissal fall within the principle of equal pay for equal work but reinstatement falls within the scope of Dir 76/207 (infra). National remedies must respect the principles of equivalence and effectiveness: see in particular Case C-78/98: *Preston v Wolverhampton Healthcare NHS Trust* [2000] All ER (EC) 714.
16 Case C-249/96: *Grant v South-West Trains* [1998] ECR I-621, paras 26-50.
17 Case C-13/94: *P v S and Cornwall County Council* [1996] ECR I-2143.

holiday entitlement, a denial of a special pension scheme available to air crews and the indignity of having to retire at the age of 40, all these having adverse financial consequences which were not experienced by her male colleagues. In the first case[18] she failed against the State of Belgium as the ECJ ruled that the right of equal pay did not cover state social and pension schemes, such schemes being outside the scope of EC Article 141 (ex Art 119). In the second case[19] Mlle Defrenne, having already obtained in the national court redress of her economic claims, namely an allowance to cover the difference which a male steward would have received if dismissed at the same age and at the same seniority, as well as arrears of salary arising from the lower remuneration received from her employers secured a confirmatory judgment from the ECJ. However, for considerations of legal certainty, the Court ordered that the judgment should have no retrospective effect. In the third case[20] the Court refused to extend the notion of equal pay to the conditions of work, especially the age limit of her contract, since neither EC Article 141 (ex Art 119) nor the Directive could be stretched that far.

The concept of equal pay has received a wide interpretation in subsequent cases such as 'equal work, as embracing not only the situation where two jobs are identical, but also the wider situation where two jobs are of equal value';[1] and pay is not confined to the basic wages but also covers all perks or special bonus payments made by employers including benefits made available to the spouse, partner or dependents of the worker.[2] However, in order to determine 'pay' it is established that there need be no contractual obligation on the employer to provide the benefit in question.[3] Similarly 'pay' is not necessarily confined to payment for the work actually done, such as a repatriation allowance.[4]

In *McCarthys Ltd v Smith*[5] a female employee who was in receipt of a lower salary than her male predecessor in the same post had the satisfaction of knowing that 'the principle that men and women should receive equal pay for equal work . . . is not confined to situations in which men and women are contemporaneously doing equal work for the same employer'. The Court acknowledged that a difference in pay between two workers occupying the same post but at different periods of time may be explained by the operation of factors which are unconnected with any discrimination on grounds of sex but this is a matter of fact which the national court has to decide.

In *Jenkins v Kingsgate*,[6] for the first time, the Court was confronted with the problem of indirect discrimination as the complainant received an hourly rate of

---

18 Case 80/70: *Defrenne v Belgium* [1971] ECR 445, [1974] 1 CMLR 494.
19 Case 43/75, supra.
20 Case 149/77: *Defrenne v SABENA* [1978] ECR 1365, [1978] 3 CMLR 312.
 1 Case 96/80: *Jenkins v Kingsgate (Clothing Production) Ltd* [1981] ECR 911 and Case 69/80: *Worrington v Lloyds Bank Ltd* [1981] ECR 767.
 2 Case 21/81: *Garland v British Rail Engineering Ltd* (rail fares) [1982] ECR 359, Case 58/81: *Commission v Luxembourg* (head of house allowance) [1982] ECR 2175, Case C-249/96: *Grant v South West Trains* [1998] ECR I-621, paras 13-14. The position regarding maternity benefits is somewhat complex because maternity is a condition peculiar to women: eg Case C-342/93: *Gillespie v Northern Health and Social Services Board* [1996] ECR I-475; Case C-411/96: *Boyle v Equal Opportunities Commission* [1998] ECR I-6401; Case C-66/96: *Handels-og Kontorfunktionaerernes Forbund i Danmark v Faeltesforeningen for Danmarks Brugsforeninger* [1998] ECR I-7327; Case C-249/97: *Gruber v Silhouette International Schmied GmbH & Co KG* [1999] ECR I-5295; Case C-218/98: *Abdoulaye v Régie Nationale des Usines Renault SA* [1999] ECR I-5723.
 3 Case 69/80, supra: Case C-333/97: *Lewen v Denda* [1999] ECR I-7243.
 4 Case 20/71: *Sabbatini v European Parliament* [1972] 2 ECR 345.
 5 Case 129/79: [1980] ECR 1275 [1980] 2 CMLR 205.
 6 Supra.

pay below that of one of her male colleagues, employed full-time on the same job. Earlier the employer had paid different wages to men and women but the hourly rate was the same whether work was paid part-time or full-time. Later the pay for full-time work became the same for male and female workers but the hourly rate for part-time workers was fixed at a lower level than for full-time workers. All of the part-time workers were women except for one male worker who, having retired, was allowed to continue working. The ECJ ruled that 'a difference in pay between full-time workers and part-time workers does not amount to discrimination prohibited by Article 119 [now Art 141] . . . unless it is in reality merely an indirect way of reducing the level of pay of part-time workers on the ground that the group of workers is composed exclusively or predominantly of women'.

In the face of criticism of the *Jenkins* decision the ECJ endeavoured to lay down guidelines, based on the principle of proportionality, for the objective justification of indirect discrimination in such cases.[7] The case involved an employer whose occupational pension scheme excluded part-time workers. Since most of the part-time workers were women the ECJ considered such a scheme to be discriminatory on the ground of sex. Thus the employer must show that, by applying a differential treatment, he is pursuing an objective which meets a genuine need for his enterprise and that the means used are suitable and, above all, necessary, for attaining that objective. National courts must determine whether the differential treatment is objectively justified.

The principle was confirmed in subsequent cases.[8] In consequence, in cases of gender-based discrimination the burden of proving justification lies upon the employer.[9]

The concept of 'pay' has received in the jurisprudence of the Court of Justice a wide meaning. 'Pay' means remuneration for work whether in cash or kind or in the form of advantage calculable in money terms arising from employment such as, for example, redundancy payments, unemployment benefits, family allowances and mortgage or credit facilities. It does not matter whether or not the employer is subject to a legal obligation (by contract or by statute) or is bound by informal arrangement.

The ECJ[10] thus defined 'pay':

'. . . the concept of pay within the meaning of the second paragraph of Article 119 [now 141] comprises any consideration, whether in cash or in kind, whether immediate or future, provided that the worker receives it, albeit indirectly, in respect of his employment from his employer, and irrespective of whether the worker receives it under a contract of employment, by virtue of legislative provisions or on a voluntary basis.'

7   Case 170/84: *Bilka-Kaufhaus GmbH v Von Hartz* [1986] ECR 1607, [1986] 2 CMLR 701. See also Case C-50/96: *Schröder v Deutsche Telekom* [2000] IRLR 353 and the cases cited there.
8   Case C-171/88: *Rinner-Kühn v FWW Spezial-Gebäudereinigung GmbH & Co KG* [1989] ECR 2743, [1993] 2 CMLR 932; Case C-33/89: *Kowalska v Freie und Hansestadt Hamburg* [1990] ECR I-2591; Case C-184/89: *Ninz v Freie und Hansestadt Hamburg* [1991] ECR I-297, [1992] 3 CMLR 699; *Enderby v Frenchay Health Authority*, re differentiation between pharmacists and speech therapists [1991] 1 CMLR 626 and Case 127/92: ibid, [1993] ECR I-5535, [1994] 1 CMLR 8.
9   The burden of proof in sex discrimination cases generally is now governed by Dir 97/80 (OJ 1998, L14/6), as amended by Dir 98/52 (OJ 1998, L205/66).
10   Case C-360/90: *Arbeiterwohlfahrt der Stadt Berlin v Bötel* [1992] ECR I-3589, [1992] IRLR 423 at para 12. See also Case 102/88: *Ruzius-Wilbrink v Bestuur vande Bedrijfsvereniging voor Overheidsdiensten* [1989] ECR 4311, [1991] 2 CMLR 202 and Case 33/89, supra.

In Case 69/80[11] a bank excluded from its retirement scheme female employees under 25 years of age but provided contributions to a scheme to its male employees. Since such contributions were paid directly by the employer the ECJ classified these benefits under the rubric of 'pay' within the meaning of EC Article 141 (ex Art 119).

In *Bilka-Kaufhaus*[12] the ECJ made a distinction between statutory and contractual pension schemes but in the *Barber* case[13] it ruled that a pension paid under a contracted-out private occupational scheme has to be considered as pay. This is important not only because the distinction between statutory and private schemes is no longer relevant but also because the rules cover both redundancy benefits and occupational pensions. Mr Barber was a member of a pension fund set up by his employer but under the scheme the pensionable age for men was 65 and 60 for women. In the event of redundancy the members of the fund were entitled to an immediate pension in the case of men at the age of 55 and women at 52. Those who did not fulfil the conditions received cash benefits computed according to their years of service and a deferred pension payable at the normal pensionable age. Mr Barber was made redundant at 52 and his employer paid to him the cash benefit due to him under the scheme, a statutory redundancy payment and an ex gratia payment. At the age of 62 he would have become entitled to a retirement pension. It was evident that, had he been a woman, he would have received an immediate retirement pension which would have been greater than the payment actually received. The ECJ ruled that the benefit paid by an employer to an employee following redundancy was within the scope of EC Article 141 (ex Art 119).

The ECJ also reminded the Member States that Directive 75/117 established the right of a worker to be 'entitled to claim before an appropriate authority that his work has the same value as other work'.[14] It is therefore not surprising that most of the ECJ's decisions in this field have originated from references under EC Article 234 (ex Art 177). However, the House of Lords without making a reference has ruled that qualifying thresholds for unfair dismissal and redundancy were discriminatory against women and thus contrary to EC Article 141 (ex Art 119).[15] Under the existing law, the criteria for unfair dismissal and redundancy were different for part-time and full-time workers. Part-time workers were required to be in continuous employment for five years to qualify whereas full-time workers were required to be in continuous employment only for two years to qualify for unfair dismissal and redundancy payments. Since 90% of part-time workers were women the UK legislation was declared to be in conflict with EC Article 141 (ex Art 119) and Directive 75/117 (equal pay) and Directive 76/207 (equal treatment). The House of Lords decision was based on weighty precedents,[16] so much so that no reference to the ECJ was considered

---

11 Supra.
12 Supra.
13 Case C-262/88: *Barber v Guardian Royal Exchange Assurance Group* [1990] ECR I-1889, [1990] 2 CMLR 513 at para 30; followed in *Jordan v Electricity Association Services* (Industrial Tribunal) [1993] 3 CMLR 586. See also Case C-152/91: *Neath v Hugh Steeper Ltd* [1993] ECR I-6935, [1994] 1 All ER 929; and Case C-50/99: *Podesta v Caisse de retraite par repartition des ingenieures cadres et assimiles* (25 May 2000, unreported) and the cases cited there.
14 Case 61/81: *Commission v United Kingdom* [1982] ECR 2601, [1982] 3 CMLR 284; see also Case 157/86: *Murphy v Bord Telecom Eireann* [1988] ECR 673 and Case 237/85: *Rummler v Dato-Druck GmbH* [1986] ECR 2101, [1987] 3 CMLR 127.
15 *R v Secretary of State for Employment, ex p Equal Opportunities Commission* [1995] 1 AC 1, [1994] 1 All ER 910, HL.
16 Esp Cases 170/84; 171/88; C-262/88; C-360/90 supra and Cases C-213/89: [1990] ECR I-2433, [1990] 3 CMLR 1; and C-221/89: *R v Secretary of State for Transport, ex p Factortame (No 3)* [1991] ECR I-3905 [1992] QB 680, [1991] 3 CMLR 589.

necessary but, in the opinion of Lord Keith of Kinkel, it would have been inappropriate to make a declaration in respect of compensation to the workers concerned on the basis of the *Francovich* cases.[17] Justice for part-time workers (predominantly women) may yet cause adverse economic consequences as far as small business is concerned.[18]

(2) DIRECTIVE 76/207[19] ON EQUAL TREATMENT IN EMPLOYMENT

Based on EC Articles 136 and 308 (ex Arts 117 and 235), Directive 76/207 purports to guarantee equal treatment as regards access to all jobs or posts irrespective of the sector or branch of activity including access to all levels of the occupational hierarchy; access to all types and levels of vocational guidance, vocational training, advanced training and retraining; and working conditions, including the conditions governing dismissal.[20]

The principle of 'equal treatment' means that there shall be no discrimination whatsoever on grounds of sex either directly or indirectly by reference in particular to marital or family status (Article 2(1)).[1] Since Article 2(3) affords protection to women particularly as regards pregnancy and maternity, case law in this area has enriched the interpretation of the Directive.

In Case C-177/88[2] the ECJ ruled that the refusal to recruit a woman to a suitable employment as an instructor at a training centre for young adults because she was pregnant, was discriminatory. Bearing in mind that only women can be refused employment on grounds of pregnancy the main reason for the exclusion of the applicant was based on a factor that would apply to one sex only and that constituted direct discrimination.

Case C-179/88[3] concerned the dismissal of a part-time cashier on the grounds of prolonged illness arising from a pregnancy a year earlier. The ECJ held that Article 2(3) of the Directive prevented dismissal of a worker because of pregnancy or during maternity leave but did not forbid dismissal for inability to work due to an illness even if the illness had been caused by complications arising from pregnancy. Equal treatment simply means that a woman cannot be dismissed for prolonged inability to work caused by illness if a man could not be dismissed in

---

17   C-6/90 and C-9/90: [1991] ECR I-5357.

18   Indeed, the consequences of the *Barber* case (supra) for privately funded pension schemes were so severe that the Member States inserted in the Maastricht Treaty a special protocol that excluded benefits under occupational social security schemes from the meaning of 'pay' for the purposes of EC Article 141 (ex Art 119), if and in so far as they were attributable to periods of employment prior to 17 May 1990 (the date of the judgment in the *Barber* case): see protocol 2. The effect of the protocol has been considered in a number of cases: see Case C-50/96: *Schröder v Deutsche Telekom* [2000] IRLR 353, and the cases cited there; Case C-166/99: *Defreyn v Sabena* (13 July 2000, unreported).

19   OJ 1976, L37/40.

20   The concept of access to employment is not limited to the stage before the employment relationship is created but encompasses benefits that act as an inducement to taking up employment: Case C-116/94: *Meyers v Adjudication Officer* [1995] ECR I-2131. The Directive also applies where an employer wrongly fails to provide references for an employee after the latter's employment has terminated: Case C-185/97: *Coote v Granada Hospitality Ltd* [1998] ECR I-5199.

1   A difference of treatment does not amount to unlawful discrimination if, for example, it is objectively justified in order to compensate for some other disadvantage suffered by the favoured person: eg Case C-79/99: *Schnorbus v Land Hessen* (7 December 2000, unreported).

2   *Dekker v Stichting Vormingscentrum voor Jong Volwassenen* [1990] ECR I-3941. See also Case C-207/98: *Mahlburg v Land Mecklenburg-Vorpommern* [2000] IRLR 276.

3   *Handels-og Kontorfunktionaerernes Forbund i Denmark v Dansk Arbejdsgiverforening, Vibeke Herz* [1990] ECR I-3979.

a similar case, whatever his illness may be. Article 2(3) of the Directive allows the Member States to adopt rules for the protection of women in connection with pregnancy and maternity but provides no guidance in this respect. The loophole was closed by Decision 92/85[4] on the safety and health at work of pregnant workers who have recently given birth or are breastfeeding.

In the *Webb* case[5] the House of Lords referred to the ECJ the problem of a lady who was specifically appointed to replace another employee who had become pregnant but, shortly after her appointment she too became pregnant and her employer decided to dismiss her. The House of Lords conceded that dismissal on the grounds of pregnancy was unlawful but, in the circumstances of the case, was aware that the employer would not have engaged a pregnant woman to replace another one during the latter's maternity leave. However it transpired that, though initially engaged as replacement for another employee, Mrs Webb was to be employed for an indefinite period.

The ECJ[6] following its decision in the *Hertz*[7] and *Habermann-Beltermann*[8] cases held that 'Directive 76/207 precludes dismissal of an employee who is recruited for an unlimited term with a view, initially, to replacing another employee during the latter's maternity leave and who cannot do so because, shortly after recruitment, she is herself found to be pregnant'.[9] In reaching that conclusion the Court relied also on Directive 92/85[10] even though its transposition into national law was delayed until 19 October 1994.

Regretfully the Court did not comment on its judgment in the *Dekker* case[11] though it cited with approval *Hertz*, the two revealing a certain inconsistency. The *Dekker* judgment suggested that the employer could justify the dismissal by distinguishing between dismissal on account of pregnancy and an absence caused by illness connected with pregnancy. Whilst the *Webb* case appears to settle the controversy where the employment was for an indefinite period it has not answered the question where the contract was entered into for a fixed term or, specifically, to cover the period of absence for a colleague on maternity leave. As far as justice for both genders is concerned, would the employer be entitled to dismiss a male employee on the grounds of sickness if he had been engaged to replace another employee during the latter's sickness? It is common ground that the law of employment ought to protect women because, generally, their condition has been ordained by nature but it should be more subtle and avoid automatism which can deter employers, especially small companies or individuals, and thus harm the prospects of women on the labour market.

In contrast with the line of judgments protecting the rights of pregnant women stands the case of a German father of a child born out of wedlock who took unpaid leave for the period extending between the expiry of the mother's obligatory maternity leave and the date at which the child would have become six months old and claimed social security benefit whilst the mother returned to work.[12] The ECJ dismissed his claim as being outside the scope of article 2(3) of the Directive and pointed out that its objective was to ensure the protection of a woman's

4   OJ 1992, L3406/1.
5   *Webb v EMO Air Cargo (UK) Ltd* [1992] 1 CMLR 793; on appeal [1993] 1 CMLR 259, HL.
6   Case C-32/93 [1994] ECR I-3567.
7   C-179/88, *supra*.
8   C-421/92: [1994] ECR I-1657, [1994] IRLR 364.
9   At para 29.
10   Supra.
11   C-177/88, *supra*.
12   Case 184/83: *Hofmann v Barmer Ersatzkasse* [1984] ECR 3047, [1986] 1 CMLR 242.

biological condition during pregnancy and thereafter until such time as her physiological and mental functions have returned to the normal. It was not concerned with the organization of the family or the sharing of parental responsibilities.

The protection of pregnant women has overshadowed other aspects of equal treatment in employment. Concerning the right of equal treatment in vocational training the ECJ held that an employer may justify a difference in the remuneration for special training since certain tasks may be more important than others and thus ought to attract a higher wage and this may be so even if the lower-paid employees have to be predominantly women.[13] Similarly, considerations of public security (though not subject to derogation within the terms of the Directive) may justify a different treatment of men and women. Thus in what might be described as a paternalist stance the ECJ confirmed that, in a particularly dangerous area, policewomen need not be assigned to duties reserved to men carrying firearms since equipping women with such weapons would expose them to terrorist activities.[14]

Article 5(1) must be interpreted as meaning that contractual provisions, which lay down the same age for dismissal of men and women under a mass redundancy scheme entailing the grant of early retirement pensions, are not discriminatory even if the normal retirement age for men and women is different and, as a result, both sexes qualify at the same age but men have advantage over women.[15]

However in employment in the public sector equal treatment means equal compulsory retirement age. Thus national legislation, which stipulates that women have to retire at 60 whilst men continue in employment until they reach the age of 65, is discriminatory.[16] The same principle applies to the private sector under the control of the state.[17] The sequel to the *Marshall* ruling was a successful claim for damages for unlawful dismissal but the award was far from satisfactory although it reflected the national statutory limit. Finally the matter was disposed of by the ECJ which ruled that since there was a choice between reinstatement and damages, if damages are awarded, they must be in full to correspond to the injury suffered by the applicant. An arbitrary upper limit of damages infringes EC Article 249(3) (ex Art 189(3)).[18]

Certain enforcement actions have exposed problems in the Member States' implementation of the Directive. Article 2(2) of the Directive provides that it shall be 'without prejudice to the right of Member States to exclude from its field of application those occupational activities and, where appropriate, the training

---

13   Case 109/88: *Handels-OG v Dansk Arbejdsverforeneng, ex p Danfoss* [1989] ECR 3199, [1990] 1 CMLR 8.
14   Case 222/84: *Johnston v Chief Constable of the Royal Ulster Constabulary* [1986] ECR 1651, [1986] 3 CMLR 240. There is, however, no general exclusion of employment in the armed forces from the scope of the Directive. Particular activities may be excluded from the principle of equal treatment by reason of their particular nature and the conditions under which they are performed. In that respect, the Member States have a broad margin of discretion so far as activities underlying public security are concerned: see Case C-273/97: *Sirdar v Army Board and Secretary of State for Defence* [1999] ECR I-7403. There are limits to that margin of discretion: see Case C-285/98: *Kreil v Bundesrepublik Deutschland* (11 January 2000, unreported).
15   Case 151/84: *Roberts v Tate &Lyle Industries Ltd* [1986] ECR 703, [1986] 1 CMLR 714. See also Case 262/84: *Beets-Proper v Van Landschot Bankiers NV* [1986] ECR 773, [1987] 2 CMLR 616.
16   Case 152/84: *Marshall v Southampton and South West Hampshire Area Health Authority* [1986] ECR 723, [1986] 1 CMLR 688.
17   Case C-188/89: *Foster v British Gas plc* [1990] ECR I-3313, [1990] 2 CMLR 833.
18   Case C-271/91: *Marshall v Southampton and South West Hampshire Area Health Authority (No 2)* [1993] ECR I-4367, [1993] 3 CMLR 293.

leading thereto, for which, by reason of their nature or the context in which they are carried out, the sex of the worker constitutes a determining factor'. The United Kingdom legislation was held incompatible with the Directive since it provided exceptions to the principle of equal treatment where:

(1) employment was in a private household;
(2) the number of persons employed by any employer did not exceed five; and
(3) the employment, promotion and training of midwives was concerned.[19]

The Commission was unsuccessful in claiming that Italian implementing legislation was discriminatory in so far as it provided, inter alia, that a woman who adopts a child under six years of age is entitled to compulsory leave and allowance during the first three months after the child enters the adoptive family while the adoptive father is not given the same rights.[20] Advocate-General Mme Rozes considered the position unfair to the father but the Court ruled that there was no discrimination in the sense of the Directive since the special treatment accorded to women strengthens their bond with a child in the early formative period of their relationship.

However, the Commission was successful in challenging the French legislation[1] which was particularly generous to women. Quite apart from allowing a special protection to be written into collective agreements it provides, inter alia, for a Mothers' Day holiday, shorter working hours for women over 59, leave days for female employees in the event of a child's illness and the beginning of the school year, allowances to mothers to cover the cost of nursery or child minders, and daily breaks for female telephone operators and typists. The ECJ held these protective measures excessive and, in particular, the child care provisions for mothers unjustified since this is a responsibility of both parents.

The Court also found that special protection of women as regards night work was no longer justified and the relevant French legislation, being discriminatory, infringed Directive 76/207[2] unless derogation is based on an international agreement.[3]

Positive discrimination in favour of women is consistent with the principle of equal treatment where there is a pre-existing imbalance that favours men and there is in other respects (such as equality in terms of the qualifications required) equal treatment of them.[4]

(3) DIRECTIVE 79/7[5] ON EQUAL TREATMENT IN SOCIAL SECURITY

Directive 79/7 on the progressive implementation of the principle of equal treatment for men and women in matters of social security purports to eliminate any discrimination on 'ground of sex directly, or indirectly, by reference in particular to marital or family status, in particular as concerns the scope of the schemes and the conditions of access thereto; the obligation to contribute and to

---

19 Case 165/82: *Commission v United Kingdom* [1983] ECR 3431, [1984] 1 CMLR 44.
20 Case 163/82: *Commission v Italy* [1983] ECR 3273, [1984] 3 CMLR 169.
 1 Case 312/86: *Commission v France* [1988] ECR 6315, [1989] 1 CMLR 408.
 2 Case C-345/89: *Stoeckel* [1991] ECR I-4047, [1993] 3 CMLR 673.
 3 Case C-13/93: *Office National de l'Emploi v Minne* [1994] ECR I-371.
 4 Case C-158/97: *Badeck v Landesanwalt bein Staatsgerichtshof des Landes Hessen* [2000] All ER (EC) 289, and the cases cited there; Case C-407/98: *Abrahamsson and Anderson v Fogelqvist* [2000] IRLR 732.
 5 OJ 1979, L6/24.

calculation of contributions; the calculation of benefits including increases due in respect of a spouse and for dependants and the conditions governing the duration and retention of entitlements to benefits' (Article 4(1)). However these provisions shall be without prejudice to the rules governing the protection of women on the grounds of maternity (Article 4(2)).

In Case 71/85[6] the ECJ, confirming the direct effect of Directive 79/7, ruled that to deny unemployment benefit to married women who are not 'head of the family' would be incompatible with Community law.

This ruling was confirmed in subsequent cases. In Case 286/85[7] the national legislation provided that married women received less in unemployment benefits than married men or single women. The Court found this to be discriminatory. Consequently married men were to receive increases in social security benefits for their spouses and children.[8] In another case[9] a non-contributory invalidity pension was wrongly denied to a woman performing normal household duties though it was available to a man in similar circumstances. The relevant British legislation had to be amended to give effect to the directly applicable Directive 79/7 but the ruling was not retrospective. The ECJ has also ruled that national procedural rules on limitation must not be used as a bar to rights secured by the *McDermott* judgment.[10]

However, though *prima facie* discriminatory, a provision which takes into account greater family responsibility which usually falls on men, and allows higher unemployment benefit than for those living with an earning person or even higher than for a worker living alone, can be justified for non-sex reasons and thus constitutes no breach of Directive 79/7.[11]

In Case 30/85[12] the ECJ held that a system of supplementary benefits which takes into consideration the family situation of a claimant with the result that a smaller proportion of women than of men are entitled to such supplements, is incompatible with Article 4(1) unless it can be objectively justified. No such objective justification was proved in a case where part-time workers (predominantly women) were entitled to a lower benefit.[13] However, Article 4(1) precludes Member States from exempting certain groups of persons, ie married women, widows and students from the payment of social contributions unless the same exemption is granted to married men or widowers.[14]

The Directive (Article 3(1)) applies specifically to:

6 *Netherlands v Federatie Nederlandse Vakbeweging* [1986] ECR 3855, [1987] 3 CMLR 767.
7 *McDermott and Cotter v Minister for Social Welfare and A-G* [1987] ECR 1453, [1987] 2 CMLR 607.
8 Case C-377/89: *Cotter and McDermott v Minister for Social Welfare and A-G* [1991] ECR 1155.
9 384/85: *Clarke v Chief Adjudication Officer* [1987] ECR 2865, [1987] 3 CMLR 277.
10 Case C-208/90: *Emmott v Minister for Social Welfare* [1991] ECR I-4269, [1991] 3 CMLR 894. In later cases, *Emmott* has been confined to its particular facts and is not authority for the more general proposition that national time limits cannot be invoked against a claimant for as long as the Member State concerned remains in breach of the Directive in question: see, for example, Case C-410/92: *Johnson v Chief Adjudication Officer* [1994] ECR I-5483.
11 Case C-229/89: *Commission v Belgium, re unemployed heads of households* [1991] ECR I-2205, [1993] 2 CMLR 403.
12 *Teuling Worm v Bedrijfsvereniging voor de Chemische Industrie* [1987] ECR 2497; see *Blaik v Department of Health and Social Security* [1991] 1 CMLR 539, CA.
13 Case C-102/88: *Ruzius-Wilbrink v Bestuur van de Bedrijfsvereniging voor Overheidsdiensten* [1989] ECR 4311, [1991] 2 CMLR 202.
14 Case 373/89: *Caisse d'Assurance Sociales pour Travailleurs Indépendants 'Integrity' v Rouvroy* [1990] ECR I-4243, [1991] IRLR 176, [1993] 3 CMLR 621.

(a) statutory schemes which provide protection against the risks of sickness; invalidity; old age; accidents at work and occupational diseases; unemployment;
(b) social assistance in so far as it is intended to supplement or replace the schemes referred to in (a).

The Directive (Article 2) applies to the working population, including self-employed persons, workers and self-employed persons whose activity is interrupted by illness, accident or involuntary unemployment and persons seeking employment, and to retired and invalided workers and self-employed persons. The ECJ has interpreted the term 'working population' in a broad sense to include a person who interrupts her work in order to care for a disabled relative. Mrs Drake was in that position as she gave up work in order to look after her invalid mother. The Social Security Act 1975 provided for the payment of invalid care allowance to a person who was regularly and substantially engaged in care for a severely disabled person. It provided that the allowance was not payable to a married woman living with her husband but was payable to a married man in similar circumstances. Since Mrs Drake did live with her husband she was disqualified. The ECJ had no difficulty in ruling that Article 4 of the Directive was infringed by the national legislation.[15]

However Article 2 applies only to persons who were working at the time when they became entitled to an old-age pension or whose working was previously interrupted by one of the events listed in Article 3 above.[16] Therefore a Dutch woman voluntarily unemployed at the time of retirement was not entitled to the protection afforded by Directive 79/7.

In Case C-243/90[17] the ECJ confirmed the principle that a benefit claimed by virtue of Directive 79/7 had to be 'directly and effectively linked to the protection provided against one of the risks specified in Article 3(1)'. Thus, a housing benefit calculated on the basis of a difference between a notional income to which the beneficiary is deemed to be entitled and his actual income was held to be outside the scope of the Directive. Similarly a supplementary allowance or income support defined by statute is not covered by the Directive.[18]

Article 7 of the Directive contains a number of exceptions providing, inter alia, that it shall be without prejudice to the right of Member States to exclude from its scope 'the determination of pensionable age for the purposes of granting old-age and retirement pensions and the possible consequences thereof, for other benefits'. The exception was tested in the *Burton* case[19] where the applicant aged 58 was considered ineligible for voluntary early retirement. The qualifying age for women was 55 but for men 60. He complained of being discriminated against on grounds of his sex. However the ECJ held that, though the voluntary early retirement scheme was within the scope of Directive 76/207, the differentials of qualifying ages were justified within Community law because they were tied up to the national rules specifying that the minimum qualifying ages for a state retirement pension were 60 for women and 65 for men.

15 Case 150/85: *Drake v Chief Adjudication Officer* [1986] ECR 1995, [1986] 3 CMLR 43.
16 Cases 48, 106, 107/88: *Achtenberg – Te Riele v Sociale Verzekeringsbank* [1989] ECR 1963, [1990] 3 CMLR 323.
17 Case C-243/90: *R v Secretary of State for Social Security, ex p Smithson* [1992] ECR I-467, [1992] 1 CMLR 1061.
18 Cases C-63, 64/91: *Jackson v Chief Adjudication Officer* [1992] ECR I-4737, [1992] 3 CMLR 389.
19 Case 19/81: *Burton v British Railways Board* [1982] ECR 555, [1982] 2 CMLR 136.

In that sense the Court held that inequality with respect to the number of years of contributions required by law to earn a full retirement pension (ie 44 years for men and 39 years for women) at the same level of benefit could be justified in terms of Article 7(1).[20] By the same token the company bridging pension for employees retiring on health grounds, topped up to notional earned pension, could be reduced by the amount of full state pension for women at age 60 and for men at 65.[1]

Where invalidity or disablement ceases when the recipient reaches the statutory retirement age but the national legislation provides for an earlier retirement age for women, the age differential is incompatible with Directive 79/7 as being discriminatory on grounds of sex but the exception under Article 7(1) is inapplicable.[2]

(4) DIRECTIVE 86/378[3] ON EQUAL TREATMENT IN OCCUPATIONAL SOCIAL SECURITY SCHEMES[4]

The object of Directive 86/378 is to complete Directive 79/7 and thus to ensure equal treatment in respect of occupational social security schemes based on private law which are not covered by the former, which are based on public law. However its effect has been reduced by the judgment in the *Barber*[5] case where the ECJ ruled that 'occupational pensions' are to be regarded as 'pay'. It follows that it applies in cases of indirect discrimination in the field of pensions which are not covered by EC Article 141 (ex Art 119).

However the Directive does not apply: (1) to individual contracts for self-employed workers; (2) to schemes for the self-employed having only one member; (3) in the case of salaried workers, to insurance contracts to which the employer is not a party; (4) to the optional provisions of occupational schemes offered to participants individually to guarantee them either additional benefits, or a choice of date on which the normal benefits will start, or a choice between several benefits; (5) to occupational schemes whose benefits are financed by voluntary contributions paid by workers (Article 2). The Directive applies to members of the working population including self-employed persons, persons whose activity is interrupted by illness, maternity, accident or involuntary unemployment, persons seeking employment, to retired and disabled workers, and to persons claiming under them in accordance with national law or practice (Article 3).

The Directive applies to occupational schemes:

---

20 Case C-9/91: *R v Secretary of State for Social Security, ex p Equal Opportunities Commission* [1992] ECR I-4297, [1992] 3 CMLR 233. It does not follow that it is possible to discriminate in other respects between men and women by reference to their pensionable age: see Case C-137/94: *R v Secretary of State for Health, ex p Richardson* [1995] ECR I-3407. Only differences that are necessarily and objectively linked to the permissible difference are acceptable: Case C-92/94: *Secretary of State for Health and Chief Adjudication Officer v Graham* [1995] ECR I-2521; Case C-154/96: *Wolfs v Office National des pensions* [1998] ECR I-6173.
1 Case C-132/92: *Birds Eye Walls Ltd v Roberts* [1993] ECR I-5579, [1993] 3 CMLR 822.
2 Case C-328/91: *Secretary of State for Social Security v Thomas* [1993] ECR I-1247, [1993] 3 CMLR 880. The same applies where there is an age difference for receiving an early retirement pension on the ground of incapacity for work: Case C-104/98: *Buchner v Sozialversicherungsanstalt der Bauern* (23 May 2000, unreported). For an illustration of a benefit falling within the exception in Art 7(1), see Case C-196/98: *Hepple v Adjudication Officer* [2000] All ER (EC) 513.
3 OJ 1986, L225/40.
4 Amended by Dir 86/97 (OJ 1997, L46/20).
5 Supra.

(a) which provide protection against sickness; invalidity; old age including early retirement; industrial accidents and occupational diseases; unemployment;
(b) which provide for other social benefits, in cash or in kind, and in particular survivors' benefits and family allowances, if such benefits are accorded to employed persons and thus constitute a consideration paid by the employer to the worker by reason of the latter's employment (Article 4).

Subject to the provisions relating to the protection of women for reason of maternity the principle of equal treatment implies that there shall be no discrimination on the basis of sex, either directly or indirectly, by reference in particular to marital or family status as regards: the scope of the schemes and conditions of access to them; the obligation to contribute and the calculation of contributions; the calculation of benefits, including supplementary benefits due in respect of a spouse or dependants, and the conditions governing the duration and retention of entitlement to benefits (Article 5).[6]

The Directive lists the following illustrations of the type of provisions that are contrary to the principle of equal treatment where they are based on sex, either directly or indirectly, such as by reference to marital or family status (Article 6) namely provisions:

(a) determining the persons who may participate in an occupational schemes;
(b) fixing the compulsory or optional nature of participation in occupational schemes;
(c) laying down different rules as regards the age of entry into the scheme or the minimum period of employment or membership of the scheme required to obtain the benefits thereof;
(d) laying down different rules, except as provided for in sub-paragraphs (h) and (i), for the reimbursement of contributions where a worker leaves a scheme without having fulfilled the conditions guaranteeing a deferred right to long-term benefits;
(e) setting different conditions for the granting of benefits or restricting such benefits to workers of one or other of the sexes;
(f) fixing different retirement ages;
(g) suspending the retention or acquisition of rights during periods of maternity leave or leave for family reasons which are granted by law or agreement and are paid by the employer;
(h) setting different levels of benefit, except in so far as may be necessary to take account of actuarial calculation factors which differ according to sex in the case of benefits designated as contribution-defined;
(i) setting different levels of worker contribution and, subject to certain acceptions, different levels of employers' contributions;
(j) laying down different standards or standards applicable only to workers of specified sex, except provided for in sub-paragraphs (h) and (i), as regards the guarantee or retention of entitlement to deferred benefits when a worker leaves a scheme.

Where the granting of benefits within the scope of this Directive is left to the discretion of the scheme's management bodies, the latter must take account of the principle of equal treatment.

---

6   The test for whether or not there has been unlawful discrimination is the same as in the context of Dir 76/207: Case C-226/98: *Jørgensen v Torenngen af Speiallaeger* [2000] IRLR 726.

The Member States are obliged to take steps to ensure that:

(1) provisions contrary to the principle of equal treatment in legally compulsory collective agreements, staff rules of undertaking or any other arrangements relating to occupational schemes are null and void, or may be declared null and void or amended; and
(2) schemes containing such provisions may not be approved or extended by administrative measures (Article 7).

They must also make sure that the provisions of occupational schemes contrary to the principle of equal treatment are revised by 1 January 1993, though the rights and obligations arising from a scheme prior to its revision may remain in force during that period (Article 8).

Member States may defer the application of the principle of equal treatment in certain cases, viz with respect to the determination of pensionable age for the purposes of granting old-age or retirement pensions, and survivors' pensions (Article 9). They were obliged to put into effect the Directive by 31 July 1989 (Article 12(1)).

(5) DIRECTIVE 86/613[7] ON EQUAL TREATMENT IN SELF-EMPLOYED CAPACITY

The object of Directive 86/613 is to extend the application of Directives 76/207 and 79/7 to self-employed persons in any activity including agriculture and the liberal professions and to extend the protection of self-employed women during pregnancy and motherhood. It covers their spouses, not being employees or partners, where they habitually, under the conditions laid down, participate in the activities of self-employed worker and perform the same tasks or ancillary tasks (Article 2).

In the scope of this Directive the principle of equal treatment implies the absence of all discrimination on grounds of sex, either directly or indirectly, in reference in particular to marital or family status (Article 3).

Member States are obliged to apply the principle of equal treatment as defined in Directive 76/207 especially in respect of the establishment, equipment or extension of a business or the launching or extension of any other form of self-employment activity including financial facilities (Article 4).

Without prejudice to the specific conditions for access to certain activities which apply to both sexes, Member States shall take the measures necessary to ensure that the conditions for the formation of a company between spouses are not more restrictive than the conditions for the formation of a company between unmarried persons (Article 5).

Where a contributory social security system for self-employed workers exists in a Member State, that state shall take the necessary measures to enable the spouses referred to in Article 2 who are not protected under the self-employed workers' social security scheme to join a contributory social security scheme voluntarily (Article 6).

Member States were obliged to put into force the Directive by 30 June 1989 though states which had to amend their laws in order to comply with Article 5 had to do this by 30 June 1991 (Article 12). The Council was to review this Directive before 31 July 1993 (Article 11).

7 OJ 1986, L359/86.

D. Protection of employees

Next to the protection of the economically weaker sex the Community turned to the protection of workers by means of the following instruments:

(1) DIRECTIVE 95/59 ON COLLECTIVE REDUNDANCIES[8]

For the purpose of this Directive 'collective redundancies' means dismissal effected by an employer for one or more reasons not related to the individual workers concerned where, according to the choice of the Member States, the number of redundancies is *either*, over a period of 30 days,

(1) at least 10 in establishments normally employing more than 20 or less than 100 workers;
(2) at least 10% of the number of workers in establishments normally employing at least 100 but less than 300 workers;
(3) at least 30 in establishments normally employing 300 workers or more;

or, over a period of 90 days, at least 20, whatever the number of workers normally employed in the establishments in question (Article 1(1)(a)).

The Directive does not apply to:

(a) collective redundancies effected under contracts of employment concluded for a limited period of time or for specific tasks except where such redundancies take place prior to the date of expiry or the completion of such contracts;
(b) workers employed by public administrative bodies or by establishments governed by public law (or, in Member States where this concept is unknown, by equivalent bodies);
(c) the crews of sea-going vessels (Article 1(2)).

The workers concerned are guaranteed information and consultations with their representatives as regards the reasons for the projected redundancies, number and categories or workers involved, the criteria for the selection of the workers to be made redundant and the method of calculating any redundancy payments other than those arising out of national legislation and/or practice (Article 2).

Article 3 provides for the procedure for collective redundancies which imposes upon the employer the duty of notifying the competent national public authority in writing of any projected collective redundancies. Employers must forward to the workers' representatives a copy of the notification and the latter may comment on the matter to the competent authority.[9]

Member States are obliged to ensure that judicial and/or administrative procedures for the enforcement of obligations contained therein are available to the workers' representatives and/or workers (Article 6). However the Directive shall not affect the right of Member States to apply or introduce measures which are more favourable to workers (Article 5).

---

8 OJ 1998, L225/26. This Directive repealed and replaced Dir 75/129 (OJ 1975, L48/29) and Dir 95/56 (OJ 1992, L245/3). The case law under the preceding directives is still relevant and the construction of similar provision in the later directive.

9 Any derogations from the procedure laid down in the Directive are to be strictly construed because the object of the Directive is to protect the workers concerned: Case C-250/97: *Dansk Metalarbejderforbund v Lønmodtagernes Garantifond* [1998] ECR I-8737.

(2) DIRECTIVE 2001/23[10] ON THE APPROXIMATION OF NATIONAL LAWS RELATING TO
EMPLOYEES' RIGHTS IN THE EVENT OF TRANSFER OF BUSINESS

Directive 2001/23 applies to the transfer of an undertaking, business or part of either to another employer as a result of a legal transfer or merger within the territorial scope of the Treaty, but it does not apply to sea-going vessels. A transfer is covered by the Directive where it involves the transfer of an economic entity which retains its identity (that is, an organized grouping of resources whose objective is the pursuit of an economic activity). The Directive applies to both public and private undertakings but not to an administrative reorganization of the public administration or to the transfer of administrative functions between different organs of the public administration.[11] (Article 1). The regime applicable to transfers is mitigated where the transferor is the subject of bankruptcy or insolvency proceedings or the like (Article 5).

Following the transfer the transferee shall continue to observe the terms and conditions agreed in any collective agreement on the same terms applicable to the transferor under that agreement until the date of termination or expiry of the collective agreement or the entry into the force or application of another collective agreement (Article 3(1) to (3)). However, employees' rights to old-age, invalidity or survivors' benefits under supplementary company or inter-company pension schemes outside the statutory social security schemes in Member States shall not be affected unless the Member State concerned so decides (Article 3(4)).

The transfer of an undertaking, business or part of them shall not in itself constitute grounds for dismissal by the transferor or the transferee though this shall not stand in the way of dismissals that may take place for economic, technological or organizational reasons entailing changes in the workforce. Moreover Member States may provide that the protection shall cover certain specific categories of employees who are not covered by the laws or practice of the Member States in respect of protection against dismissal (Article 4). Where the business or undertaking transferred retains its autonomy, the transfer must not alter the status and functions of the employees' representatives (Article 6).

The transferor and the transferee are required to inform the representatives of their respective employees concerned of the date and reasons for the transfer, the legal, economic and social implications of the transfer for the employees and measures envisaged in relation to the employees. The information must be provided and consultations take place in good time before the change in the business is effected (Article 7).

However, whilst employers are bound by the Directive the employees can opt out, in which case the effects of opting out are governed by national law.[12]

Member States, when implementing the Directive, have the right to apply or introduce measures which are more favourable to employees (Article 8).

---

10   OJ 2001, L82/16. This Directive codified and replaced Dir 77/187 (OJ 1977, L61/27), and Dir 98/50 (OJ 1998, L201/88). The case law under the earlier directives is still relevant to the interpretation of similar provisions in Dir 2001/23.
11   On the meaning of transfer and economic entity, see for example, Cases C-127/96, C-229/96 and C-74/97: *Hernendez Videl SA v Ferez* [1998] ECR I-8179; Case C-399/96: *Europieces SA v Sanders* [1998] ECR I-6965; Case C-234/98: *G C Allen v Amalgamated Construction Co* [1999] ECR I-8643; Case C-343/98: *Collino v Telecom Italie SpA* [2000] IRLR 788; Case C-175/99: *Meyeur v Association Promotion de l'Information Messine* [2000] IRLR 783.
12   Cases C-132/91 and 138/91: *Katsikas v Konstantinidis* [1992] ECR I-6577, [1993] 1 CMLR 845.

(3) DIRECTIVE 80/987,[13] AMENDED BY DIRECTIVE 87/164[14] ON THE PROTECTION OF EMPLOYEES IN THE EVENT OF INSOLVENCY OF EMPLOYERS

This Directive applies to employees' claims arising from contracts of employment or employment relationships and existing claims against employers who are in the state of insolvency but, by way of exception, Member States may exclude claims by certain categories of employee by virtue of the special nature of an employee's contract of employment offering the employee protection equivalent to that guaranteed by the Directive (Article 1). The employees in that category are listed in the Annex. In the United Kingdom such employees include the master and the members of the crew of a fishing vessel who are remunerated by a share of the profits or gross earnings of the vessel; the spouse of the employer; registered dock workers other than those who are wholly or mainly engaged in work which is not dock work, and the crews of sea-going vessels.

An employer is deemed to be in a state of insolvency:

(1) where, under the national law, a request has been made for the opening of proceedings involving the employer's assets to satisfy collectively the claims of creditors; and
(2) where the competent authority either decided to open the proceedings, or established that the employer's undertaking or business has been definitely closed down and that the available assets are insufficient to warrant the opening of the proceedings.

Member States are obliged to ensure that guarantee institutions pay the employees' outstanding claims resulting from contracts of employment relating to pay for the work done prior to a given date. At the choice of the Member States the relevant date shall be either that of the onset of the employer's insolvency,[15] or that of the notice of dismissal issued to the employee concerned on account of the employer's insolvency or that on which the contract of employment or the employment relationship with the employer concerned was discontinued on account of the employer's insolvency (Article 3).[16]

Member States have the option to limit the liability of guarantee institutions in accordance with Article 4 but to avoid the payment of sums beyond the social objective of the Directive they may set a ceiling to the liability of employees' outstanding claims.[17]

Member States must lay down rules for the organization, financing and operation of the guarantee institutions providing in particular that:

---

13   OJ 1980, L283/23.
14   OJ 1987, L66/11.
15   As to which, see Cases C-94/95 and C-95/95: *Bonifaci v INPS* [1997] ECR I-3969, paras 33-44.
16   In the case of multi-nationals, the competent guarantee institution is that of the state in which the employee was working: Case C-198/98: *Everson and Barrass v Secretary of State for Trade and Industry and Bell Lines Ltd* [1999] ECR I-8903. Otherwise it is that of the state in which it was decided to open proceedings to satisfy the creditors' claims or it was established that the employers' business had been closed down: Case C-117/96: *Mosback v Lonmodtagernes Garantifond* [1997] ECR I-5017.
17   Cf Case C-235/95: *AGS Assedic Pas-de-Calais v Dumon* [1998] ECR I-4531 on ceilings; Case C-125/97: *Regeling v Bestuur van de Bedrijfsvereniging voor de Metaalnijverheid* [1998] ECR I-4493 on the allocation of payments to claims; Case C-373/95: *Maso v INPS and Italy* [1997] ECR I-4051, paras 55-59 on aggregation with other benefits.

(1) the assets of the institutions shall be independent of the employer's operating capital and be inaccessible to proceedings for insolvency;
(2) employers shall contribute to financing, unless it is fully covered by the public authorities;
(3) institutions' liabilities shall not depend on whether or not obligations to contribute to financing have been fulfilled (Article 5).[18]

Articles 6, 7 and 8 contain no provisions safeguarding the social security rights of employees including those who have already left the employer's undertaking or business at the onset of the employer's insolvency.

Finally, Member States are at liberty to apply or introduce measures which are more favourable to employees than the provisions of the Directive.

(4) DIRECTIVE 89/391[19] ON SAFETY AND HEALTH

The objective of Directive 89/391 is to introduce measures to encourage improvements in safety and health of workers at work. It applies to all sectors of economic activity, both private and public (industrial, agricultural, commercial, administrative, service, educational, cultural, leisure, etc), except to certain specific public service activities such as the armed forces or the police (Article 2).

The Directive imposes certain obligations on employers ensuring the safety and health of workers in every aspect related to the work (Article 5) and detailing the measures which have to be taken in this respect (Article 6). Moreover employers have to organize protective and preventive services and designate to that end one or more workers to carry out activities related thereto (Article 7). They must provide for first aid and fire-fighting equipment and ensure evacuation of workers in serious and imminent danger (Article 8). Employers have to inform the workforce of the safety and health risks and protective and preventive measures concerning the undertakings as well as the workstation and/or job (Article 10). Workers and their representatives have to be consulted and allowed to take part in discussions on all questions relating to safety and health at work (Article 11). They have also the right to receive adequate training during working hours at the employer's expense (Article 12).

Workers' obligations entail responsibility for their own safety and health and, in accordance with their training and the instruction given by their employer, the correct use of machinery and equipment as well as of the personal protective equipment and safety devices. They have to inform the employer and/or the workers with specific responsibility for the safety and health of workers of any work situation which represents a serious and immediate danger to safety and health and of any shortcomings in the protection arrangements. They ought to co-operate, in accordance with national practice, with the employer and with workers with specific responsibility for the safety and health of the workforce in order to enable the requirements imposed by the competent authority to be carried out and to ensure that the working environment and working conditions are safe and pose no risk to safety and health within their field of activity (Article 13).

---

18   Although Arts 1-4 are sufficiently precise to be relied on before a national court in the event of a failure to implement the directive properly or at all, Art 5 does not make it possible to identify the person liable to provide the guarantee and so may preclude reliance upon the directive (as in Cases C-6/90 and C-9/90: *Francovich v Italy* [1991] ECR I-5357, paras 10-27) unless the state has properly implemented Art 5.
19   OJ 1989, L183/1.

Article 14 provides for measures to be introduced in accordance with national law and/or practice to ensure that workers receive health surveillance appropriate to the health and safety risks they incur at work, such measures to form part of a national health system.

The Council, acting on a proposal from the Commission based on EC Article 138 (ex Art 118a) has been charged with the enactment of Directives in areas specified in the Annex ie work places;[20] work equipment;[1] personal protective equipment;[2] work with visual display units;[3] handling heavy loads involving risk of back injury;[4] temporary or mobile work sites;[5] and fisheries and agriculture[6] (Article 16).

In the task of the purely technical adjustments to the individual directives in this field the Commission shall be assisted by a Committee consisting of the representatives of the Member States and chaired by the non-voting representative of the Commission. The Committee shall deliver its opinion on the drafts submitted by the representative of the Commission by the majority laid down in EC Article 205(2) (ex Art 148(2)) in the case of decisions which the Council is required to adopt on a proposal from the Commission. The Commission shall adopt the measures if they are in accordance with the opinion of the Committee. If they are not or if no opinion is delivered, the Commission shall submit to the Council a proposal which will be decided by a qualified majority. If on the expiry of three months from the date of the referral to the Council, the Council has not acted, the proposed measure shall be adopted by the Commission.

(5) EMPLOYER/EMPLOYEE RELATIONS

Under Directive 91/533,[7] employers are obliged to inform their employees of the essential aspects of the contract or employment relationship between them. The Directive specifies the information that must be provided and the means by which the employee must be informed. The end result is that employees are entitled to a written contract of employment or letter of engagement setting out the terms of the employment relationship, or at least to one or more other documents setting them out. Any change in the information given to the employee must be communicated in writing.

---

20   Dir 89/654 (OJ 1989, L393/1); Dir 90/394 (OJ 1990, L196/1) as amended (exposure to carcinogens – see Case C-2/97: *Società Italiana Petroli v Borsana* [1998] ECR I-8597); Dir 90/679 (OJ 1990, L374/1), as amended (exposure to biological agents); Dir 92/58 (OJ 1992, L245/23) (safety and health signs); Dir 92/85 (OJ 1992, L348/1) (pregnant workers and workers who have recently given birth or who are breastfeeding); Dir 92/91 (OJ 1992, L348/9) (mineral extraction through drilling); Dir 92/104 (OJ 1992, L404/10) (surface and underground mineral extraction); Dir 98/24 (OJ 1998, L131/11) (chemical agents).
1   Dir 89/655 (OJ 1989, L393/13); see Case C-2/97: *Società Italiana Petroli v Borsana* [1998] ECR I-8597.
2   Dir 89/656 (OJ 1989, L393/18).
3   Dir 90/270 (OJ 1990, L156/14); see Case C-11/99: *Dietrich v Westdeutscher Rundfunk* (6 July 2000, unreported).
4   Dir 90/269 (OJ 1990, L156/9).
5   Dir 92/57 (OJ 1992, L245/6) – implementing minimum health and safety requirements in this area.
6   Dir 93/103 (OJ 1993, L307/1) (fishing vessels).
7   OJ 1991, L288/32. See Cases C-253/96 to C-258/96: *Kampelmann v Landschaftsverband Westfalen-Lippe* [1997] ECR I-6907.

(6) WORKING HOURS

Directive 93/104[8] lays down minimum safety and health requirements for the organization of working time. It applies to minimum periods of daily rest, weekly rest and annual leave, to breaks and maximum weekly working time, and to certain aspects of night work, shift work and patterns of work. It applies to all sectors of activity, both public and private, to which Directive 89/391 applies,[9] with the exception of air, rail, road, sea, inland waterway and lake transport, sea fishing, other work at sea and the activities of doctors in training. However, the Directive allows Member States a broad range of derogations.

(7) INDUSTRIAL RELATIONS

Directive 94/45[10] provides for the creation of a European works council[11] or a procedure for informing and consulting employees in Community-scale undertakings and Community-scale groups of undertakings. An undertaking is of Community-scale if it has at least 1,000 employees within the Member States and there are at least 150 of them in each of at least two Member States; a group is of Community-scale if it satisfies the same criteria *mutatis mutandis* (in particular, there must be at least two group undertakings in different Member States). The central management of the undertaking or group of undertakings is responsible for setting up the works council or the information and consultation procedure. That is to be done on the initiative of the central management or at the request of the employees or their representatives by means of negotiations between central management and a special negotiating body representing the employees.

E. The Social Charter

Encouraged by the provisions of the Single European Act (Sub-section III – Social Policy) the Commission presented to the Heads of State or Government a Draft Community Charter of Fundamental Social Rights[12] comprising twelve items, ie rights to: free movement; employment and remuneration; improved living and working conditions; social security, freedom of association and collective bargaining; vocational training; equal treatment for men and women; right to information, consultation and worker participation; protection of health and safety in the workplace; protection of children and young people; protection of the elderly and of the handicapped. These were considered to be 'fundamental social rights' guaranteed to all Community citizens. However, in view of British opposition, only eleven countries agreed at the Madrid Summit in the summer of 1989 to press on with the Charter.

The resolution of the eleven was accompanied by the Commission Action Programme detailing some 47 proposals for the adoption of measures considered

---

8 OJ 1993, L307/18. See Case C-303/98: *Sindicato de médicos de Asistencia Pública v Conselleria de Sanidad y Consumo de la Generalidad Valenciana* [2000] IRLR 845.
9 See above.
10 OJ 1994, L254/64, amended by Dir 97/74 (OJ 1998, L10/22) (by which Dir 94/45 was extended to the United Kingdom).
11 This is essentially a forum for the communication of information and for consultation between employer and employees.
12 COM(89) 248 Final.

necessary for the achievement of the objectives of the Charter.[13] By the end of 1991 the Commission presented its proposal to the Council but in its First Report on the Application of the Charter[14] it recorded its disappointment. The Charter was a declaration of intent but not a legally binding instrument. The lukewarm reception of the Council apart, progress was impeded by the deliberations of the Intergovernmental Conference on the Political Union.

Since the United Kingdom was unwilling to drop its opposition to the inclusion of the Charter in the Maastricht package deal because it considered that it would have resulted in an unnecessary but considerable transfer of competence to Community institutions, including an increase of qualified majority voting, the 12 Member States agreed that the resolution of the 11 should be embodied in an Agreement signed by the 11 in the form of a Protocol annexed to the Treaty on European Union. The Protocol would be binding on the 11 Member States only.[15]

The Treaty on European Union includes among the objectives of the Union the promotion of social progress and a high level of employment.[16] It also amended the EC Treaty so as to include the promotion of a high level of employment and of social protection, the raising of the standards of living and quality of life and economic and social cohesion among the tasks of the EC.[17] EC Article 3 (ex Art 3), which lists the activities of the Community, includes a 'policy in the social sphere comprising a European Social Fund'. This brings us back to the Protocol on Social Policy on which a great deal has been written.[18]

As far as constitution-making technique is concerned, it is unfortunate that the Twelve decided to depart from the principle of unanimity which is the hallmark of the international law-making process and embarked on a byzantine device which is, at best, divisive and, at worst, may prove to be impracticable. It would have seemed to be wiser to allow the social policy to evolve on the basis of the Treaty in the light of the Commission Action Programme. Since the various measures proposed by the Commission anyway require separate legislation to deal with individual issues and bearing in mind the Council's lack of enthusiasm for legislation, there seemed to be no need to adopt at once the whole Charter.

However what we have is an 'inter-governmental agreement' signed by 11 Member States which, unlike a Community act, cannot be challenged before the Court of Justice. Unlike the Community secondary legislation it remains part of the constitution of the Union, ie a primary law. By analogy to Annexes to the Accessions Acts the ECJ has to decline jurisdiction. In the Court's view:

'The adaptations set out in Annex 1 to the Act of Accession are . . . the subject of an agreement between the Member States and the applicant State . . . They do not constitute an act of the Council but provisions of primary law which . . . may not be suspended, amended or repealed otherwise than by means of the procedure laid down for the revision of the original Treaties . . .

It follows . . .that the contested provisions, which form an integral part of the Act of Accession . . . do not constitute an act of the Council within the

---

13   COM(89) 568 Final.
14   COM(91) 511 Final.
15   To all intents and purposes, the position did not alter with the change of government in the United Kingdom in 1997. The new Labour government agreed to sign up to various directives that had been adopted in the meantime but did not commit the United Kingdom to the Social Charter.
16   TEU 2, ex B, first indent.
17   EC Art 2 (ex Art 2), as amended.
18   See especially, Philippa Watson, Social Policy after Maastricht, [1993] 30 CMLRev, 481-513.

meaning of Article 173 of the EEC Treaty [now EC Art 234] and that consequently the Court has no jurisdiction to consider the legality of such provisions.'[19]

It follows that the Protocol on Social Policy cannot be challenged and it can be amended only in accordance with TEU 48, ex N.

Since EC Article 311 (ex Art 239), provides that the Protocols form an integral part of the Treaty it can be assumed that the Agreement on Social Policy being part of the Protocol on Social Policy is also part of the Treaty. Thus the Treaty mechanism will apply to the implementation of the provisions of the Agreement subject to derogation from EC Article 205(2) (ex Art 148(2)) in view of the United Kingdom not being party to deliberations on instruments adopted by virtue of the Agreement.

Article 1 of the Agreement lists its objectives, ie the promotion of employment, improved living and working conditions, proper social protection, dialogue between management and labour, and development of human resources with a view to lasting high employment and the combating of exclusion of the handicapped from the labour market. The Community and the Member States shall implement measures in particular in the field of contractual relations and in the need of maintaining the competitiveness of the Community economy.

Article 2(1) is crucial mainly because it reflects the increased legislative powers of the 11 who are to adopt new directives in accordance with EC Article 252 (ex Art 189c) by qualified majority in respect of: improvement in particular of the working environment to protect workers' health and safety; working conditions; the information and consultation of workers; equality between men and women with regard to labour market opportunities and treatment at work; and the integration of persons excluded from the labour market (without prejudice to EC Article 150 (ex Art 127) which provides for the implementation of a vocational training policy).

However, according to Article 2(3) the principle of unanimity applies to directives concerning: social security and social protection of workers; protection of workers where their employment contract is terminated; representation and collective defence of the interests of workers and employers including co-determination subject to exceptions set out in paragraph 6 of Article 2; conditions of employment for third-country nationals legally residing in Community territory; and financial contributions for promotion of employment and job-creation, without prejudice to the provisions relating to the Social Fund.

According to Article 2(4) Member States may entrust management and labour, at their joint request, with the implementation of directives pursuant to paragraphs 2 and 3. However the provisions of this Article shall not apply to pay, the right of association, the right to strike or the right to impose lock-outs (para 6).

Article 3 entrusts the Commission with the task of promoting the consultation of management and labour at the Community level and thus enlarges the Commission's power in this respect.

Article 6 reiterates the principle of equal pay for male and female workers and enjoins the Member States to ensure that it is applied.

In brief the repetitious provisions of the TEU and the Protocol have done little to enhance the vague wording of the EC Treaty. Maastricht stands accused of failing to elaborate a coherent Community Social Policy. The credit for the enhancement of social rights goes to the Court of Justice.

---

19 Cases 31, 35/86: *Levantina Agricola Industrial SA v Council* [1988] ECR 2285, paras 12 and 18.

Chapter 33

The Policy for the Environment

A. Origins

The protection of the physical environment and the prevention of its further deterioration has become one of the major concerns of both the industrialized and non-industrialized countries. This concern has both national and international dimensions since most forms of injury to the environment (like, eg the Chernobyl disaster) do not respect any national frontiers. International nuisance sours relations between Member States[1] and leads to litigation.[2] Facing this problem the Community has reacted as initiator and executor of a common policy as well as an international body representing the Member States.

The Community's environment policy began with recognition at the Paris Summit in 1972 of the fact that economic expansion is not an end in itself but a means to obtaining an improvement in the quality of life.[3] Shortly afterwards, the Community adopted its First Action Programme for the Environment[4] in which combating pollution and nuisance and protecting the environment were bought into the Community's tasks of promoting harmonious development of economic activities and balanced expansion. However, no Treaty provision provided expressly for the adoption of legislation to protect the environment. The gap was filled by the general powers to legislate contained in EC Article 94 (ex Art 100) and EC Article 308 (ex Art 235)[5] until the adoption of the SEA, which inserted a new Title into the EC Treaty concerned with the environment. By then, the ECJ had proclaimed that environmental protection was one of the Community's essential objectives and that it could justify restrictions on the freedom of trade and competition.[6] Finally, the Amsterdam Treaty amended EC Article 2 so as

---

1   Eg the Franco-Dutch dispute over the discharge of sulphur into the Rhine, Europe, 6 December 1979, p 5.
2   Cf Case 21/76: *Handelskwekerij G J Bier BV and Stitchting Reinwater v Mines de Potasse d'Alsace* [1976] ECR 1735, [1977] 1 CMLR 284.
3   6th General Report, 1972, p 8.
4   OJ 1973, C 112/1.
5   See Case C-300/89: *Commission v Council* [1991] ECR I-2867.
6   Case 240/83: *Procureur de la République v ADBHU* [1985] ECR 531, paras 12-15. See also Case 302/86: *Commission v Denmark* [1988] ECR 4607.

to include the promotion of a high level of protection and improvement of the quality of the environment as one of the tasks of the Community.

B. The Treaty provisions

Under the EC Treaty in its current form, the Community's policy on the environment is intended to contribute to pursuit of the following objectives:

(1) preserving, protecting and improving the quality of the environment;
(2) protecting human health;
(3) prudent and rational utilization of natural resources;[7]
(4) promoting measures at international level to deal with regional or worldwide environmental problems.

The Community policy is to aim at a high level of protection (taking into account the diversity of situations in the various regions of the Community) and is based on four principles: the precautionary principle; the principle that preventative action should be taken; the principle that environmental damage should as a priority be rectified at source; and the principle that polluters should pay.[8]

The EC Treaty, as amended by the SEA, provided that the Community would take action relating to the environment 'to the extent to which the objectives [of such action] can be attained better at Community level than at the level of the individual Member States'.[9] With the emergence of environmental protection as a policy of the Community (as opposed to being a sphere in which the Community had recognized competence to act), that nod in the direction of subsidiarity has disappeared. However, EC Article 174(4) (ex Art 130r(4)), still refers to the Community and the Member States acting 'within their respective spheres of competence'. The competence of the Member States referred to expressly in EC Article 174(4) is that of negotiating in international bodies and concluding international agreements, in relation to which (and to co-operation with third countries and international organizations generally) the Community and the Member States must necessarily act together even though they retain separate competences. Nonetheless, the Treaty recognizes a wider competence on the part of the Member States: it expressly provides that protective measures adopted by the Community do not preclude Member States from maintaining or introducing more stringent measures (albeit that such measures must still be compatible with the Treaty).[10] The consequence is that, unlike other areas of EC law, the existence of a Community policy regarding the environment does not deprive the Member States of general competence to act.

The Community's environmental policy must take account of: available scientific and technical data; environmental conditions in the various regions of the Community; the potential benefits and costs of action or lack of action; the economic and social development of the Community as a whole and the balanced development of its regions.[11] The Council decides what action is to be taken in accordance with the procedure under EC Article 251 (ex Art 189b), after consulting

---

7   EC Art 174(1) (ex Art 130r(1)).
8   EC Art 174(2) (ex Art 130r(2)).
9   EC Art 130r(4), now Art 174.
10   EC Art 176 (ex Art 130t). Such measures must also be notified to the Commission.
11   EC Art 174(3) (ex Art 130r(3)).

the Economic and Social Committee and the Committee of the Regions.[12] However, in relation to the following measures, the Council is obliged to act unanimously on a proposal from the Commission and after consulting the Parliament, the Economic and Social Committee and the Committee of the Regions: provisions primarily of a fiscal nature; measures concerning town and country planning, land use with the exception of waste management and measures of a general nature, and management of water resources; measures significantly affecting a Member State's choice between different energy sources and the general structure of its energy supply.[13] In other areas, general action programmes setting out priority objectives and the measures designed to complement them are to be adopted by the Council.[14]

Although the basic principle is that the polluter should pay, the Member State's finance and implement the Community's environmental policy save where specific measures of a Community nature provide otherwise. In particular, where a measure adopted by the Community involves costs that are deemed to be disproportionate for the public authorities of a Member State, the Council shall lay down appropriate provisions in the form of a temporary derogation from the measure in question and/ or financial support.[15]

Although not obvious at first sight the Policy for the Environment, when transformed into mandatory rules, directly impinges upon manufacturing and business activities as it affects the standard of goods, the cost of production and services and the marketability and competitiveness of a product. Even when embarking on an ordinary transaction, eg taking a room in a hotel at the seaside, one would be wise to check whether the drinking and bathing water came up to the Community standard.

C. Community policy

Like all other Community policies the policy for the environment is primarily directed towards the completion of the internal market. Whilst, therefore, pursuing a general objective of the improvement of the quality of life, its main thrust is economic as it affects directly the manufacturing industry for which it lays down standards of operations and of the quality of the product.

The first programme (1973-1977) singled out the main objectives[16] to include:

(1) the protection of the aquatic environment by controlling pollution through discharge of certain dangerous substances into the environment and establishing a common procedure for the exchange of information on the quality of surface fresh water;
(2) measures to combat atmospheric pollution by controlling in particular:
    (a) air quality standards for lead;
    (b) air quality standards for sulphur dioxide; and
    (c) use of fuel oils;

---

12 EC Art 175(1) (ex Art 130s(1)).
13 EC Art 175(2) (ex Art 130s(2)). Decisions in relation to those matters may also be taken by a qualified majority if the Council so decides following the same procedure as that set out in the text. In addition, the Council can also act under EC Art 95 (ex Art 100a), where an appropriate solution lies in the approximation of national laws. For the meaning of the management of water resources, see Case C-36/98: *Spain v Council* (30 January 2001, unreported), paras 47-57.
14 EC Art 175(3) (ex Art 130s(3)).
15 EC Art 175(4)-(5) (ex Art 130s(4)-(5)).
16 OJ 1973, C 112/1.

(3) the control of noise pollution by laying down maximum permitted noise levels for different motor vehicles, construction equipment and domestic appliances;
(4) the control of chemicals in the environment; and
(5) the promotion of scientific research, information and various international environment-orientated agreements.

The principle that 'the polluter must pay for the damage caused' was to be the principal guideline.[17]

The second programme (1977-1983) was devoted to the implementation of the first programme[18] with a special emphasis on the protection of the marine environment following the pollution caused by the *Amoco Cadiz* disaster and other oil spills.[19] The emphasis also shifted to the improvement of the environment by requiring an assessment of the environmental impact of major industrial and infrastructure projects.

The third programme (1983-1987)[20] saw the implementation of the various international agreements enumerated below, transforming these into specific rules embodied in Community directives. These directives have carried into effect the promise to combat pollution of the aquatic environment as well as of the air by measures to control the discharge of harmful substances by industrial sectors. Noise abatement and the control of the movement of hazardous waste to non-Community countries also attracted a fair amount of legislation.

The fourth programme (1987-1992), to coincide with the completion of the internal market[1] reflected not only the general principles that the polluter must pay but also the consideration that the policy ought to be formulated on the basis of scientific and technical data and be related to the economic and social development of the Community as a whole. Thus the policy for the environment would no longer be pursued in isolation but rather in concert with the economic and social policies converging on the completion of the Common Market.

The fifth programme (1993-2000)[2] was designed to set out a new strategy for transforming patterns of growth within the Community in such a way as to reach a sustainable development path. It was prompted by the realization that, despite the measures taken over the previous two decades, there had been a slow but relentless deterioration in the general state of the environment in the Community. The approach then being taken and the then existing measures to protect the environment were not geared towards dealing with an expected growth in international competition and an upwards trend in Community activity and developments that would impose greater burdens on natural resources, the environment, and the quality of life. In addition, the Community's international responsibilities had been increased by global concerns about the environment, the persistence of problems of underdevelopment, and political and economic change in Central and Eastern Europe.

In 2001, the Commission proposed a sixth programme (2001-2010)[3] focusing on four priority areas: climatic change; nature and biodiversity; environment and health; and natural resources and waste. That programme is intended to continue

---

17 OJ 1975, C 92.
18 OJ 1977, C 139.
19 OJ 1978, C 162.
20 OJ 1983, C 46.
1   OJ 1987, C 328.
2   OJ 1993, C 138. See also Decision 2179/98 (OJ 1998, L275/1), in which the programme was reviewed.
3   COM 2001/31.

to pursue some of the targets left over from the fifth programme. It is also designed to achieve improvements in the four areas of primary concern by the following means: ensuring the implementation of existing environmental legislation; integrating environmental concerns into all relevant policy areas; working closely with business and consumers to identify solutions; ensuring better and more accessible information on the environment for citizens; and developing a more environmentally conscious attitude towards land use.

D. Implementation of the policy

The volume of legislation implementing the environmental programme is quite impressive. It comprises general measures such as Regulations 793/93 and 1488/94, which are concerned with evaluating and controlling the risks to human and the environment from existing substances[4] and Directive 90/313[5] on freedom of access to environmental information, to highly detailed measures concerning specific substances.[6] The elaboration of the legislation is a continuing process. It covers five broad areas: aquatic and air pollution, noise abatement, chemical pollution and the protection of the natural environment.

(1) AQUATIC POLLUTION

The principal directives are:

(1)   75/440[7] laying down standards and procedures for the quality of surface drinking water;
(2)   79/869[8] on methods of sampling and measuring of the quality of surface drinking water;
(3)   80/778[9] and 98/83[10] on the quality of water intended for human consumption;
(4)   76/160[11] on the quality of bathing water;
(5)   78/659[12] on the quality of water for the fishing industry;
(6)   79/923[13] on the quality of water for shellfish;
(7)   76/464[14] on discharge of dangerous substances into the aquatic environment;

---

4   OJ 1993, L84/1 and OJ 1994, L161/3. See also Dir 2000/60 (OJ 2000, L327/1) on water policy.
5   OJ 1990, L158/56; See Case C-217/97: *Commission v Germany* [1999] ECR I-5087.
6   Eg Decision 96/281 (OJ 1996, L107/10), on the placing on the market of genetically modified soya.
7   OJ 1975, L104, as amended.
8   OJ 1979, L271, as amended.
9   OJ 1980, L229/11, as amended. See Case C-42/89: *Commission v Belgium* [1990] ECR I-2821, [1992] 1 CMLR 22; Case C-340/96: *Commission v United Kingdom* [1999] ECR I-2023.
10 OJ 1998, L330/32.
11 OJ 1976, L31, as amended. See Case C-198/97: *Commission v Germany* [1999] ECR I-3257; Case C-307/98: *Commission v Belgium* (25 May 2000, unreported).
12 OJ 1978, L222, as amended.
13 OJ 1979, L377/48, as amended.
14 OJ 1976, L129/23, as amended. See Case C-168/95: *Arcaro* [1996] ECR I-4705; C-214/96: *Commission v Spain* [1998] ECR I-7661; Case C-207/97: *Commission v Belgium* [1999] ECR I-275; Case C-184/97: *Commission v Germany* [1999] ECR I-7837; Case C-231/97: *van Rooij v Dagelijk bestuur van het Waterschap de Dommel* [1999] ECR I-6355; Case C-232/97: *Nederhoff & Zn v Dijkgraaf en Hoogheemraden* [1999] ECR I-6385; Case C-384/97: *Commission v Greece* (25 May 2000, unreported).

(8)   77/795[15] establishing a common procedure for the exchange of information on the quality of surface fresh water;

(9)   80/68[16] against pollution of groundwater by dangerous substances;

(10)   91/271[17] on urban waste-water treatment;

(11)   91/676[18] on the protection of waters against pollution caused by nitrates from agricultural sources;

(12)   93/75[19] on minimum requirements for vessels carrying dangerous or polluted goods;

(13)   various directives setting limit values and quality objectives for certain discharges.[20]

(2) AIR POLLUTION

To reduce air pollution the following directives have been issued:

(1)   84/360[1] to control pollution from industrial plants;

(2)   92/72[2] on air pollution by ozone;

(3)   75/324[3] on the approximation of the laws on aerosol dispensers;

(4)   75/716[4] amended by 87/219[5] on the sulphur content of gas oils;

(5)   85/210,[6] on the lead content of petrol;

(6)   72/306[7] on emission of pollutants from diesel engines and 97/68[8] concerning emissions from engines in non-road mobile machinery;

(7)   87/217[9] on pollution by asbestos;

(8)   70/220,[10] 77/102,[11] 77/537,[12] 88/77[13] on emission of gaseous pollutants from various types of vehicles;[14]

(9)   88/609[15] on emission of certain pollutants from large combustion plants;

(10)   96/62[16] on ambient air quality assessment and management;

---

15   OJ 1977, L334/29, as amended.
16   OJ 1980, L20, as amended.
17   OJ 1991, L135/40, as amended.
18   OJ 1991, L375/1. See Case C-293/97: *R v Secretary of State for the Environment, ex p Standley* [1999] ECR I-2603; Case C-69/99: *Commission v United Kingdom* (7 December 2000, unreported).
19   OJ 1993, L247/19, as amended.
20   82/176 (OJ 1982, L81/29), as amended (mercury); 83/513 (OJ 1983, L291), as amended (cadmium); 84/491 (OJ 1984, L274/11), as amended (hexachlorocyclohexane); 86/280 (OJ 1986, L181/16), as amended (various).
1   OJ 1984, L188, as amended.
2   OJ 1992, L297/1.
3   OJ 1975, L147/40.
4   OJ 1975, L307.
5   OJ 1987, L91.
6   OJ 1985, L96, as amended.
7   OJ 1972, L190/1, as amended.
8   OJ 1998, L59/1.
9   OJ 1987, L85/40; OJ 1990, L59; OJ 1991, L48.
10   OJ 1970, L76/1, as amended.
11   OJ 1977, L32/32.
12   OJ 1977, L220/38, as amended.
13   OJ 1988, L36/33, as amended.
14   Other similar measures have been adopted in context of the approximation of national laws relating to type approval: see, for example, Dir 74/150 (OJ 1974, L84/10), as amended (in particular by Dir 2000/25 (OJ 2000, L173/1)).
15   OJ 1988, L336/1, as amended.
16   OJ 1996, L296/55.

(11) 89/369 and 89/429[17] to prevent air pollution from municipal incineration plants; and
(12) various directives setting limit values and air quality standards for certain pollutants.[18]

The Community has also acted by way of regulation: see, for example, Regulation 3528/86 on the protection of the Community's forests against atmospheric pollution;[19] Regulation 3093/94 on substances that deplete the ozone layer.[20]

(3) NOISE ABATEMENT

Noise abatement has attracted the following directives:

(1) 78/1015[1] amended by Directives 87/56[2] and 89/235[3] laying down the permissible sound level and exhaust systems for motorcycles;
(2) 70/157[4] on the permissible sound level and exhaust systems for motor vehicles;
(3) 79/113[5] on the noise emission of construction plant and equipment;
(4) 80/51[6] and 89/629[7] on the limitation of noise emission by subsonic aircraft based on the International Convention on Civil Aviation;
(5) various directives concerning the permitted levels of noise emissions from different types of equipment;[8]
(6) 86/188[9] on the protection of workers from noise at work.

(4) CHEMICAL AND INDUSTRIAL POLLUTION AND BIOTECHNOLOGY

National laws on the classification, packaging and labelling of dangerous substances have been approximated by Directive 67/548.[10] Directive 93/67[11] lays down the principles for assessing the risks to man and the environment presented by such substances. Directive 96/82[12] deals with the control of major

---

17 OJ 1989, L163/32 and 203/50.
18 80/779 (OJ 1980, L229/30), as amended (sulphur dioxide); 82/884 (OJ 1982, L378/15), as amended (lead); 85/203 (OJ 1985, L87/1), as amended (nitrogen dioxide); 93/76 (OJ 1993, L237/28) (carbon dioxide); 1999/13 (OJ 1999, L85/1) (volatile organic compounds); 1999/30 (OJ 1999, L163/41) (various).
19 OJ 1986, L326/2, as amended.
20 OJ 1994, L333/1; see also Reg 2037/2000 (OJ 2000, L244/1).
1 OJ 1978, L349/21.
2 OJ 1987, L24/42.
3 OJ 1989, L98/1.
4 OJ 1970, L42/16, as amended.
5 OJ 1989, L33/15, as amended.
6 OJ 1980, L18/26, as amended.
7 OJ 1989, L363/27.
8 84/533 (OJ 1984, L300/123), as amended (compressors); 84/534 (OJ 1984, L300/130), as amended (tower cranes); 84/535 (OJ 1984, L300/142), as amended (welding generators); 84/536 (OJ 1984, L300/149), as amended (power generators); 84/537 (OJ 1984, L300/156), as amended (concrete breakers and picks); 84/538 (OJ 1984, L300/171), as amended (lawn-mowers); 86/594 (OJ 1986, L344/24) (household appliances); 86/662 (OJ 1986, L384/1), as amended (excavators and the like); 2000/14 (OJ 2000, L162/1) (equipment for use outdoors).
9 OJ 1986, L137.
10 OJ 1967, L196, as amended.
11 OJ 1993, L227/9.
12 OJ 1996, L10/13.

accident hazards. National laws restricting the marketing and use of certain dangerous substances and preparations are also the subject of approximizing measures.[13] Directives 88/320[14] and 89/569[15] provide guidelines for good laboratory practice. In relation to biotechnology, the following directives have been adopted: 90/219 on the contained use of genetically modified micro-organisms;[16] 90/220 on the deliberate release of genetically modified organisms into the environment.[17]

(5) WASTE MANAGEMENT

The Community legislation distinguishes between ordinary waste management and management of dangerous and hazardous waste. The former comprises Directives:

(1) 75/439[18] on the disposal of waste oils;
(2) 86/278[19] on the use of sewage sludge in agriculture;
(3) 94/62[20] on packaging waste;
(4) 1999/31[1] on landfill of waste.

Dangerous waste is managed according to the following:

(1) Regulation 259/93[2] on the supervision and control within the Community of the trans-frontier shipment of hazardous waste;
(2) Directive 75/442[3] providing for the development of clean technologies and recycling or re-use of waste as secondary raw material or a source of energy;
(3) Directive 91/689[4] on hazardous waste;
(4) Directive 91/157[5] which deals with the disposal of batteries and accumulators containing dangerous substances;
(5) Directive 78/176[6] on waste from the titanium dioxide industry;
(6) Directive 94/67[7] on incineration of hazardous waste; and
(7) Directive 96/59[8] on the disposal of polychlorinated biphenyls and polychlorinated terphenyls.

13   Dir 76/769 (OJ 1976, L262/201), as amended. See Case C-127/97: *Burstein v Freistadt Bayern* [1998] ECR I-6005.
14   OJ 1988, L145/35, as amended.
15   OJ 1989, L315/1.
16   OJ 1990, L117/1, as amended.
17   OJ 1990, L117/15, as amended. See Case C-6/99: *Association Greenpeace France and others v Ministère de l'Agriculture et de le Pêche* (21 March 2000, unreported).
18   OJ 1975, L194/23, as amended. See Case C-102/97: *Commission v Germany* [1999] ECR I-5051.
19   OJ 1986, L181/6, as amended.
20   OJ 1994, L365/10.
 1   OJ 1999, L182/1.
 2   OJ 1993, L30/1, as amended.
 3   OJ 1975, L194/39, as amended. See Cases C-175/98 and C-177/98: *Lirusi and Bizzaro* [1999] ECR I-6881; Case C-365/97: *Commission v Italy* [1999] ECR I-7773; Case C-387/97: *Commission v Greece* (4 July 2000, unreported) (pecuniary sanctions for failure to comply).
 4   OJ 1991, L377/20, as amended. See Case C-318/98: *Fornasar* (22 June 2000, unreported).
 5   OJ 1991, L78/38, as amended. See Case C-347/97: *Commission v Belgium* [1999] ECR I-309.
 6   OJ 1978, L54/19, as amended.
 7   OJ 1994, L365/34. See also Dir 2000/76 (OJ 2000, L332/91).
 8   OJ 1996, L243/31.

(6) PROTECTION OF ANIMALS AND WILDLIFE

Animals used for experimental purposes are subject to a modicum of protection by Council Directive 86/609,[9] Council Resolutions of 24 November 1986[10] and Commission Decision 90/67.[11]

Regulation 3254/91[12] prohibits the use of leghold traps in the Community and the import into the Community of pelts and manufactured goods derived from certain wild animal species originating in countries where such animals are caught by means of methods which do not meet humane trapping standards.

The Community[13] also prohibits the importation for commercial purposes of skins of certain seal pups and products derived therefrom.

Regulation 348/81[14] prohibits importation of whales, whale products or other cetacean products.

Wildlife is further protected by:

(1) Directive 79/409 on the Protection of Wild Birds;[15]
(2) Convention on the Conservation of Migratory Species of Wild Animals;[16]
(3) Convention on the Conservation of the European Wildlife and Natural Habitats;[17]
(4) Regulation 338/97[18] on the protection of species of wild fauna and flora by regulating trade in them;
(5) Directive 1999/22[19] on keeping wild animals in zoos;
(6) Regulation 1968/1999[20] suspending the introduction into the Community of specimens of certain species of wild fauna and flora.

These measures affect hunting, farming and the use of land generally.

(7) PROTECTION OF NATURAL ENVIRONMENT

Regulations 3528/86[1] and 2158/92[2] are designed to protect forests from atmospheric pollution (acid rains) and fires.

Agriculture is the chief polluter of land and inland waters. The success story of the CAP has been tarnished by the violation of the natural environment. To

---

9   OJ 1986, L358/1.
10   OJ 1986, C 331/1 and C 331/2.
11   OJ 1990, L44/30.
12   OJ 1991, L308/1. The prohibition on importation was brought into effect by Regulation 1771/94, OJ 1994, L184/3.
13   Dir 83/129, OJ 1983, L91/30, as amended. See also Council Resolution of 5 January 1983 (OJ 1983, C 14/1).
14   OJ 1981, L39/1, as amended.
15   OJ 1979, L103/1, as amended. Case C-339/87: *Commission v Netherlands* [1990] ECR I-851, [1993] 2 CMLR 360; Case C-44/95: *R v Secretary of State, ex p RSPB* [1996] ECR I-3805; Case C-166/97: *Commission v France* [1999] ECR I-1719; Case C-96/98: *Commission v France* [1999] ECR I-8531.
16   OJ 1982, L210/11, implemented by Decision 32/461 (OJ 1982, L210/10).
17   OJ 1982, L38/1; Dir 92/43, OJ 1992, L206/7, as amended. See Case C-256/98: *Commission v France* (6 April 2000, unreported); Case C-371/98: *R v Secretary of State for the Environment, Transport and the Regions, ex p First Corporate Shipping Ltd* [2001] All ER (EC) 177.
18   OJ 1997, L61/1. Reg 338/97 implements in the Community the Washington Convention on International Trade in Endangered Species of Wild Fauna and Flora (OJ 1982, L384/1).
19   OJ 1999, L94/24.
20   OJ 1999, L244/22.
1   OJ 1986, L326/2, as amended.
2   OJ 1992, L217/3, as amended.

increase production farmers have been encouraged to disfigure the land by extending the arable surface, destroying the natural habitat of certain species of animal, bird and insect life; burning of stubble and profligate use of chemicals and fertilizers. As rain washes the land the chemicals are diverted to streams and inland water, destroying aquatic life.

Relevant to the use of land, Directive 85/337[3] provides a set of guidelines for national planning authorities which ought to assess the effects of certain public and private projects upon the environment as forming part of the procedure for planning permissions. 'Environmental assessment' is a technique and process by which information about the environmental effects of a major industrial or infrastructure project is collected both by the developer and from other sources and which is taken into account when considering a planning application. The directive is addressed to the national planning authorities but, as held by the Irish High Court,[4] has no direct effect upon private parties. It is nevertheless relevant to individual applications involved in the planning of industrial and infrastructure projects of a certain significance.

E. External dimension

In its international capacity the Community has joined or concluded in its own right or concurrently with the Member States a number of international Conventions on the environment, ie:

(1) The Helsinki Convention on the Protection of Marine Environment in the Baltic Sea Area;[5]
(2) the Berne Convention on Wild Life and Natural Habitat;[6]
(3) the Bonn Convention on the Conservation of Migratory Species of Wild Animals;[7]
(4) the Convention on Long-range Transboundary Air Pollution;[8]
(5) the Convention for the Conservation of Salmon in the North Sea;[9]
(6) the Bonn Agreement for co-operation in dealing with pollution of the North Sea;[10]
(7) the International Convention for the Conservation of Atlantic tunas;[11]
(8) the Berne Convention for the Protection of the River Rhine against Chemical Pollution;[12]

---

3 OJ 1985, L175/40, as amended. See *Twyford Parish Council v Secretary of State for the Environment* (temporal application) [1992] 1 CMLR 276, QB; Case C-72/95: *Aannemersbedrijf P K Kraaijveld v Gedeputeerde Staten van Zuid-Holland* [1996] ECR I-5403; Case C-301/95: *Commission v Germany* [1998] ECR I-6135; Case C-150/97: *Commission v Portugal* [1999] ECR I-259; Case C-435/97: *World Wildlife Fund v Autonome Provinz Bozen* [1999] ECR I-5613; Case C-392/96: *Commission v Ireland* [1999] ECR I-5901; Case C-287/98: *Luxembourg v Linster* (19 September 2000, unreported).
4 *Brown v An Bord Pleanala* [1990] 1 CMLR 3.1983, L237/9.
5 OJ 1983, L237/9; revised in 1992 (OJ 1994, L73/2); Decision 94/156 (OJ 1994, L73/1).
6 OJ 1982, L38/1.
7 OJ 1982, L210/11.
8 OJ 1986, L181/1.
9 OJ 1982, L378/25; Decision 82/886 (OJ 1982, L378/24).
10 OJ 1984, L188/9; Decision 84/358 (OJ 1984, L188/7), as amended.
11 OJ 1986, L162/34; Decision 86/238 (OJ 1986, L162/33).
12 Council Decision 77/586 (OJ 1977, L240, as supplemented OJ 1985, L240). See also Decision 2000/706 (OJ 2000, L289/30).

(9) the Barcelona Convention for the Protection of the Mediterranean Sea against Pollution;[13]

(10) the Paris Convention for the Prevention of Marine Pollution from Land-based sources;[14]

(11) the Washington Convention on International Trade in Endangered Species of Fauna and Flora;[15]

(12) the Vienna Convention for the Protection of the Ozone Layer;[16]

(13) the Montreal Protocol on Substances that Deplete the Ozone Layer;[17]

(14) the Convention on the Conservation of Antarctic Marine Living Resources (1980);[18] and

(15) the Convention on co-operation for the protection and sustainable use of the Danube.[19]

As part of its aid to Third World countries, both to prevent the export of pollution and other environmental problems, the Community supports operations to promote the conservation and sustainable management of tropical forests.[20]

The obligations arising from international Conventions are binding both upon the Community institutions and the Member States. The latter are locked in a double obligation: that to the co-signatories of the Conventions and that to the Community itself which can be enforced by the Commission in accordance with the Community enforcement procedure. Community treaties form an integral part of the Community system and as such are equivalent to acts of Community institutions. However the individual is not affected directly unless these international obligations are either directly applicable or implemented by means of Community legislation. These measures strengthen the machinery of compliance and enforcement and bind both the state and the individual. Thus, for example, the Council of Ministers adopted, on the basis of the Convention for the Protection of the Ozone Layer, a Regulation on certain chlorofluoro-carbons (CFCs) and halons that deplete the ozone layer.[1] Thereupon the Commission began a programme of legislation to control the production, sale and import into the Community the CFCs and halons and to reduce these substances in aerosols, solvents, foam plastics and refrigeration equipment.

F. Enforcement of the policy

(1) LEGALITY OF THE MEASURES

To be enforceable a measure must itself be valid according to Community law. Thus the ECJ annulled Directive 89/424 on the pollution caused by waste from the titanium dioxide manufacturing process because it was enacted, despite the European Parliament's objections, on the basis of EC Article 175 (ex Art 130s)

---

13 Council Decision 77/585 (OJ 1977, L240).
14 OJ 1985, L194.
15 Supra note 3.
16 OJ 1988, L297/10.
17 OJ 1988, L297/21.
18 OJ 1981, L252/27.
19 OJ 1997, L342/19; Decision 97/825 (OJ 1997, L342/18); Case C-36/98: *Spain v Council* (30 January 2001, unreported).
20 Regulation 3062/95 (OJ 1995, L327/9).
 1 OJ 1988, L1297; OJ 1988, C 285.

instead of EC Article 95 (ex Art 100a).[2] The Court ruled that, while EC Article 95 (ex Art 100a) requires the observance of the co-operation procedure governed by EC Article 149(2) (now repealed), EC Article 175 (ex Art 130S) requires the Council to act unanimously after merely consulting the EP. Citing its own judgments[3] the Court concluded that, bearing in mind the effect of competition in the relevant industrial sector, harmonization on the basis of EC Article 95 (ex Art 100a) is appropriate to the attainment of the internal market.[4]

Later[5] the Court changed its mind, ruling that the Directive on Waste 91/156[6] was valid and well founded on EC Article 175 (ex Art 130S) and dismissing the Commission's contention that it should have been based on EC Article 95 (ex Art 100a) and was, therefore, invalid. The two protagonists, Commission and Council, relied on the theory of the 'principal and the accessory' (ie the contents and effects of the measure in question) and the 'centre of gravity' (ie the subjective analysis of the measure), respectively, the EP (intervening) trailing behind the Commission. The Court favoured the Council's arguments as it concluded that Directive 91/156 was primarily concerned with the protection of the environment and human health and left the Member States a substantial degree of discretion in its implementation. It was not concerned with the harmonization of the conditions of competition or movement of goods. The Court ruled:

'. . . according to its aim and content, the directive at issue has the object of ensuring the management of waste, whether it is of industrial or domestic origin, in accordance with the requirements of environmental protection.'[7]

One can doubt the practical value of the institutional controversy in this respect especially as the energy expended in the exercise only adds to the uncertainty of the law. The two Articles, it seems, furnish an interchangeable authority depending on the primary object of the measure, ie whether the protection of the environment (EC Article 175 (ex Art 130S)) or harmonization of national laws relevant to the environment (EC Article 95 (ex Art 100a)).

(2) MEMBER STATES' DUTIES

Member States do endeavour to comply but occasionally they fail because of an untimely[8] implementation or inadequate transposition or failure to meet the technical standards laid down in the measures in question and, consequently, have to face an enforcement action under EC Article 226 (ex Art 169).

Considering the task of transposition the ECJ felt that:

'. . . the transposition of a directive into domestic law does not necessarily require that its provisions be incorporated formally and verbatim in express, specific legislation; a general legal context may, depending on the content of

---

2 Case C-300/89: *Commission v Council* [1991] ECR I-2867, [1993] 3 CMLR 359.
3 Cases 91/79 and 92/79: *Commission v Italy* [1980] ECR 1099, [1980] ECR 1115, [1981] 1 CMLR 331; Case 62/88: *Greece v Council* [1990] ECR I-1527.
4 Case C-300/89, supra.
5 Case C-155/91: *Commission v Council* [1993] ECR I-939.
6 OJ 1991, L78/32.
7 Case C-155/91, supra at para 10. Compare the analogous dispute in Cases C-164/97 and C-165/97: *Parliament v Council* [1999] ECR I-1139, in which the Parliament was successful.
8 Eg Cases 97/81: *Commission v Netherlands* [1982] ECR 1819; 73/81: *Commission v Belgium* [1982] ECR 189; 30-34/81: *Commission v Italy* [1981] ECR 3379, re Dir 75/440; Cases 30-34/81: *Commission v Italy* [1981] ECR 3379 and 227-230/85: *Commission v Belgium* [1988] ECR 1, [1989] 2 CMLR 797, re Dir 75/442; etc.

the directive, be adequate for the purpose provided that it does indeed guarantee the full application of the directive in a sufficiently clear and precise manner so that, where the directive is intended to create rights for individuals, the persons concerned can ascertain the full extent of their rights and, where appropriate, rely on them before the national courts.'[9]

In form transposition into national rules must embody binding provisions and not merely advisory circulars. It follows that 'mere administrative practices, which by their nature may be changed according to the whim of the authorities and which lack appropriate publicity cannot be regarded as constituting a valid implementation of the duties imposed on Member States'.[10] It must meet the requirements of legal certainty.[11]

It is not sufficient for a Member State to allege that a Directive is so vague as to be incapable of generating precise and specific rules and, therefore, content itself with a statement of a number of fairly general rules, ie provisions which do not relate specifically to its object, *in casu*, the protection of ground water. No vagueness could be read into the Directive in question which provided for two kinds of substances, each listed in the Annex. As regards substances in list I, the Member States were required to take steps to prevent their introduction into ground water and to limit the introduction into ground water of the substances in list II. Clearly transposition was inadequate where national measures failed to reflect the text of the Directive.[12]

Directives are like commands issued to the Member States which have to be faithfully passed into substance down the line; only the method of executing the message is left to the Member States. To carry out their duties they must not only institute machinery for the collection of the necessary information, the monitoring of developments and the enforcement of the measures comprised in the directives but also adjust their substantive law as appropriate. In that respect they act as agents of the Community policy and are responsible to the Community for their acts and omissions. They owe a duty to their fellow Members not only because they have to act in solidarity but also because they partake of the common Community heritage.[13]

The Member State has at its disposal administrative and repressive measures which it applies according to its own procedures. Indeed, its authorities are liable to determine whether in any particular situation the conditions of any particular directive are met. Whilst the Community institutions supervise the Member State *qua* states as far as implementation is concerned the state authorities administer the system. Thus, for example, Directive 78/659 could not directly (ie without implementation) impose criminal sanctions on individuals prosecuted for causing river pollution detrimental to fish life.[14]

However the national authorities are in charge of the execution of a directive and their choice of agents or operators (eg in the case of waste disposal) is not

---

9   Case 363/85: *Commission v Italy* [1987] ECR 1733, at para 7; Case C-14/90: *Commission v France*, re Dir 85/203, [1991] ECR I-4331; See also Case C-13/90: *Commission v France*, re Dir 82/884, [1991] ECR I-4327; Cases 131/88: *Commission v Germany* [1991] ECR I-825; Cases C-361/88 and C-59/89: *Commission v Germany* [1991] ECR I-2567 and I-2607, at para 18 resp.

10 Case 160/82: *Commission v Netherlands* [1982] ECR 4637, [1984] 1 CMLR 230, para 4; see also Case 291/84: *Commission v Netherlands*, re Ground water Dir 80/68 [1987] ECR 3483, [1989] 1 CMLR 479; Case 208/85: *Commission v Germany* [1987] ECR 4045.

11 Case 239/85: *Commission v Belgium*, re Dir 79/315 on Toxic and Dangerous Waste [1986] ECR 3645, [1988] 1 CMLR 248.

12 Case C-360/87: *Commission v Italy* [1991] ECR I-791. Case C-131/88: *Commission v Germany* [1991] ECR I-825.

13 Case 247/85: *Commission v Belgium* [1987] ECR 3029.

14 Case 14/86: *Pretore di Salò v Persons Unknown* [1987] ECR 2545, [1989] 1 CMLR 71.

restricted by Community rules as long as the objectives of the given directive are complied with,[15] and as long as the freedom of provision of services is not infringed. The procedure for the granting of permits for operators may not be adequate to satisfy the requirements of implementation.[16]

The positive response to a directive requires that 'in order to secure the full implementation of directives in law and not only in fact, Member States must establish a specific legal framework in the area in question',[17] or a plan of action especially so required by a particular directive[18] and binding provisions ensuring complete implementation of the directive.[19]

Where a directive contains definitions a Member State is not at liberty to re-draft these since such changes in the text would tamper with the substance of the directive.[20] Similarly, where a directive contains a prohibition such a prohibition must be expressly laid down in the implementing national legislation.[1]

The failure in implementing in substance can be summarized simply in that the Member State in question has failed to furnish the requisite information or has not met the technical standards laid down in the directives. For example, condemning the United Kingdom for breach of Directive 80/778 on water for human consumption the ECJ found a failure in the notification and implementation.[2] So was the judgment concerning the standard of bathing water[3] where the ECJ warned that the state was not free to imply approval of its action because of initial inaction on the part of the Commission.

Directive 80/778 allowed Member States to permit higher concentrations of controlled chemicals but must be interpreted strictly[4] whilst the conditions laid down in various other measures must be generally complied with. For example the ground water Directive 80/68;[5] Directives 75/440 and 79/869 on the quality of surface water for the abstraction of drinking water and on the measurement and frequencies of sampling and analysis of surface water, respectively;[6] Directive 80/779 fixing air quality limit values applicable to the concentration of sulphur dioxide;[7] Directive 82/88 on the limit value for lead in the air;[8] Directive 85/203 on air quality standards for nitrogen dioxide.[9]

---

15 Cases 372-374/85: *Ministère Public v Traen* [1987] ECR 2141, [1988] 3 CMLR 511.
16 See Case 291/84: *Commission v Netherlands, re Ground water Directive* [1987] ECR 3483, [1989] 1 CMLR 479; Case 1/86: *Commission v Belgium* [1987] ECR 2797, [1989] 1 CMLR 474.
17 Case C-339/87: *Commission v Netherlands* [1990] ECR I-851, at para 25; [1993] 2 CMLR 360.
18 Case C-33/90: *Commission v Italy, re Directive 75/442 on Waste and 78/319 on Toxic and Dangerous Waste* [1991] ECR I-5987, para 25.
19 Case C-337/89: *Commission v United Kingdom, re Directive 80/778* [1992] ECR I-6103.
20 See Case 359/88: *Zanetti v Ministère Public of Italy, re Directive 85/339* [1990] ECR I-1509; see also case 380/87: *Enichem Base v Commune di Cinisello Balsamo, re Directive 75/442; 76/403 and 78/319* [1989] ECR 2491, [1991] 1 CMLR 313.
1 Case 252/85: *Commission v France* [1988] ECR 2243, at paras 18 and 19; Case 339/87: *Commission v Netherlands* [1990] ECR I-851 at paras 35 and 36.
2 Case C-337/89: *Commission v United Kingdom* [1992] ECR I-6103.
3 Case C-56/90: *Commission v United Kingdom* [1993] ECR I-4109.
4 Case 228/87: *Pretura Unificata di Torino v Persons Unknown* [1988] ECR 5099, [1990] 1 CMLR 71.
5 Case 291/84: supra; Case 1/86: supra; Case C-131/88: supra.
6 Case 96/81: *Commission v Netherlands* [1982] ECR 1791; Cases 30-34/81: *Commission v Italy* [1981] ECR 3379; Case C-58/89: *Commission v Germany* [1991] ECR I-4983; Case C-290/89: *Commission v Belgium* [1991] ECR I-2851.
7 Case C-64/90: *Commission v France* [1991] ECR I-4335.
8 Case C-59/89: *Commission v Germany* [1991] ECR I-2607; Case C-13/90: *Commission v France* [1991] ECR I-4327.
9 Case C-14/90: *Commission v France* [1991] ECR I-4331.

In cases C-361/88 and C-59/89[10] the ECJ condemned a feeble implementation of Directive 80/779 and 82/884 on air pollution by sulphur dioxide and lead, respectively. Whilst the German legislation was limited in scope it was deficient in measuring techniques and effective sanctions and applied to 'exposed zones' rather than the entire territory of the state; it failed to respond to the universality of the directive.

Directives on waste have proved to be particularly troublesome in their application[11] and, as we shall see below, have penetrated other areas of Community law.

Conservation problems and the protection of wildlife have caused some difficulties especially as Member States claimed derogations to accommodate the use of land and hunting interests. The Court found deficiencies in transposition of Directive 79/409[12] and in one case[13] held that by authorizing the destruction of nests and eggs coupled with the disturbance of wild birds in the course of the normal use of land for agricultural, forestry and fishing activities the state failed to justify the derogation under the directive. Similarly prohibition on hunting was held to be insufficiently enforced under national rules.[14] However the Commission failed to establish that the construction work carried out under a coastal protection project had contravened Article 4(4) of the Directive 79/409 on the conservation of wild birds[15] as it allegedly disturbed the habitat of birds in a specially protected area. Commenting on the power of the Member States to tamper with protected areas the Court said:

'... the power of the Member States to reduce the extent of a special area can be justified only on exceptional grounds. Those grounds must correspond to a general interest which is superior to the general interest represented by the ecological objective of the directive. In that context the interests referred to in Article 2 of the directive, namely economic and recreational requirements, do not enter into consideration.'[16]

(3) HORIZONTAL APPLICATION

It is common ground that directives concerned with the protection of the environment have a vertical application or effect only. Individuals are protected from national sanctions where national rules have been superseded by a directive which, but for untimely or incorrect implementation, would have been given effect.[17]

Where a directive has been duly implemented, provisions of national law apply[18] and the litigant is not free to disregard the latter and rely instead on the

---

10 *Commission v Germany* [1991] ECR I-2567 and 2607, [1993] 2 CMLR 821.
11 See eg Case C-33/90: *Commission v Italy, re Disposal of Toxic and Dangerous Waste* [1991] ECR I-5987 and Case C-2/90: *Commission v Belgium* [1992] ECR I-4431, [1993] 1 CMLR 365.
12 Case 252/85: *Commission v France* [1988] ECR 2243; Case 236/85: *Commission v Netherlands* [1987] ECR 3989; Case 247/85: *Commission v Belgium* [1987] ECR 3029; Case 262/85: *Commission v Italy* [1987] ECR 3073.
13 Case 412/85: *Commission v Germany* [1987] ECR 3503.
14 Case C-339/87: *Commission v Netherlands, re Protection of Wild Birds* [1990] ECR I-851, [1993] 2 CMLR 360.
15 Case C-57/89: *Commission v Germany* [1991] ECR I-883.
16 Case C-57/89: at paras 21 and 22.
17 Case 148/78: *Pubblico Ministero v Ratti* [1979] ECR 1629, [1980] 1 CMLR 96; but see Case C-106/89: *Marleasing SA v La Commercial Internacional de Alimentación SA* [1990] ECR I-4135, [1992] 1 CMLR 305.
18 Case 270/81: *Felicitas Rickmers-Linie KG & Co v Finanzamt für Verkehrsteuern, Hamburg* [1982] ECR 2771, [1982] 3 CMLR 447.

provisions of the directive. Consequently, as in the case of 'new torts or wrongs' grafted on the fabric of the national systems by the Community competition law,[19] new nuisances' have been added to the existing ones by the environmental directives. Moreover, the principle 'the polluter pays' can now be regarded as a general rule of law embodied in environmental protection to form part of the enforcement process under national law.

The ECJ has intimated that individual rights may have been contemplated by the environmental directives. Thus,

'Directive 80/779 itself, moreover, provides an indication that its provisions are necessarily of such a nature as to affect the rights and obligations of individuals.'[20]

Again, referring to the same directive:

'. . . It implies, therefore, that whenever the exceeding of the limit values could endanger human health, the persons concerned must be in a position to rely on mandatory rules in order to be able to assert their rights. Furthermore, the fixing of limit values in a provision whose binding nature is undeniable is also necessary in order that all those whose activities are liable to give rise to nuisance may ascertain precisely the obligations to which they are subject.'[1]

However, where a directive merely sets out a programme to be followed, it does not confer on individuals rights that national courts must safeguard.[2]

(4) INTERACTION WITH OTHER POLICIES

The process of legal integration leads to interaction between the policy for the environment with the established Community policies;[3] notably free movement of goods and competition.

Environmental protection was considered by the Court of Justice to constitute an 'essential Community objective'[4] and required expressly as a 'mandatory requirement' capable of justifying national measures derogating from the principle of the free movement of goods.[5]

In Case 302/86, Danish legislation, which provided for marketing of beer and soft drinks only in returnable containers approved by the national Agency for the Protection of the Environment, was challenged by the Commission on the ground that it restricted freedom of movement of goods. The ECJ conceded that national measures could justify a restriction on trade (thus effectively extending the scope of the derogations under EC Article 30 (ex Art 36)) but ruled that the requirement that the containers be of an approved type was not necessary to achieve the objective of these measures.[6]

---

19 See *Applications des Gaz v Falks Veritas Ltd* [1974] 2 CMLR 75.
20 Case C-361/88: supra Opinion of AG Mischo at para 21.
1 Case C-64/90: supra Opinion of the AG Lenz at para 2.
2 Case C-236/92: *Comitato di Coordinamento per la Difesa della Cava v Regione Lombardia* [1994] ECR I-483.
3 Case C-62/88: *Greece v Council* [1990] ECR I-1527 at 1550.
4 Case 240/83: *Procureur de la République v Association de Défence de Brûleurs d'Huiles Usagées* [1985] ECR 531 at 549.
5 Case 302/86: *Commission v Denmark* [1988] ECR 4607, [1989] 1 CMLR 619; Case C-2/90 supra; Case C-155/91: *Commission v Council* [1993] ECR I-939.
6 Supra. See also Case C-288/89: *Stichting Collective Antennevoorziening v Commissariaat voor de Media* [1991] ECR I-4007.

Several cases relating to waste oil reflect an interaction between environmental policy and trade. In Case 240/83[7] the ECJ held that the measures provided by Directive 75/439 on the disposal of waste oils did not create restrictions on intra-Community trade. However where such measures may have a restrictive impact on the freedom of trade and of competition they must be neither discriminatory nor extend beyond the inevitable restrictions justified by the pursuit of the objective of environmental protection. In Case 172/82[8] the Court held that, where national law prevented export of waste oil to an authorized disposal or regenerating undertaking in another Member State, it infringed EC Article 29 (ex Art 34). In Case 173/83[9] the CJ held that, where national legislation casts doubt as to whether or not it contains a prohibition on exports, it must be construed as having a restrictive effect and, therefore, it constitutes, in fact, an obstacle to trade. Indeed the Court warned elsewhere[10] that Community regulations must not be interpreted so as to authorize national measures infringing the Treaty provisions on the movement of goods.

In the background of Case C-2/90[11] was a decree of the Walloon Regional Executive prohibiting (subject to certain exceptions) the storage, tipping and dumping of 'foreign waste' in depots in Wallonia. Storage, tipping and dumping of waste from any other Belgian region was similarly prohibited. 'Foreign waste' or waste from another region was defined as waste which is not produced in Wallonia. Since the decree did allow for derogations from the law on treating Belgian (but not foreign) waste only in case of emergency the effect of the decree was a global ban on the importation of all waste products into Wallonia. The Commission sought a declaration that by adopting the above-mentioned decree Belgium was in breach of Directive 75/442 on waste management and 84/631 on the supervision and control of the trans-frontier shipment of hazardous waste as well as EC Articles 28 and 30 (ex Arts 30 and 36). The Court found that Directive 75/442, although applicable to all forms of waste, did not regulate trade and, therefore, did not preclude an import ban. However a global ban on the importation of dangerous waste was incompatible with Directive 84/631.[12] Considering the application of EC Article 28 (ex Art 30) the Court had to determine whether waste was 'goods' for the purpose of trans-frontier transport and concluded that all types of waste (ie whether recyclable or non-recyclable waste) must be considered as goods and that their circulation, in principle, cannot be restricted.[13]

The Commission argued that 'imperative or mandatory requirements' (in reference to environmental policy) could not be invoked in favour of a measure which expressly discriminated against imports. However, the Court thought that the discriminatory nature of the restriction must be determined by the nature of the goods.[14] Now, EC Article 174(2) (ex Art 130R(2)) enables remedial action with regard to environmental damage to be taken at source which means that

7 Supra, note 4.
8 *Syndicat des Fabricants Raffineurs d'Huile de Graissage National v Groupement d'Intérêt Économique Inter-Huiles* [1983] ECR 555. See also Case 118/86: *Openbaar Ministerie v Nertsvoederfabriek Nederland, Re Slaughterhouse wastes* [1987] ECR 3883.
9 *Commission v France* [1985] ECR 491.
10 Case C-47/90: *Établissements Delhaize Frérés v Promalvin SA and AGE Bodegas Unidas SA* [1992] ECR I-3669.
11 *Commission v Belgium* [1992] ECR I-4431, [1993] 1 CMLR 365.
12 At paras 20-21.
13 At paras 26-29.
14 At para 34.

regional or local authorities are entitled to adopt measures to limit transport of hazardous waste. Therefore, taking into consideration the difference between products the contested measures cannot be regarded as discriminatory but may be justified on environmental grounds.[15] However by imposing an absolute ban on the storage, tipping and disposal of hazardous waste originating from another Member State, Belgium failed to comply with Directive 84/631.

So far we have seen a linkage between environmental policy and movement of goods and competition.[16] There is no reason to assume that economic and environmental objectives shall not converge into other areas of Community policy.[17]

---

15 Paras 35 and 36.
16 Cf the Commission's Guidelines on State aid for environmental protection (OJ 2001, C 31/3).
17 See Case C-17/90: *Pinaud Wieger v Bundesanstalt für den Güterfremdeverkehr re transport policy* [1990] ECR I-5253 at 5283 [1994] 1 481.

Chapter 34

Consumer protection

A. Introduction

The Common Market is consumer-orientated because all the economic policies of the European Community aim at the improvement of the living conditions, better standards of living, greater awareness of social needs and closer relations between the peoples of Europe. In brief, political and economic integration of Western Europe has, basically, a humanitarian objective.

In the circumstances consumerism has become a struggle between the individual and the collective forces of the market, the concessions to be achieved through agitation, pressure groups and the changes in the law recognizing consumer rights and providing a machinery for their enforcement. The Community has to respond to these pressures as it is endeavouring to create a single market. Moreover the enlarged market offers the opportunity for consumer abuse across the national frontiers. The task is quite onerous as it is necessary to take into account as many national systems as there are Member States of the Community. It is the function of the Community not only to bring into line all the Member States but also to devise a common policy and to ensure its enforcement. However, though European consumerism owes a great deal to developments in the USA, it has taken a different turn from the legal confrontation between the manufacturers and the public which seems to dominate the American scene.

B. Treaty provisions

The Coal and Steel Treaty specifically mentions consumers in relation to access to the sources of supply, standards of living for the workers in the relevant industries, unfair pricing and restrictive practices and provides that, in the Consultative Committee attached to the Commission, consumers shall be represented.[1]

---

1   ECSC Arts 3(b); 3(c); 4(d); 18(1); 60-64.

The Atomic Energy Treaty refers to the protection of the health of workers and of the general public and endeavours to eliminate discrimination between the users of source materials and fissile materials.[2]

There are a few scattered provisions relevant to consumers in the European Economic Treaty[3] but the most important sources of authority to legislate in this field are comprised in the provisions regarding the approximation of national laws relevant to the proper functioning of the Common Market[4] and the implied powers[5] enabling the Council of Ministers acting on a proposal from the Commission and after consulting the European Parliament, to take measures necessary to attain the objectives of the Community in the establishment of the Common Market.

As a result of the amendments made to the EC Treaty by the TEU, the activities of the Community now include contributing to the strengthening of consumer protection;[6] and a single article dealing with consumer protection[7] features in the part of the EC Treaty that sets out the policies of the Community. The role of the Community is stated to be to contribute to: (1) protecting the health, safety and economic interests of consumers; (2) promoting their rights to information and education; and (3) organizing consumers in order to safeguard their interests.[8] Consumer protection requirements are to be taken into account in defining and implementing other Community policies and activities.[9] The Community acts through:

(1) measures adopted pursuant to EC Article 95 (ex Art 100a) in the context of the completion of the international market; and
(2) measures adopted in accordance with EC Article 251 (ex Art 189(b)), after consulting the Economic and Social Committee, that support, supplement and monitor the policy pursued by the Member States.[10]

As we shall presently observe the Community has already embarked on a continuing programme and enacted a number of measures. However the tendency in this field is to adopt a lowest common denominator in the process of harmonizing national laws which, though securing acceptance, falls short of the sophistication of an integrated market.

The TEU expressly encourages national divergences although it requires the Commission to be informed and provides that more stringent national measures must not conflict with the tenets of the Treaty. However, in this way the territoriality of national laws is emphasized with the conceivable risk of creating conflicts of national laws.

---

2   EAEC Arts 2(b) and 30-39.
3   EC Art 33 (ex Art 39) (agricultural supplies; EC Art 30 (ex Art 36)) (health of humans animals and plants); EC Art 81(3) (ex Art 85(3)); and EC Art 82(a), (b) (ex Art 86(a) (b)) competition.
4   EC Arts 3(h) and 94-97, (ex Arts 100-102).
5   EC Art 308 (ex Art 235).
6   EC Art 3(t).
7   EC Art 153 (ex Art 129a).
8   EC Art 153(1) (ex Art 129a(1)).
9   EC Art 153(2) (ex Art 129a(2)).
10 EC Art 153(3) and (4) (ex Art 129a(3) and (4)). The adoption of measures supporting, supplementing or monitoring the policy of the Member States does not preclude the latter from introducing more stringent protective measures (as long as those measures are in all other respects compatible with the Treaty): see EC Art 153(5) (ex Art 129a(5)).

C. Consumer policy

(1) FIRST PROGRAMME (1975-1981)

The First Programme[11] expressed consumer interests in terms of five basic rights to be implemented by Community legislation, ie the right to protection of health and safety; the right to protection of legal and economic interests; the right of redress; the right of information and the right of representation.

(a) Consumer health and safety

By the end of 1976[12] some 80 directives had been issued to protect consumers' health and safety. These cover a wide range of products but mainly in the context of the CAP, ie foodstuffs, fruit and vegetables and animal health. In the context of the free movement of goods some 18 directives were adopted in July 1976[13] under the general programme for the removal of technical barriers to trade, which concerns consumers directly. Of these, of particular interest are the measures applicable to motor vehicles,[14] chemical substances such as solvents, paints and varnishes and household goods and cosmetics.

Cosmetics present a continuing problem. In 1978[15] a Scientific Committee on Cosmetology was set up with the object of providing the Commission with opinions on the toxicological effects of the use of cosmetics and thus providing a sound scientific background to further legislation.

Toy safety too has been considered and, to protect children from the dangers inherent in certain toys, the Commission drafted a directive[16] which was enacted by the Council in 1988.

(b) Legal and economic interests

The Programme[17] envisaged that 'purchasers of goods should be protected against the abuse of power by the seller, in particular against one-sided standard contracts, the unfair exclusion of essential rights in contracts, harsh conditions of credit, demands for payment for unsolicited goods and against high-pressure selling methods'. Moreover, the consumer ought to be protected against damage to his economic interests caused by defective products or unsatisfactory services.

(c) Redress

The Programme[18] postulated that consumers should receive advice and help in respect of complaints arising from purchase or use of defective goods or unsatisfactory services. They should be entitled to proper redress for injury or damage by means of prompt, effective and inexpensive procedures.

(d) Information and education

According to the Programme[19] sufficient information should be made available to the purchase of goods or services offered so that he or she could make a rational

11 Annex to Council Resolution of 14 April 1975 (OJ 1975, C 92).
12 See First Report on Consumer Protection and Information Policy (1977).
13 Tenth General Report (1976); item 116 et seq.
14 Ibid items 121 and 122.
15 OJ 1978, L13.
16 OJ 1980, C 228 amended OJ 1983, C 203; enacted OJ 1988, L187.
17 OJ 1975, C 92 art 19.
18 OJ 1975, C 92, art 32.
19 Ibid art 34.

choice between competing products and services; use these products and services safely and to his or her satisfaction; and claim redress for any resulting injury or damage. Consumer education ought to begin at school.

Several proposals have been made by the Commission to attain these objectives but so far only a directive on the indication by labelling of the energy consumption of domestic appliances has been adopted by the Council.[20]

(e) Representation

Consumers should be consulted and allowed to express their views, in particular through organizations representing their interests.[1] The Commission itself consults the Consumers' Consultative Committee established in 1973 and financially supports major European consumer organizations but has as yet produced no legislation in this field.

(2) SECOND PROGRAMME (1981-1985)

In 1981 the Council approved the Second Programme[2] which reiterated the objectives of the First Programme but underlined priorities for legislative action and added a new dimension, ie consumer protection in the field of services.[3]

The legislative activity under the Second Programme comprised several amendments to the 1976 directive on cosmetics;[4] a proposal to improve the 1978 directive on alcoholic beverages by indicating on the labels their alcoholic strength;[5] a directive on the labelling of foodstuffs;[6] a directive on misleading and unfair advertising;[7] a discussion paper on unfair contract terms;[8] and a directive to establish an information procedure for technical standards.[9]

(3) THIRD PROGRAMME (1985-1988)

A Third Programme,[10] submitted to the Council in 1985, reviewed critically the progress to date and recommended vigorous legislative action to deal with the outstanding problems in three areas, ie health and safety, economic interests and co-ordination of consumer protection with other Community policies. It singled out the reasons for the slow pace of the Community action, of which the principal one was the unanimity requirement for the enactment of harmonizing directives. It was hoped that the Single European Act,[11] by derogating from the principle and expressly giving a high profile to consumer protection, would remedy the position.

---

20 OJ 1979, L145.
1   OJ 1975, C 92, Art 46.
2   OJ 1981, C 133.
3   Ibid Arts 34-37.
4   OJ 1982, L167; OJ 1982, L63; OJ 1982, L185; OJ 183, L332; OJ 1983, L291; OJ 1984, L228.
5   OJ 1978, L33; proposal OJ 1982, C 281.
6   OJ 1983, L255.
7   OJ 1984, L250. See below.
8   COM(84) 55, Final, EC Bull Supp 2/1984, point 2.1.94.
9   OJ 1983, L109. See now Dir 98/34, OJ 1998, L204/37, as amended.
10 'A New Impetus for Consumer Protection Policy', COM(83) 314, Final. See also the Council Resolution of 23 June 1986 on the future orientation of consumer protection policy (OJ 1986, C 167/1), which envisaged that the development of consumer protection should march in step with the creation of the internal market. Later that year a resolution was adopted on the integration of consumer policy in the other common policies (OJ 1987, C 3/1).
11 Single European Act, Art 18(1), (3).

Perhaps the most important development lay in the field of Community standards aiming at the quality of products, ensuring thereby a degree of consumer protection. The task of laying down Community standards was given to independent bodies consisting of industry experts and representative of consumer organizations. Thus consumers have become directly involved.

The Community has abandoned the piecemeal approach to standardization which required legislation for every product. Instead it intends to harmonize only what is 'essential', leaving the rest to the discretion of the Member States. This new approach follows the *Cassis de Dijon* case[12] which gave rise to the principle that goods lawfully manufactured and marketed in one Member State are entitled to free circulation in the Community. It was adopted by a Council Regulation in 1985[13] and implemented by Directive 86/361[14] and Decision 87/95.[15] However, Member States are obliged to notify the Commission in advance of any newly proposed technical standards. The Commission has the power to prevent the implementation of such proposals until satisfied that they will not create any new barriers to intra-Community trade.

The programme of 'essential' harmonization was directed at the telecommunications sector, pharmaceutical sector, civil engineering and construction sector, and above all, at the food sector, which is extremely complex.

(4) FOURTH PROGRAMME (1988-1992)

The Fourth Programme represented a continuation of the process in the context of the completion of the internal market with an emphasis on the greater awareness of the protection of economic interests generally and on the greater consumer involvement in standardization, in particular.[16] In 1989 the Consumer Policy Service was set up with the object of promoting consumer interests and the Commission organized a publicity campaign on child safety. The Commission set up guidelines for the promotion of Community policy on food product quality. The Council adopted a resolution on consumer education in primary and secondary schools.[17]

The legislation activity included directives on trade in animals treated with substances having an hormonal action, foodstuffs, food labelling, cosmetics, detergents and cleaning substances, aerosol dispensers, and package holidays.

(5) THE RELAUNCHING OF CONSUMER PROTECTION POLICY

In 1989, the Council adopted a resolution on future priorities for relaunching the Community's consumer protection policy.[18] The resolution called upon the Commission to present before the end of 1989 a three-year plan for the protection and promotion of consumer interests. A three-year work programme was adopted in 1990.[19] In 1995, the Commission adopted an action plan setting out priorities for consumer policy for 1996-1998[20] and, at the end of 1998, followed that with a further action plan for 1999-2001.[1] In January 1999, the Parliament and the

---

12   Case 120/78: *Rewe-Zentral AG v Bundesmonopolverwaltung für Branntwein* [1979] ECR 649.
13   OJ 1985, C 136/1.
14   OJ 1985, L217/21.
15   OJ 1987, L36/31 (re telecommunication tenders).
16   Council Resolution OJ 1988, C 293/1.
17   Council Resolution OJ 1986, C 184/21; See 23rd General Report point 554.
18   OJ 1989, C 294/1.
19   COM (90) 88 Final, 3 May 1990.
20   1995 General Report, para 644.
 1   COM (1998) 696.

Council adopted a general framework for Community activities in favour of consumers.[2] The general framework was adopted for the period from 1999 to 2003 and was supported by Community funding. It was concerned specifically with actions in the following areas: health and safety of consumers; protection of their economic and legal interests; educating and informing them of their protection and rights; and promotion and representation of the interests of consumers. In June 1999, the Council responded to the Commission's action plan for 1999-2001 by adopting a resolution calling upon it to take account of the general framework adopted by the Council and Parliament. The Council also called upon the Commission to put special emphasis on various issues, such as the safety of products and services and maintenance of market transparency and market balance in the interests of consumers, in particular in the areas of the information society, electronic commerce, distance selling, financial services and the opening to competition of public utilities.

D. Selected legislation

(1) MISLEADING AND UNFAIR ADVERTISING

Directive 84/450[3] is intended to protect consumers, persons carrying on a trade or business or practising a craft or profession, and the interests of the public in general, against misleading advertising and any unfair consequences of it. It also lays down conditions under which comparative advertising is permitted. Misleading advertising is any advertising that deceives or is likely to deceive the persons to whom it is addressed or whom it reaches and which, by reason of its deceptive nature, is likely to affect their economic behaviour or injure competitors. Comparative advertising is advertising that expressly or implicitly identifies a competitor or goods or services offered by a competitor.[4]

In determining whether advertising is misleading, account must be taken of all its features and of the information that it contains concerning in particular: the characteristics of the goods or services, such as their availability, nature, execution, composition, method and date of manufacture or provision, fitness for purpose, uses, quantity, specification, origin, the results to be expected from their use, or the results and material features of tests or checks carried out on the goods or services; the price or manner in which the price is calculated and the conditions of contract; the nature, attributes and rights of the advertiser, such as his identity, assets, qualifications, ownership of intellectual property rights or awards and distinctions.[5]

Comparative[6] advertising is not forbidden as long as it: is not misleading, compares goods or services meeting the same needs or having the same purpose; compares objectively; does not create confusion between the advertiser and a competitor or between their trademarks etc; does not discredit or denigrate trademarks etc; relates to products with the same designation; does not take unfair advantage of the reputation of a trademark etc; does not present goods or services as imitations or replicas.

---

2 Decision 283/1999 (OJ 1999, L34/1).
3 OJ 1984, L250/17, as amended by Dir 97/55 (OJ 1997, L290/18).
4 Arts 1-2.
5 Art 3.
6 Art 3a. Case C-362/88: *GB-INNO-BV v CCL* [1990] ECR I-667.

The directive imposed upon the Member States the duty of adopting adequate and effective laws against misleading advertising and comparative advertising that does not meet the conditions laid down in the directive. Such laws must provide persons and organizations having a legitimate interest in the matter with the ability either to take legal action or to bring matters before a competent administrative authority. They must also provide legal means to stop misleading and unlawful comparative advertising and sanctions to deter infringements.[7]

The directive does not exclude voluntary control of misleading and comparative advertising or preclude Member States from giving consumers and other persons more extensive protection.[8]

(2) CONSUMER INFORMATION

Consumers ought to be better informed about their position by virtue of the directives on consumers' credit,[9] correct description of products,[10] and information on prices.[11]

(3) LEGAL PROTECTION OF CONSUMERS

Various directives are concerned with enhancing the legal protection of consumers. Directive 90/314[12] sets out basic requirements safeguarding consumers who are parties to contracts for package travel, package holidays and package tours, the basic object being to protect them in the event that the tour operator becomes unable to perform its obligations and the consumer is left stranded abroad. Directive 93/13[13] deals with unfair contract terms. Directive 94/47[14] is concerned with the protection of purchasers of the right to use immovable property on a timeshare basis. Directive 97/7[15] protects consumers who are parties to distance contracts. Directive 98/27[16] requires the Member States to put in place arrangements to ensure that bodies representing the collective interests of consumers can bring legal proceedings in order to obtain injunctive relief preventing infringement of the national provisions implementing a number of consumer protection directives. Directive 1999/44[17] is designed to ensure a minimum degree of consumer protection in relation to the sale of consumer goods and associated guarantees by providing for a basic level of rights and obligations in the contractual relationship between seller and buyer.

---

7   Arts 4 and 6.
8   Arts 5 and 7.
9   Dir 87/102 (OJ 1987, L42/48), as amended.
10   Dir 85/374 (OJ 1985, L210/29) as amended: See Case C-204/88: *Ministère Public v Paris, re labelling eggs* [1989] ECR 4361, [1991] 1 CMLR 841, and Case C-203/90: *Erzeugergemeinschaft Gutshof – Ei GmbH v Stadt Bühl* [1992] ECR I-1003, [1994] 1 CMLR 397.
11   Dir 88/314 (OJ 1988, L142/19), as amended (non-food products); Dir 98/6 (OJ 1998, L80/27).
12   OJ 1990, L158/59. See Cases C-178/94, C-179/94, C-188/94 to C-190/94: *Dillenkofer v Germany* [1996] ECR I-4845; Case C-237/97: *AFS Intercultural Programs Finland ry* [1999] ECR I-825; Case C-140/97: *Rechberger v Austria* [1999] ECR I-3499.
13   OJ 1993, L95/29. See Cases C-240/98 to C-244/98: *Oceano Grupo Editorial v Murciano Quintero* (27 June 2000, unreported).
14   OJ 1994, L280/83.
15   OJ 1997, L144/19.
16   OJ 1998, L166/51, amended by Dir 1999/44 (OJ 1999, L171/12).
17   OJ 1999, L171/12.

(4) DOOR-STEP SELLING

The door-step selling directive[18] purports to curb the hard-selling techniques which often lead to purchase of unwanted goods and the purchaser's misery. This directive applies to contracts between a consumer and a trader, and unilateral engagements, by a consumer towards a trader, where negotiations were carried out away from business premises, ie at the door of the consumer. It does not apply to contracts negotiated exclusively at the initiative of the consumer though the ordering of catalogues, patterns or samples, a request for a visit or demonstration and participation in an event organized by the trader will not be regarded as negotiations. It also does not apply to contracts negotiated solely in writing; contracts concluded before a court, a notary public or other person who is under a duty to inform both contracting parties of their rights and obligations; contracts relating to immovable property and contracts of a small value, ie up to ECU 25.

The directive is general in its scope as it leaves room for specific legislation in relation to certain types of contract, notably consumer credit, home-study courses, movable assets and insurance contracts in the contemplation of the Community legislator.

Under the sanction of nullity, door-step contracts must be made in writing and include certain specific information, ie name and address of the contracting parties, description of the goods or services involved, time limit of delivery of the goods or supply of the services, the price, the terms of payment and the notice of the right of cancellation. They must be signed by the consumer in his own hand and the consumer must receive a copy of the contract.

The consumer has a right to cancel[19] the contract by giving the trader notice within seven days from the signature in accordance with the procedure to be laid down by national law. The notice served on the trader shall release the consumer from his contractual obligation. A cancellation form, separate from the contract, must be handed to the customer when he signs the contract.

If the customer cancels the contract within the specific time any payment made must be reimbursed to him and the goods received must be returned at the expense and risk of the trader. The customer shall not have to pay for normal use of the goods during that time.

Except for any payment of a deposit required under national law, the trader is forbidden to require the customer, before the expiry of the cancellation period, to make full or partial payment of the contract price, or to sign a bill of exchange or any other negotiable instrument to that effect.

In case of dispute as to whether the contract was negotiated exclusively at the initiative of the consumer, or whether it was negotiated solely in writing, the burden of proof shall be on the trader.

Stipulations, which require the consumer to pay compensation if he exercises his right of cancellation or exclude the jurisdiction of the normally competent court, are of no effect. Indeed the object of the directive is to protect consumers rather than traders.[20]

The directive enables, however, the Member States to make special provisions in some details such as regarding the fixing of the initial date of the cancellation

---

18 Dir 85/577 (OJ 1985, L372/31). The Directive cannot be relied on directly by a consumer against a trader: Case C-91/92: *Faccini Dori v Recreb Srl* [1994] ECR I-3325. See also Case C-423/97: *Travel Vac SL v Antelm Sanchis* [1999] ECR I-2195.
19 See Case C-382/87: *Buet v Ministère Public* [1989] ECR 1235, [1993] 3 CMLR 659.
20 See Case C-361/89: *The Republic v Di Pinto* [1991] ECR I-1189, [1993] 1 CMLR 399.

period, supplementary requirements relating to the effects of cancellation, affixing the date of the contract, registering the contract and the prohibition of negotiating door-step contracts with regard to certain goods or services.

(5) CONSUMER CREDIT

The object of Directive 87/102[1] on consumer credit is to provide a minimum standard of protection to consumers entering into credit transactions. Such transactions include: any agreement whereby a creditor grants or promises to grant to a consumer credit in the form of deferred payment, a loan or other similar financial accommodations.

The transactions envisaged in the directive cover any agreement for the supply of goods or services but do not include credit agreements for the purpose of acquiring property rights in land; hiring agreements; credit granted without interest or a charge; credit agreements under which no interest is payable but the credit is repaid in a single payment; advances on a current account granted or accepted by a credit institution or financial institution, other than credit cards; credit agreements involving amounts less than 200 ECU or more than 20,000 ECU; credit agreements under which the credit is to be repaid within 3 months or by a maximum of 4 payments within a period of 12 months.[2]

All credit agreements must be made in writing and contain certain essential information, some of which is prescribed by the directive (eg information about the rate of charge, and payment details) and some of which are to be laid down by the Member States.[3]

The Member States are given discretion to regulate certain aspects of these agreements, such as the consequences of failure to respect the conditions laid down above and the conditions of the repossession of the goods. Moreover the Member States are free to improve upon the Community standard provided, of course, these improvements are not incompatible with the EC Treaty.

(6) SAFETY OF TOYS

Close to the product liability directive (see below) is the directive on the safety of toys[4] which is important not only for its contents but also for the fact that for the first time the new approach to standardization adopted as from 1985[5] was applied to a consumer product.

The directive lays down uniform basic safety requirements for toys manufactured in the Community and toys imported from abroad. Thus it is specifically directed at toy manufacturers who trade in the Community, irrespective of their origin.

A toy means 'any product or material designed or clearly intended for use in play by children of less than 14 years of age'. Annex I to the directive contains a list of 21 products which are not regarded as toys and these range from fashion jewellery for children to equipment used in playgrounds and public places (eg shopping centres) and air guns. Some of these items look obviously dangerous but others, for example puzzles with more than 500 pieces or decorative dolls for adult collectors, appear less obvious.

---

1   OJ 1987, L42/48, as amended. The Directive cannot be relied on directly by a consumer against a trader: Case C-192/94: *El Corte Inglès v Blazquez Rivero* [1996] ECR I-1281.
2   Art 2. See Case C-208/98: *Berliner Kindi Brauerei v Siepert* (23 March 2000, unreported).
3   Arts 4 and 6.
4   Dir 88/378 (OJ 1988, L187), as amended by Dir 93/68 (OJ 1993, L220/1).
5   Dir 86/361 (OJ 1986, L217/21).

Toys may be placed on the market only if they do not jeopardize the safety and/or health of users or third parties, where they are used as intended or in a foreseeable way, bearing in mind the normal behaviour of children.

Annex II lays down safety requirements which have to be met in toys and the Member States must take the necessary steps to ensure that toys which do not come up to standard are not placed on the market. The safety standards, in detail, are concerned with physical and mechanical properties of toys, flammability, chemical properties, electrical properties, hygiene and radio-activity.[6] If the safety requirements are satisfied the Member States must not impede the placing of toys on their markets. Compliance is presumed if the toy in question bears the CE marking denoting conformity with the relevant national standards which transpose the harmonized standards published in the Official Journal of the European Communities.

In addition warnings and indications of precautions to be taken when using toys must be clearly stated either on the toy itself or on the accompanying descriptions of use or literature. Annex IV provides in this respect for toys not intended for children under 36 months of age, ie slides, suspending swings and rings, trapezes, ropes and similar toys attached to a crossbeam; functional toys; toys containing dangerous substances or preparation; chemical toys; skates or skateboards for children; and toys intended for use in water.

Where a Member State or the Commission considers that the harmonized standards do not satisfy the essential requirements the matter must be referred to the Standing Committee set up under Directive 83/189 which will, in turn, inform the Commission and, through it, the European Standardization Body of its finding.

The directive on toys lays down detailed provisions regarding examination and certification of the models of toys, and the affixing and use of the CE marking which sets the seal of approval upon the product and, as such, is respected throughout the Community. By this mark the Community manufacturer or, in the case of a non-Community manufacturer, his authorized representative established in the Community, confirms that the toys comply with Community standards. This means that foreign manufacturers of toys, unless established in the Community, ought to have authorized representatives in the Community who will see to it that the products are tested according to the testing rules laid down in the directive and receive the mark of approval. This may be regarded as an obstacle to free trade, but the benefit of the CE marking obtained in one country, is that it shall be recognized in the entire Community.

(7) PRODUCT LIABILITY

The text of Directive 85/374[7] is relatively brief but the preamble which explains the philosophy and the principles underlying the directive is relatively long. It means that the directive will be limited to generalities, to the lowest common denominator which the Commission dared to propose and on which the Member States were prepared to agree. This is not a new area of the law where the Community could engage in a pioneering venture. It is an area with a long tradition of national civil liability law which has proved inadequate to cope with the problems inherent in modern technology but which is difficult to reform even at a national level. This partially explains the shortcomings of the directive.

The directive proceeds from the premise that liability without fault on the part of the producer is the sole means of adequately solving the problem peculiar

---

6 Dir 80/836/Euratom (OJ 1980, L246) applies in this respect.
7 OJ 1985, L210/29, amended by Dir 99/34 (OJ 1999, L141/20).

to our age of increasing technicality and of a fair apportionment of the risk inherent in modern technological production. This reflects the responsibility of the law to protect the more vulnerable party to the bargain who has no means of testing the product for any detrimental ingredients or latent defect and is often the victim of advertising and even of his own gullibility. The principle is stated briefly in Article 1 of the directive that 'the producer shall be liable for damage caused by a defect in his product'.

'Product' and 'producer' are defined in Articles 2 and 3. Thus 'product' means all movables, including electricity, even though incorporated into another movable or an immovable (such as heating system or lifts in office or apartment blocks). It follows that liability without fault should apply only to movables which have been industrially produced. Logically the producer ought to be responsible for his creation.

'Producer' means the manufacturer of a finished product, the producer of any raw material or the manufacturer of a component part, or any person who, by putting his name, trademark or other distinguishing feature on the product, presents himself as its producer. The definition also includes importers, ie persons who import into the Community a product for sale, hire, leasing or any form of distribution in the course of their business. Such persons are like those who represent themselves as producers by affixing their name or mark on the product. Therefore they are responsible as producers unless, of course, the real producer can be made liable.

If the producer cannot be identified each supplier of the product is treated as its producer unless he informs the consumer, in reasonable time, who the real producer or the person who supplied him with the product is. The same principle applies to an imported product, if the product does not indicate the identity of the importer even if the name of the producer is indicated. Here the onus is on the importer to identify himself for the simple reason that a consumer may not be able to pursue his claim against a foreign producer and, even if he can, he should not be put to such inconvenience because it is the importer who puts the producer on the market.

There is no straight definition of the defect of the product but Article 6 of the directive relates defectiveness of the product to the lack of safety of the product which the public at large is entitled to expect. The reference, therefore, is not to the fitness of the product for use but an objective, if not somewhat vague, notion of what the consumer is entitled to expect. The safety element or criterion should take into account the presentation of the product, the reasonable use of the product and the time when the product was put into circulation. However the Article adds that, if a better product has subsequently been put into circulation, it does not mean that the previous product must have been defective. This is reasonable because a product is a creature of its time and there ought to be progress and improvement in the product resulting from improved technology. That by itself alone does not render earlier products defective.

Article 4 requires the injured person to prove the damage, the defect and the causal connection between defect and damage. However the directive does not define the 'injured person' and does not embark on any particular theory of causation.

'Damage' according to Article 9 means:

(1) damage caused by death or by personal injuries;
(2) damage to, or destruction of, any item of property other than the defective product itself; provided that the item of property

(a) is of a type ordinarily intended for private use or consumption, and
(b) was used by the injured person mainly for his own private use or consumption.

The claim for material loss must not be lower than ECU 500, which means that claims for lower compensation can still be pursued under national law, unless, of course, the national law too applies the same limit.

The directive expressly excludes compensation for non-material or 'moral' damage (eg pain and suffering, anxiety, loss of reputation etc), leaving this matter to national legislation. One can, therefore, imagine parallel actions arising from a defective product, one under the directive (as incorporated into national law) for compensation for material damage and another one for moral damage or compensation below the threshold set by the directive. This is not a happy prospect for a directive which is meant to harmonize the national systems.

Article 9 also fails to indicate the categories or heads under which compensation can be claimed. As it is confined to generalities, ie material damage arising from death, bodily injury and destruction or injury to property, it leaves the details of specific action to national jurisdictions and thus invites forum shopping.

The injured person and, in the case of damage caused by death, the personal representative of the deceased, has to prove his claim, ie the damage and the causal connection between defect and damage. The procedure and the standard of proof are governed by national law. The injured person has to make his claim against the producer as defined in the directive. However Article 5 envisages a joint and several liability of several persons responsible for the same damage. In such cases the protection of the consumer requires that the injured person shall be able to claim full compensation for the damage sustained from any one of them subject to the provisions of national law concerning the right of contribution and recourse. Thus whilst the substantive principle of joint and several liability has been accepted as a Community rule, the procedural aspects have been left to national jurisdictions.

The Directive enables the producer to exculpate himself in accordance with Article 7 if he proves:

(1) that he did not put the product into circulation; or
(2) that in the circumstances, it is probable that the effect which caused the damage did not exist at the time when the product was put into circulation by him or that this defect came into being afterwards; or
(3) that the product was neither manufactured by him for sale or any form of distribution for economic purposes nor manufactured or distributed by him in the course of his business; or
(4) that the defect is due to compliance of the product with mandatory regulations issued by the public authorities; or
(5) that the state of scientific and technical knowledge at the time when he put the product into circulation was not such as to enable the existence of the defect to be discovered;[8] or
(6) in the case of a manufacturer of a component that the defect is attributable to the design of the product in which the component has been fitted or to the instructions given by the manufacturer of the product.

The burden of proof lies upon the producer but the grounds of exculpability include the state of 'technical knowledge' and this, clearly, restricts the scope of the

---

8   See Case C-300/95: *Commission v United Kingdom* [1997] ECR I-2649.

protection of the consumer. Therefore, to assuage objections Article 15(1)(b) provides for a derogation which enables a Member State to retain in its existing legislation or to provide in new legislation that this particular exculpating ground is not allowed. In the case of new legislation to that effect the directive provides for a stand-still period of nine months during which the Commission shall consult other Member States with a view to submitting to the Council of Ministers a proposal that the level of protection be raised in a uniform manner throughout the Community.

The principle of no-fault liability is further tempered by the provisions regarding the fault of the injured party and the intervening act of a third party. Thus contributory negligence of the injured person or of any person for whom he is responsible, will be taken into account and the producer's liability may be reduced or disallowed, depending on the circumstances of the case (Article 8(2)). However the liability of the producer remains unaffected by the acts or omissions of third parties which contribute to the cause of the damage (Article 8(1)). In such cases the liability of the producer shall not be reduced but the Member States' rules regarding contribution or recourse remain effective. It means that, depending on the national law applicable to the case in hand, the producer, who has discharged his obligation to the injured party, may seek contribution from the third party involved, or pursue his right of recovery from such a party. In this case the directive is concerned that the injured person is compensated, but the apportionment between the parties responsible for the damage is left to the Member States.

True to the principle that liability for unlawful acts is governed by law the directive does not permit any contractual derogation. Thus the liability of the producer arising from the directive cannot be limited or excluded by private arrangement (Article 12). However under the national systems, an injured person may have a claim for damages, based on a contractual or non-contractual obligation other than that provided for, in the directive. If that is so the directive shall not affect such rights (Article 13). Thus the injured person may pursue these rights independently, which means that he can elect his remedy but, of course, cannot have a concurrent right to be compensated twice for the same defective product. This undermines the directive as an effective Community instrument but is not incompatible with the idea of consumer protection. Such special protection already exists in the sector of pharmaceutical products.

For a similar reason liability for damage caused by nuclear accidents is excluded from the directive (Article 14) because of adequate special Community rules and the international conventions ratified by the Member States.

Article 16(1) permits a Member State to derogate from the principle of unlimited liability (which is clearly favoured by the Community legislator) by providing a limit for the actual liability for damage resulting from death or personal injury which is caused by identical items with the same defect to an amount which, however, cannot be less than ECU 70 million.

The action is time-barred after three years, the limitation period beginning to run from the date on which the plaintiff became aware, or should reasonably have become aware, of the damage, the defect and the identify of the product (Article 10). Whilst Article 10 introduces a uniform period of limitation for bringing the action for compensation, it nevertheless leaves the Member States at liberty to regulate suspension or interruption of the limitation period. The provision on limitation is, therefore, incomplete and there seems to be no reason why suspension or interruption should be left to the vagaries of the national laws unless this is regarded as a matter of procedure.

There is another limitation period under Article II of the directive. Bearing in mind that products age in the course of time the rights conferred by the directive shall be extinguished after ten years from the date on which the product which caused the damage has been put into circulation. This is a form of prescription, understandable in view of the nature of things, but it is not clear whether for the purpose of the prescription of rights the Community is regarded as one territory.

If it is, it would not matter in which country the product was first put on the market, unless it is expected that 'putting into circulation' means putting it on the market in the country where the damage had occurred. Such an interpretation would be contrary to the unity of the Community Market but not inconsistent with the directive which, as far as the procedure is concerned, clearly recognizes the diversity of national jurisdictions. The directive purports to promote the unity of substantive law but retains disunity of procedural law. It is also a matter of contention whether prescription, unlike limitation, is a matter of substantive or procedural law.

In view of the evident shortcomings of the directive, Article 21 enjoins the Commission to monitor its working in practice, and to report every five years to the Council of Ministers submitting, as appropriate, proposal for its amendment. It is particularly important to re-examine its impact, especially of the effects of derogations and procedural rules, to see whether the directive has effectively improved the protection of consumers, and contributed to the unity of the Common Market.

Chapter 35

Education and culture

Part I. Education

A. Treaty provisions

Jean Monnet is reported to have said that, if he were to start over again, he would have begun with education and culture as the key to European integration. Whether he actually would have is a different story. However the Treaties pay scant attention to matters of education or culture. The EAEC[1] envisages specifically the setting up of an institution of nuclear science and technology while the other Treaties referred to vocational training for workers[2] and farmers[3] as well as the recognition of diplomas and other evidence of formal qualifications necessary for the exercise of professional activities of self-employed persons.[4] EC Article 128 (as originally worded) developed the theme by charging the Council with the task of 'laying down general principles for implementing a common vocational training policy'.

From such modest elements, due to the dynamism of the Community, an Education Policy developed. It was mooted in the Resolution of the Ministers of Education of 1971. In 1974 education was considered to be 'an integral part of the overall development of the Community'[5] and in the same year the Community embarked on an Education Action Programme[6] by identifying, at first, certain priorities and, then, setting up an Education Committee and a detailed Programme of Action.[7] Various actions were set up, in particular various pilot projects and studies to evaluate and develop national educational and vocational training policies.

The 1980 assessment of the Programme gained a positive reception,[8] especially the reports on the pre-primary education and the special education of handicapped

1 EAEC Art 9.
2 ECSC Art 56; EC Art 118 (as originally worded).
3 EC Art 35 (ex Art 41).
4 EC Art 47 (ex Art 57).
5 EC Bull Supp 4/74, p 6.
6 Resolution of the Ministers of Education (OJ 1974, C 98/2).
7 Resolution of the Council and the Ministers of Education (OJ 1976, C 81/1).
8 EC Bull 6/80, pp 76-77.

children and on the preparation of girls for working life and equal opportunities for boys and girls.

Following the reorganization of the Commission in 1981 an integrated approach emerged and a greater emphasis was laid on the preparation of young people for work and their transition from education to working activity. Further Resolutions followed and guidelines were issued, inter alia, on the introduction of new information technologies in education.[9]

The Adonnino Report on a People's Europe[10] and the Commission White Paper on the Completion of the Internal Market[11] turned to education as one of the levers of European integration and the means of enhancing the social dimension of the Community, respectively. A European 'dimension to education' was accepted to be a contribution to the 'ever closer union' among the peoples of Europe and to the awareness of the European identity among young people.[12] The Commission, in its Communication to the European Parliament[13] stated that 'From now on systems of education and training must contribute to the Community's economic and social cohesion' and, as part of the investment in human resources, began working on new schemes. It issued guidelines for education and training in the medium term (1989-1991)[14] which were endorsed by the Council and the Ministers of Education,[15] thus confirming a Community policy up to 1993.

The Maastricht Treaty added to the activities of the Community 'a contribution to education and training of quality and to the flowering of the cultures of the Member States'[16] and Chapter 3 of Title VIII devoted to 'Education, Vocational Training and Youth'. Education and vocational training are not new to the Community but the TEU amplified the objectives of the policy encouraging co-operation between Member States 'while fully respecting the responsibility of the Member States for the content of teaching and the organization of educational systems and their cultural and linguistic diversity'.[17] The Community,[18] for its part, shall aim at developing the European dimension in education, particularly the teaching of the languages of the Member States; encouraging mobility of students and teachers; promoting co-operation between educational establishments; developing exchanges of information and experience on issues common to educational systems; encouraging the development of youth exchanges and of instructors; encouraging the development of distance education and fostering co-operation with third countries and the competent international organizations.

In order to achieve these objectives the Council, acting in accordance with the procedure laid down in EC Article 251 (ex Art 189b), after consulting the Economic and Social Committee and the Committee of the Regions, shall adopt incentive measures, excluding any harmonization of the laws and regulations of the Member States and, acting by a qualified majority on a proposal from the Commission, shall adopt recommendations.[19]

It is clear that, whilst there is a Community policy in the field of education, the issue is considered to be delicate and the measured language of the Treaty

 9   OJ, 1983, C 256/1.
10   EC Bull Supp 7/85.
11   COM (85) 310.
12   Council Resolution (OJ 1988, C 177/02).
13   COM (88) 331, p 13.
14   COM (89) 236.
15   OJ 1989, C 277/5.
16   EC Art 3(q).
17   EC Art 149(1) (ex Art 126(1)).
18   EC Art 149(2) and (3) (ex Art 126(2) and (3)).
19   EC Art 149(4) (ex Art 126(4)).

takes account of national susceptibilities. Thus the Community ought to 'encourage' rather than 'order' the Member States to co-operate in this field. The programmes and their financial backing by the Community budget ought to provide a sufficient incentive for the Member States; on the other hand specific measures may well come within the scope of the principle of subsidiarity.

Vocational training can be regarded not only as a collective response to the challenge of modern technology and competitiveness but also as a practical means of combating unemployment, especially among the young. Here again, as in the field of education generally, the function of the Community is to 'support and supplement the action of the Member States',[20] whilst the Community legislative measures shall be confined to initiatives and recommendations, harmonization of national laws and regulations being expressly excluded. The inclusion of the Committee of Regions in the process is well understood in view of the educational responsibilities of local governments, especially the German Länder. The Treaty takes into account the federal pretensions of the European Union.

B. Major programmes

Several programmes have been adopted since 1986 but of these the following five have had the greatest impact:

(1) *ERASMUS*: provides for co-operation between institutions of higher education in the Community. It promotes, in particular, links between organizations representing higher education institutions; short study visits of teaching, research and administrative staff; and joint programmes of study and research between institutions of Member States.

The ERAMUS scheme, based on Council Decision 87/327,[1] promoted not only co-operation between universities but also mobility of students and ensured equality of opportunity for male and female students. The Annex to the Decision ensured financial support and students' grants.

The decision was based on EC Article 128 as then worded (vocational training) and EC Article 308 (ex Art 235) (implied powers). It was challenged by the Commission[2] on the ground that Article 128 provided a sufficient authority for the measure. Whilst the Advocate-General argued that EC Article 308 (ex Art 235) had to be added to support the provisions of Article 128, the Court ruled that Article 128 contained sufficient powers to enable the Council to adopt the measure which the Court classified as 'vocational training'. Having confirmed that university education is essentially concerned with 'vocational training' the Court laid the foundations for its subsequent judgments affecting students.

(2) *COMETT*, established by Council Decision 86/365,[3] represented a programme of co-operation between universities and industry aiming, in particular, at training in the field of technology. Its objectives were: to give a European dimension to co-operation between universities and enterprises in training relating to innovation and the development and application of new technologies; to foster the joint development of training programmes and exchange of experience; to improve the supply of training at local, regional and national

---

20 EC Art 150 (ex Art 127).
1 OJ 1987, L166/20.
2 Case 242/87: *Commission v Council* [1989] ECR 1425.
3 OJ 1986, L222/17.

level; and to develop the level of training in response to technological change and social changes by identifying the resulting priorities in existing training arrangements.

The correct legal basis of the decision lay in EC Articles 128 (as originally worded) and 308 (ex Art 235). However, Decision 89/27[4] adopting COMETT II which substantially increased the funding failed to mention EC Article 308 (ex Art 235) and was therefore challenged[5] as having an insufficient legal basis because it extended beyond vocational training in so far as it included elements of research and development. The Court rejected this contention and concluded that Article 128 'is directed at a common vocational training policy and does not draw any distinction between initial training and continuing training'.

(3) *LINGUA*, established by Decision 89/489,[6] had as its principal objective 'to promote quantitative and qualitative improvement in foreign language competence with a view to developing communication skills within the Community'. The scheme was complementary to programmes promoting the in-service teaching of foreign language teachers in the Member States.

(4) *TEMPUS*, like the PHARE programme designed to aid the economic and social restructuring of the former Communist countries (except the Commonwealth of Independent States and part of former Yugoslavia), was established by Decision 90/233,[7] as subsequently amended, with the object of 'enabling students from eligible countries to spend a specific period of study at university or to undertake industry placements within the Member States, while ensuring equality of opportunity for male and female students as regards participation in such mobility'. This enabled students from the eligible countries to move to the Member States and to participate in co-operation between universities, and universities and industry. These activities were supported by mobility grants.

TEMPUS was extended by TEMPUS II and TEMPUS III[8] in order to promote 'the development of higher education systems in the eligible countries, through as balanced a co-operation as possible with partners from all the Member States of the Community'. Their objectives include curriculum development, the reform of structures of institutions and the development of training related to skills. Again, mobility is the principal aim.

(5) *SOCRATES* represents an ambitious extension of the ERASMUS and LINGUA programmes.[9] With a budget of more than ECU 1 bn over the first five years (1995-1999) and ECU 1.4 bn over the next five years (2000-2004) this programme will focus special attention on the promotion of activities between the Member States involving mobility and exchange in the field of higher education (like ERASMUS); new emphasis on development, research and exchange at school level and the extension of LINGUA, promotion of distance education and the extension of the Community education information network (EURYDICE).

---

4 OJ 1989, L13/28.
5 Joined Cases C-51/89, C-90/89 and C-94/89: *United Kingdom v Council* [1991] ECR I-2757, [1992] 1 CMLR 40, para 31.
6 OJ 1989, L239/24.
7 OJ 1990, L131/21.
8 Decision 93/246 (OJ 1993, L112/34), amended by Decision 96/663 (OJ 1996, L306/36); Decision 1999/311 (OJ 1999, L120/30).
9 Decision 819/95 (OJ 1995, L87/10), amended by Decision 98/576 (OJ 1998, L77/1).

Other Community programmes include Matthaeus[10] (vocational training of customs and tax officials); Leonardo de Vinci[11] (vocational training); and Youth for Europe[12] (to help young people in their education outside the formal school system).

C. Education as social advantage

Regulation 1612/68,[13] implementing the principle of free movement of workers, provided in Article 7 for equality of treatment with national workers and, in Article 12, for the education of foreign workers' children residing in a Member State. The latter was further amplified by Directive 77/486.[14] The Member States were obliged to take special measures to integrate these children into the educational system of the host state and to promote a European dimension in education reflected in the study of languages and of European history. The concern for the education of children was extended to the education of adolescents and mature students.

Thus in *Casagrande*[15] the Court of Justice ruled that a son of an Italian worker living in Germany was entitled to a Bavarian state scholarship like any other Bavarian citizen and a similar conclusion was reached in the case of a daughter of an Italian worker living in France.[16] In both cases the Court relied on the principle of non-discrimination and social advantage accorded to children of foreign workers.

More complex issues were involved in the *Echternach* and *Moritz* cases.[17] Echternach was resident in the Netherlands where his father moved from Germany but he was refused financial assistance for his studies on the ground that he could not be treated like a resident in the Netherlands. His father was employed by the European Space Agency and his position and that of his son was governed by an international agreement and, therefore, was not subject to Dutch legislation. Moritz lived in the Netherlands where he started his studies but moved to Germany with his father. He resumed his studies in the Netherlands and was granted a temporary residence permit. However his application for a grant was refused since under Dutch law only foreign students entitled to a permanent residence permit could be treated like Dutch students.

In both cases the ECJ found in favour of the students, indicating that Article 12 refers to the parent who 'is employed or has been employed in the territory of another Member State'. It ruled that the rights of the children of migrant workers could not be subjected to national rules applying to residence.

In *Humbel*[18] the son of a French worker living in Luxembourg refused to pay an enrolment fee as a condition of admission to a Belgian school though such

---

10 Decision 91/341 (OJ 1991, L187/41); Decision 92/39 (OJ 1992, L16/14); Decision 93/5 (OJ 1993, L10/19); Decision 93/23 (OJ 1993, L16/13); Decision 93/588 (OJ 1993, L280/27); Decision 94/844 (OJ 1994, L352/29).
11 Decision 1999/382 (OJ 1999, L146/33).
12 Decision 818/95 (OJ 1995, L87/1).
13 OJ 1968, L257/2.
14 OJ 1977, L199/32.
15 Case 9/74: *Casagrande v Landeshauptstadt München* [1974] ECR 773.
16 Case 68/74: *Alaimo v Prefét du Rhône* [1975] ECR 109.
17 389 and 390/87: *Echternach and Moritz v Minister van Onderwijs en Wetenschappen* [1989] ECR 723.
18 Case 263/86: *Belgium v Humbel* [1988] ECR 5365.

fees were not imposed on Belgian children or Luxembourg children studying in Belgium. The ECJ considered that vocational training was not involved, and ruled that Article 12 of Regulation 1612/68 'does not preclude a Member State from imposing an enrolment fee (. . .), as a condition for admission to ordinary schooling within its territory, on children of migrant workers residing in another Member State even when the nationals of that other Member State are not required to pay such a fee'.

Humbel's case has to be distinguished from *Di Leo*,[19] where the daughter of an Italian worker, who wished to study medicine, was refused admission to a medical school on the grounds of numeral restriction. Therefore she decided to study in Italy and claimed a grant to which she would have been entitled in Germany. That was refused on the ground that a grant to study abroad could be awarded only to German nationals. The ECJ, relying on Article 7 of Regulation 1612/68, ruled that she was entitled to social advantages enjoyed by national workers. Denial of that right would amount to discrimination prohibited by Article 7(2) of the Regulation.

D. Vocational training[20]

In *Forcheri*[1] the Italian wife of a Commission official, who wished to embark on a course leading to becoming a social worker, objected to the paying of an enrolment fee which was not applied to Belgian students. The ECJ considered that, though not within the competence of the Community, vocational training was nevertheless within the contemplation of the legislative power of the Council as mentioned in EC Article 128 (as then worded). If, therefore, such courses were available within a Member State to its own citizens, discrimination against Community citizens (as regards fees, *in casu*) would fall within the prohibition of EC Article 12 (ex Art 7).

Vocational training was defined by the Court in a case concerning a Frenchman who wished to study strip cartoon design in Belgium[2] and objected to the payment of the enrolment fees which were not charged to Belgian students. The ECJ said that 'any form of education which prepares for a qualification for a particular profession, trade or employment or which provides the necessary training and skills for such a profession, trade or employment is vocational training, whatever the age and level of training of the pupils or students'. Fees charged to Community citizens were, in such cases, discriminatory.

In a case involving courses in veterinary medicine which consisted of a period of general study followed by a study leading to professional qualification the Court held that the two parts taken together constituted vocational training.[3] Thus, following the *Gravier* ruling, the enrolment fee charged to French students had to be repaid.[4]

---

19 Case C-308/89: *Di Leo v Land Berlin* [1990] ECR I-4185; see also case C-3/90: *Bernini v Minister van Onderwijs en Wetenchappen* [1992] ECR I-1071.

20 See Decision 94/819, OJ 1994, L340/8, which establishes an action programme for implementing a vocational training policy.

1 Case 152/82: [1983] ECR 2323.

2 Case 293/83: *Gravier v City of Liège* [1985] ECR 593, see para 30.

3 Case 24/86: *Blaizot v University of Liège* [1988] ECR 379.

4 Case 293/85: [1988] ECR 305; see also Case 309/85: *Barra v Belgium* [1988] ECR 355.

Whilst children of migrant workers must not be discriminated against as regards maintenance grants, workers are also entitled to grants as a social advantage under Article 7(2) of the Regulation to enable them to pursue vocational courses.

In an English case[5] an Irish national, who worked for a year in England, applied for a grant to undertake a teacher-training course. He was refused on the ground that he had not been ordinarily resident in the UK for the three years preceding the first year of the course. However it was held that, since he was a worker, the three years' residence requirement was discriminatory and he was entitled to access to vocational training.

Two further cases which came before the ECJ are relevant in this context. In *Lair*[6] a French national who worked for two years in Germany before becoming redundant, applied for a grant to study languages. Her application was rejected because under German law she should have been employed for five years and have paid taxes and social security contributions. The Court dismissed her claim ruling that, to obtain a grant for university education, there must be 'some continuity between the previous occupation and the course of study'. In another case[7] the plaintiff Brown had dual French and British nationality. Before commencing his studies at Cambridge he was engaged in 'pre-university industrial training' as a trainee engineer in Scotland. His application for a grant was refused since he was not resident in the UK during the previous three years as required by British legislation. The ECJ considered Brown to be a 'worker' but, referring to its decision in *Lair*, it ruled that a national of a Member State will not be entitled to a grant for studies in another Member States by virtue of his status as a worker where it is established that he acquired that status exclusively as a result of his being accepted for admission to university to undertake the studies in question, the employment relationship being ancillary to his studies. The judgments in *Lair* and *Brown* are far from satisfactory.

Incidentally, some light on vocational training was shed in an English case[8] where a French and two Irish applicants were refused grants on the ground that they were not resident in the UK during a three-year period prior to commencing their studies and these studies were not vocational. Taylor J thought that 'if an educational establishment provides a vocational course on a substantial and continuing basis it is a vocational school, whatever else it may do'. This definition would apply to a medical school, a teacher-training college, the Bar School of Law and the Law Society's College of Law but not to a university LL.B. course for which Hinde was hoping to get a grant.

E. Mobility of students

The various programmes (especially ERASMUS and COMETT) mentioned above entail a limited freedom of movement of students but students are not in the same class as workers or self-employed. However, it should be borne in mind that Regulation 1612/68 covers children of migrant workers and workers who

---

5   *MacMahon v Department of Education and Science* [1982] 3 CMLR 91.
6   Case 39/86: *Lair v University of Hanover* [1988] ECR 3161; followed in Case C-357/89: *Raulin v Minister van Onderwijsen Wetenschappen* [1992] ECR I-1027, [1994] 1 CMLR 227.
7   Case 197/86: *Brown v Secretary of State for Scotland* [1988] ECR 3205.
8   *R v Inner London Education Authority, ex p Hinde* [1985] 1 CMLR 716.

pursue vocational training. Significantly, Directive 90/366[9] which aimed at supplementing the existing rules, in its preamble, considered the students' right of residence as one of 'related measures designed to promote vocational training'. The directive was successfully challenged by the European Parliament[10] on the ground that it was enacted on the basis of EC Article 308 (ex Art 235) which deprived the European Parliament of active participation in the process since it merely had to be consulted. The Court annulled the directive and ruled that it should have been enacted by virtue of EC Article 12 (ex Art 7). However, it declared it effective until it had been replaced by another measure. That was done by Directive 93/96.[11]

Part II. Culture

In reality, until Maastricht, there has been no policy for culture and, even so, the provisions of the TEU do not measure up to a definition of a policy in terms of an explicit statement of objectives, the means of their achievement and the mechanism of their enforcement. The founding Treaties, focusing attention on economic objectives, would regard culture as something non-economic and thus outside Community competence like, for example, the resolution of the Ministers of Culture establishing the Annual European City of Culture event.[12]

However, even within the strictly economic competences of the Community, matters of cultural concern have occasionally surfaced. Where they have, they could be tolerated as derogations justifying restrictions on the freedoms of the common market on condition that they do not serve as tools of discrimination or protection of national interests. Thus EC Article 30 (ex Art 36) expressly provides for protection of 'national treasures possessing artistic, historic or archaeological value' and, in view of the ECJ, cultural protection may constitute a mandatory requirement capable of justifying restrictions on imports otherwise prohibited by EC Article 28 (ex Art 30).[13] According to Advocate-General van Gerven[14] protection of cultural values would be included among 'mandatory requirements' in the context of Sunday trading.

On the positive side, the movement of goods Regulation 3911/92[15] on the export of cultural goods and Directive 93/7[16] on the return of cultural goods and objects exported illegally, are directly linked with the cultural heritage of the Member States but, clearly, only for the sake of completion of the internal market. The Community concept of national treasures is vague[17] but the concern for their protection was motivated by the practical needs arising from the abolition of national frontiers. The primary object of Regulation 3911/92 'is to ensure that

---

9   OJ 1990, L180/30.
10   Case C-295/90: *European Parliament v Council* [1992] ECR I-4193, [1992] 3 CMLR 281.
11   OJ 1993, L317/59.
12   OJ 1985, C 153/2; Decision 1419/1999 (OJ 1999, L166/1).
13   Cases 60 and 61/84: *Cinéthèque v Fédération National des Cinémas Français* [1985] ECR 2605, [1986] 1 CMLR 365.
14   Case C-169/91: *Stoke-on-Trent and Norwich City Council v B & Q* [1992] ECR I-6635, [1993] 1 CMLR 426; Opinion of Advocate-General.
15   OJ 1992, L395/1, amended by Reg 2469/96 (OJ 1996, L335/9).
16   OJ 1993, L74/74, amended by Dir 96/100 (OJ 1997, L60/59).
17   See Commission communication to the Council on the protection of national treasures possessing artistic, historical or archaeological values, COM (89) 594, EC Bull Supp 4/87, p 10.

exports of cultural goods are subject to uniform controls at the external borders of the EC'. Exports of such goods can be effected only by a licence valid throughout the entire EC (Article 2(1)). Such licences can be issued by the authorities in the Member States in which the cultural goods are located and they can be refused 'where the cultural goods in question are covered by legislation protecting national treasures of artistic, historical or archaeological value in the Member State concerned' (Article 2(2)). The Annex to the regulation lists the categories of objects covered by the Regulation.

Directive 93/7 complements Regulation 3911/92; Article 1(1) defines cultural objects similarly to Regulation 3911/92 and an Annex to the directive extends the list of the objects covered. The preamble of the directive provides that: '. . . under the terms and within the limits of Article 36 of the Treaty [now Article 30], Member States will, after 1992, retain the right to define their national treasures and to take the necessary measures to protect them'. On the other hand, they are no longer able to apply checks or formalities at the Community's internal frontiers to ensure the effectiveness of those measures.

However, the directive provides a guarantee that national treasures removed unlawfully shall be returned to their national habitats with the co-operation of the national authorities concerned. Where such objects have been returned the court in the state in which the object is found may order compensation to a bona fide acquirer (Article 2).

Labelling requirements may serve to protect national linguistic interests, being an aspect of national culture, but such concern can be rarely justified in the face of the principle of the freedom of movement of goods.[18]

Regulation 1612/68, which explains the right to take up employment in a Member State, nevertheless enables the host country to curtail this freedom where linguistic knowledge is required by reason of the nature of the post in question.[19] In the judgment of the ECJ,[20] though the knowledge of the language was not strictly relevant to the teaching of the particular subject, the refusal of the appointment of a Community national to a teaching post in a state vocational institution was justified if the requirement was imposed as a part of a policy for the promotion of the official national language.

Similarly, considerations of protection of national culture (incidentally recognized by Article 10 of the European Convention on Human Rights) may inhibit the freedom of providing services in the audio-visual sector[1] but have to be justified. Restrictions were held to be justified in another case.[2] Whilst it is too early to anticipate how cultural interests will fare if in conflict with economic interests, it is evident that cultural values have been degraded by the powerful industry which, in the name of the freedom of expression, fills the air with vulgarity, pornography, violence etc. Maybe the concept of 'culture' will have to be judicially defined to distinguish between what is 'objectively cultural' and commercial products which trade under the 'label of culture'. Community initiatives in this respect have not been particularly successful. If we take, for

---

18 See Case 27/80: *Fietje* [1980] ECR 3839, [1981] 3 CMLR 722; Case C-369/89: *PLAGEME v BVBA Pieters* [1991] ECR I-2971.
19 Art 3(1).
20 Case 379/87: *Groener v Minister for Education* [1989] ECR 3967, [1990] 1 CMLR 401.
1 Case C-288/89: *Stichting Collectieve Antennevoorziening Gouda v Commisariaat voor de Media* [1991] ECR I-4007.
2 Case C-148/91: *Vereniging Veronica Omroep Organisatie v Commissariaat voor de Media* [1993] ECR I-487; see also *R v Secretary of State for the National Heritage, ex p Continental Television BV* [1993] 3 CMLR 387 (CA – reference later withdrawn).

example, Directive 89/522,[3] we observe that the Community promotes the transmission of 'European works' but at the same time insists on the ideal of the single market; thus, by definition, paying lip service to cultural diversity which is the hallmark of West European civilization. One can understand the desirability of promoting 'European works' in preference to products of other cultures but it takes a great act of faith to identify European works with European 'cultural works' for what passes for 'European' does not necessarily represent a 'cultural' value.

Similarly, there is as yet not enough experience to evaluate the impact of cultural interests on the competition policy which is an essential component of the single market. The Commission, undoubtedly motivated by commercial reasons, refused exemption under EC Article 81(3) (ex Art 85(3)) to resale price agreements in the book trade and its decision was upheld by both the Court of Justice and the Court of First Instance.[4] One could argue that the cultural interest was set aside in favour of maintaining competition discipline in the internal market since, in Cases 43 and 63/82, the objects of the restrictive practice were to subsidize less popular titles by more popular ones, to help the survival of small bookshops facing competition from self-service shops and book clubs. No doubt the advantages and disadvantages of the re-sale price agreements were well balanced and one would like to see a stronger case on a cultural side.

As a result of amendments made by the TEU, the EC Treaty (Article 3(p)) includes in the activities of the Community a contribution to the 'flowering of cultures of the Member States; but does not define 'culture'. Significantly the Treaty refers to 'the European dimension in education'[5] and 'cultural heritage of European significance' and 'the culture and history of the European peoples'.[6] It seems that the authors of the Treaty have consciously taken into account education as a kind of product and service which ought to be available universally whilst the Community is a multi-cultural entity, cultural diversity reflecting the identity of states and, indeed, ethnic groups within the states. Maybe this distinction reflects the subsidiarity principle. However the Community is set on course of homogenization of the European market, though culture (witness for example Belgium) defies the trend.

The Treaty charges the Community with the task of encouraging co-operation between Member States while 'respecting their national and regional diversity' and at the same time bringing the common cultural heritage to the fore.[7] It should, 'if necessary', support and supplement national action in the 'improvement of the knowledge and dissemination of the culture and history of the European peoples; conservation and safeguarding of cultural heritage of European significance; non-commercial cultural exchanges; artistic and literary creation, including in the audio-visual sector'.[8]

As in the case of education the Community and the Member States are to foster co-operation with third countries and international organizations, in particular the Council of Europe.[9] Again, as in the case of education, the Council

---

3 OJ 1989, L298/23, amended by Dir 97/36 (OJ 1997, L202/60).
4 Cases 43 and 63/82: *VBVB v VBBB* [1984] ECR 19, [1985] 1 CMLR 87 and Case T-66/89: *Publishers' Association v Commission* [1992] ECR II-1995, [1992] 5 CMLR 120. See also the Council Decision of 22 September 1997 on cross-border fixed book prices (OJ 1997, C 305/2) and the Council Resolution of 8 February 1999 (OJ 1999, C 42/3).
5 Art 149(2) (ex Art 126(2)).
6 Art 151(2) (ex Art 128(2)).
7 Art 151(1) and (2) (ex Art 128(1) and (2)).
8 Art 151(2) (ex Art 128(2)).
9 Art 151(3) (ex Art 128(3)).

is enjoined to adopt under the procedure in EC Article 251 (ex Art 189b), on a proposal from the Commission in co-decision with the European Parliament and after consulting the Committee of the Regions, 'incentive measures', excluding any harmonization of the laws and regulations of the Member States and unanimously adopt recommendations.[10] However, unlike in education, the Community shall take cultural aspects into account in its action under other provisions of the Treaty.[11] The effect of this provision remains to be evaluated. It is broad enough to impinge upon any Community policy but being taken 'into account' implies that the obligation involved is not particularly onerous. However a new state aid said to be compatible with the Common Market includes aid to 'promote culture and heritage conservation where such aid does not affect trading conditions and competition in the Community to an extent that is contrary to the common interest'.[12]

The action of the Community in relation to culture has hitherto taken the form mainly of Council Resolutions[13] but there are also action programmes promoting particular aspects of culture.[14]

---

10 Art 151(5) (ex Art 128(5)).
11 Art 151(4) (ex Art 128(4)).
12 Art 87(3)(d) (ex Art 92(3)(d)).
13 Eg, the Resolution of 25 July 1996 on access to culture for all (OJ 1996, C 242/1) and the Resolution of 20 January 1997 on the integration of cultural aspects into Community actions (OJ 1997, C 36/4).
14 Eg, Decision 719/96 (OJ 1996, L99/20), as amended and extended (the Kaleidoscope programme); Decision 2085/97 (OJ 1997, L291/26), as amended and extended (the Aviane programme concerned books and reading); Decision 2228/97 (OJ 1997, L305/31) (the Raphael programme).

Chapter 36

Miscellaneous policies

In the life of the Community policies consequent upon the development of the Common Market have been implemented with varied speed and intensity. Maastricht added new initiatives extending the Community competence.

A. Energy[1]

A continuous supply to meet the ever growing demand for energy is one of the imperatives to sustain the industrial economy and the standard of living of the peoples of the Community. This was well understood during the 1958 crisis in the coal industry. Some initial steps to develop a Community energy policy had been taken at that time[2] and efforts continue but, so far, apart from a statement of policy objectives[3] and exhortations at the highest level[4] little has been achieved. The 1973-74 energy crisis caused by the quadrupling of oil prices by the OPEC countries[5] found the Community in disarray, each Member State endeavouring to further its own interest. At that time the Commission issued a Memorandum[6] recommending a strategy consisting in a reduction of the Community dependence on imported oil by energy saving, development of nuclear energy, stabilization of the production of solid fuels and greater security of supply. The Council[7] approved the scheme.

The Commission issued further communications on the subject, such as 'On energy objectives for 1990 and convergence of policies of Member States'[8] and

---

1 For more detailed treatment see Grazebrook, D, Rebner, G D A and Hayden, J A, 'Energy other than Coal', in *Law of the European Communities*, Part 10 (Butterworths).
2 Agreement of the Council of Ministers and the High Authority of the ECSC, JO 7 December 1958, 574.
3 EC Bull Supp 4/74.
4 Dublin communiqué of the meetings of the Heads of State or Government, *The Times*, 1 December 1979.
5 Organization of Petroleum Exporting Countries.
6 EC Bull Sup 1/74.
7 OJ 1975, C 153.
8 Communication 79/7662.

on 'Energy and economic policy',[9] the latter being concerned mainly with pricing policy.

A major step forward occurred in 1991[10] when the Commission issued general guidelines for the completion of the internal market in gas and electricity.[11] This programme was to be accomplished in three stages ie (1) by the implementation of directives on electricity transit; natural gas transit and price transparency; (2) by the abolition of exclusive rights and (3) by the review of the position in 1996. In 1990 and 1991 directives were adopted dealing with the transit of electricity and natural gas, respectively, through grids;[12] in 1996 and 1998, directives were adopted setting out common rules for the internal market in, respectively, electricity and natural gas.[13] The Commission's attempts to open up the internal market by eliminating exclusive rights were only partially successful.[14]

In the meantime, under the Thermic[15] programme the Commission established in January 1990 a network of 35 organizations for the promotion of energy technologies (the so-called Opets)[16] which cover almost all the regions of the Community. With financial assistance of the Community several projects concerning the rational utilization of energy, renewable energy sources, solid fuels and oil and gas got under way.

The Community also promoted an energy efficiency programme (SAVE)[17] concentrating attention on the efficiency of new hot-water boilers fired with liquid or gaseous fuels which enables consumers to choose the most energy-efficient domestic appliances. In the context of the SAVE programme the Council enacted a directive[18] with the object of limiting carbon dioxide emissions and improving energy efficiency in buildings, transport and industry.

Energy policy forms part of the Community cohesion plan especially that there is need for a co-ordination of the energy programmes SAVE and Thermic. It is also linked with the policy for the environment.[19]

In December 1991 the Community, the European countries, the eleven independent states of the former USSR, Australia, Canada and Japan signed the European Energy Charter[20] with the object of negotiating a legally binding Basic Agreement setting out the general rules on trade in energy, competition rules, access to capital, transmission and transit, transfer of technology, environmental protection, intellectual property, conditions for investments and the procedure for settlement of disputes.

In 1998 the Council adopted a multi-annual framework programme for actions in the energy sector.[1] The Energy Policy, as it is shaping at present, implies extension of Community competence in the negotiations with third countries

---

9　EC Bull 10-1980, points 1.2.2-1.2.4.

10　EC Bull 10-1991, point 1.2.64.

11　OJ 1990, L313; OJ 1990, L185; OJ 1992, C 100.

12　Dir 90/547 (OJ 1990, L313/30), as amended; Dir 91/296 (OJ 1991, L147/37), as amended.

13　Dir 96/92 (OJ 1997, L27/20); Dir 98/30 (OJ 1998, L204/1).

14　See Case C-157/94: *Commission v Netherlands* [1997] ECR I-5699; Case C-158/94: *Commission v Italy* [1997] ECR I-5789; Case C-159/94: *Commission v France* [1997] ECR I-5815; Case C-160/94: *Commission v Spain* [1997] ECR I-5851.

15　OJ 1990, L185.

16　XXV General Report (1991) point 751.

17　OJ 1991, L307.

18　Dir 93/76 (OJ 1993, L237).

19　Ibid.

20　XXV General Report, point 761; EC Bull 10-1993, point 1.2.80. COM (93) 542; EC Bull 11-1993, point 1.2.84.

1　Decision 1999/21 (OJ 1999, L7/16).

producing or importing energy. Relations in this field include not only nuclear co-operation but also commercial agreements and technical assistance programmes to improve the legal framework, the rational utilization of energy, the electricity and oil and gas sectors. Energy co-operation embraces not only the European countries and the former USSR republics (who have benefited from the Tacis and Phare programmes) but also certain Latin American and Asian countries including China.

B. Industry[2]

The Community, because of its nature and objectives, seems unthinkable without an industrial policy linked to economic policy and state involvement in the economy. Yet, perhaps because of the industrial nature of West European societies, the formulation and implementation of such a policy has been fraught with difficulties. An industrial policy implies a change of entrenched attitudes in the face of technological advancement and a Community approach to sectoral interests. It means, in effect, an adaptation and sometimes a drastic revision of national capacity (eg in steel, textiles, shipbuilding) to accommodate the European and world markets. Social consequences inevitably call for reflection and prudence.

There are at present a framework of industrial policies proposed in 1970,[3] as further elaborated in 1973[4] with the object of establishing '. . . a single industrial base for the Community as a whole',[5] and various Council Resolutions concerning internal trade in the internal market, the strengthening of the competitiveness of Community industry, and industrial co-operation with other regions and third countries.[6]

Industrial policy is closely connected with the establishment of the internal market, activities of undertakings, investments, state and Community aids to industry as well as scientific research and development. It requires co-ordination of policies and Community initiatives.

Due to economic recession, competition from abroad and technological changes the industrial pattern of Western Europe has been subject to revolutionary change. Certain traditional industries (eg coal and steel, shipbuilding, textiles, footwear etc) have to face the problems of restructuring and adaptation. Growth industries (eg data processing, aerospace, telecommunications, pharmaceuticals, new energy sources etc) face the problem of investment, research, development and foreign competition. A coherent Community action pooling the national resources seems the rational answer to these problems but progress to date does not seem to match the challenge.

The Community strategy as from 1990 has been mapped out in the Commission's communication to the Council[7] focusing attention on electronics and information technology, biotechnology, maritime industries and textiles and clothing. The Community policy repudiates interventionist measures in favour

---

2 For more detailed treatment see Hunnings, N M, 'Industrial Policy', in *Law of the European Communities*, Part 6 (Butterworths).
3 Commission Memorandum to the Council, Fourth General Report, 1970, item 205 et seq.
4 Council Resolution of 17 December 1973, OJ 1973, C 117/1.
5 Sixth General Report, 1972, p 12.
6 OJ 1989, C 297/2; OJ 1994, C 343/1; OJ 1996, C 203/4, respectively.
7 XXIV General Report (1990), point 212.

of an open market approach and positive adjustment. In 1992[8] the Commission addressed several communications to industries with adjustment problems, especially the motor car industry, the telecommunications equipment industry and the maritime industry. The other aspect of the policy is the stress on competitiveness in inter-relation with growth and employment.

The external aspects of the industrial policy are reflected in co-operation with Eastern Europe and the republics of the former USSR consisting of financial and technical assistance and various schemes. Competition with certain countries in certain sectors, especially the motor car sector, maritime industries, textiles and clothing is a continuing problem as the Community endeavours to reconcile its protectionist stance with the open market philosophy. Faced with Japanese imports the Community has negotiated with Japan an informal voluntary restraint agreement,[9] become involved in negotiations within the OECD for an aid to shipbuilding,[10] adopted, in the European Parliament, a resolution on the crisis in the Community textile industry,[11] communicating the same to the GATT.

Although there is an abundance of research papers, communications, study recommendations and various other paper efforts one cannot see much of a tangible result that would move from programmes to enforceable obligations.

The Maastricht Treaty breaks no new ground in the field of industry though it adds a new Article to the EC Treaty reiterating the basic principles of what is thought to be the policy of the Community. EC Article 157(1) (ex Art 130(1)) lays down four specific objectives, all intended to achieve an overall objective of ensuring that the conditions necessary for the competitiveness of Community industry exist:

(1) speeding up the adjustment to structural changes;
(2) encouraging an environment favourable to initiative and to the development of undertakings, particularly small and medium-sized undertakings;
(3) encouraging an environment favourable to co-operation between undertakings; and
(4) fostering better exploitation of industrial potential of policies and innovation, research and technological development.

Those objectives are to be achieved 'in accordance with a system of open and competitive markets', which confines industrial policy to a model derived from current Western capitalistic theories. The Member States are enjoined to consult each other and, in liaison with the Commission, co-ordinate their action, where necessary (EC Article 157(2) (ex Art 130(2)). The function of the Community is to contribute to achievement of the objectives laid down above whilst the Council, acting unanimously on a proposal from the Commission, after consulting the European Parliament and the Economic and Social Committee, may decide on specific measures in support of action taken in the Member States in this respect (EC Article 157(3) (ex Art 130(3))).

Finally, there is a warning that the above provisions must not be regarded as a basis for the introduction by the Community of any measures which could lead to a distortion of competition.[12]

---

8 XXVI General Report (1992), point 249.
9 XXV General Report (1991), point 1060.
10 XXVII General Report (1993), point 883 and Dir 93/115.
11 OJ 1993, C 150; EC Bull 4-1993, point 1.2.61.
12 Ibid.

C. The Enterprise Policy

The Enterprise Policy reflects the economic conditions of the Community in the eighties[13] especially the need for structural changes facing the industry. According to the Commission this policy has three objectives: (1) to help to create conditions in which the legal and administrative business environment meets the needs of a modern and rapidly changing economy; (2) to encourage the creation of new firms and the development of small businesses; and (3) to set up a coherent framework for the ways in which other Community policies are implemented throughout the enterprise sector.

To achieve these objectives an Action Programme for small and medium-sized enterprises (SMEs) was adopted in 1986.[14] In it a distinction was drawn between Community action to improve the business environment generally and specific measure to help to create and develop SMEs. Taking into account the fixed assets and the percentage holding of a firm's capital as well as the number of employees not exceeding 500 it is considered that 95% of companies within the EC providing more than two-thirds of total employment, approximately 60% in industry and more than 75% in services, fall into the category of SMEs. This is an important feature of the EC economy which the development of the EC policies has to take into account.

The completion of the internal market resulting in the elimination of barriers to trade and the removal of protectionism carries a risk to the SMEs. Therefore, in the view of the Commission, every proposal for regulatory or legislative measures ought to be evaluated with reference to its impact on firms and employment. Should this evaluation prove to be negative the proposals would not be proceeded with unless suitably modified. This attitude has already been taken with regard to the proposed harmonization of indirect taxes.

The Commission is also anxious to see the SMEs' participation in public procurement contracts not only nationally but also in the entire Community. Similarly, when examining state aids to industry the Commission would take into account the position of the SMEs in less favoured regions.

The Commission intends to give a favourable consideration to the SMEs in the field of competition in view of their contribution to research specialization and technological innovation. This can be done within the Community concept of competition under the de minimis[15] principle and within the policy on exemptions.

The Community has made available services to the SMEs, ie

(1) European Information Centres with access to databanks which provide information and advice and act as an internal market early-warning system;
(2) Research programmes especially with the ESPIRIT and BRITE schemes;
(3) Advisory service on innovation and technology transfer with the SPRINT programme;
(4) Training to develop cross-border co-operation in acquiring industrial and technological skills within the COMETT programme;
(5) Business Co-operation Centre (integrated into the Commission) which provides information to firms searching for business partners to engage in technical, commercial, financial or sub-contracting co-operation.

---

13   COM (88) 241 pp 9 and 10.
14   COM (86) 445.
15   See Chs 27 and 28.

Moreover, various forms of financial assistance are available to the SMEs:

(1) Community loans offered by the EIB and loans under the New Community Financial Instrument with priority for small firms;
(2) Grants by the European Regional Development Fund and, since 1986, within the Integrated Mediterranean Programme;
(3) Access to capital in the form of a loan or a grant to promote joint ventures facilitated by the Commission's participation in the European Venture Capital Association which has launched a pilot project dubbed as 'Venture Consort'.

The policy greatly assisted the integration of Eastern Germany and further is likely to help the Central and Eastern European countries in their progress towards a market economy.[16]

The Policy for Industry outlined in EC Article 157(1) (ex Art 130(1)) has emphasized the role of the SMEs in the Community strategy.

D. Tourism

Tourism,[17] for the first time dignified in EC Article 3(u) as an 'activity' to be included among the pursuits of the Community, is rapidly developing as a major leisure industry. Last of the activities mentioned in the Treaty it is tacked, as if by accident, onto energy and civil protection, the three making odd company. However tourism is also a service, the payment of which had to be liberalized even in the absence of a specific Community measure in this respect.[18] So it is within the interests of the Community irrespective of any ambition to extend the competence of the Community.

The Council, by designating 1990[19] to be 'European Tourism Year', took the opportunity of putting tourism on the agenda of the Community activities and a directive was adopted to protect tourists on package travel, package holidays and package tours.[20]

E. Public health

References to public health in the EC Treaty[1] are basically concerned with national measures which may constitute derogations from the free movement of goods, persons and services. Consideration of public health may also form part of the mandatory requirements based on case law[2] and the legislation in the agricultural

---

16 *Twenty-seventh General Report* (1993) item 167.
17 Van Kray, F, *Tourism and the Hotel and Catering Industries in the EC* (1993).
18 See Cases 286/82 and 26/83: *Luisi and Carbone v Ministero del Tresoro* [1984] ECR 377, [1987] 3 CMLR 455.
19 *Twenty-third General Report*, point 302. There had already been Council Resolutions on the subject in 1984 (OJ 1984, C 115/1-2) and subsequently.
20 Dir 90/314 (OJ 1990, L158/59).
1 EC Arts 30, 39(3), 46, 55 (ex Arts 36, 48(3), 56, 66); see Case C-62/90: *Commission v Germany* [1992] ECR I-2575.
2 See Case 120/78: *Rewe-Zentral AG v Bundesmonopolverwaltung für Branntwein (Re Cassis de Dijon)* [1979] ECR 649, [1979] 3 CMLR 494; Case 238/82: *Duphar BV v Netherlands* [1984] ECR 523, [1985] 1 CMLR 256.

sector.[3] Community legislation purports to deal with barriers to trade and the promotion of the internal market.

Positive provisions are contained within the sphere of social policy such as prevention of occupational accidents and diseases and occupational hygiene[4] but their purpose is the improvement of the working conditions for which the Member States assume responsibility.[5] The Treaty provisions are auxiliary in nature, simply encouraging the Member States' activity.

The new provisions written into the EC Treaty by the TEU[6] are more detailed and more explicit. The Treaty declares that 'a higher level of human health protection shall be ensured in the definition and implementation of all Community policies and activities' (EC Article 152(1) (ex Art 129(1))). However, Community action is to complement the action of the Member States (ibid) and must respect the responsibilities of the Member States for the organization and delivery of health services and medical care (EC Article 152(5) (ex Art 129(5))). The Treaty focuses on co-ordination and co-operation between the Member States and between the Community and the Member States, on the one hand, and third countries and international organizations on the other (EC Article 152(2) and (3) (ex Art 129(2) and (3))). The Council is authorized to issue non-binding recommendations by a qualified majority[7] and to adopt, in accordance with the procedure under EC Article 251 (ex Art 189b), measures setting high standards of quality and safety of organs and substances of human origin, blood and blood derivatives, public health measures in the veterinary and phytosanitary fields, and incentive measures excluding, however, any harmonization of national laws.[8]

Community action[9] shall be directed towards the prevention of human illness and diseases, in particular the major health scourges including drug dependence, and obviating sources of danger to human health by promoting research and education and co-operation with third countries and competent international organizations.[10]

TEU is concerned with human health only.

F. Economic and social cohesion

Economic and social cohesion, mooted in the Single European Act[11] was considered by the Commission[12] as one of the priorities leading to the completion of the internal market and the Lisbon European Council[13] endorsed it as an 'essential dimension' of the Community. The TEU included economic and social

---

3   A good example is Case C-180/96: *United Kingdom v Commission* [1998] ECR I-2265, which concerned the ban on the export of beef and beef products from the United Kingdom due to the risk to humans from BSE.

4   EC Art 137 (ex Art 118).

5   EC Art 138 (ex Art 118a).

6   EC Art 152 (ex Art 129).

7   EC Art 152(4), last subpara (ex Art 129(4), last subpara).

8   EC Art 152(4), 1st subpara (ex Art 129(4)), 1st subpara. The exclusion of harmonization of national laws cannot be circumvented by basing a measure on a different Treaty provision unless to do so is properly justified: see Case C-376/98: *Germany v Parliament and Council* [2000] All ER (EC) 769.

9   EC Art 152(1), 2nd and 3rd indents, (ex Art 129(1) 2nd and 3rd inds).

10   EC Art 152(3) (ex Art 129(3)).

11   EC Arts 130a and 130b, as then numbered.

12   The Single Act: A New Frontier for Europe, COM (87) 100.

13   EC Bull 6-92, p 11.

cohesion among the tasks[14] of the Community, once more emphasized its 'strengthening'[15] and added a new chapter[16] to amplify the policy in this respect. It is clear that the principal objectives of the Economic and Monetary Union cannot be easily achieved without a policy that would even out economic and social disparities among Member States and their regions. That is its objective, or to be more precise, the Community shall pursue its activities in order to 'promote its overall harmonious development' and, in particular, shall 'aim at reducing disparities between the levels of development of the various regions and the backwardness of the least-favoured regions or islands, including rural areas'.[17] Member States, additionally,[18] ought to conduct their economic policies in concert so as to attain the Treaty objectives.

The Community shall conduct this policy through the support of the Structural Funds (European Agricultural Guidance and Guarantee Fund, Guidance Section; European Social Fund; European Regional Development Fund), the European Investment Bank and the other existing financial instruments.[19] Moreover the Council, following the appropriate procedure, is authorized to adopt the necessary action outside the Structural Funds[20] and, in particular, to create a Cohesion Fund,[1] to provide a financial contribution to projects in the field of environment and trans-European networks in the area of transport infra-structure.[2]

The Council, unanimously, is empowered to defined the tasks, priority objectives and organization of the Structural Funds but, as observed,[3] the problem here is one of discipline since some Member States have been known to have abused funds and also because of the lack of transparency in their administration.

According to the Protocol on Economic and Social Cohesion[4] the Cohesion Fund shall be available to Member States with a per capita GNP of less than 90% of the Community average (ie Greece, Ireland, Portugal, and Spain) providing they have programmes leading to the fulfilment of the conditions of economic convergence as set out in EC Article 104 (ex Art 104c).

As far as social cohesion is concerned it is evident that the Protocol on Social Policy has introduced a jarring note in the Community concert but a great deal of cohesion can be achieved on the basis of EC Articles 136 and 137 (ex Arts 117 and 118). It is logical to suggest that the British abstention from the Social Charter ought to be revised with a view to adopting a positive approach in this matter.

G. Trans-European networks

In order to help achieve the internal market and economic and social cohesion and enable citizens of the Union, economic operators and regional and local communities to derive full benefit from the setting up of an area without internal frontiers, the EC Treaty provides that the Community shall contribute to the establishment and

---

14   EC Art 4.
15   EC Art 3(k).
16   Ch XIV, EC Arts 158-162 (ex Arts 130a-130e).
17   EC Art 158 (ex Art 130a(2)).
18   EC Art 159 (ex Art 130b).
19   EC Art 159, 1st indent, (ex Art 130b (1st ind)).
20   EC Art 159, 3rd indent, (ex Art 130b (3rd ind)).
 1   See Reg 1164/94, OJ 1994, L130/1, as amended.
 2   EC Art 161, 2nd indent (ex Art 130d (2nd ind)).
 3   Lane, R, *New Community Competences under the Maastricht Treaty*, (1993) 30 CMLR 962, 963.
 4   TEU Protocol No 15.

development of 'trans-European networks' in the areas of transport, telecommunications and energy infrastructures.[5] As in the case of industrial policy,[6] the action of the Community operates 'within the framework of a system of open and competitive markets', thus directing the approach to be followed towards solutions based on current Western capitalistic theories. The Community's action must aim at promoting the interconnection and inter-operability of national networks as well as access to such networks, taking into account the need to link island, landlocked and peripheral regions with the central regions of the Community.[7]

The particular action of the Community identified in the Treaty takes the form of the following: establishing guidelines covering the objectives, priorities and broad lines of measures envisaged in the sphere of trans-European networks (including the identification of projects of common interest); implementing measures necessary to ensure the inter-operability of networks, in particular in the field of technical standardization; and supporting projects of common interest that are supported by Member States and that are identified in the framework of any guidelines that have been adopted (the support specifically referred to in the Treaty covers feasibility studies and different forms of financial assistance but is not limited to either). The Community may also decide to co-operate with third countries to promote projects of mutual interest and to ensure the inter-operability of networks.[8] Decisions to co-operate with third countries are not made subject to any particular decision-making process; but the guidelines and other measures referred to above are to be adopted by the Council in accordance with the procedure laid down in EC Article 251 (ex Art 189b), after consulting the Economic and Social Committee and the Committee of the Regions. Where any guidelines and projects of common interest relate to the territory of a Member State, they require the approval of that state.[9]

The Treaty charges the Member States with the duty to co-ordinate among themselves (in liaison with the Commission) policies pursued at national level that may have a significant impact on the achievement of the objectives of trans-European networks. The Commission is empowered to take any useful initiative to promote such co-ordination but must act in close co-operation with the Member States.[10]

Guidelines for the various trans-European networks were laid down in 1996 and 1997.[11] In 1995, a series of guidelines was laid down for the development of an integrated services digital network as a trans-European network,[12] and, in 1999, a series of guidelines was laid down for the electronic exchange of information.[13] Measures have been adopted concerning the inter-operability of networks.[14] In the energy sector, various actions have been identified for creating a more

---

5 This was inserted in the EC Treaty by the TEU but followed on from an earlier Council Resolution of 22 January 1990 (OJ 1990, C 27/8).
6 See EC Art 157(1), 2nd indent (ex Art 130(1), 2nd indent).
7 EC Art 154 (ex Art 129b). See the Commission's 1999 annual report on trans-European networks (COM (2000) 591) and, for example, the Court of Auditors' special report on trans-European telecommunications networks (OJ 2000, C 166/1).
8 EC Art 155(1) and (3) (ex Art 129c(1) and (3)).
9 EC Art 156 (ex Art 129d).
10 EC Art 155(2) (ex Art 129c(2)).
11 Decision 1254/96 (OJ 1996, L161/47) (energy), amended by Decision 1047/97 (OJ 1997, L152/12) and Decision 2000/761 (OJ 2000, L305/22); Decision 1692/96 (OJ 1996, L228/1) (transport); Decision 1336/97 (OJ 1997, L183/12) (telecommunications).
12 Decision 95/489 (OJ 1995, L282/16).
13 Decision 1999/1719 (OJ 1999, L203/1).
14 Dir 96/48 (OJ 1996, L235/6) (the trans-European high speed rail system); Decision 1999/1720 (OJ 1999, L203/9) (electronic interchange of data between administrations, as to which, see also Decision 96/715 (OJ 1996, L327/34)).

favourable context for the development of trans-European networks;[15] and the specifications of projects of common interest have been defined.[16] Basic parameters for command-and-control and signalling systems relating to the trans-European high-speed rail system have also been identified.[17] The Community has laid down general rules for the granting of financial aid for trans-European networks.[18]

H. Regionalism

There is much in the EC Treaty, beginning with Article 2, to promote a regional policy not only to eliminate disparities between regions but also to promote a harmonious development of the Community as a whole.

The policy was initiated in 1969 but got off the ground as late as 1975 with the setting up by the relevant Regulations of the Regional Policy Committee and the European Regional Development Fund. In institutional terms, the position has changed considerably since then because the Treaty, in its current form, provides for an advisory committee, with the status of an auxiliary institution, consisting of representatives of regional and local bodies: the Committee of the Regions.[19]

The European Regional Development Fund is now also based on a Treaty provision. It is intended to correct the principal regional imbalances in the Community through participating in the development and structural adjustment of regions whose development is lagging behind and in the conversion of declining industrial regions.[20] It is financed out of the Community general budget. It does not finance projects entirely but makes a contribution to their costs supported by national resources. The main tasks of the Fund are set out in Article 2(2) of Regulation 1260/1999[1] as given further definition in Regulation 1783/1999.[2] In policy terms, regional policy has now been largely assumed into economic and social cohesion (see above).

I. Research and technology

The roots of a Community policy for research and technology are in the ECSC and EAEC Treaties.[3] The EC Treaty referred somewhat obliquely to 'technical progress' and research in agriculture.[4] However, overall Community policy began emerging only from the exhortations of the Summit Conferences culminating in

---

15 Decision 96/391 (OJ 1996, L161/154).
16 Decision 2000/761 (OJ 2000, L305/22), which replaced Decision 97/548 (OJ 1997, L225/25).
17 Decision 1999/569 (OJ 1999, L216/23).
18 Reg 2236/95 (OJ 1995, L228/1), amended by Reg 1655/99 (OJ 1999, L197/1). Various decisions have been adopted over the years dealing with measures qualifying for Community financing: see, for example, Decision 95/234 (OJ 1995, L156/80) (inter-administration telematic networks for statistics relating to the trading of goods between Member States).
19 EC Arts 263-265 (ex Arts 198a-198c). Protocol 16 provides that the Committee of the Regions shall have a common organizational structure with the Economic and Social Committee.
20 EC Art 160 (ex Art 130c).
 1 OJ 1999, L161/1.
 2 OJ 1999, L213/1.
 3 Art 55 and 411 respectively.
 4 Art 33(1)(a) (ex Art 39(1) and Art 35(a) (ex Art 41(a)).

the four guidelines adopted in 1974.[5] These four guidelines include the co-ordination of national policies, the participation in the European Science Foundation, elaboration of a Community programme of research in science and technology and a programme of research for forecasting, assessment and methodology. The resulting policy should, in particular, focus attention on the supply of resources (ie raw materials, energy, food and water), the competitiveness of the Community as a whole, the improvement of the standards of living within the Community and the protection and conservation of the environment.

The basis of the Community's policy regarding research and technological development changed when the SEA included a new title on that topic in the EC Treaty. The TEU then amended EC Article 3 to include the promotion of research and technological development as one of the activities of the Community: Article 3(n). In consequence, the Community has as one of its Treaty objectives that of strengthening the scientific and technological bases of Community industry and encouraging it to become more competitive at international level, while promoting all the research activities deemed necessary by virtue of other provisions of the Treaty.[6] To that end, the Community is to encourage undertakings, research centres and universities in their high quality research and development activities; support their efforts to co-operate with one another (aiming, in particular, at enabling undertakings to exploit the internal market to the full, such as through the opening up to competitive tender of national public contracts, the definition of common standards and the removal of legal and fiscal obstacles to that co-operation).[7] The Community is also to carry out the following activities by way of complementing the activities of the Member States: implementation of research, technological development and demonstration programmes, by promoting co-operation with and between undertakings, research centres and universities; promotion of co-operation in the field of Community research, technological development and demonstration with third countries and international organizations; dissemination and optimisation of the results of activities in Community research, technological development and demonstration; stimulation of the training and mobility of researchers in the Community.[8] The Community and the Member States are to co-ordinate their research and technological development activities so as to ensure that national and Community policies are consistent; and the Commission may take any useful initiatives to promote such co-ordination in close co-operation with the Member States.[9]

All Community activities under the EC Treaty in the area of research and technological development, including demonstration projects, must be decided upon and implemented in accordance with the provisions of Title XVIII of Part 3 of the Treaty.[10] That appears to apply to activities in that area that might be capable of being carried out otherwise than in the context of that Title. Title XVIII identifies two ways in which the Community's activities in the area of research and technological development can take shape:[11] through multi-annual framework programmes,[12] and the setting up of joint undertakings or other structures necessary

---

5 OJ 1974, C 7/4, et seq.
6 EC Art 163(1) (ex Art 130f(1)).
7 EC Art 163(2) (ex Art 130f(2)).
8 EC Art 164 (ex Art 130g).
9 EC Art 165 (ex Art 130h).
10 EC Art 163(3) (ex Art 130f(3)).
11 EC Art 173 (ex Art 130p) also refers to the making of reports by the Commission; but that does not relate to the discharge in substantive terms of the functions envisaged in Title XVIII.
12 EC Art 166 (ex Art 130i).

for the efficient execution of Community research, technological development and demonstration programmes.[13]

The EC Treaty provides that a multi-annual framework programme setting out all the activities of the Community, is to be adopted by the Council in accordance with the procedure in EC Article 251 (ex Art 189b), after consulting the Economic and Social Committee. It must establish the scientific and technological objectives to be achieved by the activities in which the Community engages, fix priorities, indicate the broad lines of such activities, fix the maximum overall amount and the detailed rules for Community financial participation, and the respective shares in each of the activities provided for. The framework programme can be adapted and supplemented as the situation changes.[14] The rules determining the participation of undertakings, research centres and universities in the implementation of the multi-annual framework programme and governing the dissemination of research results are to be laid down by the Council.[15]

The framework programme can be implemented in two ways: by specific programmes adopted by the Council acting by a qualified majority on a proposal from the Commission and after consulting the European Parliament and the Economic and Social Committee;[16] or by supplementary programmes involving the participation of certain Member States.[17] The specific programmes are to deal with a specific activity and must define detailed rules for their implementation, determine their duration and provide for the means necessary for their implementation.[18] Supplementary programmes are financed by the Member State(s) concerned (subject to the possibility of financial participation by the Community) but they are to be governed by rules adopted by the Council, in particular regarding the dissemination of knowledge and access by other Member States.[19] When implementing the multi-annual framework programme, the Community may also make provision for: (1) participation (in agreement with the Member States concerned) in research and development programmes undertaken by several Member States, including participation in the structures created for the execution of those programmes;[20] and (2) co-operation in Community research, technological development and demonstration with third countries or international organizations.[1]

---

13   EC Art 171 (ex Art 130n).
14   EC Art 166(1)-(2) (ex Art 130i(1)-(2)). See eg Decision 182/1999 (OJ 1999, L26/1) (the fifth framework programme, covering 1998-2002).
15   EC Art 167 (ex Art 130j). The Council must follow the procedure laid down in EC Art 251 (ex Art 189b), after consulting the Economic and Social Committee: see EC Art 172 (ex Art 130o, 2nd indent). For an example of the rules that may govern participation in a framework programme and the dissemination of its results, see Reg 996/1999 (OJ 1999, L122/9), and 1605/1999 (OJ 1999, L190/3).
16   EC Art 166(3)-(4) (ex Art 130i(3)-(4)).
17   EC Art 168 (ex Art 130k). Supplementary programmes must be adopted in accordance with the procedure set out in EC Art 251 (ex Art 189b), after consulting the Economic and Social Committee, and require the agreement of the Member State concerned: see EC Art 172 (ex Art 130o, 2nd indent).
18   EC Art 166(3) (ex Art 130i(3)). For an example of a specific programme, see Decision 1999/174 (OJ 1999, L64/127).
19   EC Art 168 (ex Art 130k).
20   EC Art 169 (ex Art 130l). The Council must follow the procedure laid down in EC Art 251 (ex Art 189b), after consulting the Economic and Social Committee: see EC Art 172 (ex Art 130o, 2nd indent).
 1   EC Art 170 (ex Art 130m). In the case of co-operation between the Community and third parties, the detailed arrangements for such co-operation may be subject of agreements between the Community and the third parties concerned, in which case the agreement must be negotiated and concluded in accordance with the procedure set out in EC Art 300 (ex Art 228).

The second way in which the Community's activity may take shape, the setting up of joint undertakings or other structures necessary for the efficient execution of Community research, technological development and demonstration programmes, requires the Council to act by a qualified majority on a proposal from the Commission and after consulting the European Parliament and the Economic and Social Committee.[2]

J. Approximation of laws

The approximation of the laws of the Member States is necessary for the proper functioning of the Common Market (EC Treaty, Article 3(h)). This we have already observed since the implementation of the economic freedoms of the Community depends on the degree of harmonization of national laws affecting trade and the movement of persons and services. Approximation (*rapprochement, Angleichung*) represents, by definition, a more intensive process of integration than harmonization. The problem was well understood from the inception of the Community and the difficulties of changing laws, like changing the ways of life or forsaking the national heritage, were never underestimated. There is a Community policy in this field and there is no lack of ideas or projects. The aims were thus summarized by the Commission:[3]

'... the object is not the creation of a vast European law of a unique character, but of a system of a federal type which would draw its force and authority of the conviction of history and at the same time of the plurality of the living nature of the laws of the Member States, of the common juristic heritage and of the necessity of an economic concentration.'

Community law, because of its nature and origin, should reflect the legal philosophy of the Member States and their experience. It should, at the same time, contribute towards political and economic integration by building up a federal system of law. In this respect, the objectives are limited for they are centred, at this stage, on the concept of the Common Market (or 'internal market'). In other words the mechanism of harmonization must be used for the removal of obstacles to the establishment of the Common Market.

The guidelines can be found in EC Articles 94-97 (ex Arts 100-102). EC Article 94 (ex Art 100) refers to the approximation of 'such laws, regulations or administrative provisions . . . as directly affect the establishment or functioning of the common market'. This is both a programme and its limitation. Moreover, laws are to be enacted by the Member States on the basis of directives[4] issued according to the Community procedures involving the European Parliament and the Economic and Social Committee. The power of the Council to issue such directives under EC Article 94 (ex Art 100) is limited because unanimity is required and so a Member State can veto the proposals of the Commission. Where, however, the Commission finds a distortion of the conditions of competition arising from the laws of the offending state, the Commission shall, through consultation, eliminate such distortion, but should this effort fail, the Council may be called in

---

2   EC Art 172 (ex Art 130o, 1st indent).
3   *Eighth General Report of the EEC*, 1965, para 83.
4   See Case 32/74: *Firma Friedrich Haaga GmbH* [1974] ECR 1201, [1975] CMLR 32, in which for the first time the Court had to interpret an article in a directive (ie 68/151 of 9 March 1968 (OJ L65)) on harmonization of company law.

(EC Article 96 (ex Art 101)). The Council may issue appropriate directives by a qualified majority. Where there is reason to fear that a state will create distortions through taking certain legislative or administrative measures, the Commission alone is empowered to act and shall issue appropriate recommendations (EC Article 97 (ex Art 102)). The sanction for ignoring the recommendation is that the other Member States may disregard EC Article 96 (ex Art 101) in relation to the offending state.

It appears that the above provisions proceed from the principle of the sovereign law-making power of the Member States modified by the Treaty obligation. Nevertheless there is implied coercion and sanction since failure to enact a directive into national law correctly would, as in the case of a regulation, expose the Member States to enforcement proceedings.[5] In fact, several such actions have been initiated and withdrawn when the state in default decided to implement the measure.

However the results, after nearly 50 years of the existence of the Community, proved disappointing mainly because of the cumbersome procedure and the requirement of unanimity for the enactment of directives. A new impetus was given by the Single European Act and the TEU, which provide a more flexible method of achieving the desired approximation of natural laws than the machinery originally set out in the EC Treaty. Under what is now EC Article 95 (ex Art 100a), the Council can adopt the measures for the approximation of the provisions laid down by law, regulation or administrative action in Member States which have as their object the establishment and functioning of the internal market. The Council acts by way of derogation from EC Article 94 (ex Art 100) using the procedure referred to in EC Article 251 (ex Art 189b) and after consulting the Economic and Social Committee. This derogation is limited. It does not apply to fiscal provisions, to those relating to the free movement of persons nor to those relating to the rights and interests of employed persons. In the proposals drawn up by the Commission under EC Article 95 (ex Art 100a) for the approximation of national laws concerning health, safety, environmental protection and consumer protection, the Commission must take as a base a high level of protection taking into account, in particular, any new development based on scientific facts; and the Council and the European Parliament, when exercising their powers in the adoption process, must also seek to achieve that objective. In appropriate cases, harmonizing measures adopted under EC Article 95 (ex Art 100a) must also include a safeguard clause authorizing the Member States to take provisional measures, for one or more of the non-economic reasons referred to in EC Article 30 (ex Art 36).[6] In addition, the adoption of a harmonization measure by the Council or Commission does not necessarily preclude the Member States from taking different action to that specified in the harmonization measure.

---

5 Eg Case 95/77: *Commission v Netherlands (Re Directive on Meteorology)* [1978] ECR 863; Case 100/77: *Commission v Italy (Re Directive on Meteorology)* [1978] ECR 879, [1979] 2 CMLR 655; Case 147/77: *Commission v Italy (Re Slaughter of animals)* [1978] ECR 1307, [1978] 3 CMLR 428; Case 69/77: *Commission v Italy (Re Agricultural tractors)* [1978] ECR 1749; Case 93/79: *Commission v Italy (Re Weighing Machines for Conveyor Belts)* [1979] ECR 3837, [1980] 2 CMLR 647; Case 42/80: *Commission v Italy (Re Wire-Ropes, Chains and Hooks)* [1980] ECR 3635, [1981] 2 CMLR 532; Case 133/80: *Commission v Italy (Re Public Supply Contracts Directive)* [1981] ECR 457, [1981] 3 CMLR 456; Case 163/78: *Commission v Italy (Re aerosol dispensers)* [1979] ECR 771, [1979] 2 CMLR 394; Case 43/80: *Commission v Italy (Re non-automatic weighing machines)* [1980] ECR 3643, [1981] 2 CMLR 532 and many subsequent cases.

6 EC Art 95(10) (ex Art 100a(10)).

EC Article 95(4) and (5), (ex Art 100a(4) and (5)) preserve the power of each Member State to: (1) maintain national provisions on grounds of major needs referred to in EC Article 30 (ex Art 36) or relating to the protection of the environment or the working environment; and (2) introduce national provisions based on new scientific evidence relating to the protection of the environment or the working environment concerning a problem specific to that Member State arising after the adoption of the measure in question. In both cases, which envisage permanent derogations, not simply the adoption of temporary protective measures, the Member States in question must notify the Commission of the national provisions and the reasons for their maintenance or introduction. The Commission then has six months, running from the date of notification (but extendible by a further six months when the matter is complex and there is no danger to human health), in which to approve or reject the national provision. In the absence of a decision of the Commission within that period, the provision is deemed to be approved. When deciding whether to approve or reject it, the Commission must verify whether or not the provision is a means of arbitrary discrimination or a disguised restriction of trade between Member States[7] and whether or not it constitutes an obstacle to the functioning of the internal market.[8] When a Member State is authorized to maintain or introduce a provision derogating from a harmonization measure, the Commission is also obliged to examine immediately whether or not to propose an adoption to the harmonization measure; and where a Member State raises a specific public health problem in a field that has been harmonized, it is obliged to bring the problem to the attention of the Commission for it to examine whether or not to propose appropriate measures to the Council.[9] Where the Commission or a Member State considers that a Member State is making improper use of the powers provided for in EC Article 95 (ex Art 100a) either may bring the matter directly before the ECJ (or the CFI, if it has jurisdiction), without going through the pre-litigation procedures set out in EC Articles 226 and 227 (ex Arts 169 and 170).[10]

At first sight, EC Articles 94-97 (ex Arts 100-102) might appear rather narrow in scope; but, if one considers that they are concerned not only with the 'establishment' but also with the 'functioning' of the common market, the scope widens considerably and is as wide as the concept of the common market itself.

K. Judicial co-operation in civil matters

Originally, judicial co-operation in civil matters was the subject of negotiation between the Member States, as envisaged in EC Article 293 (ex Art 220). The best known example of the action of the Member States in that area was the Brussels Convention on jurisdiction and the enforcement of judgments in civil and commercial matters (see below). The Amsterdam Treaty retained EC Article 293 (ex Art 220) as a possible basis for such action but also created a more flexible alternative in the form of EC Article 65 (ex Art 73m). Action under that provision can take the form of a Council Regulation. One illustration of that is the extension of the Brussels Convention so as to cover jurisdiction and the recognition and

---

7 Wording familiar from EC Art 30 (ex Art 36) as to which see p 471, supra.
8 EC Art 95(6) (ex Art 100a(6)).
9 EC Art 95(7) and (8) (ex Art 100a(7) and (8)).
10 EC Art 95(9) (ex Art 100a(9)).

enforcement of judgments in relation to the dissolution of marriage and the custody of children. The Brussels Convention was originally to be extended in that way by another Convention ('Brussels II') signed on 28 May 1998.[11] The Convention was not ratified and, instead, it was converted into a Council Regulation which came into force on 1 March 2001. Subsequently, the Brussels Convention was itself converted into a Regulation, which will come into effect on 1 March 2002 as between all the Member States save Denmark, in relation to which the Brussels Convention shall continue to apply.[12]

(1) CIVIL JURISDICTION AND RECOGNITION AND ENFORCEMENT OF JUDGMENTS

The Brussels Convention on 27 September 1968 on Jurisdiction and the Enforcement of Judgments in Civil and Commercial Matters,[13] was negotiated in pursuance of Article 220(4) of the EC Treaty, and entered into force between the original Member States on 1 February 1973.   As amended by various accession conventions (signed in 1978, 1982, 1989 and 1997),[14] it came into force progressively between all the Member States.[15]

The conversion of the Convention into a regulation is not intended to disrupt continuity in the interpretation and application of its terms.

By Article 1, the Regulation and the Convention apply to disputes of a civil and commercial nature, even if the proceedings are brought before a criminal court or an administrative tribunal;[16] but not to disputes between a private person and a public authority arising from the latter's acts performed in the exercise of its powers as such,[17] nor to other revenue, customs or administrative matters. There are also specific exclusions, by Article 1(2), for proceedings principally concerned with individual status or capacity, matrimonial property (as distinct from familial maintenance),[18] succession on death, bankruptcy or insolvent corporate liquidation,[19] social security, or arbitration.[20] Moreover, by Article 57,

---

11   OJ 1998, C 221/1.
12   See Reg 1347/2000 (OJ 2000, L160/19); and Reg 44/2001 (OJ 2001, L12/1), respectively.
13   For the original and 1978 versions of its text, see OJ 1978, L304; for the 1983 version, OJ 1983, C 97; for the 1989 version, OJ 1990, C 189; and the 1997 version, OJ 1998, C 27/1. For the accompanying reports, see OJ 1979, C 59; OJ 1986, C 298; OJ 1990, C 189; and OJ 1998, C 27.
14   See OJ 1978, L304; OJ 1982, L388; OJ 1989, L285; and OJ 1997, C 15/1.
15   There is also a Protocol, originally signed on 3 June 1971, empowering the ECJ to give preliminary rulings on the interpretation of the 1968 Convention (see now OJ 1998, C 27), under which a substantial case law has developed. In addition a parallel convention between the EC Member States and the EFTA countries, signed at Lugano on 16 September 1988, is currently in force between the United Kingdom and Switzerland; for its text see OJ 1998, L319.
16   See Arts 5(4) and 25, and the annexed Protocol, Art II; Case 157/80: *Rinkau* [1981] ECR 1391, [1983] 1 CMLR 205; and Case C-172/91: *Sonntag v Waidmann* [1993] ECR I-1963.
17   See Case 19/76: *LTU v Eurocontrol* [1976] ECR 1541, [1977] 1 CMLR 88; Cases 9-10/77: *Bavaria Fluggesellschaft and Germanair v Eurocontrol* [1977] ECR 1517, [1980] 1 CMLR 566; Case 814/79: *Netherlands v Rüffer* [1980] ECR 3807, [1981] 3 CMLR 293; *Sonntag v Waidmann*, supra.
18   See also Arts 5(2) and 27(4); Case 143/78: *De Cavel v De Cavel* [1979] ECR 1055, [1979] 2 CMLR 547; Case 120/79: *De Cavel v De Cavel (No 2)* [1980] ECR 731, [1980] 3 CMLR 1; Case 25/81: *CHW v GJH* [1982] ECR 1189, [1983] 2 CMLR 125; Case C-220/95: *Van den Boogaard v Laumen* [1997] ECR I-1147.
19   See Case 133/78: *Gourdain v Nadler* [1979] ECR 733, [1979] 3 CMLR 180. As to insolvency, see now Reg 1346/2000 (OJ 2000, L160/1).
20   See Case C-190/89: *Marc Rich & Co AG v Italiana Impianti PA* [1991] ECR I-3855; and [1992] 1 Lloyd's Rep 624, English CA. Also excluded are proceedings or judgments concerning the recognition or enforcement of a judgment given in a third country: Case C-129/92: *Owens Bank v Bracco (No 2)* [1994] ECR I-117.

the 1968 Convention gives way to other, existing or future, international conventions on particular subject matter (such as admiralty actions in rem, collisions at sea, and contracts of carriage).[1] With effect from 1 March 2001, the Convention was extended to cover divorce, legal separation and annulment of marriage and all matters concerning the parental responsibility of the spouses over a child of both of them.[2]

(2) DIRECT JURISDICTION

Title II of the 1968 Convention and Chapter II of the Regulation regulate the direct jurisdiction of the courts of the Member States; that is, they lay down rules which must be applied by a court of a Member State in which an original action for the decision of the merits of a dispute is brought in determining its own jurisdiction to entertain the action. Title III and Chapter III, respectively, which provide for the recognition and enforcement in a Member State of judgments given in other Member States, largely preclude the court addressed from reviewing the jurisdiction of the original court.[3] Moreover, the original court must apply Title (or Chapter) II of its own motion to the extent of declining jurisdiction if the claim principally concerns a matter within the exclusive jurisdiction of another Member State, or if it lacks jurisdiction over a defendant who is domiciled in another Member State and has not entered an appearance, or if a court of another Member State has previously been seised of a similar claim.[4]

Title (or Chapter) II is based primarily on the defendants' domicile; nationality is immaterial if the defendant is domiciled within the Union. In general, by Articles 2 and 3, where the defendant is domiciled in a Member State, the courts of that state have jurisdiction to entertain actions against him (though the distribution of such jurisdiction among its courts is remitted to its law), and the court of the other Member States lack jurisdiction over him. By Article 4, if the defendant is not domiciled in any Member State, the jurisdiction of a court of a Member State is in general remitted to its own law.

There is no uniform substantive definition of domicile; instead, its ascertainment is remitted by Articles 52 and 53 of the Convention (Articles 59 and 60 of the Regulation) to national law. The court must apply its own law to determine whether an individual is domiciled within its own State; and, if he is not so domiciled, it must apply the law of each of the other Member States to determine whether he is domiciled in that other state. In the case of a company or other legal person, its seat constitutes its domicile, but the court must ascertain the seat in accordance with its own law.

Major exceptions to Article 3 (of the Convention and the Regulation) are specified by Article 5, which confers jurisdiction in certain cases over a defendant domiciled in one Member State on courts of another Member State with which the claim has a specified connection. The plaintiff then has the option of suing either in the courts of the defendant's domicile, in accordance with Article 2, or in another Member State, in accordance with Article 5. These cases include contractual claims, where Article 5(1) confers jurisdiction on the courts for the place of performance of the obligation on which the action, or that principal claim

---

1   Case C-406/92: *The Maciej Rataj* [1994] ECR I-5439.
2   Reg 1347/2000 (OJ 2000, L160/19). As noted above, this regulation is derived from a convention signed in 1998. The Explanatory Reports on the Convention and its attached protocol were published in OJ 1998, C 221 at 27 and 65.
3   See Arts 29 and 34 of the Convention; Arts 36, 45(2) of the Regulation.
4   See Arts 19-21 of the Convention; Arts 25-27 of the Regulation.

made in the action, is based;[5] tortious claims, where Article 5(3) confers jurisdiction on the courts for the place where a harmful event occurred;[6] and claims arising from the operations of a branch, agency or other establishment, where Article 5(5) confers jurisdiction on the courts for the place in which such an establishment is situated.[7] Similarly, with a view to facilitating litigational economy and convenience by the joinder of related claims, Articles 6 and 6A of the Convention (Articles 6-7 of the Regulation) derogate from Article 3 by conferring jurisdiction over persons domiciled in other Member States in certain cases involving co-defendants, third parties, counter-claims, contracts involving land, or admiralty limitation actions.

Articles 2-6A of the Convention and 2-7 of the Regulation operate subject to Articles 17-18 and 23-24, respectively, on submission by agreement or appearance. Articles 17 and 23 are designed to ensure respect for a jurisdiction clause, agreed to by potential litigants, designating a court or courts of a Member State as competent to determine their existing or future disputes connected with a particular legal relationship. The formalities required of a jurisdiction clause have now been reduced almost to vanishing point by the developing case law[8] and the successive amendments made by the accession conventions. Its effect is usually, but not invariably, to render the chosen court or courts exclusively competent.[9] By Articles 18 and 24, respectively, a court before which the defendant appears, otherwise than solely to contest jurisdiction, thereby acquires jurisdiction.

5   See Case 12/76: *Industrie Tessili Italiana Como v Dunlop AG* [1976] ECR 1473, [1977] 1 CMLR 26; Case 14/76: *Establissements A de De Bloos Sprl v Bouyer* [1976] ECR 1497, 1 CMLR 60; Case 56/79: *Zelger v Salinitri* [1980] ECR 89, [1980] 2 CMLR 635; Case 38/81: *Effer SpA v Kantner* [1982] ECR 825, [1984] 2 CMLR 667; Case 34/82: *Peters v South Netherlands Contractors' Association* [1983] ECR 987, [1984] 2 CMLR 605; Case 226/85: *Shenavai v Kreischer* [1987] ECR 239, [1987] 3 CMLR 782; Case 9/87: *Arcado Sprl v SA Haviland* [1988] ECR 1539; Case C-26/91: *Handte v Traitements Mécano-Chimiques des Surfaces* [1992] ECR I-3967; Case C-288/92: *Custom Made Commercial Ltd v Stawa* [1994] ECR I-2913; Case C-106/95: *MSG v Les Gravières Rhénanes* [1997] ECR I-911.

6   See Case 21/76: *Handelskwkerij GJ Bier BV v Mines de Potasse d'Alsace SA* [1976] ECR 1735, [1977] 1 CMLR 284; Case 189/87: *Kalfelis v Schröder, Münchmeyer, Hengst & Co* [1988] ECR 5565; Case 220/88: *Dumez France and Tracona v Hessische Landesbank* [1990] ECR 49; Case C-261/90: *Reichert v Dresdner Bank (No 2)* [1992] ECR I-2149; Case C-68/93: *Shevill v Presse Alliance* [1995] ECR I-415; Case C-364/93: *Marinari v Lloyd's Bank* [1995] ECR I-2719.

7   See Case 14/76: *Etablissements A de De Bloos Sprl v Bouyer* [1976] ECR 1497, [1977] 1 CMLR 60; Case 33/78: *Etablissements Somafer SA v Saar-Ferngas* [1978] ECR 2183, [1979] 1 CMLR 490; Case 139/80: *Blanckaert & Willems v Trost* [1981] ECR 819, [1982] 2 CMLR 1; Case 218/86: *SAR Schotte GmbH v Parfums Rothchild SARL* [1987] ECR 4905; Case C-439/93: *Lloyd's Shipping Register v Campenon Bernard* [1995] ECR I-961. Other provisions of Art 5 deal with familial maintenance; tortious claims brought ancillarily to a criminal prosecution; trusts; and salvage: see Case C-295/95: *Farrell v Long* [1997] ECR I-1683.

8   See Case 24/76: *Colzano v RÜWA* [1976] ECR 1831, [1977] 1 CMLR 345; Case 25/76: *Galeries Segoura Sprl v Bonakdarian* [1976] ECR 1851, [1977] 1 CMLR 361; Case 784/79: *Porta-Leasing GmH v Prestige International SA* [1980] ECR 1517, [1981] 1 CMLR 135; Case 150/80: *Elefanten Shuh GmbH v Jacqmain* [1981] ECR 1671, [1982] 3 CMLR 1; Case 201/82: *Gerling v Treasury Administration* [1983] ECR 2503, [1984] 3 CMLR 638; Case 71/83: *Partenreederei ms Tilly Russ v Haven and Vervabedrijf Nova NV* [1984] ECR 2417, [1984] 3 CMLR 499; Case 221/84: *Berhoefer GmbH & Co KG v ASA* [1985] ECR 2699, [1986] 1 CMLR 13; Case 313/85: *Iveco Fiat SpA v Van Hool NV* [1986] ECR 3337, [1988] 1 CMLR 57; Case C-214/89: *Powell Duffryn plc v Petereit* [1992] ECR I-1745; Case C-106/95: *MSG v Les Gravières Rhénanes* [1997] ECR I-911; Case C-269/95 *Benincasa v Dentalkit* [1997] ECR I-3767.

9   See Case 23/78: *Meeth v Glacetal Sarl* [1978] ECR 2133, [1979] 1 CMLR 520; and Case 22/85: *Anterist v Crédit Lyonnais* [1986] ECR 1951, [1987] 1 CMLR 333.

With a view to protecting the supposedly weaker party, the Convention and the Regulation lay down particular jurisdictional rules for insurance,[10] consumer,[11] and employment[12] contracts. These offer a wide choice of fora to a protected party (such as a policyholder, consumer or employee) where he is plaintiff, and restrict the available fora where he is defendant, as well as restricting the use of a jurisdiction clause against him. Articles 16 and 19 of the Convention (22 and 25 of the Regulation) provide for the exclusive jurisdiction of the courts of a Member State over proceedings principally concerned with certain matters regarded as especially sensitive to its interest or sovereignty, such as title to or tenancies of land situated within its territory.[13] Such exclusive jurisdiction overrides the normal rules about domicile, agreement or appearance.

Title II also contains provisions designed to ensure that the defendant receives the originating document in sufficient time to enable him to defend;[14] that, where there are simultaneously pending actions in respect of similar or related claims in courts of different Member States, the court subsequently seised should decline jurisdiction or stay its proceedings in favour of the court first seised;[15] and that a court should be able to grant provisional relief even if the Convention deprives it of jurisdiction over the substance of the dispute.[16]

In relation to matrimonial matters and custody disputes to which the Convention extends, jurisdiction in relation to the former is determined by the country of residence of one or both spouses or their country of nationality. The court having jurisdiction in relation to matrimonial matters also has jurisdiction in all matters concerning parental responsibility in relation to a child of both spouses that is resident in the same state (where that is not so, the court in question may still have jurisdiction in certain circumstances). Where there are parallel

10 See Arts 7-12A of the Convention; Arts 8-14 of the Regulation.

11 See Arts 13-15 and 15-17, respectively; Case 150/77: *Société Bertrand v Paul Ott KG* [1978] ECR 1431, [1978] 3 CMLR 499; Case C-89/91: *Shearson Lehman Hutton v TVB* [1993] ECR I-139; *Benincasa v Dentalkit* (above).

12 See Arts 5(1) and 17(6) of the Convention, Arts 18-21 of the Regulation: Case 133/81: *Ivenel v Schwab* [1982] ECR 1891, [1983] 1 CMLR 538; Case 226/85: *Shenavai v Kreischer* [1987] ECR 239, [1987] 3 CMLR 782; Case 32/88: *Six Constructions Ltd v Humbert* [1989] ECR 341; Case C-125/92: *Mulox IBC Ltd v Geels* [1993] ECR I-4075, [1994] IRLR 422; Case C-294/92: *Webb v Webb* [1994] ECR I-1717; Case C-292/93: *Lieber v Göebel* [1994] ECR I-2535.

13 On title to or tenancies of land, see Arts 16(1) of the Convention and 22(1) of the Regulation; Case 73/77: *Sanders v Van der Putte* [1977] ECR 2383, [1978] 1 CMLR 331; Case 241/83: *Rösler v Rottwinkel* [1985] ECR 99, [1985] 1 CMLR 806; Case 158/87: *Scherrens v Maenhout* [1988] ECR 3791; Case C-280/90: *Hacker v Euro-Relais GmbH* [1992] ECR I-1111; Case C-294/92: *Webb v Webb* [1994] ECR I-1717; Case C-292/93: *Lieber v Goebel* [1994] ECR I-2535. Other matters subject to exclusive jurisdiction include certain aspects of company law, where jurisdiction belongs to the seat (see Arts 16(2) and 22(2), respectively); the registration or validity of patents and trademarks where it belongs to the state of registration (see Arts 16(4) and 22(4), respectively, and Case 288/82: *Duijnstee v Goderbauer* [1983] ECR 3663, [1985] 1 CMLR 220); and the enforcement of judgments, where it belongs to the state of enforcement (see Arts 16(5) and 22(5), respectively; Case 220/84: *AS-Autoteile Service GmbH v Malhé* [1985] ECR 2267, [1986] 3 CMLR 321; Case C-261/90: *Reichert v Dresdner Bank AG (No 2)* [1992] ECR I-2149; and Case C-129/92: *Owens Bank Ltd v Bracco (No 2)* [1994] QB 509, [1994] ECR I-117, ECJ).

14 See Art 20 of the Convention; Art 26 of the Regulation.

15 See Arts 21-23 of the Convention; Arts 27-30 of the Regulation; Case 129/83: *Zelger v Salinitri (No 2)* [1984] ECR 2397, [1985] 3 CMLR 366; Case 144/86: *Gubisch Maschinenfabrik AG v Palumbo* [1987] ECR 4861; Case C-406/92: *The Maciej Rataj* [1994] ECR I-5439; Case C-163/95: *Von Horn v Cinnamond* [1997] ECR I-5451.

16 See Art 24 of the Convention; Art 31 of the Regulation.

disputes in several jurisdictions, the courts later seised defer to the court seised first in point of time.

(3) RECOGNITION AND ENFORCEMENT OF JUDGMENTS

Title III of the Convention and the Regulation provides for the recognition and enforcement in a Member State of judgments given by courts of the Member States. Recognition implies giving the judgment the same effect, as regards claims and issues decided and parties affected, in the state addressed as it has in the state of origin, and enforcement refers to the taking of official action in the state addressed for the purpose of securing the performance of obligations imposed by the judgment. By Article 26 of the Convention (Article 33 of the Regulation), recognition requires no special procedure and may be invoked incidentally whenever relevant, but an interested party may utilize the enforcement procedure to obtain a declaration of recognition. Enforcement procedure is regulated in detail by Articles 31 et seq of the Convention (Articles 38 et seq of the Regulation) and this procedure is exclusive.[17] Under Title III a judgment is recognizable and enforceable despite its being open to appeal or review in the original country;[18] but, to be enforceable abroad, it must be enforceable at home.[19] Judgments awarding non-monetary relief (such as the specific performance of a contract), as well as money judgments, are enforceable under Title III.

Under Title III the judgment benefits from a strong presumption of regularity. An applicant for recognition need only prove the judgment itself, and show that it falls within the spatial, temporal and material scope of the Convention, and, in the case of a default judgment, that the original defendant was served with the originating process. An applicant for enforcement must also establish that the judgment is enforceable in the original state and has been served.[20]

Articles 29 and 34(3) of the Convention (Articles 36 and 45(2) of the Regulation) emphasize that under no circumstances may the substance of the judgment be reviewed by the court in which recognition or enforcement is sought. Moreover, by Articles 28(3) and 34(2) of the Convention (Articles 35(3) and 45(1) of the Regulation), in general the court addressed cannot review the jurisdiction of the original court, even under the guise of public policy. By way of exception, Articles 28(1)-(2), 34(2) and 59 of the Convention (Articles 35(1)-(2) and 45(1) of the Regulation) require jurisdictional review in relation to insurance or consumer contracts, and to exclusive jurisdiction, and in connection with certain conventions between the state addressed and a non-Member State; but even in these cases the court addressed is bound by the findings of fact on which the original court based its jurisdiction. Jurisdictional review is also required in transitional cases by Article 54 of the Convention and Article 66 of the Regulation.

Recognition and enforcement must, however, be refused in the limited circumstances specified by Article 27 of the Convention (Article 34 of the Regulation). These are where recognition of the judgment would contravene the public policy of the state addressed;[1] (in the case of the Convention) where the original court decided a preliminary question of individual status or capacity, matrimonial property or succession inconsistently with a conflict rule of the state

---

17 See Case 42/76: *De Wolf v Cox* [1976] ECR 1759, [1977] 2 CMLR 43.
18 See Arts 30, 38 and 43 of the Convention; Arts 37, 46 and 49 of the Regulation.
19 See Art 31 of the Convention; Art 38 of the Regulation.
20 See Arts 1, 25-26, 31, 46-47 and 54 of the Convention; Arts 1, 32-33, 38, 53-54 and 66 of the Regulation.
1   See Art 27(1) of the Convention; Art 34(1) of the Regulation.

addressed and consequently reached a different result;[2] where the defendant was not duly served with the originating process in sufficient time to defend and did not appear;[3] and in certain cases where the judgment is irreconcilable with another judgment given or recognized in the state addressed.[4]

Article 31 et seq of the Convention (Article 38 et seq of the Regulation) provide a uniform, simple, expeditious and exclusive procedure for the obtaining in a Member State of an order for the enforcement of a judgment given in another Member State. In the United Kingdom, enforcement is effected separately in England, in Scotland, and in Northern Ireland; and the enforcement order takes the form of an order that the judgment be registered for enforcement, made by the superior court (or in the case of a maintenance order, an inferior court) of the relevant territory. After an enforcement order has become final, actual execution is governed by the law of the state addressed; and in England the same measures (such as a writ of *fieri facias* against chattels, or a garnishee order against debts, belonging to the judgment debtor) are available as in the case of a similar English judgment.[5]

The initial application for an enforcement order is made ex parte, and the court applied to must give its decision without delay and without hearing the respondent.[6] If the initial application is successful, the decision is served on the respondent, who may appeal against it within a short period; in England to the court which registered the judgment.[7] The decision on the appeal is subject only to a single further appeal on a point of law, in England to either the Court of Appeal or, under the 'leapfrog' procedure, the House of Lords; except in the case of a maintenance order, where it lies to the Family Division of the High Court.[8]

By Article 38 of the Convention (Article 46 of the Regulation), if an ordinary appeal has been or may still be lodged against the judgment in the original state, the court hearing the first appeal against the enforcement order has a discretion, on application, to stay its proceedings so as to await the outcome of the appeal in

---

2   See Art 27(4) of the Convention; Art 72 of the Regulation.
3   See Art 27(2) of the Convention; Art 34(2) of the Regulation; Case 125/79: *Denilauler v SNC Couchet Frères* [1980] ECR 1553, [1981] 1 CMLR 62; Case 228/81: *Pendy Plastic Products BV v Pluspunkt* [1982] ECR 2723, [1983] 1 CMLR 665; Case 49/84: *Debaecker and Plouvier v Bouwman* [1985] ECR 1779, [1986] 2 CMLR 400; Case 166/80: *Klomps v Michel* [1981] ECR 1593, [1982] 2 CMLR 773; Case C-305/88: *Lancray v Peters and Sickert* [1990] ECR I-2725; Case C-123/91: *Minalmet v Brandeis* [1992] ECR I-5661; Case C-172/91: *Sonntag v Waidmann* [1993] ECR I-1963; Case C-474/93 *Hengst v Campese* [1995] ECR I-2113; Case C-78/95: *Hendrikman v Magenta Druck & Verlag* [1996] ECR I-4943.
4   See Art 27(3) and (5) of the Convention; Art 34(3) and (4) of the Regulation; and Case 145/86: *Hofmann v Kreig* [1988] ECR 645.
5   See Case 119/84: *Capelloni and Aquilini v Pelmans* [1985] ECR 3147; and Case 148/84: *Deutsche Genossenschaftsbank v Brasserie du Pecheur SA* [1985] ECR 1981, [1986] 2 CMLR 496; and the (UK) Civil Jurisdiction and Judgments Act 1982, ss 4 and 5.
6   See Art 34(1) of the Convention; Art 41 of the Regulation. By Arts 44 and 50, respectively, an applicant for enforcement who was granted legal aid in the original state is entitled to receive the most favourable legal aid provided for by the law of the state addressed in respect of his initial application for enforcement. See also Case 198/85: *Carron v Germany* [1986] ECR 2437, [1987] 1 CMLR 838.
7   See Arts 36 and 37(1) of the Convention; Arts 43 of the Regulation; Case 148/84: *Deutsche Genossenschaftsbank v Brasserie du Pecheur* [1985] ECR 1981, [1986] 2 CMLR 496; and Case 145/86: *Hoffmann v Krieg* [1988] ECR 645.
8   See Art 37(2) of the Convention; Art 44 of the Regulation; Case 258/83: *Calzaturificio Brennero SAS v Wendel GmbH* [1984] ECR 3971, [1986] 2 CMLR 59; Case C-183/90: *Van Dalfsen v Van Loon* [1991] ECR I-4743; Case C-172/91: *Sonntag v Waidmann* [1993] ECR I-1963; Case C-432/93: *SISRO v Ampersand* [1995] ECR I-2269 and the (UK) Civil Jurisdiction and Judgments Act 1982, s 6.

the original country.[9] There is also power to order enforcement conditionally on the provision of security.[10] By Article 39 of the Convention (Article 47(3) of the Regulation), while the first appeal against the enforcement order is possible or pending, only protective measures against the respondent's property may be taken in the state addressed, but such order entitles the applicant to take such measures.[11]

If the initial application for an enforcement order is rejected, the applicant may appeal; in the United Kingdom, to the court which rejected his application. The respondent must be summoned and is entitled to be heard.[12] The decision on the appeal is again subject only to a single further appeal on a point of law.[13]

L. Choice-of-law

After the signature of the 1968 Convention on jurisdiction and judgments, a programme was adopted for the unification within the Community, through the negotiation of conventions, of choice-of-law rules on such matters as obligations, property, form and proof, and general concepts (such as *renvoi*), and a working group was set up by the Commission, comprising representatives of the Member States. The group initially attempted to negotiate a convention covering both contractual and non-contractual obligations, but eventually decided to limit its first convention to contracts. Ultimately a Convention on the Law Applicable to Contractual Obligations, based on the efforts of the working group, was opened for signature at Rome on 19 June 1980,[14] and, after over a decade of further delay, this has now entered into force in all the Member States. Two Protocols on the Interpretation of the 1980 Convention by the European Court were eventually signed on 19 December 1988.[15] The 1980 Convention applies only to contracts concluded after its entry into force,[16] and gives way to other international conventions.[17]

The 1980 Convention regulates choice-of-law in respect of contracts, with certain exceptions in respect of such matters as individual status and capacity, family law, negotiable instruments, the internal affairs of companies, representation, and insurance.[18] It applies even if the applicable law is that of a non-Member State.[19]

Under the general rules laid down in Articles 3 and 4, a contract is governed by its proper law, and this is ascertained primarily by reference to the intention

---

9   See Case 43/77: *Industrial Diamond Supplies v Riva* [1977] ECR 2175, [1978] 1 CMLR 349; and Case C-183/90: *Van Dalfsen v Van Loon* [1991] ECR I-4743.
10 See Art 38(3) of the Convention; Art 46(3) of the Regulation; and Case 258/83: *Calzaturificio Brennero SAS v Wendel GmbH* [1984] ECR 3971, [1986] 2 CMLR 59.
11 See Case 119/84: *Capelloni and Aquilini v Pelkmans* [1985] ECR 3147, [1986] 1 CMLR 388.
12 See Art 40 of the Convention; and Case 178/83: *Firma P v Firma K* [1984] ECR 3033.
13 See Art 41 of the Convention.
14 For its text, see OJ 1980, L266. A consolidated version containing later amendments is published in OJ 1998, C 27/34. For the Guiliano and Lagarde Report thereon, OJ 1980, C 282. For the Convention of 10 April 1984 on Greek accession to the 1980 Convention, see OJ 1984, L146. For the Convention on the accession of Spain and Portugal, see OJ 1992, L333/1. For the Convention on the accession of Austria, Finland and Sweden, see OJ 1997, C 15/10. The explanatory report is published in OJ 1997, C 191/11.
15 See OJ 1989, L48 and, for the consolidated versions, OJ 1998, C 27/47 and 52. For the Tizzano Report on the 1988 Protocols, see OJ 1990, C 219.
16 Art 17.
17 Art 21.
18 See Art 1.
19 See Art 2.

of the parties. Their choice may be made by an explicit agreement, or may be inferred from other terms or circumstances which demonstrate their implied choice with reasonable certainty. In the absence of any such choice, the proper law is that of the country with which the contract is most closely connected, and there is a rebuttable presumption in favour of the residence of the characteristic performer.

Special provision is however made by Articles 5 and 6 for consumer and employment contracts, in order to protect the weaker party. More generally, Articles 7(2) and 16 make savings for the mandatory rules, and the public policy of the *lex fori*, and (subject to reservation) Article 7(1) permits mandatory rules of a third law to be applied where it has a sufficient interest. There are also specific provisions dealing with such issues as consent, capacity, formalities and proof.[20] Time limitations are characterized as substantive,[1] and *renvoi* is excluded.[2]

M. Service of judicial and extra-judicial documents

Regulation 1348/2000[3] improves and expedites the transmission of judicial and extra-judicial documents in civil or commercial matters. It came into force on 31 May 2001 and requires the Member States to designate public officers, authorities or other persons as 'transmitting' or 'receiving' agencies responsible for, respectively, sending and receiving documents. Each Member State must also designate a central agency responsible for supplying information and resolving disputes. Documents sent through the system must be served in the receiving state in accordance with the legislation of that state or in the manner requested by the transmitting agency if possible.

N. Development co-operation

The Policy for Development Co-operation is a continuation of a practice developed on the basis of EC Article 310 (ex Art 238) (international agreements) reinforced by EC Article 308 (ex Art 235) (implied powers). EC Articles 177-181 (ex Arts 130u-130y) codify the position with reference to EC Article 3(r) which mentions development co-operation as one of the activities of the Community. It corresponds to the expansion of the Community in the field of international relations and the new Title on the Common Foreign and Security Policy of the Union.[4]

The Community and the Member States are partners in Development Co-operation with developing countries, which shall be complementary to the policies of the Member States, and which aims to foster the sustainable economic and social development of developing countries; the smooth and gradual integration of the developing countries into the world economy; and the campaign against

---

20 See Arts 8, 9 and 11-14.
1 See Art 10.
2 Art 15.
3 OJ 2000, L160/37. The Regulation is based on a Convention signed in 1997: see OJ 1997, C 261/2. The Explanatory Report on the Convention was published on p 26.
4 TEU Arts 3 and 11-28 (ex Arts C and J). However, the objectives of development co-operation are to be taken into account in all the policies of the Community that are likely to affect developing countries: EC Art 178 (ex Art 130r).

poverty.[5] Development policy operates without prejudice to the co-operation between the Community and African, Caribbean and Pacific countries under the ACP-EC Convention and, after its ratification, the ACP-EC Partnership Agreement.[6]

Community policy in this area shall contribute to the general objective of developing and consolidating democracy, the rule of law and respect for human rights and fundamental freedoms.[7]

Except as regards the ACP-EC co-operation, the Council, according to the procedure laid down in EC Article 251 (ex Art 189b), shall adopt measures necessary for the implementation of the policy and the European Investment Bank shall support its objectives.[8]

The Community and the Member States shall comply with the commitments and objectives that they have approved in the context of the United Nations and other competent international organizations, co-ordinate their policies and consult each other on their aid programmes and generally act together in international organizations and at international conferences.[9]

Whilst the Commission may take any useful initiative to promote the co-ordination of the national efforts in this field,[10] the Treaty emphasized the bicephalous nature of the arrangements envisaged under this Title as the Member States' competence to negotiate with international bodies and conclude international agreements is safeguarded.[11]

---

5   EC Art 177(1) (ex Art 130u(1)).
6   EC Art 179(3) (ex Art 130w(3)).
7   EC Art 177(2) (ex Art 130u(2)). Cf Reg 975/1999 (OJ 1999, L120/1).
8   EC Art 179(1) and (2) (ex Art 130w(1) and (2)).
9   EC Arts 177(3), 180 and 181 (ex Arts 130u(3), 130x and 130y).
10 EC Art 180(2) (ex Art 130x(2)).
11 EC Art 181 (ex Art 130y), last sentence.

Appendix

The Treaty of Nice

The Treaty of Nice[1] was signed on 26 February 2001. Like the other principal Treaties (with the exception of the ECSC Treaty), it was concluded for an unlimited period.[2] The Treaty is to enter into force on the first day of the second month following that in which the last State to do so has deposited the instrument of ratification.[3] At the time of writing (March 2001), it was estimated that the ratification process would take two years. In summary, the Treaty makes various amendments to the TEU,[4] the EC Treaty,[5] the EAEC Treaty,[6] the ECSC Treaty,[7] the Protocol on the Statute of the European System of Central Banks and of the ECB,[8] and the Protocol on the privileges and immunities of the European Communities.[9] In addition, the Protocols on the Statute of the Court of Justice attached to the EC and EAEC Treaties are repealed and replaced in their entirety; the Protocol on the Statute of the Court of Justice attached to the ECSC Treaty is largely repealed and, to the extent of the repeal, is replaced by the new Protocols attached to the EC and EAEC Treaties; and Council Decision 88/591, which established the CFI, is repealed save in regard to the ECSC Treaty.[10] The Protocol on the institutions attached to the TEU and to the Treaties establishing the European Communities is repealed and replaced by a Protocol on the enlargement of the European Union. Two new protocols are attached to the EC Treaty: one on the financial consequences of the expiry of the ECSC Treaty; and a protocol consisting of only one article providing that, as from 1 May 2004, the Council shall act by a qualified majority, on a proposal from the Commission and after consulting the European Parliament, in order to adopt the measures referred to in EC Article 66. The Conference of the representatives of the Governments of

---

1   OJ 2001, C 80/1. References to the Treaty shall be to 'NT', followed by the relevant provision.
2   NT Art 11.
3   NT Art 12(2).
4   NT Art 1.
5   NT Art 2.
6   NT Art 3.
7   NT Art 4.
8   NT Art 5.
9   NT Art 6.
10 NT Arts 7-10.

the Member States also adopted 24 declarations annexed to the Final Act of the Treaty of Nice and took note of three declarations made by various Member States.

The amendments to the TEU

TEU Article 7 (ex Art F.1), which empowers the Council to take action where a Member State has committed a serious and persistent breach of principles laid down in TEU Article 6(1) (ex Art F(1)), is extended to cover the situation where there is a clear risk of a serious breach of those principles. In that event, the Council may act on a reasoned proposal put forward by one third of the Member States or by the European Parliament or by the Commission. In order to find that there is such a risk and address appropriate recommendations to the Member State concerned, the Council must act by a four-fifths majority and must have the assent of the European Parliament.[11] Before coming to a determination, the Council must hear the Member State in question and may call on independent persons to submit a report on the situation in that State.[12] Where a determination is made, the Council must regularly verify that the grounds on which it was based continue to apply.

In relation to the common foreign and security policy, the role of the WEU, as described in TEU Article 17 (ex Art J.7), has been reduced to a single reference in TEU Article 17(4). In the case of agreements with other states or international organisations (TEU Article 24 (ex Art J.14)), the principle of majority voting has been introduced, with unanimity and qualified majorities limited to specific cases. The Policy Committee provided for in TEU Article 25 (ex Art J.15), has been renamed the Policy and Security Committee. It is formally entrusted with the exercise of political control and strategic direction of crisis management operations, under the responsibility of the Council.[13] Entry into force of the Nice Treaty is not a precondition for the operation of the European security and defence policy.[14] Five new articles[15] are inserted dealing with 'enhanced co-operation' aimed at safeguarding the values and serving the interests of the Union as a whole. Enhanced co-operation relates to implementation of a joint action or common position but not to matters having military or defence implications. Member States wishing to engage in enhanced co-operation must address a request to that effect to the Council. The provisions dealing with police and judicial co-operation now include a reference to 'Eurojust', which is the European Judicial Cooperation Unit,[16] and provision for 'enhanced co-operation' similar to that applicable in the context of the common foreign and security policy.

---

11 It would appear that, even if the reasoned proposal originally came from the European Parliament, the Council must still seek the assent of the former for its conclusion that there was a risk of serious breach of the principles.

12 The Council must give the State concerned the opportunity to be heard before deciding to call on independent persons to make such a report. Those persons must be required to submit the report within a reasonable time.

13 The Council may authorize the Committee to take political control and strategic direction of an operation.

14 See the first declaration annexed to the Final Act of the Nice Treaty.

15 TEU Arts 27a-27e, as inserted by NT Art 1(5).

16 The decision to set up Eurojust was made at the European Council meeting at Tampere in October 1999: see the second declaration annexed to the Final Act of the Nice Treaty. A provisional judicial co-operation unit was set up by a Decision of 14 December 2000 (OJ 2000, L324/2) in order to pave the way for Eurojust.

Title VII of the TEU ('Provisions on closer cooperation') is renamed 'Provisions on enhanced cooperation'. Such co-operation must be aimed at furthering the objectives of both the Union and the Community (not just, at the time of writing, the interests of the Union), must remain within the limits of the powers of the Union or the Community, must not concern areas falling within the exclusive competence of the latter, and must not undermine the internal market and economic and social cohesion between the Member States or constitute a trade barrier, discrimination in trade or a distortion of competition between Member States. Enhanced co-operation must involve at least eight Member States (at the time of writing, closer co-operation must concern a majority at least of the Member States). Acts and decisions adopted in the context of enhanced co-operation do not form part of the 'Union *acquis*', that is, the legal patrimony of the Union itself. The Council and the Commission are responsible for ensuring that activities undertaken on the basis of enhanced co-operation are consistent both internally and in relation to the policies of the Union and the Community.

Finally, the jurisdiction of the ECJ is extended to the purely procedural stipulations in TEU Article 7. The ECJ acts at the request of the Member State concerned within one month of the date of the Council determination that that State has breached or risks breaching one of the principles set out in TEU Article 6(1) and that specifies the consequences. It follows that the ECJ has no jurisdiction over the substantive conclusions reached by the Council.

The amendments to the EC Treaty

The third declaration annexed to the Final Act of the Nice Treaty refers to the duty of sincere co-operation based on EC Article 10 (ex Art 5) and states that it applies also as between the Community institutions, which may conclude inter-institutional agreements between themselves in order to facilitate the application of the Treaty (but not for the purpose of amending or supplementing the Treaty). EC Article 11 (ex Art 5a), which deals with closer co-operation between the Member States, is replaced by two provisions (Articles 11 and 11a) that tie such co-operation more closely to the parallel provisions in the TEU. Where the proposed co-operation concerns an area in relation to which action by the Community must be adopted following the procedure laid down in EC Article 251 (ex Art 189b), the assent of the European Parliament is required.

In relation to measures adopted to combat discrimination under EC Article 13 (ex Art 6a), it is provided that incentive measures (excluding harmonization of national law) must be adopted in accordance with the procedure in EC Article 251 (ex Art 189b).

In relation to the rights of citizens of the Union, as defined in EC Article 18 (ex Art 8a), the Council's powers to take action are amended. The general power to take action is to be found elsewhere in the Treaty and, where it is lacking, the Council has a special power that must be exercised in accordance with the procedure laid down in EC Article 251 (ex Art 189b). That special power does not apply to provisions on passports, identity cards, residence permits and other such documents, or to provisions on social security and social protection. Measures on asylum, minimum protective standards for displaced persons and other persons in need of international protection (EC Articles 63(1) and (2)(a)) (ex Arts 73k(1) and (2)(a))) and measures in the field of judicial co-operation, with the exception of aspects relating to family law (EC Article 65 (ex Art 73m)), are to be adopted in accordance with the same procedure. A protocol attached to the Nice Treaty provides that, for the adoption of the measures referred to in EC Article 66 (ex Art 73n), the Council shall act by a qualified majority on a proposal from the Commission and after consulting the European Parliament.[17]

Unanimity has been replaced by qualified majority (or, in some instances, the procedure under EC Article 251 (ex Art 189b)) in the following provisions: EC Articles 100 (ex 103a); 111(4) (ex 109(4)); 123(4) (ex 1091(4)), third sentence; 157(3) (ex 130(3)); 159 (ex 130b), third paragraph; 161 (ex 130d), as from 1 January 2007; 190(5) (ex 138a), with the exception of rules or conditions relating to taxation; 207(2) (ex 151(2)); 214(2) (ex 158(2)); 215 (ex 159), save where the Council decides that a vacancy need not be filled; 247(3) (ex 188b(3)); 279(1) (ex 209), after 1 January 2007. In relation to EC Article 67 (ex Art 73o), the fifth declaration annexed to the Final Act sets out an agreement that the procedure referred to in EC Article 251 (ex Art 189b) will apply from 1 May 2004 or, as the case may, as from the date on which agreement is reached on the scope of the measures concerning the crossing by persons of the external frontiers of the Member States; the Council will endeavour to apply the same procedure in other areas covered by Title IV.

EC Article 133 (ex Art 113) on the common commercial policy is amended so as to extend its provisions to the negotiation and conclusion of agreements in the fields of trade in services and the commercial aspects of intellectual property (to the extent that they are not already covered). Unanimity is required for the negotiation and conclusion of such agreements. The Council's powers in that regard are limited because it may not conclude an agreement that goes beyond the Community's internal powers. Agreements relating to trade in cultural and audiovisual services, educational services and social and human health services are declared to fall within the shared competence of the Community and the Member States.

In relation to social policy, EC Article 137(1) (ex Art 118(1)) is amended so as to incorporate four of the matters previously referred to in EC Article 137(3) (ex Art 118(3)) (social security and social protection of workers, protection of workers where their employment contract is terminated, representation and defence of the interests of workers and employers and conditions of employment for third country nationals) but the requirement of unanimity for the adoption of measures in those areas remains.[18] Two further matters are added: the combating of social exclusion and the modernization of social protection systems. Any action taken by the Community shall not affect the right of Member States to define the fundamental principles of their social security systems and must not affect significantly the financial equilibrium of those systems. Article 144 (ex Art 121) is replaced by a provision that requires the Council to establish a Social Protection Committee with advisory status to promote co-operation on social protection policies between the Member States and the Commission. EC Article 157(3) (ex Art 130(3)), on industrial policy, is amended so as to provide that the Treaty does not provide a basis for Community action that affects tax provisions or provisions relating to the rights and interests of employed persons.

A new Title XXI is added to Part Three of the EC Treaty, entitled 'Economic, Financial and Technical Cooperation with Third Countries'. It consists of a single article that empowers the Community to adopt measures of that nature that are

---

17 See the Protocol on Art 67 of the Treaty establishing the European Community.
18 It may be removed by unanimous decision of the Council, acting on a proposal from the Commission and after consulting the European Parliament.

complementary to measures carried out by the Member States and consistent with the Community's development policy.[19]

The maximum number of members of the European Parliament is increased to 732 (EC Article 189 (ex Art 137)). EC Article 191 (ex Art 138a) is amended so as to empower the Council to lay down regulations governing political parties at European level.[20] EC Articles 217 and 219 (ex Arts 161 and 163) are amended so as to strengthen formally the position of the President of the Commission. He or she is formally entrusted with the task of deciding the internal organization of the Commission so as to ensure that it acts consistently, efficiently and on the basis of collegiality. That includes structuring and allocating responsibilities between the members of the Commission and reshuffling them during the Commission's term of office. The members of the Commission are subject to an express obligation to carry out the duties assigned to them by the President under his authority. The President also appoints the Vice-Presidents. A member of the Commission is obliged to resign if the President so requests after obtaining the approval of the College of Commissioners. That provides a solution to the problem that caused the whole Commission to resign in 1999 amid allegations of corruption and nepotism that centred on one or two members who were not, apparently, prepared to resign of their own accord. The number of members of the Court of Auditors is now fixed at one per Member State: Article 247(1) (ex Art 188b(1)). The maximum number of members of the Economic and Social Committee is fixed at 350: Article 258 (ex Art 194). The members are to be appointed for four years on the basis of proposals from the Member States: EC Article 259(1) (ex Art 195(1)). Similar changes are made to the Committee of the Regions: EC Article 263 (ex Art 198a).[1]

Among the more interesting changes wrought by the Nice Treaty are those that concern the ECJ and the CFI. They include the amendment and replacement of the Protocol on the Statute of the Court of Justice attached to the EC Treaty. The new Protocol consolidates that Protocol and the parallel Protocol attached to the EAEC Treaty.

The Nice Treaty brings the CFI fully into the institutional structure of the Treaty by amending EC Article 220 (ex Art 164) so as to refer expressly to the CFI. In addition, it is provided that 'judicial panels' may be attached to the CFI in order to exercise the judicial competence of the CFI in specific areas. Such 'judicial panels' may hear and determine at first instance certain classes of action or proceedings brought in specific areas. They may be created by the Council, acting unanimously on a proposal from either the Commission or the ECJ, and after consulting the European Parliament and the ECJ (in the case of a proposal from the Commission) or the Commission (in the case of a request from the ECJ).

---

19   The tenth declaration annexed to the Final Act of the Nice Treaty states that balance of payments aid to third countries falls outside the scope of the policy.

20   The 11th declaration states that EC Art 191 does not imply any transfer of powers to the EC and does not affect the application of national constitutional rules. Funding of political parties at European level may not be used to fund political parties at national level and will not discriminate between different political forces.

1   The Member States also adopted a common position in relation to their stance at any accession negotiations on the distribution of seats in the European Parliament, the weighting of votes in the Council, the composition of the Economic and Social Committee and the composition of the Committee of the Regions for a Union of 27 Member States. The position is set out in the 20th declaration annexed to the Final Act of the Nice Treaty. The 21st declaration sets out how the qualified majority threshold shall evolve according to the pace of accessions.

The decision establishing a judicial panel must define the extent of its jurisdiction, lay down the rules governing its organisation, and provide for appeals from its decisions. Under the EC Treaty (as amended), decisions of a judicial panel may be subject to a right of appeal on points of law only or on points of law and fact, to the CFI, depending upon the decision creating the judicial panel.[2] Members of judicial panels are appointed by the Council acting unanimously and must be chosen from persons whose independence is beyond doubt and who possess the ability required for appointment to judicial office. Judicial panels therefore have effectively the same status as the CFI used to have before the Nice Treaty incorporated it into the institutional structure provided for in the EC Treaty.[3] It is anticipated that judicial panels will be used for specialist litigation such as staff cases and intellectual property litigation concerning rights defined in and conferred by Community law. Indeed, one of the declarations annexed to the Final Act of the Nice Treaty implies that the Boards of Appeal set up to deal with trademarks and designs might be transformed into judicial panels.[4]

The number of members of the ECJ and CFI is now 'stabilized' at one judge per Member State for each court and eight Advocates-General for the ECJ (previously, the number of judges was a fixed number that had to be amended every time a state acceded to the Community). Members of the CFI must be eligible for 'high' judicial office. Originally, they needed to be eligible for 'judicial office'. The addition of 'high' places them between members of the ECJ (who must be eligible for the 'highest' judicial offices) and members of judicial panels.

The ECJ is to sit in chambers, in a 'Grand Chamber' or as a full court. The chambers may consist of three or five judges and each is presided over by a president elected by the judges from among their number; the presidents of the chambers of five judges are elected for three years and may be re-elected once. The Grand Chamber consists of 11 judges. The President of the Court presides. The members of the Grand Chamber include the presidents of the chambers of five judges and other judges appointed in accordance with the rules of procedure.[5] The Grand Chamber is effectively a formalized version of what used to be known as the *'petit plenum'*.[6] The quorum for the chambers of three and five judges is three; the quorum of the Grand Chamber is nine; the quorum of the full court is 11.[7] The Court must sit in a Grand Chamber when a Member State or Community

---

2   Under EC Art 225(2), as amended, the CFI has jurisdiction to hear and determine actions or proceedings brought against decisions of judicial panels and the decisions of the CFI may 'exceptionally' be subject to review by the ECJ under conditions laid down in the Protocol on the Statute of the Court 'where there is a serious risk of the unity or consistency of Community law being affected'.

3   For the provisions dealing with judicial panels, see the new EC Art 225a. The 16th declaration annexed to the Final Act of the Nice Treaty requested the ECJ and the Commission to prepare as swiftly as possible a draft decision establishing a judicial panel for staff cases.

4   See the declaration by Luxembourg. That declaration was merely one of which the conference of representatives of the governments of the Member States 'took note'. It therefore lacks the status of a declaration made by all the Member States.

5   Protocol on the Statute of the Court of Justice ('the Statute'), Art 16.

6   The *'petit plenum'* involved convening a sufficient number of judges to meet the quorum requirement for the full court, but not all the judges, thus enabling those not sitting in the *'petit plenum'* to do something else, such as sitting in a chamber. As such, it amounted to paying lip service to the notion of a full court: the ECJ could meet its obligation to hear certain cases as a full court without actually doing so. As from the 1980s, the ECJ used the *'petit plenum'* to maximize its output.

7   Ibid, Art 17.

institution that is a party to the proceedings so requests. The Court must sit as a full court either when it decides that a case before it is of exceptional importance and ought to be referred to the full court or in the case of certain specified proceedings.[8] In the result, the Member States and Community institutions may require the ECJ to sit only in a Grand Chamber and not as a full court. When a case raises no new point of law, the ECJ may, after hearing the Advocate General, decide to determine the case without an opinion from him or her.[9]

The CFI has general jurisdiction at first instance over actions for annulment, actions in respect of a failure to act, damages actions, staff cases, and actions brought under an arbitration clause, save to the extent that a matter has been assigned to a judicial panel, and subject to a right of appeal to the ECJ on points of law only. The jurisdiction of the CFI may be altered by provision in the Protocol on the Statute of the Court.[10] The CFI also has jurisdiction over references for a preliminary ruling under EC Article 234 (ex Art 177) in specific areas identified in the Protocol on the Statute of the Court.[11] In relation to such cases, the CFI has power to refer it to the ECJ if the CFI considers that the case requires a decision of principle likely to affect the unity or consistency of Community law. For the same reason, preliminary rulings given by the CFI may exceptionally be subject to review by the ECJ as provided for in the Protocol on the Statute of the Court.

The CFI is to sit in chambers of three or five judges (for which the quorum is three judges). In cases specified in the rules of procedure, it may be constituted by a single judge or sit in a Grand Chamber or as a full court. For the full court, the quorum is 11 judges. No quorum is laid down for the Grand Chamber. As in the case of the ECJ, the presidents of the chambers of five judges are elected for three years and may be re-elected once.[12] The procedure before the CFI in intellectual property disputes can diverge from the normal rules governing intervention and judgment by default.[13] Where there is a serious risk of the unity or consistency of Community being affected, the ECJ may decide to review decisions of the CFI on appeal from decisions of a judicial panel and preliminary rulings made by the CFI, on a proposal from the First Advocate General of the ECJ made within one month of the delivery of the CFI's judgment or order.[14]

An additional area of jurisdiction is created in the sense that, under a new EC Article 229a, the Council is empowered to adopt provisions conferring

---

8   Ibid, Art 16. The specified proceedings are: proceedings for the dismissal of the European Parliament's Ombudsman; compulsory retirement of a member of the Commission or deprivation of his or her pension or other benefits; compulsory retirement of a member of the Commission for breach of the conditions required for performance of his or her office or serious misconduct; deprivation of office of a member of the Court of Auditors or deprivation of his or her pension or other benefits.

9   Ibid, Art 20, 5th para.

10 See Statute, Art 51, which provides that the ECJ has jurisdiction in actions brought by the Member States, the Community institutions and the ECB 'by way of exception to' EC Art 225(1). The 12th declaration annexed to the Final Act enjoins the ECJ and the Commission 'to give overall consideration as soon as possible to the division of jurisdiction' between the ECJ and the CFI and to submit suitable proposals as soon as the Nice Treaty enters into force.

11 At the time of writing, no relevant provision appears in the Statute.

12 Statute, Arts 47 (which cross-refers to part only of Art 17) and 50.

13 Ibid, Art 53, 3rd sentence.

14 Ibid, Art 62. The 15th declaration annexed to the Final Act states that, when the ECJ reviews a preliminary ruling made by the CFI, it should act under 'an emergency procedure' (that appears to be an allusion to the summary procedure used in interim relief cases).

jurisdiction on the ECJ in disputes relating to the application of acts adopted under the Treaty that create Community industrial property rights.[15] EC Article 230 (ex Art 173) is the subject of a minor amendment that gives the European Parliament full rights to bring an action for annulment, as opposed to a limited right of action to protect its prerogatives. EC Article 300(6) (ex Art 228(6)) is amended so as to enable the European Parliament to obtain the opinion of the ECJ on the compatibility of an agreement with the Treaty.

The amendments to the EAEC Treaty

The Nice Treaty amends the institutional provisions of the EAEC Treaty[16] along the same lines as the amendments made to the corresponding provisions of the EC Treaty that are summarized above.

The amendments to the ECSC Treaty

The Nice Treaty amends the institutional provisions of the ECSC Treaty[17] along the same lines as the amendments made to the corresponding provisions of the EC Treaty that are summarized above. The bulk of the Protocol on the Statute of the Court attached to the ECSC Treaty is repealed. When the ECJ exercises its powers under the ECSC Treaty, it applies the Protocol on the Statute of the Court attached to the EC and EAEC Treaties (as amended by the Nice Treaty) save for Articles 21-43, 46 (the first paragraph only), 50, 53 and 56 of the ECSC Protocol, which remain in force.[18] In reality, only Articles 23 and 41-42 of the ECSC Protocol are any different from the EC and EAEC Protocols.

The Protocol on the enlargement of the European Union

This Protocol replaces the Protocol on the Institutions annexed to the TEU and to the EC, EAEC and ECSC Treaties. It specifies the allocation, between the Member States, of representatives in the European Parliament from the start of the 2004–2009 term of office, the weighting of votes in the Council as from 1 January 2005, and the number of members of the Commission as from the same date (one per Member State). When the number of Member States reaches 27, the number of members of the Commission shall be reduced and the members shall be chosen according to a rotation system organized on the basis of the principle of equality and designed so as to reflect satisfactorily the demographic and geographical range of all the Member States.[19]

---

15 The 16th declaration annexed to the Final Act indicates that EC Art 229a is not intended to prejudge the choice of judicial framework that may be set up to deal with disputes relating to the application of Community law provisions creating industrial property rights. It is therefore open to the Council to select other means of resolving such disputes than recourse to the ECJ (or CFI).
16 EAEC Arts 107, 108(5), 121(2), 127(2), 128, 130, 132, 136-140b, 146, 160, 160b, 160c, 163, 165, 166, 167(1), 183, 190 and 204.
17 ECSC Arts 10(2), 11-13, 20, 21(5), 30(2), 31-33, 45, 45b, 45c and 96.
18 NT Arts 8-9.
19 The rotation system will be adopted by the Council once the 27th Member State has acceded.

The Charter of Fundamental Rights

In the course of the Nice summit, the European Parliament, Council and Commission proclaimed a charter of fundamental rights.[20] The precise status of the Charter is one of the matters to be established in the course of a deeper and wider debate about the future of the European Union initiated by the agreement on the Nice Treaty. At the time of writing, appropriate initiatives for the continuation of the process were to be agreed at the European Council meeting to be held in Laeken/Brussels in December 2001.[1] The Charter is addressed to the institutions and bodies of the Union and, when they are implementing Union law, to the Member States. It does not purport to create new powers or tasks for the Community or the Union; and it is not intended to limit the degree of protection available under other instruments, in particular the European Convention for the Protection of Human Rights and Fundamental Freedoms and the constitutions of the Member States.

Its main provisions are grouped together under six chapters dealing with: human dignity (the right to life, prohibition of torture and the like); various freedoms (obvious ones such as liberty and security, respect for private and family life but also freedom of artistic and scientific expression and the right to education); equality (including equal treatment of children, the elderly and disabled persons); solidarity (ranging from collective bargaining and other rights associated with workers to environmental and consumer protection); citizen's rights (the right to vote and be a candidate in elections, the right to good administration, and so forth), justice (the right to an effective remedy and to a fair trial, as well as particular rights in connection with criminal offences).

The Charter is intended to reaffirm the fundamental rights that emerge from the constitutional traditions and international obligations common to the Member States, from the TEU, the ECSC, EC and EAEC Treaties, the Convention for the Protection of Human Rights and Fundamental Freedoms, the Social Charter and the case law of the ECJ and the Human Rights Court. Accordingly, the uncertain nature of its exact legal (or, indeed, political) status may not matter too much: it can still be regarded as a convenient summary of those rights as they currently apply in the European Union.

---

20   OJ 2000, C 363/1.
1   See the 23rd declaration annexed to the Final Act of the Nice Treaty.

Index